AN
APPROACH
TO
LITERATURE

AN
APPROACH
TO
LITERATURE

Fifth Edition

———————◆◆◆———————

CLEANTH BROOKS
Professor (Emeritus), Yale University

JOHN THIBAUT PURSER
Professor, Southeastern Louisiana College

ROBERT PENN WARREN
Professor (Emeritus), Yale University

PRENTICE-HALL, INC., ENGLEWOOD CLIFFS, NEW JERSEY

Library of Congress Cataloging in Publication Data

BROOKS, CLEANTH, 1906– ed.
An approach to literature.

1. English literature. 2. American literature.
I. Purser, John Thibaut, joint ed. II. Warren,
Robert Penn, 1905– joint ed. III. Title.
PR1109.B675 1975 808'.04275 74-30326
ISBN 0-13-043802-2

10 9 8 7 6 5

Prentice-Hall International, Inc., *London*
Prentice-Hall of Australia, Pty. Ltd., *Sydney*
Prentice-Hall of Canada, Ltd., *Toronto*
Prentice-Hall of India Private Ltd., *New Delhi*
Prentice-Hall of Japan, Inc., *Tokyo*

ACKNOWLEDGMENTS

LÉONIE ADAMS, "Ghostly Tree," from *Poems: A Selection* by Léonie Adams. Reprinted by permission of the author.

A. R. AMMONS, "The Quince Bush." Reprinted from *Collected Poems, 1951–1971* by A. R. Ammons. By permission of W. W. Norton & Company, Inc. Copyright © 1972 by A. R. Ammons.

SHERWOOD ANDERSON, "I'm a Fool," from *Horses and Men* by Sherwood Anderson. Copyright 1923. Published by The Viking Press.

JOHN ASHBERY, "Years of Indiscretion," from the book *The Double Dream of Spring* by John Ashbery. Copyright © 1970, 1969, 1968, 1967, 1966 by John Ashbery. Published by E. P. Dutton & Co., Inc., and used with their permission.

W. H. AUDEN, "Lay your sleeping head, my love" (*Another Time*), W. H. Auden. Copyright 1940 by W. H. Auden. Reprinted from *The Collected Poetry of W. H. Auden* by permission of Random House, Inc., and Faber and Faber, Ltd.

MARCEL AYMÉ, "State of Grace," from *The Walker Through Walls & Other Stories*. By permission of The Bodley Head and Harper & Row Publishers, Inc.

ISAAC BABEL, "Crossing into Poland"; "Kronkin's Prisoner." Reprinted by permission of S. G. Phillips, Inc., from *The Collected Stories*. Copyright © 1955 by S. G. Phillips, Inc.

IMAMU AMIRI BARAKA, "Poem for Halfwhite College Students," from *Black Magic Poetry 1961–1967*. Copyright © 1969 by LeRoi Jones, reprinted by permission of the publisher, The Bobbs-Merrill Company, Inc.

DONALD BARTHELME, "The Indian Uprising." Reprinted with permission of Farrar, Straus & Giroux, Inc., from *Unspeakable Practices, Unnatural Acts* by Donald Barthelme. Copyright © 1965, 1968 by Donald Barthelme, originally appeared in *The New Yorker.*

SAMUEL BECKETT, *Act Without Words I: A Mime for One Player.* Translated from the French by the author. Reprinted by permission of Grove Press, Inc. Copyright 1957 by Samuel Beckett, Copyright © 1958, 1959, 1960 by Grove Press, Inc.

JOHN BERRYMAN, "Master of Beauty." Reprinted with the permission of Farrar, Straus & Giroux, Inc., from *Love & Fame* by John Berryman. Copyright © 1970 by John Berryman.

ELIZABETH BISHOP, "Little Exercise." Reprinted with the permission of Farrar, Straus & Giroux, Inc., from *Complete Poems* by Elizabeth Bishop. Copyright renewed 1974 by Elizabeth Bishop.

JOHN PEALE BISHOP, "Experience of the West." "Experience of the West" is reprinted by permission of Charles Scribner's Sons from *The Collected Poems of John Peale Bishop*, edited by Alan Tate. Copyright 1948 by Charles Scribner's Sons.

LOUISE BOGAN, "Old Countryside." Reprinted with the permission of Farrar, Straus & Giroux, Inc., from *The Blue Estuaries* by Louise Bogan. Copyright © 1923, 1929, 1930, 1931, 1933, 1934, 1935, 1936, 1937, 1938, 1941, 1949, 1951, 1952, 1957, 1958, 1962, 1963, 1964, 1965, 1966, 1967, 1968 by Louise Bogan.

ROBERT BRIDGES, "A Passer-by," from *The Shorter Poems of Robert Bridges*, by permission of the Clarendon Press, Oxford.

JOHN CHEEVER, "O Youth and Beauty!" By permission of the author. Originally, 1954, in *The New Yorker.*

ANTON CHEKHOV, "The Lottery Ticket," from *The Wife and Other Stories*, by Anton Chekhov, translated by Constance Garnett, published by courtesy of Mr. David Garnett and Chatto & Windus, London. By permission of the Macmillan Co., Inc., and A. P. Watt & Son, Ltd.

ELEANOR CLARK, "Hurry, Hurry." Copyright 1938 by Eleanor Clark. Reprinted from *Dr. Heart: A Novella and Other Stories*, by Eleanor Clark, by permission of Pantheon Books, a Division of Random House, Inc.

JOHN COLLIER, "Wet Saturday." Copyright 1938 by John Collier. Reprinted by permission of Harold Matson Company, Inc. Originally appeared in *The New Yorker.*

JOSEPH CONRAD, "The Lagoon," from *Tales of Unrest*, by permission of J. M. Dent & Sons, Ltd.

HART CRANE, "Voyage II." From *The Collected Poems and Selected Letters and Prose of Hart Crane*. Copyright © 1933, 1958, 1966 by Liveright Publishing Corp. Reprinted by permission of the publisher.

STEPHEN CRANE, "An Episode of War." Published 1952 by Alfred A. Knopf, Inc. Reprinted from *Stephen Crane: An Omnibus* edited by Robert Wooster Stallman, by permission of Alfred A. Knopf, Inc.

E. E. CUMMINGS, "Nine Birds." Copyright 1950 by E. E. Cummings. From his volume *Complete Poems 1913–1962*. Reprinted by permission of Harcourt Brace Jovanovich, Inc.

PETER DAVISON, "The Pleaders." From *Pretending to be Asleep* by Peter Davison. Copyright © 1967, 1968 by Peter Davison. Reprinted by permission of Atheneum Publishers. Appeared originally in *The New Yorker.*

WALTER DE LA MARE, "Silver," from *Collected Poems* by Walter de la Mare. Copyright, 1920, by Holt, Rinehart & Winston, Inc. Copyright, 1948, by Walter de la Mare. Used by permission of the publishers.

PETER DE VRIES, "Afternoon of a Faun." From *Without a Stitch in Time* by Peter de Vries by permission of Little, Brown and Co., in association with The Atlantic Monthly Press.

JAMES DICKEY, "Adultery." Copyright © 1962, 1966 by James Dickey. Reprinted from *Poems 1957–1967*, by James Dickey, by permission of Wesleyan University Press.

EMILY DICKINSON, "These are the days when Birds come back"; "The Sky is low—the Clouds are mean"; "The Mountains stood in Haze"; "I could not prove the Years had feet"; "'Hope' is the thing with feathers"; "Success is counted sweetest"; "Our journey had advanced"; "Her final Summer was it"; "Because I could not stop for Death"; "I heard a Fly buzz—when I died." Reprinted by permission of the publishers from *The Poems of Emily Dickinson*, Thomas H. Johnson, Editor. Cambridge, Mass.: The Belknap Press of Harvard University Press. Copyright, 1951, '55, by The President and fellows of Harvard College.

RICHARD EBERHART, "The Fury of Aerial Bombardment"; "I Walked Out to the Graveyard." From *Collected Poems 1930–1960* by Richard Eberhart. © Richard Eberhart 1960. Reprinted by permission of Oxford University Press, Inc. and Chatto & Windus, Ltd.

T. S. ELIOT. "Preludes"; "Rhapsody on a Windy Night" from *Collected Poems 1909–1962* by T. S. Eliot, copyright 1936, by Harcourt Brace Jovanovich, Inc.; copyright © 1963, 1964, by T. S. Eliot. Reprinted by permission of Harcourt Brace Jovanovich, Inc. and Faber and Faber Ltd. *Caution:* Professionals and amateurs are hereby warned that *Murder in the Cathedral*, being fully protected under the copyright laws of the United States of America, the British Empire, including the Dominion of Canada, and all other countries of the Copyright Union, is subject to a royalty. All rights, including professional, amateur, motion pictures, recitation, public reading, radio broadcasting and the rights of translation into foreign language are strictly reserved. Amateurs may produce this play upon payment of

$35.00 for each performance one week before the play is to be given to Samuel French, at 25 W. 45th St., New York 19, N.Y., or, 7623 Sunset Boulevard, Hollywood 46, Calif., or, if in Canada, to Samuel French (Canada) Ltd., 480 University Ave., Toronto, Ont.

WILLIAM FAULKNER, "Spotted Horses." Copyright 1931 and renewed 1959 by William Faulkner. Reprinted by permission of Random House, Inc. An expanded version of this story appears as part of *The Hamlet*, by William Faulkner.

F. SCOTT FITZGERALD, "The Rich Boy," from *All the Sad Young Men* by F. Scott Fitzgerald; copyright 1925, 1926 Consolidated Magazines Corp., renewed 1953, 1954 Frances Scott Fitzgerald Lanahan, reprinted by permission of Charles Scribner's Sons.

JOHN GOULD FLETCHER, "Gulls" from "Irradiations" from *Selected Poems* by John Gould Fletcher. Copyright 1938 by John Gould Fletcher, Copyright © 1966 by Charlie May Fletcher. Reprinted by permission of Holt, Rinehart and Winston, Inc.

ROBERT FROST, "Come In"; "Desert Places"; "To Earthward"; "A Leaf Treader"; "The Need of Being Versed in Country Things"; "The Oven Bird"; "The Star-Splitter"; "Stopping by Woods on a Snowy Evening"; and "The Wood-Pile." From *The Poetry of Robert Frost* edited by Edward Connery Lathem. Copyright 1916, 1923, 1930, 1939, © 1969 by Holt, Rinehart and Winston, Inc. Copyright 1936, 1942, 1944, 1951, © 1958 by Robert Frost. Copyright © 1964, 1967, 1970 by Lesley Frost Ballantine. Reprinted by permission of Holt, Rinehart and Winston, Inc.

ALLEN GINSBERG, "A Supermarket in California." Copyright © 1956, 1959 by Allen Ginsberg. Reprinted by permission of City Lights Books.

NIKKI GIOVANNI, "The Only Song I'm Singing." From *My House* by Nikki Giovanni. Copyright © 1972 by Nikki Giovanni. Reprinted by permission of William Morrow & Company, Inc.

THOM GUNN, "Black Jackets." Reprinted by permission of Farrar, Straus & Giroux, Inc. and Faber and Faber Ltd. From *Moly and My Sad Captains* by Thom Gunn. Copyright © 1961, 1971, 1973 by Thom Gunn.

THOMAS HARDY, "Channel Firing"; "The Convergence of the Twain"; "The Man He Killed"; "Neutral Tones"; and "On an Invitation to the United States," from *The Collected Poems of Thomas Hardy*. Copyright 1925 by Thomas Hardy. By permission of the Macmillan Co., Inc., and by arrangement with the Hardy Estate and the Macmillan Company of Canada Ltd.

ANTHONY HECHT, "The Dover Bitch." From *The Hard Hours* by Anthony Hecht. Copyright © 1960 by Anthony E. Hecht. Reprinted by permission of Atheneum Publishers. Appeared originally in *Transatlantic Review*.

ERNEST HEMINGWAY, "In Another Country," from *Men Without Women* by Ernest Hemingway. Copyright 1926, 1927 by Charles Scribner's Sons; used by permission of Charles Scribner's Sons.

JOHN HOLLANDER, "Alaska Brown Bear." From *The Night Mirror* by John Hollander. Copyright © 1971 by John Hollander. Reprinted by permission of Atheneum Publishers. Appeared originally in *The New Yorker*.

A. E. HOUSMAN, "Bredon Hill"; "The True Lover"; and "The Tree of Man," from *A Shropshire Lad* (1896) by A. E. Housman, by permission of The Society of Authors as the literary representative of the Estate of the late A. E. Housman, and Jonathan Cape, Ltd., publishers of A. E. Housman's *Collected Poems*. "1887," from *A Shropshire Lad*—authorised Edition—from *The Collected Poems of A. E. Housman*. Copyright 1939, 1940 © 1965 by Holt, Rinehart and Winston, Inc. Copyright © 1967, 1968 by Robert E. Symons. Reprinted by permission of Holt, Rinehart and Winston, Inc. "Epitaph of an Army of Mercenaries," from *The Collected Poems of A. E. Housman*. Copyright 1922 by Holt, Rinehart and Winston, Inc. Copyright 1950 by Barclays Bank Ltd. Reprinted by permission of Holt, Rinehart and Winston, Inc.

RICHARD HOWARD, "Further Instructions to the Architect." Copyright © 1967 by Richard Howard. Reprinted from *Damages* by Richard Howard, by permission of Wesleyan University Press.

LANGSTON HUGHES, "Mama and Daughter." Copyright 1948 by Alfred A. Knopf, Inc. "Ku Klux." Copyright 1942 by Alfred A. Knopf, Inc., and renewed 1970 by Arna Bontemps and George Houston Bass. "Midwinter Blues." Copyright 1927 by Alfred A. Knopf, Inc., and renewed 1955 by Langston Hughes. All are reprinted from *Selected Poems* by Langston Hughes, by permission of the publisher.

RANDALL JARRELL, "Burning the Letters," reprinted with the permission of Farrar, Straus & Giroux, Inc., from *The Complete Poems* by Randall Jarrell. Copyright © 1945, 1947, 1948, 1955 by Randall Jarrell. Copyright © 1969 by Mrs. Randall Jarrell, copyright renewed 1973, 1975 by Mrs. Randall Jarrell. "Eighth Air Force," from *Losses* by Randall Jarrell. Copyright 1948, by Harcourt Brace Jovanovich, Inc., and reprinted with their permission.

JAMES JOYCE, "Araby," from *Dubliners*, included in *The Portable James Joyce*. Copyright 1946, 1947 by The Viking Press. By permission of The Viking Press.

RUDYARD KIPLING, "Danny Deever," from *Departmental Ditties and Ballads and Barrack-Room Ballads*. Reprinted by permission of Mrs. George Bambridge, Doubleday & Company, Inc. and The Macmillan Company of Canada, Ltd. "If" and "Recessional," copyright 1910 by Rudyard Kipling from *Rudyard Kipling's Verse*, Definitive Edition. Reprinted by permission of Mrs. George Bambridge and Doubleday & Company, Inc.

JUDITH KROLL, "Bed" (copyright © 1972 by Judith Kroll) is reprinted by permission of Charles Scribner's Sons from *In the Temperate Zone* by Judith Kroll.

RING LARDNER, "Haircut" (copyright 1925 Ellis A. Lardner) is reprinted by permission of Charles Scribner's Sons from *The Love Nest and Other Stories* by Ring Lardner.

D. H. LAWRENCE, "Love on the Farm," from *Collected Poems* by D. H. Lawrence. Copyright, 1929, by Jonathan Cape and Harrison Smith, Inc. Reprinted by permission of The Viking Press. "The Horse Dealer's Daughter," from *England My England* by D. H. Lawrence. Copyright 1922 by Thomas Seltzer, Inc., 1950 by Frieda Lawrence. By permission of The Viking Press.

DENISE LEVERTOV, "The Old Adam." From *O Taste and See*. Copyright © 1964 by Denise Levertov Goodman. Reprinted by permission of New Directions Publishing Corporation.

ROBERT LOWELL, "Christmas Eve under Hooker's Statue," from *Lord Weary's Castle*, copyright, 1944, 1946, by Robert Lowell. Reprinted by permission of Harcourt Brace Jovanovich, Inc. "Colonel Shaw and the Massachusetts '54th." Reprinted from *Life Studies* by Robert Lowell by permission of Farrar, Straus & Company, Inc. Copyright © 1956, 1959 by Robert Lowell.

ANDREW LYTLE, "Jerico, Jerico, Jerico," *The Southern Review*, 1936.

ARCHIBALD MACLEISH, "You, Andrew Marvell," from *Poems, 1924–1933* by Archibald MacLeish. "Ars Poetica," from *The Collected Poems of Archibald MacLeish*. Copyright © 1962 by Archibald MacLeish, reprinted by permission of the publisher, Houghton Mifflin Company.

BERNARD MALAMUD, "The Magic Barrel." Reprinted with permission of Farrar, Straus & Giroux, Inc., from *The Magic Barrel* by Bernard Malamud. Copyright © 1954, 1958 by Bernard Malamud.

THOMAS MANN, "Disorder and Early Sorrow," from *Stories of Three Decades* by Thomas Mann, by permission of Alfred A. Knopf, Inc.

EDGAR LEE MASTERS, "Lucinda Matlock," from *Spoon River Anthology* by Edgar Lee Masters. Copyright © 1914, 1915, 1916, 1942, 1944 by Edgar Lee Masters. By permission of the Estate of Edgar Lee Masters.

CLAUDE MCKAY, "If We Must Die." From *Selected Poems by Claude McKay*. Copyright 1953 by Bookman Associates. Reprinted by permission of Twayne Publishers, Inc.

JAMES ALAN MCPHERSON, "Private Domain." From *Hue and Cry* by James Alan McPherson. By permission of Little, Brown and Co. in association with The Atlantic Monthly Press.

JAMES MERRILL, "A Timepiece." From *The Country of a Thousand Years of Peace* by James Merrill. Copyright © 1953, 1970 by James Merrill. Reprinted by permission of Atheneum Publishers. "A Timepiece" appeared originally in *Shenandoah*.

W. S. MERWIN, "The Last One." From *The Lice* by W. S. Merwin. Reprinted by permission of Atheneum Publishers. Appeared originally in *Poetry*.

CHARLOTTE MEW, "The Farmer's Bride," from *The Farmer's Bride and Other Poems* by Charlotte Mew. Published by Gerald Duckworth & Co., Ltd.

EDNA ST. VINCENT MILLAY, "Wild Swans" and "The Cameo," from *Collected Poems*, Harper & Row, Publishers. Copyright 1921, 1928, 1948, 1955 by Edna St. Vincent Millay and Norma Millay Ellis.

HOWARD MOSS, "Long Island Springs." From *Selected Poems* by Howard Moss. Reprinted by permission of Atheneum Publishers. Appeared originally in *The New Yorker Quarterly*.

OGDEN NASH, "Very Like a Whale," from *Many Long Years Ago* by Ogden Nash. Copyright 1935 by Ogden Nash. By permission of Little, Brown & Co. "Kind of an Ode to Duty." Copyright 1935 by The Curtis Publishing Company. "A Visit from Dr. Fell." Copyright 1942 by The Curtis Publishing Company.

FLANNERY O'CONNOR, "Everything that Rises Must Converge." Reprinted with permission of Farrar, Straus & Giroux, Inc. Copyright © 1961, 1965 by the Estate of Mary Flannery O'Connor.

FRANK O'CONNOR, "Legal Aid." Copyright, 1951 by Frank O'Connor. Reprinted from *The Stories of Frank O'Connor* by permission of Alfred A. Knopf, Inc. Canadian rights by permission of Harold Matson Co., Inc., and A. D. Peters.

NED O'GORMAN, "Color." From *The Flag the Hawk Flies* by Ned O'Gorman. Copyright © 1972 by Ned O'Gorman. Reprinted by permission of Alfred A. Knopf, Inc.

FRANK O'HARA, "The Apricot Season." From *The Collected Poems of Frank O'Hara*, edited by Donald Allen. Copyright © 1971 by Maureen

Granville-Smith, Administratrix of the Estate of Frank O'Hara. Reprinted by permission of Alfred A. Knopf, Inc.

WILFRED OWEN, "Dulce et Decorum Est." From the Collected Poems of Wilfred Owen, edited by C. Day-Lewis. Copyright © Chatto & Windus Ltd., 1963. Reprinted by permission of New Directions Publishing Corporation, Chatto & Windus Ltd., and Mr. Harold Owen.

SYLVIA PLATH, "The Applicant." From *Ariel* by Sylvia Plath. Copyright © 1963 by Ted Hughes.

KATHERINE ANNE PORTER, "Noon Wine," copyright 1936, 1964, by Katherine Anne Porter. Reprinted from her volume *Pale Horse, Pale Rider* by permission of Harcourt Brace Jovanovich, Inc.

J. F. POWERS, "The Valiant Woman," from *Prince of Darkness and Other Stories* by J. F. Powers. Copyright 1943, 1944, 1946, 1947 by J. F. Powers. Copyright 1943, 1944, 1946, 1947 by J. F. Powers. By permission of Doubleday & Company, Inc.

JAMES PURDY, "Daddy Wolf." From *Children Is All* by James Purdy. © 1961 by James Purdy. By permission of New Directions, Publishers.

JOHN CROWE RANSOM, "Bells for John Whiteside's Daughter;" and "Philomela." Copyright 1924, by Alfred A. Knopf, Inc. Renewed, 1952, by John Crowe Ransom. Reprinted from *Selected Poems* by John Crowe Ransom, by permission of Alfred A. Knopf, Inc.

ISHMAEL REED, "The Black Cock." Reprinted by permission of Ishmael Reed and The University of Massachusetts Press from *Conjure* by Ishmael Reed, 1972.

ADRIENNE RICH, "Living in Sin." Reprinted from *Poems, Selected and New, 1950–1974* by Adrienne Rich. With permission of W. W. Norton Company, Inc. Copyright © 1975, 1973, 1971, 1969, 1966 by W. W. Norton Company, Inc. Copyright © 1967, 1963, 1962, 1961, 1960, 1959, 1958, 1957, 1956, 1955, 1954, 1953, 1952, 1951 by Adrienne Rich.

EDWIN ARLINGTON ROBINSON, "Richard Cory." From *Children of the Night*, reprinted by permission of Charles Scribner's Sons.

THEODORE ROETHKE, "The Abyss." By permission of Mrs. Theodore Roethke.

DELMORE SCHWARTZ, "For Rhoda," from *In Dreams Begin Responsibilities*. Copyright, 1938, by New Directions. "In Dreams Begin Responsibilities," from *The World Is a Wedding* by Delmore Schwartz. Copyright 1948 by Delmore Schwartz. Reprinted by permission of New Directions, Publishers. "The Heavy Bear Who Walks with Me." From *Selected Poems: Summer Knowledge*. Copyright 1938 by New Directions Publishing Corporation. Reprinted by permission of New Directions Publishing Corporation.

HUGH SEIDMAN, "The Days: Cycle"; from *Collecting Evidence*. Reprinted by permission of Yale University Press. Copyright © 1970 by Hugh Seidman. Originally published in *Chelsea*.

ANNE SEXTON, "For My Lover Returning to His Wife." From *Love Poems*, copyright © 1967, 1968, 1969 by Anne Sexton. Reprinted by permission of the publisher, Houghton Mifflin Company.

KARL SHAPIRO, "Hollywood." Copyright 1942 and renewed 1970 by Karl Shapiro. Reprinted from *Selected Poems*, by Karl Shapiro, by permission of Random House, Inc.

GEORGE BERNARD SHAW, "Saint Joan." Copyright 1924, 1930, George Bernard Shaw. Copyright 1951, 1957, The Public Trustee as Executor of the Estate of George Bernard Shaw. By permission of The Public Trustee and the Society of Authors. "Pygmalion." Reprinted by permission of The Society of Authors on behalf of the Bernard Shaw Estate.

LOUIS SIMPSON, "Doubting." From *Adventures of the Letter I* by Louis Simpson. Copyright © 1970 by Louis Simpson.

W. D. SNODGRASS, "What We Said." From *After Experience* by W. D. Snodgrass. Copyright © 1958 by W. D. Snodgrass.

GARY SNYDER, "For the Boy Who Was Dodger Point Lookout Fifteen Years Ago." From *The Back Country* by Gary Snyder. Copyright © 1966 by Gary Snyder. Reprinted by permission of New Directions Publishing Corporation.

SOPHOCLES, *The Oedipus Rex of Sophocles: An English Version by Dudley Fitts and Robert S. Fitzgerald*, copyright 1949, by Harcourt Brace Jovanovich, Inc., and reprinted with their permission.

STEPHEN SPENDER, "An Elementary School Classroom in a Slum" (*Ruins and Vision, Poems 1934–1942*), Stephen Spender. Copyright 1942 by Stephen Spender. Reprinted from *Collected Poems, 1928–1953*, by Stephen Spender, by permission of Random House, Inc., and Faber and Faber, Ltd.

JEAN STAFFORD, "Bad Characters." Reprinted with permission of Farrar, Straus & Giroux, Inc., from *Collected Stories* by Jean Stafford. Copyright © 1954, 1964 by Jean Stafford.

JOHN STEINBECK, "Flight," from *The Portable Steinbeck*. Copyright 1938, 1943 by John Steinbeck. Reprinted by permission of The Viking Press, New York.

JAMES STEPHENS, "A Glass of Beer." Copyright 1918 by the Macmillan Publishing Co., Inc. Reprinted with permission of the Macmillan Publishing Co., Inc., and Macmillan Company of Canada Ltd.

WALLACE STEVENS, "The Idea of Order at Key West." Copyright 1936 by Wallace Stevens. "Anecdote of the Jar." Copyright 1923 and renewed 1951 by Wallace Stevens. Reprinted from *The Collected Poems of Wallace Stevens* by permission of Alfred A. Knopf, Inc.

MARK STRAND, "From a Litany." From *Darker* by Mark Strand. Reprinted by permission of Atheneum Publishers. Appeared originally in *TriQuarterly*.

ALLEN TATE, "Death of Little Boys" and "Sonnets at Christmas," from *Poems—1922–1947* by Allen Tate; copyright 1932, 1948 by Charles Scribner's Sons; by permission of the publishers.

PETER TAYLOR, "Two Pilgrims." Reprinted with permission of Farrar, Straus & Giroux, Inc., from *Collected Stories* by Peter Taylor. Copyright © 1963, 1969 by Peter Taylor, originally appeared in *The New Yorker*. "A Wife of Nashville." Reprinted by permission of the author. Copyright 1949 New Yorker Magazine, Inc.

DYLAN THOMAS, "A Refusal to Mourn;" and "The force that through the green fuse." From *The Collected Poems of Dylan Thomas*. © 1957 by New Directions. Reprinted by permission of New Directions, Publishers, and J. M. Dent & Sons, Ltd. "After the Fair" and "Enemies," from *Adventures in the Skin Trade*. Copyright 1939, 1955, by New Directions Publishing Corporation. Reprinted by permission of New Directions Publishing Corporation, and J. H. Dent & Sons, Ltd.

JAMES THURBER, "The Catbird Seat." Copyright © 1945 James Thurber. Copyright © 1963 Helen W. Thurber and Rosemary Thurber Sauers. From *The Thurber Carnival* published by Harper & Row, New York. Originally printed in *The New Yorker*.

JOHN UPDIKE, "Tomorrow and Tomorrow and So Forth." Copyright, 1955 by John Updike. "Tomorrow and Tomorrow and So Forth," first appeared in the *New Yorker*. Reprinted from *The Same Door* by John Updike by permission of Alfred A. Knopf, Inc.

GIOVANNI VERGA, "La Lupa." Reprinted from *Cavalleria Rusticana* by Giovanni Verga. Translated by D. H. Lawrence. Copyright 1928 by The Dial Press, 1955 by Frieda Lawrence. By permission of The Dial Press, Jonathan Cape, Ltd., Laurence Pollinger Limited and the Estate of the late Mrs. Frieda Lawrence.

DIANE WAKOSKI, "I Lay Next to You All Night Trying Awake to Understand the Watering Places of the Moon." From *The Motorcycle Betrayal Poems* by Diane Wakoski. Copyright © 1971 by Diane Wakoski. Reprinted by permission of Simon and Schuster.

EUDORA WELTY, "Keela, The Outcast Indian Maiden," copyright 1941, 1969, by Eudora Welty. Reprinted from her volume *A Curtain of Green and Other Stories* by permission of Harcourt Brace Jovanovich, Inc.

PHILIP WHEELWRIGHT, "Metaphor and Reality." By permission of the Indiana University Press.

THORNTON WILDER, "The Skin of Our Teeth." *The Skin of Our Teeth: A Play in Three Acts.* Copyright 1942 by Thornton Wilder. Reprinted with permission of Harper & Row, Publisher.

OSCAR WILLIAMS, "The Leg in the Subway," from *Selected Poems*, copyright 1947 by Oscar Williams. By permission of the publishers, Charles Scribner's Sons.

WILLIAM CARLOS WILLIAMS, "The Red Wheelbarrow." From *The Collected Earlier Poems of William Carlos Williams*. Copyright, 1938, 1951, by William Carlos Williams. Reprinted by permission of New Directions Publishing Corporation. "The Use of Force," from *The Farmer's Daughters* by William Carlos Williams. Copyright 1938 by William Carlos Williams, by permission of New Directions Publishing Corporation.

JAMES WRIGHT, "At the Slackening of the Tide." Copyright © 1959 by James Wright. Reprinted from *Saint Judas* by James Wright, by permission of Wesleyan University Press.

RICHARD WRIGHT, "The Man Who Was Almost a Man." Reprinted by permission of The World Publishing Company from *Eight Men* by Richard Wright. Copyright © 1961, 1940 by Richard Wright.

WILLIAM BUTLER YEATS, "The Wild Swans at Coole," from *The Wild Swans at Coole;* "That the Night Come," from *Responsibilities;* and "A Prayer for My Daughter," from *Later Poems* by William Butler Yeats, 1922. By permission of the Macmillan Company. "In Memory of Major Roberts Gregory," from *Collected Poems of William Butler Yeats*, copyright 1937. By permission of Mrs. W. B. Yeats and A. P. Watt & Son, Ltd.

PREFACE

This fifth edition is the sixth version of a book for courses in the introduction to literature that was first published in 1936. The method of that book of long ago was uncompromisingly inductive; that is, the student was to proceed by examining one specific instance after another in order to discover the nature of literature — from what impulses it springs, what needs it satisfies, what interests it nourishes, what forms it may assume. In each division of literature (basically, fiction, poetry, and drama, though some editions included essays and biography), the book was designed to move from the simple to the complex, from examples that might appeal immediately to the student to those demanding more experience and training. The progression, then, was not characteristically chronological (though in the division of drama, for special reasons, it happens to be so); the examples were drawn from various periods to illustrate to the student that historical differences, in language, style, attitude, and theme, are significant, and that literature, in general, is a human development in time. For instance, in the sections on poetry (where, because of the relatively small scale of each unit, variety can be greatest) early folk ballads, Victorian poems, Elizabethan songs, and twentieth-century poems would appear cheek by jowl.

We should emphasize, however, that in spite of the differences among the basic modes of literature, and in spite of the variety of selections within a mode, we conceived of our book as a unit. We hoped that the study of fiction would prepare the student for poetry, and that both would provide a basis for drama. More specifically, we tried to build into the book many interrelations of method and theme, sometimes specified, sometimes not. To sum up, we constantly held in mind that our final concern has to do with what we may call the literary imagination, and not merely aspects of a particular literary mode.

What differences appear in this new edition?

Though our experience with this book, and that of a massive number of other teachers, has not persuaded us to alter the basic principles from which we started, we have striven, in each revision, but especially in this, to refine our methods, to sharpen our formulations, to absorb benefits from on-going scholarship and criticism, and to broaden the base of appeal in our selections.

For instance, as a refinement of the inductive method, we have now dropped the general Introduction, with its elaborate theoretical discussion, and have tried to absorb those ideas, bit by bit, into later commentaries as they seemed relevant; and this process has meant, most immediately, a re-casting of the treatment of fiction. (It should be added that among the thirty-nine stories and novelettes here included, fifteen selections are new.)

The poetry sections have a completely new introduction and, though retaining the general basic divisions (narrative, tone, imagery, theme, and so forth), have been completely restructured. The most obvious novelty involves the thorniest and most recalcitrant of subjects: metrics and other technical questions. The last of the poetry sections provides a continuing and heavily illustrated discussion of such matters, but experience suggests that students should not be subjected to massive doses. By the new plan, as need arises and occasion fruitfully presents itself, students are given small doses — that is, they are referred to a topic (and subsection) in the technical discussion that has some special relation to what they have just been reading. Well before students have finished reading all works in the poetry sections, they will have absorbed, we hope, the principles of meter and other technical matters. The full and coherent discussion, however, is always available for reference or for such special study as a teacher may feel desirable.

We have retained the backlog of traditional poems, but have, from the opening pages, introduced a number of poems from the first half of this century. The section on individual poets (Keats, Dickinson, and Frost) is retained. We have added, however, an entirely new section, "Some Poets of This Time," which contains work by twenty-eight writers, some of them very young, who are representative of the variety of poetic impulses found in the last decade or so and at this moment. These pieces are presented without comment, with the idea that if students have deepened their sense of poetry, they may now venture into the poetry of the world of their own time. To summarize changes in the contents of the poetry sections: total number of entries, 219; number of entries new to this edition, 99; number of entries by twentieth-century poets, 84. It should be remarked that among the 219 entries there are several very long selections: Eliot's *The Waste Land,* Gray's "Elegy in a Country Churchyard," and 310 lines of Whitman's "Song of Myself."

The student's earlier study of fiction and poetry prepares for, and feeds into, the final section, that on drama. Drama obviously shares with fiction problems and terms, such as exposition, motivation, and denouement; and the study of poetry ought to have quickened the student's appreciation of the finer verbal effects of drama. Besides, three of the plays we include are actually in verse. But in our presentation we have not neglected the special characteristics of drama. The eight plays, in their chronological range and in their variety of spirit, mode, and method, provide a splendid introduction to the genre. Not least in our justification of the choice of plays is their intrinsic quality: we seriously doubt that this list could be bettered.

An Approach to Literature provides a very liberal selection of fiction, poetry, and drama, and it is scarcely to be expected that the book will be regularly used from cover to cover. What we have tried to do, now more positively than ever, is to give teachers room to maneuver, a range of choices out of which they can tailor a course to their special needs and to the tastes and capacities of their students. But there is one more thought that we have held in mind: the surplus of reading material will not necessarily be wasted. Every class is uneven, and in a class in which the whole book is not used, there will always be a certain number of students with an intellectual curiosity and taste for reading that will lure them into the unassigned material so readily available.

This revision has been a long and arduous task, and could scarcely have been completed without help from many quarters. Our gratitude is deep-felt to those teachers who, as the fruit of their experience with the book, have offered criticisms and suggestions. More specifically, we wish to thank David Milch of Yale University, Marilyn Brauer and Robb Reavill of Prentice-Hall, and Claude Conyers, whose notations and suggestions have often raised copyediting to a form of literary criticism.

C.B.
R.P.W.

CONTENTS

FICTION

Section 9 Scale, Pace, and Time, 205

Section 10 Stories, 261

POETRY

Section 15   **Imagery,** 400

GROUP 1:   FROM IMAGE TO SYMBOL, *401*

GROUP 2:   DISCOURSE AND COMPLEXITY OF METAPHOR, *411*

GROUP 3: IMAGES—OR SYMBOLS—TO EXPLORE, *428*

Section 16   Theme, 432

GROUP 1: THE CONDUCT OF LIFE, *433*

DRAMA

AN
APPROACH
TO
LITERATURE

FICTION

Section 1

INTRODUCTION

THE NATURE OF FICTION

Why do we like fiction?

The most obvious and fundamental answer is that we like it because we like it. The hairy brutes of prehistory huddling around the night fire of the cave were bemused by a tale, and the telling of tales, in one form or another, has not ceased since then. To like a story seems as natural to us as to like food or drink. It is an attribute of our nature.

We can, however, go beyond that fundamental answer to our question. As civilized, self-conscious human beings, we want to see what aspects of our nature are involved in our apparently instinctive liking. In other words, we want to know more about our own nature, more about the nature of fiction, and more about the way in which the two are related.

Even the hairy brute by the cave fire was a human being. In fact, we might say that he had become truly human just at that moment when he could become bemused by a tale—when, that is, he could escape by the magic of imagination* from the bonds of time, place, and, even, the self. And since the hairy brute had reached the stage of being truly human, for him the appetite for a tale must now have been far from simple. He was, already, the most complex thing in nature, and in one dimension—insofar as he had language—had left nature behind.

We can't know exactly what passed through our ancestor's unbarbered, low-browed, and jut-jawed head as he listened to a tale, but it is a safe guess that the underlying reason he listened was that the tale enhanced his sense of life. The hunt or the battle was relived, with the evocation of all the emotions associated with the literal event—but now without the literal risks, so that those emotions, even the terror and despair, might be savored and, in some sense, understood. The tale was of conflict—that is, something was at stake in the events narrated; and conflict, as we shall see, with its awakening, imaginatively, of our emotions and the enhancing of our sense of life, remains the great central fact of our fiction, from the simplest tale to the most complex and sophisticated novel.

Such must have been the underlying reason for the attention to the tale, but for even the most primitive auditor other reasons must have been present, and, from folklore, myths, and fairy tales preserved into our age, we can get some hints of what they were. For one thing, threatened by beasts and other men, darkness, floods, inexplicable thunderstorms, and all the murderously whimsical powers that ruled the world, and aware of his own weakness, the poor creature in the cave longed to be bigger, stronger, and grander than he was. And he could be—for as long as the tale of hero or demigod lasted—or even the tale of some fellow who, though little, was very cunning, or very lucky. So we have the epics of heroes, such as Achilles and Aeneas and Beowulf, and fairy tales such as Hans Christian Andersen's "The Tinder Box," which we give here in summary:

---

* The anthropologist Carleton S. Coon describes such a group by the tribal fire: "Fire has four basic uses: frightening off predators, keeping people warm and dry, cooking food, and providing a spatial nucleus or center for the home territory of a group of people. Here they can sit at night, warm and secure, seeing one another's faces in the firelight, talking over what they did during the day while they were separated, acting out scenes of the hunt, planning for the next day's adventures, discussing matrimonial prospects, and generally getting to know one another so well that friction can be kept at a minimum. They may also dance by firelight, and conduct ceremonies. It is difficult to see how, without fire, human society could have risen much above the level of that of baboons." *The Origin of Races* (New York: Alfred A. Knopf, 1962).

On the highroad a soldier meets an ugly old witch, who indicates an old tree in which, she tells him, is a hole that will let him go down into an underground corridor. There he will find three doors. Behind one is a chest on which sits a dog with eyes as big as saucers and in the chest copper coins; behind the second, a dog with eyes as big as millwheels, on a chest full of silver coins; and behind the third, a dog with eyes as big as the Round Tower, on a chest full of gold coins. If he takes her blue-checked apron, ties a rope round himself so that she can pull him back up, and goes boldly in to each dog in turn and sets him on the apron, he can help himself to all the money he wants. Only he must bring back up an old tinder box, which, she says, her mother had left down there.

The soldier does as directed, comes back loaded with, of course, gold, and when the witch won't tell him what she wants with the tinder box, slashes off her head with his sword and leaves her in the road, while he goes on to the city. At the city he sets up fine quarters in a hotel and leads the life of a gentleman, dreaming meanwhile of the local princess, whose father keeps her locked up in a copper castle, all because there's a prophecy that she will marry a common soldier. Meanwhile his money runs out, he goes into mean quarters, and one night, trying to light his last bit of candle, he strikes the flint on the steel of his tinder box, and suddenly the dog with eyes as big as saucers appears, and asks his command. "Money," the soldier says, and the dog comes back with a bag full of copper coins in his mouth. Strike once, he discovers, and the first dog comes with copper; twice, the dog with silver; and three times, the horrid big dog with gold.

Now the soldier has the power to have the princess brought at night to the grand chambers that he again inhabits, but when the princess next morning reports that she has had a fine dream of riding on the back of a great dog and being kissed by a soldier, the king orders a lady-in-waiting to keep watch by her bed. The lady, seeing the princess taken off by the dog, pursues them to the doorway of a great house, which she marks with chalk. But the next morning, when she leads the king and his court to find the door, all doors are marked with chalk, thanks to the cleverness of the faithful dog.

The next night the dog comes again, but this time the lady has tied a little bag of seed around the neck of the princess, with a tiny hole in the bag so that a trail will be left. So the soldier is found and is condemned to be hanged. On the morning of the execution, he sees, from the window of his cell, a lad hurrying past to be on time for the sport. He hails the lad and promises him a penny to fetch the tinder box from the hotel.

With the box in his pocket, the soldier is led to the great gallows, where the king and queen and all the court wait in state to watch. The soldier asks the boon of smoking a last pipe. When the king kindly grants this request, the little soldier strikes on the tinder box and summons up all the dogs, who kill the king and queen and all the councilors. So the people hail the soldier as their king and the princess delightedly marries him, and they rule happily forever afterward.

The tale is like a daydream. All wishes are here fulfilled with the effortlessness of dream. There is no ordinary logic. The little soldier is not virtuous, industrious, wise, good, or kind. He is not even very clever. He has no quality that would merit success. He is merely lucky, and the only logic in his story is that of the naked wish. So now in our time, not merely for children but for adults, there is a great body of fiction (as well as movies and plays) that, behind the façade of some ordinary logic of plot, simply provides the satisfaction of the same old daydreams—of money, sex, power, status.

Sometimes, however, a dream may be of a less self-aggrandizing sort. Even when we read what is called "escape fiction," we may not be trying to escape into another grander self, but into a world resembling one that our own poor, limited self once inhabited and enjoyed, as when an aging woman turns to stories of young love; or into a world that we have never had and can never have, as when a middle-aged, balding, family-trapped man in straitened circumstances reads stories of travel or adventure in far and glamorous places.

To all of us, that is what, in one sense, fiction is—a daydream. It is, in other words, an imaginative enactment. In it we find, in imagination, not only the pleasure of recognizing the world we have known and of reliving the past, but also the pleasure of entering worlds we do not know and of experimenting with experiences which we deeply crave but which the limitations of life, the fear of consequences, or the severity of our principles forbid to us. Fiction can give us this pleasure. In fiction we escape limitations and penalties. But fiction gives us not only what we want; more importantly, it may give us things we hadn't even known we wanted.

As a daydream—a mere daydream—fiction may be for us, as for our hairy progenitor in the cave, a very crude and simple enriching of our lives, enlarging the self and its experiences. But if fiction is—as it clearly is for some readers—merely a fantasy to redeem the liabilities of our private fate, it is a flight from reality and therefore, paradoxically, the enemy of growth, of the very life process. But is it necessarily such a stultifying flight?

For the intelligent reader, the daydream that is fiction differs from the ordinary daydream in being publicly available. This fact has consequences. In the purely private daydream you remain yourself—though nobler, stronger, more fortunate, more beautiful than in life. But when a spindly youth, for instance, settles cozily with his thriller by Mickey Spillane, he is likely to find that the granite-jawed hero is not Slim Willett after all—as poor Slim, with his thin chest and low mark in algebra, longs for him to be.

In other words, to enter into the publicly available daydream that fiction is, you have to accept, if you are intelligent, the fact that the name of the hero will never quite be your own. The publicly available daydream is not exquisitely cut to your secret longings, and the identification can never be complete. In fact, only the very naïve reader tries to make it thrillingly complete. The more sophisticated reader plays a deep double game with himself; one part of him is identified with a character—or even with several in turn, if he is very adept at the double game—while another part holds aloof to respond, interpret, and judge. How often have we heard some sentimental old lady say of a book: "I just loved the heroine. I mean, I just went through everything with her, and I knew

exactly how she felt. Then when she died, I just really cried." The sweet old lady, even if she isn't very sophisticated, is instinctively playing the double game, too: she identifies with the heroine, but she also survives the heroine's death to shed delicious tears.

Even the old lady knows how to make the most of what we call her role-taking. She knows that doubleness, in the very act of identification, is of the essence of role-taking. Part of the self remains the old self, and part takes the role. Fiction is, in imaginative enactment, a role-taking.

For some people—those who fancy themselves hardheaded and realistic—the business of role-taking is as reprehensible as indulgence in a daydream. But in trying to understand our appetite for fiction, we can see that the process of role-taking not only stems from, but also affirms, the life process. It is an essential part of growth.

To begin with, role-taking is at the very center of children's play. In it begins the child's long process of adaptation to others, for only by feeling himself into another person's skin can he predict behavior; and the stakes in the game are high, for only thus does he learn how to expect the kiss or the slap. In this process of role-taking we find, too, the roots of many of the massive intellectual structures we later rear—most obviously psychology and ethics; for it is only by role-taking that the child comes to know, to know "inwardly" in the only way that finally counts, that other people really exist and are, in fact, persons with needs, hopes, fears, and, even, rights. So the role-taking of fiction, at the same time that it gratifies our deep need to extend and enrich our experience, continues this long discipline in human sympathy. And this discipline in sympathy, through the imaginative enactment of role-taking, gratifies another deep need in us: our yearning to enter and feel at ease in the human community.

It is by role-taking that we go far beyond the satisfactions afforded by the merely personal daydream to those fuller satisfactions of discovering selves other than what we ordinarily regard as our own. We may enter the skin of saint or sinner, humanitarian or murderer, aristocrat or guttersnipe. We discover, that is, the complex and contradictory possibilities of our own self—our "official" self.

The official self emerges as the child grows up, but the soul, as Plato long ago put it, remains full of "ten thousand opposites occurring at the same time," and modern psychology has said nothing to contradict him. All our submerged selves, our outlaw selves, the old rejected possibilities and desires, are lurking deep in us, sleepless and eager to have another go. There is knife-fighting in the inner dark. The fact that most of the time we are not aware of trouble does not mean that trouble is any the less present and significant; and fiction, most often in subtly disguised forms, liberatingly reenacts for us such inner conflicts. We feel the pleasure of liberation even when we cannot specify the source of the pleasure.

In experiencing, even though unconsciously, the complexity of the self, we feel better prepared to deal with that self. As a matter of fact, our entering into the fictional process helps to redefine the dominant self—even, as it were, to re-create it on a sounder basis, sounder because better understood. As the philosopher Henri Bergson says, fiction "brings us back into our own presence"—the presence in which we must make our final terms with life and death. And this process, too, means a sense of liberation.

Let us return to our hairy progenitor. It is true that what primarily makes him listen to the telling of the tale is, presumably, the yearning to dream a grander self—a yearning that may end, generations later, in the imaginative penetration into the inner selves of others and into the secrets of our own selfhood. But this, with all its consequences, is only one of our progenitor's yearnings. It is very important for him to make what sense he can of the mysterious and inimical world he lives in, to get the hang of it, to under-stand the logic by which the shadowy powers around him conduct the affairs of the world. So we find the myths in which man has sought to explain how his world came to exist, to understand the nature of gods and the nature of his own relation to them. And the element of the mythic—to strain the word somewhat—remains in fiction to this day.

For most of our explanations of the world, society and ourselves, we now turn to scientists, sociologists, and historians, but allowing for all the margins of certainty that, mistakenly or not, we pride ourselves on having achieved, the fate of man, like the nature of man, remains veiled. So every piece of fiction, whether the writer is conscious of the fact or not, whether the fiction is trivial or not, represents an attempt to make some sense of man's lot, to demonstrate some logic in his experience. And on this point, fiction enhances—and reflects—our awareness of life.

Even in childhood we begin the attempt to make some sense of our lives, to think of some pattern of cause and effect, to try to see ourselves in significant relation to other people; and the older we grow, the more the part of life already lived challenges us to make sense of it, the more it resembles, to borrow the phrase the Book of Common Prayer applies to the finished life, "a tale told." Long before life is finished, however, and the tale is told, we yearn to understand the logic, the meaning—the "theme" shall we say—of our individual lives, just as we thrust on, in reading a story, to understand the logic inherent in it, and the theme that in the end brings that logic to focus.*

THE STRUCTURE OF FICTION

Thus far we have been generally concerned not with the form of fiction, but with the content, not with the "telling" of a story,

---

* Here it may be objected that some fiction denies logic (which is very different, however, from failing in logic—for example, in presenting the motivation of a character). It is true that some fiction does emphasize the irony of the irrational element in experience; or we have in recent years what is called the literature of the "absurd" (see section 21), in which meaninglessness is taken to be the central fact of existence; or we have what is called "black humor," which may merge with the literature of the absurd. But even in such work the issue of logic is simply pushed back a stage. The issue reappears in the question: in a world of irony, absurdity, or black humor (that is, of illogicality), what attitude may a man ("logically") take toward life, to assert himself as real? And in asking this question, we should remember, too, that to assert "illogicality" is a "logical" act—as in *Alice in Wonderland*.

but with "what is told." But a piece of fiction basically represents the writer's ideas and feelings about life and its meaning—in short, what we may call his vision of life. This vision, we must insist, as vitally penetrates and informs the "telling" as it does the "told."

The story, in a fictional sense, is not, we must remember, something that exists of and by itself, out in the world, like a stone or a tree or a person. The *materials* of fiction—certain objects and persons—may exist out in the world, but they are not fictionally meaningful to us until a human mind has shaped them. In other words, we are like the princess in one of Hans Christian Andersen's fairy tales: she refuses her suitor when she discovers that the bird with the ravishing song he has offered as a token of love is only a real bird after all. We, like the princess, want an *artificial* bird with a *real* song. Ultimately we go to fiction because it is a *created* thing.

Because fiction is a created thing, it draws us, as human beings, by its human significance. The material, existing out in the world, does indeed have its human significance, but both the general fact of its being shaped and the particular way of the shaping have a significance perhaps even deeper. They represent the effort of a human mind to seize on the inner nature of experience. In trying to do this, the author must give the material an expressive structure, must discover a relation among all the elements of the material to embody his vision—or, we may even say, to discover his vision, for the vision may not become clear to him except as he struggles toward a formulation of it, an embodiment.

In our discussion of the structure of fiction we must begin by emphasizing that every successful example of fiction is an expressive *unity*, that the structural elements that can be distinguished and analyzed are, in actuality, parts of an organic unity, just as hands, feet, liver and lights, circulatory system, brain cells, and so forth are parts of the organic unity we call the body, intimately related in the ongoing life process. In our discussion of structure we must continually hold this fact in mind, for we are, ultimately, concerned with the elements of fictional structure *only insofar as they function in the vital unity of an individual story or novel.*

There is another thing to hold in mind as we proceed. Even if, at moments, the discussion of structure may seem abstract and academic, it is the only systematic way of really answering the natural and spontaneous questions that spring to mind about a piece of fiction. Take, for instance, the questions that the city editor of a newspaper tells the cub reporter he must answer for any news story: *What? Who? Where? When?* These questions, for the news story, concern the hard objective facts; but sometimes, when information is available, the news story may even consider another and more subjective question: *Why?*

These are the same questions that we must ask about a piece of fiction. We want to know how it answers them. But we are instinctively aware that the kinds of answers we expect from a piece of fiction are, in the end, more complex than those offered by a news story. Furthermore, even the most trivial piece of fiction provokes a question that the city editor never tells the cub reporter he must answer: *What does it mean?* And the answer to that is the most complex of all. Our discussion must deal with the kind of complexity that the nature of fiction dictates, but it must be remembered that behind the complexity lie the natural and spontaneous questions, and that those questions shape the order of our discussion.

Most obviously, fiction is a kind of narrative. But there are many kinds of narrative that are not fiction. The husband returning from work asks his wife, "What happened today?" She says, "Oh, nothing. Not really. I just got the children off to school, then I went shopping. Oh, yes, your mother called, just to see how we are. Oh, nothing really." So far we have a narrative—a mere sequence of events in time—and the husband will be listening, if at all, merely out of politeness. But just let his wife say, "Oh, yes, something did happen! Mrs. Harris came over here crying her eyes out. The police picked up Danny—you know what a fine-looking, polite boy he is, and how fine the Harrises are. Well, it seems that Danny . . ."

The husband is all ears now. He is listening because something has "happened"—

the kind of happening that fiction involves: what is called an *action*. We have at least the beginning of an action. By action we mean not a particular act, deed, or event, not a mere sequence of such items, but a *sequence of items bearing a significant and developing relation to one another*.* To understand what is meant by such a significantly developing relation we must consider the logical stages of an action as ordinarily described: the *Beginning*, the *Middle*, and the *End*.

The key fact of the Beginning is that it presents a conflict. There may be a collision between one person and another, between one group and another, between a person (or group) and some element in the world around, or between various needs, impulses, or values within a person. Conflict is the essential germ of an action: *no conflict, no action*. The Beginning must adequately present the nature of the conflict, and give some indication of what is at stake in it. It presents, that is, an unstable situation from which an action must move toward a moment of stability. Conflict is the dynamic of action. The Middle consists of the stages by which the conflict moves toward its resolution, by which instability gives place to stability. If we have only the Beginning and then, immediately, the End, there is no action, or at least only an aborted one. The End exhibits the achievement of stability, the resolution of whatever forces were in conflict.

The Nature of an Action

Thus far we have regarded an action as primarily representing a way of regarding events in the external world. And here it is important to realize that only by being able to recognize an action are we able to live effectively in the real world. If we simply look at the multitudinous events of the world streaming past us, they make no sense. They make sense only insofar as we can isolate certain groups from the blurred mass, and recognize

them—*interpret* them—as an action. Such interpretation may be applied to the past, present, or future. An old woman looking back to assess her past life, a lad in the middle of a tennis match trying to assess his opponent's strategy, a businessman planning a sales program—all are trying to recognize in the welter of events the logical structure of an action, large or small, with its tripartite division.

A historian, for example, would see the American Revolution as an action. He might regard the Beginning as the events leading up to the Declaration of Independence, by which the issue was sharply defined; the Middle, as the events of military, political, and social importance leading up to the surrender of Cornwallis; the End, as the movement toward the ratification of the Constitution in 1788, the event establishing the new nation. Another historian dealing with the same subject, might, however, define his action differently, for instance, by seeing the End as the movement toward the adopting of the Articles of Confederation in 1781. We must realize, too, that the events a particular historian takes to constitute his action are still connected with other events coming before and after, and that another historian (or even this one with another purpose) might take another perspective. For instance, the American Revolution itself might be regarded as merely an episode (in the Middle, say) of an action involving the rise of modern democracy, or of one involving the rise of the British Empire.

In all of the instances we have referred to, great and small, we have thought of the action as existing out in the world—a sequence of events logically related to one another in time. This notion of an action as existing in the external world underlies fiction, too. The writer of fiction *may* base his work on an action drawn, literally, from the external world—that is, from events in the external world that he has recognized as constituting an action—or from an imagined ac-

---

* In relation to fiction an action must involve human beings. Even in stories about animals, say in Beatrix Potter's *The Tale of Peter Rabbit* or Jack London's *The Call of the Wild*, the animal is a human being in disguise.

tion. *What is important here is that the action, whether literal or imagined, is assumed to have existed prior to, and independent of, the finished fiction.* In either case, the action is thought of as, in a sense, the "raw material" to be manipulated in what we call the *plot.*

The Nature of Plot

The writer's process of manipulation involves two aspects: *selection* and *ordering.* As for selection, we must recall that an action involves (theoretically, at least, for the imagined one), the infinite mass of details characteristic of events in the real world. Since, clearly, the writer could not, and should not try to, reproduce this massiveness of actuality, he must select the details that he thinks important because *relevant* or *suggestive.* Here the relevant items may be understood as those essential to establishing the logic of the action —that is, the impression of cause and effect and of a meaningful conclusion. The suggestive are those that provoke the imagination to attribute the density and immediacy of events in the actual world to those in the fiction. Such suggestive detail in fiction is one of the things that gives the impression of lifelikeness, that help to sustain the *illusion* of reality, that imply the massivenests of actuality. With the question of ordering, we are dealing, in one sense, with selectivity again, for certainly all details of action cannot be accommodated in a plot. But more specially, the writer often finds it necessary in creating his plot to violate the strict logical and chronological sequence characteristic of the action that is his raw material. From early times, storytellers have, for various reasons, felt free to distort the sequence of an underlying action. For instance, we find as early as Homer the practice of beginning the plot *in medias res*—that is, "in the middle of things."

This means, of course, that the action, in its chronological order, has begun at a point earlier than the first event given in the actual piece of narrative. For instance, the first episode of the story "The Tinder Box" might be that in which the Little Soldier, still in his old uniform, goes into a fine hotel and, to general surprise, asks for the best room in the establishment. Then, at some later point, the narrator, to make the story make sense, would have to go back to the episode of the meeting with the witch—that is, to the beginning of the action. (Below is a chart to illustrate both selection and ordering in the projection of action into plot.*)

The action, then, is the raw material of plot. It is the story behind the story as we find it formed into fiction. The plot is the action as we find it projected, by whatever selection of event and distortion of chronology, into the fiction that we actually confront.

The plot is the final shaping of the action, and the key to the distinction between action and plot is that the writer manipulates the action in accordance with two (interrelated) impulses, or needs: to engage the reader imaginatively as well as intellectually, and to render his own vision. These impulses make for certain changes in the structure of plot as compared with that of the action. So in plot the divisions of structure as described for action may, as we have suggested in our chart, interpenetrate to a greater or lesser degree. And the interpenetration of structural elements makes it convenient in talking about plot to think in new structural terms, terms that do not merely describe the parts of an action, but emphasize the writer's role in manipulation.

Exposition refers to such elements as inform the reader of *facts necessary to understand the plot,* for instance, facts of time, persons, the preliminary condition of affairs,

*Sequence of action:

a b c d e f g h i j k l m n o p q r s t u v w x y z

SEQUENCE OF PLOT: *etc.*

H I N A B K L M N X Z

and what will be at stake in the basic motivations impelling the plot. Such elements are precisely the same that appear in the Beginning of an action, but in plot they may be, and often are, differently *distributed*. In his exposition, the writer deals the cards for the game, but we must remember that he may hold some back for another round—as does the dealer in stud poker.

The *complication* roughly corresponds to the stages by which, in the Middle of an action, the conflict moves toward resolution. Here we must emphasize that complication implies resistance to the movement toward solution of the problem from which the plot stems. It implies uncertainty, mounting intensity, as the conflict is being developed through complication toward the *climax*, the point at which the forces in conflict reach their moment of greatest concentration, the moment at which, as it develops subsequently, the apparently dominant force becomes the subordinate. It is the moment of the plot which is called the *turn*, the *reversal*, such as the moment when Pepé, in John Steinbeck's story "Flight" (sec. 3), after the posse has pursued him into the hills like an animal, stands erect, silhouetted against the sky, to receive the death-bullet and, in doing so, dies like a man.

Some pieces of fiction, such as "Wet Saturday," by John Collier (sec. 5), demonstrate very obviously this movement through complication toward what we call the *denouement*—literally, the "unknotting." There are, of course, stories of greater subtlety or complexity than the two described, such as "An Episode of War" by Stephen Crane (sec. 2), or "Keela, the Outcast Indian Maiden" by Eudora Welty (sec. 7), but we must remember that in all cases of effective fiction, the principle remains the same.

As has been implied in our discussion, without some development of complication there can be no body for a story. Consider, for instance:

SOMEBODY: I've got a story to tell you.
YOU: Fine, tell me.
SOMEBODY: You remember how Jim Hawkins wouldn't study and got kicked out of college?
YOU: Yes.

SOMEBODY: And wouldn't work, and took to drinking and was going to the dogs.
YOU: Sure, I remember.
SOMEBODY: Well, he met a girl at a dance and married her and settled down and now he's vice president of the bank in Murrayton.

It is clear that "Somebody" does not have a story to tell. Here we have the exposition (Jim is a drunken bum and meets the girl), and the next we know there is the denouement (he has married and is a banker). Was there no conflict? Was it love at first sight on both sides, and then no struggle to conquer the Demon Rum? Did Hawkins just walk into the Murrayton bank and get made a vice president next morning? Did everything work out, with no uncertainty, no resistance? But if there was, in fact, a conflict developing through various stages, then "Somebody" simply doesn't know how to tell a story. Here the dealer merely deals the cards face up, and there is no game.

Thus it is important to remember that the complication does not necessarily appear neatly between the exposition and the denouement, that, as we have earlier suggested in relation to Homer, the writer may, in his plot, distort the chronological order of an action. He may, as we have said, even start "in the middle of things"—that is, with what would actually be one of the elements of complication—and then return, by what is called a *cutback*, to introduce items of exposition. Indeed, a skillful writer may actually be able to interfuse so subtly complication and exposition that they can scarcely be distinguished, as in the first scene of Shakespeare's *Romeo and Juliet*, or—to turn again to a clever, but unpretentious, story—as in "Wet Saturday" by John Collier (sec. 5). But however it is worked out, in complication the writer puts the cards into play; but again, as in stud poker, the actual playing may start long before all cards are dealt.

The *denouement* is the end of the plot, literally, as we have said, the "unknotting" of the tangle of the complications. Here the conflict is resolved, stability is restored, Jack marries Jill, or the giant gets killed. The game is over and the stakes are claimed. But the full nature of what is at stake in the denouement we shall come to later, when we discuss *theme*.

Character

Up to this point we have discussed both action and plot abstractly, almost as though out of place and time and involving only robots or ghosts. But, as we have suggested earlier, fiction appeals to us because it is concerned with human beings, alive and fully fleshed. It must have, to begin with, the sense of the physical presence of persons, in a specific place and at a specific time. Necessary as is the sense of physical presence, however, it is not the final aspect of our concern with the persons appearing in fiction. Such persons, as we know, are called *characters*, and the term points to the importance of the essential nature of a person, of inner being and inner life.

Even in the kind of fiction called "action stories," such as adventure or detective fiction, the sense of character is crucial. In a fiction, however simple and rudimentary, the characters call our sympathies or antipathies into play. They invite us to identify with them, even gratifying our daydreams. Or they may, of course, repel us. Furthermore, even the crudest detective story, which may seem to engage our interest only because of the puzzle of the plot, depends on human character, human desires and fears, for the very existence of that plot. The story is not about X, Y, and Z, but about Archibald Donaldson, the polished and suave gentleman who commits seven murders before detection; Henry Milton, the gruff police inspector who has a softer side after all and collects old china; and Isabel Ravenal, the sweet-natured and high-spirited heiress whom the inspector saves from Mr. Donaldson. The personalities of X, Y, and Z must be established as Donaldson, Milton, and Ravenal, and they must interact with one another before we can have a plot at all.

A story is, in a sense, like a pinball game. Nobody cares whether a small metal ball bounces off a certain number of obstacles that ring bells and then falls into a slot in a polished board. We care only when some values can be attached to the operation. So when we turn X, Y, and Z into characters we assign values, human values. That an interest in mere plot cannot exist by itself, even in the detective story or adventure story, is amply indicated by the fact that the most successful and popular writers in those genres have a gift for characterization and can make the reader believe, for the moment anyway, in their people.

In the detective or adventure story, character not only "humanizes" the action, as we may say; it must also, in that process, motivate the action; it must provide a logic of action. The writer of a detective story who makes his criminal a mere lunatic has cheated the reader, and, no doubt, lost him for good. The reader of fiction wants to know the *why* of an action just as much as the *what*. Even in fiction that seems to be primarily concerned with portraying character—in what is called the character story, where the emphasis is primarily on the *who*—the reader wants to see the character in action, for action is the flowering of character. It is, indeed, the best way of knowing character; pretty is as pretty does, the old saying goes.

We may go a step further. Characters not only act, but are acted upon by other people, by circumstances, by the results, at some remove, of their own acts. People change with time and experience. A young man grows old. The degree in which he influences his own development may be great or small. We know how physical weaklings have, by force of will, made themselves, as Theodore Roosevelt did, into vigorous and effective men; but we also know how vigorous and effective men have been ruined by circumstances apparently beyond their control. But whatever a man, living through time, becomes, we feel that what he is cannot be thought of except in terms of his past, and that his final condition bears some relation, however shadowy, to his earlier character. There is a logic, hard to define as it sometimes is, of character as well as of action, and a logic of their interrelation; and the change of character in terms of such interrelation, may sometimes constitute the central fact of the plot of fiction. We see this most obviously and powerfully in certain large works, such as Shakespeare's *Hamlet* or *King Lear*, or in

Theodore Dreiser's novel *An American Tragedy*; but we see it, too, in a simple story such as "Flight," by John Steinbeck, which, as we have said, shows Pepé's growth into manhood, or, in a more complex fashion, in the discovery of love in D. H. Lawrence's "The Horse Dealer's Daughter" (sec. 8). Change is the essence of fiction, and the change of fortunes is certainly not less important than the change of self.

To summarize: *character is action, and action is character.*

In discussing the plot and character, we have been concerned with what may seem to be content, not form, with the "told," not the "telling." We have just said "seem to be," because, in actuality, in the organic unity of a piece of fiction, content and form interfuse. This is most obvious in the case of plot. On the one hand, it comes to us as the "story" we literally get—that is, as content. But on the other, it is, by definition, the writer's way of manipulating, shaping, or forming the massive raw action (which, however, we know only through plot). In the same sense, even though we think of character as content, we literally know it only as presented—that is, as it appears formed for us in the general structure. As with action, which is a raw material, we only get a sense of the "raw" character through what is fictionally formed.

Scene and Atmosphere

We often think of the *scene* of a piece of fiction—if we think of it at all—as little more than a detail, mechanically necessary of course, but without further significance. Sometimes, after we have finished a good story or novel, we do become aware that it has a characteristic "feel," that the world it has created carries a characteristic "atmosphere," and we become aware, too, that this atmosphere is a component of the whole effect.

A story occurs, after all, in a particular place, and places provoke, however minimally, certain feelings. A dingy alley provokes a feeling different from that naturally associated with a green field, a luxurious room, or a tropical jungle. Not only the

scene in itself, but the associations, enter into the characteristic feeling: we are depressed by the dingy alley, not merely because it is ugly and dirty, but because with it we associate, consciously or unconsciously, the poverty, misery, and struggle of the human beings forced to live there. So with the scene, the setting, of a story. We expect a kind of story from the jungle or merchant ship of Joseph Conrad (sec. 10) very different from that in the backcountry Mississippi of Faulkner's "Spotted Horses" (sec. 6). Sometimes, in fact, a writer may make the scene itself the very beginning of his work, as in Thomas Hardy's novel *The Return of the Native*, with the desolate vastness of the moor. But even when the writer does not insist on the scene, the effect may be there. In Verga's "La Lupa" (sec. 9), the image of the sexually insatiable woman wandering the sun-blazing paths of open country in Sicily is the very center of the story. Such a woman may exist anywhere, say in a poor slum or a rich drawing room, but here, in this fiercely lit emptiness of the Sicilian landscape, the woman seems merely an extension of nature, with nature, somehow, her fate. Again, could the story "The Gentleman from San Francisco" (sec. 8) really exist in another setting? Less obviously, the scene of "The Horse Dealer's Daughter" interpenetrates the story itself. Think of the blankness of the house about to be abandoned, and of the somnolent, rich, slow motion of the great shire horses being led past. Could we have such a story as "The Indian Uprising," by Donald Barthelme (sec. 8), except in the setting of a great modern city?

Again: *the scene is the story, and the story the scene.*

We have used the term *atmosphere.* Some critics tend to equate scene and atmosphere, but it is useful to distinguish them, even if they do have an intimate connection. The scene is a quite specifically identifiable place; atmosphere is a metaphor for a feeling or impression that we *may associate with a place but that may be created by other means.* We say that an old farmhouse set among large maples on a smooth lawn has an "atmosphere of peace," or that a cataract shadowed by lichened cliffs has a "romantic atmosphere." What we mean is that the house, by reason of the look of quietness *and* by reason of a number of associations we have with the kind of life characteristically lived in such a place remote from the hurrying world, stirs a certain response in our imagination, and so with the cataract. As with the various examples of stories included here, the scene does provoke a certain atmosphere.

But atmosphere does not necessarily depend on the scene or setting. The kind of vocabulary and the figures of speech used affect the atmosphere of a story. For instance, compare "The Gentleman from San Francisco" in this respect with "Spotted Horses" or "The Indian Uprising." The very rhythm of a prose style contributes to atmosphere; it may be short, brisk, and clipped or long and swinging, strongly accentuated or weakly, simple or complicated, and however unconsciously, such differences condition the reader's response. But atmosphere depends, too, on plot and character, even as it contributes to our reactions to them.

In short, we may say that the atmosphere of fiction is the pervasive, general feeling, created by a number of factors, that is characteristic of a given story or novel. That feeling, that atmosphere, which we associate with a good story (or other literary work) is really a kind of pervasive meaning, like electricity in a gathering storm. In recognizing it, we sense some kind of unity between the physical and the psychological, even the moral, spheres. It may even be a kind of circumambient metaphor, as is the atmosphere in "La Lupa," or, on a grander scale, in Shakespeare's *Macbeth*. In *Macbeth* the brooding darkness *is* the play.

Point of View

Our discussion of plot, character, and scene will serve as a preamble to our treatment of certain other elements of fictional structure that, at first glance, seem to be purely formal but that actually have a relation to content, too, in that they are indissolubly associated with, are aspects of, the meaning of a work.

The first of these elements is *point of view.*

When a writer approaches his story, he cannot set down a single word until he has answered the question "Who tells the story?" On the answer to this question hinges the control and arrangement of material—in short, the nature of the plot—and to a large degree, the style. Let us regard the possibilities that, in a general sense, may present themselves.

First, there is the fictional first person. Here the narrator (who may or may not resemble the author) tells us all that we are to know. But there are various possibilities within this general point of view. The narrator may tell his own story, may, in fact, be the central character, as in "The Use of Force" by William Carlos Williams (sec. 2), "I'm a Fool" by Sherwood Anderson (sec. 7), and "Araby" by James Joyce (sec. 7). The narrator may, however, be merely an observer, as in "The Rich Boy" by F. Scott Fitzgerald (sec. 9) and "Haircut" by Ring Lardner (sec. 7), or a character involved in the action, as in "Kronkin's Prisoner" by Isaac Babel (sec. 10) and "In Another Country" by Ernest Hemingway (sec. 8).

The first-person narrator is, presumably, in a position to speak with special, immediate authority about all he himself thinks and feels and sees around him. His narrative carries the impression of truth, total conviction. It can sometimes be a positive asset in establishing the *illusion necessary for fiction*—for illusion is what fiction always is; but the first-person narrator, though he may help to establish the illusion, certainly cannot, in any literal sense, be believed. He himself is merely a part of the illusion, is merely a fictional character, too. Even so, the illusion of authority, of intimacy, possible with the first-person narrator can sometimes have special effectiveness. How could a writer otherwise get the sense of immediacy and involvement found in "Daddy Wolf" by James Purdy (sec. 10)? Or, to turn to novels, in *A Farewell to Arms* by Ernest Hemingway or *Moll Flanders* by Daniel Defoe?

Certain other advantages may accrue through the first-person narrator. A first-person narrator observer (and even as main character) is, naturally, limited in his range of observation, and in certain complex fictions this fact may disqualify him; he simply would not be able to see and feel enough. But in other instances he may provide the built-in principle of selectivity—that is, when what he is privileged to see includes the crucial events of the story. Furthermore, his special sensibility, his degree of awareness as conditioned by class, education, temperament, and experience, may also serve as a principle of selectivity. Clearly, the effect of "Kronkin's Prisoner" depends, in large part, on the fact that the narrator is a Communist, and a soldier, and is, in the end, the killer of the prisoner: he tells what is relevant to his own nature and role.

"Kronkin's Prisoner" leads us to another possible advantage in the first-person narrator: the special sensibility of the narrator may be crucially involved in the effect and meaning of a story. The clipped, detached, almost incredulous way in which Kronkin, the Communist soldier, narrates the episode of the old general's clinging to his antiquated conception of "honor"—the very ambivalence in Kronkin's relation to the episode—makes the pathos of the general more acceptable and, at the same time, more acute than would be possible in a version given by a narrator of the general's old, aristocratic world committed wholeheartedly to the general's views. There is an irony in the ambivalence of Kronkin's attitude toward his victim, but another kind of irony, again based on the nature of the narrator, is found in such a story as "Haircut," by Ring Lardner (sec. 7). Here the irony derives from the fact that the narrator thinks the meaning of his account is one thing, while we, the readers, see it as quite another. The barber, who tells the story, thinks that the practical joker of the town is great, is wonderfully amusing, is a "card," while we recognize him as a monster.

Thus far, in discussing the nature of the first-person narrator we have emphasized an irony based primarily on his limitation. But we should not forget that a first-person narrator may be unusually perceptive and intelligent, that he may, in fact, be a conscious interpreter and guide for the reader. The narrator of "Araby," looking back on his own boyhood experience, is clearly a man of great psychological penetration, and his purpose is not to exploit the pathos or comedy of puppy love but to see it, poetically, as an image of human fate. The narrator in "The Use of Force" can analyze what is at stake in his own experience, and in that of the child. The narrator may, we find, allow himself a range of commentary and an openness of feeling that would ordinarily seem intrusive or excessive in a third-person narrative.

The omniscient third-person point of view is the exact opposite of that of the first-person in that it suffers from none of the limitations (and enjoys none of the advantages) found in that method. The most obvious form of the omniscient third-person point of view is the panoramic; here the narrator sweeps the field with his all-seeing eye, in simultaneous command of the most minute objective events and the secrets of every heart. This method can give the epic sweep of Tolstoy's *War and Peace,* but it can be used somewhat more modestly in novels such as Thackeray's *Vanity Fair.* Even more modestly the method appears in certain short stories, for clearly in such instances the panorama must be severely restricted; the nearest approach here to the method appears in "The Gentleman from San Francisco" by Ivan Bunin (sec. 8).

The omniscient third-person point of view lays the burden of selectivity clearly on the writer; he has no ready-made scheme, no principle, by which to organize his material. Thus we find certain variants that represent different self-imposed limitations to provide a principle of selectivity. For instance, a writer may refuse the privilege of entering into the consciousness of any character, and work more or less strictly in *scenic* terms, treating his material as though in a play, using only description and dialogue, as in "Wet Saturday" (sec. 5). Again, as in "Jerico, Jerico, Jerico," by Andrew Lytle (sec. 10), the omniscient author, presenting only a minimum of objective action, may work exclusively through the consciousness of one character, giving the effect of a shadowy first-person narrator. As a variant of this practice, the author may enter into the consciousness of several characters significantly involved in the story, a method especially effective when the work depends primarily on the interplay of personalities, as in "The Horse Dealer's Daughter" by D. H. Lawrence (sec. 8). In such instances, the author may actually dip into the consciousness of minor characters, too, to hint at a panoramic effect, at a context for the central concern.

In the story by Lytle mentioned above, the consciousness entered is that of the main character, but an author may enter into the consciousness of a minor character to use that character as a device of observation (and sometimes of response and interpretation) for the story; doing so, he may reserve the privilege of omniscience and occasionally withdraw from the consciousness of his observer to develop a scene, to comment on the observer's response, or even to evaluate events at a level beyond the observer's capacities. This particular method is sometimes known as that of the "central intelligence."

These instances do not exhaust the variations of point of view possible in fiction. Most short stories, because of the limitations of length, keep to one point of view, but many novels shift the method from time to time, not only mixing different types of the omniscient point of view, but sometimes using some variety of first-person narration as, in a limited sense, does "Keela, the Outcast Indian Maiden" by Eudora Welty (sec. 7). There is, in fact, no rule to bind a writer to one practice. Probably the only rule is so general as to be no rule: the writer must not confuse the reader by capricious shifts from one point of view to another, but must work from some self-consistent basis. He should, in short, keep in mind the overall effect he wishes the completed work to give.

For instance, the use of a narrator whose consciousness the omniscient author might use as a vehicle for the story would undoubtedly weaken the effect of "The Gentleman from San Francisco" (sec. 8). The author does, indeed, enter into the mind of this character or that, but he does so only sparingly, and never commits himself consistently to any character's inward response, as does Lytle in his story (sec. 10). The dominant effect Bunin aims at is the tone of a learned historian, as if he were writing about a period and class that have long since disappeared. For instance: "The class of people to which he belonged was in the habit of beginning its enjoyment of life by a trip to Europe, India, Egypt." Notice that the main character does not even have a name, he is only the "gentleman from San Francisco"— the term by which he would be identified by hotel keepers, no doubt. He is representative, rather than personal, even if he does have at least a limited personal story.* Bunin, in accordance with this assumption, writes from an impersonal and all-judging "distance," as though the very name of his main character had been lost in time. So when Bunin enters the mind of an individual, he does so by approaching from his "distance," seizing on the one idea or response relevant to his need, and then again withdrawing into that distance.

Style

We began the discussion of point of view by saying that a writer could not set down a single word until he has answered the question "Who tells the story?" We then had in mind the function of point of view in controlling the arrangement of material, but there is another reason, too. The writer can't put down a single word until he knows the kind of word the speaker would utter. So point of view conditions style. And if we, as readers, are to understand a work of fiction, are to fully appreciate it, we must sense the deeper expressive function of style.

First, we must ask whether the writer is using his own voice, a personal style, or whether, in a greater or lesser degree, he is fully playing the ventriloquist, using the voice of a specific character, or is modifying

---

* We should note that Bunin's story is peculiarly lacking in conflict; the gentleman from San Francisco travels, observes, dies. This is consistent with the author's use of him as an example of a class rather than a person. Here the conflict, and the suspense, derives from the development of the ideas, the theme.

and flavoring the style with the language of a world he is writing about, or with the language of a character who is not, strictly speaking, a narrator, but whose consciousness is being penetrated. To reverse matters, let us begin, not with examples of work in a personal style, but with "I'm a Fool" (sec. 7), which is pure ventriloquism:

> It was a peachey time for me, I'll say that. Sometimes now I think that boys who are raised regular in houses, and never have a fine nigger like Burt for best friend, and go to high schools and college, and never steal anything, or get drunk a little, or learn to swear from fellows who know how, or come walking up in front of a grand stand in their shirt sleeves and with dirty horsy pants on when the races are going on and the grand stand is full of people all dressed up— What's the use of talking about it? Such fellows don't know nothing at all. They've never had no opportunity.

We can easily see that here the vocabulary and grammar are appropriate for a boy raised without much education. We realize, too, that almost any writer could go this far in verisimilitude. But only a very good writer could capture the movement and rhythm of the boy's speech, and by this do what Anderson has done: through the very rhythm help to give the impression of the boy's sensitivity on which the story depends. In "Jerico, Jerico, Jerico" (sec. 10), however, the style is merely flavored; the purpose here is not, primarily, to suggest the special quality of an individual, but that of a world, the world the whole story is drawn from and whose death is implied in the death of the old woman. Technically speaking, what we find here is basically the writer's style absorbing certain phrases directly, such as "no-count" or "of a winter's night," or answering echoes, as below:

> She could not see but she could feel the heavy cluster of mahogany grapes that tumbled from the center of the head board— out of its vines curling down the sides it tumbled. How much longer would these never-picked grapes hang above her head?

> How much longer would she, rather, hang to the vine of this world, she who lay beneath as dry as any raisin.

And:

> She could smell her soul burning and see it. What a fire it would make below, dripping with sin, like a rag soaked in kerosene.

Both passages are only indirectly referred to the woman's mind, and are not quoted but written, as it were, on the author's own responsibility; but the biblical flavor of "the vine of the world" and the homely similes of the raisin and the rag soaked in kerosene belong to the world of the story.

In both "I'm a Fool" and "Jerico, Jerico, Jerico," we have dealt with the use of vernacular, but in "Araby," which, like "I'm a Fool," is a first-person narrative, the style is formal and literary. Even so, as in "I'm a Fool," the style in "Araby" indicates the special sensitivity of the narrator: the boy, unlike the hero of Anderson's story, is educated and has a poetic awareness of his role, awareness in contrast to the world of his family, and both the awareness and the contrast are heightened by the fact that the story is told in retrospect, after the boy has grown up and developed the literary powers that enable him to realize and suggest the full meaning of the experience narrated.

To turn to the opposite extreme, a story in which the style has no connection with the language of the character being presented, we may consider "The Gentleman from San Francisco." Here, as we have pointed out, the distance of the omniscient narrator, with his tone of historical authority, from the almost anonymous "Gentleman" is of the very essence of the story. The range of historical and philosophical reference and the literary elaboration in metaphor and rhythm* are far beyond the reach of the limited, self-absorbed, and essentially trivial Gentleman—and are, in fact, a method of emphasizing his triviality.

To sum up: According to the French critic Buffon, style is the man. The "man," in Buffon's dictum, is the author. But the

---

* Since this is a translation, we can only assume that the English style corresponds to a degree at least with the original.

"man" may also be a character. To go further: *style is meaning, and meaning is style.*

Theme

In turning to the consideration of meaning —of *interpretation*, or *theme*—in the structure of fiction, let us think, first, of meaning in its most general function. The most obvious factor in humanizing fiction is, of course, the presence of characters, but there is another, less obvious but equally important. The creature crouching by the fire in the cave longed, as we have said, to hear the tale make some sort of sense of his world, to explain his fate to him. The writer is a human being, too, and his work, as we have said long back, represents, directly or indirectly, his own attempt to make sense of life, his vision of human life, his own attitudes and values as absorbed into his treatment of plot and character in the story. The story itself, as a whole, is an interpretation of the world beyond the story. The story is not a mere report, it is a creation. And *to create is, inevitably, to interpret.*

More specifically, however, the story itself may be interpreted. It has what we ordinarily call a theme, *the governing idea implicit in the original situation of conflict that becomes, in the end, the focal idea— that is, what we take to be the "meaning" of the whole.* For instance, in the story "Young Goodman Brown" by Hawthorne (sec. 4) it is easy to see how the meaning comes to focus at the moment when Brown, at the foul ritual of witches in the forest, sees his own sweet and pure bride among the congregation. In this moment, it becomes clear to him that the soul of every human being is compounded of evil *and* good. The story is, then, one of initiation, in this case of the coming to full awareness of the nature of man and of the necessity for self-knowledge that is at the center of the moral life—a knowledge that, however, Goodman Brown can't bear.

"Young Goodman Brown" is relatively simple, with its idea presented in a transparent allegory. Many stories are much more complex—for instance, the apparently simple fairy tale "The Fir Tree" (sec. 3). Here the theme derives from a contrast between immediate experience and past experience— the fact, tragic or pathetic, that man, caught in his expectant thrust toward the future, fails to appreciate the present until it is past and beyond him. The theme arising from this contrast may seem, at first glance, to be indicated in the cry of the fir tree at the end: "Had I but rejoiced when I could have done so!" It seems at first, then, that we have the theme: "Appreciate life while it is being lived." Actually, such an idea is involved in the story. But does it exhaust the meaning of the story?

Let us look at the last paragraph. The first important fact there is that the youngest child, excited and happy in burning the now "ugly old fir tree," wears on his breast the golden star the tree had worn on the happiest moment of its life, on Christmas Eve. But that evening had gone by without proper appreciation, and now, since the boy, not appreciating the present moment, wears the same golden star, we take it that he (like all men) will fail in the same way to seize the full impact of life as it passes.

But there remains to be considered the very last sentence of the story, ending, "past! past!—and that's the way with all stories." And the way with all lives, which cannot be fully appreciated and understood until they become, shall we say, stories—until they become the embodied resolution of all their contradictory forces. So we are approaching some such ironical, but consolatory, theme as this: "Since life cannot, in the living, be fully appreciated, man, to find meaning in life, must seek it by his inspection of the total process re-created in memory and by the act of imagination." We have, then, something close to Socrates' remark that "the uninspected life is not worth living." Or should we go beyond this to the theme that reality lies neither in the seizing of the particular moment nor in the re-created image, but in a tension between these two poles of experience?

In many stories that resist a simple statement of theme, we may find that the complexity, range, and contrasts of possibilities offer, in themselves, an aspect of the theme—that is, these facts must be recognized in any statement. And in such cases, the mere recognition of the complexity may be basically what we need, after all.

The greatest mistake possible in dealing with fiction is to assume that the theme of a story is like a moral tag to hang on the wall, such as "Honesty is the best policy" or "Honor thy father and thy mother." In Shakespeare's *King Lear*, Cordelia's trouble, and the whole tragic upset of her death and her father's, flows from the fact that she can't tell a lie; here, in one sense, honesty is the worst policy, or is, at least, in conflict with other values. Cordelia, further, won't tell a lie even to honor her father, at least in the way he wants to be "honored." One thing the play does—and all serious literature does— is to affirm, by implication at least, that life is more complex than any maxim would lead us to believe. Reality must be sought beneath the kind of mentality that deals in maxims.

The theme of serious literature cannot be sought in maxims. Nor is it hortatory; it does not say "Do this" or "Do that." Rather, it shows that to know what to do in life is probably harder than we had thought, that we must work to understand the world and ourselves, and that solutions are never simple. The reader, in fact, instinctively objects when a writer seems to be using fiction as a disguise for preaching at him. He instinctively realizes that the basic truth implicit in fiction is that man must struggle for his "truth," for knowledge of the world and of the self and to ground his values firmly enough to make action possible. The very movement of a story is toward such an end. It may be, of course, embodied in the experience of a character in the story, who comes to increased awareness, as with the boy (and the boy grown up into narrator) in James Joyce's "Araby" (sec. 7), but it may be embodied merely in the story itself, taken as a whole as in "The Horse Dealer's Daughter" (sec. 8) or "Noon Wine" by Katherine Anne Porter (sec. 8). In fact, in all instances, we must consult the whole story, its total import, for the theme.

Clearly, if a story embodies an author's attitudes and values, there must be great differences in theme from story to story, and the reader can't be expected to find them all congenial to him. If the theme of a story is, then, unacceptable to him—if he can't believe in it—can he still enjoy the fiction in question? And if so, in what way, to what degree? This is a very complicated problem, and there is no solution that covers all readers. But we do know that most people have a fairly wide range of acceptance. The same person can enjoy the novels of Sir Walter Scott, which are based on a romantic, simple, and chivalric idea of human conduct, as well as the stories of de Maupassant, which are based on an ironic and realistic view of life. Scott's heroes are very heroic and are suitably rewarded. De Maupassant has no heroes in this sense, and in his stories accident plays a more important part than justice. If we enjoy "The Gentleman from San Francisco," we are not forbidden enjoyment of the pathos of Katharine Anne Porter's tale of rural Texas, "Noon Wine."

Perhaps we can say that, with theme, as with plot and character, our reading of fiction is often provisional and experimental. With attitudes and values, we are here reaching out to enlarge ourselves, to experiment with life, to understand ourselves more fully. If the fiction is good enough—if the characters seem real, if the plot is convincing, and if the theme seems to emerge from the body of the story—we are prepared to experience the world as the writer conceives it to be. We demand, however, that the writer's themes shall not be trivial or ridiculous; even the themes of the most delicate comedy must brush reality in order to be really funny. And above all, we demand that the world offered by a piece of fiction be coherent, that it be fundamentally logical in its own way to its premises, and that it be true to the life it professes to express.

But there is another way in which we accept the meaning of fiction, a way more general and fundamental than our way of accepting a particular theme. The mere fact that a story is fulfilled as story, that it coherently moves to its end, serves as an image of the possibility of making sense of life, of meaningfully ordering experience. It is an image of what we most deeply desire in our life process. The basic promise made by fiction is that life makes sense—or can be made to make sense.

We have earlier said that a piece of fiction, insofar as it is successful, possesses an organic unity, and that, in this unity, form and content interfuse. This idea cannot be overemphasized, for in this sense of unity, of a dynamic interfusion, the power of the fictional illusion inheres. This idea, however, is especially difficult to grasp in relation to theme. The theme of a story seems to be something at the end of the story, something like the piece of chewing gum that comes out when the penny is put into the machine. Certainly the chewing gum is not the machine. But the theme *is* the story. Only in so far as the theme is implicit in the other elements and in the dynamic progression, can the story be said, in the fictional sense, to exist at all. That is, just as easily as we conceive of the theme as content, can we conceive of it as the principle of form by which other elements are vitally related.

So, after all, *the story is theme*, and *the theme, story.*

Section 2

FICTIONAL POINT

We might approach the study of fiction by taking some highly developed, complex stories, but there are certain advantages in beginning with simple narratives, mere episodes that, at first glance, scarcely seem to be stories at all, that seem to be little more than events without point. If such an episode becomes a story, it does so because the writer finds in it a conflict that may be meaningfully resolved. Here we try to understand what might have been the writer's interest in the original situation (real or imagined); that is, what made him feel that he had a story, after all.

THE USE OF FORCE
William Carlos Williams (1883–1963)

They were new patients to me, all I had was the name, Olson. Please come down as soon as you can, my daughter is very sick.

When I arrived I was met by the mother, a big startled looking woman, very clean and apologetic who merely said, Is this the doctor? and let me in. In the back, she added. You must excuse us, doctor, we have her in the kitchen where it is warm. It is very damp here sometimes.

The child was fully dressed and sitting on her father's lap near the kitchen table. He tried to get up, but I motioned for him not to bother, took off my overcoat and started to look things over. I could see that they were all very nervous, eyeing me up and down distrustfully. As often, in such cases, they weren't telling me more than they had to, it was up to me to tell them: that's why they were spending three dollars on me.

The child was fairly eating me up with her cold, steady eyes, and no expression to her face whatever. She did not move and seemed, inwardly, quiet; an unusually attractive little thing, and as strong as a heifer in appearance. But her face was flushed, she was breathing rapidly, and I realized that she had a high fever. She had magnificent blonde hair, in profusion. One of those picture children often reproduced in advertising leaflets and the photogravure sections of the Sunday papers.

She's had a fever for three days, began the father and we don't know what it comes from. My wife has given her things, you know, like people do, but it don't do no good. And there's been a lot of sickness around. So we tho't you'd better look her over and tell us what is the matter.

As doctors often do I took a trial shot at it as a point of departure. Has she had a sore throat?

Both parents answered me together, No . . . No, she says her throat don't hurt her.

Does your throat hurt you? added the mother to the child. But the little girl's expression didn't change nor did she move her eyes from my face.

Have you looked?

I tried to, said the mother, but I couldn't see.

As it happens we have been having a number of cases of diphtheria in the school to which this child went during that month and we were all, quite apparently, thinking of that, though no one had as yet spoken of the thing.

Well, I said, suppose we take a look at the throat first. I smiled in my best professional manner and asking for the child's first name I said, come on, Mathilda, open your mouth and let's take a look at your throat.

Nothing doing.

Aw, come on, I coaxed, just open your mouth wide and let me take a look. Look, I said opening both hands wide, I haven't anything in my hands. Just open up and let me see.

Such a nice man, put in the mother. Look how kind he is to you. Come on, do what he tells you to. He won't hurt you.

At that I ground my teeth in disgust. If only they wouldn't use the word "hurt" I might be able to get somewhere. But I did not allow myself to be hurried or disturbed but speaking quietly and slowly I approached the child again.

As I moved my chair a little nearer suddenly with one catlike movement both her hands clawed instinctively for my eyes and she almost reached them too. In fact she knocked my glasses flying and they fell, though unbroken, several feet away from me on the kitchen floor.

Both the mother and father almost turned themselves inside out in embarrassment and apology. You bad girl, said the mother, taking her and shaking her by one arm. Look what you've done. The nice man. . . .

For heaven's sake, I broke in. Don't call me a nice man to her. I'm here to look at her throat on the chance that she might have diphtheria and possibly die of it. But that's nothing to her. Look here, I said to the child, we're going to look at your throat. You're old enough to understand what I'm saying. Will you open it now by yourself or shall we have to open it for you?

Not a move. Even her expression hadn't changed. Her breaths however were becoming faster and faster. Then the battle began. I had to do it. I had to have a throat culture for her own protection. But first I told the parents that it was entirely up to them. I explained the danger but said that I would not insist on a throat examination so long as they would take the responsibility.

If you don't do what the doctor says you'll have to go to the hospital, the mother admonished her severely.

Oh yeah? I had to smile to myself. After all. I had already fallen in love with the savage brat, the parents were contemptible to me. In the ensuing struggle they grew more and more abject, crushed, exhausted while she surely rose to magnificent heights of insane fury of effort bred of her terror of me.

The father tried his best, and he was a big man but the fact that she was his daughter, his shame at her behavior and his dread of hurting her made him release her just at the critical times when I had almost achieved success, till I wanted to kill him. But his dread also that she might have diphtheria made him tell me to go on, go on though he himself was almost fainting, while the mother moved back and forth behind us raising and lowering her hands in an agony of apprehension.

Put her in front of you on your lap, I ordered, and hold both her wrists.

But as soon as he did the child let out a scream. Don't, you're hurting me. Let go of my hands. Let them go I tell you. Then she shrieked terrifyingly, hysterically. Stop it! Stop it! You're killing me!

Do you think she can stand it, doctor! said the mother.

You get out, said the husband to his wife. Do you want her to die of diphtheria?

Come on now, hold her, I said.

Then I grasped the child's head with my left hand and tried to get the wooden tongue depressor between her teeth. She fought, with clenched teeth, desperately! But now I also had grown furious—at a child. I tried to hold myself down but I couldn't. I know how to expose a throat for inspection. And I did my best. When finally I got the wooden spatula behind the last teeth and just the point of it into the mouth cavity, she opened up for an instant but before I could see anything she came down again and gripping the wooden blade between her molars she reduced it to splinters before I could get it out again.

Aren't you ashamed, the mother yelled at her. Aren't you ashamed to act like that in front of the doctor?

Get me a smooth-handled spoon of some sort, I told the mother. We're going through with this. The child's mouth was already bleeding. Her tongue was cut and she was screaming in wild hysterical shrieks. Perhaps I should have desisted and come back in an hour or more. No doubt it would have been better. But I have seen at least two children lying dead in bed of neglect in such cases, and feeling that I must get a diagnosis now or never I went at it again. But the worst of it was that I too had got beyond reason. I could have torn the child apart in my own fury and enjoyed it. It was a pleasure to attack her. My face was burning with it.

The damned little brat must be protected against her own idiocy, one says to one's self at such times. Others must be protected against her. It is a social necessity. And all these things are true. But a blind fury, a feeling of adult shame, bred of a longing for muscular release are the operatives. One goes on to the end.

In a final unreasoning assault I overpowered the child's neck and jaws. I forced the heavy silver spoon back of her teeth and down her throat till she gagged. And there it was—both tonsils covered with membrane. She had fought valiantly to keep me from knowing her secret. She had been hiding that sore throat for three days at least and lying to her parents in order to escape just such an outcome as this.

Now truly she was furious. She had been on the defensive before but now she attacked. Tried to get off her father's lap and fly at me while tears of defeat blinded her eyes.

The obvious conflict here is between the doctor, who must try to make a diagnosis, and the child, who resists him. But the conflict, in itself, has little fictional significance —that is, no conflict of what we may call, in the broadest sense, moral values. To create a satisfying story, the writer must find a more significant conflict beneath the obvious situation. He must interpret it. Furthermore, he must resolve the conflict significantly; he must bring it to a point of equilibrium.

The title of the story gives us the lead to the significant conflict beneath the obvious situation. What is at stake in the use of force? Force is, clearly, necessary here, for the good of the child and that of society: "The damned little brat must be protected against her own idiocy. . . . Others must be protected against her. It is a social necessity." But at the same time the child instinctively recognizes that the use of force is a fundamental affront, a violation, and so resists with all her powers. So both the doctor and the child are, in a sense, "right." Both appeal to our sympathies, and even the doctor recognizes the child's rightness and sympathizes with her: "After all, I had already fallen in love with the savage brat"—really with her "savagery," her courage and integrity. With this division of feeling, the doctor must continue his effort to pry open the patient's jaws.

In the end the doctor succeeds, and discovers that the child does have diphtheria. Is this fact the resolution, the point, of the story? No, for what we—including the doctor—learn is something about the use of force. The real point is the unmasking of something deep in human nature. The use of force, even in a good cause, opens up some dark, primitive depth of our nature, "a blind fury," a will to conquest, a delight in cruelty. The doctor admits: "I could have torn the child apart in my own fury and enjoyed it. It was a pleasure to attack her." That is the terrifying revelation the story comes to, that and the corollary realization that, ironically, the very savagery of the assault finds justification in a "good" cause.

The objective fact that the symptoms of the disease are, in the end, revealed is not, as we have said earlier, the significant element in the resolution. It is significant only insofar as the symptoms of diphtheria stand as an echo of, as a kind of image of, the real disease revealed—that other kind of disease in our nature that the use of force releases.

EXERCISES

1. The story is not, simply, dealing with the relation of "bad means" and "good ends," however important may be such an idea and however powerful may be certain pieces of fiction embodying it. The issue here is not that the doctor uses force. He must use force; it is necessary, as the story clearly states. Force, we may say, is neither good nor bad, in itself. What issue lies in the doctor's use of force?

2. Read "Daddy Wolf," by James Purdy (sec. 10). This story is much longer than "The Use of Force," but may seem to some readers almost as pointless. Draw up a set of questions that might lead to a statement of the point. You may not be able to answer all your own questions, but being able to ask the right questions about a thing is half way to an understanding of it. Compare your questions with those framed by other students.

AN EPISODE OF WAR
Stephen Crane (1871–1900)

The lieutenant's rubber blanket lay on the ground, and upon it had been poured the company's supply of coffee. Corporals and other representatives of the grimy and hot-throated men who lined the breastwork had come for each squad's portion.

The lieutenant was frowning and serious at this task of division. His lips pursed as he drew with his sword various crevices in the heap until brown squares of coffee, astoundingly equal in size, appeared on the blanket. He was on the verge of a great triumph in mathematics, and the corporals were thronging forward, each to reap a little square, when suddenly the lieutenant cried out and looked quickly at a man near him as if he suspected it was a case of personal assault. The other cried out also when they saw blood upon the lieutenant's sleeve.

He had winced like a man stung, swayed dangerously, and then straightened. The sound of his hoarse breathing was plainly audible. He looked sadly, mystically, over the breastwork at the green face of a wood, where now were many little puffs of white smoke. During this moment the men about him gazed statue-like and silent, astonished and awed by this catastrophe which happened when catastrophes were not expected—when they had leisure to observe it.

As the lieutenant stared at the wood, they too swung their heads, so that for another instance all hands, still silent, contemplated the distant forest as if their minds were fixed upon the mystery of a bullet's journey.

The officer had, of course, been compelled to take his sword into his left hand. He did not hold it at the hilt. He gripped it at the middle of the blade, awkwardly. Turning his eyes from the hostile wood, he looked at the sword as he held it there, and seemed puzzled as to what to do with it, where to put it. In short, this weapon had of a sudden become a strange thing to him. He looked at it in a kind of stupefaction, as if he had been endowed with a trident, a sceptre, or a spade.

Finally he tried to sheath it. To sheath a sword held by the left hand, at the middle of the blade, in a scabbard hung at the left hip, is a feat worthy of a sawdust ring. This wounded officer engaged in a desperate struggle with the sword and the wobbling scabbard, and during the time of it he breathed like a wrestler.

But at this instant the men, the spectators, awoke from their stone-like poses and crowded forward sympathetically. The orderly-sergeant took the sword and tenderly placed it in the scabbard. At the time, he leaned nervously backward, and did not allow even his finger to brush the body of the lieutenant. A wound gives strange dignity to him who bears it. Well men shy from this new and terrible majesty. It is as if the wounded man's hand is upon the curtain which hangs before the revelations of all existence—the meaning of ants, potentates, wars, cities, sunshine, snow, a feather dropped from a bird's wing; and the power of it sheds radiance upon a bloody form, and makes the other men understand sometimes that they are little. His comrades look at him with large eyes thoughtfully. Moreover, they fear vaguely that the weight of a finger upon him might send him headlong, precipitate the tragedy, hurl him at once into the dim, gray unknown. And so the orderly-sergeant, while sheathing the sword, leaned nervously backward.

There were others who proffered assistance. One timidly presented his shoulder and asked the lieutenant if he cared to lean upon it, but the latter waved him away mournfully. He wore the look of one who knows he is the victim of a terrible disease and understands his helplessness. He again stared over the breastwork at the forest, and then turning went slowly rearward. He held his right wrist tenderly in his left hand as if the wounded arm was made of very brittle glass.

And the men in silence stared at the wood, then at the departing lieutenant—then at the wood, then at the lieutenant.

As the wounded officer passed from the line of battle, he was enabled to see many things which as a participant in the fight were unknown to him. He saw a general on a black horse gazing over the lines of blue infantry at the green woods which veiled his problems. An aide galloped furiously, dragged his horse suddenly to a halt, saluted, and presented a paper. It was, for a wonder, precisely an historical painting.

To the rear of the general and his staff a group, composed of a bugler, two or three orderlies, and the bearer of the corps standard, all upon maniacal horses, were working like slaves to hold their ground, preserve their respectful interval, while the shells boomed in the air about them, and caused their chargers to make furious quivering leaps.

A battery, a tumultuous and shining mass, was swirling toward the right. The wild thud of hoofs, the cries of the riders shouting blame and praise, menace and encouragement, and, last, the roar of the wheels, the slant of the glistening guns, brought the lieutenant to an intent pause. The battery swept in curves that stirred the heart; it made halts as dramatic as the crash of a wave on the rocks, and when it fled onward, this aggregation of wheels, lever, motors, had a beautiful unity, as if it were a missile. The sound of it was a war-chorus that reached into the depths of man's emotion.

The lieutenant, still holding his arm as if it were of glass, stood watching the battery until all detail of it was lost, save the figures of the riders, which rose and fell and waved lashes over the black mass.

Later, he turned his eyes toward the battle where the shooting sometimes crackled like bush-fires, sometimes sputtered with exasperating irregularity, and sometimes reverberated like the thunder. He saw the smoke rolling upward and saw crowds of men who ran and cheered, or stood and blazed away at the inscrutable distance.

He came upon some stragglers, and they told him how to find the field hospital. They described its exact location. In fact, these men, no longer having part in the battle, knew more of it than others. They told the performance of every corps, every division, the opinion of every general. The lieutenant, carrying his wounded arm rearward, looked upon them with wonder.

At the roadside a brigade was making coffee and buzzing with talk like a girls' boarding-school. Several officers came out to him and inquired concerning things of which he knew nothing. One, seeing his arm, began to scold. "Why, man, that's no way to do. You want to fix that thing." He appropriated the lieutenant and the lieutenant's wound. He cut the sleeve and laid bare the arm, every nerve of which softly fluttered under his touch. He bound his handkerchief over the wound, scolding away in the meantime. His tone allowed one to think that he was in the habit of being wounded every day. The lieutenant hung his head, feeling, in this presence, that he did not know how to be correctly wounded.

The low white tents of the hospital were grouped around an old school-house. There was here a singular commotion. In the foreground two ambulances interlocked wheels in the deep mud. The drivers were tossing the blame of it back and forth, gesticulating and berating, while from the ambulances, both crammed with wounded, there came an occasional groan. An interminable crowd of bandaged men were coming and going. Great numbers sat under the trees nursing heads or arms or legs. There was a dispute of some kind raging on the steps of the school-house. Sitting with his back against a tree a man with a face as gray as a new army blanket was serenely smoking a corn-cob pipe. The lieutenant wished to rush forward and inform him that he was dying.

A busy surgeon was passing near the lieutenant. "Good morning," he said, with a friendly smile. Then he caught sight of the lieutenant's arm and his face at once changed. "Well, let's have a look at it." He seemed possessed suddenly of a great contempt for the lieutenant. This wound evidently placed the latter on a very low social plane. The doctor cried out impatiently, "What mutton-head had tied it up that way anyhow?" The lieutenant answered, "Oh, a man."

When the wound was disclosed the doctor fingered it disdainfully. "Humph," he said. "You come along with me and I'll tend to you." His voice contained the same scorn as if he were saying, "You will have to go to jail."

The lieutenant had been very meek, but now his face flushed, and he looked into the doctor's eyes. "I guess I won't have it amputated," he said.

"Nonsense, man! Nonsense! Nonsense!" cried the doctor. "Come along, now. I won't amputate it. Come along. Don't be a baby."

"Let go of me," said the lieutenant, holding back wrathfully, his glance fixed upon the door of the old school-house, as sinister to him as the portals of death.

And this is the story of how the lieutenant lost his arm. When he reached home, his sisters, his mother, his wife, sobbed for a long time at the sight of the flat sleeve. "Oh, well," he said, standing shamefaced amid these tears, "I don't suppose it matters so much as all that."

EXERCISES

At first glance this seems a mere sketch. The plot element is slight; there is an objective conflict, but it is of a most elementary sort, and the resolution is, at best, vague. Is it possible to make a case for this narrative as fiction? In examining this possibility, attempt to answer the following questions:

1. What is the function of the relatively large amount of description here? In what way, if any, can the apparently descriptive elements be said to introduce thematic considerations?

2. The writer has taken pains to indicate how the wound sets the lieutenant apart from his fellows. How do the men regard him? The officers? The surgeon? Is there a progression of complication here? Do these elements help to define a theme?

3. What elements of contrast are used in the narrative?

4. What is the "turn"—the reversal—in the piece? (See sec. 1.)

5. What do you make of the lieutenant's reaction to his wife's grief? What is brought to focus here? How does the tone of the first sentence of the last paragraph relate to the attitude of the lieutenant?

6. Is there any reason for the writer's refusal to give the lieutenant a distinguishing name?

7. What phrases and comparisons make for immediacy and vividness? Now comparing your original answer to question 1, what phrases and comparisons have significance thematically?

8. Read "Kronkin's Prisoner" by Isaac Babel (sec. 10), which recounts an episode in the war between Russians and Poles just after the Communist Revolution of 1917. Frame a set of questions that might lead to a statement of the fictional point.

AFTER THE FAIR
Dylan Thomas (1914–1953)

The fair was over, the lights in the cocoanut stalls were put out, and the wooden horses stood still in the darkness, waiting for the music and the hum of the machines that would set them trotting forward. One by one, in every booth, the naphtha jets were turned down and the canvases pulled over the little gambling tables. The crowd went home, and there were lights in the windows of the caravans.

Nobody had noticed the girl. In her black clothes she stood against the side of the roundabouts, hearing the last feet tread upon the sawdust and the last voices die into the distance. Then, all alone on the deserted ground, surrounded by the shapes of wooden horses and cheap fairy boats, she looked for a place to sleep. Now here and now there, she raised the canvas that shrouded the cocoanut stalls and peered into the warm darkness. She was frightened to step inside, and as a mouse scampered across the littered shavings on the floor, or as the canvas creaked and a rush of wind set it dancing, she ran away and hid again near the roundabouts. Once she stepped on the boards; the bells round a horse's throat jingled and were still; she did not dare breathe until all was quiet again and the darkness had forgotten the noise of the bells. Then here and there she went peeping for a bed, into each gondola, under each tent. But there was nowhere, nowhere in all the fair for her to sleep. One place was too silent, and in another was the noise of mice. There was straw in the corner of the Astrologer's tent, but it moved as she touched it; she knelt by its side and put out her hand; she felt a baby's hand upon her own.

Now there was nowhere; so slowly she turned towards the caravans, and reaching them where they stood on the outskirts of the field, found all but two to be unlit. She stood, clutching her empty bag, and wondering which caravan she should disturb. At last she decided to knock upon the window of the little, shabby one near her, and standing on tiptoe, she looked in. The fattest man she had ever seen was sitting in front of the stove, toasting a piece of bread. She tapped three times on the glass, then hid in the shadows. She heard him come to the top of the steps and call out Who? Who? but she dared not answer. Who? Who? he called again; she laughed at his voice which was as thin as he was fat. He heard her laughter and turned to where the darkness concealed her. First you tap, he said. Then you hide, then, by jingo, you laugh. She stepped into the circle of light, knowing she need no longer hide herself. A girl, he said, Come in and wipe your feet. He did not wait but retreated into his caravan, and she could do nothing but follow him up the steps and into the crowded room. He was seated again, and toasting the same piece of bread. Have you come in? he said, for his back was towards her. Shall I close the door? she asked, and closed it before he replied.

She sat on the bed and watched him toasting the bread until it burnt. I can toast better than you, she said. I don't doubt it, said the Fat Man. She watched him put down the charred toast upon a plate by his side, take another round of bread and hold that, too, in front of the stove. It burnt very quickly. Let me toast it for you, she said. Ungraciously he handed her the fork and the loaf. Cut it, he said, Toast it, and eat it, by jingo. She sat on the chair. See the dent you've made on my bed, said the Fat Man. Who are you to come in and dent my bed? My name is Annie, she told him. Soon all the bread was toasted and buttered, so she put it in the centre of the table and arranged two chairs. I'll have mine on the bed, said the Fat Man. You'll have it here.

When they had finished their supper, he pushed back his chair and stared at her across the table. I am the Fat Man, he said. My home is Treorchy; the Fortune Teller next door is Aberdare. I am nothing to do with the fair—I am Cardiff, she said. There's a town, agreed the Fat Man. He asked her why she had come away. Money, said Annie. I have one and three, said the Fat Man. I have nothing, said Annie.

Then he told her about the fair and the places he had been to and the people he had met. He told her his age and his weight and the names of his brothers and what he would call his son. He showed her a picture of Boston Harbour and the photograph of his mother who lifted weights. He told her how summer looked in Ireland. I've always been a fat man, he said, And now I'm *the* Fat Man; there's nobody to touch me for fatness. He told her of a heat wave in Sicily and of the Mediterranean Sea and of the wonders of the South stars. She told him of the baby in the Astrologer's tent.

That's the stars again, by jingo; looking at the stars doesn't do anybody any good.

The baby'll die, said Annie. He opened the door and walked out into the darkness. She looked about her but did not move, wondering if he had gone to fetch a policeman. It would never do to be caught by the policeman again. She stared through the open door into the inhospitable night and drew her chair closer to the stove. Better to be caught in the warmth, she said. But she trembled at the sound of the Fat Man approaching, and pressed her hands upon her thin breast, as he climbed up the steps like a walking mountain. She could see him smile in the darkness. See what the stars have done, he said, and brought in the Astrologer's baby in his arms.

After she had nursed it against her and it had cried on the bosom of her dress, she told him how she had feared his going. What should I be doing with a policeman? She told him that the policeman wanted her. What have you done for a policeman to be wanting you? She did not answer but took the child nearer again to her wasted breast. If it was money, I could have given you one and three, he said. Then he understood her and begged her pardon. I'm not quick, he told her. I'm just fat; sometimes I think I'm almost too fat. She was feeding the child; he saw her thinness. You must eat, Cardiff, he said.

Then the child began to cry. From a little wail its crying rose into a tempest of despair. The girl rocked it to and fro on her lap, but nothing soothed it. All the woe of a child's world flooded its tiny voice. Stop it, stop it, said the Fat Man, and the tears increased. Annie smothered it in kisses, but its wild cry broke on her lips like water upon rocks. We must do something, she said. Sing it a lullabee. She sang, but the child did not like her singing.

There's only one thing, said Annie, we must take it on the roundabouts. With the child's arm around her neck, she stumbled down the steps and ran towards the deserted fair, the Fat Man panting behind her. She found her way through the tents and stalls into the centre of the ground where the wooden horses stood waiting, and clambered up on to a saddle. Start the engine, she called out. In the distance the Fat Man could be heard cranking up the antique machine that drove the horses all the day into a wooden gallop. She heard the sudden spasmodic humming of the engine; the boards rattled under the horses' feet. She saw the Fat Man clamber up by her side, pull the central lever and climb on to the saddle of the smallest horse of all. As the roundabout started, slowly at first and slowly gaining speed, the child at the girl's breast stopped crying, clutched its hands together, and crowed with joy. The night wind tore through its hair, the music jangled in its ears. Round and round the wooden horses sped, drowning the cries of the wind with the beating of their wooden hooves.

And so the men from the caravans found them, the Fat Man and the girl in black with a baby in her arms, racing round and round on their mechanical steeds to the ever-increasing music of the organ.

———————◆·◆◆▷·◆———————

This story presents the encounter of two derelicts, the Fat Man of a carnival and a waif, both outsiders to ordinary, normal human society. In this encounter each gives, and finds, the kind of acceptance not possible to them in the ordinary world. But if the story stopped at this point would it be a story? Scarcely; because it would not come to focus, would give no impression of coming to a moment of revelation, of resolution. The episode of the baby provides such a moment, in the weird picture of a sort of family outing, as it were, with father, mother, and child, an outing which the misfits can enjoy only at night and can enjoy only up to the moment when the normal world breaks in upon them.

EXERCISES

1. Locate the "turn" in the development of the story. (See sec. 1.)
2. Can you distinguish stages leading up to it?
3. If ordinary people had discovered such an abandoned baby, what would they have done? What is indicated by the contrast between such ordinary behavior and that of the misfits?
4. Is the story only a comment on the value and behavior of such misfits, or does it have a bearing on all humanity? That is, is the theme one of general applicability?

CROSSING INTO POLAND

Isaac Babel (1894–1941)

The Commander of the VI Division reported: Novograd-Volynsk was taken at dawn today. The Staff had left Krapivno, and our baggage train was spread out in a noisy rearguard over the highroad from Brest to Warsaw built by Nicholas I upon the bones of peasants.

Fields flowered around us, crimson with poppies; a noontide breeze played in the yellowing rye; on the horizon virginal buckwheat rose like the wall of a distant monastery. The Volyn's peaceful stream moved away from us in sinuous curves and was lost in the pearly haze of the birch groves; crawling between flowery slopes, it wound weary arms through a wilderness of hops. The orange sun rolled down the sky like a lopped-off head, and mild light glowed from the cloud gorges. The standards of the sunset flew above our heads. Into the cool of evening dripped the smell of yesterday's blood, of slaughtered horses. The blackened Zbruch roared, twisting itself into foamy knots at the falls. The bridges were down, and we waded across the river. On the waves rested a majestic moon. The horses were in to the cruppers, and the noisy torrent gurgled among hundreds of horses' legs. Somebody sank, loudly defaming the Mother of God. The river was dotted with the square black patches of the wagons, and was full of confused sounds, of whistling and singing, that rose above the gleaming hollows, the serpentine trails of the moon.

Far on in the night we reached Novograd. In the house where I was billeted I found a pregnant woman and two red-haired, scraggy-necked Jews. A third, huddled to the wall with his head covered up, was already asleep. In the room I was given I discovered turned-out wardrobes, scraps of women's fur coats on the floor, human filth, fragments of the occult crockery the Jews use only once a year, at Eastertime.

"Clear this up," I said to the woman. "What a filthy way to live!" The two Jews rose from their places and, hopping on their felt soles, cleared the mess from the floor. They skipped about noiselessly, monkey-fashion, like Japs in a circus act, their necks swelling and twisting. They put down for me a feather bed that had been disemboweled, and I lay down by the wall next to the third Jew, the one who was asleep. Faint-hearted poverty closed in over my couch.

Silence overcame all. Only the moon, clasping in her blue hands her round, bright, carefree face, wandered like a vagrant outside the window.

I kneaded my numbed legs and, lying on the ripped-open mattress, fell asleep. And in my sleep the Commander of the VI Division appeared to me; he was pursuing the Brigade Commander on a heavy stallion, fired at him twice between the eyes. The bullets pierced the Brigade Commander's head, and both his eyes dropped to the ground. "Why did you turn back the brigade?" shouted Savitsky, the Divisional Commander, to the wounded man—and here I woke up, for the pregnant woman was groping over my face with her fingers.

"Good sir," she said, "you're calling out in your sleep and you're tossing to and fro. I'll make you a bed in another corner, for you're pushing my father about."

She raised her thin legs and rounded belly from the floor and removed the blanket from the sleeper. Lying on his back was an old man, a dead old man. His throat had been torn out and his face cleft in two; in his beard blue blood was clotted like a lump of lead.

"Good sir," said the jewess, shaking up the feather bed, "the Poles cut his throat, and he begging them: 'Kill me in the yard so that my daughter shan't see me die.' But they did as suited them. He passed away in this room, thinking of me.—And now I should wish to know," cried the woman with sudden and terrible violence, "I should wish to know where in the whole world you could find another father like my father?"

EXERCISES

1. If "Crossing into Poland" ended merely with the discovery of the fact that the old Jew was dead, would there be a story? What point does the present ending provide?
2. In the early part of the story we find a contrast between the violent human world of war and the striking beauty of the natural world around it. For what more significant contrast to come does this prepare us? To be more specific, what relation does this early contrast have to the lament of the pregnant young woman for her father?
3. To return to "Kronkin's Prisoner" (sec. 10), what similarities do you find between the two stories by Babel, in both method and meaning?

Section 3

THE TALE: TIME AND THE TELLING

The pieces in this group are not simple episodes. They are, in fact, rather long narratives, involving a series of events. But these narratives do not have the close organization of events and the kind of interrelation of characters we expect in a highly developed piece of fiction. Such a "tale" as "The Tinder Box" by Hans Christian Andersen (sec. 1), to take a rather extreme example, can scarcely be said to have characters at all; the soldier, the witch, the princess, and the others are merely conventional figures the events are pegged to. Furthermore, as we have said earlier, the tale can scarcely be said to have a theme—to make any comment on the logic of life or the values of life. We simply follow the events in the chronological sequence, marveling at them as they appear, led on by the most rudimentary suspense—what happens next? and next?

In a tale, too, the sense of being "told" is strong with the impression of the immediacy and informality of a voice and of casualness and improvisation characteristic of such an occasion. The tale affords, too, the sense of events moving through time, in the simple order of time, with the interest very slight on character, logic, and meaning, with little emphasis on dramatically developed scenes connected and interpreted in a tissue of narrative, such as we find in ordinary modern fiction.

Only one of the selections offered here, "The Fir Tree," is literally a tale, and it is, as we shall see, far more sophisticated than "The Tinder Box." Nevertheless, all three selections exhibit the simple chronological approach of a tale, with the impression of casualness, even of oral narration, and the meaning, the theme, seems to emerge naturally from the narration rather than to be dramatically brought to focus as in the more complex stories to be found later in this book.

THE FIR TREE

Hans Christian Andersen (1805–1875)

Out in the forest stood a pretty little Fir Tree. It had a good place; it could have sunlight, air there was in plenty, and all around grew many larger comrades—pines as well as firs. But the little Fir Tree was in such a hurry to grow. It did not care for the warm sun and the fresh air; it took no notice of the peasant children, who went about talking together, when they had come out to look for strawberries and raspberries. Often they came with a whole pot-full, or had strung berries on a straw; then they would sit down by the little Fir Tree and say, 'How pretty and small that one is!' and the Tree did not like to hear that at all.

Next year it had grown a great joint, and the following year it was longer still, for in fir trees one can always tell by the number of joints they have how many years they have been growing.

'Oh, if I were only as great a tree as the others!' sighed the little Fir, 'then I would spread my branches far around, and look out from my crown into the wide world. The birds would then build nests in my boughs, and when the wind blew I could nod just as grandly as the others yonder.'

It took no pleasure in the sunshine, in the birds, and in the red clouds that went sailing over it morning and evening.

When it was winter, and the snow lay all around, white and sparkling, a hare would often come jumping along, and spring right over the little Fir Tree. Oh! this made it so angry. But two winters went by, and when the third came the little Tree had grown so tall that the hare was obliged to run round it.

'Oh! to grow, to grow, and become old; that's the only thing in the world,' thought the Tree.

In the autumn woodcutters always came and felled a few of the largest trees; that happened every year, and the little Fir Tree, that was now quite well grown, shuddered with fear, for the great stately trees fell to the ground with a crash, and their branches were cut off, so that the trees looked quite naked, long, and slender—they could hardly be recognized. But then they were laid upon wagons, and horses dragged them away out of the wood. Where were they going? What destiny awaited them?

In the spring, when Swallows and the Stork came, the Tree asked them, 'Do you know where they were taken? Did you not meet them?'

The Swallows knew nothing about it, but the Stork looked thoughtfully, nodded his head, and said,

'Yes, I think so. I met many new ships

when I flew out of Egypt; on the ships were stately masts; I fancy that these were the trees. They smelt like fir. I can assure you they're stately—very stately.'

'Oh that I were only big enough to go over the sea! What kind of thing is this sea, and how does it look?'

'It would take too long to explain all that,' said the Stork, and went away.

'Rejoice in thy youth,' said the Sunbeams; 'rejoice in thy fresh growth, and in the young life that is within thee.'

And the wind kissed the Tree, and the dew wept tears upon it; but the Fir Tree did not understand that.

When Christmas-time approached, quite young trees were felled, sometimes trees which were neither so old nor so large as this Fir Tree, that never rested but always wanted to go away. These young trees, which were just the most beautiful, kept all their branches; they were put upon wagons, and horses dragged them away out of the wood.

'Where are they all going?' asked the Fir Tree. 'They are not greater than I—indeed, one of them was much smaller. Why do they keep all their branches? Whither are they taken?'

'We know that! We know that!' chirped the Sparrows. 'Yonder in the town we looked in at the windows. We know where they go. Oh! they are dressed up in the greatest pomp and splendour that can be imagined. We have looked in at the windows, and have perceived that they are planted in the middle of the warm room, and adorned with the most beautiful things—gilt apples, honeycakes, playthings, and many hundreds of candles.'

'And then?' asked the Fir Tree, and trembled through all its branches. 'And then? What happens then?'

'Why, we have not seen anything more. But it was incomparable.'

'Perhaps I may be destined to tread this glorious path one day!' cried the Fir Tree rejoicingly. 'That is even better than travelling across the sea. How painfully I long for it! If it were only Christmas now! Now I am great and grown up, like the rest who were led away last year. Oh, if I were only on the carriage! If I were only in the warm room, among all the pomp and splendour! And then? Yes, then something even better will come, something far more charming, or else why should they adorn me so? There must be something grander, something greater still to come; but what? Oh! I'm suffering, I'm longing! I don't know myself what is the matter with me!'

'Rejoice in us,' said Air and Sunshine. 'Rejoice in thy fresh youth here in the woodland.'

But the Fir Tree did not rejoice at all, but it grew and grew; winter and summer it stood there, green, dark green. The people who saw it said, 'That's a handsome tree!' and at Christmas-time it was felled before any one of the others. The axe cut deep into its marrow, and the Tree fell to the ground with a sigh: it felt a pain, a sensation of faintness, and could not think at all of happiness, for it was sad at parting from its home, from the place where it had grown up: it knew that it should never again see the dear old companions, the little bushes and flowers all around—perhaps not even the birds. The parting was not at all agreeable.

The Tree only came to itself when it was unloaded in a yard, with other trees, and heard a man say,

'This one is famous; we only want this one!'

Now two servants came in gay liveries, and carried the Fir Tree into a large beautiful saloon. All around the walls hung pictures, and by the great stove stood large Chinese vases with lions on the covers; there were rocking-chairs, silken sofas, great tables covered with picture-books, and toys worth a hundred times a hundred dollars, at least the children said so. And the Fir Tree was put into a great tub filled with sand; but no one could see that it was a tub, for it was hung round with green cloth, and stood on a large many-coloured carpet. Oh, how the Tree trembled! What was to happen now? The servants, and the young ladies also, decked it out. On one branch they hung little nets, cut out of coloured paper; every net was filled with sweetmeats; golden apples and walnuts hung down as if they grew there, and more than a hundred little candles, red, white, and blue, were fastened to the different boughs. Dolls that looked exactly like real people—the Tree had never seen such before—swung among the foliage, and high on the summit of the Tree was fixed a tinsel star. It was splendid, particularly splendid.

'This evening,' said all, 'this evening it will shine.'

'Oh,' thought the Tree, 'that it were evening already! Oh that the lights may be soon lit up! What will happen then? I wonder if trees will come out of the forest to look at me? Will the sparrows fly against the panes? Shall I grow fast here, and stand adorned in summer and winter?'

Yes, it knew all about it. But it had a regular bark-ache from mere longing, and the bark-ache is just as bad for a Tree as the headache for a person.

At last the candles were lighted. What a brilliance, what splendour! The Tree trembled so in all its branches that one of the candles set fire to a green twig, and it was really painful.

'Heaven preserve us!' cried the young ladies; and they hastily put the fire out.

Now the Tree might not even tremble. Oh, that was terrible! It was so afraid of losing any of its ornaments, and it was quite bewildered with all the brilliance. And now the folding doors were thrown open, and a number of children rushed in as if they would have overturned the whole Tree; the older people followed more deliberately. The little ones stood quite silent, but only for a minute; then they shouted till the room rang; they danced gleefully round the Tree, and one present after another was plucked from it.

'What are they about?' thought the Tree. 'What's going to be done?'

And the candles burned down to the twigs, and as they burned down they were extinguished, and then the children received permission to plunder the Tree. Oh! they rushed in upon it, so that every branch cracked again: if it had not been fastened by the top and by the golden star to the ceiling, it would have fallen down.

The children danced about with their pretty toys. No one looked at the Tree except the old nursemaid, who came up and peeped among the branches, but only to see if a fig or an apple had not been forgotten.

'A story! a story!' shouted the children; and they drew a little fat man towards the Tree; and he sat down just beneath it,—'for then we shall be in the green wood,' said he, 'and the tree may have the advantage of listening to my tale. But I can only tell one. Will you hear the story of Ivede-Avede, or of Humpty-Dumpty, who fell downstairs, and still was raised up to honour and married the Princess?'

'Ivede-Avede!' cried some, 'Humpty-Dumpty!' cried others, and there was a great crying and shouting. Only the Fir Tree was quite silent, and thought, 'Shall I not be in it? shall I have nothing to do in it?' But it had been in the evening's amusement, and had done what was required of it.

And the fat man told about Humpty-Dumpty, who fell downstairs, and yet was raised to honour and married the Princess. And the children clapped their hands, and cried, 'Tell another! tell another!' for they wanted to hear about Ivede-Avede; but they only got the story of Humpty-Dumpty. The Fir Tree stood quite silent and thoughtful; never had the birds in the wood told such a story as that. Humpty-Dumpty fell downstairs, and yet came to honour and married the Princess!

'Yes, so it happens in the world!' thought the Fir Tree, and believed it must be true, because that was such a nice man who told it. 'Well, who can know? Perhaps I shall fall downstairs too, and marry a Princess!' And it looked forward with pleasure to being adorned again, the next evening, with candles and toys, gold and fruit. 'To-morrow

I shall not tremble,' it thought. 'I will rejoice in all my splendour. To-morrow I shall hear the story of Humpty-Dumpty again, and, perhaps, that of Ivede-Avede too.'

And the tree stood all night quiet and thoughtful.

In the morning the servants and the chambermaid came in.

'Now my splendour will begin afresh,' thought the Tree. But they dragged it out of the room, and upstairs to the garret, and here they put it in a dark corner where no daylight shone.

'What's the meaning of this?' thought the Tree. 'What am I to do here? What am I to get to know here?'

And he leaned against the wall, and thought, and thought. And he had time enough, for days and nights went by, and nobody came up; and when at length some one came, it was only to put some great boxes in a corner. Now the Tree stood quite hidden away, and one would think that it was quite forgotten.

'Now it's winter outside,' thought the Tree. 'The earth is hard and covered with snow, and people cannot plant me; therefore I suppose I'm to be sheltered here until spring comes. How considerate that is! How good people are! If it were only not so dark here, and so terribly solitary!—not even a little hare! It was pretty out there in the wood, when the snow lay thick and the hare sprang past; yes, even when he jumped over me, although I did not like that at the time. It is terribly lonely up here!'

'Piep! piep!' said a little Mouse, and crept forward, and then came another little one. They smelt at the Fir Tree, and then slipped among the branches.

'It's horribly cold,' said the two little Mice, 'or else it would be comfortable here. Don't you think so, you old Fir Tree?'

'I'm not old at all,' said the Fir Tree. 'There are many much older than I.'

'Where do you come from?' asked the Mice. 'And what do you know?' They were dreadfully inquisitive. 'Tell us about the most beautiful spot on earth. Have you been there? Have you been in the store-room, where cheeses lie on the shelves, and hams hang from the ceiling, where one dances on tallow candles, and goes in thin and comes out fat?'

'I don't know that!' replied the Tree; 'but I know the wood, where the sun shines, and where the birds sing.'

And then it told all about its youth.

And the little Mice had never heard anything of the kind; and they listened and said,

'What a number of things you have seen! How happy you must have been!'

'I?' said the Fir Tree; and it thought about what it had told. 'Yes, those were really quite happy times.' But then it told of the Christmas-eve, when it had been hung with sweetmeats and candles.

'Oh!' said the little Mice, 'how happy you have been, you old Fir Tree!'

'I'm not old at all,' said the Tree. 'I only came out of the wood this winter. I'm in my very best years.'

'What splendid stories you can tell!' said the little Mice.

And next night they came with four other little Mice, to hear what the Tree had to relate; and the more it said, the more clearly did it remember everything, and thought, 'Those were quite merry days! But they may come again. Humpty-Dumpty fell downstairs, and yet he married the Princess. Perhaps I may marry a Princess too!' And then the Fir Tree thought of a pretty little birch tree that grew out in the forest, for the Fir Tree, that birch was a real Princess.

'Who's Humpty-Dumpty?' asked the little Mice.

And then the Fir Tree told the whole story. It could remember every single word; and the little Mice were ready to leap to the very top of the tree with pleasure. Next night a great many more Mice came, and on Sunday two Rats even appeared; but these thought the story was not pretty, and the little Mice were sorry for that, for now they also did not like it so much as before.

'Do you only know one story?' asked the Rats.

'Only that one,' replied the Tree. 'I heard that on the happiest evening of my life; I did not think then how happy I was.'

'That's an exceedingly poor story. Don't you know any about bacon and tallow candles—a store-room story?'

'No,' said the Tree.

'Then we'd rather not hear you,' said the Rats.

And they went back to their own people. The little Mice at last stayed away also; and then the Tree sighed and said,

'It was very nice when they sat around me, the merry little Mice, and listened when I spoke to them. Now that's past too. But I shall remember to be pleased when they take me out.'

But when did that happen? Why, it was one morning that people came and rummaged in the garret: the boxes were put away, and the Tree brought out; they certainly threw it rather roughly on the floor, but a servant dragged it away at once to the stairs, where the daylight shone.

'Now life is beginning again,' thought the Tree.

It felt the fresh air and the first sunbeams, and now it was out in the courtyard. Everything passed so quickly that the Tree quite forgot to look at itself, there was so much to look at all round. The courtyard was close to a garden, and here everything was blooming; the roses hung fresh and fragrant over the little paling, the linden trees were in blossom, and the swallows cried, 'Quirre-virre-vit! my husband's come!' But it was not the Fir Tree that they meant.

'Now I shall live!' said the Tree, rejoicingly, and spread its branches far out; but, alas! they were all withered and yellow; and it lay in the corner among nettles and weeds. The tinsel star was still upon it, and shone in the bright sunshine.

In the courtyard a couple of the merry children were playing, who had danced round the tree at Christmas-time, and had rejoiced over it. One of the youngest ran up and tore off the golden star.

'Look what is sticking to the ugly old fir tree,' said the child, and he trod upon the branches till they cracked again under his boots.

And the Tree looked at all the blooming flowers and the splendour of the garden, and then looked at itself, and wished it had remained in the dark corner of the garret; it thought of its fresh youth in the wood, of the merry Christmas-eve, and of the little Mice which had listened so pleasantly to the story of Humpty-Dumpty.

'Past! past!' said the poor Tree. 'Had I but rejoiced when I could have done so! Past! past!'

And the servant came and chopped the Tree into little pieces; a whole bundle lay there: it blazed brightly under the great brewing copper, and it sighed deeply, and each sigh was like a little shot: and the children who were at play there ran up and seated themselves at the fire, looked into it, and cried, 'Puff! puff!' But at each explosion, which was a deep sigh, the tree thought of a summer day in the woods, or of a winter night there, when the stars beamed; it thought of Christmas-eve and of Humpty-Dumpty, the only story it had ever heard or knew how to tell; and then the Tree was burned.

The boys played in the garden, and the youngest had on his breast a golden star, which the Tree had worn on its happiest evening. Now that was past, and the Tree's life was past, and the story is past too: past! past!—and that's the way with all stories.

EXERCISES

1. What is the conflict, if any, in this story? Is it basically internal or external? What idea emerges at the end of the story?
2. Though "The Fir Tree" is presumably intended for children, the adult reader finds something here too. What is it? And is it the same thing

that the child finds? If "The Fir Tree" were re-written with more sophisticated handling of the narrative and in a more sophisticated style, would it have a more powerful effect on the mature reader?

Is not the very fact that the story is designed for children important in creating the effect on the adult reader? That is, is not the adult reader looking, as it were, over the shoulder of the child reader? To answer this question, try to imagine what a child would find here, and try to contrast it with your response. Can it be said that the effect on the adult reader depends on the ironical (see Glossary) discrepancy between the response of the child, who has little sense of the human fate in time, and who, though perhaps troubled by the tale, is primarily caught by the imaginative details of action, and the response of the adult, who, from his height of experience, can look down on the child's ignorance of life, with pity and tenderness? In any case, the effect here, however you may define it, is dependent on the point of view from which the tale is told and the audience to which it is ostensibly directed.

FLIGHT
John Steinbeck (1902–1968)

About fifteen miles below Monterey, on the wild coast, the Torres family had their farm, a few sloping acres above a cliff that dropped to the brown reefs and to the hissing white waters of the ocean. Behind the farm the stone mountains stood up against the sky. The farm buildings huddled like little clinging aphids on the mountain skirts, crouched low to the ground as though the wind might blow them into the sea. The little shack, the rattling, rotting barn were gray-bitten with sea salt, beaten by the damp wind until they had taken on the color of the granite hills. Two horses, a red cow and a red calf, half a dozen pigs and a flock of lean, multi-colored chickens stocked the place. A little corn was raised on the sterile slope, and it grew short and thick under the wind, and all the cobs formed on the landward side of the stalks.

Mama Torres, a lean, dry woman with ancient eyes, had ruled the farm for ten years, ever since her husband tripped over a stone

in the field one day and fell full length on a rattle-snake. When one is bitten on the chest there is not much that can be done.

Mama Torres had three children, two undersized black ones of twelve and fourteen, Emilio and Rosy, whom Mama kept fishing on the rocks below the farm when the sea was kind and when the truant officer was in some distant part of Monterey County. And there was Pepé, the tall smiling son of nineteen, a gentle, affectionate boy, but very lazy. Pepé had a tall head, pointed at the top, and from its peak, coarse black hair grew down like a thatch all around. Over his smiling little eyes Mama cut a straight bang so he could see. Pepé had sharp Indian cheekbones and an eagle nose, but his mouth was as sweet and shapely as a girl's mouth, and his chin was fragile and chiseled. He was loose and gangling, all legs and feet and wrists, and he was very lazy. Mama thought him fine and brave, but she never told him so. She said, "Some lazy cow must have gone into thy father's family, else how could I have a son like thee." And she said, "When I carried thee, a sneaking lazy coyote came out of the brush and looked at me one day. That must have made thee so."

Pepé smiled sheepishly and stabbed at the ground with his knife to keep the blade sharp and free from rust. It was his inheritance, that knife, his father's knife. The long heavy blade folded back into the black handle. There was a button on the handle. When Pepé pressed the button, the blade leaped out ready for use. The knife was with Pepé always, for it had been his father's knife.

One sunny morning when the sea below the cliff was glinting and blue and the white surf creamed on the reef, when even the stone mountains looked kindly, Mama Torres called out the door of the shack, "Pepé, I have a labor for thee."

There was no answer. Mama listened. From behind the barn she heard a burst of laughter. She lifted her full long skirt and walked in the direction of the noise.

Pepé was sitting on the ground with his

back against a box. His white teeth glistened. On either side of him stood the two black ones, tense and expectant. Fifteen feet away a redwood post was set in the ground. Pepé's right hand lay limply in his lap, and in the palm the big black knife rested. The blade was closed back into the handle. Pepé looked smiling at the sky.

Suddenly Emilio cried, "Ya!"

Pepé's wrist flicked like the head of a snake. The blade seemed to fly open in midair, and with a thump the point dug into the redwood post, and the black handle quivered. The three burst into excited laughter. Rosy ran to the post and pulled out the knife and brought it back to Pepé. He closed the blade and settled the knife carefully in his listless palm again. He grinned self-consciously at the sky.

"Ya!"

The heavy knife lanced out and sunk into the post again. Mama moved forward like a ship and scattered the play.

"All day you do foolish things with the knife, like a toy-baby," she stormed. "Get up on thy huge feet that eat up shoes. Get up!" She took him by one loose shoulder and hoisted at him. Pepé grinned sheepishly and came half-heartedly to his feet. "Look!" Mama cried. "Big lazy, you must catch the horse and put on him thy father's saddle. You must ride to Monterey. The medicine bottle is empty. There is no salt. Go thou now, Peanut! Catch the horse."

A revolution took place in the relaxed figure of Pepé. "To Monterey, me? Alone? *Si,* Mama."

She scowled at him. "Do not think, big sheep, that you will buy candy. No, I will give you only enough for the medicine and the salt."

Pepé smiled. "Mama, you will put the hatband on the hat?"

She relented then. "Yes, Pepé. You may wear the hatband."

His voice grew insinuating, "And the green handkerchief, Mama?"

"Yes, if you go quickly and return with no trouble, the silk green handkerchief will go. If you make sure to take off the handkerchief when you eat so no spot may fall on it. . . ."

"*Si,* Mama. I will be careful. I am a man."

"Thou? A man? Thou art a peanut."

He went into the rickety barn and brought out a rope, and he walked agilely enough up the hill to catch the horse.

When he was ready and mounted before the door, mounted in his father's saddle that was so old that the oaken frame showed through torn leather in many places, then Mama brought out the round black hat with the tooled leather band, and she reached up and knotted the green silk handkerchief about his neck. Pepé's blue denim coat was much darker than his jeans, for it had been washed much less often.

Mama handed up the big medicine bottle and the silver coins. "That for the medicine," she said, "and that for the salt. That for a candle to burn for the papa. That for *dulces* for the little ones. Our friend Mrs. Rodriguez will give you dinner and maybe a bed for the night. When you go to the church say only ten Paternosters and only twenty-five Ave Marias. Oh! I know, big coyote. You would sit there flapping your mouth over Aves all day while you looked at the candles and the holy pictures. That is not good devotion to stare at the pretty things."

The black hat, covering the high pointed head and black thatched hair of Pepé, gave him dignity and age. He sat the rangy horse well. Mama thought how handsome he was, dark and lean and tall. "I would not send thee now alone, thou little one, except for the medicine," she said softly. "It is not good to have no medicine, for who knows when the toothache will come, or the sadness of the stomach. These things are."

"Adios, Mama," Pepé cried. "I will come back soon. You may send me often alone. I am a man."

"Thou art a foolish chicken."

He straightened his shoulders, flipped the reins against the horse's shoulder and rode away. He turned once and saw that they still watched him, Emilio and Rosy and Mama. Pepé grinned with pride and gladness and lifted the tough buckskin horse to a trot.

When he had dropped out of sight over a little dip in the road, Mama turned to the black ones, but she spoke to herself. "He is nearly a man now," she said. "It will be a nice thing to have a man in the house again." Her eyes sharpened on the children. "Go to the rocks now. The tide is going out. There will be abalones to be found." She put the iron hooks into their hands and saw them down the steep trail to the reefs. She brought the smooth stone *metate* to the doorway and sat grinding her corn to flour and looking occasionally at the road over which Pepé had gone. The noonday came and then the afternoon, when the little ones beat the abalones on a rock to make them tender and Mama patted the tortillas to make them thin. They ate their dinner as the red sun was plunging down toward the ocean. They sat on the doorsteps and watched the big white moon come over the mountain tops.

Mama said, "He is now at the house of our friend Mrs. Rodriguez. She will give him nice things to eat and maybe a present."

Emilio said, "Some day I too will ride to Monterey for medicine. Did Pepé come to be a man today?"

Mama said wisely, "A boy gets to be a man when a man is needed. Remember this thing. I have known boys forty years old because there was no need for a man."

Soon afterwards they retired, Mama in her big oak bed on one side of the room, Emilio and Rosy in their boxes full of straw and sheepskins on the other side of the room.

The moon went over the sky and the surf roared on the rocks. The roosters crowed the first call. The surf subsided to a whispering surge against the reef. The moon dropped toward the sea. The roosters crowed again.

The moon was near down to the water when Pepé rode on a winded horse to his home flat. His dog bounced out and circled the horse yelping with pleasure. Pepé slid off the saddle to the ground. The weathered little shack was silver in the moonlight and the square shadow of it was black to the north and east. Against the east the piling mountains were misty with light; their tops melted into the sky.

Pepé walked wearily up the three steps and into the house. It was dark inside. There was a rustle in the corner.

Mama cried out from her bed. "Who comes? Pepé, is it thou?"

"*Si*, Mama."

"Did you get the medicine?"

"*Si*, Mama."

"Well, go to sleep, then. I thought you would be sleeping at the house of Mrs. Rodriguez." Pepé stood silently in the dark room. "Why do you stand there, Pepé? Did you drink wine?"

"*Si*, Mama."

"Well, go to bed then and sleep out the wine."

His voice was tired and patient, but very firm. "Light the candle, Mama. I must go away into the mountains."

"What is this, Pepé? You are crazy." Mama struck a sulphur match and held the little blue burr until the flame spread up the stick. She set light to the candle on the floor beside her bed. "Now, Pepé, what is this you say?" She looked anxiously into his face.

He was changed. The fragile quality seemed to have gone from his chin. His mouth was less full than it had been, the lines of the lips were straighter, but in his eyes the greatest change had taken place. There was no laughter in them any more nor any bashfulness. They were sharp and bright and purposeful.

He told her in a tired monotone, told her everything just as it had happened. A few people came into the kitchen of Mrs. Rodriguez. There was wine to drink. Pepé drank dark wine. The little quarrel—the man started toward Pepé and then the knife —it went almost by itself. It flew, it darted before Pepé knew it. As he talked, Mama's face grew stern, and it seemed to grow more lean. Pepé finished. "I am a man now, Mama. The man said names to me I could not allow."

Mama nodded. "Yes, thou art a man, my poor little Pepé. Thou art a man. I have seen it coming on thee. I have watched you throwing the knife into the post, and I have been afraid." For a moment her face had softened, but now it grew stern again. "Come! We must get you ready. Go. Awaken Emilio and Rosy. Go quickly."

Pepé stepped over to the corner where his brother and sister slept among the sheepskins. He leaned down and shook them gently. "Come, Rosy! Come, Emilio! The mama says you must arise."

The little black ones sat up and rubbed their eyes in the candlelight. Mama was out of bed now, her long black skirt over her nightgown. "Emilio," she cried. "Go up and catch the other horse for Pepé. Quickly, now! Quickly." Emilio put his legs in his overalls and stumbled sleepily out the door.

"You heard no one behind you on the road?" Mama demanded.

"No, Mama. I listened carefully. No one was on the road."

Mama darted like a bird about the room. From a nail on the wall she took a canvas water bag and threw it on the floor. She stripped a blanket from her bed and rolled it into a tight tube and tied the ends with string. From a box beside the stove she lifted a flour sack half full of black stringy jerky. "Your father's black coat, Pepé. Here, put it on."

Pepé stood in the middle of the floor watching her activity. She reached behind the door and brought out the rifle, a long 38-56, worn shiny the whole length of the

barrel. Pepé took it from her and held it in the crook of his elbow. Mama brought a little leather bag and counted the cartridges into his hand. "Only ten left," she warned. "You must not waste them."

Emilio put his head in the door. "'Qui 'st 'l caballo, Mama."

"Put on the saddle from the other horse. Tie on the blanket. Here, tie the jerky to the saddle horn."

Still Pepé stood silently watching his mother's frantic activity. His chin looked hard, and his sweet mouth was drawn and thin. His little eyes followed Mama about the room almost suspiciously.

Rosy asked softly, "Where goes Pepé?"

Mama's eyes were fierce. "Pepé goes on a journey. Pepé is a man now. He has a man's thing to do."

Pepé straightened his shoulders. His mouth changed until he looked very much like Mama.

At last the preparation was finished. The loaded horse stood outside the door. The water bag dripped a line of moisture down the bay shoulder.

The moonlight was being thinned by the dawn and the big white moon was near down to the sea. The family stood by the shack. Mama confronted Pepé. "Look, my son! Do not stop until it is dark again. Do not sleep even though you are tired. Take care of the horse in order that he may not stop of weariness. Remember to be careful with the bullets—there are only ten. Do not fill thy stomach with jerky or it will make thee sick. Eat a little jerky and fill thy stomach with grass. When thou comest to the high mountains, if thou seest any of the dark watching men, go not near to them nor try to speak to them. And forget not thy prayers." She put her lean hands on Pepé's shoulders, stood on her toes and kissed him formally on both cheeks, and Pepé kissed her on both cheeks. Then he went to Emilio and Rosy and kissed both of their cheeks.

Pepé turned back to Mama. He seemed

to look for a little softness, a little weakness in her. His eyes were searching, but Mama's face remained fierce. "Go now," she said. "Do not wait to be caught like a chicken."

Pepé pulled himself into the saddle. "I am a man," he said.

It was the first dawn when he rode up the hill toward the little canyon which let a trail into the mountains. Moonlight and daylight fought with each other, and the two warring qualities made it difficult to see. Before Pepé had gone a hundred yards, the outlines of his figure were misty; and long before he entered the canyon, he had become a gray, indefinite shadow.

Mama stood stiffly in front of her doorstep, and on either side of her stood Emilio and Rosy. They cast furtive glances at Mama now and then.

When the gray shape of Pepé melted into the hillside and disappeared, Mama relaxed. She began the high, whining keen of the death wail. "Our beautiful—our brave," she cried. "Our protector, our son is gone." Emilio and Rosy moaned beside her. "Our beautiful—our brave, he is gone." It was the formal wail. It rose to a high piercing whine and subsided to a moan. Mama raised it three times and then she turned and went into the house and shut the door.

Emilio and Rosy stood wondering in the dawn. They heard Mama whimpering in the house. They went out to sit on the cliff above the ocean. They touched shoulders. "When did Pepé come to be a man?" Emilio asked.

"Last night," said Rosy. "Last night in Monterey." The ocean clouds turned red with the sun that was behind the mountains.

"We will have no breakfast," said Emilio. "Mama will not want to cook." Rosy did not answer him. "Where is Pepé gone," he asked.

Rosy looked around at him. She drew her knowledge from the quiet air. "He has gone on a journey. He will never come back."

"Is he dead? Do you think he is dead?"

Rosy looked back at the ocean again. A little steamer, drawing a line of smoke sat on the edge of the horizon. "He is not dead," Rosy explained. "Not yet."

Pepé rested the big rifle across the saddle in front of him. He let the horse walk up the hill and he didn't look back. The stony slope took on a coat of short brush so that Pepé found the entrance to a trail and entered it.

When he came to the canyon opening, he swung once in his saddle and looked back, but the houses were swallowed in the misty light. Pepé jerked forward again. The high shoulder of the canyon closed in on him. His horse stretched out its neck and sighed and settled to the trail.

It was a well-worn path, dark soft leaf-mold earth strewn with broken pieces of sandstone. The trail rounded the shoulder of the canyon and dropped steeply into the bed of the stream. In the shallows the water ran smoothly, glinting in the first morning sun. Small round stones on the bottom were as brown as rust with sun moss. In the sand along the edges of the stream the tall, rich wild mint grew, while in the water itself the cress, old and tough, had gone to heavy seed.

The path went into the stream and emerged on the other side. The horse sloshed into the water and stopped. Pepé dropped his bridle and let the beast drink of the running water.

Soon the canyon sides became steep and the first giant sentinel redwoods guarded the trail, great round red trunks bearing foliage as green and lacy as ferns. Once Pepé was among the trees, the sun was lost. A perfumed and purple light lay in the pale green of the underbrush. Gooseberry bushes and blackberries and tall ferns lined the stream, and overhead the branches of the redwoods met and cut off the sky.

Pepé drank from the water bag, and he reached into the flour sack and brought out a black string of jerky. His white teeth gnawed at the string until the tough meat parted. He chewed slowly and drank occasionally from the water bag. His little eyes were slumberous and tired, but the muscles of his face were hard set. The earth of the trail was black now. It gave up a hollow sound under the walking hoofbeats.

The stream fell more sharply. Little waterfalls splashed on the stones. Five-fingered ferns hung over the water and dripped spray from their fingertips. Pepé rode half over in his saddle, dangling one leg loosely. He picked a bay leaf from a tree beside the way and put it into his mouth for a moment to flavor the dry jerky. He held the gun loosely across the pommel.

Suddenly he squared in his saddle, swung the horse from the trail and kicked it hurriedly up behind a big redwood tree. He pulled up the reins tight against the bit to keep the horse from whinnying. His face was intent and his nostrils quivered a little.

A hollow pounding came down the trail, and a horseman rode by, a fat man with red cheeks and a white stubble beard. His horse put down its head and blubbered at the trail when it came to the place where Pepé had turned off. "Hold up!" said the man and he pulled up his horse's head.

When the last sound of the hoofs died away, Pepé came back into the trail again. He did not relax in the saddle any more. He lifted the big rifle and swung the lever to throw a shell into the chamber, and then he let down the hammer to half cock.

The trail grew very steep. Now the redwood trees were smaller and their tops were dead, bitten dead where the wind reached them. The horse plodded on; the sun went slowly overhead and started down toward the afternoon.

Where the stream came out of a side canyon, the trail left it. Pepé dismounted and watered his horse and filled up his water bag. As soon as the trail had parted from the stream, the trees were gone and only the thick brittle sage and manzanita and chaparral edged the trail. And the soft black earth was gone, too, leaving only the light tan broken rock for the trail bed. Lizards scampered away into the brush as the horse rattled over the little stones.

Pepé turned in his saddle and looked back. He was in the open now: he could be seen from a distance. As he ascended the trail the country grew more rough and terrible and dry. The way wound about the bases of great square rocks. Little gray rabbits skittered in the brush. A bird made a monotonous high creaking. Eastward the bare rock mountaintops were pale and powder-dry under the dropping sun. The horse plodded up and up the trail toward a little V in the ridge which was the pass.

Pepé looked suspiciously back every minute or so, and his eyes sought the tops of the ridges ahead. Once, on a white barren spur, he saw a black figure for a moment, but he looked quickly away, for it was one of the dark watchers. No one knew who the watchers were, nor where they lived, but it was better to ignore them and never to show interest in them. They did not bother one who stayed on the trail and minded his own business.

The air was parched and full of light dust blown by the breeze from the eroding mountains. Pepé drank sparingly from his bag and corked it tightly and hung it on the horn again. The trail moved up the dry shale hillside, avoiding rocks, dropping under clefts, climbing in and out of old water scars. When he arrived at the little pass he stopped and looked back for a long time. No dark watchers were to be seen now. The trail behind was empty. Only the high tops of the redwoods indicated where the stream flowed.

Pepé rode on through the pass. His little eyes were nearly closed with weariness, but his face was stern, relentless and manly. The high mountain wind coasted sighing through the pass and whistled on the edges of the big blocks of broken granite. In the air, a red-tailed hawk sailed over close to the ridge and screamed angrily. Pepé went slowly through the broken jagged pass and looked down on the other side.

The trail dropped quickly, staggering

among broken rock. At the bottom of the slope there was a dark crease, thick with brush, and on the other side of the crease a little flat, in which a grove of oak trees grew. A scar of green grass cut across the flat. And behind the flat another mountain rose, desolate with dead rocks and starving little black bushes. Pepé drank from the bag again for the air was so dry that it encrusted his nostrils and burned his lips. He put the horse down the trail. The hooves slipped and struggled on the steep way, starting little stones that rolled off into the brush. The sun was gone behind the westward mountain now, but still it glowed brilliantly on the oaks and on the grassy flat. The rocks and the hillsides still sent up waves of the heat they had gathered from the day's sun.

Pepé looked up to the top of the next dry withered ridge. He saw a dark form against the sky, a man's figure standing on top of a rock, and he glanced away quickly not to appear curious. When a moment later he looked up again, the figure was gone.

Downward the trail was quickly covered. Sometimes the horse floundered for footing, sometimes set his feet and slid a little way. They came at last to the bottom where the dark chaparral was higher than Pepé's head. He held up his rifle on one side and his arm on the other to shield his face from the sharp brittle fingers of the brush.

Up and out of the crease he rode, and up a little cliff. The grassy flat was before him, and the round comfortable oaks. For a moment he studied the trail down which he had come, but there was no movement and no sound from it. Finally he rode out over the flat, to the green streak, and at the upper end of the damp he found a little spring welling out of the earth and dropping into a dug basin before it seeped out over the flat.

Pepé filled his bag first, and then he let the thirsty horse drink out of the pool. He led the horse to the clump of oaks, and in the middle of the grove, fairly protected from sight on all sides, he took off the saddle and the bridle and laid them on the ground. The horse stretched his jaws sideways and yawned. Pepé knotted the lead rope about the horse's neck and tied him to a sapling among the oaks, where he could graze in a fairly large circle.

When the horse was gnawing hungrily at the dry grass, Pepé went to the saddle and took a black string of jerky from the sack and strolled to an oak tree on the edge of the grove, from under which he could watch the trail. He sat down in the crisp dry oak leaves and automatically felt for his big black knife to cut the jerky, but he had no knife. He leaned back on his elbow and gnawed at the tough strong meat. His face was blank, but it was a man's face.

The bright evening light washed the eastern ridge, but the valley was darkening. Doves flew down from the hills to the spring, and the quail came running out of the brush and joined them, calling clearly to one another.

Out of the corner of his eye Pepé saw a shadow grow out of the bushy crease. He turned his head slowly. A big spotted wildcat was creeping toward the spring, belly to the ground, moving like thought.

Pepé cocked his rifle and edged the muzzle slowly around. Then he looked apprehensively up the trail and dropped the hammer again. From the ground beside him he picked an oak twig and threw it toward the spring. The quail flew up with a roar and the doves whistled away. The big cat stood up: for a long moment he looked at Pepé with cold yellow eyes, and then fearlessly walked back into the gulch.

The dusk gathered quickly in the deep valley. Pepé muttered his prayers, put his head down on his arm and went instantly to sleep.

The moon came up and filled the valley with cold blue light, and the wind swept rustling down from the peaks. The owls worked up and down the slopes looking for rabbits. Down in the brush of the gulch a coyote gabbled. The oak trees whispered softly in the night breeze.

Pepé started up, listening. His horse had whinnied. The moon was just slipping behind the western ridge, leaving the valley in darkness behind it. Pepé sat tensely gripping his rifle. From far up the trail he heard an answering whinny and the crash of shod hooves on the broken rock. He jumped to his feet, ran to his horse and led it under the trees. He threw on the saddle and clinched it tight for the steep trail, caught the unwilling head and forced the bit into the mouth. He felt the saddle to make sure the water bag and the sack of jerky were there. Then he mounted and turned up the hill.

It was velvet dark. The horse found the entrance to the trail where it left the flat, and started up, stumbling and slipping on the rocks. Pepé's hand rose up to his head. His hat was gone. He had left it under the oak tree.

The horse had struggled far up the trail when the first change of dawn came into the air, a steel grayness as light mixed thoroughly with dark. Gradually the sharp snaggled edge of the ridge stood out above them, rotten granite tortured and eaten by the wind of time. Pepé had dropped his reins on the horn, leaving direction to the horse. The brush grabbed at his legs in the dark until one knee of his jeans was ripped.

Gradually the light flowed down over the ridge. The starved brush and rocks stood out in the half light, strange and lonely in high perspective. Then there came warmth into the light. Pepé drew up and looked back, but he could see nothing in the darker valley below. The sky turned blue over the coming sun. In the waste of the mountainside, the poor dry brush grew only three feet high. Here and there, big outcroppings of unrotted granite stood up like moldering houses. Pepé relaxed a little. He drank from his water bag and bit off a piece of jerky. A single eagle flew over, high in the light.

Without warning Pepé's horse screamed and fell on its side. He was almost down before the rifle crash echoed up from the valley. From a hole behind the struggling shoulder, a stream of bright crimson blood pumped and stopped and pumped and stopped. The hooves threshed on the ground. Pepé lay half stunned beside the horse. He looked slowly down the hill. A piece of sage clipped off beside his head and another crash echoed up from side to side of the canyon. Pepé flung himself frantically behind a bush.

He crawled up the hill on his knees and on one hand. His right hand held the rifle up off the ground and pushed it ahead of him. He moved with the instinctive care of an animal. Rapidly he wormed his way toward one of the big outcroppings of granite on the hill above him. Where the brush was high he doubled up and ran, but where the cover was slight he wriggled forward on his stomach, pushing the rifle ahead of him. In the last little distance there was no cover at all. Pepé poised and then he darted across the space and flashed around the corner of the rock.

He leaned panting against the stone. When his breath came easier he moved along behind the big rock until he came to a narrow split that offered a thin section of vision down the hill. Pepé lay on his stomach and pushed the rifle barrel through the slit and waited.

The sun reddened the western ridges now. Already the buzzards were settling down toward the place where the horse lay. A small brown bird scratched in the dead sage leaves directly in front of the rifle muzzle. The coasting eagle flew back toward the rising sun.

Pepé saw a little movement in the brush far below. His grip tightened on the gun. A little brown doe stepped daintily out on the trail and crossed it and disappeared into the brush again. For a long time Pepé waited. Far below he could see the little flat and the oak trees and the slash of green. Suddenly his eyes flashed back at the trail again. A quarter of a mile down there had been a quick movement in the chaparral. The rifle swung over. The front sight nestled in the V of the rear sight. Pepé studied for a moment and then raised the rear sight a notch. The little movement in the brush came again. The sight settled on it. Pepé squeezed the trigger. The explosion crashed down the mountain and up the other side, and came rattling back. The whole side of the slope grew still. No more movement. And then a white streak cut into the granite of the slit and a bullet whined away and a crash sounded up from below. Pepé felt a sharp pain in his right hand. A sliver of granite was sticking out from between his first and second knuckles and the point protruded from his palm. Carefully he pulled out the sliver of stone. The wound bled evenly and gently. No vein nor artery was cut.

Pepé looked into a little dusty cave in the rock and gathered a handful of spider web, and he pressed the mass into the cut, plastering the soft web into the blood. The flow stopped almost at once.

The rifle was on the ground. Pepé picked it up, levered a new shell into the chamber. And then he slid into the brush on his stomach. Far to the right he crawled, and then up the hill, moving slowly and carefully, crawling to cover and resting and then crawling again.

In the mountains the sun is high in its arc before it penetrates the gorges. The hot face looked over the hill and brought instant heat with it. The white light beat on the rocks and reflected from them and rose up quivering from the earth again, and the rocks and bushes seemed to quiver behind the air.

Pepé crawled in the general direction of the ridge peak, zig-zagging for cover. The deep cut between his knuckles began to throb. He crawled close to a rattlesnake before he saw it, and when it raised its dry head and made a soft beginning whirr, he backed up and took another way. The quick gray lizards flashed in front of him, raising a tiny line of dust. He found another mass of spider web and pressed it against his throbbing hand.

Pepé was pushing the rifle with his left hand now. Little drops of sweat ran to the ends of his coarse black hair and rolled down his cheeks. His lips and tongue were growing thick and heavy. His lips writhed to draw saliva into his mouth. His little dark eyes were uneasy and suspicious. Once when a gray lizard paused in front of him on the parched ground and turned its head sideways he crushed it flat with a stone.

When the sun slid past noon he had not gone a mile. He crawled exhaustedly a last hundred yards to a patch of high sharp manzanita, crawled desperately, and when the patch was reached he wriggled in among the tough gnarly trunks and dropped his head on his left arm. There was little shade in the meager brush, but there was cover and safety. Pepé went to sleep as he lay and the sun beat on his back. A few little birds hopped close to him and peered and hopped away. Pepé squirmed in his sleep and he raised and dropped his wounded hand again and again.

The sun went down behind the peaks and the cool evening came, and then the dark. A coyote yelled from the hillside, Pepé started awake and looked about with misty eyes. His hand was swollen and heavy; a little thread of pain ran up the inside of his arm and settled in a pocket in his armpit. He peered about and then stood up, for the mountains were black and the moon had not yet risen. Pepé stood up in the dark. The coat of his father pressed on his arm. His tongue was swollen until it nearly filled his mouth. He wriggled out of the coat and dropped it in the brush, and then he struggled up the hill, falling over rocks and tearing his way through the brush. The rifle knocked against stones as he went. Little dry avalanches of gravel and shattered stone went whispering down the hill behind him.

After a while the old moon came up and showed the jagged ridge top ahead of him. By moonlight Pepé traveled more easily. He bent forward so that his throbbing arm hung away from his body. The journey uphill was made in dashes and rests, a frantic rush up a few yards and then a rest. The wind coasted down the slope rattling the dry stems of the bushes.

The moon was at meridian when Pepé

came at last to the sharp backbone of the ridge top. On the last hundred yards of the rise no soil had clung under the wearing winds. The way was on solid rock. He clambered to the top and looked down on the other side. There was a draw like the last below him, misty with moonlight, brushed with dry struggling sage and chaparral. On the other side the hill rose up sharply and at the top the jagged rotten teeth of the mountain showed against the sky. At the bottom of the cut the brush was thick and dark.

Pepé stumbled down the hill. His throat was almost closed with thirst. At first he tried to run, but immediately he fell and rolled. After that he went more carefully. The moon was just disappearing behind the mountains when he came to the bottom. He crawled into the heavy brush feeling with his fingers for water. There was no water in the bed of the stream, only damp earth. Pepé laid his gun down and scooped up a handful of mud and put it in his mouth, and then he spluttered and scraped the earth from his tongue with his finger, for the mud drew at his mouth like a poultice. He dug a hole in the stream bed with his fingers, dug a little basin to catch water; but before it was very deep his head fell forward on the damp ground and he slept.

The dawn came and the heat of the day fell on the earth, and still Pepé slept. Late in the afternoon his head jerked up. He looked slowly around. His eyes were slits of wariness. twenty feet away in the heavy brush a big tawny mountain lion stood looking at him. Its long thick tail waved gracefully, its ears erect with interest, not laid back dangerously. The lion squatted down on its stomach and watched him.

Pepé looked at the hole he had dug in the earth. A half inch of muddy water had collected in the bottom. He tore the sleeve from his hurt arm, with his teeth ripped out a little square, soaked it in the water and put it in his mouth. Over and over he filled the cloth and sucked it.

Still the lion sat and watched him. The evening came down but there was no move-ment on the hills. No birds visited the dry bottom of the cut. Pepé looked occasionally at the lion. The eyes of the yellow beast drooped as though he were about to sleep. He yawned and his long thin red tongue curled out. Suddenly his head jerked around and his nostrils quivered. His big tail lashed. He stood up and slunk like a tawny shadow into the thick brush.

A moment later Pepé heard the sound, the faint far crash of horses' hooves on gravel. And he heard something else, a high whining yelp of a dog.

Pepé took his rifle into his left hand and he glided into the brush almost as quietly as the lion had. In the darkening evening he crouched up the hill toward the next ridge. Only when the dark came did he stand up. His energy was short. Once it was dark he fell over the rocks and slipped to his knees on the steep slope, but he moved on and on up the hill, climbing and scrabbling over the broken hillside.

When he was far up toward the top, he lay down and slept for a little while. The withered moon, shining on his face, awakened him. He stood up and moved up the hill. Fifty yards away he stopped and turned back, for he had forgotten his rifle. He walked heavily down and poked about in the brush, but he could not find his gun. At last he lay down to rest. The pocket of pain in his armpit had grown more sharp. His arm seemed to swell out and fall with every heartbeat. There was no position lying down where the heavy arm did not press against his armpit.

With the effort of a hurt beast, Pepé got up and moved again toward the top of the ridge. He held his swollen arm away from his body with his left hand. Up the steep hill he dragged himself, a few steps and a rest, and a few more steps. At last he was nearing the top. The moon showed the uneven sharp back of it against the sky.

Pepé's brain spun in a big spiral up and away from him. He slumped to the ground and lay still. The rock ridge top was only a hundred feet above him.

The moon moved over the sky. Pepé

half turned on his back. His tongue tried to make words, but only a thick hissing came from between his lips.

When the dawn came, Pepé pulled himself up. His eyes were sane again. He drew his great puffed arm in front of him and looked at the angry wound. The black line ran up from his wrist to his armpit. Automatically he reached in his pocket for the big black knife, but it was not there. His eyes searched the ground. He picked up a sharp blade of stone and scraped at the wound, sawed at the proud flesh and then squeezed the green juice out in big drops. Instantly he threw back his head and whined like a dog. His whole right side shuddered at the pain, but the pain cleared his head.

In the gray light he struggled up the last slope to the ridge and crawled over and lay down behind a line of rocks. Below him lay a deep canyon exactly like the last, waterless and desolate. There was no flat, no oak trees, not even heavy brush in the bottom of it. And on the other side a sharp ridge stood up, thinly brushed with starving sage, littered with broken granite. Strewn over the hill there were giant outcroppings, and on the top the granite teeth stood out against the sky.

The new day was light now. The flame of sun came over the ridge and fell on Pepé where he lay on the ground. His coarse black hair was littered with twigs and bits of spider web. His eyes had retreated back into his head. Between his lips the tip of his black tongue showed.

He sat up and dragged his great arm into his lap and nursed it, rocking his body and moaning in his throat. He threw back his head and looked up into the pale sky. A big black bird circled nearly out of sight, and far to the left another was sailing near.

He lifted his head to listen, for a familiar sound had come to him from the valley he had climbed out of; it was the crying yelp of hounds, excited and feverish, on a trail.

Pepé bowed his head quickly. He tried to speak rapid words but only a thick hiss came from his lips. He drew a shaky cross on his breast with his left hand. It was a long struggle to get to his feet. He crawled slowly and mechanically to the top of a big rock on the ridge peak. Once there, he arose slowly, swaying to his feet, and stood erect. Far below he could see the dark brush where he had slept. He braced his feet and stood there, black against the morning sky.

There came a ripping sound at his feet. A piece of stone flew up and a bullet droned off into the next gorge. The hollow crash echoed up from below. Pepé looked down for a moment and then pulled himself straight again.

His body jarred back. His left hand fluttered helplessly toward his breast. The second crash sounded from below. Pepé swung forward and toppled from the rock. His body struck and rolled over and over, starting a little avalanche. And when at last he stopped against a bush, the avalanche slid slowly down and covered up his head.

EXERCISES

1. Clearly, there is a conflict between Pepé and the unseen pursuers, and the most obvious suspense of the story is based on this fact. But is there another dimension to the conflict? To answer this, think of the kind of world in which Pepé and his family live and the values of that world.

2. It is clear that the story is, in a way, the account of the growing up of Pepé. How does this fact relate to the deeper conflict of the story? That is, according to what set of values does Pepé die, that of his own world or of the unseen pursuers?

3. Characterize the mother. What is her attitude toward Pepé's situation? How does this relate to the main idea of the story?

4. Is it significant that the pursuers are never seen?

5. What is the significance of the next to the last paragraph?

One critic has pointed out that during the flight Pepé becomes more and more identified with the natural world, that he seems to be gradually absorbed into it. How does the author's use of the various wild creatures support this notion? What other indications are there for the identification of Pepé with nature? What connection would this identification have with the conflict between Pepé's world and that of the pursuers?

7. Steinbeck has vividly presented the country through which Pepé flees. Select certain details that strike you as especially vivid. Why is such vividness important for the story?

8. What is the significance of the last paragraph of the story? What does it add beyond the fact that Pepé has had his mortal wound?

9. Read "La Lupa" by Giovanni Verga (sec. 9). What similarity is there in the backgrounds of the two stories? Can we imagine either story occur-

ring in a large modern city? If so, what differences can you imagine? What would the absence of the natural background imply? What is the fictional point—the theme—of "La Lupa"?

10. What is gained by keeping the impression of translated language in the dialogue between Pepé and his mother rather than rendering it in ordinary English? Compare this quality of "translation English" in the dialogue here with the style of "The Fir Tree." (We are not concerned here with the fact that the fairy tale literally is a translation; remember, rather, that the story as we have remarked, is addressed to children.)

Section 4

FABLE: ACTION AS MEANING

As the word *tale* implies the process of "telling," so the word *fable* implies the meaning of the thing "told." A fable is, traditionally, a narrative directed to a moral or prudential point—that is, to a point concerned with right and wrong or prudence and imprudence. The tale primarily gives us a sense of the motion and texture of experience; it quickens our sense of wonder, of marvel, of curiosity, of, in short, life. The fable gives us precepts, ideas, by which to conduct life, or understand life.* Against a fairy tale, such as "The Tinder Box," set a fable of Aesop:

> One day a dog carrying a nice piece of meat in his mouth was crossing a bridge over a stream. Looking down, he saw his reflection, another dog with what he thought was a nicer piece of meat. Drop-

* A parable resembles a fable in that it, too, is a narrative, usually very concise, to illustrate a "truth," as in the parables of Jesus. For instance, in Luke 8:5–15:

A sower went out to sow his seed; and as he sowed some fell by the wayside; and it was trodden down, and the fowls of the air devoured it.

And some fell upon a rock; and as soon as it was sprung up, it withered away because it lacked moisture.

And some fell among thorns; and the thorns sprung up with it, and choked it.

And other fell on good ground, and sprang up, and bare fruit a hundred fold. And when Jesus had said these things, he cried, He that hath ears to hear, let him hear.

And his disciples asked him saying, What might this fable be?

And he said, Unto you it is given to know the mysteries of the kingdom of God: but to others in parables; that seeing they might not see, and hearing they might not understand.

Now the parable is this: The seed is the word of God.

Those by the wayside are they that hear; then cometh the devil, and taketh away the word out of their hearts, lest they should believe and be saved.

They on the rock are they, which, when they hear, receive the word with joy; and these have no root, which for a while believe, and in time of temptation fall away.

And that which fell among thorns are they, which, when they have heard, go forth, and are choked with cares and riches and pleasures of this life, and bring no fruit to perfection.

But that on the good ground are they, which in an honest and good heart, having heard the word, keep it, and bring forth fruit with patience.

So some pieces of fiction that emphasize the action as primarily an embodiment of meaning are said to be "parabolic" or to be parables. In the same sense the plot of a piece of fiction is, in old-fashioned usage, sometimes called the "fable," implying that the plot is the carrier of the meaning.

ping what was in his mouth, he plunged at the other dog to get his meat. Meanwhile, of course, his own piece had fallen into the stream and had been carried away.

The action is minimal. It is the precept that stands out, that in fact really makes the action seem important to us. As for the precept in this instance, it is: Don't give up the substance for the shadow.

We do not suggest, however, that a tale has no meaning, no theme, and offers no comment on life. Quite the contrary; our undertaking in section 3 has been to interpret the tales there presented. Nor do we suggest that the fable does not appeal to our interest in experience as such, and does not quicken the sense of life. Again, quite the contrary, for the mere fact of narrative implies these appeals. What is important here is a matter of emphasis, not a matter of absolute distinction. In the contrast between tale and fable, then, we may find the two poles of fiction: the emphasis of the one is on the sense of life as lived, of the other, on the meaning of life. All fiction, to be fiction, must involve, to some degree, both a sense of life as lived and a sense of the meaning of life, but the degree is constantly shifting from story to story, just as the way in which the two concerns interpenetrate in fiction is constantly varying.

The stories here are not, strictly speaking, fables, but all except the last distort the actual world (which is commonly the concern of fiction) in order to emphasize meaning— a "truth" symbolized in the distorted and, in the literal sense, unbelievable action. We must remember, however, that the use of distortion and fantasy is not necessary to the fable, and certainly not to the fabulous element in fiction. What is at stake here is the *emphasis* on the element of meaning.

YOUNG GOODMAN BROWN
Nathaniel Hawthorne (1804–1864)

Young Goodman Brown came forth at sunset into the street at Salem village; but put his head back, after crossing the threshold, to exchange a parting kiss with his young wife. And Faith, as the wife was aptly named, thrust her own pretty head into the street, letting the wind play with the pink ribbons of her cap while she called to Goodman Brown.

"Dearest heart," whispered she, softly and rather sadly, when her lips were close to his ear, "prithee put off your journey until sunrise and sleep in your own bed to-night. A lone woman is troubled with such dreams and such thoughts that she's afeard of herself sometimes. Pray tarry with me this night, dear husband, of all nights in the year."

"My love and my Faith," replied young Goodman Brown, "of all nights in the year, this one night must I tarry away from thee. My journey, as thou callest it, forth and back again, must needs be done 'twixt now and sunrise. What, my sweet, pretty wife, dost thou doubt me already, and we but three months married?"

"Then God bless you!" said Faith, with the pink ribbons; "and may you find all well when you come back."

"Amen!" cried Goodman Brown. "Say thy prayers, dear Faith, and go to bed at dusk, and no harm will come to thee."

So they parted; and the young man pursued his way until, being about to turn the corner by the meeting-house, he looked back and saw the head of Faith still peeping after him with a melancholy air, in spite of her pink ribbons.

"Poor little Faith!" thought he, for his heart smote him. "What a wretch am I to leave her on such an errand! She talks of dreams, too. Methought as she spoke there was trouble in her face, as if a dream had warned her what work is to be done tonight. But no, no; 't would kill her to think it. Well, she's a blessed angel on earth; and after this one night I'll cling to her skirts and follow her to heaven."

With this excellent resolve for the future, Goodman Brown felt himself justified in making more haste on his present evil purpose. He had taken a dreary road, darkened by all the gloomiest trees of the forest, which barely stood aside to let the narrow path creep through, and closed immediately behind. It was all as lonely as could be; and there is this peculiarity in such a solitude, that the traveller knows not who may be concealed by the innumerable trunks and the thick boughs overhead; so that with lonely footsteps he may yet be passing through an unseen multitude.

"There may be a devilish Indian behind every tree," said Goodman Brown to himself; and he glanced fearfully behind him as he added, "What if the devil himself should be at my very elbow!"

His head being turned back, he passed a crook of the road, and, looking forward again, beheld the figure of a man, in grave and decent attire, seated at the foot of an old tree. He arose at Goodman Brown's approach and walked onward side by side with him.

"You are late, Goodman Brown," said he. "The clock of the Old South was striking as I came through Boston, and that is full fifteen minutes agone."

"Faith kept me back a while," replied the young man, with a tremor in his voice, caused by the sudden appearance of his companion, though not wholly unexpected.

It was now deep dusk in the forest, and deepest in that part of it where these two were journeying. As nearly as could be discerned, the second traveller was about fifty years old, apparently in the same rank of life as Goodman Brown, and bearing a considerable resemblance to him, though perhaps more in expression than features. Still they might have been taken for father and son. And yet, though the elder person was as simply clad as the younger, and as simple in manner too, he had an indescribable air of one who knew the world, and who would not have felt abashed at the governor's dinner table or in King William's court, were it possible that his affairs should call him thither. But the only thing about him that could be fixed upon as remarkable was his staff, which bore the likeness of a great black snake, so curiously wrought that it might almost be seen to twist and wriggle itself like a living serpent.

This, of course, must have been an ocular deception, assisted by the uncertain light.

"Come, Goodman Brown," cried his fellow-traveller, "this is a dull place for the beginning of a journey. Take my staff, if you are so soon weary."

"Friend," said the other, exchanging his slow pace for a full stop, "having kept covenant by meeting thee here, it is my purpose now to return whence I came. I have scruples touching the matter thou wot'st of."

"Sayest thou so?" replied he of the serpent, smiling apart. "Let us walk on, nevertheless, reasoning as we go; and if I convince thee not thou shalt turn back. We are but a little way in the forest yet."

"Too far! too far!" exclaimed the goodman, unconsciously resuming his walk. "My father never went into the woods on such an errand, nor his father before him. We have been a race of honest men and good Christians since the days of the martyrs; and shall I be the first of the name of Brown that ever took this path and kept"—

"Such company, thou wouldst say," observed the elder person, interpreting his pause. "Well said, Goodman Brown! I have been as well acquainted with your family as with ever a one among the Puritans; and that's no trifle to say. I helped your grandfather, the constable, when he lashed the Quaker woman so smartly through the streets of Salem; and it was I that brought your father a pitch-pine knot, kindled at my own hearth, to set fire to an Indian village, in King Philip's war. They were my good friends, both; and many a pleasant walk have we had along this path, and returned merrily after midnight. I would fain be friends with you for their sake."

"If it be as thou sayest," replied Goodman Brown, "I marvel they never spoke of these matters; or, verily, I marvel not, seeing that the least rumor of the sort would have driven them from New England. We are a people of prayer, and good works to boot, and abide no such wickedness."

"Wickedness or not," said the traveller

with the twisted staff, "I have a very general acquaintance here in New England. The deacons of many a church have drunk the communion wine with me; the selectmen of divers towns make me their chairman; and a majority of the Great and General Court are firm supporters of my interest. The governor and I, too—But these are state secrets."

"Can this be so?" cried Goodman Brown, with a stare of amazement at his undisturbed companion. "Howbeit, I have nothing to do with the governor and council; they have their own ways, and are no rule for a simple husbandman like me. But, were I to go on with thee, how should I meet the eye of that good old man, our minister, at Salem village? Oh, his voice would make me tremble both Sabbath day and lecture day."

Thus far the elder traveller had listened with due gravity; but now burst into a fit of irrepressible mirth, shaking himself so violently that his snake-like staff actually seemed to wriggle in sympathy.

"Ha! ha! ha!" shouted he again and again; then composing himself, "Well, go on, Goodman Brown, go on; but, prithee, don't kill me with laughing."

"Well, then, to end the matter at once," said Goodman Brown, considerably nettled, "there is my wife, Faith. It would break her dear little heart; and I'd rather break my own."

"Nay, if that be the case," answered the other, "e'en go thy ways, Goodman Brown. I would not for twenty old women like the one hobbling before us that Faith should come to any harm."

As he spoke he pointed his staff at a female figure on the path, in whom Goodman Brown recognized a very pious and exemplary dame, who had taught him his catechism in youth, and was still his moral and spiritual adviser, jointly with the minister and Deacon Gookin.

"A marvel, truly, that Goody Cloyse should be so far in the wilderness at night-fall," said he. "But with your leave, friend, I shall take a cut through the woods until we have left this Christian woman behind. Being a stranger to you, she might ask whom I was consorting with and whither I was going."

"Be it so," said his fellow-traveller. "Betake you the woods, and let me keep the path."

Accordingly the young man turned aside, but took care to watch his companion, who advanced softly along the road until he had come within a staff's length of the old dame. She, meanwhile, was making the best of her way, with singular speed for so aged a woman, and mumbling some indistinct words —a prayer, doubtless—as she went. The traveller put forth his staff and touched her withered neck with what seemed the serpent's tail.

"The devil!" screamed the pious old lady.

"Then Goody Cloyse knows her old friend?" observed the traveller, confronting her and leaning on his writhing stick.

"Ah, forsooth, and is it your worship indeed?" cried the good dame. "Yea, truly is it, and in the very image of my old gossip, Goodman Brown, the grandfather of the silly fellow that now is. But—would your worship believe it?—my broomstick hath strangely disappeared, stolen, as I suspect, by that unhanged witch, Goody Cory, and that, too, when I was all anointed with the juice of smallage, and cinquefoil, and wolf's bane"—

"Mingled with fine wheat and the fat of a new-born babe," said the shape of old Goodman Brown.

"Ah, your worship knows the recipe," cried the old lady, cackling aloud. "So, as I was saying, being all ready for the meeting, and no horse to ride on, I made up my mind to foot it; for they tell me there is a nice young man to be taken into communion tonight. But now your good worship will lend me your arm, and we shall be there in a twinkling."

"That can hardly be," answered her friend. "I may not spare you my arm, Goody Cloyse; but here is my staff, if you will."

So saying, he threw it down at her feet, where, perhaps, it assumed life, being one of the rods which its owner had formerly lent to the Egyptian magi. Of this fact, however, Goodman Brown could not take cognizance. He has cast up his eyes in astonishment, and, looking down again, beheld neither Goody Cloyse nor the serpentine staff, but this fellow-traveller alone, who waited for him as calmly as if nothing had happened.

"That old woman taught me my catechism," said the young man; and there was a world of meaning in this simple comment.

They continued to walk onward, while the elder traveller exhorted his companion to make good speed and persevere in the path, discoursing so aptly that his arguments seemed rather to spring up in the bosom of his auditor than to be suggested by himself. As they went, he plucked a branch of maple to serve for a walking stick, and began to strip it of the twigs and little boughs, which were wet with evening dew. The moment his fingers touched them they became strangely withered and dried up as with a week's sunshine. Thus the pair proceeded, at a good free pace, until suddenly, in a gloomy hollow of the road, Goodman Brown sat himself down on the stump of a tree and refused to go any farther.

"Friend," said he, stubbornly, "my mind is made up. Not another step will I budge on this errand. What if a wretched old woman do choose to go to the devil when I thought she was going to heaven: is that any reason why I should quit my dear Faith and go after her?"

"You will think better of this by and by," said his acquaintance, composedly. "Sit here and rest yourself a while; and when you feel like moving again, there is my staff to help you along."

Without more words, he threw his companion the maple stick, and was as speedily out of sight as if he had vanished into the deepening gloom. The young man sat a few moments by the roadside, applauding himself greatly, and thinking with how clear a conscience he should meet the minister in his morning walk, nor shrink from the eye of good old Deacon Gookin. And what calm sleep would be his that very night, which was to have been spent so wickedly, but so purely and sweetly now, in the arms of Faith! Amidst these pleasant and praiseworthy meditations, Goodman Brown heard the tramp of horses along the road, and deemed it advisable to conceal himself within the verge of the forest, conscious of the guilty purpose that had brought him thither, though now so happily turned from it.

On came the hoof tramps and the voices of the riders, two grave old voices, conversing soberly as they drew near. These mingled sounds appeared to pass along the road, within a few yards of the young man's hiding-place; but, owing doubtless to the depth of the gloom at that particular spot, neither the travellers nor their steeds were visible. Though their figures brushed the small boughs by the wayside, it could not be seen that they intercepted, even for a moment, the faint gleam from the strip of bright sky athwart which they must have passed. Goodman Brown alternately crouched and stood on tiptoe, pulling aside the branches and thrusting forth his head as far as he durst without discerning so much as a shadow. It vexed him the more, because he could have sworn, were such a thing possible, that he recognized the voices of the minister and Deacon Gookin, jogging along quietly, as they were wont to do, when bound to some ordination or ecclesiastical council. While yet within hearing, one of the riders stopped to pluck a switch.

"Of the two, reverend sir," said the voice like the deacon's, "I had rather miss an ordination dinner than to-night's meeting. They tell me that some of our community are to be here from Falmouth and beyond, and others from Connecticut and Rhode Island, besides several of the Indian pow-wows, who, after their fashion, know almost as much deviltry as the best of us. Moreover, there is a goodly young woman to be taken into communion."

"Mighty well, Deacon Gookin!" replied the solemn old tones of the minister. "Spur up, or we shall be late. Nothing can be done, you know, until I get on the ground."

The hoofs clattered again; and the voices, talking so strangely in the empty air, passed on through the forest, where no church had ever been gathered or solitary Christian prayed. Whither, then, could these holy men be journeying so deep into the heathen wilderness? Young Goodman Brown caught hold of a tree for support, being ready to sink down on the ground, faint and over-burdened with the heavy sickness of his heart. He looked up to the sky, doubting whether there really was a heaven above him. Yet there was the blue arch, and the stars brightening in it.

"With heaven above and Faith below, I will yet stand firm against the devil!" cried Goodman Brown.

While he still gazed upward into the deep arch of the firmament and had lifted his hands to pray, a cloud, though no wind was stirring, hurried across the zenith and hid the brightening stars. The blue sky was still visible, except directly overhead, where this black mass of cloud was sweeping swiftly northward. Aloft in the air, as if from the depths of the cloud, came a confused and doubtful sound of voices. Once the listener fancied that he could distinguish the accents of towns-people of his own, men and women, both pious and ungodly, many of whom he had met at the communion table, and had seen others rioting at the tavern. The next moment, so indistinct were the sounds, he doubted whether he had heard aught but the murmur of the old forest, whispering without a wind. Then came a stronger swell of those familiar tones, heard daily in the sunshine at Salem village, but never until now from a cloud of night. There was one voice, of a young woman, uttering lamentations, yet with an uncertain sorrow, and entreating for some favor, which, perhaps, it would grieve her to obtain; and all the unseen multitude, both saints and sinners, seemed to encourage her onward.

"Faith!" shouted Goodman Brown, in a voice of agony and desperation; and the echoes of the forest mocked him, crying, "Faith! Faith!" as if bewildered wretches were seeking her all through the wilderness.

The cry of grief, rage, and terror was yet piercing the night, when the unhappy husband held his breath for a response. There was a scream, drowned immediately in a louder murmur of voices, fading into far-off laughter, as the dark cloud swept away, leaving the clear and silent sky above Goodman Brown. But something fluttered lightly down through the air and caught on the branch of a tree. The young man seized it, and beheld a pink ribbon.

"My Faith is gone!" cried he, after one stupefied moment. "There is no good on earth; and sin is but a name. Come, devil; for to thee is this world given."

And, maddened with despair, so that he laughed loud and long, did Goodman Brown grasp his staff and set forth again, at such a rate that he seemed to fly along the forest path rather than to walk or run. The road grew wilder and drearier and more faintly traced, and vanished at length, leaving him in the heart of the dark wilderness, still rushing onward with the instinct that guides mortal man to evil. The whole forest was peopled with frightful sounds—the creaking of the trees, the howling of wild beasts, and the yell of Indians; while sometimes the wind tolled like a distant church bell, and sometimes gave a broad roar around the traveller, as if all Nature were laughing him to scorn. But he was himself the chief horror of the scene and shrank not from its other horrors.

"Ha! ha! ha!" roared Goodman Brown when the wind laughed at him. "Let us hear which will laugh loudest. Think not to frighten me with your deviltry. Come witch, come wizard, come Indian powwow, come devil himself, and here comes Goodman Brown. You may as well fear him as he fear you."

In truth, all through the haunted forest there could be nothing more frightful than the figure of Goodman Brown. On he flew among the black pines, brandishing his staff with frenzied gestures, now giving vent to an inspiration of horrid blasphemy, and now shouting forth such laughter as set all the echoes of the forest laughing like demons around him. The fiend in his own shape is less hideous than when he rages in the breast of man. Thus sped the demoniac on his course, until, quivering among the trees, he saw a red light before him, as when the felled trunks and branches of a clearing have been set on fire, and throw up their lurid blaze against the sky, at the hour of midnight. He paused, in a lull of the tempest that had driven him onward, and heard the swell of what seemed a hymn, rolling solemnly from a distance with the weight of many voices. He knew the tune; it was a familiar one in the choir of the village meeting-house. The verse died heavily away, and was lengthened by a chorus, not of human voices, but of all the sounds of the benighted wilderness pealing in awful harmony together. Goodman Brown cried out, and his cry was lost to his own ear by its unison with the cry of the desert.

In the interval of silence he stole forward until the light glared full upon his eyes. At one extremity of an open space, hemmed in by the dark wall of the forest, arose a rock, bearing some rude, natural resemblance either to an altar or a pulpit, and surrounded by four blazing pines, their tops aflame, their stems untouched, like candles at an evening meeting. The mass of foliage that had overgrown the summit of the rock was all on fire, blazing high into the night and fitfully illuminating the whole field. Each pendent twig and leafy festoon was in a blaze. As the red light arose and fell, a numerous congregation alternately shone forth, then disappeared in shadow, and again grew, as it were, out of the darkness, peopling the heart of the solitary woods at once.

"A grave and dark-clad company," quoth Goodman Brown.

In truth they were such. Among them, quivering to and fro between gloom and splendor, appeared faces that would be seen next day at the council board of the province, and others which, Sabbath after Sabbath, looked devoutly heavenward, and benignantly over the crowded pews, from the holiest pulpits in the land. Some affirm that the lady of the governor was there. At least there were high dames well known to her, and wives of honored husbands, and widows, a great multitude, and ancient maidens, all of excellent repute, and fair young girls, who trembled lest their mothers should espy them. Either the sudden gleams of light flashing over the obscure field bedazzled Goodman Brown, or he recognized a score of the church members of Salem village famous for their especial sanctity. Good old Deacon Gookin had arrived, and waited at the skirts of that venerable saint, his revered pastor. But, irreverently consorting with these grave, reputable, and pious people, these elders of the church, these chaste dames and dewy virgins, there were men of dissolute lives and women of spotted fame, wretches given over to all mean and filthy vice, and suspected even of horrid crimes. It was strange to see that the good shrank not from the wicked, nor were the sinners abashed by the saints. Scattered also among their pale-faced enemies were the Indian priests, or powwows, who had often scared their native forest with more hideous incantations than any known to English witchcraft.

"But where is Faith?" thought Goodman Brown; and, as hope came into his heart, he trembled.

Another verse of the hymn arose, a slow and mournful strain, such as the pious love, but joined to words which expressed all that our nature can conceive of sin, and darkly hinted at far more. Unfathomable to mere mortals is the lore of fiends. Verse after verse was sung; and still the chorus of the desert swelled between like the deepest tone of a mighty organ; and with the final peal of that dreadful anthem there came a sound, as if the roaring wind, the rushing streams, the howling beasts, and every other voice of the unconcerted wilderness were mingling and according with the voice of guilty man in homage to the prince of all. The four blazing pines threw up a loftier flame, and obscurely discovered shapes and visages of horror on the smoke wreaths above the impious assembly. At the same moment the fire on the rock shot redly forth and formed a glowing arch above its base, where now appeared a figure. With reverence be it spoken, the figure bore no slight similitude, both in garb and manner, to some grave divine of the New England churches.

"Bring forth the converts!" cried a voice that echoed through the field and rolled into the forest.

At the word, Goodman Brown stepped forth from the shadow of the trees and approached the congregation, with whom he felt a loathful brotherhood by the sympathy of all that was wicked in his heart. He could have well-nigh sworn that the shape of his own dead father beckoned him to advance, looking downward from a smoke wreath, while a woman, with dim features of despair, threw out her hand to warn him back. Was it his mother? But he had no power to retreat one step, nor to resist, even in thought, when the minister and good old Deacon Gookin seized his arms and led him to the blazing rock. Thither came also the slender form of a veiled female, led between Goody Cloyse, that pious teacher of the catechism, and Martha Carrier, who had received the devil's promise to be queen of hell. A rampant hag was she. And there stood the proselytes beneath the canopy of fire.

"Welcome, my children," said the dark figure, "to the communion of your race. Ye

have found thus young your nature and your destiny. My children, look behind you!"

They turned; and flashing forth, as it were, in a sheet of flame, the fiend worshippers were seen; the smile of welcome gleamed darkly on every visage.

"There," resumed the sable form, "are all whom ye have reverenced from youth. Ye deemed them holier than yourselves, and shrank from your own sin, contrasting it with their lives of righteousness and prayerful aspirations heavenward. Yet here are they all in my worshipping assembly. This night it shall be granted you to know their secret deeds: how hoary-bearded elders of the church have whispered wanton words to the young maids of their households; how many a woman, eager for widows' weeds, has given her husband a drink at bedtime and let him sleep his last sleep in her bosom; how beardless youths have made haste to inherit their fathers' wealth; and how fair damsels—blush not, sweet ones—have dug little graves in the garden, and bidden me, the sole guest, to an infant's funeral. By the sympathy of your human hearts for sin ye shall scent out all the places—whether in church, bed-chamber, street, field, or forest—where crime has been committed, and shall exult to behold the whole earth one stain of guilt, one mighty blood spot. Far more than this. It shall be yours to penetrate, in every bosom, the deep mystery of sin, the fountain of all wicked arts, and which inexhaustibly supplies more evil impulses than human power—than my power at its utmost—can make manifest in deeds. And now, my children, look upon each other."

They did so; and, by the blaze of the hell-kindled torches, the wretched man beheld his Faith, and the wife her husband, trembling before that unhallowed altar.

"Lo, there ye stand, my children," said the figure, in a deep and solemn tone, almost sad with its despairing awfulness, as if his once angelic nature could yet mourn for our miserable race. "Depending upon one another's hearts, ye had still hoped that virtue were not all a dream. Now are ye undeceived. Evil is the nature of mankind. Evil must be your only happiness. Welcome again, my children, to the communion of your race."

"Welcome," repeated the fiend worshippers, in one cry of despair and triumph.

And there they stood, the only pair, as it seemed, who were yet hesitating on the verge of wickedness in this dark world. A basin was hollowed, naturally, in the rock. Did it contain water, reddened by the lurid light? or was it blood? or, perchance, a liquid flame? Herein did the shape of evil dip his hand and prepare to lay the mark of baptism upon their foreheads, that they might be partakers of the mystery of sin, more conscious of the secret guilt of others, both in deed and thought, than they could now be of their own. The husband cast one look at his pale wife, and Faith at him. What polluted wretches would the next glance show them to each other, shuddering alike at what they disclosed and what they saw!

"Faith! Faith!" cried the husband, "look up to heaven, and resist the wicked one."

Whether Faith obeyed he knew not. Hardly had he spoken when he found himself amid calm night and solitude, listening to a roar of the wind which died heavily away through the forest. He staggered against the rock, and felt it chill and damp; while a hanging twig, that had been all on fire, besprinkled his cheek with the coldest dew.

The next morning young Goodman Brown came slowly into the street of Salem village, staring around him like a bewildered man. The good old minister was taking a walk along the graveyard to get an appetite for breakfast and meditate his sermon, and bestowed a blessing, as he passed, on Goodman Brown. He shrank from the venerable saint as if to avoid an anathema. Old Deacon Gookin was at domestic worship, and the holy words of his prayer were heard through the open window. "What God doth the wizard pray to?" quoth Goodman Brown. Goody Cloyse, that excellent old Christian, stood in the early sunshine at her own lattice, catechizing a little girl who had brought her a pint of morning's milk. Goodman Brown snatched away the child as from the grasp of the fiend himself. Turning the corner by the meeting-house, he spied the head of Faith, with the pink ribbons, gazing anxiously forth, and bursting into such joy at sight of him that she skipped along the street and almost kissed her husband before the whole village. But Goodman Brown looked sternly and sadly into her face, and passed on without a greeting.

Had Goodman Brown fallen asleep in the forest and only dreamed a wild dream of a witch-meeting?

Be it so if you will; but, alas! it was a dream of evil omen for young Goodman Brown. A stern, a sad, a darkly meditative, a distrustful, if not a desperate man did he become from the night of that fearful dream. On the Sabbath day, when the congregation were singing a holy psalm, he could not listen because an anthem of sin rushed loudly upon his ear and drowned all the blessed strain. When the minister spoke from the pulpit with power and fervid eloquence, and, with his hand on the open Bible, of the sacred truths of our religion, and of saint-like lives and triumphant deaths, and of future bliss or misery unutterable, then did Goodman Brown turn pale, dreading lest the roof should thunder down upon the gray blasphemer and his hearers. Often, awaking suddenly at midnight, he shrank from the bosom of Faith; and at morning or eventide, when the family knelt down at prayer, he scowled and muttered to himself, and gazed sternly at his wife, and turned away. And when he had lived long, and was borne to his grave, a hoary corpse, followed by Faith, an aged woman, and children and grandchildren, a goodly procession, besides neighbors not a few, they carved no hopeful verse upon his tombstone, for his dying hour was gloom.

EXERCISES

1. The story begins in a quite literal New England village of colonial times, but with the same air of factuality (which, by the way, would not have seemed strange to that age in which men believed in devils and witches) moves into the realm of the supernatural. Try to identify the stages by which the transition takes place.

2. The discovery that the young bride Faith—whose name, clearly selected for the sake of the "fable" is allegorical (see Glossary)—is capable of coming to the Witches' Sabbath in the woods is the climax of the story. By what stages is this climax approached?

3. The point of the fable is clearly that all human beings, even the best, have evil in their nature. But certain questions are raised by the young husband's reaction to the discovery. If so many of the "good" had come, why should he have been so totally and disastrously surprised to find his wife there in the woods? Do you think that his complete idealization of her was reasonable in the first place? Could it represent, in fact, a self-indulgent sentimentality on his part? Is his shock, at the end, a wise and humane response? Or does it have a morbid, even a pathological, element? What view do you think Hawthorne takes of the matter? Or can we be sure? What view do you take? What, if you were Goodman Brown in this situation, would you do? What are the sexual implications of this story? In spite of differences in sexual attitudes between colonial times and ours, in what sense is this story one for us?

THE ENEMIES
Dylan Thomas (1914–1953)

It was morning in the green acres of the Jarvis valley, and Mr. Owen was picking the weeds from the edges of his garden path. A great wind pulled at his beard, the vegetable world roared under his feet. A rook had lost itself in the sky, and was making a noise to its mate; but the mate never came, and the rook flew into the west with a woe in its beak. Mr. Owen, who had stood up to ease his shoulders and look at the sky, observed how dark the wings beat against the red sun. In her draughty kitchen Mrs. Owen grieved over the soup. Once, in past days, the valley had housed the cattle alone; the farm-boys came down from the hills to holla at the cattle and to drive them to be milked; but no stranger set foot in the valley. Mr. Owen, walking lonely through the country, had come upon it at the end of a late summer evening when the cattle were lying down still, and the stream that divided it was speaking over the pebbles. Here, thought Mr. Owen, I will build a small house with one storey, in the middle of the valley, set around by a garden. And, remembering clearly the way he had come along the winding hills, he returned to his village and the questions of Mrs. Owen. So it came about that a house with one storey was built in the green fields; a garden was dug and planted, and a low fence put up around the garden to keep the cows from the vegetables.

That was early in the year. Now summer and autumn had gone over; the garden had blossomed and died; there was frost at the weeds. Mr. Owen bent down again, tidying the path, while the wind blew back the heads of the nearby grasses and made an oracle of each green mouth. Patiently he strangled the weeds; up came the roots, making war in the soil around them; insects were busy in the holes where the weeds had sprouted, but, dying between his fingers, they left no stain. He grew tired of their death, and tireder of the fall of the weeds. Up came the roots, down went the cheap, green heads.

Mrs. Owen, peering into the depths of her crystal, had left the soup to bubble on unaided. The ball grew dark, then lightened as a rainbow moved within it. Growing hot like a sun, and cooling again like an arctic star, it shone in the folds of her dress where she held it lovingly. The tea leaves in her cup at breakfast had told of a dark stranger. What would the crystal tell her? Mrs. Owen wondered.

Up came the roots, and a crooked worm, disturbed by the probing of the fingers, wriggled blind in the sun. Of a sudden the valley filled all its hollows with the wind, with the voice of the roots, with the breathing of the nether sky. Not only a mandrake screams;

torn roots have their cries; each weed Mr. Owen pulled out of the ground screamed like a baby. In the village behind the hill the wind would be raging, the clothes on the garden lines would be set to strange dances. And women with shapes in their wombs would feel a new knocking as they bent over the steamy tubs. Life would go on in the veins, in the bones, the binding flesh, that had their seasons and their weathers even as the valley binding the house about with the flesh of the green grass.

The ball, like an open grave, gave up its dead to Mrs. Owen. She stared on the lips of women and the hairs of men that wound into a pattern on the face of the crystal world. But suddenly the patterns were swept away, and she could see nothing but the shapes of the Jarvis hills. A man with a black hat was walking down the paths into the invisible valley beneath. If he walked any nearer he would fall into her lap. There's a man with a black hat walking on the hills, she called through the window. Mr. Owen smiled and went on weeding.

It was at this time that the Reverend Mr. Davies lost his way; he had been losing it most of the morning, but now he had lost it altogether, and stood perturbed under a tree on the rim of the Jarvis hills. A great wind blew through the branches, and a great grey-green earth moved unsteadily beneath him. Wherever he looked the hills stormed up to the sky, and wherever he sought to hide from the wind he was frightened by the darkness. The farther he walked, the stranger was the scenery around him; it rose to undreamed-of heights, and then fell down again into a valley no bigger than the palm of his hand. And the trees walked like men. By a divine coincidence he reached the rim of the hills just as the sun reached the centre of the sky. With the wide world rocking from horizon to horizon, he stood under a tree and looked down into the valley. In the fields was a little house with a garden. The valley roared around it, the wind leapt at it like a boxer, but the house stood still. To Mr. Davies it

seemed as though the house had been carried out of a village by a large bird and placed in the very middle of the tumultuous universe.

But as he climbed over the craggy edges and down the side of the hill, he lost his place in Mrs. Owen's crystal. A cloud displaced his black hat, and under the cloud walked a very old phantom, a shape of air with stars all frozen in its beard, and a half-moon for a smile. Mr. Davies knew nothing of this as the stones scratched his hands. He was old, he was drunk with the wine of the morning, but the stuff that came out of his cuts was a human blood.

Nor did Mr. Owen, with his face near the soil and his hands on the necks of the screaming weeds, know of the transformation in the crystal. He had heard Mrs. Owen prophesy the coming of the black hat, and had smiled as he always smiled at her faith in the powers of darkness. He had looked up when she called, and, smiling, had returned to the clearer call of the ground. Multiply, multiply, he had said to the worms disturbed in their channelling, and had cut the brown worms in half so that the halves might breed and spread their life over the garden and go out, contaminating, into the fields and bellies of the cattle.

Of this Mr. Davies knew nothing. He saw a young man with a beard bent industriously over the garden soil; he saw that the house was a pretty picture, with the face of a pale young woman pressed up against the window. And, removing his black hat, he introduced himself as the rector of a village some ten miles away.

You are bleeding, said Mr. Owen.

Mr. Davies's hands, indeed, were covered in blood.

When Mrs. Owen had seen to the rector's cuts, she sat him down in the armchair near the window, and made him a strong cup of tea.

I saw you on the hill, she said, and he asked her how she had seen him, for the hills are high and a long way off.

I have good eyes, she answered.

He did not doubt her. Her eyes were the strangest he had seen.

It is quiet here, said Mr. Davies.

We have no clock, she said, and laid the table for three.

You are very kind.

We are kind to those that come to us.

He wondered how many came to the lonely house in the valley, but did not question her for fear of what she would reply. He guessed she was an uncanny woman loving the dark because it was dark. He was too old to question the secrets of darkness, and now, with the black suit torn and wet and his thin hands bound with the bandages of the stranger woman, he felt older than ever. The winds of the morning might blow him down, and the sudden dropping of the dark be blind in his eyes. Rain might pass through him as it passes through the body of a ghost. A tired, white-haired old man, he sat under the window, almost invisible against the panes and the white cloth of the chair.

Soon the meal was ready, and Mr. Owen came in unwashed from the garden.

Shall I say grace? asked Mr. Davies when all three were seated around the table.

Mrs. Owen nodded.

O Lord God Almighty, bless this our meal, said Mr. Davies. Looking up as he continued his prayer, he saw that Mr. and Mrs. Owen had closed their eyes. We thank Thee for the bounties that Thou hast given us. And he saw that the lips of Mr. and Mrs. Owen were moving softly. He could not hear what they said, but he knew that the prayers they spoke were not his prayers.

Amen, said all three together.

Mr. Owen, proud in his eating, bent over the plate at he had bent over the complaining weeds. Outside the window was the brown body of the earth, the green skin of the grass, and the breasts of the Jarvis hills; there was a wind that chilled the animal earth, and a sun that had drunk up the dews on the fields; there was creation sweating out of the pores of the trees; and the grains of sand on faraway seashores would be multiplying as the sea rolled over them. He felt the coarse foods on his tongue; there was a meaning in the rind of the meat, and a purpose in the lifting of food to mouth. He saw, with a sudden satisfaction, that Mrs. Owen's throat was bare.

She, too, was bent over her plate, but was letting the teeth of her fork nibble at the corners of it. She did not eat, for the old powers were upon her, and she dared not lift up her head for the greenness of her eyes. She knew by the sound which way the wind blew in the valley; she knew the stage of the sun by the curve of the shadows on the cloth. Oh, that she could take her crystal, and see within it the stretches of darkness covering up this winter light. But there was a darkness gathering in her mind, drawing in the light around her. There was a ghost on her left; with all her strength she drew in the intangible light that moved around him, and mixed it in her dark brains.

Mr. Davies, like a man sucked by a bird, felt desolation in his veins, and, in a sweet delirium, told of his adventures on the hills, of how it had been cold and blowing, and how the hills went up and down. He had been lost, he said, and had found a dark retreat to shelter from the bullies in the wind; but the darkness had frightened him, and he had walked again on the hills where the morning tossed him about like a ship on the sea. Wherever he went he was blown in the open or frightened in the narrow shades. There was nowhere, he said pityingly, for an old man to go. Loving his parish, he had loved the surrounding lands, but the hills had given under his feet or plunged him into the air. And, loving his God, he had loved the darkness where men of old had worshipped the dark invisible. But now the hill caves were full of shapes and voices that mocked him because he was old.

He is frightened of the dark, thought Mrs. Owen, the lovely dark.

With a smile, Mr. Owen thought, He

is frightened of the worm in the earth, of the copulation in the tree of the living grease in the soil.

They looked at the old man, and saw that he was more ghostly than ever. The window behind him cast a ragged circle of light round his head.

Suddenly Mr. Davies knelt down to pray. He did not understand the cold in his heart nor the fear that bewildered him as he knelt, but, speaking his prayers for deliverance, he stared up at the shadowed eyes of Mrs. Owen and at the smiling eyes of her husband. Kneeling on the carpet at the head of the table, he stared in bewilderment at the dark mind and the gross dark body. He stared and he prayed, like an old god beset by his enemies.

———————— ◆·◄◆►·◆ ————————

Unlike "Young Goodman Brown," this story seems, at first sight, to remain in the world of actuality. But an air, an atmosphere, of strangeness does hover over this world. The house is lonely in the wide landscape. As Mr. Owen works in his garden, "a great wind pulled at his beard, the vegetable world roared under his feet." He is weeding the edges of his garden path: "Up came the roots, and a crooked worm, disturbed by the probing of the fingers, wriggled blind in the sun. Of a sudden the valley filled all its hollows with the wind, with the voice of the roots, with the breathing of the nether sky." Clearly, something is going on here beyond merely realistic description.

Meanwhile, in the cottage, Mrs. Owen stares into her crystal ball; and her claim to clairvoyance is vindicated when she actually sees there "the man with a black hat" moving down the hills into the valley. In other words, though the story seems to be founded on actuality, on a real valley in Wales, there is a teasing ambiguity about it that prepares the reader for the ending.

This ambiguity appears when we see for ourselves "the man with the black hat," the Reverend Mr. Davies, who has lost his way in the hills:

> A great wind blew through the branches, and a great grey-green earth moved unsteadily beneath him. Wherever he looked the hills stormed up to the sky, and wherever he sought to hide from the wind he was frightened by the darkness. The farther he walked, the stranger was the scenery around him; it rose to undreamed-of heights, and then fell down again into a valley no bigger than the palm of his hand. And the trees walked like men.

Out of this natural, and preternatural, landscape, "the man in the black hat"—who, we must remember, is a Christian priest, with the Christian view of nature—descends to the cottage, and now we expect a conflict to develop toward a climax that will, as in an ordinary story, bring the events into focus and give a point to the whole. The strange Mrs. Owen binds up the wounds the clergyman has suffered in his scrambling and sets him down to a meal with his two hosts. That single external event leads to the climax when the clergyman suddenly slips from his chair and kneels to pray.

EXERCISES

1. What is the meaning of Mr. Davies's act? To understand what is at stake here, look back over the story for hints. Images of light and dark run throughout the story, but where does the writer give us something more specific? What we have here is a confrontation of opposing forces, but what, in this "fable," do the various characters "stand for"? Be sure to make a distinction between Mr. and Mrs. Owen. Suppose we say that he represents a sunny, matter-of-fact "naturalism"—then what is her view? Does the confrontation offer us necessary, though opposing, views of life, or aspects of reality?
2. Does this fable have the same basic point as "Young Goodman Brown"? Take into account the fact that both Goodman Brown and the Reverend Mr. Davies enter a world so much at variance with their beliefs that they are revolted and horrified. But do the two stories end the same way?

THE STATE OF GRACE
Marcel Aymé (1902–1967)

In the year 1939 the best Christian in the Rue Gabrielle, and indeed in all Montmartre, was a certain Monsieur Duperrier, a man of such piety, uprightness and charity that God, without awaiting his death, and while he was still in the prime of life, crowned his head with a halo which never left it by day or by night. Like those in Paradise this halo, although made of some immaterial substance, manifested itself in the form of a whitish ring which looked as though it might have been cut out of fairly stiff cardboard, and shed a tender light. M. Duperrier wore it gratefully, with devout thanks to Heaven for a distinction which, however, his modesty did not permit him to regard as a formal undertaking in respect of the hereafter. He would have been unquestionably the happiest of men had his wife, instead of rejoicing in this signal mark of the Divine approval, not received it with outspoken resentment and exasperation.

'Well really, upon my word,' the lady said, 'what do you think you look like going around in a thing like that, and what do you suppose the neighbours and the tradespeople will say, not to mention my cousin Léopold? I never in my life saw anything so ridiculous. You'll have the whole neighbourhood talking.'

Mme Duperrier was an admirable woman, of outstanding piety and impeccable conduct, but she had not yet understood the vanity of the things of this world. Like so many people whose aspirations to virtue are marred by a certain lack of logic, she thought it more important to be esteemed by her concierge than by her Creator. Her terror lest she should be questioned on the subject of the halo by one of the neighbours or by the milkman had from the very outset an embittering effect upon her. She made repeated attempts to snatch away the shimmering plate of light that adorned her husband's cranium, but with no more effect than if she had tried to grasp a sunbeam, and without altering its position by a hair's-breadth. Girdling the top of his forehead where the hair began, the halo hung low over the back of his neck, with a slight tilt which gave it a coquettish look.

The foretaste of beatitude did not cause Duperrier to overlook the consideration he owed to his wife's peace of mind. He himself possessed too great a sense of discretion and modesty not to perceive that there were grounds for her disquiet. The gifts of God, especially when they wear a somewhat gratuitous aspect, are seldom accorded the respect they deserve, and the world is all too ready to find in them a subject of malicious gossip. Duperrier did his utmost, so far as the thing was possible, to make himself at all times inconspicuous. Regretfully putting aside the bowler hat which he had hitherto regarded as an indispensable attribute of his accountant's calling, he took to wearing a large felt hat, light in colour, of which the wide brim exactly covered the halo provided he wore it rakishly on the back of his head. Thus clad, there was nothing startlingly out-of-the-way in his appearance to attract the attention of the passer-by. The brim of his hat merely had a slight phosphorescence which by daylight might pass for the sheen on the surface of smooth felt. During office hours he was equally successful in avoiding the notice of his employer and fellow-workers. His desk, in the small shoe factory in Ménilmontant where he kept the books, was situated in a glass-paned cubby-hole between two workshops, and his state of isolation saved him from awkward questions. He wore the hat all day, and no one was sufficiently interested to ask him why he did so.

But these precautions did not suffice to allay his wife's misgivings. It seemed to her that the halo must already be a subject of comment among the ladies of the district, and she went almost furtively about the streets adjoining the Rue Gabrielle, her buttocks contracted and her heart wrung with agonising suspicions, convinced that she heard the echo of mocking laughter as she passed. To this worthy woman who had never had any ambition other than to keep her place in a social sphere ruled by the cult of the absolute norm, the glaring eccentricity with which her husband had been afflicted rapidly assumed catastrophic proportions. Its very improbability made it monstrous. Nothing would have induced her to accompany him out of doors. The evenings and Sunday afternoons which they had previously devoted to small outings and visits to friends were now passed in a solitary intimacy which became daily more oppressive. In the living-room of light oak where between meals the long leisure hours dragged by, Mme Duperrier, unable to knit a single stitch, would sit bitterly contemplating the halo, while Duperrier, generally reading some work of devotion and feeling the brush of angels' wings, wore an expression of beatific rapture which added to her fury. From time to time, however, he would glance solicitously at her, and noting the expression of angry disapproval on her face would feel a regret which was incompatible with the gratitude he owed to Heaven, so that this in its turn inspired him with a feeling of remorse at one remove.

So painful a state of affairs could not long continue without imperilling the unhappy woman's mental equilibrium. She began presently to complain that the light of the halo, bathing the pillows, made it impossible for her to sleep at nights. Duperrier, who sometimes made use of the divine illumination to read a chapter of the Scriptures, was obliged to concede the justice of this grievance, and he began to be afflicted with a sense of guilt. Finally, certain events, highly deplorable in their consequences, transformed this state of unease into one of acute crisis.

Upon setting out for the office one morning, Duperrier passed a funeral in the Rue Gabrielle, within a few yards of their house. He had become accustomed, outrageous though it was to his natural sense of courtesy, to greet acquaintances by merely raising a hand to his hat; but being thus confronted by the near presence of the dead he decided, after thinking the matter over, that nothing could relieve him of the obligation to uncover himself entirely. Several shopkeepers, yawning in their doorways, blinked at the sight of the halo, and gathered together to discuss the phenomenon. When she came out to do her shopping Mme Duperrier was assailed with questions, and in a state of extreme agitation uttered denials whose very vehemence appeared suspect. Upon his return home at midday her husband found her in a state of nervous crisis which caused him to fear for her reason.

'Take off that halo!' she cried. 'Take it off instantly! I never want to see it again!'

Duperrier gently reminded her that it was not in his power to remove it, whereupon she cried still more loudly:

'If you had any consideration for me you'd find some way of getting rid of it. You're simply selfish, that's what you are!'

These words, to which he prudently made no reply, gave Duperrier much food for thought. And on the following day a second incident occurred to point to the inevitable conclusion. Duperrier never missed early morning Mass, and since he had become endowed with the odour of sanctity he had taken to hearing it at the Basilica of the Sacré-Cœur. Here he was obliged to remove his hat, but the church is a large one and at that hour of the morning the congregation was sufficiently sparse to make it a simple matter for him to hide behind a pillar. On this particular occasion, however, he must have been less circumspect than usual. As he was leaving the church after the service an elderly spinster flung herself at his feet crying, 'St. Joseph! St. Joseph!', and kissed the hem of his overcoat. Duperrier beat a hasty retreat, flattered but considerably put out at recognising his adorer, who lived only a few doors away. A few hours later the devoted creature burst into the apartment, where Mme Duperrier was alone, uttering cries of —'St. Joseph! I want to see St. Joseph!'

Although somewhat lacking in brilliant

and picturesque qualities, St. Joseph is never-theless an excellent saint: but his unsensa-tional merits, with their flavour of solid craftsmanship and passive goodwill, seem to have brought upon him some degree of in-justice. There are indeed persons, some of the utmost piety, who, without even being conscious of it, associate the notion of naïve complaisance with the part he played in the Nativity. This impression of simple-minded-ness is further enhanced by the habit of super-imposing upon the figure of the saint the recollection of that other Joseph who resisted the advances of Potiphar's wife. Mme Duperrier had no great respect for the pre-sumed sanctity of her husband, but this fer-vour of adoration which with loud cries in-voked him by the name of St. Joseph seemed to her to add the finishing touch to his shame and absurdity. Goaded into a state of almost demented fury, she chased the visitor out of the apartment with an umbrella and then smashed several piles of plates. Her first act upon her husband's return was to have hys-terics, and when finally she had regained her self-control she said in a decided voice:

'For the last time I ask you to get rid of that halo. You can do it if you choose. You know you can.'

Duperrier hung his head, not daring to ask how she thought he should go about it, and she went on:

'It's perfectly simple. You only have to sin.'

Uttering no word of protest, Duperrier withdrew to the bedroom to pray.

'Almighty God,' he said in substance, 'you have granted me the highest reward that man may hope for upon earth, excepting martyrdom. I thank you, Lord, but I am married and I share with my wife the bread of tribulation which you deign to send us, no less than the honey of your favour. Only thus can a devout couple hope to walk in your footsteps. And it so happens that my wife cannot endure the sight or even the thought of my halo, not at all because it is a gift be-stowed by Heaven but simply because it's a

halo. You know what women are. When some unaccustomed happening does not chance to kindle their enthusiasm it is likely to upset all the store of rules and harmonies which they keep lodged in their little heads. No one can prevent this, and though my wife should live to be a hundred there will never be any place for my halo in her scheme of things. Oh God, you who see into my heart, you know how little store I set by my personal tranquility and the evening slippers by the fireside. For the rapture of wearing upon my head the token of your goodwill I would gladly suffer even the most violent domestic upheavals. But, alas, it is not my own peace of mind that is imperilled. My wife is losing all taste for life. Worse still, I can see the day approaching when her hatred of my halo will cause her to revile Him who bestowed it upon me. Am I to allow the life-companion you chose for me to die and damn her soul for all eternity without making an effort to save her? I find myself today at the parting of the ways, and the safe road does not appear to me to be the more merciful. That your spirit of in-finite justice may talk to me with the voice of my conscience is the prayer which in this hour of my perplexity I lay at your radiant feet, oh Lord.'

Scarcely had Duperrier concluded this prayer than his conscience declared itself in favour of the way of sin, making of this an act of duty demanded by Christian charity. He returned to the living-room, where his wife awaited him, grinding her teeth.

'God is just,' he said, with his thumbs in the armholes of his waistcoat. 'He knew what he was doing when he gave me my halo. The truth is that I deserve it more than any man alive. They don't make men like me in these days. When I reflect upon the vileness of the human herd and then consider the manifold perfections embodied in myself I am tempted to spit in the faces of the people in the street. God has rewarded me, it is true, but if the Church had any regard for justice I should be an archbishop at the very least.'

Duperrier had chosen the sin of pride,

which enabled him, while exalting his own merits, in the same breath to praise God, who had singled him out. His wife was not slow to realize that he was sinning deliberately and at once entered into the spirit of the thing.

'My angel,' she said, 'you will never know how proud I am of you. My cousin Léopold, with his car and his villa at Vesinet, is not worthy to unloose the latchet of your shoe.'

'That is precisely my own opinion. If I had chosen to concern myself with sordid matters I could have amassed a fortune as easily as any man, and a much bigger one than Léopold's, but I chose to follow a different road and my triumph is of another kind. I despise his money as I despise the man himself and all the countless other half-wits who are incapable of perceiving the grandeur of my modest existence. They have eyes and see not.'

The utterance of sentiments such as these, spoken at first from half-closed lips, his heart rent with shame, became within a short time a simple matter for Duperrier, a habit costing him no effort at all. And such is the power of words over the human mind that it was not long before he accepted them as valid currency. His wife, however, anxiously watching the halo, and seeing that its lustre showed no sign of diminishing, began to suspect that her husband's sin was lacking in weight and substance. Duperrier readily agreed with this.

'Nothing could be more true,' he said. 'I thought I was giving way to pride when in fact I was merely expressing the most simple and obvious of truths. When a man has attained to the uttermost degree of perfection, as I have done, the word "pride" ceases to have any meaning.'

This did not prevent him from continuing to extol his merits, but at the same time he recognized the necessity for embarking upon some other form of sin. It appeared to him that gluttony was, of the Deadly Sins, the one most suited to his purpose, which was

to rid himself of the halo without too far forfeiting the goodwill of Heaven. He was supported in this conclusion by the recollection, from his childhood days, of gentle scoldings for excessive indulgence in jam or chocolate. Filled with hope his wife set about the preparation of rich dishes whose variety enhanced their savour. The Duperriers' dinner-table was loaded with game, pâté, river-trout, lobsters, sweets, pastries and vintage wines. Their meals lasted twice as long as hitherto, if not three times. Nothing could have been more hideous and revolting than the spectacle of Duperrier, his napkin tied round his neck, his face crimson and his eyes glazed with satiation, loading his plate with a third helping, washing down roast and stuffing with great gulps of claret, belching, dribbling sauce and gravy, and perspiring freely under his halo. Before long he had developed such a taste for good cooking and rich repasts that he frequently rebuked his wife for an over-cooked joint or an unsuccessful mayonnaise. One evening, annoyed by his incessant grumbling, she said sharply:

'Your halo seems to be flourishing. Anyone would think it was growing fat on my cooking, just as you are. It looks to me as though gluttony isn't a sin after all. The only thing against it is that it costs money, and I can see no reason why I shouldn't put you back on vegetable soup and spaghetti.'

'That's enough of that!' roared Duperrier. 'Put me back on vegetable soup and spaghetti, will you? By God, I'd like to see you try! Do you think I don't know what I'm doing? Put me back on spaghetti, indeed! The insolence! Here am I, wallowing in sin just to oblige you, and that's the way you talk. Don't let me hear another word. It would serve you right if I slapped your face.'

One sin leads to another, in short, and thwarted greed, no less than pride, promotes anger. Duperrier allowed himself to fall into this new sin without really knowing whether he was doing it for his wife's sake or because he enjoyed it. This man who had hitherto been distinguished by the gentleness and equability of his nature now became given to thunderous rages; he smashed the crockery and on occasions went so far as to strike his wife. He even swore, invoking the name of his Creator. But his outbursts, growing steadily more frequent, did not save him from being both arrogant and gluttonous. He was, in fact, now sinning in three different ways, and Mme Duperrier mused darkly on God's infinite indulgence.

The fact is that the noblest of virtues can continue to flourish in a soul sullied by sin. Proud, gluttonous and choleric, Duperrier nevertheless remained steeped in Christian charity, nor had he lost anything of his lofty sense of duty as a man and a husband. Finding that Heaven remained unmoved by his anger, he resolved to be envious as well. To tell the truth, without his knowing it, envy had already crept into his soul. Rich feeding, which puts a burden on the liver, and pride, which stirs the sense of injustice, may dispose even the best of men to envy his neighbour. And anger lent a note of hatred to Duperrier's envy. He became jealous of his relations, his friends, his employer, the shopkeepers of the neighbourhood and even the stars of sport and screen whose photographs appeared in the papers. Everything infuriated him, and he was known to tremble with ignoble rage at the thought that the people next door possessed a cutlery service with silver handles, whereas his own were only of bone. But the halo continued to glow with undiminished brightness. Instead of being dismayed by this, he concluded that his sins were lacking in reality, and he had no difficulty in reasoning that his supposed gluttony did not in fact exceed the natural demands of a healthy appetite, while his anger and his envy merely bore witness to a lofty craving for justice. It was the halo itself, however, which furnished him with the most solid arguments.

'I'm bound to say I would have expected Heaven to be a little more fussy,' his wife said. 'If all your gluttony and boasting and brutality have done nothing to dim your halo, it doesn't look as though I need worry about *my* place in Paradise.'

'Hold your jaw!' roared the furious man. 'How much longer have I got to listen to your nagging? I'm fed up with it. You think it funny, do you, that a saintly character like myself should have to plunge into sin for the sake of your blasted peace of mind? Stow it, d'you hear me?'

The tone of these replies was clearly lacking in that suavity which may rightly be looked for in a man enhaloed by the glory of God. Since he had entered upon the paths of sin Duperrier had become increasingly given to strong language. His formerly ascetic countenance was becoming bloated with rich food. Not only was his vocabulary growing coarse, but a similar vulgarity was invading his thoughts. His vision of Paradise, for example, had undergone a notable transformation. Instead of appearing to him as a symphony of souls in robes of cellophane, the dwelling-place of the elect came to look more and more like a vast dining-room. Mme Duperrier did not fail to observe the changes that were overtaking her husband and even to feel some anxiety for the future. Nevertheless, the thought of his possible descent into the abyss still did not outweigh in her mind the horror of singularity. Rather than an enhaloed Duperrier she would have preferred a husband who was an atheist, a debauchee and as crude of speech as her cousin Léopold. At least she would not then have to blush for him before the milkman.

No especial decision was called for on the part of Duperrier for him to lapse into the sin of sloth. The arrogant belief that he was required at the office to perform tasks unworthy of his merits, together with the drowsiness caused by heavy eating and drinking, made him naturally disposed to be idle; and since he had sufficient conceit to believe that he must excel in all things, even the worst, he very soon became a model of indolence. The day his indignant employer sacked him, he received the sentence with his hat in his hand.

'What's that on your head?' his employer asked.

'A halo,' said Duperrier.

'Is it indeed? And I suppose that's what you've been fooling around with when you were supposed to be working?'

When he told his wife of his dismissal, she asked him what he intended to do next.

'It seems to me that this would be a good moment to try the sin of avarice,' he answered gaily.

Of all the Deadly Sins, avarice was the one that called for the greatest effort of will-power on his part. To those not born avaricious it is the vice offering the fewest easy allurements, and when it is adopted on principle there is nothing to distinguish it, at least in the early stages, from that most sterling of all virtues, thrift. Duperrier subjected himself to severe disciplines, such as confining himself to gluttony, and thus succeeded in gaining a solid reputation for avarice among his friends and acquaintances. He really liked money for its own sake, and was better able than most people to experience the malicious thrill which misers feel at the thought that they control a source of creative energy and prevent it from functioning. Counting up his savings, the fruit of a hitherto laborious existence, he came by degrees to know the hideous pleasure of harming others by damming a current of exchange and of life. This outcome, simply because it was painfully achieved, filled Mme Duperrier with hope. Her husband had yielded so easily to the seductions of the other sins that God, she thought, could not condemn him very severely for an innocent, animal surrender which made him appear rather a victim deserving of compassion. His deliberate and patient progress along the road of avarice, on the other hand, could only be the fruit of a perverse desire which was like a direct challenge to Heaven. Nevertheless, although Duperrier became miserly to the point of putting trouser-buttons in the collection-bag, the brilliance and size of the halo remained unimpaired. This new setback,

duly noted, plunged husband and wife into despair.

Proud, gluttonous, angry, envious, slothful and avaricious, Duperrier felt that his soul was still perfumed with innocence. Deadly though they were, the six sins he had thus far practised were nevertheless such as a first communicant may confess to without despairing. The deadliest of all, lust, filled him with horror. The others, it seemed to him, might be said to exist almost outside the sphere of God's notice. In the case of each, sin or peccadillo, it all depended on the size of the dose. But lust, the sin of the flesh, meant unqualified acceptance of the Devil's work. The enchantments of thē night were a foretaste of the burning shades of Hell, the darting tongues were like the flames of eternity, the moans of ecstasy, the writhing bodies, these did but herald the wailing of the damned and the convulsions of flesh racked by endless torment. Duperrier had not deliberately reserved the sin of the flesh to the last: he had simply refused to contemplate it. Mme Duperrier herself could not think of it without disquiet. For many years the pair had lived in a state of delicious chastity, their nightly rest attended, until the coming of the halo, by dreams as pure as the driven snow. As she thought of it, the recollection of those years of continence was a source of considerable annoyance to Mme Duperrier, for she did not doubt that the halo was the result. Plainly that lily-white nimbus could be undone by lust alone.

Duperrier, after obstinately resisting his wife's persuasions, at length allowed himself to be overborne. Once again his sense of duty cast out fear. Having reached the decision he was embarrassed by his ignorance; but his wife, who thought of everything, bought him a revolting book in which all the essentials were set forth in the form of plain and simple instruction. The night-time spectacle of that saintly man, the halo encircling his head, reading a chapter of the abominable work to his wife, was a poignant one indeed. Often his voice trembled at some infamous word or some image more hideously evocative than the rest. Having thus achieved a theoretical mastery of the subject, he still delayed while he considered whether this last sin should be consummated in domestic intimacy or elsewhere. Mme Duperrier took the view that it should all be done at home, adducing reasons of economy which did not fail to weigh with him; but having considered all the pros and cons he concluded that he had no need to involve her in vile practices which might be prejudicial to her own salvation. As a loyal husband he valiantly resolved that he alone should run the risks.

Thereafter Duperrier spent most of his nights in disreputable hotels where he pursued his initiation in company with the professionals of the quarter. The halo, which he could not conceal from these wretched associates, led to his finding himself in various odd situations, sometimes embarrassing and sometimes advantageous. In the beginning, owing to his anxiety to conform to the instructions in his manual, he sinned with little exaltation but rather with the methodical application of a dancer learning a new step or figure of choreography. However, the desire for perfection to which his pride impelled him soon achieved its lamentable reward in the notoriety which he gained among the women with whom he consorted. Although he came to take the liveliest pleasure in these pursuits, Duperrier nevertheless found them expensive and was cruelly afflicted in his avarice. One evening on the Place Pigalle he made the acquaintance of a creature twenty years of age, already a lost soul, whose name was Marie-Jannick. It was for her, so it is believed, that the poet Maurice Fombeure wrote the charming lines:

> C'est Marie-Jannick
> De Landivisiau
> Qui tue les moustiques
> Avec son sabot.

Marie-Jannick had come from Brittany six months previously to go into service as maid-of-all-work in the home of a municipal councillor who was both a socialist and an atheist. Finding herself unable to endure the life of this godless household, she had given notice and was now courageously earning her living on the Boulevard de Clichy. As was to be expected, the halo made a deep impression on that little religious soul. To Marie-Jannick, Duperrier seemed the equal of St. Yves and St. Ronan, and he, on his side, was not slow to perceive the influence he had over her and to turn it to profit.

Thus it is that on this very day, the 22nd February of the year 1944, amid the darkness of winter and of war, Marie-Jannick, who will shortly be twenty-five, may be seen walking her beat on the Boulevard de Clichy. During the black-out hours the stroller between the Place Pigalle and the Rue des Martyrs may be startled to observe, floating and swaying in the darkness, a mysterious circle of light that looks rather like a ring of Saturn. It is Duperrier, his head adorned with the glorious halo which he no longer seeks to conceal from the curiosity of all and sundry; Duperrier, burdened with the weight of the seven Deadly Sins, who, lost to all shame, supervises the labours of Marie-Jannick, administering a smart kick in the pants when her zeal flags, and waiting at the hotel door to count her takings by the light of the halo. But from the depths of his degradation, through the dark night of his conscience, a murmur yet rises from time to time to his lips, a prayer of thanksgiving for the absolute gratuity of the gifts of God.

———◆•◀▶•◆———

With "The State of Grace," we have a comic story. It is based on certain theological questions that have been debated since the early days of Christianity. Can man, who is a fallen creature, ever become virtuous enough, no matter how hard he tries, to be worthy of salvation? Or does salvation come only gratuitously—unearned? That is, does the "state of grace" bear any relation to man's deserts? What is the connection, if any, between "works" and "grace"? For example, the Calvinistic churches, such as the Congregational and the Presbyterian, have held that salvation comes only through "election"—that certain souls, from the beginning of time, have been "predestined" by God for salvation, and that the "elect" cannot be damned, that their behavior on earth has no relevance. On the other hand, certain churches, most notably the Catholic, have held that "works" are significant, and that man's conduct is the result of his "free will" and is to be judged.

Such questions are, clearly, part of the overarching question of what constitutes divine justice. How can human ideas of justice be squared with God's apparent management of the universe? Milton, in *Paradise Lost*, declared that he sought to "justify God's ways to man," but it is a far cry from Milton's endeavor to Marcel Aymé's little comedy. In fact, the comedy of "The State of Grace" depends, finally, on the contrast between the gravity of the Church Fathers and theologians and such theological poets as Dante and Milton on the one hand, and the realism of Aymé's tight little world on the other. In Aymé's world the great questions are reduced to the humdrum life of the petty bourgeois, and we have a theological farce, a sort of theological high jinks.

We must insist, however, that the story does not deny the seriousness of the concern on which its comic effect is based. A devout Christian might find the story even funnier than would the unbeliever; and even if we take the story purely in nontheological terms, it clearly recognizes the mysterious and paradoxical aspects of life with which the theologians had struggled in sweat and prayer. For example, the final butt of Aymé's wit is not the famous theologians, or even poor Monsieur Duperrier, but Madame Duperrier, "who had never had any ambition other than to keep her place in a social sphere ruled by the cult of the absolute norm."

EXERCISES

1. What do you think are the funniest touches or episodes in the story. Why?
2. How can it be said that Marie-Jannick, the poor little girl from Brittany, gives a new dimension to the comedy? What would be the difference if she were an ordinary, cynical prostitute?
3. How would you describe the tone of the story? That is, what attitude does Aymé seem to take toward the event presented? To put the matter another way, how would you describe his style? Is it cool and detached? Boisterous and insisting on the absurdity of the story? Satirical?
4. Can you imagine how Aymé might have treated the material used by Hawthorne in "Young Goodman Brown"? What kind of comedy might he have developed at the end?

Section 5

PLOT: THE SIMPLE TURN

In the stories of this group there is a sudden turn of plot, a surprising reversal, which opens our eyes to a new meaning, and on which the effect of the story rests. We can see how different this emphasis on plot is from the handling of event in a story such as "Flight" (sec. 3). In such a story there may be elements of suspense, even of surprise, but the effect is primarily achieved by the gradual accumulation of detail, the delineation of a personality, the creation of a certain feeling and atmosphere. In the tale, we may say, the sequence of events is its own excuse for being—the "teller" presumably is telling what happens; he washes his hands, as it were, of the responsibility for what happens. In fact, there is the implied defense: "It happened this way, I'm just telling it."

The stories in this section differ, also, from those in section 4. In the fable, the sense of the "happening" is subordinated to the management of events to make a point, and, as we have seen, the use of fantasy may give a justification for a management that violates the demands of actuality.

In this section we are dealing with stories that can be thought of as more nearly representative of modern fiction than those in sections 3 and 4. In such stories the mere sequence of events ("I'm just telling how it really happened") does not justify, as in a tale, the story; here we find a more obvious concern with the organization of events in a pattern of cause and effect—that is, with plot. At the same time, unlike the fable, the stories here insist on verisimilitude. They do present action as embodying meaning, as making a point, but the action must be justified in the actual world.

We must again insist, however, that the distinctions made here are merely a matter of emphasis. The tale and the fable may, in a sense, be taken as the poles of fiction, and the actual story must always partake, in varying degrees, of the nature of both.

The stories that follow are very simple in organization, moving through a fairly clear set of complications to the single turn that provides the denouement. These are, in fact, more simple than some of the stories we have already looked at, but their very simplicity, now that we are about to consider various complicated modes of fictional organization, may give us a firm basis for further exploration of fiction.

WET SATURDAY
John Collier (b. 1901)

It was July. In the large, dull house they were imprisoned by the swish and the gurgle and all the hundred sounds of rain. They were in the drawing-room, behind four tall and weeping windows, in a lake of damp and faded chintz.

This house, ill-kept and unpreposses-

sing, was necessary to Mr. Princey, who detested his wife, his daughter, and his hulking son. His life was to walk through the village, touching his hat, not smiling. His cold pleasure was to recapture snapshot memories of the infinitely remote summers of his childhood—coming into the orangery and finding his lost wooden horse, the tunnel in the box hedge, and the little square of light at the end of it. But now all this was threatened—his austere pride of position in the village, his passionate attachment to the house—and all because Millicent, his cloddish daughter Millicent, had done this shocking and incredibly stupid thing. Mr. Princey turned from her in revulsion and spoke to his wife.

"They'd send her to a lunatic asylum," he said. "A criminal-lunatic asylum. We should have to move away. It would be impossible."

His daughter began to shake again. "I'll kill myself," she said.

"Be quiet," said Mr. Princey. "We have very little time. No time for nonsense. I intend to deal with this." He called to his son, who stood looking out of the window. "George, come here. Listen. How far did you get with your medicine before they threw you out as hopeless?"

"You know as well as I do," said George.

"Do you know enough—did they drive enough into your head for you to be able to guess what a competent doctor could tell about such a wound?"

"Well, it's a—it's a knock or blow."

"If a tile fell from the roof? Or a piece of the coping?"

"Well, guv'nor, you see, it's like this ——"

"Is it possible?"

"No."

"Why not?"

"Oh, because she hit him several times."

"I can't stand it," said Mrs. Princey.

"You have got to stand it, my dear," said her husband. "And keep that hysterical note out of your voice. It might be overheard. We are talking about the weather. If he fell down the well, George, striking his head several times?"

"I really don't know, guv'nor."

"He'd have had to hit the sides several times in thirty or forty feet, and at the correct angles. No, I'm afraid not. We must go over it all again. Millicent."

"No! No!"

"Millicent, we must go over it all again. Perhaps you have forgotten something. One tiny irrelevant detail may save or ruin us. Particularly you, Millicent. You don't *want* to be put in an asylum, do you? Or be hanged? They might hang you, Millicent. You must stop that shaking. You must keep your voice quiet. We are talking of the weather. Now."

"I can't. I . . . I . . ."

"Be quiet, child. Be quiet." He put his long cold face very near to his daughter's. He found himself horribly revolted by her. Her features were thick, her jaw heavy, her whole figure repellently powerful. "Answer me," he said. "You were in the stable?"

"Yes."

"One moment, though. Who knew you were in love with this wretched curate?"

"No one. I've never said a——"

"Don't worry," said George. "The whole god-damned village knows. They've been sniggering about it in the Plough for three years past."

"Likely enough," said Mr. Princey. "Likely enough. What filth!" He made as if to wipe something off the backs of his hands. "Well, now, we continue. You were in the stable?"

"Yes."

"You were putting the croquet set into its box?"

"Yes."

"You heard someone crossing the yard?"

"Yes."

"It was Withers?"

"Yes."

"So you called him?"

"Yes."

"Loudly? Did you call him loudly? Could anyone have heard?"

"No, Father. I'm sure not. I didn't call him. He saw me as I went to the door. He just waved his hand and came over."

"How *can* I find out from you whether there was anyone about? Whether he *could* have been seen?"

"I'm sure not, Father. I'm quite sure."

"So you both went into the stable?"

"Yes. It was raining hard."

"What did he say?"

"He said 'Hullo, Milly.' And to excuse him coming in the back way, but he'd set out to walk over to Bass Hill."

"Yes."

"And he said, passing the park, he'd seen the house and suddenly thought of me, and he thought he'd just look in for a minute, just to tell me something. He said he was so happy, he wanted me to share it. He'd heard from the Bishop he was to have the vicarage. And it wasn't only that. It meant he could marry. And he began to stutter. And I thought he meant me."

"Don't tell me what you thought. Exactly what he said. Nothing else."

"Well . . . Oh dear!"

"Don't cry. It is a luxury you cannot afford. Tell me."

"He said no. He said it wasn't me. It's Ella Brangwyn-Davies. And he was sorry. And all that. Then he went to go."

"And then?"

"I went mad. He turned his back. I had the winning post of the croquet set in my hand——"

"Did you shout or scream? I mean, as you hit him?"

"No. I'm sure I didn't."

"Did he? Come on. Tell me."

"No, Father."

"And then?"

"I threw it down. I came straight into the house. That's all. I wish I were dead!"

"And you met none of the servants. No

one will go into the stable. You see, George, he probably told people he was going to Bass Hill. Certainly no one knows he came here. He might have been attacked in the woods. We must consider every detail . . . A curate, with his head battered in——"

"Don't, Father!" cried Millicent.

"Do you want to be hanged? A curate, with his head battered in, found in the woods. Who'd want to kill Withers?"

There was a tap on the door, which opened immediately. It was little Captain Smollett, who never stood on ceremony. "Who'd kill Withers?" he said. "I would, with pleasure. How d'you do, Mrs. Princey. I walked right in."

"He heard you, Father," moaned Millicent.

"My dear, we can all have our little joke," said her father. "Don't pretend to be shocked. A little theoretical curate-killing, Smollett. In these days we talk nothing but thrillers."

"Parsonicide," said Captain Smollett. "Justifiable parsonicide. Have you heard about Ella Brangwyn-Davies? I shall be laughed at."

"Why?" said Mr. Princey. "Why should you be laughed at?"

"Had a shot in that direction myself," said Smollett, with careful sang-froid. "She half said yes, too. Hadn't you heard? She told most people. Now it'll look as if I got turned down for a white rat in a dog collar."

"Too bad!" said Mr. Princey.

"Fortune of war," said the little captain.

"Sit down," said Mr. Princey. "Mother, Millicent, console Captain Smollett with your best light conversation. George and I have something to look to. We shall be back in a minute or two, Smollett. Come, George."

It was actually five minutes before Mr. Princey and his son returned.

"Excuse me, my dear," said Mr. Princey to his wife. "Smollett, would you care to see something rather interesting? Come out to the stables for a moment."

They went into the stable yard. The buildings were now unused except as odd sheds. No one ever went there. Captain Smollett entered, George followed him, Mr. Princey came last. As he closed the door he took up a gun which stood behind it. "Smollett," said he, "we have come out to shoot a rat which George heard squeaking under that tub. Now, you must listen to me very carefully or you will be shot by accident. I mean that."

Smollett looked at him. "Very well," said he. "Go on."

"A very tragic happening has taken place this afternoon," said Mr. Princey. "It will be even more tragic unless it is smoothed over."

"Oh?" said Smollett.

"You heard me ask," said Mr. Princey, "who would kill Withers. You heard Millicent make a comment, an unguarded comment."

"Well?" said Smollett. "What of it?"

"Very little," said Mr. Princey. "Unless you heard that Withers had met a violent end this very afternoon. And that, my dear Smollett, is what you are going to hear."

"Have you killed him?" cried Smollett.

"Millicent has," said Mr. Princey.

"Hell!" said Smollett.

"It *is* hell," said Mr. Princey. "You would have remembered—and guessed."

"Maybe," said Smollett. "Yes. I suppose I should."

"Therefore," said Mr. Princey, "you constitute a problem."

"Why did she kill him?" said Smollett.

"It is one of these disgusting things," said Mr. Princey. "Pitiable, too. She deluded herself that he was in love with her."

"Oh, of course," said Smollett.

"And he told her about the Brangwyn-Davies girl."

"I see," said Smollett.

"I have no wish," said Mr. Princey, "that she should be proved either a lunatic or a murderess. I could hardly live here after that."

"I suppose not," said Smollett.

"On the other hand," said Mr. Princey, *"you* know about it."

"Yes," said Smollett. "I am wondering if I could keep my mouth shut. If I promised you——"

"I am wondering if I could believe you," said Mr. Princey.

"If I promised," said Smollett.

"If things went smoothly," said Mr. Princey. "But not if there was any sort of suspicion, any questioning. You would be afraid of being an accessory."

"I don't know," said Smollett.

"I do," said Mr. Princey. "What are we going to do?"

"I can't see anything else," said Smollett. "You'd never be fool enough to do me in. You can't get rid of two corpses."

"I regard it," said Mr. Princey, "as a better risk than the other. It could be an accident. Or you and Withers could both disappear. There are possibilities in that."

"Listen," said Smollett. "You can't ——"

"Listen," said Mr. Princey. "There may be a way out. There *is* a way out, Smollett. You gave me the idea yourself."

"Did I?" said Smollett. "What?"

"You said you would kill Withers," said Mr. Princey. "You have a motive."

"I was joking," said Smollett.

"You are always joking," said Mr. Princey. "People think there must be something behind it. Listen, Smollett, I can't trust you, therefore you must trust me. Or I will kill you now, in the next minute. I mean that. You can choose between dying and living."

"Go on," said Smollett.

"There is a sewer here," said Mr. Princey, speaking fast and forcefully. "That is where I am going to put Withers. No outsider knows he has come up here this afternoon. No one will ever look there for him unless you tell them. You must give me evidence that you have murdered Withers."

"Why?" said Smollett.

"So that I shall be dead sure that you will never open your lips on the matter," said Mr. Princey.

"What evidence?" said Smollett.

"George," said Mr. Princey, "hit him in the face, hard."

"Good God!" said Smollett.

"Again," said Mr. Princey. "Don't bruise your knuckles."

"Oh!" said Smollett.

"I'm sorry," said Mr. Princey. "There must be traces of a struggle between you and Withers. Then it will not be altogether safe for you to go to the police."

"Why don't you take my word?" said Smollett.

"I will when we've finished," said Mr. Princey. "George, get that croquet post. Take your handkerchief to it. As I told you. Smollett, you'll just grasp the end of this croquet post. I shall shoot you if you don't."

"Oh, hell," said Smollett. "All right."

"Pull two hairs out of his head, George," said Mr. Princey, "and remember what I told you to do with them. Now, Smollett, you take that bar and raise the big flagstone with the ring in it. Withers is in the next stall. You've got to drag him through and dump him in."

"I won't touch him," said Smollett.

"Stand back, George," said Mr. Princey, raising his gun.

"Wait a minute," cried Smollett. "Wait a minute." He did as he was told.

Mr. Princey wiped his brow. "Look here," said he. "Everything is perfectly safe. Remember, no one knows that Withers came here. Everyone thinks he walked over to Bass Hill. That's five miles of country to search. They'll never look in our sewer. Do you see how safe it is?"

"I suppose it is," said Smollett.

"Now come into the house," said Mr. Princey. "We shall never get that rat."

They went into the house. The maid was bringing tea into the drawing-room. "See, my dear," said Mr. Princey to his wife, "we went to the stable to shoot a rat and we found Captain Smollett. Don't be offended, my dear fellow."

"You must have walked up the back drive," said Mrs. Princey.

"Yes. Yes. That was it," said Smollett in some confusion.

"You've cut your lip," said George, handing him a cup of tea.

"I . . . I just knocked it."

"Shall I tell Bridget to bring some iodine?" said Mrs. Princey. The maid looked up, waiting.

"Don't trouble, please," said Smollett. "It's nothing."

"Very well, Bridget," said Mrs. Princey. "That's all."

"Smollett is very kind," said Mr. Princey. "He knows all our trouble. We can rely on him. We have his word."

"Oh, have we, Captain Smollett?" cried Mrs. Princey. "You *are* good."

"Don't worry, old fellow," Mr. Princey said. "They'll never find anything."

Pretty soon Smollett took his leave. Mrs. Princey pressed his hand very hard. Tears came into her eyes. All three of them watched him go down the drive. Then Mr. Princey spoke very earnestly to his wife for a few minutes and the two of them went upstairs and spoke still more earnestly to Millicent. Soon after, the rain having ceased, Mr. Princey took a stroll round the stable yard.

He came back and went to the telephone. "Put me through to Bass Hill police station," said he. "Quickly . . . Hullo, is that the police station? This is Mr. Princey, of Abbott's Laxton. I'm afraid something rather terrible has happened up here. Can you send someone at once?"

The structure of this little story is very simple. The exposition (see Glossary), consists in the revelation that Mr. Princey likes his house and position in the village but detests his family, that his daughter Millicent has committed a murder, and that he must save her, not because he likes her, but because he can't continue to live here if there is a scandal. The complication (see Glossary) discloses that Captain Smollett had a grudge against the curate whom Millicent had murdered, and presents the gradual involvement of Smollett to the point where he has been forced to incriminate himself as a safeguard against betraying the Princey family. With the denouement (see Glossary), Mr. Princey has succeeded in making all safe for himself. Smollett, at gun point to be sure, is now necessarily committed to the Princey's side. A solution has been reached for the original problem—the original conflict—from which the story arises: the struggle of Mr. Princey to escape the consequences of Millicent's act. This could be the end of the story, even if a rather tame and falling-away end.

But it is not the end. We have the sharp turn in the last paragraph, when Mr. Princey calls the police. Mr. Smollett is not merely going to keep quiet about the murder: he is going to hang for it! There is, in this turn, a shock—the revelation of the completeness of Mr. Princey's cold-blooded isolation from life.

How do we react to the story? What sort of sympathies do we have or what identifications do we make? We start out committed—dramatically, at least—to the solution of Mr. Princey's problem. The reservation implied by the word *dramatically* is important. That is, this is not simply a moral question—a question of who is right and who is wrong. For instance, in Shakespeare's play *Macbeth* we have some commitment with Macbeth in his ambition that leads him to the murder of Duncan, and some commitment with him in his struggle to avoid the consequences. In "Wet Saturday," in a much more modest way, our sympathies are involved with Mr. Princey in his effort to solve his problem.

But we can go a little further. Millicent is made pathetic, perhaps in some deep, long-range way, the victim of her father's cold egotism. The curate whom she murders is made heartless and unattractive; in a way, he "deserves" his fate. As for the second victim,

Captain Smollett, we are given no hint of any human qualities to make us feel for him. In fact, he walks into it, the stupe. Against him, we tend to identify ourselves with the cold ruthless cunning of Mr. Princey—for that represents one of our own potentialities, too.

The reader's general identification with Mr. Princey carries along with it a general attitude toward the events of the story. What is this attitude? What is the tone of this story? To understand "tone" in this sense, it may be useful to reflect on how the tone of one's voice may modify the meaning of what is being said—how, for instance, the word *yes* changes its meaning in a kind of spectrum from enthusiastic agreement through acceptance, warm or cool, on to a sarcastic utterance of the word that means exactly the opposite of the literal meaning of the word, the "oh yeah?" of denial. Tone, then, implies the attitude of the speaker or writer toward what is said and, we may add, toward the audience.

In this connection it is significant that Collier gives a detached factual narrative. He does not aim for—in fact, he tries to suppress—emotional effects. He is treating the plot like a mechanism, with the human values kept in the background.

By implication he is saying that if you look at life with a certain cool detachment, things feel somewhat different. Think how different we should feel if the anguish of Millicent were developed. Or, if, for example, Mr. Princey did have a profound feeling for his daughter and at the same time a deep moral sense. Or if he should discover in this moment a tragic revelation about himself. But no, Collier gives us the coldly mechanical working out of Mr. Princey's plan. It is a splendid plan, beautifully conceived, accurately worked out. Bravo!

The story is a very good illustration of what the French philosopher Bergson takes to be the basis of comedy—the contrast between the mechanical and the vital—Mr. Princey's plan set against all the human issues; it merely gives a perspective on them, in this story a coldly ironical one. Comedy, even in this cold irony, is another way for us to learn something about ourselves.

EXERCISES

Read "Tomorrow and Tomorrow and So Forth," by John Updike (sec. 10). What elements do you find there that might be regarded as comic?

THE LOTTERY TICKET
Anton Chekhov (1860–1904)

Ivan Dmitritch, a middle-class man who lived with his family on an income of twelve hundred a year and was very well satisfied with his lot, sat down on the sofa after supper and began reading the newspaper.

"I forgot to look at the newspaper today," his wife said to him as she cleared the table. "Look and see whether the list of drawings is there."

"Yes, it is," said Ivan Dmitritch; "but hasn't your ticket lapsed?"

"No; I took the interest on Tuesday."

"What is the number?"

"Series 9,499, number 26."

"All right . . . we will look . . . 9,499 and 26."

Ivan Dmitritch had no faith in lottery luck, and would not, as a rule, have consented to look at the lists of winning numbers, but now, as he had nothing else to do and as the newspaper was before his eyes, he passed his finger downwards along the column of numbers. And immediately, as though in mockery of his scepticism, no further than the second line from the top, his eye was caught by the figure 9,499! Unable to believe his eyes, he hurriedly dropped the paper on his knees without looking to see the number of the ticket, and, just as though some one had given him a douche of cold water, he felt an agreeable chill in the pit of the stomach; tingling and terrible and sweet!

"Masha, 9,499 is there!" he said in a hollow voice.

His wife looked at his astonished and panic-stricken face, and realized that he was not joking.

"9,499?" she asked, turning pale and dropping the folded tablecloth on the table.

"Yes, yes . . . it really is there!"

"And the number of the ticket?"

"Oh, yes! There's the number of the ticket too. But stay . . . wait! No, I say! Anyway, the number of our series is there! Anyway, you understand. . . ."

Looking at his wife, Ivan Dmitritch gave a broad, senseless smile, like a baby when a bright object is shown it. His wife smiled too; it was as pleasant to her as to him that he only mentioned the series, and did not try to find out the number of the winning ticket. To torment and tantalize oneself with hopes of possible fortune is so sweet, so thrilling!

"It is our series," said Ivan Dmitritch, after a long silence. "So there is a probability that we have won. It's only a probability, but there it is!"

"Well, now look!"

"Wait a little. We have plenty of time to be disappointed. It's on the second line from the top, so the prize is seventy-five thousand. That's not money, but power, capital! And in a minute I shall look at the list, and there—26! Eh? I say, what if we really have won?"

The husband and wife began laughing and staring at one another in silence. The possibility of winning bewildered them; they could not have said, could not have dreamed, what they both needed that seventy-five thousand for, what they would buy, where they would go. They thought only of the figures 9,499 and 75,000 and pictured them in their imagination, while somehow they could not think of the happiness itself which was so possible.

Ivan Dmitritch, holding the paper in his hand, walked several times from corner to corner, and only when he had recovered from the first impression began dreaming a little.

"And if we have won," he said—"why, it will be a new life, it will be a transformation! The ticket is yours, but if it were mine I should, first of all, of course, spend twenty-five thousand on real property in the shape of an estate; ten thousand on immediate expenses, new furnishing . . . travelling . . . paying debts, and so on. . . . The other forty thousand I would put in the bank and get interest on it."

"Yes, an estate, that would be nice," said his wife, sitting down and dropping her hands in her lap.

"Somewhere in the Tula or Oryol provinces. . . . In the first place we shouldn't need a summer villa, and besides, it would always bring in an income."

And pictures came crowding on his imagination, each more gracious and poetical than the last. And in all these pictures he saw himself well-fed, serene, healthy, felt warm, even hot! Here, after eating a summer soup, cold as ice, he lay on his back on the burning sand close to a stream or in the garden under a lime-tree. . . . It is hot. . . . His little boy and girl are crawling about near him, digging in the sand or catching ladybirds in the grass. He dozes sweetly, thinking of nothing, and feeling all over that he need not go to the office today, tomorrow, or the day after. Or, tired of lying still, he goes to the hayfield, or to the forest for mushrooms, or watches the peasants catching fish with a net. When the sun sets he takes a towel and soap and saunters to the bathing shed, where he undresses at his leisure, slowly rubs his bare chest with his hands, and goes into the water. And in the water, near the opaque soapy circles, little fish flit to and fro and green water-weeds nod their heads. After bathing there is tea with cream and milk rolls. . . . In the evening a walk or *vint* with the neighbors.

"Yes, it would be nice to buy an estate," said his wife, also dreaming, and from her face it was evident that she was enchanted by her thoughts.

Ivan Dmitritch pictured to himself autumn with its rains, its cold evenings, and its St. Martin's summer. At that season he would have to take longer walks about the garden and beside the river, so as to get thoroughly chilled, and then drink a big glass of vodka and eat a salted mushroom or a soused cucumber, and then—drink another. . . . The children would come running from the kitchen-garden, bringing a carrot and a radish smelling of fresh earth. . . . And then, he would lie stretched full length on the sofa, and in leisurely fashion turn over the pages of some illustrated magazine, or, covering his face with it and unbuttoning his waistcoat, give himself up to slumber.

The St. Martin's summer is followed by cloudy, gloomy weather. It rains day and night, the bare trees weep, the wind is damp and cold. The dogs, the horses, the fowls— all are wet, depressed, downcast. There is nowhere to walk; one can't go out for days together; one has to pace up and down the room, looking despondently at the grey window. It is dreary!

Ivan Dmitritch stopped and looked at his wife.

"I should go abroad, you know, Masha," he said.

And he began thinking how nice it would be in late autumn to go abroad somewhere to the South of France . . . to Italy . . . to India!

"I should certainly go abroad too," his wife said. "But look at the number of the ticket!"

"Wait, wait! . . ."

He walked about the room and went on thinking. It occurred to him: what if his wife really did go abroad? It is pleasant to travel alone, or in the society of light, careless women who live in the present, and not such as think and talk all the journey about nothing but their children, sigh, and tremble with dismay over every farthing. Ivan Dmitritch imagined his wife in the train with a multitude of parcels, baskets, and bags; she would be sighing over something, complaining that the train made her head ache, that she had spent so much money. . . . At the stations he would continually be having to run for boiling water, bread and butter. . . . She wouldn't have dinner because of its being too dear. . . .

"She would begrudge me every farthing," he thought, with a glance at his wife.

"The lottery ticket is hers, not mine! Besides, what is the use of her going abroad? What does she want there? She would shut herself up in the hotel, and not let me out of her sight . . . I know!"

And for the first time in his life his mind dwelt on the fact that his wife had grown elderly and plain, and that she was saturated through and through with the smell of cooking, while he was still young, fresh, and healthy, and might well have got married again.

"Of course, all that is silly nonsense," he thought; "but . . . why should she go abroad? What would she make of it? And yet she would go, of course. . . . I can fancy. . . . In reality it is all one to her, whether it is Naples or Klin. She would only be in my way. I should be dependent upon her. I can fancy how, like a regular woman, she will lock the money up as soon as she gets it. . . . She will look after her relations and grudge me every farthing."

Ivan Dmitritch thought of her relations. All those wretched brothers and sisters and aunts and uncles would come crawling about as soon as they heard of the winning ticket, would begin whining like beggars, and fawning upon them with oily, hypocritical smiles. Wretched, detestable people! If they were given anything, they would ask for more; while if they were refused, they would swear at them, slander them, and wish them every kind of misfortune.

Ivan Dmitritch remembered his own relations, and their faces, at which he had looked impartially in the past, struck him now as repulsive and hateful.

"They are such reptiles!" he thought.

And his wife's face, too, struck him as repulsive and hateful. Anger surged up in his heart against her, and he thought malignantly:

"She knows nothing about money, and so she is stingy. If she won it she would give me a hundred roubles, and put the rest away under lock and key."

And he looked at his wife, not with a smile now, but with hatred. She glanced at him too, and also with hatred and anger. She had her own daydreams, her own plans, her own reflections; she understood perfectly well what her husband's dreams were. She knew who would be the first to try to grab her winnings.

"It's very nice making daydreams at other people's expense!" is what her eyes expressed. "No, don't you dare!"

Her husband understood her look; hatred began stirring again in his breast, and in order to annoy his wife he glanced quickly, to spite her at the fourth page on the newspaper and read out triumphantly:

"Series 9,499, number 46! Not 26!"

Hatred and hope both disappeared at once, and it began immediately to seem to Ivan Dmitritch and his wife that their rooms were dark and small and low-pitched, that the supper they had been eating was not doing them good, but lying heavy on their stomachs, that the evenings were long and wearisome. . . .

"What the devil's the meaning of it?" said Ivan Dmitritch, beginning to be ill-humored. "Wherever one steps there are bits of paper under one's feet, crumbs, husks. The rooms are never swept! One is simply forced to go out. Damnation take my soul entirely! I shall go and hang myself on the first aspen-tree!"

EXERCISES

1. Locate the exposition, the complication, and the denouement of this story. Compare its structure with that of "Wet Saturday."
2. What is the question, problem, or conflict on which this story is based? Or can we say that it begins with one question, a fairly objective superficial one, and ends with a deep subjective one? Working from this matter of the conflict, state the theme of the story.
3. In working on exercise 2 you may find it desirable to consider the following questions. Have new facts of the past life of the husband and wife been revealed? Or has, merely, their idea of the facts been changed? Have they previously deceived themselves about their relationship, or can

we say that, under the earlier circumstances, they had been sincere in their humdrum affection and mutual acceptance? Is it logical and credible that out of the dream of winning the lottery should come the change of attitude? Are we to suppose that later on, long after the events recounted in the story, the husband and wife may again find their old comfortable relationship? Do we find in the story any indication of an answer to this question? Or is the question itself relevant to the effectiveness or even to the meaning of the story?
4. This story may be said to be based on an extraordinary coincidence, an accident. Does this invalidate the story? If not, why not?

LEGAL AID
Frank O'Connor (1903–1966)

Delia Carty came of a very respectable family. It was going as maid to the O'Grady's of Pouladuff that ruined her. That whole family was slightly touched. The old man, a national teacher, was hardly ever at home, and the daughters weren't much better. When they weren't away visiting, they had people visiting them, and it was nothing to Delia to come in late at night and find one of them plastered round some young fellow on the sofa.

That sort of thing isn't good for any young girl. Like mistress like maid; inside six months she was smoking, and within a year she was carrying on with one Tom Flynn, a farmer's son. Her father, a respectable, hard-working man, knew nothing about it, for he would have realized that she was no match for one of the Flynns, and even if Tom's father, Ned, had known, he would never have thought it possible that any labourer's daughter could imagine herself a match for Tom.

Not, God knows, that Tom was any great catch. He was a big uncouth galoot who was certain that lovemaking, like drink, was one of the simple pleasures his father tried to deprive him of, out of spite. He used to call at the house while the O'Gradys were away, and there would be Delia in one of Eileen O'Grady's frocks and with Eileen

O'Grady's lipstick and powder on, doing the lady over the tea things in the parlour. Throwing a glance over his shoulder in case anyone might spot him, Tom would heave himself onto the sofa with his boots over the end.

"Begod, I love sofas," he would say with simple pleasure.

"Put a cushion behind you," Delia would say.

"Oh, begod," Tom would say, making himself comfortable, "if ever I have a house of my own 'tis unknown what sofas and cushions I'll have. Them teachers must get great money. What the hell do they go away at all for?"

Delia loved making the tea and handing it out like a real lady, but you couldn't catch Tom out like that.

"Ah, what do I want tay for?" he would say with a doubtful glance at the cup. "Haven't you any whisky? Ould O'Grady must have gallons of it. . . . Leave it there on the table. Why the hell don't they have proper mugs with handles a man could get a grip on? Is that taypot silver? Pity I'm not a teacher!"

It was only natural for Delia to show him the bedrooms and the dressing-tables with the three mirrors, the way you could see yourself from all sides, but Tom, his hands under his head, threw himself with incredulous delight on the low double bed and cried: "Springs! Begod, 'tis like a car!"

What the springs gave rise to was entirely the O'Grady's fault since no one but themselves would have left a house in a lonesome part to a girl of nineteen to mind. The only surprising thing was that it lasted two years without Delia showing any signs of it. It probably took Tom that time to find the right way.

But when he did he got into a terrible state. It was hardly in him to believe that a harmless poor devil like himself whom no one ever bothered his head about could achieve such unprecedented results on one girl, but when he understood it he knew only

too well what the result of it would be. His father would first beat hell out of him and then throw him out and leave the farm to his nephews. There being no hope of conciliating his father, Tom turned his attention to God, who, though supposed to share Ned Flynn's views about fellows and girls, had some nature in Him. Tom stopped seeing Delia, to persuade God that he was reforming and to show that anyway it wasn't his fault. Left alone he could be a decent, good-living young fellow, but the Carty girl was a forward, deceitful hussy who had led him on instead of putting him off the way any well-bred girl would do. Between lipsticks, sofas, and tay in the parlour, Tom put it up to God that it was a great wonder she hadn't got him into worse trouble.

Delia had to tell her mother, and Mrs. Carty went to Father Corcoran to see could he induce Tom to marry her. Father Corcoran was a tall, testy old man who, even at the age of sixty-five, couldn't make out for the life of him what young fellows saw in girls, but if he didn't know much about lovers he knew a lot about farmers.

"Wisha, Mrs. Carty," he said crankily, "how could I get him to marry her? Wouldn't you have a bit of sense? Some little financial arrangement, maybe, so that she could leave the parish and not be a cause of scandal—I might be able to do that."

He interviewed Ned Flynn, who by this time had got Tom's version of the story and knew financial arrangements were going to be the order of the day unless he could put a stop to them. Ned was a man of over six foot with a bald brow and a smooth unlined face as though he never had a care except his general concern for the welfare of humanity which made him look so abnormally thoughtful. Even Tom's conduct hadn't brought a wrinkle to his brow.

"I don't know, father," he said, stroking his bald brow with a dieaway air, "I don't know what you could do at all."

"Wisha, Mr. Flynn," said the priest who, when it came to the pinch, had more nature than twenty Flynns, "wouldn't you do the handsome thing and let him marry her before it goes any farther?"

"I don't see how much farther it could go, father," said Ned.

"It could become a scandal."

"I'm afraid 'tis that already, father."

"And after all," said Father Corcoran, forcing himself to put in a good word for one of the unfortunate sex whose very existence was a mystery to him, "is she any worse than the rest of the girls that are going? Bad is the best of them, from what I see, and Delia is a great deal better than most."

"That's not my information at all," said Ned, looking like "The Heart Bowed Down."

"That's a very serious statement, Mr. Flynn," said Father Corcoran, giving him a challenging look.

"It can be proved, father," said Ned gloomily. "Of course I'm not denying the boy was foolish, but the cleverest can be caught."

"You astonish me, Mr. Flynn," said Father Corcoran who was beginning to realize that he wasn't even going to get a subscription. "Of course I can't contradict you, but 'twill cause a terrible scandal."

"I'm as sorry for that as you are, father," said Ned, "but I have my son's future to think of."

Then, of course, the fun began. Foolish to the last, the O'Gradys wanted to keep Delia on till it was pointed out to them that Mr. O'Grady would be bound to get the blame. After this, her father had to be told. Dick Carty knew exactly what became a devoted father, and he beat Delia till he had to be hauled off her by the neighbours. He was a man who loved to sit in his garden reading his paper; now he felt he owed it to himself not to be seen enjoying himself, so instead he sat over the fire and brooded. The more he brooded the angrier he became. But seeing that, with the best will in the world, he could not beat Delia every time he got angry, he turned his attention to the Flynns. Ned

Flynn, that contemptible bosthoon, had slighted one of the Carty's in a parish where they had lived for hundreds of years with unblemished reputations; the Flynns, as everyone knew, being mere upstarts and outsiders without a date on their gravestones before 1850—nobodies!

He brought Delia to see Jackie Canty, the solicitor in town. Jackie was a little jenny-ass of a man with thin lips, a pointed nose, and a pince-nez that wouldn't stop in place, and he listened with grave enjoyment to the story of Delia's misconduct. "And what happened then, please?" he asked in his shrill singsong, looking at the floor and trying hard not to burst out into a giggle of delight. "The devils!" he thought. "The devils!" It was as close as Jackie was ever likely to get to the facts of life, an opportunity not to be missed.

"Anything in writing?" he sang, looking at her over the pince-nez. "Any letters? Any documents?"

"Only a couple of notes I burned," said Delia, who thought him a very queer man, and no wonder.

"Pity!" Jackie said with an admiring smile. "A smart man! Oh, a very smart man!"

"Ah, 'tisn't that at all," said Delia uncomfortably, "only he had no occasion for writing."

"Ah, Miss Carty," cried Jackie in great indignation, looking at her challengingly through the specs while his voice took on a steely ring, "a gentleman in love always finds plenty of occasion for writing. He's a smart man; your father might succeed in an action for seduction, but if 'tis defended 'twill be a dirty case."

"Mr. Canty," said her father solemnly, "I don't mind how dirty it is so long as I get justice." He stood up, a powerful man of six feet, and held up his clenched fish. "Justice is what I want," he said dramatically. "That's the sort I am. I keep myself to myself and mind my own business, but give me a cut, and I'll fight in a bag, tied up."

"Don't forget that Ned Flynn has the money, Dick," wailed Jackie.

"Mr. Canty," said Dick with a dignity verging on pathos, "you know me?"

"I do, Dick, I do."

"I'm living in this neighbourhood, man and boy, fifty years, and I owe nobody a ha-penny. If it took me ten years, breaking stones by the road, I'd pay it back, every penny."

"I know, Dick, I know," moaned Jackie. "But there's other things as well. There's your daughter's reputation. Do you know what they'll do? They'll go into court and swear someone else was the father."

"Tom could never say that," Delia cried despairingly. "The tongue would rot in his mouth."

Jackie had no patience at all with this chit of a girl, telling him his business. He sat back with a weary air, his arm over the back of his chair.

"That statement has no foundation," he said icily. "There is no record of any such thing happening a witness. If there was, the inhabitants of Ireland would have considerably less to say for themselves. You would be surprised the things respectable people will say in the witness box. Rot in their mouths indeed! Ah, dear me, no. With documents, of course, it would be different, but it is only our word against theirs. Can it be proved that you weren't knocking round with any other man at this time, Miss Carty?"

"Indeed, I was doing nothing of the sort," Delia said indignantly. "I swear to God I wasn't, Mr. Canty. I hardly spoke to a fellow the whole time, only when Tom and myself might have a row and I'd go out with Timmy Martin."

"Timmy Martin!" Canty cried dramatically pointing an accusing finger at her. "There is their man!"

"But Tom did the same with Betty Daly," cried Delia on the point of tears, "and he only did it to spite me. I swear there was nothing else in it, Mr. Canty, nor he never accused me of it."

"Mark my words," chanted Jackie with a mournful smile, "he'll make up for lost time now."

In this he showed considerably more foresight than Delia gave him credit for. After the baby was born and the action begun, Tom and his father went to town to see their solicitor, Peter Humphreys. Peter, who knew all he wanted to know about the facts of life, liked the case much less than Jackie. A crosseyed, full-blooded man who had made his money when law was about land, not love, he thought it a terrible comedown. Besides, he didn't think it nice to be listening to such things.

"And so, according to you, Timmy Martin is the father?" he asked Tom.

"Oh, I'm not swearing he is," said Tom earnestly, giving himself a heave in his chair and crossing his legs. "How the hell could I? All I am saying is that I wasn't the only one, and what's more she boasted about it. Boasted about it, begod!" he added with a look of astonishment at such female depravity.

"Before witnesses?" asked Peter, his eyes doing a double cross with hopelessness.

"As to that," replied Tom with great solemnity, looking over his shoulder for an open window he could spit through, "I couldn't swear."

"But you understood her to mean Timmy Martin?"

"I'm not accusing Timmy Martin at all," said Tom in great alarm, seeing how the processes of law were tending to involve him in a row with the Martins, who were a turbulent family with ways of getting their own back unknown to any law. "Timmy Martin is one man she used to be round with. It might be Timmy Martin or it might be someone else, or what's more," he added with the look of a man who has had a sudden revelation, "it might be more than one." He looked from Peter to his father and back again to see what effect the revelation was having, but like other revelations it didn't seem to be going down too well. "Begod," he said, giving himself another heave, "it might be any God's number. . . . But, as to that," he added cautiously, "I wouldn't like to swear."

"Nor indeed, Tom," said his solicitor with a great effort at politeness, "no one would advise you. You'll want a good counsel."

"Begod, I suppose I will," said Tom with astonished resignation before the idea that there might be people in the world bad enough to doubt his word.

There was great excitement in the village when it became known that the Flynns were having the Roarer Cooper as counsel. Even as a first-class variety turn Cooper could always command attention, and everyone knew that the rights and wrongs of the case would be relegated to their proper position while the little matter of Eileen O'Grady's best frock received the attention it deserved.

On the day of the hearing the court was crowded. Tom and his father were sitting at the back with Peter Humphreys, waiting for Cooper, while Delia and her father were talking to Jackie Canty and their own counsel, Ivers. He was a well-built young man with a high brow, black hair, and half-closed, red-tinged sleepy eyes. He talked in a bland drawl.

"You're not worrying, are you?" he asked Delia kindly. "Don't be a bit afraid. . . . I suppose there's no chance of them settling, Jackie?"

"Musha, what chance would there be?" Canty asked scoldingly. "Don't you know yourself what sort they are?"

"I'll have a word with Cooper myself," said Ivers. "Dan isn't as bad as he looks." He went to talk to a coarse-looking man in wig and gown who had just come in. To say he wasn't as bad as he looked was no great compliment. He had a face that was almost a square, with a big jaw and blue eyes in wicked little slits that made deep dents across his cheekbones.

"What about settling this case of ours, Dan?" Ivers asked gently.

Cooper didn't even return his look; apparently he was not responsive to charm.

"Did you ever know me to settle when I could fight?" he growled.

"Not when you could fight your match," Ivers said, without taking offence. "You don't consider that poor girl your match?"

"We'll soon see what sort of girl she is," replied Cooper complacently as his eyes fell on the Flynns. "Tell me," he whispered, "what did she see in my client?"

"What you saw yourself when you were her age, I suppose," said Ivers. "You don't mean there wasn't a girl in a tobacconist's shop that you thought came down from heaven with the purpose of consoling you?"

"She had nothing in writing," Cooper replied gravely. "And, unlike your client, I never saw double."

"You don't believe that yarn, do you?"

"That's one of the things I'm going to inquire into."

"I can save you the trouble. She was too fond of him."

"Hah!" snorted Cooper as though this were a good joke. "And I suppose that's why she wants the cash."

"The girl doesn't care if she never got a penny. Don't you know yourself what's behind it? A respectable father. Two respectable fathers! The trouble about marriage in this country, Dan Cooper, is that the fathers always insist on doing the courting."

"Hah!" grunted Cooper, rather more uncertain of himself. "Show me this paragon of the female sex, Ivers."

"There in the brown hat beside Canty," said Ivers without looking round. "Come on, you old devil, and stop trying to pretend you're Buffalo Bill. It's enough going through what she had to go through. I don't want her to go through any more."

"And why in God's name do you come to me?" Cooper asked in sudden indignation. "What the hell do you take me for? A society for Protecting Fallen Women? Why didn't the priest make him marry her?"

"When the Catholic Church can make a farmer marry a labourer's daughter the Kingdom of God will be at hand," said Ivers. "I'm surprised at you, Dan Cooper, not knowing better at your age."

"And what are the neighbours doing here if she has nothing to hide?"

"Who said she had nothing to hide?" Ivers asked lightly, throwing in his hand. "Haven't you daughters of your own? You know she played the fine lady in the O'Gradys' frocks. If 'tis any information to you she wore their jewellery as well."

"Ivers, you're a young man of great plausibility," said Cooper, "but you can spare your charm on me. I have my client's interests to consider. Did she sleep with the other fellow?"

"She did not."

"Do you believe that?"

"As I believe in my own mother."

"The faith that moves mountains," Cooper said despondently. "How much are ye asking?"

"Two hundred and fifty," replied Ivers, shaky for the first time.

"Merciful God Almighty!" moaned Cooper, turning his eyes to the ceiling. "As if any responsible Irish court would put that price on a girl's virtue. Still, it might be as well. I'll see what I can do."

He moved ponderously across the court and with two big arms outstretched like wings shepherded out the Flynns.

"Two hundred and fifty pounds?" gasped Ned, going white. "Where in God's name would I get that money?"

"My dear Mr. Flynn," Cooper said with coarse amiability, "that's only half the yearly allowance his Lordship makes the young lady that obliges him, and she's not a patch on that girl in court. After a lifetime of experience I can assure you that for two years' fornication with a fine girl like that you won't pay a penny less than five hundred."

Peter Humphreys's eyes almost grew straight with the shock of such reckless slander on a blameless judge. He didn't know what had come over the Roarer. But that wasn't the worst. When the settlement was announced and the Flynns were leaving he went up to them again.

"You can believe me when I say you did the right thing, Mr. Flynn," he said. "I never like cases involving good-looking girls. Gentlemen of his Lordship's age are terribly susceptible. But tell me, why wouldn't your son marry her now as he's about it?"

"Marry her?" echoed Ned, who hadn't yet got over the shock of having to pay two hundred and fifty pounds and costs for a little matter he could have compounded for with Father Corcoran for fifty. "A thing like that!"

"With two hundred and fifty pounds, man?" snarled Cooper. " 'Tisn't every day you'll pick up a daughter-in-law with that. . . . What do you say to the girl yourself?" he asked Tom.

"Oh, begod, the girl is all right," said Tom.

Tom looked different. It was partly relief that he wouldn't have to perjure himself, partly astonishment at seeing his father so swiftly overthrown. His face said: "The world is wide."

"Ah, Mr. Flynn, Mr. Flynn," whispered Cooper scornfully, "sure you're not such a fool as to let all that good money out of the family?"

Leaving Ned gasping, he went on to where Dick Carty, aglow with pride and malice, was receiving congratulations. There were no congratulations for Delia who was standing near him. She felt a big paw on her arm and looked up to see the Roarer.

"Are you still fond of that boy?" he whispered.

"I have reason to be, haven't I?" she retorted bitterly.

"You have," he replied with no great sympathy. "The best. I got you that money so that you could marry him if you wanted to. Do you want to?"

Her eyes filled with tears as she thought of the poor broken china of an idol that was being offered her now.

"Once a fool, always a fool," she said sullenly.

"You're no fool at all, girl," he said, giving her arm an encouraging squeeze. "You might make a man of him yet. I don't know what the law in this country is coming to. Get him away to hell out of this till I find Michael Ivers and get him to talk to your father."

The last two lawyers made the match themselves at Johnny Desmond's pub, and Johnny said it was like nothing in the world so much as a mission, with the Roarer roaring and threatening hell-fire on all concerned, and Michael Ivers piping away about the joys of heaven. Johnny said it was the most instructive evening he ever had. Ivers was always recognized as a weak man so the marriage did him no great harm, but of course it was a terrible comedown for a true Roarer, and Cooper's reputation has never been the same since then.

EXERCISES

1. This story seems much more complicated than "Wet Saturday" or "The Lottery Ticket," but on inspection we may find that what seems complication is, rather, a development of detail and not a change of basic structure. What is the basic structure? Here, as in the previous stories of this group, does the story depend on a single final turn?

2. We have, clearly, an objective conflict between the two families. The issue may be put in the question, "Will Delia win her law suit?" Somewhat in the background is another question,

"Will Delia get her man?" But there is another deeper and more pervasive conflict, one between the assumptions of romantic love and the views of love and sex that belong to the society portrayed in the story. How would you state this conflict?

3. This deeper, more pervasive conflict is the basis of the humor of the story. Locate examples of this sort of humorous effect. But there is another humor mingled with this. At bottom the story is about calling in legal aid to avoid payment, the whole question of payment arising in turn from the desire of the farmer to avoid the marriage of his son to the dowryness daughter of a laborer. But, humorously enough, and ironically enough, the calling in of legal aid ends in a marriage—the trap has been sprung. How is this humor of someone trapping himself related to the pervasive conflict?

The pervasive humor here stems from the author's general attitude toward the world he depicts. His feeling, his attitude, is what comes through and dominates the story. It is what gives the plot mechanism (the "trap") its final fictional significance. For as we have said, the sense of a special, personal vision of life is what, in the end, makes a story good. A good story is more than plot, character, setting, symbols, theme—or any mechanically conceived set of relations among such things. It involves such things, but involves them as unified and interpenetrating, as the embodiment of the author's special vision of life.

4. What is the tone of the story?

5. Read "O Youth and Beauty!" by John Cheever (sec. 10). Though this story is rather long and full of detail it ends with a sharp turn, with what might be called a "trick ending" (see Glossary). Is the shooting of Cash merely a trick—a way to end the story with a shock of irony? Or does the accidental and ironical quality of the end have some relation to the meaning of the story? Can it be said of this story, as of "Legal Aid," that the world depicted here, and the author's feeling about that world, is fundamental to the effect of the story? That Cash, though a well-developed character of interest as an individual, is primarily significant in relation to his world?

Section 6

PEOPLE AND PLACES

Character, as we have insisted in section 1, is always involved in fiction, even in the stories that apparently appeal only to our interest in action. We have insisted, too, that the germ of fiction is conflict, conflict eventuating in significant action, and that character is always a dynamic of action, even in stories that, apparently, appeal only to our interest in action and our curiosity about the outcome of action.

Here we may go even further, and point out that we, as human beings, are naturally and intensely interested in our own kind. Ordinary gossip is as much concerned with the character of this neighbor or that as with their goings on. And when we do discuss their goings on, amusing or deplorable, we inevitably set the deed in the context of our expectations of character; that is, we express surprise that so-and-so would do such a thing, or nod sagely and opine that it is just what we had expected. And all our lives we marvel that Nature has, in Shakespeare's phrase, framed such strange creatures in her time. To return to the idea that, as we have said, *character is action*, we must add that action is also the demonstration of character.

Taking another perspective on character in fiction, we may say that, even if it may seem to be the interest in action that sustains fiction and carries us to the end, the end itself represents a shift in, or a clarification of, human values. And the question of human values inevitably raises the question of human character.

Furthermore, a character does not exist in a vacuum. The person has an environment; he inhabits a place with special physical and social qualities. The degree of importance of place, like that of the importance of character, may vary from instance to in-

stance, sometimes immediate and compelling and sometimes recessive and scarcely visible. But almost always there is a relation between people and places. After reading each story in this section, one may well ask himself what part place has played in the whole effect—and meaning. For instance, could the very first story, "The Catbird Seat," be given any other setting than the bustling, dehumanizing office of a thriving business in a big city? Place is, in one sense, person.

THE CATBIRD SEAT
James Thurber (1894–1961)

Mr. Martin bought the pack of Camels on Monday night in the most crowded cigar store on Broadway. It was theatre time and seven or eight men were buying cigarettes. The clerk didn't even glance at Mr. Martin, who put the pack in his overcoat pocket and went out. If any of the staff at F & S had seen him buy the cigarettes, they would have been astonished, for it was generally known that Mr. Martin did not smoke, and never had. No one saw him.

It was just a week to the day since Mr. Martin had decided to rub out Mrs. Ulgine Barrows. The term "rub out" pleased him because it suggested nothing more than the correction of an error—in this case an error of Mr. Fitweiler. Mr. Martin had spent each night of the past week working out his plan and examining it. As he walked home now he went over it again. For the hundredth time he resented the element of imprecision, the margin of guesswork that entered into the business. The project as he had worked it out was casual and bold, the risks were considerable. Something might go wrong anywhere along the line. And therein lay the cunning of his scheme. No one would ever see in it the cautious, painstaking hand of Erwin Martin, head of the filing department at F & S, of whom Mr. Fitweiler had once said, "Man is fallible but Martin isn't." No one would see his hand, that is, unless it were caught in the act.

Sitting in his apartment, drinking a glass of milk, Mr. Martin reviewed his case against Mrs. Ulgine Barrows, as he had every night for seven nights. He began at the beginning. Her quacking voice and braying laugh had first profaned the halls of F & S on March 7, 1941 (Mr. Martin had a head for dates). Old Roberts, the personnel chief, had introduced her as the newly appointed special adviser to the president of the firm, Mr. Fitweiler. The woman had appalled Mr. Martin instantly, but he hadn't shown it. He had given her his dry hand, a look of studious concentration, and a faint smile. "Well," she had said, looking at the papers on his desk, "are you lifting the oxcart out of the ditch?" As Mr. Martin recalled that moment, over his milk, he squirmed slightly. He must keep his mind on her crimes as a special adviser, not on her peccadillos as a personality. This he found difficult to do, in spite of entering an objection and sustaining it. The faults of the woman as a woman kept chattering on in his mind like an unruly witness. She had, for almost two years now, baited him. In the halls, in the elevator, even in his own office, into which she romped now and then like a circus horse, she was constantly shouting these silly questions at him. "Are you lifting the oxcart out of the ditch? Are you tearing up the pea patch? Are you hollering down the rain barrel? Are you scraping around the bottom of the pickle barrel? Are you sitting in the catbird seat?"

It was Joey Hart, one of Mr. Martin's two assistants, who had explained what the gibberish meant. "She must be a Dodger fan," he had said. "Red Barber announces the Dodger games over the radio and he uses those expressions—picked 'em up down South." Joey had gone on to explain one or two. "Tearing up the pea patch" meant going on a rampage; "sitting in the catbird seat" meant sitting pretty, like a batter with three balls and no strikes on him. Mr. Martin dismissed all this with an effort. It had been annoying, it had driven him near to distraction, but he was too solid a man to be moved to murder by anything so childish. It was fortunate, he reflected as he passed on to the important charges against Mrs. Barrows, that he had stood up under it so well. He had maintained always an outward appearance of polite tolerance. "Why, I even believe you like the woman," Miss Paird, his other assistant, had once said to him. He had simply smiled.

A gavel rapped in Mr. Martin's mind and the case proper was resumed. Mrs. Ulgine Barrows stood charged with willful, blatant, and persistent attempts to destroy the efficiency and system of F & S. It was competent, material, and relevant to review her advent and rise to power. Mr. Martin had got the story from Miss Paird, who seemed always able to find things out. According to her, Mrs. Barrows had met Mr. Fitweiler at a party, where she had rescued him from the embraces of a powerfully built drunken man who had mistaken the president of F & S for a famous retired Middle Western football coach. She had led him to a sofa and somehow worked upon him a monstrous magic. The aging gentleman had jumped to the conclusion there and then that this was a woman of singular attainments, equipped to bring out the best in him and in the firm. A week later he had introduced her into F & S as his special adviser. On that day confusion got its foot in the door. After Miss Tyson, Mr. Brundage, and Mr. Bartlett had been fired and Mr. Munson had taken his hat and stalked out, mailing in his resignation later, old Roberts had been emboldened to speak to Mr. Fitweiler. He mentioned that Mr.

Munson's department had been "a little disrupted" and hadn't they perhaps better resume the old system there? Mr. Fitweiler had said certainly not. He had the greatest faith in Mrs. Barrows' ideas. "They require a little seasoning, a little seasoning, is all," he had added. Mr. Roberts had given it up. Mr. Martin reviewed in detail all the changes wrought by Mrs. Barrows. She had begun chipping at the cornices of the firm's edifice and now she was swinging at the foundation stones with a pickaxe.

Mr. Martin came now, in his summing up, to the afternoon of Monday, November 2, 1942—just one week ago. On that day, at 3 P.M., Mrs. Barrows had bounced into his office. "Boo!" she had yelled. "Are you scraping around the bottom of the pickle barrel?" Mr. Martin had looked at her from under his green eyeshade, saying nothing. She had begun to wander about the office, taking it in with her great, popping eyes. "Do you really need *all* these filing cabinets?" she had demanded suddenly. Mr. Martin's heart had jumped. "Each of these files," he had said, keeping his voice even, "plays an indispensable part in the system of F & S." She had brayed at him, "Well, don't tear up the pea patch!" and gone to the door. From there she had bawled, "But you sure have got a lot of fine scrap in here!" Mr. Martin could no longer doubt that the finger was on his beloved department. Her pickaxe was on the upswing, poised for the first blow. It had not come yet; he had received no blue memo from the enchanted Mr. Fitweiler bearing nonsensical instructions deriving from the obscene woman. But there was no doubt in Mr. Martin's mind that one would be forthcoming. He must act quickly. Already a precious week had gone by. Mr. Martin stood up in his living room, still holding his milk glass. "Gentlemen of the jury," he said to himself, "I demand the death penalty for this horrible person."

The next day Mr. Martin followed his routine, as usual. He polished his glasses more often and once sharpened an already sharp pencil, but not even Miss Paird noticed. Only once did he catch sight of his victim; she swept past him in the hall with a patronizing "Hi!" At five-thirty he walked home, as usual, and had a glass of milk, as usual. He had never drunk anything stronger in his life—unless you could count ginger ale. The late Sam Schlosser, the S of F & S, had praised Mr. Martin at a staff meeting several years before for his temperate habits. "Our most efficient worker neither drinks nor smokes," he had said. "The results speak for themselves." Mr. Fitweiler had sat by, nodding approval.

Mr. Martin was still thinking about that red-letter day as he walked over to the Schrafft's on Fifth Avenue near Forty-sixth Street. He got there, as he always did, at eight o'clock. He finished his dinner and the financial page of the *Sun* at a quarter to nine, as he always did. It was his custom after dinner to take a walk. This time he walked down Fifth Avenue at a casual pace. His gloved hands felt moist and warm, his forehead cold. He transferred the Camels from his overcoat to a jacket pocket. He wondered, as he did so, if they did not represent an unnecessary note of strain. Mrs. Barrows smoked only Luckies. It was his idea to puff a few puffs on a Camel (after the rubbing-out), stub it out in the ashtray holding her lipstick-stained Luckies, and thus drag a small red herring across the trail. Perhaps it was not a good idea. It would take time. He might even choke, too loudly.

Mr. Martin had never seen the house on West Twelfth Street where Mrs. Barrows lived, but he had a clear enough picture of it. Fortunately, she had bragged to everybody about her ducky first-floor apartment in the perfectly darling three-story red-brick. There would be no doorman or other attendants; just the tenants of the second and third floors. As he walked along, Mr. Martin realized that he would get there before nine-thirty. He had considered walking north on Fifth Avenue from Schrafft's to a point from which it would take him until ten o'clock to reach the house. At that hour people were less likely to be coming in or going out. But the procedure would have made an awkward loop in the straight thread of his casualness, and he had abandoned it. It was impossible to figure when people would be entering or leaving the house, anyway. There was a great risk at any hour. If he ran into anybody, he would simply have to place the rubbing-out of Ulgine Barrows in the inactive file forever. The same thing would hold true if there were someone in her apartment. In that case he would just say that he had been passing by, recognized her charming house and thought to drop in.

It was eighteen minutes after nine when Mr. Martin turned into Twelfth Street. A man passed him, and a man and a woman talking. There was no one within fifty paces when he came to the house, halfway down the block. He was up the steps and in the small vestibule in no time, pressing the bell under the card that said "Mrs. Ulgine Barrows." When the clicking in the lock started, he jumped forward against the door. He got inside fast, closing the door behind him. A bulb in a lantern hung from the hall ceiling on a chain seemed to give a monstrously bright light. There was nobody on the stair, which went up ahead of him along the left wall. A door opened down the hall in the wall on the right. He went toward it swiftly, on tiptoe.

"Well, for God's sake, look who's here!" bawled Mrs. Barrows, and her braying laugh rang out like the report of a shotgun. He rushed past her like a football tackle, bumping her. "Hey, quit shoving!" she said, closing the door behind them. They were in her living room, which seemed to Mr. Martin to be lighted by a hundred lamps. "What's after you?" she said. "You're as jumpy as a goat." He found he was unable to speak. His heart was wheezing in his throat. "I— yes," he finally brought out. She was jabbering and laughing as she started to help him off with his coat. "No, no," he said. "I'll

put it here." He took it off and put it on a chair near the door. "Your hat and gloves, too," she said. "You're in a lady's house." He put his hat on top of the coat. Mrs. Barrows seemed larger than he had thought. He kept his gloves on. "I was passing by," he said. "I recognized—is there anyone here?" She laughed louder than ever. "No," she said, "we're all alone. You're as white as a sheet, you funny man. Whatever *has* come over you? I'll mix you a toddy." She started toward a door across the room. "Scotch-and-soda be all right? But say, you don't drink, do you?" She turned and gave him her amused look. Mr. Martin pulled himself together. "Scotch-and-soda will be all right," he heard himself say. He could hear her laughing in the kitchen.

Mr. Martin looked quickly around the living room for the weapon. He had counted on finding one there. There were andirons and a poker and something in a corner that looked like an Indian club. None of them would do. It couldn't be that way. He began to pace around. He came to a desk. On it lay a metal paper knife with an ornate handle. Would it be sharp enough? He reached for it and knocked over a small brass jar. Stamps spilled out of it and it fell to the floor with a clatter. "Hey," Mrs. Barrows yelled from the kitchen, "are you tearing up the pea patch?" Mr. Martin gave a strange laugh. Picking up the knife, he tried its point against his left wrist. It was blunt. It wouldn't do.

When Mrs. Barrows reappeared, carrying two highballs, Mr. Martin, standing there with his gloves on, became acutely conscious of the fantasy he had wrought. Cigarettes in his pocket, a drink prepared for him—it was all too grossly improbable. It was more than that; it was impossible. Somewhere in the back of his mind a vague idea stirred, sprouted. "For heaven's sake, take off those gloves," said Mrs. Barrows. "I always wear them in the house," said Mr. Martin. The idea began to bloom, strange and wonderful.

She put the glasses on a coffee table in front of a sofa and sat on the sofa. "Come over here, you odd little man," she said. Mr. Martin went over and sat beside her. It was difficult getting a cigarette out of the pack of Camels, but he managed it. She held a match for him, laughing. "Well," she said, handing him his drink, "this is perfectly marvelous. You with a drink and a cigarette."

Mr. Martin puffed, not too awkwardly, and took a gulp of the highball. "I drink and smoke all the time," he said. He clinked his glass against hers. "Here's nuts to that old windbag, Fitweiler," he said, and gulped again. The stuff tasted awful, but he made no grimace. "Really, Mr. Martin," she said, her voice and posture changing, "you are insulting our employer." Mrs. Barrows was now all special adviser to the president. "I am preparing a bomb," said Mr. Martin, "which will blow the old goat higher than hell." He had only had a little of the drink, which was not strong. It couldn't be that. "Do you take dope or something?" Mrs. Barrows asked coldly. "Heroin," said Mr. Martin. "I'll be coked to the gills when I bump that old buzzard off." "Mr. Martin!" she shouted, getting to her feet. "That will be all of that. You must go at once." Mr. Martin took another swallow of his drink. He tapped his cigarette out in the ashtray and put the pack of Camels on the coffee table. Then he got up. She stood glaring at him. He walked over and put on his hat and coat. "Not a word about this," he said, and laid an index finger against his lips. All Mrs. Barrows could bring out was "Really!" Mr. Martin put his hand on the doorknob. "I'm sitting in the catbird seat," he said. He stuck his tongue out at her and left. Nobody saw him go.

Mr. Martin got to his apartment, walking, well before eleven. No one saw him go in. He had two glasses of milk after brushing his teeth, and he felt elated. It wasn't tipsiness, because he hadn't been tipsy. Anyway, the walk had worn off all effects of the whiskey. He got in bed and read a magazine for a while. He was asleep before midnight.

Mr. Martin got to the office at eight-thirty the next morning, as usual. At a quarter to nine, Ulgine Barrows, who had never before arrived at work before ten, swept into his office. "I'm reporting to Mr. Fitweiler now!" she shouted. "If he turns you over to the police, it's no more than you deserve!" Mr. Martin gave her a look of shocked surprise. "I beg your pardon?" he said. Mrs. Barrows snorted and bounced out of the room, leaving Miss Paird and Joey Hart staring after her. "What's the matter with that old devil now?" asked Miss Paird. "I have no idea," said Mr. Martin, resuming his work. The other two looked at him and then at each other. Miss Paird got up and went out. She walked slowly past the closed door of Mr. Fitweiler's office. Mrs. Barrows was yelling inside, but she was not braying. Miss Paird could not hear what the woman was saying. She went back to her desk.

Forty-five minutes later, Mrs. Barrows left the president's office and went into her own, shutting the door. It wasn't until half an hour later that Mr. Fitweiler sent for Mr. Martin. The head of the filing department, neat, quiet, attentive, stood in front of the old man's desk. Mr. Fitweiler was pale and nervous. He took his glasses off and twiddled them. He made a small, bruffing sound in his throat. "Martin," he said, "you have been with us more than twenty years." "Twenty-two, sir," said Mr. Martin. "In that time," pursued the president, "your work and your —uh—manner have been exemplary." "I trust so, sir," said Mr. Martin. "I have understood, Martin," said Mr. Fitweiler, "that you have never taken a drink or smoked." "That is correct, sir," said Mr. Martin. "Ah, yes." Mr. Fitweiler polished his glasses. "You may describe what you did after leaving the office yesterday, Martin," he said. Mr. Martin allowed less than a second for his bewildered pause. "Certainly, sir," he said. "I walked home. Then I went to Schrafft's for dinner. Afterward I walked home again. I went to bed early, sir, and read a magazine for a while. I was asleep before eleven." "Ah, yes," said Mr. Fitweiler again. He was silent for a moment, searching for the proper words to say to the head of the filing department. "Mrs. Barrows," he said finally, "Mrs. Barrows has worked hard, Martin, very hard. It grieves me to report that she has suffered a severe breakdown. It has taken the form of a persecution complex accompanied by distressing hallucinations." "I am very sorry, sir," said Mr. Martin. "Mrs. Barrows is under the delusion," continued Mr. Fitweiler, "that you visited her last evening and behaved yourself in an—uh—unseemly manner." He raised his hand to silence Mr. Martin's little pained outcry. "It is the nature of these psychological diseases," Mr. Fitweiler said, "to fix upon the least likely and most innocent party as the—uh—source of persecution. These matters are not for the lay mind to grasp, Martin. I've just had my psychiatrist, Doctor Fitch, on the phone. He would not, of course, commit himself, but he made enough generalizations to substantiate my suspicions. I suggested to Mrs. Barrows when she had completed her—uh—story to me this morning, that she visit Doctor Fitch, for I suspected a condition at once. She flew, I regret to say, into a rage, and demanded— uh—requested that I call you on the carpet. You may not know, Martin, but Mrs. Barrows had planned a reorganization of your department—subject to my approval, of course, subject to my approval. This brought you, rather than anyone else, to her mind— but again that is a phenomenon for Doctor Fitch and not for us. So, Martin, I am afraid Mrs. Barrows' usefulness here is at an end." "I am dreadfully sorry, sir," said Mr. Martin.

It was at this point that the door to the office blew open with the suddenness of a gas-main explosion and Mrs. Barrows catapulted through it. "Is the little rat denying it?" she screamed. "He can't get away with that!" Mr. Martin got up and moved discreetly to a point beside Mr. Fitweiler's chair. "You

drank and smoked at my apartment," she bawled at Mr. Martin, "and you know it! You called Mr. Fitweiler an old windbag and said you were going to blow him up when you got coked to the gills on your heroin!" She stopped yelling to catch her breath and a new glint came into her popping eyes. "If you weren't such a drab, ordinary little man," she said. "I'd think you'd planned it all. Sticking your tongue out, saying you were sitting in the catbird seat, because you thought no one would believe me when I told it! My God, it's really too perfect!" She brayed loudly and hysterically, and the fury was on her again. She glared at Mr. Fitweiler. "Can't you see how he has tricked us, you old fool? Can't you see his little game?" But Mr. Fitweiler had been surreptitiously pressing all the buttons under the top of his desk and employees of F & S began pouring into the room. "Stockton," said Mr. Fitweiler, "you and Fishbein will take Mrs. Barrows to her home. Mrs. Powell, you will go with them." Stockton, who had played a little football in high school, blocked Mrs. Barrows as she made for Mr. Martin. It took him and Fishbein together to force her out of the door into the hall, crowded with stenographers and office boys. She was still screaming imprecations at Mr. Martin, tangled and contradictory imprecations. The hubbub finally died out down the corridor.

"I regret that this has happened," said Mr. Fitweiler. "I shall ask you to dismiss it from your mind, Martin." "Yes, sir," said Mr. Martin, anticipating his chief's "That will be all" by moving to the door. "I will dismiss it." He went out and shut the door, and his step was light and quick in the hall. When he entered his department he had slowed down to his customary gait, and he walked quietly across the room to the W20 file, wearing a look of studious concentration.

———————◆·◄◆►·◆———————

"The Catbird Seat" is the old story of the worm that turns, of the ugly duckling that becomes the swan, of the stone that the builders rejected becoming the head of the corner, of the race not being to the swift nor the battle unto the strong, of David and Goliath, of Br'er Rabbit and Br'er Fox. It is a story based on surprise and reversal. Poor, dim, recessive Mr. Martin is not so pitiable and defenseless after all.

The shadow of old fables, folk tales, and sayings rises, it is true, behind the modern story, and in these archetypes there is an ironical humor, that of the unexpected joke played on the self-confident and overbearing contender in life's contest, and, too, a joke on the expectations of the audience. But Thurber is a great humorist and can find new dimensions of irony in his rehandling of the old idea. For one thing, the simple turn of the traditional plot, which provides the basic irony, does not satisfy him. He demands more than one turn, more than one reversal, as he plays with his audience. We are led to accept the idea that the worm has turned, that Mr. Martin is out to exact vengeance, and when, before entering the apartment of Mrs. Ulgine Barrows, he methodically pauses to put on gloves, we know that the moment has come when he will execute his decision to "rub out" * the monster. But, once he enters, the joke is on us. He scrutinizes the poker and andirons, and handles a paper knife, but suddenly becomes "acutely conscious of the fantasy." He won't "rub her out," after all. Then "a vague idea" stirs— an idea as yet undefined. Nothing happens, nothing at least beyond Mr. Martin's one drink and the blurted-out remark about his employer. He has lost his nerve, it seems— poor fellow, a worm after all. Just as we expected, we decide, and congratulate ourselves on our perspicacity.

But just as Thurber has been toying with us, so Mr. Martin, as we soon learn, has been toying with his victim. She, full of glee at what she regards as her certain conquest, sticks her head into Mr. Martin's office the next morning, gloats over him, and passes on to settle his hash with the president of the firm. But in her interview with the president, she signs her own death warrant. For when Mr. Martin is summoned to the president's office and asked to recount how he had spent the previous evening, who could fail to believe the lie he tells? That lie is true of every other evening in his drearily blameless life. His whole life has been his alibi. So it is Mrs. Barrows who is sacked, and Mr. Martin returns happily to his irreproachable, unimpeachable filing system.

Thus far we have been speaking of Thurber's expert handling of the turns of plot and the jokes on our expectations that give the story irony (see Glossary). But the mere turn of plot or mere defeat of expectations, though ironical, does not necessarily create a humorous effect. The turn is characteristic of all fiction, in one form or another, even the most serious works, even tragedy. But let us look, for instance, at the defeat of expectations in the reversal in "The Lottery Ticket," by Chekhov (sec. 5), where we find the clear-cut reversal, which, though ironical, cannot be called humorous, or comic, except in some mordant fashion: the final joke involves human misery. Or take Shakespeare's *Macbeth*, in which the whole development of the plot depends on the joke, if we wish to call it one, that the Weird Sisters play on the ambition-blinded king; the joke here is, of course, merely the frame of the tragedy, the shape of a joke with the content of tragedy.

Our idea here is that the turn that makes Mrs. Barrows the butt of the joke, though essential to the humor of the story, is not the final turning of the story. The real and final butt of the joke is the reader. It is our expectations that are turned topsy-turvy, and finally, and most importantly, in a way we have not yet touched on. To explain what we mean, we must return to Mr. Martin's character. It is indeed the action. Only the dimness, the pitiable recessiveness, makes the story possible at all, finally in the fact that because of such traits the president believes his lie. Not only the action, the plot, depends on this character, but the humor lies here, too. Certainly the humor of the worm's turning depends on Mr. Martin's being a worm, but the humor is more complex than

---

* Mr. Martin has, it is suggested, used that phrase in meditating his plans, and what a touch of humor to put it in the mind of apparently the most mild of men, this phrase suggesting all the casualness and callous impersonality of gangsterdom as well as his professional practice of making corrections by erasure.

that. We pity Mr. Martin for his drab life, we feel immensely superior to him, and suddenly proud of our own exciting lives, we condescendingly think that if the poor fellow knew how drab his life is, he wouldn't be able to endure it.

But he does know precisely how drab his life is, and surprisingly, even gleefully, makes a weapon of our belief, and the president's belief, that his life is hopelessly drab. The joke is on us, in the end, and Mr. Martin returns triumphantly to his files, triumphant most of all in his self-knowledge and knowledge of exactly what he wants in life. He is fulfilled far more completely than we may be. If Mrs. Barrows gets a glorious comeuppance, we get an even more glorious one. But at the same time we feel liberated, relieved from the burden of pity for Mr. Martin. He can take care of himself. And we can in our own discomfiture at being the butt of a joke, forget it by laughing at the fate of Mrs. Barrows, that horrid creature and unnatural bully, trying to take over a man's world. For that element, too, is in the joke.

Let us return, for a moment, to our earlier distinction between the shape of a joke (with the attendant factors of reversal and irony) and the possibly serious, or even tragic, content of that shape. Would "The Catbird Seat" be funny if Mrs. Barrows should go home and shoot herself through the head? Certainly in one perspective, she is deserving of pity, a blundering, arrogant, unfulfilled creature, with her own little tragedy suffered at the hands of Mr. Martin.

But that is *not* the concern of the story. Every story has its own special perspective of feeling. Every story, big or little, has its own special control of emotional lighting to set the tone, to direct the attention of the audience, to obscure the unwanted elements and accent the essential. Behind every comedy lurks a tragedy, and every joke involves pain in the background. But we can reverse this idea. After all, Macbeth is, as we have said, the butt of a joke, and Hamlet, too, can be construed as a blundering oaf. All we need to do is to change the lighting.

Again to sum up our main point: character is action, and here it is humorous action.

EXERCISES

1. Let us suppose that Mr. Barrows is still alive, a paraplegic in a wheel chair. Suppose we see Mrs. Barrows, after being fired, arrive at her apartment, pretending cheerfulness after an affectionate greeting from the invalid, and then going to her room to work up courage enough to tell him the truth? What kind of story would we then have?
2. Let us suppose that you are discussing this story with two members of Woman's Lib. The first finds this story funny, the second is enraged. Which would you think more intelligent?

BAD CHARACTERS
Jean Stafford (b. 1915)

Up until I learned my lesson in a very bitter way, I never had more than one friend at a time, and my friendships, though ardent, were short. When they ended and I was sent packing in unforgetting indignation, it was always my fault; I would swear vilely in front of a girl I knew to be pious and prim (by the time I was eight, the most grandiloquent gangster could have added nothing to my vocabulary—I had an awful tongue), or I would call a Tenderfoot Scout a sissy or make fun of athletics to the daughter of the high-school coach. These outbursts came without plan; I would simply one day, in the middle of a game of Russian bank or a hike or a conversation, be possessed with a passion to be by myself, and my lips instantly and without warning would accommodate me. My friend was never more surprised than I was when this irrevocable slander, this terrible, talented invective, came boiling out of my mouth.

Afterward, when I had got the solitude I had wanted, I was dismayed, for I did not like it. Then I would sadly finish the game of cards as if someone were still across the table from me; I would sit down on the mesa and through a glaze of tears would watch my friend departing with outraged strides; mournfully, I would talk to myself. Because I had already alienated everyone I knew, I then had nowhere to turn, so a famine set in and I would have no companion but Muff, the cat, who loathed all human beings except, significantly, me—truly. She bit and scratched the hands that fed her, she arched her back like a Halloween cat if someone kindly tried to pet her, she hissed, laid her ears flat to her skull, growled, fluffed up her tail into a great bush and flailed it like a bullwhack. But she purred for me, she patted me with her paws, keeping her claws in their velvet scabbards. She was not only an ill-natured cat, she was also badly dressed. She was a calico, and the distribution of her colors was a mess; she looked as if she had been left out in the rain and her paint had run. She had a Roman nose as the result of some early injury, her tail was skinny, she had a perfectly venomous look in her eye. My family said—my family discriminated against me—that I was much closer kin to Muff than I was to any of them. To tease me into a tantrum, my brother Jack and my sister Stella often called me Kitty instead of Emily. Little Tess did not dare, because she knew I'd chloroform her if she did. Jack, the meanest boy I have ever known in my life, called me Polecat and talked about my mania for fish, which, it so happened, I despised. The name would have been far more appropriate for *him*, since he trapped skunks up in the foothills—we lived in Adams, Colorado—and quite often, because he was careless and foolhardy, his clothes had to be buried, and even when that was done, he sometimes was sent home from school on the complaint of girls sitting next to him.

Along about Christmastime when I was eleven, I was making a snowman with Virgil Meade in his back yard, and all of a sudden, just as we had got around to the right arm, I had to be alone. So I called him a son of a sea cook, said it was common knowledge that his mother had bedbugs and that his father, a dentist and the deputy marshal, was a bootlegger on the side. For a moment, Virgil was too aghast to speak—a little earlier we had agreed to marry someday and become mil-

lionaires—and then, with a bellow of fury, he knocked me down and washed my face in snow. I saw stars, and black balls bounced before my eyes. When finally he let me up, we were both crying, and he hollered that if I didn't get off his property that instant, his father would arrest me and send me to Canon City. I trudged slowly home, half frozen, critically sick at heart. So it was old Muff again for me for quite some time. Old Muff, that is, until I met Lottie Jump, although "met" is a euphemism for the way I first encountered her.

I saw Lottie for the first time one afternoon in our kitchen, stealing a chocolate cake. Stella and Jack had not come home from school yet—not having my difficult disposition, they were popular, and they were at their friends' houses, pulling taffy, I suppose, making popcorn balls, playing casino, having fun—and my mother had taken Tess with her to visit a friend in one of the T.B. sanitariums. I was alone in the house, and making a funny-looking Christmas card, although I had no one to send it to. When I heard someone in the kitchen, I thought it was Mother home early, and I went out to ask her why the green pine tree I had pasted on a square of red paper looked as if it were falling down. And there, instead of Mother and my baby sister, was this pale, conspicuous child in the act of lifting the glass cover from the devil's-food my mother had taken out of the oven an hour before and set on the plant shelf by the window. The child had her back to me, and when she heard my footfall, she wheeled with an amazing look of fear and hatred on her pinched and pasty face. Simultaneously, she put the cover over the cake again, and then stood motionless as if she were under a spell.

I was scared, for I was not sure what was happening, and anyhow it gives you a turn to find a stranger in the kitchen in the middle of the afternoon, even if the stranger is only a skinny child in a moldy coat and sopping-wet basketball shoes. Between us there was a lengthy silence, but there was a great deal of noise in the room: the alarm clock ticked smugly; the teakettle simmered patiently on the back of the stove; Muff, cross at having been waked up, thumped her tail against the side of the flower box in the window where she had been sleeping—contrary to orders—among the geraniums. This went on, it seemed to me, for hours and hours while that tall, sickly girl and I confronted each other. When, after a long time, she did open her mouth, it was to tell a prodigious lie. "I came to see if you'd like to play with me," she said. I think she sighed and stole a sidelong and regretful glance at the cake.

Beggars cannot be choosers, and I had been missing Virgil so sorely, as well as all those other dear friends forever lost to me, that in spite of her flagrance (she had never clapped eyes on me before, she had had no way of knowing there was a creature of my age in the house—she had come in like a hobo to steal my mother's cake), I was flattered and consoled. I asked her name and, learning it, believed my ears no better than my eyes: Lottie Jump. What on earth! What on earth—you surely will agree with me—and yet when I told her mine, Emily Vanderpool, she laughed until she coughed and gasped. "Beg pardon," she said. "Names like them always hit my funny bone. There was this towhead boy in school named Delbert Saxonfield." I saw no connection and I was insulted (what's so funny about Vanderpool, I'd like to know), but Lottie Jump was, technically, my guest and I *was* lonesome, so I asked her, since she had spoken of playing with me, if she knew how to play Andy-I-Over. She said "Naw." It turned out that she did not know how to play any games at all; she couldn't do anything and didn't want to do anything; her only recreation and her only gift was, and always had been, stealing. But this I did not know at the time.

As it happened, it was too cold and snowy to play outdoors that day anyhow, and after I had run through my list of indoor games and Lottie had shaken her head at all of them (when I spoke of Parcheesi, she went

"Ugh!" and pretended to be sick), she suggested that we look through my mother's bureau drawers. This did not strike me as strange at all, for it was one of my favorite things to do, and I led the way to Mother's bedroom without a moment's hesitation. I loved the smell of the lavender she kept in gauze bags among her chamois gloves and linen handkerchiefs and filmy scarves; there was a pink fascinator knitted of something as fine as spider's thread, and it made me go quite soft—I wasn't soft as a rule. I was as hard as nails and I gave my mother a rough time—to think of her wearing it around her head as she waltzed on the ice in the bygone days. We examined stockings, nightgowns, camisoles, strings of beads, and mosaic pins, keepsake buttons from dresses worn on memorial occasions, tortoiseshell combs, and a transformation made from Aunt Joey's hair when she had racily had it bobbed. Lottie admired particularly a blue cloisonné perfume flask with ferns and peacocks on it. "Hey," she said, "this sure is cute. I like thing-daddies like this here." But very abruptly she got bored and said, "Let's talk instead. In the front room." I agreed, a little perplexed this time, because I had been about to show her a remarkable powder box that played "The Blue Danube." We went into the parlor, where Lottie looked at her image in the pier glass for quite a while and with great absorption, as if she had never seen herself before. Then she moved over to the window seat and knelt on it, looking out at the front walk. She kept her hands in the pockets of her thin dark-red coat; once she took out one of her dirty paws to rub her nose for a minute and I saw a bulge in that pocket, like a bunch of jackstones. I know now that it wasn't jackstones, it was my mother's perfume flask; I thought at the time her hands were cold and that was why she kept them put away, for I had noticed that she had no mittens.

Lottie did most of the talking, and while she talked, she never once looked at me but kept her eyes fixed on the approach to our house. She told me that her family had come to Adams a month before from Muskogee, Oklahoma, where her father, before he got tuberculosis, had been a brakeman on the Frisco. Now they lived down by Arapahoe Creek, on the west side of town, in one of the cottages of a wretched settlement made up of people so poor and so sick—for in nearly every ramshackle house someone was coughing himself to death—that each time I went past I blushed with guilt because my shoes were sound and my coat was warm and I was well. I wished that Lottie had not told me where she lived, but she was not aware of any pathos in her family's situation, and, indeed, it was with a certain boastfulness that she told me her mother was the short-order cook at the Comanche Café (she pronounced this word in one syllable), which I knew was the dirtiest, darkest, smelliest place in town, patronized by coal miners who never washed their faces and sometimes had such dangerous fights after drinking dago red that the sheriff had to come. Laughing, Lottie told me that her mother was half Indian, and, laughing even harder, she said that her brother didn't have any brains and had never been to school. She herself was eleven years old, but she was only in the third grade, because teachers had always had it in for her— making her go to the blackboard and all like that when she was tired. She hated school— she went to Ashton, on North Hill, and that was why I had never seen her, for I went to Carlyle Hill—and she especially hated the teacher, Miss Cudahy, who had a head shaped like a pine cone and who had killed several people with her ruler. Lottie loved the movies ("Not them Western ones or the ones with apes in," she said. "Ones about hugging and kissing. I love it when they die in that big old soft bed with the curtains up top, and he comes in and says 'Don't leave me, Marguerite de la Mar' ''), and she loved to ride in cars. She loved Mr. Goodbars, and if there was one thing she despised worse than another it was tapioca. ("Pa calls it fish eyes. He calls floating island horse spit. He's a big piece of cheese. I hate him.") She did not

like cats (Muff was now sitting on the mantelpiece, glaring like an owl); she kind of liked snakes—except cottonmouths and rattlers— because she found them kind of funny; she had once seen a goat eat a tin can. She said that one of these days she would take me downtown—it was a slowpoke town, she said, a one-horse burg (I had never heard such gaudy, cynical talk and was trying to memorize it all)—if I would get some money for the trolley fare; she hated to walk, and I ought to be proud that she had walked all the way from Arapahoe Creek today for the sole solitary purpose of seeing me.

Seeing our freshly baked dessert in the window was a more likely story, but I did not care, for I was deeply impressed by this bold, sassy girl from Oklahoma and greatly admired the poise with which she aired her prejudices. Lottie Jump was certainly nothing to look at. She was tall and made of skin and bones; she was evilly ugly, and her clothes were a disgrace, not just ill-fitting and old and ragged but dirty, unmentionably so; clearly she did not wash much or brush her teeth, which were notched like a saw, and small and brown (it crossed my mind that perhaps she chewed tobacco); her long, lank hair looked as if it might have nits. But she had personality. She made me think of one of those self-contained dogs whose home is where his handout is and who travels alone but, if it suits him to, will become the leader of a pack. She was aloof, never looking at me, but amiable in the way she kept calling me "kid." I liked her enormously, and presently I told her so.

At this, she turned around and smiled at me. Her smile was the smile of a jack-o'-lantern—high, wide, and handsome. When it was over, no trace of it remained. "Well, that's keen, kid, and I like you, too," she said in her downright Muskogee accent. She gave me a long, appraising look. Her eyes were the color of mud. "Listen, kid, how much do you like me?"

"I like you loads, Lottie," I said. "Better than anybody else, and I'm not kidding."

"You want to be pals?"

"Do I!" I cried. So *there*, Virgil Meade, you big fat hootnanny, I thought.

"All right, kid, we'll be pals." And she held out her hand for me to shake. I had to go and get it, for she did not alter her position on the window seat. It was a dry, cold hand, and the grip was severe, with more a feeling of bones in it than friendliness.

Lottie turned and scanned our path and scanned the sidewalk beyond, and then she said, in a lower voice, "Do you know how to lift?"

"Lift?" I wondered if she meant to lift *her*. I was sure I could do it, since she was so skinny, but I couldn't imagine why she would want me to.

"Shoplift, I mean. Like in the five-and-dime."

I did not know the term, and Lottie scowled at my stupidity.

"*Steal*, for crying in the beer!" she said impatiently. This she said so loudly that Muff jumped down from the mantel and left the room in contempt.

I was thrilled to death and shocked to pieces. "Stealing is a sin," I said. "You get put in jail for it."

"Ish ka bibble! I should worry if it's a sin or not," said Lottie, with a shrug. "And they'll never put a smart old whatsis like *me* in jail. It's fun, stealing is—it's a picnic. I'll teach you if you want to learn, kid." Shamelessly she winked at me and grinned again. (That grin! She could have taken it off her face and put it on the table.) And she added, "If you don't, we can't be pals, because lifting is the only kind of playing I like. I hate those dumb games like Statues, Kick-the-Can—phooey!"

I was torn between agitation (I went to Sunday School and knew already about morality; Judge Bay, a crabby old man who loved to punish sinners, was a friend of my father's and once had given Jack a lecture on the criminal mind when he came to call and found Jack looking up an answer in his arithmetic book) and excitement over the

daring invitation to misconduct myself in so perilous a way. My life, on reflection, looked deadly prim; all I'd ever done to vary the monotony of it was to swear. I knew that Lottie Jump meant what she said—that I could have her friendship only on her terms (plainly, she had gone it alone for a long time and could go it alone for the rest of her life)—and although I trembled like an aspen and my heart went pitapat, I said, "I want to be pals with you, Lottie."

"All right, Vanderpool," said Lottie, and got off the window seat. "I wouldn't go braggin' about it if I was you. I wouldn't go telling my ma and pa and the next-door neighbor that you and Lottie Jump are going down to the five-and-dime next Saturday aft and lift us some nice rings and garters and things like that. I mean it, kid." And she drew the back of her forefinger across her throat and made a dire face.

"I won't. I promise I won't. My *gosh*, why would I?"

"That's the ticket," said Lottie, with a grin. "I'll meet you at the trolley shelter at two o'clock. You have the money. For both down and up. I ain't going to climb up that ornery hill after I've had my fun."

"Yes, Lottie," I said. Where was I going to get twenty cents? I was going to have to start stealing before she even taught me how. Lottie was facing the center of the room, but she had eyes in the back of her head, and she whirled around back to the window; my mother and Tess were turning in our front path.

"Back way," I whispered, and in a moment Lottie was gone; the swinging door that usually squeaked did not make a sound as she vanished through it. I listened and I never heard the back door open and close. Nor did I hear her, in a split second, lift the glass cover and remove that cake designed to feed six people.

I was restless and snappish between Wednesday afternoon and Saturday. When Mother found the cake was gone, she scolded me for not keeping my ears cocked. She assumed, naturally, that a tramp had taken it, for she knew I hadn't eaten it; I never ate anything if I could help it (except for raw potatoes, which I loved) and had been known as a problem feeder from the beginning of my life. At first it occurred to me to have a tantrum and bring her around to my point of view; my tantrums scared the living daylights out of her because my veins stood out and I turned blue and couldn't get my breath. But I rejected this for a more sensible plan. I said, "It just so happens I didn't hear anything. But if I had, I suppose you wish I had gone out in the kitchen and let the robber cut me up into a million little tiny pieces with his sword. You wouldn't even bury me. You'd just put me on the dump. *I* know who's wanted in this family and who isn't." Tears of sorrow, not of anger, came in powerful tides and I groped blindly to the bedroom I shared with Stella, where I lay on my bed and shook with big, silent *weltschmerzlich* sobs. Mother followed me immediately, and so did Tess, and both of them comforted me and told me how much they loved me. I said they didn't; they said they did. Presently, I got a headache, as I always did when I cried, so I got to have an aspirin and a cold cloth on my head, and when Jack and Stella came home, they had to be quiet. I heard Jack say, "Emily Vanderpool is the biggest polecat in the U.S.A. Whyn't she go in the kitchen and say, 'Hands up'? He woulda lit out." And Mother said, "Sh-h-h! You don't want your sister to be sick, do you?" Muff, not realizing that Lottie had replaced her, came in and curled up at my thigh, purring lustily; I found myself glad that she had left the room before Lottie Jump made her proposition to me, and in gratitude I stroked her unattractive head.

Other things happened. Mother discovered the loss of her perfume flask and talked about nothing else at meals for two whole days. Luckily, it did not occur to her that it had been stolen—she simply thought she had mislaid it—but her monomania got

on my father's nerves and he lashed out at her and at the rest of us. And because I was the cause of it all and my conscience was after me with red-hot pokers, I finally *had* to have a tantrum. I slammed my fork down in the middle of supper on the second day and yelled, "If you don't stop fighting, I'm going to kill myself. Yammer, yammer, nag, nag!" And I put my fingers in my ears and squeezed my eyes tight shut and screamed so the whole county could hear, "Shut *up!*" And then I lost my breath and began to turn blue. Daddy hastily apologized to everyone, and Mother said she was sorry for carrying on so about a trinket that had been nothing but sentimental value—she was just vexed with herself for being careless, that was all, and she wasn't going to say another word about it.

I never heard so many references to stealing and cake, and even to Oklahoma (ordinarily no one mentioned Oklahoma once in a month of Sundays) and the ten-cent store as I did throughout those next days. I myself once made a ghastly slip and said something to Stella about "the five-and-dime." "The five-and-*dime!*" she exclaimed. "Where'd you get *that* kind of talk? Do you by any chance have reference to the *ten-cent store?*"

The worst of all was Friday night—the very night before I was to meet Lottie Jump —when Judge Bay came to play two-handed pinochle with Daddy. The Judge, a giant in intimidating haberdashery—for some reason, the white piping on his vest bespoke, for me, handcuffs and prison bars—and with an aura of disapproval for almost everything on earth except what pertained directly to himself, was telling Daddy, before they began their game, about the infamous vandalism that had been going on among the college students. "I have reason to believe that there are girls in this gang as well as boys," he said. "They ransack vacant houses and take everything. In one house on Pleasant Street, up there by the Catholic Church, there wasn't anything to take, so they took the kitchen sink. Wasn't a question of taking everything *but*—they took the kitchen sink."

"What ever would they want with a kitchen sink?" asked my mother.

"Mischief," replied the Judge. "If we ever catch them and if they come within my jurisdiction, I can tell you I will give them no quarter. A thief, in my opinion, is the lowest of the low."

Mother told about the chocolate cake. By now, the fiction was so factual in my mind that each time I thought of it I saw a funny-paper bum in baggy pants held up by rope, a hat with holes through which tufts of hair stuck up, shoes from which his toes protruded, a disreputable stubble on his face; he came up beneath the open window where the devil's food was cooling and he stole it and hotfooted it for the woods, where his companion was frying a small fish in a beat-up skillet. It never crossed my mind any longer that Lottie Jump had hooked that delicious cake.

Judge Bay was properly impressed. "If you will steal a chocolate cake, if you will steal a kitchen sink, you will steal diamonds and money. The small child who pilfers a penny from his mother's pocketbook has started down a path that may lead him to holding up a bank."

It was a good thing I had no homework that night, for I could not possibly have concentrated. We were all sent to our rooms, because the pinochle players had to have absolute quiet. I spent the evening doing cross-stitch. I was making a bureau runner for a Christmas present; as in the case of the Christmas card, I had no one to give it to, but now I decided to give it to Lottie Jump's mother. Stella was reading *Black Beauty*, crying. It was an interminable evening. Stella went to bed first; I saw to that, because I didn't want her lying there awake listening to me talking in my sleep. Besides, I didn't want her to see me tearing open the cardboard box—the one in the shape of a church, which held my Christmas Sunday School offering. Over the door of the church was this

shaming legend: "My mite for the poor widow." When Stella had begun to grind her teeth in her first deep sleep, I took twenty cents away from the poor widow, whoever she was (the owner of the kitchen sink, no doubt), for the trolley fare, and secreted it and the remaining three pennies in the pocket of my middy. I wrapped the money well in a handkerchief and buttoned the pocket and hung my skirt over the middy. And then I tore the paper church into bits—the heavens opened and Judge Bay came toward me with a double-barreled shotgun—and hid the bits under a pile of pajamas. I did not sleep one wink. Except that I must have, because of the stupendous nightmares that kept wrenching the flesh off my skeleton and caused me to come close to perishing of thirst; once I fell out of bed and hit my head on Stella's ice skates. I would have waked her up and given her a piece of my mind for leaving them in such a lousy place, but then I remembered: I wanted *no* commotion of any kind.

I couldn't eat breakfast and I couldn't eat lunch. Old Johnny-on-the-spot Jack kept saying, *"Poor* Polecat. Polecat wants her fish for dinner."* Mother made an abortive attempt to take my temperature. And when all that hullabaloo subsided, I was nearly in the soup because Mother asked me to mind Tess while she went to the sanitarium to see Mrs. Rogers, who, all of a sudden, was too sick to have anyone but grownups near her. Stella couldn't stay with the baby, because she had to go to ballet, and Jack couldn't because he had to go up to the mesa and empty his traps. ("No, they *can't* wait. You want my skins to rot in this hot-one-day-cold-the-next weather?") I was arguing and whining when the telephone rang. Mother went to answer it and came back with a look of great sadness; Mrs. Rogers, she had learned, had had another hemorrhage. So Mother would not be going to the sanitarium after all and I needn't stay with Tess.

By the time I left the house, I was as cross as a bear. I felt awful about the widow's mite and I felt awful for being mean about staying with Tess, for Mrs. Rogers was a kind old lady, in a cozy blue hug-me-tight and an old-fangled boudoir cap, dying here all alone; she was a friend of Grandma's and had lived just down the street from her in Missouri, and all in the world Mrs. Rogers wanted to do was go back home and lie down in her own big bedroom in her own big, high-ceilinged house and have Grandma and other members of the Eastern Star come in from time to time to say hello. But they wouldn't let her go home; they were going to kill or cure her. I could not help feeling that my hardness of heart and evil of intention had had a good deal to do with her new crisis; right at the very same minute I had been saying "Does that old Mrs. Methuselah *always* have to spoil my fun?" the poor wasted thing was probably coughing up her blood and saying to the nurse, "Tell Emily Vanderpool not to mind me, she can run and play."

I had a bad character, I know that, but my badness never gave me half the enjoyment Jack and Stella thought it did. A good deal of the time I wanted to eat lye. I was certainly having no fun now, thinking of Mrs. Rogers and depriving that poor widow of bread and milk; what if this penniless woman without a husband had a dog to feed, too? Or a baby? And besides, I didn't want to go downtown to steal anything from the ten-cent store; I didn't want to see Lottie Jump again—not really, for I knew in my bones that that girl was trouble with a capital T. And still, in our short meeting she had mesmerized me; I would think about her style of talking and the expert way she had made off with the perfume flask and the cake (how had she carried the cake through the streets without being noticed?) and be bowled over, for the part of me that did not love God was a black-hearted villain. And apart from these considerations, I had some sort of idea that if I did not keep my appointment with Lottie Jump, she would somehow get revenge; she had seemed a girl of purpose. So, revolted and fascinated, brave and lily-

livered, I plodded along through the snow in my flopping galoshes up toward the Chautauqua, where the trolley stop was. On my way, I passed Virgil Meade's house; there was not just a snowman, there was a whole snow family in the back yard, and Virgil himself was throwing a stick for his dog. I was delighted to see that he was alone.

Lottie, who was sitting on a bench in the shelter eating a Mr. Goodbar, looked the same as she had the other time except that she was wearing an amazing hat. I think I had expected her to have a black handkerchief over the lower part of her face or be wearing a Jesse James waistcoat. But I had never thought of a hat. It was felt; it was the color of cooked meat; it had some flowers appliquéd on the front of it; it had no brim, but rose straight up to a very considerable height, like a monument. It sat so low on her forehead and it was so tight that it looked, in a way, like part of her.

"How's every little thing, bub?" she said, licking her candy wrapper.

"Fine, Lottie," I said, freshly awed.

A silence fell. I drank some water from the drinking fountain, sat down, fastened my galoshes, and unfastened them again.

"My mother's teeth grow wrong way to," said Lottie, and showed me what she meant: the lower teeth were in front of the upper ones. "That so-called trolley car takes its own sweet time. This town is blah."

To save the honor of my home town, the trolley came scraping and groaning up the hill just then, its bell clanging with an idiotic frenzy, and groaned to a stop. Its broad, proud cowcatcher was filled with dirty snow, in the middle of which rested a tomato can, put there, probably, by somebody who was bored to death and couldn't think of anything else to do—I did a lot of pointless things like that on lonesome Saturday afternoons. It was the custom of this trolley car, a rather mysterious one, to pause at the shelter for five minutes while the conductor, who was either Mr. Jansen or Mr. Peck, depending on whether it was the A.M. run or the P.M., got out and stretched and smoked and spit. Sometimes the passengers got out, too, acting like sightseers whose destination was this sturdy stucco gazebo instead of, as it really was, the Piggly Wiggly or the Nelson Dry. You expected them to take snapshots of the drinking fountain or of the Chautauqua meeting house up on the hill. And when they all got back in the car, you expected them to exchange intelligent observations on the aborigines and the ruins they had seen.

Today there were no passengers, and as soon as Mr. Peck got out and began staring at the mountains as if he had never seen them before while he made himself a cigarette, Lottie, in her tall hat (was it something like the Inspector's hat in the Katzenjammer Kids?), got into the car, motioning me to follow. I put our nickels in the empty box and joined her on the very last double seat. It was only then that she mapped out the plan for the afternoon, in a low but still insouciant voice. The hat—she did not apologize for it, she simply referred to it as "my hat"—was to be the repository of whatever we stole. In the future, it would be advisable for me to have one like it. (How? Surely it was unique. The flowers, I saw on closer examination, were tulips, but they were blue, and a very unsettling shade of blue.) I was to engage a clerk on one side of the counter, asking her the price of, let's say, a tube of Daggett & Ramsdell vanishing cream, while Lottie would lift a round comb or a barrette or a hair net or whatever on the other side. Then, at a signal, I would decide against the vanishing cream and would move on to the next counter that she indicated. The signal was interesting; it was to be the raising of her hat from the rear—"like I've got the itch and gotta scratch," she said. I was relieved that I was to have no part in the actual stealing, and I was touched that Lottie, who was going to do all the work, said we would "go halvers" on the take. She asked me if there was anything in particular I wanted—she herself had nothing special in mind and was going

to shop around first—and I said I would like some rubber gloves. This request was entirely spontaneous; I had never before in my life thought of rubber gloves in one way or another, but a psychologist—or Judge Bay—might have said that this was most significant and that I was planning at that moment to go on from petty larceny to bigger game, armed with a weapon on which I wished to leave no fingerprints.

On the way downtown, quite a few people got on the trolley, and they all gave us such peculiar looks that I was chicken hearted until I realized it must be Lottie's hat they were looking at. No wonder. I kept looking at it myself out of the corner of my eye; it was like a watermelon standing on end. No, it was like a tremendous test tube. On this trip—a slow one, for the trolley pottered through that part of town in a desultory, neighborly way, even going into areas where no one lived—Lottie told me some of the things she had stolen in Muskogee and here in Adams. They included a white satin prayer book (think of it!), Mr. Goodbars by the thousands (she had probably never paid for a Mr. Goodbar in her life), a dinner ring valued at two dollars, a strawberry emery, several cans of corn, some shoelaces, a set of poker chips, countless pencils, four spark plugs ("Pa had this old car, see, and it was broke, so we took 'er to get fixed; I'll build me a radio with 'em sometime—you know? Listen in on them ear muffs to Tulsa?"), a Boy Scout knife, and a Girl Scout folding cup. She made a regular practice of going through the pockets of the coats in the cloakroom every day at recess, but she had never found anything there worth a red cent and was about to give that up. Once, she had taken a gold pencil from a teacher's desk and had got caught—she was sure that this was one of the reasons she was only in the third grade. Of this unjust experience, she said, "The old hoot owl! If I was drivin' in a car on a lonesome stretch and she was settin' beside me, I'd wait till we got to a pile of gravel and then I'd stop and say, 'Git out, Miss Priss.' She'd git out, all right."

Since Lottie was so frank, I was emboldened at last to ask her what she had done with the cake. She faced me with her grin; this grin, in combination with the hat, gave me a surprise from which I have never recovered. "I ate it up," she said. "I went in your garage and sat on your daddy's old tires and ate it. It was pretty good."

There were two ten-cent stores side by side in our town, Kresge's and Woolworth's, and as we walked down the main street toward them, Lottie played with a Yo-Yo. Since the street was thronged with Christmas shoppers and farmers in for Saturday, this was no ordinary accomplishment; all in all, Lottie Jump was someone to be reckoned with. I cannot say that I was proud to be seen with her; the fact is that I hoped I would not meet anyone I knew, and I thanked my lucky stars that Jack was up in the hills with his dead skunks, because if he had seen her with that lid and that Yo-Yo, I would never have heard the last of it. But in another way I *was* proud to be with her; in a smaller hemisphere, in one that included only her and me, I was swaggering—I felt like Somebody, marching along beside this lofty Somebody from Oklahoma who was going to hold up the dime store.

There is nothing like Woolworth's at Christmastime. It smells of peanut brittle and terrible chocolate candy, Djer-Kiss talcum powder and Ben Hur Perfume—smells sourly of tinsel and waxily of artificial poinsettias. The crowds are made up largely of children and women, with here and there a deliberative old man; the women are buying ribbons and wrappings and Christmas cards, and the children are buying asbestos pot holders for their mothers and, for their fathers, suède bookmarks with a burnt-in design that says "A good book is a good friend" or "Souvenir from the Garden of the Gods." It is very noisy. The salesgirls are forever ringing their bells and asking the floor-walker to bring them change for a five; babies in go-carts are screaming as parcels fall on their heads; the women, waving rolls of red tissue paper, try to attract the attention of the harried girl behind the counter. ("Miss! All I want is this one batch of the red. Can't I just give you the dime?" And the girl, beside herself, mottled with vexation, cries back, "Has to be rung up, Moddom, that's the rule.") There is pandemonium at the toy counter, where things are being tested by the customers—wound up, set off, tooted, pounded, made to say "Maaaah-Maaaah!" There is very little gaiety in the scene and, in fact, those baffled old men look as if they were walking over their own dead bodies, but there is an atmosphere of carnival, nevertheless, and as soon as Lottie and I entered the doors of Woolworth's golden-and-vermilion bedlam, I grew giddy and hot—not pleasantly so. The feeling, indeed, was distinctly disagreeable, like the beginning of a stomach upset.

Lottie gave me a nudge and said softly, "Go look at the envelopes. I want some rubber bands."

This counter was relatively uncrowded (the seasonal stationery supplies—the Christmas cards and wrapping paper and stickers —were at a separate counter), and I went around to examine some very beautiful letter paper; it was pale pink and it had a border of roses all around it. The clerk here was a cheerful middle-aged woman wearing an apron, and she was giving all her attention to a seedy old man who could not make up his mind between mucilage and paste. "Take your time, Dad," she said. "Compared to the rest of the girls, I'm on my vacation." The old man, holding a tube in one hand and a bottle in the other, looked at her vaguely and said, "I want it for stamps. Sometimes I write a letter and stamp it and then don't mail it and steam the stamp off. Must have ninety cents' worth of stamps like that." The woman laughed. "I know what you mean," she said. "I get mad and write a letter and then I tear it up." The old man gave her a condescending look and said, "That so? But I don't suppose yours are of a political nature." He bent his gaze again to the choice of adhesives.

This first undertaking was duck soup for Lottie. I did not even have to exchange a word with the woman; I saw Miss Fagin lift up *that hat* and give me the high sign, and we moved away, she down one aisle and I down the other, now and again catching a glimpse of each other through the throngs. We met at the foot of the second counter, where notions were sold.

"Fun, huh?" said Lottie, and I nodded, although I felt wholly dreary. "I want some crochet hooks," she said. "Price the rickrack."

This time the clerk was adding up her receipts and did not even look at me or at a woman who was angrily and in vain trying to buy a paper of pins. Out went Lottie's scrawny hand, up went her domed chimney. In this way for some time she bagged sitting birds: a tea strainer (there was no one at all at that counter), a box of Mrs. Carpenter's All Purpose Nails, the rubber gloves I had said I wanted, and four packages of mixed seeds. Now you have some idea of the size of Lottie Jump's hat.

I was nervous, not from being her accomplice but from being in this crowd on an empty stomach, and I was getting tired— we had been in the store for at least an hour —and the whole enterprise seemed pointless. There wasn't a thing in her hat I wanted— not even the rubber gloves. But in exact proportion as my spirits descended, Lottie's rose; clearly she had only been target-practicing and now she was moving in for the kill.

We met beside the books of paper dolls, for reconnaissance. "I'm gonna get me a pair of pearl beads," said Lottie. "You go fuss with the hairpins, hear?"

Luck, combined with her skill, would have stayed with Lottie, and her hat would have been a cornucopia by the end of the afternoon if, at the very moment her hand went out for the string of beads, the idiosyn-crasy of mine had not struck me full force. I had never known it to come with so few preliminaries; probably this was so because I was oppressed by all the masses of bodies poking and pushing me, and all the open mouths breathing in my face. Anyhow, right then, at the crucial time, I *had to be alone*.

I stood staring down at the bone hairpins for a moment, and when the girl behind the counter said, "What kind does Mother want, hon? What color is Mother's hair?" I looked past her and across at Lottie and I said, "Your brother isn't the only one in your family that doesn't have any brains." The clerk, astonished, turned to look where I was looking and caught Lottie in the act of lifting up her hat to put the pearls inside. She had unwisely chosen a long strand and was having a little trouble; I had the nasty thought that it looked as if her brains were leaking out.

The clerk, not able to deal with this emergency herself, frantically punched her bell and cried, "Floorwalker! Mr. Bellamy! I've caught a thief!"

Momentarily there was a violent hush —then such a clamor as you have never heard. Bells rang, babies howled, crockery crashed to the floor as people stumbled in their rush to the arena.

Mr. Bellamy, nineteen years old but broad of shoulder and jaw, was instantly standing beside Lottie, holding her arm with one hand while with the other he removed her hat to reveal to the overjoyed audience that incredible array of merchandise. Her hair was wild, her face a mask of innocent bewilderment, Lottie Jump, the scurvy thing, pretended to be deaf and dumb. She pointed at the rubber gloves and then she pointed at me, and Mr. Bellamy, able at last to prove his mettle, said "Aha!" and, still holding Lottie, moved around the counter to me and grabbed *my* arm. He gave the hat to the clerk and asked her kindly to accompany him and his redhanded catch to the manager's office.

I don't know where Lottie is now— whether she is on the stage or in jail. If her performance after our arrest meant anything, the first is quite as likely as the second. (I never saw her again, and for all I know she lit out of town that night on a freight train. Or perhaps her whole family decamped as suddenly as they had arrived; ours was a most transient population. You can be sure I made no attempt to find her again, and for months I avoided going anywhere near Arapahoe Creek or North Hill.) She never said a word but kept making signs with her fingers, ad-libbing the whole thing. They tested her hearing by shooting off a popgun right in her ear and she never batted an eyelid.

They called up my father, and he came over from the Safeway on the double. I heard very little of what he said because I was crying so hard, but one thing I did hear him say was, "Well, young lady, I guess you've seen to it that I'll have to part company with my good friend Judge Bay." I tried to defend myself, but it was useless. The manager, Mr. Bellamy, the clerk, and my father patted Lottie on the shoulder, and the clerk said, "Poor afflicted child." For being a poor, afflicted child, they gave her a bag of hard candy, and she gave them the most fraudulent smile of gratitude, and slobbered a little, and shuffled out, holding her empty hat in front of her like a beggar-man. I hate Lottie Jump to this day, but I have to hand it to her—she was a genius.

The floorwalker would have liked to see me sentenced to the reform school for life, I am sure, but the manager said that, considering this was my first offense, he would let my father attend to my punishment. The old-maid clerk, who looked precisely like Emmy Schmalz, clucked her tongue and shook her head at me. My father hustled me out of the office and out of the store and into the car and home, muttering the entire time; now and again I'd hear the words "morals" and "nowadays."

What's the use of telling you the rest? You know what happened. Daddy on second thoughts decided not to hang his head in front of Judge Bay but to make use of his friendship in this time of need, and he took me to see the scary old curmudgeon at his house. All I remember of that long declamation, during which the Judge sat behind his desk never taking his eyes off me, was the warning: "I want you to give this a great deal of thought, miss. I want you to search and seek in the innermost corners of your conscience and root out every bit of badness." Oh, *him!* Why, listen, if I'd rooted out all the badness in me, there wouldn't have been anything left of me. My mother cried for days because she had nurtured an outlaw and was ashamed to show her face at the neighborhood store; my father was silent, and he often looked at me. Stella, who was a prig, said, "And to think you did it at *Christmas-time!*" As for Jack—well, Jack a couple of times did not know how close he came to seeing glory when I had a butcher knife in my hand. It was Polecat this and Polecat that until I nearly went off my rocker. Tess, of course, didn't know what was going on and asked so many questions that finally I told her to go to Helen Hunt Jackson in a savage tone of voice.

Good old Muff.

It is not true that you don't learn by experience. At any rate, I did that time. I began immediately to have two or three friends at a time—to be sure, because of the stigma on me, they were by no means the elite of Carlyle Hill Grade—and never again when that terrible need to be alone arose did I let fly. I would say, instead, "I've got a headache. I'll have to go home and take an aspirin," or "Gosh all hemlocks, I forgot— I've got to go to the dentist."

After the scandal died down, I got into the Camp Fire Girls. It was through pull, of course, since Stella had been a respected member for two years and my mother was a friend of the leader. But it turned out all right. Even Muff did not miss our periods of companionship, because about that time she grew up and started having literally millions of kittens.

EXERCISES

1. On what trait in the main character does this story depend? The main character is, we are told even by the title, "bad," and Lottie is even "badder." But what is the nature of the "badness" in the story? What leads the heroine to her "badness"—what makes her always feel compelled to shock her friend and ruin a friendship? Why, to cut back, does she have only one friend at a time?

    As a help in answering the questions above, let us ask what the family of the heroine is like. What are the values of the mother and father, of the other children, especially Stella (see the last paragraph)? What is the role of the Judge in the story? What, that is, does he thematically embody? This comes clear if we see him in contrast to Lottie, against whose world he is pitted. But this leads us to Lottie. How does she differ from the heroine? In the beginning, they seem to be two against the world, two "outlaws," but in the end they go their separate ways. What is suggested here? For instance, though Lottie, unlike the heroine, is presumed to go her independent way, it is a way that may lead in either of two directions. What are they? How are artists like criminals, as seems to be suggested here?

2. What, in the light of your answers to the questions above, is the story about? Is it about "evil" (even at a childish level) or does the "badness" spring from a basic and even admirable human need that is somehow being thwarted? If so, what is that need? Review all the questions and your answers under exercise 1, and try to make a general statement about the theme of the story.

3. Without insisting on an essential relation, can you see any relation between the setting in "Bad Characters" and the substance of the story?

THE VALIANT WOMAN
J. F. Powers (b. 1917)

They had come to the dessert in a dinner that was a shambles. "Well, John," Father Nulty said, turning away from Mrs. Stoner and to Father Firman, long gone silent at his own table. "You've got the bishop coming for confirmations next week."

"Yes," Mrs. Stoner cut in, "and for dinner. And if he don't eat any more than he did last year—"

Father Firman, in a rare moment, faced it. "Mrs. Stoner, the bishop is not well. You know that."

"And after I fixed that fine dinner and all." Mrs. Stoner pouted in Father Nulty's direction.

"I wouldn't feel bad about it, Mrs. Stoner," Father Nulty said. "He never eats much anywhere."

"It's funny. And that new Mrs. Allers said he ate just fine when he was there," Mrs. Stoner argued, and then spit out, "but she's a damned liar!"

Father Nulty, unsettled but trying not to show it, said, "Who's Mrs. Allers?"

"She's at Holy Cross," Mrs. Stoner said.

"She's the housekeeper," Father Firman added, thinking Mrs. Stoner made it sound as though Mrs. Allers were the pastor there.

"I swear I don't know what to do about the dinner this year," Mrs. Stoner said.

Father Firman moaned. "Just do as you've always done, Mrs. Stoner."

"Huh! And have it all to throw out! Is that any way to do?"

"Is there any dessert?" Father Firman asked coldly.

Mrs. Stoner leapt up from the table and bolted into the kitchen, mumbling. She came back with a birthday cake. She plunged it in the center of the table. She found a big wooden match in her apron pocket and thrust it at Father Firman.

"I don't like this bishop," she said. "I never did. And the way he went and cut poor Ellen Kennedy out of Father Doolin's will!"

She went back into the kitchen.

"Didn't they talk a lot of filth about Doolin and the housekeeper?" Father Nulty asked.

"I should think they did," Father Firman said. "All because he took her to the movies on Sunday night. After he died and the bishop cut her out of the will, though I hear he gives her a pension privately, they talked about the bishop."

"I don't like this bishop at all," Mrs. Stoner said, appearing with a cake knife. "Bishop Doran—there was the man!"

"We know," Father Firman said. "All man and all priest."

"He did know real estate," Father Nulty said.

Father Firman struck the match.

"Not on the chair!" Mrs. Stoner cried, too late.

Father Firman set the candle burning —it was suspiciously large and yellow, like a blessed one, but he could not be sure. They watched the fluttering flame.

"I'm forgetting the lights!" Mrs. Stoner said, and got up to turn them off. She went into the kitchen again.

The priests had a moment of silence in the candle-light.

"Happy birthday, John," Father Nulty said softly. "Is it fifty-nine you are?"

"As if you didn't know, Frank," Father Firman said, "and you the same but one."

Father Nulty smiled, the old gold of his incisors shining in the flickering light, his collar whiter in the dark, and raised his glass of water, which would have been wine or better in the bygone days, and toasted Father Firman.

"Many of 'em, John."

"Blow it out," Mrs. Stoner said, returning to the room. She waited by the light switch for Father Firman to blow out the candle.

Mrs. Stoner, who ate no desserts, began to clear the dishes into the kitchen, and the priests, finishing their cake and coffee in a hurry, went to sit in the study.

Father Nulty offered a cigar.

"John?"

"My ulcers, Frank."

"Ah, well, you're better off." Father Nulty lit the cigar and crossed his long black legs. "Fish Frawley has got him a Filipino, John. Did you hear?"

Father Firman leaned forward, interested. "He got rid of the woman he had?"

"He did. It seems she snooped."

"Snooped, eh?"

"She did. And gossiped. Fish introduced two town boys to her, said, 'Would you think these boys were my nephews?' That's all, and the next week the paper had it that his two nephews were visiting him from Erie. After that, he let her believe he was going East to see his parents, though both are dead. The paper carried the story. Fish returned and made a sermon out of it. Then he got the Filipino."

Father Firman squirmed with pleasure in his chair. "That's like Fish, Frank. He can do that." He stared at the tips of his fingers bleakly. "You could never get a Filipino to come to a place like this."

"Probably not," Father Nulty said. "Fish is pretty close to Minneapolis. Ah, say, do you remember the trick he played on us all in Marmion Hall!"

"That I'll not forget!" Father Firman's eyes remembered. "Getting up New Year's morning and finding the toilet seats all painted!"

"*Happy Circumcision!* Hah!" Father Nulty had a coughing fit.

When he had got himself together again, a mosquito came and sat on his wrist. He watched it a moment before bringing his heavy hand down. He raised his hand slowly, viewed the dead mosquito, and sent it spinning with a plunk of his middle finger.

"Only the female bites," he said.

"I didn't know that," Father Firman said.

"Ah, yes . . ."

Mrs. Stoner entered the study and sat down with some sewing—Father Firman's black socks.

She smiled pleasantly at Father Nulty. "And what do you think of the atom bomb, Father?"

"Not much," Father Nulty said.

Mrs. Stoner had stopped smiling. Father Firman yawned.

Mrs. Stoner served up another: "Did you read about this communist convert, Father?"

"He's been in the Church before," Father Nulty said, "and so it's not a conversion, Mrs. Stoner."

"No? Well, I already got him down on my list of Monsignor's converts."

"It's better than a conversion, Mrs. Stoner, for there is more rejoicing in heaven over the return of . . . uh, he that was lost, Mrs. Stoner, is found."

"And that congresswoman, Father?"

"Yes. A convert—she."

"And Henry Ford's grandson, Father. I got him down."

"Yes, to be sure."

Father Firman yawned, this time audibly, and held his jaw.

"But he's one only by marriage, Father," Mrs. Stoner said. "I always say you got to watch those kind."

"Indeed you do, but a convert nonetheless, Mrs. Stoner. Remember, Cardinal Newman himself was one."

Mrs. Stoner was unimpressed. "I see where Henry Ford's making steering wheels out of soybeans, Father."

"I didn't see that."

"I read it in the *Reader's Digest* or some place."

"Yes, well . . ." Father Nulty rose and held his hand out to Father Firman. "John," he said. "It's been good."

"I heard Hirohito's next," Mrs. Stoner said, returning to converts.

"Let's wait and see, Mrs. Stoner," Father Nulty said.

The priests walked to the door.

"You know where I live, John."

"Yes. Come again, Frank. Good night."

Father Firman watched Father Nulty go down the walk to his car at the curb. He hooked the screen door and turned off the porch light. He hesitated at the foot of the stairs, suddenly moved to go to bed. But he went back into the study.

"Phew!" Mrs. Stoner said. "I thought he'd never go. Here it is after eight o'clock."

Father Firman sat down in his rocking chair. "I don't see him often," he said.

"I give up!" Mrs. Stoner exclaimed, flinging the holey socks upon the horsehair sofa. "I'd swear you had a nail in your shoe."

"I told you I looked."

"Well, you ought to look again. And cut your toenails, why don't you? Haven't I got enough to do?"

Father Firman scratched in his coat pocket for a pill, found one, swallowed it. He let his head sink back against the chair and closed his eyes. He could hear her moving about the room, making the preparations; and how he knew them—the fumbling in the drawer for a pencil with a point, the rip of the page from his daily calendar, and finally the leg of the card table sliding up against his leg.

He opened his eyes. She yanked the floor lamp alongside the table, setting the bead fringe tinkling on the shade, and pulled up her chair on the other side. She sat down and smiled at him for the first time that day. Now she was happy.

She swept up the cards and began to shuffle with the abandoned virtuosity of an old riverboat gambler, standing them on end, fanning them out, whirling them through her fingers, dancing them halfway up her arms, cracking the whip over them. At last they lay before him tamed into a neat deck.

"Cut?"

"Go ahead," he said. She liked to go first.

She gave him her faint, avenging smile and drew a card, cast it aside for another which he thought must be an ace from the way she clutched it face down.

She was getting all the cards, as usual, and would have been invincible if she had possessed his restraint and if her cunning had been of a higher order. He knew a few things about leading and lying back that she would never learn. Her strategy was attack, forever attack, with one baffling departure: she might sacrifice certain tricks as expendable if only she could have the last ones, the heartbreaking ones, if she could slap them down one after another, shatteringly.

She played for blood, no bones about it,

but for her there was no other way; it was her nature, as it was the lion's, and for this reason he found her ferocity pardonable, more a defect of the flesh, venial, while his own trouble was all in the will, mortal. He did not sweat and pray over each card as she must, but he did keep an eye out for reneging and demanded a cut now and then just to aggravate her, and he was always secretly hoping for aces.

With one card left in her hand, the telltale trick coming next, she delayed playing it, showing him first the smile, the preview of defeat. She laid it on the table—so! She held one more trump than he had reasoned possible. Had she palmed it from somewhere? No, she would not go that far; that would not be fair, was worse than reneging, which so easily and often happened accidentally, and she believed in being fair. Besides he had been watching her.

God smote the vines with hail, the sycamore trees with frost, and offered up the flocks to the lightning—but Mrs. Stoner! What a cross Father Firman had from God in Mrs. Stoner! There were other housekeepers as bad, no doubt, walking the rectories of the world, yes, but . . . yes. He could name one and maybe two priests who were worse off. One, maybe two. Cronin. His scraggly blonde of sixty—take her, with her everlasting banging on the grand piano, the gift of the pastor; her proud talk about the goiter operation at the Mayo Brothers', also a gift; her honking the parish Buick at passing strange priests because they were all in the game together. She was worse. She was something to keep the home fires burning. Yes sir. And Cronin said she was not a bad person really, but what was he? He was quite a freak himself.

For that matter, could anyone say that Mrs. Stoner was a bad person? No. He could not say it himself, and he was no freak. She had her points, Mrs. Stoner. She was clean. And though she cooked poorly, could not play the organ, would not take up the collec-

tion in an emergency, and went to card parties, and told all—even so, she was clean. She washed everything. Sometimes her underwear hung down beneath her dress like a paratrooper's pants, but it and everything she touched was clean. She washed constantly. She was clean.

She had her other points, to be sure—her faults, you might say. She snooped—no mistake about it—but it was not snooping for snooping's sake; she had a reason. She did other things, always with a reason. She overcharged on rosaries and prayer books, but that was for the sake of the poor. She censored the pamphlet rack, but that was to prevent scandal. She pried into the baptismal and matrimonial records, but there was no other way if Father was out, and in this way she had once uncovered a bastard and flushed him out of the rectory, but that was the perverted decency of the times. She held her nose over bad marriages in the presence of the victims, but that was her sorrow and came from having her husband buried in a mine. And he had caught her telling a bewildered young couple that there was only one good reason for their wanting to enter into a mixed marriage—the child had to have a name, and that—that was what?

She hid his books, kept him from smoking, picked his friends (usually the pastors of her colleagues), bawled out people for calling after dark, had no humor, except at cards, and then it was grim, very grim, and she sat hatchet-faced every morning at Mass. But she went to Mass, which was all that kept the church from being empty some mornings. She did annoying things all day long. She said annoying things into the night. She said she had given him the best years of her life. Had she? Perhaps—for the miner had her only a year. It was too bad, sinfully bad, when he thought of it like that. But all talk of best years and life was nonsense. He had to consider the heart of the matter, the essence. The essence was that housekeepers were hard to get, harder to get than ushers, than willing workers, than organists, than secretaries—yes, harder to get than assistants or vocations.

And she was a *saver*—saved money, saved electricity, saved string, bags, sugar, saved—him. That's what she did. That's what she said she did, and she was right, in a way. In a way, she was usually right. In fact, she was always right—in a way. And you could never get a Filipino to come way out here and live. Not a young one anyway, and he had never seen an old one. Not a Filipino. They liked to dress up and live.

Should he let it drop about Fish having one, just to throw a scare into her, let her know he was doing some thinking? No. It would be a perfect cue for the one about a man needing a woman to look after him. He was not up to that again, not tonight.

Now she was doing what she liked most of all. She was making a grand slam, playing it out card for card, though it was in the bag, prolonging what would have been cut short out of mercy in gentle company. Father Firman knew the agony of losing.

She slashed down the last card, a miserable deuce trump, and did in the hapless king of hearts he had been saving.

"Skunked you!"

She was awful in victory. Here was the bitter end of their long day together, the final murderous hour in which all they wanted to say—all he wouldn't and all she couldn't— came out in the cards. Whoever won at honeymoon won the day, slept on the other's scalp, and God alone had to help the loser.

"We've been at it long enough, Mrs. Stoner," he said, seeing her assembling the cards for another round.

"Had enough, huh!"

Father Firman grumbled something.

"No?"

"Yes."

She pulled the table away and left it against the wall for the next time. She went out of the study carrying the socks, content and clucking. He closed his eyes after her

and began to get under way in the rocking chair, the nightly trip to nowhere. He could hear her brewing a cup of tea in the kitchen and conversing with the cat. She made her way up the stairs, carrying the tea, followed by the cat, purring.

He waited, rocking out to sea, until she would be sure to be through in the bathroom. Then he got up and locked the front door (she looked after the back door) and loosened his collar going upstairs.

In the bathroom he mixed a glass of antiseptic, always afraid of pyorrhea, and gargled to ward off pharyngitis.

When he turned on the light in his room, the moths and beetles began to batter against the screens, the lighter insects humming. . . .

Yes, and she had the guest room. How did she come to get that? Why wasn't she in the back room, in her proper place? He knew, if he cared to remember. The screen in the back room—it let in mosquitoes, and if it didn't do that she'd love to sleep back there, Father, looking out at the steeple and the blessed cross on top, Father, if it just weren't for the screen, Father. Very well, Mrs. Stoner, I'll get it fixed or fix it myself. Oh, could you now, Father? I could, Mrs. Stoner, and I will. In the meantime you take the guest room. Yes, Father, and thank you, Father, the house ringing with amenities then. Years ago, all that. She was a pie-faced girl then, not really a girl perhaps, but not too old to marry again. But she never had. In fact, he could not remember that she had even tried for a husband since coming to the recovery, but, of course, he could be wrong, not knowing how they went about it. God! God save us! Had she got her wires crossed and mistaken him all these years for *that*? *That!* Him! Suffering God! No. That was going too far. That was getting morbid. No. He must not think of that again, ever. No.

But just the same she had got the guest room and she had it yet. Well, did it matter? Nobody ever came to see him any more, nobody to stay overnight anyway, nobody to stay very long . . . not any more. He knew how they laughed at him. He had heard Frank humming all right—before he saw how serious and sad the situation was and took pity—humming, "Wedding Bells Are Breaking Up That Old Gang of Mine." But then they'd always laughed at him for something—for not being an athlete, for wearing glasses, for having kidney trouble . . . and mail coming addressed to Rev. and Mrs. Stoner.

Removing his shirt, he bent over the table to read the volume left open from last night. He read, translating easily, "Eisdem licet cum illis . . . Clerics are allowed to reside only with women about whom there can be no suspicion, either because of a natural bond (as mother, sister, aunt) or of advanced age, combined in both cases with good repute."

Last night he had read it, and many nights before, each time as though this time to find what was missing, to find what obviously was not in the paragraph, his problem considered, a way out. She was not mother, not sister, not aunt, and *advanced age* was a relative term (why, she was younger than he was) and so, eureka, she did not meet the letter of the law—but, alas, how she fulfilled the spirit! And besides it would be a slimy way of handling it after all her years of service. He could not afford to pension her off, either.

He slammed the book shut. He slapped himself fiercely on the back, missing the wily mosquito, and whirled to find it. He took a magazine and folded it into a swatter. Then he saw it—oh, the preternatural cunning of it!—poised in the beard of St. Joseph on the bookcase. He could not hit it there. He teased it away, wanting it to light on the wall, but it knew his thoughts and flew high away. He swung wildly, hoping to stun it, missed, swung back, catching St. Joseph across the neck. The statue fell to the floor and broke.

Mrs. Stoner was panting in the hall outside his door.

"What is it!"

"Mosquitoes!"

"What is it, Father? Are you hurt?"

"Mosquitoes—damn it! And only the female bites!"

Mrs. Stoner, after a moment, said, "Shame on you, Father. She needs the blood for her eggs."

He dropped the magazine and lunged at the mosquito with his bare hand.

She went back to her room, saying, "Pshaw, I thought it was burglars murdering you in your bed."

He lunged again.

This is a comic story, a humorous story. What gives it this quality? We usually say that the comic effect involves some kind of contrast, the expected in contrast with the unexpected, the pretension in contrast with the reality, a sudden upset.

Let us take an example. A man slips on a banana peel and comes crashing down. If the man is an inoffensive, ordinary fellow going quietly down the street, the situation is not nearly so funny as if he were pompous and lordly and condescending, with a top hat. The comedy, then, involves the contrast between the man's pretension and what actually happens to him. This, of course, is a very simple situation, but it may give us a way into the discussion of more complicated comedy.

What contrast do we find in "The Valiant Woman"? The basic situation is a standard one, that of the henpecked man. A man who sets up as the lord and master finds himself under female tyranny and can vent his protest and rebellion only by killing a mosquito: "And only the female bites!" We can imagine a comic story with the main characters husband and wife, but, as we have said, that situation is a standard one and a story based on it would run the risk of being somewhat hackneyed. Here, however, the standard situation of the henpecked man receives a new twist. The situation does not involve man and wife, but a priest and his housekeeper. A priest is celibate. He is supposed to be removed from the cares and distractions of domestic life. Ideally, his thoughts and energies go into the duties of his high calling. But, in contrast to all this we find the poor Father Firman just as henpecked as the butcher or baker or candlestick maker down the street. Mrs. Stoner has him under her thumb, and writhe and twist and rebel as he may, he can never escape. Even her piety and her good works and her economies and her attentions are simply a mask for her tyranny. Poor Father Firman might as well be married to some dragon of a wife, for the situation is a kind of parody of domestic life—even to Mrs. Stoner's words that she had given the best years of her life to Father Firman, the very words of an angry or aggrieved wife.

Are we to conclude from this that when we get a contrast we automatically get a comic effect? No, that does not follow. Let us return to our example of the man who slips on the banana peel. The situation will be comic only if we don't worry sympathetically about the poor fellow's broken leg, or neck. There must be some degree of detachment from the victim of the comic situation. We must feel ourselves not too deeply involved in the possible seriousness of things. This, of course, does not depend merely on the situation but also on ourselves. A gross, insensitive person may laugh at the man falling on the banana peel where another person might run to help him up. But sometimes we are able to see the funny element even in a serious situation or in a situation set in a larger context that is serious.

This last statement leads us to a question: is "The Valiant Woman" disrespectful to the Catholic church and the priesthood? Only a completely humorless person would think so. In fact, insofar as one had respect for the church and the priesthood, the more fully he would appreciate the contrast between Father Firman's role as priest and his human condition. In other words, we are aware of the funny element in a situation that is set in a serious context, the context of the church and the priest's function. Let us look at it this way: if we had no notion of the church and the priesthood there would be no contrast to give comic salt to the story.

We have said that we must have some detachment in order to appreciate the comedy of a situation. We may add that for a thing to be comic, in real life or in fiction, there must be some speed, some quickness. We must grasp the situation immediately. In a story, for example, there is never the comic effect if the author belabors the point, if he systematically analyzes the situation for us. No, he must arrange things so that the significance flashes on us, out of the very texture of personality or event. Let us look at a passage of conversation from "The Valiant Woman":

> Mrs. Stoner served up another: "Did you read about this communist convert, Father?"
>
> "He's been in the Church before," Father Nulty said, "and so it's not a conversion, Mrs. Stoner."
>
> "No? Well, I already got him down on my list of Monsignor's converts."
>
> "It's better than a conversion, Mrs. Stoner, for there is more rejoicing in heaven over the return of . . . uh, he that was lost, Mrs. Stoner, is found."
>
> "And that congresswoman, Father?"
>
> "Yes. A convert—she."
>
> "And Henry Ford's grandson, Father. I got him down."
>
> "Yes, to be sure."
>
> Father Firman yawned, this time audibly, and held his jaw.
>
> "But he's one only by marriage, Father," Mrs. Stoner said. "I always say you got to watch those kind."
>
> "Indeed you do, but a convert nonetheless, Mrs. Stoner. Remember, Cardinal Newman himself was one."
>
> Mrs. Stoner was unimpressed. "I see where Henry Ford's making steering wheels out of soybeans, Father."
>
> "I didn't see that."
>
> "I read it in the *Reader's Digest* or some place."
>
> "Yes, well . . ." Father Nulty rose and held his hand out to Father Firman. "John," he said. "It's been good."
>
> "I hear Hirohito's next," Mrs. Stoner said, returning to converts.

We get it all—Mrs. Stoner's domination of the conversation, her churchiness, which we know does not have a shred of real piety in it, just a kind of gossipy clubbiness, her scatterbrained irrelevancy (from converts to soybeans), Father Nulty's strained politeness to his friend's housekeeper, Father Firman's yawn. It all comes over directly, in a flash, without discussion or preparation.

EXERCISES

1. How would you treat this story in terms of exposition, complication, and denouement? Does it break up rather neatly into these divisions or is there a general interpenetration? What is the basic conflict?

2. Comment on the comic elements in the following passages:

(a) "I don't like this bishop at all," Mrs. Stoner said, appearing with a cake knife. "Bishop Doran —there was the man!"
"We know," Father Firman said. "All man and all priest."
"He did know real estate," Father Nulty said.
Father Firman struck the match.
"Not on the chair!" Mrs. Stoner cried, too late.
Father Firman set the candle burning—it was suspiciously large and yellow, like a blessed one, but he could not be sure. They watched the fluttering flame.

(b) She swept up the cards and began to shuffle with the abandoned virtuosity of an old river-boat gambler, standing them on end, fanning them out, whirling them through her fingers, dancing them halfway up her arms, cracking the whip over them. At last they lay before him tamed into a neat deck.

(c) He could name one or maybe two priests who were worse off. One, maybe two. Cronin. His scraggly blonde of sixty—take her, with her everlasting banging on the grand piano, the gift of the pastor; her proud talk about the goiter operation at the Mayo Brothers', also a gift; her honking the parish Buick at passing strange priests because they were all in the game together.

3. When Mrs. Stoner hears Father Firman say that he is trying to kill a mosquito, she calls back: "Shame on you, Father. She needs the blood for her eggs." What is the point of this in the story?

4. Can you locate the basic divisions of this story? What is accomplished in each?

5. In what sense does the comedy of this story depend on the "place"—which, in this case, implies the profession of the men?

SPOTTED HORSES
William Faulkner (1897–1962)

I

Yes sir. Flem Snopes has filled that whole country full of spotted horses. You can hear folks running them all day and all night, whooping and hollering, and the horses running back and forth across them little wooden bridges ever now and then kind of like thunder. Here I was this morning pretty near half way to town, with the team ambling along and me setting in the buckboard about half asleep, when all of a sudden something come swurging up outen the bushes and jumped the road clean, without touching hoof to it. It flew right over my team big as a billboard and flying through the air like a hawk. It taken me thirty minutes to stop my team and untangle the harness and the buckboard and hitch them up again.

That Flem Snopes. I be dog if he ain't a case, now. One morning about ten years ago the boys was just getting settled down on Varner's porch for a little talk and tobacco, when here come Flem out from behind the counter, with his coat off and his hair all parted, like he might have been clerking for Varner for ten years already. Folks all knowed him; it was a big family of them about five miles down the bottom. That year, at least. Share-cropping. They never stayed on any place over a year. Then they would move on to another place, with the chap or maybe the twins of that year's litter. It was a regular nest of them. But Flem. The rest of them stayed tenant farmers, moving ever year, but here come Flem one day, walking out from behind Jody Varner's counter like he owned it. And he wasn't there but a year or two before folks knowed that if him and Jody was both still in that store in ten years more it would be Jody clerking for Flem Snopes. Why, that fellow could make a nickel where it wasn't but four cents to begin with. He skun me in two trades, myself, and the fellow that can do that, I just hope he'll get rich before I do; that's all.

All right. So here Flem was, clerking at Varner's, making a nickel here and there and not telling nobody about it. No, sir. Folks never knowed when Flem got the better of somebody lessen the fellow he beat told it. He'd just set there in the store-chair, chewing his tobacco and keeping his own business to hisself, until about a week later we'd find out it was somebody else's business he was keeping to hisself—provided the fellow he trimmed was mad enough to tell it. That's Flem.

We give him ten years to own ever thing Jody Varner had. But he never waited no ten years. I reckon you-all know that gal of Uncle Billy Varner's, the youngest one; Eula. Jody's sister. Ever Sunday ever yellow-wheeled buggy and curried riding horse in that country would be hitched to Bill Varner's fence, and the young bucks setting on the porch, swarming around Eula like bees around a honey pot. One of these here kind of big, soft-looking gals that could giggle richer than plowed new-ground. Wouldn't none of them leave before the others, and so they would set there on the porch until time to go home, with some of them with nine and ten miles to ride and then get up tomorrow and go back to the field. So they would all leave together and they would ride in a clump down to the creek ford and hitch them curried horses and yellow-wheeled buggies and get out and fight one another. Then they would get in the buggies again and go home.

Well, one day about a year ago, one of them yellow-wheeled buggies and one of them curried saddle-horses quit this country. We heard they was heading for Texas. The next day Uncle Billy and Eula and Flem come in to town in Uncle Bill's surrey, and when they come back, Flem and Eula was married. And on the next day we heard that two more of them yellow-wheeled buggies had left the country. They mought have gone to Texas, too. It's a big place.

Anyway, about a month after the wedding, Flem and Eula went to Texas, too. They was gone pretty near a year. Then one day last month, Eula come back, with a baby. We figured up, and we decided that it was as well-growed a three-months-old baby as we ever see. It can already pull up on a chair. I reckon Texas makes big men quick, being a big place. Anyway, if it keeps on like it started, it'll be chewing tobacco and voting time it's eight years old.

And so last Friday here come Flem himself. He was on a wagon with another fellow. The other fellow had one of these two-gallon hats and a ivory-handled pistol and a box of ginger snaps sticking out of his hind pocket, and tied to the tail-gate of the wagon was about two dozen of them Texas ponies, hitched to one another with barbed wire. They was colored like parrots and they was quiet as doves, and ere a one of them would kill you quick as a ratlesnake. Nere a one of them had two eyes the same color, and nere a one of them had ever see a bridle, I reckon; and when that Texas man got down offen the wagon and walked up to them to show how gentle they was, one of them cut his vest clean offen him, same as with a razor.

Flem had done already disappeared; he had went on to see his wife, I reckon, and to see if that ere baby had done gone on to the field to help Uncle Billy plow, maybe. It was the Texas man that taken the horses on to Mrs. Littlejohn's lot. He had a little trouble at first, when they come to the gate, because they hadn't never seen a fence before, and when he finally got them in and taken a pair of wire cutters and unhitched them and got them into the barn and poured some shell corn into the trough, they durn nigh tore down the barn. I reckon they thought that shell corn was bugs, maybe. So he left them in the lot and he announced that the auction would begin at sunup tomorrow.

That night we was setting on Mrs. Littlejohn's porch. You-all mind the moon was nigh full that night, and we could watch them spotted varmints swirling along the fence and back and forth across the lot same as minnows in a pond. And then now and then they would all kind of huddle up against the barn and rest themselves by biting and kicking one another. We would hear a squeal, and then a set of hoofs would go Bam! against the barn, like a pistol. It sounded just like a fellow with a pistol, in a nest of cattymounts, taking his time.

II

It wasn't ere a man knowed yet if Flem owned them things or not. They just knowed one thing: that they wasn't never going to know for sho if Flem did or not, or if maybe he didn't just get on the wagon at the edge of town, for the ride or not. Even Eck Snopes didn't know, Flem's own cousin. But wasn't nobody surprised at that. We knowed that Flem would skin Eck quick as he would ere a one of us.

They was there by sunup next morning, some of them come twelve and sixteen miles, with seed-money tied up in tobacco sacks in their overalls, standing along the fence, when the Texas man come out of Mrs. Littlejohn's after breakfast and clumb onto the gate post with that ere white pistol butt sticking outen his hind pocket. He taken a new box of gingersnaps outen his pocket and bit the end offen it like a cigar and spit out the paper, and said the auction was open. And still they was coming up in wagons and a horse- and mule-back and hitching the teams across the road and coming to the fence. Flem wasn't nowhere in sight.

But he couldn't get them started. He begun to work on Eck, because Eck holp him last night to get them into the barn and feed them that shell corn. Eck got out just in time. He come outen that barn like a chip on the crest of a busted dam of water, and clumb into the wagon just in time.

He was working on Eck when Henry Armstid come up in his wagon. Eck was saying he was skeered to bid on one of them, because he might get it, and the Texas man says, "Them ponies? Them little horses?" He clumb down offen the gate post and went toward the horses. They broke and run, and

him following them, kind of chirping to them, with his hand out like he was fixing to catch a fly, until he got three or four of them cornered. Then he jumped into them, and then we couldn't see nothing for a while because of the dust. It was a big cloud of it, and them blare eyed, spotted things swoaring outen it twenty foot to a jump, in forty directions without counting up. Then the dust settled and there they was, that Texas man and the horse. He had its head twisted clean around like a owl's head. Its legs was braced and it was trembling like a new bride and groaning like a saw mill, and him holding its head wrung clean around on its neck so it was snuffing sky. "Look it over," he says, with his heels dug too and that white pistol sticking outen his pocket and his neck swole up like a spreading adder's until you could just tell what he was saying, cussing the horse and talking to us all at once: "Look him over, the fiddle headed son of fourteen fathers. Try him, buy him; you will get the best—" Then it was all dust again, and we couldn't see nothing but spotted hide and mane, and that ere Texas man's boot-heels like a couple of walnuts on two strings, and after a while that two-gallon hat come sailing out like a fat old hen crossing a fence.

When the dust settled again, he was just getting outen the far fence corner, brushing himself off. He come and got his hat and brushed it off and come and clumb onto the gate post again. He was breathing hard. The hammer-head horse was still running round and round the lot like a merry-go-round at a fair. That was when Henry Armstid come shoving up to the gate in them patched overalls and one of them dangle-armed shirts of hisn. Hadn't nobody noticed him until then. We was all watching the Texas man and the horses. Even Mrs. Littlejohn; she had done come out and built a fire under the wash-pot in her back yard, and she would stand at the fence a while and then go back into the house and come out again with a arm full of wash and stand at the fence again. Well, here come Henry shoving up, and then we see Mrs.

Armstid right behind him, in that ere faded wrapper and sunbonnet and them tennis shoes. "Git on back to that wagon," Henry says.

"Henry," she says.

"Here, boys," the Texas man says; "make room for missus to git up and see. Come on Henry," he says; "here's your chance to buy that saddle-horse missus has been wanting. What about ten dollars, Henry?"

"Henry," Mrs. Armstid says. She put her hand on Henry's arm. Henry knocked her hand down.

"Git on back to that wagon, like I told you," he says.

Mrs. Armstid never moved. She stood behind Henry, with her hands rolled into her dress, not looking at nothing. "He hain't no more despair than to buy one of them things," she says. "And us not five dollars ahead of the pore house, he hain't no more despair." It was the truth, too. They ain't never made more than a bare living offen that place of theirs, and them with four chaps and the very clothes they wears she earns by weaving by the firelight at night while Henry's asleep.

"Shut your mouth and git on back to that wagon," Henry says. "Do you want I taken a wagon stake to you here in the big road?"

Well, that Texas man taken one look at her. Then he begun on Eck again; like Henry wasn't even there. But Eck was skeered. "I can git me a snapping turtle or a water moccasin for nothing. I ain't going to buy none."

So the Texas man said he would give Eck a horse. "To start the auction, and because you holp me last night. If you'll start the bidding on the next horse," he says, "I'll give you that fiddle-head horse."

I wish you could have seen them, standing there with their seed-money in their pockets, watching that Texas man give Eck Snopes a live horse, all fixed to call him a fool if he taken it or not. Finally Eck says

he'll take it. "Only I just starts the bidding," he says. "I don't have to buy the next one lessen I ain't overtopped." The Texas man said all right, and Eck bid a dollar on the next one, with Henry Armstid standing there with his mouth already open, watching Eck and the Texas man like a mad-dog or something. "A dollar," Eck says.

The Texas man looked at Eck. His mouth was already open too, like he had started to say something and what he was going to say had up and died on him. "A dollar? You mean, *one* dollar, Eck?"

"Durn it," Eck says; "two dollars, then."

Well, sir, I wish you could a seen that Texas man. He taken out that gingersnap box and held it up and looked into it, careful, like it might have been a diamond ring in it, or a spider. Then he throwed it away and wiped his face with a bandanna. "Well," he says. "Well. Two dollars. Is your pulse all right, Eck?" he says. "Do you have agersweats at night, maybe?" he says. "Well," he says, "I got to take it. But are you boys going to stand there and see Eck get two horses at a dollar a head?"

That done it. I be dog if he wasn't nigh as smart as Flem Snopes. He hadn't no more than got the words outen his mouth before here was Henry Armstid, waving his hand. "Three dollars," Henry says. Mrs. Armstid tried to hold him again. He knocked her hand off, shoving up to the gate post.

"Mister," Mrs. Armstid says, "we got chaps in the house and not corn to feed the stock. We got five dollars I earned my chaps a-weaving after dark, and him snoring in the bed. And he hain't no more despair."

"Henry bids three dollars," the Texas man says. "Raise him a dollar, Eck, and the horse is yours."

"Henry," Mrs. Armstid says.

"Raise him, Eck," the Texas man says.

"Four dollars," Eck says.

"Five dollars," Henry says, shaking his fist. He shoved up right under the gate post. Mrs. Armstid was looking at the Texas man too.

"Mister," she says, "if you take that five dollars I earned my chaps a-weaving for one of them things, it'll be a curse onto you and yourn during all the time of man."

But it wasn't no stopping Henry. He had shoved up, waving his fist at the Texas man. He opened it; the money was in nickels and quarters, and one dollar bill that looked like a cow's cud. "Five dollars," he says. "And the man that raises it'll have to beat my head off, or I'll beat hisn."

"All right," the Texas man says. "Five dollars is a bid. But don't you shake your hand at me."

III

It taken till nigh sundown before the last one was sold. He got them hotted up once and the bidding got up to seven dollars and a quarter, but most of them went around three or four dollars, him setting on the gate post and picking the horses out one at a time by mouthword, and Mrs. Littlejohn pumping up and down at the tub and stopping and coming to the fence for a while and going back to the tub again. She had done got done too, and the wash was hung on the line in the back yard, and we could smell supper cooking. Finally they was all sold; he swapped the last two and the wagon for a buckboard.

We was all kind of tired, but Henry Armstid looked more like a mad-dog than ever. When he bought, Mrs. Armstid had went back to the wagon, setting in it behind them two rabbit-sized, bone-pore mules, and the wagon itself looking like it would fall all to pieces soon as the mules moved. Henry hadn't even waited to pull it outen the road; it was still in the middle of the road and her setting in it, not looking at nothing, ever since this morning.

Henry was right up against the gate. He went up to the Texas man. "I bought a horse and I paid cash," Henry says. "And yet you expect me to stand around here until they are all sold before I can get my horse. I'm going to take my horse outen that lot."

The Texas man looked at Henry. He talked like he might have been asking for a cup of coffee at the table. "Take your horse," he says.

Then Henry quit looking at the Texas man. He begun to swallow, holding onto the gate. "Ain't you going to help me?" he says.

"It ain't my horse," the Texas man says.

Henry never looked at the Texas man again, he never looked at nobody. "Who'll help me catch my horse?" he says. Never nobody said nothing. "Bring the plowline," Henry says. Mrs. Armstid got outen the wagon and brought the plowline. The Texas man got down offen the post. The woman made to pass him, carrying the rope.

"Don't you go in there, missus," the Texas man says.

Henry opened the gate. He didn't look back. "Come on here," he says.

"Don't you go in there, missus," the Texas man says.

Mrs. Armstid wasn't looking at nobody, neither, with her hands across her middle, holding the rope. "I reckon I better," she says. Her and Henry went into the lot. The horses broke and run. Henry and Mrs. Armstid followed.

"Get him into the corner," Henry says. They got Henry's horse cornered finally, and Henry taken the rope, but Mrs. Armstid let the horse get out. They hemmed it up again, but Mrs. Armstid let it get out again, and Henry turned, and hit her with the rope. "Why didn't you head him back?" Henry says. He hit her again. "Why didn't you?" It was about that time I looked around and see Flem Snopes standing there.

It was the Texas man that done something. He moved fast for a big man. He caught the rope before Henry could hit the third time, and Henry whirled and make like he would jump at the Texas man. But he never jumped. The Texas man went and taken Henry's arm and led him outen the lot. Mrs. Armstid come behind them and the Texas man taken some money outen his pocket and he give it into Mrs. Armstid's hand. "Get him into the wagon and take him on home," the Texas man says, like he might have been telling them he enjoyed his supper.

Then here come Flem. "What's that for Buck?" Flem says.

"Thinks he bought one of them ponies," the Texas man says. "Get him on away, missus."

But Henry wouldn't go. "Give him back that money," he says. "I bought that horse and I aim to have him if I have to shoot him."

And there was Flem, standing there with his hands in his pockets, chewing, like he had just happened to be passing.

"You take your money and I take my horse," Henry says. "Give it back to him," he says to Mrs. Armstid.

"You don't own no horse of mine," the Texas man says. "Get him on home, missus."

Then Henry sees Flem. "You got something to do with these horses," he says. "I bought one. Here's the money for it." He taken the bill outen Mrs. Armstid's hand. He offered it to Flem. "I bought one. Ask him. Here. Here's the money," he says, giving the bill to Flem.

When Flem taken the money, the Texas man dropped the rope he had snatched outen Henry's hand. He had done sent Eck Snope's boy up to the store for another box of gingersnaps, and he taken the box outen his pocket and looked into it. It was empty and he dropped it on the ground. "Mr. Snopes will have your money for you tomorrow," he says to Mrs. Armstid. "You can get it from him tomorrow. He don't own no horse. You get him into the wagon and get him on home." Mrs. Armstid went back to the wagon and got in. "Where's that ere buckboard I bought?" the Texas man says. It was after sundown then. And then Mrs. Littlejohn come out on the porch and rung the supper bell.

IV

I come on in and et supper. Mrs. Littlejohn would bring in a pan of bread or something, then she would go out to the porch a minute and come back and tell us. The Texas man had hitched his team to the buckboard he had swapped them last two horses for, and him and Flem had gone, and then she told that the rest of them that never had ropes had went back to the store with I. O. Snopes to get some ropes, and wasn't nobody at the gate but Henry Armstid, and Mrs. Armstid setting in the wagon in the road, and Eck Snopes and the boy of hisn. "I don't care how many of them fool men gets killed by them things," Mrs. Littlejohn says, "but I ain't going to let Eck Snopes take that boy into that lot again." So she went down to the gate, but she come back without the boy or Eck neither.

"It ain't no need to worry about that boy," I says. "He's charmed." He was right behind Eck last night when Eck went to help feed them. The whole drove of them jumped clean over that boy's head and never touched him. It was Eck that touched him. Eck snatched him into the wagon and taken a rope and frailed the tar outen him.

So I had done et and went to my room and was undressing, long as I had a long trip to make next day; I was trying to sell a machine to Mrs. Bundren up past Whiteleaf; when Henry Armstid opened that gate and went in by hisself. They couldn't make him wait for the balance of them to get back with their ropes. Eck Snopes said he tried to make Henry wait, but Henry wouldn't do it. Eck said Henry walked right up to them and that when they broke, they run clear over Henry like a haymow breaking down. Eck said he snatched that boy of hisn out of the way just in time and that them things went through that gate like a creek flood and into the wagons and teams hitched side the road, busting wagon tongues and snapping harness like it was fishing-line, with Mrs. Armstid still setting in their wagon in the middle of it like something carved outen wood. Then they scattered, wild horses and tame mules with pieces of harness and single trees dangling offen them, both ways up and down the road.

"There goes ourn, paw!" Eck says his boy said. "There it goes, into Mrs. Littlejohn's house." Eck says it run right up the steps and into the house like a boarder late for supper. I reckon so. Anyway, I was in my room, in my underclothes, with one sock on and one sock in my hand, leaning out the window when the commotion busted out, when I heard something run into the melodeon in the hall; it sounded like a railroad engine. Then the door to my room come sailing in like when you throw a tin bucket into the wind and I looked over my shoulder and see something that looked like a fourteen-foot pinwheel a-blaring its eyes at me. It had to blare them fast, because I was already done jumped out the window.

I reckon it was anxious, too. I reckon it hadn't never seen barbed wire or shell corn before, but I know it hand't never seen underclothes before, or maybe it was a sewing-machine agent it hadn't never seen. Anyway, it whirled and turned to run back up the hall and outen the house, when it met Eck Snopes and that boy just coming in, carrying a rope. It swirled again and run down the hall and out the back door just in time to meet Mrs. Littlejohn. She had just gathered up the clothes she had washed, and she was coming onto the back porch with a armful of washing in one hand and a scrubbing-board in the other, when the horse skidded up to her, trying to stop and swirl again. It never taken Mrs. Littlejohn no time a-tall.

"Git outen here, you son," she says. She hit it across the face with the scrubbing-board; that ere scrubbing-board split as neat as ere a axe could have done it, and when the horse swirled to run back up the hall, she hit it again with what was left of the scrubbing-board, not on the head this time. "And stay out," she says.

Eck and that boy was half-way down the hall by this time. I reckon that horse looked like a pinwheel to Eck too. "Git to hell outen here, Ad!" Eck says. Only there wasn't time. Eck dropped flat on his face, but the boy never moved. The boy was about a yard tall

maybe, in overalls just like Eck's; that horse swoated over his head without touching a hair. I saw that, because I was just coming back up the front steps, still carrying that ere sock and still in my underclothes, when the horse come onto the porch again. It taken one look at me and swirled again and run to the end of the porch and jumped the banisters and the lot fence like a hen-hawk and lit in the lot running and went out the gate again and jumped eight or ten upside-down wagons and went on down the road. It was a full moon then. Mrs. Armstid was still setting in the wagon like she had done been carved outen wood and left there and forgot.

That horse. It ain't never missed a lick. It was going about forty miles a hour when it come to the bridge over the creek. It would have had a clear road, but it so happened that Vernon Tull was already using the bridge when it got there. He was coming back from town; he hadn't heard about the auction; him and his wife and three daughters and Mrs. Tull's aunt, all setting in chairs in the wagon bed, and all asleep, including the mules. They waked up when the horse hit the bridge one time, but Tull said the first he knew was when the mules tried to turn the wagon around in the middle of the bridge and he seen that spotted varmint run right twixt the mules and run up the wagon tongue like a squirrel. He said he just had time to hit it across the face with his whip-stock, because about that time the mules turned the wagon around on that ere one-way bridge and that horse clumb across onto the bridge again and went on, with Vernon standing up in the wagon and kicking at it.

Tull said the mules turned in the harness and clumb back into the wagon too, with Tull trying to beat them out again, with the reins wrapped around his wrist. After that he says all he seen was overturned chairs and womenfolks' legs and white drawers shining in the moonlight, and his mules and that spotted horse going on up the road like a ghost.

The mules jerked Tull outen the wagon

and drug him a spell on the bridge before the reins broke. They thought at first that he was dead, and while they was kneeling around him, picking the bridge splinters outen him, here come Eck and that boy, still carrying the rope. They was running and breathing a little hard. "Where'd he go?" Eck says.

V

I went back and got my pants and shirt and shoes on just in time to go and help get Henry Armstid outen the trash in the lot. I be dog if he didn't look like he was dead, with his head hanging back and his teeth showing in the moonlight, and a little rim of white under his eye-lids. We could still hear them horses, here and there; hadn't none of them got more than four—five miles away yet, not knowing the country, I reckon. So we could hear them and folks yelling now and then: "Whooey. Head him!"

We toted Henry into Mrs. Littlejohn's. She was in the hall; she hadn't put down the armful of clothes. She taken one look at us, and she laid down the busted scrubbing-board and taken up the lamp and opened a empty door. "Bring him in here," she says.

We toted him in and laid him on the bed. Mrs. Littlejohn set the lamp on the dresser, still carrying the clothes. "I'll declare, you men," she says. Our shadows was way up the wall, tiptoeing too; we could hear ourselves breathing. "Better get his wife," Mrs. Littlejohn says. She went out, carrying the clothes.

'I reckon we had," Quick says. "Go get her, somebody."

"Whyn't you go?" Winterbottom says.

"Let Ernest git her," Durley says. "He lives neighbors with them."

Ernest went to fetch her. I be dog if Henry didn't look like he was dead. Mrs. Littlejohn come back, with a kettle and some towels. She went to work on Henry, and then Mrs. Armstid and Ernest come in. Mrs. Armstid come to the foot of the bed and stood there, with her hands rolled into her apron, watching what Mrs. Littlejohn was doing, I reckon.

"You men get outen the way," Mrs. Littlejohn says. "Git outside," she says. "See if you can't find something else to play with that will kill some more of you."

"Is he dead?" Winterbottom says.

"It ain't your fault if he ain't," Mrs. Littlejohn says. "Go tell Will Varner to come up here. I reckon a man ain't so difference from a mule, come long come short. Except maybe a mule's got more sense."

We went to get Uncle Billy. It was a full moon. We could hear them, now and then, four miles away: "Whooey. Head him." The country was full of them, one on ever wooden bridge in the land, running across it like thunder: "Whooey. There he goes. Head him."

We hadn't got far before Henry began to scream. I reckon Mrs. Littlejohn's water had brung him to; anyway, he wasn't dead. We went on to Uncle Billy's. The house was dark. We called to him, and after a while the window opened and Uncle Billy put his head out, peart as a peckerwood, listening. "Are they still trying to catch them durn rabbits?" he says.

He come down, with his britches on over his night-shirt and his suspenders dangling, carrying his horse-doctoring grip. "Yes, sir," he says, cocking his head like a woodpecker; "they're still a-trying."

We could hear Henry before we reached Mrs. Littlejohn's. He was going Ah-Ah-Ah. We stopped in the yard. Uncle Billy went on in. We could hear Henry. We stood in the yard, hearing them on the bridges, this-a-way and that: "Whooey. Whooey."

"Eck Snopes ought to caught hisn," Ernest says.

"Looks like he ought," Winterbottom said.

Henry was going Ah-Ah-Ah steady in the house; then he begun to scream. "Uncle Billy's started," Quick says. We looked into the hall. We could see the light where the door was. Then Mrs. Littlejohn come out.

"Will needs some help," she says. "You, Ernest. You'll do." Ernest went into the house.

"Hear them?" Quick said. "That one was on Four Mile bridge." We could hear them; it sounded like thunder a long way off; it didn't last long:

"Whooey."

We could hear Henry: "Ah-Ah-Ah-Ah-Ah."

"They are both started now," Winterbottom says. "Ernest too."

That was early in the night. Which was a good thing, because it taken a long night for folks to chase them things right and for Henry to lay there and holler, being as Uncle Billy never had none of this here chloryfoam to set Henry's leg with. So it was considerate in Flem to get them started early. And what do you reckon Flem's comment was?

That's right. Nothing. Because he wasn't there. Hadn't nobody see him since that Texas man left.

VI

That was Saturday night. I reckon Mrs. Armstid got home about daylight, to see about the chaps. I don't know where they thought her and Henry was. But lucky the oldest one was a gal, about twelve, big enough to take care of the little ones. Which she did for the next two days. Mrs. Armstid would nurse Henry all night and work in the kitchen for hern and Henry's keep, and in the afternoon she would drive home (it was about four miles) to see to the chaps. She would cook up a pot of victuals and leave it on the stove, and the gal would bar the house and keep the little ones quiet. I would hear Mrs. Littlejohn and Mrs. Armstid talking in the kitchen. "How are the chaps making out?" Mrs. Littlejohn says.

"All right," Mrs. Armstid says.

"Don't they git skeered at night?" Mrs. Littlejohn says.

"Ina May bars the door when I leave," Mrs. Armstid says. "She's got the axe in bed with her. I reckon she can make out."

I reckon they did. And I reckon Mrs. Armstid was waiting for Flem to come back to town; hadn't nobody seen him until this morning; to get her money the Texas man said Flem was keeping for her. Sho. I reckon she was.

Anyway, I heard Mrs. Armstid and Mrs. Littlejohn talking in the kitchen this morning while I was eating breakfast. Mrs. Littlejohn had just told Mrs. Armstid that Flem was in town. "You can ask him for that five dollars," Mrs. Littlejohn says.

"You reckon he'll give it to me?" Mrs. Armstid says.

Mrs. Littlejohn was washing dishes, washing them like a man, like they was made out of iron. "No," she says. "But asking him won't do no hurt. It might shame him. I don't reckon it will, but it might."

"If he wouldn't give it back, it ain't no use to ask," Mrs. Armstid says.

"Suit yourself," Mrs. Littlejohn says. "It's your money."

I could hear the dishes.

"Do you reckon he might give it back to me?" Mrs. Armstid says. "That Texas man said he would. He said I could get it from Mr. Snopes later."

"Then go and ask him for it," Mrs. Littlejohn says.

I could hear the dishes.

"He won't give it back to me," Mrs. Armstid says.

"All right," Mrs. Littlejohn says. "Don't ask him for it, then."

I could hear the dishes; Mrs. Armstid was helping. "You don't reckon he would, do you?" she says. Mrs. Littlejohn never said nothing. It sounded like she was throwing the dishes at one another. "Maybe I better go and talk to Henry about it," Mrs. Armstid says.

"I would," Mrs. Littlejohn says. I be dog if it didn't sound like she had two plates

in her hands, beating them together. "Then
Henry can buy another five-dollar horse with
it. Maybe he'll buy one next time that will
out and out kill him. If I thought that, I'd
give you back the money, myself."

"I reckon I better talk to him first,"
Mrs. Armstid said. Then it sounded like
Mrs. Littlejohn taken up all the dishes and
throwed them at the cook-stove, and I come
away.

That was this morning. I had been up
to Bundren's and back, and I thought that
things would have kind of settled down. So
after breakfast, I went up to the store. And
there was Flem, setting in the store chair and
whittling, like he might not have ever moved
since he come to clerk for Jody Verner.
I. O. was leaning in the door, in his shirt
sleeves and with his hair parted too, same as
Flem was before he turned the clerking job
over to I. O. It's a funny thing about them
Snopes: they all looks alike, yet there ain't ere
a two of them that claims brothers. They're
always just cousins, like Flem and Eck and
Flem and I. O. Eck was there too, squatting
against the wall, him and that boy, eating
cheese and crackers outen a sack; they told
me that Eck hadn't been home a-tall. And
that Lon Quick hadn't got back to town,
even. He followed his horse clean down to
Samson's Bridge, with a wagon and a camp
outfit. Eck finally caught one of hisn. It run
into a blind lane at Freeman's and Eck and
the boy taken and tied their rope across the
end of the lane, about three foot high. The
horse come to the end of the lane and whirled
and run back without ever stopping. Eck says
it never seen the rope a-tall. He says it looked
just like one of these here Christmas pin-
wheels. "Didn't it try to run again?" I says.

"No," Eck says, eating a bite of cheese
offen his knife blade. "Just kicked some."

"Kicked some?" I says.

"It broke its neck," Eck says.

Well, they were squatting there, about
six of them, talking, talking at Flem; never
nobody knowed yet if Flem had ere a interest

in them horses or not. So finally I come right
out and asked him. "Flem's done skun all of
us so much," I says, "that we're proud of him.
Come on, Flem," I says, "how much did you
and that Texas man make offen them horses?
You can tell us. Ain't nobody here but Eck
that bought one of them; the others ain't got
back to town yet, and Eck's your own cousin;
he'll be proud to hear, too. How much did
you-all make?"

They was all whittling, not looking at
Flem, making like they were studying. But
you could a heard a pin drop. And I. O. He
had been rubbing his back up and down on
the door, but he stopped now, watching Flem
like a pointing dog. Flem finished cutting the
silver offen his stick. He spit across the porch,
into the road. "Twarn't none of my horses,"
he says.

I. O. cackled, like a hen, slapping his
legs with both hands. "You boys might just
as well quit trying to get ahead of Flem," he
said.

Well, about that time I see Mrs. Armstid come outen Mrs. Littlejohn's gate, coming up the road. I never said nothing. I says,
"Well, if a man can't take care of himself i
a trade, he can't blame the man that trims
him."

Flem never said nothing, trimming at
the stick. He hadn't seen Mrs. Armstid.
"Yes, sir," I says. "A fellow like Henry Armstid ain't got nobody but hisself to blame."

"Course he ain't," I. O. says. He ain't
seen her, either. "Henry Armstid's a born
fool. Always is been. If Flem hadn't a got
his money, somebody else would."

We looked at Flem. He never moved.
Mrs. Armstid come on up the road.

"That's right," I says. "But come to
think of it, Henry never bought no horse."
We looked at Flem; you could a heard a
match drop. "That Texas man told her to
get five dollars back from Flem next day. I
reckon Flem's done already taken that money
to Mrs. Littlejohn's and give it to Mrs. Armstid."

We watched Flem. I. O. quit rubbing his back against the door again. After a while Flem raised his head and spit across the porch, into the dust. I. O. cackled, just like a hen. "Ain't he a beating fellow, now?" I. O. says.

Mrs. Armstid was getting closer, so I kept on talking, watching to see if Flem would look up and see her. But he never looked up. I went on talking about Tull, about how he was going to sue Flem, and Flem setting there, whittling his stick, not saying nothing else after he said they wasn't none of his horses.

Then I. O. happened to look around. He seen Mrs. Armstid. "Psssst!" he says. Flem looked up. "Here she comes!" I. O. says. "Go out the back. I'll tell her you done went in to town today."

But Flem never moved. He just set there, whittling, and we watched Mrs. Armstid come up onto the porch, in that ere faded sunbonnet and wrapper and them tennis shoes that made a kind of hissing noise on the porch. She come onto the porch and stopped, her hands rolled into her dress in front, not looking at nothing.

"He said Saturday," she says, "that he wouldn't sell Henry no horse. He said I could get the money from you."

Flem looked up. The knife never stopped. It went on trimming off a sliver same as if he was watching it. "He taken that money off with him when he left," Flem says.

Mrs. Armstid never looked at nothing. We never looked at her, neither, expect that boy of Eck's. He had a half-et cracker in his hand, watching her, chewing.

"He said Henry hadn't bought no horse," Mrs. Armstid says. "He said for me to get the money from you today."

"I reckon he forgot about it," Flem said. "He taken that money off with him Saturday." He whittled again. I. O. kept on rubbing his back, slow. He licked his lips. After a while the woman looked up the road, where it went on up the hill, toward the graveyard.

She looked up that way for a while, with that boy of Eck's watching her and I. O. rubbing his back slow against the door. Then she turned back toward the steps.

"I reckon it's time to get dinner started," she says.

"How's Henry this morning, Mrs. Armstid?" Winterbottom says.

She looked at Winterbottom; she almost stopped. "He's resting, I thank you kindly," she says.

Flem got up, outen the chair, putting his knife away. He spit across the porch. "Wait a minute, Mrs. Armstid," he says. She stopped again. She didn't look at him. Flem went on into the store, with I. O. done quit rubbing his back now, with his head craned after Flem, and Mrs. Armstid standing there with her hands rolled into her dress, not looking at nothing. A wagon come up the road and passed; it was Freeman, on the way to town. Then Flem come out again, with I. O. still watching him. Flem had one of these little striped sacks of Jody Varner's candy; I bet he still owes Jody that nickel, too. He put the sack into Mrs. Armstid's hand, like he would have put it into a hollow stump. He spit again across the porch. "A little sweetening for the chaps," he says.

"You're right kind," Mrs. Armstid says. She held the sack of candy in her hand, not looking at nothing. Eck's boy was watching the sack, the half-et cracker in his hand; he wasn't chewing now. He watched Mrs. Armstid roll the sack into her apron. "I reckon I better get on back and help with dinner," she says. She turned and went back across the porch. Flem set down in the chair again and opened his knife. He spit across the porch again, past Mrs. Armstid where she hadn't went down the steps yet. Then she went on, in that ere sunbonnet and wrapper all the same color, back down the road toward Mrs. Littlejohn's. You couldn't see her dress move, like a natural woman walking. She looked like a old snag still standing up and moving along on a high water. We watched her turn in at Mrs. Littlejohn's and go outen sight. Flem was whittling. I. O. begun to rub his back on the door. Then he begun to cackle, just like a durn hen.

"You boys might just as well quit trying," I. O. says. "You can't git ahead of Flem. You can't touch him. Ain't he a sight, now?"

I be dog if he ain't. If I had brung a herd of wild cattymounts into town and sold them to my neighbors and kinfolks, they would have lynched me. Yes, sir.

EXERCISES

1. Describe the character of Flem Snopes. Describe the other important characters in this story. Does this lead you to some idea of the basic conflict?
2. What is the attitude of the narrator toward Flem?
3. What is the quality of the humor here? Is it subtle? Ironical? Extravagant? Satirical? Indulgent and sympathetic? If sympathetic, then sympathetic to whom? How is the quality of the humor (which may, in fact, be mixed of various kinds) related to the society of the story? Contrast the humor here to that in James Purdy's "Daddy Wolf" (sec. 10).

4. Imagine this story as related by the objective omniscient third-person narrator (see sec. 1). What would be the difference in effect? How might this change modify the humor? What is the present narrator's evaluation of Flem? Does it differ from the evaluation any other characters may have of Flem? Does it differ from your own evaluation of him?
5. Is this story merely a piece of humor—of rural high jinks? If not, what else do you find in it, what other feelings and attitudes? Does the humor run counter to such feelings and attitudes? If so, is this an ineptitude on the part of the author? Compare "Spotted Horses" with "Daddy Wolf" in this respect.
6. Mrs. Armstid is a pathetic figure. She has suffered real loss in the injury of her husband, and she is so poor that she cannot afford to lose the $5. Why has the author put her into the story and made her appearance the more emphatic by putting her at the end of the story? What effect does it have upon the humor? What effect does it have upon the meaning of the story as a whole?
7. Can it be said that "Spotted Horses" might, as far as the general feel and the structure are concerned, be grouped with the stories in section 3? What points of similarity do you find with "Jerico, Jerico, Jerico" (sec. 10)? With "The Lagoon," by Joseph Conrad (sec. 10)?
8. How intimately is "place" connected with this story? Explain in detail. What about the events and the reaction to the events? What about the language? What about the tone of the telling?

Section 7

PLOT AND COMPLEXITY OF MOVEMENT: POINT OF VIEW AND MEANING

The stories in this section do not move in a more or less straight line toward a single decisive turn to mark the denouement, as in, for instance, "The Use of Force." There is, instead, a complexity in their very conception. Our concern here is to see how such complexities are related to the meaning of a story. Especially, we are concerned with the relation of the point of view to the meaning.

I'M A FOOL
Sherwood Anderson (1876–1941)

It was a hard jolt for me, one of the most bitterest I ever had to face. And it all came about through my own foolishness, too. Even yet sometimes, when I think of it, I want to cry or swear or kick myself. Perhaps, even now, after all this time, there will be a kind of satisfaction in making myself look cheap by telling of it.

It began at three o'clock one October afternoon as I sat in the grand stand at the fall trotting and pacing meet at Sandusky, Ohio.

To tell the truth, I felt a little foolish that I should be sitting in the grand stand at all. During the summer before I had left my home town with Harry Whitehead and, with a nigger named Burt, had taken a job as swipe with one of the two horses Harry was campaigning through the fall race meets that year. Mother cried and my sister Mildred, who wanted to get a job as a school teacher in our town that fall, stormed and scolded about the house all during the week before I left. They both thought it was something disgraceful that one of our family should take a place as a swipe with race horses. I've an idea Mildred thought my taking the place would stand in the way of her getting the job she'd been working so long for.

But after all I had to work, and there was no other work to be got. A big lumbering fellow of nineteen couldn't just hang around the house and I had got too big to mow people's lawns and sell newspapers. Little chaps who could get next to people's sympathies by their sizes were always getting jobs away from me. There was one fellow who kept saying to everyone who wanted a lawn mowed or a cistern cleaned, that he was saving money to work his way through college, and I used to lay awake nights thinking up ways to injure him without being found out. I kept thinking of wagons running over him and bricks falling on his head as he walked along the street. But never mind him.

I got the place with Harry and I liked Burt fine. We got along splendid together. He was a big nigger with a lazy sprawling body and soft, kind eyes, and when it came to a fight he could hit like Jack Johnson. He had Bucephalus, a big black pacing stallion that could do 2.09 or 2.10, if he had to, and I had a little gelding named Doctor Fritz that never lost a race all fall when Harry wanted him to win.

We set out from home late in July in a box car with the two horses and after that, until late November, we kept moving along to the race meets and the fairs. It was a peachey time for me, I'll say that. Sometimes now I think that boys who are raised regular in houses, and never have a fine nigger like Burt for best friend, and go to high schools and college, and never steal anything, or get drunk a little, or learn to swear from fellows who know how, or come walking up in front of a grand stand in their shirt sleeves and with dirty horsy pants on when the races are going on and the grand stand is full of people all dressed up—What's the use of talking about it? Such fellows don't know nothing at all. They've never had no opportunity.

But I did. Burt taught me how to rub down a horse and put the bandages on after a race and steam a horse out and a lot of valuable things for any man to know. He could wrap a bandage on a horse's leg so smooth that if it had been the same color you would think it was his skin, and I guess he'd have been a big driver, too, and got to the top like Murphy and Walter Cox and the others if he hadn't been black.

Gee whizz, it was fun. You got to a county seat town, maybe say on a Saturday or Sunday, and the fair began the next Tuesday and lasted until Friday afternoon. Doctor Fritz would be, say in the 2.25 trot on Tuesday afternoon and on Thursday afternoon Bucephalus would knock 'em cold in the "free-for-all" pace. It left you a lot of time to hang around and listen to horse talk, and see Burt knock some yap cold that got too gay, and you'd find out about horses and men and pick up a lot of stuff you could use all the rest of your life, if you had some sense and salted down what you heard and felt and saw.

And then at the end of the week when the race meet was over, and Harry had run home to tend up to his livery stable business, you and Burt hitched the two horses to carts and drove slow and steady across country, to the place for the next meeting, so as to not overheat the horses, etc., etc., you know.

Gee whizz, Gosh amighty, the nice hickory-nut and beechnut and oaks and other kinds of trees along the roads, all brown and red, and the good smells, and Burt singing a song that was called Deep River, and all the country girls at the windows of houses and everything. You can stick your colleges up your nose for all me. I guess I know where I got my education.

Why, one of those little burgs of towns you come to on the way, say now on a Saturday afternoon, and Burt says, "let's lay up here." And you did.

And you took the horses to a livery stable and fed them, and you got your good clothes out of a box and put them on.

And the town was full of farmers gaping, because they could see you were race horse people, and the kids maybe never see a nigger before and was afraid and run away when the two of us walked down their main street.

And that was before prohibition and all that foolishness, and so you went into a saloon, the two of you, and all the yaps come and stood around, and there was always someone pretended he was horsy and knew things and spoke up and began asking questions, and all you did was to lie and lie all you could about what horses you had, and I said I owned them, and then some fellow said, "Will you have a drink of whiskey" and Burt knocked his eye out the way he could say, off-hand like, "Oh well, all right, I'm agreeable to a little nip. I'll split a quart with you." Gee whizz.

But that isn't what I want to tell my story about. We got home late in November and I promised mother I'd quit the race horses for good. There's a lot of things you've got to promise a mother because she don't know any better.

And so, there not being any work in our town any more than when I left there to go to the races, I went off to Sandusky and got a pretty good place taking care of horses for a man who owned a teaming and delivery and storage and coal and real estate business there. It was a pretty good place with good eats, and a day off each week, and sleeping on a cot in a big barn, and mostly just shovelling in hay and oats to a lot of big good-enough skates of horses, that couldn't have trotted a race with a toad. I wasn't dissatisfied and I could send money home.

And then, as I started to tell you, the fall races come to Sandusky and I got the day off and I went. I left the job at noon and had on my good clothes and my new brown derby hat, I'd just bought the Saturday before, and a stand-up collar.

First of all I went down-town and walked about with the dudes. I've always thought to myself, "put up a good front" and so I did it. I had forty dollars in my pocket and so I went into the West House, a big hotel, and walked up to the cigar stand. "Give me three twenty-five cent cigars," I said. There was a lot of horsemen and strangers and dressed-up people from other towns standing around in the lobby and in the bar, and I mingled amongst them. In the bar there was a fellow with a cane and a Windsor tie on, that it made me sick to look at him. I like a man to be a man and dress up, but not to go put on that kind of airs. So I pushed him aside, kind of rough, and had me a drink of whiskey. And then he looked at me, as though he thought maybe he'd get gay, but he changed his mind and didn't say anything. And then I had another drink of whiskey, just to show him something, and went out and had a hack out to the races, all to myself, and when I got there I bought myself the best seat I could get up in the grand stand, but didn't go in for any of these boxes. That's putting on too many airs.

And so there I was, sitting up in the grand stand as gay as you please and looking down on the swipes coming out with their horses, and with their dirty horsy pants on and the horse blankets swung over their shoulders, same as I had been doing all the year before. I liked one thing about the same as the other, sitting up there and feeling grand and being down there and looking up at the yaps and feeling grander and more important, too. One thing's about as good as another, if you take it just right. I've often said that.

Well, right in front of me, in the grand stand that day, there was a fellow with a couple of girls and they was about my age. The young fellow was a nice guy all right. He was the kind maybe that goes to college and then comes to be a lawyer or maybe a newspaper editor or something like that, but he wasn't stuck on himself. There are some of that kind are all right and he was one of the ones.

He had his sister with him and another girl and the sister looked around over his shoulder, accidental at first, not intending to start anything—she wasn't that kind—and her eyes and mine happened to meet.

You know how it is. Gee, she was a peach! She had on a soft dress, kind of a blue stuff and it looked carelessly made, but was well sewed and made and everything. I knew that much. I blushed when she looked right at me and so did she. She was the nicest girl I've ever seen in my life. She wasn't stuck on herself and she could talk proper grammar without being like a school teacher or something like that. What I mean, is, she was O.K. I think maybe her father was well-to-do, but not rich to make her chesty because she was his daughter, as some are. Maybe he owned a drug store or a dry-goods store in their home town, or something like that. She never told me and I never asked.

My own people are all O.K. too, when you come to that. My grandfather was Welsh and over in the old country, in Wales he was ——But never mind that.

The first heat of the first race came off and the young fellow setting there with the two girls left them and went down to make a bet. I knew what he was up to, but he didn't talk big and noisy and let everyone around know he was a sport, as some do. He wasn't that kind. Well, he come back and I heard him tell the two girls what horse he'd bet on, and when the heat trotted they all half got to their feet and acted in the excited, sweaty way people do when they've got money down on a race, and the horse they bet on is up there pretty close at the end, and they think maybe he'll come on with a rush, but he never does because he hasn't got the old juice in him, come right down to it.

And then, pretty soon, the horses came out for the 2.18 pace and there was a horse in it I knew. He was a horse Bob French had in his string but Bob didn't own him. He was a horse owned by a Mr. Mathers down at Marietta, Ohio.

This Mr. Mathers had a lot of money and owned some coal mines or something and he had a swell place out in the country, and he was struck on race horses, but was a Presbyterian or something, and I think more than likely his wife was one, too, maybe a stiffer one than himself. So he never raced his horses hisself, and the story round the Ohio race tracks was that when one of his horses got ready to go to the races he turned him over to Bob French and pretended to his wife he was sold.

So Bob had the horses and he did pretty much as he pleased and you can't blame Bob, at least, I never did. Sometimes he was out to win and sometimes he wasn't. I never cared much about that when I was swiping a horse. What I did want to know was that my horse had the speed and could go out in front, if you wanted him to.

And, as I'm telling you, there was Bob in this race with one of Mr. Mathers' horses, was named "About Ben Ahem" or something like that, and was fast as a streak. He was a gelding and had a mark of 2.21, but could step in .08 or .09.

Because when Burt and I were out, as I've told you, the year before, there was a nigger, Burt knew, worked for Mr. Mathers and we went out there one day when we didn't have no race on at the Marietta Fair and our boss Harry was gone home.

And so everyone was gone to the fair but just this one nigger and he took us all through Mr. Mathers' swell house and he and Burt tapped a bottle of wine Mr. Mathers had hid in his bedroom, back in a closet, without his wife knowing, and he showed us this Ahem horse. Burt was always struck on being a driver but didn't have much chance to get to the top, being a nigger, and he and the other nigger gulped the whole bottle of wine and Burt got a little lit up.

So the nigger let Burt take this About Ben Ahem and step him a mile in a track Mr. Mathers had all to himself, right there on the farm. And Mr. Mathers had one child, a daughter, kinda sick and not very good looking, and she came home and we had to hustle and get About Ben Ahem stuck back in the barn.

I'm only telling you to get everything straight. At Sandusky, that afternoon I was at the fair, this young fellow with the two girls was fussed, being with the girls and losing his bet. You know how a fellow is that way. One of them was his girl and the other his sister. I had figured that out.

"Gee whizz," I says to myself, "I'm going to give him the dope."

He was mighty nice when I touched him on the shoulder. He and the girls were nice to me right from the start and clear to the end. I'm not blaming them.

And so he leaned back and I give him the dope on About Ben Ahem. "Don't bet a cent on this first heat because he'll go like an oxen hitched to a plow, but when the first heat is over go right down and lay on your pile." That's what I told him.

Well, I never saw a fellow treat any one sweller. There was a fat man sitting beside the little girl, that had looked at me twice by this time, and I at her, and both blushing, and what did he do but have the nerve to turn and ask the fat man to get up and change places with me so I could set with his crowd.

Gee whizz, craps amighty. There I was. What a chump I was to go and get gay up there in the West House bar, and just because that dude was standing there with a cane and that kind of a necktie on, to go and get all balled up and drink that whiskey, just to show off.

Of course she would know, me setting right beside her and letting her smell of my breath. I could have kicked myself right down out of that grand stand and all around that race track and made a faster record than most of the skates of horses they had there that year.

Because that girl wasn't any mutt of a girl. What wouldn't I have give right then for a stick of chewing gum to chew, or a lozenger, or some licorice, or most anything. I was glad I had those twenty-five cent cigars in my pocket and right away I give that fellow one and lit one myself. Then that fat man got up and we changed places and there I was, plunked right down beside her.

They introduced themselves and the fellow's best girl, he had with him, was named Miss Elinor Woodbury, and her father was a manufacturer of barrels from a place called Tiffin, Ohio. And the fellow himself was named Wilbur Wessen and his sister was Miss Lucy Wessen.

I suppose it was their having such swell names that got me off my trolley. A fellow, just because he has been a swipe with a race horse, and works taking care of horses for a man in the teaming, delivery, and storage business isn't any better or worse than any one else. I've often thought that, and said it too.

But you know how a fellow is. There's something in that kind of nice clothes, and the kind of nice eyes she had, and the way she had looked at me, awhile before, over her brother's shoulder, and me looking back at her, and both of us blushing.

I couldn't show her up for a boob, could I?

I made a fool of myself, that's what I did. I said my name was Walter Mathers from Marietta, Ohio, and then I told all three of them the smashingest lie you ever heard. What I said was that my father owned the horse About Ben Ahem and that he had let him out to this Bob French for racing purposes, because our family was proud and had never gone into racing that way, in our own name, I mean. Then I had got started and they were all leaning over and listening, and Miss Lucy Wessen's eyes were shining, and I went the whole hog.

I told about our place down at Marietta, and about the big stables and the grand brick house we had on a hill, up above the Ohio River, but I knew enough not to do it in no bragging way. What I did was to start things and then let them drag the rest out of me. I acted just as reluctant to tell as I could. Our family hasn't got any barrel factory, and since I've known us, we've always been pretty poor, but not asking anything of any one at that, and my grandfather, over in Wales—but never mind that.

We set there talking like we had known each other for years and years, and I went and told them that my father had been expecting maybe this Bob French wasn't on the square, and had sent me up to Sandusky on the sly to find out what I could.

And I bluffed it through I had found out all about the 2.18 pace, in which About Ben Ahem was to start.

I said he would lose the first heat by pacing like a lame cow and then he would come back and skin 'em alive after that. And to back up what I said I took thirty dollars out of my pocket and handed it to Mr. Wilbur Wessen and asked him, would he mind, after the first heat, to go down and place it on About Ben Ahem for whatever odds he could get. What I said was that I didn't want Bob French to see me and none of the swipes.

Sure enough the first heat come off and About Ben Ahem went off his stride, up the back stretch, and looked like a wooden horse or a sick one, and come in to be last. Then this Wilbur Wessen went down to the betting place under the grand stand and there I was

with the two girls, and when that Miss Woodbury was looking the other way once, Lucy Wessen kinda, with her shoulder you know, kinda touched me. Not just tucking down, I don't mean. You know how a woman can do. They get close, but not getting gay either. You know what they do. Gee whizz.

And then they give me a jolt. What they had done, when I didn't know, was to get together, and they had decided Wilbur Wessen would bet fifty dollars, and the two girls had gone and put in ten dollars each, of their own money, too. I was sick then, but I was sicker later.

About the gelding, About Ben Ahem, and their winning their money, I wasn't worried a lot about that. It come out O.K. Ahem stepped the next three heats like a bushel of spoiled eggs going to market before they could be found out, and Wilbur Wessen had got nine to two for the money. There was something else eating at me.

Because Wilbur come back, after he had bet the money, and after that he spent most of his time talking to that Miss Woodbury, and Lucy Wessen and I was left alone together like on a desert island. Gee, if I'd only been on the square or if there had been any way of getting myself on the square. There ain't any Walter Mathers, like I said to her and them, and there hasn't ever been one, but if there was, I bet I'd go to Marietta, Ohio, and shoot him tomorrow.

There I was, big boob that I am. Pretty soon the race was over, and Wilbur had gone down and collected our money, and we had a hack down-town, and he stood us a swell supper at the West House, and a bottle of champagne beside.

And I was with that girl and she wasn't saying much, and I wasn't saying much either. One thing I know. She wasn't stuck on me because of the lie about my father being rich and all that. There's a way you know. . . . Craps amighty. There's a kind of girl, you see just once in your life, and if you don't get busy and make hay, then you're gone for good and all, and might as well go jump off a bridge. They give you a look from inside of them somewhere, and it ain't no vamping, and what it means is—you want that girl to be your wife, and you want nice things around her like flowers and swell clothes, and you want her to have the kids you're going to have, and you want good music played and no rag time. Gee whizz.

There's a place over near Sandusky, across a kind of bay, and it's called Cedar Point. And after we had supper we went over to it in a launch, all by ourselves. Wilbur and Miss Lucy and that Miss Woodbury had to catch a ten o'clock train back to Tiffin, Ohio, because, when you're out with girls like that you can't get careless and miss any trains and stay out all night, like you can with some kinds of Janes.

And Wilbur blowed himself to the launch and it cost him fifteen cold plunks, but I wouldn't never have knew if I hadn't listened. He wasn't no tin horn kind of a sport.

Over at the Cedar Point place, we didn't stay around where there was a gang of common kind of cattle at all.

There was big dance halls and dining places for yaps, and there was a beach you would walk along and get where it was dark, and we went there.

She didn't talk hardly at all and neither did I, and I was thinking how glad I was my mother was all right, and always made us kids learn to eat with a fork at table, and not swill soup, and not be noisy and rough like a gang you see around a race track that way.

Then Wilbur and his girl went away up the beach and Lucy and I sat down in a dark place, where there was some roots of old trees, the water had washed up, and after that the time, till we had to go back in the launch and they had to catch their trains, wasn't nothing at all. It went like winking your eye.

Here's how it was. The place we were setting in was dark, like I said, and there was the roots from that old stump sticking up like arms, and there was a watery smell, and the

night was like—as if you could put your hand out and feel it—so warm and soft and dark and sweet like an orange.

I most cried and I most swore and I most jumped up and danced, I was so mad and happy and sad.

When Wilbur come back from being alone with his girl, and she saw him coming, Lucy she says, "we got to go to the train now," and she was most crying too, but she never knew nothing I knew, and she couldn't be so all busted up. And then, before Wilbur and Miss Woodbury got up to where we was, she put her face up and kissed me quick and put her head up against me and she was all quivering and—Gee whizz.

Sometimes I hope I have cancer and die. I guess you know what I mean. We went in the launch across the bay to the train like that, and it was dark, too. She whispered and said it was like she and I could get out of the boat and walk on the water, and it sounded foolish, but I knew what she meant.

And then quick we were right at the depot, and there was a big gang of yaps, the kind that goes to the fairs, and crowded and milling around like cattle, and how could I tell her? "It won't be long because you'll write and I'll write to you." That's all she said.

I got a chance like a haybarn afire. A swell chance I got.

And maybe she would write me, down at Marietta that way, and the letter would come back, and stamped on the front of it by the U.S.A. "there ain't any such guy," or something like that, whatever they stamp on a letter that way.

And me trying to pass myself off for a big-bug and a swell—to her, as decent a little body as God ever made. Craps amighty—a swell chance I got!

And then the train come in, and she got on it, and Wilbur Wessen, he come and shook hands with me, and that Miss Woodbury was nice too and bowed to me, and I at her, and the train went and I busted out and cried like a kid.

Gee, I could have run after that train and made Dan Patch look like a freight train after a wreck but, socks amighty, what was the use? Did you ever see such a fool?

I'll bet you what—if I had an arm broke right now or a train had run over my foot—I wouldn't go to no doctor at all. I'd go set down and let her hurt and hurt—that's what I'd do.

I'll bet you what—if I hadn't a drunk that booze I'd a never been such a boob as to go tell such a lie—that couldn't never be made straight to a lady like her.

I wish I had that fellow right here that had on a Windsor tie and carried a cane. I'd smash him for fair. Gosh darn his eyes. He's a big fool—that's what he is.

And if I'm not another you just go find me one and I'll quit working and be a bum and give him my job. I don't care nothing for working, and earning money, and saving it for no such boob as myself.

EXERCISES

1. "I'm a Fool" shows a boy being brought to a poignant moment of self-knowledge. What does the boy find out about himself? And what are the stages through which he passes on the way to self-knowledge?
2. For this story to be effective we must have a sympathy with the boy, an awareness, too, of the subtle stages through which he reaches his self-knowledge. That is, his character must be felt in its inwardness. In what ways does the fact that "I'm a Fool" is told in the first person help to achieve this effect? How much does the idiom in which the boy speaks promote the effect desired? What other elements are involved?

Try to imagine the story told by the objective omniscient narrator (see "points of view" in the Glossary), such as we find in "La Lupa" and "The Lottery Ticket." What might be the difference in effect? For one thing, what might be the difference in our feeling of identification with the character, and in our sense of place and society? For another, the difference in the amount of objective exposition required?

What is gained by the fact that the boy's self-knowledge is not clearly stated, by the fact that, in a way, he is only fumbling to come to

grips with it? We see here, then, a case in which the reader sees more clearly, and could articulate more readily, what the hero is struggling to understand. What is the effect of this ironical situation?
3. Again read "Daddy Wolf" by James Purdy (sec. 10). What is our attitude toward the main character?

ARABY

James Joyce (1882–1941)

North Richmond Street, being blind, was a quiet street except at the hour when the Christian Brothers' School set the boys free. An uninhabited house of two stories stood at the blind end, detached from its neighbors in a square ground. The other houses of the street, conscious of decent lives within them, gazed at one another with brown imperturbable faces.

The former tenant of our house, a priest, had died in the back drawing-room. Air, musty from having been long enclosed, hung in all the rooms, and the waste room behind the kitchen was littered with old useless papers. Among these I found a few paper-covered books, the pages of which were curled and damp: *The Abbot*, by Walter Scott, *The Devout Communicant*, and *The Memoirs of Vidocq*. I liked the last best, because its leaves were yellow. The wild garden behind the house contained a central apple tree and a few straggling bushes, under one of which I found the late tenant's rusty bicycle-pump. He had been a very charitable priest; in his will he had left all his money to institutions and the furniture of his house to his sister.

When the short days of winter came, dusk fell before we had well eaten our dinners. When we met in the street, the houses had grown sombre. The space of sky above us was the color of ever-changing violet, and towards it the lamps of the street lifted their feeble lanterns. The cold air stung us and we played till our bodies glowed. Our shouts echoed in the silent street. The career of our play brought us through the dark muddy lanes behind the houses where we ran the gauntlet of the rough tribes from the cottages, to the back doors of the dark dripping gardens where odors arose from the ashpits, to the dark odorous stables where a coachman smoothed and combed the horse or shook music from the buckled harness. When we returned to the street, if uncle was seen turning the corner, we hid in the shadow until we had seen him safely housed. Or if Mangan's sister came out on the doorstep to call her brother in to his tea, we watched her from our shadow peer up and down the street. We waited to see whether she would remain or go in, and, if she remained, we left our shadow and walked up to Mangan's steps resignedly. She was waiting for us, her figure defined by the light from the half-opened door. Her brother always teased her before he obeyed, and I stood by the railings looking at her. Her dress swung as she moved her body, and the soft rope of her hair tossed from side to side.

Every morning I lay on the floor in the front parlor watching her door. The blind was pulled down to within an inch of the sash, so that I could not be seen. When she came out on the doorstep my heart leaped. I ran to the hall, seized my books, and followed her. I kept her brown figure always in my eye, and, when we came near the point at which our ways diverged, I quickened my pace and passed her. This happened morning after morning. I had never spoken to her, except for a few casual words, and yet her name was like a summons to all my foolish blood.

Her image accompanied me even in places the most hostile to romance. On Saturday evenings, when my aunt went marketing, I had to go to carry some of the parcels. We walked through the flaring streets, jostled by drunken men and bargaining women, amid the curses of laborers, the shrill litanies of shop-boys, who stood on guard by the barrels of pigs' cheeks, the nasal chanting of street-singers, who sang a *come-all-you* about

O'Donovan Rossa, or a ballad about the troubles in our native land. These noises converged in a single sensation of life for me: I imagined that I bore my chalice safely through a throng of foes. Her name sprang to my lips at moments in strange prayers and praises which I myself did not understand. My eyes were often full of tears (I could not tell why) and at times a flood from my heart seemed to pour itself out into my bosom. I thought little of the future. I did not know whether I would ever speak to her or not, or, if I spoke to her, how I could tell her of my confused adoration. But my body was like a harp, and her words and gestures were like fingers running upon the wires.

One evening I went into the back drawing-room, in which the priest had died. It was a dark rainy evening, and there was no sound in the house. Through one of the broken panes I heard the rain impinge upon the earth, the fine incessant needles of water playing in the sodden beds. Some distant lamp or lighted window gleamed below me. I was thankful that I could see so little. All my senses seemed to desire to veil themselves, and, feeling that I was about to slip from them, I pressed the palms of my hands together until they trembled, murmuring: *"O love! O love!"* many times.

At last she spoke to me. When she addressed the first words to me, I was so confused that I did not know what to answer. She asked me was I going to *Araby*. I forget whether I answered yes or no. It would be a splendid bazaar; she said she would love to go.

"And why can't you?" I asked.

While she spoke, she turned a silver bracelet round and round her wrist. She could not go, she said, because there would be a retreat that week in her convent. Her brother and two other boys were fighting for their caps, and I was alone at the railings. She held one of the spikes, bowing her head towards me. The light from the lamp opposite our door caught the white curve of her neck, lit up her hair that rested there, and, falling, lit up the hand upon the railing. It fell over one side of her dress and caught the white border of a petticoat, just visible as she stood at ease.

"It's well for you," she said.

"If I go," I said, "I will bring you something."

What innumerable follies laid waste my waking and sleeping thoughts after that evening! I wished to annihilate the tedious intervening days. I chafed against the work of school. At night in my bedroom and by day in the classroom her image came between me and the page I strove to read. The syllables of the word *Araby* were called to me through the silence in which my soul luxuriated and cast an Eastern enchantment over me. I asked for leave to go to the bazaar on Saturday night. My aunt was surprised and hoped it was not some Freemason affair. I answered few questions in class. I watched my master's face pass from amiability to sternness; he hoped I was not beginning to idle. I could not call my wandering thoughts together. I had hardly any patience with the serious work of life, which, now that it stood between me and my desire, seemed to me child's play, ugly monotonous child's play.

On Saturday morning I reminded my uncle that I wished to go to the bazaar in the evening. He was fussing at the hallstand looking for the hat-brush, and answered me curtly:

"Yes, boy, I know."

As he was in the hall, I could not go into the front parlor and lie at the window. I left the house in bad humor and walked slowly towards the school. The air was pitilessly raw, and already my heart misgave me.

When I came home to dinner, my uncle had not yet been home. Still, it was early. I sat staring at the clock for some time, and, when its ticking began to irritate me, I left the room. I mounted the staircase and gained the upper part of the house. The high cold empty gloomy rooms liberated me and I went from room to room singing. From the front window I saw my companions playing below in the street. Their cries reached me weakened and indistinct, and, leaning my forehead against the cool glass, I looked over at the dark house where she lived. I may have stood there for an hour, seeing nothing but the brown-clad figure cast by my imagination, touched discreetly by the lamplight at the curved neck, at the hand upon the railings, and at the border below the dress.

When I came downstairs again, I found Mrs. Mercer sitting at the fire. She was an old garrulous woman, a pawn-broker's widow, who collected used stamps for some pious purpose. I had to endure the gossip of the tea-table. The meal was prolonged beyond an hour, and still my uncle did not come. Mrs. Mercer stood up to go: she was sorry she couldn't wait any longer, but it was after eight o'clock and she did not like to be out late, as the night air was bad for her. When she had gone, I began to walk up and down the room, clenching my fists. My aunt said:

"I'm afraid you may put off your bazaar for this night of Our Lord."

At nine o'clock I heard my uncle's latch-key in the hall-door. I heard him talking to himself and heard the hallstand rocking when it had received the weight of his overcoat. I could interpret these signs. When he was midway through his dinner, I asked him to give me the money to go to the bazaar. He had forgotten.

"The people are in bed and after their first sleep now," he said.

I did not smile. My aunt said to him energetically:

"Can't you give him the money and let him go? You've kept him late enough as it is."

My uncle said he was very sorry he had forgotten. He said he believed in the old saying: "All work and no play makes Jack a dull boy." He asked me where I was going, and, when I had told him a second time, he asked me did I know *The Arab's Farewell to His Steed*. When I left the kitchen, he was about to recite the opening lines of the piece to my aunt.

I held a florin tightly in my hand as I strode down Buckingham Street towards the station. The sight of the streets thronged with buyers and glaring with gas recalled to me the purpose of my journey. I took my seat in a third-class carriage of a deserted train. After an intolerable delay the train moved out of the station slowly. It crept onward among ruinous houses and over the twinkling river. At Westland Row Station a crowd of people pressed to the carriage doors; but the porters moved them back, saying that it was a special train for the bazaar. I remained alone in the bare carriage. In a few minutes the train drew up beside an improvised wooden platform. I passed out on to the road and saw by the lighted dial of a clock that it was ten minutes to ten. In front of me was a large building which displayed the magical name.

I could not find any sixpenny entrance, and, fearing that the bazaar would be closed, I passed in quickly through a turnstile, handing a shilling to a weary-looking man. I found myself in a big hall girdled at half its height by a gallery. Nearly all the stalls were closed and the greater part of the hall was in darkness. I recognized a silence like that which pervades a church after a service. I walked into the center of the bazaar timidly. A few people were gathered about the stalls which were still open. Before a curtain, over which the words *Café Chantant* were written in colored lamps, two men were counting money on a salver. I listened to the fall of the coins.

Remembering with difficulty why I had come, I went over to one of the stalls and examined porcelain vases and flowered tea-sets. At the door of the stall a young lady was talking and laughing with two young gentlemen. I remarked their English accents and listened vaguely to their conversation.

"O, I never said such a thing!"
"O, but you did!"
"O, but I didn't!"
"Didn't she say that?"
"Yes. I heard her."
"O, there's a . . . fib!"

Observing me, the young lady came over and asked me did I wish to buy anything. The tone of her voice was not encouraging; she seemed to have spoken to me out of a sense of duty. I looked humbly at the great jars that stood like eastern guards at either side of the dark entrance to the stall and murmured:

"No, thank you."

The young lady changed the position of one of the vases and went back to the two young men. They began to talk of the same subject. Once or twice the young lady glanced at me over her shoulder.

I lingered before her stall, though I knew my stay was useless, to make my interest in her wares seem the more real. Then I turned away slowly and walked down the middle of the bazaar. I allowed the two pennies to fall against the sixpence in my pocket. I heard a voice call from one end of the gallery that the light was out. The upper part of the hall was now completely dark.

Gazing up into the darkness, I saw myself as a creature driven and derided by vanity; and my eyes burned with anguish and anger.

EXERCISES

1. What do you think accounts for the fact that the editors of this book place "Araby" with "I'm a Fool"? Allowing for differences, what elements, in content or method, make the association logical?
2. This section, as we have said, presents relatively complex stories. But at first glance, "Araby" seems simple, a story with few and obvious stages of complication: the growth of the boy's secret feeling for the girl, then the trip to the bazaar, to which the story has been directed from early on, and then the disappointment when he stands in the great empty building as the lights go down. This is all we have if we take the story at the time of the event—that is, if it were related, as in the case of "I'm a Fool," by the hero at the age when the story occurs. In fact, it would be hard to find much meaning in the story if it were presented in that way. It would be little more than an anecdote of disappointment in calf love, with no general reference of meaning.

But the story, though in the first person, is not in the language of the schoolboy who has fallen in love with the girl next door. The story is written with a full range of sophisticated literary effects, presumably long after the event, when the narrator has grown up, become a writer of achievement, and has passed through experiences of adult manhood. In other words, we have here a complex variant of the first-person narrator, very different in function from that in "I'm a Fool" or "Spotted Horses" (sec. 6).

How, then, does this particular use of the first-person narrator relate to the meaning of the story? In other words, what significance does the boyhood event now have for the man? What does it stand for?

3. One of the sophisticated literary effects here depends on the use of imagery and metaphor. There is a religious background for the story (it is Catholic Ireland), and much of the imagery is religious. Locate such items. What is their significance for the meaning of the story? In what way does the narrator associate religion and love? For one thing, the bazaar is like a temple. In that case, what does the counting of money signify? It is, in fact, a biblical allusion. What, too, are we to make of the banal conversation of the girl and the young men in the "temple"? How does this relate to the general meaning?

4. In "Bad Characters," as in "Araby," the lapse of time between the event narrated and the time of narration is important. Explain. Furthermore, what is gained by the use of a narrator in both these stories as a device for selecting elements from the action on which the story is based?

5. Read "In Dreams Begin Responsibilities" by Delmore Schwartz (sec. 10). Here, in the form of a dream, the main character looks back, not on an episode of his own early youth, but on the story of his parents when they were young. What is the meaning of this story? How would you compare it to "Araby" in method and meaning?

6. Return to "Legal Aid" (sec. 5). It, like "Araby," is a story about love. But how does its meaning compare with that of "Araby"? Could "Legal Aid" have well been told by one of the main characters in the first person and keep the same meaning and the same attitude toward love?

HAIRCUT

Ring Lardner (1885–1933)

I got another barber that comes over from Carterville and helps me out Saturdays, but the rest of the time I can get along all right alone. You can see for yourself that this ain't no New York City and besides that, the most of the boys works all day and don't have no leisure to drop in here and get themselves prettied up.

You're a newcomer, ain't you? I thought I hadn't seen you round before. I hope you like it good enough to stay. As I say, we ain't no New York City or Chicago, but we have pretty good times. Not as good, though, since Jim Kendall got killed. When he was alive, him and Hod Meyers used to keep this town in an uproar. I bet they was more laughin' done here than any town its size in America.

Jim was comical, and Hod was pretty near a match for him. Since Jim's gone, Hod tries to hold his end up just the same as ever, but it's tough goin' when you ain't got nobody to kind of work with.

They used to be plenty fun in here Saturdays. This place is jam-packed Saturdays, from four o'clock on. Jim and Hod would show up right after their supper, round six o'clock. Jim would set himself down in that big chair, nearest the blue spittoon. Whoever had been settin' in that chair, why they'd get up when Jim come in and give it to him.

You'd have thought it was a reserved seat like they have sometimes in a theayter. Hod would generally always stand or walk up and down, or some Saturdays, of course, he'd be settin' in this chair part of the time, gettin' a haircut.

Well, Jim would set there a'wile without openin' his mouth only to spit, and then finally he'd say to me, "Whitey,"—my right name, that is, my right first name, is Dick, but everybody round here calls me Whitey —Jim would say, "Whitey, your nose looks like a rosebud tonight. You must of been drinkin' some of your aw de cologne."

So I'd say, "No, Jim, but you look like you'd been drinkin' somethin' of that kind or somethin' worse."

Jim would have to laugh at that, but then he'd speak up and say, "No, I ain't had nothin' to drink, but that ain't sayin' I wouldn't like somethin'. I wouldn't even mind if it were alcohol."

Then Hod Meyers would say, "Neither would your wife." That would set everybody to laughin' because Jim and his wife wasn't on very good terms. She'd of divorced him only they wasn't no chance to get alimony and she didn't have no way to take care of herself and the kids. She couldn't never understand Jim. He *was* kind of rough, but a good fella at heart.

Him and Hod had all kinds of sport with Milt Sheppard. I don't suppose you've seen Milt. Well, he's got an Adam's apple that looks more like a mushmelon. So I'd be shavin' Milt and when I'd start to shave down here on his neck, Hod would holler, "Hey, Whitey, wait a minute! Before you cut into it, let's make up a pool and see who can guess closest to the number of seeds."

And Jim would say, "If Milt hadn't of been so hoggish, he'd of ordered a half a cantaloupe instead of a whole one and it might not of stuck in his throat."

All the boys would roar at this and Milt himself would force a smile, though the joke was on him. Jim certainly was a card!

There's his shavin' mug, settin' on the shelf, right next to Charley Vail's. "Charles M. Vail." That's the druggist. He comes in regular for his shave, three times a week. And Jim's is the cup next to Charley's. "James H. Kendall." Jim won't need no shavin' mug no more, but I'll leave it there just the same for old time's sake. Jim certainly was a character!

Years ago, Jim used to travel for a canned goods concern over in Carterville. They sold canned goods. Jim had the whole northern half of the State and was on the road five days out of every week. He'd drop in here Saturdays and tell his experiences for that week. It was rich.

I guess he paid more attention to playin' jokes than makin' sales. Finally the concern let him out and he come right home here and told everybody he'd been fired instead of sayin' he'd resigned like most fellas would of.

It was a Saturday and the shop was full and Jim got up out of that chair and says, "Gentlemen, I got an important announcement to make. I been fired from my job."

Well, they asked him if he was in earnest and he said he was and nobody could think of nothin' to say till Jim finally broke the ice himself. He says, "I been sellin' canned goods and now I'm canned goods myself."

You see, the concern he'd been workin' for was a factory that made canned goods. Over in Carterville. And now Jim said he was canned himself. He was certainly a card!

Jim had a great trick that he used to play w'ile he was travelin'. For instance, he'd be ridin' on a train and they'd come to some little town like, well, we'll say, like Benton. Jim would look out the train window and read the signs on the stores.

For instance, they'd be a sign, "Henry Smith, Dry Goods." Well, Jim would write down the name and the name of the town and when he got to wherever he was goin' he'd mail back a postal card to Henry Smith at Benton and not sign no name to it, but he'd write on the card, well, somethin' like "Ask your wife about that book agent that spent the afternoon last week," or "Ask your Missus who kept her from gettin' lonesome the last time you was in Carterville." And he'd sign the card, "A Friend."

Of course, he never knew what really come of none of these jokes, but he could picture what *probably* happened and that was enough.

Jim didn't work very steady after he lost his position with the Carterville people. What he did earn, doin' odd jobs round town, why he spent pretty near all of it on gin and his family might of starved if the stores hadn't of carried them along. Jim's wife tried her hand at dressmakin', but they ain't nobody goin' to get rich makin' dresses in this town.

As I say, she'd of divorced Jim, only she seen that she couldn't support herself and the kids and she was always hopin' that some day Jim would cut out his habits and give her more than two or three dollars a week.

They was a time when she would go to whoever he was workin' for and ask them to give her his wages, but after she done this once or twice, he beat her to it by borrowin' most of his pay in advance. He told it all round town, how he had outfoxed his Missus. He certainly was a caution!

But he wasn't satisfied with just outwittin' her. He was sore the way she had acted, tryin' to grab off his pay. And he made up his mind he'd get even. Well, he waited till Evans's Circus was advertised to come to town. Then he told his wife and two kiddies that he was goin' to take them to the circus. The day of the circus, he told them he would get the tickets and meet them outside the entrance to the tent.

Well, he didn't have no intentions of bein' there or buyin' tickets or nothin'. He got full of gin and laid round Wright's pool-room all day. His wife and the kids waited and waited and of course he didn't show up. His wife didn't have a dime with her, or no-where else, I guess. So she finally had to tell the kids it was all off and they cried like they wasn't never goin' to stop.

Well, it seems, w'ile they was cryin', Doc Stair came along and he asked what was the matter, but Mrs. Kendall was stubborn and wouldn't tell him, but the kids told him and he insisted on takin' them and their mother in the show. Jim found this out after-wards and it was one reason why he had it in for Doc Stair.

Doc Stair come here about a year and a half ago. He's a mighty handsome young fella and his clothes always look like he has them made to order. He goes to Detroit two or three times a year and w'ile he's there he must have a tailor take his measure and then make him a suit to order. They cost pretty near twice as much, but they fit a whole lot better than if you just bought them in a store.

For a w'ile everybody was wonderin' why a young doctor like Doc Stair should come to a town like this where we already got old Doc Gamble and Doc Foote that's both been here for years and all the practice in the town was always divided between the two of them.

Then they was a story got round that Doc Stair's gal had throwed him over, a gal up in the Northern Peninsula somewheres, and the reason he come here was to hide him-self away and forget it. He said himself that he thought they wasn't nothin' like general practice in a place like ours to fit a man to be a good all round doctor. And that's why he'd came.

Anyways, it wasn't long before he was makin' enough to live on, though they tell me that he never dunned nobody for what they owed him, and the folks here certainly has got the owin' habit, even in my business. If I had all that was comin' to me for just shaves alone, I could go to Carterville and put up at the Mercer for a week and see a different picture every night. For instance, they's old George Purdy—but I guess I shouldn't ought to be gossipin'.

Well, last year our coroner died, died of the flu. Ken Beatty, that was his name. He was the coroner. So they had to choose an-other man to be coroner in his place and they picked Doc Stair. He laughed at first and said he didn't want it, but they made him take it. It ain't no job that anybody would fight for and what a man makes out of it in a year would just about buy seeds for their garden. Doc's the kind, though, that can't say no to nothin' if you keep at him long enough.

But I was goin' to tell you about a poor boy we got here in town—Paul Dickson. He fell out of a tree when he was about ten years old. Lit on his head and it done somethin' to him and he ain't never been right. No harm in him, but just silly. Jim Kendall used to call him cuckoo; that's a name Jim had for anybody that was off their head, only he called people's head their bean. That was another of his gags, callin' head bean and callin' crazy people cuckoo. Only poor Paul ain't crazy, but just silly.

You can imagine that Jim used to have all kinds of fun with Paul. He'd send him to the White Front Garage for a left-handed monkey wrench. Of course they ain't no such a thing as a left-handed monkey wrench.

And once we had a kind of a fair here and they was a baseball game between the fats and the leans and before the game started Jim called Paul over and sent him way down to Schrader's hardware store to get a key for the pitcher's box.

They wasn't nothin' in the way of gags that Jim couldn't think up, when he put his mind to it.

Poor Paul was always kind of suspicious of people, maybe on account of how Jim had kept foolin' him. Paul wouldn't have much to do with anybody only his own mother and Doc Stair and a girl here in town named Julie Gregg. That is, she ain't a girl no more, but pretty near thirty or over.

When Doc first come to town, Paul seemed to feel like here was a real friend and he hung round Doc's office most of the w'ile; the only time he wasn't there was when he'd go home to eat or sleep or when he seen Julie Gregg doin' her shoppin'.

When he looked out Doc's window and seen her, he'd run downstairs and join her and tag along with her to the different stores. The poor boy was crazy about Julie and she always treated him mighty nice and made him feel like he was welcome, though of course it wasn't nothin' but pity on her side.

Doc done all he could to improve Paul's mind and he told me once that he really thought the boy was gettin' better, that they was times when he was as bright and sensible as anybody else.

But I was goin' to tell you about Julie Gregg. Old Man Gregg was in the lumber business, but got to drinkin' and lost the most of his money and when he died, he didn't leave nothin' but the house and just enough insurance for the girl to skimp along on.

Her mother was a kind of half invalid and didn't hardly ever leave the house. Julie wanted to sell the place and move somewheres else after the old man died, but the mother said she was born here and would die here. It was tough on Julie, as the young people round this town—well, she's too good for them.

She's been away to school and Chicago and New York and different places and they ain't no subject she can't talk on, where you take the rest of the young folks here and you mention anything to them outside of Gloria Swanson or Tommy Meighan and they think you're delirious. Did you see Gloria in Wages of Virtue? You missed somethin'!

Well, Doc Stair hadn't been here more than a week when he come in one day to get shaved and I recognized who he was as he had been pointed out to me, so I told him about my old lady. She's been ailin' for a couple of years and either Doc Gamble or Doc Foote, neither one, seemed to be helpin' her. So he said he would come out and see her, but if she was able to get out herself, it would be better to bring her to his office where he could make a completer examination.

So I took her to his office and w'ile I was waitin' for her in the reception room, in come Julie Gregg. When somebody comes in Doc Stair's office, they've a bell that rings in his inside office so as he can tell they's somebody to see him.

So he left my old lady inside and come out to the front office and that's the first time him and Julie met and I guess it was what they call love at first sight. But it wasn't fifty-fifty. This young fella was the slickest lookin' fella she'd ever seen in this town and she went wild over him. To him she was just a young lady that wanted to see the doctor.

She'd came on about the same business I had. Her mother had been doctorin' for years with Doc Gamble and Doc Foote and without no results. So she'd heard they was a new doc in town and decided to give him a try. He promised to call and see her mother that same day.

I said a minute ago that it was love at

first sight on her part. I'm not only judgin' by how she acted afterwards but how she looked at him that first day in his office. I ain't no mind reader, but it was wrote all over her face that she was gone.

Now Jim Kendall, besides bein' a joke-smith and a pretty good drinker, well, Jim was quite a lady-killer. I guess he run pretty wild durin' the time he was on the road for them Carterville people, and besides that, he'd had a couple of little affairs of the heart right here in town. As I say, his wife could of divorced him, only she couldn't.

But Jim was like the majority of men, and women, too, I guess. He wanted what he couldn't get. He wanted Julie Gregg and worked his head off tryin' to land her. Only he'd of said bean instead of head.

Well, Jim's habits and his jokes didn't appeal to Julie and of course he was a married man, so he didn't have no more chance than, well, than a rabbit. That's an expression of Jim's himself. When somebody didn't have no chance to get elected or somethin', Jim would always say they didn't have no more chance than a rabbit.

He didn't make no bones about how he felt. Right in here, more than once, in front of the whole crowd, he said he was stuck on Julie and anybody that could get her for him was welcome to his house and his wife and kids included. But she wouldn't have nothin' to do with him; wouldn't even speak to him on the street. He finally seen he wasn't gettin' nowheres with his usual line so he decided to try the rough stuff. He went right up to her house one evenin' and when she opened the door he forced his way in and grabbed her. But she broke loose and before he could stop her, she run in the next room and locked the door and phoned to Joe Barnes. Joe's the marshal. Jim could hear who she was phonin' to and he beat it before Joe got there.

Joe was an old friend of Julie's pa. Joe went to Jim the next day and told him what would happen if he ever done it again.

I don't know how the news of this little affair leaked out. Chances is that Joe Barnes told his wife and she told somebody else's wife and they told their husband. Anyways, it did leak out and Hod Meyers had the nerve to kid Jim about it, right here in this shop. Jim didn't deny nothin' and kind of laughed it off and said for us all to wait; that lots of people had tried to make a monkey out of him, but he always got even.

Meanw'ile everybody in town was wise to Julie's being wild mad over the Doc. I don't suppose she had any idear how her face changed when him and her was together; of course she couldn't of, or she'd of kept away from him. And she didn't know that we was all noticin' how many times she made excuses to go up to his office or pass it on the other side of the street and look up in his window to see if he was there. I felt sorry for her and so did most other people.

Hod Meyers kept rubbin' it into Jim about how the Doc had cut him out. Jim didn't pay no attention to the kiddin' and you could see he was plannin' one of his jokes.

One trick Jim had was the knack of changin' his voice. He could make you think he was a girl talkin' and he could mimic any man's voice. To show you how good he was along this line, I'll tell you the joke he played on me once.

You know, in most towns of any size, when a man is dead and needs a shave, why the barber that shaves him soaks him five dollars for the job; that is, he don't soak *him*, but whoever ordered the shave. I just charge three dollars because personally I don't mind much shavin' a dead person. They lay a whole lot stiller than live customers. The only thing it that you don't feel like talkin' to them and you get kind of lonesome.

Well, about the coldest day we ever had here, two years ago last winter, the phone rung at the house w'ile I was home to dinner and I answered the phone and it was a woman's voice and she said she was Mrs. John Scott and her husband was dead and would I come out and shave him.

Old John had always been a good customer of mine. But they live seven miles out in the country, on the Streeter road. Still I didn't see how I could say no.

So I said I would be there, but would have to come in a jitney and it might cost three or four dollars besides the price of the shave. So she, or the voice, it said that was all right, so I got Frank Abbott to drive me out to the place and when I got there, who should open the door but old John himself! He wasn't no more dead than, well, than a rabbit.

It didn't take no private detective to figure out who had played me this little joke. Nobody could of thought it up but Jim Kendall. He certainly was a card!

I tell you this incident just to show you how he could disguise his voice and make you believe it was somebody else talkin'. I'd of swore it was Mrs. Scott had called me. Anyways, some woman.

Well, Jim waited till he had Doc Stair's voice down pat; then he went after revenge.

He called Julie up on a night when he knew Doc was over in Carterville. She never questioned but what it was Doc's voice. Jim said he must see her that night; he couldn't wait no longer to tell her somethin'. She was all excited and told him to come to the house. But he said he was expectin' an important long distance call and wouldn't she please forget her manners for once and come to his office. He said they couldn't nothin' hurt her and nobody would see her and he just *must* talk to her a little w'ile. Well, poor Julie fell for it.

Doc always keeps a night light in his office, so it looked to Julie like they was somebody there.

Meanw'ile Jim Kendall had went to Wright's poolroom, where they was a whole gang amusin' themselves. The most of them had drank plenty of gin, and they was a rough bunch even when sober. They was always strong for Jim's jokes and when he told them to come with him and see some fun they give up their card games and pool games and followed along.

Doc's office is on the second floor. Right outside his door they's a flight of stairs leadin'

to the floor above. Jim and his gang hid in the dark behind these stairs.

Well, Julie come up to Doc's door and rung the bell and they was nothin' doin'. She rung it again and she rung it seven or eight times. Then she tried the door and found it locked. Then Jim made some kind of a noise and she heard it and waited a minute, and then she says, "Is that you, Ralph?" Ralph is Doc's first name.

They was no answer and it must of came to her all of a sudden that she'd been bunked. She pretty near fell downstairs and the whole gang after her. They chased her all the way home, hollerin', "Is that you, Ralph?" and "Oh, Ralphie, dear, is that you?" Jim says he couldn't holler it himself, as he was laughin' too hard.

Poor Julie! She didn't show up here on Main Street for a long, long time afterward.

And of course Jim and his gang told everybody in town, everybody but Doc Stair. They were scared to tell him, and he might of never knowed only for Paul Dickson. The poor cuckoo, as Jim called him, he was here in the shop one night when Jim was still gloatin' yet over what he'd done to Julie. And Paul took in as much of it as he could understand and he run to Doc with the story.

It's a cinch Doc went up in the air and swore he'd make Jim suffer. But it was a kind of a delicate thing, because if it got out that he had beat Jim up, Julie was bound to hear of it and then she'd know that Doc knew and of course knowin' that he knew would make it worse for her than ever. He was goin' to do somethin', but it took a lot of figurin'.

Well, it was a couple of days later when Jim was here in the shop again, and so was the cuckoo. Jim was goin' duck-shootin' the next day and had come in lookin' for Hod Meyers to go with him. I happened to know that Hod had went over to Carterville and wouldn't be home till the end of the week. So Jim said he hated to go alone and he guessed he would call it off. Then poor Paul spoke up and said if Jim would take him he would go along. Jim thought a w'ile and then he said, well, he guessed a half-wit was better than nothin'.

I suppose he was plottin' to get Paul out in the boat and play some joke on him, like pushin' him in the water. Anyways, he said Paul could go. He asked him had he ever shot a duck and Paul said no, he'd never even had a gun in his hands. So Jim said he could set in the boat and watch him and if he behaved himself, he might lend him his gun for a couple of shots. They made a date to meet in the mornin' and that's the last I seen if Jim alive.

Next mornin', I hadn't been open more than ten minutes when Doc Stair come in. He looked kind of nervous. He asked me had I seen Paul Dickson. I said no, but I knew where he was, out duck-shootin' with Jim Kendall. So Doc says that's what he had heard, and he couldn't understand it because Paul had told him he wouldn't never have no more to do with Jim as long as he lived.

He said Paul had told him about the joke Jim had played on Julie. He said Paul had asked him what he thought of the joke and the Doc had told him that anybody that would do a thing like that ought not to be let live.

I said it had been a kind of a raw thing, but Jim just couldn't resist no kind of a joke, no matter how raw. I said I thought he was all right at heart, but just bubblin' over with mischief. Doc turned and walked out.

At noon he got a phone call from old John Scott. The lake where Jim and Paul had went shootin' is on John's place. Paul had came runnin' up to the house a few minutes before and said they'd been an accident. Jim had shot a few ducks and then give the gun to Paul and told him to try his luck. Paul hadn't never handled a gun and he was nervous. He was shakin' so hard that he couldn't control the gun. He let fire and Jim sunk back in the boat, dead.

Doc Stair, bein' the coroner, jumped in Frank Abbott's flivver and rushed out to Scott's farm. Paul and old John was down on the shore of the lake. Paul had rowed the boat to shore, but they'd left the body in it, waitin' for Doc to come.

Doc examined the body and said they might as well fetch it back to town. They was no use leavin' it there or callin' a jury, as it was a plain case of accidental shootin'.

Personally I wouldn't never leave a person shoot a gun in the same boat I was in unless I was sure they knew somethin' about guns. Jim was a sucker to leave a new beginner have his gun, let alone a half-wit. It probably served Jim right, what he got. But still we miss him round here. He certainly was a card!

Comb it wet or dry?

———◆·◀▶·◆———

In two preceding stories, "I'm a Fool" and "Araby," we have just seen examples of first-person narration in which the narrator is the principal character. In "Haircut," we again encounter an example of first-person narration, but with an important difference. Here the narrator is merely a narrator, not the principal character, not even one peripherally involved in the objective events. But we should ask ourselves if he has another kind of involvement in the story as a whole—if he is something more than a convenience for the author, a device for controlling the presentation of the material.

One way to get an answer to our question is to think of the story of Jim Kendall, Doc Stair, Julie, and Poor Paul as told by a third-person narrator—as in "The Lottery Ticket." There is, indeed, a simple, objective plot: Kendall has tortured the simpleminded Paul; Doc Stair and Julie have befriended him; as a result of the brutal joke Kendall plays on Julie, Doc Stair bursts out with the enraged remark that such a fellow should not be allowed to live; Paul shoots Kimball; Stair, as coroner, pronounces the death accidental; presumably Stair and Julie marry and live happily ever after.

Basically, we have here an ironical story of the biter bit, of the joker whose joke backfires, lethally, on him—with, of course, virtue triumphant in the end.

This objective account is simple, crude,

and, worse, very predictable. We must ask ourselves what, in Lardner's version, redeems this account. What, in other words, is gained by the use of the barber? The barber adds a whole new dimension of complication, interest, and meaning. The objective version is too obvious to engage us; we find, simply, the picture of a brutal, stupid jokester who, in the midst of his own blunderings and failure, comforts his ego with a series of pain-giving pranks on defenseless people. From the start we are appalled by the "card's" brutality; we emotionally predict the story. At the same time, the lack of complication in our own attitude robs the account of interest; it has, for us, no "insides." But when the barber is introduced as narrator, we encounter a competing attitude, an attitude quite different from our own. He admires the "card" and, in his admiration, vicariously participates in the sadistic jokes and is, thus, a kind of accomplice; this fact sets up, in Lardner's version, a pervasive and functional, even if rather obvious, irony. The barber's attitude is, clearly, set in contrast to the author's attitude—and to our own. The barber's evaluation of the events belies what we take to be the meaning of the tale he tells, and in the process heightens our own feeling, irritating us, we may say, to fuller awareness of what is at stake here. Furthermore, it is not only the attitude of the barber we are set against; the barber appears as a spokesman for a large segment of the community, for Jim Kendall has a large audience of admirers. We can't, that is, simply lull ourselves with our easy assent to the fact that the biter will be bit. Evil is broadly afoot and connivance is constant. We may even be stung to some awareness of the possibility of our own connivance in such situations. To sum up, it is the barber who provides a dramatic center for the story, and the telling here—as many times elsewhere—is more significant than what is told.

EXERCISES

1. Compare the function of the narrator in "Haircut" with that of the narrator in "Kronkin's Prisoner" (sec. 10).

2. We have said that "Haircut" is basically an ironical story in that there is a great discrepancy between the meaning that the narrator attributes to his story and the meaning the reader gets from it. Contrast this story with "Spotted Horses" (sec. 6) in relation to irony.

KEELA, THE OUTCAST INDIAN MAIDEN
Eudora Welty (b. 1909)

One morning in summertime, when all his sons and daughters were off picking plums and Little Lee Roy was all alone, sitting on the porch and only listening to the screech owls away down in the woods, he had a surprise.

First he heard white men talking. He heard two white men coming up the path from the highway. Little Lee Roy ducked his head and held his breath; then he patted all around back of him for his crutches. The chickens all came out from under the house and waited attentively on the steps.

The men came closer. It was the young man who was doing all of the talking. But when they got through the fence, Max, the older man, interrupted him. He tapped him on the arm and pointed his thumb toward Little Lee Roy.

He said, "Bud? Yonder he is."

But the younger man kept straight on talking, in an explanatory voice.

"Bud?" said Max again. "Look, Bud, yonder's the only little clubfooted nigger man was ever around Cane Springs. Is he the party?"

They came nearer and nearer to Little Le Roy and then stopped and stood there in the middle of the yard. But the young man was so excited he did not seem to realize that they had arrived anywhere. He was only about twenty years old, very sunburned. He talked constantly, making only one gesture—raising his hand stiffly and then moving it a little to one side.

"They dressed it in a red dress, and it ate chickens alive," he said. "I sold tickets and I thought it was worth a dime, honest. They gimme a piece of paper with the thing wrote off I had to say. That was easy. 'Keela, the Outcast Indian Maiden!' I call it out through a pasteboard megaphone. Then ever' time it was fixin' to eat a live chicken, I blowed the siren out front."

"Just tell me, Bud," said Max, resting back on the heels of his perforated tan-and-white sports shoes. "Is this nigger the one? Is that him sittin' there?"

Little Lee Roy sat huddled and blinking, a smile on his face. . . . But the young man did not look his way.

"Just took the job that time. I didn't mean to—I mean, I meant to go to Port Arthur because my brother was on a boat," he said. "My name is Steve, mister. But I worked with this show selling tickets for three months, and I never would of knowed it was like that if it hadn't been for that man." He arrested his gesture.

"Yeah, what man?" said Max in a hopeless voice.

Little Lee Roy was looking from one white man to the other, excited almost beyond respectful silence. He trembled all over, and a look of amazement and sudden life came into his eyes.

"Two years ago," Steve was saying impatiently. "And we was travelin' through Texas in those ole trucks.—See, the reason nobody ever come clost to it before was they give it a iron bar this long. And tole it if anybody come near, to shake the bar good at 'em, like this. But it couldn't say nothin'. Turned out they'd tole it it couldn't say nothin' to anybody ever, so it just kind of mumbled and growled, like a animal."

"Hee! hee!" This from Little Lee Roy, softly.

"Tell me again," said Max, and just from his look you could tell that everybody knew old Max. "Somehow I can't get it straight in my mind. Is this the boy? Is this little nigger boy the same as this Keela, the Outcast Indian Maiden?"

Up on the porch, above them, Little

Lee Roy gave Max a glance full of hilarity, and then bent the other way to catch Steve's next words.

"Why, if anyone was to even come near it or even bresh their shoulder against the rope it'd growl and take on and shake its iron rod. When it would eat the live chickens it'd growl somethin' awful—you ought to heard it."

"Hee! hee!" It was a soft, almost incredulous laugh that began to escape from Little Lee Roy's tight lips, a little mew of delight.

"They'd throw it this chicken, and it would reach out an' grab it. Would sort of rub over the chicken's neck with its thumb an' press on it good, an' then it would bite its head off."

"O.K.," said Max.

"It skint back the feathers and stuff from the neck and sucked the blood. But ever'body said it was still alive." Steve drew closer to Max and fastened his light-colored, troubled eyes on his face.

"O.K."

"Then it would pull the feathers out easy and neat-like, awful fast, an' growl the whole time, kind of moan, an' then it would commence to eat all the white meat. I'd go in an' look at it. I reckon I seen it a thousand times."

"That was you, boy?" Max demanded of Little Lee Roy unexpectedly.

But Little Lee Roy could only say, "Hee! hee!" The little man at the head of the steps where the chickens sat, one on each step, and the two men facing each other below made a pyramid.

Steve stuck his hand out for silence. "They said—I mean, I said it, out front through the megaphone, I said it myself, that it wouldn't eat nothin' but only live meat. It was supposed to be a Indian woman, see, in this red dress an' stockin's. It didn't have on no shoes, so when it drug its foot ever body could see. . . . When it come to the chicken's heart, it would eat that too, real fast, and the heart would still be **jumpin'**."

"Wait a second, Bud," said Max briefly. "Say, boy, is this white man here crazy?"

Little Lee Roy burst into hysterical, deprecatory giggles. He said, "Naw suh, don't think so." He tried to catch Steve's eye, seeking appreciation, crying, "Naw suh, don't think he crazy, mista."

Steve gripped Max's arm. "Wait! Wait!" he cried anxiously. "You ain't listenin'. I want to tell you about it. You didn't catch my name—Steve. You never did hear about that little nigger—all that happened to him? Lived in Cane Springs, Miss'ippi?"

"Bud," said Max, disengaging himself, "I don't hear anything. I got a juke box, see, so I don't have to listen."

"Look—I was really the one," said Steve more patiently, but nervously, as if he had been slowly breaking bad news. He walked up and down the bare-swept ground in front of Little Lee Roy's porch, along the row of princess feathers and snow-on-the-mountain. Little Lee Roy's turning head followed him. "I was the one—that's what I'm tellin' you."

"Suppose I was to listen to what every dope comes in Max's Place got to say, *I'd* be nuts," said Max.

"It's all me, see," said Steve. "I know that. I was the one was the cause for it goin' on an' on an' not bein' found out—such an awful thing. It was me, what I said out front through the megaphone."

He stopped still and stared at Max in despair.

"Look," said Max. He sat on the steps, and the chickens hopped off. "I know I ain't nobody but Max. I got Max's Place. I only run a place, understand, fifty yards down the highway. Liquor buried twenty feet from the premises, and no trouble yet. I ain't ever been up here before. I don't claim to been anywhere. People come to my place. Now. You're the hitchhiker. You're tellin' me, see. You claim a lot of information. If I don't get it I don't get it and I ain't complaining about it, see. But I think you're nuts, and did from the first. I only come up here with you because I figured you's crazy."

"Maybe you don't believe I remember every word of it even now," Steve was saying gently. "I think about it at night—that an' drums on the midway. You ever hear any drums on the midway?" He paused and stared politely at Max and Little Le Roy.

"Yeh," said Max.

"Don't it make you feel sad. I remember how the drums was goin' and I was yellin', 'Ladies and gents! Do not try to touch Keela, the Outcast Indian Maiden— she will only beat your brains out with her iron rod, and eat them alive!'" Steve waved his arm gently in the air, and Little Lee Roy drew back and squealed. "'Do not go near her, ladies and gents! I'm warnin' you!' So nobody ever did. Nobody ever come near her. Until that man."

"Sure," said Max. "That fella." He shut his eyes.

"Afterwards when he come up so bold, I remembered seein' him walk up an' buy the ticket an' go in the tent. I'll never forget that man as long as I live. To me he's a sort of—well—"

"Hero," said Max.

"I wish I could remember what he looked like. Seem like he was a tallish man with a sort of white face. Seem like he had bad teeth, but I may be wrong. I remember he frowned a lot. Kept frownin'. Whenever he'd buy a ticket, why, he'd frown."

"Ever seen him since?" asked Max cautiously, still with his eyes closed. "Ever hunt him up?"

"No, never did," said Steve. Then he went on. "He'd frown an' buy a ticket ever' day we was in these two little smelly towns in Texas, sometimes three-four times a day, whether it was fixin' to eat a chicken or not."

"O.K., so he gets in the tent," said Max.

"Well, what the man finally done was, he walked right up to the little stand where it was tied up and laid his hand out open on the planks in the platform. He just laid his hand out open there and said, 'Come here,' real low and quick, that-a-way."

Steve laid his open hand on Little Lee

Roy's porch and held it there, frowning in concentration.

"I get it," said Max. "He'd caught on it was a fake."

Steve straightened up. "So ever'body yelled to git away, git away," he continued, his voice rising, "because it was growlin' an' carryin' on an' shakin' its iron bar like they tole it. When I heard all that commotion—boy! I was scared."

"You didn't know it was a fake."

Steve was silent for a moment, and Little Lee Roy held his breath, for fear everything was all over.

"Look," said Steve finally, his voice trembling. "I guess I was supposed to feel bad like this, and you wasn't. I wasn't supposed to ship out on that boat from Port Arthur and all like that. This other had to happen to me—not you all. Feelin' responsible. You'll be O.K., mister, but I won't. I feel awful about it. That poor little old thing."

"Look, you got him right here," said Max quickly. "See him? Use your eyes. He's O.K., ain't he? Looks O.K. to me. It's just you. You're nuts, is all."

"You know—when that man laid out his open hand on the boards, why, it just let go the iron bar," continued Steve, "let it fall down like that—bang—and act like it didn't know what to do. Then it drug itself over to where the fella was standin' an' leaned down an' grabbed holt onto that white man's hand as tight as it could an' cried like a baby. It didn't want to hit him!"

"Hee! hee! hee!"

"No sir, it didn't want to hit him. You know what it wanted?"

Max shook his head.

"It wanted him to help it. So the man said, 'Do you wanta get out of this place, whoever you are?' An' it never answered—none of us knowed it could talk—but it just wouldn't let that man's hand a-loose. It hung on, cryin' like a baby. So the man says, 'Well, wait here till I come back.'"

"Uh-huh?" said Max.

"Went off an' come back with the sheriff. Took us all to jail. But just the man owned the show and his son got took to the pen. They said I could go free. I kep' tellin' 'em I didn't know it wouldn't hit me with the iron bar an' kep' tellin' 'em I didn't know it could tell what you was sayin' to it."

"Yeh, guess you told 'em," said Max.

"By that time I felt bad. Been feelin' bad ever since. Can't hold onto a job or stay in one place for nothin' in the world. They made it stay in jail to see if it could talk or not, and the first night it wouldn't say nothin'. Some time it cried. And they undressed it an' found out it wasn't no outcast Indian woman a-tall. It was a little clubfooted nigger man."

"Hee! hee!"

"You mean it was this boy here—yeh. It was him."

"Washed its face, and it was paint all over it made it look red. It all come off. And it could talk—as good as me or you. But they'd tole it not to, so it never did. They'd tole it if anybody was to come near it they was comin' to git it—and for it to hit 'em quick with that iron bar an' growl. So nobody ever come near it—until that man. I was yellin' outside, tellin' 'em to keep away, keep away. You could see where they'd whup it. They had to whup it some to make it eat all the chickens. It was awful dirty. They let it go back home free, to where they got it in the first place. They made them pay its ticket from Little Oil, Texas, to Cane Springs, Miss'ippi."

"You got a good memory," said Max.

"The way it *started* was," said Steve, in a wondering voice, "the show was just travelin' along in ole trucks through the country, and just seen this little deformed nigger man, sittin' on a fence, and just took it. It couldn't help it."

Little Lee Roy tossed his head back in a frenzy of amusement.

"I found it all out later. I was up on the Ferris wheel with one of the boys—got to talkin' up yonder in the peace an' quiet—an' said they just kind of happened up on it. Like a cyclone happens: it wasn't nothin' it could do. It was just took up." Steve suddenly paled through his sunburn. "An' they found out that back in Miss'ippi it had it a little bitty pair of crutches an' could just go runnin' on 'em!"

"And there they are," said Max.

Little Lee Roy held up a crutch and turned it about, and then snatched it back like a monkey.

"But if it hadn't been for that man, I wouldn't of knowed it till yet. If it wasn't for him bein' so bold. If he hadn't knowed what he was doin'."

"You remember that man this fella's talkin' about, boy?" asked Max, eyeing Little Lee Roy.

Little Lee Roy, in reluctance and shyness, shook his head gently.

"Naw suh, I can't say as I remembas that ve'y man, suh," he said softly, looking down where just then a sparrow alighted on his child's shoe. He added happily, as if on inspiration, "Now I remembas *this* man."

Steve did not look up, but when Max shook with silent laughter, alarm seemed to seize him like a spasm in his side. He walked painfully over and stood in the shade for a few minutes, leaning his head on a sycamore tree.

"Seemed like that man just studied it out an' knowed it was somethin' wrong," he said presently, his voice coming more remotely than ever. "But I didn't know. I can't look at nothin' an' be sure what it is. Then afterwards I know. Then I see how it was."

"Yeh, but you're nuts," said Max affably.

"You wouldn't of knowed it either!" cried Steve in sudden boyish, defensive anger. Then he came out from under the tree and stood again almost pleadingly in the sun, facing Max where he was sitting below Little Lee Roy on the steps. "You'd of let it go on an' on when they made it do those things— just like I did."

"Bet I could tell a man from a woman and an Indian from a nigger though," said Max.

Steve scuffed the dust into little puffs with his worn shoe. The chickens scattered, alarmed at last.

Little Lee Roy looked from one man to the other radiantly, his hands pressed over his grinning gums.

Then Steve sighed, and as if he did not know what else he could do, he reached out and without any warning hit Max in the jaw with his fist. Max fell off the steps.

Little Lee Roy suddenly sat as still and dark as a statue, looking on.

"Say! Say!" cried Steve. He pulled shyly at Max where he lay on the ground, with his lips pursed up like a whistler, and then stepped back. He looked horrified. "How you feel?"

"Lousy," said Max thoughtfully. "Let me alone." He raised up on one elbow and lay there looking all around, at the cabin, at Little Lee Roy sitting cross-legged on the porch, and at Steve with his hand out. Finally he got up.

"I can't figure out how I could of ever knocked down an athaletic guy like you. I had to do it," said Steve. "But I guess you don't understand. I had to hit you. First you didn't believe me, and then it didn't bother you."

"That's all O.K., only hush," said Max, and added, "some dope is always giving me the lowdown on something, but this is the first time one of 'em ever got away with a thing like this. I got to watch out."

"I hope it don't stay black long," said Steve.

"I got to be going," said Max. But he waited. "What you want to transact with Keela? You come a long way to see him." He stared at Steve with his eyes wide open now, and interested.

"Well, I was goin' to give him some money or somethin', I guess, if I ever found him, only now I ain't got any," said Steve defiantly.

"O.K.," said Max. "Here's some change for you, boy. Just take it. Go on back in the house. Go on."

Little Lee Roy took the money speechlessly, and then fell upon his yellow crutches and hopped with miraculous rapidity away through the door. Max stared after him for a moment.

"As for you"—he brushed himself off, turned to Steve and then said, "When did you eat last?"

"Well, I'll tell you," said Steve.

"Not here," said Max. "I didn't go to ask you a question. Just follow me. We serve eats at Max's Place, and I want to play the juke box. You eat, and I'll listen to the juke box."

"Well . . ." said Steve. "But when it cools off I got to catch a ride some place."

"Today while all you all was gone, and not a soul in de house," said Little Lee Roy at the supper table that night, "two white mens come heah to de house. Wouldn't come in. But talks to me about de ole times when I use to be wid de circus—"

"Hush up, Pappy," said the children.

EXERCISES

Write an essay analyzing and interpreting this story. In studying the story it may be useful to use the following questions and topics as a kind of guide:

1. In the first two paragraphs what impression do we get of Lee Roy and of the writer's attitude toward him? Notice how the story opens almost with the simplicity of a tale told to children: "One morning in summertime . . ." Notice Lee Roy's occupation—listening to the screech owls—and the way the subsequent events are defined as a "surprise," the notion of something pleasantly falling across the vacancy of the morning. How does the fact that the chickens come out and wait "attentively" for the arrival of the strangers relate to the general impression we get of Lee Roy?

2. In the early stages of the story, how does the writer build up suspense? That is, how are interests stimulated but not gratified?

3. In the first description of Steve how is it indicated that he is under some nervous compulsion?

4. Why has Steve come to seek out the "outcast Indian maiden"?

5. If the central fact of a story is a conflict, how would you define the conflict here? We see, of course, that it exists between Steve and Max. Why does Steve finally strike Max? And why doesn't Max, a big, strong man, defend himself? Does the fact that he doesn't defend himself indicate that he has accepted Steve's view, or has begun to understand it? Why does Max give the money to Lee Roy? And why does he ask Steve to come and have a meal?

6. We see the structure of the story involves an omniscient narrator in whose account is set a first-person narration. Why is this inserted first-person narration necessary? Or rather, why must it be in the first person? Without the first-person narrator would we lose the sense of Steve's struggle with his own experience? Would we lose the dramatic development of the awareness by Max of the meaning of the story for him? Read "Kronkin's Prisoner" (sec. 10) and indicate the parallel in method between it and "Keela, the Outcast Indian Maiden."

7. What is Lee Roy's attitude during the encounter between the white men? Does he understand why Steve is here? How does the very end of the story relate to this question? From the fact that the children try to hush up their father when he begins to talk about "de ole times when I use to be wid de circus," what do we learn of Lee Roy's present attitude toward what had been a pitiful and degrading experience? Is this ending intended to make the story less serious in its impact? Or is Lee Roy's attitude a way of intensifying the pitiful aspect of the whole situation?

8. If you have read Coleridge's poem "The Ancient Mariner," how would you compare the story with the poem in regard to theme? In what sense can we say that Steve has committed a crime similar to that of the Mariner and must expiate his crime in much the same way?

9. Read "The Lagoon," by Joseph Conrad (sec. 10). This, like "Keela," is a story within a story —that is, a story told by a character who has an actual fictional presence and a relation to the story he narrates. You have no doubt determined what is the relation of the narrator in "Keela" to the story he narrates. What is that of the narrator in "The Lagoon"? What is the attitude of the white man who hears the story? What is his place and importance in the story? How does his role compare with that of the hearer in "Keela"? Is he there merely to provoke the story? Does he have any relation to the underlying conflict? To the theme?

THEME AND METHOD

Every story, of course, has a theme, and we have often used the word. To state the matter negatively, if a narrative means nothing it isn't a story. We have not selected stories for this group because their themes are presented more obviously than those of the stories in previous groups. In fact, in some of the stories in this group, the meaning is merely hinted at. Rather we are concerned here in illustrating some more of the various methods by which narrative may move toward meaning. Some of the stories have what, as far as a general statement goes, might be called the same theme, for instance, "The Horse Dealer's Daughter" (sec. 8) and "Araby" (sec. 7). But the fact that two stories are similar in theme does not mean that they mean the same thing. The attitude toward the theme may be very different; the tone of treatment may be, for example, either comic or tragic, ironic or straightforward. The writer's vision of life, as we have said, is the special underlying fact of any story, and a theme, abstractly stated, is not the same thing as a vision of life.

IN ANOTHER COUNTRY
Ernest Hemingway (1899–1961)

In the fall the war was always there, but we did not go to it any more. It was cold in the fall in Milan and the dark came very early. Then the electric lights came on, and it was pleasant along the streets looking in the windows. There was much game hanging outside the shops, and the snow powdered in the fur of the foxes and the wind blew their tails. The deer hung stiff and heavy and empty, and small birds blew in the wind and the wind turned their feathers. It was a cold fall and the wind came down from the mountains.

We were all at the hospital every afternoon, and there were different ways of walking across the town through the dusk to the hospital. Two of the ways were alongside canals, but they were long. Always, though, you crossed a bridge across a canal to enter the hospital. There was a choice of three bridges. On one of them a woman sold roasted chestnuts. It was warm, standing in front of her charcoal fire, and the chestnuts were warm afterward in your pocket. The hospital was very old and very beautiful, and you entered through a gate and walked across a courtyard and out a gate on the other side. There were usually funerals starting from the courtyard. Beyond the old hospital were the new brick pavilions, and there we met every afternoon and were all very polite and interested in what was the matter, and sat in the machines that were to make so much difference.

The doctor came up to the machine where I was sitting and said: "What did you like best to do before the war? Did you practice a sport?"

I said: "Yes, football."

"Good," he said. "You will be able to play football again better than ever."

My knee did not bend and the leg dropped straight from the knee to the ankle without a calf, and the machine was to bend the knee and make it move as in riding a tricycle. But it did not bend yet, and instead the machine lurched when it came to the bending part. The doctor said: "That will all pass. You are a fortunate young man. You will play football again like a champion."

In the next machine was a major who had a little hand like a baby's. He winked at me when the doctor examined his hand, which was between two leather straps that bounced up and down and flapped the stiff fingers, and said: "And will I too play football, captain-doctor?" He had been a very great fencer, and before the war the greatest fencer in Italy.

The doctor went to his office in a back room and brought a photograph which showed a hand that had been withered almost as small as the major's, before it had taken a machine course, and after was a little larger. The major held the photograph with his good hand and looked at it very carefully. "A wound?" he asked.

"An industrial accident," the doctor said.

"Very interesting, very interesting," the major said, and handed it back to the doctor.

"You have confidence?"

"No," said the major.

There were three boys who came each day who were about the same age I was. They were all three from Milan, and one of them was to be a lawyer, and one was to be a painter, and one had intended to be a soldier, and after we were finished with the machines, sometimes we walked back together to the Café Cova, which was next door to the Scala. We walked the short way through the communist quarter because we were four together. The people hated us because we were officers, and from a wine-shop someone called out, "A basso gli ufficiali!" as we passed. Another boy who walked with us sometimes and made us five wore a black silk handkerchief across his face because he had no nose then and his face was to be rebuilt. He had gone out to the front from the military academy and been wounded within an hour after he had gone into the front line for the first time. They rebuilt his face, but he came

from a very old family and they could never get the nose exactly right. He went to South America and worked in a bank. But this was a long time ago, and then we did not any of us know how it was going to be afterward. We only knew then that there was always the war, but that we were not going to it any more.

We all had the same medals, except the boy with the black silk bandage across his face, and he had not been at the front long enough to get any medals. The tall boy with a very pale face who was to be a lawyer had been a lieutenant of Arditi and had three medals of the sort we each had only one of. He had lived a very long time with death and was a little detached. We were all a little detached, and there was nothing that held us together except that we met every afternoon at the hospital. Although, as we walked to the Cova through the tough part of town, walking in the dark, with light and singing coming out of the wineshops, and sometimes having to walk into the street when the men and women would crowd together on the sidewalk so that we would have had to jostle them to get by, we felt held together by there being something that had happened that they, the people who disliked us, did not understand.

We ourselves all understood the Cova, where it was rich and warm and not too brightly lighted, and noisy and smoky at certain hours, and there were always girls at the tables and the illustrated papers on a rack on the wall. The girls at the Cova were very patriotic, and I found that the most patriotic people in Italy were the café girls —and I believe they are still patriotic.

The boys at first were very polite about my medals and asked me what I had done to get them. I showed them the papers, which were written in very beautiful language and full of *fratellanza* and *abnegazione*, but which really said, with the adjectives removed, that I had been given the medals because I was an American. After that their manner changed a little toward me, although I was their friend against outsiders. I was a friend, but I was never really one of them after they had read the citations, because it had been different with them and they had done very different things to get their medals. I had been wounded, it was true; but we all knew that being wounded, after all, was really an accident. I was never ashamed of the ribbons, though, and sometimes, after the cocktail hour, I would imagine myself having done all the things they had done to get their medals; but walking home at night through the empty streets with the cold wind and all the shops closed, trying to keep near the street lights, I knew that I would never have done such things, and I was very much afraid to die, and often lay in bed at night by myself, afraid to die and wondering how I would be when I went back to the front again.

The three with the medals were like hunting-hawks; and I was not a hawk, although I might seem a hawk to those who had never hunted; they, the three, knew better and so we drifted apart. But I stayed good friends with the boy who had been wounded his first day at the front, because he would never know now how he would have turned out; so he could never be accepted either, and I liked him because I thought he would not have turned out to be a hawk either.

The major, who had been the great fencer, did not believe in bravery, and spent much time while we sat in the machines correcting my grammar. He had complimented me on how I spoke Italian, and we talked together very easily. One day I had said that Italian seemed such an easy language to me that I could not take a great interest in it; everything was so easy to say. "Ah, yes," the major said. "Why, then, do you not take up the use of grammar?" So we took up the use of grammar, and soon Italian was such a difficult language that I was afraid to talk to him until I had the grammar straight in my mind.

The major came very regularly to the hospital. I do not think he ever missed a day, although I am sure he did not believe in the machines. There was a time when none of us believed in the machines, and one day the major said it was all nonsense. The machines were new then and it was we who were to prove them. It was an idiotic idea, he said, "a theory like another." I had not learned my grammar, and he said I was a stupid impossible disgrace, and he was a fool to have bothered with me. He was a small man and he sat straight up in his chair with his right hand thrust into the machine and looked straight ahead at the wall while the straps thumped up and down with his fingers in them.

"What will you do when the war is over if it is over?" he asked me. "Speak grammatically!"

"I will go to the States."

"Are you married?"

"No, but I hope to be."

"The more of a fool you are," he said. He seemed very angry. "A man must not marry."

"Why, Signor Maggiore?"

"Don't call me 'Signor Maggiore.'"

"Why must not a man marry?"

"He cannot marry. He cannot marry," he said angrily. "If he is to lose everything, he should not place himself in a position to lose that. He should not place himself in a position to lose. He should find things he cannot lose."

He spoke very angrily and bitterly, and looked straight ahead while he talked.

"But why should he necessarily lose it?"

"He'll lose it," the major said. He was looking at the wall. Then he looked down at the machine and jerked his little hand out from between the straps and slapped it hard against his thigh. "He'll lose it," he almost shouted. "Don't argue with me!" Then he called to the attendant who ran the machines. "Come and turn this damned thing off."

He went back into the other room for the light treatment and the massage. Then I heard him ask the doctor if he might use his telephone and he shut the door. When he came back into the room, I was sitting in another machine. He was wearing his cape and had his cap on, and he came directly toward my machine and put his arm on my shoulder.

"I am sorry," he said, and patted me on the shoulder with his good hand. "I would not be rude. My wife has just died. You must forgive me."

"Oh—" I said, feeling sick for him. "I am so sorry."

He stood there biting his lower lip. "It is very difficult," he said. "I cannot resign myself."

He looked straight past me and out through the window. Then he began to cry. "I am utterly unable to resign myself," he said and choked. And then crying, his head up looking at nothing, carrying himself straight and soldierly, with tears on both his cheeks and biting his lips, he walked past the machines and out the door.

The doctor told me that the major's wife, who was very young and whom he had not married until he was definitely invalided out of the war, had died of pneumonia. She had been sick only a few days. No one expected her to die. The major did not come to the hospital for three days. Then he came at the usual hour, wearing a black band on the sleeve of his uniform. When he came back, there were large framed photographs around the wall, of all sorts of wounds before and after they had been cured by the machines. In front of the machine the major used there were three photographs of hands like his that were completely restored. I do not know where the doctor got them. I always understood we were the first to use the machines. The photographs did not make much difference to the major because he only looked out of the window.

———————◆·◀▶·◆———————

The student may at first be puzzled to decide what this story is about. Indeed, a first reading, if it be hasty, may yield little more than some excellent description of walks through

a North Italian city in the winter, followed by an incident the narrator witnessed in an Italian hospital. The incident does not concern the narrator directly. The last paragraph is quiet and neutral in tone; the significance of the incident is not pointed up so much as deliberately played down. The student, therefore, may be pardoned for feeling that the story is almost pointless.

It is true that the American boy who tells the story has nothing in particular happen to him in the story, and it is further true that the Italian major to whom something does happen does not come into sharp focus until the story is two-thirds over. Yet "In Another Country" is a highly unified story after all; and, as we shall see, it does not lack drama.

Is it the boy's story? Or is it the major's? The answer to this question is best postponed until we have seen toward what the story is building; and once we have seen that, the answer will perhaps appear to be not so important after all. In any case, we must begin by asking what is the boy's state of mind, and what is the situation in which he finds himself; for unless we understand these things, we shall scarcely see why the major and what happens to the major make so powerful an impact upon him—and through him upon us.

The narrator is evidently a boy of keen and alert senses. The sights and sounds and smells of wartime Milan register upon him very vividly. There are, for instance, such details as "The deer hung stiff and heavy and empty, and small birds blew in the wind and the wind turned their feathers," and "The chestnuts were warm afterward in your pocket." Indeed the boy's description of what he sees and hears is so vividly factual that we may not at first realize how much concerned he is with the problem of bravery.

He has been given a medal, but he suspects that the medal has been given him, not because he has been brave but because he is an American fighting in the Italian army. He is not at all sure that he really would be brave under a supreme test, and therefore feels closer to the boy who "had not been at the front long enough to get any medals" than he does to the three boys whom he calls "hunting hawks." He feels that he "was never really one of them after they had read the citations"; and his isolation here is reinforced by his being in a foreign country, and by the hostility of the common people toward all officers in general.

The first half of the story, then, does much more than merely describe a place and time with its appropriate atmosphere. It suggests the peculiar alienation of the narrator, though it does this quietly, and relates his sense of alienation to his own lack of confidence in himself. On one level this prepares us for his response to the attention that the major pays to him. On a deeper level, however, it points to the more special interest that the major holds for him, for the major, though he has three medals, does not believe in bravery. Moreover, the major has no confidence in the machines. He pays little attention to them; he does not discuss the war; he spends his time correcting the boy's grammar. He is dry, civil, commonsensical, and apparently even cynical.

For all of these reasons, the major's sudden outburst against marriage and his bitterness and anger evidently shock the boy as they shock us. We, no more than the boy, understand this emotional explosion so much out of character until the major comes back to apologize and to say "I would not be rude. My wife has just died. You must forgive me." The momentary outbreak, however, actually underlines the iron control with which the major habitually disciplines himself. It suggests, furthermore, in what kind of personal philosophy this discipline is rooted: the major dreads all posturing and posing; he dreads anything that would possibly suggest personal indulgence of emotion. He prefers to keep his own deeds of bravery and his own sense of loss to himself. The man who does not believe in bravery is actually the bravest man of all, though his bravery is grounded not upon hope but upon despair.

Stated in these terms, the story might seem too obviously a little tract on bravery. Hemingway, of course, has not stated it in these terms. The story has been kept as dry and factual and understated as the major's own characteristic utterance. The kind of description given in the first half of the story plays its part in corroborating this quality of feeling. It also helps to undercut any sense

of the author's having sentimentalized the major's tragedy. In the last paragraph, we get, for example, a few sentences that fill out the exposition—the facts that the major's wife had been sick for only a few days and that her death had been shockingly unexpected. We get also a final picture of the major: the discreet black mourning band, the machine bearing three photographs of hands that had been "completely restored," and the major himself, not noticing them but looking "out of the window."

The major in his grief had said, "I am utterly unable to resign myself." But after three days he is, if not resigned, at least outwardly calm; if he despairs, he is surely not self-pitying.

At this point the student might try to answer for himself two questions raised by this last paragraph: (1) Where would the doctor have got three photographs of hands after treatment? (2) Why does the major, though obviously not believing in the curative power of the machines, return to the machine? We may add, as a third question, the question raised earlier: is this the major's story? Or is it the boy's story—the impact of the incident upon the boy?

This story is typical of Hemingway's work. The situations and characters of his fictional world are usually violent. There is the hard-drinking and sexually promiscuous world in *The Sun Also Rises*; the chaotic and brutal world of war in *A Farewell to Arms, For Whom the Bell Tolls*, many of the inserted sketches of *In Our Time*, the play *The Fifth Column*, and some of the stories; the world of sport in "Fifty Grand," "My Old Man," "The Undefeated," and "The Snows of Kilimanjaro"; the world of crime in "The Killers," "The Gambler, the Nun, and the Radio," and *To Have and To Have Not*. Even when the situation of a story does not fall into one of these categories, it usually involves a desperate risk, and behind it is the shadow of ruin, physical or spiritual. As for the typical characters, they are usually tough men, experienced in the hard worlds they inhabit, and not obviously given to emotional display or sensitive shrinking, men like Rinaldi or Frederick Henry of *A Farewell to Arms*, Robert Jordan of *For Whom the*

Bell Tolls, Harry Morgan of *To Have and To Have Not*, the big-game hunter of "The Snows of Kilimanjaro," the old bullfighter of "The Undefeated," or the pugilist of "Fifty Grand." Or if the typical character is not of this seasoned order, he is a very young man, or boy, first entering the violent world and learning his first adjustment to it. Both typical characters are obviously to be found in "In Another Country": the tough experienced man who knows the hard world, and the boy who is being initiated into that world.

In the shadow of ruin that colors the typical Hemingway situation, the typical Hemingway character faces defeat or death. But out of defeat or death he usually manages to salvage something. And here we discover Hemingway's special interest in such situations and such characters. His heroes are not defeated except upon their own terms. They are not squealers, welchers, compromisers, or cowards, and when they confront defeat, they realize that the stance they take, the stoic endurance, the stiff upper lip, mean a kind of victory. Defeated upon their own terms, some of them hold, even in the practical defeat, an ideal of themselves, some definition of how a man should behave, formulated or unformulated, by which they have lived. They represent some notion of a code, some notion of honor, that makes a man a man, and that distinguishes him from people who merely follow their random impulses and who are, by consequence, "messy."

Most writers—one is tempted to say all good writers—have a characteristic "world" in their fiction. The "world" may be a literal place—as the "South" of Faulkner, Katherine Anne Porter, or Eudora Welty. But if it is such a place, that place will be inhabited by a special kind of character in a special kind of situation. For example, the South of Faulkner is not at all the South of Katherine Anne Porter, for the "South" of each is to some extent the projection of the author. One can push this notion further still; the world of Ernest Hemingway cannot be located on any map: it is the world defined in great part by the special kind of character in the special kind of situation that engages his imagination.

This leads to the notion that the special "world" of a writer is neither accidental nor arbitrary. The kind of world a writer knows, in the literal sense, is, of course, an accident of his birth and experience. Yet on reflection, we must modify even this statement. The world of a writer depends upon the accident of his birth, but not, in a final sense, upon the accident of his experience. For any man's experience is, within limits, a projection of himself: as his character develops in time (a development modified, of course, by accidents and limitations of experience), it rejects or accepts, flees from or seeks, certain kinds of experience. So even the world of factual experience available to a writer, including his world of observation, the world on which he must necessarily base his imaginatively projected world, is not merely accidental; it is in itself, in part at least, a creative expression of his own process of living.

Nor is the "world" of a writer arbitrary. A good writer does not deliberately, and by an act of will, select a world he thinks will be popular among his readers. He turns, more or less instinctively, to the world that not only is available to him in the factual sense but is, we may say, *expressively available to him*—that is, *to a world that will embody and dramatize the issues that he feels significant in experience.*

To sum up this point, the special world of a writer has some aura of significance in itself. Such a world embodies significantly the conflict that underlies the specific conflicts in the individual works of fiction (or poems or plays, for that matter), and the problem of values that underlies the specific themes treated in the individual works.

EXERCISES

1. In the story "In Another Country," locate the paragraph beginning: "There were three boys who came each day who were about the same age I was," and ending, "We only knew then that there was always the war, but that we were not going to it any more." What is the significance of this paragraph for the story?

2. Do you find any points of similarity in either theme or treatment between this story and "The Lagoon" by Conrad (sec. 10).

3. What similarities do you find between "In Another Country" and "Crossing into Poland" (sec. 2)?

THE HORSE DEALER'S DAUGHTER

D. H. Lawrence (1885–1930)

"Well, Mabel, and what are you going to do with yourself?" asked Joe, with foolish flippancy. He felt quite safe himself. Without listening for an answer, he turned aside, worked a grain of tobacco to the tip of his tongue, and spat it out. He did not care about anything, since he felt safe himself.

The three brothers and the sister sat round the desolate breakfast table, attempting some sort of desultory consultation. The morning's post had given the final tap to the family fortune, and all was over. The dreary dining-room itself, with its heavy mahogany furniture, looked as if it were waiting to be done away with.

But the consulation amounted to nothing. There was a strange air of ineffectuality about the three men, as they sprawled at table, smoking and reflecting vaguely on their own condition. The girl was alone, a rather short, sullen-looking young woman of twenty-seven. She did not share the same life as her brothers. She would have been good-looking, save for the impassive fixity of her face, "bulldog," as her brothers called it.

There was a confused tramping of horses' feet outside. The three men all sprawled round in their chairs to watch. Beyond the dark holly-bushes that separated the strip of lawn from the highroad, they could see a cavalcade of shire horses swinging out of their own yard, being taken for exercise. This was the last time. These were the last horses that would go through their hands. The young men watched with critical, callous look. They were all frightened at the collapse of their lives, and the sense of disaster in which they were involved left them no inner freedom.

Yet they were three fine, well-set fellows enough. Joe, the eldest, was a man of thirty-three, broad and handsome in a hot, flushed way. His face was red, he twisted his black moustache over a thick finger, his eyes were shallow and restless. He had a sensual way of uncovering his teeth when he laughed, and his bearing was stupid. Now he watched the horses with a glazed look of helplessness in his eyes, a certain stupor of downfall.

The great draught-horses swung past. They were tied head to tail, four of them, and they heaved along to where a lane branched off from the highroad, planting their great hoofs floutingly in the fine black mud, swinging their great rounded haunches sumptuously, and trotting a few sudden steps as they were led into the lane, round the corner. Every movement showed a massive, slumbrous strength, and a stupidity which held them in subjection. The groom at the head looked back, jerking the leading rope. And the cavalcade moved out of sight up the lane, the tail of the last horse, bobbed up tight and stiff, held out taut from the swinging great haunches as they rocked behind the hedges in a motion like sleep.

Joe watched with glazed hopeless eyes. The horses were almost like his own body to him. He felt he was done for now. Luckily he was engaged to a woman as old as himself, and therefore her father, who was steward of a neighbouring estate, would provide him with a job. He would marry and go into harness. His life was over, he would be a subject animal now.

He turned uneasily aside, the retreating steps of the horses echoing in his ears. Then, with foolish restlessness, he reached for the scraps of bacon-rind from the plates, and making a faint whistling sound, flung them to the terrier that lay against the fender. He watched the dog swallow them, and waited till the creature looked into his eyes. Then a faint grin came on his face, and in a high, foolish voice he said:

"You won't get much more bacon, shall you, you little bitch?"

The dog faintly and dismally wagged its tail, then lowered its haunches, circled round, and lay down again.

There was another helpless silence at the table. Joe sprawled uneasily in his seat, not willing to go till the family conclave was dissolved. Fred Henry, the second brother, was erect, clean-limbed, alert. He had watched the passing of the horses with more sang-froid. If he was an animal, like Joe, he was an animal which controls, not one which is controlled. He was master of any horse, and he carried himself with a well-tempered air of mastery. But he was not master of the situations of life. He pushed his coarse brown moustache upwards, off his lip, and glanced irritably at his sister, who sat impassive and inscrutable.

"You'll go and stop with Lucy for a bit, shan't you?" he asked. The girl did not answer.

"I don't see what else you can do," persisted Fred Henry.

"Go as a skivvy," Joe interpolated laconically.

The girl did not move a muscle.

"If I was her, I should go in for training for a nurse," said Malcolm, the youngest of them all. He was the baby of the family, a young man of twenty-two, with a fresh, jaunty *museau*.

But Mabel did not take any notice of him. They had talked at her and round her for so many years, that she hardly heard them at all.

The marble clock on the mantelpiece softly chimed the half-hour, the dog rose uneasily from the hearthrug and looked at the party at the breakfast table. But still they sat on in ineffectual conclave.

"Oh, all right," said Joe suddenly, apropos of nothing. "I'll get a move on."

He pushed back his chair, straddled his knees with a downward jerk, to get them free, in horsey fashion, and went to the fire. Still he did not go out of the room; he was curious to know what the others would do or say. He

began to charge his pipe, looking down at the dog and saying, in a high, affected voice:

"Going wi' me? Going wi' me are ter? Tha'rt goin' further tha that counts on just now, dost hear?"

The dog faintly wagged its tail, the man stuck out his jaw and covered his pipe with his hands, and puffed intently, losing himself in the tobacco, looking down all the while at the dog with an absent brown eye. The dog looked up at him in mournful distrust. Joe stood with his knees stuck out, in real horsey fashion.

"Have you had a letter from Lucy?" Fred Henry asked of his sister.

"Last week," came the neutral reply.

"And what does she say?"

There was no answer.

"Does she *ask* you to go and stop there?" persisted Fred Henry.

"She says I can if I like."

"Well, then, you'd better. Tell her you'll come on Monday."

This was received in silence.

"That's what you'll do then, is it?" said Fred Henry, in some exasperation.

But she made no answer. There was a silence of futility and irritation in the room. Malcolm grinned fatuously.

"You'll have to make up your mind between now and next Wednesday," said Joe loudly, "or else find yourself lodgings on the kerbstone."

The face of the young woman darkened, but she sat on immutable.

"Here's Jack Fergusson!" exclaimed Malcolm, who was looking aimlessly out of the window.

"Where?" exclaimed Joe, loudly.

"Just gone past."

"Coming in?"

Malcolm craned his neck to see the gate.

"Yes," he said.

There was a silence. Mabel sat on like one condemned, at the head of the table. Then a whistle was heard from the kitchen. The dog got up and barked sharply. Joe opened the door and shouted:

"Come on."

After a moment a young man entered. He was muffled up in overcoat and a purple woollen scarf, and his tweed cap, which he did not remove, was pulled down on his head. He was of medium height, his face was rather long and pale, his eyes looked tired.

"Hello, Jack! Well, Jack!" exclaimed Malcolm and Joe. Fred Henry merely said, "Jack."

"What's doing?" asked the newcomer, evidently addressing Fred Henry.

"Same. We've got to be out by Wednesday. Got a cold?"

"I have—got it bad, too."

"Why don't you stop in?"

"*Me* stop in? When I can't stand on my legs, perhaps I shall have a chance." The young man spoke huskily. He had a slight Scotch accent.

"It's a knock-out, isn't it," said Joe, boisterously, "if a doctor goes round croaking with a cold. Looks bad for the patients, doesn't it?"

The young doctor looked at him slowly.

"Anything the matter with *you*, then?" he asked sarcastically.

"Not as I know of. Damn your eyes, I hope not. Why?"

"I thought you were very concerned about the patients, wondered if you might be one yourself."

"Damn it, no, I've never been patient to no flaming doctor, and hope I never shall be," returned Joe.

At this point Mabel rose from the table, and they all seemed to become aware of her existence. She began putting the dishes together. The young doctor looked at her, but did not address her. He had not greeted her. She went out of the room with the tray, her face impassive and unchanged.

"When are you off then, all of you?" asked the doctor.

"I'm catching the eleven-forty," replied Malcolm. "Are you goin' down wi' th' trap, Joe?"

"Yes, I've told you I'm going down wi' th' trap, haven't I?"

"We'd better be getting her in then. So long, Jack, if I don't see you before I go," said Malcolm, shaking hands.

He went out, followed by Joe, who seemed to have his tail between his legs.

"Well, this is the devil's own," exclaimed the doctor, when he was left alone with Fred Henry. "Going before Wednesday, are you?"

"That's the orders," replied the other.

"Where, to Northampton?"

"That's it."

"The devil!" exclaimed Fergusson, with quiet chagrin.

And there was silence between the two.

"All settled up, are you?" asked Fergusson.

"About."

There was another pause.

"Well, I shall miss yer, Freddy, boy," said the young doctor.

"And I shall miss thee, Jack," returned the other.

"Miss you like hell," mused the doctor.

Fred Henry turned aside. There was nothing to say. Mabel came in again, to finish clearing the table.

"What are *you* going to do, then, Miss Pervin?" asked Fergusson. "Going to your sister's, are you?"

Mabel looked at him with her steady, dangerous eyes, that always made him uncomfortable, unsettling his superficial ease.

"No," she said.

"Well, what in the name of fortune *are* you going to do? Say what you mean to do," cried Fred Henry, with futile intensity.

But she only averted her head, and continued her work. She folded the white table-cloth, and put on the chenille cloth.

"The sulkiest bitch that ever trod!" muttered her brother.

But she finished her task with perfectly impassive face, the young doctor watching her interestedly all the while. Then she went out.

Fred Henry stared after her, clenching his lips, his blue eyes fixing in sharp antagonism, as he made a grimace of sour exasperation.

"You could bray her into bits, and that's all you'd get out of her," he said in a small, narrowed tone.

The doctor smiled faintly.

"What's she *going* to do, then?" he asked.

"Strike me if *I* know!" returned the other.

There was a pause. Then the doctor stirred.

"I'll be seeing you to-night, shall I?" he said to his friend.

"Ay—where's it to be? Are we going over to Jessdale?"

"I don't know. I've got such a cold on me. I'll come round to the Moon and Stars, anyway."

"Let Lizzie and May miss their night for once, eh?"

"That's it—if I feel as I do now."

"All's one—"

The two young men went through the passage and down to the back door together. The house was large, but it was servantless now, and desolate. At the back was a small bricked house-yard, and beyond that a big square, gravelled fine and red, and having stables on two sides. Sloping, dank, winter-dark fields stretched away on the open sides.

But the stables were empty. Joseph Pervin, the father of the family, had been a man of no education, who had become a fairly large horse dealer. The stables had been full of horses, there was a great turmoil and come-and-go of horses and of dealers and grooms. Then the kitchen was full of servants. But of late things had declined. The old man had married a second time, to retrieve his fortunes. Now he was dead and everything was gone to the dogs, there was nothing but debt and threatening.

For months, Mabel had been servantless in the big house, keeping the home together in penury for her ineffectual brothers. She had kept house for ten years. But previously it was with unstinted means. Then, however

brutal and coarse everything was, the sense of money had kept her proud, confident. The men might be foul-mouthed, the women in the kitchen might have bad reputations, her brothers might have illegitimate children. But so long as there was money, the girl felt herself established, and brutally proud, reserved.

No company came to the house, save dealers and coarse men. Mabel had no associates of her own sex, after her sister went away. But she did not mind. She went regularly to church, she attended to her father. And she lived in the memory of her mother, who had died when she was fourteen, and whom she had loved. She had loved her father, too, in a different way, depending upon him, and feeling secure in him, until at the age of fifty-four he married again. And then she had set hard against him. Now he had died and left them all hopelessly in debt.

She had suffered badly during the period of poverty. Nothing, however, could shake the curious sullen, animal pride that dominated each member of the family. Now, for Mabel, the end had come. Still she would not cast about her. She would follow her own way just the same. She would always hold the keys of her own situation. Mindless and persistent, she endured from day to day. Why should she think? Why should she answer anybody? It was enough that this was the end, and there was no way out. She need not pass any more darkly along the main street of the small town, avoiding every eye. She need not demean herself any more, going into the shops and buying the cheapest food. This was at an end. She thought of nobody, not even of herself. Mindless and persistent, she seemed in a sort of ecstasy to be coming nearer to her fulfilment, her own glorification, approaching her dead mother, who was glorified.

In the afternoon she took a little bag, with shears and sponge and a small scrubbing brush, and went out. It was a grey, wintry day, with saddened, dark green fields and an atmosphere blackened by the smoke of foundries not far off. She went quickly, darkly along the causeway, heeding nobody, through the town to the churchyard.

There she always felt secure, as if no one could see her, although as a matter of fact she was exposed to the stare of every one who passed along under the churchyard wall. Nevertheless, once under the shadow of the great looming church, among the graves, she felt immune from the world, reserved within the thick churchyard wall as in another country.

Carefully she clipped the grass from the grave, and arranged the pinky white, small chrysanthemums in the tin cross. When this was done, she took an empty jar from a neighbouring grave, brought water, and carefully, most scrupulously sponged the marble headstone and the coping-stone.

It gave her sincere satisfaction to do this. She felt in immediate contact with the world of her mother. She took minute pains, went through the park in a state bordering on pure happiness, as if in performing this task she came into a subtle, intimate connection with her mother. For the life she followed here in the world was far less real than the world of death she inherited from her mother.

The doctor's house was just by the church. Fergusson, being a mere hired assistant, was slave to the country-side. As he hurried now to attend to the outpatients in the surgery, glancing across the graveyard with his quick eye, he saw the girl at her task at the grave. She seemed so intent and remote, it was like looking into another world. Some mystical element was touched in him. He slowed down as he walked, watching her as if spell-bound.

She lifted her eyes, feeling him looking. Their eyes met. And each looked away again at once, each feeling, in some way, found out by the other. He lifted his cap and passed on down the road. There remained distinct in his consciousness, like a vision, the memory of her face, lifted from the tombstone in the churchyard, and looking at him with slow, large, portentous eyes. It *was* portentous, her face. It seemed to mesmerize him. There was a heavy power in her eyes which laid hold of his whole being, as if he had drunk some powerful drug. He had been feeling weak and done before. Now the life came back into him, he felt delivered from his own fretted, daily self.

He finished his duties at the surgery as quickly as might be, hastily filling up the bottle of the waiting people with cheap drugs. Then, in perpetual haste, he set off again to visit several cases in another part of his round, before teatime. At all times he preferred to walk if he could, but particularly when he was not well. He fancied the motion restored him.

The afternoon was falling. It was grey, deadened, and wintry, with a slow, moist, heavy coldness sinking in and deadening all the faculties. But why should he think or notice? He hastily climbed the hill and turned across the dark green fields, following the black cindertrack. In the distance, across a shallow dip in the country, the small town was clustered like smouldering ash, a tower, a spire, a heap of low, raw, extinct houses. And on the nearest fringe of the town, sloping into the dip, was Oldmeadow, the Pervins' house. He could see the stables and the outbuildings distinctly, as they lay towards him on the slope. Well, he would not go there many more times! Another resource would be lost to him, another place gone: the only company he cared for in the alien, ugly little town he was losing. Nothing but work, drudgery, constant hastening from dwelling to dwelling among the colliers and the iron-workers. It wore him out, but at the same time he had a craving for it. It was a stimulant to him to be in the homes of the working people, moving as it were through the innermost body of their life. His nerves were excited and gratified. He could come so near, into the very lives of the rough, inarticulate, powerfully emotional men and women. He grumbled, he said he hated the hellish hole. But as a matter of fact it excited him, the contact with the rough, strongly-feeling people was a stimulant applied direct to his nerves.

Below Oldmeadow, in the green, shallow, soddened hollow of fields, lay a square, deep pond. Roving across the landscape, the doctor's quick eye detected a figure in black passing through the gate of the field, down towards the pond. He looked again. It would be Mabel Pervin. His mind suddenly became alive and attentive.

Why was she going down there? He pulled up on the path on the slope above, and stood staring. He could just make sure of the small black figure moving in the hollow of the failing day. He seemed to see her in the midst of such obscurity, that he was like a clairvoyant, seeing rather with the mind's eye than with ordinary sight. Yet he could see her positively enough, whilst he kept his eye attentive. He felt, if he looked away from her, in the thick, ugly falling dusk, he would lose her altogether.

He followed her minutely as she moved, direct and intent, like something transmitted rather than stirring in voluntary activity, straight down the field towards the pond. There she stood on the bank for a moment. She never raised her head. Then she waded slowly into the water.

He stood motionless as the small black figure walked slowly and deliberately towards the centre of the pond, very slowly, gradually moving deeper into the motionless water, and still moving forward as the water got up to her breast. Then he could see her no more in the dusk of the dead afternoon.

"There!" he exclaimed. "Would you believe it?"

And he hastened straight down, running over the wet, soddened fields, pushing through the hedges, down into the depression of callous wintry obscurity. It took him several minutes to come to the pond. He stood on the bank, breathing heavily. He

could see nothing. His eyes seemed to penetrate the dead water. Yes, perhaps that was the dark shadow of her black clothing beneath the surface of the water.

He slowly ventured into the pond. The bottom was deep, soft clay, he sank in, and the water clasped dead cold round his legs. As he stirred he could smell the cold, rotten clay that fouled up into the water. It was objectionable in his lungs. Still, repelled and yet not heeding, he moved deeper into the pond. The cold water rose over his thighs, over his loins, upon his abdomen. The lower part of his body was all sunk in the hideous cold element. And the bottom was so deeply soft and uncertain, he was afraid of pitching with his mouth underneath. He could not swim, and was afraid.

He crouched a little, spreading his hands under the water and moving them round, trying to feel for her. The dead cold pond swayed upon his chest. He moved again, a little deeper, and again, with his hands underneath, he felt all around under the water. And he touched her clothing. But it evaded his fingers. He made a desperate effort to grasp it.

And so doing he lost his balance and went under, horribly, suffocating in the foul earthy water, struggling madly for a few moments. At last, after what seemed an eternity, he got his footing, rose again into the air, and looked around. He gasped, and knew he was in the world. Then he looked at the water. She had risen near him. He grasped her clothing, and drawing her nearer, turned to take his way to land again.

He went very slowly, carefully, absorbed in the slow progress. He rose higher, climbing out of the pond. The water was now only about his legs; he was thankful, full of relief to be out of the clutches of the pond. He lifted her and staggered on to the bank, out of the horror of wet, grey clay.

He laid her down on the bank. She was quite unconscious and running with water. He made the water come from her mouth, he worked to restore her. He did not have to work very long before he could feel the breathing begin again in her; she was breathing naturally. He worked a little longer. He could feel her live beneath his hands; she was coming back. He wiped her face, wrapped her in his overcoat, looked round into the dim, dark grey world, then lifted her and staggered down the bank and across the fields.

It seemed an unthinkably long way, and his burden so heavy he felt he would never get to the house. But at last he was in the stable-yard, and then in the house-yard. He opened the door and went into the house. In the kitchen he laid her down on the hearthrug, and called. The house was empty. But the fire was burning in the grate.

Then again he kneeled to attend to her. She was breathing regularly, her eyes were wide open and as if conscious, but there seemed something missing in her look. She was conscious in herself, but unconscious of her surroundings.

He ran upstairs, took blankets from a bed, and put them before the fire to warm. Then he removed her saturated, earthy-smelling clothing, rubbed her dry with a towel, and wrapped her naked in the blankets. Then he went into the dining-room, to look for spirits. There was a little whisky. He drank a gulp himself, and put some into her mouth.

The effect was instantaneous. She looked full into his face, as if she had been seeing him for some time, and yet had only just become conscious of him.

"Dr. Fergusson?" she said.

"What?" he answered.

He was divesting himself of his coat, intending to find some dry clothing upstairs. He could not bear the smell of the dead, clayey water, and he was mortally afraid for his own health.

"What did I do?" she asked.

"Walked into the pond," he replied. He had begun to shudder like one sick, and could hardly attend to her. Her eyes remained full on him, he seemed to be going dark in his mind, looking back at her helplessly. The shuddering became quieter in him, his life came back in him, dark and unknowing, but strong again.

"Was I out of my mind?" she asked, while her eyes were fixed on him all the time.

"Maybe, for the moment," he replied. He felt quiet, because his strength had come back. The strange fretful strain had left him.

"Am I out of my mind now?" she asked.

"Are you?" he reflected a moment. "No," he answered truthfully, "I don't see that you are." He turned his face aside. He was afraid now, because he felt dazed, and felt dimly that her power was stronger than his, in this issue. And she continued to look at him fixedly all the time. "Can you tell me where I shall find some dry things to put on?" he asked.

"Did you dive into the pond for me?" she asked.

"No," he answered. "I walked in. But I went in overhead as well."

There was silence for a moment. He hesitated. He very much wanted to go upstairs to get into dry clothing. But there was another desire in him. And she seemed to hold him. His will seemed to have gone to sleep, and left him, standing there slack before her. But he felt warm inside himself. He did not shudder at all, though his clothes were sodden on him.

"Why did you?" she asked.

"Because I didn't want you to do such a foolish thing," he said.

"It wasn't foolish," she said, still gazing at him as she lay on the floor, with a sofa cushion under her head. "It was the right thing to do. *I* knew best, then."

"I'll go and shift these wet things," he said. But still he had not the power to move out of her presence, until she sent him. It was as if she had the life of his body in her hands, and he could not extricate himself. Or perhaps he did not want to.

Suddenly she sat up. Then she became aware of her own immediate condition. She felt the blankets about her, she knew her own limbs. For a moment it seemed as if her reason were going. She looked round, with wild eye, as if seeking something. He stood still with fear. She saw her clothing lying scattered.

"Who undressed me?" she asked, her eyes resting full and inevitable on his face.

"I did," he replied, "to bring you round."

For some moments she sat and gazed at him awfully, her lips parted.

"Do you love me, then?" she asked.

He only stood and stared at her, fascinated. His soul seemed to melt.

She shuffled forward on her knees, and put her arms round him, round his legs, as he stood there, pressing her breasts against his knees and thighs, clutching him with strange, convulsive certainty, pressing his thighs against her, drawing him to her face, her throat, as she looked up at him with flaring, humble eyes of transfiguration, triumphant in first possession.

"You love me," she murmured, in strange transport, yearning and triumphant and confident. "You love me. I know you love me, I know."

And she was passionately kissing his knees, through the wet clothing, passionately and indiscriminately kissing his knees, his legs, as if unaware of everything.

He looked down at the tangled wet hair, the wild, bare animal shoulders. He was amazed, bewildered, and afraid. He had never thought of loving her. He had never wanted to love her. When he rescued her and restored her, he was a doctor, and she was a patient. He had had no single personal thought of her. Nay, this introduction of the personal element was very distasteful to him, a violation of his professional honour. It was horrible to have her there embracing his knees. It was horrible. He revolted from it, violently. And yet—and yet—he had not the power to break away.

She looked at him again, with the same supplication of powerful love, and that same transcendent, frightening light of triumph. In view of the delicate flame which seemed to come from her face like a light, he was powerless. And yet he had never intended to love her. He had never intended. And something stubborn in him could not give way.

"You love me," she repeated, in a murmur of deep, rhapsodic assurance. "You love me."

Her hands were drawing him, drawing him down to her. He was afraid, even a little horrified. For he had, really, no intention of loving her. Yet her hands were drawing him towards her. He put out his hand quickly to steady himself, and grasped her bare shoulder. A flame seemed to burn the hand that grasped her soft shoulder. He had no intention of loving her: his whole will was against his yielding. It was horrible. And yet wonderful was the touch of her shoulders, beautiful the shining of her face. Was she perhaps mad? He had a horror of yielding to her. Yet something in him ached also.

He had been staring away at the door, away from her. But his hand remained on her shoulder. She had gone suddenly very still. He looked down at her. Her eyes were now wide with fear, with doubt, the light was dying from her face, a shadow of terrible greyness was returning. He could not bear the touch of her eyes' question upon him, and the look of death behind the question.

With an inward groan he gave way, and let his heart yield towards her. A sudden gentle smile came on his face. And her eyes, which never left his face, slowly, slowly filled with tears. He watched the strange water rise in her eyes, like some slow fountain coming up. And his heart seemed to burn and melt away in his breast.

He could not bear to look at her any more. He dropped on his knees and caught her head with his arms and pressed her face against his throat. She was very still. His heart, which seemed to have broken, was burning with a kind of agony in his breast. And he felt her slow, hot tears wetting his throat. But he could not move.

He felt the hot tears wet his neck and the hollows of his neck, and he remained motionless, suspended through one of man's eternities. Only now it had become indispensable to him to have her face pressed close to him; he could never let her go again. He could never let her head go away from the close clutch of his arm. He wanted to remain like that for ever, with his heart hurting him in a pain that was also life to him. Without knowing, he was looking down on her damp, soft brown hair.

Then, as it were suddenly, he smelt the horrid stagnant smell of that water. And at the same moment she drew away from him and looked at him. Her eyes were wistful and unfathomable. He was afraid of them, and he fell to kissing her, not knowing what he was doing. He wanted her eyes not to have that terrible, wistful, unfathomable look.

When she turned her face to him again, a faint delicate flush was glowing, and there was again dawning that terrible shining of joy in her eyes, which really terrified him, and yet which he now wanted to see, because he feared the look of doubt still more.

"You love me?" she said, rather faltering.

"Yes." The word cost him a painful effort. Not because it wasn't true. But because it was too newly true, the *saying* seemed to tear open again his newly-torn heart. And he hardly wanted it to be true, even now.

She lifted her face to him, and he bent forward and kissed her on the mouth, gently, with the one kiss that is an eternal pledge. And as he kissed her his heart strained again in his breast. He never intended to love her. But now it was over. He had crossed over the gulf to her, and all that he had left behind had shrivelled and become void.

After the kiss, her eyes again slowly filled with tears. She sat still, away from him, with her face drooped aside, and her hands folded in her lap. The tears fell very slowly. There was complete silence. He too sat there motionless and silent on the hearthrug. The

strange pain of his heart that was broken seemed to consume him. That he should love her? That this was love! That he should be ripped open in this way! Him, a doctor! How they would all jeer if they knew! It was agony to him to think they might know.

In the curious naked pain of the thought he looked again to her. She was sitting there drooped into a muse. He saw a tear fall, and his heart flared hot. He saw for the first time that one of her shoulders was quite uncovered, one arm bare, he could see one of her small breasts; dimly, because it had become almost dark in the room.

"Why are you crying?" he asked, in an altered voice.

She looked up at him, and behind her tears the consciousness of her situation for the first time brought a dark look of shame to her eyes.

"I'm not crying, really," she said, watching him half frightened.

He reached his hand, and softly closed it on her bare arm.

"I love you! I love you!" he said in a soft, low vibrating voice, unlike himself.

She shrank, and dropped her head. The soft, penetrating grip of his hand on her arm distressed her. She looked up at him.

"I want to go," she said. "I want to go and get you some dry things."

"Why?" he said. "I'm all right."

"But I want to go," she said. "And I want you to change your things."

He released her arm, and she wrapped herself in the blanket, looking at him rather frightened. And still she did not rise.

"Kiss me," she said wistfully.

He kissed her, but briefly, half in anger.

Then, after a second, she rose nervously, all mixed up in the blanket. He watched her in her confusion, as she tried to extricate herself and wrap herself up so that she could walk. He watched her relentlessly, as she knew. And as she went, the blanket trailing, and as he saw a glimpse of her feet and her white leg, he tried to remember her as she was when he had wrapped her in the blanket.

But then he didn't want to remember, because she had been nothing to him then, and his nature revolted from remembering her as she was when she was nothing to him.

A tumbling, muffled noise from within the dark house startled him. Then he heard her voice:—"There are clothes." He rose and went to the foot of the stairs, and gathered up the garments she had thrown down. Then he came back to the fire, to rub himself down and dress. He grinned at his own appearance when he had finished.

The fire was sinking, so he put on coal. The house was now quite dark, save for the light of a street-lamp that shone in faintly from beyond the holly trees. He lit the gas with matches he found on the mantelpiece. Then he emptied the pockets of his own clothes, and threw all his wet things in a heap into the scullery. After which he gathered up her sodden clothes, gently, and put them in a separate heap on the copper-top in the scullery.

It was six o'clock on the clock. His own watch had stopped. He ought to go back to the surgery. He waited, and still she did not come down. So he went to the foot of the stairs and called:

"I shall have to go."

Almost immediately he heard her coming down. She had on her best dress of black voile, and her hair was tidy, but still damp. She looked at him—and in spite of herself, smiled.

"I don't like you in those clothes," she said.

"Do I look a sight?" he answered.

They were shy of one another.

"I'll make you some tea," she said.

"No, I must go."

"Must you?" And she looked at him again with the wide, strained, doubtful eyes. And again, from the pain of his breast, he knew how he loved her. He went and bent to kiss her, gently, passionately, with his heart's painful kiss.

"And my hair smells so horrible," she murmured in distraction. "And I'm so awful,

I'm so awful! Oh, no, I'm too awful." And she broke into bitter, heart-broken sobbing. "You can't want to love me, I'm horrible."

"Don't be silly, don't be silly," he said, trying to comfort her, kissing her, holding her in his arms. "I want you, I want to marry you, we're going to be married, quickly, quickly—tomorrow if I can."

But she only sobbed terribly, and cried:

"I feel awful. I feel awful. I feel I'm horrible to you."

"No, I want you, I want you," was all he answered, blindly, with that terrible intonation which frightened her almost more than her horror lest he should *not* want her.

———— ◆ ◆ ◆ ————

This story is an interpretation of love, of the paradoxical quality of love, which in its shocking and distressing destruction of the old, accustomed self is a kind of death, and in its awakening of new hopes and powers is a kind of birth. Since the story is primarily about the nature of love, and not about the nature of individual persons, it presents two quite diverse people being surprised into the same experience. That is, we may say that it is scarcely more the story of the horse dealer's daughter than of Dr. Fergusson. True, we approach the story through her, but at the crisis his consciousness dominates the action until the very end.

"Well, Mabel, and what are you going to do with yourself?" one of the brothers asks in the opening sentence, and that question sets the line for the story. The question of Mabel's future is the main topic of discussion, but it is a discussion into which she does not enter. It is a question that Dr. Fergusson himself repeats at the end of what we may consider the first section, or movement, of the story. But the question is more than a practical one, a question about her plans for occupation and so on; we, the readers, know that it concerns her fundamental fate, the kind of being she will achieve.

The whole temper of the first section is one of heaviness and futility. The dining room is "dreary." The men reflect "vaguely on their own condition," each one locked within himself. They all feel the lack of "inner freedom." The horses that move past swing their haunches sumptuously and show a massive, slumbrous strength, but they are held in subjection by their own "stupidity," and they rock behind the hedges in a "motion like sleep." Mabel's face wears an "impassive fixity," and later on, after the arrival of Dr. Fergusson, she sits "like one condemned." And from the big, cheerless house, "sloping, dank, winter-dark fields" stretch away. The world of the story is a deathly, unawakened, wintry world. The awakening and regeneration of this world will constitute the action.

The second section has to do with Mabel's life in the past and her identification with the dead mother: "Mindless and persistent, she seemed in a sort of ecstasy to be coming nearer to her fulfilment, her own glorification, approaching her dead mother, who was glorified." At the graveyard she feels "immune from the world," and "the life she followed here in the world was far less real than the world of death she inherited from her mother." In one sense, this section prepares us for the attempted suicide, but in another sense it foreshadows the symbolic death through love that will lead to Mabel's "glorification." In this section, the diffuse atmosphere of unfulfillment and death that had characterized the first section is now associated with Mabel herself. But this section ends when Mabel lifts her eyes to the eyes of Dr. Fergusson, and each feels, "in some way, found out by the other."

The third section shifts into the consciousness of Dr. Fergusson. It begins with his discovery of the "heavy power in her eyes" and the reviving effect on him: "Now the life came back into him, he felt delivered from his own fretted, daily self." This, then, corresponds to the foreshadowing of Mabel's "glorification." But he is still caught in the "gray, deadened, wintry" world, so "why should he think or notice?" The only life he now has is the stimulation he gets from his contact with the "rough, inarticulate, powerfully emotional men and women" who are his poor patients. He has no life of his own. This section ends with the moment

when he sees Mabel pass and feels that if he looks away from her, "in the thick, ugly falling dusk," he will "lose her altogether."

The fourth section shows Mabel entering the pond with the intention of suicide, and Dr. Fergusson's rescue. The pond is "cold," "rotten," "fouled," and "earthy," with the "horror of wet, grey clay." It is the pond of death that they both enter, symbolically the risk of the destruction of self. Perhaps, too, the pond with its repellent qualities symbolizes the aspects of sexuality that may seem "unclean." The pond remains, of course, a real pond in a real world, a pond of dirty water in which a person can really drown, but in the pattern of meaning in the story we see that it has also other significances.

The fifth section shows the consequences of the crucial decision to enter the pond, a decision made by Mabel and then by Dr. Fergusson. This is the section of the awakening, the regeneration, the "glorification." Mabel, who has more fully accepted the idea of death (she had actually intended suicide), is therefore the more ready of the two for the awakening: she had already renounced the self. Dr. Fergusson, however, had entered the pond with fear and revulsion, and even now "something stubborn in him could not give way," and even now, as she embraces him, he smells "the horrid stagnant smell of that water." But the pain he now experiences is "also life to him," and in the end he accepts that life, and the past becomes nothing: he does not even want to remember Mabel as she had been before when she "was nothing to him."

The last part of this section (or shall we call it another section?) shows their return to the ordinary world. Dr. Fergusson must go to the surgery. Mabel changes clothes. She offers to make him some tea. They are shy of each other. But in the midst of this ordinary life, their new sense of the world bursts out again with joy and terror.

Looking back over the story, we can see how vividly the real world is presented, how strongly felt and visualized are the scenes. But we can also see how almost every detail, details that at first may seem merely descriptive and casual, are related to the main line of the story, that is, how they tend to move from description to symbolism. The details of the brooding, deathly, winter world apply also to the condition of the lovers before their awakening. The horror of the real pond applies also to an emotional experience. In other words, the story is strongly integrated: we sense meaningfulness in even the smallest details.

EXERCISES

1. After the rescue from the pond, the following sentence about Mabel appears: "She was conscious in herself, but unconscious of her surroundings." What is the significance of this in relation to the theme? A little later there is the sentence about Dr. Fergusson: "He could not bear the smell of the dead, clayey water, and he was mortally afraid for his own health." What is the significance of this?

2. What is the gain in having Dr. Fergusson discover the attempted suicide rather than in having the reader follow the process with Mabel? Do we grasp enough of Mabel's motivation to be able to leave her before the decision is made and yet not be surprised when we discover the results of the decision?

3. We have said of this story that some of the details that are quite realistic in their presentation tend to take on a symbolic (see Glossary) relation to the theme of the story, or at the least generate an atmosphere (see Glossary) that is significant for the story. Can you locate some such details?

4. Compare the conception of love in this story with that in "Araby" (sec. 7). In "Legal Aid" (sec. 5).

THE MAN WHO WAS ALMOST A MAN

Richard Wright (1908–1960)

Dave struck out across the fields, looking homeward through paling light. Whut's the use talkin wid em niggers in the field? Anyhow, his mother was putting supper on the table. Them niggers can't understan nothing. One of these days he was going to get a gun and practice shooting, then they couldn't talk to him as though he were a little boy. He slowed, looking at the ground. Shucks, Ah ain scareda them even ef they are biggern me! Aw, Ah know whut Ahma do. Ahm going by ol Joe's sto n git that Sears Roebuck catlog n look at them guns. Mebbe Ma will lemme buy one when she gits mah pay from ol man Hawkins. Ahma beg her t gimme some money. Ahm ol ernough to hava gun. Ahm seventeen. Almost a man. He strode, feeling his long loose-jointed limbs. Shucks, a man oughta hava little gun aftah he done worked hard all day.

He came in sight of Joe's store. A yellow lantern glowed on the front porch. He mounted steps and went through the screen door, hearing it bang behind him. There was a strong smell of coal oil and mackerel fish. He felt very confident until he saw fat Joe walk in through the rear door, then his courage began to ooze.

"Howdy, Dave! Whutcha want?"

"How yuh, Mistah Joe? Aw, Ah don wanna buy nothing. Ah jus wanted t see ef yuhd lemme look at tha catlog erwhile."

"Sure! You wanna see it here?"

"Nawsuh. Ah wans t take it home wid me. Ah'll bring it back termorrow when Ah come in from the fiels."

"You plannin on buying something?"

"Yessuh."

"Your ma lettin you have your own money now?"

"Shucks. Mistah Joe, Ahm gittin t be a man like anybody else!"

Joe laughed and wiped his greasy white face with a red bandanna.

"Whut you plannin on buyin?"

Dave looked at the floor, scratched his head, scratched his thigh, and smiled. Then he looked up shyly.

"Ah'll tell yuh, Mistah Joe, ef yuh promise yuh won't tell."

"I promise."

"Waal, Ahma buy a gun."

"A gun? Whut you want with a gun?"

"Ah wanna keep it."

"You ain't nothing but a boy. You don't need a gun."

"Aw, lemme have the catlog, Mistah Joe. Ah'll bring it back."

Joe walked through the rear door. Dave was elated. He looked around at barrels of sugar and flour. He heard Joe coming back. He craned his neck to see if he were bringing the book. Yeah, he's got it. Gawd-dog, he's got it!

"Here, but be sure you bring it back. It's the only one I got."

"Sho, Mistah Joe."

"Say, if you wanna buy a gun, why don't you buy one from me? I gotta gun to sell."

"Will it shoot?"

"Sure it'll shoot."

"Whut kind is it?"

"Oh, it's kinda old . . . a left-hand Wheeler. A pistol. A big one."

"Is it got bullets in it?"

"It's loaded."

"Kin Ah see it?"

"Where's your money?"

"Whut yuh wan fer it?"

"I'll let you have it for two dollars."

"Just two dollahs? Shucks, Ah could buy tha when Ah git mah pay."

"I'll have it here when you want it."

"Awright, suh. Ah be in fer it."

He went through the door, hearing it slam again behind him. Ahma git some money from Ma n buy me a gun! Only two dollahs! He tucked the thick catalogue under his arm and hurried.

"Where yuh been, boy?" His mother held a steaming dish of black-eyed peas.

"Aw, Ma, Ah jus stopped down the road t talk wid the boys."

"Yuh know bettah t keep suppah waitin."

He sat down, resting the catalogue on the edge of the table.

"Yuh git up from there and git to the well n wash yosef! Ah ain feedin no hogs in mah house!"

She grabbed his shoulder and pushed him. He stumbled out of the room, then came back to get the catalogue.

"Whut this?"

"Aw, Ma, it's jusa catlog."

"Who yuh git it from?"

"From Joe, down at the sto."

"Waal, thas good. We kin use it in the outhouse."

"Naw, Ma." He grabbed for it. "Gimme ma catlog, Ma."

She held onto it and glared at him.

"Quit hollerin at me! Whut's wrong wid yuh? Yuh crazy?"

"But Ma, please. It ain mine! It's Joe's! He tol me t bring it back t im termorrow."

She gave up the book. He stumbled down the back steps, hugging the thick book under his arm. When he had splashed water on his face and hands, he groped back to the kitchen and fumbled in a corner for the towel. He bumped into a chair; it clattered to the floor. The catalogue sprawled at his feet. When he had dried his eyes he snatched up the book and held it again under his arm. His mother stood watching him.

"Now, ef yuh gonna act a fool over that ol book, Ah'll take it n burn it up."

"Naw, Ma, please."

"Waal, set down n be still!"

He sat down and drew the oil lamp close. He thumbed page after page, unaware of the food his mother set on the table. His father came in. Then his small brother.

"Whutcha got there, Dave?" his father asked.

"Jusa catlog," he answered, not looking up.

"Yeah, here they is!" His eyes glowed at blue-and-black revolvers. He glanced up, feeling sudden guilt. His father was watching him. He eased the book under the table and rested it on his knees. After the blessing was asked, he ate. He scooped up peas and swallowed fat meat without chewing. Buttermilk helped to wash it down. He did not want to mention money before his father.

He would do much better by cornering his mother when she was alone. He looked at his father uneasily out of the edge of his eye.

"Boy, how come yuh don quit foolin wid tha book n eat yo suppah?"

"Yessuh."

"How you n ol man Hawkins gitten erlong?"

"Suh?"

"Can't yuh hear? Why don yuh lissen? Ah ast yu how wuz yuh n ol man Hawkins gittin erlong?"

"Oh, swell, Pa. Ah plows mo lan than anybody over there."

"Waal, yuh oughta keep yo mind on whut yuh doin."

"Yessuh."

He poured his plate full of molasses and sopped it up slowly with a chunk of cornbread. When his father and brother had left the kitchen, he still sat and looked again at the guns in the catalogue, longing to muster courage enough to present his case to his mother. Lawd, ef Ah only had tha pretty one! He could almost feel the slickness of the weapon with his fingers. If he had a gun like that he would polish it and keep it shining so it would never rust. N Ah'd keep it loaded, by Gawd!

"Ma?" His voice was hesitant.

"Hunh?"

"Ol man Hawkins give yuh mah money yit?"

"Yeah, but ain no usa yuh thinking bout throwin nona it erway. Ahm keepin tha money sos yuh kin have cloes t go to school this winter."

He rose and went to her side with the open catalogue in his palms. She was washing dishes, her head bent low over a pan. Shyly he raised the book. When he spoke, his voice was husky, faint.

"Ma, Gawd knows Ah wans one of these."

"One of whut?" she asked, not raising her eyes.

"One of these," he said again, not dar-

ing even to point. She glanced up at the page, then at him with wide eyes.

"Nigger, is yuh gone plumb crazy?"

"Aw, Ma—"

"Git outta here! Don yuh talk t me bout no gun! Yuh a fool!"

"Ma, Ah kin buy one fer two dollahs."

"Not ef Ah knows it, yuh ain!"

"But yuh promised me one—"

"Ah don care whut Ah promised! Yuh ain nothing but a boy yit!"

"Ma, ef yuh lemme buy one Ah'll *never* ast yuh fer nothing no mo."

"Ah tol yuh t git outta here! Yuh ain gonna toucha penny of tha money fer no gun! Thas how come Ah has Mistah Hawkins t pay yo wages t me, cause Ah knows yuh ain got no sense."

"But, Ma, we needa gun. Pa ain got no gun. We needa gun in the house. Yuh kin never tell whut might happen."

"Now don yuh try to maka fool outta me, boy! Ef we did hava gun, yuh wouldn't have it!"

He laid the catalogue down and slipped his arm around her waist.

"Aw, Ma, Ah done worked hard alla summer n ain ast yuh fer nothin, is Ah, now?"

"Thas whut yuh spose t do!"

"But Ma, Ah wans a gun. Yuh kin lemme have two dollahs outta mah money. Please, Ma. I kin give it to Pa . . . Please, Ma! Ah loves yuh, Ma."

When she spoke her voice came soft and low.

"Whut yu wan wida gun, Dave? Yuh don need no gun. Yuh'll git in trouble. N ef yo pa jus thought Ah let yuh have money t buy a gun he'd hava fit."

"Ah'll hide it, Ma. It ain but two dollahs."

"Lawd, chil, whut's wrong wid yuh?"

"Ain nothin wrong, Ma. Ahm almos a man now. Ah wans a gun."

"Who gonna sell yuh a gun?"

"Ol Joe at the sto."

"N it don cos but two dollahs?"

"Thas all, Ma. Jus two dollahs. Please, Ma."

She was stacking the plates away; her hands moved slowly, reflectively. Dave kept an anxious silence. Finally, she turned to him.

"Ah'll let yuh git tha gun ef yuh promise me one thing."

"Whut's tha, Ma?"

"Yuh bring it straight back t me, yuh hear? It be fer Pa."

"Yessum! Lemme go now, Ma."

She stooped, turned slightly to one side, raised the hem of her dress, rolled down the top of her stocking, and came up with a slender wad of bills.

"Here," she said. "Lawd knows yuh don need no gun. But yer pa does. Yuh bring it right back t me, yuh hear? Ahma put it up. Now ef yuh don, Ahma have yuh pa lick yuh so hard yuh won fergit it."

"Yessum."

He took the money, ran down the steps, and across the yard.

"Dave! Yuuuuuh Daaaaave!"

He heard, but he was not going to stop now. "Naw, Lawd!"

The first movement he made the following morning was to reach under his pillow for the gun. In the gray light of dawn he held it loosely, feeling a sense of power. Could kill a man with a gun like this. Kill anybody, black or white. And if he were holding his gun in his hand, nobody could run over him; they would have to respect him. It was a big gun, with a long barrel and a heavy handle. He raised and lowered it in his hand, marveling at its weight.

He had not come straight home with it as his mother had asked; instead he had stayed out in the fields, holding the weapon in his hand, aiming it now and then at some imaginary foe. But he had not fired it; he had been afraid that his father might hear. Also he was not sure he knew how to fire it.

To avoid surrendering the pistol he had not come into the house until he knew that they were all asleep. When his mother had tiptoed to his bedside late that night and demanded the gun, he had first played possum; then he had told her that the gun was hidden outdoors, that he would bring it to her in the morning. Now he lay turning it slowly in his hands. He broke it, took out the cartridges, felt them, and then put them back.

He slid out of bed, got a long strip of old flannel from a trunk, wrapped the gun in it, and tied it to his naked thigh while it was still loaded. He did not go in to breakfast. Even though it was not yet daylight, he started for Jim Hawkins' plantation. Just as the sun was rising he reached the barns where the mules and plows were kept.

"Hey! That you, Dave?"

He turned. Jim Hawkins stood eying him suspiciously.

"What're yuh doing here so early?"

"Ah didn't know Ah wuz gittin up so early, Mistah Hawkins. Ah wuz fixin t hitch up ol Jenny n take her t the fiels."

"Good. Since you're so early, how about plowing that stretch down by the woods?"

"Suits me, Mistah Hawkins."

"O.K. Go to it!"

He hitched Jenny to a plow and started across the fields. Hot dog! This was just what he wanted. If he could get down by the woods, he could shoot his gun and nobody would hear. He walked behind the plow, hearing the traces creaking, feeling the gun tied tight to his thigh.

When he reached the woods, he plowed two whole rows before he decided to take out the gun. Finally, he stopped, looked in all directions, then untied the gun and held it in his hand. He turned to the mule and smiled.

"Know whut this is, Jenny? Naw, yuh wouldn know! Yuhs jusa ol mule! Anyhow, this is a gun, n it kin shoot, by Gawd!"

He held the gun at arm's length. Whut t hell, Ahma shoot this thing! He looked at Jenny again.

"Lissen here, Jenny! When Ah pull this ol trigger, Ah don wan yuh t run n acka fool now!"

Jenny stood with head down, her short ears pricked straight. Dave walked off about twenty feet, held the gun far out from him at arm's length, and turned his head. Hell, he told himself, Ah ain afraid. The gun felt loose in his fingers; he waved it wildly for a moment. Then he shut his eyes and tightened his forefinger. Bloom! A report half deafened him and he thought his right hand was torn from his arm. He heard Jenny whinnying and galloping over the field, and he found himself on his knees, squeezing his fingers hard between his legs. His hand was numb; he jammed it into his mouth, trying to warm it, trying to stop the pain. The gun lay at his feet. He did not quite know what had happened. He stood up and stared at the gun as though it were a living thing. He gritted his teeth and kicked the gun. Yuh almos broke mah arm! He turned to look for Jenny; she was far over the fields, tossing her head and kicking wildly.

"Hol on there, ol mule!"

When he caught up with her she stood trembling, walling her big white eyes at him. The plow was far away; the traces had broken. Then Dave stopped short, looking, not believing. Jenny was bleeding. Her left side was red and wet with blood. He went closer. Lawd, have mercy! Wondah did Ah shoot this mule? He grabbed for Jenny's mane. She flinched, snorted, whirled, tossing her head.

"Hol on now! Hol on."

Then he saw the hole in Jenny's side, right between the ribs. It was round, wet, red. A crimson stream streaked down the front leg, flowing fast. Good Gawd! Ah wuzn't shootin at tha mule. He felt panic. He knew he had to stop that blood, or Jenny would bleed to death. He had never seen so much blood in all his life. He chased the mule for half a mile, trying to catch her. Finally she stopped, breathing hard, stumpy tail half

arched. He caught her mane and led her back to where the plow and gun lay. Then he stooped and grabbed handfuls of damp black earth and tried to plug the bullet hole. Jenny shuddered, whinnied, and broke from him.

"Hol on! Hol on now!"

He tried to plug it again, but blood came anyhow. His fingers were hot and sticky. He rubbed dirt into his palms, trying to dry them. Then again he attempted to plug the bullet hole, but Jenny shied away, kicking her heels high. He stood helpless. He had to do something. He ran at Jenny; she dodged him. He watched a red stream of blood flow down Jenny's leg and form a bright pool at her feet.

"Jenny . . . Jenny," he called weakly.

His lips trembled. She's bleeding t death! He looked in the direction of home, wanting to go back, wanting to get help. But he saw the pistol lying in the damp black clay. He had a queer feeling that if he only did something, this would not be; Jenny would not be there bleeding to death.

When he went to her this time, she did not move. She stood with sleepy, dreamy eyes; and when he touched her she gave a low-pitched whinny and knelt to the ground, her front knees slopping in blood.

"Jenny . . . Jenny . . ." he whispered.

For a long time she held her neck erect; then her head sank, slowly. Her ribs swelled with a mighty heave and she went over.

Dave's stomach felt empty, very empty. He picked up the gun and held it gingerly between his thumb and forefinger. He buried it at the foot of a tree. He took a stick and tried to cover the pool of blood with dirt—but what was the use? There was Jenny lying with her mouth open and her eyes walled and glassy. He could not tell Jim Hawkins he had shot his mule. But he had to tell something. Yeah, Ah'll tell em Jenny started gittin wil n fell on the joint of the plow. . . . But that would hardly happen to a mule. He walked across the field slowly, head down.

It was sunset. Two of Jim Hawkins' men were over near the edge of the woods digging a hole in which to bury Jenny. Dave was surrounded by a knot of people, all of whom were looking down at the dead mule.

"I don't see how in the world it happened," said Jim Hawkins for the tenth time.

The crowd parted and Dave's mother, father, and small brother pushed into the center.

"Where Dave?" his mother called.

"There he is," said Jim Hawkins.

His mother grabbed him.

"Whut happened, Dave? Whut yuh done?"

"Nothin."

"Cmon, boy, talk," his father said.

Dave took a deep breath and told the story he knew nobody believed.

"Waal," he drawled. "Ah brung ol Jenny down here sos Ah could do mah plowin. Ah plowed bout two rows, just like yuh see." He stopped and pointed at the long rows of upturned earth. "Then somethin musta been wrong wid ol Jenny. She wouldn ack right a-tall. She started snortin n kickin her heels. Ah tried t hol her, but she pulled erway, rearin n goin in. Then when the point of the plow was stickin up in the air, she swung erroun n twisted herself back on it . . . She stuck herself n started t bleed. N fo Ah could do anything, she wuz dead."

"Did you ever hear of anything like that in all your life?" asked Jim Hawkins.

There were white and black standing in the crowd. They murmured. Dave's mother came close to him and looked hard into his face. "Tell the truth, Dave," she said.

"Looks like a bullet hole to me," said one man.

"Dave, whut yuh do wid the gun?" his mother asked.

The crowd surged in, looking at him. He jammed his hands into his pockets, shook his head slowly from left to right, and backed away. His eyes were wide and painful.

"Did he hava gun?" asked Jim Hawkins.

"By Gawd, Ah tol yuh tha wuz a gun wound," said a man, slapping his thigh.

His father caught his shoulders and shook him till his teeth rattled.

"Tell whut happened, yuh rascal! Tell whut . . ."

Dave looked at Jenny's stiff legs and began to cry.

"Whut yuh do wid tha gun?" his mother asked.

"Whut wuz he doin wida gun?" his father asked.

"Come on and tell the truth," said Hawkins. "Ain't nobody going to hurt you . . ."

His mother crowded close to him.

"Did yuh shoot tha mule, Dave?"

Dave cried, seeing blurred white and black faces.

"Ahh ddinn gggo tt sshooot hher . . . Ah ssswear ffo Gawd Ahh ddin. . . . Ah wuz a-tryin t sssee ef the old gggun would sshoot—"

"Where yuh git the gun from?" his father asked.

"Ah got it from Joe, at the sto."

"Where yuh git the money?"

"Ma give it t me."

"He kept worryin me, Bob. Ah had t. Ah tol im t bring the gun right back t me . . . It was fer yuh, the gun."

"But how yuh happen to shoot that mule?" asked Jim Hawkins.

"Ah wuzn shootin at the mule, Mistah Hawkins. The gun jumped when Ah pulled the trigger . . . N fo Ah knowed anythin Jenny was there a-bleedin."

Somebody in the crowd laughed. Jim Hawkins walked close to Dave and looked into his face.

"Well, looks like you have bought you a mule, Dave."

"Ah swear fo Gawd, Ah didn go t kill the mule, Mistah Hawkins!"

"But you killed her!"

All the crowd was laughing now. They stood on tiptoe and poked heads over one another's shoulders.

"Well, boy, looks like yuh done bought a dead mule! Hahaha!"

"Ain tha ershame."

"Hohohohoho."

Dave stood, head down, twisting his feet in the dirt.

"Well, you needn't worry about it, Bob," said Jim Hawkins to Dave's father. "Just let the boy keep on working and pay me two dollars a month."

"Whut yuh wan fer yo mule, Mistah Hawkins?"

Jim Hawkins screwed up his eyes.

"Fifty dollars."

"Whut yuh do wid tha gun?" Dave's father demanded.

Dave said nothing.

"Yuh wan me t take a tree n beat yuh till yuh talk!"

"Nawsuh!"

"Whut yuh do wid it?"

"Ah throwed it erway."

"Where?"

"Ah . . . Ah throwed it in the creek."

"Waal, c mon home. N firs thing in the mawnin git to tha creek n fin tha gun."

"Yessuh."

"Whut yuh pay fer it?"

"Two dollahs."

"Take tha gun n git yo money back n carry it t Mistah Hawkins, yuh hear? N don fergit Ahma lam you black bottom good fer this! Now march yosef on home, suh!"

Dave turned and walked slowly. He heard people laughing. Dave glared, his eyes welling with tears. Hot anger bubbled in him. Then he swallowed and stumbled on.

That night Dave did not sleep. He was glad that he had gotten out of killing the mule so easily, but he was hurt. Something hot seemed to turn over inside him each time he remembered how they had laughed. He tossed on his bed, feeling his hard pillow. N Pa says he's gonna beat me . . . He remembered other beatings, and his back quivered. Naw, naw, Ah sho don wan im t beat me tha way no mo. Dam em all! Nobody ever gave him anything. All he did was work. They treat me like a mule, n then they beat me. He gritted his teeth. N Ma had t tell on me.

Well, if he had to, he would take old man Hawkins that two dollars. But that meant selling the gun. And he wanted to keep that gun. Fifty dollars for a dead mule.

He turned over, thinking how he had fired the gun. He had an itch to fire it again. Ef other men kin shoota gun, by Gawd, Ah kin! He was still, listening. Mebbe they all sleepin now. The house was still. He heard the soft breathing of his brother. Yes, now! He would go down and get that gun and see if he could fire it! He eased out of bed and slipped into overalls.

The moon was bright. He ran almost all the way to the edge of the woods. He stumbled over the ground, looking for the spot where he had buried the gun. Yeah, here it is. Like a hungry dog scratching for a bone, he pawed it up. He puffed his black cheeks and blew dirt from the trigger and barrel. He broke it and found four cartridges unshot. He looked around; the fields were filled with silence and moonlight. He clutched the gun stiff and hard in his fingers. But, as soon as he wanted to pull the trigger, he shut his eyes and turned his head. Naw, Ah can't shoot wid mah eyes closed n mah head turned. With effort he held his eyes open; then he squeezed. *Blooooom!* He was stiff, not breathing. The gun was still in his hands. Dammit, he'd done it! He fired again. *Bloooom!* He smiled. *Bloooom! Blooooom! Click, click.* There! It was empty. If anybody could shoot a gun, he could. He put the gun into his hip pocket and started across the fields.

When he reached the top of a ridge he stood straight and proud in the moonlight, looking at Jim Hawkins' big white house, feeling the gun sagging in his pocket. Lawd, ef Ah had just one mo bullet Ah'd taka shot at tha house. Ah'd like t scare ol man Hawkins jusa little . . . Jusa enough t let im know Dave Saunders is a man.

To his left the road curved, running to the tracks of the Illinois Central. He jerked his head, listening. From far off came a faint *hoooof-hoooof; hoooof-hoooof; hoooof-hoooof.* . . . He stood rigid. Two dollahs a mont. Les see now . . . Tha means it'll take bout two years. Shucks! Ah'll be dam!

He started down the road, toward the tracks. Yeah, here she comes! He stood beside the track and held himself stiffly. Here she comes, erroun the ben . . . C mon, yuh slow poke! C mon! He had his hand on his gun; something quivered in his stomach. Then the train thundered past, the gray and brown box cars rumbling and clinking. He gripped the gun tightly; then he jerked his hand out of his pocket. Ah betcha Bill wouldn't do it! Ah betcha . . . The cars slid past, steel grinding upon steel. Ahm ridin yuh ternight, so hep me Gawd! He was hot all over. He hesitated just a moment; then he grabbed, pulled atop of a car, and lay flat. He felt his pocket; the gun was still there. Ahead the long rails were glinting in the moonlight, stretching away, away to somewhere, somewhere where he could be a man . . .

———◆·◀▶·◆———

This story, like "I'm a Fool" (sec. 7), is an account of growing up, of initiation into life, and the pistol is, of course, a symbol of masculinity, in both the specific and the general sense. Dave, like any normal seventeen-year-old boy, feels the need to assert himself, to enter the world and be a man, and opposing his need he finds the pressure of the family and of society. More specifically, this story deals with the growing up of a black boy in backcountry Mississippi some half-century ago; absorbed into the story of the boy's struggle is that of his race.

To respond to the full resonance of the story we should examine the stages by which it develops. In the first stage, there has already been, as we learn from the exposition, some sort of quarrel between Dave and the other "hands"—other black laborers—in the field, who hold the boy in contempt on account of his youth. At first, the potential tar-

gets of the gun he hopes to get are these older and bigger blacks; if he gets a gun, he thinks, he won't be "scareda them even ef they are biggern me." In the second stage we see, fleetingly, an enlargement of the possible target, when Dave, in the morning after he has bought the old pistol, thinks: "Could kill a man with a gun like this. Kill anybody, black or white." So Dave, almost unconsciously, has taken the white man for a target, too. In the third stage, the general, natural pressure of his family against him increases after the mule is killed, and his family, especially his father, become the agents, as it were, of the white world, siding with Mr. Hawkins. His father, in fact, is going to beat him. But it is not only Dave's family, it is the whole crowd of the other field hands, laughing at him and contemptuous of him, who are arrayed against him. In the last stage, after Dave has dug up the gun and now successfully fired it and finds himself truly a man, he sees the house of Mr. Hawkins, white in the moonlight, and thinks: "Lawd, ef Ah had just one mo bullet Ah'd taka shot at tha house. Ah'd like t scare ol man Hawkins jusa little . . . Jusa enough t let im know Dave Saunders is a man."

He has, in short, located his ultimate target.

EXERCISES

1. When Dave, pistol in pocket, hops the northbound freight, what destiny is he riding toward? Is he riding toward maturity and fulfillment? Or whatever happens, will he remain the victim? Try to imagine what may happen in the future for Dave.
2. What attitude does the author take—and expect us to take—toward Dave and his fate? In this connection, what importance do you think the title has?

PRIVATE DOMAIN
James Alan McPherson (b. 1943)

I

Rodney finished his beer in slow, deliberate swallows, peering over the rim of his mug at the other black who, having polished off three previous mugs of draft, now sat watching Rodney expectantly, being quite obvious with his eyes that he held no doubt that more beer was forthcoming. Rodney ignored his eyes. He licked his lips. He tabled the empty mug. "Now give it to me again," he said to the heavily bearded, beer-hungry black still eyeing him, now demandingly, from across the small booth. "Let me see if I have it all down."

"How 'bout throwing some more suds on me?" said the black.

"In a minute," said Rodney.

The black considered. "I'm dry again. Another taste."

Rodney sighed, considered his position from behind the sigh, made himself look annoyed and then grudgingly raised his hand until the cigar-chewing bartender noticed, stopped his stooped, glass-washing dance behind the counter, and nodded to the waitress, sitting on a stool at the bar, to replenish them. She was slow about getting up. It was a lazy day: the two men in the booth were the only customers.

"Now," said Rodney, "give it to me again."

The other man smiled. He had won again. "It's this way," he said to Rodney.

Rodney ignored the waitress as she pushed the two fresh mugs onto the table while his companion paused to consider her ass bouncing beneath the cloth of her blue dress. Lighting another cigarette, Rodney observed that the waitress wore no stockings and felt himself getting uncomfortable.

"Well?" he said.

"It's this way," his companion said again. "Your *bag* is where you keep whatever you do best. Whatever is in your bag is your *thing*. Some cats call it your *stick*, but it means the same. Now when you know you got your thing going all right, you say 'I got myself together' or 'I got my game together.'"

"All right, all right," said Rodney. "I've got it down now." He was growing very irritated at the other man, who smiled all the time in a superior way and let the beer wet his gold tooth before he swallowed, as if expecting Rodney to be impressed with its gleam. Rodney was not impressed. He disliked condescension, especially from Willie, whom he regarded in most respects as his inferior.

"Anything else I should know?" Rodney snapped.

"Yeah, baby-boy," Willie said slow and matter-of-factly, implying, in his accents, a whole world of essential instruction being overlooked for want of beer and money and mind and other necessities forever beyond Rodney's reach. "There's lots. There's lots and lots."

"Like what?"

Willie drained his mug. "You know about the big 'I Remember Rock 'n Roll' Memorial in Cleveland last week?"

"No." Rodney was excited. "Who was there?"

"All the cats from the old groups."

"Anything special happen?"

"Hell yes!" Willie smiled again and looked very pleased with himself. "Fatso Checkers didn't show. The cats would have tore the place down but Dirty Rivers filled in for him. He made up a song right on stage. Man, the cats dug it, they went wild they dug it so."

"What's the song?"

"I donno."

"Is it on record?"

"Not yet. He just made it up."

"There's no place I can check it out?"

Again Willie smiled. "You can follow the other squares and check out this week's issue of *Soul*. They might have a piece on it."

"I don't have *time*," Rodney said. "I've got my studies to do."

"You don't have to, then; just be cool."

Rodney got up. "That's it," he said to Willie. "I'll check you out later." He put two dollars down on the table and turned to go. Willie reached over and picked up the bills. "That's for the beer," Rodney cautioned him.

"Sure," said Willie.

Rodney walked towards the door. "Be cool," he heard Willie say from behind him.

He did not look back. He knew that Willie and possibly the waitress and even the bartender would be smiling.

Although he felt uncomfortable in that area of the city, Rodney decided to walk around and digest all that he had been told before driving back to the University. He had parked and locked his car on a small side street and felt relatively protected from the rows and rows of aimless men who lined the stoops of houses and posts and garbage cans on either side of the street, their eyes seemingly shifty, their faces dishonest, their broad black noses alert and sniffing, feeling the air for the source of the smell which Rodney half believed rose from the watch and the wallet and the valuables stored in his pocket. He walked faster. He felt their eyes on his back and he was very uncomfortable being there, in the rising heat from the sidewalk, amid the smells of old food and wine and urine which rose with the heat.

He passed two boys with gray-black, ashy faces and running noses who laughed as they chased a little black girl up and down the steps of a tenement. "Little Tommy Tucker was a bad motherfucker," one of the boys half sang, half spoke, and they all laughed. Rodney thought it obscene and a violation of a protective and sacred barrier between two distinctively different age groups. But after a few more steps he began to think that it was very clever. He stopped. He looked back. He began to memorize it. Then he began to walk back towards them, still at play on the steps, having already forgotten the inventiveness of a moment before. Rodney was about to call to them to repeat the whole verse when a robust and short-haired dark woman in a tight black dress that was open at the side came out of the tenement and down the stairs and began to undulate her way, sensually, toward him. The three children followed her, laughing as they each attempted to imitate her walk. Just when he was about to pass her, a light blue Ford pulled over to the curb next to her and a bald-headed white man leaned, questioning-

ly, out of the driver's window toward the big woman. She stopped, and looking the man directly in the eye with a hint of professional irritation on her round, hard face, asked, "How much?"

"Ten," the man said.

"Hell no," she said turning to go in a way that, while sharp and decisive, also suggested that there was a happy chance that, upon the occurrence of certain conditions, as yet unnamed, she might not go at all.

"Twelve," said the man.

The woman looked at Rodney for a moment; then she looked the leaning man full in the face with fierce eyes. "Fuck you!" she said matter-of-factly.

"Well, damn if you're worth more than that," the man said, ignoring Rodney and the children.

"Get the hell on," said the woman, and began to walk slowly and sensually in the direction in which the car was pointed.

"She ain't got no drawers on," exclaimed one of the children.

"Can you see her cunt?"

"Yeah" was the answer. They all ran after her and the car, which was now trailing her, leaving Rodney alone on that part of the hot sidewalk. But he was not minding the heat now, or the smells, or the lounging men, or even Willie's condescension; he only minded that he had not thought to bring a notebook because he was having difficulty arranging all this in his head for memorization.

Returning to his car at last, Rodney paused amid afternoon traffic to purchase a copy of *Muhammad Speaks* from a conservatively dressed, cocoa-brown Muslim on a street corner. Rodney tried to be very conspicuous about the transaction, doing his absolute best to engage the fellow in conversation while the homebound cars, full of black and white workers, passed them. "What made you join?" he asked the Muslim, a striking fellow who still retained the red eyes of an alcoholic or drug addict.

"Come to see us and find out for yourself," said the fellow, his eyes not on Rodney but on the moving traffic lest he should miss the possibility of a sale.

"Are you happy being a Muslim?" asked Rodney.

"Come to our mosque, brother, and find out."

"I should think you'd get tired of selling papers all the time."

The Muslim, not wanting to insult Rodney and lose a possible conversion and at the same time more than slightly irritated, struck a compromise with himself, hitched his papers under his arms and moved out into the street between the two lanes of traffic. "Come to our mosque, brother, and gain all knowledge from the lips of the Messenger," he called back to Rodney. Rodney turned away and walked to his car. It was safe; the residents had not found it yet. Still, he inspected the doors and windows and keyholes for jimmy marks, just to feel secure.

II

"Where have you been?" Lynn asked as he opened the door to his apartment. She was sitting on the floor, her legs crossed, her panties showing—her favorite position, which always embarrassed Rodney when they relaxed with other people. He suspected that she did it on purpose. He had developed the habit of glancing at all the other fellows in a room, whenever she did it, until they saw him watching them discovering her and directing their eyes elsewhere in silent respect for his unexpressed wish. This always made Rodney feel superior and polished.

"Put your legs down," he told her.

"For what?" she said.

"You'll catch cold."

"Nobody's looking. Where you been?"

Rodney stood over her and looked down. He looked severe. He could not stand irritation at home too. "Go sit on the sofa," he ordered her. "Only white girls expose themselves in public."

"You prude," she said. "This isn't pub-

lic." But she got up anyway and reclined on the sofa.

"That's better," said Rodney, pulling off his coat. "If sitting like that is your thing, you should put it in a separate bag and bury it someplace."

"What do you know about *my thing*?" Lynn said.

Rodney did not answer her.

"Where you been, *bay-bee*?"

Rodney said nothing. He hated her when she called him that in private.

"We're going to be late for dinner, *bay-bee*," she said again.

"I've been out studying," Rodney finally said.

"What?"

"Things."

"Today's Saturday."

"So? God made Saturdays for students."

"Crap," she said. Then she added: *"Bay-bee!"*

"Oh, shut up," said Rodney.

"You can give me orders when we're married," said Lynn.

"That'll be the day," Rodney muttered.

"Yeah," Lynn repeated. "That'll be the day."

Rodney looked at her, legs miniskirted but sufficiently covered, hair natural but just a little too straight to be that way, skin nut-brown and smooth and soft to touch and feel against his mouth and arms and legs, body well built and filled, very noticeable breasts and hips, also good to touch and feel against his body at night. Rodney liked to make love at night, in the dark. He especially did not like to make sounds while making love, although he felt uneasy if the girl did not make any. He was considering whether or not it was dark enough in the room to make love when the telephone rang. Lynn did not move on the sofa so he answered it himself. It was Charlie Pratt.

"What's happening, baby?" said Rodney.

"Not much," said Charlie. "Listen, can you make dinner around seven? We got some other cats coming over at nine we don't want to feed nothin' but beer."

"Cool," said Rodney. He looked at his watch. "We can make it as soon as Lynn gets herself together." He glanced over at Lynn still stretched out on the sofa.

"Great," said Charlie Pratt. "Later."

Rodney hung up. "What do you have to do to get ready?" he asked Lynn.

"Nothing."

"You *could* put on another skirt."

"Go to hell," she said, not lifting her head from the sofa. "This skirt's fine."

"You could at least comb your hair or something."

Lynn ignored him. Rodney began to reconsider the sufficiency of the darkness in the room. Then he thought better of the idea. Instead, he went out of the room to shave and take a bath.

These days Rodney found himself coming close to hating everyone. Still, he never allowed himself to recognize it, or call what he felt toward certain people genuine hate. He preferred to call it differing degrees of dislike, an emotion with two sides like a coin, which was constantly spinning in his mind. Sometimes it landed, in his brain, heads up, signifying a certain affinity; sometimes it landed tails up, signifying a slight distaste or perhaps a major objection to a single person and his attitudes. He refused to dislike absolutely because, he felt, dislike was uncomfortably close to bigotry and Rodney knew too many different people to be a practicing bigot. Sometimes, very frequently in fact, he disliked Willie immensely. On the other hand, he sometimes felt a bit of admiration for the fellow and, occasionally, footnoted that admiration by purchasing an extra beer for him. This gesture served to stamp those rare moments onto his memory, a reminder that, because he had done this on enough occasions in the past, there would always be a rather thick prophylactic between how he really felt and how Willie assumed he felt.

Talking to Willie was informative and amusing to Rodney up to the point when

Willie began to smile and to seem to know that what he was telling Rodney had some value. After he could see when that point was reached in Willie's face, Rodney was not amused any more. Sometimes he was annoyed and sometimes, when Willie smiled confidently and knowledgeably and condescendingly, Rodney began to almost hate him. He felt the same about Lynn and her panties and her *bay-bee* and the loose ways she had, Rodney assumed, picked up from living among whites for too long. Sometimes she made him feel really uncomfortable and scared. He began to say *bay-bee, bay-bee* to himself in the shower. Thinking about it, he suddenly realized that he felt exactly the same way about Charlie Pratt.

Pratt made Rodney feel uncomfortable because he did not fit either side of the coin. The fellow had well over two thousand records: some rhythm and blues, some jazz, some folk, some gospels, but all black. And Charlie Pratt was not. He knew the language and was proud to use the vocabulary Rodney had been trying to forget all his life. He was pleasantly chubby with dark blond hair and a fuzzy Genghis Khan moustache which hung down on either side of his chin. Sometimes the ends dangled when he moved. And sometimes Pratt dangled when he moved. Sometimes Charlie Pratt, his belly hanging over his belt and his chin going up and down in talk, dangled when he did not move. Drying his legs with a towel, Rodney thought of himself and Charlie in mortal combat. Rodney had no doubt that he would win; he was slim and wiry, he was quick, he had a history of natural selection in his ancestry. Besides, Charlie was fat. He never used his body. Thinking about him, Rodney realized that he had never seen Charlie dance or move to the rhythm of any one of his two thousand records. He had never seen him snap his fingers once, or voluntarily move any part of his body besides his arms and legs; and even these movements were not rhythmic but something close to an unnatural shuffle.

Rodney did a quick step with his feet as he brushed his teeth in front of the mirror.

He moved back from the mirror in order to see his feet. He did the step again, grinning at himself and at the white-foamed toothbrush hanging loosely from his mouth. The foam covered his lips and made them white, and, remembering a fast song in his head, Rodney snapped his fingers and did the step again. And again.

III

"When you finish," said Charlie Pratt in between chews on a pork-chop bone, "I'll let you hear some of the stuff I picked up yesterday."

Rodney wiped his mouth carefully before answering. "What'd you get this time?" he asked, knowing what to expect.

"Some vintage Roscoe and Shirley stuff," said Charlie. "We found it in Markfield's back room. It was just lying there under a stack of oldies full of dust. We figure it must be their only L.P. Jesus, what a find!" Both Charlie and his wife smiled pridefully.

"How about that," said Rodney. But he did not say it with enthusiasm.

Charlie stood up from the table and began to shift his bulk from foot to foot, a sort of safe dance, but more like the movements of someone who wants desperately to go to the bathroom.

"Whatever happened to them?" asked Lynn.

Both the Pratts smiled together. "They broke up in '52 because the girl was a lesbian," his wife said. She had gone to Vassar, and Rodney always noticed how small and tight her mouth became whenever she took the initiative from her husband, which was, Rodney had noticed over a period of several dinners and many beer parties with them, very, very often. She was aggressive, in keeping with the Vassar tradition, and seemed to play a very intense, continuous game of one-upmanship with her husband.

"That's not what happened at all," her husband said. "After they hit the big time with 'I Want to Do It,' it was in '53, Roscoe started sleeping around. One night she caught him in a hotel room with a chick and

razored his face. His face was so cut up he couldn't go on stage any more. I saw him in Newark in '64 when he was trying to make a comeback. He still looked razored. He looked bad."

Rodney felt tight inside, remembering that in '64 he had been trying desperately to make up for a lifetime of not knowing anything about Baroque. Now he knew all about it and he had never heard of Roscoe and Shirley. "There was an 'I Remember Rock 'n Roll' Memorial in Cleveland last week," he said.

"Yeah," said Charlie. "Too bad Fatso couldn't make it. But that was one hell of a song Dirty Rivers made up. Jesus, right on the spot too! Jesus, right on the stage! He sang for almost two hours. Christ! I was lucky to get it taped, the cats went wild. They almost overran the stage."

"How did you get the tape?" asked Rodney, now vaguely disgusted.

"We knew about the show for months," Peggy Pratt broke in. "We planned to go but there was an Ashy Williamson Revue in the Village that same night. We couldn't make both so we called up this guy in Cleveland and got him to tape the show for us." She paused. "Want to hear it?"

"No," said Rodney, somewhat flatly. Then he added: "Not right now."

"Want to hear the Roscoe and Shirley?"

"No."

"I got a new Baptist group," said Charlie Pratt. "Some new freedom songs. Lots of finger-poppin' and hand jive."

"That's not my stick," said Rodney.

"You mean that ain't your *thing*," said Charlie.

"Yeah," said Rodney. "That's what I mean."

IV

They were drinking beer and listening to the Dirty Rivers tape when the other people came in. Rodney had been sitting on the sofa, quietly, too heavy to keep time with his feet and too tight inside to care if the Pratts did. Lynn was in her best position, on the floor.

crosslegged. The two girls with names he did not catch sat in chairs and crossed their legs, keeping time to the music and smoking. Looking at Lynn on the floor and looking at them on the chairs made Rodney mad. Listening to the Pratts recount, to the two white fellows, how they got the Cleveland tape made Rodney mad too. He drained his beer can and then began to beat time to the music with his foot and both hands on the arm of the sofa with a heavy, controlled deliberation that was really off the beat. Still, he knew that, since he was the only black male in the room, the others would assume that he alone knew the proper beat, even if it was out of time with their own perception of it, and would follow him. The two bearded fellows did just that when they sat down on the floor with Lynn; but the two girls maintained their original perception of the beat. Nevertheless, watching the fellows, Rodney felt the return of some sense of power.

"Some more suds," he said to Peggy Pratt.

She went out of the room.

"You've had enough," said Lynn.

Rodney looked at her spitefully. "Just be cool," he told her. "You just play your own game and stay cool."

The two girls looked at him and smiled. Their dates looked at Lynn. They did not smile. Dirty Rivers was moaning, *"Help me! Help me! Help me!"* now, and Rodney felt that he had to feel more from the music than any of them. *"Mercy! mercy! mercy!"* he exclaimed as Peggy Pratt handed him another can of beer. "This cat is *together!"*

The girls agreed and smiled again. One of them even reconciled her beat to Rodney's. Lynn just looked at him.

"He's just a beautiful man," the reconciled girl said.

"He's got more soul than anybody," said Rodney. "Nobody can touch him." He got up from the sofa, put his hands in his pockets and began to exercise a slow, heavy grind to the music without moving his feet. Charlie, who had been standing by the recorder all this time with his hands locked

together, smiled his Genghis Khan smile. "Actually," he said rather slowly, "I think Ashy Williamson is better."

"You jivetime cat," said Rodney. "Williamson couldn't touch Dirty Rivers with a stick."

"Rivers couldn't adapt," said Charlie.

"What do you mean?"

"He's just an old man now, playing the toilets, doing his same thing. Williamson's got class. He's got a new sound everybody digs. Even the squares."

"What do you know?" said Rodney.

Charlie Pratt smiled. "Plenty," he said.

After more beer and argument all around, and after playing Williamson's oldest and latest LP's by way of proof, it was decided that they should put it to a vote. Both the Pratts were of the same mind: Ashy Williamson was better than Dirty Rivers. The two fellows on the floor agreed with them. And also one of the girls. The other girl, however, the skinny brunette who had reconciled her beat to Rodney's, observed that she had been raised on Rivers and felt, absolutely, that he had had in the past, and still had now, a very good thing going for him. But Rodney was not impressed. She had crooked teeth and was obviously out to flatter her date with her maintenance of an independent mind in spite of her looks. Rodney turned to Lynn, still sitting cross-legged and exposed on the floor, but saving Rodney from utilizing his cautioning eye by having the beer can conveniently placed between her open legs. "Well, what do you say?" he asked, standing over her in his usual way.

She looked up at him. Casually sipping her beer, she considered for a long moment. The room was now very quiet, the last cut having been played on the Williamson record. The only sound was Lynn sipping her beer. It grated in Rodney's mind. The only movement was Charlie Pratt doing his rubber shift from foot to foot. That also irritated Rodney. "Well?" he said.

Lynn placed the can between her legs

again, very carefully and neatly. "Dirty Rivers is an old man," she said.

"What the hell does that mean?"

"He's got nothing new going for him, *bay-bee*," she said in a way that told Rodney she had made up her mind about it long before her opinion had been asked. She looked up at Rodney, her face resolved and, it seemed to him, slightly victorious.

"There you go, mother," Charlie said.

Rodney could see them all smiling at him, even Lynn, even the ugly brunette who had reconciled. He sat down on the sofa and said nothing.

"Now I'll play my new Roscoe and Shirley for you," Charlie told the others.

"Wasn't she a lesbian?" one of the fellows asked.

"Absolutely not!" said Charlie Pratt.

Rodney was flipping the coin in his mind again now. He flipped it faster and faster. After a while it was spinning against Willie and the cigar-chewing bartender and Lynn and especially the Pratts. Finishing the beer, Rodney found that the coin had stopped spinning; and from where his mind hung on the bad side of it, somewhere close to the place where he kept his bigotry almost locked away, he could hear the Pratts battling back and forth for the right to tell the others about a famous movie star who sued her parents when she found out that she was a mulatto. He got to his feet and walked over to the stacks and stacks of records that lined the wall. Aimlessly going through them, he considered all the black faces on their covers and all the slick, praising language by white disc jockeys and white experts and white managers on their backs. Then he commenced to stare at the brunette who had agreed with him. She avoided his eyes. He stared at Lynn too; but she was looking at Charlie Pratt, very intentionally. Only once did she glance up at him and smiled in a way that said *"bay-bee."* And then she looked away again.

Rodney leaned against the wall of records, put his hands in his pockets and wet his lips. Then he said: "Little Tommy Tucker was a *bad* motherfucker!"

They all looked up at him.

"What?" said Peggy Pratt, smiling.

He repeated it.

V

Driving home, Rodney went slower than required and obeyed traffic signals on very quiet, very empty streets. Lynn sat against the door, away from him. She had her legs crossed.

"You were pretty good tonight," she said at last.

Rodney was looking at a traffic light changing back to red.

"You were the life of the party."

Rodney inspected a white line of bird shit running down the top of the window, between him and the red light. It would have to come off in the morning.

"I knew you would let that color come through if you had enough beer," Lynn said.

"Oh shut the hell up!" said Rodney. He was not mad. She had just interrupted his thinking. He was thinking of going over to buy some more beer for Willie and talk some more before the usual Saturday time. He was thinking about building up his collection of Ashy Williamson LP's. He was thinking about driving Lynn directly home and not going up with her to make love to her in bed, which was much wider than his own, no matter how much she apologized later and no matter how dark and safe and inviting her room would be.

EXERCISES

1. "Private Domain," like "The Man Who Was Almost a Man," is the work of a black writer and deals with racial conflict. McPherson's story, however, differs significantly from Wright's; written more than a generation later, it is set in a world that would have been unthinkable in the time and place of "The Man Who Was Almost a Man" —an urban world of educated people, living in a society that, superficially at least, is racially integrated. What, in such a world, is the conflict that generates the story?

2. To what extent is the conflict objective (between Rodney and others) and to what extent is

it subjective (between elements of Rodney's own nature)? To what extent is it resolved?
3. Read "The Lagoon" by Joseph Conrad (sec. 10), which, too, involves the question of race. What is the significance of the fact that Arsat's story is told to a white man? What would be the difference in meaning if it were simply told from an omniscient point of view, with no white man in it at all?

EVERYTHING THAT RISES MUST CONVERGE
Flannery O'Connor (1925–1964)

Her doctor had told Julian's mother that she must lose twenty pounds on account of her blood pressure, so on Wednesday nights Julian had to take her downtown on the bus for a reducing class at the Y. The reducing class was designed for working girls over fifty, who weighed from 165 to 200 pounds. His mother was one of the slimmer ones, but she said ladies did not tell their age or weight. She would not ride the buses by herself at night since they had been integrated, and because the reducing class was one of her few pleasures, necessary for her health, and *free*, she said Julian could at least put himself out to take her, considering all she did for him. Julian did not like to consider all she did for him, but every Wednesday night he braced himself and took her.

She was almost ready to go, standing before the hall mirror, putting on her hat, while he, his hands behind him, appeared pinned to the door frame, waiting, like Saint Sebastian for the arrows to begin piercing him. The hat was new and had cost her seven dollars and a half. She kept saying, "Maybe I shouldn't have paid that for it. No, I shouldn't have. I'll take it off and return it tomorrow. I shouldn't have bought it."

Julian raised his eyes to heaven. "Yes, you should have bought it," he said. "Put it on and let's go." It was a hideous hat. A purple velvet flap came down on one side of it and stood up on the other; the rest of it was green and looked like a cushion with the stuffing out. He decided it was less comical than jaunty and pathetic. Everything that gave her pleasure was small and depressed him.

She lifted the hat one more time and set it down slowly on top of her head. Two wings of gray hair protruded on either side of her florid face, but her eyes, sky-blue, were as innocent and untouched by experience as they must have been when she was ten. Were it not that she was a widow who had struggled fiercely to feed and clothe and put him through school and who was supporting him still, "until he got on his feet," she might have been a little girl that he had to take to town.

"It's all right, it's all right," he said. "Let's go." He opened the door himself and started down the walk to get her going. The sky was a dying violet and the houses stood out darkly against it, bulbous liver-colored monstrosities of a uniform ugliness though no two were alike. Since this had been a fashionable neighborhood forty years ago, his mother persisted in thinking they did well to have an apartment in it. Each house had a narrow collar of dirt around it in which sat, usually, a grubby child. Julian walked with his hands in his pockets, his head down and thrust forward and his eyes glazed with the determination to make himself completely numb during the time he would be sacrificed to her pleasure.

The door closed and he turned to find the dumpy figure, surmounted by the atrocious hat, coming toward him. "Well," she said, "you only live once and paying a little more for it, I at least won't meet myself coming and going."

"Some day I'll start making money," Julian said gloomily—he knew he never would—"and you can have one of those jokes whenever you take the fit." But first they would move. He visualized a place where the nearest neighbors would be three miles away on either side.

"I think you're doing fine," she said, drawing on her gloves. "You've only been out of school a year. Rome wasn't built in a day."

She was one of the few members of the Y reducing class who arrived in hat and gloves and who had a son who had been to college. "It takes time," she said, "and the world is in such a mess. This hat looked better on me than any of the others, though when she brought it out I said, 'Take that thing back. I wouldn't have it on my head,' and she said, 'Now wait till you see it on,' and when she put it on me, I said, 'We-ull,' and she said, 'If you ask me, that hat does something for you and you do something for the hat, and besides,' she said, 'with that hat, you won't meet yourself coming and going.' "

Julian thought he could have stood his lot better if she had been selfish, if she had been an old hag who drank and screamed at him. He walked along, saturated in depression, as if in the midst of his martyrdom he had lost his faith. Catching sight of his long, hopeless, irritated face, she stopped suddenly with a grief-stricken look, and pulled back on his arm. "Wait on me," she said. "I'm going back to the house and take this thing off and tomorrow I'm going to return it. I was out of my head. I can pay the gas bill with that seven-fifty."

He caught her arm in a vicious grip. "You are not going to take it back," he said. "I like it."

"Well," she said, "I don't think I ought . . ."

"Shut up and enjoy it," he muttered, more depressed than ever.

"With the world in the mess it's in," she said, "it's a wonder we can enjoy anything. I tell you, the bottom rail is on the top."

Julian sighed.

"Of course," she said, "if you know who you are, you can go anywhere." She said this every time he took her to the reducing class. "Most of them in it are not our kind of people," she said, "but I can be gracious to anybody. I know who I am."

"They don't give a damn for your graciousness," Julian said savagely. "Knowing who you are is good for one generation only. You haven't the foggiest idea where you stand now or who you are."

She stopped and allowed her eyes to flash at him. "I most certainly do know who I am," she said, "and if you don't know who you are, I'm ashamed of you."

"Oh hell," Julian said.

"Your great-grandfather was a former governor of this state," she said. "Your grandfather was a prosperous landowner. Your grandmother was a Godhigh."

"Will you look around you," he said tensely, "and see where you are now?" and he swept his arm jerkily out to indicate the neighborhood, which the growing darkness at least made less dingy.

"You remain what you are," she said. "Your great-grandfather had a plantation and two hundred slaves."

"There are no more slaves," he said irritably.

"They were better off when they were," she said. He groaned to see that she was off on that topic. She rolled onto it every few days like a train on an open track. He knew every stop, every junction, every swamp along the way, and knew the exact point at which her conclusion would roll majestically into the station: "It's ridiculous. It's simply not realistic. They should rise, yes, but on their own side of the fence."

"Let's skip it," Julian said.

"The ones I feel sorry for," she said, "are the ones that are half white. They're tragic."

"Will you skip it?"

"Suppose we were half white. We would certainly have mixed feelings."

"I have mixed feelings now," he groaned.

"Well let's talk about something pleasant," she said. "I remember going to Grandpa's when I was a little girl. Then the house had double stairways that went up to what was really the second floor—all the cooking was done on the first. I used to like to stay down in the kitchen on account of the way the walls smelled. I would sit with my nose pressed against the plaster and take deep breaths. Actually the place belonged to the Godhighs but your grandfather Chestny paid the mortgage and saved it for them. They were in reduced circumstances," she said, "but reduced or not, they never forgot who they were."

"Doubtless that decayed mansion reminded them," Julian muttered. He never spoke of it without contempt or thought of it without longing. He had seen it once when he was a child before it had been sold. The double stairways had rotted and been torn down. Negroes were living in it. But it remained in his mind as his mother had known it. It appeared in his dreams regularly. He would stand on the wide porch, listening to the rustle of oak leaves, then wander through the high-ceilinged hall into the parlor that opened onto it and gaze at the worn rugs and faded draperies. It occurred to him that it was he, not she, who could have appreciated it. He preferred its threadbare elegance to anything he could name and it was because of it that all the neighborhoods they had lived in had been a torment to him— whereas she had hardly known the difference. She called her insensitivity "being adjustable."

"And I remember the old darky who was my nurse, Caroline. There was no better person in the world. I've always had a great respect for my colored friends," she said. "I'd do anything in the world for them and they'd . . ."

"Will you for God's sake get off that subject?" Julian said. When he got on a bus by himself, he made it a point to sit down beside a Negro, in reparation as it were for his mother's sins.

"You're mighty touchy tonight," she said. "Do you feel all right?"

"Yes I feel all right," he said. "Now lay off."

She pursed her lips. "Well, you certainly are in a vile humor," she observed. "I just won't speak to you at all."

They had reached the bus stop. There was no bus in sight and Julian, his hands still jammed in his pockets and his head thrust forward, scowled down the empty street. The frustration of having to wait on the bus as well as ride on it began to creep up his neck like a hot hand. The presence of his mother was borne in upon him as she gave a pained sigh. He looked at her bleakly. She was holding herself very erect under the preposterous hat, wearing it like a banner of her imaginary dignity. There was in him an evil urge to break her spirit. He suddenly unloosened his tie and pulled it off and put it in his pocket.

She stiffened. "Why must you look like *that* when you take me to town?" she said. "Why must you deliberately embarrass me?"

"If you'll never learn where you are," he said, "you can at least learn where I am."

"You look like a—thug," she said.

"Then I must be one," he murmured.

"I'll just go home," she said. "I will not bother you. If you can't do a little thing like that for me . . ."

Rolling his eyes upward, he put his tie back on. "Restored to my class," he muttered. He thrust his face toward her and hissed, "True culture is in the mind, the *mind*," he said, and tapped his head, "the mind."

"It's in the heart," she said, "and in how you do things and how you do things is because of who you *are*."

"Nobody in the damn bus cares who you are."

"I care who I am," she said icily.

The lighted bus appeared on top of the next hill and as it approached, they moved out into the street to meet it. He put his hand under her elbow and hoisted her up on the creaking step. She entered with a little smile, as if she were going into a drawing room where everyone had been waiting for her. While he put in the tokens, she sat down on one of the broad front seats for three which faced the aisle. A thin woman with protruding teeth and long yellow hair was sitting on the end of it. His mother moved up beside her and left room for Julian beside herself. He sat down and looked at the floor across the aisle where a pair of thin feet in red and white canvas sandals were planted.

His mother immediately began a general conversation meant to attract anyone who felt like talking. "Can it get any hotter?" she said and removed from her purse a folding fan, black with a Japanese scene on it, which she began to flutter before her.

"I reckon it might could," the woman with the protruding teeth said, "but I know for a fact my apartment couldn't get no hotter."

"It must get the afternoon sun," his mother said. She sat forward and looked up and down the bus. It was half filled. Everybody was white. "I see we have the bus to ourselves," she said. Julian cringed.

"For a change," said the woman across the aisle, the owner of the red and white canvas sandals. "I come on one the other day and they were thick as fleas—up front and all through."

"The world is in a mess everywhere," his mother said. "I don't know how we've let it get in this fix."

"What gets my goat is all those boys from good families stealing automobile tires," the woman with the protruding teeth said. "I told my boy, I said you may not be rich but you been raised right and if I ever catch you in any such mess, they can send you on to the reformatory. Be exactly where you belong."

"Training tells," his mother said. "Is your boy in high school?"

"Ninth grade," the woman said.

"My son just finished college last year. He wants to write but he's selling typewriters until he gets started," his mother said.

The woman leaned across and peered at Julian. He threw her such a malevolent look that she subsided against the seat. On the floor across the aisle there was an abandoned newspaper. He got up and got it and opened it out in front of him. His mother discreetly continued the conversation in a lower tone but the woman across the aisle said in a loud voice, "Well that's nice. Selling typewriters is close to writing. He can go right from one to the other."

"I tell him," his mother said, "that Rome wasn't built in a day."

Behind the newspaper Julian was withdrawing into the inner compartment of his mind where he spent most of his time. This was a kind of mental bubble in which he established himself when he could not bear to be a part of what was going on around him. From it he could see out and judge but in it he was safe from any kind of penetration from without. It was the only place where he felt free of the general idiocy of his fellows. His mother had never entered it but from it he could see her with absolute clarity.

The old lady was clever enough and he thought that if she had started from any of the right premises, more might have been expected of her. She lived according to the laws of her own fantasy world, outside of which he had never seen her set foot. The law of it was to sacrifice herself for him after she had first created the necessity to do so by making a mess of things. If he had permitted her sacrifices, it was only because her lack of foresight had made them necessary. All of her life had been a struggle to act like a Chestny without the Chestny goods, and to give him everything she thought a Chestny ought to have; but since, said she, it was fun to struggle, why complain? And when you had won, as she had won, what fun to look back on the hard times! He could not forgive her that she had enjoyed the struggle and that she thought *she* had won.

What she meant when she said she had won was that she had brought him up successfully and had sent him to college and that he had turned out so well—good looking (her teeth had gone unfilled so that his could be straightened), intelligent (he realized he was too intelligent to be a success), and with a future ahead of him (there was of course no future ahead of him). She excused his gloominess on the grounds that he was still growing up and his radical ideas on his lack of practical experience. She said he didn't yet know a thing about "life," that he hadn't even entered the real world—when already he was as disenchanted with it as a man of fifty.

The further irony of all this was that in spite of her, he had turned out so well. In spite of going to only a third-rate college, he had, on his own initiative, come out with a first-rate education; in spite of growing up dominated by a small mind, he had ended up with a large one; in spite of all her foolish views, he was free of prejudice and unafraid to face facts. Most miraculous of all, instead of being blinded by love for her as she was for him, he had cut himself emotionally free of her and could see her with complete objectivity. He was not dominated by his mother.

The bus stopped with a sudden jerk and shook him from his meditation. A woman from the back lurched forward with little steps and barely escaped falling in his newspaper as she righted herself. She got off and a large Negro got on. Julian kept his paper lowered to watch. It gave him a certain satisfaction to see injustice in daily operation. It confirmed his view that with a few exceptions there was no one worth knowing within a radius of three hundred miles. The Negro was well dressed and carried a briefcase. He looked around and then sat down on the other end of the seat where the woman with the red and white canvas sandals was sitting. He immediately unfolded a newspaper and obscured himself behind it. Julian's mother's elbow at once prodded insistently into his ribs. "Now you see why I won't ride on these buses by myself," she whispered.

The woman with the red and white canvas sandals had risen at the same time the Negro sat down and had gone further back in the bus and taken the seat of the woman who had got off. His mother leaned forward and cast her an approving look.

Julian rose, crossed the aisle, and sat down in the place of the woman with the canvas sandals. From this position, he looked serenely across at his mother. Her face had turned an angry red. He stared at her, making his eyes the eyes of a stranger. He felt his tension suddenly lift as if he had openly declared war on her.

He would have liked to get in conversation with the Negro and to talk with him about art or politics or any subject that would be above the comprehension of those around them, but the man remained entrenched behind his paper. He was either ignoring the change of seating or had never noticed it. There was no way for Julian to convey his sympathy.

His mother kept her eyes fixed reproachfully on his face. The woman with the protruding teeth was looking at him avidly as if he were a type of monster new to her.

"Do you have a light?" he asked the Negro.

Without looking away from his paper, the man reached in his pocket and handed him a packet of matches.

"Thanks," Julian said. For a moment he held the matches foolishly. A NO SMOKING sign looked down upon him from over the door. This alone would not have deterred him; he had no cigarettes. He had quit smoking some months before because he could not afford it. "Sorry," he muttered and handed back the matches. The Negro lowered the paper and gave him an annoyed look. He took the matches and raised the paper again.

His mother continued to gaze at him but she did not take advantage of his momentary discomfort. Her eyes retained their battered look. Her face seemed to be unnaturally red, as if her blood pressure had risen. Julian allowed no glimmer of sympathy to show on his face. Having got the advantage, he wanted desperately to keep it and carry it through. He would have liked to teach her a lesson that would last her a while, but there seemed no way to continue the point. The Negro refused to come out from behind his paper.

Julian folded his arms and looked stolidly before him, facing her but as if he did not see her, as if he had ceased to recognize her existence. He visualized a scene in which, the bus having reached their stop, he would remain in his seat and when she said, "Aren't you going to get off?" he would look at her as at a stranger who had rashly addressed him. The corner they got off on was usually deserted, but it was well lighted and it would not hurt her to walk by herself the four blocks to the Y. He decided to wait until the time came and then decide whether or not he would let her get off by herself. He would have to be at the Y at ten to bring her back, but he could leave her wondering if he was going to show up. There was no reason for her to think she could always depend on him.

He retired again into the high-ceilinged room sparsely settled with large pieces of antique furniture. His soul expanded momentarily but then he became aware of his mother across from him and the vision shriveled. He studied her coldly. Her feet in little pumps dangled like a child's and did not quite reach the floor. She was training on him an exaggerated look of reproach. He felt completely detached from her. At that moment he could with pleasure have slapped her as he would have slapped a particularly obnoxious child in his charge.

He began to imagine various unlikely ways by which he could teach her a lesson. He might make friends with some distinguished Negro professor or lawyer and bring him home to spend the evening. He would be entirely justified but her blood pressure would rise to 300. He could not push her to the extent of making her have a stroke, and moreover, he had never been successful at making any Negro friends. He had tried to strike up an acquaintance on the bus with some of the better types, with ones that looked like professors or ministers or lawyers. One morning he had sat down next to a distinguished-looking dark brown man who had answered his questions with a sonorous solemnity but who had turned out to be an undertaker. Another day he had sat down beside a cigar-smoking Negro with a diamond ring on his finger, but after a few stilted pleasantries, the Negro had rung the buzzer and risen, slipping two lottery tickets into

Julian's hand as he climbed over him to leave.

He imagined his mother lying desperately ill and his being able to secure only a Negro doctor for her. He toyed with that idea for a few minutes and then dropped it for a momentary vision of himself participating as a sympathizer in a sit-in demonstration. This was possible but he did not linger with it. Instead, he approached the ultimate horror. He brought home a beautiful suspiciously Negroid woman. Prepare yourself, he said. There is nothing you can do about it. This is the woman I've chosen. She's intelligent, dignified, even good, and she's suffered and she hasn't thought it *fun*. Now persecute us, go ahead and persecute us. Drive her out of here, but remember, you're driving me too. His eyes were narrowed and through the indignation he had generated, he saw his mother across the aisle, purple-faced, shrunken to the dwarf-like proportions of her moral nature, sitting like a mummy beneath the ridiculous banner of her hat.

He was tilted out of his fantasy again as the bus stopped. The door opened with a sucking hiss and out of the dark a large, gaily dressed, sullen-looking colored woman got on with a little boy. The child, who might have been four, had on a short plaid suit and a Tyrolean hat with a blue feather in it. Julian hoped that he would sit down beside him and that the woman would push in beside his mother. He could think of no better arrangement.

As she waited for her tokens, the woman was surveying the seating possibilities—he hoped with the idea of sitting where she was least wanted. There was something familiar-looking about her but Julian could not place what it was. She was a giant of a woman. Her face was set not only to meet opposition but to seek it out. The downward tilt of her large lower lip was like a warning sign: DON'T TAMPER WITH ME. Her bulging figure was encased in a green crepe dress and her feet overflowed in red shoes. She had on a hideous hat. A purple velvet flap came down on one side of it and stood up on the other; the rest of it was green and looked like a cushion with the stuffing out. She carried a mammoth red pocketbook that bulged throughout as if it were stuffed with rocks.

To Julian's disappointment, the little boy climbed up on the empty seat beside his mother. His mother lumped all children, black and white, into the common category, "cute," and she thought little Negroes were on the whole cuter than little white children. She smiled at the little boy as he climbed on the seat.

Meanwhile the woman was bearing down upon the empty seat beside Julian. To his annoyance, she squeezed herself into it. He saw his mother's face change as the woman settled herself next to him and he realized with satisfaction that this was more objectionable to her than it was to him. Her face seemed almost gray and there was a look of dull recognition in her eyes, as if suddenly she had sickened at some awful confrontation. Julian saw that it was because she and the woman had, in a sense, swapped sons. Though his mother would not realize the symbolic significance of this, she would feel it. His amusement showed plainly on his face

The woman next to him muttered something unintelligible to herself. He was conscious of a kind of bristling next to him, a muted growling like that of an angry cat. He could not see anything but the red pocketbook upright on the bulging green thighs. He visualized the woman as she had stood waiting for her tokens—the ponderous figure, rising from the red shoes upward over the solid hips, the mammoth bosom, the haughty face, to the green and purple hat.

His eyes widened.

The vision of the two hats, identical, broke upon him with the radiance of a brilliant sunrise. His face was suddenly lit with joy. He could not believe that Fate had thrust upon his mother such a lesson. He gave a loud chuckle so that she would look at him and see that he saw. She turned her eyes on him slowly. The blue in them seemed to have turned a bruised purple. For a mo-

ment he had an uncomfortable sense of her innocence, but it lasted only a second before principle rescued him. Justice entitled him to laugh. His grin hardened until it said to her as plainly as if he were saying aloud: Your punishment exactly fits your pettiness. This should teach you a permanent lesson.

Her eyes shifted to the woman. She seemed unable to bear looking at him and to find the woman preferable. He became conscious again of the bristling presence at his side. The woman was rumbling like a volcano about to become active. His mother's mouth began to twitch slightly at one corner. With a sinking heart, he saw incipient signs of recovery on her face and realized that this was going to strike her suddenly as funny and was going to be no lesson at all. She kept her eyes on the woman and an amused smile came over her face as if the woman were a monkey that had stolen her hat. The little Negro was looking up at her with large fascinated eyes. He had been trying to attract her attention for some time.

"Carver!" the woman said suddenly. "Come heah!"

When he saw that the spotlight was on him at last, Carver drew his feet up and turned himself toward Julian's mother and giggled.

"Carver!" the woman said. "You heah me? Come heah!"

Carver slid down from the seat but remained squatting with his back against the base of it, his head turned slyly around toward Julian's mother, who was smiling at him. The woman reached a hand across the aisle and snatched him to her. He righted himself and hung backwards on her knees, grinning at Julian's mother. "Isn't he cute?" Julian's mother said to the woman with the protruding teeth.

"I reckon he is," the woman said without conviction.

The Negress yanked him upright but he eased out of her grip and shot across the aisle and scrambled, giggling wildly, onto the seat beside his love.

"I think he likes me," Julian's mother

said, and smiled at the woman. It was the smile she used when she was being particularly gracious to an inferior. Julian saw everything lost. The lesson had rolled off her like rain on a roof.

The woman stood up and yanked the little boy off the seat as if she were snatching him from contagion. Julian could feel the rage in her at having no weapon like his mother's smile. She gave the child a sharp slap across his leg. He howled once and then thrust his head into her stomach and kicked his feet against her shins. "Be-have," she said vehemently.

The bus stopped and the Negro who had been reading the newspaper got off. The woman moved over and set the little boy down with a thump between herself and Julian. She held him firmly by the knee. In a moment he put his hands in front of his face and peeped at Julian's mother through his fingers.

"I see yoooooooo!" she said and put her hand in front of her face and peeped at him.

The woman slapped his hand down. "Quit yo' foolishness," she said, "before I knock the living Jesus out of you!"

Julian was thankful that the next stop was theirs. He reached up and pulled the cord. The woman reached up and pulled it at the same time. Oh my God, he thought. He had the terrible intuition that when they got off the bus together his mother would open her purse and give the little boy a nickel. The gesture would be as natural to her as breathing. The bus stopped and the woman got up and lunged to the front, dragging the child, who wished to stay on, after her. Julian and his mother got up and followed. As they neared the door, Julian tried to relieve her of her pocketbook.

"No," she murmured, "I want to give the little boy a nickel."

"No!" Julian hissed. "No!"

She smiled down at the child and opened her bag. The bus door opened and the woman picked him up by the arm and descended with him, hanging at her hip.

Once in the street she set him down and shook him.

Julian's mother had to close her purse while she got down the bus step but as soon as her feet were on the ground, she opened it again and began to rummage inside. "I can't find but a penny," she whispered, "but it looks like a new one."

"Don't do it!" Julian said fiercely between his teeth. There was a streetlight on the corner and she hurried to get under it so that she could better see into her pocketbook. The woman was heading off rapidly down the street with the child still hanging backward on her hand.

"Oh little boy!" Julian's mother called and took a few quick steps and caught up with them just beyond the lamp-post. "Here's a bright new penny for you," and she held out the coin, which shone bronze in the dim light.

The huge woman turned and for a moment stood, her shoulders lifted and her face frozen with frustrated rage, and stared at Julian's mother. Then all at once she seemed to explode like a piece of machinery that had been given one ounce of pressure too much. Julian saw the black fist swing out with the red pocketbook. He shut his eyes and cringed as he heard the woman shout, "He don't take nobody's pennies!" When he opened his eyes, the woman was disappearing down the street with the little boy staring wide-eyed over her shoulder. Julian's mother was sitting on the sidewalk.

"I told you not to do that," Julian said angrily. "I told you not to do that!"

He stood over her for a minute, gritting his teeth. Her legs were stretched out in front of her and her hat was on her lap. He squatted down and looked her in the face. It was totally expressionless. "You got exactly what you deserved," he said. "Now get up."

He picked up her pocketbook and put what had fallen out back in it. He picked the hat up off her lap. The penny caught his eye on the sidewalk and he picked that up and let it drop before her eyes into the purse. Then he stood up and leaned over and held his hands out to pull her up. She remained immobile. He sighed. Rising above them on either side were black apartment buildings, marked with irregular rectangles of light. At the end of the block a man came out of a door and walked off in the opposite direction. "All right," he said, "suppose somebody happens by and wants to know why you're sitting on the sidewalk?"

She took the hand and, breathing hard, pulled heavily up on it and then stood for a moment, swaying slightly as if the spots of light in the darkness were circling around her. Her eyes, shadowed and confused, finally settled on his face. He did not try to conceal his irritation. "I hope this teaches you a lesson," he said. She leaned forward and her eyes raked his face. She seemed trying to determine his identity. Then, as if she found nothing familiar about him, she started off with a headlong movement in the wrong direction.

"Aren't you going on to the Y?" he asked.

"Home," she muttered.

"Well, are we walking?"

For answer she kept going. Julian followed along, his hands behind him. He saw no reason to let the lesson she had had go without backing it up with an explanation of its meaning. She might as well be made to understand what had happened to her. "Don't think that was just an uppity Negro woman," he said. "That was the whole colored race which will no longer take your condescending pennies. That was your black double. She can wear the same hat as you, and to be sure," he added gratuitously (because he thought it was funny), "it looked better on her than it did on you. What all this means," he said, "is that the old world is gone. The old manners are obsolete and your graciousness is not worth a damn." He thought bitterly of the house that had been lost for him. "You aren't who you think you are," he said.

She continued to plow ahead, paying no attention to him. Her hair had come un-

done on one side. She dropped her pocketbook and took no notice. He stooped and picked it up and handed it to her but she did not take it.

"You needn't act as if the world had come to an end," he said, "because it hasn't. From now on you've got to live in a new world and face a few realities for a change. Buck up," he said, "it won't kill you."

She was breathing fast.

"Let's wait on the bus," he said.

"Home," she said thickly.

"I hate to see you behave like this," he said. "Just like a child. I should be able to expect more of you." He decided to stop where he was and make her stop and wait for a bus. "I'm not going any farther," he said, stopping. "We're going on the bus."

She continued to go on as if she had not heard him. He took a few steps and caught her arm and stopped her. He looked into her face and caught his breath. He was looking into a face he had never seen before. "Tell Grandpa to come get me," she said.

He stared, stricken.

"Tell Caroline to come get me," she said.

Stunned, he let her go and she lurched forward again, walking as if one leg were shorter than the other. A tide of darkness seemed to be sweeping her from him. "Mother!" he cried. "Darling, sweetheart, wait!" Crumpling, she fell to the pavement. He dashed forward and fell at her side, crying, "Mamma, Mamma!" He turned her over. Her face was fiercely distorted. One eye, large and staring, moved slightly to the left as if it had become unmoored. The other remained fixed on him, raked his face again, found nothing and closed.

"Wait here, wait here!" he cried and jumped up and began to run for help toward a cluster of lights he saw in the distance ahead of him. "Help, help!" he shouted, but his voice was thin, scarcely a thread of sound. The lights drifted farther away the faster he ran and his feet moved numbly as if they carried him nowhere. The tide of darkness seemed to sweep him back to her, postponing from moment to moment his entry into the world of guilt and sorrow.

———————◆—◆◆◆—◆—————————

In "The Man Who Was Almost a Man," Richard Wright, by recording the psychological development of an adolescent boy, is attacking an objective social situation. In "Private Domain," the author is primarily concerned with the analysis of a subjective situation. In "Everything That Rises Must Converge," a racial conflict, as in the two previous stories, provides the dynamic of the action. But here the problem of race is not thematically central; the conflict manifests itself in the contrasting attitudes of the mother and son on this point, but the point itself is only one of many that might bring them to loggerheads. The story, in fact, undertakes to go beneath the problem of race, as merely a particular precipitant of the conflict, to the fundamentals of the conflict.

To understand the story, we may begin by asking ourselves whose side we are on—the mother's or the son's. On the son's, we no doubt feel—at first glance, anyway. No wonder the son is irritated by his mother. She is the victim of stupid vanities and delusions. Poor, and feeling herself declassed, she can cling only to the comforting thought of her breeding and gentility. To her, the world is "a mess," and the "bottom rail" (in her metaphor, that of a rail fence, which aptly evokes the old agrarian regime of her origins) is "on the top." Most of the people she is now compelled to associate with are not her "kind of people," but she, as she affirms out of what she would no doubt call noblesse oblige, "can be gracious to anybody." She can do this, for, as she puts it, "I know who I am." It emerges, however, that when she is being what she calls "gracious," she is merely asserting her outraged sense of superiority. But on what is her sense of superiority based? On delusions, for she is "untouched by experience," incapable of assessing reality.

Her son is acutely aware of her every failing. He suffers from the absurdity of her pretensions in the midst of her poverty, her flights into delusion, her general ignorance, her lack of aesthetic taste, and her social and racial prejudices; and he realizes that all these failings stem from the basic one that she cannot, or will not, recognize the facts of life. Toward the end, he is viciously hoping that she will learn something from the encounter on the bus.

We are invited, in this perspective at least, to be on the son's side. But there are other elements in the story. Are we supposed to take the same attitude toward the episode of the absurd hat as the son takes? What is in the episode that the son does not see, or at least refuses to accept at its full value? Can it be that her worry about the hat as an extravagance reminds him (unconsciously, shall we say?) of her long schooling in self-denial that has made possible his own advantages, his orthodontic treatments and his college education? What attitude, in fact, does he take toward her years of sacrifice?

There are many questions we should probe. The mother dreams about past glories of the Godhigh plantation house, but what is his own secret feeling about those glories? In what sense does he feel himself entitled to them, while she is not? He sneers, justifiably of course, at her lack of a sense of reality, but what about his own? Can he cope with the world as it is? If he cannot, does he have his own compensatory dreams in addition to that of past glories?

To return to the matter of race in the story: Let us grant that the son does have some generous understanding of the plight of the black man in American (in this instance, southern) society, and grant that he is "right" in his social attitudes while his mother, trapped in the past and in vanity and delusions, is "wrong." But is this a complete account of the son's attitude? How much is his attitude not one of generosity but a result of his own sense of failure and of being an outsider in society? Are we supposed to admire and sympathize with the way in which he is "right"? For instance, how much self-righteousness is there in his "rightness"? How much sense of self-justifying virtue in a world in which he finds himself a failure? How much vengeful (vengeful for what?) aggression in his relation to his mother? What do his wishes and fantasies about his relations to blacks indicate? How much, in a final analysis, is his attitude similar to his mother's? To come to the climactic action of the story, what complication of attitude do we find in him in the encounter between his mother and the black woman who strikes her? In what sense, can it be said that the black woman fulfills his secret wish?

After considering all these questions, do you think it can be said that Flannery O'Connor is here attempting to show how complex is the problem of good and evil, and how "rightness" in attitudes is meaningless—or even evil—when taken abstractly, that is, outside a context of imaginative understanding, and outside what, in old-fashioned language, is called Christian charity?

EXERCISES

1. If the idea that abstract "rightness" in attitudes is meaningless is central to the story, what are we to make of the end of the story—of the son's cry for help, of the lights drifting away into distance? What, to summarize the story, are we to make of the last sentence? How can the tide of darkness, by sweeping the son back to the mother, postpone "his entry into the world of guilt and sorrow"? Can it be said that, for this instant, at her death, the son is restored to filial piety and human sympathy?

2. Study the following exchange between mother and son:

"True culture is in the mind, the *mind*," he said, and tapped his head, "the mind."

"It's in the heart," she said, "and in how you do things and how you do things is because of who you *are*."

"Nobody in the damn bus cares who you are."

"I care who I am," she said icily.

It might be said that here both mother and son are "right" and both are "wrong." Discuss this notion. Can it be maintained that neither understands the true meaning of what is said? Can this passage be taken, in its irony, as the key of the thematic interpretation of the story?

3. Would the mother have given a bright new penny to a little white child? What is implied by the son's vague disappointment when the black man with whom he has developed a conversation turns out to be an undertaker rather than a physician or a college professor?

4. As a kind of footnote to all three questions that have been asked in discussing the story, one last one: what attitude are we supposed to take toward the black woman who strikes the mother down? Certainly we understand the provocation, but how are we to judge this act in the pattern of the story? What, by the way, is the significance of the fact that both the mother and the black woman wear identical hats?

5. Can you imagine this story being told by Julian in the first person? If it could be successfully done—that is, with the same basic meaning as in the present version—would Julian as narrator have to resemble the narrator in "Araby" (sec. 7) or that in "Haircut" (sec. 7)? In other words, how full a degree of awareness of the meaning of the story would be permitted him?

THE GENTLEMAN FROM SAN FRANCISCO
Ivan Bunin (1870–1953)

Translated by A. Yarmolinsky

"Alas, Alas, that great city Babylon, that mighty city!"—*Revelation of St. John*

The Gentleman from San Francisco—neither at Naples nor on Capri could any one recall his name—with his wife and daughter, was on his way to Europe, where he intended to stay for two whole years, solely for the pleasure of it.

He was firmly convinced that he had a full right to a rest, enjoyment, a long comfortable trip, and what not. This conviction had a two-fold reason: first he was rich, and second, despite his fifty-eight years, he was just about to enter the stream of life's pleasures. Until now he had not really lived, but simply existed, to be sure—fairly well, yet putting off his fondest hopes for the future. He toiled unweariedly—the Chinese, whom he imported by thousands for his works, knew full well what it meant—and finally he saw that he had made much, and that he had nearly come up to the level of those whom he had once taken as a model, and he decided to catch his breath. The class of people to which he belonged was in the habit of beginning its enjoyment of life with a trip to

Europe, India, Egypt. He made up his mind to do the same. Of course, it was first of all himself that he desired to reward for the years of toil, but he was also glad for his wife and daughter's sake. His wife was never distinguished by any extraordinary impressionability, but then, all elderly American women are ardent travelers. As for his daughter, a girl of marriageable age, and somewhat sickly—travel was the very thing she needed. Not to speak of the benefit to her health, do not happy meetings occur during travels? Abroad, one may chance to sit at the same table with a prince, or examine frescoes side by side with a multi-millionaire.

The itinerary the Gentleman from San Francisco planned out was an extensive one. In December and January he expected to relish the sun of southern Italy, monuments of antiquity, the tarantella, serenades of wandering minstrels, and that which at his age is felt most keenly—the love, not entirely disinterested though, of young Neapolitan girls. The Carnival days he planned to spend at Nice and Monte Carlo, which at that time of the year is the meeting-place of the choicest society, the society upon which depend all the blessings of civilization: the cut of dress suits, the stability of thrones, the declaration of wars, the prosperity of hotels. Some of these people passionately give themselves over to automobile and boat races, others to roulette, others, again, busy themselves with what is called flirtation, and others shoot pigeons, which soar so beautifully from the dovecote, hover awhile over the emerald lawn, on the background of the forget-me-not colored sea, and then suddenly hit the ground, like little white lumps. Early March he wanted to devote to Florence, and at Easter, to hear the Miserere in Paris. His plans also included Venice, Paris, bull-baiting at Seville, bathing on the British Islands, also Athens, Constantinople, Palestine, Egypt, and even Japan, of course, on the way back. . . . And at first things went very well indeed.

It was the end of November, and all the way to Gibraltar the ship sailed across seas which were either clad by icy darkness or swept by storms carrying wet snow. But there were no accidents, and the vessel did not even roll. The passengers—all people of consequence—were numerous, and the steamer, the famous *Atlantis*, resembled the most expensive European hotel with all improvements: a night refreshment-bar, Oriental baths, even a newspaper of its own. The manner of living was a most aristocratic one; passengers rose early, awakened by the shrill voice of a bugle, filling the corridors at the gloomy hour when the day broke slowly and sulkily over the grayish-green watery desert, which rolled heavily in the fog. After putting on their flannel pajamas, they took coffee, chocolate, cocoa; they seated themselves in marble baths, went through their exercises, whetting their appetites and increasing their sense of well-being, dressed for the day, and had their breakfast. Till eleven o'clock they were supposed to stroll on the deck, breathing in the chill freshness of the ocean, or they played table-tennis, or other games which arouse the appetite. At eleven o'clock a collation was served consisting of sandwiches and bouillon, after which people read their newspapers, quietly waiting for luncheon, which was more nourishing and varied than the breakfast. The next two hours were given to rest; all the decks were crowded then with steamer chairs, on which the passengers, wrapped in plaids, lay stretched, dozing lazily, or watching the cloudy sky and the foamy-fringed water hillocks flashing beyond the sides of the vessel. At five o'clock, refreshed and gay, they drank strong, fragrant tea; at seven the sound of the bugle announced a dinner of nine courses. . . . Then the Gentleman from San Francisco, rubbing his hands in an onrush of vital energy, hastened to his luxurious stateroom to dress.

In the evening, all the decks of the *Atlantis* yawned in the darkness, shone with their innumerable fiery eyes, and a multitude of servants worked with increased feverishness in the kitchen, dish-washing compartments, and wine-cellars. The ocean, which heaved about the sides of the ship, was dreadful, but no one thought of it. All had faith in the controlling power of the captain, a red-headed giant, heavy and very sleepy, who, clad in a uniform with broad golden stripes, looked like a huge idol, and but rarely emerged, for the benefit of the public, from his mysterious retreat. On the forecastle, the siren gloomily roared or screeched in a fit of mad rage, but few of the diners heard the siren: its hellish voice was covered by the sounds of an excellent string orchestra, which played ceaselessly and exquisitely in a vast hall, decorated with marble and spread with velvety carpets. The hall was flooded with torrents of light, radiated by crystal lustres and gilt chandeliers; it was filled with a throng of bejeweled ladies in low-necked dresses, of men in dinner-coats, graceful waiters, and deferential maîtres'hôtel. One of these—who accepted wine orders exclusively—wore a chain on his neck like some lord mayor. The evening dress, and the ideal linen, made the Gentleman from San Francisco look very young. Dry-skinned, of average height, strongly, though irregularly built, glossy with thorough washing and cleaning, and moderately animated, he sat in the golden splendor of this palace. Near him stood a bottle of amber-colored Johannisberg, and goblets of most delicate glass and of varied sizes, surmounted by a frizzled bunch of fresh hyacinths. There was something Mongolian in his yellowish face with its trimmed silvery moustache; his large teeth glimmered with gold fillings, and his strong, bald head had a dull glow, like old ivory. His wife, a big, broad and placid woman, was dressed richly, but in keeping with her age. Complicated, but light, transparent, and innocently immodest was the dress of his daughter, tall and slender, with magnificent hair gracefully combed; her breath was sweet with violet-scented tablets, and she had a number of tiny and most delicate pink pimples near her lips and between her slightly-powdered shoulder blades. . . .

The dinner lasted two whole hours, and was followed by dances in the dancing hall, while the men—the Gentleman from San Francisco among them—made their way to the refreshment bar, where negroes in red jackets and with eye-balls like shelled hard-boiled eggs, waited on them. There, with their feet on tables, smoking Havana cigars, and drinking themselves purple in the face, they settled the destinies of nations on the basis of the latest political and stock exchange news. Outside, the ocean tossed up black mountains with a thud; and the snowstorm hissed furiously in the rigging grown heavy with slush; the ship trembled in every limb, struggling with the storm and ploughing with difficulty the shifting and seething mountainous masses that threw far and high their foaming tails; the siren groaned in agony, choked by storm and fog; the watchmen in their towers froze and almost went out of their minds under the superhuman stress of attention. Like the gloomy and sultry mass of the inferno, like its last, ninth circle, was the submersed womb of the steamer, where monstrous furnaces yawned with red-hot open jaws, and emitted deep, hooting sounds, and where the stokers, stripped to the waist, and purple with reflected flames, bathed in their own dirty, acid sweat. And here, in the refreshment bar, carefree men, with their feet, encased in dancing shoes, on the table, sipped cognac and liquers, swam in waves of spiced smoke, and exchanged subtle remarks, while in the dancing hall everything sparkled and radiated light, warmth, and joy. The couples now turned around in a waltz, now swayed in the tango; and the music, sweetly shameless and sad, persisted in its ceaseless entreaties. . . . There were many persons of note in this magnificent crowd: an ambassador, a dry, modest old man; a great millionaire, shaved, tall, of an indefinite age, who, in his old-fashioned dress-coat looked like a prelate; also a famous Spanish writer, and an international belle, already slightly faded and of dubious morals. There was also among them a loving pair, exquisite and refined, whom everybody watched with curiosity and who did not conceal their bliss; he danced only with her, sang —with great skill—only to her accompaniment, and they were so charming, so graceful. The captain alone knew that they had been hired by the company at a good salary to play at love, and that they had been sailing now on one, now on another steamer, for quite a long time.

In Gibraltar everybody was gladdened by the sun, and by the weather which was like early spring. A new passenger appeared aboard the *Atlantis* and aroused everybody's interest. It was the crown-prince of an Asiatic state, who traveled incognito, a small man, very nimble, though looking as if made of wood, broad-faced, narrow-eyed, in gold-rimmed glasses, somewhat disagreeable because of his long black moustache, which was sparse like that of a corpse, but otherwise—charming, plain, modest. In the Mediterranean the breath of winter was again felt. The seas were heavy and motley like a peacock's tail and the waves, stirred up by the gay gusts of the tramontane, tossed their white crests under a sparkling and perfectly clear sky. Next morning, the sky grew paler and the skyline misty. Land was near. Then Ischia and Capri came in sight and one could descry, through an opera-glass, Naples, looking like pieces of sugar strewn at the foot of an indistinct dove-colored mass, and above them, a snow-covered chain of distant mountains. The decks were crowded, many ladies and gentlemen put on light fur-coats; Chinese servants, bandy-legged youths—with pitch black braids down to the heels and with girlish, thick eyelashes—always quiet and speaking in a whisper, were carrying to the foot of the staircases plaid wraps, canes, and crocodile-leather valises and hand-bags. The daughter of the Gentleman from San Francisco stood near the prince, who, by a happy chance, had been introduced to her the evening before, and feigned to be looking steadily at something far-off, which he was pointing out to her, while he was, at the same time, explaining something, saying some-

thing rapidly and quietly. He was so small that he looked like a boy among other men, and he was not handsome at all. And then there was something strange about him; his glasses, derby, and coat were most commonplace, but there was something horse-like in the hair of his sparse moustache, and the thin, tanned skin of his flat face looked as though it were somewhat stretched and varnished. But the girl listened to him, and so great was her excitement that she could hardly grasp the meaning of his words, her heart palpitated with incomprehensible rapture and with pride that he was standing and speaking with her and nobody else. Everything about him was different: his dry hands, his clean skin, under which flowed ancient kingly blood, even his light shoes and his European dress, plain, but singularly tidy— everything hid an inexplicable fascination and engendered thoughts of love. And the Gentleman from San Francisco himself, in a silk-hat, gray leggings, patent leather shoes, kept eyeing the famous beauty who was standing near him, a tall, stately blonde, with eyes painted according to the latest Parisian fashion, and a tiny, hunched-up, hairless pet-dog, to whom she addressed herself. And the daughter, in a kind of vague perplexity, tried not to notice him.

Like all wealthy Americans he was very liberal when traveling, and believed in the complete sincerity and goodwill of those who so painstakingly fed him, served him day and night, anticipating his slightest desire, protected him from dirt and disturbance, hauled things for him, hailed carriers, and delivered his luggage to hotels. So it was everywhere, and it had to be so at Naples. Meanwhile, Naples grew and came nearer. The musicians, with their shining brass instruments, had already formed a group on the deck, and all of a sudden deafened everybody with the triumphant sounds of a rag-time march. The giant captain, in his full uniform, appeared on the bridge and, like a gracious pagan idol, waved his hands to the passengers—and it seemed to the Gentleman from San Francisco, as it did to all the rest, that for him alone thundered the march, so greatly loved by proud America, and that him alone did the captain congratulate on the safe arrival. And when the *Atlantis* had finally entered the port and all its many-decked mass leaned against the quay, and the gang-plank began to rattle heavily—what a crowd of porters, with their assistants, in caps with golden galloons, what a crowd of various boys and husky ragamuffins with pads of colored postal cards attacked the Gentleman from San Francisco, offering their services! With kindly contempt he grinned at these beggars, and, walking towards the automobile of the hotel where the prince might stop, muttered between his teeth, now in English, now in Italian—"Go away! *Via. . . ."*

Immediately, life at Naples began to follow a set routine. Early in the morning breakfast was served in the gloomy dining-room, swept by a wet draught from the open windows looking upon a stony garden, while outside the sky was cloudy and cheerless, and a crowd of guides swarmed at the door of the vestibule. Then came the first smiles of the warm roseate sun, and from the high suspended balcony, a broad vista unfolded itself: Vesuvius, wrapped to its base in radiant morning vapors; the pearly ripple, touched to silver, of the bay, the delicate outline of Capri on the skyline; tiny asses dragging two-wheeled buggies along the soft, sticky embankment, and detachments of little soldiers marching somewhere to the tune of cheerful and defiant music.

Next on the day's program was a slow automobile ride along crowded, narrow, and damp corridors of streets, between high, many-windowed buildings. It was followed by visits to museums, lifelessly clean and lighted evenly and pleasantly, but as though with the dull light cast by snow; then to churches, cold, smelling of wax, always alike: a majestic entrance, closed by a ponderous, leather curtain, and inside—a vast, void, silence, quiet flames of seven-branched candlesticks, sending forth a red glow from

where they stood at the farther end, on the bedecked altar—a lonely, old woman lost among the dark wooden benches, slippery gravestones under the feet, and somebody's "Descent from the Cross," infallibly famous. At one o'clock—luncheon, on the mountain of San-Martius, where at noon the choicest people gathered, and where the daughter of the Gentleman from San Francisco once almost fainted with joy, because it seemed to her that she saw the prince in the hall, although she had learned from the newspapers that he had temporarily left for Rome. At five o'clock it was customary to take tea at the hotel, in a smart salon, where it was far too warm because of the carpets and the blazing fireplaces; and then came dinner-time —and again did the mighty, commanding voice of the gong resound throughout the building, again did silk rustle and the mirrors reflect files of ladies in low-necked dresses ascending the staircases, and again the splendid palatial dining hall opened with broad hospitality, and again the musicians' jackets formed red patches on the estrade, and the black figures of the waiters swarmed around the maître-d'hôtel, who, with extra-ordinary skill, poured a thick pink soup into plates. . . . As everywhere, the dinner was the crown of the day. People dressed for it as for a wedding, and so abundant was it in food, wines, mineral waters, sweets and fruits, that about eleven o'clock in the evening chamber-maids would carry to all the rooms hot-water bags.

That year, however, December did not happen to be a very propitious one. The doormen were abashed when people spoke to them about the weather, and shrugged their shoulders guiltily, mumbling that they could not recollect such a year, although, to tell the truth, that it was not the first year they mumbled those words, usually adding that "things are terrible everywhere"; that unprecedented showers and storms had broken out on the Riviera, that it was snowing in Athens, that Ætna, too, was all blocked up with snow, and glowed brightly at night, and that tourists were fleeing from Paler-

mo to save themselves from the cold spell.
. . .

That winter, the morning sun daily deceived Naples; toward noon the sky would invariably grow gray, and a light rain would begin to fall, growing thicker and duller. Then the palms at the hotel porch glistened disagreeably like wet tin, the town appeared exceptionally dirty and congested, the museums too monotonous, the cigars of the drivers in their rubber raincoats, which flattened in the wind like wings, intolerably stinking, and the energetic flapping of their whips over their thin-necked nags—obviously false. The shoes of the signors, who cleaned the street-car tracks, were in a frightful state; the women who splashed in the mud, with black hair unprotected from the rain, were ugly and short-legged, and the humidity mingled with the foul smell of rotting fish, that came from the foaming sea, was simply disheartening. And so, early-morning quarrels began to break out between the Gentleman from San Francisco and his wife; and their daughter now grew pale and suffered from headaches, and now became animated, enthusiastic over everything, and at such times was lovely and beautiful. Beautiful were the tender, complex feelings which her meeting with the ungainly man aroused in her—the man in whose veins flowed unusual blood, for, after all, it does not matter what in particular stirs up a maiden's soul: money, or fame, or nobility of birth. . . . Everybody assured the tourists that it was quite different at Sorrento and on Capri, that lemon trees were blossoming there, that it was warmer and sunnier there, the morals purer, and the wine less adulterated. And the family from San Francisco decided to set out with all their luggage for Capri. They planned to settle down at Sorrento, but first to visit the island, tread the stones where stood Tiberius's palaces, examine the fabulous wonders of the Blue Grotto, and listen to the bagpipes of Abruzzi, who roam about the island during the whole month preceding Christmas and sing the praises of the Madonna.

On the day of departure—a very memorable day for the family from San Francisco—the sun did not appear even in the morning. A heavy winter fog covered Vesuvius down to its very base and hung like a gray curtain low over the leaden surge of the sea, hiding it completely at a distance of half a mile. Capri was completely out of sight, as though it had never existed on this earth. And the little steamboat which was making for the island tossed and pitched so fiercely that the family lay prostrated on the sofas in the miserable cabin of the little steamer, with their feet wrapped in plaids and their eyes shut because of their nausea. The older lady suffered, as she thought, most; several times she was overcome with sea-sickness, and it seemed to her then she was dying, but the chambermaid, who repeatedly brought her the basin, and who for many years, in heat and in cold, had been tossing on these waves, ever on the alert, ever kindly to all—the chambermaid only laughed. The lady's daughter was frightfully pale and kept a slice of lemon between her teeth. Not even the hope of an unexpected meeting with the prince at Sorrento, where he planned to arrive at Christmas, served to cheer her. The Gentleman from San Francisco, who was lying on his back, dressed in a large overcoat and a big cap, did not loosen his jaws throughout the voyage. His face grew dark, his moustache white, and his head ached heavily; for the last few days, because of the bad weather, he had drunk far too much in the evenings.

And the rain kept on beating against the rattling window panes, and water dripped down from them on the sofas; the howling wind attacked the masts, and sometimes, aided by a heavy sea, it laid the little steamer on its side, and then something below rolled about with a rattle.

While the steamer was anchored at Castellamare and Sorrento, the situation was more cheerful; but even here the ship rolled terribly, and the coast with all its precipices, gardens and pines, with its pink and white hotels and hazy mountains clad in curling verdure, flew up and down as if it were on swings. The row-boats hit against the sides of the steamer, the sailors and the deck passengers shouted at the top of their voices, and somewhere a baby screamed as if it were being crushed to pieces. A wet wind blew through the door, and from a wavering barge flying the flag of the Hotel Royal, an urchin kept on unwearyingly shouting "Kgoyal-al! Hotel Kgoyal-al! . . ." inviting tourists. And the Gentleman from San Francisco felt like the old man that he was, and it was with weariness and animosity that he thought of all these "Royals," "Splendids," "Excelsiors," and of all those greedy bugs, reeking with garlic, who are called Italians. Once, during a stop, having opened his eyes and half-risen from the sofa, he noticed in the shadow of the rock beach a heap of stone huts, miserable, mildewed through and through, huddled close by the water, near boats, rags, tin-boxes, and brown fishing nets, and as he remembered that this was the very Italy he had come to enjoy, he felt a great despair. . . . Finally, in twilight, the black mass of the island began to grow nearer, as though burrowed through at the base by red fires, the wind grew softer, warmer, more fragrant; from the dock-lanterns huge golden serpents flowed down the tame waves which undulated like black oil. . . . Then, suddenly, the anchor rumbled and fell with a splash into the water, the fierce yells of the boatmen filled the air—and at once everyone's heart grew easy. The electric lights in the cabin grew more brilliant, and there came a desire to eat, drink, smoke, move. . . . Ten minutes later the family from San Francisco found themselves in a large ferry-boat; fifteen minutes later they trod the stones of the quay, and then seated themselves in a small lighted car, which, with a buzz, started to ascend the slope, while vineyard stakes, half-ruined stone fences, and wet, crooked lemon trees, in spots shielded by straw sheds, with their glimmering orange-colored fruit and thick glossy foliage, were sliding down past the open car windows. . . . After rain, the earth smells sweet in Italy, and each of her islands has a fragrance of its own.

The island of Capri was dark and damp on that evening. But for a while it grew animated and lit up, in spots, as always in the hour of the steamer's arrival. On the top of the hill, at the station of the *funiculaire*, there stood already the crowd of those whose duty it was to receive properly the Gentleman from San Francisco. The rest of the tourists hardly deserved any attention. There were a few Russians, who had settled on Capri, untidy, absent-minded people, absorbed in their bookish thoughts, spectacled, bearded, with the collars of their cloth overcoats raised. There was also a company of long-legged, long-necked, round-headed German youths in Tyrolean costume, and with linen bags on their backs, who need no one's services, are everywhere at home, and are by no means liberal in their expenses. The Gentleman from San Francisco, who kept quietly aloof from both the Russians and the Germans, was noticed at once. He and his ladies were hurriedly helped from the car, a man ran before them to show them the way, and they were again surrounded by boys and those thickset Caprean peasant women, who carry on their heads the trunks and valises of wealthy travelers. Their tiny, wooden footstools rapped against the pavement of the small square, which looked almost like an opera square, and over which an electric lantern swung in the damp wind; the gang of urchins whistled like birds and turned somersaults, and as the Gentleman from San Francisco passed among them, it all looked like a stage scene; he went first under some kind of medieval archway, beneath houses huddled close together, and then along a steep echoing lane which led to the hotel entrance, flooded with light. At the left, a palm tree raised its tuft above the flat roofs, and higher up, blue stars burned in the black sky. And again things looked as though it was in honor of the guests from San Francisco that the stony damp little town had awakened on its rocky island in the Mediterranean, that it was they who had made the owner of the hotel so happy and beaming, and that the Chinese gong, which had sounded the call to dinner through all the floors as soon as they entered the lobby, had been waiting only for them.

The owner, an elegant young man, who met the guests with a polite and exquisite bow, for a moment startled the Gentleman from San Francisco. Having caught sight of him, the Gentleman from San Francisco suddenly recollected that on the previous night, among other confused images which disturbed his sleep, he had seen this very man. His vision resembled the hotel keeper to a dot, had the same head, the same hair, shining and scrupulously combed, and wore the same frock-coat with rounded skirts. Amazed, he almost stopped for a while. But as there was not a mustard seed of what is called mysticism in his heart, his surprise subsided at once; in passing the corridor of the hotel he jestingly told his wife and daughter about this strange coincidence of dream and reality. His daughter alone glanced at him with alarm; longing suddenly compressed her heart, and such a strong feeling of solitude on this strange, dark island seized her that she almost began to cry. But, as usual, she said nothing about her feelings to her father.

A person of high dignity, Rex XVII, who had spent three entire weeks on Capri, had just left the island, and the guests from San Francisco were given the apartments he had occupied. At their disposal was put the most handsome and skillful chambermaid, a Belgian, with a figure rendered slim and firm by her corset, and with a starched cap, shaped like a small, indented crown; and they had the privilege of being served by the most well-appearing and portly footman, a black, fiery-eyed Sicilian, and by the quickest waiter, the small stout Luigi, who was a fiend at cracking jokes and had changed many places in his life. Then the maître-d'hôtel, a Frenchman, gently rapped at the door of the American gentleman's room. He came to ask whether the gentleman and the ladies would dine, and in case they would, which he did not doubt, to report that there was to be had that day lobsters, roast beef, asparagus, pheasants, etc., etc.

The floor was still rocking under the Gentleman from San Francisco—so sea-sick had the wretched Italian steamer made him —yet, he slowly, though awkwardly, shut the window which had banged when the maître-d'hôtel entered, and which let in the smell of the distant kitchen and wet flowers in the garden, and answered with slow distinctness, that they would dine, that their table must be placed farther away from the door, in the depth of the hall, that they would have local wine and champagne, moderately dry and but slightly cooled. The maître-d'hôtel approved the words of the guest in various intonations, which all meant, however, only one thing; there is and can be no doubt that the desires of the Gentleman from San Francisco are right, and that everything would be carried out, in exact conformity with his words. At last he inclined his head and asked delicately:

"Is that all, sir?"

And having received in reply a slow "Yes," he added that today they were going to have the tarantella danced in the vestibule by Carmella and Giuseppe, known to all Italy and to "the entire world of tourists."

"I saw her on post card pictures," said the Gentleman from San Francisco in a tone of voice which expressed nothing. "And this Giuseppe, is he her husband?"

"Her cousin, sir," answered the maître-d'hôtel.

The Gentleman from San Francisco tarried a little, evidently musing on something, but said nothing, then dismissed him with a nod of his head.

Then he started making preparations, as though for a wedding: he turned on all the electric lamps, and filled the mirrors with reflections of light and the sheen of furniture, and opened trunks; he began to shave and to wash himself, and the sound of his bell was heard every minute in the corridor, crossing with other impatient calls which came from the rooms of his wife and daughter. Luigi, in his red apron, with the ease characteristic of stout people, made funny faces at the chambermaids, who were dashing by with tile buckets in their hands, making them laugh until the tears came. He rolled head over heels to the door, and, tapping with his knuckles, asked with feigned timidity and with an obsequiousness which he knew how to render idiotic:

"*Ha sonato, Signore?*" (Did you ring, sir?)

And from behind the door a slow, grating, insultingly polite voice, answered:

"Yes, come in."

What did the Gentleman from San Francisco think and feel on that evening forever memorable to him? It must be said frankly: absolutely nothing exceptional. The trouble is that everything on this earth appears too simple. Even had he felt anything deep in his heart, a premonition that something was going to happen, he would have imagined that it was not going to happen so soon, at least not at once. Besides, as is usually the case just after sea-sickness is over, he was very hungry, and he anticipated with real delight the first spoonful of soup, and the first gulp of wine; therefore, he was performing the habitual process of dressing, in a state of excitement which left no time for reflection.

Having shaved and washed himself, and dexterously put in place a few false teeth, he then, standing before the mirror, moistened and vigorously plastered what was left of his thick pearly-colored hair, close to his tawny-yellow skull. Then he put on, with some effort, a tight-fitting undershirt of cream-colored silk, fitted tight to his strong, aged body with its waist swelling out because of an abundant diet; and he pulled black silk socks and patent leather dancing shoes on his dry feet with their fallen arches. Squatting down, he set right his black trousers, drawn high by means of silk suspenders, adjusted his snow-white shirt with its bulging front, put the buttons into the shining cuffs, and began the painful process of hunting up the front button under the hard collar. The floor was still swaying under him, the tips of his fingers hurt terribly, the button at times painfully pinched the flabby skin in the depression under his Adam's apple, but he persevered, and finally, with his eyes shining from the effort, his face blue because of the narrow collar which squeezed his neck, he triumphed over the difficulties—and all exhausted, he sat down before the pier glass, his reflected image repeating itself in all the mirrors.

"It's terrible!" he muttered, lowering his strong, bald head and making no effort to understand what was terrible; then, with a careful and habitual gesture, he examined his short fingers with gouty callosities in the joints, and their large, convex, almond-colored nails, and repeated with conviction, "It's terrible!"

But here the stentorian voice of the second gong sounded throughout the house, as in a heathen temple. And having risen hurriedly, the Gentleman from San Francisco drew his tie more taut and firm around his collar and pulled together his abdomen by means of a tight waistcoat, put on a dinner-coat, set to right the cuffs, and for the last time he examined himself in the mirror. . . . This Carmella, tawny as a mulatto, with fiery eyes, in a dazzling dress in which orange-color predominated, must be an extraordinary dancer—it occurred to him. And cheerfully leaving his room, he walked on the carpet, to his wife's chamber, and asked in a loud tone of voice if they would be long.

"In five minutes, papa!" answered cheerfully and gaily a girlish voice. "I am combing my hair."

"Very well," said the Gentleman from San Francisco.

And thinking of her wonderful hair, streaming on her shoulders, he slowly walked down along corridors and staircases, spread with red velvet carpets, looking for the library. The servants he met hugged the walls, and he walked by as if not noticing them. An old lady, late for dinner, already bowed with years, with milk-white hair, yet bare-necked, in a light-gray silk dress, hurried at top speed, but she walked in a mincing, funny, hen-like manner, and he easily overtook her. At the glass door of the dining hall where the guests had already gathered and started eating, he stopped before the table crowded with boxes of matches and Egyptian cigarettes, took a great Manila cigar, and threw three liras on the table. On the winter veranda he glanced into the open window; a stream of soft air came to him from the darkness, the top of the old palm loomed up before him afar-off, with its boughs spread among the stars and looking gigantic, and the distant even noise of the sea reached his ear. In the library-room, snug, quiet, a German in round silver-bowed glasses and with crazy, wondering eyes stood turning the rustling pages of a newspaper. Having coldly eyed him, the Gentleman from San Francisco seated himself in a deep leather armchair near a lamp under a green hood, put on his pince-nez and twitching his head because of the collar which choked him, hid himself from view behind a newspaper. He glanced at a few headlines, read a few lines about the interminable Balkan war, and turned over the page with an habitual gesture. Suddenly, the lines blazed up with a glassy sheen, the veins of his neck swelled, his eyes bulged out, the pince-nez fell from his nose. . . . He dashed forward, wanted to swallow air—and made a wild, rattling noise; his lower jaw dropped, dropped on his shoulder and began to shake, the shirt-front bulged out—and the whole body, writhing, the heels catching in the carpet, slowly fell to the floor in a desperate struggle with an invisible foe. . . .

Had not the German been in the library, this frightful accident would have been quickly and adroitly hushed up. The body of the Gentleman from San Francisco would have been rushed away to some far corner—and none of the guests would have known of the occurrence. But the German dashed out of the library with outcries and spread the alarm all over the house. And many rose from their meal, upsetting chairs, others growing pale, ran along the corridors to the library, and the question, asked in many languages, was heard; "What is it? What has happened?" And no one was able to answer it clearly, no one understood anything, for until this very day men still wonder most at death and most absolutely refuse to believe in it. The owner rushed from one guest to another, trying to keep back those who were running and soothe them with hasty assurances, that this was nothing, a mere trifle, a little fainting-spell by which a Gentleman from San Francisco had been overcome. But no one listened to him, many saw how the footmen and waiters tore from the gentleman his tie, collar, waistcoat, the rumpled evening coat, and even—for no visible reason—the dancing shoes from his black silk-covered feet. And he kept on writhing. He obstinately struggled with death, he did not want to yield to the foe that attacked him so unexpectedly and grossly. He shook his head, emitted rattling sounds like one throttled, and turned up his eye-balls like one drunk with wine. When he was hastily brought into Number Forty-three—the smallest, worst, dampest, and coldest room at the end of the lower corridor—and stretched on the bed—his daughter came running, her hair falling over her shoulders, the skirts of her dressing-gown thrown open, with bare breasts raised by the corset. Then came his wife, big, heavy, almost completely dressed for dinner, her mouth round with terror.

In a quarter of an hour all was again in good trim at the hotel. But the evening was irreparably spoiled. Some tourists returned to the dining hall and finished their dinner, but they kept silent, and it was obvious that they took the accident as a personal insult, while the owner went from one guest to another, shrugging his shoulders in impotent and appropriate irritation, feeling like one innocently victimized, assuring everyone that he understood perfectly well "how disagreeable this is," and giving his word that he would take all "the measures that are within his power" to do away with the trouble. Yet it was found necessary to cancel the tarantella. The unnecessary electric lamps were put out, most of the guests left for the beer hall, and it grew so quiet in the hotel that one could distinctly hear the tick-tock of the clock in the lobby, where a lonely parrot babbled something in its expression-less manner, stirring in its cage, and trying to fall asleep with its claw clutching the upper perch in a most absurd manner. The Gentleman from San Francisco lay stretched in a cheap iron bed, under coarse woolen blankets, dimly lighted by a single gas-burner fastened in the ceiling. An ice bag slid down on his wet, cold forehead. His blue, already lifeless face grew gradually cold; the hoarse, rattling noise which came from his mouth, lighted by the glimmer of the golden fillings, gradually weakened. It was not the Gentleman from San Francisco that was emitting those weird sounds; he was no more—someone else did it. His wife and daughter, the doctor, the servants were stand-ing and watching him apathetically. Sud-denly, that which they expected and feared happened. The rattling sound ceased. And slowly, slowly, in everybody's sight a pallor stole over the face of the dead man, and his features began to grow thinner and more luminous, beautiful with the beauty that he had long shunned and that became him well.

The proprietor entered. *"Gia é morto,"* whispered the doctor to him. The proprietor shrugged his shoulders indifferently. The older lady, with tears slowly running down her cheeks, approached him and said timidly that now the deceased must be taken to his room.

"O no, madam," answered the propri-etor politely, but without any amiability and not in English, but in French. He was no longer interested in the trifle which the guests from San Francisco could now leave at his cash-office. "This is absolutely impossible," he said, and added in the form of an ex-planation that he valued this apartment highly, and if he satisfied her desire, this would become known over Capri and the tourists would begin to avoid it.

The girl, who had looked at him strangely, sat down, and with her handker-chief to her mouth, began to cry. Her mother's tears dried up at once, and her face flared up. She raised her tone, began to de-mand, using her own language and still un-able to realize that the respect for her was absolutely gone. The proprietor, with polite dignity, cut her short: "If madam does not like the ways of this hotel, he dare not detain her." And he firmly announced that the corpse must leave the hotel that very day, at dawn, that the police had been informed, that an agent would call immediately and attend to all the necessary formalities. . . . "Is it possible to get on Capri at least a plain coffin?" madam asks. . . . Unfortunately not; by no means, and as for making one, there will be no time. It will be necessary to ar-range things some other way. . . . For instance, he gets English soda-water in big, oblong boxes. . . . The partitions could be taken out from such a box. . . .

By night, the whole hotel was asleep. A waiter opened the window in Number 43 —it faced a corner of the garden where a consumptive banana tree grew in the shadow of a high stone wall set with broken glass on the top—turned out the electric light, locked the door, and went away. The deceased re-mained alone in the darkness. Blue stars looked down at him from the black sky, the cricket in the wall started his melancholy, carefree song. In the dimly lighted corridor two chambermaids were sitting on the win-dow-sill mending something. Then Luigi came in, in slippered feet, with a heap of clothes on his arm.

"Pronto?"—he asked in a stage whisper, as if greatly concerned, directing his eyes to-ward the terrible door, at the end of the corridor. And waving his free hand in that direction, *"Partenza!"* he cried out in a whis-per, as if seeing off a train—and the cham-bermaids, choking with noiseless laughter, put their heads on each other's shoulders.

Then, stepping softly, he ran to the door, slightly rapped at it, and inclining his ear, asked most obsequiously in a subdued tone of voice:

"Ha sonato, Signore?"

And, squeezing his throat and thrusting his lower jaw forward, he answered himself in a drawling, grating, sad voice, as if from behind the door:

"Yes, come in. . . ."

At dawn, when the window panes in Number Forty-three grew white, and a damp wind rustled in the leaves of the banana tree, when the pale-blue morning sky rose and stretched over Capri, and the sun, rising from behind the distant mountains of Italy, touched into gold the pure, clearly outlined summit of Monte Solaro, when the masons, who mended the paths for the tourists on the island, went out to their work—an oblong box was brought to room Number Forty-three. Soon it grew very heavy and painfully pressed against the knees of the assistant doorman who was conveying it in a one-horse carriage along the white high-road which winded on the slopes, among stone fences and vineyards, all the way down to the seacoast. The driver, a sickly man, with red eyes, in an old short-sleeved coat and in worn-out shoes, had a drunken headache; all night long he had played dice at the eatinghouse—and he kept on flogging his vigorous little horse. According to Sicilian custom, the animal was heavily burdened with decorations: all sorts of bells tinkled on the bridle, which was ornamented with colored woolen fringes; there were bells also on the edges of the high saddle; and a bird's feather, two feet long, stuck in the trimmed crest of the horse, nodded up and down. The driver kept silence: he was depressed by his wrong-headedness and vices, by the fact that last night he had lost in gambling all the copper coins with which his pockets had been full—neither more nor less than four liras and forty centesimi. But on such a morning, when the air is so fresh, and the sea stretches near by, and the sky is serene with a morning serenity, a headache passes rapidly and one becomes carefree again. Besides, the driver was also somewhat cheered by the unexpected earnings which the Gentleman from San Francisco, who bumped his dead head against the walls of the box behind his back, had

brought him. The little steamer, shaped like a great bug, which lay far down, on the tender and brilliant blue filling to the brim the Neapolitan bay, was blowing the signal of departure, and the sounds swiftly resounded all over Capri. Every bend of the island, every ridge and stone was seen as distinctly as if there were no air between heaven and earth. Near the quay the driver was overtaken by the head doorman who conducted in an auto the wife and daughter of the Gentleman from San Francisco. Their faces were pale and their eyes sunken with tears and a sleepless night. And in ten minutes the little steamer was again stirring up the water and picking its way toward Sorrento and Castellamare, carrying the American family away from Capri forever. . . . Meanwhile, peace and rest were restored on the island.

Two thousand years ago there had lived on that island a man who became utterly entangled in his own brutal and filthy actions. For some unknown reason he usurped the rule over millions of men and found himself bewildered by the absurdity of this power, while the fear that someone might kill him unawares, made him commit deeds inhuman beyond all measure. And mankind has forever retained his memory, and those who, taken together, now rule the world, as incomprehensibly and, essentially, as cruelly as he did—come from all the corners of the earth to look at the remnants of the stone house he inhabited, which stands on one of the steepest cliffs of the island. On that wonderful morning the tourists, who had come to Capri for precisely that purpose, were still asleep in the various hotels, but tiny long-eared asses under red saddles were already being led to the hotel entrances. Americans and Germans, men and women, old and young, after having arisen and breakfasted heartily, were to scramble on them, and the old beggarwomen of Capri, with sticks in their sinewy hands, were again to run after them along stony, mountainous paths, all the way up to the summit of Monte Tiberia. The dead old man from San Francisco, who had planned to keep the tourists company but who had, instead, only scared them by reminding them of death, was already shipped to Naples, and soothed by this, the travelers slept soundly, and silence reigned over the island. The stores in the little town were still closed, with the exception of the fish and greens market on the tiny square. Among the plain people who filled it, going about their business, stood idly by, as usual, Lorenzo, a tall old boatman, a carefree reveller and once a handsome man, famous all over Italy, who had many times served as a model for painters. He had brought and already sold—for a song—two big sea-crawfish, which he had caught at night and which were rustling in the apron of Don Cataldo, the cook of the hotel where the family from San Francisco had been lodged, and now Lorenzo could stand calmly until nightfall, wearing princely airs, showing off his rags, his clay pipe with its long reed mouth-piece, and his red woolen cap, tilted on one ear. Meanwhile, among the precipices of Monte Solare, down the ancient Phoenician road, cut in the rocks in the form of a gigantic staircase, two Abruzzi mountaineers were coming from Anacapri. One carried under his leather mantle a bagpipe, a large goat's skin with two pipes; the other, something in the nature of a wooden flute. They walked, and the entire country, joyous, beautiful, sunny, stretched below them; the rocky shoulders of the island, which lay at their feet, the fabulous blue in which it swam, the shining morning vapors over the sea, westward, beneath the dazzling sun, and the wavering masses of Italy's mountains, both near and distant, whose beauty human word is powerless to render. . . . Midway they slowed up. Overshadowing the road stood, in a grotto of the rock wall of Monte Solare, the Holy Virgin, all radiant, bathed in the warmth and the splendor of the sun. The rust of her snow-white plaster-of-Paris vestures and queenly crown was touched into gold, and there were meekness and mercy in her eyes raised toward the heavens, toward the eternal and beatific abode of her thrice-blessed Son. They bared their heads, applied

the pipes to their lips, and praises flowed on, candid and humbly-joyous, praises to the sun and the morning, to Her, the Immaculate Intercessor for all who suffer in this evil and beautiful world, and to Him who had been born of her womb in the cavern of Bethlehem, in a hut of lowly shepherds in distant Judea.

As for the body of the dead Gentleman from San Francisco, it was on its way home, to the shores of the New World, where a grave awaited it. Having undergone many humiliations and suffered much human neglect, having wandered about a week from one port warehouse to another, it finally got on that same famous ship which had brought the family, such a short while ago and with such a pomp, to the Old World. But now he was concealed from the living: in a tar-coated coffin he was lowered deep into the black hold of the steamer. And again did the ship set out on its far sea journey. At night it sailed by the island of Capri, and, for those who watched it from the islands, its lights slowly disappearing in the dark sea, it seemed infinitely sad. But there, on the vast steamer, in its lighted halls shining with brilliance and marble, a noisy dancing party was going on, as usual.

On the second and the third night there was again a ball—this time in mid-ocean, during the furious storm sweeping over the ocean, which roared like a funeral mass and rolled up mountainous seas fringed with mourning silvery foam. The Devil, who from the rocks of Gibraltar, the stony gateway of two worlds, watched the ship vanish into night and storm, could hardly distinguish from behind the snow the innumerable fiery eyes of the ship. The Devil was as huge as a cliff, but the ship was even bigger, a many-storied, many-stacked giant, created by the arrogance of the New Man with the old heart. The blizzard battered the ship's rigging and its broad-necked stacks, whitened with snow, but it remained firm, majestic—and terrible. On its uppermost deck, amidst a snowy whirlwind there loomed up in a loneliness the cozy, dimly lighted cabin, where, only half awake, the vessel's ponderous pilot reigned over its entire mass, bearing the semblance of a pagan idol. He heard the wailing moans and the furious screeching of the siren, choked by the storm, but the nearness of that which was behind the wall and which in the last account was incomprehensible to him, removed his fears. He was reassured by the thought of the large, armored cabin, which now and then was filled with mysterious rumbling sounds and with the dry creaking of blue fires, flaring up and exploding around a man with a metallic headpiece, who was eagerly catching the indistinct voices of the vessels that hailed him, hundreds of miles away. At the very bottom, in the underwater womb of the *Atlantis*, the huge masses of tanks and various other machines, their steel parts shining dully, wheezed with steam and oozed hot water and oil; here was the gigantic kitchen, heated by hellish furnaces, where the motion of the vessel was being generated; here seethed those forces terrible in their concentration which were transmitted to the keel of the vessel, and into that endless round tunnel, which was lighted by electricity, and looked like a gigantic cannon barrel, where slowly, with a punctuality and certainty that crushes the human soul, a colossal shaft was revolving in its oily nest, like a living monster stretching in its lair. As for the middle part of the *Atlantis*, its warm, luxurious cabins, dining rooms, and halls, they radiated light and joy, were astir with a chattering smartly dressed crowd, were filled with the fragrance of fresh flowers, and resounded with a string orchestra. And again did the slender supple pair of hired lovers painfully turn and twist and at times clash convulsively amid the splendor of lights, silks, diamonds, and bare feminine shoulders: she—a sinfully modest pretty girl, with lowered eyelashes and an innocent hair-dressing, he—a tall, young man, with black hair, looking as if it were pasted, pale with powder, in most exquisite patent leather shoes, in a narrow, long-skirted dress-coat,—a beautiful man resembling a leech. And no one knew that this couple had long since been weary of

torturing themselves with a feigned beatific torture under the sounds of shamefully melancholy music; nor did anyone know what lay deep, deep, beneath them, on the very bottom of the hold, in the neighborhood of the gloomy and sultry maw of the ship, that heavily struggled with the ocean, the darkness, and the storm.

At first glance "The Gentleman from San Francisco" seems a very puzzling story. The main character, the Gentleman, goes on a trip, he amuses himself with his dissipations, he dies of a stroke while staying at a fashionable hotel, his body is hurried out of the hotel, ignominiously crated in a box designed for the shipment of soda water, and sent back to America by the same liner by which he had come to Europe. This simple narrative would, as we have suggested in section 1, seem merely to unfold a process and therefore scarcely deserve to be called a plot. The narrative itself is surrounded by a number of characters and episodes, most of which have little if any direct relation to the personal story of the Gentleman. What are such characters and episodes doing here? What holds the story together? What, in other words, serves the same function here that plot does in the ordinary story?

We may say that, though the Gentleman's story does provide a kind of spine for the whole, and is to be taken as the most important single element, the real principle of progression is the development of an idea, through its various complications. Here thematic organization exists with only the most tenuous connection with organization by action. We see the relation of parts to the whole only as related to the idea, not as related to the action. As for the theme, the epigraph from Revelation indicates that it involves pride and the fall of pride, and statements in the story, most explicitly in the comparison of the modern ruling class to the emperor Tiberius, indicate that it involves the question of social justice. Let us turn back to the story itself and try to see how these ideas are developed.

We may start with the Gentleman himself—the proud man who is struck down in the moment of his pride. He is the central character. But we know astonishingly little about him: he is proud, he is self-indulgent, he is contemptuous of others, especially those of inferior economic and social station, he is a complete materialist without even "a mustard seed of what is called mysticism in his heart." There are only two moments when we get some hint of an inner life: when he tells his daughter the dream and when, dressing for dinner on his last night of life, he is struck by a nameless distress. We do not even know his name—"neither at Naples nor on Capri could any one recall his name." In other words, as Bunin seems to imply, his individuality, his name, is not important. It is not important because the Gentleman as a person is not important; he is important only as a type, as a member of a class, the class who "taken together, now rule the world, as incomprehensibly and, essentially, as cruelly" as the Roman emperor Tiberius once did. This namelessness, then, points us beyond the individual to the development of an idea.

In support of this we find the method of the story. Bunin takes the tone of a historian, as it were, as if he were giving an account long afterward of the way life had existed at a certain period. He says, for example: "The class of people to which he belonged was in the habit. . . ." Furthermore, observe the great detail devoted to the life of that class, the class upon which, Bunin ironically says, "depend all the blessings of civilization: the cut of dress suits, the stability of thrones, the declaration of wars, the prosperity of hotels."

Once we have accepted the development of a theme, an idea, as the principle of organization of this story, we understand, too, the significance of many digressions involving minor characters, such as the hired lovers on the ship, the Asiatic prince and the Gentleman's daughter, the valet Luigi, the boatman Lorenzo, the cab driver, the emperor Tiberius, the Abruzzi pipers, the hotel proprietor on Capri. A few of these characters belong to the class that rules the world, but most of them belong to the class that, in one way or another, serves the Gentleman and his kind.

We may now notice what at first glance may appear a peculiar fact in a story that has an important element of protest against social injustice: the fact that we do not have a simple arrangement of the rulers as bad and the ruled as good. The daughter of the Gentleman, though she belongs to the class of the rulers and though her notion of love has been corrupted, is yet presented with a certain sympathy: she has some sensitivity, some awareness of her isolation, as we understand from her reaction when her father tells about his dream. On the other hand, most of the class of the ruled—for example, Lorenzo, the cabman, and the valet Luigi—are presented as corrupted in one way or another. Lorenzo has been spoiled and turned into an idler and reveller by others' admiration for his picturesque good looks. The cabman is a drunkard and gambler. Luigi has been so embittered by his condition that his satiric humor appears even after the Gentleman's death. The general point here seems to be that the system spreads corruption downward as well as upward, that the stain spreads in all directions, and that injustice has persisted, as is indicated by the references to Tiberius, from the ancient to the modern world.

Let us lay aside for the moment the theme of social justice. We can see that many of the elements in the story do not seem to be accommodated to it. For instance, the various references to love, the Gentleman's relations with prostitutes, the young couple who are hired to pose as lovers on the liner, the love of the daughter for the Asiatic prince, the figure of the Virgin on the road to Monte Solare. We have here a scale from a degraded form of human love up to divine love. In between the two extremes there are the hired lovers and the daughter. They imply the same thing: even in the corrupted world people want to believe in love, to have at least the illusion of love. The hired lovers provide a romantic atmosphere by their pretended devotion. The daughter, though she is drawn to the prince merely by social snobbery (personally he is described as very unattractive), must convert this into the emotion of love. Bunin says: "Beautiful were the tender, complex feelings which her meeting with the ungainly man aroused in her—the man in whose veins flowed unusual blood, for after all, it does not matter what in particular stirs up a maiden's soul: money, or fame, or nobility of birth." Bunin has put the matter ironically—"it does not matter." But it does matter, for all human beings have some yearning for meaning in life and some awareness of possibilities beyond the physical routines of life. For instance, we may recall the two moments when even the Gentleman exhibits, in a confused way, his sense of an inner life. So with the daughter, Bunin is implying that the human being, even when the victim of his system, when accepting the false values of money, fame, and birth, must still try to maintain the illusion of love. That is, against the injustice of the world there is the idea of love, culminating in divine love.

A second set of elements that does not seem to be readily accounted for by the theme of injustice centers on the ship and the captain. It is true that the ship first appears as an easily interpreted symbol for society—the Gentleman and his kind take their ease in the dining room or bar, while the stokers sweat before the furnaces and the lookouts freeze in the crow's nest. But we begin to sense that more is meant. The darkness and the storm are outside the ship, but people ignore that terror, for they "trust" the captain who is presented as a "pagan idol." We can begin now to read the symbolism. The modern world worships its "pagan idol," the technician, the scientist, the administrator, the man who has apparently conquered nature and made irrelevant any concern with the mysteries of life and death. But we see that death does strike down the Gentleman—even though "men still wonder most at death and most absolutely refuse to believe in it." The mystery of death remains despite the skills of all the pagan idols. And even the pagan idol himself who reigns over the ship would be afraid of the darkness and mystery of the sea if he did not have the comfort of the wireless. But let us notice that the wireless is put down as a mystery, a thing "in the last account incomprehensible to him," and notice that the wireless shack is described as a kind of shrine or temple: "the large armored cabin, which now and then filled with mysterious rumbling sounds and with the dry creaking of blue fires." So in the end the idol, the man who is supposed to know the solution to all problems and who is supposed to bring all to safety, must trust a "mystery."

Before we try to relate this idea to the theme of justice, we may look at the last paragraph of the story, the scene where the Devil leans on Gibraltar and watches the great ship disappear in the dark and storm toward America. What is the Devil doing in this story? There are several details to be observed before we frame an answer. Gibraltar is defined as the "gateway of two worlds," the Old World and the New World, Europe and America. The ship is bigger than the Devil and leaves him behind, staring after it. The ship is a "giant created by the arrogance of the New Man with the old heart."

To put these details together into a pattern, we may begin by taking the Devil as the embodiment of evil, a quite conventional and usual equation. Then we may say that the Devil is left behind in the Old World because the New World doesn't believe in evil. The spirit of modernism, it is sometimes said, takes it that all difficulties are merely difficulties of adjustment of one kind or another. If there is injustice in society, simply change the system. Moral problems, by such reasoning, are not really moral problems, they are problems in "conditioning." The chief concern is not with right and wrong, good and evil, but with what will work. To sum up this point, the modern spirit, which in the story is taken as characteristically American, ignores evil; it thinks that it can solve all problems by the application of technical skills. Therefore the ship, the symbol of the achievement of the modern spirit, is "bigger" than the Devil.

Now for the second point. The ship is a "giant created by the arrogance of the New Man with the old heart." To interpret, we must say that the New Man, with all his skills, has not solved the final problem, the problem of the heart. There can be no justice by merely changing systems, by tinkering machines, either literal machines or social machines. The problem is, in the end, a problem of a change of heart, a birth of moral awareness, a spiritual redemption. Systems *must* be changed, machines *must* be tinkered —but without "redemption" no final gain can be expected. With this idea, which is the central and final theme of the story, we can now see how the elements concerning love and the elements concerning the captain as idol are related to the rest of the story. Love may be taken as the redeeming power, the beneficent mystery as opposed to the terrible mystery of death. Then the captain—that is, the technician, the scientist, the administrator, the being whom all men trust—must himself finally trust a mystery. There is always the mystery of nature and man's fate (the sea outside the hull of the ship, we may say, the night, the storm), for there are always love and death; there is the mystery of the human heart.

We must not conclude this interpretation without a word of caution. We must not be too ready to read the story as an attack on the achievements of the modern spirit. We might even go so far as to say that the story is not an attack at all, but a warning, rather, against a misinterpretation of the modern spirit, an oversimplification of it. The story provides, as it were, a perspective on a problem, not an absolute and dogmatic solution to it.

EXERCISES

1. Why are the museums visited by the Gentleman described as "lifelessly clean"? Does Bunin mean to imply that the objects in those museums never had any relation to life, or that they have now lost it? Why is there irony in the description of the interior of the churches—for instance, in the phrase, "somebody's 'Descent from the Cross,' infallibly famous"? Is this irony a sneer at either painting or religion? If not, at what is the irony directed? Contrast this with the tone adopted toward the simple pipers who honor the Virgin with their music.
2. What is the thematic significance of the hotel proprietor's change of attitude after the death of the Gentleman?
3. Why does Bunin make the Gentleman say while dressing on his last night, "It's terrible"? What does this signify psychologically? Thematically?
4. Why is the male dancer on shipboard compared, at the end of the story, to a leech?
5. Does the fact that the Gentleman is from San Francisco have any significance?
6. Read "In Dreams Begin Responsibilities" by Delmore Schwartz (sec. 10). What similarities of method do you find in that story and this one?

THE INDIAN UPRISING
Donald Barthelme (b. 1931)

We defended the city as best we could. The arrows of the Comanches came in clouds. The war clubs of the Comanches clattered on the soft, yellow pavements. There were earthworks along the Boulevard Mark Clark and the hedges had been laced with sparkling wire. People were trying to understand. I spoke to Sylvia. "Do you think this is a good life?" The table held apples, books, long-playing records. She looked up. "No."

Patrols of paras and volunteers with armbands guarded the tall, flat buildings. We interrogated the captured Comanche. Two of us forced his head back while another poured water into his nostrils. His body jerked, he choked and wept. Not believing a hurried, careless, and exaggerated report of the number of casualties in the outer districts where trees, lamps, swans had been reduced to clear fields of fire we issued entrenching tools to those who seemed trustworthy and turned the heavy-weapons companies so that we could not be surprised from that direction. And I sat there getting drunker and drunker and more in love and more in love. We talked.

"Do you know Fauré's 'Dolly'?"

"Would that be Gabriel Fauré?"

"It would."

"Then I know it," she said. "May I say that I play it at certain times, when I am sad, or happy, although it requires four hands."

"How is that managed?"

"I accelerate," she said, "ignoring the time signature."

And when they shot the scene in the bed I wondered how you felt under the eyes of the cameramen, grips, juicers, men in the mixing booth: excited? stimulated? And when they shot the scene in the shower I sanded a hollow-core door working carefully against the illustrations in texts and whispered instructions from one who had already solved the problem. I had made after all other tables, one while living with Nancy, one while living with Alice, one while living with Eunice, one while living with Marianne.

Red men in waves like people scattering in a square startled by something tragic or a sudden, loud noise accumulated against the barricades we had made of window dummies, silk, thoughtfully planned job descriptions (including scales for the orderly progress of other colors), wine in demi-johns, and robes. I analyzed the composition of the barricade nearest me and found two ashtrays, ceramic, one dark brown and one dark brown with an orange blur at the lip; a tin frying pan; two-litre bottles of red wine; three-quarter-litre bottles of Black and White, aquavit, cognac, vodka, gin, Fad #6 sherry; a hollow-core door in birch veneer on black wrought-iron legs; a blanket, red-orange with faint blue stripes; a red pillow and a blue pillow; a woven straw wastebasket; two glass jars for flowers; corkscrews and can openers; two plates and two cups, ceramic, dark brown; a yellow-and-purple poster; a Yugoslavian carved flute, wood, dark brown; and other items. I decided I knew nothing.

The hospitals dusted wounds with powders the worth of which was not quite established, other supplies having been exhausted early in the first day. I decided I knew nothing. Friends put me in touch with a Miss R., a teacher, unorthodox they said, excellent they said, successful with difficult cases, steel shutters on the windows made the house safe. I had just learned via an International Distress Coupon that Jane had been beaten up by a dwarf in a bar on Tenerife but Miss R. did not allow me to speak of it. "You know nothing," she said, "you feel nothing, you are locked in a most savage and terrible ignorance, I despise you, my boy, *mon cher*, my heart. You may attend but you must not attend now, you must attend later, a day or a week or an hour, you are making me ill. . . ." I nonevaluated these remarks as Korzybski instructed. But it was difficult. Then they pulled back in a feint near the river and we rushed into that sector with a reinforced battalion hastily formed among the Zouaves and

cabdrivers. This unit was crushed in the afternoon of a day that began with spoons and letters in hallways and under windows where men tasted the history of the heart, cone-shaped muscular organ that maintains *circulation of the blood.*

But it is you I want now, here in the middle of this Uprising, with the streets yellow and threatening, short, ugly lances with fur at the throat and inexplicable shell money lying in the grass. It is when I am with you that I am happiest, and it is for you that I am making this hollow-core door table with black wrought-iron legs. I held Sylvia by her bear-claw necklace. "Call off your braves," I said. "We have many years left to live." There was a sort of muck running in the gutters, yellowish, filthy stream suggesting excrement, or nervousness, a city that does not know what it has done to deserve baldness, errors, infidelity. "With luck you will survive until matins," Sylvia said. She ran off down the Rue Chester Nimitz, uttering shrill cries.

Then it was learned that they had infiltrated our ghetto and that the people of the ghetto instead of resisting had joined the smooth, well-coördinated attack with zipguns, telegrams, lockets, causing that portion of the line held by the I.R.A. to swell and collapse. We sent more heroin into the ghetto, and hyacinths, ordering another hundred thousand of the pale, delicate flowers. On the map we considered the situation with its strung-out inhabitants and merely personal emotions. Our parts were blue and their parts were green. I showed the blue-and-green map to Sylvia. "Your parts are green," I said. "You gave me heroin first a year ago," Sylvia said. She ran off down George C. Marshall Allée, uttering shrill cries. Miss R. pushed me into a large room painted white (jolting and dancing in the soft light, and I was excited! and there were people watching!) in which there were two chairs. I sat in one chair and Miss R. sat in the other. She wore a blue dress containing a red figure. There was nothing exceptional about her. I was disappointed by her plainness, by the bareness of the room, by the absence of books.

The girls of my quarter wore long blue mufflers that reached to their knees. Sometimes the girls hid Comanches in their rooms, the blue mufflers together in a room creating a great blue fog. Block opened the door. He was carrying weapons, flowers, loaves of bread. And he was friendly, kind, enthusiastic, so I related a little of the history of torture, reviewing the technical literature quoting the best modern sources, French, German, and American, and pointing out the flies which had gathered in anticipation of some new, cool color.

"What is the situation?" I asked.

"The situation is liquid," he said. "We hold the south quarter and they hold the north quarter. The rest is silence."

"And Kenneth?"

"That girl is not in love with Kenneth," Block said frankly. "She is in love with his coat. When she is not wearing it she is huddling under it. Once I caught it going down the stairs by itself. I looked inside. Sylvia."

Once I caught Kenneth's coat going down the stairs by itself but the coat was a trap and inside a Comanche who made a thrust with his short, ugly knife at my leg which buckled and tossed me over the balustrade through a window and into another situation. Not believing that your body brilliant as it was and your fat, liquid spirit distinguished and angry as it was were stable quantities to which one could return on wires more than once, twice, or another number of times I said: "See the table?"

In Skinny Wainwright Square the forces of green and blue swayed and struggled. The referees ran out on the field trailing chains. And then the blue part would be enlarged, the green diminished. Miss R. began to speak. "A former king of Spain, a Bonaparte, lived for a time in Bordentown, New Jersey. But that's no good." She paused. "The ardor aroused in men by the beauty of women can only be satisfied by God. That is *very* good (it is Valéry) but it is not what I have to teach you, goat, muck, filth, heart of

my heart." I showed the table to Nancy. "See the table?" She stuck out her tongue red as a cardinal's hat. "I made such a table once," Block said frankly. "People all over America have made such tables. I doubt very much whether one can enter an American home without finding at least one such table, or traces of its having been there, such as faded places in the carpet." And afterward in the garden the men of the 7th Cavalry played Gabrieli, Albinoni, Marcello, Vivaldi, Boccherini. I saw Sylvia. She wore a yellow ribbon, under a long blue muffler. "Which side are you on," I cried, "after all?"

"The only form of discourse of which I approve," Miss R. said in her dry, tense voice, "is the litany. I believe our masters and teachers as well as plain citizens should confine themselves to what can safely be said. Thus when I hear the words *pewter, snake, tea, Fad #6 sherry, serviette, fenestration, crown, blue* coming from the mouth of some public official, or some raw youth, I am not disappointed. Vertical organization is also possible," Miss R. said, "as in

> pewter
> snake
> tea
> Fad #6 sherry
> serviette
> fenestration
> crown
> blue.

I run to liquids and colors," she said, "but you, you may run to something else, my virgin, my darling, my thistle, my poppet, my own. Young people," Miss R. said, "run to more and more unpleasant combinations as they sense the nature of our society. Some people," Miss R. said, "run to conceits or wisdom but I hold to the hard, brown, nutlike word. I might point out that there is enough aesthetic excitement here to satisfy anyone but a damned fool." I sat in solemn silence.

Fire arrows lit my way to the post office in Patton Place where members of the Abraham Lincoln Brigade offered their last, exhausted letters, postcards, calendars. I opened a letter but inside was a Comanche flint arrowhead played by Frank Wedekind in an elegant gold chain and congratulations. Your earring rattled against my spectacles when I leaned forward to touch the soft, ruined place where the hearing aid had been. "Pack it in! Pack it in!" I urged, but the men in charge of the Uprising refused to listen to reason or to understand that it was real and that our water supply had evaporated and that our credit was no longer what it had been, once.

We attached wires to the testicles of the captured Comanche. And I sat there getting drunker and drunker and more in love and more in love. When we threw the switch he spoke. His name, he said, was Gustave Aschenbach. He was born at L—, a country town in the province of Silesia. He was the son of an upper official in the judicature, and his forebears had all been officers, judges, departmental functionaries. . . . And you can never touch a girl in the same way more than once, twice, or another number of times however much you may wish to hold, wrap, or otherwise fix her hand, or look, or some other quality, or incident, known to you previously. In Sweden the little Swedish children cheered when we managed nothing more remarkable than getting off a bus burdened with packages, bread and liver-paste and beer. We went to an old church and sat in the royal box. The organist was practicing. And then into the graveyard next to the church. *Here lies Anna Pedersen, a good woman.* I threw a mushroom on the grave. The officer commanding the garbage dump reported by radio that the garbage had begun to move.

Jane! I heard via an International Distress Coupon that you were beaten up by a dwarf in a bar on Tenerife. That doesn't sound like you, Jane. Mostly you kick the dwarf in his little dwarf groin before he can get his teeth into your tasty and nice-looking leg, don't you, Jane? Your affair with Harold is reprehensible, you know that, don't you, Jane? Harold is married to Nancy. And there is Paula to think about (Harold's kid), and Billy (Harold's other kid). I think your

values are peculiar, Jane! Strings of language extend in every direction to bind the world into a rushing, ribald whole.

And you can never return to felicities in the same way, the brilliant body, the distinguished spirit recapitulating moments that occur once, twice, or another number of times in rebellions, or water. The rolling consensus of the Comanche nation smashed our inner defenses on three sides. Block was firing a greasegun from the upper floor of a building designed by Emery Roth & Sons. "See the table?" "Oh, pack it in with your bloody table!" The city officials were tied to trees. Dusky warriors padded with their forest tread into the mouth of the mayor. "Who do you want to be?" I asked Kenneth and he said he wanted to be Jean-Luc Godard but later when time permitted conversations in large, lighted rooms, whispering galleries with black-and-white Spanish rugs and problematic sculpture on calm, red catafalques. The sickness of the quarrel lay thick in the bed. I touched your back, the white, raised scars.

We killed a great many in the south suddenly with helicopters and rockets but we found that those we had killed were children and more came from the north and from the east and from other places where there are children preparing to live. "Skin," Miss R. said softly in the white, yellow room. "This is the Clemency Committee. And would you remove your belt and shoelaces." I removed my belt and shoelaces and looked (rain shattering from a great height the prospects of silence and clear, neat rows of houses in the sub-divisions) into their savage black eyes, paint, feathers, beads.

———————— ◆ ◀◆▶ ◆ ————————

The most obvious fact about "The Indian Uprising" is that the writer does *not* mean for us to take it literally. Just as certain events in "Young Goodman Brown" (sec. 4) and the atmosphere of "The Enemies" (sec. 4) signal us to expect something beyond the ordinary—some level of interpretation not found in the realistic story—so here we early get signals that this is a fantasy. And we are early aware, too, that this fantasy, like "Young Goodman Brown" and "The Enemies," is devised not merely for diversion and marvel, as with "The Tinder Box" (sec. 1), but to make a point about real life.

The point made by "The Indian Uprising" is, however, very different from the points made by the previous stories in this section, and is made by a different method. The earlier stories quite directly and seriously illustrate a truth about our moral and spiritual life: for the first, that the human soul harbors both good and evil and that it is the locus of moral struggle, and for the second, that life involves certain opposing and irreconcilable principles. "The Indian Uprising" involves, as we soon also discover, quite serious ideas, but the difference in method is great; and this difference is most obviously one of tone (see Glossary).

The difference of tone is implied in the fact that "The Indian Uprising" is satirical, a satirical fantasy such as *Gulliver's Travels* by Jonathan Swift. Satire is never direct, and no matter how biting and savage it may be, it is never mere condemnation or naked invective or vituperation. Some distortion always appears in satire, some irony of understatement or overstatement, some element of parody. Satire, however severe, bears some relation to comedy—in fact, it may be said to be a form of comedy considered as a general literary mode, and comedy, even though the intention underlying it may be deadly earnest, always has a surface effect that, apparently at least, modifies, or even denies, that underlying earnestness.

Let us look at the story. Factually, we are presented with the absurdity of a large modern city's being attacked by Indians armed with bows and war clubs. Absurdity* is, indeed, the most obvious characteristic of the piece.

At first, the Comanches, even with their primitive armament, are fairly successful against the city with its "heavy-weapons companies"; but this situation, in its very absur-

dity, suggests the violent revolutionary, or anarchistic, potential in the modern world, with angry minorities, undeveloped nations, underprivileged classes, economic injustices, and sadistic maniacs. In the absurdity, the quite literal world finds its image.

In the fourth sentence, with the earthworks in the city street and the "sparkling wire" strung like a deadly decoration, we might be reading a report from a correspondent dealing with any war, but more probably some civil war or revolutionary uprising in which street fighting would be characteristic. The fact that the attack is being staged by Comanches (with their traditional weapons), along with the name of Mark Clark for the street, sets the mysterious struggle in an American city that is, however, in sharp contrast to the unity and power of the victorious and confident United States of World War II, in which Clark was a famous general.

Then we find the sentence "People were trying to understand." The fact that the verb "to understand" is used intransitively leaves a range of mysterious possibilities. Understand what? How things could so soon have changed from victorious confidence? How this could happen to us? How the primitive could conquer the civilized? Many questions are suggested, even the big general, sentimental, and foggy one, "What is the meaning of life?"

This last possibility is one of the clichés of our time. The phrase "to try to understand" belongs to the world of serious and liberal-minded but often addle-pated "seekers." The same connotation extends to the question to Sylvia, with the cliché "good life," which echoes not only the tone of the "seekers" but, paradoxically enough, that of advertisements—the "good life" with a certain brand of refrigerator or a vacation in the Virgin Islands or a European sports car.

But the question, we note on second thought, concerns the emotional relation of the young couple, the narrator and Sylvia (whoever they are), and here we are back to a stock topic of "sexual adjustment," "marriage counseling," "communicating," "empathiz-

---

* The story clearly springs from the same impulse that has produced the "theater of the absurd" (see sec. 21).

ing," "sharing," and "honesty," that fill the pages of popular magazines, Sunday supplements of newspapers, marriage manuals, and lovelorn columns. In any case, the reference of the phrase remains unclear, one possibility flowing into another; but the bit of description of the table indicates something of the world from which the question arises: apples, books, and long-playing records (on tables made from hollow-core doors) are objects sacred to young couples in not very luxurious apartments, young couples educated (more or less), earnest, and probably full of social consciousness or artiness. We can shut our eyes and see the other objects in such an apartment, or shut our ears and hear the conversations about current topics—cocaine, sexism, racism, pollution, pornography, economic justice, plastic jewelry—whatever is news at the moment. The point here is not that the writer is denying the seriousness of some of those topics. He is not necessarily satirizing the topics, he is satirizing the triviality of the people to whom serious topics are merely fads, or who, for all their gabble, are sunk in apathy or self-indulgence.

To return to the text, the reference of the question ("Do you think this is a good life?") remains unclear. In fact, there are too many confusing answers possible; and they flow into one another and blur so that the question becomes a sort of pretentious nonsense without direction. Sylvia's answer is simply "No." But, no to what? Is her answer specific? Or is it merely a general negative, an echo of the absurdity and meaninglessness of the world she inhabits?

In the first paragraph we have the pattern of the story. On the one hand, we find an objective action, the world of the "uprising," and on the other, the subjective realm of private experience, the vague hints of personal relationships and individual stories. These two realms bear some mysterious relation to each other; they may be shockingly juxtaposed or may flow into each other, as in this paragraph:

In Skinny Wainwright Square [Wainwright was another American commander in World War II] the forces of green and blue swayed and struggled.* The referees ran out on the field trailing chains. And then the blue part would be enlarged, the green diminished. Miss R. began to speak. "A former king of Spain, a Bonaparte, lived for a time in Bordentown, New Jersey. But that's no good." She paused. "The ardor aroused in men by the beauty of women can only be satisfied by God. That is *very* good (it is Valéry) but it is not what I have to teach you, goat, muck, filth, heart of my heart." I showed the table to Nancy [the table made from a hollow-core door on which the narrator was earlier working]. "See the table?" She stuck out her tongue red as a cardinal's hat. "I made such a table once," Block said frankly. "People all over America have made such tables. I doubt very much whether one can enter an American home without finding at least one such table, or traces of its having been there, such as faded places in the carpet." And afterward in the garden the men of the 7th Cavalry played Gabrieli, Albinoni, Marcello, Vivaldi, Boccherini. I saw Sylvia. She wore a yellow ribbon, under a long blue muffler. "Which side are you on," I cried, "after all?"

"The Indian Uprising" is, then, a satirical parody of the modern world. By its incoherence, in the midst of hints of never specified coherences and logical relationships, it affirms that the modern world, for all its pretentions to science, rationality, system, and organization, is finally incomprehensible. This parody affirms, too, that the modern world, for all its pretensions to humanitarianism and idealism, is dehumanizing and brutal.

The reader may feel that Barthelme, the author, is overinsistent and unfair, that he distorts the facts of his world, and overstates his case. Indeed, he does overstate it, but the overstatement, by its very distortion, is a device of satire, a way of saying that if we dare to penetrate the mask of plausibilities of

---

* In ancient Byzantium the two great factions of the populace, who bet on horse races and sometimes engaged each other in bloody street fights, were the blues and the greens. Barthelme presumably sees such a situation as a symptom in all decadent civilizations.

the actual world, this is the wild and wicked absurdity we find.

Let us look more closely at some of the devices of parody used here. Take the sentence "Then it was learned that they [the Comanches] had infiltrated our ghetto and that the people of the ghetto instead of resisting had joined the smooth well-coördinated attack with zipguns, telegrams, lockets, causing that portion of the line held by the I.R.A. to swell and collapse."

The sentence starts like a straightforward military account of street fighting, an account that faintly reminds us of many factual accounts encountered elsewhere, but the allusions transmute it into fantasy. The word *ghetto* (the very word has become a kind of cliché in recent years) echoes the dire predictions of sociologists and journalists of race war; but notice how this reference moves through the actuality of zipguns (a weapon characteristic of the ghetto) and leads quite deadpan to the absurdity of telegrams and lockets as weapons (with some hint of a love affair, the sentiment of lockets, the urgency of telegrams). Then, with the allusion to the I.R.A. (the Irish Republican Army, a secret nationalist organization opposed to the partition of Ireland and active in anti-British terrorism) we find the crowning absurdity: why should the I.R.A. be fighting in this race war in America?

There are, however, other kinds of allusion in the parody. For instance, in the same paragraph as the sentence quoted above, Sylvia (whoever she is) remarks, "You gave me heroin first a year ago," thus echoing the line "You gave me hyacinths first a year ago," spoken by the Hyacinth Girl in T. S. Eliot's famous poem *The Waste Land*. The poem itself deals with the decay and collapse of Western civilization, and the allusion is a way of indicating that "The Indian Uprising," too, is on the same subject.

Another such literary allusion (and cliché) appears in an exchange between the narrator and Block:

> "What is the situation?" I asked.
> "The situation is liquid," he said. "We hold the south quarter and they hold the north quarter. The rest is silence." *

The last sentence here is a quotation from the dying speech of Hamlet, and the allusion suggests (as do many allusions in *The Waste Land*) an ironical contrast between the grandeur and heroism possible in the past and the confusion and decay in the present world. But the line from Shakespeare has long since become a cliché, an almost comic cliché. †

EXERCISES

1. Compare "The Indian Uprising" with "The Gentleman from San Francisco" in regard to theme. Specify similarities and differences. Describe the difference in tone. How do these differences relate to differences in meaning?
2. How would you compare "The Indian Uprising" with "Hurry, Hurry," by Eleanor Clark (sec. 10) in regard to theme? In regard to method?

---

* Another element of parody appears here. The normal word for an uncertain situation is *fluid*. Here the unexpected substitution of the synonym *liquid* gives a peculiar shock of literalism; it "wakes up" the metaphor, suggesting that things are really, direly, uncertain.

† *The Waste Land*, as we have suggested, lies behind this story. But the story reminds us, not only of Eliot, but of Franz Kafka and of James Joyce. Kafka is the great modern master of the symbolical fable, and his novels *The Trial* and *The Castle* paint a world of dehumanized incoherence and brutality. As for Joyce, his famous novel *Ulysses* presents, in modern Dublin, an image of the world disintegrating into meaninglessness. Here, two generations earlier than Barthelme's work, we find the method of cliché and allusion—clichés wittily and masterfully used to show the hardening of the arteries of thought and feeling in a culture that may be slipping back toward barbarism.

Section 9

SCALE, PACE, AND TIME

Here we present one story very much shorter than ordinary, and two very much longer. We shall ask ourselves how, in the light of the materials involved, we may account for the scale. In this connection, we are necessarily led to consider the relation of summary treatment of narratives to dramatically developed treatment, in other words, to consider shifts of pace in the treatment of time. Summary treatment moves swiftly over time, dramatic treatment slowly. The shift from one kind of treatment to the other is connected, of course, with the question of selectivity: on what basis does a writer summarize material here and present it there? And the answer to this question is finally related to the dominant interest the writer finds in his material—the interest that gives a story its thematic and emotional focus.

LA LUPA *

Giovanni Verga (1840–1922)

Translated by D. H. Lawrence

She was tall, and thin; but she had the firm, vigorous bosom of a grown woman, though she was no longer young. Her face was pale, as though she had the malaria always on her, and in her pallor, two great dark eyes and fresh, red lips that seemed to eat you.

In the village they called her La Lupa, because she had never had enough—of anything. The women crossed themselves when they saw her go by, alone like a roving she-dog, with that ranging, suspicious motion of a hungry wolf. She bled their sons and their husbands dry in a twinkling, with those red lips of hers, and she had merely to look at them with her great evil eyes to have them running after her skirts, even if they'd been kneeling at the altar of Saint Agrippina. Fortunately, La Lupa never entered the church, neither at Easter nor at Christmas, nor to hear Mass, nor to confess. Fra Angiolino, of Santa Maria di Jesu, who had been a true servant of God, had lost his soul because of her.

Maricchia, poor thing, was a good girl and a nice girl, and she wept in secret because she was La Lupa's daughter, and nobody would take her in marriage, although she had her marriage chest full of linen, and her piece of fertile land in the sun, as good as any other girl in the village.

Then one day La Lupa fell in love with a handsome lad who'd just come back from serving as a soldier and was cutting the hay alongside her in the closes belonging to the lawyer: but really what you'd call falling in love, feeling your body burn under your stuff bodice, and suffering, when you stared into his eyes, the thirst that you suffer in the hot hours of June, away in the burning plains. But he went on mowing quietly, with his nose bent over his swath, and he said to her: "Why, what's wrong with you, Mrs. Pina?" —In the immense fields, where only the grasshoppers crackled into flight, when the sun beat down like lead, La Lupa gathered armful after armful together, tied sheaf after

---

* La lupa means "the she-wolf" but also "the prostitute."

sheaf, without ever wearying, without straightening her back for a moment, without putting her lips to the flask, so that she could keep at Nanni's heels, as he mowed and mowed, and asked her from time to time: "Why, what do you want, Mrs. Pina?"

One evening she told him, while the men were dozing in the stackyard, tired from the long day, and the dogs were howling away in the vast, dark, open country: "You! I want you! Thou'rt handsome as the day, and sweet as honey to me. I want thee, lad!"

"Ah! I'd rather have your daughter, who's a filly," replied Nanni, laughing.

La Lupa clutched her hands in her hair and tore her temples, without saying a word, and went away and was seen no more in the yard. But in October she saw Nanni again, when they were getting the oil out of the olives, because he worked next her house, and the screeching of the oil press didn't let her sleep at night.

"Take the sack of olives," she said to her daughter, "and come with me."

Nanni was throwing the olives under the millstone with the shovel, in the dark chamber like a cave, where the olives were ground and pressed, and he kept shouting Ohee! to the mule, so it shouldn't stop.

"Do you want my daughter Maricchia?" Mrs. Pina asked him.

"What are you giving your daughter Maricchia?" replied Nanni.

"She has what her father left, and I'll give her my house into the bargain; it's enough for me if you'll leave me a corner in the kitchen, where I can spread myself a bit of a straw mattress to sleep on."

"All right! If it's like that, we can talk about it at Christmas," said Nanni.

Nanni was all greasy and grimy with the oil and the olives set to ferment, and Maricchia didn't want him at any price; but her mother seized her by the hair, at home in front of the fireplace, and said to her between

her teeth: "If thou doesn't take him, I'll lay thee out!"

La Lupa was almost ill, and the folks were saying that the devil turns hermit when he gets old. She no longer went roving round; she no longer sat in the doorway, with those eyes of one possessed. Her son-in-law, when she fixed on him those eyes of hers, would start laughing and draw out from his breast the bit of Madonna's dress,* to cross himself. Maricchia stayed at home nursing the children, and her mother went to the fields, to work with the men, just like a man, weeding, hoeing, tending the cattle, pruning the vines, whether in the northeast wind or the east winds of January, or in the hot, stifling African wind of August, when the mules let their heads hang in dead weight, and the men slept face downward under the wall, on the north side. Between vesper bell and the night bell's sound, when no good woman goes roving around, Mrs. Pina was the only soul to be seen wandering through the countryside, on the ever-burning stones of the little roads, through the parched stubble of the immense fields, which lost themselves in the sultry haze of the distance, far off, far off, toward misty Etna, where the sky weighed down upon the horizon, in the afternoon heat.

"Wake up!" said La Lupa to Nanni, who was asleep in the ditch, under the dusty hedge, with his arms around his head. "Wake up! I've brought thee some wine to cool thy throat."

Nanni opened his eyes wide like a disturbed child, half-awake, seeing her erect above him, pale, with her arrogant bosom, and her eyes black as coals, and he stretched out his hand gropingly, to keep her off.

"No! No good woman goes roving around between vespers and night," sobbed Nanni, pressing his face down again in the dry grass of the ditch bottom, away from her, clutching his hair with his hands. "Go away!

* When the dress of the Madonna in the church is renewed, the old dress is divided in tiny fragments among the parishioners; the fragment is sewn in a tiny heart-shaped or locket-shaped sack and worn around the neck on a cord, hidden in the breast, to ward off evil.

Go away! Don't you come into the stackyard again!"

She did indeed go away, La Lupa, but fastening up again the coils of her superb black hair, staring straight in front of her, as she stepped over the hot stubble, with eyes black as coals.

And she came back into the stackyard time and again, and Nanni no longer said anything; and when she was late coming, in the hour between evensong and night, he went to the top of the white, deserted little road to look for her, with sweat on his forehead; and afterward, he clutched his hair in his hand and repeated the same thing every time: "Go away! Go away! Don't you come into the stackyard again!"

Maricchia wept night and day; and she glared at her mother with eyes that burned with tears and jealousy; like a young she-wolf herself now, when she saw her coming in from the fields, every time silent and pallid.

"Vile woman!" she said to her. "Vile, vile mother!"

"Be quiet!"

"Thief! Thief that you are!"

"Be quiet!"

"I'll go to the Sergeant, I will."

"Then go!"

And she did go, finally, with her child in her arms, went fearless and without shedding a tear, like a madwoman, because now she also was in love with that husband of hers, whom they'd forced her to accept, greasy and grimy from the olives set to ferment.

The Sergeant went for Nanni and threatened him with jail and the gallows. Nanni began to sob and to tear his hair; he denied nothing, he didn't try to excuse himself. —"It's the temptation," he said. "It's the temptation of hell!" and he threw himself at the feet of the Sergeant, begging to be sent to jail.

"For pity's sake, Sergeant, get me out of this hell! Have me hung, or send me to prison; but don't let me see her again, never, never!"

"No!" replied La Lupa to the Sergeant. "I kept myself a corner in the kitchen, to sleep in, when I gave her my house for her dowry. The house is mine. I won't be turned out."

A little later, Nanni got a kick in the chest from a mule and was likely to die; but the parish priest wouldn't bring the Host to him, unless La Lupa left the house. La Lupa departed, and then her son-in-law could prepare himself to depart also, like a good Christian; he confessed and took the communion with such evident signs of repentance and contrition that all the neighbors and the busybodies wept round the bed of the dying man.

And better for him if he had died that time, before the devil came back to tempt him and to get a grip on his body and his soul, when he was well.

"Leave me alone!" he said to La Lupa. "For God's sake, leave me in peace! I've been face to face with death. Poor Maricchia is only driven wild. Now all the place knows about it. If I never see you again, it's better for you and for me."

And he would have liked to tear his eyes out so as not to see again those eyes of La Lupa, which, when they fixed themselves upon his, made him lose both body and soul. He didn't know what to do, to get free from the spell she put on him. He paid for Masses for the souls in Purgatory, and he went for help to the priest and to the Sergeant. At Easter he went to confession, and he publicly performed the penance of crawling on his belly and licking the stones of the sacred threshold before the church for a length of six feet.

After that, when La Lupa came back to tempt him: "Hark here!" he said. "Don't you come again into the stackyard; because if you keep on coming after me, as sure as God's above I'll kill you."

"Kill me, then," replied La Lupa. "It doesn't matter to me; I'm not going to live without thee."

He, when he perceived her in the distance, amid the fields of green young wheat, he left off hoeing the vines and went to take the ax from the elm tree. La Lupa saw him advancing toward her, pale and wild-eyed, with the ax glittering in the sun, but she did not hesitate in her step, nor lower her eyes, but kept on her way to meet him, with her hands full of red poppies, and consuming him with her black eyes.

"Ah! Curse your soul!" stammered Nanni.

———————— •◄◆► • ————————

Though the action of "La Lupa" covers some years, not even counting the time before Nanni comes back from military service, and could conceivably have furnished the basic material for a novel, the narrative here is, in fact, a marvel of compression, marvelous especially in that it gives no impression of a mere summary, and suggests the depth and fullness of actual life. Here the whole is far greater than the sum of the parts, for the simple reason that a particular part is always freighted with a burden of suggestion.

For one thing, the vividness of the presentation of La Lupa herself is remarkable— the "vigorous bosom," the "two great dark eyes and fresh, red lips that seemed to eat you," the restless roving of the countryside, with that ranging, questing motion of a "hungry wolf." We know all we need to know about her and her obsessive, insatiable desire. She is like a natural force. She seems, indeed, an extension of the natural background, the blazing, parched land, where grasshoppers "crackled into flight," where in the noontide men lay face down in the shadow on the north side of a wall, and where at night dogs howled in "the vast, dark, open country." Not only does she seem a natural extension of that world; it seems to possess and victimize her, as when she cannot sleep at night for the screeching of the oil press operated by Nanni, that screech an image of her lustful yearnings in the hot darkness. In sum, as a natural force, she requires no explanation or psychological analysis, no fictional development in the ordinary sense. She requires only recognition.

Not only is La Lupa firmly set in nature. She is firmly set, too, in the social world, the world of simple peasant life in the remote interior of Sicily. Here, too, a few vivid strokes suggest all: the women crossing themselves as she ranges past in her characteristic prowling, Nanni's confident laughter as he draws out from his breast "the bit of Madonna's dress" to ward off her power, the priest's refusal to bring the Host to the presumably dying Nanni as long as La Lupa is in the house.

But this is not mere background. The story of La Lupa seems an extension of the social world in which she moves. It is told in the simple, direct, unanalyzed fashion of a folk tale or a folk ballad (see Glossary). A gesture or a burst of dialogue without a formal context may suddenly appear, the very suddenness suggesting the dramatic urgency of the story. For instance, in the scene at the oil press:

> But in October she saw Nanni again, when they were getting oil out of the olives, because he worked next her house, and the screeching of the oil press didn't let her sleep at night.
>
> "Take the sack of olives," she said to her daughter, "and come with me."
>
> Nanni was throwing the olives under the millstone, in the dark chamber like a cave, where the olives were ground and pressed, and he kept shouting Ohee! to the mule, so it shouldn't stop.

The order to the daughter follows the night-screech of the press as an emotional extension of it and La Lupa's feelings; and then, as though transported by magic, we are in the dark, cavelike chamber, where the crying of Nanni keeps the mill in constant motion—and this constant, grinding motion hints at the remorseless process in which all are caught.

The key scenes and dramatic moments flick past, yet with the authority of fully perceived and experienced events, until we come to the extraordinary climax. Observe how that final scene represents a leap from the preceding scene in the stackyard, when La Lupa had said to Nanni, "Kill me, then." The final scene is, in the number of words, very brief, but even so, with its precision of selectivity, it gives the sense of almost painful duration. La Lupa is "perceived" (not "seen" —"perceived" insists upon the formality of the act) in the distance, over intervening fields; Nanni gets the ax (from "the elm tree" we are told—the irrelevance of that information certifying the actuality of the scene and the sense of portentousness in every detail suggesting the retardation of action). Then he is moving toward her. But he moves, we know, across distance; the motion takes time, and there is no sense of hysterical haste on the part of either: "she did not hesitate in her step, nor lower her eyes, but kept on her way to meet him, with her hands full of red poppies, and consuming him with her black eyes."

But what happens? Does the ax fall? To relieve her, of course, from her bondage? Does she even welcome the stroke? Perhaps there is no stroke, for in the weakness and uncertainty implied by the word *stammered,* Nanni's resolution may fail him and he may again, and forever, surrender to La Lupa. It doesn't really matter, however. If he surrenders again, he is lost. If he splits her skull, he is lost, too. The scene, in its very ambiguity, is a frozen moment in which fate is fulfilled, a ritualistic, symbolic moment, somehow brought to focus by the red poppies the woman clutches and the gleam of the ax-blade, timelessly summarizing the ambiguity of love, its destructive and its creative aspects. The whole story drives toward this moment, and in its compression the story prepares the effect of the concluding scene.

EXERCISE

Compare this story with "Araby" (sec. 7) in regard to the method of presentation and the theme.

NOON WINE
Katherine Anne Porter (b. 1890)

Time: 1896–1905
Place: Small South Texas Farm

I

The two grubby small boys with tow-colored hair who were digging among the ragweed in the front yard sat back on their heels and said, "Hello," when the tall bony man with straw-colored hair turned in at their gate. He did not pause at the gate; it had swung back, conveniently half open, long ago, and was now sunk so firmly on its broken hinges no one thought of trying to close it. He did not even glance at the small boys, much less give them good-day. He just clumped down his big square dusty shoes one after the other steadily, like a man following a plow, as if he knew the place well and knew where he was going and what he would find there. Rounding the right-hand corner of the house under the row of chinaberry trees, he walked up to the side porch where Mr. Thompson was pushing a big swing churn back and forth.

Mr. Thompson was a tough weather-beaten man with stiff black hair and a week's growth of black whiskers. He was a noisy proud man who held his neck so straight his whole face stood level with his Adam's apple, and the whiskers continued down his neck and disappeared into a black thatch under his open collar. The churn rumbled and swished like the belly of a trotting horse, and Mr. Thompson seemed somehow to be driving a horse with one hand, reining it in and urging it forward; and every now and then he turned halfway around and squirted a tremendous spit of tobacco juice out over the steps. The door stones were brown and gleaming with fresh tobacco juice. Mr. Thompson had been churning quite a while and he was tired of it. He was just fetching a mouthful of juice to squirt again when the stranger came around the corner and stopped. Mr. Thompson saw a narrow-chested man with blue eyes so pale they were almost white, looking and not looking at him from a long gaunt face, under white eyebrows. Mr. Thompson judged him to be another of these Irishmen, by his long upper lip.

"Howdy do, sir," said Mr. Thompson politely, swinging his churn.

"I need work," said the man, clearly enough but with some kind of foreign accent Mr. Thompson couldn't place. It wasn't Cajun and it wasn't Nigger and it wasn't

Dutch, so it had him stumped. "You need a man here?"

Mr. Thompson gave the churn a great shove and it swung back and forth several times on its own momentum. He sat on the steps, shot his quid into the grass, and said, "Set down. Maybe we can make a deal. I been kinda lookin' round for somebody. I had two niggers but they got into a cutting scrape up the creek last week, one of 'em dead now and the other in the hoosegow at Cold Springs. Neither one of 'em worth killing, come right down to it. So it looks like I'd better get somebody. Where'd you work last?"

"North Dakota," said the man, folding himself down on the other end of the steps, but not as if he were tired. He folded up and settled down as if it would be a long time before he got up again. He never had looked at Mr. Thompson, but there wasn't anything sneaking in his eye, either. He didn't seem to be looking anywhere else. His eyes sat in his head and let things pass by them. They didn't seem to be expecting to see anything worth looking at. Mr. Thompson waited a long time for the man to say something more, but he had gone into a brown study.

"North Dakota," said Mr. Thompson, trying to remember where that was. "That's a right smart distance off, seems to me."

"I can do everything on farm," said the man; "cheap. I need work."

Mr. Thompson settled himself to get down to business. "My name's Thompson, Mr. Royal Earle Thompson," he said.

"I'm Mr. Helton," said the man, "Mr. Olaf Helton." He did not move.

"Well, now," said Mr. Thompson in his most carrying voice, "I guess we'd better talk turkey."

When Mr. Thompson expected to drive a bargain he always grew very hearty and jovial. There was nothing wrong with him except that he hated like the devil to pay wages. He said so himself. "You furnish grub and a shack," he said, "and then you got to pay 'em besides. It ain't right. Besides the wear and tear on your implements," he said, "they just let everything go to rack and ruin." So he began to laugh and shout his way through the deal.

"Now, what I want to know is, how much you fixing to gouge outa me?" he brayed, slapping his knee. After he had kept it up as long as he could, he quieted down, feeling a little sheepish, and cut himself a chew. Mr. Helton was staring out somewhere between the barn and the orchard, and seemed to be sleeping with his eyes open.

"I'm good worker," said Mr. Helton as from the tomb. "I get dollar a day."

Mr. Thompson was so shocked he forgot to start laughing again at the top of his voice until it was nearly too late to do any good. "Haw, haw," he bawled. "Why, for a dollar a day I'd hire out myself. What kinda work is it where they pay you a dollar a day?"

"Wheatfields, North Dakota," said Mr. Helton, not even smiling.

Mr. Thompson stopped laughing. "Well, this ain't any wheatfield by a long shot. This is more of a dairy farm," he said, feeling apologetic. "My wife, she was set on a dairy, she seemed to like working around with cows and calves, so I humored her. But it was a mistake," he said. "I got nearly everything to do, anyhow. My wife ain't very strong. She's sick today, that's a fact. She's been porely for the last few days. We plant a little feed, and a corn patch, and there's the orchard, and a few pigs and chickens, but our main hold is the cows. Now just speakin' as one man to another, there ain't any money in it. Now I can't give you no dollar a day because ackshally I don't make that much out of it. No, sir, we get along on a lot less than a dollar a day, I'd say, if we figger up everything in the long run. Now, I paid seven dollars a month to the two niggers, three-fifty each, and grub, but what I say is, one middlin'-good white man ekals a whole passel of niggers any day in the week, so I'll give you seven dollars and you eat at the table with us, and you'll be treated like a white man, as the feller says—"

"That's all right," said Mr. Helton. "I take it."

"Well, now I guess we'll call it a deal, hey?" Mr. Thompson jumped up as if he had remembered important business. "Now, you just take hold of that churn and give it a few swings, will you, while I ride to town on a coupla little errands. I ain't been able to leave the place all week. I guess you know what to do with butter after you get it, don't you?"

"I know," said Mr. Helton without turning his head. "I know butter business." He had a strange drawling voice, and even when he spoke only two words his voice waved slowly up and down and the emphasis was in the wrong place. Mr. Thompson wondered what kind of foreigner Mr. Helton could be.

"Now just where did you say you worked last?" he asked, as if he expected Mr. Helton to contradict himself.

"North Dakota," said Mr. Helton.

"Well, one place is good as another once you get used to it," said Mr. Thompson, amply. "You're a forriner, ain't you?"

"I'm a Swede," said Mr. Helton, beginning to swing the churn.

Mr. Thompson let forth a booming laugh, as if this was the best joke on somebody he'd ever heard. "Well, I'll be damned," he said at the top of his voice. "A Swede: well, now, I'm afraid you'll get pretty lonesome around here. I never seen any Swedes in this neck of the woods."

"That's all right," said Mr. Helton. He went on swinging the churn as if he had been working on the place for years.

"In fact, I might as well tell you, you're practically the first Swede I ever laid eyes on."

"That's all right," said Mr. Helton.

II

Mr. Thompson went into the front room where Mrs. Thompson was lying down, with the green shades drawn. She had a bowl of water by her on the table and a wet cloth over her eyes. She took the cloth off at the sound of Mr. Thompson's boots and said, "What's all the noise out there? Who is it?"

"Got a feller out there says he's a Swede, Ellie," said Mr. Thompson, "says he knows how to make butter."

"I hope it turns out to be the truth," said Mrs. Thompson. "Looks like my head never will get any better."

"Don't you worry," said Mr. Thompson. "You fret too much. Now I'm gointa ride into town and get a little order of groceries."

"Don't you linger, now, Mr. Thompson," said Mrs. Thompson. "Don't go to the hotel." She meant the saloon; the proprietor also had rooms for rent upstairs.

"Just a coupla little toddies," said Mr. Thompson, laughing loudly, "never hurt anybody."

"I never took a dram in my life," said Mrs. Thompson, "and what's more I never will."

"I wasn't talking about the women-folks," said Mr. Thompson.

The sound of the swinging churn rocked Mrs. Thompson first into a gentle doze, then a deep drowse from which she waked suddenly knowing that the swinging had stopped a good while ago. She sat up shading her weak eyes from the flat strips of late summer sunlight between the sill and the lowered shades. There she was, thank God, still alive, with supper to cook but no churning on hand, and her head still bewildered, but easy. Slowly she realized she had been hearing a new sound even in her sleep. Somebody was playing a tune on the harmonica, not merely shrilling up and down making a sickening noise, but really playing a pretty tune, merry and sad.

She went out through the kitchen, stepped off the porch, and stood facing the east, shading her eyes. When her vision cleared and settled, she saw a long, pale-haired man in blue jeans sitting in the doorway of the hired man's shack, tilted back in a kitchen chair, blowing away at the harmonica with his eyes shut. Mrs. Thompson's heart fluttered and sank. Heavens, he looked lazy and worthless, he did, now. First a lot of no-count fiddling darkies and then a no-count white man. It was just like Mr. Thompson to take on that kind. She did wish he would be more considerate, and take a little trouble with his business. She wanted to believe in her husband, and there were too many times when she couldn't. She wanted to believe that tomorrow, or at least the day after, life, such a battle at best, was going to be better.

She walked past the shack without glancing aside, stepping carefully, bent at the waist because of the nagging pain in her side, and went to the springhouse, trying to harden her mind to speak very plainly to that new hired man if he had not done his work.

The milk house was only another shack of weather-beaten boards nailed together hastily years before because they needed a milk house; it was meant to be temporary, and it was; already shapeless, leaning this way and that over a perpetual cool trickle of water that fell from a little grot, almost choked with pallid ferns. No one else in the whole countryside had such a spring on his land. Mr. and Mrs. Thompson felt they had a fortune in that spring, if ever they got around to doing anything with it.

Rickety wooden shelves clung at hazard in the square around the small pool where the larger pails of milk and butter stood, fresh and sweet in the cold water. One hand supporting her flat, pained side, the other shading her eyes, Mrs. Thompson leaned over and peered into the pails. The cream had been skimmed and set aside, there was a rich roll of butter, the wooden molds and shallow pans had been scrubbed and scalded for the first time in who knows when, the barrel was full of buttermilk ready for the pigs and the weanling calves, the hard packed-dirt floor had been swept smooth. Mrs. Thompson straightened up again, smiling tenderly. She had been ready to scold him, a poor man

who needed a job, who had just come there and who might not have been expected to do things properly at first. There was nothing she could do to make up for the injustice she had done him in her thoughts but to tell him how she appreciated his good clean work, finished already, in no time at all. She ventured near the door of the shack with her careful steps; Mr. Helton opened his eyes, stopped playing, and brought his chair down straight, but did not look at her, or get up. She was a little frail woman with long thick brown hair in a braid, a suffering patient mouth and diseased eyes which cried easily. She wove her fingers into an eyeshade, thumbs on temples, and, winking her tearful lids, said with a polite little manner, "Howdy do, sir. I'm Miz Thompson, and I wanted to tell you I think you did real well in the milk house. It's always been a hard place to keep."

He said, "That's all right," in a slow voice, without moving.

Mrs. Thompson waited a moment. "That's a pretty tune you're playing. Most folks don't seem to get much music out of a harmonica."

Mr. Helton sat humped over, long legs sprawling, his spine in a bow, running his thumb over the square mouth-stops; except for his moving hand he might have been asleep. The harmonica was a big shiny new one, and Mrs. Thompson, her gaze wandering about, counted five others, all good and expensive, standing in a row on the shelf beside his cot. "He must carry them around in his jumper pocket," she thought, and noted there was not a sign of any other possession lying about. "I see you're mighty fond of music," she said. "We used to have an old accordion, and Mr. Thompson could play it right smart, but the little boys broke it up."

Mr. Helton stood up rather suddenly, the chair clattered under him, his knees straightened though his shoulders did not, and he looked at the floor as if he were listening carefully. "You know how little boys are," said Mrs. Thompson. "You'd better set them harmonicas on a high shelf or they'll be after them. They're great hands for getting into things. I try to learn 'em, but it don't do much good."

Mr. Helton, in one wide gesture of his long arms, swept his harmonicas up against his chest, and from there transferred them in a row to the ledge where the roof joined to the wall. He pushed them back almost out of sight.

"That's do, maybe," said Mrs. Thompson. "Now I wonder," she said, turning and closing her eyes helplessly against the stronger western light. "I wonder what became of them little tads. I can't keep up with them." She had a way of speaking about her children as if they were rather troublesome nephews on a prolonged visit.

"Down by the creek," said Mr. Helton, in his hollow voice. Mrs. Thompson, pausing confusedly, decided he had answered her question. He stood in silent patience, not exactly waiting for her to go, perhaps, but pretty plainly not waiting for anything else. Mrs. Thompson was perfectly accustomed to all kinds of men full of all kinds of cranky ways. The point was, to find out just how Mr. Helton's crankiness was different from any other man's, and then get used to it, and let him feel at home. Her father had been cranky, her brothers and uncles had all been set in their ways and none of them alike; and every hired man she'd ever seen had quirks and crotchets of his own. Now here was Mr. Helton, who was a Swede, who wouldn't talk, and who played the harmonica besides.

"They'll be needing something to eat," said Mrs. Thompson in a vague friendly way, "pretty soon. Now I wonder what I ought to be thinking about for supper? Now what do you like to eat, Mr. Helton? We always have plenty of good butter and milk and cream, that's a blessing. Mr. Thompson says we ought to sell all of it, but I say my family comes first." Her little face went all out of shape in a pained blind smile.

"I eat anything," said Mr. Helton, his words wandering up and down.

He *can't* talk, for one thing, thought Mrs. Thompson; it's a shame to keep at him when he don't know the language good. She took a slow step away from the shack, looking back over her shoulder. "We usually have cornbread except on Sundays," she told him. "I suppose in your part of the country you don't get much good cornbread."

Not a word from Mr. Helton. She saw from her eye-corner that he had sat down again, looking at his harmonica, chair tilted. She hoped he would remember it was getting near milking time. As she moved away, he started playing again, the same tune.

Milking time came and went. Mrs. Thompson saw Mr. Helton going back and forth between the cow barn and the milk house. He swung along in an easy lope, shoulders bent, head hanging, the big buckets balancing like a pair of scales at the ends of his bony arms. Mr. Thompson rode in from town sitting straighter than usual, chin in, a towsack full of supplies swung behind the saddle. After a trip to the barn, he came into the kitchen full of good will, and gave Mrs. Thompson a hearty smack on the cheek after dusting her face off with his tough whiskers. He had been to the hotel, that was plain. "Took a look around the premises, Ellie," he shouted. "That Swede sure is grinding out the labor. But he is the closest mouthed feller I ever met up with in all my days. Looks like he's scared he'll crack his jaw if he opens his front teeth."

Mrs. Thompson was stirring up a big bowl of buttermilk cornbread. "You smell like a toper, Mr. Thompson," she said with perfect dignity. "I wish you'd get one of the little boys to bring me in an extra load of firewood. I'm thinking about baking a batch of cookies tomorrow."

Mr. Thompson, all at once smelling the liquor on his own breath, sneaked out, justly rebuked, and brought in the firewood himself. Arthur and Herbert, grubby from thatched head to toes, from skin to shirt, came stamping in yelling for supper. "Go wash your faces and comb your hair," said Mrs. Thompson, automatically. They retired to the porch. Each one put his hand under the pump and wet his forelock, combed it down with his fingers, and returned at once to the kitchen, where all the fair prospects of life were centered. Mrs. Thompson set an extra plate and commanded Arthur, the eldest, eight years old, to call Mr. Helton for supper.

Arthur, without moving from the spot, bawled like a bull calf, "Saaaaaay, Helllllll-ton, suuuuuupper's ready!" and added in a lower voice, "You big Swede!"

"Listen to me," said Mrs. Thompson, "that's no way to act. Now you go out there and ask him decent, or I'll get your daddy to give you a good licking."

Mr. Helton loomed, long and gloomy, in the doorway. "Sit right there," boomed Mr. Thompson, waving his arm. Mr. Helton swung his square shoes across the kitchen in two steps, slumped onto the bench and sat. Mr. Thompson occupied his chair at the head of the table, the two boys scrambled into place opposite Mr. Helton, and Mrs. Thompson sat at the end nearest the stove. Mrs. Thompson clasped her hands, bowed her head and said aloud hastily, "Lord, for all these and Thy other blessings we thank Thee in Jesus' name, amen," trying to finish before Herbert's rusty little paw reached the nearest dish. Otherwise she would be duty-bound to send him away from the table, and growing children need their meals. Mr. Thompson and Arthur always waited, but Herbert, aged six, was too young to take training yet.

Mr. and Mrs. Thompson tried to engage Mr. Helton in conversation, but it was a failure. They tried first the weather, and then the crops, and then the cows, but Mr. Helton simply did not reply. Mr. Thompson then told something funny he had seen in town. It was about some of the other old grangers at the hotel, friends of his, giving beer to a goat, and the goat's subsequent behavior. Mr. Helton did not seem to hear. Mrs. Thompson laughed dutifully, but she didn't think it was very funny. She had heard it often before, though Mr. Thompson, each time he told it, pretended it had happened that self-same day. It must have happened years ago if it ever happened at all, and it had never been a story that Mrs. Thompson thought suitable for mixed company. The whole thing came of Mr. Thompson's weakness for a dram too much now and then, though he voted for local option at every election. She passed the food to Mr. Helton, who took a helping of everything, but not much, not enough to keep him up to his full powers if he expected to go on working the way he had started.

At last, he took a fair-sized piece of cornbread, wiped his plate up as clean as if it had been licked by a hound dog, stuffed his mouth full, and, still chewing, slid off the bench and started for the door.

"Good night, Mr. Helton," said Mrs. Thompson, and the other Thompsons took it up in a scattered chorus. "Good night, Mr. Helton!"

"Good night," said Mr. Helton's wavering voice grudgingly from the darkness.

"Gude not," said Arthur, imitating Mr. Helton.

"Gude not," said Herbert, the copy-cat.

"You don't do it right," said Arthur. "Now listen to me. Guuuuuude naht," and he ran a hollow scale in a luxury of successful impersonation. Herbert almost went into a fit with joy.

"Now you *stop* that," said Mrs. Thompson. "He can't help the way he talks. You ought to be ashamed of yourselves, both of you, making fun of a poor stranger like that. How'd you like to be a stranger in a strange land?"

"I'd like it," said Arthur. "I think it would be fun."

"They're both regular heathens, Ellie," said Mr. Thompson. "Just plain ignoramuses." He turned the face of awful fatherhood upon his young. "You're both going to get sent to school next year, and that'll knock some sense into you."

"I'm going to git sent to the 'formatory when I'm old enough," piped up Herbert. "That's where I'm goin'."

"Oh, you are, are you?" asked Mr. Thompson. "Who says so?"

"The Sunday School Supintendant," said Herbert, a bright boy showing off.

"You see?" said Mr. Thompson, staring at his wife. "What did I tell you?" He became a hurricane of wrath. "Get to bed, you two," he roared until his Adam's apple shuddered. "Get now before I take the hide off you!" They got, and shortly from their attic bedroom the sounds of scuffling and snorting and giggling and growling filled the house and shook the kitchen ceiling.

Mrs. Thompson held her head and said in a small uncertain voice, "It's no use picking on them when they're so young and tender. I can't stand it."

"My goodness, Ellie," said Mr. Thompson, "we've got to raise 'em. We can't just let 'em grow up hog wild."

She went on in another tone. "That Mr. Helton seems all right, even if he can't be made to talk. Wonder how he comes to be so far from home."

"Like I said, he isn't no whamper-jaw," said Mr. Thompson, "but he sure knows how to lay out the work. I guess that's the main thing around here. Country's full of fellers trampin' round looking for work."

Mrs. Thompson was gathering up the dishes. She now gathered up Mr. Thompson's plate from under his chin. "To tell you the honest truth," she remarked, "I think it's a mighty good change to have a man round the place who knows how to work and keep his mouth shut. Means he'll keep out of our business. Not that we've got anything to hide, but it's convenient."

"That's a fact," said Mr. Thompson. "Haw, haw," he shouted suddenly. "Means you can do all the talking, huh?"

"The only thing," went on Mrs. Thompson, "is this: he don't eat hearty enough to suit me. I like to see a man set

down and relish a good meal. My granma used to say it was no use putting dependence on a man who won't set down and make out his dinner. I hope it won't be that way this time."

"Tell *you* the truth, Ellie," said Mr. Thompson, picking his teeth with a fork and leaning back in the best of good humors, "I always thought your granma was a ter'ble ole fool. She'd just say the first thing that popped into her head and call it God's wisdom."

"My granma wasn't anybody's fool. Nine times out of ten she knew what she was talking about. I always say, the first thing you think is the best thing you can say."

"Well," said Mr. Thompson, going into another shout, "you're so *ree*fined about that goat story, you just try speaking out in mixed comp'ny sometime! You just try it. S'pose you happened to be thinking about a hen and a rooster, hey? I reckon you'd shock the Babtist preacher!" He gave her a good pinch on her thin little rump. "No more meat on you than a rabbit," he said, fondly. "Now I like 'em cornfed."

Mrs. Thompson looked at him open-eyed and blushed. She could see better by lamplight. "Why, Mr. Thompson, sometimes I think you're the evilest-minded man that ever lived." She took a handful of hair on the crown of his head and gave it a good, slow pull. "That's to show you how it feels, pinching so hard when you're supposed to be playing," she said, gently.

III

In spite of his situation in life, Mr. Thompson had never been able to outgrow his deep conviction that running a dairy and chasing after chickens was woman's work. He was fond of saying that he could plow a furrow, cut sorghum, shuck corn, handle a team, build a corn crib, as well as any man. Buying and selling, too, were man's work. Twice a week he drove the spring wagon to market with the fresh butter, a few eggs, fruits in their proper season, sold them, pocketed the change, and spent it as seemed best, being careful not to dig into Mrs. Thompson's pin money.

But from the first the cows worried him, coming up regularly twice a day to be milked, standing there reproaching him with their smug female faces. Calves worried him, fighting the rope and strangling themselves until their eyes bulged, trying to get at the teat. Wrestling with a calf unmanned him, like having to change a baby's diaper. Milk worried him, coming bitter sometimes, drying up, turning sour. Hens worried him, cackling, clucking, hatching out when you least expected it and leading their broods into the barnyard where the horses could step on them; dying of roup and wryneck and getting plagues of chicken lice; laying eggs all over God's creation so that half of them were spoiled before a man could find them, in spite of a rack of nests Mrs. Thompson had set out for them in the feed room. Hens were a blasted nuisance.

Slopping hogs was hired man's work, in Mr. Thompson's opinion. Killing hogs was a job for the boss, but scraping them and cutting them up was for the hired man again; and again woman's proper work was dressing meat, smoking, pickling, and making lard and sausage. All his carefully limited fields of activity were related somehow to Mr. Thompson's feeling for the appearance of things, his own appearance in the sight of God and man. "It don't *look* right," was his final reason for not doing anything he did not wish to do.

It was his dignity and his reputation that he cared about, and there were only a few kinds of work manly enough for Mr. Thompson to undertake with his own hands. Mrs. Thompson, to whom so many forms of work would have been becoming, had simply gone down on him early. He saw, after a while, how short-sighted it had been of him to expect much from Mrs. Thompson; he had fallen in love with her delicate waist and lace-trimmed petticoats and big blue eyes, and, though all those charms had disappeared, she had in the meantime become Ellie to him,

not at all the same person as Miss Ellen Bridges, popular Sunday School teacher in the Mountain City First Baptist Church, but his dear wife, Ellie, who was not strong. Deprived as he was, however, of the main support in life which a man might expect in marriage, he had almost without knowing it resigned himself to failure. Head erect, a prompt payer of taxes, yearly subscriber to the preacher's salary, land owner and father of a family, employer, a hearty good fellow among men, Mr. Thompson knew, without putting it into words, that he had been going steadily down hill. God amighty, it did look like somebody around the place might take a rake in hand now and then and clear up the clutter around the barn and the kitchen steps. The wagon shed was so full of broken-down machinery and ragged harness and old wagon wheels and battered milk pails and rotting lumber you could hardly drive in there any more. Not a soul on the place would raise a hand to it, and as for him, he had all he could do with his regular work. He would sometimes in the slack season sit for hours worrying about it, squirting tobacco on the ragweeds growing in a thicket against the wood pile, wondering what a fellow could do, handicapped as he was. He looked forward to the boys growing up soon; he was going to put them through the mill just as his own father had done with him when he was a boy; they were going to learn how to take hold and run the place right. He wasn't going to overdo it, but those two boys were going to earn their salt, or he'd know why. Great big lubbers sitting around whittling! Mr. Thompson sometimes grew quite enraged with them, when imagining their possible future, big lubbers sitting around whittling or thinking about fishing trips. Well, he'd put a stop to that, mighty damn quick.

As the seasons passed, and Mr. Helton took hold more and more, Mr. Thompson began to relax in his mind a little. There seemed to be nothing the fellow couldn't do, all in the day's work and as a matter of course. He got up at five o'clock in the morning, boiled his own coffee and fried his own bacon and was out in the cow lot before Mr. Thompson had even begun to yawn, stretch, groan, roar and thump around looking for his jeans. He milked the cows, kept the milk house, and churned the butter; rounded the hens up and somehow persuaded them to lay in the nests, not under the house and behind the haystacks; he fed them regularly and they hatched out until you couldn't set a foot down for them. Little by little the piles of trash around the barns and house disappeared. He carried buttermilk and corn to the hogs, and curried cockleburs out of the horses' manes. He was gentle with the calves, if a little grim with the cows and hens; judging by his conduct, Mr. Helton had never heard of the difference between man's and woman's work on a farm.

In the second year, he showed Mr. Thompson the picture of a cheese press in a mail order catalogue, and said, "This is a good thing. You buy this, I make cheese." The press was bought and Mr. Helton did make cheese, and it was sold, along with the increased butter and the crates of eggs. Sometimes Mr. Thompson felt a little contemptuous of Mr. Helton's ways. It did seem kind of picayune for a man to go around picking up half a dozen ears of corn that had fallen off the wagon on the way from the field, gathering up fallen fruit to feed to the pigs, storing up old nails and stray parts of machinery, spending good time stamping a fancy pattern on the butter before it went to market. Mr. Thompson, sitting up high on the spring-wagon seat, with the decorated butter in a five-gallon lard can wrapped in wet towsack, driving to town, chirruping to the horses and snapping the reins over their backs, sometimes thought that Mr. Helton was a pretty meeching sort of fellow; but he never gave way to these feelings, he knew a good thing when he had it. It was a fact the hogs were in better shape and sold for more money. It was a fact that Mr. Thompson stopped buying feed, Mr. Helton managed the crops so well. When beef- and hog-slaugh-

tering time came, Mr. Helton knew how to save the scraps that Mr. Thompson had thrown away, and wasn't above scraping guts and filling them with sausages that he made by his own methods. In all, Mr. Thompson had no grounds for complaint. In the third year, he raised Mr. Helton's wages, though Mr. Helton had not asked for a raise. The fourth year, when Mr. Thompson was not only out of debt but had a little cash in the bank, he raised Mr. Helton's wages again, two dollars and a half a month each time.

"The man's worth it, Ellie," said Mr. Thompson, in a glow of self-justification for his extravagance. "He's made this place pay, and I want him to know I appreciate it."

Mr. Helton's silence, the pallor of his eyebrows and hair, his long, glum jaw and eyes that refused to see anything, even the work under his hands, had grown perfectly familiar to the Thompsons. At first, Mrs. Thompson complained a little. "It's like sitting down at the table with a disembodied spirit," she said. "You'd think he'd find something to say, sooner or later."

"Let him alone," said Mr. Thompson. "When he gets ready to talk, he'll talk."

The years passed, and Mr. Helton never got ready to talk. After his work was finished for the day, he would come up from the barn or the milk house or the chicken house, swinging his lantern, his big shoes clumping like pony hoofs on the hard path. They, sitting in the kitchen in the winter, or on the back porch in summer, would hear him drag out his wooden chair, hear the creak of it tilted back, and then for a little while he would play his single tune on one or another of his harmonicas. The harmonicas were in different keys, some lower and sweeter than the others, but the same changeless tune went on, a strange tune, with sudden turns in it, night after night, and sometimes even in the afternoons when Mr. Helton sat down to catch his breath. At first the Thompsons liked it very much, and always stopped to listen. Later there came a time when they were fairly sick of it, and began to wish to each other that he would learn a new one. At last they did not hear it any more, it was as natural as the sound of the wind rising in the evenings, or the cows lowing, or their own voices.

Mrs. Thompson pondered now and then over Mr. Helton's soul. He didn't seem to be a church-goer, and worked straight through Sunday as if it were any common day of the week. "I think we ought to invite him to go to hear Dr. Martin," she told Mr. Thompson. "It isn't very Christian of us not to ask him. He's not a forward kind of man. He'd wait to be asked."

"Let him alone," said Mr. Thompson. "The way I look at it, his religion is every man's own business. Besides, he ain't got any Sunday clothes. He wouldn't want to go to church in them jeans and jumpers of his. I don't know what he does with his money. He certainly don't spend it foolishly."

Still, once the notion got into her head, Mrs. Thompson could not rest until she invited Mr. Helton to go to church with the family next Sunday. He was pitching hay into neat little piles in the field back of the orchard. Mrs. Thompson put on smoked glasses and a sunbonnet and walked all the way down there to speak to him. He stopped and leaned on his pitchfork, listening, and for a moment Mrs. Thompson was almost frightened at his face. The pale eyes seemed to glare past her, the eyebrows frowned, the long jaw hardened. "I got work," he said bluntly, and lifting his pitchfork he turned from her and began to toss the hay. Mrs. Thompson, her feelings hurt, walked back thinking that by now she should be used to Mr. Helton's ways, but it did seem like a man, even a foreigner, could be just a little polite when you gave him a Christian invitation. "He's not polite, that's the only thing I've got against him," she said to Mr. Thompson. "He just can't seem to behave like other people. You'd think he had a grudge against the world," she said. "I sometimes don't know what to make of it."

In the second year something had hap-pened that made Mrs. Thompson uneasy, the kind of thing she could not put into words, hardly into thoughts, and if she had tried to explain to Mr. Thompson it would have sounded worse than it was, or not bad enough. It was that kind of queer thing that seems to be giving a warning, and yet, nearly always nothing comes of it. It was on a hot, still spring day, and Mrs. Thompson had been down to the garden patch to pull some new carrots and green onions and string beans for dinner. As she worked, sunbonnet low over her eyes, putting each kind of vege-table in a pile by itself in her basket, she noticed how neatly Mr. Helton weeded, and how rich the soil was. He had spread it all over with manure from the barns, and worked it in, in the fall, and the vegetables were coming up fine and full. She walked back under the nubbly little fig trees where the unpruned branches leaned almost to the ground, and the thick leaves made a cool screen. Mrs. Thompson was always looking for shade to save her eyes. So she, looking idly about, saw through the screen a sight that struck her as very strange. If it had been a noisy spectacle, it would have been quite natural. It was the silence that struck her. Mr. Helton was shaking Arthur by the shoulders, ferociously, his face most terribly fixed and pale. Arthur's head snapped back and forth and he had not stiffened in resis-tance, as he did when Mrs. Thompson tried to shake him. His eyes were rather fright-ened, but surprised, too, probably more sur-prised than anything else. Herbert stood by meekly, watching. Mr. Helton dropped Arthur, and seized Herbert, and shook him with the same methodical ferocity, the same face of hatred. Herbert's mouth crumpled as if he would cry, but he made no sound. Mr. Helton let him go, turned and strode into the shack, and the little boys ran, as if for their lives, without a word. They disappeared around the corner to the front of the house.

Mrs. Thompson took time to set her basket on the kitchen table, to push her sun-bonnet back on her head and draw it forward again, to look in the stove and make certain the fire was going, before she followed the boys. They were sitting huddled together under a clump of chinaberry trees in plain sight of her bedroom window, as if it were a safe place they had discovered.

"What are you doing?" asked Mrs. Thompson.

They looked hang-dog from under their foreheads and Arthur mumbled, "Nothin'."

"Nothing *now*, you mean," said Mrs. Thompson, severely. "Well, I have plenty for you to do. Come right in here this minute and help me fix vegetables. This minute."

They scrambled up very eagerly and followed her close. Mrs. Thompson tried to imagine what they had been up to; she did not like the notion of Mr. Helton taking it on himself to correct her little boys, but she was afraid to ask them for reasons. They might tell her a lie, and she would have to overtake them in it, and whip them. Or she would have to pretend to believe them, and they would get in the habit of lying. Or they might tell her the truth, and it would be something she would have to whip them for. The very thought of it gave her a headache. She supposed she might ask Mr. Helton, but it was not her place to ask. She would wait and tell Mr. Thompson, and let him get at the bottom of it. While her mind ran on, she kept the little boys hopping. "Cut those carrot tops closer, Herbert, you're just being careless. Arthur, stop breaking up the beans so little. They're little enough already. Herbert, you go get an armload of wood. Arthur, you take these onions and wash them under the pump. Herbert, as soon as you're done here, you get a broom and sweep out this kitchen. Arthur, you get a shovel and take up the ashes. Stop picking your nose, Herbert. How often must I tell you? Arthur, you go look in the top drawer of my bureau, left-hand side, and bring me the vaseline for Herbert's nose. Herbert, come here to me. . . ."

They galloped through their chores,

their animal spirits rose with activity, and shortly they were out in the front yard again, engaged in a wrestling match. They sprawled and fought, scrambled, clutched, rose and fell shouting, as aimlessly, noisily, monotonously as two puppies. They imitated various animals, not a human sound from them, and their dirty faces were streaked with sweat. Mrs. Thompson, sitting at her window, watched them with baffled pride and tenderness, they were so sturdy and healthy and growing so fast; but uneasily, too, with her pained little smile and the tears rolling from her eyelids that clinched themselves against the sunlight. They were so idle and careless, as if they had no future in this world, and no immortal souls to save, and oh, what had they been up to that Mr. Helton had shaken them, with his face positively dangerous?

In the evening before supper, without a word to Mr. Thompson of the curious fear the sight had caused her, she told him that Mr. Helton had shaken the little boys for some reason. He stepped out to the shack and spoke to Mr. Helton. In five minutes he was back, glaring at his young. "He says them brats been fooling with his harmonicas, Ellie, blowing in them and getting them all dirty and full of spit and they don't play good."

"Did he say all that?" asked Mrs. Thompson. "It doesn't seem possible."

"Well, that's what he meant, anyhow," said Mr. Thompson. "He didn't say it just that way. But he acted pretty worked up about it."

"That's a shame," said Mrs. Thompson, "a perfect shame. Now we've got to do something so they'll remember they mustn't go into Mr. Helton's things."

"I'll tan their hides for them," said Mr. Thompson. "I'll take a calf rope to them if they don't look out."

"Maybe you'd better leave the whipping to me," said Mrs. Thompson. "You haven't got a light enough hand for children."

"That's just what's the matter with them now," shouted Mr. Thompson, "rotten

spoiled and they'll wind up in the penitentiary. You don't half whip 'em. Just little
love taps. My pa used to knock me down
with a stick of stove wood or anything else
that came handy."

"Well, that's not saying it's right," said
Mrs. Thompson. "I don't hold with that way
of raising children. It makes them run away
from home. I've seen too much of it."

"I'll break every bone in 'em," said Mr.
Thompson, simmering down, "if they don't
mind you better and stop being so bull-
headed."

"Leave the table and wash your face
and hands," Mrs. Thompson commanded the
boys, suddenly. They slunk out and dabbled
at the pump and slunk in again, trying to
make themselves small. They had learned
long ago that their mother always made
them wash when there was trouble ahead.
They looked at their plates. Mr. Thompson
opened up on them.

"Well, now, what you got to say for
yourselves about going into Mr. Helton's
shack and ruining his harmonicas?"

The two little boys wilted, their faces
drooped into the grieved hopeless lines of
children's faces when they are brought to the
terrible bar of blind adult justice; their eyes
telegraphed each other in panic, "Now we're
really going to catch a licking"; in despair,
they dropped their buttered cornbread on
their plates, their hands lagged on the edge
of the table.

"I ought to break your ribs," said
Mr. Thompson, "and I'm a good mind to
do it."

"Yes, sir," whispered Arthur, faintly.

"Yes, sir," said Herbert, his lip trembling.

"Now, papa," said Mrs. Thompson in a
warning tone. The children did not glance
at her. They had no faith in her good will.
She had betrayed them in the first place.
There was no trusting her. Now she might
save them and she might not. No use depending on her.

"Well, you ought to get a good thrash-
ing. You deserve it, don't you, Arthur?"

Arthur hung his head. "Yes, sir."

"And the next time I catch either of
you hanging around Mr. Helton's shack, I'm
going to take the hide off *both* of you, you
hear me, Herbert?"

Herbert mumbled and choked, scattering his cornbread. "Yes, sir."

"Well, now sit up and eat your supper
and not another word out of you," said Mr.
Thompson, beginning on his own food. The
little boys perked up somewhat and started
chewing, but every time they looked around
they met their parents' eyes, regarding them
steadily. There was no telling when they
would think of something new. The boys ate
warily, trying not to be seen or heard, the
cornbread sticking, the buttermilk gurgling,
as it went down their gullets.

"And something else, Mr. Thompson,"
said Mrs. Thompson after a pause. "Tell
Mr. Helton he's to come straight to us when
they bother him, and not to trouble shaking
them himself. Tell him we'll look after
that."

"They're so mean," answered Mr.
Thompson, staring at them. "It's a wonder
he don't just kill 'em off and be done with
it." But there was something in the tone that
told Arthur and Herbert that nothing more
worth worrying about was going to happen
this time. Heaving deep sighs, they sat up,
reaching for the food nearest them.

"Listen," said Mrs. Thompson, suddenly. The little boys stopped eating. "Mr.
Helton hasn't come for his supper. Arthur,
go and tell Mr. Helton he's late for supper.
Tell him nice, now."

Arthur, miserably depressed, slid out of
his place and made for the door, without a
word.

IV

There were no miracles of fortune to be
brought to pass on a small dairy farm. The
Thompsons did not grow rich, but they kept
out of the poor house, as Mr. Thompson was
fond of saying, meaning he had got a little
foothold in spite of Ellie's poor health, and
unexpected weather, and strange declines in

market prices, and his own mysterious handicaps which weighed him down. Mr. Helton was the hope and the prop of the family, and all the Thompsons became fond of him, or at any rate they ceased to regard him as in any way peculiar, and looked upon him, from a distance they did not know how to bridge, as a good man and a good friend. Mr. Helton went his way, worked, played his tune. Nine years passed. The boys grew up and learned to work. They could not remember the time when Ole Helton hadn't been there: a grouchy cuss, Brother Bones; Mr. Helton, the dairymaid; that Big Swede. If he had heard them, he might have been annoyed at some of the names they called him. But he did not hear them, and besides they meant no harm —or at least such harm as existed was all there, in the names; the boys referred to their father as the Old Man, or the Old Geezer, but not to his face. They lived through by main strength all the grimy, secret, oblique phases of growing up and got past the crisis safely if anyone does. Their parents could see they were good solid boys with hearts of gold in spite of their rough ways. Mr. Thompson was relieved to find that, without knowing how he had done it, he had succeeded in raising a set of boys who were not trifling whittlers. They were such good boys Mr. Thompson began to believe they were born that way, and that he had never spoken a harsh word to them in their lives, much less thrashed them. Herbert and Arthur never disputed his word.

V

Mr. Helton, his hair wet with sweat, plastered to his dripping forehead, his jumper streaked dark and light blue and clinging to his ribs, was chopping a little firewood. He chopped slowly, struck the ax into the end of the chopping log, and piled the wood up neatly. He then disappeared round the house into his shack, which shared with the wood pile a good shade from a row of mulberry trees. Mr. Thompson was lolling in a swing chair on the front porch, a place he had never liked. The chair was new, and

Mrs. Thompson had wanted it on the front porch, though the side porch was the place for it, being cooler; and Mr. Thompson wanted to sit in the chair, so there he was. As soon as the new wore off of it, and Ellie's pride in it was exhausted, he would move it round to the side porch. Meantime the August heat was almost unbearable, the air so thick you could poke a hole in it. The dust was inches thick on everything, though Mr. Helton sprinkled the whole yard regularly every night. He even shot the hose upward and washed the tree tops and the roof of the house. They had laid waterpipes to the kitchen and an outside faucet. Mr. Thompson must have dozed, for he opened his eyes and shut his mouth just in time to save his face before a stranger who had driven up to the front gate. Mr. Thompson stood up, put on his hat, pulled up his jeans, and watched while the stranger tied his team, attached to a light spring wagon, to the hitching post. Mr. Thompson recognized the team and wagon. They were from a livery stable in Buda. While the stranger was opening the gate, a strong gate that Mr. Helton had built and set firmly on its hinges several years back, Mr. Thompson strolled down the path to greet him and find out what in God's world a man's business might be that would bring him out at this time of day, in all this dust and welter.

He wasn't exactly a fat man. He was more like a man who had been fat recently. His skin was baggy and his clothes were too big for him, and he somehow looked like a man who should be fat, ordinarily, but who might have just got over a spell of sickness. Mr. Thompson didn't take to his looks at all, he couldn't say why.

The stranger took off his hat. He said in a loud hearty voice, "Is this Mr. Thompson, Mr. Royal Earle Thompson?"

"That's my name," said Mr. Thompson, almost quietly, he was so taken aback by the free manner of the stranger.

"My name is Hatch," said the stranger, "Mr. Homer T. Hatch, and I've come to see you about buying a horse."

"I reckon you've been misdirected," said Mr. Thompson. "I haven't got a horse for sale. Usually if I've got anything like that to sell," he said, "I tell the neighbors and tack up a little sign on the gate."

The fat man opened his mouth and roared with joy, showing rabbit teeth brown as shoeleather. Mr. Thompson saw nothing to laugh at, for once. The stranger shouted, "That's just an old joke of mine." He caught one of his hands in the other and shook hands with himself heartily. "I always say something like that when I'm calling on a stranger, because I've noticed that when a feller says he's come to buy something nobody takes him for a suspicious character. You see? Haw, haw, haw."

His joviality made Mr. Thompson nervous, because the expression in the man's eyes didn't match the sounds he was making. "Haw, haw," laughed Mr. Thompson obligingly, still not seeing the joke. "Well, that's all wasted on me because I never take any man for a suspicious character 'til he shows hisself to be one. Says or does something," he explained. "Until that happens, one man's as good as another, so far's *I'm* concerned."

"Well," said the stranger, suddenly very sober and sensible, "I ain't come neither to buy nor sell. Fact is, I want to see you about something that's of interest to us both. Yes, sir, I'd like to have a little talk with you, and it won't cost you a cent."

"I guess that's fair enough," said Mr. Thompson, reluctantly. "Come on around the house where there's a little shade."

They went round and seated themselves on two stumps under a chinaberry tree.

"Yes, sir, Homer T. Hatch is my name and America is my nation," said the stranger. "I reckon you must know the name? I used to have a cousin named Jameson Hatch lived up the country a ways."

"Don't think I know the name," said Mr. Thompson. "There's some Hatchers settled somewhere around Mountain City."

"Don't know the old Hatch family," cried the man in deep concern. He seemed to be pitying Mr. Thompson's ignorance. "Why, we came over from Georgia fifty years ago. Been here long yourself?"

"Just all my whole life," said Mr. Thompson, beginning to feel peevish. "And my pa and my grampap before me. Yes, sir, we've been right here all along. Anybody wants to find a Thompson knows where to look for him. My grampap immigrated in 1836."

"From Ireland, I reckon?" said the stranger.

"From Pennsylvania," said Mr. Thompson. "Now what makes you think we came from Ireland?"

The stranger opened his mouth and began to shout with merriment, and he shook hands with himself as if he hadn't met himself for a long time. "Well, what I always says is, a feller's got to come from *somewhere*, ain't he?"

While they were talking, Mr. Thompson kept glancing at the face near him. He certainly did remind Mr. Thompson of somebody, or maybe he really had seen the man himself somewhere. He couldn't just place the features. Mr. Thompson finally decided it was just that all rabbit-teethed men looked alike.

"That's right," acknowledged Mr. Thompson, rather sourly, "but what I always say is, Thompsons have been settled here for so long it don't make much difference any more *where* they come from. Now a course, this is the slack season, and we're all just laying round a little, but nevertheless we've all got our chores to do, and I don't want to hurry you, and so if you've come to see me on business maybe we'd better get down to it."

"As I said, it's not in a way, and again in a way it is," said the fat man. "Now I'm looking for a man named Helton, Mr. Olaf Eric Helton, from North Dakota, and I was told up around the country a ways that I might find him here, and I wouldn't mind having a little talk with him. No, siree, I sure wouldn't mind, if it's all the same to you."

"I never knew his middle name," said

Mr. Thompson, "but Mr. Helton is right here, and been here now for going on nine years. He's a mighty steady man, and you can tell anybody I said so."

"I'm glad to hear that," said Mr. Homer T. Hatch. "I like to hear of a feller mending his ways and settling down. Now when I knew Mr. ⁔ ⁘on he was pretty wild, yes, sir, wild is what he was, he didn't know his own mind atall. Well, now, it's going to be a great pleasure to me to meet up with an old friend and find him all settled down and doing well by hisself."

"We've all got to be young once," said Mr. Thompson. "It's like the measles, it breaks out all over you, and you're a nuisance to yourself and everybody else, but it don't last, and it usually don't leave no ill effects." He was so pleased with this notion he forgot and broke into a guffaw. The stranger folded his arms over his stomach and went into a kind of fit, roaring until he had tears in his eyes. Mr. Thompson stopped shouting and eyed the stranger uneasily. Now he liked a good laugh as well as any man, but there ought to be a little moderation. Now this feller laughed like a perfect lunatic, that was a fact. And he wasn't laughing because he really thought things were funny, either. He was laughing for reasons of his own. Mr. Thompson fell into a moody silence, and waited until Mr. Hatch settled down a little.

Mr. Hatch got out a very dirty blue cotton bandanna and wiped his eyes. "That joke just about caught me where I live," he said, almost apologetically. "Now I wish I could think up things as funny as that to say. It's a gift. It's . . ."

"If you want to speak to Mr. Helton, I'll go and round him up," said Mr. Thompson, making motions as if he might get up. "He may be in the milk house and he may be setting in his shack this time of day." It was drawing towards five o'clock. "It's right around the corner," he said.

"Oh, well, there ain't no special hurry," said Mr. Hatch. "I've been wanting to speak to him for a good long spell now and I guess a few minutes more won't make no difference. I just more wanted to locate him, like. That's all."

Mr. Thompson stopped beginning to stand up, and unbuttoned one more button of his shirt, and said, "Well, he's here, and he's this kind of man, that if he had any business with you he'd like to get it over. He don't dawdle, that's one thing you can say for him."

Mr. Hatch appeared to sulk a little at these words. He wiped his face with the bandanna and opened his mouth to speak, when round the house there came the music of Mr. Helton's harmonica. Mr. Thompson raised a finger. "There he is," said Mr. Thompson. "Now's your time."

Mr. Hatch cocked an ear towards the east side of the house and listened for a few seconds, a very strange expression on his face.

"I know that tune like I know the palm of my own hand," said Mr. Thompson, "but I never heard Mr. Helton say what it was."

"That's a kind of Scandahoovian song," said Mr. Hatch. "Where I come from they sing it a lot. In North Dakota, they sing it. It says something about starting out in the morning feeling so good you can't hardly stand it, so you drink up all your likker before noon. All the likker, y' understand, that you was saving for the noon lay-off. The words ain't much, but it's a pretty tune. It's a kind of drinking song." He sat there drooping a little, and Mr. Thompson didn't like his expression. It was a satisfied expression, but it was more like the cat that et the canary.

"So far as I know," said Mr. Thompson, "he ain't touched a drop since he's been on the place, and that's nine years this coming September. Yes, sir, nine years, so far as I know, he ain't wetted his whistle once. And that's more than I can say for myself," he said, meekly proud.

"Yes, that's a drinking song," said Mr. Hatch. "I used to play 'Little Brown Jug' on the fiddle when I was younger than I am now," he went on, "but this Helton, he just keeps it up. He just sits and plays it by himself."

"He's been playing it off and on for nine years right here on the place," said Mr. Thompson, feeling a little proprietary.

"And he was certainly singing it as well, fifteen years before that, in North Dakota," said Mr. Hatch. "He used to sit up in a straitjacket, practically, when he was in the asylum—"

"What's that you say?" said Mr. Thompson. "What's that?"

"Shucks, I didn't mean to tell you," said Mr. Hatch, a faint leer of regret in his drooping eyelids. "Shucks, that just slipped out. Funny, now I'd made up my mind I wouldn' say a word, because it would just make a lot of excitement, and what I say is, if a man has lived harmless and quiet for nine years it don't matter if he *is* loony, does it? So long's he keeps quiet and don't do nobody harm."

"You mean they had him in a straitjacket?" asked Mr. Thompson, uneasily. "In a lunatic asylum?"

"They sure did," said Mr. Hatch. "That's right where they had him, from time to time."

"They put my Aunt Ida in one of them things in the State asylum," said Mr. Thompson. "She got vi'lent, and they put her in one of these jackets with long sleeves and tied her to an iron ring in the wall, and Aunt Ida got so wild she broke a blood vessel and when they went to look after her she was dead. I'd think one of them things was dangerous."

"Mr. Helton used to sing his drinking song when he was in a straitjacket," said Mr. Hatch. "Nothing ever bothered him, except if you tried to make him talk. That bothered him, and he'd get vi'lent, like your Aunt Ida. He'd get vi'lent and then they'd put him in the jacket and go off and leave him, and he'd lay there perfickly contented, so far's you could see, singing his song. Then one night he just disappeared. Left, you might say, just went, and nobody ever saw hide or hair of him again. And then I come along and find

him here," said Mr. Hatch, "all settled down and playing the same song."

"He never acted crazy to me," said Mr. Thompson. "He always acted like a sensible man, to me. He never got married, for one thing, and he works like a horse, and I bet he's got the first cent I paid him when he landed here, and he don't drink, and he never says a word, much less swear, and he don't waste time runnin' around Saturday nights, and if he's crazy," said Mr. Thompson, "why, I think I'll go crazy myself for a change."

"Haw, ha," said Mr. Hatch, "heh, he, that's good! Ha, ha, ha, I hadn't thought of it jes like that. Yeah, that's right! Let's all go crazy and get rid of our wives and save our money, hey?" He smiled unpleasantly, showing his little rabbit teeth.

Mr. Thompson felt he was being misunderstood. He turned around and motioned toward the open window back of the honeysuckle trellis. "Let's move off down here a little," he said. "I oughta thought of that before." His visitor bothered Mr. Thompson. He had a way of taking the words out of Mr. Thompson's mouth, turning them around and mixing them up until Mr. Thompson didn't know himself what he had said. "My wife's not very strong," said Mr. Thompson. "She's been kind of invalid now goin' on fourteen years. It's mighty tough on a poor man, havin' sickness in the family. She had four operations," he said proudly, "one right after the other, but they didn't do any good. For five years handrunnin', I just turned every nickel I made over to the doctors. Upshot is, she's a mighty delicate woman."

"My old woman," said Mr. Homer T. Hatch, "had a back like a mule, yes, sir. That woman could have moved the barn with her bare hands if she'd ever took notion. I used to say, it was a good thing she didn't know her own stren'th. She's dead now, though. That kind wear out quicker than the puny ones. I never had much use for a woman always complainin'. I'd get rid of her mighty quick, yes, sir, mighty quick. It's just as you say: a dead loss, keepin' one of 'em up."

This was not at all what Mr. Thompson had heard himself say; he had been trying to explain that a wife as expensive as his was a credit to a man. "She's a mighty reasonable woman," said Mr. Thompson, feeling baffled, "but I wouldn't answer for what she'd say or do if she found out we'd had a lunatic on the place all this time." They had moved away from the window; Mr. Thompson took Mr. Hatch the front way, because if he went the back way they would have to pass Mr. Helton's shack. For some reason he didn't want the stranger to see or talk to Mr. Helton. It was strange, but that was the way Mr. Thompson felt.

Mr. Thompson sat down again, on the chopping log, offering his guest another tree stump. "Now, I mighta got upset myself at such a thing, once," said Mr. Thompson, "but now I *deefy* anything to get me lathered up." He cut himself an enormous plug of tobacco with his horn-handled pocketknife, and offered it to Mr. Hatch, who then produced his own plug and, opening a huge bowie knife with a long blade sharply whetted, cut off a large wad and put it in his mouth. They then compared plugs and both of them were astonished to see how different men's ideas of good chewing tobacco were.

"Now, for instance," said Mr. Hatch, "mine is lighter colored. That's because, for one thing, there ain't any sweetenin' in this plug. I like it dry, natural leaf, medium strong."

"A little sweetenin' don't do no harm so far as I'm concerned," said Mr. Thompson, "but it's got to be mighty little. But with me, now, I want a strong leaf, I want it heavy-cured, as the feller says. There's a man near here, named Williams, Mr. John Morgan Williams, who chews a plug—well, sir, it's black as your hat and soft as melted tar. It fairly drips with molasses, jus' plain molasses, and it chews like licorice. Now, I don't call that a good chew."

"One man's meat," said Mr. Hatch, "is another man's poison. Now, such a chew would simply gag me. I couldn't begin to put it in my mouth."

"Well," said Mr. Thompson, a tinge of apology in his voice, "I jus' barely tasted it myself, you might say. Just took a little piece in my mouth and spit it out again."

"I'm dead sure I couldn't even get that far," said Mr. Hatch. "I like a dry natural chew without any artificial flavorin' of any kind."

Mr. Thompson began to feel that Mr. Hatch was trying to make out he had the best judgment in tobacco, and was going to keep up the argument until he proved it. He began to feel seriously annoyed with the fat man. After all, who was he and where did he come from? Who was he to go around telling other people what kind of tobacco to chew?

"Artificial flavorin'," Mr. Hatch went on, doggedly, "is jes put in to cover up a cheap leaf and make a man think he's gettin' somethin' more than he *is* gettin'. Even a little sweetenin' is a sign of cheap leaf, you can mark my words."

"I've always paid a fair price for my plug," said Mr. Thompson, stiffly. "I'm not a rich man and I don't go round settin' myself up for one, but I'll say this, when it comes to such things as tobacco, I buy the best on the market."

"Sweetenin', even a little," began Mr. Hatch, shifting his plug and squirting tobacco juice at a dry-looking little rose bush that was having a hard enough time as it was, standing all day in the blazing sun, its roots clenched in the baked earth, "is the sign of—"

"About this Mr. Helton, now," said Mr. Thompson, determinedly, "I don't see no reason to hold it against a man because he went loony once or twice in his lifetime and so I don't expect to take no steps about it. Not a step. I've got nothin' against the man, he's always treated me fair. They's things and people," he went on, " 'nough to drive any man loony. The wonder to me is, more men don't wind up in straitjackets, the way things are going these days and times."

"That's right," said Mr. Hatch, promptly, entirely too promptly, as if he were turning Mr. Thompson's meaning back on him. "You took the words right out of my mouth. There ain't every man in a straitjacket that ought to be there. Ha, ha, you're right all right. You got the idea."

Mr. Thompson sat silent and chewed steadily and stared at a spot on the ground about six feet away and felt a slow muffled resentment climbing from somewhere deep down in him, climbing and spreading all through him. What was this fellow driving at? What was he trying to say? It wasn't so much his words, but his looks and his way of talking: that droopy look in the eye, that tone of voice, as if he was trying to mortify Mr. Thompson about something. Mr. Thompson didn't like it, but he couldn't get hold of it either. He wanted to turn around and shove the fellow off the stump, but it wouldn't look reasonable. Suppose something happened to the fellow when he fell off the stump, just for instance, if he fell on the ax and cut himself, and then someone should ask Mr. Thompson why he shoved him, and what could a man say? It would look mighty funny, it would sound mighty strange to say, Well, him and me fell out over a plug of tobacco. He might just shove him anyhow and then tell people he was a fat man not used to the heat and while he was talking he got dizzy and fell off by himself, or something like that, and it wouldn't be the truth either, because it wasn't the heat and it wasn't the tobacco. Mr. Thompson made up his mind to get the fellow off the place pretty quick, without seeming to be anxious, and watch him sharp till he was out of sight. It doesn't pay to be friendly with strangers from another part of the country. They're always up to something, or they'd stay at home where they belong.

"And they's some people," said Mr. Hatch, "would jus' as soon have a loonatic around their house as not, they can't see no

difference between them and anybody else. I always say, if that's the way a man feels, don't care who he associates with, why, why, that's his business, not mine. I don't wanta have a thing to do with it. Now back home in North Dakota, we don't feel that way. I'd like to a seen anybody hiring a loonatic there, aspecially after what he done."

"I didn't understand your home was North Dakota," said Mr. Thompson. "I thought you said Georgia."

"I've got a married sister in North Dakota," said Mr. Hatch, "married a Swede, but a white man if ever I saw one. So I say *we* because we got into a little business together out that way. And it seems like home, kind of."

"What did he do," asked Mr. Thompson, feeling very uneasy again.

"Oh, nothin' to speak of," said Mr. Hatch, jovially, "jus' went loony one day in the hayfield and shoved a pitchfork right square through his brother, when they was makin' hay. They was goin' to execute him, but they found out he had went crazy with the heat, as the feller says, and so they put him in the asylum. That's all he done. Nothin' to get lathered up about, ha, ha, ha!" he said, and taking out his sharp knife he began to slice off a chew as carefully as if he were cutting cake.

"Well," said Mr. Thompson, "I don't deny that's news. Yes, sir, news. But I still say somethin' must have drove him to it. Some men make you feel like giving 'em a good killing just by lookin' at you. His brother may a been a mean ornery cuss."

"Brother was going to get married," said Mr. Hatch; "used to go courtin' his girl nights. Borrowed Mr. Helton's harmonica to give her a serenade one evenin', and lost it. Brand new harmonica."

"He thinks a heap of his harmonicas," said Mr. Thompson. "Only money he ever spends, now and then he buys hisself a new one. Must have a dozen in that shack, all kinds and sizes."

"Brother wouldn't buy him a new one,"

said Mr. Hatch, "so Mr. Helton just ups, as I says, and runs his pitchfork through his brother. Now you know he musta been crazy to get all worked up over a little thing like that."

"Sounds like it," said Mr. Thompson, reluctant to agree in anything with this intrusive and disagreeable fellow. He kept thinking he couldn't remember when he had taken such a dislike to a man on first sight.

"Seems to me you'd get pretty sick of hearin' the same tune year in, year out," said Mr. Hatch.

"Well, sometimes I think it wouldn't do no harm if he learned a new one," said Mr. Thompson, "but he don't, so there's nothin' to be done about it. It's a pretty good tune, though."

"One of the Scandahoovians told me what it meant, that's how I come to know," said Mr. Hatch. "Especially that part about getting so gay you jus' go ahead and drink up all the likker you got on hand before noon. It seems like up in them Swede countries a man carries a bottle of wine around with him as a matter of course, at least that's the way I understood it. Those fellers will tell you anything, though—" He broke off and spat.

The idea of drinking any kind of liquor in this heat made Mr. Thompson dizzy. The idea of anybody feeling good on a day like this, for instance, made him tired. He felt he was really suffering from the heat. The fat man looked as if he had grown to the stump; he slumped there in his damp, dark clothes too big for him, his belly slack in his pants, his wide black felt hat pushed off his narrow forehead red with prickly heat. A bottle of good cold beer, now, would be a help, thought Mr. Thompson, remembering the four bottles sitting deep in the pool at the springhouse, and his dry tongue squirmed in his mouth. He wasn't going to offer this man anything, though, not even a drop of water. He wasn't even going to chew any more tobacco with him. He shot out his quid suddenly, and wiped his mouth on the back of his hand, and studied the head near him

attentively. The man was no good, and he was there for no good, but what was he up to? Mr. Thompson made up his mind he'd give him a little more time to get his business, whatever it was, with Mr. Helton over, and then if he didn't get off the place he'd kick him off.

Mr. Hatch, as if he suspected Mr. Thompson's thoughts, turned his eyes, wicked and piglike, on Mr. Thompson. "Fact is," he said, as if he had made up his mind about something, "I might need your help in the little matter I've got on hand, but it won't cost you any trouble. Now, this Mr. Helton here, like I tell you, he's a dangerous escaped loonatic, you might say. Now fact is, in the last twelve years or so I musta rounded up twenty-odd escaped loonatics, besides a couple of escaped convicts that I just run into by accident, like. I don't make a business of it, but if there's a reward, and there usually is a reward, of course, I get it. It amounts to a tidy little sum in the long run, but that ain't the main question. Fact is, I'm for law and order, I don't like to see lawbreakers and loonatics at large. It ain't the place for them. Now I reckon you're bound to agree with me on that, aren't you?"

Mr. Thompson said, "Well, circumstances alters cases, as the feller says. Now, what I know of Mr. Helton, he ain't dangerous, as I told you." Something serious was going to happen, Mr. Thompson could see that. He stopped thinking about it. He'd just let this fellow shoot off his head and then see what could be done about it. Without thinking he got out his knife and plug and started to cut a chew, then remembered himself and put them back in his pocket.

"The law," said Mr. Hatch, "is solidly behind me. Now this Mr. Helton, he's been one of my toughest cases. He's kept my record from being practically one hundred per cent. I knew him before he went loony, and I know the fam'ly, so I undertook to help out rounding him up. Well, sir, he was gone slick as a whistle, for all we knew the man was as good as dead long while ago. Now we never might have caught up with him, but do you know what he did? Well, sir, about two weeks ago his old mother gets a letter from him, and in that letter, what do you reckon she found? Well, it was a check on that little bank in town for eight hundred and fifty dollars, just like that; the letter wasn't nothing much, just said he was sending her a few little savings, she might need something, but there it was, name, postmark, date, everything. The old woman practically lost her mind with joy. She's gettin' childish, and it looked like she kinda forgot that her only living son killed his brother and went loony. Mr. Helton said he was getting along all right, and for her not to tell nobody. Well, natchally, she couldn't keep it to herself, with that check to cash and everything. So that's how I come to know." His feelings got the better of him. "You coulda knocked me down with a feather." He shook hands with himself and rocked, wagging his head, going "Heh, heh," in his throat. Mr. Thompson felt the corners of his mouth turning down. Why, the dirty low-down hound, sneaking around spying into other people's business like that. Collecting blood money, that's what it was! Let him talk!

"Yea, well, that musta been a surprise all right," he said, trying to hold his voice even. "I'd say a surprise."

"Well, siree," said Mr. Hatch, "the more I got to thinking about it, the more I just come to the conclusion that I'd better look into the matter a little, and so I talked to the old woman. She's pretty decrepit, now, half blind and all, but she was all for taking the first train out and going to see her son. I put it up to her square—how she was too feeble for the trip, and all. So, just as a favor to her, I told her for my expenses I'd come down and see Mr. Helton and bring her back all the news about him. She gave me a new shirt she made herself by hand, and a big Swedish kind of cake to bring to him, but I musta mislaid them along the road somewhere. It don't reely matter, though, he prob'ly ain't in any state of mind to appreciate 'em."

Mr. Thompson sat up and turning round on the log looked at Mr. Hatch and asked as quietly as he could, "And now what are you aiming to do? That's the question."

Mr. Hatch slouched up to his feet and shook himself. "Well, I come all prepared for a little scuffle," he said. "I got the handcuffs," he said, "but I don't want no violence if I can help it. I didn't want to say nothing around the countryside, making an uproar. I figured the two of us could overpower him." He reached into his big inside pocket and pulled them out. Handcuffs, for God's sake, thought Mr. Thompson. Coming round on a peaceable afternoon worrying a man, and making trouble, and fishing handcuffs out of his pocket on a decent family homestead, as if it was all in the day's work.

Mr. Thompson, his head buzzing, got up too. "Well," he said, roundly, "I want to tell you I think you've got a mighty sorry job on hand, you sure must be hard up for something to do, and now I want to give you a good piece of advice. You just drop the idea that you're going to come here and make trouble for Mr. Helton, and the quicker you drive that hired rig away from my front gate the better I'll be satisfied."

Mr. Hatch put one handcuff in his outside pocket, the other dangling down. He pulled his hat down over his eyes, and reminded Mr. Thompson of a sheriff, somehow. He didn't seem in the least nervous, and didn't take up Mr. Thompson's words. He said, "Now listen just a minute, it ain't reasonable to suppose that a man like yourself is going to stand in the way of getting an escaped loonatic back to the asylum where he belongs. Now I know it's enough to throw you off, coming sudden like this, but fact is I counted on your being a respectable man and helping me out to see that justice is done. Now a course, if you won't help, I'll have to look around for help somewheres else. It won't look very good to your neighbors that you was harbring an escaped loonatic who killed his own brother, and then you refused to give him up. It will look mighty funny."

Mr. Thompson knew almost before he heard the words that it would look funny. It would put him in a mighty awkward position. He said, "But I've been trying to tell you all along that the man ain't loony now. He's been perfectly harmless for nine years. He's—he's—"

Mr. Thompson couldn't think how to describe how it was with Mr. Helton. "Why, he's been like one of the family," he said, "the best standby a man ever had." Mr. Thompson tried to see his way out. It was a fact Mr. Helton might go loony again any minute, and now this fellow talking around the country would put Mr. Thompson in a fix. It was a terrible position. He couldn't think of any way out. "You're crazy," Mr. Thompson roared suddenly, "you're the crazy one around here, you're crazier than he ever was! You get off this place or I'll handcuff you and turn you over to the law. You're trespassing," shouted Mr. Thompson. "Get out of here before I knock you down!"

He took a step towards the fat man, who backed off, shrinking. "Try it, try it, go ahead!" and then something happened that Mr. Thompson tried hard afterwards to piece together in his mind, and in fact it never did come straight. He saw the fat man with his long bowie knife in his hand, he saw Mr. Helton come round the corner on the run, his long jaw dropped, his arms swinging, his eyes wild. Mr. Helton came in between them, fists doubled up, then stopped short, glaring at the fat man, his big frame seemed to collapse, he trembled like a shied horse; and then the fat man drove at him, knife in one hand, handcuffs in the other. Mr. Thompson saw it coming, he saw the blade going into Mr. Helton's stomach, he knew he had the ax out of the log in his own hands, felt his arms go up over his head and bring the ax down on Mr. Hatch's head as if he were stunning a beef.

Mrs. Thompson had been listening uneasily for some time to the voices going on, one of them strange to her, but she was too tired at first to get up and come out to see what was going on. The confused shouting that rose so suddenly brought her up to her feet and out across the front porch without her slippers, hair half-braided. Shading her eyes, she saw first Mr. Helton, running all stooped over through the orchard, running like a man with dogs after him; and Mr. Thompson supporting himself on the ax handle was leaning over shaking by the shoulder a man Mrs. Thompson had never seen, who lay doubled up with the top of his head smashed and the blood running away in a greasy-looking puddle. Mr. Thompson without taking his hand from the man's shoulder, said in a thick voice, "He killed Mr. Helton, he killed him, I saw him do it. I had to knock him out," he called loudly, "but he won't come to."

Mrs. Thompson said in a faint scream, "Why, yonder goes Mr. Helton," and she pointed. Mr. Thompson pulled himself up and looked where she pointed. Mrs. Thompson sat down slowly against the side of the house and began to slide forward on her face; she felt as if she were drowning, she couldn't rise to the top somehow, and her only thought was she was glad the boys were not there, they were out, fishing at Halifax, oh, God, she was glad the boys were not there.

VI

Mr. and Mrs. Thompson drove up to their barn about sunset. Mr. Thompson handed the reins to his wife, got out to open the big door, and Mrs. Thompson guided old Jim in under the roof. The buggy was gray with dust and age, Mrs. Thompson's face was gray with dust and weariness, and Mr. Thompson's face, as he stood at the horse's head and began unhitching, was gray except for the dark blue of his freshly shaven jaws and chin, gray and blue and caved in, but patient, like a dead man's face.

Mrs. Thompson stepped down to the hard packed manure of the barn floor, and shook out her light flower-sprigged dress. She wore her smoked glasses, and her wide shady leghorn hat with the wreath of exhausted pink and blue forget-me-nots hid her forehead, fixed in a knot of distress.

The horse hung his head, raised a huge sigh and flexed his stiffened legs. Mr. Thompson's words came up muffled and hollow. "Poor ole Jim," he said, clearing his throat, "he looks pretty sunk in the ribs. I guess he's had a hard week." He lifted the harness up in one piece, slid it off and Jim walked out of the shafts halting a little. "Well, this is the last time," Mrs. Thompson said, still talking to Jim. "Now you can get a good rest."

Mrs. Thompson closed her eyes behind her smoked glasses. The last time, and high time, and they should never have gone at all. She did not need her glasses any more, now the good darkness was coming down again, but her eyes ran full of tears steadily, though she was not crying, and she felt better with the glasses, safer, hidden away behind them. She took out her handkerchief with her hands shaking as they had been shaking ever since *that day,* and blew her nose. She said, "I see the boys have lighted the lamps. I hope they've started the stove going."

She stepped along the rough path holding her thin dress and starched petticoats around her, feeling her way between the sharp small stones, leaving the barn because she could hardly bear to be near Mr. Thompson, advancing slowly towards the house because she dreaded going there. Life was all one dread, the faces of her neighbors, of her boys, of her husband, the face of the whole world, the shape of her own house in the darkness, the very smell of the grass and the trees were horrible to her. There was no place to go, only one thing to do, bear it somehow—but how? She asked herself that question often. How was she going to keep on living now? Why had she lived at all? She wished now she had died one of those times when she had been so sick, instead of living on for this.

The boys were in the kitchen; Herbert was looking at the funny pictures from last Sunday's newspapers, the Katzenjammer Kids and Happy Hooligan. His chin was in his hands and his elbows on the table, and he was really reading and looking at the pictures, but his face was unhappy. Arthur was building the fire, adding kindling a stick at a time, watching it catch and blaze. His face was heavier and darker than Herbert's, but he was a little sullen by nature; Mrs. Thompson thought, he takes things harder, too. Arthur said, "Hello, Momma," and went on with his work. Herbert swept the papers together and moved over on the bench. They were big boys—fifteen and seventeen, and Arthur as tall as his father. Mrs. Thompson sat down beside Herbert, taking off her hat. She said, "I guess you're hungry. We were late today. We went the Log Hollow road, it's rougher than ever." Her pale mouth drooped with a sad fold on either side.

"I guess you saw the Mannings, then," said Herbert.

"Yes, and the Fergusons, and the Allbrights, and that new family McClellan."

"Anybody say anything?" asked Herbert.

"Nothing much, you know how it's been all along, some of them keeps saying, yes, they know it was a clear case and a fair trial and they say how glad they are your papa came out so well, and all that, some of 'em do, anyhow, but it looks like they don't really take sides with him. I'm about wore out," she said, the tears rolling again from under her dark glasses." "I don't know what good it does, but your papa can't seem to rest unless he's telling how it happened. I don't know."

"I don't think it does any good, not a speck," said Arthur, moving away from the stove. "It just keeps the whole question stirred up in people's minds. Everybody will go round telling what he heard, and the whole thing is going to get worse mixed up than ever. It just makes matters worse. I wish you could get Papa to stop driving round the country talking like that."

"Your papa knows best," said Mrs. Thompson. "You oughtn't to criticize him.

He's got enough to put up with without that."

Arthur said nothing, his jaw stubborn. Mr. Thompson came in, his eyes hollowed out and dead-looking, his thick hands gray white and seamed from washing them clean every day before he started out to see the neighbors to tell them his side of the story. He was wearing his Sunday clothes, a thick pepper-and-salt-colored suit with a black string tie.

Mrs. Thompson stood up, her head swimming. "Now you-all get out of the kitchen, it's too hot in here and I need room. I'll get us a little bite of supper, if you'll just get out and give me some room."

They went as if they were glad to go, the boys outside, Mr. Thompson into his bedroom. She heard him groaning to himself as he took off his shoes, and heard the bed creak as he lay down. Mrs. Thompson opened the icebox and felt the sweet coldness flow out of it; she had never expected to have an icebox, much less did she hope to afford to keep it filled with ice. It still seemed like a miracle, after two or three years. There was the food, cold and clean, all ready to be warmed over. She would never have had that icebox if Mr. Helton hadn't happened along one day, just by the strangest luck; so saving, and so managing, so good, thought Mrs. Thompson, her heart swelling until she feared she would faint again, standing there with the door open and leaning her head upon it. She simply could not bear to remember Mr. Helton, with his long sad face and silent ways, who had always been so quiet and harmless, who had worked so hard and helped Mr. Thompson so much, running through the hot fields and woods, being hunted like a mad dog, everybody turning out with ropes and guns and sticks to catch and tie him. Oh, God, said Mrs. Thompson in a long dry moan, kneeling before the icebox and fumbling inside for the dishes, even if they did pile mattresses all over the jail floor and against the walls, and five men there to hold him to keep him from hurting him-self any more, he was already hurt too badly, he couldn't have lived anyway. Mr. Barbee, the sheriff, told her about it. He said, well, they didn't aim to harm him but they had to catch him, he was crazy as a loon; he picked up rocks and tried to brain every man that got near him. He had two harmonicas in his jumper pocket, said the sheriff, but they fell out in the scuffle, and Mr. Helton tried to pick 'em up again, and that's when they finally got him. "They *had* to be rough, Miz Thompson, he fought like a wildcat." Yes, thought Mrs. Thompson again with the same bitterness, of course, they had to be rough. They always have to be rough. Mr. Thompson can't argue with a man and get him off the place peaceably; no, she thought, standing up and shutting the icebox, he has to kill somebody, he has to be a murderer and ruin his boys' lives and cause Mr. Helton to be killed like a mad dog.

Her thoughts stopped with a little soundless explosion, cleared and began again. The rest of Mr. Helton's harmonicas were still in the shack, his tune ran in Mrs. Thompson's head at certain times of the day. She missed it in the evenings. It seemed so strange she had never known the name of that song, nor what it meant, until after Mr. Helton was gone. Mrs. Thompson, trembling in the knees, took a drink of water at the sink and poured the red beans into the baking dish, and began to roll the pieces of chicken in flour to fry them. There was a time, she said to herself, when I thought I had neighbors and friends, there was a time when we could hold up our heads, there was a time when my husband hadn't killed a man and I could tell the truth to anybody about anything.

VII

Mr. Thompson, turning on his bed, figured that he had done all he could, he'd just try to let the matter rest from now on. His lawyer, Mr. Burleigh, had told him right at the beginning, "Now you keep calm and collected. You've got a fine case, even if you haven't got witnesses. Your wife must sit in court, she'll be a powerful argument with the jury. You just plead not guilty and I'll do the rest. The trial is going to be a mere formality, you haven't got a thing to worry about. You'll be clean out of this before you know it." And to make talk Mr. Burleigh had got to telling about all the men he knew around the country who for one reason or another had been forced to kill somebody, always in self-defense, and there just wasn't anything to it at all. He even told about how his own father in the old days had shot and killed a man just for setting foot inside his gate when he told him not to. "Sure, I shot the scoundrel," said Mr. Burleigh's father, "in self-defense; I *told* him I'd shoot him if he set his foot in my yard, and he did, and I did." There had been bad blood between them for years, Mr. Burleigh said, and his father had waited a long time to catch the other fellow in the wrong, and when he did he certainly made the most of his opportunity.

"But Mr. Hatch, as I told you," Mr. Thompson had said, "made a pass at Mr. Helton with his bowie knife. That's why I took a hand."

"All the better," said Mr. Burleigh. "That stranger hadn't any right coming to your house on such an errand. Why, hell," said Mr. Burleigh, "that wasn't even manslaughter you committed. So now you just hold your horses and keep your shirt on. And don't say one word without I tell you."

Wasn't even manslaughter. Mr. Thompson had to cover Mr. Hatch with a piece of wagon canvas and ride to town to tell the sheriff. It had been hard on Ellie. When they got back, the sheriff and the coroner and two deputies, they found her sitting beside the road, on a low bridge over a gulley, about half a mile from the place. He had taken her up behind his saddle and got her back to the house. He had already told the sheriff that his wife had witnessed the whole business, and now he had time, getting her to her room

and in bed, to tell her what to say if they asked anything. He had left out the part about Mr. Helton being crazy all along, but it came out at the trial. By Mr. Burleigh's advice Mr. Thompson had pretended to be perfectly ignorant; Mr. Hatch hadn't said a word about that. Mr. Thompson pretended to believe that Mr. Hatch had just come looking for Mr. Helton to settle old scores, and the two members of Mr. Hatch's family who had come down to try to get Mr. Thompson convicted didn't get anywhere at all. It hadn't been much of a trial, Mr. Burleigh saw to that. He had charged a reasonable fee, and Mr. Thompson had paid him and felt grateful, but after it was over Mr. Burleigh didn't seem pleased to see him when he got to dropping into the office to talk it over, telling him things that had slipped his mind at first: trying to explain what an ornery low hound Mr. Hatch had been, anyhow. Mr. Burleigh seemed to have lost his interest; he looked sour and upset when he saw Mr. Thompson at the door. Mr. Thompson kept saying to himself that he'd got off, all right, just as Mr. Burleigh had predicted, but, but—and it was right there that Mr. Thompson's mind stuck, squirming like an angleworm on a fishhook: he had killed Mr. Hatch, and he was a murderer. That was the truth about himself that Mr. Thompson couldn't grasp, even when he said the word to himself. Why, he had not even once *thought* of killing anybody, much less Mr. Hatch, and if Mr. Helton hadn't come out so unexpectedly, hearing the row, why, then— but then, Mr. Helton had come on the run that way to help him. What he couldn't understand was what happened next. He had seen Mr. Hatch go after Mr. Helton with the knife, he had seen the point, blade up, go into Mr. Helton's stomach and slice up like you slice a hog, but when they finally caught Mr. Helton there wasn't a knife scratch on him. Mr. Thompson knew he had the ax in his own hands and felt himself lifting it, but he couldn't remember hitting Mr. Hatch. He couldn't remember it. He couldn't. He remembered only that he had been determined to stop Mr. Hatch from cutting Mr. Helton. If he was given a chance he could explain the whole matter. At the trial they hadn't let him talk. They just asked questions and he answered yes or no, and they never did get to the core of the matter. Since the trial, now, every day for a week he had washed and shaved and put on his best clothes and had taken Ellie with him to tell every neighbor he had that he never killed Mr. Hatch on purpose, and what good did it do? Nobody believed him. Even when he turned to Ellie and said, "You was there, you saw it, didn't you?" and Ellie spoke up, saying, "Yes, that's the truth. Mr. Thompson was trying to save Mr. Helton's life," and he added, "If you don't believe me, you can believe my wife. She won't lie," Mr. Thompson saw something in all their faces that disheartened him, made him feel empty and tired out. They didn't believe he was not a murderer.

Even Ellie never said anything to comfort him. He hoped she would say finally, "I remember now, Mr. Thompson, I really did come round the corner in time to see everything. It's not a lie, Mr. Thompson. Don't you worry." But as they drove together in silence, with the days still hot and dry, shortening for fall, day after day, the buggy jolting in the ruts, she said nothing; they grew to dread the sight of another house, and the people in it: all houses looked alike now, and the people—old neighbors or new—had the same expression when Mr. Thompson told them why he had come and began his story. Their eyes looked as if someone had pinched the eyeball at the back; they shriveled and the light went out of them. Some of them sat with fixed tight smiles trying to be friendly. "Yes, Mr. Thompson, we know how you must feel. It must be terrible for you, Mrs. Thompson. Yes, you know, I've about come to the point where I believe in such a thing as killing in self-defense. Why, certainly, we believe you, Mr. Thompson, why shouldn't we believe you? Didn't you have a perfectly fair and above-board trial? Well, now, natchally, Mr. Thompson, we think you done right."

Mr. Thompson was satisfied they didn't think so. Sometimes the air around him was so thick with their blame he fought and pushed with his fists, and the sweat broke out all over him, he shouted his story in a dust-choked voice, he would fairly bellow at last: "My wife, here, you know her, she was there, she saw and heard it all, if you don't believe me, ask her, she won't lie!" and Mrs. Thompson, with her hands knotted together, aching, her chin trembling, would never fail to say: "Yes, that's right, that's the truth—"

The last straw had been laid on today, Mr. Thompson decided. Tom Allbright, an old beau of Ellie's, why, he had squired Ellie around a whole summer, had come out to meet them when they drove up, and standing there bareheaded had stopped them from getting out. He had looked past them with an embarrassed frown on his face, telling them his wife's sister was there with a raft of young ones, and the house was pretty full and everything upset, or he'd ask them to come in. "We've been thinking of trying to get up to your place one of these days," said Mr. Allbright, moving away trying to look busy, "we've been mighty occupied up here of late." So they had to say, "Well, we just happened to be driving this way," and go on. "The Allbrights," said Mrs. Thompson, "always was fair-weather friends." "They look out for number one, that's a fact," said Mr. Thompson. But it was cold comfort to them both.

Finally Mrs. Thompson had given up. "Let's go home," she said. "Old Jim's tired and thirsty, and we've gone far enough."

Mr. Thompson said, "Well, while we're out this way, we might as well stop at the McClellans'." They drove in, and asked a little cotton-haired boy if his mamma and papa were at home. Mr. Thompson wanted to see them. The little boy stood gazing with his mouth open, then galloped into the house shouting, "Mommer, Popper, come out hyah. That man that kilt Mr. Hatch has come ter see yer!"

The man came out in his sock feet, with one gallus up, the other broken and dangling, and said, "Light down, Mr. Thompson, and come in. The ole woman's washing, but she'll git here." Mrs. Thompson, feeling her way, stepped down and sat in a broken rocking-chair on the porch that sagged under her feet. The woman of the house, barefooted, in a calico wrapper, sat on the edge of the porch, her fat sallow face full of curiosity. Mr. Thompson began, "Well, as I reckon you happen to know, I've had some strange troubles lately, and, as the feller says, it's not the kind of trouble that happens to a man every day in the year, and there's some things I don't want no misunderstanding about in the neighbors' minds, so—" He halted and stumbled forward, and the two listening faces took on a mean look, a greedy, despising look, a look that said plain as day, "My, you must be a purty sorry feller to come round worrying about what *we* think, *we* know you wouldn't be here if you had anybody else to turn to—my, I wouldn't lower myself that much, myself." Mr. Thompson was ashamed of himself, he was suddenly in a rage, he'd like to knock their dirty skunk heads together, the low-down white trash—but he held himself down and went on to the end. "My wife will tell you," he said, and this was the hardest place, because Ellie always without moving a muscle seemed to stiffen as if somebody had threatened to hit her; "ask my wife, she won't lie."

"It's true, I saw it—"

"Well, now," said the man, drily, scratching his ribs inside his shirt, "that sholy is too bad. Well, now, I kaint see what we've got to do with all this here, however. I kaint see no good reason for us to git mixed up in these murder matters, I shore kaint. Whichever way you look at it, it ain't none of my business. However, it's mighty nice of you-all to come around and give us the straight of it,

fur we've heerd some mighty queer yarns about it, mighty queer, I golly you couldn't hardly make head ner tail of it."

"Evvybody goin' round shootin' they heads off," said the woman. "Now we don't hold with killin'; the Bible says—"

"Shet yer trap," said the man, "and keep it shet 'r I'll shet it fer yer. Now it shore looks like to me—"

"We mustn't linger," said Mrs. Thompson, unclasping her hands. "We've lingered too long now. It's getting late, and we've far to go." Mr. Thompson took the hint and followed her. The man and the woman lolled against their rickety porch poles and watched them go.

Now lying on his bed, Mr. Thompson knew the end had come. Now, this minute, lying in the bed where he had slept with Ellie for eighteen years; under this roof where he had laid the shingles when he was waiting to get married; there as he was with his whiskers already sprouting since his shave that morning; with his fingers feeling his bony chin, Mr. Thompson felt he was a dead man. He was dead to his other life, he had got to the end of something without knowing why, and he had to make a fresh start, he did not know how. Something different was going to begin, he didn't know what. It was in some way not his business. He didn't feel he was going to have much to do with it. He got up, aching, hollow, and went out to the kitchen where Mrs. Thompson was just taking up the supper.

"Call the boys," said Mrs. Thompson. They had been down to the barn, and Arthur put out the lantern before hanging it on a nail near the door. Mr. Thompson didn't like their silence. They had hardly said a word about anything to him since that day. They seemed to avoid him, they ran the place together as if he wasn't there, and attended to everything without asking him for any advice. "What you boys been up to?" he asked, trying to be hearty. "Finishing your chores?"

"No, sir," said Arthur, "there ain't

much to do. Just greasing some axles." Herbert said nothing. Mrs. Thompson bowed her head: "For these and all Thy blessings. . . . Amen," she whispered weakly, and the Thompsons sat there with their eyes down and their faces sorrowful, as if they were at a funeral.

VIII

Every time he shut his eyes, trying to sleep, Mr. Thompson's mind started up and began to run like a rabbit. It jumped from one thing to another, trying to pick up a trail here or there that would straighten out what had happened that day he killed Mr. Hatch. Try as he might, Mr. Thompson's mind would not go anywhere that it had not already been, he could not see anything but what he had seen once, and he knew that was not right. If he had not seen straight that first time, then everything about his killing Mr. Hatch was wrong from start to finish, and there was nothing more to be done about it, he might just as well give up. It still seemed to him that he had done, maybe not the right thing, but the only thing he could do, that day, but had he? *Did he have to kill Mr. Hatch?* He had never seen a man he hated more, the minute he laid eyes on him. He knew in his bones the fellow was there for trouble. What seemed so funny now was this: Why hadn't he just told Mr. Hatch to get out before he ever even got in?

Mrs. Thompson, her arms crossed on her breast, was lying beside him, perfectly still, but she seemed awake, somehow. "Asleep, Ellie?"

After all, he might have got rid of him peaceably, or maybe he might have had to overpower him and put those handcuffs on him and turn him over to the sheriff for disturbing the peace. The most they could have done was to lock Mr. Hatch up while he cooled off for a few days, or fine him a little something. He would try to think of things he might have said to Mr. Hatch. Why, let's see, I could just have said, Now look here, Mr. Hatch, I want to talk to you as man to man. But his brain would go empty. What could he have said or done? But if he *could* have done anything else almost except kill Mr. Hatch, then nothing would have happened to Mr. Helton. Mr. Thompson hardly ever thought of Mr. Helton. His mind just skipped over him and went on. If he stopped to think about Mr. Helton he'd never in God's world get anywhere. He tried to imagine how it might all have been, this very night even, if Mr. Helton were still safe and sound out in his shack playing his tune about feeling so good in the morning, drinking up all the wine so you'd feel even better; and Mr. Hatch safe in jail somewhere, mad as hops, maybe, but out of harm's way and ready to listen to reason and to repent of his meanness, the dirty, yellow-livered hound coming around persecuting an innocent man and ruining a whole family that never harmed him! Mr. Thompson felt the veins of his forehead start up, his fists clutched as if they seized an ax handle, the sweat broke out on him, he bounded up from the bed with a yell smothered in his throat, and Ellie started up after him, crying out, "Oh, oh, don't! Don't! Don't!" as if she were having a nightmare. He stood shaking until his bones rattled in him, crying hoarsely, "Light the lamp, light the lamp, Ellie."

Instead, Mrs. Thompson gave a shrill weak scream, almost the same scream he had heard on that day she came around the house when he was standing there with the ax in his hand. He could not see her in the dark, but she was on the bed, rolling violently. He felt for her in horror, and his groping hands found her arms, up, and her own hands pulling her hair straight out from her head, her neck strained back, and the tight screams strangling her. He shouted out for Arthur, for Herbert. "Your mother!" he bawled, his voice cracking. As he held Mrs. Thompson's arms, the boys came tumbling in, Arthur with the lamp above his head. By this light Mr. Thompson saw Mrs. Thompson's eyes, wide open, staring dreadfully at him, the tears pouring. She sat up at sight of the boys, and held out one arm towards them, the hand wagging in a crazy circle, then dropped on her back again, and suddenly went limp. Arthur set the lamp on the table and turned on Mr. Thompson. "She's scared," he said, "she's scared to death." His face was in a knot of rage, his fists were doubled up, he faced his father as if he meant to strike him. Mr. Thompson's jaw fell, he was so surprised he stepped back from the bed. Herbert went to the other side. They stood on each side of Mrs. Thompson and watched Mr. Thompson as if he were a dangerous wild beast. "What did you do to her?" shouted Arthur, in a grown man's voice. "You touch her again and I'll blow your heart out!" Herbert was pale and his cheek twitched, but he was on Arthur's side; he would do what he could to help Arthur.

Mr. Thompson had no fight left in him. His knees bent as he stood, his chest collapsed. "Why, Arthur," he said, his words crumbling and his breath coming short. "She's fainted again. Get the ammonia." Arthur did not move. Herbert brought the bottle, and handed it, shrinking, to his father.

Mr. Thompson held it under Mrs. Thompson's nose. He poured a little in the palm of his hand and rubbed it on her forehead. She gasped and opened her eyes and turned her head away from him. Herbert began a doleful hopeless sniffling. "Mamma," he kept saying, "Mamma, don't die."

"I'm all right," Mrs. Thompson said. "Now don't you worry around. Now Herbert, you mustn't do that. I'm all right." She closed her eyes. Mr. Thompson began pulling on his best pants; he put on his socks and shoes. The boys sat on each side of the bed, watching Mrs. Thompson's face. Mr. Thompson put on his shirt and coat. He said, "I reckon I'll ride over and get the doctor. Don't look like all this fainting is a good sign. Now you just keep watch until I get back." They listened, but said nothing. He said, "Don't you get any notions in your head. I never did your mother any harm in my life, on purpose." He went out, and, looking back, saw Herbert staring at him from under his brows, like a stranger. "You'll know how to look after her," said Mr. Thompson.

Mr. Thompson went through the kitchen. There he lighted the lantern, took a thin pad of scratch paper and a stub pencil from the shelf where the boys kept their schoolbooks. He swung the lantern on his arm and reached into the cupboard where he kept the guns. The shotgun was there to his hand, primed and ready, a man never knows when he may need a shotgun. He went out of the house without looking around, or looking back when he had left it, passed his barn without seeing it, and struck out to the farthest end of his fields, which ran for half a mile to the east. So many blows had been struck at Mr. Thompson and from so many directions he couldn't stop any more to find out where he was hit. He walked on, over plowed ground and over meadow, going through barbed wire fences cautiously, putting his gun through first; he could almost see in the dark, now his eyes were used to it. Finally he came to the last fence; here he sat down, back against a post, lantern at his side, and, with the pad on his knee, moistened the stub pencil and began to write:

"Before Almighty God, the great judge of all before who I am about to appear, I do hereby solemnly swear that I did not take the life of Mr. Homer T. Hatch on purpose. It was done in defense of Mr. Helton. I did not aim to hit him with the ax but only to keep him off Mr. Helton. He aimed a blow at Mr. Helton who was not looking for it. It was my belief at the time that Mr. Hatch would of taken the life of Mr. Helton if I did not interfere. I have told all this to the judge and the jury and they let me off but nobody believes it. This is the only way I can prove I am not a cold blooded murderer like everybody seems to think. If I had been in Mr. Helton's place he would of done the same for me. I still think I done the only thing there was to do. My wife—"

Mr. Thompson stopped here to think a while. He wet the pencil point with the tip of his tongue and marked out the last two words. He sat a while blacking out the words until he had made a neat oblong patch where they had been, and started again:

"It was Mr. Homer T. Hatch who came to do wrong to a harmless man. He caused all this trouble and he deserved to die but I am sorry it was me who had to kill him."

He licked the point of his pencil again, and signed his full name carefully, folded the paper and put it in his outside pocket. Taking off his right shoe and sock, he set the butt of the shotgun along the ground with the twin barrels pointed towards his head. It was very awkward. He thought about this a little, leaning his head against the gun mouth. He was trembling and his head was drumming until he was deaf and blind, but he lay down flat on the earth on his side, drew the barrel under his chin and fumbled for the trigger with his great toe. That way he could work it.

———————◆·◆◆·◆———————

This story, for all its length, is essentially simple. A stranger turns up as a hand on a poor Texas farm, and makes the place pay for the first time. Nine years later, another stranger appears and reveals that the hand is a murderer and a lunatic. The farmer, for reasons he himself cannot define, kills the second stranger who would arrest the hand, and then when he finds that, first, his neighbors, and finally his family, believe him guilty, kills himself. But the story is fleshed out with considerable detail. What justifies this detail? What justifies the scale of the story?

First, we may say that the very vividness and richness provide some justification for the detail. The world of the Thompsons is set up with great completeness, and we enjoy the precision with which it is presented, the recognition of the world. We know the springhouse, the kitchen, the stumps in the yard. But more, we get the whole "feel" of the place, the sense of the kind of life lived there. Then we have the Thompsons themselves,

and poor Mr. Helton. They are visualized very fully, but we realize before we have gone far into the story that all the details of their appearance begin to have some bearing on our understanding of their characters and on our feeling for them.

We first see Mr. Thompson: "He was a noisy proud man who held his neck so straight his whole face stool level with his Adam's apple, and the whiskers continued down his neck and disappeared into a black thatch under his open collar." Later, looking back, we can see that the story is the story of a noisy, proud, stiff-necked man, whose pride has constantly suffered from failures, who salves his hurt pride by harmless bluster with his children and by his refusal to do anything but proper "man's work," and who, in the end, stumbles into a situation that takes the last prop of certainty from his life. In a sense, he finally kills himself out of pride. He can't stand the moral uncertainty of his situation and the isolation when even his family turns against him, and pulls the trigger as a way of justifying himself before the world.

So, with our first glimpse of Mrs. Thompson lying down in the "front room" with the green shades down and a wet cloth over her poor weak eyes, we get a pointed indication of her pitiful story. The constant shading of her eyes from the light, the constant weeping, the waiting for the cool darkness—all these details lead to our conception of her inward as well as her outward being.

The same principle applies to certain episodes that at first glance seem to be unrelated to the main line of the story, for instance, the conversation between Mr. and Mrs. Thompson at the beginning of section II, the episode of the pinch at the end of section II, and the episode toward the end of section III, after the boys have tampered with the Swede's harmonicas. All of these episodes establish the quality of the life lived on the Thompson place. Let us look at the second:

"Tell *you* the truth, Ellie," said Mr. Thompson, picking his teeth with a fork and leaning back in the best of good humors, "I always thought your granma was a ter'ble ole fool. She'd just say the first thing that popped into her head and call it God's wisdom."

"My granma wasn't anybody's fool. Nine times out of ten she knew what she was talking about. I always say, the first thing you think is the best thing you can say."

"Well," said Mr. Thompson, going into another shout, "You're so reefined about that goat story, you just try speaking out in mixed comp'ny sometime! You just try it. S'pose you happened to be thinking about a hen and a rooster, hey? I reckon you'd shock the Baptist preacher!" He gave her a good pinch on her thin little rump. "No more meat on you than a rabbit," he said, fondly. "Now I like 'em cornfed."

Mrs. Thompson looked at him open-eyed and blushed. She could see better by lamplight. "Why, Mr. Thompson, sometimes I think you're the evilest-minded man that ever lived." She took a handful of hair on the crown of his head and gave it a good, slow pull. "That's to show you how it feels, pinching so hard when you're supposed to be playing," she said, gently.

This little glimpse of their secret life together, Mr. Thompson's masculine, affectionate bragging and bullying and teasing, Mrs. Thompson's shy and embarrassed playfulness, comes as a surprise in the middle of their drab world, a sudden brightness and warmth. Without this episode we should not get the full force of Mr. Thompson's bafflement and anger when Mr. Hatch misinterprets Mr. Thompson's talk of Mrs. Thompson's ill health and says he'd get rid of a puny wife mighty quick. And without it we would not have the same sense of pity when the terrible end comes to their life together. What seems at first glance to be a casual, incidental episode really gives the emotional charge to the conclusion: it makes us believe in Mr. and Mrs. Thompson as people.

But let us come back to the main idea of the story. We have said that the story is the story of a noisy, proud, stiff-necked man whose bluster really conceals a sense of failure, and who in the end stumbles into a situation that takes the last prop of certainty from his life. Is he innocent or guilty? He himself doesn't really know. He is sure that he had seen the stranger's knife enter the body of Mr. Helton, but then, that is proved to be a delusion. He had felt himself to be acting to protect Mr. Helton, but before the act of violence he had experienced a long building up of a mysterious anger against the stranger. Furthermore, we know that Mr. Helton has made life possible for the Thompsons and now that support is about to be snatched away. Poor Mr. Thompson is both innocent and guilty. He can't sort out the facts, the complex of motives working within himself. So he takes refuge in a lie, the lie his wife must tell. But the lie isn't enough, least of all for him, and so nothing is left but the last act of pride and justification.

The story, then, is about the difficult definition of guilt and innocence: because Mr. Thompson had not been able to trust his own sense of innocence he had taken refuge in the lie, and the lie, in the end, kills him. We must remember, however, that it is not the abstract idea that is important here. Rather, it is the human warmth and sympathy that the writer has managed to create as the context of the idea. We see the terrible ruin of the lives of good, decent people, a ruin brought about not so much by actual faults of their own as by a striving to be good and decent. That is all the Thompsons want.

But let us come back to the point where we started, the question of scale, the justification of the elaborate detail. We have commented on its vividness and the richness of the reader's pleasure in that; but the deeper justification lies in the creation of a little world, a world so fully realized that the events that come to shake it come with terrific emotional force. This story has a complex and strongly articulated plot (a fact that in itself does something to account for the scale), but the plot is not obtruded; we are concerned, as the writer is, with the emotional complications around the facts of the plot. And this concern is the determining factor in the scale.

EXERCISES

1. "Noon Wine" is divided into eight sections. What is the point of each section?
2. The story covers nine years. Are the transitions from one time to another made arbitrarily or are they absorbed into narrative? If they are absorbed, how does the writer succeed in giving this effect?

3. Katherine Anne Porter is famous for vividness of style. Indicate bits of description of places and people and actions in "Noon Wine" that seem especially good.

4. Can you think of a reason why the writer did not use one point of view but several? Why, since she uses several, does she never give us a glimpse of things as Mr. Helton sees them? Or Mr. Hatch?

5. Can you tell how suspense is maintained in this story?

6. What qualities does this story share with Eudora Welty's "Keela, the Outcast Indian Maiden" (sec 7)?

7. Verga's "La Lupa" is, as we have seen, very short, yet covers a long span of time. On the basis of scale and pace, compare it with "Noon Wine." What are the differences of method? How do you relate them to the differences in interest the two writers find in their material? To differences in tone?

THE RICH BOY

F. Scott Fitzgerald (1896–1940)

I

Begin with an individual, and before you know it you find that you have created a type; begin with a type, and you find that you have created—nothing. That is because we are all queer fish, queerer behind our faces and voices than we want any one to know or than we know ourselves. When I hear a man proclaiming himself an "average, honest, open fellow," I feel pretty sure that he has some definite and perhaps terrible abnormality which he has agreed to conceal—and his protestation of being average and honest and open is his way of reminding himself of his misprision.

There are no types, no plurals. There is a rich boy, and this is his and not his brothers' story. All my life I have lived among his brothers but this one has been my friend. Besides, if I wrote about his brothers I should have to begin by attacking all the lies that the poor have told about the rich and the rich have told about themselves— such a wild structure they have erected that when we pick up a book about the rich, some instinct prepares us for unreality. Even the intelligent and impassioned reporters of life have made the country of the rich as unreal as fairy-land.

Let me tell you about the very rich. They are different from you and me. They possess and enjoy early, and it does something to them, makes them soft where we are hard, and cynical where we are trustful, in a way that, unless you were born rich, it is very difficult to understand. They think, deep in their hearts, that they are better than we are because we had to discover the compensations and refuges of life for ourselves. Even when they enter deep into our world or sink below us, they still think that they are better than we are. They are different. The only way I can describe young Anson Hunter is to approach him as if he were a foreigner and cling stubbornly to my point of view. If I accept his for a moment I am lost—I have nothing to show but a preposterous movie.

II

Anson was the eldest of six children who would some day divide a fortune of fifteen million dollars, and he reached the age of reason—is it seven?—at the beginning of the century when daring young women were already gliding along Fifth Avenue in electric "mobiles." In those days he and his brother had an English governess who spoke the language very clearly and crisply and well, so that the two boys grew to speak as she did— their words and sentences were all crisp and clear and not run together as ours are. They didn't talk exactly like English children but acquired an accent that is peculiar to fashionable people in the city of New York.

In the summer the six children were moved from the house on Seventy-first Street to a big estate in northern Connecticut. It was not a fashionable locality—Anson's father wanted to delay as long as possible his children's knowledge of that side of life. He was a man somewhat superior to his class, which composed New York society, and to his period, which was the snobbish and formalized vulgarity of the Gilded Age, and he wanted his sons to learn habits of concentration and have sound constitutions and grow up into right-living and successful men. He and his wife kept an eye on them as well as they were able until the two older boys went away to school, but in huge establishments this is difficult—it was much simpler in the series of small and medium-sized houses in which my own youth was spent—I was never far out of the reach of my mother's voice, of the sense of her presence, her approval or disapproval.

Anson's first sense of his superiority came to him when he realized the half-grudging American deference that was paid to him in the Connecticut village. The parents of the boys he played with always inquired after his father and mother, and were vaguely excited when their own children were asked to the Hunters' house. He accepted this as the natural state of things, and a sort of impatience with all groups of which he was not the center—in money, in position, in authority —remained with him for the rest of his life. He disdained to struggle with other boys for precedence—he expected it to be given him freely, and when it wasn't he withdrew into his family. His family was sufficient, for in the East money is still a somewhat feudal thing, a clanforming thing. In the snobbish West, money separates families to form "sets."

At eighteen, when he went to New Haven, Anson was tall and thick-set, with a clear complexion and a healthy color from the ordered life he had led in school. His hair was yellow and grew in a funny way on his head, his nose was beaked—these two things kept him from being handsome—but he had a confident charm and a certain brusque style, and the upper-class men who passed him on the street knew without being told that he was a rich boy and had gone to one of the best schools. Nevertheless, his very superiority kept him from being a success in college— the independence was mistaken for egotism, and the refusal to accept Yale standards with the proper awe seemed to belittle all those who had. So, long before he graduated, he began to shift the center of his life to New York.

He was at home in New York—there was his own house with "the kind of servants you can't get any more"—and his own family, of which, because of his good humor and a certain ability to make things go, he was rapidly becoming the centre, and the débutante parties, and the correct manly world of the men's clubs, and the occasional wild spree with the gallant girls whom New Haven only knew from the fifth row. His aspirations were conventional enough—they included even the irreproachable shadow he would some day marry, but they differed from the aspirations of the majority of young men in that there was no mist over them, none of that quality which is variously known as "idealism" or "illusion." Anson accepted without reservation the world of high finance and high extravagance, of divorce and dissipation, of snobbery and of privilege. Most of our lives end as a compromise—it was as a compromise that his life began.

He and I first met in the late summer of 1917 when he was just out of Yale, and, like the rest of us, was swept up into the systematized hysteria of the war. In the blue-green uniform of the naval aviation he came down to Pensacola, where the hotel orchestras played "I'm sorry, dear," and we young officers danced with the girls. Everyone liked him, and though he ran with the drinkers and wasn't an especially good pilot, even the instructors treated him with a certain respect. He was always having long talks with them in his confident, logical voice—talks which ended by his getting himself, or, more frequently, another officer, out of some impending trouble. He was convivial, bawdy, robustly avid for pleasure, and we were all surprised when he fell in love with a conservative and rather proper girl.

Her name was Paula Legendre, a dark, serious beauty from somewhere in California. Her family kept a winter residence just outside of town, and in spite of her primness she was enormously popular; there is a large class of men whose egotism can't endure humor in a woman. But Anson wasn't that sort, and I couldn't understand the attraction of her "sincerity"—that was the thing to say about her—for his keen and somewhat sardonic mind.

Nevertheless, they fell in love—and on her terms. He no longer joined the twilight gathering at the De Sota bar, and whenever they were seen together they were engaged in a long, serious dialogue, which must have gone on several weeks. Long afterward he told me that it was not about anything in particular but was composed on both sides of immature and even meaningless statements —the emotional content that gradually came to fill it grew up not out of the words but out of its enormous seriousness. It was a sort of hypnosis. Often it was interrupted, giving way to that emasculated humor we call fun; when they were alone it was resumed again, solemn, low-keyed, and pitched so as to give each other a sense of unity in feeling and thought. They came to resent any interruptions of it, to be unresponsive to facetiousness about life, even to the mild cynicism of their contemporaries. They were only happy when the dialogue was going on, and its seriousness bathed them like the amber glow of an open fire. Toward the end there came an interruption they did not resent—it began to be interrupted by passion.

Oddly enough, Anson was as engrossed in the dialogue as she was and as profoundly affected by it, yet at the same time aware that on his side much was insincere, and on hers much was merely simple. At first, too, he despised her emotional simplicity as well, but with his love her nature deepened and blossomed, and he could despise it no longer. He felt that if he could enter into Paula's warm safe life he would be happy. The long preparation of the dialogue removed any constraint—he taught her some of what he had learned from more adventurous women, and she responded with a rapt holy intensity. One evening after a dance they agreed to marry, and he wrote a long letter about her

to his mother. The next day Paula told him that she was rich, that she had a personal fortune of nearly a million dollars.

III

It was exactly as if they could say "Neither of us has anything: we shall be poor together"—just as delightful that they should be rich instead. It gave them the same communion of adventure. Yet when Anson got leave in April, and Paula and her mother accompanied him North, she was impressed with the standing of his family in New York and with the scale on which they lived. Alone with Anson for the first time in the rooms where he had played as a boy, she was filled with a comfortable emotion, as though she were preëminently safe and taken care of. The pictures of Anson in a skull cap at his first school, of Anson on horseback with the sweetheart of a mysterious forgotten summer, of Anson in a gay group of ushers and bridesmaids at a wedding, made her jealous of his life apart from her in the past, and so completely did his authoritative person seem to sum up and typify these possessions of his that she was inspired with the idea of being married immediately and returning to Pensacola as his wife.

But an immediate marriage wasn't discussed—even the engagement was to be secret until after the war. When she realized that only two days of his leave remained, her dissatisfaction crystallized in the intention of making him as unwilling to wait as she was. They were driving to the country for dinner, and she determined to force the issue that night.

Now a cousin of Paula's was staying with them at the Ritz, a severe, bitter girl who loved Paula but was somewhat jealous of her impressive engagement, and as Paula was late in dressing, the cousin, who wasn't going to the party, received Anson in the parlor of the suite.

Anson had met friends at five o'clock and drunk freely and indiscreetly with them for an hour. He left the Yale Club at a proper time, and his mother's chauffeur drove him to the Ritz, but his usual capacity was not in evidence, and the impact of the steam-heated sitting-room made him suddenly dizzy. He knew it, and he was both amused and sorry.

Paula's cousin was twenty-five, but she was exceptionally naïve, and at first failed to realize what was up. She had never met Anson before, and she was surprised when he mumbled strange information and nearly fell off his chair, but until Paula appeared it didn't occur to her that what she had taken for the odor of a dry-cleaned uniform was really whisky. But Paula understood as soon as she appeared; her only thought was to get Anson away before her mother saw him, and at the look in her eyes the cousin understood too.

When Paula and Anson descended to the limousine they found two men inside, both asleep; they were the men with whom he had been drinking at the Yale Club, and they were also going to the party. He had entirely forgotten their presence in the car. On the way to Hempstead they awoke and sang. Some of the songs were rough, and though Paula tried to reconcile herself to the fact that Anson had few verbal inhibitions, her lips tightened with shame and distaste.

Back at the hotel the cousin, confused and agitated, considered the incident, and then walked into Mrs. Legendre's bedroom, saying: "Isn't he funny?"

"Who is funny?"

"Why—Mr. Hunter. He seemed so funny."

Mrs. Legendre looked at her sharply.

"How is he funny?"

"Why, he said he was French. I didn't know he was French."

"That's absurd. You must have mis-understood." She smiled: "It was a joke."

The cousin shook her head stubbornly.

"No. He said he was brought up in France. He said he couldn't speak any En-glish, and that's why he couldn't talk to me. And he couldn't!"

Mrs. Legendre looked away with impa-tience just as the cousin added thoughtfully, "Perhaps it was because he was so drunk," and walked out of the room.

This curious report was true. Anson, finding his voice thick and uncontrollable, had taken the unusual refuge of announcing that he spoke no English. Years afterward he used to tell that part of the story, and he invariably communicated the uproarious laughter which the memory aroused in him.

Five times in the next hour Mrs. Leg-endre tried to get Hempstead on the phone. When she succeeded, there was a ten-minute delay before she heard Paula's voice on the wire.

"Cousin Jo told me Anson was intoxi-cated."

"Oh, no. . . ."

"Oh, yes. Cousin Jo says he was intoxi-cated. He told her he was French, and fell off his chair and behaved as if he was very intoxicated. I don't want you to come home with him."

"Mother, he's all right! Please don't worry about——"

"But I do worry. I think it's dreadful. I want you to promise me not to come home with him."

"I'll take care of it, mother. . . ."

"I don't want you to come home with him."

"All right, mother. Good-by."

"Be sure now, Paula. Ask some one to bring you."

Deliberately Paula took the receiver from her ear and hung it up. Her face was flushed with helpless annoyance. Anson was stretched out asleep in a bedroom upstairs, while the dinner party below was proceeding lamely toward conclusion.

The hour's drive had sobered him some-what—his arrival was merely hilarious—and Paula hoped that the evening was not spoiled, after all, but two imprudent cock-tails before dinner completed the disaster. He talked boisterously and somewhat offen-sively to the party at large for fifteen minutes, and then slid silently unler the table; like a man in an old print—but, unlike an old print, it was rather horrible without being at all quaint. None of the young girls present remarked upon the incident—it seemed to merit only silence. His uncle and two other men carried him upstairs, and it was just after this that Paula was called to the phone.

An hour later Anson awoke in a fog of nervous agony, through which he perceived after a moment the figure of his Uncle Robert standing by the door.

". . . I said are you better?"

"What?"

"Do you feel better, old man?"

"Terrible," said Anson.

"I'm going to try you on another Bromoseltzer. If you can hold it down, it'll do you good to sleep."

With an effort Anson slid his legs from the bed and stood up.

"I'm all right," he said dully.

"Take it easy."

"I thin' if you gave me a glassbrandy I could go downstairs."

"Oh, no——"

"Yes, that's the only thin'. I'm all right now. . . . I suppose I'm in dutch dow' there."

"They know you're a little under the weather," said his uncle deprecatingly. "But don't worry about it. Schuyler didn't even get here. He passed away in the locker-room over at the Links."

Indifferent to any opinion, except Paula's, Anson was nevertheless determined to save the débris of the evening, but when after a cold bath he made his appearance most of the party had already left. Paula got up immediately to go home.

In the limousine the old serious dialogue began. She had known that he drank, she admitted, but she had never expected anything like this—it seemed to her that perhaps they were not suited to each other, after all. Their ideas about life were too different, and so forth. When she finished speaking, Anson spoke in turn, very soberly. Then Paula said she'd have to think it over; she wouldn't decide tonight; she was not angry but she was terribly sorry. Nor would she let him come into the hotel with her, but just before she got out of the car she leaned and kissed him unhappily on the cheek.

The next afternoon Anson had a long talk with Mrs. Legendre while Paula sat listening in silence. It was agreed that Paula was to brood over the incident for a proper period and then, if mother and daughter thought it best, they would follow Anson to Pensacola. On his part he apologized with sincerity and dignity—that was all; with every card in her hand Mrs. Legendre was unable to establish any advantage over him. He made no promises, showed no humility, only delivered a few serious comments on life which brought him off with rather a moral superiority at the end. When they came South three weeks later, neither Anson in his satisfaction nor Paula in her relief at the reunion realized that the psychological moment had passed forever.

IV

He dominated and attracted her, and at the same time filled her with anxiety. Confused by his mixture of solidity and self-indulgence, of sentiment and cynicism—incongruities which her gentle mind was unable to resolve—Paula grew to think of him as two alternating personalities. When she saw him alone, or at a formal party, or with his casual inferiors, she felt a tremendous pride in his strong, attractive presence, the paternal, understanding stature of his mind. In other company she became uneasy when what had been a fine imperviousness to mere gentility showed its other face. The other face was gross, humorous, reckless of everything but pleasure. It startled her mind temporarily away from him, even led her into a short covert experiment with an old beau, but it was no use—after four months of Anson's enveloping vitality there was an anæmic pallor in all other men.

In July he was ordered abroad, and their tenderness and desire reached a crescendo.

Paula considered a last-minute marriage—decided against it only because there were always cocktails on his breath now, but the parting itself made her physically ill with grief. After his departure she wrote him long letters of regret for the days of love they had missed by waiting. In August Anson's plane slipped down into the North Sea. He was pulled onto a destroyer after a night in the water and sent to hospital with pneumonia; the armistice was signed before he was finally sent home.

Then, with every opportunity given back to them, with no material obstacle to overcome, the secret weavings of their temperaments came between them, drying up their kisses and their tears, making their voices less loud to one another, muffling the intimate chatter of their hearts until the old communication was only possible by letters, from far away. One afternoon a society reporter waited for two hours in the Hunters' house for a confirmation of their engagement. Anson denied it; nevertheless an early issue carried the report as a leading paragraph—they were "constantly seen together at Southampton, Hot Springs, and Tuxedo Park." But the serious dialogue had turned a corner into a long-sustained quarrel, and the affair was almost played out. Anson got drunk flagrantly and missed an engagement with her, whereupon Paula made certain behavioristic demands. His despair was helpless before his pride and his knowledge of himself: the engagement was definitely broken.

"Dearest," said their letters now, "Dearest, Dearest, when I wake up in the middle of the night and realize that after all it was not to be, I feel that I want to die. I can't go on living any more. Perhaps when we meet this summer we may talk things over and decide differently—we were so excited and sad that day, and I don't feel that I can live all my life without you. You speak of other people. Don't you know there are no other people for me, but only you. . . ."

But as Paula drifted here and there around the East she would sometimes mention her gaieties to make him wonder. Anson was too acute to wonder. When he saw a man's name in her letters he felt more sure of her and a little disdainful—he was always superior to such things. But he still hoped that they would some day marry.

Meanwhile he plunged vigorously into all the movement and glitter of post-bellum New York, entering a brokerage house, joining half a dozen clubs, dancing late, and moving in three worlds—his own world, the world of young Yale graduates, and that section of the half-world which rests one end on Broadway. But there was always a thorough and infractible eight hours devoted to his work in Wall Street, where the combination of his influential family connection, his sharp intelligence, and his abundance of sheer physical energy brought him almost immediately forward. He had one of those invaluable minds with partitions in it; sometimes he appeared at his office refreshed by less than an hour's sleep, but such occurrences were rare. So early as 1920 his income in salary and commission exceeded twelve thousand dollars.

As the Yale tradition slipped into the past he became more and more of a popular figure among his classmates in New York, more popular than he had ever been in college. He lived in a great house, and had the means of introducing young men into other great houses. Moreover, his life already seemed secure, while theirs, for the most part, had arrived again at precarious beginnings. They commenced to turn to him for amusement and escape, and Anson responded readily, taking pleasure in helping people and arranging their affairs.

There were no men in Paula's letters now, but a note of tenderness ran through them that had not been there before. From several sources he heard that she had "a heavy beau," Lowell Thayer, a Bostonian of wealth and position, and though he was sure she still loved him, it made him uneasy to think that he might lose her, after all. Save for one unsatisfactory day she had not been in New

York for almost five months, and as the rumors multiplied he became increasingly anxious to see her. In February he took his vacation and went down to Florida.

Palm Beach sprawled plump and opulent between the sparkling sapphire of Lake Worth, flawed here and there by houseboats at anchor, and the great turquoise bar of the Atlantic Ocean. The huge bulks of the Breakers and the Royal Poinciana rose as twin paunches from the bright level of the sand, and around them clustered the Dancing Glade, Bradley's House of Chance, and a dozen modistes and milliners with goods at triple prices from New York. Upon the trellissed veranda of the Breakers two hundred women stepped right, stepped left, wheeled, and slid in that then celebrated calisthenic known as the double-shuffle, while in half-time to the music two thousand bracelets clicked up and down on two hundred arms.

At the Everglades Club after dark Paula and Lowell Thayer and Anson and a casual fourth played bridge with hot cards. It seemed to Anson that her kind, serious face was wan and tired—she had been around now for four, five, years. He had known her for three.

"Two spades."

"Cigarette? . . . Oh, I beg your pardon. By me."

"By."

"I'll double three spades."

There were a dozen tables of bridge in the room, which was filling up with smoke. Anson's eyes met Paula's, held them persistently even when Thayer's glance fell between them. . . .

"What was bid?" he asked abstractedly.

Rose of Washington Square

sang the young people in the corners:

> *I'm withering there*
> *In basement air——.*

The smoke banked like fog, and the opening of a door filled the room with blown swirls of ectoplasm. Little Bright Eyes streaked past the tables seeking Mr. Conan Doyle among the Englishmen who were posing as Englishmen about the lobby.

"You could cut it with a knife."

". . . cut it with a knife."

". . . a knife."

At the end of the rubber Paula suddenly got up and spoke to Anson in a tense, low voice. With scarcely a glance at Lowell Thayer, they walked out the door and descended a long flight of stone steps—in a moment they were walking hand in hand along the moonlit beach.

"Darling, darling. . . ." They embraced recklessly, passionately, in a shadow. . . . Then Paula drew back her face to let his lips say what she wanted to hear—she could feel the words forming as they kissed again. . . . Again she broke away, listening, but as he pulled her close once more she realized that he had said nothing—only *Darling! Darling!* in that deep, sad whisper that always made her cry. Humbly, obediently, her emotions yielded to him and the tears streamed down her face, but her heart kept on crying: "Ask me—oh, Anson, dearest, ask me!"

"Paula. . . . *Paula!*"

The words wrung her heart like hands, and Anson, feeling her tremble, knew that emotion was enough. He need say no more, commit their destinies to no practical enigma. Why should he, when he might hold her so, biding his own time, for another year—forever? He was considering them both, her more than himself. For a moment, when she said suddenly that she must go back to her hotel, he hesitated, thinking, first, "This is the moment, after all," and then: "No, let it wait—she is mine. . . ."

He had forgotten that Paula too was worn away inside with the strain of three years. Her mood passed forever in the night.

He went back to New York next morning filled with a certain restless dissatisfaction. Late in April, without warning, he received a telegram from Bar Harbor in which Paula told him that she was engaged to Lowell Thayer, and that they would be married immediately in Boston. What he never really believed could happen had happened at last.

Anson filled himself with whisky that morning, and going to the office, carried on his work without a break—rather with a fear of what would happen if he stopped. In the evening he went out as usual, saying nothing of what had occurred; he was cordial, humorous, unabstracted. But one thing he could not help—for three days, in any place, in any company, he would suddenly bend his head into his hands and cry like a child.

V

In 1922 when Anson went abroad with the junior partner to investigate some London loans, the journey intimated that he was to be taken into the firm. He was twenty-seven now, a little heavy without being definitely stout, and with a manner older than his years. Old people and young people liked him and trusted him, and mothers felt safe when their daughters were in his charge, for he had a way, when he came into a room, of putting himself on a footing with the oldest and most conservative people there. "You and I," he seemed to say, "we're solid. We understand."

He had an instinctive and rather charitable knowledge of the weaknesses of men and women, and, like a priest, it made him the more concerned for the maintenance of outward forms. It was typical of him that every Sunday morning he taught in a fashionable Episcopal Sunday school—even though a cold shower and a quick change into a cutaway coat were all that separated him from the wild night before.

After his father's death he was the practical head of his family, and, in effect, guided the destinies of the younger children. Through a complication his authority did not extend to his father's estate, which was administered by his Uncle Robert, who was the horsy member of the family, a good-natured, hard-drinking member of that set which centers about Wheatley Hills.

Uncle Robert and his wife, Edna, had been great friends of Anson's youth, and the former was disappointed when his nephew's superiority failed to take a horsy form. He backed him for a city club which was the most difficult in America to enter—one could only join if one's family had "helped to build up New York" (or, in other words, were rich before 1880)—and when Anson, after his election, neglected it for the Yale Club, Uncle Robert gave him a little talk on the subject. But when on top of that Anson declined to enter Robert Hunter's own conservative and somewhat neglected brokerage house, his manner grew cooler. Like a primary teacher who has taught all he knew, he slipped out of Anson's life.

There were so many friends in Anson's life—scarcely one for whom he had not done some unusual kindness and scarcely one whom he did not occasionally embarrass by his bursts of rough conversation or his habit of getting drunk whenever and however he liked. It annoyed him when any one else blundered in that regard—about his own lapses he was always humorous. Odd things happened to him and he told them with infectious laughter.

I was working in New York that spring, and I used to lunch with him at the Yale Club, which my university was sharing until the completion of our own. I had read of Paula's marriage, and one afternoon, when I asked him about her, something moved him to tell me the story. After that he frequently invited me to family dinners at his house and behaved as though there was a special relation between us, as though with his confidence a little of that consuming memory had passed into me.

I found that despite the trusting mothers, his attitude toward girls was not indiscriminately protective. It was up to the girl—if she showed an inclination toward looseness, she must take care of herself, even with him.

"Life," he would explain sometimes, "has made a cynic of me."

By life he meant Paula. Sometimes, especially when he was drinking, it became a little twisted in his mind, and he thought that she had callously thrown him over.

This "cynicism," or rather his realization that naturally fast girls were not worth sparing, led to his affair with Dolly Karger. It wasn't his only affair in those years, but it came nearest to touching him deeply, and it had a profound effect upon his attitude toward life.

Dolly was the daughter of a notorious "publicist" who had married into society. She herself grew up into the Junior League, came out at the Plaza, and went to the Assembly; and only a few old families like the Hunters could question whether or not she "belonged," for her picture was often in the papers, and she had more enviable attention than many girls who undoubtedly did. She was dark-haired, with carmine lips and a high, lovely color, which she concealed under pinkish-gray powder all through the first year out, because high color was unfashionable—Victorian-pale was the thing to be. She wore black, severe suits and stood with her hands in her pockets leaning a little forward, with a humorous restraint on her face. She danced exquisitely—better than anything she liked to dance—better than anything except making love. Since she was ten she had always been in love, and, usually, with some boy who didn't respond to her. Those who did—and there were many—bored her after a brief encounter, but for her failures she reserved the warmest spot in her heart. When she met them she would always try once more —sometimes she succeeded, more often she failed.

It never occurred to this gypsy of the unattainable that there was a certain resemblance in those who refused to love her—they shared a hard intuition that saw through to her weakness, not a weakness of emotion but a weakness of rudder. Anson perceived this when he first met her, less than a month after Paula's marriage. He was drinking rather heavily, and he pretended for a week that he was falling in love with her. Then he dropped her abruptly and forgot—immediately he took up the commanding position in her heart.

Like so many girls of that day Dolly was slackly and indiscreetly wild. The unconventionality of a slightly older generation had been simply one facet of a postwar movement to discredit obsolete manners—Dolly's was both older and shabbier, and she saw in Anson the two extremes which the emotionally shiftless woman seeks, an abandon to indulgence alternating with a protective strength. In his character she felt both the sybarite and the solid rock, and these two satisfied every need of her nature.

She felt that it was going to be difficult, but she mistook the reason—she thought that Anson and his family expected a more spectacular marriage, but she guessed immediately that her advantage lay in his tendency to drink.

They met at the large débutante dances, but as her infatuation increased they managed to be more and more together. Like most mothers, Mrs. Karger believed that Anson was exceptionally reliable, so she allowed Dolly to go with him to distant country clubs and suburban houses without inquiring closely into their activities or questioning her explanations when they came in late. At first these explanations might have been accurate, but Dolly's worldly ideas of capturing Anson were soon engulfed in the rising sweep of her emotion. Kisses in the back of taxis and motor-cars were no longer enough; they did a curious thing:

They dropped out of their world for a while and made another world just beneath it where Anson's tippling and Dolly's irregular hours would be less noticed and commented on. It was composed, this world, of varying elements—several of Anson's Yale friends and their wives, two or three young brokers and bond salesmen and a handful of unattached men, fresh from college, with money and a propensity to dissipation. What this world lacked in spaciousness and scale it made up for by allowing them a liberty that it scarcely permitted itself. Moreover, it centered around them and permitted Dolly the pleasure of a faint condescension—a pleasure which Anson, whose whole life was a condescension from the certitudes of his childhood, was unable to share.

He was not in love with her, and in the long feverish winter of their affair he frequently told her so. In the spring he was weary—he wanted to renew his life at some other source—moreover, he saw that either he must break with her now or accept the responsibility of a definite seduction. Her family's encouraging attitude precipitated his decision—one evening when Mr. Karger knocked discreetly at the library door to announce that he had left a bottle of old brandy in the dining-room, Anson felt that life was hemming him in. That night he wrote her a short letter in which he told her that he was going on his vacation, and that in view of all the circumstances they had better meet no more.

It was June. His family had closed up the house and gone to the country, so he was living temporarily at the Yale Club. I had heard about his affair with Dolly as it developed—accounts salted with humor, for he despised unstable women, and granted them no place in the social edifice in which he believed—and when he told me that night that he was definitely breaking with her I was glad. I had seen Dolly here and there, and each time with a feeling of pity at the hopelessness of her struggle, and of shame at knowing so much about her that I had no right to know. She was what is known as "a pretty little thing," but there was a certain recklessness which rather fascinated me. Her dedication to the goddess of waste would have been less obvious had she been less spirited—she would most certainly throw herself away, but I was glad when I heard that the sacrifice would not be consummated in my sight.

Anson was going to leave the letter of farewell at her house next morning. It was one of the few houses left open in the Fifth Avenue district, and he knew that the Kargers, acting upon erroneous information from Dolly, had foregone a trip abroad to give their daughter her chance. As he stepped out the door of the Yale Club into Madison Avenue the postman passed him, and he followed back inside. The first letter that caught his eye was in Dolly's hand.

He knew what it would be—a lonely and tragic monologue, full of the reproaches he knew, the invoked memories, the "I wonder if's"—all the immemorial intimacies that he had communicated to Paula Legendre in what seemed another age. Thumbing over some bills, he brought it on top again and opened it. To his surprise it was a short, somewhat formal note, which said that Dolly would be unable to go to the country with him for the week-end, because Perry Hull from Chicago had unexpectedly come to town. It added that Anson had brought this on himself: "—if I felt that you loved me as I love you I would go with you at any time, any place, but Perry is *so* nice, and he so much wants me to marry him——"

Anson smiled contemptuously—he had had experience with such decoy epistles. Moreover, he knew how Dolly had labored over this plan, probably sent for the faithful Perry and calculated the time of his arrival —even labored over the note so that it would make him jealous without driving him away. Like most compromises, it had neither force nor vitality but only a timorous despair.

Suddenly he was angry. He sat down in the lobby and read it again. Then he went to the phone, called Dolly and told her in his clear, compelling voice that he had received her note and would call for her at five o'clock as they had previously planned. Scarcely waiting for the pretended uncertainty of her "Perhaps I can see you for an hour," he hung up the receiver and went down to his office. On the way he tore his own letter into bits and dropped it in the street.

He was not jealous—she meant nothing to him—but at her pathetic ruse everything stubborn and self-indulgent in him came to the surface. It was a presumption from a mental inferior and it could not be over-looked. If she wanted to know to whom she belonged she would see.

He was on the door-step at quarter past five. Dolly was dressed for the street, and he listened in silence to the paragraph of "I can only see you for an hour," which she had begun on the phone.

"Put on your hat, Dolly," he said, "we'll take a walk."

They strolled up Madison Avenue and over to Fifth while Anson's shirt dampened upon his portly body in the deep heat. He talked little, scolding her, making no love to her, but before they had walked six blocks she was his again, apologizing for the note, offering not to see Perry at all as an atone-ment, offering anything. She thought that he had come because he was beginning to love her.

"I'm hot," he said when they reached 71st Street. "This is a winter suit. If I stop by the house and change, would you mind waiting for me downstairs? I'll only be a minute."

She was happy; the intimacy of his be-ing hot, of any physical fact about him, thrilled her. When they came to the iron-grated door and Anson took out his key she experienced a sort of delight.

Downstairs it was dark, and after he ascended in the lift Dolly raised a curtain and looked out through opaque lace at the houses over the way. She heard the lift machinery stop, and with the notion of teasing him pressed the button that brought it down. Then on what was more than an impulse she got into it and sent it up to what she guessed was his floor.

"Anson," she called, laughing a little.

"Just a minute," he answered from his bedroom . . . then after a brief delay: "Now you can come in."

He had changed and was buttoning his vest. "This is my room," he said lightly. "How do you like it?"

She caught sight of Paula's picture on the wall and stared at it in fascination, just as Paula had stared at the pictures of Anson's childish sweethearts five years before. She knew something about Paula—sometimes she tortured herself with fragments of the story.

Suddenly she came close to Anson, rais-ing her arms. They embraced. Outside the area window a soft artificial twilight already hovered, though the sun was still bright on a back roof across the way. In half an hour the room would be quite dark. The uncalculated opportunity overwhelmed them, made them both breathless, and they clung more closely. It was eminent, inevitable. Still holding one another, they raised their heads—their eyes fell together upon Paula's picture, staring down at them from the wall.

Suddenly Anson dropped his arms, and sitting down at his desk tried the drawer with a bunch of keys.

"Like a drink?" he asked in a gruff voice.

"No, Anson."

He poured himself half a tumbler of whisky, swallowed it, and then opened the door into the hall.

"Come on," he said.

Dolly hesitated.

"Anson—I'm going to the country with you tonight, after all. You understand that, don't you?"

"Of course," he answered brusquely.

In Dolly's car they rode on to Long Island, closer in their emotions than they had ever been before. They knew what would happen—not with Paula's face to remind them that something was lacking, but when they were alone in the still, hot Long Island night they did not care.

The estate in Port Washington where they were to spend the week-end belonged to a cousin of Anson's who had married a Mon-tana copper operator. An interminable drive began at the lodge and twisted under im-ported poplar saplings toward a huge, pink, Spanish house. Anson had often visited there before.

After dinner they danced at the Linx Club. About midnight Anson assured himself that his cousins would not leave before two—then he explained that Dolly was tired; he would take her home and return to the dance later. Trembling a little with excitement, they got into a borrowed car together and drove to Port Washington. As they reached the lodge he stopped and spoke to the night-watchman.

"When are you making a round, Carl?"

"Right away."

"Then you'll be here till everybody's in?"

"Yes, sir."

"All right. Listen: if any automobile, no matter whose it is, turns in at this gate, I want you to phone the house immediately." He put a five-dollar bill into Carl's hand. "Is that clear?"

"Yes, Mr. Anson." Being of the Old World, he neither winked nor smiled. Yet Dolly sat with her face turned slightly away.

Anson had a key. Once inside he poured a drink for both of them—Dolly left hers untouched—then he ascertained definitely the location of the phone, and found that it was within easy hearing distance of their rooms, both of which were on the first floor.

Five minutes later he knocked at the door of Dolly's room.

"Anson?" He went in, closing the door behind him. She was in bed, leaning up anxiously with elbows on the pillow; sitting beside her he took her in his arms.

"Anson, darling."

He didn't answer.

"Anson. . . . Anson! I love you. . . . Say you love me. Say it now—can't you say it now? Even if you don't mean it?"

He did not listen. Over her head he perceived that the picture of Paula was hanging here upon this wall.

He got up and went close to it. The frame gleamed faintly with thrice-reflected moonlight—within was a blurred shadow of a face that he saw he did not know. Almost

sobbing, he turned around and stared with abomination at the little figure on the bed.

"This is all foolishness," he said thickly. "I don't know what I was thinking about. I don't love you and you'd better wait for somebody that loves you. I don't love you a bit, can't you understand?"

His voice broke, and he went hurriedly out. Back in the salon he was pouring himself a drink with uneasy fingers, when the front door opened suddenly, and his cousin came in.

"Why, Anson, I hear Dolly's sick," she began solicitously. "I hear she's sick. . . ."

"It was nothing," he interrupted, raising his voice so that it would carry into Dolly's room. "She was a little tired. She went to bed."

For a long time afterward Anson believed that a protective God sometimes interfered in human affairs. But Dolly Karger, lying awake and staring at the ceiling, never again believed in anything at all.

VI

When Dolly married during the following autumn, Anson was in London on business. Like Paula's marriage, it was sudden, but it affected him in a different way. At first he felt that it was funny, and had an inclination to laugh when he thought of it. Later it depressed him—it made him feel old.

There was something repetitive about it—why, Paula and Dolly had belonged to different generations. He had a foretaste of the sensation of a man of forty who hears that the daughter of an old flame has married. He wired congratulations and, as was not the case with Paula, they were sincere—he had never really hoped that Paula would be happy.

When he returned to New York, he was made a partner in the firm, and, as his responsibilities increased, he had less time on his hands. The refusal of a life-insurance company to issue him a policy made such an impression on him that he stopped drinking for a year, and claimed that he felt better physically, though I think he missed the convivial recounting of those Celliniesque adventures which, in his early twenties, had played such a part of his life. But he never abandoned the Yale Club. He was a figure there, a personality, and the tendency of his class, who were now seven years out of college, to drift away to more sober haunts was checked by his presence.

His day was never too full nor his mind too weary to give any sort of aid to any one who asked it. What had been done at first through pride and superiority had become a habit and a passion. And there was always something—a younger brother in trouble at New Haven, a quarrel to be patched up between a friend and his wife, a position to be found for this man, an investment for that. But his specialty was the solving of problems for young married people. Young married people fascinated him and their apartments were almost sacred to him—he knew the story of their love-affair, advised them where to live and how, and remembered their babies' names. Toward young wives his attitude was circumspect: he never abused the trust which their husbands—strangely enough in view of his unconcealed irregularities—invariably reposed in him.

He came to take a vicarious pleasure in happy marriages, and to be inspired to an almost equally pleasant melancholy by those that went astray. Not a season passed that he did not witness the collapse of an affair that perhaps he himself had fathered. When Paula was divorced and almost immediately remarried to another Bostonian, he talked about her to me all one afternoon. He would never love any one as he had loved Paula, but he insisted that he no longer cared.

"I'll never marry," he came to say; "I've seen too much of it, and I know a happy marriage is a very rare thing. Besides, I'm too old."

But he did believe in marriage. Like all men who spring from a happy and successful marriage, he believed in it passionately

—nothing he had seen would change his belief, his cynicism dissolved upon it like air. But he did really believe he was too old. At twenty-eight he began to accept with equanimity the prospect of marrying without romantic love; he resolutely chose a New York girl of his own class, pretty, intelligent, congenial, above reproach—and set about falling in love with her. The things he had said to Paula with sincerity, to other girls with grace, he could no longer say at all without smiling, or with the force necessary to convince.

"When I'm forty," he told his friends, "I'll be ripe. I'll fall for some chorus girl like the rest."

Nevertheless, he persisted in his attempt. His mother wanted to see him married, and he could now well afford it—he had a seat on the Stock Exchange, and his earned income came to twenty-five thousand a year. The idea was agreeable: when his friends—he spent most of his time with the set he and Dolly had evolved—closed themselves in behind domestic doors at night, he no longer rejoiced in his freedom. He even wondered if he should have married Dolly. Not even Paula had loved him more, and he was learning the rarity, in a single life, of encountering true emotion.

Just as this mood began to creep over him a disquieting story reached his ear. His Aunt Edna, a woman just this side of forty, was carrying on an open intrigue with a dissolute hard-drinking young man named Cary Sloane. Every one knew of it except Anson's Uncle Robert, who for fifteen years had talked long in clubs and taken his wife for granted.

Anson heard the story again and again with increasing annoyance. Something of his old feeling for his uncle came back to him, a feeling that was more than personal, a reversion toward that family solidarity on which he had based his pride. His intuition singled out the essential point of the affair, which was that his uncle shouldn't be hurt. It was his first experiment in unsolicited meddling, but with his knowledge of Edna's character he felt that he could handle the matter better than a district judge or his uncle.

His uncle was in Hot Springs. Anson traced down the sources of the scandal so that there should be no possibility of mistake and then he called Edna and asked her to lunch with him at the Plaza next day. Something in his tone must have frightened her, for she was reluctant, but he insisted, putting off the date until she had no excuse for refusing.

She met him at the appointed time in the Plaza lobby, a lovely, faded, gray-eyed blonde in a coat of Russian sable. Five great rings, cold with diamonds and emeralds, sparkled on her slender hands. It occurred to Anson that it was his father's intelligence and not his uncle's that had earned the fur and the stones, the rich brilliance that buoyed up her passing beauty.

Though Edna scented his hostility, she was unprepared for the directness of his approach.

"Edna, I'm astonished at the way you've been acting," he said in a strong, frank voice. "At first I couldn't believe it."

"Believe what?" she demanded sharply.

"You needn't pretend with me, Edna. I'm talking about Cary Sloane. Aside from any other consideration, I didn't think you could treat Uncle Robert——"

"Now look here, Anson—" she began angrily, but his peremptory voice broke through hers:

"—and your children in such a way. You've been married eighteen years, and you're old enough to know better."

"You can't talk to me like that! You ——"

"Yes, I can. Uncle Robert has always been my best friend." He was tremendously moved. He felt a real distress about his uncle, about his three young cousins.

Edna stood up, leaving her crab-flake cocktail untasted.

"This is the silliest thing——"

"Very well, if you won't listen to me I'll go to Uncle Robert and tell him the whole story—he's bound to hear it sooner or later.

And afterward I'll go to old Moses Sloane."

Edna faltered back into her chair.

"Don't talk so loud," she begged him. Her eyes blurred with tears. "You have no idea how your voice carries. You might have chosen a less public place to make all these crazy accusations."

He didn't answer.

"Oh, you never liked me, I know," she went on. "You're just taking advantage of some silly gossip to try and break up the only interesting friendship I've ever had. What did I ever do to make you hate me so?"

Still Anson waited. There would be the appeal to his chivalry, then to his pity, finally to his superior sophistication—when he had shouldered his way through all these there would be admissions, and he could come to grips with her. By being silent, by being impervious, by returning constantly to his main weapon, which was his own true emotion, he bullied her into frantic despair as the luncheon hour slipped away. At two o'clock she took out a mirror and a handkerchief, shined away the marks of her tears and powdered the slight hollows where they had lain. She had agreed to meet him at her own house at five.

When he arrived she was stretched on a chaise longue which was covered with cretonne for the summer, and the tears he had called up at luncheon seemed still to be standing in her eyes. Then he was aware of Cary Sloane's dark anxious presence upon the cold hearth.

"What's this idea of yours?" broke out Sloane immediately. "I understand you invited Edna to lunch and then threatened her on the basis of some cheap scandal."

Anson sat down.

"I have no reason to think it's only scandal."

"I hear you're going to take it to Robert Hunter, and to my father."

Anson nodded.

"Either you break it off—or I will," he said.

"What God damned business is it of yours, Hunter?"

"Don't lose your temper, Cary," said Edna nervously. "It's only a question of showing him how absurd——"

"For one thing, it's my name that's being handed around," interrupted Anson. "That's all that concerns you, Cary."

"Edna isn't a member of your family."

"She most certainly is!" His anger mounted. "Why—she owes this house and the rings on her fingers to my father's brains. When Uncle Robert married her she didn't have a penny."

They all looked at the rings as if they had a significant bearing on the situation. Edna made a gesture to take them from her hand.

"I guess they're not the only rings in the world," said Sloane.

"Oh, this is absurd," cried Edna. "Anson, will you listen to me? I've found out how the silly story started. It was a maid I discharged who went right to the Chilicheffs —all these Russians pump things out of their servants and then put a false meaning on them." She brought down her fist angrily on the table: "And after Tom lent them the limousine for a whole month when we were South last winter——"

"Do you see?" demanded Sloane eagerly. "This maid got hold of the wrong end of the thing. She knew that Edna and I were friends, and she carried it to the Chilicheffs. In Russia they assume that if a man and a woman——"

He enlarged the theme to a disquisition upon social relations in the Caucasus.

"If that's the case it better be explained to Uncle Robert," said Anson dryly, "so that when the rumors do reach him he'll know they're not true."

Adopting the method he had followed with Edna at luncheon he let them explain it all away. He knew that they were guilty and that presently they would cross the line from explanation into justification and convict themselves more definitely than he could ever do. By seven they had taken the desperate step of telling him the truth—Robert Hunter's neglect, Edna's empty life, the casual dalliance that had flamed up into passion—but like so many true stories it had the misfortune of being old, and its enfeebled body beat helplessly against the armor of Anson's will. The threat to go to Sloane's father sealed their helplessness, for the latter, a retired cotton broker out of Alabama, was a notorious fundamentalist who controlled his son by a rigid allowance and the promise that at his next vagary the allowance would stop forever.

They dined at a small French restaurant, and the discussion continued—at one time Sloane resorted to physical threats, a little later they were both imploring him to give them time. But Anson was obdurate. He saw that Edna was breaking up, and that her spirit must not be refreshed by any renewal of their passion.

At two o'clock in a small night-club on 53d Street, Edna's nerves suddenly collapsed, and she cried to go home. Sloane had been drinking heavily all evening, and he was faintly maudlin, leaning on the table and weeping a little with his face in his hands. Quickly Anson gave them his terms. Sloane was to leave town for six months, and he must be gone within forty-eight hours. When he returned there was to be no resumption of the affair, but at the end of a year Edna might, if she wished, tell Robert Hunter that she wanted a divorce and go about it in the usual way.

He paused, gaining confidence from their faces for his final word.

"Or there's another thing you can do," he said slowly, "if Edna wants to leave her children, there's nothing I can do to prevent your running off together."

"I want to go home!" cried Edna again. "Oh, haven't you done enough to us for one day?"

Outside it was dark, save for a blurred glow from Sixth Avenue down the street. In that light those two who had been lovers looked for the last time into each other's tragic faces, realizing that between them there was not enough youth and strength to avert their eternal parting. Sloane walked suddenly off down the street and Anson tapped a dozing taxi-driver on the arm.

It was almost four; there was a patient flow of cleaning water along the ghostly pavement of Fifth Avenue, and the shadows of two night women fitted over the dark façade of St. Thomas's church. Then the desolate shrubbery of Central Park where Anson had often played as a child, and the mounting numbers, significant as names, of the marching streets. This was his city, he thought, where his name had flourished through five generations. No change could alter the permanence of its place here, for change itself was the essential substratum by which he and those of his name identified themselves with the spirit of New York. Resourcefulness and a powerful will—for his threats in weaker hands would have been less than nothing—had beaten the gathering dust from his uncle's name, from the name of his family, from even this shivering figure that sat beside him in the car.

Cary Sloane's body was found next morning on the lower shelf of a pillar of Queensboro Bridge. In the darkness and in his excitement he had thought that it was the water flowing black beneath him, but in less than a second it made no possible difference —unless he had planned to think one last thought of Edna, and call out her name as he struggled feebly in the water.

VII

Anson never blamed himself for his part in this affair—the situation which brought it about had not been of his making. But the just suffer with the unjust, and he found that his oldest and somehow his most precious friendship was over. He never knew what distorted story Edna told, but he was welcome in his uncle's house no longer.

Just before Christmas Mrs. Hunter retired to a select Episcopal heaven, and Anson became the responsible head of his family. An unmarried aunt who had lived with them for years ran the house, and attempted with helpless inefficiency to chaperone the younger girls. All the children were less self-reliant than Anson, more conventional both in their virtues and in their shortcomings. Mrs. Hunter's death had postponed the début of one daughter and the wedding of another. Also it had taken something deeply material from all of them, for with her passing the quiet, expensive superiority of the Hunters came to an end.

For one thing, the estate, considerably diminished by two inheritance taxes and soon to be divided among six children, was not a notable fortune any more. Anson saw a tendency in his youngest sisters to speak rather respectfully of families that hadn't "existed" twenty years ago. His own feeling of precedence was not echoed in them—sometimes they were conventionally snobbish, that was all. For another thing, this was the last summer they would spend on the Connecticut estate; the clamor against it was too loud: "Who wants to waste the best months of the year shut up in that dead old town?" Reluctantly he yielded—the house would go into the market in the fall, and next summer they would rent a smaller place in Westchester County. It was a step down from the expensive simplicity of his father's idea, and, while he sympathized with the revolt, it also annoyed him; during his mother's lifetime he had gone up there at least every other week-end—even in the gayest summers.

Yet he himself was part of this change, and his strong instinct for life had turned him in his twenties from the hollow obsequies of that abortive leisure class. He did not see this clearly—he still felt that there was a norm, a standard of society. But there was no norm, it was doubtful if there had ever been a true norm in New York. The few who still paid and fought to enter a particular set succeeded only to find that as a society it scarcely functioned—or, what was more alarming, that the Bohemia from which they fled sat above them at table.

At twenty-nine Anson's chief concern was his own growing loneliness. He was sure now that he would never marry. The number of weddings at which he had officiated as best man or usher was past all counting—there was a drawer at home that bulged with the official neckties of this or that wedding-party, neckties standing for romances that had not endured a year, for couples who had passed completely from his life. Scarf-pins, gold pencils, cuff-buttons, presents from a generation of grooms had passed through his jewel-box and been lost—and with every ceremony he was less and less able to imagine himself in the groom's place. Under his hearty good-will toward all those marriages there was despair about his own.

And as he neared thirty he became not a little depressed at the inroads that marriage, especially lately, had made upon his friendships. Groups of people had a disconcerting tendency to dissolve and disappear. The men from his own college—and it was upon them he had expended the most time and affection—were the most elusive of all. Most of them were drawn deep into domesticity, two were dead, one lived abroad, one was in Hollywood writing continuities for pictures that Anson went faithfully to see.

Most of them, however, were permanent commuters with an intricate family life centering around some suburban country club, and it was from these that he felt his estrangement most keenly.

In the early days of their married life they had all needed him; he gave them advice about their slim finances, he exorcised their doubts about the advisability of bringing a baby into two rooms and a bath, especially he stood for the great world outside. But now their financial troubles were in the past and the fearfully expected child had evolved into an absorbing family. They were always glad to see old Anson, but they dressed up for him and tried to impress him with their present importance, and kept their troubles to themselves. They needed him no longer.

A few weeks before his thirtieth birthday the last of his early and intimate friends was married. Anson acted in his usual rôle of best man, gave his usual silver tea-service, and went down to the usual *Homeric* to say good-by. It was a hot Friday afternoon in May, and as he walked from the pier he realized that Saturday closing had begun and he was free until Monday morning.

"Go where?" he asked himself.

The Yale Club, of course; bridge until dinner, then four or five raw cocktails in somebody's room and a pleasant confused evening. He regretted that this afternoon's groom wouldn't be along—they had always been able to cram so much into such nights: they knew how to attach women and how to get rid of them, how much consideration any girl deserved from their intelligent hedonism. A party was an adjusted thing—you took certain girls to certain places and spent just so much on their amusement; you drank a little, not much, more than you ought to drink, and at a certain time in the morning you stood up and said you were going home. You avoided college boys, sponges, future engagements, fights, sentiment, and indiscretions. That was the way it was done. All the rest was dissipation.

In the morning you were never violently sorry—you made no resolutions, but if you had overdone it and your heart was slightly out of order, you went on the wagon for a few days without saying anything about it, and waited until an accumulation of nervous boredom projected you into another party.

The lobby of the Yale Club was unpopulated. In the bar three very young alumni looked up at him, momentarily and without curiosity.

"Hello there, Oscar," he said to the bartender. "Mr. Cahill been around this afternoon?"

"Mr. Cahill's gone to New Haven."

"Oh . . . that so?"

"Gone to the ball game. Lot of men gone up."

Anson looked once again into the lobby, considered for a moment, and then walked out and over to Fifth Avenue. From the broad window of one of his clubs—one that he had scarcely visited in five years—a gray man with watery eyes stared down at him. Anson looked quickly away—that figure sitting in vacant resignation, in supercilious solitude, depressed him. He stopped and, retracing his steps, started over 47th Street toward Teak Warden's apartment. Teak and his wife had once been his most familiar friends—it was a household where he and Dolly Karger had been used to go in the days of their affair. But Teak had taken to drink, and his wife had remarked publicly that Anson was a bad influence on him. The remark reached Anson in an exaggerated form—when it was finally cleared up, the delicate spell of intimacy was broken, never to be renewed.

"Is Mr. Warden at home?" he inquired.

"They've gone to the country."

The fact unexpectedly cut at him. They were gone to the country and he hadn't known. Two years before he would have known the date, the hour, come up at the last moment for a final drink, and planned his first visit to them. Now they had gone without a word.

Anson looked at his watch and considered a week-end with his family, but the only train was a local that would jolt through the aggressive heat for three hours. And tomorrow in the country, and Sunday—he was in no mood for porch-bridge with polite undergraduates, and dancing after dinner at a rural road-house, a diminutive of gaiety which his father had estimated too well.

"Oh, no," he said to himself. . . . "No."

He was a dignified, impressive young man, rather stout now, but otherwise unmarked by dissipation. He could have been cast for a pillar of something—at times you were sure it was not society, at others nothing else—for the law, for the church. He stood for a few minutes motionless on the sidewalk in front of a 47th Street apartment-house; for almost the first time in his life he had nothing whatever to do.

Then he began to walk briskly up Fifth Avenue, as if he had just been reminded of an important engagement there. The necessity of dissimulation is one of the few characteristics that we share with dogs, and I think of Anson on that day as some well-bred specimen who had been disappointed at a familiar back door. He was going to see Nick, once a fashionable bartender in demand at all private dances, and now employed in cooling non-alcoholic champagne among the labyrinthine cellars of the Plaza Hotel.

"Nick," he said, "what's happened to everything?"

"Dead," Nick said.

"Make me a whisky sour." Anson handed a pint bottle over the counter. "Nick, the girls are different; I had a little girl in Brooklyn and she got married last week without letting me know."

"That a fact? Ha-ha-ha," responded Nick diplomatically. "Slipped it over on you."

"Absolutely," said Anson. "And I was out with her the night before."

"Ha-ha-ha," said Nick, "ha-ha-ha!"

"Do you remember the wedding, Nick, in Hot Springs where I had the waiters and the musicians singing 'God save the King'?"

"Now where was that, Mr. Hunter?" Nick concentrated doubtfully. "Seems to me that was——"

"Next time they were back for more, and I began to wonder how much I'd paid them," continued Anson.

"—seems to me that was at Mr. Trenholm's wedding."

"Don't know him," said Anson decisively. He was offended that a strange name should intrude upon his reminiscences; Nick perceived this.

"Naw—aw—" he admitted, "I ought to know that. It was one of *your* crowd—Brakins. . . . Baker——"

"Bicker Baker," said Anson responsively. "They put me in a hearse after it was over and covered me up with flowers and drove me away."

"Ha-ha-ha," said Nick. "Ha-ha-ha."

Nick's simulation of the old family servant paled presently and Anson went upstairs to the lobby. He looked around—his eyes met the glance of an unfamiliar clerk at the desk, then fell upon a flower from the morning's marriage hesitating in the mouth of a brass cuspidor. He went out and walked slowly toward the blood-red sun over Columbus Circle. Suddenly he turned around and, retracing his steps to the Plaza, immured himself in a telephone-booth.

Later he said that he tried to get me three times that afternoon, that he tried every one who might be in New York—men and girls he had not seen for years, an artist's model of his college days whose faded number was still in his address book—Central told him that even the exchange existed no longer. At length his quest roved into the country, and he held brief disappointing conversations with emphatic butlers and maids. So-and-so was out, riding, swimming, playing golf, sailed to Europe last week. Who shall I say phoned?

It was intolerable that he should pass the evening alone—the private reckonings which one plans for a moment of leisure lose every charm when the solitude is enforced. There were always women of a sort, but the ones he knew had temporarily vanished, and to pass a New York evening in the hired company of a stranger never occurred to him—he would have considered that that was something shameful and secret, the diversion of a traveling salesman in a strange town.

Anson paid the telephone bill—the girl tried unsuccessfully to joke with him about its size—and for the second time that afternoon started to leave the Plaza and go he knew not where. Near the revolving door the figure of a woman, obviously with child, stood sideways to the light—a sheer beige cape fluttered at her shoulders when the door turned and, each time, she looked impatiently toward it as if she were weary of waiting. At the first sight of her a strong nervous thrill of familiarity went over him, but not until he

was within five feet of her did he realize that it was Paula.

"Why, Anson Hunter!"

His heart turned over.

"Why, Paula——"

"Why, this is wonderful. I can't believe it, *Anson!*"

She took both his hands, and he saw in the freedom of the gesture that the memory of him had lost poignancy to her. But not to him—he felt that old mood that she evoked in him stealing over his brain, that gentleness with which he had always met her optimism as if afraid to mar its surface.

"We're at Rye for the summer. Pete had to come East on business—you know of course I'm Mrs. Peter Hagerty now—so we brought the children and took a house. You've got to come out and see us."

"Can I?" he asked directly. "When?"

"When you like. Here's Peter." The revolving door functioned, giving up a fine tall man of thirty with a tanned face and a trim mustache. His immaculate fitness made a sharp contrast with Anson's increasing bulk, which was obvious under the faintly tight cutaway coat.

"You oughtn't to be standing," said Hagerty to his wife. "Let's sit down here." He indicated lobby chairs, but Paula hesitated.

"I've got to go right home," she said. "Anson, why don't you—why don't you come out and have dinner with us tonight? We're just getting settled, but if you can stand that ——"

Hagerty confirmed the invitation cordially.

"Come out for the night."

Their car waited in front of the hotel, and Paula with a tired gesture sank back against silk cushions in the corner.

"There's so much I want to talk to you about," she said, "it seems hopeless."

"I want to hear about you."

"Well"—she smiled at Hagerty—"that would take a long time too. I have three children—by my first marriage. The oldest is five, then four, then three." She smiled again. "I didn't waste much time having them, did I?"

"Boys?"

"A boy and two girls. Then—oh, a lot of things happened, and I got a divorce in Paris a year ago and married Pete. That's all —except that I'm awfully happy."

In Rye they drove up to a large house near the Beach Club, from which there issued presently three dark, slim children who broke from an English governess and approached them with an esoteric cry. Abstractedly and with difficulty Paula took each one into her arms, a caress which they accepted stiffly, as they had evidently been told not to bump into Mummy. Even against their fresh faces Paula's skin showed scarcely any weariness— for all her physical languor she seemed younger than when he had last seen her at Palm Beach seven years ago.

At dinner she was preoccupied, and afterward, during the homage to the radio, she lay with closed eyes on the sofa, until Anson wondered if his presence at this time were not an intrusion. But at nine o'clock, when Hagerty rose and said pleasantly that he was going to leave them by themselves for a while, she began to talk slowly about herself and the past.

"My first baby," she said—"the one we call Darling, the biggest little girl—I wanted to die when I knew I was going to have her, because Lowell was like a stranger to me. It didn't seem as though she could be my own. I wrote you a letter and tore it up. Oh, you were *so* bad to me, Anson."

It was the dialogue again, rising and falling. Anson felt a sudden quickening of memory.

"Weren't you engaged once?" she asked —"a girl named Dolly something?"

"I wasn't ever engaged. I tried to be engaged, but I never loved anybody but you, Paula."

"Oh," she said. Then after a moment: "This baby is the first one I ever really wanted. You see, I'm in love now—at last."

He didn't answer, shocked at the treachery of her remembrance. She must have seen that the "at last" bruised him, for she continued:

"I was infatuated with you, Anson— you could make me do anything you liked. But we wouldn't have been happy. I'm not smart enough for you. I don't like things to be complicated like you do." She paused. "You'll never settle down," she said.

The phrase struck at him from behind —it was an accusation that of all accusations he had never merited.

"I could settle down if women were different," he said. "If I didn't understand so much about them, if women didn't spoil you for other women, if they had only a little pride. If I could go to sleep for a while and wake up into a home that was really mine— why, that's what I'm made for, Paula, that's what women have seen in me and liked in me. It's only that I can't get through the preliminaries any more."

Hagerty came in a little before eleven; after a whisky Paula stood up and announced that she was going to bed. She went over and stood by her husband.

"Where did you go, dearest?" she demanded.

"I had a drink with Ed Saunders."

"I was worried. I thought maybe you'd run away."

She rested her head against his coat.

"He's sweet, isn't he, Anson?" she demanded.

"Absolutely," said Anson, laughing.

She raised her face to her husband.

"Well, I'm ready," she said. She turned to Anson: "Do you want to see our family gymnastic stunt?"

"Yes," he said in an interested voice.

"All right. Here we go!"

Hagerty picked her up easily in his arms.

"This is called the family acrobatic stunt," said Paula. "He carries me upstairs Isn't it sweet of him?"

"Yes," said Anson.

Hagerty bent his head slightly until his face touched Paula's.

"And I love him," she said. "I've just been telling you, haven't I, Anson?"

"Yes," he said.

"He's the dearest thing that ever lived in this world; aren't you, darling? . . . Well, good night. Here we go. Isn't he strong?"

"Yes," Anson said.

"You'll find a pair of Pete's pajamas laid out for you. Sweet dreams—see you at breakfast."

"Yes," Anson said.

VIII

The older members of the firm insisted that Anson should go abroad for the summer. He had scarcely had a vacation in seven years, they said. He was stale and needed a change. Anson resisted.

"If I go," he declared, "I won't come back any more."

"That's absurd, old man. You'll be back in three months with all this depression gone. Fit as ever."

"No." He shook his head stubbornly. "If I stop, I won't go back to work. If I stop, that means I've given up—I'm through."

"We'll take a chance on that. Stay six months if you like—we're not afraid you'll leave us. Why, you'd be miserable if you didn't work."

They arranged his passage for him. They liked Anson—every one liked Anson—and the change that had been coming over him cast a sort of pall over the office. The enthusiasm that had invariably signaled up business, the consideration toward his equals and his inferiors, the lift of his vital presence —within the past four months his intense nervousness had melted down these qualities into the fussy pessimism of a man of forty. On every transaction in which he was involved he acted as a drag and a strain.

"If I go I'll never come back," he said.

Three days before he sailed Paula Legendre Hagerty died in childbirth. I was with him a great deal then, for we were crossing together, but for the first time in our friendship he told me not a word of how he felt, nor did I see the slightest sign of emotion. His chief preoccupation was with the fact that he was thirty years old—he would turn the conversation to the point where he could remind you of it and then fall silent, as if he assumed that the statement would start a chain of thought sufficient to itself. Like his partners, I was amazed at the change in him, and I was glad when the *Paris* moved off into the wet space between the worlds, leaving his principality behind.

"How about a drink?" he suggested.

We walked into the bar with that defiant feeling that characterizes the day of departure and ordered four Martinis. After one cocktail a change came over him—he suddenly reached across and slapped my knee with the first joviality I had seen him exhibit for months.

"Did you see that girl in the red tam?" he demanded, "the one with the high color who had the two police dogs down to bid her good-by."

"She's pretty," I agreed.

"I looked her up in the purser's office and found out that she's alone. I'm going down to see the steward in a few minutes. We'll have dinner with her tonight."

After a while he left me, and within an hour he was walking up and down the deck with her, talking to her in his strong, clear voice. Her red tam was a bright spot of color against the steel-green sea, and from time to time she looked up with a flashing bob of her head, and smiled with amusement and interest, and anticipation. At dinner we had champagne, and were very joyous—afterward Anson ran the pool with infectious gusto, and several people who had seen me with him asked me his name. He and the girl were talking and laughing together on a lounge in the bar when I went to bed.

I saw less of him on the trip than I had hoped. He wanted to arrange a foursome, but there was no one available, so I saw him only at meals. Sometimes, though, he would have a cocktail in the bar, and he told me about the girl in the red tam, and his adventures with her, making them all bizarre and amusing, as he had a way of doing, and I was glad that he was himself again, or at least the self that I knew, and with which I felt at home. I don't think he was ever happy unless some one was in love with him, responding to him like filings to a magnet, helping him to explain himself, promising him something. What it was I do not know. Perhaps they promised that there would always be women in the world who would spend their brightest, freshest, rarest hours to nurse and protect that superiority he cherished in his heart.

------◆·◄►·◆------

This novelette has something of the range and complexity of a novel. It is really what the word *novelette* implies: a little novel. In time it covers some thirty years, the period from Anson's childhood to the moment when his character is fully defined. The main element in the story is the love affair with Paula, which runs through various stages, but there is also the story of Dolly Karger, the story of Anson's interference with his aunt's love affair, and various minor episodes, such as the conversation with Nick, the barman, and the encounter with the girl on shipboard. All of this is not to say that "The Rich Boy" is necessarily better than a long story—for instance, "The Gentleman from San Francisco," which runs over ten thousand words, but which is very simple in organization—or better than a simpler kind of novelette, such as "Noon Wine." It is merely to indicate a difference.

If "The Rich Boy" has this range and complexity, how does Fitzgerald manage the material so that there is no impression of mere summary? For one thing, the use of a narrator permits what we may call a foreshortening of time. If the author himself were telling the story on his own responsibility as author, with the assumption of complete knowledge of his characters and their lives, we should expect some filling out of the

narrative: we should be inclined to ask, "If he knows all, why doesn't he tell more?" But when the narrator appears in the story, we recognize the limitations of his knowledge; he can tell only what he knows. This difference is purely conventional; that is, in the final analysis we understand, of course, that the author is responsible for his story and the method used to tell it, but we accept the narrator and his function in the same sense that we accept any character in the story. And his presence is a device for controlling the material and giving it the desired scale.

The presence of the narrator is, however, not the only thing that allows Fitzgerald to manage his material so that it does not give the impression of a mere summary. We notice that section I does not really begin the action of the story. It is concerned with establishing the attitude of the narrator to his material—the attitude of the "poor" narrator to the rich boy—and through this attitude the general proposition about the rich on which the story depends:

> They possess and enjoy early, and it does something to them, makes them soft where we are hard, and cynical where we are trustful, in a way that, unless you were born rich, it is very difficult to understand. They think, deep in their hearts, that they are better than we are because we had to discover the compensations and refuges of life for ourselves.

The story, then, is an analysis of Anson's life and development as an illustration of the proposition. By treating the story as an illustration, Fitzgerald (through his narrator, of course) is able to practice another kind of foreshortening: he needs to tell only what is relevant to the proposition, what significantly illustrates the proposition. This means that he can summarize or omit at will without breaking the line of interest—the interest we have in the development of the proposition. The air of detachment, of authority, of almost scientific analysis all go with the method of illustration. Fitzgerald is not trying, this air seems to imply, to make us realize the full quality of Anson's life; he is interested only in what supports the proposition, in what makes Anson a specimen. For Anson is a specimen. Even though Fitzgerald says in the second paragraph of the story that "There are no types, no plurals," his proposition in the end deals with a type, the "very rich," and Anson is presented as an example of what inherited wealth may do to human personality and character.

What is that effect on Anson Hunter? As Arthur Mizener, the biographer of Fitzgerald, puts it, the story is "primarily one of how Anson's queer, rich-boy's pride deprived him of what he wanted most, a home and an ordered life. Hating not to dominate, Anson cannot love those whom he does dominate, cannot commit himself to the human muddle as he must if he is to have the life he wants."* Anson must finally live by that sense of superiority that has robbed him of what he really wants. As the last lines of the story put it:

> I don't think he was ever happy unless some one was in love with him, responding to him like filings to a magnet, helping him to explain himself, promising him something. What it was I do not know. Perhaps they promised that there would always be women in the world who would spend their brightest, freshest, rarest hours to nurse and protect that superiority he cherished in his heart.

EXERCISES

1. "The Rich Boy" is divided into eight sections. Study these divisions as units of the structure of the story. That is, try to answer the question "What point is made in each section in relation to the theme behind the story?" Section I is clearly a kind of prologue. In what sense is section VIII a kind of epilogue, a way of summing up what has already been established by the story? Can you state why Anson's rejection of Paula should come at the middle of the story (end of section IV) and not near the end?

2. Why was Anson's day "never too full nor his mind too weary to give any sort of aid to any one who asked it" (section VI)?

3. When Anson is talking with his uncle's wife (section VI) about her love affair, we find the following passage: " 'Yes, I can. Uncle Robert has been my best friend.' He was tremendously moved. He felt a real distress about his uncle, about his three young cousins." Is Anson's distress to be taken as completely sincere? Or do we understand that there is some self-deception, some shallowness, in it? Argue this question.

4. Why did Anson never blame himself for his part in the death of Cary Sloane, the lover of his uncle's wife? Does the author imply that in some sense he might have properly blamed himself?

5. Toward the middle of section VII, when Anson finds himself idle and without plans on a Friday afternoon, we read the following passage: "Anson looked once again into the lobby, considered for a moment, and then walked out and over to Fifth Avenue. From the broad window of one of his clubs—one that he had scarcely visited in five years—a gray man with watery eyes stared down at him. Anson looked quickly away—that figure sitting in vacant resignation, in supercilious solitude, depressed him." What is the point of this passage?

6. Read Fitzgerald's story "Winter Dreams" or his novel *The Great Gatsby*. What points of similarity do you find between these and "The Rich Boy"? How would you describe the "world" of Fitzgerald? The basic conflict in that world?

Section 10

STORIES

The stories in this section represent a variety of topics, themes, conventions, and techniques. In our comments on stories in the earlier sections we have often referred to stories in this "pool" for purposes of comparison and clarification. But here we refrain

* The Far Side of Paradise (Boston: Houghton Mifflin Company, 1951), pp. 193–194.

from adding further comments and analyses. We hope, in fact, that the student will approach these stories as freshly as possible, ready to make his own explorations and evaluations.

KRONKIN'S PRISONER
Isaac Babel (1894–1941)

We was wiping out the Poles up Belaya Tserkov way. We was wiping them out and making a clean job of it, so that even the trees bent. I got a scratch in the morning, but managed to get about somehow. The day was getting on for evening, I remember, and I'd got away from the Brigade Commander with only five Cossacks of the proletariat to stick with me. All around there's hand to hand fighting going on, all going at one another like cats and dogs. Blood's trickling down from me and my horse. You know the sort of thing.

I and Spirka Zabuty got away together, further away from the forest, and lo and behold—a lucky break—three hundred yards off, not more, dust what may be from a Staff, or from transport wagons. If it's Staff—all right, and if it's transport wagons—better still. The kids were going about in rags, and their shirts didn't reach down to their little bottoms.

"Zabuty," says I to Spirka, "you damned so-and-so, one way and another, I call upon you as the speaker—up and doing, man! That must be their Staff lighting out."

"I don't say no," says Spirka, "only there's two of us and eight of them."

"Puff away, Spirka," I says, "anyway, I'll go and dirty their chasubles. Come along and die for a pin and the World Revolution!"

Well, we went for them. There were eight swordsmen among 'em. Two we put out of action with our rifles. The third, I see, Spirka's gone and done in. And I takes aim at a big pot, boys, with a gold watch and chain. I got him up against a farm, all over apple trees and cherries. My big pot's mount

was a regular beauty, but he was fagged. Then the Pan General drops his bridle, points his Mauser at me, and makes a hole in my leg.

"All right," I thinks, "I'll get you to kick your legs up all right."

So I got busy and put two bullets in the little horse. I was sorry about the stallion. He was a little Bolshevik—a regular little Bolshevik that stallion was, all chestnut, like a copper coin, with a good brush of tail and hocks like cords. I thought to myself: I'll take it alive to Lenin. But it didn't come off: I went and did that little horse in. It plumped down all of a heap like a bride, and my big pot fell out of the saddle. He jerked to one side and turned around and made a draft in my face again. So now I've got three distinctions in action.

"Jesus," I thinks, "he's as like as not to go and kill me by mistake."

So I galloped up to him, and he'd already got his sword out, and tears were running down his cheeks—white tears, real human milk.

"I'll get the Order of the Red Banner through you," I shouts. "Hands up, as I'm alive, Your Worship!"

"I can't, Pan," the old fellow answers. "You'll do me in."

Then suddenly up comes Spirka from nowhere, all bathed in sweat and his eyes hanging from his mug by threads.

"Vasily," he shouts to me, "you'll never believe the amount I've finished off! As for that general with trimmings all over him, I wouldn't mind finishing him off too."

"Go to blazes!" I says to Zabuty, losing my temper. "The trimmings cost me blood, I can tell you!"

And I got my mare to drive the general into a shed with hay in it or something. It was quiet in there and dark and cool.

"Pan," I says, "go steady in your old age. Now hands up, for the love of Mike, and we'll have a talk together."

He puffs away with his back to the wall and wipes his forehead with his red fingers.

"I can't," he says, "you'll do me in. I'll only give up my sword to Budenny."

Go and fetch him Budenny! That's gone and torn it! I see the old guy's had his day.

"Pan," I shouts, crying and grinding my teeth, "I'll give you my proletarian word that I'm myself commander-in-chief here. You needn't go looking for trimmings on me, but I've got the title all right. Here's my title; musical entertainer and drawing-room ventriloquist from the town of Nizhni—Nizhny Novogorod on the Volga River."

And a devil in me worked me up. The general's eyes were blinking like lanterns. A red sea opened up in front of me. The offense was like putting salt in a wound, because I could see the old fellow didn't believe me. So I shut my mouth, lads, squeezed in my belly in the old way, in our way, in the Nizhni-town way, and proved to the Pole that I was a ventriloquist.

And the old chap went quite white and clutched at his heart and sat down on the ground.

"Now d'you believe Vasily the Entertainer, Commissar of the 3rd Invincible Cavalry Brigade?"

"Commissar?" he cries.

"Commissar," I says.

"Communist?" he cries.

"Communist," I says.

"In my last hour," he cries, "as I draw my last breath, tell me, Cossack friend, are you really a Communist, or are you lying?"

"I'm a Communist all right," I says.

Then my old fellow sits there on the ground and kisses some amulet or other and breaks his sword in two, while two lamps light up in his eyes—two lanterns over the dark steppe.

"Forgive me," he says, "I can't surrender to a Communist." And he shakes me by the hand. "Forgive me," says he. "And kill me like a true soldier."

This story was related to us some time ago, during a halt, and in the customary farcical manner, by Kronkin, the political commissar of the N. Cavalry Brigade, thrice Knight of the Order of the Red Banner.

"And what came of your talk with the general, Vasily?"

"Could anything come of it with a chap like that, full of his sense of honor? I bowed to him again, but he would stick to it, so then we took the papers that were on him, the queer old bird, and his Mauser and the saddle that's under me now. And then I noticed my strength's all ebbing away and a terrible sleepiness is descending upon me— well, and I couldn't be bothered with him any more. . . ."

"So the old fellow was put out of his misery?"

" 'Fraid so."

TOMORROW AND TOMORROW AND SO FORTH
John Updike (b. 1932)

Whirling, talking, 11D began to enter Room 109. From the quality of their excitement Mark Prosser guessed it would rain. He had been teaching high school for three years, yet his students still impressed him; they were such sensitive animals. They reacted so infallibly to merely barometric pressure.

In the doorway, Brute Young paused while little Barry Snyder giggled at his elbow. Barry's stagy laugh rose and fell, dipping down toward some vile secret that had to be tasted and retasted, then soaring artificially to proclaim that he, little Barry, shared such a secret with the school's fullback. Being Brute's stooge was precious to Barry. The fullback paid no attention to him; he twisted his neck to stare at something not yet coming through the door. He yielded heavily to the procession pressing him forward.

Right under Prosser's eyes, like a murder suddenly appearing in an annalistic frieze of kings and queens, someone stabbed a girl in the back with a pencil. She ignored the assault saucily. Another hand yanked out

Geoffrey Langer's shirt-tail. Geoffrey, a bright student, was uncertain whether to laugh it off or defend himself with anger, and made a weak, half-turning gesture of compromise, wearing an expression of distant arrogance that Prosser instantly coördinated with feelings of fear he used to have. All along the line, in the glitter of key chains and the acute angles of turned-back shirt cuffs, an electricity was expressed which simple weather couldn't generate.

Mark wondered if today Gloria Angstrom wore that sweater, an ember-pink angora, with very brief sleeves. The virtual sleevelessness was the disturbing factor: the exposure of those two serene arms to the air, white as thighs against the delicate wool.

His guess was correct. A vivid pink patch flashed through the jiggle of arms and shoulders as the final knot of youngsters entered the room.

"Take your seats," Mr. Prosser said. "Come on. Let's go."

Most obeyed, but Peter Forrester, who had been at the center of the group around Gloria, still lingered in the doorway with her, finishing some story, apparently determined to make her laugh or gasp. When she did gasp, he tossed his head with satisfaction. His orange hair bobbed. Redheads are all alike, Mark thought, with their white eyelashes and pale puffy faces and thyroid eyes, their mouths always twisted with preposterous self-confidence. Bluffers, the whole bunch.

When Gloria, moving in a considered, stately way, had taken her seat, and Peter had swerved into his, Mr. Prosser said, "Peter Forrester."

"Yes?" Peter rose, scrabbling through his book for the right place.

"Kindly tell the class the exact meaning of the words 'Tomorrow, and tomorrow, and tomorrow/Creeps in this petty pace from day to day.' "

Peter glanced down at the high-school edition of *Macbeth* lying open on his desk. One of the duller girls tittered expectantly

from the back of the room. Peter was popular with the girls; girls that age had minds like moths.

"Peter. With your book shut. We have all memorized this passage for today. Remember?" The girl in the back of the room squealed in delight. Gloria laid her own book face-open on her desk, where Peter could see it.

Peter shut his book with a bang and stared into Gloria's. "Why," he said at last, "I think it means pretty much what it says."

"Which is?"

"Why, that tomorrow is something we often think about. It creeps into our conversation all the time. We couldn't make any plans without thinking about tomorrow."

"I see. Then you would say that Macbeth is here referring to the, the date-book aspect of life?"

Geoffrey Langer laughed, no doubt to please Mr. Prosser. For a moment, he *was* pleased. Then he realized he had been playing for laughs at a student's expense.

His paraphrase had made Peter's reading of the lines seem more ridiculous than it was. He began to retract. "I admit—"

But Peter was going on; redheads never know when to quit. "Macbeth means that if we quit worrying about tomorrow, and just lived for today, we could appreciate all the wonderful things that are going on under our noses."

Mark considered this a moment before he spoke. He would not be sarcastic. "Uh, without denying that there is truth in what you say, Peter, do you think it likely that Macbeth, in his situation, would be expressing such"—he couldn't help himself—"such sunny sentiments?"

Geoffrey laughed again. Peter's neck reddened; he studied the floor. Gloria glared at Mr. Prosser, the anger in her face clearly meant for him to see.

Mark hurried to undo his mistake. "Don't misunderstand me, please," he told Peter. "I don't have all the answers myself. But it seems to me the whole speech, down to

'Signifying nothing,' is saying that life is—well, a *fraud*. Nothing wonderful about it.''

"Did Shakespeare really think that?" Geoffrey Langer asked, a nervous quickness pitching his voice high.

Mark read into Geoffrey's question his own adolescent premonitions of the terrible truth. The attempt he must make was plain. He told Peter he could sit down and looked through the window toward the steadying sky. The clouds were gaining intensity. "There is," Mr. Prosser slowly began, "much darkness in Shakespeare's work, and no play is darker than 'Macbeth.' The atmosphere is poisonous, oppressive. One critic has said that in this play, humanity suffocates." This was too fancy.

"In the middle of his career, Shakespeare wrote plays about men like Hamlet and Othello and Macbeth—men who aren't allowed by their society, or bad luck, or some minor flaw in themselves, to become the great men they might have been. Even Shakespeare's comedies of this period deal with a world gone sour. It is as if he had seen through the bright, bold surface of his earlier comedies and histories and had looked upon something terrible. It frightened him, just as some day it may frighten some of you." In his determination to find the right words, he had been staring at Gloria, without meaning to. Embarrassed, she nodded, and, realizing what had happened, he smiled at her.

He tried to make his remarks gentler, even diffident. "But then I think Shakespeare sensed a redeeming truth. His last plays are serene and symbolical, as if he had pierced through the ugly facts and reached a realm where the facts are again beautiful. In this way, Shakespeare's total work is a more complete image of life than that of any other writer, except perhaps for Dante, an Italian poet who wrote several centuries earlier." He had been taken far from the Macbeth soliloquy. Other teachers had been happy to tell him how the kids made a game of getting him talking. He looked toward Geoffrey. The boy was doodling on his tablet, indifferent.

Mr. Prosser concluded, "The last play Shakespeare wrote is an extraordinary poem called 'The Tempest.' Some of you may want to read it for your next book reports—the ones due May 10th. It's a short play."

The class had been taking a holiday. Barry Snyder was snicking BBs off the blackboard and glancing over at Brute Young to see if he noticed. "Once more, Barry," Mr. Prosser said, "and out you go." Barry blushed, and grinned to cover the blush, his eyeballs sliding toward Brute. The dull girl in the rear of the room was putting on lipstick. "Put that away, Alice," Mr. Prosser commanded. She giggled and obeyed. Sejak, the Polish boy who worked nights, was asleep at his desk, his cheek white with pressure against the varnished wood, his mouth sagging sidewise. Mr. Prosser had an impulse to let him sleep. But the impulse might not be true kindness, but just the self-congratulatory, kindly pose in which he sometimes discovered himself. Besides, one breach of discipline encouraged others. He strode down the aisle and shook Sejak awake. Then he turned his attention to the mumble growing at the front of the room.

Peter Forrester was whispering to Gloria, trying to make her laugh. The girl's face, though, was cool and solemn, as if a thought had been provoked in her head. Perhaps at least *she* had been listening to what Mr. Prosser had been saying. With a bracing sense of chivalrous intercession, Mark said, "Peter. I gather from this noise that you have something to add to your theories."

Peter responded courteously. "No, sir. I honestly don't understand the speech. Please, sir, what *does* it mean?"

This candid admission and odd request stunned the class. Every white, round face, eager, for once, to learn, turned toward Mark. He said, "I don't know. I was hoping *you* would tell *me*."

In college, when a professor made such a remark, it was with grand effect. The professor's humility, the necessity for creative interplay between teacher and student were dramatically impressed upon the group. But to 11D, ignorance in an instructor was as wrong as a hole in a roof. It was as if he had held forty strings pulling forty faces taut toward him and then had slashed the strings. Heads waggled, eyes dropped, voices buzzed. Some of the discipline problems, like Peter Forrester, smirked signals to one another.

"Quiet!" Mr. Prosser shouted. "All of you. Poetry isn't arithmetic. There's no single right answer. I don't want to force my own impression on you, even if I *have* had much more experience with literature." He made this last clause very loud and distinct, and some of the weaker students seemed reassured. "I know none of *you* want that," he told them.

Whether or not they believed him, they subsided, somewhat. Mark judged he could safely reassume his human-among-humans attitude again. He perched on the edge of the desk and leaned forward beseechingly. "Now, honestly. Don't any of you have some personal feeling about the lines that you would like to share with the class and me?"

One hand, with a flowered handkerchief balled in it, unsteadily rose. "Go ahead, Teresa," Mr. Prosser said encouragingly. She was a timid, clumsy girl whose mother was a Jehovah's Witness.

"It makes me think of cloud shadows," Teresa said.

Geoffrey Langer laughed. "Don't be rude, Geoff," Mr. Prosser said sideways, softly, before throwing his voice forward: "Thank you, Teresa. I think that's an interesting and valid impression. Cloud movement has something in it of the slow, monotonous rhythm one feels in the line 'Tomorrow, and tomorrow, and tomorrow.' It's a very gray line, isn't it, class?" No one agreed or disagreed.

Beyond the windows actual clouds were bunching rapidly, and erratic sections of sunlight slid around the room. Gloria's arm, crooked gracefully above her head, turned gold. "Gloria?" Mr. Prosser asked.

She looked up from something on her desk with a face of sullen radiance. "I think what Teresa said was very good," she said, glaring in the direction of Geoffrey Langer. Geoffrey chuckled defiantly. "And I have a question. What does 'petty pace' mean?"

"It means the trivial day-to-day sort of life that, say, a bookkeeper or a bank clerk leads. Or a schoolteacher," he added, smiling.

She did not smile back. Thought wrinkles irritated her perfect brow. "But Macbeth has been fighting wars, and killing kings, and being a king himself, and all," she pointed out.

"Yes, but it's just these acts Macbeth is condemning as 'nothing.' Can you see that?"

Gloria shook her head. "Another thing I worry about—isn't it silly for Macbeth to be talking to himself right in the middle of this war, with his wife just dead, and all?"

"I don't think so, Gloria. No matter how fast events happen, thought is faster."

His answer was weak; everyone knew it, even if Gloria hadn't mused, supposedly to herself, but in a voice the entire class could hear, "It seems so *stupid*."

Mark winced, pierced by the awful clarity with which his students saw him. Through their eyes, how queer he looked, with his long hands, and his horn-rimmed glasses, and his hair never slicked down, all wrapped up in "literature," where, when things get rough, the king mumbles a poem nobody understands. The delight Mr. Prosser took in such crazy junk made not only his good sense but his masculinity a matter of doubt. It was gentle of them not to laugh him out of the room. He looked down and rubbed his fingertips together, trying to erase the chalk dust. The class noise sifted into unnatural quiet. "It's getting late," he said finally. "Let's start the recitations of the memorized passage. Bernard Amilson, you begin."

Bernard had trouble enunciating, and his rendition began " 'T'mau 'n' t'mau 'n' t'mau.' " It was reassuring, the extent to which the class tried to repress its laughter. Mr. Prosser wrote "A" in his marking book opposite Bernard's name. He always gave Bernard A on recitations, despite the school nurse, who claimed there was nothing organically wrong with the boy's mouth.

It was the custom, cruel but traditional, to deliver recitations from the front of the room. Alice, when her turn came, was reduced to a helpless state by the first funny face Peter Forrester made at her. Mark let her hang up there a good minute while her face ripened to cherry redness, and at last forgave her. She may try it later. Many of the youngsters knew the passage gratifyingly well, though there was a tendency to leave out the line "To the last syllable of recorded time" and to turn "struts and frets" into "frets and struts" or simply "struts and struts." Even Sejak, who couldn't have looked at the passage before he came to class, got through it as far as "And then is heard no more."

Geoffrey Langer showed off, as he always did, by interrupting his own recitation with bright questions. " 'Tomorrow, and tomorrow, and tomorrow,' " he said, " 'creeps in'—shouldn't that be '*creep* in,' Mr. Prosser?"

"It is 'creeps.' The trio is in effect singular. Go on." Mr. Prosser was tired of coddling Langer. If you let them, these smart students will run away with the class. "Without the footnotes."

" 'Creep*sss* in this petty pace from day to day, to the last syllable of recorded time, and all our yesterdays have lighted fools the way to dusty death. Out, out—' "

"No, no!" Mr. Prosser jumped out of his chair. "This is poetry. Don't mushmouth it! Pause a little after 'fools.' " Geoffrey looked genuinely startled this time, and Mark himself did not quite understand his annoyance and, mentally turning to see what was behind him, seemed to glimpse in the humid undergrowth the two stern eyes of the indignant look Gloria had thrown Geoffrey. He glimpsed himself in the absurd position

of acting as Gloria's champion in her private war with this intelligent boy. He sighed apologetically. "Poetry is made up of lines," he began, turning to the class. Gloria was passing a note to Peter Forrester.

The rudeness of it! To pass notes during a scolding that she herself had caused! Mark caged in his hand the girl's frail wrist and ripped the note from her fingers. He read it to himself, letting the class see he was reading it, though he despised such methods of discipline. The note went:

> Pete— I think you're *wrong* about Mr. Prosser. I think he's wonderful and I get a lot out of his class. He's heavenly with poetry. I think I love him. I really do *love* him. So there.

Mr. Prosser folded the note once and slipped it into his side coat pocket. "See me after class, Gloria," he said. Then, to Geoffrey, "Let's try it again. Begin at the beginning."

While the boy was reciting the passage, the buzzer sounded the end of the period. It was the last class of the day. The room quickly emptied, except for Gloria. The noise of lockers slamming open and books being thrown against metal and shouts drifted in.

"Who has a car?"

"Lend me a cig, pig."

"We can't have practice in this slop."

Mark hadn't noticed exactly when the rain started, but it was coming down fast now. He moved around the room with the window pole, closing windows and pulling down shades. Spray bounced in on his hands. He began to talk to Gloria in a crisp voice that, like his device of shutting the windows, was intended to protect them both from embarrassment.

"About note passing." She sat motionless at her desk in the front of the room, her short, brushed-up hair like a cool torch. From the way she sat, her naked arms folded at her breasts and her shoulders hunched, he felt she was chilly. "It is not only rude to scribble when a teacher is talking, it is stupid to put one's words down on paper, where they look much more foolish than they might have sounded if spoken." He leaned the window pole in its corner and walked toward his desk.

"And about love. 'Love' is one of those words that illustrate what happens to an old, overworked language. These days, with movie stars and crooners and preachers and psychiatrists all pronouncing the word, it's come to mean nothing but a vague fondness for something. In this sense, I love the rain, this blackboard, these desks, you. It means nothing, you see, whereas once the word signified a quite explicit thing—a desire to share all you own and are with someone else. It is time we coined a new word to mean that, and when you think up the word *you* want to use, I suggest that you be economical with it. Treat it as something you can spend only once—if not for your own sake, for the good of the language." He walked over to his own desk and dropped two pencils on it, as if to say, "That's all."

"I'm sorry," Gloria said.

Rather surprised, Mr. Prosser said, "Don't be."

"But you don't understand."

"Of course I don't. I probably never did. At your age, I was like Geoffrey Langer."

"I bet you weren't." The girl was almost crying; he was sure of that.

"Come on, Gloria. Run along. Forget it." She slowly cradled her books between her bare arm and her sweater, and left the room with that melancholy shuffling teen-age gait, so that her body above her thighs seemed to float over the desks.

What was it, Mark asked himself, these kids were after? What did they want? Glide, he decided, the quality of glide. To slip along, always in rhythm, always cool, the little wheels humming under you, going nowhere special. If Heaven existed, that's the way it would be there. "He's heavenly with poetry." They loved the word. Heaven was in half their songs.

"Christ, he's humming." Strunk, the physical ed teacher, had come into the room without Mark's noticing. Gloria had left the door ajar.

"Ah," Mark said, "a fallen angel, full of grit."

"What the hell makes you so happy?"

"I'm not happy, I'm just serene. I don't know why you don't appreciate me."

"Say." Strunk came up an aisle with a disagreeably effeminate waddle, pregnant with gossip. "Did you hear about Murchison?"

"No." Mark mimicked Strunk's whisper.

"He got the pants kidded off him today."

"Oh dear."

Strunk started to laugh, as he always did before beginning a story. "You know what a goddam lady's man he thinks he is?"

"You bet," Mark said, although Strunk said that about every male member of the faculty.

"You have Gloria Angstrom, don't you?"

"You bet."

"Well, this morning Murky intercepts a note she was writing, and the note says what a damn neat guy she thinks Murchison is and how she *loves* him!" Strunk waited for Mark to say something, and then, when he didn't, continued, "You could see he was tickled pink. But—get this—it turns out at lunch that the same damn thing happened to Fryeburg in history yesterday!" Strunk laughed and cracked his knuckles viciously. "The girl's too dumb to have thought it up herself. We all think it was Peter Forrester's idea."

"Probably was," Mark agreed. Strunk followed him out to his locker, describing Murchison's expression when Fryeburg (in all innocence, mind you) told what had happened to him.

Mark turned the combination of his locker, 18–24–3. "Would you excuse me, Dave?" he said. "My wife's in town waiting."

Strunk was too thick to catch Mark's anger. "I got to get over to the gym. Can't take the little darlings outside in the rain; their mommies'll write notes to teacher." He clattered down the hall and wheeled at the far end, shouting, "Now don't tell You-know-who!"

Mr. Prosser took his coat from the locker and shrugged it on. He placed his hat upon his head. He fitted his rubbers over his shoes, pinching his fingers painfully, and lifted his umbrella off the hook. He thought of opening it right there in the vacant hall, as a kind of joke, and decided not to. The girl had been almost crying; he was sure of that.

DADDY WOLF
James Purdy (b. 1923)

You aren't the first man to ask me what I am doing so long in the phone booth with the door to my flat open and all. Let me explain something, or if you want to use the phone, I'll step out for a minute, but I am trying to get Operator to re-connect me with a party she just cut me off from. If you're not in a big hurry would you let me just try to get my party again.

See I been home 2 days now just looking at them 2 or 3 holes in the linoleum in my flat, and those holes are so goddam big now —you can go in there and take a look—those holes are so goddam big that I bet my kid, if he was still here, could almost put his leg through the biggest one.

Maybe of course the rats don't use the linoleum holes as entrances or exits. They could come through the calcimine in the wall. But I kind of guess and I bet the super for once would back me up on this, the rats are using the linoleum holes. Otherwise what is the meaning of the little black specks in and near each hole in the linoleum. I don't see how you could ignore the black specks there. If they were using the wall holes you would expect black specks there, but I haven't found a single one.

The party I was just talking to on the phone when I got cut off was surprised when I told her how the other night after my wife and kid left me I came in to find myself staring right head-on at a fat, I guess a Mama rat, eating some of my uncooked cream of wheat. I was so took by surprise that I did not see which way she went out. She ran, is all I can say, the minute I come into the room.

I had no more snapped back from seeing the Mama rat when a teeny baby one run right between my legs and disappeared ditto.

I just stood looking at my uncooked cream of wheat knowing I would have to let it go to waste.

It was too late that evening to call the super or anybody and I know from a lot of sad experience how sympathetic he would be, for the rats, to quote him, is a *un-avoidable probability* for whatever party decides to rent one of these you-know-what linoleum apartments.

If you want something better than some old you-know-what linoleum-floor apartments, the super says, *you got the map of Newyorkcity to hunt with.*

Rats and linoleum go together, and when you bellyache about rats, remember you're living on linoleum.

I always have to go to the hall phone when I get in one of these states, but tonight instead of calling the super who has gone off by now anyhow to his night job (he holds down 2 jobs on account of, he says, the high cost of chicken and peas), I took the name of the first party my finger fell on in the telephone book.

This lady answered the wire.

I explained to her the state I was in, and that I was over in one of the linoleum apartments and my wife and kid left me.

She cleared her throat and so on.

Even for a veteran, I told her, this is rough.

She kind of nodded over the phone in her manner.

I could feel she was sort of half-friendly, and I told her how I had picked her name out from all the others in the telephone book.

It was rough enough, I explained to her, to be renting an apartment in the linoleum district and to not know nobody in Newyorkcity, and then only the other night after my wife and kid left me this Mama rat was in here eating my uncooked cream of wheat, and before I get over this, her offspring run right between my legs.

This lady on the wire seemed to say *I see* every so often but I couldn't be sure on account of I was talking so fast myself.

I would have called the super of the building, I explained to her, in an emergency like this, but he has 2 jobs, and as it is after midnight now he is on his night job. But it would be just as bad in the daytime as then usually he is out inspecting the other linoleum apartments or catching up on his beauty sleep and don't answer the door or phone.

When I first moved into this building, I told her, I had to pinch myself to be sure I was actually seeing it right. I seen all the dirt before I moved in, but once I was in, I really SEEN: all the traces of the ones who had been here before, people who had died or lost their jobs or found they was the wrong race or something and had had to vacate all of a sudden before they could clean the place up for the next tenant. A lot of them left in such a hurry they just give you a present of some of their belongings and underwear along with their dirt. But then after one party left in such a hurry, somebody else from somewhere moved in, found he could not make it in Newyorkcity, and lit out somewhere or maybe was taken to a hospital in a serious condition and never returned.

I moved in just like the others on the linoleum.

Wish you could have seen it then. Holes everywhere and that most jagged of the holes I can see clear over here from the phone booth is where the Mama rat come through, which seems now about 3,000 years ago to me.

I told the lady on the phone how polite she was to go on listening and I hoped I was not keeping her up beyond her bedtime or from having a nightcap before she did turn in.

I don't object to animals, see. If it had been a Mama bird, say, which had come out of the hole, I would have had a start, too, as a Mama bird seldom is about and around at that hour, not to mention it not nesting in a linoleum hole, but I think I feel the way I do just because you think of rats along with neglect and lonesomeness and not having nobody near or around you.

See my wife left me and took our kid with her. They could not take any more of Newyorkcity. My wife was very scared of disease, and she had heard the radio in a shoe-repair store telling that they were going to raise the V.D. rate, and she said to me just a few hours before she left, *I don't think I am going to stay on here, Benny, if they are going to have one of them health epidemics.* She didn't have a disease, but she felt she would if the city officials were bent on raising the V.D. rate. She said it would be her luck and she would be no exception to prove the rule. She packed and left with the kid.

Did I feel sunk with them gone, but Jesus it was all I could do to keep on here myself. A good number of times at night I did not share my cream of wheat with them. I told them to prepare what kind of food they had a yen for and let me eat my cream of wheat alone with a piece of warmed-over oleo and just a sprinkle of brown sugar on that.

My wife and kid would stand and watch me eat the cream of wheat, but they was entirely indifferent to food. I think it was partly due to the holes in the linoleum, and them knowing what was under the holes of course.

We have only the one chair in the flat, and so my kid never had any place to sit when I was to home.

I couldn't help telling this party on the phone then about my wife and DADDY WOLF.

I was the one who told my wife about DADDY WOLF and the TROUBLE PHONE in the first place, but at first she said she didn't want any old charity no matter if it was money or advice or just encouraging words.

Then when things got so rough, my wife did call DADDY WOLF. I think the number is CRack 8-7869 or something like that, and only ladies can call. You phone this number and say *Daddy Wolf, I am a lady in terrible trouble. I am in one of the linoleum apartments, and just don't feel I can go on another day. Mama rats are coming in and out of their holes with their babies, and all we have had to eat in a month is cream of wheat.*

DADDY WOLF would say he was listening and to go on, and then he would ask her if she was employed anywhere.

DADDY WOLF, *yes and no. I just do not seem to have the willpower to go out job-hunting any more or on these house-to-house canvassing jobs that I have been holding down lately, and if you could see this linoleum flat, I think you would agree,* DADDY WOLF, *that there is very little incentive for me and Benny.*

Then my wife would go on about how surprised we had both been, though she was the only one surprised, over the high rate of V.D. in Newyorkcity.

You see, DADDY WOLF, *I won't hold a thing back, I have been about with older men in order to tide my husband over this rough financial situation we're in. My husband works in the mitten factory, and he just is not making enough for the three of us to live on. He has to have his cream of wheat at night or he would not have the strength to go back to his day-shift, and our linoleum apartment costs 30 smackers a week.*

I leave the kid alone here and go out to try and find work, DADDY WOLF, *but I'm telling you, the only job I can find for a woman of my education and background is this house-to-house canvassing of Queen Bee royal jelly which makes older women look so much more appealing, but I hardly sell more than a single jar a day and am on my feet 12 hours at a stretch.*

The kid is glad when I go out to sell as *he can have the chair to himself then. You see when I and his Daddy are home he either has to sit down on my lap, if I am sitting, or if his Daddy is sitting, just stand because I won't allow a little fellow like him to sit on that linoleum, it's not safe, and his Daddy will not let him sit on his lap because he is too dead-tired from the mitten factory.*

That was the way she explained to DADDY WOLF on the TROUBLE PHONE, and that went on every night, night after night, until she left me.

DADDY WOLF always listened, I will give him credit for that. He advised Mabel too: *go to Sunday school and church and quit going up to strange men's hotel rooms. Devote yourself only to your husband's need, and you don't ever have to fear the rise in the V.D. rate.*

My wife, though, could just not take Newyorkcity. She was out selling that Queen Bee royal jelly every day, but when cold weather come she had only a thin coat and she went out less and less and that all added up to less cream of wheat for me in the evening.

It is funny thing about cream of wheat, you don't get tired of it. I think if I ate, say, hamburger and chop suey every night, I would get sick and tired of them. Not that I ever dine on them. But if I did, I would—get sick and tired, I mean. But there's something about cream of wheat, with just a daub of warm oleo on it, and a sprinkle of brown sugar that makes you feel you might be eatin' it for the first time.

My wife don't care for cream of wheat nearly so much as I do.

Our kid always ate with the old gentleman down the hall with the skullcap. He rung a bell when it was supper time, and the kid went down there and had his meal. Once in a while, he brought back something or other for us.

It's funny talking to you like this, Mister, and as I told this lady I am waiting to get reconnected with on the phone, if I didn't know any better I would think either one of you was DADDY WOLF on the TROUBLE PHONE.

Well, Mabel left me, then, and took the kid with her.

It was her silly fear of the V.D. rate that really made her light out. She could have stayed here indefinitely. She loved this here city at first. She was just crazy about Central Park.

Newyorkcity was just the place for me to find work in. I had a good job with the Singer sewing-machine people in one of their spareparts rooms, then I got laid off and was without a thing for over 6 months and then was lucky to find this job at the mitten factory. I raise the lever that sews the inner lining to your mittens.

I don't think it is Mabel and the kid leaving me so much sometimes as it is the idea of that Mama rat coming through the holes in the linoleum that has got me so down-in-the-dumps today. I didn't even go to the mitten factory this A.M., and I have, like I say, got so down-in-the-dumps I almost felt like calling DADDY WOLF myself on the TROUBLE PHONE like she did all the time. But knowing he won't talk to nobody but ladies, as a kind of next-best-thing I put my finger down haphazard on top of this lady's name in the phone book, and I sure appreciated having that talk with her.

See DADDY WOLF would only talk with my wife for about one and a half minutes on account of other women were waiting to tell him their troubles. He would always say *Go back to your affiliation with the Sunday school and church of your choice, Mabel, and you'll find your burdens lighter in no time.*

DADDY said the same thing to her every night, but she never got tired hearing it, I guess.

DADDY WOLF told Mabel she didn't have to have any fear at all of the V.D. rate on account of she was a married woman and therefore did not have to go out for that relationship, but if she ever felt that DESIRE coming over her when her husband was gone,

to just sit quiet and read an uplifting book.

Mabel has not had time, I don't think, to write me yet, taking care of the kid and all, and getting settled back home, and I have, well, been so goddam worried about everything. They are talking now about a shut-down at the mitten factory so that I hardly as a matter of fact have had time to think about my wife and kid, let alone miss them. There is, as a matter of fact, more cream of wheat now for supper, and I splurged today and bought a 5-pound box of that soft brown sugar that don't turn to lumps, which I wouldn't ever have done if they was still here.

The old gent down the hall with the skull-cap misses my kid, as he almost entirely kept the boy in eats.

He never speaks to me in the hall, the old man. They said, I heard this somewhere, he don't have linoleum on his floor, but carpets, but I have not been invited in to see.

This building was condemned two years ago, but still isn't torn down, and the old man is leaving as soon as he can find the right neighborhood for his married daughter to visit him in.

Wait a minute. No, I thought I seen some action from under that one hole there in the linoleum.

Excuse me if I have kept you from using the phone with my talk but all I can say is you and this lady on the phone have been better for me tonight than DADDY WOLF on the TROUBLE PHONE ever was for my wife.

Up until now I have usually called the super when I was in one of these down-moods, but all he ever said was *Go back where you and Mabel got your own people and roots, Benny. You can't make it here in a linoleum apartment with your background and education.*

He has had his eyes opened—the super. He has admitted himself that he never thought Mabel and me could stick it out this long. (He don't know she is gone.)

But I won't give up. I WILL NOT give

up. Mabel let a thing like the hike in the V.D. rates chase her out. I tried to show her that that was just statistics, but she always was superstitious as all get-out.

I judge when this scare I've had about the Mama rat dies down and I get some sleep and tomorrow if I go back to the mitten factory I will then really and truly begin to miss Mabel and the kid. The old man down the hall already misses the kid. That kid ate more in one meal with him than Mabel and me eat the whole week together. I don't begrudge it to him, though, because he was growing.

Well, Mister, if you don't want to use the phone after all, I think I will try to have Operator re-connect me with that party I got disconnected from. I guess as this is the hour that Mabel always called DADDY WOLF I have just automatically caught her habit, and anyhow I sure felt in the need of a talk.

Do you hear that funny clicking sound? Here, I'll hold you the receiver so as you can hear it. Don't go away just yet: I think Operator is getting me that party again, so stick around awhile yet.

No, they cut us off again, hear? there is a bad connection or something.

Well, like I say, anyhow Mabel and the kid did get out of here, even if it was superstition. Christ, when I was a boy I had every one of those diseases and it never did me no hurt. I went right into the army with a clean bill of health, Korea, home again, and now Newyorkcity.

You can't bullshit me with a lot of statistics.

Mabel, though, goddam it, I could knock the teeth down her throat, running out on me like this and taking the kid.

WHERE IS THAT GODDAM OPERATOR?

Hello. Look, Operator, what number was that I dialed and talked so long. Reconnect me please. That number I just got through talking with so long. I don't know the party's name or number. Just connect me back, will you please. This here is an emergency phone call, Operator.

TWO PILGRIMS
Peter Taylor (b. 1917)

We were on our way from Memphis to a small town in northern Alabama, where my uncle, who was a cotton broker, had a lawsuit that he hoped could be settled out of court. Mr. Lowder, my uncle's old friend and lawyer, was traveling with him. I had just turned seventeen, and I had been engaged to come along in the capacity of chauffeur. I sat alone in the front seat of the car. The two men didn't discuss the lawsuit along the way, as I would have expected them to do. I don't know to this day exactly what was involved, or even whether or not Mr. Lowder managed to settle the matter on that trip. From the time we left the outskirts of Memphis, the two men talked instead about how good the bird hunting used to be there in our section of the country. During the two hours while we were riding through the big cotton counties of West Tennessee, they talked of almost nothing but bird dogs and field trials, interrupting themselves only when we passed through some little town or settlement to speak of the fine people they knew who had once lived there. We went through Collierville, La Grange, Grand Junction, Saulsbury. At La Grange, my uncle pointed out a house with a neo-classic portico and said he had once had a breakfast there that lasted three hours. At Saulsbury, Mr. Lowder commented that it somehow did his soul good to see the name spelled that way. Though it was November, not all the trees had lost their leaves yet. There was even some color still—dull pinks and yellows mixed with reddish browns—and under a bright, limitless sky the trees and the broad fields of grayish cotton stalks, looking almost lavender in places, gave a kind of faded-tapestry effect.

After we crossed the Tennessee River at Savannah, the country changed. And it was as if the new kind of country we had got into depressed the two men. But it may have been only the weather, because the weather changed, too, after we crossed the river. The sky became overcast, and everything seemed rather closed in. Soon there was intermittent rain of a light, misty sort. I kept switching my windshield wiper on and off, until presently my uncle asked me in a querulous tone why I didn't just let the thing run. For thirty or forty miles, the two men had little to say to each other. Finally, as we were passing through a place called Waynesboro—a hard-looking hill town with a cement-block jail-house dominating the public square—my uncle said that this town was where General Winfield Scott had made one of his halts on the notorious Trail of Tears, when he was rounding up the Cherokees to move them west, in 1838. The two men spoke of what a cruel thing that had been, but they agreed that one must not judge the persons responsible too harshly, that one must judge them by the light of their times and remember what the early settlers had suffered at the hands of the Indians.

Not very long after we had left Waynesboro, Mr. Lowder remarked that we were approaching the old Natchez Trace section and that the original settlers there had been a mighty rough lot of people. My uncle added that from the very earliest days the whole area had been infested with outlaws and robbers and that even now it was said to be a pretty tough section. They sounded as though they were off to a good start; I thought the subject might last them at least until lunchtime. But just as this thought occurred to me, they were interrupted.

We came over the brow of one of the low-lying hills in that country of scrub oaks and pinewoods, and there before us—in a clearing down in the hollow ahead—was a house with smoke issuing from one window toward the rear and with little gray geysers rising at a half-dozen points on the black-shingled roof. It was an unpainted, one-story house set close to the ground and with two big stone end chimneys. All across the front was a kind of lean-to porch. There was an old log barn beyond the house. Despite my uncle's criticism, I had switched off the windshield wiper a mile or so up the road, and then I had had to switch it on again just as we came over the hill. Even with the wiper going, visibility was not very good, and my first thought was that only the misty rain in the air was keeping the roof of that house from blazing up. Mr. Lowder and my uncle were so engrossed in their talk that I think it was my switching the wiper on again that first attracted their attention. But instantly upon seeing the smoke, my uncle said, "Turn in down there!"

"But be careful how you slow down," Mr. Lowder warned. "This blacktop's slick." Already he and my uncle were perched on the edge of the back seat, and one of them had put a hand on my shoulder as if to steady me.

The little house was in such a clearing as must have been familiar to travelers in pioneer days. There were stumps everywhere, even in the barn lot and among the cabbages in the garden. I suppose I particularly noticed the stumps because a good number were themselves smoldering and sending up occasional wisps of smoke. Apparently, the farmer had been trying to rid himself of the stumps in the old-fashioned way. There was no connection between these fires and the one at the house, but the infernal effect of the whole scene was inescapable. One felt that the entire area within the dark ring of pinewoods might at any moment burst into flame.

I turned the car off the macadam pavement, and we bumped along some two hundred feet, following wagon ruts that led more toward the barn than toward the house. The wide barn door stood open, and I could see the figure of a man inside herding a couple of animals through a door at the other end, where the barn lot was. Then I heard Mr. Lowder and my uncle open the back doors of the car. While the car was still moving, they leaped out onto the ground. They both were big men, more than six feet tall and with sizable stomachs that began just below the breastbone, but they sprinted off in the direction of the house. As they ran, I saw them hurriedly putting on their black gloves. Next, they began stripping off their topcoats. By the time I had stopped the car and got out, they had pulled their coats over their heads, and I realized then that each had tossed his hat onto the back seat before leaping from the car. Looking like a couple of hooded night riders, they were now mounting the shallow porch steps. It was just as they gained the porch that I saw the woman appear from around the far side of the house. At the sight of the hooded and begloved men on her porch—the porch of her burning house—the woman threw one hand to her forehead and gave such an alarmed and alarming cry that I felt something turn over inside me. Even the two intruders halted for an instant on the porch and looked at her.

I thought at first glance that she was an old woman, she was so stooped. Then something told me—I think it was the plaintive sounds she was making—that she was more young than old. After her first outcry, she continued a kind of girlish wailing, which, it seemed to me, expressed a good deal more than mere emotional shock. The noises she made seemed to say that all this *couldn't* be happening to *her*. Not hooded bandits added to a house-burning! It wasn't right; life *couldn't* be so hard, *couldn't* be as evil as this; it was more than she should be asked to bear!

"Anybody inside, Miss?" my uncle called out to the girl.

She began shaking her head frantically.

"Well, we'll fetch out whatever we can!" he called. Glancing back at me—I was trying to make a hood of my own topcoat and preparing to join them—my uncle shouted, "Don't you come inside! Stay with that girl! And calm her down!" With that, he followed Mr. Lowder through the doorway and into the house.

Presently, they were hurling bedclothes and homemade-looking stools and chairs through the side windows. Then one or the other of them would come dashing out across the porch and into the yard, deposit on the ground a big pitcher and washbasin or a blurry old mirror with a carved wooden frame, and then dash back inside again. Now and then when one of them brought something out, he would pause for just the briefest moment, not to rest but to examine the rescued object before he put it down. It was comical to see the interest they took in the old things they brought out of that burning house.

When I came up to where the woman was standing, she seemed to have recovered completely from her first fright. She looked at me a little shamefacedly, I thought. Her deep-socketed eyes were almost freakishly large. And I noticed at once that they were of two different colors. One was a mottled brown, the other a gray-green. When finally she spoke, she turned her eyes away and toward the house. "Who are you-all?" she asked.

"We were just passing by," I said.

She looked at me and then turned away again. I felt she was skeptical, that she suspected we had been sent by someone. Each time she directed her eyes at me, I read deceit or guilt or suspicion in them.

"Where you coming from?" she asked in an idle tone, craning her neck to see what some object was that had come flying out the window. She seemed abundantly calm now. Without answering her question, I yanked my coat over my head and ran off toward the house. My uncle met me on the porch steps. He handed me a dresser drawer he was carrying, not failing to give the contents a quick inventory. Then he gave me a rather heavy punch on the chest. "*You* stay out there and keep that girl calm," he said. "You hear what I say! She's apt to go to pieces any minute."

The woman was taking a livelier interest in matters now. I set the drawer on a stump, and when I looked up, she peered over me to see which drawer it was I had brought and what extra odds and ends my uncle might have swept into it. On top lay a rusty fire poker and a couple of small picture frames with the glass so smashed up you couldn't make out the pictures. Underneath, there was a jumble of old cloth scraps and paper dress patterns and packages of garden seeds. Seeing all this, the woman opened her mouth and smiled vacantly, perhaps a little contemptuously. She was so close to me that I became aware of the sweetness of her breath! I could not have imagined that her breath would be sweet. Though the skin on her forehead and on her high cheekbones was clear and very fair, there were ugly pimples on her chin and at the corners of her mouth. Her dark hair was wet from the drizzle of rain and was pushed behind her ears and hung in clumps over the collar of her soiled denim jacket. She was breathing heavily through her parted lips. Presently, when our eyes met, I thought I detected a certain momentary gleefulness in her expression. But her glance darted back toward the house at once.

The two men had pressed on beyond the front rooms and into the ell of the house. Now the woman took a couple of steps in order to look through one of the front windows and perhaps catch a glimpse of them back there.

"We were coming from Memphis," I said. "We're *from* Memphis." But she seemed no longer interested in that subject.

"It's no use what they're doing," she said. "Unless they like it."

"It's all right," I said, still hoping to distract her. "We're on our way to a place in Alabama."

"They your bosses?" she asked. She couldn't take her eyes off the window.

"No, it's my uncle and his lawyer."

"Well, they're right active," she commented. "But there ain't nothing in there worth their bustle and bother. Yet some folks like to take chances. It's just the worst lot of junk in there. We heired this place from my grandma when she passed on last spring; the junk was all hern."

Just then, Mr. Lowder and my uncle came running from the house. Each of them was carrying a coal-oil lamp, his right hand supporting the base of the lamp and his left clamped protectively on the fragile chimney. I almost burst out laughing.

"It's gotten too hot in there," Mr. Lowder said. "We'll have to stop."

When they had set down their lamps, they began examining each other's coats, making sure they weren't on fire. Next, they tossed their coats on the bare ground and set about pulling some of the rescued articles farther from the house. I went forward to help, and the woman followed. She didn't follow to help, however. Apparently, she was only curious to see which of her possessions these men had deemed worth saving. She looked at everything she came to with almost a disappointed expression. Then Mr. Lowder picked up an enameled object, and I noticed that as he inspected it a deep frown appeared on his brow. He held the thing up for my uncle to see, and I imagined for a moment that he was trying to draw laughter from all of us. It was a child's chamber pot, not much larger than a beer mug. "Did you bring this out?" Mr. Lowder asked my uncle.

My uncle nodded, and, still bending over, he studied the pot for a second, showing that he had not really identified it before. Then he looked at the woman. "Where's your child, ma'am?" he asked in a quiet voice.

The woman gaped at him as though she didn't understand what he was talking about. She shifted her eyes to the tiny pot that Mr. Lowder was still holding aloft. Now her mouth dropped wide open, and at the same time her lips drew back in such a way that her bad teeth were exposed for the first time. It was impossible not to think of a death's-head. At that instant, the whole surface of the shingled roof on the side of the house where we were standing burst into flames.

A few minutes before this, the rain had ceased altogether, and now it was as though someone had suddenly doused the roof with kerosene. My back was to the house, but I heard a loud "swoosh" and I spun around in that direction. Then I heard the woman cry out and I spun back again. Mr. Lowder set the chamber pot on the ground and began moving rather cautiously toward her. My uncle stood motionless, watching her as though she were an animal that might bolt. As Mr. Lowder came toward her, she took a step backward, and then she wailed, "My baby! Oh, Lord, my baby! He's in thar!" Mr. Lowder seized her by the wrist and simultaneously gave us a quick glance over his shoulder.

My uncle snatched up a ragged homespun blanket from the ground and threw it over his head. I seized a patchwork quilt that had been underneath the blanket, and this time I followed him inside the house. Even in the two front rooms it was like a blast furnace, and I felt I might faint. The smoke was so dense that you couldn't see anything an arm's length away. But my uncle had been in those two front rooms and he knew there was no baby there. With me at his heels, he ran right on through and into the first room in the ell, where there wasn't so much smoke —only raw flames eating away at the wall toward the rear. The window lights had burst from the heat in there, and there was a hole in the ceiling, so that you could look right up through the flames to the sky. But my eyes were smarting so that I couldn't really see anything in the room, and I was coughing so hard that I couldn't stand up straight. My uncle was coughing, too, but he could still manage to look about. He made two complete turns around the room and then he headed us on into the kitchen. There wasn't anything recognizable to me in the kitchen except the black range. One of the two window frames fell in as we ran through. The next instant, after we had leaped across the burning floorboards and had jumped off the back stoop of the house, the rafters and the whole roof above the kitchen came down.

There must have been a tremendous crash, though I hardly heard it. Even before my uncle and I could shed our smoldering blankets, we saw the man coming toward us from the barn. "You're afire!" he called out to us. But we had already dropped the blankets before I understood what he was saying. He was jogging along toward us. One of his legs was shorter than the other, and he couldn't move very fast. Under one arm he was carrying a little towheaded child of not more than two years. He held it exactly as though it might be a sack of corn meal he was bringing up from the barn.

"Do you have another baby?" my uncle shouted at him.

"No, narry other," the man replied.

My uncle looked at me. He was coughing still, but at the same time he was smiling and shaking his head. "You all right?" he asked me. He gave my clothes a quick once-over, and I did the same for him. We had somehow got through the house without any damage, even to our shoes or our trouser legs.

By the time the man came up to the house, my uncle had dashed off to tell the woman her baby was safe. I tried to explain to the man about the mistake his wife had made. "Your wife thought your baby was in the house," I said.

He was a stocky, black-haired man, wearing overalls and a long-sleeved undershirt. "She *whut?*" he said, looking at me darkly. He glanced up briefly at the flames, which were now leaping twenty or thirty feet above the framework of the kitchen. Then he set out again, in the same jogging pace, toward the front of the house. I caught a glimpse of the baby's intense blue eyes gazing up at the smoke and flames.

"She thought the baby was inside the house," I said, following the man at a trot.

"Like hell she did!" he said under his breath but loud enough for me to hear.

As we rounded the corner of the house, I heard my uncle call out to the woman that her baby was safe. She was seated on a stump with her face hidden in her hands. My uncle and Mr. Lowder once again began pulling rescued objects farther away from the house.

As the man passed him, Mr. Lowder looked up and said, "Did you get all the stock out?"

"Yup," said the man.

"I guess you're lucky there's no wind," Mr. Lowder said.

And my uncle said, "It must have started in the kitchen and spread through the attic. You didn't have any water drawn?"

The man stopped for a second and looked at my uncle. He shifted the baby from one hip to the other. "The pump's broke," he said. "It was about wore out, and *she* broke it for good this morning."

"Isn't that the way it goes," my uncle said sympathetically, shaking his head.

Then, still carrying the baby, the man shuffled on toward his wife. The woman kept her face hidden in her hands, but I think she heard him coming. Neither of them seemed to have any awareness that their house and most of their possessions were at that moment going up in flames. I was watching the man when he got to her. He still had the baby under his arm. I saw him draw back his free hand, and saw the hand come down in a resounding slap on the back of her head. It knocked her right off the stump. She hit the ground in a sitting position and still she didn't look up at her husband. "J'you aim to git them fellows burned alive?" he thundered.

Mr. Lowder and my uncle must have been watching, too, because we all three ran forward at the same moment. "Lay off that!" Mr. Lowder bellowed. "Just lay off, now!"

"She knowed this here young'un warn't in no house!" the man said, twisting the baby to his shoulder. "I reckoned she'd like as not lose her head. That's how come I carried him with me, and I told her plain as daylight I was a-goin' to."

"Now, you look here, mister," my uncle said, "the girl was just scared. She didn't know what she was saying."

"Probably she couldn't remember, in her fright," Mr. Lowder said.

The man stood staring down at his wife. "She's feared of her own shadow, and that's how come I carried him to the barn."

"Well, you're not going to beat her with us here," Mr. Lowder said firmly. "She was scared out of her wits, that's all."

"Who sent y' all out here?" the man asked my uncle, turning his back on Mr. Lowder. "Ain't they goan send no fire engine?"

It was as he spoke the word that we heard the fire truck coming. The whine of the siren must have first reached us from a point three or four miles distant, because at least five minutes elapsed before the fire truck and the two carloads of volunteers arrived. It turned out that somebody else had stopped by before we did and had hurried on to the next town to give the alarm. I thought it strange that the woman hadn't told us earlier that they were expecting help from town. But, of course, there was little about the woman's behavior that didn't seem passing strange to me.

As soon as we heard the siren, she began pushing herself up from the ground. Without a glance at any of the rest of us, she went directly to her husband and snatched the baby from him. The baby's little face was dirty, and there were wide streaks on it, where some while earlier there must have been a flow of tears. But his eyes were dry now and wore a glazed look. He seemed to stare up at the flaming house with total indifference. Almost as soon as he was in his mother's arms, he placed his chin on the shoulder of her denim jacket and quietly closed his eyes. He seemed to have fallen asleep at once. With her baby in her arms, the woman strode away into the adjoining field, among the smoking stumps and toward the edge of the pinewoods. There she stopped, at the edge of the woods, and there she remained standing, with her back turned toward the house and toward us and toward all the activity that ensued after the fire truck and the other cars arrived. She was still standing there, with the baby on her shoulder, when we left the scene.

We stayed on for only a few minutes after the local fire brigade arrived. Mr. Lowder and my uncle could see that their work here was done and they were mindful of the pressing business that they hoped to transact in Alabama that afternoon. We lingered just long enough to see most of the articles they had rescued from the flames thoroughly soaked with water. The sight must have been disheartening to them, but they didn't speak of it. The inexpert firemen couldn't control the pressure from their tank, and whenever there came a great spurt of water they lost their grip on the hose. They seemed bound to spray everything but the burning house. We withdrew a little way in the direction of our car and joined a small group of spectators who had now come on the scene.

I didn't tell my uncle or Mr. Lowder what I was thinking during the time that we stood there with the local people who had gathered. I could still see the woman down in the field, and I wondered if my uncle or Mr. Lowder were not going to tell some local person how suspicious her behavior had been —and her husband's, too, for that matter. Surely there was some mystery, I said to myself, some questions that ought to be answered or asked. But no question of any kind seemed to arise in the minds of my two companions. It was as if such a fire were an everyday occurrence in their lives and as if they lived always among such queer people as that afflicted poor-white farmer and his simple wife.

Once we had got back into the car and were on our way again, I was baffled by the quiet good humor—and even serenity—of those two men I was traveling with. The moment they had resettled themselves on the back seat of the car, after giving their overcoats a few final brushings and after placing their wide-brimmed fedoras firmly on their heads again, they began chatting together with the greatest ease and nonchalance. I could not see their faces; I had to keep my eyes on the road. But I listened and presently I heard my uncle launch upon a reminiscence. "I did the damndest thing once," he said. "It was when I was a boy of just eight or nine. The family have kidded me about it all my life. One morning after I had been up to mischief of some kind, Father took me into

the kitchen and gave me a switching on my legs with a little shoot he had broken off the privet hedge. When I came outside again, I was still yowling, and the other children who were playing there in the house lot commenced guying me about it. All at once, I burst out at them: 'You'd cry, too, if he beat *you* with the shovel handle!' I hadn't aimed to say it; I just said it. My brothers kid me about it to this day."

"Yes," said Mr. Lowder. "It's like that —the things a person will say." He liked my uncle's story immensely. He said it sounded so true. As he spoke, I could hear one of them striking a match. It wasn't long before I caught the first whiff of cigar smoke. Then another match was struck. They were both smoking now. Pretty soon their conversation moved on to other random topics.

Within the next half hour, we got out of that hill country along the Tennessee River and entered the rich and beautiful section to the east of it, near the fine old towns of Pulaski and Fayetteville. I could not help remarking on the change to my uncle. "Seems good to have finally got out of that godforsaken-looking stretch back there," I said over my shoulder.

"How do you mean 'godforsaken'?" my uncle replied. I recognized a testiness in his tone, and his reply had come so quickly that I felt he had been waiting for me to say exactly what I had said.

"It's just ugly, that's all," I mumbled, hoping that would be the end of it.

But Mr. Lowder joined in the attack, using my uncle's tone. "I wouldn't say one kind of country's any better-looking than another—not really."

And then my uncle again: "To someone *your* age, it just depends on what kind of country—if any—you happen to be used to."

"Maybe so," said I, not wanting to say more but unable to stop myself. "Maybe so, but I could live for a hundred years in that scrubby-looking country without ever getting used to it."

No doubt the rolling pasture land on both sides of the highway now—still green in

November, and looking especially green after recent rain—caused me to put more feeling into my statement than I might otherwise have done. And it may also have had its effect on the two men in the back seat.

There was a brief pause, and then my uncle fired away again. "Every countryside has its own kind of beauty. It's up to you to learn to see it, that's all."

Then Mr. Lowder: "And if you don't see it, it's just your loss. Because it's *there*."

"Besides, a lot you know about that country," my uncle went on, in what seemed to me an even more captious spirit than before. "And how could you? How could you judge, flying along the highway at fifty miles an hour, flapping that damned wiper off and on?"

"More than that," said Mr. Lowder with renewed energy, "you would have to have seen that country thirty years ago to understand why it looks the way it does now. That was when they cut out the last of the old timber. I've heard it said that when the first white men came through that section it had the prettiest stand of timber on the continent!"

Suddenly I blurted out, "But what's that got to do with it?" I was so irritated that I could feel the blood rising in my cheeks and I knew that the back of my neck was already crimson. "It's how the country looks now I'm talking about. Anyway, I'm only here as your driver. I don't *have* to like the scenery, do I?"

Both men broke into laughter. It was a kind of laughter that expressed both apology and relief. My uncle bent forward, thumped me on the shoulder with his knuckle, and said, "Don't be so touchy, boy." Almost at once, they resumed their earlier dialogue. One of them lowered a window a little way to let out some of the smoke, but the aroma of their cigars continued to fill the car, and they spoke in the same slow cadences as before and in the same tranquil tone.

We reached the town in Alabama toward the middle of the afternoon and we spent the night in an old clapboard hotel on the courthouse square. After dinner that night, the two men sat in the lobby and talked to other men who were staying there in the hotel. I found myself a place near the stove and sat there with my feet on the fender, sometimes dozing off. But even when I was half asleep I was still listening to see whether, in their talk, either Mr. Lowder or my uncle would make any reference to our adventure that morning. Neither did. Instead, as the evening wore on they got separated and were sitting with two different groups of men, I heard them both repeating the very stories they had told in the car before we crossed the Tennessee River—stories about bird hunting and field trials and about my uncle's three-hour breakfast in the old house with the neo-classic portico.

THE LAGOON
Joseph Conrad (1857–1924)

The white man, leaning with both arms over the roof of the little house in the stern of the boat, said to the steersman:

"We will pass the night in Arsat's clearing. It is late."

The Malay only grunted, and went on looking fixedly at the river. The white man rested his chin on his crossed arms and gazed at the wake of the boat. At the end of the straight avenue of forests cut by the intense glitter of the river, the sun appeared unclouded and dazzling, poised low over the water that shone smoothly like a band of metal. The forests, somber and dull, stood motionless and silent on each side of the broad stream. At the foot of big, towering trees, trunkless nipa palms rose from the mud of the bank, in bunches of leaves enormous and heavy, that hung unstirring over the brown swirl of eddies. In the stillness of the air every tree, every leaf, every bough, every tendril of creeper and every petal of minute blossoms seemed to have been bewitched into an immobility perfect and final. Nothing moved on the river but the eight paddles that rose flashing regularly, dipped together with a single splash; while the steersman swept right and left with a periodic and sudden flourish of his blade describing a glinting semicircle above his head. The churned-up water frothed alongside with a confused murmur. And the white man's canoe, advancing upstream in the short-lived disturbance of its own making, seemed to enter the portals of a land from which the very memory of motion had forever departed.

The white man, turning his back upon the setting sun, looked along the empty and broad expanse of the sea-reach. For the last three miles of its course the wandering, hesitating river, as if enticed irresistibly by the freedom of an open horizon, flows straight into the sea, flows straight to the east—to the east that harbors both light and darkness. Astern of the boat the repeated call of some bird, a cry discordant and feeble, skipped along over the smooth water and lost itself, before it could reach the other shore, in the breathless silence of the world.

The steersman dug his paddle into the stream, and held hard with stiffened arms, his body thrown forward. The water gurgled aloud; and suddenly the long straight reach seemed to pivot on its center, the forests swung in a semicircle, and the slanting beams of sunset touched the broadside of the canoe with a fiery glow, throwing the slender and distorted shadows of its crew upon the streaked glitter of the river. The white man turned to look ahead. The course of the boat had been altered at right angles to the stream, and the carved dragon head of its prow was pointing now at a gap in the fringing bushes of the bank. It glided through, brushing the overhanging twigs, and disappeared from the river like some slim and amphibious creature leaving the water for its lair in the forests.

The narrow creek was like a ditch: tortuous, fabulously deep; filled with gloom under the thin strip of pure and shining blue of the heaven. Immense trees soared up, invisible behind the festooned draperies of creep-

ers. Here and there, near the glistening blackness of the water, a twisted root of some tall tree showed amongst the tracery of small ferns, black and dull, writhing and motionless, like an arrested snake. The short words of the paddlers reverberated loudly between the thick and somber walls of vegetation. Darkness oozed out from between the trees, through the tangled maze of the creepers, from behind the great fantastic and unstirring leaves; the darkness mysterious and invincible; the darkness scented and poisonous of impenetrable forests.

The men poled in the shoaling water. The creek broadened, opening out into a wide sweep of a stagnant lagoon. The forests receded from the marshy bank, leaving a level strip of bright green, reedy grass to frame the reflected blueness of the sky. A fleecy pink cloud drifted high above, trailing the delicate coloring of its image under the floating leaves and the silvery blossoms of the lotus. A little house, perched on high piles, appeared black in the distance. Near it, two tall nibong palms, that seemed to have come out of the forests in the background, leaned slightly over the ragged roof, with a suggestion of sad tenderness and care in the droop of their leafy and soaring heads.

The steersman, pointing with his paddle, said, "Arsat is there. I see his canoe fast between the piles."

The polers ran along the sides of the boat glancing over their shoulders at the end of the day's journey. They would have preferred to spend the night somewhere else than on this lagoon of weird aspect and ghostly reputation. Moreover, they disliked Arsat, first as a stranger, and also because he who repairs a ruined house, and dwells in it, proclaims that he is not afraid to live amongst the spirits that haunt the places abandoned by mankind. Such a man can disturb the course of fate by glances or words; while his familiar ghosts are not easy to propitiate by casual wayfarers upon whom they long to wreak the malice of their human master. White men care not for such things, being un-

believers and in league with the Father of
Evil, who leads them unharmed through the
invisible dangers of this world. To the warnings of the righteous they oppose an offensive
pretense of disbelief. What is there to be
done?

So they thought, throwing their weight
on the end of their long poles. The big
canoe glided on swiftly, noiselessly, and
smoothly, towards Arsat's clearing, till, in a
great rattling of poles thrown down, and the
loud murmurs of "Allah be praised!" it came
with a gentle knock against the crooked piles
below the house.

The boatmen with uplifted faces shouted discordantly, "Arsat! O Arsat!" Nobody
came. The white man began to climb the
rude ladder giving access to the bamboo platform before the house. The juragan of the
boat said sulkily, "We will cook in the sampan, and sleep on the water."

"Pass my blankets and the basket," said
the white man, curtly.

He knelt on the edge of the platform to
receive the bundle. Then the boat shoved
off, and the white man, standing up, confronted Arsat, who had come out through the low
door of his hut. He was a man young, powerful, with broad chest and muscular arms. He
had nothing on but his sarong. His head was
bare. His big, soft eyes stared eagerly at the
white man, but his voice and demeanor were
composed as he asked, without any words of
greeting:

"Have you medicine, Tuan?"

"No," said the visitor in a startled tone.
"No. Why? Is there sickness in the house?"

"Enter and see," replied Arsat, in the
same calm manner, and turning short round,
passed again through the small doorway.
The white man, dropping his bundles, followed.

In the dim light of the dwelling he
made out on a couch of bamboos a woman
stretched on her back under a broad sheet of
red cotton cloth. She lay still, as if dead; but
her big eyes, wide open, glittered in the
gloom, staring upwards at the slender rafters,
motionless and unseeing. She was in a high
fever, and evidently unconscious. Her cheeks
were sunk slightly, her lips were partly open,
and on the young face there was the ominous
and fixed expression—the absorbed, contemplating expression of the unconscious who
are going to die. The two men stood looking
down at her in silence.

"Has she been long ill?" asked the traveler.

"I have not slept for five nights," answered the Malay, in a deliberate tone. "At
first she heard voices calling her from the
water and struggled against me who held her.
But since the sun of today rose she hears nothing—she hears not me. She sees nothing. She
sees not me—ME!"

He remained silent for a minute, then
asked softly:

"Tuan, will she die?"

"I fear so," said the white man, sorrow-
fully. He had known Arsat years ago, in a
far country in times of trouble and danger,
when no friendship is to be despised. And
since his Malay friend had come unexpectedly to dwell in the hut on the lagoon with a
strange woman, he had slept many times
there, in his journeys up and down the river.
He liked the man who knew how to keep
faith in council and how to fight without fear
by the side of his white friend. He liked him
—not so much perhaps as a man likes his
favorite dog—but still he liked him well
enough to help and ask no questions, to think
sometimes vaguely and hazily in the midst of
his own pursuits, about the lonely man and
the long-haired woman with audacious face
and triumphant eyes, who lived together hidden by the forests—alone and feared.

The white man came out of the hut in
time to see the enormous conflagration of
sunset put out by the swift and stealthy shadows that, rising like a black and impalpable
vapor above the treetops, spread over the
heaven, extinguishing the crimson glow of
floating clouds and the red brilliance of de-

parting daylight. In a few moments all the stars came out above the intense blackness of the earth and the great lagoon gleaming suddenly with reflected lights resembled an oval patch of night sky flung down into the hopeless and abysmal night of the wilderness. The white man had some supper out of the basket, then collecting a few sticks that lay about the platform, made up a small fire, not for warmth, but for the sake of the smoke, which would keep off the mosquitoes. He wrapped himself in the blankets and sat with his back against the reed wall of the house, smoking thoughtfully.

Arsat came through the doorway with noiseless steps and squatted down by the fire. The white man moved his outstretched legs a little.

"She breathes," said Arsat in a low voice, anticipating the expected question. "She breathes and burns as if with a great fire. She speaks not; she hears not—and burns!"

He paused for a moment, then asked in a quiet, incurious tone:

"Tuan . . . will she die?"

The white man moved his shoulders uneasily and muttered in a hesitating manner:

"If such is her fate."

"No, Tuan," said Arsat, calmly. "If such is my fate. I hear, I see, I wait. I remember. . . . Tuan, do you remember the old days? Do you remember my brother?"

"Yes," said the white man. The Malay rose suddenly and went in. The other, sitting still outside, could hear the voice in the hut. Arsat said: "Hear me! Speak!" His words were succeeded by a complete silence. "O Diamelen!" he cried, suddenly. After that cry there was a deep sigh. Arsat came out and sank down again in his old place.

They sat in silence before the fire. There was no sound within the house, there was no sound near them; but far away on the lagoon they could hear the voices of the boatmen ringing fitful and distinct on the calm water. The fire in the bows of the sampan

shone faintly in the distance with a hazy red glow. Then it died out. The voices ceased. The land and the water slept invisible, unstirring and mute. It was as though there had been nothing left in the world but the glitter of stars streaming, ceaseless and vain through the black stillness of the night.

The white man gazed straight before him in the darkness with wide-open eyes. The fear and fascination, the inspiration and the wonder of death—of death near, unavoidable, and unseen, soothed the unrest of his race and stirred the most indistinct, the most intimate of his thoughts. The ever-ready suspicion of evil, the gnawing suspicion that lurks in our hearts, flowed out into the stillness round him—into the stillness profound and dumb, and made it appear untrustworthy and infamous, like the placid and impenetrable mask of an unjustifiable violence. In that fleeting and powerful disturbance of his being the earth enfolded in the starlight peace became a shadowy country of inhuman strife, a battlefield of phantoms terrible and charming, august or ignoble, struggling ardently for the possession of our helpless hearts. An unquiet and mysterious country of inextinguishable desires and fears.

A plaintive murmur rose in the night; a murmur saddening and startling, as if the great solitudes of surrounding woods had tried to whisper into his ear the wisdom of their immense and lofty indifference. Sounds hesitating and vague floated in the air round him, shaped themselves slowly into words; and at last flowed on gently in a murmuring stream of soft and monotonous sentences. He stirred like a man waking up and changed his position slightly. Arsat, motionless and shadowy, sitting with bowed head under the stars was speaking in a low and dreamy tone:

". . . for where can we lay down the heaviness of our trouble but in a friend's heart? A man must speak of war and of love. You, Tuan, know what war is, and you have seen me in time of danger seek death as other men seek life! A writing may be lost; a lie may be written; but what the eye has seen is truth and remains in the mind!"

"I remember," said the white man, quietly. Arsat went on with mournful composure:

"Therefore I shall speak to you of love. Speak in the night. Speak before both night and love are gone—and the eye of day looks upon my sorrow and my shame; upon my blackened face; upon my burnt-up heart."

A sigh, short and faint, marked an almost imperceptible pause, and then his words flowed on, without a stir, without a gesture.

"After the time of trouble and war was over and you went away from my country in the pursuit of your desires, which we, men of the islands, cannot understand, I and my brother became again, as we had been before, the sword bearers of the Ruler. You know we were men of family, belonging to a ruling race, and more fit than any to carry on our right shoulder the emblem of power. And in the time of prosperity Si Dendring showed us favor, as we, in time of sorrow, had showed to him the faithfulness of our courage. It was a time of peace. A time of deer hunts and cock fights; of idle talks and foolish squabbles between men whose bellies are full and weapons are rusty. But the sower watched the young rice shoots grow up without fear, and the traders came and went, departed lean and returned fat into the river of peace. They brought news, too. Brought lies and truth mixed together, so that no man knew when to rejoice and when to be sorry. We heard from them about you also. They had seen you here and had seen you there. And I was glad to hear, for I remembered the stirring times, and I always remembered you, Tuan, till the time came when my eyes could see nothing in the past, because they had looked upon the one who is dying there—in the house."

He stopped to exclaim in an intense whisper, "O Mara bahia! O Calamity!" then went on speaking a little louder:

"There's no worse enemy and no better friend than a brother, Tuan, for one brother knows another, and in perfect knowledge is strength for good or evil. I loved my brother. I went to him and told him that I could see nothing but one face, hear nothing but one voice. He told me: 'Open your heart so that she can see what is in it—and wait. Patience is wisdom. Inchi Midah may die or our Ruler may throw off his fear of a woman!' . . . I waited! . . . You remember the lady with the veiled face, Tuan, and the fear of our Ruler before her cunning and temper. And if she wanted her servant, what could I do? But I fed the hunger of my heart on short glances and stealthy words. I loitered on the path to the bathhouses in the daytime, and when the sun had fallen behind the forest I crept along the jasmine hedges of the women's courtyard. Unseeing, we spoke to one another through the scent of flowers, through the veil of leaves, through the blades of long grass that stood still before our lips; so great was our prudence, so faint was the murmur of our great longing. The time passed swiftly . . . and there were whispers amongst women—and our enemies watched—my brother was gloomy, and I began to think of killing and of a fierce death. . . . We are of a people who take what they want—like you whites. There is a time when a man should forget loyalty and respect. Might and authority are given to rulers, but to all men is given love and strength and courage. My brother said, 'You shall take her from their midst. We are two who are like one.' And I answered, 'Let it be soon, for I find no warmth in sunlight that does not shine upon her.' Our time came when the Ruler and all the great people went to the mouth of the river to fish by torchlight. There were hundreds of boats, and on the white sand, between the water and the forests, dwellings of leaves were built for the households of the Rajahs. The smoke of cooking fires was like a blue mist of the evening, and many voices rang in it joyfully. While they were making the boats ready to beat up the fish, my brother came to me and said, 'Tonight!' I looked to my weapons, and when the time came our canoe took its place in the circle of boats carrying the torches. The lights blazed on the water, but behind the boats there was darkness. When the shouting began and the excitement made them like mad we dropped out. The water swallowed our fire, and we floated back to the shore that was dark with only here and there the glimmer of embers. We could hear the talk of slave girls amongst the sheds. Then we found a place deserted and silent. We waited there. She came. She came running along the shore, rapid and leaving no trace, like a leaf driven by the wind into the sea. My brother said gloomily, 'Go and take her; carry her into our boat.' I lifted her in my arms. She panted. Her heart was beating against my breast. I said, 'I take you from those people. You came to the cry of my heart, but my arms take you into my boat against the will of the great!' 'It is right,' said my brother. 'We are men who take what we want and can hold it against many. We should have taken her in daylight.' I said, 'Let us be off'; for since she was in my boat I began to think of our Ruler's many men. 'Yes. Let us be off,' said my brother. 'We are cast out and this boat is our country now— and the sea is our refuge.' He lingered with his foot on the shore, and I entreated him to hasten, for I remembered the strokes of her heart against my breast and thought that two men cannot withstand a hundred. We left, paddling downstream close to the bank; and as we passed by the creek where they were fishing, the great shouting had ceased, but the murmur of voices was loud like the humming of insects flying at noonday. The boats floated, clustered together, in the red light of torches, under a black roof of smoke; and men talked of their sport. Men that boasted, and praised, and jeered—men that would have been our friends in the morning, but on that night were already our enemies. We paddled swiftly past. We had no more friends in the country of our birth. She sat in the middle of the canoe with covered face; silent as she is now; unseeing as she is now— and I had no regret at what I was leaving be-

cause I could hear her breathing close to me —as I can hear her now."

He paused, listened with his ear turned to the doorway, then shook his head and went on:

"My brother wanted to shout the cry of challenge—one cry only—to let the people know we were freeborn robbers who trusted our arms and the great sea. And again I begged him in the name of our love to be silent. Could I not hear her breathing close to me? I knew the pursuit would come quick enough. My brother loved me. He dipped his paddle without a splash. He only said, 'There is half a man in you now—the other half is in that woman. I can wait. When you are a whole man again, you will come back with me here to shout defiance. We are sons of the same mother.' I made no answer. All my strength and all my spirit were in my hands that held the paddle—for I longed to be with her in a safe place beyond the reach of men's anger and of women's spite. My love was so great, that I thought it could guide me to a country where death was unknown, if I could only escape from Inchi Midah's fury and from our Ruler's sword. We paddled with haste, breathing through our teeth. The blades bit deep into the smooth water. We passed out of the river; we flew in clear channels amongst the shallows. We skirted the black coast; we skirted the sand beaches where the sea speaks in whispers to the land; and the gleam of white sand flashed back past our boat, so swiftly she ran upon the water. We spoke not. Only once I said, 'Sleep, Diamelen, for soon you may want all your strength.' I heard the sweetness of her voice, but I never turned my head. The sun rose and still we went on. Water fell from my face like rain from a cloud. We flew in the light and heat. I never looked back, but I knew that my brother's eyes, behind me, were looking steadily ahead, for the boat went as straight as a bushman's dart, when it leaves the end of the sumpitan. There was no better paddler, no better steersman than my brother. Many times, together, we had won races in that canoe. But we never had put out our strength as we did then—then, when for the last time we paddled together! There was no braver or stronger man in our country than my brother. I could not spare the strength to turn my head and look at him, but every moment I heard the hiss of his breath getting louder behind me. Still he did not speak. The sun was high. The heat clung to my back like a flame of fire. My ribs were ready to burst, but I could no longer get enough air into my chest. And then I felt I must cry out with my last breath. 'Let us rest!' . . . 'Good!' he answered; and his voice was firm. He was strong. He was brave. He knew not fear and no fatigue . . . My brother!"

A murmur powerful and gentle, a murmur vast and faint; the murmur of trembling leaves, of stirring boughs, ran through the tangled depths of the forests, ran over the starry smoothness of the lagoon, and the water between the piles lapped the slimy timber once with a sudden splash. A breath of warm air touched the two men's faces and passed on with a mournful sound—a breath loud and short like an uneasy sigh of the dreaming earth.

Arsat went on in an even, low voice.

"We ran our canoe on the white beach of a little bay close to a long tongue of land that seemed to bar our road; a long wooded cape going far into the sea. My brother knew that place. Beyond the cape a river has its entrance, and through the jungle of that land there is a narrow path. We made a fire and cooked rice. Then we lay down to sleep on the soft sand in the shade of our canoe, while she watched. No sooner had I closed my eyes than I heard her cry of alarm. We leaped up. The sun was half-way down the sky already, and coming in sight in the opening of the bay we saw a prau manned by many paddlers. We knew it at once; it was one of our Rajah's praus. They were watching the shore, and saw us. They beat the gong, and turned the head of the prau into the bay. I felt my heart become weak within my breast. Diamelen sat

on the sand and covered her face. There was no escape by sea. My brother laughed. He had the gun you had given him, Tuan, before you went away, but there was only a handful of powder. He spoke to me quickly: 'Run with her along the path. I shall keep them back, for they have no firearms, and landing in the face of a man with a gun is certain death for some. Run with her. On the other side of that wood there is a fisherman's house—and a canoe. When I have fired all the shots I will follow. I am a great runner, and before they can come up we shall be gone. I will hold out as long as I can, for she is but a woman—that can neither run nor fight, but she has your heart in her weak hands.' He dropped behind the canoe. The prau was coming. She and I ran, and as we rushed along the path I heard shots. My brother fired—once—twice—and the booming of the gong ceased. There was silence behind us. That neck of land is narrow. Before I heard my brother fire the third shot I saw the shelving shore, and I saw the water again; the mouth of a broad river. We crossed a grassy glade. We ran down to the water. I saw a low hut above the black mud, and a small canoe hauled up. I heard another shot behind me. I thought, 'That is his last charge.' We rushed down to the canoe; a man came running from the hut, but I leaped on him, and we rolled together in the mud. Then I got up, and he lay still at my feet. I don't know whether I had killed him or not. I and Diamelen pushed the canoe afloat. I heard yells behind me, and I saw my brother run across the glade. Many men were bounding after him. I took her in my arms and threw her into the boat, then leaped in myself. When I looked back I saw that my brother had fallen. He fell and was up again, but the men were closing round him. He shouted, 'I am coming!' The men were close to him. I looked. Many men. Then I looked at her. Tuan, I pushed the canoe! I pushed it into deep water. She was kneeling forward looking at me, and I said, 'Take your paddle,' while I struck the water with mine. Tuan, I heard him cry. I heard him cry my name twice; and I heard voices shouting, 'Kill! Strike!' I never turned back. I heard him calling my name again with a great shriek, as when life is going out together with the voice —and I never turned my head. My own name! . . . My brother! Three times he called —but I was not afraid of life. Was she not there in that canoe? And could I not with her find a country where death is forgotten— where death is unknown!"

The white man sat up. Arsat rose and stood, an indistinct and silent figure above the dying embers of the fire. Over the lagoon a mist drifting and low had crept, erasing slowly the glittering images of the stars. And now a great expanse of white vapor covered the land: it flowed cold and gray in the darkness eddied in noiseless whirls round the tree trunks and about the platform of the house, which seemed to float upon a restless and impalpable illusion of a sea. Only far away the tops of the trees stood outlined on the twinkle of heaven, like a somber and forbidding shore —a coast deceptive, pitiless and black.

Arsat's voice vibrated loudly in the profound peace.

"I had her there! I had her! To get her I would have faced all mankind. But I had her—and—"

His words went out ringing into the empty distances. He paused, and seemed to listen to them dying away very far—beyond help and beyond recall. Then he said quietly:

"Tuan, I loved my brother."

A breath of wind made him shiver. High above his head, high above the silent sea of mist the drooping leaves of the palms rattled together with a mournful and expiring sound. The white man stretched his legs. His chin rested on his chest, and he murmured sadly without lifting his head:

"We all love our brothers."

Arsat burst out with an intense whispering violence:

"What did I care who died? I wanted peace in my own heart."

He seemed to hear a stir in the house— listened—then stepped in noiselessly. The white man stood up. A breeze was coming in fitful puffs. The stars shone paler as if they had retreated into the frozen depths of immense space. After a chill gust of wind there were a few seconds of perfect calm and absolute silence. Then from behind the black and wavy line of the forests a column of golden light shot up into the heavens and spread over the semicircle of the eastern horizon. The sun had risen. The mist lifted, broke into drifting patches, vanished into thin flying wreaths; and the unveiled lagoon lay, polished and black, in the heavy shadows at the foot of the wall of trees. A white eagle rose over it with a slanting and ponderous flight, reached the clear sunshine and appeared dazzlingly brilliant for a moment, then soaring higher, became a dark and motionless speck before it vanished into the blue as if it had left the earth forever. The white man, standing gazing upwards before the doorway, heard in the hut a confused and broken murmur of distracted words ending with a loud groan. Suddenly Arsat stumbled out with outstretched hands, shivered, and stood still for some time with fixed eyes. Then he said:

"She burns no more."

Before his face the sun showed its edge above the treetops rising steadily. The breeze freshened; a great brilliance burst upon the lagoon, sparkled on the rippling water. The forests came out of the clear shadows of the morning, became distinct, as if they had rushed nearer—to stop short in a great stir of leaves, of nodding boughs, of swaying branches. In the merciless sunshine the whisper of unconscious life grew louder, speaking in an incomprehensible voice round the dumb darkness of that human sorrow. Arsat's eyes wandered slowly, then stared at the rising sun.

"I can see nothing," he said half aloud to himself.

"There is nothing," said the white man, moving to the edge of the platform and waving his hand to his boat. A shout came faintly over the lagoon and the sampan began to glide towards the abode of the friend of ghosts.

"If you want to come with me, I will wait all the morning," said the white man, looking away upon the water.

"No, Tuan," said Arsat softly. "I shall not eat or sleep in this house, but I must first see my road. Now I can see nothing—see nothing! There is no light and no peace in the world; but there is death—death for many. We are sons of the same mother—and I left him in the midst of enemies; but I am going back now."

He drew a long breath and went on in a dreamy tone:

"In a little while I shall see clear enough to strike—to strike. But she has died, and . . . now . . . darkness."

He flung his arms wide open, let them fall along his body, then stood still with unmoved face and stony eyes, staring at the sun. The white man got down into his canoe. The polers ran smartly along the sides of the boat, looking over their shoulders at the beginning of a weary journey. High in the stern, his head muffled up in white rags, the juragan sat moody, letting his paddle trail in the water. The white man, leaning with both arms over the grass roof of the little cabin, looked back at the shining ripple of the boat's wake. Before the sampan passed out of the lagoon into the creek he lifted his eyes. Arsat had not moved. He stood lonely in the searching sunshine; and he looked beyond the great light of a cloudless day into the darkness of a world of illusions.

AFTERNOON OF A FAUN
Peter De Vries (b. 1910)

This is only a story about how I became engaged, but the nature and ingredients of that event and of the emotional transactions that immediately preceded it are so of a piece with what went before, and so depend on it for illumination, that a lick of autobiography is indicated.

I think I can say that my childhood was as unhappy as the next braggart's. I was read to sleep with the classics and spanked with obscure quarterlies. My father was a man steeped in the heavyweight German philosophers; his small talk ran to the likes of "I believe is was Hegel who defined love as the ideality of the relativity of the reality of an infinitesimal portion of the absolute totality of the Infinite Being." I don't think I need dwell further on the influence which, more than any other single factor in my life, inspired in me my own conversational preference: the light aphorism.

I belonged, in my late adolescence, which I spent in Scranton, Pennsylvania, to a clique of pimpled boulevardiers who met at a place called the Samothrace, a restaurant and ice-cream parlor run by a Greek who let us pull tables out on the sidewalk and talk funny. Andropoulos, which was his name, was a prickly sort who was forever complaining—especially when his trade was slack and the lack of money in the till made him more irritable than usual—that this country was materialistic. Be that as it may, we expatriates-at-home could be seen at the Samothrace almost every evening, loitering over pastry and coffee, or toying with a little of what the Greek called his fruit compost. I often wore my topcoat with the sleeves hanging loose, so that the effect was like that of an Inverness cape, when it was not like that of two broken arms. An earnest youth on the high-school debating squad, who got in with our set by mistake one *soir*, tried to interest me in politics by speaking of the alarming layoffs then occurring in the Department of Agriculture. "I had thought," I said, smiling around at my disciples as I tapped a Melachrino on the lid of its box, "that the Department of Agriculture slaughtered its surplus employees."

This attitude grew into a *fin-de-siècle* one of cultivated fatigue and bored aestheticism, marked by amusement with the colloquial main stream. I would lie full-length around the house and with a limp hand wave life away. My mother took this as an indication that I had "no pep," and urged a good tonic to fix me up.

"No, no, no," my father said. "That isn't what the trouble is. It's what they call Decadence. It's an attitude toward life." He looked at the horizontal product of their union, disposed on the living-room sofa with a cigarette. "He'll come to his senses."

"Instead of coming to one's senses," I airily returned, "how much more delightful to let one's senses come to one."

My mother, a slender woman with a nimbus of fluffy gray hair, next tried to get me interested in "healthy" books, like the jumbo three-generation novels she herself "couldn't put down."

"The books Mother cannot put down," I said, "are the ones I cannot pick up."

"He *is* run-down—now, I don't *care!*" my mother said.

My father stamped his foot, for he was becoming as vexed with her as he was with me. "It has nothing to do with his health," he explained again. "This is a literary and aesthetic pose. He's precious."

"Mother has always thought so," I said, and laughed, for there were things that brought out my heartier side.

Such is my memory of seventeen.

I was slightly above medium height, reedy, with clothes either too casual or too studied. I had a pinched-in, pendulous underlip, rather like the lip of a pitcher, which must have conferred on me an air of jocularity somewhat at odds with my intention to be "dry." My best friend was a high-school— and, later, junior-college—classmate named Nickie Sherman. He needed a good tonic, too, being if anything even more *fin-de-siècle* than I. "Thomas Wolfe was a genius without talent," he asserted between sips of hot chocolate at the Greek's one evening, speaking in a drawl suited to the paradox of the statement, which was not meant to be un-

derstood by more than three or four of those who heard it. The double dose of nuance entailed by Nickie's visiting my house, as he did sometimes for dinner or even overnight, drove my father to distraction, and he literally took to sending me upstairs to my room for making epigrams and paradoxes. He said that he was thinking not so much of himself as of my mother, to whom he considered these subtleties disrespectful, because they were hopelessly over her head.

One evening just after dinner, for example, my younger sister Lila got to teasing me about a girl named Crystal Chickering, whom I had been dating. My mother remarked that she'd have guessed I'd have preferred Jessie Smithers, because "Jessie laughs at absolutely everything a person says."

"That is because she has no sense of humor," I said.

My father made a truncheon of his *Yale Review.* "I'll ask you to apologize to your mother for that remark," he said.

"Why?" I protested.

"Because we don't engage in repartee with the mother who gave us life," he said in a florid burst of chivalry that in part arose, I think, out of his own sense of guilt at having neglected her, leaving her to what he eruditely called her "needle-pwah" while he sat with his nose in Schopenhauer or went off on vacation by himself. "Apologize!"

"Oh, don't worry about it, Roebuck," my mother put in. "Let him talk over my head the same as I talked over my father's. That's progress."

Feeling perfidy in the form of aphorisms to be uncoiling everywhere about him, my father became angrier still. "Explain to her what that last so-called paradox means," he said, his face red from a lifetime of bad claret and plain damn exasperation. "My father would have given me short shrift if I'd insulted my mother with language fit for nothing but a Mayfair drawing room. All this confounded lint-picking. Upstairs!" he ordered with a flourish of the *Yale Review.*

"Go on up to your room, please, until you can learn to talk to your family in considerate English."

"But I've got a date," I objected.

"You should have thought of that sooner," said my father.

Rather than waste precious time arguing, I hurried upstairs to start serving my sentence. It wasn't until nine o'clock, after apologizing for the subtlety of my rejoinder and promising to engage in more normal intercourse, that I was let out. By that time, of course, I was late for my date with Crystal Chickering, toward whose house I legged it, as a consequence, with commendable pep.

Crystal was a girl of my own age who lived about a mile from my house. She was one of the milk-white daughters of the moon, and it goes without saying that I pursued the amorous life with the same easy, half-spectatorial air of inconsequence that I did the intellectual—or tried to. It wasn't easy, for more reasons than one. First, the atmosphere around Crystal's house wasn't right. Her father was a sort of home-spun philosopher, who conducted an advice-to-the-troubled column in the local evening paper. He ran readers' letters and his own counsel, which was usually packaged in maxims. He had volumes of these, all (in notebooks of his own) cross-indexed under types of trouble. That he was my favorite character goes without saying, and I was careful not to say it either to him or to his daughter. I felt that one had a lot of work to do on her before she would understand *why* he was one's favorite character; why he was like those Currier and Ives prints which, having outgrown them, one laps the field of Sensibility to approach again from behind and see as "wonderful." Crystal was often, not to make any bones about it, pretty wonderful herself, in those days. The first time I dropped the name Baudelaire to her, I had the queer suspicion that she thought it was the name of a refrigerator or air-conditioner. But I eventually got *The Flowers of Evil* across by reading the bulk of

it to her aloud. On the night my confinement made me late, our fare was to be something more conventional: I was taking along a new album of *Boris Godunov*.

Setting the records on the family phonograph, for her parents were upstairs and we had the parlor to ourselves, I asked, "Do you like *Godunov?*"

"Yes," she answered from the sofa, where she was settling herself with a cigarette. "Which composition of his is it?"

I heard the great ships baying at the harbor's mouth, and chuckled, already aboard—clean out of this. I had that exhilarating sense of being a misfit that I could taste almost anywhere in Scranton and that was, in a way, my birthright.

Crystal closed her eyes and listened to the music. When the album had been played through and duly enjoyed, we forgot about music and got on a variety of other subjects, among them marriage and families. "I suppose most people want that sort of thing," I said. "You know—the eternal severities."

"Everybody wants children, certainly," Crystal answered. "Don't you think it would be awful to go through life without them?"

"Yes," I said. "There is only one thing worse than not having children, and that is having them."

"Just what do you mean?" she asked.

"I don't want to get married," I said, in clear enough tones. "I just—don't—want to get married."

She looked thoughtfully at the floor. "We're having our first quarrel," she said, as though noting a milestone in our progress.

To kiss into silence the lips from which such bromides fell, and turn them to the laughter and sighs for which they were intended, seemed precisely the formula for tinkling pleasures, for caught felicities, for which we were so sumptuously cued by nature. One evening in midsummer, I was early for a date we were to spend at her house with nobody home at all, even upstairs. Her folks were at a testimonial dinner for the editor of the paper Mr. Chickering worked for. There was no answer when I rang the front door-bell, and, following the strains of the love duet from *Tristan*, which seemed to be coming from somewhere in back, I walked around the house and found Crystal in the back yard with a portable phonograph on a chair. She herself was stretched out in a hammock with her eyes closed and one hand outflung above her head. I had a feeling that she had seen me coming, quickly set the record going, and hurried back to the hammock in time for me to find her lying on it in a trance of appreciation.

She was wearing yellow shorts and a red halter, for the weather was very warm. Her hair was gathered at the back and knotted with a red silk ribbon. On the grass beneath her was an empty Coke bottle with a bent straw in it. She appeared at length to become aware of me standing there, and she rolled her head toward me, her eyes fluttering open.

"Oh, hello," she said.

I snapped a burning cigarette into the grass and walked up to her, my nerves in a trembling knot. She extended a white hand, which I took in both of mine and ate like cake. She rolled her head away with a sigh.

"This music. Lawrence Melchior," she said.

On persuasions from myself, she eased out of the hammock and onto a blanket lying on the ground nearby. She pulled the grass and, as one who knew good music, my hair. "This night." It was darkening, the air wreathed with the musks of summer, as of something crushed from the grape of Dusk. A moon hung like a gong above the grove of birches behind the house.

The night was a success, and I went home ill with fear. I spent the next days scorching myself with one speculation. The sight of perambulators sent galvanic shocks through me. I was to wheel one through an eternity of ridicule because I had succumbed to a single folly—and that to the music of a composer whose works I had termed mucilaginous. The great ships would bay at the harbor's mouth nevermore for me. I heard, in-

stead, voices, local in origin and of an almost hallucinatory force: "Shotgun wedding, you know." "You mean Charles Swallow? That guy who was always—?" "Yes, the old *flâneur* himself." (*Flâneur:* One who strolls aimlessly; hence, an intellectual trifler.) Think of a boulevardier pushing a baby carriage!

I hid in my room with the door locked most of the time. Once I stood before my dresser mirror and looked at myself. My face was drawn. It was the face of an alien. I contorted it into deliberately gruesome expressions of woe, so as to give everything an exaggerated and theatrical aspect, and, by this means, make what I was worrying about seem to have no basis in fact. My grimaces did create an atmosphere of relative absurdity, and I smiled bravely. Of course all this would blow over! Six months from now I would be laughing at it. I had about convinced myself of that when the idea of tallied months struck me with fresh horror, and I was back where I started.

The voices came again. I tried at first to drown them out with a phonograph I had in my room, but there were no compositions that could not, by deplorable associations, return me swiftly to my *crise*. And the voices continued: "You mean that guy who was always knocking convention?" "The same." "He seemed to be that type they call the carriage trade. Ha! I guess *now* he—" Never. I would go to Lethe first. I would twist wolfsbane. I would slip into the hospitable earth, and among her dumb roots and her unscandalizing boulders make my bed.

I was walking down the street, one afternoon during the cooling-off period, when I saw a sight that gave the winch of agony a fresh turn. Nickie Sherman was approaching. He had our *Zeitgeist* well at heel, for, one hand in his trouser pocket and the other swinging a blackthorn stick he was affecting those days, he drifted up and said "Hi."

Stark, staring mad, I answered "Hi."

"What cooketh?"

Suddenly, instead of dreading the encounter, I saw a way of turning it to advantage. I would remove the sting from having to get married (if such was the pass things came to) by taking the line that that was what I wanted. This would need a little groundwork, and to lay it I suggested we drop in at the Greek's, which was a block from there, for some coffee. We did.

The tables at which it was our wont to dally in the cool of the evening were in their places outside (Andropoulos himself now cultivated the Continental touch we had introduced, and kept a few tables in the open air), but this was the heat of the day and we went inside. Several women gabbled at a table about a movie they had been to.

"Matinee idle," I murmured to Nickie as we took chairs ourselves.

We ordered coffee. Then Nickie, who had laid the blackthorn across an empty chair, asked, *"Was ist los?"*

Glancing around with a matter-of-factness into which some note of furtiveness must also have crept, I drew out cigarettes and answered negligently, "I've been having an affair."

"And?"

I shrugged. "It gets to be rather a nuisance. We pay for security with boredom, for adventure with bother. It's six of one and half a dozen of the other, really." I lit the cigarette and waved the match out. "Shaw makes matrimony sound rather attractive, with that puritanical definition he has of it somewhere. I'm sure you remember it."

Nickie watched Andropoulos shamble over with our coffee.

"Shaw is great, up to a point," he said, "and then one suddenly finds oneself thinking, Oh, pshaw!"

"He describes marriage as combining a maximum of temptation with a maximum of opportunity. He's quite right, of course. It's the most sensual of our institutions," I said. "I've half a notion to get married myself," I added vagrantly, stirring my coffee.

Nickie's problem was to get back into the conversation. I could sense him mulling my gambit as he sipped his own coffee, keep-ing his dark eyes casually averted. He set his cup down and cleared his throat, appearing at last to have worked something out, and I knew that what he said next would determine whether I would have to blow my brains out or not.

"Yes. The logistics of adultery are awful. Matrimony is a garrison, but one that has its appeal to a man out bivouacking every night," said that probable virgin.

Freeze it there, I told myself. I knew that if a neat way of putting a rebuttal had occurred to him first, instead of a concurrence, he would have rebutted, but it hadn't, and I was to that extent in luck. My object was to get Nickie into as good a frame of mind as possible for my armed nupitals, if any—to give him a viewpoint from which he would see me not as a ridiculous bourgeois casualty going down the aisle but heathen to the end. I had to come out of this making sense as a boulevardier who had said "I do." So I said appreciatively, "That's neat, Nickie. By God, that's neatly put."

Next to be prepared were, of course, my parents.

They knew only that I'd been seeing Crystal Chickering for about a year, and talk of wedding bells would fall rather unexpectedly on their ears, aside from sorely disillusioning them about my plans to matriculate at Dartmouth in the fall.Therefore it seemed wise to pave the way a little by giving them to understand that this girl and I were "serious." I let drop this intelligence when they and I were sitting in the living room shortly after dinner on the day of my passage with Nickie at the Greek's.

"I've fallen in love with a girl I rather like," I said. "I suppose I shall marry eventually. One does that. One drifts into stability."

"Upstairs!" said my father.

But my mother clapped her hands. "That's wonderful!" she exclaimed. She was pleased as Punch when I assured her it was the Chickering girl, whom she liked best after Jessie Smithers, and told her that we were informally engaged. The act of betrothal showed pep. It showed downright spunk, she declared, especially considering that I had no prospects whatever and had to finish school first in any case. "Come and sit by me," she said.

I jollied my mother by joining her on the sofa, where she straightway hauled my long legs up across hers, so that I was half-way sitting on her lap, and rummaged in my hair for old times' sake. "I remember when you were a little shaver how you'd crawl across the floor to where I was talking on the phone, and kink the cord," she said. "As though you could stop the conversation coming through it, the way you can the water in a hose. We never knew whether you were joking or serious. Did you really think that cut off the electricity in the wire?"

"Doesn't it?" I inquired with wide eyes. She gave me a hug that squeezed a groan out of me, like a note out of an accordion.

"We thought for a while you might be feebleminded," my father put in wistfully from the mantel, against which he had backed to scratch a perennially itching spot between his shoulder blades. "Well, all those things come back in a flood at a time like this is what your mother means. I've done my best for you—I believe God will bear me out on that—but you cannot force values on one who will not have them." He fingered an onion wisp of beard, which, together with his harried features and embedded eyes, made him surprisingly resemble the illustrations of depleted sensibility in the very literature with which I outraged him—Baudelaire, Huys-mans, and the rest. "I had some standing in the community once, under other spiritual weathers and skies, and cut a fine figure, too, if I do say so myself. Why, the little tots would come out of Sunday school and say, 'There goes Jesus.'" He drew a deep breath, and resumed almost immediately. "And hu-mor—where is *it* today? In my day, we would get up to speak at Thanksgiving banquets, and begin: 'A moment ago you could have said the sage was in the turkey. Now the tur-

key is in the sage.' *That* was humor, I wish to submit. Well, I've tried to do my best."

"And you have, Popper," I said, look-ing over at him from my mother's lap. "I ap-preciate everything you've done for me."

"It's a tradition I've tried to give you, not bread alone," he said. "The rest is up to you. You have brains, imagination—but have you the brains and imagination to ap-prehend that these in themselves are not enough?" He squared himself a little, and we understood more was coming. "Imagina-tion without discipline," he said, looking the young aphorist steadily in the eye, "is like a pillow without the ticking."

My cries of praise and thumps on his back declared him to be a success. He pinch-ed his nose and smiled modestly at the floor. "Ah, well, perhaps we can manage a wedding gift of a thousand dollars when the time comes," he said. More thumps and outcries attested to the tide of good feeling created by his knack for the right words, and afterward he opened a bottle of Madeira and toasted my eventual departure from his board in lambent words.

So everything, on my end at least, was in readiness; as much in readiness, certainly, as I could make it. There remained now only to await zero hour, as I thought of the time when I was to learn my fate. That was pre-sumably the following Tuesday evening, when I had a date with Crystal. Then I would learn whether it was Heaven or Hell for which I was to leave Purgatory.

Crystal was upstairs dressing when I ar-rived at the Chickering house that night, so I sat down in the living room to wait. Her father was there, in a Cogswell chair, wearing slippers and reading the evening paper. He was in shirtsleeves, but then, after all, he was the local shirtsleeve philosopher. He put the paper down and regarded me with a deep frown. "I'd like to talk to you," he said.

He was a red-haired man of medium size, with green eyes magnified by the heavy-lensed glasses he wore. He had been sunbathing recently, and his was the kind of skin that never tans but only turns the pink of mouthwashes. He removed his glasses and chewed on their bows. I was twiddling my thumbs at a rate not normally associated with that act. "What about, Mr. Chickering?" I asked.

"I think you know."

I met this with a gulp and the word "What?" brought out in a dry treble. The ceiling creaked as under a footstep upstairs. That foolish girl had confessed her condition to her parents, I thought with panic. Even now, she and her mother were up there, hysterically promenading. Paralyzed, I watched Chickering thoughtfully revolve a cockleshell ashtray on a table beside his chair. The cockleshell was—like the resort pillows and the wall thermometers in the shape of keys to cities, which also heavily garnished the living room—a souvenir of some past family holiday. Together, they left me ill with premonition. Now I would never board the great ships. Now I would never bicycle down the Palatinate sampling wines, never sit at the captain's table opposite a woman returning to the States after some years spent in a novel by Henry James. At best, I would see Niagara Falls from the air; it would look like a kitchen sink running over.

"I think we can safely say that now you're a young man with a problem," Chickering said. "And there are some folks who think that's my field."

"There are? I mean, I am? What's my problem?"

"Why, you're about to enter college without any clear idea, I might even say without the *least* idea, what you want to be when you come out of it—butcher, baker or candlestick maker," he said, in the American grain. "Now, wait a minute. I know education is for the mind, and all that. But at the same time a person ought to have *some* notion of where he wants to head. And I just want to leave this thought with you for what it may be worth."

I was spared whatever piece of free wisdom he may have had prepared for me by the arrival of Crystal, who just then slowly descended the stairway. She was wearing a new dress, and she looked singularly radiant.

"Ah, there you are," I said, rising. "Shall we go? We're probably late for the party as it is."

We were going to a housewarming only three blocks away, so we walked. As we strolled toward our destination, Crystal slipped a hand into mine, and from time to time turned to smile at me. "This night," she said, and took a deep breath. What I died to hear I feared to ask.

At last she said, "I suppose you're anxious to know."

"Know?" I said.

She stopped and turned to face me on the sidewalk. "You must be out of your mind with worry, the same as I've been, so I won't keep you on pins and needles any longer. Everything is all right."

I was free—free! The very word went winging and singing through my head, like a bird sprung from a cage. Chains fell away from me, doors opened in every direction. Flowers that had withered leaped to life. The hours in Purgatory were almost worth it, for the joy of this release. I that had been dead lived again, the master of my fate. I was absolutely and completely Free!

I turned, seized her in my arms, and, in an ecstasy of gratitude, asked her to marry me.

JERICO, JERICO, JERICO
Andrew Lytle (b. 1903)

She opened her eyes. She must have been asleep for hours or months. She could not reckon; she could only feel the steady silence of time. She had been Joshua and made it swing suspended in her room. Forever she had floated above the counterpane, between the tester and the counterpane she had floated until her hand, long and bony, its speckled-dried skin drawing away from the bulging blue veins, had reached and drawn her body under the covers. And now she was resting, clearheaded and quiet, her thoughts clicking like a new-greased mower. All creation could not make her lift her thumb or cross it over her finger. She looked at the bed, the bed her mother had died in, the bed her children had been born in, her marriage bed, the bed the General had drenched with his blood. Here it stood where it had stood for seventy years, square and firm on the floor, wide enough for three people to lie comfortable in, if they didn't sleep restless; but not wide enough for her nor long enough when her conscience scorched the cool wrinkles in the sheets. The two foot posts, octagonal-shaped and mounted by carved pieces that looked like absurd flowers, stood up to comfort her when the world began to crumble. Her eyes followed down the posts and along the basket-quilt. She had made it before her marriage to the General, only he wasn't a general then. He was a slight, tall young man with a rolling mustache and perfume in his hair. A many a time she had seen her young love's locks dripping with scented oil, down upon his collar . . . She had cut the squares for the baskets in January, and for stuffing had used the letters of old lovers, fragments of passion cut to warm her of a winter's night. The General would have his fun. *Miss Kate, I didn't sleep well last night. I heard Sam Buchanan make love to you out of that farthest basket. If I hear him again, I mean to toss this piece of quilt in the fire.* Then he would chuckle in his round, soft voice; reach under the covers and pull her over to his side of the bed. On a cold and frosting night he would sleep with his nose against her neck. His nose was so quick to turn cold, he said, and her neck was so warm. Sometimes her hair, the loose, unruly strands at the nape, would tickle his nostrils and he would wake up with a sneeze. This had been so long ago, and there had been so many years of trouble and worry. Her eyes, as apart from her as the mirror on the bureau, rested upon the half-tester, upon the enormous button that caught the rose-

colored canopy and shot its folds out like the rays of the morning sun. She could not see but she could feel the heavy cluster of mahogany grapes that tumbled from the center of the head board—out of its vines curling down the sides it tumbled. How much longer would these never-picked grapes hang above her head? How much longer would she, rather, hang to the vine of this world, she who lay beneath as dry as any raisin. Then she remembered. She looked at the blinds. They were closed.

"You, Ants, where's my stick? I'm a great mind to break it over your trifling back."

"Awake? What a nice long nap you've had," said Doctor Ed.

"The boy? Where's my grandson? Has he come?"

"I'll say he's come. What do you mean taking to your bed like this? Do you realize, beautiful lady, that this is the first time I ever saw you in bed in my whole life? I believe you've taken to bed on purpose. I don't believe you want to see me."

"Go long, boy, with your foolishness."

That's all she could say, and she blushed as she said it—she blushing at the words of a snip of a boy, whom she had diapered a hundred times and had washed as he stood before the fire in the round tin tub, his little back swayed and his little belly sticking out in front, rosy from the scrubbing he had gotten. *Mammy, what for I've got a hole in my stummick; what for, Mammy?* Now he was sitting on the edge of the bed calling her beautiful lady, an old hag like her, beautiful lady. A good-looker the girls would call him, with his bold, careless face and his hands with their fine, long fingers. Soft, how soft they were, running over her rough, skinny bones. He looked a little like his grandpa, but somehow there was something missing . . .

"Well, boy, it took you a time to come home to see me die."

"Nonsense. Cousin Edwin, I wouldn't wait on a woman who had so little faith in my healing powers."

"There an't nothing strange about dying. But I an't in such an all-fired hurry. I've got a heap to tell you about before I go."

The boy leaned over and touched her gently. "Not even death would dispute you here, on Long Gourd, Mammy."

He was trying to put her at ease in his carefree way. It was so obvious a pretending, but she loved him for it. There was something nice in its awkwardness, the charm of the young's blundering and of their efforts to get along in the world. Their pretty arrogance, their patronizing airs, their colossal unknowing of what was to come. It was a quenching drink to a sin-thirsty old woman. Somehow his vitality had got crossed in her blood and made a dry heart leap, her blood that was almost water. Soon now she would be all water, water and dust, lying in the burying ground between the cedar—and fire. She could smell her soul burning and see it. What a fire it would make below, dripping with sin, like a rag soaked in kerosene. But she had known what she was doing. And here was Long Gourd, all its fields intact, ready to be handed on, in better shape than when she took it over. Yes, she had known what she was doing. How long, she wondered, would his spirit hold up under the trials of planting, of cultivating, and of the gathering time, year in and year out—how would he hold up before so many springs and so many autumns. The thought of him giving orders, riding over the place, or rocking on the piazza, and a great pain would pin her heart to her backbone. She had wanted him by her to train—there was so much for him to know: how the south field was cold and must be planted late, and where the orchards would best hold their fruit, and where the frosts crept soonest—that now could never be. She turned her head—who was that woman, that strange woman standing by the bed as if she owned it, as if . . .

"This is Eva, Mammy."

"Eva?"

"We are going to be married."

"I wanted to come and see—to meet Dick's grandmother . . ."

I wanted to come to see her die. That's what she meant. Why didn't she finish and say it out. She had come to lick her chops and see what she would enjoy. That's what she had come for, the lying little slut. The richest acres in Long Gourd valley, so rich hit'd make yer feet greasy to walk over'm, Saul Oberly at the first tollgate had told the peddler once, and the peddler had told it to her, knowing it would please and make her trade. *Before you die.* Well, why didn't you finish it out? You might as well. You've given yourself away.

Her fierce thoughts dried up the water in her eyes, tired and resting far back in their sockets. They burned like a smothered fire stirred up by the wind as they traveled over the woman who would lie in her bed, eat with her silver, and caress her flesh and blood. The woman's body was soft enough to melt and pour about him. She could see that; and her firm, round breasts, too firm and round for any good to come from them. And her lips, full and red, her eyes bright and cunning. The heavy hair crawled about her head to tangle the poor, foolish boy in its ropes. She might have known he would do something foolish like this. He had a foolish mother. There wasn't any way to avoid it. But look at her belly, small and no-count. There wasn't a muscle the size of a worm as she could see. And those hips—

And then she heard her voice: "What did you say her name was, son? Eva? Eva Callahan, I'm glad to meet you, Eva. Where'd your folks come from, Eva? I knew some Callahans who lived in the Goosepad settlement. They couldn't be any of your kin, could they?

"Oh, no, indeed. My people . . ."

"Right clever people they were. And good farmers, too. Worked hard. Honest—that is, most of 'm. As honest as that run of people go. We always gave them a good name."

"My father and mother live in Birmingham. Have always lived there."

"Birmingham," she hear herself say with contempt. They could have lived there all their lives and still come from somewhere. I've got a mule older 'n Birmingham. "What's your pa's name?"

"Her father is Mister E. L. Callahan, Mammy."

"First name not Elijah by any chance? Lige they called him."

"No. Elmore, Mammy."

"Old Mason Callahan had a son they called Lige. Somebody told me he moved to Elyton. So you think you're going to live with the boy here."

"We're to be married . . . that is, if Eva doesn't change her mind."

And she saw his arm slip possessively about the woman's waist. "Well, take care of him, young woman, or I'll come back and han't you. I'll come back and claw your eyes out."

"I'll take very good care of him, Mrs. McCowan."

"I can see that." She could hear the threat in her voice, and Eva heard it.

"Young man," spoke up Doctor Edwin, "you should feel powerful set up, two such women pestering each other about you."

The boy kept an embarrassed silence.

"All of you get out now. I want to talk to him by himself. I've got a lot to say and precious little time to say it in. And he's mighty young and helpless and ignorant."

"Why, Mammy, you forget I'm a man now. Twenty-six. All teeth cut. Long trousers."

"It takes a heap more than pants to make a man. Throw open them blinds, Ants."

"Yes'm."

"You don't have to close the door so all-fired soft. Close it naturally. And you can

tip about all you want to—later. I won't be hurried to the burying ground. And keep your head away from that door. What I've got to say to your new master is private."

"Listen at you, Mistiss."

"You listen to me. That's all. No, wait. I had something else on my mind—what is it? Yes. How many hens has Melissy set? You don't know? Find out. A few of the old hens ought to be setting. Tell her to be careful to turn the turkey eggs every day. No, you bring them and set them under my bed. I'll make sure. We got a mighty pore hatch last year. You may go now. I'm plumb worn out, boy, worn out thinking for these people. It's that that worries a body down. But you'll know all about it in good time. Stand out there and let me look at you good. You don't let me see enough of you, and I almost forgot how you look. Not really, you understand. Just a little. It's your own fault. I've got so much to trouble me that you, when you're not here, naturally slip back in my mind. But that's all over now. You are here to stay, and I'm here to go. There will always be Long Gourd, and there must always be a McCowan on it. I had hoped to have you by me for several years, but you would have your fling in town. I thought it best to clear your blood of it, but as God is hard, I can't see what you find to do in town. And now you've gone and gotten you a woman. Well, they all have to do it. But do you reckon you've picked the right one—you must forgive the frankness of an old lady who can see the bottom of her grave—I had in mind one of the Carlisle girls. The Carlisle place lies so handy to Long Gourd and would give me a landing on the river. Have you seen Anna Belle since she's grown to be a woman? I'm told there's not a better housekeeper in the valley."

"I'm sure Anna Belle is a fine girl. But, Mammy, I love Eva."

"She'll wrinkle up on you, Son; and the only wrinkles land gets can be smoothed out by the harrow. And she looks sort of puny to me, Son. She's powerful small in the waist and walks about like she had worms."

"Gee, Mammy, you're not jealous are you? That waist is in style."

"You want to look for the right kind of style in a woman. Old Mrs. Penter Matchem had two daughters with just such waists, but 'twarnt natural. She would tie their corset strings to the bed posts and whip'm out with a buggy whip. The poor girls never drew a hearty breath. Just to please that old woman's vanity. She got paid in kind. It did something to Eliza's bowels and she died before she was twenty. The other one never had any children. She used to whip'm out until they cried. I never liked that woman. She thought a whip would do anything."

"Well, anyway, Eva's small waist wasn't made by any corset strings. She doesn't wear any."

"How do you know, sir?"

"Well . . . I . . . What a question for a respectable woman to ask."

"I'm not a respectable woman. No woman can be respectable and run four thousand acres of land. Well, you'll have it your own way. I suppose the safest place for a man to take his folly is to bed."

"Mammy!"

"You must be lenient with your Cousin George. He wanders about night times talking about the War. I put him off in the west wing where he won't keep people awake, but sometimes he gets in the yard and gives orders to his troops. 'I will sweep that hill, General' —and many's the time he's done it when the battle was doubtful—'I'll sweep it with my iron brooms'; then he shouts out his orders, and pretty soon the dogs commence to barking. But he's been a heap of company for me. You must see that your wife humors him. It won't be for long. He's mighty feeble."

"Eva's not my wife yet, Mammy."

"You won't be free much longer—the way she looks at you, like a hungry hound."

"I was just wondering," he said hurriedly. "I hate to talk about anything like this . . ."

"Everybody has a time to die, and I'll have no maudlin nonsense about mine."

"I was wondering about Cousin George . . . if I could get somebody to keep him. You see, it will be difficult in the winters. Eva will want to spend the winters in town . . ."

He paused, startled, before the great bulk of his grandmother rising from her pillows, and in the silence that frightened the air, his unfinished words hung suspended about them.

After a moment he asked if he should call the doctor.

It was some time before she could find words to speak.

"Get out of the room."

"Forgive me, Mammy. You must be tired."

"I'll send for you," sounded the dead voice in the still room, "when I want to see you again. I'll send for you and—the woman."

She watched the door close quietly on his neat square back. Her head whirled and turned like a flying jennet. She lowered and steadied it on the pillows. Four thousand acres of the richest land in the valley he would sell and squander on that slut, and he didn't even know it and there was no way to warn him. This terrifying thought rushed through her mind, and she felt the bed shake with her pain, while before the footboard the spectre of an old sin rose up to mock her. How she had struggled to get this land and keep it together—through the War, the Reconstruction, and the pleasanter after days. For eighty-seven years she had suffered and slept and planned and rested and had pleasure in this valley, seventy of it, almost a turning century, on this place; and now that she must leave it . . .

The things she had done to keep it together. No. The one thing . . . from the dusty stacks the musty odor drifted through the room, met the tobacco smoke over the long table piled high with records, reports. Iva Louise stood at one end, her hat clinging perilously to the heavy auburn hair, the hard blue eyes and the voice:

"You promised Pa to look after me"— she had waited for the voice to break and scream—"and you have stolen my land!"

"Now, Miss Iva Louise," the lawyer dropped his empty eyes along the floor, "you don't mean . . ."

"Yes, I do mean it."

Her own voice had restored calm to the room: "I promised your pa his land would not be squandered."

"My husband won't squander my property. You just want it for yourself."

She cut through the scream with the sharp edge of her scorn: "What about that weakling's farm in Madison? Who pays the taxes now?"

The girl had no answer to that. Desperate, she faced the lawyer: "Is there no way, sir, I can get my land from the clutches of this unnatural woman?"

The man coughed; the red rim of his eyes watered with embarrassment: "I'm afraid," he cleared his throat, "you say you can't raise the money . . . I'm afraid—"

That trapped look as the girl turned away. It had come back to her, now trapped in her bed. As a swoon spreads, she felt the desperate terror of weakness, more desperate where there had been strength. Did the girl see right? Had she stolen the land because she wanted it?

Suddenly, like the popping of a thread in a loom, the struggles of the flesh stopped, and the years backed up and covered her thoughts like the spring freshet she had seen so many times creep over the dark soil. Not in order but, as if they were stragglers trying to catch up, the events of her life passed before her sight that had never been so clear. Sweeping over the mounds of her body rising beneath the quilts came the old familiar

odors—the damp, strong, penetrating smell of a new-turned ground; the rank, clinging, resistless odor of green-picked feathers stuffed in a pillow by Guinea Nell, thirty-odd years ago; tobacco on the mantel, clean and sharp like smelling salts; her father's sweat, sweet like stale oil; the powerful ammonia of manure turned over in a stall; curing hay in the wind; the polecat's stink on the night air, almost pleasant, a sort of commingled scent of all the animals, man and beast; the dry smell of dust under a rug; the over-strong scent of too-sweet fruit trees blooming; the inhospitable wet ashes of a dead fire in a poor white's cabin; black Rebeccah in the kitchen; a wet hound steaming before a fire. There were other odors she could not identify, over-whelming her, making her weak, taking her body and drawing out of it a choking longing to hover over all that she must leave, the animals, the fences, the crops growing in the fields, the houses, the people in them . . .

It was early summer, and she was standing in the garden after dark—she had heard something after the small chickens. Mericy and Yellow Jane passed beyond the paling fence. Dark shadows—gay, full voices. *Where you gwine, gal? I dunno. Jest a-gwine. Where you? To the frolic, do I live. Well, stay off'n yoe back tonight.* Then out of the rich, gushing laughter: *All right, you stay off'n yourn. I done caught de stumbles.* More laughter.

The face of Uncle Ike, head man in slavery days, rose up. A tall Senegalese, he was standing in the crib of the barn unmoved before the bushwhackers. *Nigger, whar is that gold hid? You better tell us, nigger. Down in the well; in the far-place. By God, you black son of a bitch, we'll roast ye alive if you air too contrary to tell. Now, listen ole nigger, Miss McCowan ain't nothen to you no more. You been set free. We'll give ye some of it, a whole sack. Come on, now—* out of the dribbling, leering mouth—*whar air it?* Ike's tall form loomed towards the shadows. In the lamp flame his forehead shone like the point, the core of night. He stood there with no word for answer. As she saw the few white beads of sweat on his forehead, she spoke.

She heard her voice reach through the dark—*you turn that black man loose. A pause and then*—*I know your kind. In better days you'd slip around and set people's barns afire. You shirked the War to live off the old and weak. You don't spare me because I'm a woman. You'd shoot a woman quicker because she has the name of being frail. Well, I'm not frail, and my Navy Six ain't frail. Ike, take their guns.* Ike moved and one of them raised his pistol arm. He dropped it, and the acrid smoke stung her nostrils. *Now, Ike, get the rest of their weapons. Their knives, too. One of us might turn our backs.*

On top of the shot she heard the soft pat of her servants' feet. White eyeballs shining through the cracks in the barn. Then: *Caesar, Al, Zebedee, step in here and lend a hand to Ike.* By sun the people had gathered in the yard. Uneasy, silent, they watched her on the porch. She gave the word, and the whips cracked. The mules strained, trotted off, skittish and afraid, dragging the white naked bodies bouncing and cursing over the sod: *Turn us loose. We'll not bother ye no more, lady. You ain't no woman, you're a devil.* She turned and went into the house. It is strange how a woman gets hard when trouble comes a-gobbling after her people.

Worn from memory, she closed her eyes to stop the whirl, but closing her eyes did no good. She released the lids and did not resist. Brother Jack stood before her, handsome and shy, but ruined from his cradle by a cleft palate, until he came to live only in the fire of spirits. And she understood, so clear was life, down to the smallest things. She had often heard tell of this clarity that took a body whose time was spending on the earth. Poor Brother Jack, the gentlest of men, but because of his mark, made the butt and wit of the valley. She saw him leave for school,

where he was sent to separate him from his drinking companions, to a church school where the boys buried their liquor in the ground and sipped it up through straws. His letters: *Dear Ma, quit offering so much advice and send me more money. You send barely enough to keep me from stealing.* His buggy wheels scraping the gravel, driving up as the first roosters crowed. *Katharine, Malcolm, I thought you might want to have a little conversation.* Conversation two hours before sun! And down she would come and let him in, and the General would get up, stir up the fire, and they would sit down and smoke. Jack would drink and sing. *If the Little Brown Jug was mine, I'd be drunk all the time and I'd never be sob-er a-gin*—or, *Hog drovers, hog drovers, hog drovers we air, a-courting your darter so sweet and so fair.* They would sit and smoke and drink until she got up to ring the bell.

He stayed as long as the whiskey held out, growing more violent towards the end. She watered his bottles; begged whiskey to make camphor—*Gre't God, Sis Kate, do you sell camphor? I gave you a pint this morning.* Poor Brother Jack, killed in Breckinridge's charge at Murfreesboro, cut in two by a chain shot from an enemy gun. All night long she had sat up after the message came. His body scattered about a splintered black gum tree. She had seen that night, as if she had been on the field, the parties moving over the dark field hunting the wounded and dead. Clyde Bascom had fallen near Jack with a bad hurt. They were messmates. He had to tell somebody; and somehow she was the one he must talk to. The spectral lanterns, swinging towards the dirge of pain and the monotonous cries of *Water,* caught by the river dew on the before-morning air and held suspended over the field in its acrid quilt. There death dripped to mildew the noisy throats . . . and all the while relief parties, or maybe it was the burial parties, moving, blots of night, sullenly moving in the viscous blackness.

Her eyes widened, and she looked across the foot posts into the room. There was some mistake, some cruel blunder; for there now, tipping about the carpet, hunting in her wardrobe, under the bed, blowing down the fire to the ashes until they glowed in their dryness, stalked the burial parties. They stepped out of the ashes in twos and threes, hunting, hunting and shaking their heads. Whom were they searching for? Jack had long been buried. They moved more rapidly; looked angry. They crowded the room until she gasped for breath. One, gaunt and haggard, jumped on the foot of her bed; rose to the ceiling; gesticulated; argued in animated silence. He leaned forward pressed his hand upon her leg. She tried to tell him to take it off. Cold and crushing heavy, it pressed her down to the bowels of the earth. Her lips trembled, but no sound came forth. Now the hand moved up to her stomach; and the haggard eyes looked gravely at her, alert, as if they were waiting for something. Her head turned giddy. She called to Dick, to Ants, to Doctor Ed; but the words struck her teeth and fell back in her throat. She concentrated on lifting the words, and the burial parties sadly shook their heads. Always the cries struck her teeth and fell back down. She strained to hear the silence they made. At last from a great distance she thought she heard . . . *too late* . . . *too late*. How exquisite the sound, like a bell swinging without ringing. Suddenly it came to her. She was dying.

How slyly death slipped up on a body, like sleep moving over the vague boundary. How many times she had lain awake to trick the unconscious there. At last she would know . . . But she wasn't ready. She must first do something about Long Gourd. That slut must not eat it up. She would give it to the hands first. He must be brought to understand this. But the spectres shook their heads. Well let them shake. She'd be damned if she would go until she was ready to go. She'd be damned all right, and she smiled at the meaning the word took on now. She gathered together all the particles of her will; the spectres faded; and there about her were the anxious faces of kin and servants. Edwin had

his hands under the cover feeling her legs. She made to raise her own hand to the boy. It did not go up. Her eyes wanted to roll upward and look behind her forehead, but she pinched them down and looked at her grandson.

"You want to say something, Mammy?" —she saw his lips move.

She had a plenty to say, but her tongue had somehow got glued to her lips. Truly it was now too late. Her will left her. Life withdrawing gathered like a frosty dew on her skin. The last breath blew gently past her nose. The dusty nostrils tingled. She felt a great sneeze coming. There was a roaring; the wind blew through her head once, and a great cotton field bent before it, growing and spreading, the bolls swelling as big as cotton sacks and bursting white as thunderheads. From a distance, out of the far end of the field, under a sky so blue that it was painful-bright, voices came singing, *Joshua fit the battle of Jerico, Jerico, Jerico—Joshua fit the battle of Jerico, and the walls came a-tumbling down.*

O YOUTH AND BEAUTY!
John Cheever (b. 1912)

At the tag end of nearly every long, large Saturday-night party in the suburb of Shady Hill, when almost everybody who was going to play golf or tennis in the morning had gone home hours ago and the ten or twelve people remaining seemed powerless to bring the evening to an end although the gin and whiskey were running low, and here and there a woman who was sitting out her husband would have begun to drink milk; when everybody had lost track of time, and the baby sitters who were waiting at home for these diehards would have long since stretched out on the sofa and fallen into a deep sleep, to dream about cooking-contest prizes, ocean voyages, and romance; when the bellicose drunk, the crapshooter, the pianist, and the woman faced with the expiration of her hopes had all expressed themselves; when every proposal—to go to the Farquarsons' for breakfast, to go swimming, to go and wake up the Townsends, to go here and go there—died as soon as it was made, then Trace Bearden would begin to chide Cash Bentley about his age and thinning hair. The chiding was preliminary to moving the living-room furniture. Trace and Cash moved the tables and the chairs, the sofas and the fire screen, the woodbox and the footstool; and when they had finished, you wouldn't know the place. Then if the host had a revolver, he would be asked to produce it. Cash would take off his shoes and assume a starting crouch behind a sofa. Trace would fire the weapon out of an open window, and if you were new to the community and had not understood what the preparations were about, you would then realize that you were watching a hurdle race. Over the sofa went Cash, over the tables, over the fire screen and the woodbox. It was not exactly a race, since Cash ran it alone, but it was extraordinary to see this man of forty surmount so many obstacles so gracefully. There was not a piece of furniture in Shady Hill that Cash could not take in his stride. The race ended with cheers, and presently the party would break up.

Cash was, of course, an old track star, but he was never aggressive or tiresome about his brilliant past. The college where he had spent his youth had offered him a paying job on the alumni council, but he had refused it, realizing that that part of his life was ended. Cash and his wife, Louise, had two children, and they lived in a medium-cost ranchhouse on Alewives Lane. They belonged to the country club, although they could not afford it, but in the case of the Bentleys nobody ever pointed this out, and Cash was one of the best-liked men in Shady Hill. He was still slender—he was careful about his weight —and he walked to the train in the morning with a light and vigorous step that marked him as an athlete. His hair was thin, and there were mornings when his eyes looked bloodshot, but this did not detract much from

a charming quality of stubborn youthfulness.

In business Cash had suffered reverses and disappointments, and the Bentleys had many money worries. They were always late with their tax payments and their mortgage payments, and the drawer of the hall table was stuffed with unpaid bills; it was always touch and go with the Bentleys and the bank. Louise looked pretty enough on Saturday night, but her life was exacting and monotonous. In the pockets of her suits, coats, and dresses there were little wads and scraps of paper on which was written: "Oleomargarine, frozen spinach, Kleenex, dog biscuit, hamburger, pepper, lard . . ." When she was still half awake in the morning, she was putting on the water for coffee and diluting the frozen orange juice. Then she would be wanted by the children. She would crawl under the bureau on her hands and knees to find a sock for Toby. She would lie flat on her belly and wriggle under the bed (getting dust up her nose) to find a shoe for Rachel. Then there were the housework, the laundry, and the cooking, as well as the demands of the children. There always seemed to be shoes to put on and shoes to take off, snowsuits to be zipped and unzipped, bottoms to be wiped, tears to be dried, and when the sun went down (she saw it set from the kitchen window) there was the supper to be cooked, the baths, the bedtime story, and the Lord's Prayer. With the sonorous words of the Our Father in a darkened room the children's day was over, but the day was far from over for Louise Bentley. There were the darning, the mending, and some ironing to do, and after sixteen years of housework she did not seem able to escape her chores even while she slept. Snowsuits, shoes, baths, and groceries seemed to have permeated her subconscious. Now and then she would speak in her sleep—so loudly that she woke her husband. "I can't *afford* veal cutlets," she said one night. Then she sighed uneasily and was quiet again.

By the standards of Shady Hill, the Bentleys were a happily married couple, but they had their ups and downs. Cash could be very touchy at times. When he came home after a bad day at the office and found that Louise, for some good reason, had not started supper, he would be ugly. "Oh, for Christ sake!" he would say, and go into the kitchen and heat up some frozen food. He drank some whiskey to relax himself during this ordeal, but it never seemed to relax him, and he usually burned the bottom out of a pan, and when they sat down for supper the dining space would be full of smoke. It was only a question of time before they were plunged into a bitter quarrel. Louise would run upstairs, throw herself onto the bed, and sob. Cash would grab the whiskey bottle and dose himself. These rows, in spite of the vigor with which Cash and Louise entered into them, were the source of a great deal of pain for both of them. Cash would sleep downstairs on the sofa, but sleep never repaired the damage, once the trouble had begun, and if they met in the morning, they would be at one another's throats in a second. Then Cash would leave for the train, and, as soon as the children had been taken to nursery school, Louise would put on her coat and cross the grass to the Beardens' house. She would cry into a cup of warmed-up coffee and tell Lucy Bearden her troubles. What was the meaning of marriage? What was the meaning of love? Lucy always suggested that Louise get a job. It would give her emotional and financial independence, and that, Lucy said, was what she needed.

The next night, things would get worse. Cash would not come home for dinner at all, but would stumble in at about eleven, and the whole sordid wrangle would be repeated, with Louise going to bed in tears upstairs and Cash again stretching out on the living-room sofa. After a few days and nights of this, Louise would decide that she was at the end of her rope. She would decide to go and stay with her married sister in Mamaroneck. She usually chose a Saturday, when Cash would be at home, for her departure. She would pack a suitcase and get her War Bonds from the desk. Then she would take a bath

and put on her best slip. Cash, passing the bedroom door, would see her. Her slip was transparent, and suddenly he was all repentance, tenderness, charm, wisdom, and love. "Oh, my darling!" he would groan, and when they went downstairs to get a bite to eat about an hour later, they would be sighing and making cow eyes at one another; they would be the happiest married couple in the whole Eastern United States. It was usually at about this time that Lucy Bearden turned up with the good news that she had found a job for Louise. Lucy would ring the doorbell, and Cash, wearing a bathrobe, would let her in. She would be brief with Cash, naturally, and hurry into the dining room to tell poor Louise the good news. "Well that's very nice of you to have looked," Louise would say wanly, "but I don't think that I want a job any more. I don't think that Cash wants me to work, do you, sweetheart?" Then she would turn her big dark eyes on Cash, and you could practically smell smoke. Lucy would excuse herself hurriedly from this scene of depravity, but she never left with any hard feelings, because she had been married for nineteen years herself and she knew that every union has its ups and downs. She didn't seem to leave any wiser, either; the next time the Bentleys quarreled, she would be just as intent as ever on getting Louise a job. But these quarrels and reunions, like the hurdle race, didn't seem to lose their interest through repetition.

On a Saturday night in the spring, the Farquarsons gave the Bentleys an anniversary party. It was their seventeenth anniversary. Saturday afternoon, Louise Bentley put herself through preparations nearly as arduous as the Monday wash. She rested for an hour, by the clock, with her feet high in the air, her chin in a sling, and her eyes bathed in some astringent solution. The clay packs, the too tight girdle, and the plucking and curling and painting that went on were all aimed at rejuvenation. Feeling in the end that she had not been entirely successful, she tied a piece of veiling over her eyes—but she was a lovely woman, and all the cosmetics that she had struggled with seemed, like her veil, to be drawn transparently over a face where mature beauty and a capacity for wit and passion were undisguisable. The Farquarsons' party was nifty, and the Bentleys had a wonderful time. The only person who drank too much was Trace Bearden. Late in the party, he began to chide Cash about his thinning hair and Cash good-naturedly began to move the furniture around. Harry Farquarson had a pistol, and Trace went out onto the terrace to fire it up at the sky. Over the sofa went Cash, over the end table, over the arms of the wing chair and the fire screen. It was a piece of carving on a chest that brought him down, and down he came like a ton of bricks.

Louise screamed and ran to where he lay. He had cut a gash in his forehead, and someone made a bandage to stop the flow of blood. When he tried to get up, he stumbled and fell again, and his face turned a terrible green. Harry telephoned Dr. Parminter, Dr. Hopewell, Dr. Altman, and Dr. Barnstable, but it was two in the morning and none of them answered. Finally, a Dr. Yerkes—a total stranger—agreed to come. Yerkes was a young man—he did not seem old enough to be a doctor—and he looked around at the disordered room and the anxious company as if there was something weird about the scene. He got off on the wrong foot with Cash. "What seems to be the matter, old-timer?" he asked.

Cash's leg was broken. The doctor put a splint on it, and Harry and Trace carried the injured man out to the doctor's car. Louise followed them in her own car to the hospital, where Cash was bedded down in a ward. The doctor gave Cash a sedative, and Louise kissed him and drove home in the dawn.

Cash was in the hospital for two weeks, and when he came home he walked with a crutch and his broken leg was in a heavy cast. It was another ten days before he could limp to the morning train. "I won't be able to run the hurdle race any more, sweetheart," he told Louise sadly. She said that it didn't matter, but while it didn't matter to her, it seemed to matter to Cash. He had lost weight in the hospital. His spirits were low. He seemed discontented. He did not himself understand what had happened. He, or everything around him, seemed subtly to have changed for the worse. Even his senses seemed to conspire to damage the ingenuous world that he had enjoyed for so many years. He went into the kitchen late one night to make himself a sandwich, and when he opened the icebox door he noticed a rank smell. He dumped the spoiled meat into the garbage, but the smell clung to his nostrils. A few days later he was in the attic, looking for his old varsity sweater. There were no windows in the attic and his flashlight was dim. Kneeling on the floor to unlock a trunk, he broke a spider web with his lips. The frail web covered his mouth as if a hand had been put over it. He wiped it impatiently, but also with the feeling of having been gagged. A few nights later, he was walking down a New York side street in the rain and saw an old whore standing in a doorway. She was so sluttish and ugly that she looked like a cartoon of Death, but before he could appraise her—the instant his eyes took an impression of her crooked figure—his lips swelled, his breathing quickened, and he experienced all the other symptoms of erotic excitement. A few nights later, while he was reading *Time* in the living room, he noticed that the faded roses Louise had brought in from the garden smelled more of earth than of anything else. It was a putrid, compelling smell. He dropped the roses into a wastebasket, but not before they had reminded him of the spoiled meat, the whore, and the spider web.

He had started going to parties again, but without the hurdle race to run, the parties of his friends and neighbors seemed to him interminable and stale. He listened to their dirty jokes with an irritability that was hard for him to conceal. Even their countenances discouraged him, and, slumped in a chair, he would regard their skin and their teeth narrowly, as if he were himself a much younger man.

The brunt of his irritability fell on Louise, and it seemed to her that Cash, in losing the hurdle race, had lost the thing that preserved his equilibrium. He was rude to his friends when they stopped in for a drink. He was rude and gloomy when he and Louise went out. When Louise asked him what was the matter, he only murmured, "Nothing, nothing, nothing," and poured himself some bourbon. May and June passed, and then the first part of July, without his showing any improvement.

Then it is a summer night, a wonderful summer night. The passengers on the eight-fifteen see Shady Hill—if they notice it at all—in a bath of placid golden light. The noise of the train is muffled in the heavy foliage, and the long car windows look like a string of lighted aquarium tanks before they flicker out of sight. Up on the hill, the ladies say to one another, "Smell the grass! Smell the trees!" The Farquarsons are giving another party, and Harry has hung a sign, WHISKEY GULCH, from the rose arbor, and is wearing a chef's white hat and an apron. His guests are still drinking, and the smoke from his meat fire rises, on this windless evening, straight up into the trees.

In the clubhouse on the hill, the first of the formal dances for the young people begins around nine. On Alewives Lane sprinklers continue to play after dark. You can smell the water. The air seems as fragrant as it is dark—it is a delicious element to walk through—and most of the windows on Alewives Lane are open to it. You can see Mr. and Mrs. Bearden, as you pass, looking at their television. Joe Lockwood, the young lawyer who lives on the corner, is practicing a speech to the jury before his wife. "I intend to show you," he says, "that a man of probity, a man whose reputation for honesty and reliability . . ." He waves his bare arms as he speaks. His wife goes on knitting. Mrs. Carver—Harry Farquarson's mother-in-law —glances up at the sky and asks, "*Where* did all the stars come from?" She is old and foolish, and yet she is right: Last night's stars seem to have drawn to themselves a new range of galaxies, and the night sky is not dark at all, except where there is a tear in the membrane of light. In the unsold house lots near the track a hermit thrush is singing.

The Bentleys are at home. Poor Cash has been so rude and gloomy that the Farquarsons have not asked him to their party. He sits on the sofa beside Louise, who is sewing elastic into the children's underpants. Through the open window he can hear the pleasant sounds of the summer night. There is another party, in the Rogerses' garden, behind the Bentleys'. The music from the dance drifts down the hill. The band is sketchy—saxophone, drums, and piano—and all the selections are twenty years old. The band plays "Valencia," and Cash looks tenderly toward Louise, but Louise, tonight, is a discouraging figure. The lamp picks out the gray in her hair. Her apron is stained. Her face seems colorless and drawn. Suddenly, Cash begins frenziedly to beat his feet in time to the music. He sings some gibberish— Jabajabajabajaba—to the distant saxophone. He sighs and goes into the kitchen.

Here a faint, stale smell of cooking clings to the dark. From the kitchen window Cash can see the lights and figures of the Rogerses' party. It is a young people's party. The Rogers girl has asked some friends in for dinner before the dance, and now they seem to be leaving. Cars are driving away. "I'm covered with grass stains," a girl says. "I hope the old man remembered to buy gasoline," a boy says, and a girl laughs. There is nothing on their minds but the passing summer night. Taxes and the elastic in underpants—all the unbeautiful facts of life that threaten to crush the breath out of Cash— have not touched a single figure in this garden. Then jealousy seizes him—such savage and bitter jealousy that he feels ill.

He does not understand what separates him from these children in the garden next door. He has been a young man. He has been a hero. He has been adored and happy and full of animal spirits, and now he stands in a dark kitchen, deprived of his athletic prowess, his impetuousness, his good looks— of everything that means anything to him. He feels as if the figures in the next yard are the specters from some party in that past where all his tastes and desires lie, and from which he has been cruelly removed. He feels like a ghost of the summer evening. He is sick with longing. Then he hears voices in the front of the house. Louise turns on the kitchen light. "Oh, here you are," she says. "The Beardens stopped in. I think they'd like a drink."

Cash went to the front of the house to greet the Beardens. They wanted to go up to the club, for one dance. They saw, at a glance, that Cash was at loose ends, and they urged the Bentleys to come. Louise got someone to stay with the children and then went upstairs to change.

When they got to the club, they found a few friends of their age hanging around the bar, but Cash did not stay in the bar. He seemed restless and perhaps drunk. He banged into a table on his way through the lounge to the ballroom. He cut in on a young girl. He seized her too vehemently and jigged her off in an ancient two-step. She signaled openly for help to a boy in the stag line, and Cash was cut out. He walked angrily off the dance floor onto the terrace. Some young couples there withdrew from one another's arms as he pushed open the screen door. He walked to the end of the terrace, where he hoped to be alone, but here he surprised another young couple, who got up from the lawn, where they seemed to have been lying, and walked off in the dark toward the pool.

Louise remained in the bar with the Beardens. "Poor Cash is tight," she said. And then, "He told me this afternoon that he was going to paint the storm windows," she said. "Well, he mixed the paint and washed the brushes and put on some old fatigues and went into the cellar. There was a telephone call for him at around five, and when I went down to tell him, do you know what he was doing? He was just sitting there in the dark with a cocktail shaker. He hadn't touched the storm windows. He was just sitting there in the dark, drinking Martinis."

"Poor Cash," Trace said.

"You ought to get a job," Lucy said. "That would give you emotional and financial independence." As she spoke, they all heard the noise of furniture being moved around in the lounge.

"Oh, my God!" Louise said. "He's going to run the race. Stop him, Trace, stop him! He'll hurt himself. He'll kill himself!"

They all went to the door of the lounge. Louise again asked Trace to interfere, but she could see by Cash's face that he was way beyond remonstrating with. A few couples left the dance floor and stood watching the preparations. Trace didn't try to stop Cash— he helped him. There was no pistol, so he slammed a couple of books together for the start.

Over the sofa went Cash, over the coffee table, the lamp table, the fire screen, and the hassock. All his grace and strength seemed to have returned to him. He cleared the big sofa at the end of the room and instead of stopping there, he turned and started back over the course. His face was strained. His mouth hung open. The tendons of his neck protruded hideously. He made the hassock, the fire screen, the lamp table, and the coffee table. People held their breath when he approached the final sofa, but he cleared it and landed on his feet. There was some applause. Then he groaned and fell. Louise ran to his side. His clothes were soaked with sweat and he gasped for breath. She knelt down beside him and took his head in her lap and stroked his thin hair.

Cash had a terrible hangover on Sunday, and Louise let him sleep until it was nearly time for church. The family went off to Christ Church together at eleven, as they always did. Cash sang, prayed, and got to his knees, but the most he ever felt in church was that he stood outside the realm of God's infinite mercy, and, to tell the truth, he no more believed in the Father, the Son, and the Holy Ghost than does my bull terrier. They returned home at one to eat the overcooked meat and stony potatoes that were their customary Sunday lunch. At around five, the Parminters called up and asked them over for a drink. Louise didn't want to go, so Cash went alone. (Oh, those suburban Sunday nights, those Sunday-night blues! Those departing weekend guests, those stale cocktails, those half-dead flowers, those trips to Harmon to catch the Century, those post-mortems and pickup suppers!) It was sultry and overcast. The dog days were beginning. He drank gin with the Parminters for an hour or two and then went over to the Townsends' for a drink. The Farquarsons called up the Townsends and asked them to come over and bring Cash with them, and at the Farquarsons' they had some more drinks and ate the leftover party food. The Farquarsons were glad to see that Cash seemed like himself again. It was half past ten or eleven when he got home. Louise was upstairs, cutting out of the current copy of *Life* those scenes of mayhem, disaster, and violent death that she felt might corrupt her children. She always did this. Cash came upstairs and spoke to her and then went down again. In a little while, she heard him moving the living-room furniture around. Then he called to her, and when she went down, he was standing at the foot of the stairs in his stocking feet, holding the pistol out to her. She had never fired it before, and the directions he gave her were not much help.

"Hurry up," he said. "I can't wait all night."

He had forgotten to tell her about the safety, and when she pulled the trigger nothing happened.

"It's that little lever," he said. "Press that little lever." Then, in his impatience, he hurdled the sofa anyhow.

The pistol went off and Louise got him in midair. She shot him dead.

THE MAGIC BARREL
Bernard Malamud (b. 1914)

Not long ago there lived in uptown New York, in a small, almost meager room, though crowded with books, Leo Finkle, a rabbinical student in the Yeshivah University. Finkle, after six years of study, was to be ordained in June and had been advised by an acquaintance that he might find it easier to win himself a congregation if he were married. Since he had no present prospects of marriage, after two tormented days of turning it over in his mind, he called in Pinye Salzman, a marriage broker whose two-line advertisement he had read in the *Forward*.

The matchmaker appeared one night out of the dark fourth-floor hallway of the graystone rooming house where Finkle lived, grasping a black, strapped portfolio that had been worn thin with use. Salzman, who had been long in the business, was of slight but dignified build, wearing an old hat, and an overcoat too short and tight for him. He smelled frankly of fish, which he loved to eat, and although he was missing a few teeth, his presence was not displeasing, because of an amiable manner curiously contrasted with mournful eyes. His voice, his lips, his wisp of beard, his bony fingers were animated, but give him a moment of repose and his mild blue eyes revealed a depth of sadness, a characteristic that put Leo a little at ease although the situation, for him, was inherently tense.

He at once informed Salzman why he had asked him to come, explaining that his home was in Cleveland, and that but for his parents, who had married comparatively late in life, he was alone in the world. He had for six years devoted himself almost entirely to his studies, as a result of which, understandably, he had found himself without time for a social life and the company of young women. Therefore he thought it the better part of trial and error—of embarrassing fumbling—to call in an experienced person to advise him on these matters. He remarked in passing that the function of the marriage broker was ancient and honorable, highly approved in the Jewish community, because it made practical the necessary without hindering joy. Moreover, his own parents had been brought together by a matchmaker. They had made, if not a financially profitable marriage—since neither had possessed any worldly goods to speak of—at least a successful one in the sense of their everlasting devotion to each other. Salzman listened in embarrassed surprise, sensing a sort of apology. Later, however, he experienced a glow of pride in his work, an emotion that had left him years ago, and he heartily approved of Finkle.

The two went to their business. Leo had led Salzman to the only clear place in the room, a table near a window that overlooked the lamp-lit city. He seated himself at the matchmaker's side but facing him, attempting by an act of will to suppress the unpleasant tickle in his throat. Salzman eagerly unstrapped his portfolio and removed a loose rubber band from a thin packet of much-handled cards. As he flipped through them, a gesture and sound that physically hurt Leo, the student pretended not to see and gazed steadfastly out the window. Although it was still February, winter was on its last legs, signs of which he had for the first time in years begun to notice. He now observed the round white moon, moving high in the sky through a cloud menagerie, and watched with half-open mouth as it penetrated a huge hen, and dropped out of her like an egg laying itself. Salzman, though pretending through eyeglasses he had just slipped on, to be engaged in scanning the writing on the cards, stole occasional glances at the young man's distinguished face, noting with pleasure the long, severe scholar's nose, brown eyes heavy with learning, sensitive yet ascetic lips, and a certain, almost hollow quality of the dark cheeks. He gazed around at shelves upon shelves of books and let out a soft, contented sigh.

When Leo's eyes fell upon the cards, he counted six spread out in Salzman's hand.

"So few?" he asked in disappointment.

"You wouldn't believe me how much cards I got in my office," Salzman replied.

"The drawers are already filled to the top, so I keep them now in a barrel, but is every girl good for a new rabbi?"

Leo blushed at this, regretting all he had revealed of himself in a curriculum vitae he had sent to Salzman. He had thought it best to acquaint him with his strict standards and specifications, but in having done so, felt he had told the marriage broker more than was absolutely necessary.

He hesitantly inquired, "Do you keep photographs of your clients on file?"

"First comes family, amount of dowry, also what kind promises," Salzman replied, unbuttoning his tight coat and settling himself in the chair. "After comes pictures, rabbi."

"Call me Mr. Finkle. I'm not yet a rabbi."

Salzman said he would, but instead called him doctor, which he changed to rabbi when Leo was not listening too attentively.

Salzman adjusted his horn-rimmed spectacles, gently cleared his throat and read in an eager voice the contents of the top card:

"Sophie P. Twenty four years. Widow one year. No children. Educated high school and two years college. Father promises eight thousand dollars. Has wonderful wholesale business. Also real estate. On the mother's side comes teachers, also one actor. Well known on Second Avenue."

Leo gazed up in surprise. "Did you say a widow?"

"A widow don't mean spoiled, rabbi. She lived with her husband maybe four months. He was a sick boy she made a mistake to marry him."

"Marrying a widow has never entered my mind."

"This is because you have no experience. A widow, especially if she is young and healthy like this girl, is a wonderful person to marry. She will be thankful to you the rest of her life. Believe me, if I was looking now for a bride, I would marry a widow."

Leo reflected, then shook his head.

Salzman hunched his shoulders in an almost imperceptible gesture of disappointment. He placed the card down on the wooden table and began to read another:

"Lily H. High school teacher. Regular. Not a substitute. Has savings and new Dodge car. Lived in Paris one year. Father is successful dentist thirty-five years. Interested in professional man. Well Americanized family. Wonderful opportunity."

"I knew her personally," said Salzman. "I wish you could see this girl. She is a doll. Also very intelligent. All day you could talk to her about books and theyater and what not. She also knows current events."

"I don't believe you mentioned her age?"

"Her age?" Salzman said, raising his brows. "Her age is thirty-two years."

Leo said after a while, "I'm afraid that seems a little too old."

Salzman let out a laugh. "So how old are you, rabbi?"

"Twenty-seven."

"So what is the difference, tell me, between twenty-seven and thirty-two? My own wife is seven years older than me. So what did I suffer?—Nothing. If Rothschild's a daughter wants to marry you, would you say on account her age, no?"

"Yes," Leo said dryly.

Salzman shook off the no in the yes. "Five years don't mean a thing. I give you my word that when you will live with her for one week you will forget her age. What does it mean five years—that she lived more and knows more than somebody who is younger? On this girl, God bless her, years are not wasted. Each one that it comes makes better the bargain."

"What subject does she teach in high school?"

"Languages. If you heard the way she speaks French, you will think it is music. I am in the business twenty-five years, and I recommend her with my whole heart. Believe me, I know what I'm talking, rabbi."

"What's on the next card?" Leo said abruptly.

Salzman reluctantly turned up the third card:

"Ruth K. Nineteen years. Honor student. Father offers thirteen thousand cash to the right bridegroom. He is a medical doctor. Stomach specialist with marvelous practice. Brother in law owns own garment business. Particular people."

Salzman looked as if he had read his trump card.

"Did you say nineteen?" Leo asked with interest.

"On the dot."

"Is she attractive?" He blushed. "Pretty?"

Salzman kissed his finger tips. "A little doll. On this I give you my word. Let me call the father tonight and you will see what means pretty."

But Leo was troubled. "You're sure she's that young?"

"This I am positive. The father will show you the birth certificate."

"Are you positive there isn't something wrong with her?" Leo insisted.

"Who says there is wrong?"

"I don't understand why an American girl her age should go to a marriage broker."

A smile spread over Salzman's face.

"So for the same reason you went, she comes."

Leo flushed. "I am pressed for time."

Salzman, realizing he had been tactless, quickly explained. "The father came, not her. He wants she should have the best, so he looks around himself. When we will locate the right boy he will introduce him and encourage. This makes a better marriage than if a young girl without experience takes for herself. I don't have to tell you this."

"But don't you think this young girl believes in love?" Leo spoke uneasily.

Salzman was about to guffaw but caught himself and said soberly, "Love comes with the right person, not before."

Leo parted dry lips but did not speak. Noticing that Salzman had snatched a glance at the next card, he cleverly asked, "How is her health?"

"Perfect," Salzman said, breathing with difficulty. "Of course, she is a little lame on her right foot from an auto accident that it happened to her when she was twelve years, but nobody notices on account she is so brilliant and also beautiful."

Leo got up heavily and went to the window. He felt curiously bitter and upbraided himself for having called in the marriage broker. Finally, he shook his head.

"Why not?" Salzman persisted, the pitch of his voice rising.

"Because I detest stomach specialists."

"So what do you care what is his business? After you marry her do you need him? Who says he must come every Friday night in your house?"

Ashamed of the way the talk was going, Leo dismissed Salzman, who went home with heavy, melancholy eyes.

Though he had felt only relief at the marriage broker's departure, Leo was in low spirits the next day. He explained it as arising from Salzman's failure to produce a suitable bride for him. He did not care for his type of clientele. But when Leo found himself hesitating whether to seek out another matchmaker, one more polished than Pinye, he wondered if it could be—his protestations to the contrary, and although he honored his father and mother—that he did not, in essence, care for the matchmaking institution? This thought he quickly put out of mind yet found himself still upset. All day he ran around in the woods—missed an important appointment, forgot to give out his laundry, walked out of a Broadway cafeteria without paying and had to run back with the ticket in his hand; had even not recognized his landlady in the street when she passed with a friend and courteously called out, "A good evening to you, Doctor Finkle." By nightfall, however, he had regained sufficient calm to sink his nose into a book and there found peace from his thoughts.

Almost at once there came a knock on the door. Before Leo could say enter, Salzman, commercial cupid, was standing in the room. His face was gray and meager, his expression hungry, and he looked as if he would expire on his feet. Yet the marriage broker managed, by some trick of the muscles, to display a broad smile.

"So good evening. I am invited?"

Leo nodded, disturbed to see him again, yet unwilling to ask the man to leave.

Beaming still, Salzman laid his portfolio on the table. "Rabbi, I got for you tonight good news."

"I've asked you not to call me rabbi. I'm still a student."

"Your worries are finished. I have for you a first-class bride."

"Leave me in peace concerning this subject." Leo pretended lack of interest.

"The world will dance at your wedding."

"Please, Mr. Salzman, no more."

"But first must come back my strength," Salzman said weakly. He fumbled with the portfolio straps and took out of the leather case an oily paper bag, from which he extracted a hard, seeded roll and a small, smoked white fish. With a quick motion of his hand he stripped the fish out of its skin and began ravenously to chew. "All day in a rush," he muttered.

Leo watched him eat.

"A sliced tomato you have maybe?" Salzman hesitantly inquired.

"No."

The marriage broker shut his eyes and ate. When he had finished he carefully cleaned up the crumbs and rolled up the remains of the fish, in the paper bag. His spectacled eyes roamed the room until he discovered, amid some piles of books, a one-burner gas stove. Lifting his hat he humbly asked, "A glass tea you got, rabbi?"

Conscience-stricken, Leo rose and brewed the tea. He served it with a chunk of lemon and two cubes of lump sugar, delighting Salzman.

After he had drunk his tea, Salzman's strength and good spirits were restored.

"So tell me, rabbi," he said amiably, "you considered some more the three clients I mentioned yesterday?"

"There was no need to consider."

"Why not?"

"None of them suits me."

"What then suits you?"

Leo let it pass because he could give only a confused answer.

Without waiting for a reply, Salzman asked, "You remember this girl I talked to you—the high school teacher?"

"Age thirty-two?"

But, surprisingly, Salzman's face lit in a smile. "Age twenty-nine."

Leo shot him a look. "Reduced from thirty-two?"

"A mistake," Salzman avowed. "I talked today with the dentist. He took me to his safety deposit box and showed me the birth certificate. She was twenty-nine years last August. They made her a party in the mountains where she went for her vacation. When her father spoke to me the first time I forgot to write the age and I told you thirty-two, but now I remember this was a different client, a widow."

"The same one you told me about? I thought she was twenty-four?"

"A different. Am I responsible that the world is filled with widows?"

"No, but I'm not interested in them, nor for that matter, in school teachers."

Salzman pulled his clasped hands to his breast. Looking at the ceiling he devoutly exclaimed, "Yiddishe kinder, what can I say to somebody that he is not interested in high school teachers? So what then you are interested?"

Leo flushed but controlled himself.

"In what else will be you interested," Salzman went on, "if you not interested in this fine girl that she speaks four languages and has personally in the bank ten thousand dollars? Also her father guarantees further twelve thousand. Also she has a new car, wonderful clothes, talks on all subjects, and she will give you a first-class home and children. How near do we come in our life to paradise?"

"If she's so wonderful, why wasn't she married ten years ago?"

"Why?" said Salzman with a heavy laugh. "—Why? Because she is *partikiler*. This is why. She wants the *best*."

Leo was silent, amused at how he had entangled himself. But Salzman had aroused his interest in Lily H., and he began seriously to consider calling on her. When the marriage broker observed how intently Leo's mind was at work on the facts he had supplied, he felt certain they would soon come to an agreement.

Late Saturday afternoon, conscious of Salzman, Leo Finkle walked with Lily Hirschorn along Riverside Drive. He walked briskly and erectly, wearing with distinction the black fedora he had that morning taken with trepidation out of the dusty hat box on his closet shelf, and the heavy black Saturday coat he had thoroughly whisked clean. Leo also owned a walking stick, a present from a distant relative, but quickly put temptation aside and did not use it. Lily, petite and not unpretty, had on something signifying the approach of spring. She was au courant, animatedly, with all sorts of subjects, and he weighed her words and found her surprisingly sound—score another for Salzman, whom he uneasily sensed to be somewhere around, hiding perhaps high in a tree along the street, flashing the lady signals with a pocket mirror; or perhaps a cloven-hoofed Pan, piping nuptial ditties as he danced his invisible way before them, strewing wild buds on the walk and purple grapes in their path, symbolizing fruit of a union, though there was of course still none.

Lily startled Leo by remarking, "I was thinking of Mr. Salzman, a curious figure, wouldn't you say?"

Not certain what to answer, he nodded.

She bravely went on, blushing, "I for one am grateful for his introducing us. Aren't you?"

He courteously replied, "I am."

"I mean," she said with a little laugh—and it was all in good taste, or at least gave the effect of being not in bad—"do you mind that we came together so?"

He was not displeased with her honesty, recognizing that she meant to set the relationship aright, and understanding that it took a certain amount of experience in life, and courage, to want to do it quite that way. One had to have some sort of past to make that kind of beginning.

He said that he did not mind. Salzman's function was traditional and honorable—valuable for what it might achieve, which, he pointed out, was frequently nothing.

Lily agreed with a sigh. They walked on for a while and she said after a long silence, again with a nervous laugh, "Would you mind if I asked you something a little bit personal? Frankly, I find the subject fascinating." Although Leo shrugged, she went on half embarrassedly, "How was it that you came to your calling? I mean was it a sudden passionate inspiration?"

Leo, after a time, slowly replied, "I was always interested in the Law."

"You saw revealed in it the presence of the Highest?"

He nodded and changed the subject. "I understand that you spent a little time in Paris, Miss Hirschorn?"

"Oh, did Mr. Salzman tell you, Rabbi Finkle?" Leo winced but she went on, "It was ages ago and almost forgotten. I remember I had to return for my sister's wedding."

And Lily would not be put off. "When," she asked in a trembly voice, "did you become enamored of God?"

He stared at her. Then it came to him that she was talking not about Leo Finkle, but of a total stranger, some mystical figure, perhaps even passionate prophet that Salzman had dreamed up for her—no relation to the living or dead. Leo trembled with rage and weakness. The trickster had obviously sold her a bill of goods, just as he had him, who'd expected to become acquainted with a young lady of twenty-nine, only to behold, the moment he laid eyes upon her strained and anxious face, a woman past thirty-five and aging rapidly. Only his self control had kept him this long in her presence.

"I am not," he said gravely, "a talented religious person," and in seeking words to go on, found himself possessed by shame and fear. "I think," he said in a strained manner, "that I came to God not because I loved Him, but because I did not."

This confession he spoke harshly because its unexpectedness shook him.

Lily wilted. Leo saw a profusion of loaves of bread go flying like ducks high over his head, not unlike the winged loaves by which he had counted himself to sleep last night. Mercifully, then, it snowed, which he would not put past Salzman's machinations.

He was infuriated with the marriage broker and swore he would throw him out of the room the minute he reappeared. But Salzman did not come that night, and when Leo's anger had subsided, an unaccountable despair grew in its place. At first he thought this was caused by his disappointment in Lily, but before long it became evident that he had involved himself with Salzman without a true knowledge of his own intent. He gradually realized—with an emptiness that seized him with six hands—that he had called in the broker to find him a bride because he was incapable of doing it himself. This terrifying insight he had derived as a result of his meeting and conversation with Lily Hirschorn. Her probing questions had somehow irritated him into revealing—to himself more than her—the true nature of his relationship to God, and from that it had come upon him, with shocking force, that apart from his parents, he had never loved anyone. Or perhaps it went the other way, that he did not love God so well as he might, because he had not loved man. It seemed to Leo that his whole life stood starkly revealed and he saw himself for the first time as he truly was—unloved and loveless. This bitter but somehow not fully unexpected revelation brought him to a point of panic, controlled only by extraordinary effort. He covered his face with his hands and cried.

The week that followed was the worst

of his life. He did not eat and lost weight. His beard darkened and grew ragged. He stopped attending seminars and almost never opened a book. He seriously considered leaving the Yeshivah, although he was deeply troubled at the thought of the loss of all his years of study—saw them like pages torn from a book, strewn over the city—and at the devastating effect of this decision upon his parents. But he had lived without knowledge of himself, and never in the Five Books and all the Commentaries—mea culpa—had the truth been revealed to him. He did not know where to turn, and in all this desolating loneliness there was no *to whom*, although he often thought of Lily but not once could bring himself to go downstairs and make the call. He became touchy and irritable, especially with his landlady, who asked him all manner of personal questions; on the other hand, sensing his own disagreeableness, he waylaid her on the stairs and apologized abjectly, until mortified, she ran from him. Out of this, however, he drew the consolation that he was a Jew and that a Jew suffered. But gradually, as the long and terrible week drew to a close, he regained his composure and some idea of purpose in life: to go on as planned. Although he was imperfect, the ideal was not. As for his quest of a bride, the thought of continuing afflicted him with anxiety and heartburn, yet perhaps with this new knowledge of himself he would be more successful than in the past. Perhaps love would now come to him and a bride to that love. And for this sanctified seeking who needed a Salzman?

The marriage broker, a skeleton with haunted eyes, returned that very night. He looked, withal, the picture of frustrated expectancy—as if he had steadfastly waited the week at Miss Lily Hirschorn's side for a telephone call that never came.

Casually coughing, Salzman came immediately to the point: "So how did you like her?"

Leo's anger rose and he could not refrain from chiding the matchmaker: "Why did you lie to me, Salzman?"

Salzman's pale face went dead white, the world had snowed on him.

"Did you not state that she was twenty-nine?" Leo insisted.

"I give you my word—"

"She was thirty-five, if a day. *At least* thirty-five."

"Of this don't be too sure. Her father told me—"

"Never mind. The worst of it was that you lied to her."

"How did I lie to her, tell me?"

"You told her things about me that weren't true. You made me out to be more, consequently less than I am. She had in mind a totally different person, a sort of semi-mystical Wonder Rabbi."

"All I said, you was a religious man."

"I can imagine."

Salzman sighed. "This is my weakness that I have," he confessed. "My wife says to me I shouldn't be a salesman, but when I have two fine people that they would be wonderful to be married, I am so happy that I talk too much." He smiled wanly. "This is why Salzman is a poor man."

Leo's anger left him. "Well, Salzman, I'm afraid that's all."

The marriage broker fastened hungry eyes on him.

"You don't want any more a bride?"

"I do," said Leo, "but I have decided to seek her in a different way. I am no longer interested in an arranged marriage. To be frank, I now admit the necessity of premarital love. That is, I want to be in love with the one I marry."

"Love?" said Salzman, astounded. After a moment he remarked, "For us, our love is our life, not for the ladies. In the ghetto they—"

"I know, I know," said Leo. "I've thought of it often. Love, I have said to myself, should be a by-product of living and worship rather than its own end. Yet for myself I find it necessary to establish the level of my need and fulfill it."

Salzman shrugged but answered, "Listen, rabbi, if you want love, this I can find for you. I have such beautiful clients that you will love them the minute your eyes will see them."

Leo smiled unhappily. "I'm afraid you don't understand."

But Salzman hastily unstrapped his portfolio and withdrew a manila packet from it.

"Pictures," he said, quickly laying the envelope on the table.

Leo called after him to take the pictures away, but as if on the wings of the wind, Salzman had disappeared.

March came. Leo had returned to his regular routine. Although he felt not quite himself yet—lacked energy—he was making plans for a more active social life. Of course it would cost something, but he was an expert in cutting corners; and when there were no corners left he would make circles rounder. All the while Salzman's pictures had lain on the table, gathering dust. Occasionally as Leo sat studying, or enjoying a cup of tea, his eyes fell on the manila envelope, but he never opened it.

The days went by and no social life to speak of developed with a member of the opposite sex—it was difficult, given the circumstances of his situation. One morning Leo toiled up the stairs to his room and stared out the window at the city. Although the day was bright his view of it was dark. For some time he watched the people in the street below hurrying along and then turned with a heavy heart to his little room. On the table was the packet. With a sudden relentless gesture he tore it open. For a half-hour he stood by the table in a state of excitement, examining the photographs of the ladies Salzman had included. Finally, with a deep sigh he put them down. There were six, of varying degrees of attractiveness, but look at them long enough and they all became Lily Hir-

schorn: all past their prime, all starved behind bright smiles, not a true personality in the lot. Life, despite their frantic yoohooings, had passed them by; they were pictures in a brief case that stank of fish. After a while, however, as Leo attempted to return the photographs into the envelope, he found in it another, a snapshot of the type taken by a machine for a quarter. He gazed at it a moment and let out a cry.

Her face deeply moved him. Why, he could at first not say. It gave him the impression of youth—spring flowers, yet age—a sense of having been used to the bone, wasted; this came from the eyes, which were hauntingly familiar, yet absolutely strange. He had a vivid impression that he had met her before, but try as he might he could not place her although he could almost recall her name, as if he had read it in her own handwriting. No, this couldn't be; he would have remembered her. It was not, he affirmed, that she had an extraordinary beauty—no, though her face was attractive enough; it was that *something* about her moved him. Feature for feature, even some of the ladies of the photographs could do better; but she leaped forth to his heart—had *lived*, or wanted to—more than just wanted, perhaps regretted how she had lived—had somehow deeply suffered: it could be seen in the depths of those reluctant eyes, and from the way the light enclosed and shone from her, and within her, opening realms of possibility: this was her own. Her he desired. His head ached and eyes narrowed with the intensity of his gazing, then as if an obscure fog had blown up in the mind, he experienced fear of her and was aware that he had received an impression, somehow, of evil. He shuddered, saying softly, it is thus with us all. Leo brewed some tea in a small pot and sat sipping it without sugar, to calm himself. But before he had finished drinking, again with excitement he examined the face and found it good: good for Leo Finkle. Only such a one could understand him and help him seek whatever he was seeking. She might, perhaps, love him. How she had happened to be among the discards in Salzman's barrel he could never guess, but he knew he must urgently go find her.

Leo rushed downstairs, grabbed up the Bronx telephone book, and searched for Salzman's home address. He was not listed, nor was his office. Neither was he in the Manhattan book. But Leo remembered having written down the address on a slip of paper after he had read Salzman's advertisement in the "personals" column of the *Forward*. He ran up to his room and tore through his papers, without luck. It was exasperating. Just when he needed the matchmaker he was nowhere to be found. Fortunately Leo remembered to look in his wallet. There on a card he found his name written and a Bronx address. No phone number was listed, the reason—Leo now recalled—he had originally communicated with Salzman by letter. He got on his coat, put a hat on over his skull cap and hurried to the subway station. All the way to the far end of the Bronx he sat on the edge of his seat. He was more than once tempted to take out the picture and see if the girl's face was as he remembered it, but he refrained, allowing the snapshot to remain in his inside coat pocket, content to have her so close. When the train pulled into the station he was waiting at the door and bolted out. He quickly located the street Salzman had advertised.

The building he sought was less than a block from the subway, but it was not an office building, nor even a loft, nor a store in which one could rent office space. It was a very old tenement house. Leo found Salzman's name in pencil on a soiled tag under the bell and climbed three dark flights to his apartment. When he knocked, the door was opened by a thin, asthmatic, gray-haired woman, in felt slippers.

"Yes?" she said, expecting nothing. She listened without listening. He could have sworn he had seen her, too, before but knew it was an illusion.

"Salzman—does he live here? Pinye Salzman," he said, "the matchmaker?"

She stared at him a long minute. "Of course."

He felt embarrassed. "Is he in?"

"No." Her mouth, though left open, offered nothing more.

"The matter is urgent. Can you tell me where his office is?"

"In the air." She pointed upward.

"You mean he has no office?" Leo asked.

"In his socks."

He peered into the apartment. It was sunless and dingy, one large room divided by a half-open curtain, beyond which he could see a sagging metal bed. The near side of a room was crowded with rickety chairs, old bureaus, a three-legged table, racks of cooking utensils, and all the apparatus of a kitchen. But there was no sign of Salzman or his magic barrel, probably also a figment of the imagination. An odor of frying fish made Leo weak to the knees.

"Where is he?" he insisted. "I've got to see your husband."

At length she answered, "So who knows where he is? Every time he thinks a new thought he runs to a different place. Go home, he will find you."

"Tell him Leo Finkle."

She gave no sign she had heard.

He walked downstairs, depressed.

But Salzman, breathless, stood waiting at his door.

Leo was astounded and overjoyed. "How did you get here before me?"

"I rushed."

"Come inside."

They entered. Leo fixed tea, and a sardine sandwich for Salzman. As they were drinking he reached behind him for the packet of pictures and handed them to the marriage broker.

Salzman put down his glass and said expectantly, "You found somebody you like?"

"Not among these."

The marriage broker turned away.

"Here is the one I want." Leo held forth the snapshot.

Salzman slipped on his glasses and took the picture into his trembling hand. He turned ghastly and let out a groan.

"What's the matter?" cried Leo.

"Excuse me. Was an accident this picture. She isn't for you."

Salzman frantically shoved the manila packet into his portfolio. He thrust the snapshot into his pocket and fled down the stairs.

Leo, after momentary paralysis, gave chase and cornered the marriage broker in the vestibule. The landlady made hysterical outcries but neither of them listened.

"Give me back the picture, Salzman."

"No." The pain in his eyes was terrible.

"Tell me who she is then."

"This I can't tell you. Excuse me."

He made to depart, but Leo, forgetting himself, seized the matchmaker by his tight coat and shook him frenziedly.

"Please," sighed Salzman. *"Please."*

Leo ashamedly let him go. "Tell me who she is," he begged. "It's very important for me to know."

"She is not for you. She is a wild one —wild, without shame. This is not a bride for a rabbi."

"What do you mean wild?"

"Like an animal. Like a dog. For her to be poor was a sin. This is why to me she is dead now."

"In God's name, what do you mean?"

"Her I can't introduce to you," Salzman cried.

"Why are you so excited?"

"Why, he asks," Salzman said, bursting into tears. "This is my baby, my Stella, she should burn in hell."

Leo hurried up to bed and hid under the covers. Under the covers he thought his life through. Although he soon fell asleep he could not sleep her out of his mind. He woke, beating his breast. Though he prayed to be rid of her, his prayers went unanswered.

Through days of torment he endlessly struggled not to love her; fearing success, he escaped it. He then concluded to convert her to goodness, himself to God. The idea alternately nauseated and exalted him.

He perhaps did not know that he had come to a final decision until he encountered Salzman in a Broadway cafeteria. He was sitting alone at a rear table, sucking the bony remains of a fish. The marriage broker appeared haggard, and transparent to the point of vanishing.

Salzman looked up first without recognizing him. Leo had grown a pointed beard and his eyes were weighted with wisdom.

"Salzman," he said, "love has at last come to my heart."

"Who can love from a picture?" mocked the marriage broker.

"It is not impossible."

"If you can love her, then you can love anybody. Let me show you some new clients that they just sent me their photographs. One is a little doll."

"Just her I want," Leo murmured.

"Don't be a fool, doctor. Don't bother with her."

"Put me in touch with her, Salzman," Leo said humbly. "Perhaps I can be of service."

Salzman had stopped eating and Leo understood with emotion that it was now arranged.

Leaving the cafeteria, he was, however, afflicted by a tormenting suspicion that Salzman had planned it all to happen this way.

Leo was informed by letter that she would meet him on a certain corner, and she was there one spring night, waiting under a street lamp. He appeared, carrying a small bouquet of violets and rosebuds. Stella stood by the lamp post, smoking. She wore white with red shoes, which fitted his expectations, although in a troubled moment he had imagined the dress red, and only the shoes white. She waited uneasily and shyly. From afar he saw that her eyes—clearly her father's

—were filled with desperate innocence. He pictured, in her, his own redemption. Violins and lit candles revolved in the sky. Leo ran forward with flowers outthrust.

Around the corner, Salzman, leaning against a wall, chanted prayers for the dead.

HURRY, HURRY
Eleanor Clark (b. 1913)

No one was there when the house began to fall. It was a beautiful June day, warmer than it had been. I remember that people had been particularly expansive that morning as after a thunder storm. They had gathered on the porch steps of the store at mail-time, exclaiming over and over on the warmth of the sun and the color of the tiger-lilies that had just sprung out all over town. One of the ladies, receiving a long-awaited letter from her nephew, had suddenly become very witty and had kissed everyone in the store, and this could never have happened on an ordinary day. Naturally it occurred to no one that a disaster was about to take place.

The only creature that might have given some warning was the French poodle, de Maupassant, who had been locked in the house and should have sensed that everything was not quite right, but he gave no sign of life until the end. Probably my mother had spoiled him too much by that time. Certainly she loved the dog, especially since the accident that paralyzed one of his paws, so that it was hard for her to deny him anything. People laughed at her for this, and she laughed at herself, but she could always find something in him to excuse her behavior. She loved the aristocracy of him, the way he tossed his luxurious black mane—Louis Quatorze she called it—or drew his shoulders a little together and pointed up his slender glossy snout. In the evening he snuggled at her feet, and then, though in the daytime her profile was too sharp and her green-flecked eyes leapt too quickly to the defense, there was something almost of a madonna in my mother's face. But she had spoiled the dog. In the end he was incapable of serious thought and must have played or slept through the whole catastrophe. The servant spent most of his time writing love letters to the village saxophonist.

I too was of no use, partly because I was walking on the hill about half a mile from the house. The other reason is simply that I was not interested. Later when I saw all my mother's property tumbling to ruin I did try to concentrate on the tragedy of it: shook myself, rubbed my arms and legs, even kicked my shins and jumped up and down as if my feet were asleep, but with no effect. I spent the entire time—two or three hours it must have been—under a maple tree, and rescued nothing but one silver-backed hand mirror which fell out of an upper window and happened to land in my lap. I think that I was also the last person in the village to be aware that the house, where I was born and spent most of my childhood, was beginning to collapse. I noticed it quite by accident from the hill. The house was swaying very gently, the top of the cobblestone chimney with a graceful and independent motion, rather like the tail of a fish, and the foundations with a more irregular ebb and swell as if the stones were offering a futile resistance to their downfall. The kitchen ell and the woodshed had already gone down, tearing an ugly wound in the north wall and leaving the servants' quarters exposed.

Naturally I made my way back as quickly as possible, but the lane had become so overgrown with sumach and brambles that it was almost half an hour before I reached the road. By that time the whole town was present and the lawn was already clotted with little groups of people (in one place the ladies of the Altar Guild, in another the three families that lived off the town, and so on) debating the causes of the collapse and the possibilities of doing something about it. My mother was running from one group to another, shaking hands with everyone, receiving advice and expressions of sympathy. She had been at a cocktail party and cut an especially charming figure, with her white picture hat and her flowered print. So much so that for some time—until the front wall actually began to bulge out over the lawn, like a paper bag slowly surcharged with water—most of the people were unable to keep their minds on the disaster and acted as if they were attending an ordinary funeral or tea.

Now and then my mother paused in her rounds as hostess, tucking the minister's arm under hers, and while appearing to cast down her eyes, with one of her green calculating upward Victorian glances managed to caress his face. "Ah Padre," she sighed, plucking at the black cloth under her fingers, "what a good friend you are," and added, turning to the church ladies, "He's the best Democrat any of us has ever seen." The minister, who had also been at the cocktail party and whose cheeks were somewhat flushed, gazed with sly benevolence over his flock, laughed his deep-bellied indifferent laugh, and kissed my mother's hand. "Ha ha ha," rattled the church ladies, and with one motion, as from a released spring, began to run in tiny circles around him, pointing delightedly at his full chest and the rather uncouth vigor of his jaw. "Always joking," said the minister, "here her house is on the verge of collapse and she talks about democracy! What a woman!" At this the church ladies could no longer control themselves, they rolled and pivoted with laughter, poking each other's corsets and smacking their lips enviously toward my mother. "It's true, upon my word it's true!" she cried, one arm to the sky. "He treats us all the same, rich and poor alike! Here's to Padre!" and she raised her empty hand still higher in a toast. "The best friend this community has ever had!"

In the meantime the disintegration of the house was becoming more and more apparent. From the upstairs bedrooms, and even in the pantry and dining-room, beams could be heard falling, and already a wide crack was beginning to open diagonally across the front living-room wall, exposing the dust-covered leaves of books, first the historical works and later the vellum-bound editions of Dante, Baudelaire and Racine. It was this, I think, that first awoke my mother to a real awareness of what was happening. It was not only that the books were threatened with destruction: it was also obvious to everyone that their pages had not been cut. Even the town servants noticed it, even Myrtle who was hired for the lowest and heaviest form of cleaning, but Myrtle was a poor half-deformed creature and she would not have dared to smile behind her fingers as the others did.

One by one the books fell among the barberry bushes, raising a cloud of greyish powder so stifling that the people nearest were forced to stumble back over the flower-beds, holding handkerchiefs to their mouths. "Oh good Lord! the books! the books!" my mother gasped. She ran up under the crack in the wall, and holding her white hat with one hand, with the other attempted to catch the volumes as they toppled from their shelves. But they were coming too fast. Many of them, too, fell apart immediately against the outer air, leaving only something like silica dust midway to the ground, so that my mother was soon taken with a violent fit of coughing. At last, reeling and choking under the rain of classics that were now striking her head and breasts and shoulders, she was obliged to stagger back toward the road. "A wonderful woman," the ladies said, and they began to scamper to and fro, picking little bunches of sweet william, wild roses and delphinium for my mother's hair. Gratefully she closed her eyes and was nestling her grey curls more warmly against the Padre's ample lap, when the cobblestone chimney tore itself loose from the main beams of the house and crashed through the lower branches of the elms and across the lawn.

Immediately my mother sprang up.

"George! Burt! Albert!" she called. "Somebody's got to save my things! Where's the Fire Department? Fire Department!" The Fire Department was not really a department at all, but a group of farmers who no longer farmed, so they had nothing better to do than to jump on the fire engine as it went by. They were now lying on the grass passing around a bottle of beer and laughing at some story or joke. "George!" my mother wheedled. "Albert! Burt!" and she ran from one to another, prodding and kicking them with her white pointed toe. The firemen looked up slowly at the waving roof and the colonial columns which were beginning to bend like wax candles in the sun, then hoisting their quids all together to the other side of their faces they announced, "It ain't a fire," and lay down again, covering their necks against the afternoon sun. "But the highboy!" my mother cried. "The highboy! It belonged to my grandfather, it's been in my family for two hundred years, my little old Aunt Mary left it to me in her will. She was so weak she could hardly hold up her head, and she whispered to me"—here my mother's voice broke —"she said, 'I want you to have it, because it's the loveliest thing I have, and you're the only one that's stood by me all these years.' "

This recital so moved my mother that for a full minute she stood with her face in her hands, sobbing, but perceiving that she had still had no effect on the Fire Department she whipped away the last traces of her grief and turned to hunt out Cedric the servant. Cedric, however, was in no condition to be called upon. The collapse of the kitchen ell, taking with it the entire outer wall of his room, had revealed him stark naked playing pinochle with one of the summer residents, an incident that he was now trying to explain to the saxophonist. "Cedric!" my mother shouted. "Come here at once!" But just then a shutter fell on Cedric from the attic window and with a moan he dropped to the ground, followed by his friend. Fortunately my mother was spared this scene. She had just remembered de Maupassant and was threatening to run into the house for him when she was assured that someone had seen someone taking him away.

In the end it was Myrtle who went in

for the highboy. She was not at all anxious to go, even cried a little when it was first suggested, which was rather a surprise because everyone knew that her life was not worth anything. She had lost four fingers in a meat-chopper, so perhaps it was the pain she was afraid of, or the noise: it was hard to tell. At any rate, as soon as she heard that the Selectmen had chosen her for the job she began to whimper and for several minutes stood twisting her fingers in her apron, made out of an old pair of bloomers my mother had given her, and chewing her hair. "Oh no," she muttered to herself, "you don't see *me* going in there"—she had the habit of talking to herself while she worked, even told herself long stories sometimes as she cleaned out the toilets—"Not me, nossir! They come up to me all together and they says, 'Now Myrtle,' they says, 'you just run along in there and bring out that hairloom. 'Taint as heavy as it looks,' they says, kind of coaxing-like, 'and mind you don't smash it on the way out.' I like that! Mind you don't smash it, they says, on the way out! And there was the whole house rolling around and a crack in the front big enough to drive a Ford through. Why you could watch the ceiling come down in the parlor, and all the upstairs furniture coming down too, bang! bang! bang! Mind you don't smash it, they says, on the way out! And do you want to know what I said?" Myrtle placed her crippled hands on her hips and with her eyes fiercely lit up she went on, raising her voice to a scream in order to hear herself above the splintering and crashing of the house. "I says to them, 'No!' I stood right up to them and I says, 'I ain't going into that house, not if you give me a million dollars I ain't!' And as for what I think of *you* . . . Yes," her lower lip began to twitch and her voice dropped suddenly, "as for what I think of you. . . ." But she was now surrounded by all the important people in town, including my mother, the minister, and the schoolteacher—a tiny knifish man with a cone-shaped head and glasses—and realizing that she had been overheard she was taken by a fit of trembling and was unable to go on. "I just got the habit of talking to myself," she apologized, letting out a choked laugh, and then she began to cry again, with her head hanging and her red stubs pressed into the hair over her eyes.

"I have no sympathy with any of them," said the school-teacher. "They ought to be horse-whipped, they don't want to work." He strode through the crowd, receiving with a wrinkling of his beagle's nose their murmurs of agreement, tore off a stout black cherry switch and with little nasal shouts, like a cheer-leader, began to slash at Myrtle's ankles. "Oh mercy," said Cedric. He giggled a little, then with a sob turned back to hide his face. "Oh darling," he moaned, waving his fingers in the direction of Myrtle who was now hobbling toward the doorway, "It has such dreadful feet!"

My mother was not wholly in sympathy with the school-teacher's tactics. She pushed her arm under Myrtle's, and half dragging, half comforting her, pressed a dollar bill between her thumb and what was left of her forefinger. "I want you to take this, my dear, and get yourself something pretty." Without raising her eyes Myrtle took the money and poked it in her shoe.

In the doorway a new difficulty arose, the columns and the door-frame itself having already collapsed, leaving only an irregular space no bigger than the entrance to a small kennel for Myrtle to pass through. However several white-flanneled husbands now sprang into action, lifted Myrtle over the debris on the stoop, and twisted and heaved her head first into the hall. In less than a minute there was nothing to be seen of her but one soleless shoe with the crisp corner of a dollar bill sticking out at the side. "It seems rather a pity," the minister murmured, looking at my mother. "Yes," she hesitated. "Poor dear Myrtle, she's such a pitiful little creature really and she has so little. . . . But of course I can make it up to her." She smiled, grabbed the dollar, and with a hidden ladylike ges-

ture forced it into the Padre's reluctant hand. "For the new altar cloths," she whispered. "I have so little these days, but this much I *can* do for the community."

For almost half an hour Myrtle fought her way through the wreckage inside the house, trying to reach the highboy in the downstairs guest-room. From time to time we could see her face in an upstairs window, perspiration dropping from her hair, or her arm through one of the cracks that were now widening on every wall. "Hurry!" my mother shouted, with increasing anger as one by one her treasures—a Russian ikon, the Dresden china coffee cups, the Renaissance desk brought so tenderly from Florence—fell and were crushed. "Hurry up, Myrtle! Hurry up! Hurry up!" And every time a part of Myrtle came into view the school-teacher's eyes brightened and he danced back and forth cracking the black cherry whip above his head. "She's a good worker but terribly slow," the ladies agreed, twisting their handkerchiefs and criticizing Myrtle's progress through the house. Some of them, the old New England stock, filled the time more usefully: dusted the grass and bushes where the books had fallen and arranged those that had remained intact in neat piles along the flagstone walk.

During this time the front of the house had been bellying more and more out toward the lawn so that it was no longer possible to see into the guest-room. "It's gone!" my mother cried. "Ah, Padre!" and she leaned against the minister. But a moment later Myrtle appeared again, this time on all fours, crawling up the circular staircase with the highboy on her back. "Bring it down! *Down*, Myrtle!" All the downstairs exits, however, were blocked: the lower half of the staircase too was caving in, leaving Myrtle hanging by two fingers while with the other hand she struggled to keep the massive piece of furniture from slipping back into the pit. Now and then over the sounds of falling timber we could hear her groaning and crying out, "Oh Holy Virgin, help. . . . Oh blessed mother of God. . . ." Then the whole front of the house squeezed down slowly, and we heard nothing more but the breaking of beams and an underground commotion of water as heavy objects fell through to the cellar.

The next and last time we saw Myrtle she was trying to reach one of the attic windows, still struggling under what must have been a part of the highboy, though it was bashed to a skeleton. Her face was dreadfully distorted, as if she had been pinned under some heavy weight and in freeing herself had pulled her features half off. Of her nose there was nothing left but a bloody splinter of bone, and her chin, which had been rather underhung, now stuck out in sharp diagonal, forcing her mouth into an enormous grin. Yet in spite of this it seemed as if she were trying to smile, perhaps out of pride in having salvaged as much as she had. She kept pointing at the mahogany ruin on her back, nodding continually and working her mangled features in an effort at communication. "I can't bear it," Cedric said, "they oughtn't to allow such things," and he turned yellow and vomited in a patch of lilies. Everyone else was shouting at Myrtle—"Don't throw it!" "Wrap it in a blanket!" "Let it down here!"—but she had suddenly let go her load. Even from the ground one could see the wild look that came into her eyes, a brilliant hatred aimed down at the crowd. Yet perhaps there was some confusion in it too, for before the wall crashed her face changed again—for a moment she resembled a small wounded animal crying for its life—and she fell with her torn-off wrists lifted up in prayer.

The rest of what happened was so sudden that I have no clear recollection of it. I remember that shortly after Myrtle's death the ladies set to gathering flowers again and made a kind of tiny monument of them on the grass, with **POOR MYRTLE** written in English daisies across the top. The schoolteacher scoffed at this, saying there might

have been some sense to it if she had done what she was sent for, but the general opinion was that the ladies had been very kind to think of such a thing. "She was very bitter," the minister said, "but a good soul too," and he took the carnation from his buttonhole and tossed it on the mound.

I think it was at about that time that the French poodle suddenly clawed its way up to the window of my mother's bedroom, the only part of the house that was still standing. Yapping and rolling his eyes he perched on the swaying sill, his bandaged paw held up and a large drop of yellow liquid rolling down his aristocratic nose. "Moppy! Moppy!" my mother cried, running up under the wall. "Did you think your mummy had forgotten you? Oh Moppy you did, you're crying! he's crying," she repeated, almost crying herself. "He thought I was going to leave him there all by himself. Come to me, my darling, come to your mummy, jump!" I remember the two of them that way: the dog afraid to jump, tossing his ruff and his long silken ears, and my mother in a new flowered print and a picture hat, holding up her arms, with an expression of love, almost—I thought at that moment but I am not sure now—almost a look of fulfillment in her face, which at times made one think of a madonna though the profile was too sharp. And then the last of the house fell and buried them.

IN DREAMS BEGIN RESPONSIBILITIES

Delmore Schwartz (1913–1966)

I

I think it is the year 1909. I feel as if I were in a moving-picture theater, the long arm of light crossing the darkness and spinning, my eyes fixed upon the screen. It is a silent picture, as if an old Biograph one, in which the actors are dressed in ridiculously old-fashioned clothes, and one flash succeeds another, with sudden jumps, and the actors, too, seem to jump about, walking too fast. The shots are full of rays and dots, as if it had been raining when the picture was photographed. The light is bad.

It is Sunday afternoon, June 12th, 1909, and my father is walking down the quiet streets of Brooklyn on his way to visit my mother. His clothes are newly pressed, and his tie is too tight in his high collar. He jingles the coins in his pocket, thinking of the witty things he will say. I feel as if I had by now relaxed entirely in the soft darkness of the theater; the organist peals out the obvious approximate emotions on which the audience rocks unknowingly. I am anonymous. I have forgotten myself: it is always so when one goes to a movie, it is, as they say, a drug.

My father walks from street to street of trees, lawns and houses, once in a while coming to an avenue on which a street-car skates and gnaws, progressing slowly. The motorman, who has a handle-bar mustache, helps a young lady wearing a hat like a feathered bowl onto the car. He leisurely makes change and rings his bell as the passengers mount the car. It is obviously Sunday, for everyone is wearing Sunday clothes and the street-car's noises emphasize the quiet of the holiday (Brooklyn is said to be the city of churches). The shops are closed and their shades drawn but for an occasional stationery store or drugstore with great green balls in the window.

My father has chosen to take this long walk because he likes to walk and think. He thinks about himself in the future and so arrives at the place he is to visit in a mild state of exaltation. He pays no attention to the houses he is passing, in which the Sunday dinner is being eaten, nor to the many trees which line each street, now coming to their full green and the time when they will enclose the whole street in leafy shadow. An occasional carriage passes, the horses' hooves falling like stones in the quiet afternoon, and once in a while an automobile, looking like an enormous upholstered sofa, puffs and passes.

My father thinks of my mother, of how ladylike she is, and of the pride which will be his when he introduces her to his family. They are not yet engaged and he is not yet sure that he loves my mother, so that, once in a while, he becomes panicky about the bond already established. But then he reassures himself by thinking of the big men he admires who are married: William Randolph Hearst and William Howard Taft, who has just become the President of the United States.

My father arrives at my mother's house. He has come too early and so is suddenly embarrassed. My aunt, my mother's younger sister, answers the loud bell with her napkin in her hand, for the family is still at dinner. As my father enters, my grandfather rises from the table and shakes hands with him. My mother has run upstairs to tidy herself. My grandmother asks my father if he has had dinner and tells him that my mother will be down soon. My grandfather opens the conversation by remarking about the mild June weather. My father sits uncomfortably near the table, holding his hat in his hand. My grandmother tells my aunt to take my father's hat. My uncle, twelve years old, runs into the house, his hair tousled. He shouts a greeting to my father, who has often given him nickels, and then runs upstairs, as my grandmother shouts after him. It is evident that the respect in which my father is held in this house is tempered by a good deal of mirth. He is impressive, but also very awkward.

II

Finally my mother comes downstairs and my father, being at the moment engaged in conversation with my grandfather, is made uneasy by her entrance, for he does not know whether to greet my mother or to continue the conversation. He gets up from his chair clumsily and says "Hello" gruffly. My grandfather watches this, examining their congruence, such as it is, with a critical eye, and meanwhile rubbing his bearded cheek roughly, as he always does when he reasons. He is worried; he is afraid that my father will not make a good husband for his oldest daughter. At this point something happens to the film, just as my father says something funny to my mother: I am awakened to myself and my unhappiness just as my interest has become most intense. The audience begins to clap impatiently. Then the trouble is attended to, but the film has been returned to a portion just shown, and once more I see my grandfather rubbing his bearded cheek, pondering my father's character. It is difficult to get back into the picture once more and forget myself, but as my mother giggles at my father's words, the darkness drowns me.

My father and mother depart from the house, my father shaking hands with my grandfather once more, out of some unknown uneasiness. I stir uneasily also, slouched in the hard chair of the theater. Where is the older uncle, my mother's older brother? He is studying in his bedroom upstairs, studying for his final examinations at the College of the City of New York, having been dead of double pneumonia for the last twenty-one years. My mother and father walk down the same quiet streets once more. My mother is holding my father's arm and telling him of the novel she has been reading and my father utters judgments of the characters as the plot is made clear to him. This is a habit which he very much enjoys, for he feels the utmost superiority and confidence when he is approving or condemning the behavior of other people. At times he feels moved to utter a brief "Ugh," whenever the story becomes what he would call sugary. This tribute is the assertion of his manliness. My mother feels satisfied by the interest she has awakened; and she is showing my father how intelligent she is and how interesting.

They reach the avenue, and the street-car leisurely arrives. They are going to Coney Island this afternoon, although my mother really considers such pleasures inferior. She has made up her mind to indulge only in a walk on the boardwalk and a pleasant dinner, avoiding the riotous amusements as being beneath the dignity of so dignified a couple.

My father tells my mother how much money he has made in the week just past, exaggerating an amount which need not have been exaggerated. But my father has always felt that actualities somehow fall short, no matter how fine they are. Suddenly I begin to weep. The determined old lady who sits next to me in the theater is annoyed and looks at me with an angry face, and being intimidated, I stop. I drag out my handkerchief and dry my face, licking the drop which has fallen near my lips. Meanwhile I have missed something, for here are my father and mother alighting from the street-car at the last stop, Coney Island.

III

They walk toward the boardwalk and my mother commands my father to inhale the pungent air from the sea. They both breathe in deeply, both of them laughing as they do so. They have in common a great interest in health, although my father is strong and husky, and my mother is frail. They are both full of theories about what is good to eat and not good to eat, and sometimes have heated discussions about it, the whole matter ending in my father's announcement, made with a scornful bluster, that you have to die sooner or later anyway. On the boardwalk's flagpole, the American flag is pulsing in an intermittent wind from the sea.

My father and mother go to the rail of the boardwalk and look down on the beach where a good many bathers are casually walking about. A few are in the surf. A peanut whistle pierces the air with its pleasant and active whine, and my father goes to buy peanuts. My mother remains at the rail and stares at the ocean. The ocean seems merry to her; it pointedly sparkles and again and again the pony waves are released. She notices the children digging in the wet sand, and the bathing costumes of the girls who are her own age. My father returns with the peanuts. Overhead the sun's lightning strikes and strikes, but neither of them are at all aware of it. The boardwalk is full of people dressed in their Sunday clothes and casually strolling. The tide does not reach as far as the boardwalk, and the strollers would feel no danger if it did. My father and mother lean on the rail of the boardwalk and absently stare at the ocean. The ocean is becoming rough; the waves come in slowly, tugging strength from far back. The moment before they somersault, the moment when they arch their backs so beautifully, showing white veins in the green and black, that moment is intolerable. They finally crack, dashing fiercely upon the sand, actually driving, full force downward, against it, bouncing upward and forward, and at last petering out into a small stream of bubbles which slides up the beach and then is recalled. The sun overhead does not disturb my father and my mother. They gaze idly at the ocean, scarcely interested in its harshness. But I stare at the terrible sun which breaks up sight, and the fatal merciless passionate ocean. I forget my parents. I stare fascinated, and finally, shocked by their indifference, I burst out weeping once more. The old lady next to me pats my shoulder and says: "There, there, young man, all of this is only a movie, only a movie," but I look up once more at the terrifying sun and the terrifying ocean, and being unable to control my tears I get up and go to the men's room, stumbling over the feet of the other people seated in my row.

IV

When I return, feeling as if I had just awakened in the morning sick for lack of sleep, several hours have apparently passed and my parents are riding on the merry-go-round. My father is on a black horse, my mother on a white one, and they seem to be making an eternal circuit for the single purpose of snatching the nickel rings which are attached to an arm of one of the posts. A hand organ is playing; it is inseparable from the ceaseless circling of the merry-go-round.

For a moment it seems that they will never get off the carousel, for it will never stop, and I feel as if I were looking down from the fiftieth story of a building. But at length they do get off; even the hand-organ has ceased for a moment. There is a sudden and sweet stillness, as if the achievement of so much motion. My mother has acquired only two rings, my father, however, ten of them, although it was my mother who really wanted them.

They walk on along the boardwalk as the afternoon descends by imperceptible degrees into the incredible violet of dusk. Everything fades into a relaxed glow, even the ceaseless murmuring from the beach. They look for a place to have dinner. My father suggests the best restaurant on the boardwalk and my mother demurs, according to her principles of economy and housewifeliness.

However they do go to the best place, asking for a table near the window so that they can look out upon the boardwalk and the mobile ocean. My father feels omnipotent as he places a quarter in the waiter's hand in asking for a table. The place is crowded and here too there is music, this time from a kind of string trio. My father orders with a fine confidence.

As their dinner goes on, my father tells of his plans for the future and my mother shows with an expressive face how interested she is, and how impressed. My father becomes exultant, lifted up by the waltz that is being played and his own future begins to intoxicate him. My father tells my mother that he is going to expand his business, for there is a great deal of money to be made. He wants to settle down. After all, he is twenty-nine, he has lived by himself since his thirteenth year, he is making more and more money, and he is envious of his friends when he visits them in the security of their homes, surrounded, it seems, by the calm domestic pleasures, and by delightful children, and then as the waltz reaches the moment when the dancers all swing madly, then, then with awful daring, then he asks my mother to marry him, although awkwardly enough and puzzled as to how he had arrived at the question, and she, to make the whole business worse, begins to cry, and my father looks nervously about, not knowing at all what to do now, and my mother says: "It's all I've wanted from the first moment I saw you," sobbing, and he finds all of this very difficult, scarcely to his taste, scarcely as he thought it would be, on his long walks over Brooklyn Bridge in the revery of a fine cigar, and it was then, at that point, that I stood up in the theater and shouted: "Don't do it! It's not too late to change your minds, both of you. Nothing good will come of it, only remorse, hatred, scandal, and two children whose characters are monstrous." The whole audience turned to look at me, annoyed, the usher came hurrying down the aisle flashing his searchlight, and the old lady next to me tugged me down into my seat, saying: "Be quiet. You'll be put out, and you paid thirty-five cents to come in." And so I shut my eyes because I could not bear to see what was happening. I sat there quietly.

V

But after a while I begin to take brief glimpses and at length I watch again with thirsty interest, like a child who tries to maintain his sulk when he is offered a bribe of candy. My parents are now having their picture taken in a photographer's booth along the boardwalk. The place is shadowed in the mauve light which is apparently necessary. The camera is set to the side on its tripod and looks like a Martian man. The photographer is instructing my parents in how to pose. My father has his arm over my mother's shoulder, and both of them smile emphatically. The photographer brings my mother a bouquet of flowers to hold in her hand, but she holds it at the wrong angle. Then the photographer covers himself with the black cloth which drapes the camera and all that one sees of him is one protruding arm and his hand with which he holds tightly to the rubber ball which he squeezes when the picture is taken. But he is not satisfied with their appearance. He feels that somehow there is something wrong in their pose. Again and again he comes out from his hiding place with new directions. Each suggestion merely makes matters worse. My father is becoming impatient. They try a seated pose. The photographer explains that he has his pride, he wants to make beautiful pictures, he is not merely interested in all of this for the money. My father says: "Hurry up, will you? We haven't got all night." But the photographer only scurries about apologetically, issuing new directions. The photographer charms me, and I approve of him with all my heart, for I know exactly how he feels, and as he criticizes each revised pose according to some obscure idea of rightness, I become quite hopeful. But then my father says angrily: "Come on, you've had enough time, we're not going to wait any longer." And the photographer, sighing unhappily, goes back into the black covering, and holds out his hand, saying: "One, two, three, Now!" and the picture is taken, with my father's smile turned to a grimace and my mother's bright and false. It takes a few minutes for the picture to be developed and as my parents sit in the curious light they become depressed.

VI

They have passed a fortune-teller's booth and my mother wishes to go in, but my father does not. They begin to argue about it. My mother becomes stubborn, my father once more impatient. What my father would like to do now is walk off and leave my mother there, but he knows that that would never do. My mother refuses to budge. She is near tears, but she feels an uncontrollable desire to hear what the palm-reader will say. My father consents angrily and they both go into the booth which is, in a way, like the photographer's, since it is draped in black cloth and its light is colored and shadowed. The place is too warm, and my father keeps saying that this is all nonsense, pointing to the crystal ball on the table. The fortune-teller, a short, fat woman garbed in robes supposedly exotic, comes into the room and greets them, speaking with an accent, but suddenly my father feels that the whole thing is intolerable; he tugs at my mother's arm but my mother refuses to budge. And then, in terrible anger, my father lets go of my mother's arm and strides out, leaving my mother stunned. She makes a movement as if to go after him, but the fortune-teller holds her and begs her not to do so, and I in my seat in the darkness am shocked and horrified. I feel as if I were walking a tight-rope one hundred feet over a circus audience and suddenly the rope is showing signs of breaking, and I get up from my seat and begin to shout once more the first words I can think of to communicate my terrible fear, and once more the usher comes hurrying down the aisle flashing his searchlight, and the old lady pleads with me, and the shocked audience has turned to stare at me, and I keep shouting: "What are they doing? Don't they know what they are doing? Why doesn't my mother go after my father and beg him not to be angry? If she does not do that, what will she do? Doesn't my father know what he is doing?" But the usher has seized my arm, and is dragging me away, and as he does so, he says: "What are *you* doing? Don't you know you can't do things like this, you can't do whatever you want to do, even if other people aren't about? You will be sorry if you do not do what you should do. You can't carry on like this, it is not right, you will find that out soon enough, everything you do matters too much," and as he said that, dragging me through the lobby of the theater, into the cold light, I woke up into the bleak winter morning of my twenty-first birthday, the window-sill shining with its lip of snow, and the morning already begun.

POETRY

The word *poetry* is slippery, and is applied in many different contexts and senses. Here, however, we are using the word in, basically, two senses. The first, and the most common, is as a generic term for the collective body of compositions called poems. This statement leaves untouched the matter of what a poem is, but that is involved in our second sense of the word. Poetry, in this second sense, is the verbal expression of the imaginative view of the world.

As for the imaginative view of the world, we may most readily understand it in contrast with the practical and scientific views, which are concerned with the nature of the objective world.* The directions for finding an address, the recipe for making a cake, the diagnosis offered by a physician, the explanation of nuclear fission, a textbook on psychology—these examples all convey information about the objective world; but when we refer to the imaginative view of the world, as distinguished from other acts of imagination that lead, say, to a scientific theory, we mean imagination applied, not to the objective structure of the world, but to the world as experienced and evaluated in experience—that is, as experienced and responded to sensorially, intellectually, *and* emotionally.

The imaginative view of the world underlies all the arts, not only poetry.† But more than any other art, poetry, the art of language, makes us feel what it means to be alive in the world, and such "feeling what it means" may involve and fuse all sorts of responses, from sensations and perceptions to

general ideas. What does it "feel like," for instance, to be in love, to hate somebody, to be conscience-stricken, to watch a sunset or to stand at a deathbed, to be willing to die for a cause? Only poetry—in the broadest sense —can answer such questions. Poetry is concerned with experience—with the "lived" fullness of the world. We, as living creatures, have an appetite for life, and poetry enriches our sense of life. And one of the things that poetry does by way of such enrichment is to give us a deeper sense of our own possibilities—that is, of our selves.

If we say that only poetry can answer such questions as we have asked above, it may be immediately objected that prose fiction— for instance, the short stories that you have just been reading in this book—are expressions of the imaginative view of the world and are not poems. That is, indeed, true: stories are not necessarily poems—though some poems, as we shall soon see, are stories. What, then, does distinguish a poem—even a poem telling a story—from a piece of prose fiction? We may answer that a special formality and intensity of language and structure as the embodiment of the imaginative view of the world are the characteristic qualities of the poem—and, if we want to use the word *poetry* in a restrictive way, of poetry.

But what are the special formality and special intensity that we have just referred to as distinguishing a poem from a prose fiction?

Suppose we turn to the ordinary, more or less uneducated man in the street and ask him what poetry is. In all likelihood he

---

* This is not to imply that the practical and the scientific views are identical. They spring from quite different impulses. The practical view springs from the desire to get something done in the world, the scientific from the desire to understand the world. Although the understanding of the world may itself make it possible to get things done, there remains the basic distinction of the imaginative view from both the scientific and the practical views, as we shall see.

† It is important to realize that the imaginative view of the world is shared, in some degree or another, by most human beings, even by those who haven't the slightest interest in the arts as such. It is an aspect of human nature.

would say: "Poetry—well, it goes sort of umpety-umpety along. It's a sort of jingle too." Rhythm, and rime, then, might strike him offhand as fundamental for poetry.

To take rhythm: Rhythm may be defined as a more or less regularly patterned flow of sound or movement. The whole world, including the human body, is a texture of rhythms of various kinds. The heart beats and the moon waxes and wanes, the lungs inhale and exhale and the seasons repeat themselves. Our whole feeling of life is associated with rhythm, and speech embodies this feeling for life. The rhythm of poetry, then, is merely a specialization of an inherent and vital characteristic of speech, and especially of speech charged with emotion. We all know how the impassioned sermon, the utterance of a person afflicted by grief, or the tirade of a pedestrian who has been splashed by a passing truck all tend to achieve a pronounced rhythmic pattern.

To take rime: Unlike rhythm, rime is *not* a fundamental characteristic of poetry. The poetry of some languages does not use rime at all (that of classical Latin, for instance), and often English poetry does not (in blank verse, for instance). But when the man in the street thinks of poetry as having a jingle, he is, after all, touching on a root characteristic. Long before he can speak, the baby in his crib plays delightedly with sounds, and such lalling, as it is called, prepares him for speech; and primitive people and children are fascinated by intricate sound patterns (of which rime, as we shall see, is only one possibility). Making sense isn't necessarily important to the fascinated primitive or child. In fact, children seem to enjoy most of all the glitter and play of sound in the most extravagant nonsense verse:

HUMPTY DUMPTY
Anonymous

> Humpty Dumpty sat on a wall,
> Humpty Dumpty had a great fall;
> All the King's horses and all the King's men
> Cannot put Humpty together again.

HINX, MINX
Anonymous

> Hinx, minx, the old witch winks,
> The fat begins to fry,
> Nobody at home but Jumping Joan
> Father, Mother, and I.*

We may, however, go a step beyond these fundamental and intrinsic pleasures in the manipulation of sounds. Let us look at another example:

THIRTY DAYS
Anonymous

> Thirty days hath September,
> April, June, and November;
> All the rest have thirty-one,
> Excepting February alone,
> And that has twenty-eight days clear
> And twenty-nine in each leap year.

This composition is not nonsense, with emphasis on the mere pleasure in verbal manipulation. It gives, in fact, some useful information. But why not say the information straight out? For instance:

> All months of the year have thirty-one days except April, June, September, and November, which have thirty, and February, which normally has twenty-eight, but acquires another in leap year.

But the man in the street, even if he doesn't take much interest in poetry, might, after all, prefer the first version, admitting that here the rime and meter help him to remember it. What he is saying is that in the jingle the material is given a *form,* a *structure,* and that because of this the mind readily grasps and remembers it.

Man is, indeed, the form-making and form-grasping animal par excellence. Even in the act of simple perception, the data perceived must be put into a meaningful form: the splotches of light and color that are the data of perception took on for the caveman

---

* The teasing possibility of sense behind the nonsense may also be part of the appeal of such verses—a pleasant spur to the imagination, a sort of riddle. Why did Humpty Dumpty fall? Why did the old witch wink? And so on. But nonsense does isolate the quality of sound—purify it, as it were, for inspection and enjoyment.

the form of a rabbit or a sabertooth tiger, and he reacted appropriately, running to catch his dinner or running to avoid becoming a dinner. At the other end of the scale from this automatic making of form in perception is the deliberate drawing of an image on the cave wall or the composition of a chant or narrative. Undoubtedly the origin of poetic form (as of art in general) did have, in pre-history, an aspect of utility. The rhythmical form did assist the tribe in remembering and transmitting certain things it deemed essential. But a deeper meaning of this *"utility"* of form emerges if we think of what the tribe felt it necessary to remember and transmit— its history, its wisdom, its myths and rituals, in fact, its very identity and sense of life and values.

In the origin of rhythm and in its continuing appeal and significance, there is, however, another and even deeper factor. It indeed has an aspect of utility, but it sprang, as we have said, from man's basic nature. The human body is an organism of rhythms; the rhythm of language echoes our very life process and tends to vitalize the material it deals with. As a corollary to this fact, we find that different rhythms are fundamentally associated with different emotional states, different feelings, different attitudes; and this association, as we shall be constantly aware, is at the root of the function of rhythm in poetry. Rhythm is indissolubly associated with meaning, as with form. It is expressive.

We have been saying, in short, that poetry is rhythmical. And the objection will immediately be forthcoming: "But so is ordinary speech, and if both ordinary speech and poetry are rhythmical, then what is the difference between them?" This objection points to a fundamentally important fact. Poetry is indeed like ordinary speech. It is a projection of ordinary speech and has the same elements. The difference inheres, simply, in the nature of the projection, in the way the common elements are used. They are used, as we have suggested, with *special formality* and with *special intensity*. For instance, rhythms are put into patterns to give special forms—most obviously metrical forms.

Rhythms are used, too, to intensify certain moods and feelings, and, even, to emphasize certain ideas and attitudes.

Rhythm, rime, and other elements of sound are not the only things that enter into the special formality and special intensification that characterize poetry. Our man in the street has said that the "umpety-umpety" and the jingle are what make poetry, but we may push him a little further and ask if there isn't something else, too. And he may well reply: "Yes, I guess so—it's full of fancy talk, a fancy way of putting things. It doesn't just say what it means." By which he means that poetry works by suggestion, by connotation and not merely denotation of word, and is full of unexplained images, comparisons, similes, metaphors, symbols, figures of speech.

True, poetry often does not say what it means. What, for instance, does the following little poem mean?

BY A FLAT ROCK

Anonymous

> By a flat rock on the shore of the sea
> My dear one spoke to me. Wild thyme
> Now grows by the rock
> And a sprig of rosemary.*

This little poem clearly doesn't say what it means, but just as clearly *it means more than it says*. It *suggests* a story: the loss of love (how, we do not know), the passage of time, some sense of continuing life that, ironically, may make loss more poignant. The emotion of the poem is not specified; it springs from this bare, factual presentation.

EXERCISE

The following short poem is "The Tuft of Kelp" by Herman Melville (1819–1891).

> All dripping in tangles green,
>   Cast up by a lonely sea,
> If purer for that, O Weed,
>   Bitterer, too, are ye?

What does it suggest?

---

* From the Welsh, quoted in *The Cherry Tree*, ed. Geoffrey Grigson (New York: Vanguard Press), p. 71.

Sometimes the single word, because of its aura of connotation, may make a line come to life. "The Woodspurge" by Dante Gabriel Rossetti (sec. 13) is a little poem in which the speaker, numb with grief, once crouched on a hillside staring fixedly at the blossom of the little plant; one of its lines reads "My naked ears heard the day pass." Here the word *naked* carries a whole group of connotations—"bare," "bereft," "defenseless," "vulnerable," "stripped," "deprived," perhaps "ignorant" and "innocent." If we try to substitute another word, one that in itself might seem exact enough, we lose something: for instance, *listening, open, attentive*. What these words lack is, it seems on first thought, the rich suggestiveness of *naked*. They seem to be too exact, and limiting. But then, on second thought, they do not seem exact enough. Something has indeed been done to all the senses of the griefstricken speaker—to his total being—and it is only the complex of apparently indeterminate meanings that can truly convey the nature of the experience. A single word may thus bring to life not only a line; one key word may control the effect of a whole poem—as does the word *astonishes* or *vexed* in "Bells for John Whiteside's Daughter" by John Crowe Ransom (sec. 14), the word *die* in "Song" by Edmund Waller (sec. 14), or the word *scare* in "Desert Places" by Robert Frost (sec. 15).

EXERCISE

Turn to the three poems mentioned above, and to our associated comments and questions; try to see what, in each instance, is at stake in the key words.

There are many means by which suggestiveness works in poetry (see *Denotation, Diction, Imagery*, and *Symbol* in the Glossary), but it may be said that the use of simile, metaphor, and symbol—all aspects of what we may call metaphorical thinking—is central. At this point we must, as a matter of clearing the ground for discussion, sharply distinguish comparisons made for purposes of illustration or decoration from those that have a truly poetic function—even when in, say, prose fiction. If in a physiology textbook

the heart is compared to a machine, the purpose is purely expository; the author wants to make something logically clear. If in a poem—almost inevitably a bad poem—the author uses comparisons merely to prettify his subject, the poetic function is not being served.

It is true that the frame of illustration is often used in poetry (it may have an important place in the structure of a poem, for example); and it is true that the material in similes, metaphors, and symbols may sometimes be beautiful or ennobling in themselves, but what is to be remembered is that, *in its poetic function*, metaphorical thinking involves the enriching of the subject, a broadening of the subject sensorially, intellectually, or emotionally—or all three. It works to sharpen and deepen experience, not necessarily to prettify it.

Let us take a famous soliloquy from Shakespeare's *Macbeth*. This comes toward the end of the play when Macbeth knows that he has been tricked by the prophecies of the Weird Sisters, has turned himself into a blood-drenched traitor for nothing, and, after seeing his wife walking in her sleep and trying to wash the imagined stains of guilty blood from her hands, has just had word that she is dead. He is speaking of what future awaits him:

From MACBETH

(Act 5, scene 5)

William Shakespeare (1564–1616)

Tomorrow, and tomorrow, and tomorrow
Creeps in this petty pace from day to day
To the last syllable of recorded time;
And all our yesterdays have lighted fools
The way to dusty death. Out, out, brief candle;
Life's but a walking shadow; a poor player
That struts and frets his hour upon the stage,
And then is heard no more: it is a tale
Told by an idiot, full of sound and fury,
Signifying nothing.

Of the various things mentioned in this passage for the purpose of comparison, only one, the candle, might be termed "pretty" or ornamental, but it is not the prettiness, as such, that counts. If the flame is pretty and bright and cheerful, what comes over to us is the fact of the surrounding darkness it does so little to dissipate, its feebly flickering light, its "brevity." In other words, the expressiveness of the image is what is important. As for the other images that follow, the shadow, the poor player, the idiot, they involve no prettiness or ornament at all; they are definitely ugly or unpleasant. The stories that idiots tell are not pretty, but this passage of poetry is universally recognized as one of the high points of Shakespeare's poetry. Therefore, if we can discover what general and fundamental function the figurative language serves in this case, we may arrive at a statement of the real function of metaphorical thinking in poetry.

That function is to express not only idea but feeling, feeling not restricted to the narrow scope it has in primarily decorative or ornamental comparisons. Macbeth says that life is a tale told by an idiot. Why? The idea, of course, is that life is meaningless. Macbeth feels, as his wife dies and all his plans begin to go to pieces, that life is meaningless. What else does the comparison tell us that the statement "Life is meaningless" does not?

In the first place, the picture of the idiot, raging and gibbering meaningless syllables, adds a horror and loathsomeness to the statement. It gives us something of the horror Macbeth feels at his discovery that life has no meaning. But the figure also tells us more accurately than the mere abstract statement does just what kind of horror Macbeth feels. Though we do not expect a beast to utter intelligible speech, we do expect intelligible speech—a statement that has a meaning— from a human being. The incoherence of the idiot has a special horror, therefore, for the idiot is, after all, a human being. The idiot's babbling is felt, thus, as a hideous travesty on human nature. Macbeth feels, as do all human beings, that life *ought* to have a meaning. His horror at finding that his own life does not is therefore the sort of horror one might feel at the babbling of an idiot.

It should be clear that the function of the comparison in the case just discussed is not merely that of making an idea clearer and simpler (the function of mere illustration); the poet is using his comparison in order to form and make expressible something that otherwise would not be available to the reader. This function of *intrinsic expressiveness* (the communication of idea *plus* the attitude toward and feeling about the idea by means of embodiment in an image) is the great primary function of figurative language. Perhaps because it is expressive we sometimes say that it is impossible to transpose what a good poet says into prose—that is, it is impossible to give the experience in any way other than by reading the poetry itself.

EXERCISE

Here are the first four lines of one of Shakespeare's most famous sonnets:

That time of year thou mayst in me behold
When yellow leaves, or none, or few, do hang
Upon those boughs which shake against the cold,
Bare ruined choirs where late the sweet birds sang.

Take out the images used metaphorically here (such as "yellow leaves") and what do you have left? What are the images implying about the poet's attitude toward getting old? Give the question some thought—and feeling—before you frame an answer.

Our man in the street, as we remember, says that "a fancy way of putting things"— figures of speech—distinguishes poetry. But he is only half right. All language, except highly developed technical language, such as that of mathematics or philosophy, is finally figurative. Obvious figures of speech are often used, as in the instance of the comparison of a heart to a pump, which we have already referred to, but the figurative element permeates language in an even deeper and more pervasive way. We use constantly many terms that are clearly figurative in their origin. Thus we speak of the eye of a needle or the mouth of a river. We do not, of course, think of these objects as being eyes or mouths in any human sense as we use the terms today, but clearly the terms originated because the small hole in a needle was thought to be like a human eye and the entrance to a river like a human mouth.

In saying that all language is at basis figurative, we come very close to saying that at basis all language is *poetic*. It will be easy to show why. We have already said that poetry tends toward concentration and intensification. But so does figurative language, particularly when the images are not worn out but are fresh and new. Compare the two statements "He is a distinctly unpleasant fellow" and "He is a swine." The latter is much sharper and more emphatic. It carries more force because it implies the figure of a hog with all the unpleasant attributes of that creature. The general idea of the "unpleasant" takes form, becomes an image, and the image evokes a body of feelings and attitudes.

This need for immediacy and vividness in language is constant, and at the very center of language. The need is, for instance, constantly manifesting itself in the development of slang, and the poetic impulse appears as vitally at that end of the spectrum as in poetry at the other. In fact, slang and poetry have more in common, in one sense, than either has with most language in between. And each historical moment has the need to refresh its sense of experience with a new slang and a new poetry. Both are expressions of a vital growth and of the human need to grasp the world as fully as possible.

Poetry has the same basic impulse to figurative expression that appears in ordinary language, but this fact involves a characteristic difference, too. What is often incidental in speech, and even in ordinary prose, is central and specialized in poetry. The intensification of effect characteristic of poetry is significantly achieved through the metaphoric process.

The way in which this occurs, and the relation of the metaphoric process to other aspects of poetry will be one of our continuing concerns in all divisions of our book. Metaphor intensifies effect; it may massively, if indirectly, widen the range and increase the complexity of intellectual implications and, at the same time suggest depth and complication of emotion. But it also may contribute to the formal structure of a poem. The relation among images (similes, metaphors, symbols) is one of the principles by which poetry is characteristically organized. And the way in which this occurs will, too, be one of our continuing concerns.

A metaphor, as we have said, embodies

meaning. It expresses meaning by embodiment. Rhythm, too, embodies meaning. Its own quality is an expression. A poem, taken as a whole, is an embodiment. It does not merely make a statement about something. It may make a statement, but, as we shall see, such overt statements in a poem are never to be equated with the meaning, which inheres in the complex of the particular qualities of the particular poem. The poem is, in the end, the meaning. To put the matter another way, a *poem is a dramatization of meaning*.

Somewhat more specifically, it is helpful to think of the dramatic aspect of a poem in another and more limited fashion. A poem implies a speaker, perhaps the unspecified "I" of the poet, perhaps the specified "I," perhaps an identified character quite different from the poet, as in Browning's "My Last Duchess" (sec. 12), which is, in the dramatic sense, spoken by an Italian duke of the period of the Renaissance.

If a poem implies, or specifies, a speaker, the speaker has some reason for speaking. An occasion provokes the poem because the speaker has some stake in it, some feeling about it, some attitude toward it, some idea about it. And the feeling, attitude, and idea provoked in the speaker by the occasion are implicit in the very tone of the poem, in the texture of the whole, just as feelings, attitudes, and ideas are implicit in any speaker's choice of words and tone of voice.

Furthermore, a reason for speaking suggests an audience for what is said. The audience may be specified, or merely implied. Robert Herrick, in his poem "To the Virgins, to Make Much of Time" (sec. 14), specifies his audience—coy and reluctant young ladies. Shakespeare, in many of his sonnets, directly addresses a young nobleman, not fictitious but quite real if not absolutely identified. John Donne, in "Batter My Heart, Three-Personed God" (sec. 16), is, obviously, uttering a prayer, addressing God. But even in poems where no audience is specified, we assume one—for we the readers are the audience, and in one way or another we, too, have a stake in the proceedings, however minimal.

This notion of the poem as a drama is of crucial importance. We shall soon see that the very reason for a poem's being the particular way it is stems from the fact of its being a drama, specified or implicit. Furthermore, if we cling to the notion, we have a start to the appreciation and understanding of a new poem. We have a way into it, and a way that links the poem directly to our ordinary human interests. Human nature, human conduct, and human fate—these are of perennial interest to us, and they lie behind all poems, as behind all fiction. For this reason, the poems with which we start, those in section 12, are, directly or by implication, stories, poems in which the question of human nature, conduct, and fate are in the foreground.

A NOTE ON THE TEXTS. Because archaic English may be a stumbling block to the novice student of poetry, we have elected to present many of our selections of poems from the sixteenth and seventeenth centuries with modern, American spelling and punctuation. We have, however, retained archaic or irregular spellings and punctuation that in any way affect the metrics, the rime, or the tone of these poems. And we have, too, for the charm of them, included a few poems from these centuries with archaic spellings and all. Poems of earlier centuries are given in traditionally accepted forms—lest modernization wring the poetry out of them altogether—and poems of later centuries are given as nearly as we can determine as their authors wrote them.

Section 12

NARRATIVE

All of the poems in this section involve, directly or indirectly, a story. In group 1 we are concerned with poems that, though they do not always give the sort of detail we are accustomed to in prose fiction, always strongly indicate the action that underlies the poem. In group 2 are poems in which the action, though suggested rather than presented, is still essential to the poem. In group 3, we find poems that deal with actions much more complicated than in groups 1 and 2, the sort of complication that we may find in fully developed prose fiction; but in these pieces presentation and implication are subtly intertwined, and, too, the themes tend to be more complex than in the earlier groups.

There is no sharp distinction between the kinds of interest and satisfaction we take in prose fiction and what we find in such poems as these. As human beings, we are interested in human nature, human experience and conduct, and human values, and such things constitute the stuff of both prose fiction and the poems presented here. These poems, like the short stories we have been reading, move to some significant climax, a moment in which action is fulfilled in meaning. We may go further, in fact, to say that there is no distinct line between prose fiction and any kind of poem. Even the most lyrical poem, one that seems to be merely an outburst of emotion, implies, as we have said above, a situation, and therefore a potential story. A poem is an utterance; there is always an utterer and some provocation for the utterance—and, usually, some hearer of it, too, is at least implied. A poem has a situation, and a situation is a potential story—or drama, as we have earlier put it. So, in considering the story poems in this section, we are considering issues that are involved in all poetry.

Even if there is no sharp and distinct line between prose fiction and poetry—even if poetry, along with short stories and novels, may be set under the more inclusive head of "fiction" in general—there are differences between the categories. The short story and the story poem, or the novel and the epic, are not identical, and our expectations when we approach them are different. Obviously, any poem differs, as we have insisted before, from a straight prose account of the action it involves.

Most prominent, of course, is the difference of meter or some other form of more or less highly organized rhythm. In the second place, there is the difference in the principle of organization: the treatment of the actual events in a poem is usually different from that one would ordinarily find in a prose account. In approaching the poems in this section, the reader should constantly ask himself this question: "In what ways might a prose account of this material differ from what is here?" The reader might well prepare a prose account of a given poem, a retelling of the story and in his own words, and compare it with the poem itself. A good prose paraphrase will give a mastery of the facts. The poem, however, does not attempt to give merely the facts; it attempts to use the facts in a certain way and for a certain purpose. What poetry does attempt is best appreciated by a long soaking in poem after poem—and a thoughtful soaking. And a thoughtful soaking implies the attempt to feel the rhythm of a poem and to relate that rhythm to the material presented and to the idea suggested by that material.

GROUP 1: SIMPLE NARRATIVE

SIR PATRICK SPENS
Anonymous

The king sits in Dumferling toune,
　　Drinking the blude-reid wine:
"O whar will I get guid sailor,
　　To sail this schip of mine."

Up and spake an eldern knicht,[1]　　　　5
　　Sat at the kings richt kne:

"Sir Patrick Spens is the best sailor,
　　That sails upon the se."

The king has written a braid[2] letter,
　　And signd it wi his hand,　　　　10
And sent it to Sir Patrick Spens,
　　Was walking on the sand.

The first line that Sir Patrick red,
　　A loud lauch[3] lauchèd he;
The next line that Sir Patrick red,　　　15
　　The teir blinded his ee.

"O wha[4] is this has don this deid,
　　This ill deid don to me,
To send me out this time o' the yeir,
　　To sail upon the se!　　　　20

"Mak hast, mak hast, my mirry men all,
　　Our guid ship sails the morne:"
"O say na sae,[5] my master deir,
　　For I feir a deadlie storme."

"Late, late yestreen I saw the new moone,　25
　　Wi the auld[6] moone in hir arme,
And I feir, I feir, my deir master,
　　That we will cum to harme."

O our Scots nobles wer richt laith[7]
　　To weet their cork-heild schoone;[8]　　30
Bot lang owre a'[9] the play wer playd,
　　Thair hats they swam aboone.[10]

O lang, lang may their ladies sit,
　　Wi their fans into their hand,
Or eir[11] they se Sir Patrick Spens　　　35
　　Cum sailing to the land.

O lang, lang may the ladies stand,
　　Wi thair gold kems[12] in their hair,
Waiting for thair ain[13] deir lords,
　　For they'll se thame na mair.[14]　　　40

Haf owre, haf owre to Aberdour,[15]
　　It's fiftie fadom deip,
And thair lies guid Sir Patrick Spens,
　　Wi the Scots lords at his feit.

This poem is a *ballad* (see Glossary), that is, it is a song that tells a story. But it is important to notice *how* it tells the story. In the first place, the poem is not so much a detailed and ordered narrative as a *drama*. The

---

[1] knight　[2] broad　[3] laugh　[4] who　[5] so　[6] old　[7] loath　[8] cork-heeled shoes　[9] all　[10] above　[11] ere　[12] combs　[13] own
[14] more　[15] Aberdeen

poem is actually made up of little dramatic scenes. The first of these scenes portrays the king inquiring for the name of a good sailor, learning of Sir Patrick, and writing a letter to Sir Patrick, ordering him to undertake a voyage for him. There is no transition from this to the second scene, which begins abruptly with Sir Patrick pacing the seashore. He receives the letter, and though he is shocked at the folly of attempting a voyage at this time of year, he passes on the order to his men. It is only when we come to the eighth stanza that we find the straight dramatic form abandoned in favor of comment on the situation by the poet, and even this comment is still close to drama.

The eighth stanza pictures—again without any transition—the hats of the Scottish lords floating on the sea. The ninth and tenth stanzas picture the ladies in their fine houses waiting for their lords to return to them. Not until the last stanza does the poem state explicitly that the ship was lost, and even here the poet does not say "The ship foundered." Instead, he paints a picture of the brave sailor lying on the sea floor with the Scottish lords at his feet.

From this account one can see how much the poem, simple though it may appear, differs from flat prose statement. The prose statement would probably go something like this: "The king, deciding that a voyage had to be made, found upon inquiry that Sir Patrick Spens was the best sailor to be had, and ordered him to make the voyage. Sir Patrick, though realizing that a storm was brewing and that the trip was likely to be disastrous, carried out the order. The ship sank, and Sir Patrick went down with the crew of noble passengers who had been entrusted to his care."

Now, is the poem better than the prose statement? We can draw up a sort of balance sheet for the poem against our prose version. On the debit side of the poem's account we must first set down this: the prose statement seems, at first glance, the clearer of the two. If one is in a hurry to give the facts and if he merely wishes to pass on the facts, he will naturally prefer to use prose. But here we do not need to learn the facts for their practical importance, as one needs to learn the price of eggs or the weather forecast. And moreover, the tragedy as given in the poem is clear enough—there is no great difficulty in finding out what really happened.

Now what is to be put to the credit side of the account? What is gained by telling the story in the form of the poem? In the first place, everything is much more *vivid* in the poem. Even the strongly marked rhythms of the poem tend to set the details off, making them more vivid, and to give the action a frame and shape. By giving the story in little flashes or scenes, we have a sharpness of detail—the sense of reality—which would otherwise be missed. The prose method is to make the flat statement that the king was thoughtless and foolhardy, knowing nothing of the sea, whereas Sir Patrick was an experienced sailor. The method of the poem is, on the other hand, to show the king actually in his characteristic surroundings. The poem shows him sitting in his palace and drinking his wine at his ease, in contrast to Sir Patrick walking on the beach, within sight of his ship, then uttering a scornful laugh at the folly of the king's orders.

In the same way, the ominous sense of disaster is given, and given vividly, by having the sailor tell of the warning in the weather signs. The new moon with the old moon in her arms is the folk way of describing what is sometimes seen at the new moon: a thin crescent whose tips are joined by an arc of light outlining the rest of the circle of the moon. The picture is very effective here, for it is not only concrete; it has associations of mystery and foreboding. To analyze a little more closely, there is an ironical contrast embedded in the figure itself. The image of the new moon holding the old moon in her arms seems to be an image that suggests affectionate care; but to those who know the weather signs, it means just the opposite—it means storms and disaster for those at sea.

Does the reader have to analyze consciously in such detail in order for the figure to be effective for him? No, much of the expressiveness of poetry depends upon effects made on the *unconscious* mind of the reader —effects that the reader may not consciously analyze and explain and that are, therefore, accounted for under some such phrase as "the magic of poetry." And the reader loses a great deal that poetry has to give him if he is willing to accept only what he can immediately account for. But a reader's sensitivity to such "magic" may be vastly increased if he tries to see how the "magic" actually works. And in this process the "magic" becomes not less but more magical.

The way in which this poem builds up to a climax at the end is a good example of the method of implication. There is a quality of suspense that the prose summary lacks. Not only does the poem avoid telling us what actually happened until we come to the last line; there is a connection of the tragic end with the forebodings of tragedy given in the earlier stanzas. For instance, after mentioning the consternation of the sailors, the poem brings us back to the Scottish lords for ironical comment. They didn't like to wet even the heels of their fine shoes, but before matters were over, their hats floated above them. Then the poem takes up the ladies, waiting for their husbands' return. They are pictured in their finery with their fans and their golden combs. But all their high birth and wealth could not bring their husbands back again. The irony built up here into a comment on the vanity of earthly power and riches is all the stronger for being merely hinted rather than stated in so many words in a moralizing fashion.

In the last stanza this rather generalized irony involving the lords and their ladies is brought to a sharp focus on Sir Patrick Spens himself. But with an important difference. The irony before the last stanza involves the ignorance of the lords and ladies; it is irony at their expense. The irony of the last stanza is not at the expense of Sir Patrick. He is a seasoned sailor. He knows the sea, and one feels that he knows life too. He knows that one can't beat the sea or nature or life. And he knows this because, unlike the fine lords, he has actually battled with life. In the end, of course, the disaster to the lords is his own disaster. As a loyal subject, he has to obey the king, even against his better knowledge. But he has his part in the general tragedy with a difference. At least he goes into it open-eyed. The tragic situation is the conflict between his loyalty and his knowledge.

On the basis of the last paragraphs, one may mention one more way in which the poem differs sharply from its prose paraphrase: the poem implies some kind of "meaning" in the experience and "feeling" about the experience. The paraphrase is interested in relating the facts. The poem is interested not merely in the facts, but in the way the author feels about the facts and the *meaning* of the facts.

EXERCISE

Read the poem out loud several times. Do you sense any difference in the quality of feeling and in the rhythms between the last stanza and the earlier part of the poem? Do you think that there is some connection between this fact (if you take it to be a fact) and the meaning of the poem?

FRANKIE AND JOHNNY

Anonymous

Frankie and Johnny were lovers, great God how they could love!
Swore to be true to each other, true as the stars up above.
He was her man, but he done her wrong.

Frankie she was his woman, everybody knows.
She spent her forty dollars for Johnny a suit of clothes.   5
He was her man, but he done her wrong.

Frankie and Johnny went walking, Johnny in his brand new suit.
"O good Lawd," said Frankie, "but don't my Johnny look cute?"
He was her man, but he done her wrong.

Frankie went down to the corner, just for a bucket of beer.   10
Frankie said, "Mr. Bartender, has my loving Johnny been here?
He is my man, he wouldn't do me wrong."

"I don't want to tell you no story, I don't want to tell you no lie,
But your Johnny left here an hour ago with that lousy Nellie Blye.
He is your man, but he's doing you wrong."   15

Frankie went back to the hotel, she didn't go there for fun,

For under her red kimono she toted a forty-four
  gun.
He was her man, but he done her wrong.

Frankie went down to the hotel and looked in the
  window so high,
And there was her loving Johnny a-loving up
  Nellie Blye.   20
He was her man, but he was doing her wrong.

Frankie threw back her kimono, took out that old
  forty-four.
Root-a-toot-toot, three times she shot, right
  through the hardwood door.
He was her man, but he was doing her wrong.

Johnny grabbed off his Stetson, crying, "O Frankie
  don't shoot!"   25
Frankie pulled that forty-four, went root-a-toot-
  toot-toot-toot.
He was her man, but he done her wrong.

"Roll me over gently, roll me over slow,
Roll me on my right side, for my left side hurts me
  so,
I was her man, but I done her wrong."   30

With the first shot Johnny staggered, with the
  second shot he fell;
When the last bullet got him, there was a new
  man's face in hell.
He was her man, but he done her wrong.

"O, bring out your rubber-tired hearses, bring out
  your rubber-tired hacks;
Gonna take Johnny to the graveyard and ain't
  gonna bring him back.   35
He was my man, but he done me wrong.

"O, put me in that dungeon, put me in that cell,
Put me where the northeast wind blows from the
  southeast corner of hell.
I shot my man, cause he done me wrong!"

This poem is a modern product of the same impulse that produced "Sir Patrick Spens" hundreds of years earlier. Frankie was a prostitute in St. Louis, several generations ago, with a kept boy some ten years younger than herself (a boy named Albert, seventeen years old, in the original version); when she discovered that he was unfaithful, she killed him. So much for the facts. But people want more than mere facts; they want something that will appeal to their emotions, and the sordid little tale of Frankie and her kept boy had some basic emotional appeal that eventuated in a song—the ballad we now know.

"Frankie and Johnny," like "Sir Patrick Spens," grows out of a simple and unsophisticated society, and in its makeup, resembles closely the older ballad. "Frankie and Johnny" raises at once for us, therefore, two important questions: (1) Can poetry grow out of the present rather than merely the past? and (2) can poetry deal with sordid materials; can it use the subject matter of the backstreets of an American city, material we are inclined to associate with tabloid headlines rather than with poetry? Any reader can imagine how a newspaper, whose function is to give the essential facts, would treat such a story as the murder of Johnny by his sweetheart. Since the answer to such questions rests on what we think of the poem, let us consider the poem first. In what ways is it like "Sir Patrick Spens"?

In the first place, this poem, though not so dramatic as the older poem, is told in terms of little scenes. The links between the scenes are left up to the reader's imagination, and quite properly. The poem continually focuses attention on the essential elements. First there is the statement of Frankie's love for Johnny; then the scene of their walk together; the scene at the saloon where Frankie learns that her lover is unfaithful; then last, the scene in which she kills him.

The scenes in themselves, moreover, are vivid. Notice how concrete they are. A *hat* is a "Stetson"; a *gun*, a "forty-four." The poem, crude as it may seem, shows a mastery of this point: that if you give the reader a few details sharply and vividly enough, his imagination will do the rest. The same holds true of the understatement in the poem. We have the given understatement of Frankie's intention: "she didn't go there for fun." Or that about Johnny's burial: the hearse and hacks may take Johnny to the graveyard, but "they ain't gonna bring him back." Understatement, rather than exaggeration, puts the imagination to work, involves the reader in the process of the poem.

Moreover, the poem is not only real; it has a certain dignity. That is, it accepts the human values the poem is based on. The poem is not interested in providing a great deal of dissection of motives, nor is it interested in moralizing comment. The focus is kept where it should be here: on the core of the action itself but on the action as based on the observance of a strict code of honor. The code of honor is assumed throughout the poem; and it is the code that holds the poem together: It is right to kill the person who proves unfaithful. Johnny, himself, after he has been shot, admits it: "I was her man, but I done her wrong."

In this connection, notice how important the refrain is in binding the poem together, and the effect of the variations that occur in it: "He is my man, he wouldn't do me wrong," "He is your man, but he's doing you wrong," and so on. The refrain affirms the idea from which the action springs.

EXERCISE

"Frankie and Johnny" was originally a song, and is usually known in that form. (Ballads have generally been sung long before they have been discovered as "literature.") If you have heard the song—or now have access to a recording—what does the musical rendering suggest to you about the difference between the poetic treatment of the action and the factual prose treatment? Does the "poem" version seem closer to the song or to a prose treatment? Whatever your opinion, why do you hold it?

LUCINDA MATLOCK
Edgar Lee Masters (1869–1950)

I went to the dances at Chandlerville,
And played snap-out at Winchester.
One time we changed partners,
Driving home in the moonlight of middle June,
And then I found Davis.   5
We were married and lived together for seventy years,
Enjoying, working, raising the twelve children,
Eight of whom we lost
Ere I had reached the age of sixty.
I spun, I wove, I kept the house, I nursed the sick,   10
I made the garden, and for holiday
Rambled over the fields where sang the larks,
And by Spoon River gathering many a shell,
And many a flower and medicinal weed—

Shouting to the wooded hills, singing to the green valleys.   15
At ninety-six I had lived enough, that is all,
And passed to a sweet repose.
What is this I hear of sorrow and weariness,
Anger, discontent and drooping hopes?
Degenerate sons and daughters,   20
Life is too strong for you—
It takes life to love Life.

Spoon River Anthology, from which this poem is taken, purports to be a collection of epitaphs from the cemetery of a small midwestern town. The author imagines that in each such epitaph the character epitomizes his own life.

EXERCISES

1. What is Lucinda Matlock's character? Are the details given in the poem well chosen to present that character? What, for instance, does the fact that Lucinda had lost eight of her twelve children add to the poem? Why, and in what spirit, would she mention it here?
2. To whom does she address the last five lines? In what sense are the sons and daughters she addresses "degenerate"?
3. This poem is in free verse (see subsec. 19.13), and its rhythms are not very emphatic—less so than in most other free verse poems. Try to imagine this poem put into a regular verse form—for instance, the four-line stanzas of "Sir Patrick Spens." What do you think would be the difference in effect?

THE STAR-SPLITTER
Robert Frost (1874–1963)

"You know Orion always comes up sideways.
Throwing a leg up over our fence of mountains,
And rising on his hands, he looks in on me
Busy outdoors by lantern-light with something
I should have done by daylight, and indeed,   5
After the ground is frozen, I should have done
Before it froze, and a gust flings a handful
Of waste leaves at my smoky lantern chimney
To make fun of my way of doing things,
Or else fun of Orion's having caught me.   10
Has a man, I should like to ask, no rights
These forces are obliged to pay respect to?"
To Brad McLaughlin mingled reckless talk
Of heavenly stars with hugger-mugger farming,
Till having failed at hugger-mugger farming   15

He burned his house down for the fire insurance
And spent the proceeds on a telescope
To satisfy a life-long curiosity
About our place among the infinities.

"What do you want with one of those blame
    things?" 20
I asked him well beforehand. "Don't you get one!"
"Don't call it blamed; there isn't anything
More blameless in the sense of being less
A weapon in our human fight," he said.
"I'll have one if I sell my farm to buy it." 25
There where he moved the rocks to plow the
    ground
And plowed between the rocks he couldn't move,
Few farms changed hands; so rather than spend
    years
Trying to sell his farm and then not selling,
He burned his house down for the fire insurance 30
And bought the telescope with what it came to.
He had been heard to say by several:
"The best thing that we're put here for's to see;
The strongest thing that's given us to see with's
A telescope. Someone in every town 35
Seems to me owes it to the town to keep one.
In Littleton it may as well be me."
After such loose talk it was no surprise
When he did what he did and burned his house
    down.

Mean laughter went about the town that day 40
To let him know we weren't the least imposed on,
And he could wait—we'd see to him to-morrow.
But the first thing next morning we reflected
If one by one we counted people out
For the least sin, it wouldn't take us long 45
To get so we had no one left to live with.
For to be social is to be forgiving.
Our thief, the one who does the stealing from us,
We don't cut off from coming to church suppers,
But what we miss we go to him and ask for. 50
He promptly gives it back, that is if still
Uneaten, unworn out, or undisposed of.
It wouldn't do to be too hard on Brad
About his telescope. Beyond the age
Of being given one for Christmas gift, 55
He had to take the best way he knew how
To find himself in one. Well, all we said was
He took a strange thing to be roguish over.
Some sympathy was wasted on the house,
A good old-timer dating back along; 60
But a house isn't sentient; the house
Didn't feel anything. And if it did,
Why not regard it as a sacrifice,
And an old-fashioned sacrifice by fire?
Instead of a new-fashioned one at auction? 65

Out of a house and so out of a farm
At one stroke (of a match), Brad had to turn
To earn a living on the Concord railroad,
As under-ticket-agent at a station
Where his job, when he wasn't selling tickets, 70
Was setting out, up track and down, not plants
As on a farm, but planets, evening stars
That varied in their hue from red to green.

He got a good glass for six hundred dollars.
His new job gave him leisure for stargazing. 75
Often he bid me come and have a look
Up the brass barrel, velvet black inside,
At a star quaking in the other end.
I recollect a night of broken clouds
And underfoot snow melted down to ice, 80
And melting further in the wind to mud.
Bradford and I had out the telescope.
We spread our two legs as we spread its three,
Pointed our thoughts the way we pointed it,
And standing at our leisure till the day broke, 85
Said some of the best things we ever said.
That telescope was christened the Star-Splitter,
Because it didn't do a thing but split
A star in two or three the way you split
A globule of quicksilver in your hand 90
With one stroke of your finger in the middle.
It's a star-splitter if there ever was one
And ought to do some good if splitting stars
'S a thing to be compared with splitting wood.

We've looked and looked, but after all where are
    we? 95
Do we know any better where we are,
And how it stands between the night to-night
And a man with a smoky lantern chimney?
How different from the way it ever stood?

EXERCISES

1. What kind of man is the narrator? How do you
know? What kind of man is Brad? How do you
know?

2. Define as carefully as you can the narrator's
attitude toward Brad. The community's. What
attitude is the reader invited to take?

3. Is the narrator simply telling an amusing story?
Are there any glances at serious issues?

4. Is Brad "justified" in taking the means he does
in order to get his telescope? In this connection,
consider lines 79–86 and 93–99.

5. How close does the language of the poem seem
to the kind of world it describes? Frost was famous
for being able to catch the accent of ordinary

colloquial speech in his verse. Do you think that "The Star-Splitter" supports that reputation?

6. The language and rhythms of "The Star-Splitter" are close to the world in which the story occurs; the language of "Frankie and Johnny," as far as idiom and vocabulary are concerned, is also that of the world of the story. But where Frost caught the rhythms of speech, the nameless poet who composed "Frankie and Johnny" wrote in rhythms far more strongly marked than speech ordinarily admits, in regular line-lengths, and with rime. Frost's poem is, we may say, more realistic. But does this fact suggest that "The Star-Splitter" —or "Lucinda Matlock"—is necessarily better than "Frankie and Johnny" or "Sir Patrick Spens"? Or do we have mere differences of effect? What qualities do the two kinds of poem share? What do they aim to do? What kind of interest and response do all four poems evoke?

THE MAN HE KILLED
Thomas Hardy (1840–1928)

> "Had he and I but met,
> By some old ancient inn,
> We should have sat us down to wet
> Right many a nipperkin! [1]
>
> "But ranged as infantry,   5
> And staring face to face,
> I shot at him as he at me,
> And killed him in his place.
>
> "I shot him dead because—
> Because he was my foe,   10
> Just so: my foe of course he was;
> That's clear enough; although
>
> "He thought he'd 'list, perhaps
> Off-hand-like—just as I—
> Was out of work—had sold his traps—   15
> No other reason why.
>
> "Yes; quaint and curious war is!
> You shoot a fellow down
> You'd treat if met where any bar is,
> Or help to half-a-crown."   20

[1] a small wine and beer measure, a "nip"

EXERCISES

1. The objective story behind this poem is quite clearly stated: the speaker, an infantryman, has killed one of the enemy and is now somewhat puzzled about the logic of what he has done. Why do we use the word *logic* here? Why don't we say that his conscience was troubled? State in your own words the nature of the problem that the soldier proposes to himself.

2. The soldier is troubled—but not painfully, we may say—about the discrepancy between the values that institutions, great social organizations, society itself, propose and those proposed by individuals; or to put it in another way, by the difference in behavior accepted as proper for a state or nation and that accepted as proper for an individual. This problem is what the poem states; it is the theme of the poem. But certainly this idea has no great originality; it is no news to anybody, except a small child; it is a cliché. Why may it be acceptable in this poem? And interesting?

3. We have referred to the "objective story" behind this poem. Is that the only action involved here? What about the story of the man who was killed? What is the relation of that story to the meaning of the poem? Is there any particular reason why one man gets killed and not the other? Can it be said that this question has an ironical relation to the theme of the poem?

4. It can be said that in addition to the objective story narrated in the poem, the poem itself involves a subjective action, a subjective story—the speaker's effort to fumble through to the meaning of his experience. No such effort is involved in, say, "Sir Patrick Spens"; in the ballad we get only the objective narrative ending in an image of the sea floor with its aura of symbolic significance. But the speaker of this poem is concerned with his own personal problem—with what sense his experience makes. Is this the basis of the drama of this poem? Explain. Could it be said that this dramatization is what makes the cliché acceptable?

5. What elements of language and what turns of the speaker's mind account for the effectiveness of the dramatization? In connection with this, what degree of education do you think the speaker has? Is he extremely intelligent? Do you imagine that he has ever given thought to the sort of problem that now his own experience proposes to him? How does the method of this poem, and the language, compare to that of "The Star-Splitter"? To that of "Frankie and Johnny"? Is this poem singable?

RICHARD CORY
Edwin Arlington Robinson (1869–1935)

> Whenever Richard Cory went down town,
>   We people on the pavement looked at him:
> He was a gentleman from sole to crown,
>   Clean favored and imperially slim.

And he was always quietly arrayed,
   And he was always human when he talked;
But still he fluttered pulses when he said,
   "Good-morning," and he glittered when he
     walked.

And he was rich—yes, richer than a king—
   And admirably schooled in every grace:
In fine, we thought that he was everything
   To make us wish that we were in his place.

So on we worked, and waited for the light,
   And went without the meat, and cursed the
     bread;
And Richard Cory, one calm summer night,
   Went home and put a bullet through his head.

EXERCISE

Prepare a set of questions involving the method of
this poem and its meaning.

Rhythm and Meter

You should give yourself a good soaking in
the poems just presented, and try to feel the
rhythm as related to the general effect of the
particular poems. Now, to sharpen your
capacity for attending to rhythm, you should
turn to subsection 19.1 and thoughtfully read
our general remarks on metrics.

EXERCISE

Turn back to "Richard Cory," and read it aloud
several times to catch the pattern of accents. Then
mark the accents. Do the same with stanza 1 of
"The Man He Killed." After you have proceeded
a little further in the study of metrics, come back
and check what you now do.

GROUP 2: SUGGESTED NARRATIVE

EDWARD
Anonymous

"Why dois your brand[1] sae[2] drap wi bluid,
   Edward, Edward?

"Why dois your brand sae drap wi bluid,
   And why sae sad gang[3] yee O?"
"O I hae killed my hauke[4] sae guid,   5
   Mither, mither,
O I hae killed my hauke sae guid,
   And I had nae mair bot hee O."

"Your haukis bluid was nevir sae reid,
   Edward, Edward,   10
Your haukis bluid was never sae reid,
   My deir son I tell thee O."
"O I hae killed my reid-roan steid,[5]
   Mither, mither,
O I hae killed my reid-roan steid,   15
   That erst was sae fair and frie O."
"Your steid was auld,[6] and ye hae gat mair,[7]
   Edward, Edward,
Your steid was auld, and ye hae gat mair;
   Sum other dule[8] ye drie[9] O."   20
"O I hae killed my fadir[10] deir,
   Mither, mither
O I hae killed by fadir deir,
   Alas, and wae is mee I!"

"And whatten penance wul ye drie for that,   25
   Edward, Edward?
And whatten penance wul ye drie, for that?
   My deir son, now tell me O."
"Ile set my feit in yonder boat,
   Mither, mither   30
Ile set my feit in yonder boat,
   And Ile fare ovir the sea O."

"And what wul ye doe wi your towirs and your
   ha,[11]
   Edward, Edward?
And what wul ye doe wi your towirs and your
   ha,   35
   That were sae fair to see O?"
"Ile let thame stand tul they doun fa,
   Mither, mither
Ile let thame stand tul they doun fa,
   For here nevir mair maun I bee O."   40

"And what wul ye leive to your bairns[12] and your
   wife,
   Edward, Edward?
And what wul ye leive to your bairns and your
   wife,
   Whan ye gang ovir the sea O?"
"The warldis[13] room, late them beg thrae life,   45
   Mither, mither
The warldis room, late them beg thrae life,
   For thame nevir mair wul I see O."

---

[1] sword   [2] so   [3] go   [4] hawk   [5] steed   [6] old   [7] more   [8] grief   [9] undergo   [10] father   [11] hall, manorhouse
[12] children   [13] world's

"And what wul ye leive to your ain mither deir,
          Edward, Edward?   50
And what wul ye leive to your ain mither deir?
  My deir son, now tell me O."
"The curse of hell frae me sall[14] ye beir,
          Mither, mither
The curse of hell frae me sall ye beir,   55
  Sic counseils ye gave to me O."

In the poems we have thus far read, we find a fairly clear action with the parts in chronological order. In the present group we find poems in which the action is suggested or implied rather than presented—that is, poems in which the interest in narrative as such is less emphasized than are other elements.* "Edward," for example, is a traditional ballad, as is "Sir Patrick Spens" in group 1, but the stories of the two poems are told in quite different manners.

In "Sir Patrick Spens" the story is given in the normal chronological order: the action begins with the old knight's telling the king about Sir Patrick and ends with the picture of Sir Patrick on the sea floor. It has been pointed out in the discussion of "Sir Patrick Spens" that the story is not treated by a simple, unemphasized forward movement, as in ordinary narrative, but is presented by a series of scenes, glimpses of the key situations, significant flashes of action that fire the reader's imagination to fill in the continuity. The method is that of a little drama composed of several scenes. But "Edward" does not tell its story in chronological order; it has only one scene, a scene after the real action, and the content of that action has to be handled by implication. It is therefore more economical and unified.

"Sir Patrick Spens" is told from an omniscient point of view. The teller is not a person in any real sense, but he can see and describe a scene such as the sea floor, as no real person could ever do. But the story of "Edward" is not "told" at all. It is, rather, presented in direct form as a dialogue be-

tween the two principal persons of the story. It is therefore even more dramatic and objective than "Sir Patrick Spens," and makes even more exciting demands on the reader's imagination.

The action of "Sir Patrick Spens" is accounted for at the very first, when the king takes the advice of the old knight; and the conclusion is foreshadowed several times, once when Sir Patrick opens the letter and gives his sardonic laugh, and again when the new moon has the old moon in her arms. The method is exactly the opposite in "Edward." We know what has actually happened long before the end, but we do not know the reason, the motivation, until the very last line. There is a sense of foreboding and inevitability about "Sir Patrick Spens," and of surprise and shock about "Edward."

The psychological interest in "Edward" is more important than in "Sir Patrick Spens." Each question and answer in "Edward" brings out some new fact, not only of the story, but of the characters involved. In "Sir Patrick Spens" we learn at the very beginning all we ever know about the characters. This does not mean that "Edward" is necessarily superior to "Sir Patrick Spens"; it merely means that there is a different kind of effect.

In regard to the matter of the technique and structure of "Edward," one can observe that its stanza form is more complicated than that of "Sir Patrick Spens." It has, too, a very elaborate use of refrain and repetition. The very action of the ballad, as a matter of fact, is carried and emphasized by these two devices. The refrains of "Edward" and "mither" define the structure of each stanza, the question and answer arrangement. Further, the question and answer arrangement is well adapted to the building up of suspense, in regard to the nature of the crime, and to prepare for the surprise, in regard to the motivation of the crime, which comes at

[14] shall

* There is no hard and fast line, however, between these two groups. "Richard Cory," for instance, is a borderline case, and might well go into group 2. It does have a specific narrative, that of the townspeople. But the narrative concerning Cory himself—the motivation for his suicide—is suggested rather than specified. Our concern, finally, is not with Cory but with the irony of the event, and its effect on the townspeople.

the end. We have here, then, a fairly clear example of how a form may be adapted to an effect.

Let us return to the details of the story of "Edward," and try to reconstruct the implied action.

Edward, the hero of the ballad, is a knight. His mother and father have presumably had a deadly quarrel. In any case we know of the desire of the mother to dispose of the father. The mother has gradually played on the son's feelings until he works himself up to the point of killing the father. The mother has therefore accomplished her purpose without making herself actually guilty of murder. She discovers her son with a bloody sword in his hand; and in a mixture of curiosity, gratification, and horror, now that the deed is actually accomplished, she questions Edward on two points: why does the blade drip and why is he so sad? He at first says that he has killed his hawk. But she says the blood is too red (a reference to the first of her questions). Then he says that he has killed his steed. But she says in such a case he would not be sad because he has other and better ones (a reference to the second of her questions). Then, overcome with his growing remorse, he confesses to the crime. She then asks a question that seems to establish her detachment from the crime, but she does not express grief. What penance will *he* do? Indicating a boat in the harbor, he answers that he will sail away and become a wanderer. To the question about his estate he says that the tower and hall may fall into decay. And to that about his wife and children he says that they may beg through life. Then at the climax she asks him what he will leave to his own dear mother. He will leave her the curse of hell, he says, because she has been responsible for the crime.

But how do we know all this?

How do we know that Edward is a knight or nobleman? Because of the reference to his towers and hall.

How do we know of the relation of father and mother? The last line of the poem established the mother's desire to get rid of the father.

How do we know that Edward is suffer-

ing remorse before he confesses? He refers to his "hawk so good," his only one, and to his "redroan steed," that before was "fair and free"; but this regret for loss is really a statement of regret for the loss of the father, who may be taken to have been "so good" and "fair and free." There would have been no more reason for killing the father than for butchering the hawk or the horse that had served him well.

How do we know that the woman is a hard and calculating woman? Naturally, we know it from the accusation at the end. But there are three significant indications that do something to define her earlier in the poem and to give an effect of mounting suspense. First, when Edward says that he grieves over the horse, she says, "why, the horse was old," ignoring any sentiment a person might feel for a faithful animal. To her it is only a piece of property. Second, she asks, "what penance will *you* do?" She attempts by the way she frames the question to separate herself from all responsibility. The normal reaction would have been one of grief or at least momentary astonishment, but she is so cold and self-controlled that she first attempts to clear her own skirts. Third, when she addresses him in the last stanza she refers to herself as his "own mother dear," trying to ingratiate herself with him, when she is really his worst enemy and has ruined him.

What is the meaning of the poem? We know the story, but what kind of effect does the story give? It gives an effect of tragic irony. A crime has been committed; and presumably the person most guilty, the mother, will suffer. But the son, whose moral nature is much superior to that of his mother but who has been influenced by her to commit the crime, must suffer too. Even the absolutely innocent persons, the wife and children, must suffer, for they will be abandoned to beg through life. The same question lies behind this story that lies behind the great tragedies: what is the nature of justice? But the ironical effect is not single, for it has certain cross-references, as it were, within the situation. First, only when the father is dead does Edward realize the father's virtues and his own better nature that brings him to remorse and penance. Second, the mother, who should be the greatest guardian of the son, has ruined him. Third, the mother, who expected some profit or satisfaction from the crime, is left with only a curse from the son whom, in her way, she loves. Fourth, the wife and children, who are innocent, must suffer too. The irony of "Sir Patrick Spens" is more simple.

EXERCISES

1. With what feelings, what attitudes, does Edward say of his wife and children that he leaves them the whole world's space in which they may beg through life?

2. What are your feelings about Edward? Do you have a sense of pity, of tragic waste in human life, of the chancey, mysterious quality of experience? Or what? What is the final effect of the poem? Try to assess your own responses. But give the poem a chance to work on you. Immerse yourself in it. Try to imagine a modern equivalent of the story.

LORD RANDALL

Anonymous

"O where hae ye been, Lord Randall, my son?
O where hae ye been, my handsome young man?"
"I hae been to the wild wood; mother, make my
    bed soon,
For I'm weary wi hunting, and fain wald[1] lie
    down."

"Where gat ye your dinner, Lord Randall, my
    son?   5
Where gat ye your dinner, my handsome young
    man?"
"I dined wi my true-love; mother, make my bed
    soon,
For I'm weary wi hunting, and fain wald lie
    down."

"What gat ye to your dinner, Lord Randall, my
    son?
What gat ye to your dinner, my handsome young
    man?"   10
"I gat eels boiled in broo; mother, make my bed
    soon,
For I'm weary wi hunting, and fain wald lie
    down."

"What became of your bloodhounds, Lord Randall, my son?
What became of your bloodhounds, my handsome
    young man?"
"O they swelld and they died; mother, make my
    bed soon,   15
For I'm weary wi hunting, and fain wald lie
    down."

"O I fear ye are poisond, Lord Randall, my son!
O I fear ye are poisond, my handsome young
    man!"
"O yes! I am poisond; mother, make my bed soon,
For I'm sick at the heart, and I fain wald lie
    down."   20

EXERCISE

Prepare a set of questions that you think might lead to a fuller understanding and appreciation of this poem. Compare your questions with those prepared by other students.

THE TRUE LOVER

A. E. Housman (1859–1936)

The lad came to the door at night,
    When lovers crown their vows,
And whistled soft and out of sight
    In shadow of the boughs.

'I shall not vex you with my face   5
    Henceforth, my love, for aye;
So take me in your arms a space
    Before the east is grey.

'When I from hence away am past
    I shall not find a bride,   10
And you shall be the first and last
    I ever lay beside.'

She heard and went and knew not why;
    Her heart to his she laid;
Light was the air beneath the sky   15
    But dark under the shade.

'Oh do you breathe, lad, that your breast
    Seems not to rise and fall,
And here upon my bosom prest
    There beats no heart at all?'   20

'Oh loud, my girl, it once would knock,
    You should have felt it then;

[1] would

> But since for you I stopped the clock
>   It never goes again.'

> 'Oh lad, what is it, lad, that drips   25
>   Wet from your neck on mine?
> What is falling on my lips,
>   My lad, that tastes of brine?'

> 'Oh like enough 'tis blood, my dear,
>   For when the knife has slit   30
> The throat across from ear to ear
>   'Twill bleed because of it.'

> Under the stars the air was light
>   But dark below the boughs,
> The still air of the speechless night,   35
>   When lovers crown their vows.

Housman's poem gives a single incident of a story, the climax, and implies the rest of the story. What is implied is, in summary, this much: a lover who has been constantly rejected by his sweetheart is prepared to go on a long journey. When the poem begins, he has come to her house at night and has whistled for her to come out to tell him goodbye. He says:

> So take me in your arms a space
>   Before the east is grey.

To that point the story may be taken as a real story which, like the preceding poems in this section, might be understood as an actual incident. But in the third stanza the reader begins to suspect that the journey the young man is to take is not a real journey, for he says:

> 'When I from hence away am past
>   I shall not find a bride,
> And you shall be the first and last
>   I ever lay beside.'

In other words, he asks his sweetheart to give him her love so that his life may have some meaning before he has to leave it.

But consider the speech of the girl in the fifth stanza:

> 'Oh do you breathe, lad, that your breast
>   Seems not to rise and fall. . . .'

With that, and with the lad's answer, the reader knows that the lover is already dead. The further question and answer merely make more emphatic an ironic fact.

The story, then, is an impossible one, and must not be understood as being realistic. To take it as realistic might make it too disgusting and horrible. It is a story invented by the poet to present more dramatically the meaning of a certain human relationship—the pathos and horror of realizing too late that one has rejected a love that can never be recovered. One need not even interpret the poem as meaning that the "true lover" has actually committed suicide or died. The love is merely lost beyond any recovery; and something within the lover has died, never to be revived. The story of the poem then stands for something beyond itself; that is, it stands as a concentrated representation of the feeling one might have about many stories that were different in their circumstantial incident and detail. It has a symbolic force.

How is the story told? The poem gives the same impression as a ballad. It uses a very simple stanza form, one that is common in the folk ballads. Further, it uses devices of repetition (observe how the questions are built up) and dialogue as do "Edward" and "Lord Randall." These devices have helped to concentrate the presentation of the story so that it is unnecessary to tell it in full. The same kind of ironic understatement appears in "The True Lover" as in "Sir Patrick Spens." For instance, the "true lover" says:

> 'But since for you I stopped the clock
>   It never goes again.'

and:

> 'Oh like enough 'tis blood, my dear,
>   For when the knife has slit
> The throat across from ear to ear
>   'Twill bleed because of it.'

This is the same effect one finds in "Sir Patrick Spens" in the stanza:

> O our Scots nobles wer richt laith
>   To weet their cork-heild schoone;
> Bot lang owre a' the play wer playd,
>   Thair hats they swam aboone.

But there are certain obvious differences from the folk ballads. The folk ballads usually tell or imply a story that is to be taken as literal; at the end of "Sir Patrick Spens" a real wreck lies on a real sea floor. In Housman's ballad, however, the action is a symbolic one; it is not likely that a man would cut his throat in the act of making love. Here an action "stands for" another action, suggesting the meaning of the literal action. It is true, of course, that the last stanza of "Sir Patrick Spens" also suggests, or embodies, the meaning, the interpretation, of the action. But the scene is, as we have said, in itself literal.

EXERCISES

1. Try to imagine a literal story for which Housman's ballad might be taken as the symbolic equivalent.
2. Do you think that Housman's story would be as readily acceptable if presented in the style of "Lucinda Matlock"? Try to transpose it into such a style.

THE BONNY EARL OF MURRAY
Anonymous

Ye Highlands, and ye Lawlands,
  Oh where have you been?
They have slain the Earl of Murray,
  And they layd him on the green.

"Now wae be to thee, Huntly!   5
  And wherefore did you sae?
I bade you bring him wi you,
  But forbade you him to slay."

He was a braw[1] gallant,
  And he rid at the ring;   10
And the bonny Earl of Murray,
  Oh he might have been a king!

He was a braw gallant,
  And he playd at the ba[2];
And the bonny Earl of Murray,   15
  Was the flower amang them a'.

He was a braw gallant,
  And he playd at the glove;

And the bonny Earl of Murray,
  Oh he was the Queen's love!   20

Oh lang will his lady
  Look o'er the castle Down,
E'er she see the Earl of Murray
  Come sounding[3] thro the town.

This ballad is based upon an actual incident in Scottish history. But nothing of the complicated events leading up to the murder are here recounted; the ballad begins after the earl has been killed, and limits itself to the speaker's (and others') reactions to the event.

EXERCISES

1. Has the poem left too much to implication? Or does it gain force by this limitation? Upon what effect is the poem centered? Would further details enhance that effect?
2. What sort of person was the dead man? How do the details serve to define his character?
3. Does the last stanza provide a fitting climax to the poem? If you think it does, why do you think so?

BREDON HILL
A. E. Housman (1859–1936)

In summertime on Bredon[1]
  The bells they sound so clear;
Round both the shires they ring them
  In steeples far and near,
    A happy noise to hear   5

Here of a Sunday morning
  My love and I would lie,
And see the coloured counties,
  And hear the larks so high
    About us in the sky.   10

The bells would ring to call her
  In valleys miles away:
'Come all to church, good people;
  Good people, come and pray.'
    But here my love would stay.   15

---

[1] brave   [2] ball   [3] riding

[1] Pronounced Breedon.

And I would turn and answer
  Among the springing thyme,
'Oh, peal upon our wedding,
And we will hear the chime,
And come to church in time.'   20

But when the snows at Christmas
  On Bredon top were strown,
My love rose up so early
  And stole out unbeknown
And went to church alone.   25

They tolled the one bell only,
  Groom there was none to see,
The mourners followed after,

And so to church went she,
  And would not wait for me.   30

The bells they sound on Bredon,
  And still the steeples hum.
'Come all to church, good people,'—
  Oh, noisy bells, be dumb;
I hear you, I will come.   35

EXERCISE

Prepare a set of questions for "Bredon Hill." Write an essay (300–500 words) based on your questions.

DANNY DEEVER

Rudyard Kipling (1865–1936)

'What are the bugles blowin' for?' said Files-on-Parade.
'To turn you out, to turn you out,' the Colour-Sergeant said.
'What makes you look so white, so white?' said Files-on-Parade.
'I'm dreadin' what I've got to watch,' the Colour-Sergeant said.
    For they're hangin' Danny Deever, you can 'ear the Dead March play,   5
    The regiment's in 'ollow square—they're hangin' him today;
    They've taken of his buttons off an' cut his stripes away,
    An' they're hangin' Danny Deever in the mornin'.

'What makes the rear-rank breathe so 'ard?' said Files-on-Parade.
'It's bitter cold, it's bitter cold,' the Colour-Sergeant said.   10
'What makes that front-rank man fall down?' said Files-on-Parade.
'A touch of sun, a touch of sun,' the Colour-Sergeant said.
    They are hangin' Danny Deever, they are marchin' of 'im round
    They 'ave 'alted Danny Deever by 'is coffin on the ground:
    And 'e'll swing in 'arf a minute for a sneakin' shootin' hound—   15
    O they're hangin' Danny Deever in the mornin'!

' 'Is cot was right-'and cot to mine,' said Files-on-Parade.
' 'E's sleepin' out an' far tonight,' the Colour-Sergeant said.
'I've drunk 'is beer a score o' times,' said Files-on-Parade.
' 'E's drinkin' bitter beer alone,' the Colour-Sergeant said.   20
    They are hangin' Danny Deever, you must mark 'im to 'is place,
    For 'e shot a comrade sleepin'—you must look 'im in the face;
    Nine 'undred of 'is county an' the regiment's disgrace,
    While they're hangin' Danny Deever in the mornin'.

'What's that so black agin the sun?' said Files-on-Parade.   25
'It's Danny fightin' 'ard for life,' the Colour-Sergeant said.
'What's that that whimpers over'ead?' said Files-on-Parade.
'It's Danny's soul that's passin' now,' the Colour-Sergeant said.
    For they're done with Danny Deever, you can 'ear the quickstep play,
    The regiment's in column, an' they're marchin' us away;   30
    Ho! the young recruits are shakin', an' they'll want their beer today,
    After hangin' Danny Deever in the mornin'.

EXERCISES

1. The two men who carry on the conversation in this poem are noncommissioned officers in the British Army. What is their attitude toward Danny Deever? What sort of person was he? How do you know? What relation does his character have to the meaning of the poem? Is the poem primarily concerned with the plight of Danny Deever as such, or with the effect of the military execution upon the typical soldier in the regiment?

2. May the poem be said to set against each other the pathos of a weak and all-too-human man and the grim and necessarily inhuman world of military regulations? How is this contrast developed in the details of the poem? As one example we may note that the poet never refers to the two cockney soldiers by name but as the Colour-Sergeant and as Files-on-Parade. What are other examples?

3. The regiment will, as a matter of fact, march away from the execution at quick step. How is this sense of a brisk movement away from the scene reflected in the last four lines? Does this sense of brisk cheerfulness contradict the feeling built up in the poem, or does it actually serve to enforce it? Can you detect, in each stanza, a difference between the rhythm of the first four lines and that of the second four? Can it be said that this contrast in rhythm sets the frame for the contrast between the painful scene of human degradation and death and the impersonal efficiency of the military?

4. Suppose that the execution were a matter of civil, not military, justice, and that the scene were the execution room of a penitentiary with only official spectators present—the warden, guards, a physician, newspapermen, and so forth. Would there be a difference in meaning, or simply a difference in the degree of clarity and intensity in the dramatization? If the execution were a civil one, would you expect a poem in this rhythm?

MEETING AT NIGHT

Robert Browning (1812–1889)

I

The grey sea and the long black land;
And the yellow half-moon large and low;
And the startled little waves that leap
In fiery ringlets from their sleep,
As I gain the cove with pushing prow,   5
And quench its speed i' the slushy sand.

II

Then a mile of warm sea-scented beach;
Three fields to cross till a farm appears;
A tap at the pane, the quick sharp scratch
And blue spurt of a lighted match,   10
And a voice less loud, thro' its joys and fears,
Than the two hearts beating each to each!

EXERCISE

Do you find this poem incomplete? If not, why not?

MAMA AND DAUGHTER

Langston Hughes (1902–1967)

Mama, please brush off my coat.
I'm going down the street.

Where're you going, daughter?

To see my sugar-sweet.

Who is your sugar, honey?
Turn around—I'll brush behind.

He is that young man, mama,
I can't get off my mind.

Daughter, once upon a time—
Let me brush the hem—
Your father, yes, he was the one!
I felt that way about him.

But it was a long time ago
He up and went his way.
I hope that wild young son-of-a-gun
Rots in hell today!

Mama, dad couldn't be still young.

He *was* young yesterday.
He *was* young when he—
Turn around!
So I can brush your back, I say!

EXERCISES

1. Do we need to know more than we are told about the relationship of the mother and father? If not, why not? If so, why?

2. What bearing does the title of the poem have on its meaning? Suppose the mother had recollections of a long, happy marriage. What difference would that make in the meaning of the poem?

3. Comment on the use of standard ballad techniques in this poem. What dramatic devices for economy are used? What devices of suggestion and implication? What examples of understatement? What tone of voice might the mother use in speaking the last line? What is the significance of the last line?

4. Does this poem more resemble in method "Lucinda Matlock" or "Sir Patrick Spens"?

Meter

To resume the study of the technical aspects of poetry, turn to subsection 19.2 and carefully read our discussion of "Meter: The General Consideration."

EXERCISE

Scan stanza 1 of "Lord Randall," stanza 1 of "The True Lover," and stanza 3 of "Bredon Hill."

GROUP 3: COMPLEX NARRATIVE

MY LAST DUCHESS

Ferrara

Robert Browning (1812–1889)

That's my last Duchess painted on the wall
Looking as if she were alive. I call
That piece a wonder, now: Frà Pandolf's hands
Worked busily a day, and there she stands.
Will't please you sit and look at her? I said   5
"Frà Pandolf" by design, for never read
Strangers like you that pictured countenance,
The depth and passion of its earnest glance,
But to myself they turned (since none puts by
The curtain I have drawn for you, but I)
And seemed as they would ask me, if they durst,
How such a glance came there; so, not the first
Are you to turn and ask thus. Sir, 'twas not
Her husband's presence only, called that spot
Of joy into the Duchess' cheek: perhaps   15
Frà Pandolf chanced to say, "Her mantle laps
Over my lady's wrist too much," or "Paint
Must never hope to reproduce the faint
Half-flush that dies along her throat." Such stuff

Was courtesy, she thought, and cause enough   20
For calling up that spot of joy. She had
A heart—how shall I say?—too soon made glad.
Too easily impressed; she liked whate'er
She looked on, and her looks went everywhere
Sir, 'twas all one! My favor at her breast,   25
The dropping of the daylight in the West,
The bough of cherries some officious fool
Broke in the orchard for her, the white mule
She rode with round the terrace—all and each
Would draw from her alike the approving
   speech,   30
Or blush, at least. She thanked men,—good! but
   thanked
Somehow—I know not how—as if she ranked
My gift of a nine-hundred-years-old name
With anybody's gift. Who'd stoop to blame
This sort of trifling? Even had you skill   35
In speech—(which I have not)—to make your will
Quite clear to such an one, and say, "Just this
Or that in you disgusts me; here you miss,
Or there exceed the mark"—and if she let
Herself be lessoned so, nor plainly set   40
Her wits to yours, forsooth, and made excuse,
—E'en then would be some stooping; and I choose
Never to stoop. Oh, sir, she smiled, no doubt,
When'er I passed her; but who passed without
Much the same smile? This grew; I gave com-
   mands;   45
Then all smiles stopped together. There she
   stands
As if alive. Will't please you rise? We'll meet
The company below then. I repeat,
The Count your master's known munificence
Is ample warrant that no just pretence   50
Of mine for dowry will be disallowed;
Though his fair daughter's self, as I avowed
At starting, is my object. Nay, we'll go
Together down, sir. Notice Neptune, though,
Taming a sea-horse, thought a rarity,   55
Which Claus of Innsbruck cast in bronze for me!

With "My Last Duchess," we move into a selection of poems much more complex in psychology, action, and method than those in the first two groups. But the basic problems and issues are the same.

In this poem we have the duke of Ferrara entertaining an emissary from an unnamed count. The purpose of their business is to arrange a marriage between the duke and the count's daughter. The events actually begin with the duke's pointing out a full-length portrait of his "last duchess." He tells the story behind the painting: the artist portrayed a "certain look" in the duchess' face. "The depth and passion of its earnest glance" displeased the duke because he thought that that particular look should have been reserved for him alone. The duchess, however, bestowed it upon any "officious fool" who happened to be courteous. The duke "gave commands" (either to have the duchess killed or sent to a convent) and "all smiles stopped."

The duke's story is apparently ended. The two start to leave the room, and the duke remarks on the dowry of the count's daughter, protesting, however, that it is of minor importance. He insists that the emissary accompany rather than follow him; and he comments on another work of art, a bronze, "Neptune . . . taming a sea-horse."

The situation is dramatic. The emissary has come to arrange a marriage, although this point is not revealed until the end of the poem—a legitimate device for securing suspense. The success of the poem lies not so much in what is actually told by the poet as in the implications that the reader can draw from what is said.

We must realize that the poet faced at least two major difficulties: First, he was trying to reconstruct an incident, a crisis in the lives of several people, he himself not one of them, of another place and time. Second, the form chosen, the dramatic monologue, is not the simplest technical form. Only one person actually speaks in the poem, and he must not only bear his own side of the drama, but imply in his speech certain questions, gestures, and even attitudes of the person we infer to be present. The result is a compression that is difficult to obtain.

Suppose we examine the poem and see just how the duke reveals his character. We know that he is proud; he refers continually to "my duchess," "my favor at her breast," "my gift of a nine-hundred-years-old name." He is proud in another sense, proud of his possessions. His interest in the portrait is not that it is of his wife but that it is a masterpiece of Frà Pandolf's. He is proud in the same material way of a bronze by Claus of Innsbruck. And this pride, or vanity, lies behind the fate of the duchess. Whether he had the duchess killed or simply sent her away

and let her die from humiliation and disgrace makes little difference. The smiles stopped, and he makes no apology or further explanation. He had not been able, in his cold egotism, to abide, much less appreciate, innocence. His jealousy was not caused by the loss of something but by his failure to possess completely every phase of his wife's life. As for his intelligence, we find him a shrewd, but superficial, person. He is interested in art, not for any relation that it might bear to his life, but as material possessions. He is desirous of a wife, not as a companion, but as a necessary ornament for his palace.

As for the duchess, all we know of her is what we learn from the duke. We assume that any information from him is likely to be derogatory, if only to justify himself. He, however, is not interested in justification but in revealing what he expects of a wife. She must have been of high rank, or the duke would not have married her. She had a heart

> too soon made glad,
> Too easily impressed; she liked whate'er
> She looked on, and her looks went everywhere.

She was, then, a natural, innocent woman whom the duke could not bend into the conventional form he thought his wife should have.

Two questions now arise. First, what was the impulse behind the writing of the poem, and second, why the indirection and compression rather than a straightforward presentation?

As for question one, the author had as his purpose the presentation of a scene of Renaissance Italy. He was not interested primarily in telling an incident, or he might have used another medium. He was not interested in presenting an accurate historical account and evaluating that period for us; therefore he even uses fictitious names. He is interested in presenting people to us at a crisis in their lives. He wishes to present a dramatic situation for its own sake and for the relation to experience it might promote. Notice that in the entire poem no direct judgments are passed on anyone or on the actions of anyone. The elements are arranged so that we, as it were, make the judgment.

As for question two, the monologue and indirection serve to compress the story, to create suspense, and to enrich the presentation. The poet cannot set the scene by means of elaborate description and exposition. He has to have the surface story and the real story behind it fused, moment by moment, in the duke's words. For instance, the lines

> I said
> "Frà Pandolf" by design, for never read
> Strangers like you that pictured countenance—

tells us several things. First, we know that the emissary made some definite comment about the portrait or at least by some gesture revealed an interest greater than that usually expressed by guests. Second, we see the character of the duke and his pride in presenting a masterpiece by a renowned artist. And we may justly see flattery and condescension in "never read strangers like you."

Notice the duke's ironic disclaimer of any skill in speech:

> Even had you skill
> In speech (which I have not)—

It is true that he failed to make his will known to his first wife but that is only the surface of the matter. The real purpose of the entire story is to inform the emissary just what he expects of his wife. The duke does not do his powers of speech justice. He tells the story subtly but it unmistakably conveys his image of a proper wife. It also conveys something he does not intend: a clear impression of his monstrous and inhuman vanity.

The success of the poem depends on this indirection and compression. In fact, the interest in character, the conversational tone, the suspense, and the clever phrasing of paradoxical statements give the poem its power.

EXERCISES

1. We have noted that Robert Frost gives the impression of conversation in the language and rhythms of "The Star-Splitter." We have also noted that "My Last Duchess" is a dramatic monologue, one side of a conversation, as it were. Does Browning give the impression of direct speech? Try to identify some of the elements related to this question.

2. Point out examples of irony and understatement. What is the effect of these instances? What elements in the background story does the duke suggest and not state?

3. What is revealed of the emissary's character?

4. Is there any evidence in the poem to suppose, as one critic has suggested, that the emissary and the count's daughter were in love?

THE FARMER'S BRIDE

Charlotte Mew (1869–1928)

Three Summers since I chose a maid,
Too young maybe—but more's to do
At harvest-time than bide and woo.
   When us was wed she turned afraid
Of love and me and all things human;   5
Like the shut of a winter's day.
Her smile went out, and 'twasn't a woman—
   More like a little frightened fay.
     One night, in the Fall, she runned away.

"Out 'mong the sheep, her be," they said,   10
'Should properly have been abed;
But sure enough she wasn't there
Lying awake with her wide brown stare.
So over seven-acre field and up-along across the
    down
We chased her, flying like a hare   15
Before our lanterns. To Church-Town
   All in a shiver and a scare
We caught her, fetched her home at last
   And turned the key upon her, fast.

She does the work about the house   20
As well as most, but like a mouse:
   Happy enough to chat and play
   With birds and rabbits and such as they,
   So long as men-folk keep away.
"Not near, not near!" her eyes beseech   25
When one of us comes within reach.
   The women say that beasts in stall
   Look round like children at her call.
   I've hardly heard her speak at all.

Shy as a leveret, swift as he,   30
Straight and slight as a young larch tree,
Sweet as the first wild violets, she
To her wild self. But what to me?

The short days shorten and the oaks are brown,
   The blue smoke rises to the low gray sky,   35
One leaf in the still air falls slowly down,
   A magpie's spotted feathers lie

On the black earth spread white with rime,
The berries redden up to Christmas-time.
What's Christmas-time without there be   40
   Some other in the house than we!
   She sleeps up in the attic there
   Alone, poor maid. 'Tis but a stair
Betwixt us. Oh! my God! the down,
The soft young down of her, the brown,   45
The brown of her—her eyes, her hair, her hair . . .

EXERCISES

1. This poem, like "My Last Duchess," is spoken by a husband who cannot understand or sympathize with a young, sensitive wife. What differences do you find in character between the duke of Ferrara and the husband in this poem?
2. In "My Last Duchess," the young wife, kind and openhearted, has offended the ego of the duke. But the situation may be more complicated with the farmer's young wife. How do you interpret her attitude? Is she morbidly and neurotically afraid of men in general? Or has the husband been brutal and insensitive in dealing with her? Can you be sure of an answer? If the husband has been insensitive in dealing with the girl, would that fact, in your opinion, necessarily reflect a hard and brutal nature? Or simply lack of imagination and tact—limitations of his personality and world?
3. How does the poem accent the pathos of the girl's situation? But what about the husband? Does he have a legitimate claim on our sympathy? If he does, does one claim on our sympathy cancel the other? Does this circumstance lead to the basic idea and feeling of the poem?
4. How successful do you think the poet has been in catching the sense of colloquial speech? That is, in dramatizing the poem? How does it compare, do you think, with "The Star-Splitter," in method and effect? Study lines 30–33. Does the style here seem to be inconsistent with that of the rest of the poem? Does this passage seem characteristic in language and feeling with the character of the farmer as you get it elsewhere? If there is some inconsistency here, what was the poet trying to do in this passage? Might this passage represent merely a lapse, or a sound intention poorly executed?
5. Do you think that the poem would be more effective without the last four lines? Suppose it ended:

     She sleeps up in the attic there
     Alone. And betwixt us 'tis but a stair.

What would you think of the poem then?
6. Do you see any relation between the last two lines of the poem as it stands and lines 30–33?

LOVE ON THE FARM

D. H. Lawrence (1885–1930)

What large, dark hands are those at the window
Grasping in the golden light
Which weaves its way through the evening wind
   At my heart's delight?

Ah, only the leaves! But in the west   5
I see a redness suddenly come
Into the evening's anxious breast—
   'Tis the wound of love goes home!

The woodbine creeps abroad
Calling low to her lover: 10
   The sun-lit flirt who all the day
   Has poised above her lips in play
   And stolen kisses, shallow and gay
   Of pollen, now has gone away—
     She woos the moth with her sweet, low word;   15
And when above her his moth-wings hover
Then her bright breast she will uncover
And yield her honey-drop to her lover.
Into the yellow, evening glow
Saunters a man from the farm below;   20
Leans, and looks in at the low-built shed
Where the swallow has hung her marriage bed.
   The bird lies warm against the wall.
   She glances quick her startled eyes
   Towards him, then she turns away   25
   Her small head, making warm display
   Of red upon the throat. Her terrors sway
   Her out of the nest's warm, busy ball,
   Whose plaintive cry is heard as she flies
   In one blue stoop from out the sties   30
   Into the twilight's empty hall.
Oh, water-hen, beside the rushes,
Hide your quaintly scarlet blushes,
Still your quick tail, lie still as dead,
Till the distance folds over his ominous tread!   35

The rabbit presses back her ears,
Turns back her liquid, anguished eyes
And crouches low; then with wild spring
Spurts from the terror of his oncoming;
To be choked back, the wire ring   40
Her frantic effort throttling:
   Piteous brown ball of quivering fears!
Ah, soon in his large, hard hands she dies,
And swings all loose from the swing of his walk!

Yet calm and kindly are his eyes 45
And ready to open in brown surprise
Should I not answer to his talk
Or should he my tears surmise.

I hear his hand on the latch, and rise from my
    chair
Watching the door open; he flashes bare 50
His strong teeth in a smile, and flashes his eyes
In a smile like triumph upon me; then careless-
    wise
He flings the rabbit soft on the table board
And comes toward me: he! the uplifted sword
Of his hand against my bosom! and oh, the
    broad 55
Blade of his glance that asks me to applaud
His coming! With his hand he turns my face to
    him
And caresses me with his fingers that still smell
    grim
Of rabbit's fur! God, I am caught in a snare!
I know not what fine wire is round my throat; 60
I only know I let him finger there
My pulse of life, and let him nose like a stoat
Who sniffs with joy before he drinks the blood.
And down his mouth comes to my mouth! and
    down
His bright dark eyes come over me, like a hood 65
Upon my mind! his lips meet mine, and a flood
Of sweet fire sweeps across me, so I drown
Against him, die, and find death good.

    In "The Farmer's Bride," the speaker is the farmer; in Lawrence's poem, the speaker is the farmer's wife. Notice that in the former poem the style is a more or less realistic rendering of the farmer's way of speech (with certain lapses that we have pointed out), but that here the language, metaphors, and rhythms are not those of a typical farmer's wife. What is Lawrence trying to do that is different from the intention of Charlotte Mew? At this point you may not be sure of your answer to the question. But keep it in mind as you proceed to investigate the poem. It may be a good guide for your thinking, and the answer may, finally, involve the whole matter of the poem's meaning.

EXERCISES

1. Could Lawrence's farmer have been the speaker in this poem? Would he necessarily know anything about the subject matter of the poem? Would he necessarily suspect that his wife was anything but a woman who responded to his passion and kept his house?

2. Compare the speaker in this poem with the young bride in Mew's poem. Could lines 1–44 here have been spoken by the young bride? Could she, do you think, have voiced the whole poem except the last two lines? Or does it contain elements not appropriate to the young bride? In other words, has the poet prepared the reader for the climax of the poem?

3. Notice that lines 1–44 are concerned with images of love, fertility, fear, and death. Is it appropriate for the farmer's wife to see the objects of nature in these terms? Would a housewife in a city apartment think in the same terms? Would the same images necessarily have the same associations or rouse the same attitudes in the city housewife as in the farmer's wife? Can it be said that all the poem leads up to the cry "I am caught in a snare"? What snare? Why does the wife compare her husband to a stoat? (If you don't know what a stoat is, use a dictionary.)

4. Are the last two lines a sudden reversal of the woman's feelings, or have we been prepared for her final emotion?

    On this point let us go back to exercise 3 concerning the early images of fertility, fear, and death.* Now we may see that the image of the rabbit, which first appears in the process of being strangled in the snare (lines 36–44), runs throughout the poem; the wife's identification with the rabbit becomes more and more marked until it becomes quite specific in lines 59–60. But we must note how the poem moves from this specific identification back into a complex image: as the husband presses his mouth down on the wife's mouth, his "bright dark eyes" seem to come over her "like a hood." With the preparation of the rabbit's strangulation, and the reference to the wife's strangulation in line 60, we sense that the "hood" here is the hangman's hood that is put over the head of the victim in an execution. In the background of this image of an execution lurks the

---

    * Imagery is so important for poetry that later on in this book we devote a special section (15) to it. Though "Love on the Farm" is a narrative poem, the images carry so much of the meaning of the poem that we shall scarcely come to understand it unless we see what the images are and what they do. Anticipations of this sort—of topics such as imagery, tone, and theme—are inevitable in these early sections on poetry; they have the merit of reminding us that many or all of the elements of poetry are commonly present in a poem.

distinction between an execution and a mere killing. The essence of the difference inheres in the
notion of law or principle; an execution involves
some such element of justification for the killing.
What might such a law or principle be in this
poem? And how might it be connected with the
paradoxical notion that runs throughout the poem
and literally, in a sexual sense, comes to a climax
in the last line? (There, "death" is found to be
"good"—ecstatic and fulfilling—the notion that
death and love are deeply related in experience.)

In connection with the implications of the
image of the hood, what are we to make of the
fact that it is the "bright dark eyes" that constitute
the hood? How can brightness be a "hood," giving
darkness? And what is at stake in the description
of the eyes as both bright and dark?

5. In exercise 4 we have been considering the
metaphorical meaning of the preparation for the
climax of the poem in the various images of fertility, fear, and death. But we must also note how
the development of those images—particularly
that of the rabbit—provides a principle of structure for the poem. In a sense, they "contain" the
poem. If we subtracted the images, what would, in
fact, be left of the poem? How much of the "story"
would be clear?

6. Return to the short story "The Horse-Dealer's
Daughter" (sec. 8) and refresh your memory of it.
What qualities does Lawrence's story share with
his "Love on a Farm"? How can it be said that the
story and the poem have the same theme and same
basic attitude toward life?

7. In the light of this poem, what new feelings or
insights do you have concerning Mew's "The
Farmer's Bride"? Concerning Housman's "The
True Lover"?

BURNING THE LETTERS
Randall Jarrell (1914–1965)

*(The wife of a pilot killed in the Pacific is speaking
several years after his death. She was once a Christian,
a Protestant.)*

Here in my head, the home that is left for you,
You have not changed; the flames rise from the sea
And the sea changes: the carrier, torn in two,
Sinks to its planes—the corpses of the carrier
Are strewn like ashes on the star-reflecting sea;   5
Are gathered, sewn with weights, are sunk.
The gatherers disperse.
                        Here to my hands
From the sea's dark, incalculable calm,
The unchanging circle of the universe,   10
The letters float: the set yellowing face
Looks home to me, a child's at last,

From the cut-out paper; and the licked
Lips part in their last questioning smile.
The poor labored answers, still unanswering;   15
The faded questions—questioning so much.
I thought then—questioning so little;
Grew younger, younger, as my eyes grew old,
As that dreamed-out and wept-for wife,
Your last unchanging country, changed   20
Out of your own rejecting life—a part
Of accusation and of loss, a child's eternally—
Into my troubled separate being.

A child has her own faith, a child's.
In its savage figures—worn down, now, to
    death—   25
Men's one life issues, neither out of earth
Nor from the sea, the last dissolving sea,
But out of death: by man came death
And his Life wells from death, the death of Man.
The hunting flesh, the broken blood   30
Glimmer within the tombs of earth, the food
Of the lives that burrow under the hunting wings
Of the light, of the darkness: dancing, dancing,
The flames grasp flesh with their last searching
    grace—
Grasp as the lives have grasped: the hunted   35
Pull down the hunter for his unused life
Parted into the blood, the dark, veined bread
Later than all law. The child shudders, aging:
The peering savior, stooping to her clutch,
His talons cramped with his own bartered flesh,   40
Pales, flickers, and flares out. In the darkness—
    darker
With the haunting after-images of light—
The dying God, the eaten Life
Are the nightmare I awaken from to night.

(The flames dance over life. The mourning
    slaves   45
In their dark secrecy, come burying
The slave bound in another's flesh, the slave
Freed once, forever, by another's flesh:
The Light flames, flushing the passive face
With its eternal life.)   50
                    The lives are fed
Into the darkness of their victory;
The ships sink, forgotten; and the sea
Blazes to darkness: the unsearchable
Death of the lives lies dark upon the life   55
That, bought by death, the loved and tortured
    lives,
Stares westward, passive, to the blackening sea.
In the tables of the dead, in the unopened
    almanac,
The head, charred, featureless—the unknown
    mean—
Is thrust from the waters like a flame, is torn   60

From its last being with the bestial cry
Of its pure agony. O death of all my life
Because of you, because of you, I have not died,
By your death I have lived.
                   The sea is empty   65
As I am empty, stirring the charred and answered
Questions about your home, your wife, your cat
That stayed at home with me—that died at home
Gray with the years that gleam above you there
In the great green grave where you are young   70
And unaccepting still. Bound in your death,
I choose between myself and you, between your
    life
And my own life: it is finished.
                   Here in my head
There is room for your black body in its shroud 75
The dog-tags welded to your breastbone, and the
    flame
That winds above your death and my own life
And the world of my life. The letters and the face
That stir still, sometimes, with your fiery breath—
Take them, O grave! Great grave of all my
    years,   80
The unliving universe in which all life is lost,
Make yours the memory of that accepting
And accepted life whose fragments I cast here.

It is important in reading this poem to keep the dramatic situation in mind. The wife is burning the letters and throughout the poem there are references to the letters with their questions and answers, and to the flames leaping up as the letters burn. For example, see lines 32–33, 45–50, or 78–79. But the flames have another reference, for they refer to the flaming aircraft carrier on which her husband has died. In the same way her vision of the sea in which he has been buried becomes the sea of death and oblivion to which she now finally consigns her husband, still young and unchanged in her memory, though she feels that in the meantime she has grown old.

EXERCISES

1. Why has the wife decided now to burn the letters? Note particularly lines 63–64 and 71–73.
2. What is the meaning of the first line—the statement that her head is the only "home that is left for you"? Note also that she calls herself in line 20 "your last unchanging country." How can she say, as she does in lines 9–11, that the letters float to her "from the sea's dark, incalculable calm"?

3. The third section of the poem deals with her childhood faith that she has (see the poet's note at the beginning of the poem) now lost. In that faith man lives, man's life issues from the death of man, from the Savior's death, "the eaten life" (1. 43). What light, if any, is thrown upon her decision to burn the letters by the statement she makes in lines 43–44?
4. What does she mean by saying that she is "bound in [his] death" (1. 71) and that she now chooses between his life and her own life? Connect this passage with lines 45–50.
5. What is the meaning of lines 74–75? Does it mean that she is now ready to accept him as dead —that she is ready to accept reality as she could not earlier accept it? In her head (see line 1) he has heretofore had a country in which he has not changed. Now he still has a "home" there, but a burial place merely—not a place in which to live unchanged, but a place in which his dead body, his death now accepted, can rest. Does the last section of the poem mean that she has ceased to love him? Or does it mean something else?

Metrical Variation

Having familiarized yourself with the basic principles of meter, you are now to consider how it works in practice. This concern will be always present, directly or indirectly, as we continue our approach to poetry, but to begin your special study of metrics turn to subsection 19.3 and read our discussion of the subtleties involved in metrical variation.

EXERCISES

1. Return to Robinson's "Richard Cory." The poem is, of course, very regular in its metrics, but in the last stanza there is one instance of a secondary accent. Locate it. In subsection 19.3, which you have just read, we have not discussed the relation of metrical variation to meaning or dramatic effect, but in reflecting on the secondary accent here, in this poem of unusual regularity, do you think that it plays some significant part? In this connection, what difference do you find between the line in the original version and this rewriting: "And Richard Cory on a summer night"? Certainly, we have omitted the word *calm*, but is that the only factor to consider?
2. As an exercise for "Bredon Hill" by A. E. Housman, you were asked to prepare a set of questions. To those questions now add one on

secondary accents in the poem and their possible significance. You should, of course, have some notion of an answer for your own questions.

3. In Frost's "The Star-Splitter," scan lines 28–30, giving special attention to secondary accents.

4. Reread "Burning the Letters" by Randall Jarrell to get a general sense of the rhythm and the emotional quality of the poem. Now scan lines 51–64. The poem is prevailingly iambic pentameter, with metrical variations and an occasional tetrameter or hexameter line. In this passage, for instance, lines 58 and 62 are hexameter, and it may be best to take line 59 in the same way. There is one unavoidable secondary accent in the passage and one in line 59 if it is taken as hexameter. Do you have any comment on any of the variations?

Section 13

DESCRIPTION

In section 12, in dealing with poems based on story, we have been primarily concerned with *action as meaning*. Now, turning from poems based on narrative to those based on description, we are concerned with the *object as meaning*. We are now concerned, that is, with the function of *imagery* in poetry—an image, in this sense, being the verbal rendering of an object, or rather with the sensory recognition of it. Ordinarily we think of imagery as visual; we imagine a thing —we "see it in the mind's eye." But we know that we can also summon up in imagination —the image-making faculty—other objects of sense. We can imagine the feel of an object touched, an odor, a taste. Poetry may also use other imagery, but, since visual imagery is the most usual and most obvious kind in poetry, we shall, for the moment, be primarily concerned with it.

Perhaps the best way to begin a discussion of imagery in poetry is to consider the question of who sees the object. Here we may think of a sort of scale. At one end, we find the direct rendering of an object (simple or complex) with no clue given as to the presence of an observer. Take, for example:

THE GULLS

John Gould Fletcher (1886–1950)*

White stars scattering,
Pale rain of spray-drops,
Delicate flesh of smoke wind-drifted low and high.
Silver upon dark purple,
The gulls quiver   5
In a noiseless flight, far out across the sky.

Here the image of gulls in flight is the central fact of the poem; the other images—those of stars, spray-drops, smoke—are metaphorically identified with the gulls and enrich our perception of them. We, the readers, make what we can of the scene. No observer is here specified.

Let us take another example:

PEAR TREE

H. D. (1886–1961)†

Silver dust
lifted from the earth,
higher than my arms reach,
you have mounted.
O silver,   5

---

* Fletcher was one of a group of poets called Imagists, which included Amy Lowell, Hilda Doolittle, and, briefly, Ezra Pound and William Carlos Williams. Their theory was that the image is the key of poetry and should be rendered as accurately as possible, with no comment or philosophizing. They were in reaction against the rhetorical expansiveness, pretentious vocabulary, and moralizing of much of the poetry of the late nineteenth century. In addition they refused to use formal verse, considering this an artificiality that cut off the poet—and the reader—from the immediate perception of the image.

† H.D. was the signature adopted by Hilda Doolittle, just mentioned as one of the Imagists.

higher than my arms reach
you front us with great mass;
no flower ever opened
so staunch a white leaf,
no flower ever parted silver   10
from such rare silver;

O white pear,
your flower-tufts,
thick on the branch,
bring summer and ripe fruits   15
in their purple hearts.

Here an observer is subtly introduced by the line: "higher than my arms reach." We have, in fact, not only the image of the tree in blossom, but of a person—a woman, presumably the poet—confronting the tree with arms lifted in awe or admiration, or in some such emotion. With this specified observer, a new element enters the poem. The reader of "The Gulls" reacts to the scene with what feeling is natural to him; the scene, that is, is rendered with what seems total objectivity. But with "Pear Tree," the reader's response is not simply to the object but to the transaction between the observer in the poem and the object. Presumably, the reader is expected to accept the observer in the poem—here the woman with her arms raised to the blossoming tree—as a sort of model for his own response.*

Let us turn to a passage from a much more elaborate poem:

From THE LOTOS-EATERS
Alfred, Lord Tennyson (1809–1892)

'Courage!' he said, and pointed toward the land,
'This mounting wave will roll us shoreward soon.'
In the afternoon they came unto a land
In which it seemed always afternoon.
All round the coast the languid air did swoon,   5
Breathing like one that hath a weary dream,
Full-faced above the valley stood the moon;
And, like a downward smoke, the slender stream
Along the cliff to fall and pause and fall did
seem.

A land of streams! some, like a downward
smoke,   10

Slow-dropping veils of thinnest lawn, did go;
And some through wavering lights and shadows
broke,
Rolling a slumbrous sheet of foam below.
They saw the gleaming river seaward flow
From the inner land: far off, three mountain-
tops,   15
Three silent pinnacles of aged snow,
Stood sunset-flush'd; and, dew'd with showery
drops,
Up-clomb the shadowy pine above the woven
copse.

The charmed sunset linger'd low adown
In the red West: through mountain clefts the
dale   20
Was seen far inland, and the yellow down
Border'd with palm, and many a winding vale
And meadow, set with slender galingale;
A land where all things always seem'd the same!
And round about the keel with faces pale,   25
Dark faces pale against that rosy flame,
The mild-eyed melancholy Lotos-eaters came.

Branches they bore of that enchanted stem,
Laden with flower and fruit, whereof they gave
To each, but whoso did receive of them   30
And taste, to him the gushing of the wave
Far far away did seem to mourn and rave
On alien shores; and if his fellow spake,
His voice was thin, as voices from the grave;
And deep-asleep he seemed, yet all awake.   35
And music in his ears his beating heart did
make.

They sat them down upon the yellow sand,
Between the sun and moon upon the shore;
And sweet it was to dream of Fatherland,
Of child, and wife, and slave; but evermore   40
Most weary seem'd the sea, weary the oar,
Weary the wandering fields of barren foam.
Then some one said, 'We will return no more;'
And all at once they sang, 'Our island home
Is far beyond the wave; we will no longer
roam.'   45

Tennyson's poem has a strong element of narrative, drawn from an episode in Homer's *Odyssey*. Odysseus (or Ulysses) and his long-wandering companions, seeking to return home to their island of Ithaca after the Trojan War, make a landfall on the island of

---

* As we shall see, however, the relation between reader and observer may sometimes be more complicated than this. We have seen such complications in stories, for instance, in "Haircut" (sec. 7), in which the reader's response is exactly opposite to that of the narrator.

the Lotos-eaters, a people constantly be-drugged by a fruit that induces a delicious, dreamy torpor.

In the opening lines Odysseus speaks, but immediately after his words we find a long description of the land and a shorter description of the inhabitants and their soporific fruit. At the very end of the long "Choric Song" that concludes the poem (sec. 14) we have the words of Odysseus' companions as they renounce their heroic enterprise and sink into torpor. Substantially, then, the poem is a series of images, all of which work to create an atmosphere—an effect that corresponds to that of the fruit on the "observers" in the poem.

Later, for other poems, we shall discuss how such effects are achieved, for instance how certain technical features of the verse are associated with the atmosphere (see Glossary). For the moment, however, the reader should immerse himself in the poem, reading it over and over, aloud. He should try, then, to locate the specific details that affect him, words, images, and rhythms. He might ask himself, for instance, how the phrase "weary dream" (l. 6) sets the tone for all description that follows. Why is the description of the land as one "in which it seemed always afternoon" peculiarly appropriate? In the first lines the sea is associated with courageous effort, but what has become of it in the last stanza? Or the reader may turn to two other poems in this section by Tennyson, "The Eagle" and "The Bugle Song," and try to define the difference in effect between them and "The Lotos-Eaters."

In discussing the role of an observer in a poem, we must remember that the final effect—the total effect of the poem—is always on the reader, and that one of the things the reader observes may be the observer in the poem. The reader sees the companions of Odysseus succumbing to the charm of the lotos island and, within limits, he himself feels the spell, but this is not to say that the poet expects the reader to take the attitude toward life presented here. The lotos island is given in all its seductiveness, but in contrast there is always the ardor, endurance, and energy of heroic enterprise. The poem, fin-

ally, is "about" the contrast between these poles of experience.

There are, then, in different poems different degrees of identification with an observer in a poem. Consider, for comparison's sake:

THE WILD SWANS AT COOLE

W. B. Yeats (1865–1939)

> The trees are in their autumn beauty,
> The woodland paths are dry,
> Under the October twilight the water
> Mirrors a still sky;
> Upon the brimming water among the stones   5
> Are nine-and-fifty swans.
>
> The nineteenth autumn has come upon me
> Since I first made my count;
> I saw, before I had well finished,
> All suddenly mount   10
> And scatter wheeling in great broken rings
> Upon their clamorous wings.
>
> I have looked upon those brilliant creatures,
> And now my heart is sore.
> All's changed since I, hearing at twilight,   15
> The first time on this shore,
> The bell-beat of their wings above my head,
> Trod with a lighter tread.
>
> Unwearied still, lover by lover,
> They paddle in the cold   20
> Companionable streams or climb the air.
> Their hearts have not grown old;
> Passion or conquest, wander where they will,
> Attend upon them still.
>
> But now they drift on the still water   25
> Mysterious, beautiful;
> Among what rushes will they build,
> By what lake's edge or pool
> Delight men's eyes, when I awake some day
> To find they have flown away?   30

The most marked difference here from Tennyson's poem is that the experience of the observer—of the poet himself—constitutes the total poem, while the experience of the mariners and the Lotos-eaters is set in the context of a larger world and other values, including those of heroic struggle. In Tennyson's poem we are scarcely invited to full identification, but in Yeats's poem we are. With this thought in mind, let us look more closely at the poem.

The poem begins as an apparently objective and simple bit of description. One notices, however, the exactitude of it. It is autumn, at twilight. The paths through the woods are dry, and this suggests that the poet on a walk through the woods has just stepped out on the shore of the still pool, and has stood there long enough to count the swans. There are fifty-nine of them. It has been nineteen years since he counted them for the first time. At that time too it was the autumn of the year, and there was a particular incident connected with that first sight of the swans that may have impressed the whole scene on his memory and that may help account for his remembering it so exactly: the swans rose in flight on that occasion almost before he had finished counting them.

But the poet remembers other things connected with that first experience—how he responded to that first hearing of their wings with a resilience of step—of what he was then as compared to what he is now. And the swans, unchanged since that first meeting, become a sort of yardstick against which the poet may measure the changes that have taken place in his own life.

The exactitude of description in the first stanzas—the poet's knowledge of the precise number of the swans, the reason for his having remembered them, and so on—is significant. These are particular swans; indeed, they are the poet's own swans because he has watched for them year after year. Because of this fact, there is no suggestion of affectation when the poet proceeds to contrast the immortality of the swans with his own mortality and change.

If the poet's words "my heart is sore" had been prompted by some accidental or chance-met scene, we would be inclined to believe his grief was an easy or trivial one. Actually, we feel in the scene the implicit recollection of all griefs that the poet might have experienced in the nineteen years that have passed, and the simple statement he makes comes, it seems, as an understatement: the poet is content to describe the reasons for his soreness of heart and the quality of it by implied contrasts between himself and the swans. Upon first seeing the swans nineteen years before, he had been able to identify himself to some extent with them. His step became lighter in exultation with them. Now "All's changed," he tells us, and what has changed for him is suggested by what has remained unchanged with the swans: they are still unwearied; they are still lover beside lover; their hearts have not become old; they still find themselves at home in their world.*

Notice how the poet has been able to suggest a great deal by his choice of words. Consider, for example, the phrase "Companionable streams." *Companionable* suggests to us the qualities of security and comfort in a spacious, well-lighted room, with perhaps a great fire burning on the hearth. At first it may not seem appropriate to apply such a word to streams, especially since they have just been called "cold." And yet the adjective fits. The swans are at home in nature; they are not aliens in nature, but part of nature in a way in which the poet is not. The swans are not only at home in their world, they dominate it; "passion" and "conquest" wait upon them like servants wherever they choose to wander.

Indeed, the swans themselves are used as a symbol for the beautiful, mysterious, unwearied immortality of nature itself. The poem is an excellent example of the poet's making a bit of natural description carry emotional intensity by relating the description to his own feelings. But he does this by telling us about the swans and not about himself. He does not "pour out his heart" to us. We learn about his own loneliness in the world and his defeat by the implied contrast with the swans. This restraint of the poet gives an impression of intensity and manliness.

---

* But we must remember that Yeats cannot well be referring to the identical swans seen nineteen years earlier, any more than Keats, in his "Ode to a Nightingale" (sec. 17), is referring to an individual bird when he describes its song as the "self-same" that was heard by Ruth, in the Bible, "amid the alien corn" (1. 67). Both Keats and Yeats are suggesting, *symbolically*, an existence outside time, unlike that of man, who is trapped in time, and in memory.

As we have said above, the final effect of a poem is on the reader, and this effect, in the broadest sense, is the meaning of a poem. The elements of a poem—events, imagery, rhythms, ideas—are vitally, significantly, interrelated in a way that implies a certain attitude toward experience, toward life. This fact leads us to the question of how imagery—our immediate concern—is related to the meaning of a poem. Here, again, we may think of the scale we set up earlier with the unobserved image at one end and the image with an interpreting observer at the other.

At one end of the scale, the effect of the image may be the meaning of the poem. In "The Gulls," for instance, we find only the image of the gulls set against a dark purple sky, drawing into themselves, metaphorically, the images of stars, spray-drops, and smoke. The poem offers no comment, no interpretation, no overt "meaning." It does, however, evoke a mood in the reader—a sense of excitement, the vitality of stars, spray-drops, wind-borne smoke, absorbed into the central image of the gull-flight—a mood clearly in contrast to that of "The Lotos-Eaters" with its languorous and dreamy torpor. The gulls move imperially into distance, masters of their element, beautiful and fulfilled—an image of what man, for all his earthboundness, aspires to in spirit. The "meaning" of the poem is simply the energizing recognition, and the affirmation, of a possibility of life. This meaning is close, in fact, to that of "The Wild Swans at Coole," but in the latter poem, which would stand far up our scale, the meaning is not left implicit in an image, but is given to us in the contrast between the poet, who knows his earthbound condition and his entrapment in time, and what he takes the swans to represent. That is, the swans have become symbols (see Glossary) of what the poet aspires to be.

In many poems, some fine ones indeed, the meaning may be as recessive and implicit as in "The Gulls"—for example, "Silver" by Walter de la Mare and "The Lamb" by William Blake, both reprinted in this section. At the other end of our scale, even beyond the method used in "The Wild Swans at Coole," we find poems that are very explicit in establishing the meaning of their imagery—for instance, Shakespeare's Sonnet 73, also in this section, in which the relation is clearly indicated between the images of autumn and sunset and the condition of the aging poet. Or to take another example, turn to "God's Grandeur" by Gerard Manley Hopkins (sec. 16), in which the first line unequivocally states the basic idea, the theme, of the poem. The images that follow do not merely illustrate the idea; they develop it, elaborate it, charge it with specific realizations and intensities. In short, they make the idea "come true" in perception and feeling. Here, too, we may note a technical feature not found in the earlier examples. The poem is not focused on a single image or scene. There are a number of images, "shook foil," "ooze of oil," and so on. These have no immediate relation to each other; each springs individually from some stage in what the poet is saying. The frame of the poem is a discourse, and the images spring from this. Later, we come to much more complicated examples of this method, but even now the distinction is important as an aspect of poetic structure.

Here is another poem concerning swans:

WILD SWANS
Edna St. Vincent Millay (1892–1950)

I looked in my heart while the wild swans went
    over.
And what did I see I had not seen before?
Only a question less or a question more;
Nothing to match the flight of wild birds flying.
Tiresome heart, forever living and dying,   5
House without air, I leave you and lock your door.
Wild swans, come over the town, come over
The town again, trailing your legs and crying!

EXERCISES

1. What "question less" or "question more" may be involved here? What evidence for your answer do you find in the poem?
2. Would a flock of starlings or grackles have served as well for this poem? Explain.
3. Turn to "To Autumn" by Keats (sec. 15). The poem ends, you notice, with an image of a flock

of swallows gathering for migration. Would swans have suited the poem better?

4. Compare Millay's poem with "The Wild Swans at Coole" in regard to theme. Which, do you think, is more precise?

Let us remind ourselves again that even when an observer is set into a poem, the final effect is always on the reader. This leads to another distinction, that between the effect of an image conceived as out in nature—in the objective world—and its effect once it is absorbed into a poem. Objects in nature may indeed, as we have said in connection with "The Gulls," provoke certain feelings and moods; a quiet pastoral scene and a storm at sea have very different emotional charges. Such charges do persist into a poem, and we may even take pleasure in merely recognizing objects, whether pleasing or painful, that suggest actuality. But once an object enters a poem it acquires a special focus of meaning; the poem is, in a sense, a manipulation, a focusing, of whatever charge of feeling and meaning the object may have had in actuality. This manipulation can become enormously complicated, but for the moment let us suggest what happens in the progression in this section.

What the poet expresses may be, as in the early poems in this section, a very vague and general feeling or mood. But the reader will observe that in this section the feeling becomes more and more closely defined and that the poems, more and more, tend to present an idea as well as a mood. That is, the objects the poet has chosen from nature tend to have more and more the force of a *symbol*. Sometimes the poet states definitely what an image is to signify or symbolize. Sometimes, however, he merely gives clues so that the reader may discover the meaning for himself. Yeats does this in "The Wild Swans at Coole," in which he, though pretending to be merely telling about an encounter with the wild swans, is really telling a truth about his own life. And Blake does it in "The Tyger," in which one quickly discovers that he is not writing about an ordinary tiger, but about a beast that stands for something, for the power of evil in the world. One must remember that when a genuine poet gives description, that description inevitably comes with an expressive force: the image implies a feeling about life, and a feeling implies an idea.

THE EAGLE
Alfred, Lord Tennyson (1809–1892)

> He clasps the crag with crooked hands;
> Close to the sun in lonely lands,
> Ringed with the azure world, he stands.
>
> The wrinkled sea beneath him crawls;
> He watches from his mountain walls,   5
> And like a thunderbolt he falls.

This short poem comes about as close to the completely *objective* account of nature as a poem can. The poet is not using his description to illustrate a moral truth, or even a personal mood. He is giving a picture of an eagle, but we shall learn something about the aims and the method of poetry if we compare carefully this description with other possible descriptions. A dictionary definition of *eagle* reads as follows: "Any of various large diurnal birds of prey of the falcon family, noted for their strength, size, graceful figure, keenness of vision, and powers of flight. The typical eagles constitute a genus *Aquila* in which the legs are feathered to the toes." A scientific description might give such information as that in the last sentence, and would probably have much to tell us about the eagle's diet, habitat, and biological structure. A poetic description would more likely deal with such matters as the "graceful figure, keenness of vision, and powers of flight."

Notice in this poem that, although the poet emphasizes the elements given in the dictionary definition, he does so by presenting them vividly through concrete figures. As for the eagle's strength: "He clasps the crag with crooked hands." The poet shows us the eagle actually exhibiting his strength, strength in this instance in repose but its latent powers suggested by its powerful talons, the crooked hands. As for the keenness of vision and powers of flight: "Close to the sun in lonely lands." One of the common folk-beliefs for a long time was that the eagle could look steadily at the sun. This is suggested by the phrase "close to the sun." But the loneliness and rugged power of the eagle are also suggested, "in lonely lands."

And in the next line the poet actually adopts the eagle's point of vantage. He does not describe the eagle as a man might look up at him, but describes the world as the eagle looks *down* on it: "Ringed with the azure world, he stands." When one is on a high place, the world seems to spread out in a ring around him, and in this case a distant ring; and *azure* indicates the bluish quality of far-off distances.

The next line continues from the eagle's vantage point—an eagle's eye view: "The wrinkled sea beneath him crawls." Why *wrinkled?* Because seen from high above, the waves give the appearance of mere wrinkles, and as they move into shore, the sea seems to be a live thing with movement of its own.

The eagle's keenness of vision and terrible power are given an almost dramatic emphasis in the last two lines. The eagle is evidently watching for prey far below him, on the lower cliffs, or probably in the sea, and perceiving it, swoops toward it with the speed of lightning. And the swift and characteristic exit of the eagle from the poet's little picture of him affords the poet an appropriate ending for his poem.

But this is not the whole story. In interpreting, in trying to get the *meaning* of an experience, the poet, being a human being writing for human beings, is certain to interpret in human terms. The eagle, even in this objective poem, becomes something of a human being. He is, one might say, like a robber baron, exulting in his own liberty and fierceness and strength. Unassailable in his own castle perched on the cliffs, he exacts toll at pleasure from the country below him.

This is, as a matter of fact, what Tennyson does suggest to the reader. It is implied in the fact that he gives his eagle *hands* and in that he has him watch from his mountain *walls*. *Walls* is a human word. A wall is a fabric built by men. And so the phrase "his mountain walls" implies a connection between the eagle and his human counterparts who owned rocky fastnesses that were indeed often as inaccessible as an eagle's aerie. Not least important is the word *his*. Animals do not properly own property. Tennyson's eagle owns his crag; and the bird becomes human enough for us, even in such a relatively objective poem, to feel a sort of understanding of it, and therefore a sense of *meaning* to the whole. And in the poem one participates in the exhilaration of the eagle's distant view and the furious but controlled plunge downward. Observe how the poet has made the word *falls* the climatic (see Glossary) point of the poem, the word on which the whole effect of the poem is finally concentrated.

What are we to make of this poem? Are we to rest on the notion that this is merely some sort of poetic equating of eagles and robber barons? No, the poem is a celebration of power and grandeur, but a lonely power and an independent grandeur—a release of spirit into an ennobling moment.

The instant we begin to analyze and interpret a poem, a certain question always comes to mind: how do we know that the poet "intended" this? We shall discuss this question more fully a little later, but for the moment we may say that our concern is with the poem as it exists and not as it was "intended" to be. We put quotation marks around the word *intended* here to indicate that we must use it in a special sense. We can't use it about a poem in the way we use it about a house. An architect may draw the blueprint for a house and that blueprint represents his intention, his plan. Then the builder proceeds to execute the plan: a man trained to read a blueprint can predict the house. That is not true of the "intention" of a poem—or, for that matter, of a novel or story or picture or piece of music. The artist, whatever kind he is, may have many ideas for his work, and many images in his head, and a kind of hunch about how he wants the finished work to feel. In his imagination he may—and to some degree must—project himself forward to the finished work. But the thing can't exist until it exists. That is, Tennyson could not "plan" the phrase "wrinkled sea." He may have an image in his mind of the sea as viewed from a great height, but that is not a "plan" or "intention" for the phrase. As soon as he has the phrase he does not have a plan, he has the thing itself. In poetry, the phrase, the rhythm, the associative relations of words are part of the meaning. Till we have them we do not have the full meaning.

This is not to say that a poet works only blindly and instinctively. It is simply to say that for the poet the composition of a poem may well be a process of exploration of his meaning, of creation of his meaning, and not the execution of a plan or intention. *Therefore, to put the matter somewhat paradoxically, we may say that, in the end, we go to the poem for the meaning of the poet and not to the poet for the meaning of the poem.* We must, of course, find out all we can about the poet and the world he lived in, what ideas and materials were available to him, what his experiences and concerns were. That information will undoubtedly help us in our reading of his poetry. But we can never take the poetry as a mere mechanical projection, the fulfillment of a plan, an intention, a blueprint.

SILVER
Walter De La Mare (1873–1956)

Slowly, silently, now the moon
Walks the night in her silver shoon;
This way, and that, she peers, and sees
Silver fruit upon silver trees;
One by one the casements catch   5
Her beams beneath the silvery thatch;
Couched in his kennel, like a log,
With paws of silver sleeps the dog;
From their shadowy cote the white breasts peep
Of doves in a silver-feathered sleep;   10
A harvest mouse goes scampering by,
With silver claws and a silver eye;
And moveless fish in the water gleam,
By silver reeds in a silver stream.

EXERCISES

1. Is this poem merely objective description—a scene such as anyone could see upon a moonlit night—and presented without bias or interpretation?

2. Who is it that "sees" this world touched with silver? (See lines 1–3.)

3. Granted that the moon is a special observer—

she herself *makes* the silver world that she *sees*—but is it true that any observer colors the world that he sees in some degree by his very act of looking at it? Is it too farfetched to say that the poem is finally about the creative quality of the human mind and imagination? Perhaps it is, but isn't that idea implicit here?

4. Notice, in line 2, the archaic form, *shoon*, of *shoes*. Ordinarily (and perhaps here), such a form seems to represent an attempt to get a "poetical" effect by illegitimate—and mechanical—means. (See *Denotation* and *Diction* in the Glossary.) Can you see any justification for *shoon* in this particular poem?

5. Suppose the first four lines had been written as follows:

> How slowly, silently, the moon
> Now walks the night in her silver shoon;
> And peering this way and that, she sees
> The silver fruit on silver trees.

What would be the difference in effect?

6. Here are two scansions for the first four lines:

A.

Slowly̆, | si̅lent̆ly̆, | now the̅ | moon ∧
Walks the̅ | night i̅n hĕr | sĭlver | shoon;
This way, | and that, | she peers, | and sees
Sĭlver | fruit upon | sĭlver | trees. ∧

B.

∧ Slow- | ly̆, sĭ- | lent̆ly̆ now | the̅ moon
∧ Walks | the̅ night | i̅n hĕr sĭl- | vĕr shoon;
This way, | and that, | she peers, | and sees
∧ Sil- | vĕr fruit | upon sil- | vĕr trees.

Both versions might be defended, but which do you prefer? If you prefer B, do you nevertheless feel that A represents an aspect of the versification that should be recognized—in other words, that the rising and falling movements are not absolutely resolved? Inspect the whole poem to see whether a rising or falling movement seems to prevail.

7. Can you relate the above question to the general "feel" of the poem, its dreamy indeterminateness as contrasted with the positiveness of daylight?

OLD COUNTRYSIDE

Louise Bogan (1897–1970)

Beyond the hour we counted rain that fell
On the slant shutter, all has come to proof.
The summer thunder, like a wooden bell,
Rang in the storm above the mansard roof,

And mirrors cast the cloudy day along   5
The attic floor; wind made the clapboards creak.
You braced against the wall to make it strong,
A shell against your cheek.

Long since, we pulled brown oak-leaves to the
            ground
In a winter of dry trees; we heard the cock   10
Shout its unplaceable cry, the axe's sound
Delay a moment after the axe's stroke.

Far back, we saw, in the stillest of the year,
The scrawled vine shudder, and the rose-branch
            show
Red to the thorns, and, sharp as sight can bear, 15
The thin hound's body arched against the snow.

EXERCISE

This poem, like "Silver," is composed of a series
of images. What emotion, what attitude, dominates it?

THE RED WHEELBARROW

William Carlos Williams (1883–1962)

        so much depends
        upon

        a red wheel
        barrow

        glazed with rain   5
        water

        beside the white
        chickens

The critic Philip Wheelwright makes
the following comment upon this poem:

    A classical case (and apparently a clas-
    sical failure) of the attempt to convey a
    simple experience through sheer simplicity
    of statement is to be found in Section xxi of

William Carlos Williams' *Spring and All.*
The eight short lines of the section, although they bear no distinguishing title,
form an independent unit with no imagistic
or thematic outside connections, and it may
therefore be treated (as its author has, in
fact, publicly spoken of it) as a single poem.
. . . To most readers it will be accepted as a
pleasant pastiche [see Glossary], with no
more than a fanciful justification for the
opening words. To Dr. Williams, however,
as he has repeatedly declared, the small remembered scene is of arresting and retaining importance. But quite obviously the
personal associations and bubbles of memory that have stirred the poet's sensitive
recollections are not shared by a reader
whose only clues are to be found in the
poem itself. The trouble is that in these
lines the poet has tried to convey the simplicity of the remembered experience by a
plain simplicity of utterance—by a simple
simplicity, one might say, as opposed to a
contextual simplicity. The attempt was
bound to fail. Simplicity, when it is fresh
and not banal, can scarcely be conveyed to
another mind, except in rare instances
where, by happy accident, two diverse sen-
sitivities happen to be attuned in just that
respect.*

Certainly, Wheelwright indicates a severe
limitation of the imagistic method when practiced in isolation—as was the custom of the
Imagists in many cases. But let us ask in
what sense Williams meant that "so much
depends" upon the wheelbarrow. Is he aiming to do more than make—perhaps in a
whimsical fashion—the claim that we must
not divorce ourselves from the world of perception, from the "thingness" of things? Is
he not saying that life is grounded in the
world and that we must not lose ourselves in
abstractions and intellectual bemusement?
Elsewhere he said, "No ideas but in things."
Williams, a physician with the scientific
training of that profession, could have intended that slogan only in a special context; as a
reminder of the fundamental concreteness of
poetry. It is true that in adhering to his
slogan as closely as he often did, Williams cut
himself off from some of the great resources
and materials of poetry; the perception of
"things" is only part of vital human experi-

___
* *Metaphor and Reality* (Bloomington: Indiana University Press, 1962), pp. 159–60.

ence, and even ideas can provoke burning passions. But let us accept Williams—and other imagists—in terms of their effects, not their theories.

This poem, which is sometimes thought of as free verse, is actually in a very strict metrical form. Each stanza can be scanned as dimeter, monometer:

$$\overset{//}{\text{So}} \overset{/}{\text{much}} \overset{\smile}{\text{de}} \overset{/}{\text{pends}}$$
$$\overset{\smile}{\text{u}} \overset{/}{\text{pon}}$$

As we point out in subsection 19.2, meter can be thought of as a kind of frame into which the material of a poem is put. "The Red Wheelbarrow" is metrical, and it thus has a kind of frame, as do all poems in ordinary verse; in the framework of its lining, however, it differs in a very marked way from almost all poems in ordinary verse.

We ordinarily find some kind of relation between the lining of a poem and what is being said, and some kind of relation between the overall rhythm and the meaning and emotion of a poem. But what strikes us here is the extreme arbitrariness, the extreme abstractness of the lining. We feel compelled to ask by what logic the poet divides his lines in this way? The answer may be that the clear lack of any obvious logic in the content (what "depends," or can depend, on what the poem proceeds to present?) accounts for the arbitrariness of the structure. The arbitrary division, that is, would be the very point—by refusing to consider syntax, phrase structure, or idea as related to the line division, Williams asserts the minimal, sharply focused "things" and aspects of things so that they stand forth clearly in their own right, whatever their own right may be. Even the word *upon*—which is certainly not a "thing"—is isolated in its own special "thing-y" significance. We focus upon "upon-ness" as it were; for this is what Williams uses as the key of his poem.

EXERCISES

1. In what sense can it be argued that anything does "depend upon" the wheelbarrow and its special setting? Could it be said that the fact that we can think of nothing—of no idea and no practical consequence—that follows from what we see here, is, in itself, the importance that "depends." If Williams intends to point to some importance beyond "idea" or "practical consequence," what can that be?

2. When Wheelwright says that Williams is trying to convey an experience by a "plain simplicity of utterance," what does he mean? Is this also true of Tennyson in "The Eagle"? What elements does Tennyson introduce into his poem that are not found in "The Red Wheelbarrow"?

3. Compare, in any way that seems significant to you, "The Red Wheelbarrow" with "Silver" by Walter de la Mare.

THE WOODSPURGE
Dante Gabriel Rossetti (1828–1882)

The wind flapped loose, the wind was still,
Shaken out dead from tree and hill:
I had walked on at the wind's will,—
I sat now, for the wind was still.

Between my knees my forehead was,—   5
My lips drawn in, said not Alas!
My hair was over in the grass,
My naked ears heard the day pass.

My eyes, wide open, had the run
Of some ten weeds to fix upon;   10
Among those few, out of the sun,
The woodspurge flowered, three cups in one.

From perfect grief there need not be
Wisdom or even memory:
One thing then learnt remains to me,—   15
The woodspurge has a cup of three.

The first three stanzas of "The Woodspurge" give a very simple bit of narrative. The speaker of the poem (unidentified), suffering from shock and grief, wanders aimlessly about, and then, when the wind stops, sinks down in total abandonment, and stares at the ground. The speaker's gaze happens to fall on one small plant there, the woodspurge. In such moments of great grief a person may fix attention on some perfectly irrelevant object, as a sort of escape from pain or a way of hanging onto reality. But the last stanza gives another dimension to the poem: nothing may come out of grief, the poet says, not "Wisdom or even memory," but grief demands some sort of objective focus for its meaning. To put matters another way, the griefstricken speaker has made the blossom of woodspurge an image that seems to stand for, to embody, to symbolize, the emotion felt long ago. We may, in fact, see this poem not only as a poem in its own right, one that catches an emotion in expressive form, but as a poem also involving the human need to objectify emotion in imagery and symbol. It is a poem about how a poetic symbol may come to exist—or rather, about the fundamental impulse that underlies poetic symbolism.

EXERCISES

1. We have said that this poem involves a narrative. Why do we not demand more explanation than is here given?
2. What advantage is there in withholding such explanation as is to be given until the last stanza? Suppose we rewrite line 2 as "In my wild grief, by vale and hill." What effect would this have on the poem, and on your interest in the poem?
3. Turn to "Neutral Tones" by Thomas Hardy (sec. 14). What fundamental connection do you see between that poem and "The Woodspurge"?
4. Dismissing the fact that the author of this poem was a man, what is the sex of the speaker of the poem? What evidence do you find in the text?
5. Return to James Joyce's story "Araby" (sec. 7) and the discussion. What similarity do you note between the story and this poem?

SONNET 18

William Shakespeare (1564–1616)

Shall I compare thee to a summer's day?
Thou art more lovely and more temperate:
Rough winds do shake the darling buds of
    May,
And summer's lease hath all too short a date:
Sometime too hot the eye of heaven shines,   5
And often is his gold complexion dimmed;
And every fair from fair sometime declines,
By chance, or nature's changing course, un-
    trimmed;
But thy eternal summer shall not fade,
Nor lose possession of that fair thou owest;   10
Nor shall Death brag thou wander'st in his
    shade,
When in eternal lines to time thou growest:
  So long as men can breathe, or eyes can see,
  So long lives this, and this gives life to thee.

In the poems offered thus far in this section (with the exception of the passage from "The Lotos-Eaters" and "The Wild Swans at Coole"), images have been more or less boldly presented in their own right, and even in those exceptions the image has been central. But with this sonnet, the imagery is invoked *to elaborate a discourse.* Paraphrased, the discourse runs something like this: I will not compare "you" (the poet's friend) to a summer's day, because a summer's day is variable and fleeting; instead I will commemorate your quality in poetry that will outlast death and time and that will endow you with immortality.

This discourse is, in itself, very dull and *conventional* (see Glossary). It is conventional in the strict sense: poets of the Renaissance repeat this idea over and over. Some poets may have actually had some degree of conviction in saying such a thing, but in any case, it was a fashionable thing to say, a literary convention.

Of the countless sonnets using this convention, a few survive as powerful poetry, this one among them. What gives power to the conventional discourse is the vividness of the imagery and the emotional resonance of its combination with the expressive rhythms and musicality of the verse.

EXERCISES

1. If the poet is serious in asking himself whether he should compare the friend to a summer's day, why does he go on to elaborate the comparison through the first eight lines of the sonnet?
2. After immersing yourself in the rhythms of the poem, what differences in rhythm do you feel between lines 8 and 11 on the one hand and the rest of the poem on the other?

SONNET 73

William Shakespeare (1564–1616)

That time of year thou mayst in me behold
When yellow leaves, or none, or few, do hang
Upon those boughs which shake against the
    cold,
Bare ruined choirs, where late the sweet birds
    sang.
In me thou seest the twilight of such day   5

As after sunset fadeth in the west;
Which by and by black night doth take away,
Death's second self, that seals up all in rest.
In me thou seest the glowing of such fire,
That on the ashes of his youth doth lie,   10
As the death-bed whereon it must expire,
Consum'd with that which it was nourished
   . by.
    This thou perceiv'st, which makes thy love
     more strong,
    To love that well which thou must leave
     ere long.

EXERCISES

1. The poet offers three basic images to describe his condition, each in a quatrain (group of four lines). What enrichment or progression justifies this accumulation of imagery around the single topic "I grow old"?

2. In the previous sonnet the closing couplet (pair of lines) seems merely a perfunctory summary of what has already been said, merely a kind of mechanical "clincher" for the poem. Does the final couplet here do more than that? Has it some organic—and emotional—relation to the body of the poem? To begin with, what is it that the friend "perceiv'st"?

WE WEAR THE MASK

Paul Laurence Dunbar (1872–1906)

We wear the mask that grins and lies,
It hides our cheeks and shades our eyes,
This debt we pay to human guile;
With torn and bleeding hearts we smile,
And mouth with myriad subtleties.   5

Why should the world be overwise,
In counting all our tears and sighs?
Nay, let them only see us, while
    We wear the mask.

We smile, but, O great Christ, our cries   10
To thee from tortured souls arise.
We sing, but oh, the clay is vile
Beneath our feet, and long the mile;
But let the world dream otherwise,
    We wear the mask.

EXERCISE

The author here is black. Interpret the "mask."

TO DAFFADILLS

Robert Herrick (1591–1674)

Faire Daffadills, we weep to see
    You haste away so soone:
As yet the early-rising Sun
    Has not attain'd his Noone.
      Stay, stay,   5
     Until the hasting day
      Has run
     But to the Even-song;
And, having pray'd together, wee
    Will goe with you along.   10

We have short time to stay, as you,
    We have as short a Spring;
As quick a growth to meet Decay,
    As you, or any thing.
      We die,   15
     As your hours doe, and drie
      Away,
    Like to the Summers raine;
Or as the pearles of Mornings dew
    Ne'er to be found againe.   20

EXERCISES

1. The speaker addresses the daffodils as if they were human beings. Does he justify this device in the analogies he develops between the daffodils and men?

2. Note that "Even-song" technically means an evening church service and thus prepares for line 9. What is the effect—and meaning—of this fact?

3. As the poem ends, is the emphasis upon the frailty of the flowers or of man?

4. What is the poet's attitude toward death? And, indeed, toward life? Bitter, despairing, or what? How does his attitude relate to the various images he uses?

THE BUGLE SONG

Alfred, Lord Tennyson (1809–1892)

The splendour falls on castle walls
    And snowy summits old in story:
The long light shakes across the lakes,
    And the wild cataract leaps in glory.
Blow, bugle, blow, set the wild echoes flying,   5
Blow, bugle; answer, echoes, dying, dying,
    dying.

O hark, O hear! how thin and clear,
    And thinner, clearer, farther going!
O sweet and far from cliff and scar

The horns of Elfland faintly blowing!   10
Blow, let us hear the purple glens replying,
Blow, bugle; answer, echoes, dying, dying,
     dying.

O love, they die in yon rich sky,
     They faint on hill or field or river;
Our echoes roll from soul to soul,   15
     And grow for ever and for ever.
Blow, bugle, blow, set the wild echoes flying,
And answer, echoes, answer, dying, dying,
     dying.

The first two stanzas of this poem describe a bugle call at sunset. The poet, who is apparently standing on some high place, describes the country about him in the light of sunset, the castle in the distance, the waterfall. Evidently, the country is mountainous, and not only are there the rich tones of the bugle, the hills throw back the echoes that gradually die away and become at last so faint that one might imagine them as notes blown from the horns of "Elfland." But an idea comes into the poet's mind as he listens to the dying echoes: these echoes of the bugle die away into nothingness, but the spiritual echoes that roll back and forth between him and his beloved do not decrease but actually increase as time goes on; that is, the poet seems to be saying, love does not become less with the years but grows greater.

It is easy to see why the poem has been very popular. The images are pretty and "poetical"; the rhythm is emphatic; and there is a great deal of rime. The rich, even gaudy, description of the bugle call at sunset is made to serve true love. Beautiful as all this is, the poet seems to say, love is more beautiful, more enduring.

Suppose we read the poem carefully, however, and explore further the poet's experience. Does the idea in the last stanza grow out of what has preceded it, or has it been added as a sort of moralizing comment?

The first stanza contains some beautiful and dramatic rhythmic effects and some brilliant and arresting imagery and phrasing. For instance, "the long light shakes." *Long* suggests, vividly, the level beams of the setting sun, and *shakes* suggests a kind of dazzling quality, as if the light itself vibrated, shimmering over the water. But in addition to the visual element, the word *shakes* invokes the taut, vibrant quality of the bugle note. So sound and sight fuse, and in that fusion excite our senses. Phrasings such as these more than make up for the rather vague and conventional phrase "old in story" in line 2.

The second stanza, after the effective image of "cliff and scar," indulges a pleasant fancy: the sound of the bugle call, diminished by echo, causes the observer to imagine that he is hearing horns blown by the elves. But what about elves? Isn't there something inevitably trivial and cute associated with them, to our modern mind at least, that debases the effect of the poem? And in any case, isn't the use of Elfland a kind of lazy shorthand for something the poet can achieve directly and powerfully in such phrases as "the long light shakes"?

Thus far, the poet has juxtaposed elements of sight and sound—the sunset gleam as reflected on faraway castle walls and mountain summits, and the notes of the bugle as "reflected"—that is, echoed back—from these same distant points of the landscape. The experience is invested with a special kind of magical glamor—despite the reference to Elfland. But the poet apparently felt that it was insufficient to let his poem stop with this kind of evocation and that he needed to bind the various descriptive elements together and to relate them to some assertion of obvious significance. He has attempted to bring this about in his last stanza.

EXERCISES

1. Has the analogy—or contrast—between the echoes of the bugle and those that "roll from soul to soul" been adequately prepared for? Note that the romantic aura associated with the echoes of the bugle call comes from the fact that they are faint and are indeed "dying," but the lover surely would not admit that the spiritual "echoes" playing between him and his sweetheart will die away. It is possible that the poet wanted to make a point of the very difference between the echoes, but in that case, has he made enough of the shock of contrast? Has he boldly dismissed the pretty magic of dying echoes in favor of the spiritual "echo"?
2. What is the sense of the word *grow* in line 16?

Grow in intensity? In volume? Or grow in some way that would leave these echoes of the soul richer yet not deafening—magical yet ever and ever stronger?

3. How effectively does the poet use the refrain? It is an obvious means of tying the three stanzas together, but why does he want to have the "wild echoes" set flying in stanza 1? In stanza 2? And finally in stanza 3. Or is there any meaningful application in each case?

4. Granted that we are not to measure poetry by strictly logical standards, is not some kind of imaginative logic—some kind of coherence—called for in the poet's management of his images? If so, is there sufficient coherence of this kind manifested in "The Bugle Song"?

THE TREE OF MAN

A. E. Housman (1859–1936)

On Wenlock Edge the wood's in trouble,
  His forest fleece the Wrekin heaves;[1]
The gale, it plies the saplings double,
  And thick on Severn[2] snow the leaves.

'Twould blow like this through holt and hanger 5
  When Uricon the city stood:
'Tis the old wind in the old anger,
  But then it threshed another wood.

Then, 'twas before my time, the Roman
  At yonder heaving hill would stare: 10
The blood that warms an English yeoman,
  The thoughts that hurt him, they were there.

There, like the wind through woods in riot,
  Through him the gale of life blew high;
The tree of man was never quiet: 15
  Then 'twas the Roman, now 'tis I.

The gale, it plies the saplings double,
  It blows so hard, 'twill soon be gone;
To-day the Roman and his trouble
  Are ashes under Uricon.   20

EXERCISES

1. This is a piece of description with an application of the scene to the poet's own life. In the description, does the wind stand for anything else? What?

2. What does the wood stand for?

3. Compare and contrast this poem with Herrick's "To Daffadills." With Shakespeare's Sonnet 97 (sec. 15). Is the use of imagery in this poem more subtle or less subtle than in the other two poems?

4. What attitude toward life and death is expressed in this poem? How do you arrive at your answer?

NULLA FIDES

Patrick Carey (fl. 1651)

For God's sake mark that fly:
See what a poor, weak, little thing it is.
When thou has marked and scorned it, know that
  this,
This little, poor, weak fly
Has killed a pope; can make an emp'ror die.   5

Behold yon spark of fire;
How little hot! how near to nothing 'tis!
When thou hast done despising, know that this,
This contemned spark of fire,
Has burnt whole towns; can burn a world
  entire.   10

That crawling worm there see:
Ponder how ugly, filthy, vile it is.
When thou hast seen and loathed it, know that
  this,
This base worm thou dost see,
Has quite devoured thy parents; shall eat thee. 15

Honour, the world, and man,
What trifles are they; since most true it is
That this poor fly, this little spark, this
So much abhorred worm, can
Honour destroy; burn worlds; devour up man. 20

EXERCISES

1. Is the description of the fly, the spark, and the worm sufficiently vivid? It could be argued that these objects are described in rather vague, general terms. If so, does this fact lessen the force of the poem? If not, why not?

2. Does the poem simply versify an obvious generalization? Is it therefore flat and trite?

3. What is the meaning of "For God's sake" (l. 1)? Is the phrase used merely to intensify the imperative? Or what is its function? What relation does the title have to the end of the poem?

[1] Wenlock Edge and the Wrekin are hills in Shropshire. [2] The Severn is a river in the west of England.

THE LAMB
William Blake (1757–1827)

Little Lamb, who made thee?
Dost thou know who made thee?
Gave thee life, & bid thee feed,
By the stream & o'er the mead;
Gave thee clothing of delight,   5
Softest clothing, wooly, bright;
Gave thee such a tender voice,
Making all the vales rejoice?
Little Lamb, who made thee?
Dost thou know who made thee?   10

Little Lamb, I'll tell thee,
Little Lamb, I'll tell thee:
He is callèd by thy name,
For he calls himself a Lamb.
He is meek, & he is mild;   15
He became a little child.
I a child, & thou a lamb,
We are callèd by his name.
Little Lamb, God bless thee!
Little Lamb, God bless thee!   20

EXERCISES

1. Is this poem concerned primarily with a description of the lamb, or with a description of the mind of the child, who speaks the poem?
2. The child speaks to the lamb as if the lamb were a younger child. How does this dramatic device support the meaning of the poem? How are lamb and child related to God (incarnate in Christ)? What facts does the child make the basis of the relationship?

THE TYGER
William Blake (1757–1827)

Tyger! Tyger! burning bright
In the forests of the night,
What immortal hand or eye
Could frame thy fearful symmetry?

In what distant deeps or skies   5
Burnt the fire of thine eyes?
On what wings dare he aspire?
What the hand dare seize the fire?

And what shoulder, & what art,
Could twist the sinews of thy heart?   10
And when thy heart began to beat,
What dread hand? & what dread feet?

What the hammer? what the chain?
In what furnace was thy brain?

What the anvil? what dread grasp   15
Dare its deadly terrors clasp?

When the stars threw down their spears,
And water'd heaven with their tears,
Did he smile his work to see?
Did he who made the Lamb make thee?   20

Tyger! Tyger! burning bright
In the forests of the night,
What immortal hand or eye,
Dare frame thy fearful symmetry?

EXERCISES

1. Like "The Lamb," from Blake's *Songs of Innocence,* this poem from his *Songs of Experience* is concerned with creation. Lamb and tiger symbolize, as it were, opposite poles in creation. But does this mean that the two poems—or the two principles here symbolized—cancel each other? Or do they illuminate each other? Do they complete each other? Could one be conceivable without the other?
2. Can you see how the idea involved in the questions above might be said to apply to the reader's attitude in confronting, in general, poems that contradict each other, directly or by implication, that offer competing values or moods?
3. Can you see how it might be said that the principle behind Blake's pair of poems might be said to apply to artistic creation or authorship as well as to God's creation of the world?
4. Can you justify dramatically the unfinished sentences and the abrupt phrases of stanzas 3, 4, and 5? Who is speaking? Out of what emotional state is he speaking?
5. Are we made to "see" the tiger? Is this a realistic description? Are we made to sense the terrible power of the tiger? Is the tiger more than a literal animal? What does the tiger come to stand for?
6. What is this poem "about"? Compare this poem with "The Eagle," by Tennyson. In which poem is the thing signified by the image more specific? What qualities, objectively considered, do the images share? If the poem about the lamb did not exist, would "The Tyger" seem more like "The Eagle"? Why?

ODE TO THE WEST WIND
Percy Bysshe Shelley (1792–1822)

I

O Wild West Wind, thou breath of Autumn's
being,

Thou, from whose unseen presence the leaves
dead
Are driven, like ghosts from an enchanter fleeing,

Yellow, and black, and pale, and hectic red,
Pestilence-stricken multitudes: O thou,   5
Who chariotest to their dark wintry bed

The wingèd seeds, where they lie cold and low,
Each like a corpse within its grave, until
Thine azure sister of the Spring shall blow

Her clarion o'er the dreaming earth, and fill 10
(Driving sweet buds like flocks to feed in air)
With living hues and odours plain and hill:

Wild Spirit, which art moving everywhere;
Destroyer and preserver; hear, oh, hear!

II

Thou on whose stream, mid the steep sky's
commotion, 15
Loose clouds like earth's decaying leaves are shed,
Shook from the tangled boughs of Heaven and
Ocean,

Angels of rain and lightning: there are spread
On the blue surface of thine aëry surge,
Like the bright hair uplifted from the head 20

Of some fierce Maenad, even from the dim verge
Of the horizon to the zenith's height,
The locks of the approaching storm. Thou dirge

Of the dying year, to which this closing night
Will be the dome of a vast sepulchre, 25
Vaulted with all thy congregated might

Of vapours, from whose solid atmosphere
Black rain, and fire, and hail, will burst: oh, hear!

III

Thou who didst waken from his summer dreams
The blue Mediterranean, where he lay, 30
Lull'd by the coil of his crystàlline streams,

Beside a pumice isle in Baiae's bay,
And saw in sleep old palaces and towers
Quivering within the wave's intenser day,

All overgrown with azure moss and flowers 35
So sweet, the sense faints picturing them! Thou
For whose path the Atlantic's level powers

Cleave themselves into chasms, while far below
The sea-blooms and the oozy woods which wear
The sapless foliage of the ocean, know 40

Thy voice, and suddenly grow gray with fear,
And tremble and despoil themselves: oh, hear!

IV

If I were a dead leaf thou mightest bear;
If I were a swift cloud to fly with thee;
A wave to pant beneath thy power, and share 45

The impulse of thy strength, only less free
Than thou, O uncontrollable! If even
I were as in my boyhood, and could be

The comrade of thy wanderings over Heaven,
As then, when to outstrip thy skiey speed 50
Scarce seemed a vision; I would ne'er have striven

As thus with thee in prayer in my sore need.
Oh, lift me as a wave, a leaf, a cloud!
I fall upon the thorns of life! I bleed!

A heavy weight of hours has chained and bowed 55
One too like thee: tameless, and swift, and proud.

V

Make me thy lyre, even as the forest is:
What if my leaves are falling like its own!
The tumult of thy mighty harmonies

Will take from both a deep, autumnal tone, 60
Sweet though in sadness. Be thou, Spirit fierce,
My spirit! Be thou me, impetuous one!

Drive my dead thoughts over the universe
Like withered leaves to quicken a new birth;
And, by the incantation of this verse, 65

Scatter, as from an unextinguished hearth
Ashes and sparks, my words among mankind!
Be through my lips to unawakened earth

The trumpet of a prophecy! O, Wind,
If Winter comes, can Spring be far behind? 70

EXERCISES

1. After a number of careful readings of the poem
—some of them aloud to get the feel of the
rhythms—draw up a set of questions that might
lead to an interpretative study of the poem. You
need not know the answer to a question before
you set it down. In fact, the best way to start might

be to set down the questions that you can't answer but that you feel are crucial. Remember that the use of imagery might be central to meaning. Remember, too, that the process of asking questions often leads to finding answers: question number 2 may provide the answer to question number 1.

2. When the sets of questions are ready, students should exchange them for discussion. Pooling your questions should, in fact, lead to answers and to a richer sense of the poem.

3. It might be said that "Ode to the West Wind" expresses the same basic attitude toward life that we find in Blake's paired poems. Do you accept this idea? Defend your position.

4. Recall "Lucinda Matlock," "The Farmer's Bride," and "Burning the Letters" in section 12. Which of the women in these poems do you think might like Shelley's poem? Why?

5. The verse form used here, called terza rima, is very complicated. Let us observe that Shelley does not obtrude the form on our attention with full or partial stops after most lines. Rather, he lets many lines run on, so that even the impact of rime is diminished, and the sense of the metrical unity of the line is subordinated to the overall thrust of syntax. Do you see any relation here between this technique and the meaning of the poem?

Rhetorical Variation

Turn to subsection 19.4 and carefully read our discussion of rhetorical variation. Pay particular attention to our charts of the rhetorical movement of various lines of poetry; if you don't see the sense of them at first, read the lines aloud until you do. Give some thoughtful attention, too, to our explanations of the ways that rhetoric can affect the meter of a poem.

EXERCISES

1. You have read the comment on the relation of the meter to the word *disobedience* in the first line of Milton's *Paradise Lost*. Return to Tennyson's "The Eagle." In what line do you find a similar grouping of metrical accents in one word to give a dramatic effect?

2. Write out as prose the first four lines of Shakespeare's Sonnet 73 and make a rhetorical chart of the sentence. Now scan the quatrain.

3. Turn back to the passage from Tennyson's "The Lotos-Eaters." Scan lines 5–9 and comment on the metrical and rhetorical variations. Notice that the last line is hexameter. Is the rhetorical variation rather flattened here? That is, does it tend to follow the metrical pattern rather than to pull strongly against it? Can you make any comment here on the expressive quality of the line? Examine line 27. What comments do you think appropriate here?

4. Examine lines 9–16 of Hardy's "The Man He Killed" (sec. 12). What difference in general rhythm do you find here in comparison to the rest of the poem? How does the rhetorical difference here reflect the movement of the speaker's mind? In this connection, return to exercise 5 following the poem.

5. Carefully reread "The Woodspurge," by Dante Gabriel Rossetti. Scan the first quatrain, noting metrical and rhetorical variations. Do you find the quatrain dramatically effective? Explain. Now compare the scansion here with that of the last quatrain. What is the difference? Can you justify the difference?

6. In Herrick's "To Daffadills," comment on variations in lines 15–20.

7. Comment on lines 5–12 of "The Tyger" by William Blake.

8. Scan and comment on lines 60–70 of Shelley's "Ode to the West Wind."

Section 14

TONE

The spoken word *yes* may mean agreement, willingness, acceptance—all the things that the dictionary says it means. But a slight change of voice may make it mean a very grudging, dubious agreement, and a further change may turn it into a humorous, ironic denial, or, again, a bitter, sarcastic refusal.

The tone of the speaker's voice, then,

indicates a range of meaning beyond what words, literally considered, mean. It indicates the speaker's *attitude*. But his attitude toward what? It may be toward the situation that prompts his speech—which does, of course, condition his attitude toward the literal words he uses. It may be toward the audience—for example, we know how irony may be playful or aggressive. It may, further, be toward himself. And, of course, the attitude involved in a particular case may be complex.

To know the meaning of an utterance we may be compelled, then, to go beyond the literal words, and this holds as true for poetry as for speech in ordinary life. When we see a poem on the page, however, we cannot hear a voice. The word *tone* is, in our sense here, metaphorical. What, we must ask ourselves, serves the same function in a poem that a literal voice may serve in speech? The answer to that question is sometimes subtle and complex, and will involve all that we have been discussing in previous sections, from the situation stated or implied in a poem to matters of imagery and rhythm. What we now undertake is to explore the truth in that statement.

GROUP 1: DISLIKE AND OUTRAGE

MR CROMEK
William Blake (1757–1827)

> A pretty sneaking knave I knew—
> O Mr Cromek, how do ye do?

A VISIT FROM DR. FELL
Ogden Nash (1902–1971)

> Dr. Fell is at the door and my *mens sana* is about to depart from my *corpore sano*,
> For this is the hour of the chocolate fingerprints in the books and the coconut-marshmallow icing on the piano.
> Dr. Fell is notable for the southern-central section of his silhouette,
> And he lands in your frailest chair like somebody from the ninth floor of a burning hotel landing in a net.
> Hitherto, the plumbing has functioned as sweetly as a hungry mosquito lapping up citronella,   5
> But the plumbing is where Dr. Fell disposes of any unwanted object, from an old cigar to an old umbrella.
> Dr. Fell's little finger projecting from his glass as he drinks couldn't possibly be genteeler or archer,
> But whatever glasses you had a dozen of on his arrival you only have eleven of on his departure.

EXERCISE

What keeps this composition from being merely a statement of dislike? What, in other words, makes it a poem?

DR. FELL
Thomas Brown (1663–1704)

> I do not love you, Dr. Fell;
> But why I cannot tell;
> But this I know full well,
> I do not love you, Dr. Fell.

Dr. Fell was dean of Christ Church College, Oxford, Bishop of Oxford, and an early promoter and benefactor of Oxford University Press. The poem, a translation of one of Martial's epigrams, was made by an undergraduate of his college. Clearly, Brown did not like Dr. Fell.

EXERCISES

1. What is the tone of Brown's statement of dislike? Is his dislike violent? Spiteful? Somewhat embarrassed and shamefaced? Is it mixed with amused contempt? Try to describe the attitude expressed here.

2. Let us put the facts of the case into a plain prose statement: "Even though I can give no reason, the fact is that I simply do not like you, Dr. Fell." What difference in tone do you find between this and the jingle? How much depends on content and how much on the mere fact of the jingle's being a jingle?

Every man but Dr. Fell has his own conception of enough;
Dr. Fell will not only nonchalantly knock a half-completed jigsaw puzzle onto the
    floor but nonchalantly carry off a key piece buried in his cuff.   10
Come on in Dr. Fell, you must take pot-luck with us, no, wait a minute, I forgot,
Today we can only offer you kettle-luck, last time you were here you ran the ice-pick
    through the pot.

If Thomas Brown couldn't tell why he disliked Dr. Fell of Oxford—his is a nameless and perhaps irrational aversion—Ogden Nash can and does tell why his "Dr. Fell" is unwelcome in his house. In fact, his poem is a rather full bill of particulars.

EXERCISES

1. What kind of person is Nash's "Dr. Fell"? A wicked man? A coldblooded monster? A kook? Or a rather jovial, Falstaffian man? Explain your view.
2. Fell's sins seem to have more to do with furniture and glassware than with human beings. What bearing does this fact have on the matter?
3. Is it possible that the speaker in Nash's poem actually has a sneaking admiration for Fell?

ON A YOUNG HEIR'S COMING OF AGE

Samuel Johnson (1709–1784)

Long expected one-and-twenty,
  Ling'ring year, at length is flown;
Pride and pleasure, pomp and plenty,
  Great ———, are now your own.

Loosened from the minor's tether,   5
  Free to mortgage or to sell;
Wild as wind, and light as feather,
  Bid the sons of thrift farewell.

Call the Betseys, Kates, and Jennies,
  All the names that banish care;   10
Lavish of your grandsire's guineas,
  Show the spirit of an heir.

All that prey on vice or folly
  Joy to see their quarry fly:
There the gamester light and jolly,   15
  There the lender grave and sly.

Wealth, my lad, was made to wander,
  Let it wander as it will;
Call the jockey, call the pander,
  Bid them come, and take their fill.   20

When the bonny blade carouses,
  Pockets full and spirits high—
What are acres? what are houses?
  Only dirt, or wet or dry.

Should the guardian, friend, or mother   25
  Tell the woes of wilful waste:
Scorn their counsel, scorn their pother,
  You can hang or drown at last.

EXERCISES

1. The poem is ostensibly addressed to the young heir himself. The speaker pretends, part of the time at least, to urge the young man on to his pleasures and dissipations, pretending, even, to adopt the same carefree, high-spirited, devil-may-care attitude that the heir has. The poem is, then, ironical. But what is the prevailing quality of the irony? Heavy-handed? Bitter? Cynical? Self-righteous? Secretly envious? Or is there a certain pity behind the irony? In any case, try to adduce evidence for your view.
2. Perhaps you will decide that the speaker's attitude changes during the course of the poem. For instance, it might be argued that stanza 4 is different from those preceding. In the first three stanzas the speaker presumably adopts the young man's own attitude. But from whose point of view are the girls, the gamester, and the lender viewed in stanza 4? In stanza 5, the point of view again changes, ironically accepting the heir's values. But what of stanza 6?
3. Clearly the last stanza is very different in tone from the body of the poem. Describe the difference. Is the speaker sarcastically saying, "Go ahead, and see what happens to you, and be damned"? Is he actually gloating ahead of time over the fate of the young fellow who won't take his—or other people's—advice. Comment on the difference in tone—and therefore meaning—if the last stanza were revised as follows:

Should the guardian friend, or mother
  Warn you that your path leads down,
Scorn their counsel, scorn their pother,
  For who cares if you hang or drown?

4. Suppose we change the last line to "You can always hang or drown." Now the heavily sarcastic "who cares" has been dropped, and the line seems to mean precisely what it meant in the original version. But on second thought we may see that the last phrase of the poem, "at last," rhetorically set off from the preceding part of the line, and of the poem, really introduces a new note, a new tone. Can it be argued that the effect here is to modify the irony, which has already run through certain variations? Perhaps in this way: The end will not merely be a well-deserved punishment for a stupid or wicked young spendthrift; it will also involve the sad waste of a human being and the grief of those attached to him. Do you accept this view?

5. The rhythm here is brisk and sharply defined, with almost all lines end-stopped. How does this fact relate to the tone of the poem?

KU KLUX

Langston Hughes (1902–1967)

> They took me out
> To some lonesome place.
> They said, "Do you believe
> In the great white race?"
>
> I say, "Mister,   5
> To tell you the truth,
> I'd believe in anything
> If you'd just turn me loose."
>
> The white man said, "Boy,
> Can it be   10
> You're a-standin' there
> A-sassin' me?"
>
> They hit me in the head
> And knocked me down.
> And then they kicked me   15
> On the ground.
>
> A klansman said, "Nigger,
> Look me in the face—
> And tell me you believe in
> The great white race."   20

In Dr. Johnson's "On a Young Heir's Coming of Age," the speaker is not very clearly identified. He, presumably the poet, is simply an older, more experienced, and wiser man, who, even as he rebukes the young wastrel, is not devoid of sympathy and pity for the human situation. In Hughes's "Ku Klux," the speaker is more sharply identified, and the situation is dramatically rendered; the speaker is an ordinary black man, presumably of meager education, who has been beaten up by klansmen. The poem is in his voice, for the most part quoting the dialogue between himself and the klansmen, with the natural, colloquial quality of language and rhythm preserved.

EXERCISES

1. What is the key irony here? How does it differ from that of Dr. Johnson's poem? There the ironies depend on the attitude of the older and wiser man who speaks. On what does it depend here? How fully, in fact, does the speaker recognize the irony? What is the attitude of the speaker?

2. What is gained by this first-person presentation? Does it help us, for instance, to accept an irony that otherwise might be too obvious? In what short stories in this book do we find the same effect?

3. What is the prevailing number of accents in a line? If some lines seem to defy an attempt to describe them in any standard foot, can you still resolve such lines by accents? Scan lines 4 and 20. What about secondary accents here?

A GLASS OF BEER

James Stephens (1882–1950)

The lanky hank of a she in the inn over there
Nearly killed me for asking the loan of a glass of
    beer;
May the devil grip the whey-faced slut by the hair,
And beat the bad manners out of her skin for a
    year.

That parboiled ape, with the toughest jaw you
    will see   5
On virtue's path, and a voice that would rasp the
    dead,
Came roaring and raging the minute she looked
    at me,
And threw me out of the house on the back of my
    head!

If I asked her master he'd give me a cask a day;
But she, with the beer at hand, not a gill would
    arrange!   10
May she marry a ghost and bear him a kitten, and
    may
The High King of Glory permit her to get the
    mange.

EXERCISES

1. In "Ku Klux" we clearly feel that there is justification for the sense of outrage voiced by the speaker. But what about the situation in "A Glass of Beer"? Reconstruct the event behind the poem, not as the speaker relates it but as you assume it to have actually happened. (Of course, the whole poem is, in one sense, a fiction, but even so, there are two versions of the event involved here: that presented by the speaker and that of the "fictional" actuality.) How does this consideration affect what you assume to have been the actual speaking voice of the would-be client of the inn? Comment on the use of the word *loan*, the phrase "bad manners," the phrase "On virtue's path," and the appeal to "The High King of Glory."
2. What kinds of irony are involved in the last line of the poem?
3. How many lies do you think the speaker has told or implied?
4. If we assume the story the outraged client tells to be true, what value would the poem have then? Some? None?
5. Comment on rhetorical variation here in relation to the tone of the poem.

THE CHIMNEY SWEEPER
William Blake (1757–1827)

When my mother died I was very young,
And my father sold me while yet my tongue
Could scarcely cry " 'weep! 'weep! 'weep! 'weep!"
So your chimneys I sweep, and in soot I sleep.

There's little Tom Dacre, who cried when his
    head,   5
That curled like a lamb's back, was shaved; so I
    said,
"Hush, Tom! never mind it, for, when your head's
    bare,
You know that the soot cannot spoil your white
    hair."

And so he was quiet, and that very night,
As Tom was asleeping, he had such a sight!   10
That thousands of sweepers, Dick, Joe, Ned, and
    Jack,
Were all of them locked up in coffins of black.

And by came an Angel who had a bright key,
And he opened the coffins and set them all free;
Then down a green plain leaping, laughing, they
    run,   15
And wash in a river, and shine in the sun.

Then naked and white, all their bags left behind,
They rise upon clouds and sport in the wind;
And the Angel told Tom, if he'd be a good boy,
He'd have God for his father, and never want
    joy.   20

And so Tom awoke, and we rose in the dark,
And got with our bags and our brushes to work.
Though the morning was cold, Tom was happy
    and warm;
So if all do their duty they need not fear harm.

One of the most obvious abuses in Blake's time was the plight of the chimney sweeps, boys who were sometimes bought and were generally treated like slaves. Their cry announcing their trade—" 'weep, 'weep"—was common in the streets of London. Like "Ku Klux," "The Chimney Sweeper" has a fundamental element of social protest. Similarly, the irony of the poem depends on the fact that it is spoken in the first person.

EXERCISES

1. Describe the basic irony here.
2. What is the particular, incidental irony in line 3? How might it be argued that the effect, though startling, is not too broad?
3. What elements in language and rhythm tend to preserve the impression of natural speech?

LONDON
William Blake (1757–1827)

I wander thro' each charter'd street,
Near where the charter'd Thames does flow,
And mark in every face I meet
Marks of weakness, marks of woe.

In every cry of every Man,   5
In every Infant's cry of fear,
In every voice; in every ban,
The mind-forg'd manacles I hear.

How the Chimney-sweeper's cry
Every black'ning Church appalls,   10
And the hapless Soldier's sigh
Runs in blood down Palace walls.

But most thro' midnight streets I hear
How the youthful Harlot's curse
Blasts the new born Infant's tear,   15
And blights with plagues the Marriage hearse.

LONDON, 1802

William Wordsworth (1770–1850)

Milton! thou should'st be living at this hour:
England hath need of thee: she is a fen
Of stagnant waters: altar, sword, and pen,
Fireside, the heroic wealth of hall and bower,
Have forfeited their ancient English dower   5
Of inward happiness. We are selfish men:
Oh! raise us up, return to us again;
And give us manners, virtue, freedom, power.
Thy soul was like a Star, and dwelt apart:
Thou hadst a voice whose sound was like the
    sea: 10
Pure as the naked heavens, majestic, free,
So didst thou travel on life's common way,
In cheerful godliness; and yet thy heart
The lowliest duties on herself did lay.

Both Blake and Wordsworth are here writing of the degradation which had befallen London near the turn of the eighteenth century. The degradation is not only physical but spiritual: the fetters that London wears, according to Blake, are "mind-forged"; the happiness Wordsworth wishes restored is an "inward happiness." And both poets think of the degradation as a loss of power: Blake regards the city as corrupted; Wordsworth thinks of the city as a marsh full of stagnant waters. In both cases energy, whether bound or reduced to torpor, is not able to exert itself. So far the poems run parallel, but in other respects they diverge widely. A comparison of their differences will indicate vividly the fact that poetry does not reside in a particular subject but in a treatment of the subject.

A comparison of method will tell much about the meanings of the poems, and more particularly about that aspect of meaning we call tone. Blake's poem is essentially simpler than Wordsworth's. Blake organized his poem on this scheme: what the poet sees, and more important, what he hears as he traverses London. Wordsworth made his scheme of organization an appeal to Milton to return with his life-giving power to restore England to its spiritual health.

Blake's method is not inherently superior to Wordsworth's, but is more dramatic. In the first place, notice the climactic order in Blake's poem: it "goes somewhere." Stanza 1 is introductory, but though it is introductory, it has its own forceful structure that dramatizes the key idea of the poem. The word *chartered*, repeated in the first two lines, is used in two senses that mutually reinforce each other: first, in the sense of "laid out, bound by a chart or plan"; and second, in the sense of "hired," or "bought up." It is possible to read even a third meaning into *chartered*: charters are documents that originally guarantee liberties to men but that in the course of time become means of enslavement; the thwarting of natural freedom is the fundamental evil against which the poem is directed. The streets, the people, and the river itself, which normally is taken as an image of free movement, are all "charter'd"; the repetition of the word emphasizes the key idea of the poem.

But the statement of an idea as such is not enough to make poetry. So here it is dramatized in the act of being observed, here in the threefold repetition of the word *mark*; and we should note that there is an assonantal echo in *mark* of the repeated word *charter*, suggesting that both are involved in the same act of "marking" the evil "marks" that result from being "chartered"—that result, in fact, from the violation of natural freedom:

> And mark in every face I meet
> Marks of weakness, marks of woe.

More than this, however, is accomplished by the repetition, which here is akin to a child's way of speaking: "I marked a mark" or "I bled blood." Thus the elemental simplicity and directness of the child becomes a device not only of emphasis but for importing that elemental directness and simplicity —and urgency—into the perception of a complex and adult idea.

With stanza 2, the poet adds to the things seen as degradation the things heard, with, we note, the repetition of the word *cry* to emphasize the meaning of the sounds. Now things both seen and heard enter into the climactic progression, as the poet, after the general statement in stanza 1, moves into a list of particular perceptions. Stanza 2 states that in every cry the poet hears, he hears the clanking of fetters. In stanzas 3 and 4, he goes on to give specific examples of particular cries and their particular meanings—all of them aspects of the great general meaning of self-enslavement.

The chimney sweeper's cry appalls the church. Why? Because the fact of the enslavement of the little chimney sweeper in a deadening and disagreeable trade shakes the church, the institution consecrated to fight against things so unchristian. Why "black'ning Church"? London churches are, as a matter of fact, blackened by soot, but the poet seizes upon this detail for a special reason: he suggests that they share in the degradation of the boys whom they should protect—both are blackened by the soot. In the same way, the soldier's sigh runs like blood down the palace walls. Sighs do not literally flow like blood, of course, but Blake is justified in saying so; for what he is really saying is this: that soldiers mistreated by the state place a blood-guilt on the state.

Blake's indictment of London builds up to a terrific climax in stanza 4. Up to this, the poet has revealed an enslaved town, with the exploitation of both children and adults. In the last stanza he indicates that the very roots of life itself are poisoned. The fact that love is so misused that it can be bought and sold proclaims a curse on the child in the cradle and on love itself. The union of the sexes is the wellspring of life. To find poison there is the logical climax of the indictment, and Blake has pointed up the climax for us. "But most," he says, as this stanza begins. The phrase is not finished, and the fact that it is not and the resulting ambiguity are made use of by the poet. He may mean "but most frequent of all these cries," or "but most damning of all the cries of woe" or some other such phrase, and since he might mean any of them, and since he does not particularize any single one, the effect we receive is that of all of them combined. The ambiguity itself is *rich*. The phrase as it stands is ungrammatical, it is true, but it gives the impression of a man speaking rapidly and forcefully, eager to hurry on to something tremendously important, and so leaving unfinished an introductory phrase. And this is just the effect appropriate to the power of the climax of the poem.

We have commented upon the organic and climactic quality of the structure of Blake's "London," but we may now comment upon its economy as well; the sharp particularity of the images focuses the idea and the emotion. For instance, though the phrase "midnight streets" applies literally, we ask why the poet is wandering the city at that hour, and given the implications of even stanza 1, we feel that he must be a man driven forth by the urgency of his own agitation about the condition of men in London. At midnight the powers of evil are most abroad, and the harlot's curse is a summarizing image of the evil. To take another detail, the word *youthful* may apply literally to the harlot, but the usual connotations—"freshness," "joyfulness," "tenderness," "sympathy"—certainly do not. Blake is bringing those associations ironically into juxtaposition with the "Harlot's curse," with the curse that bears upon her and the curse that she utters. The curse, we are told, "blights." But blights what or whom? We do not know precisely. She may be cursing some particular person or event, merely cursing out of a blind rage at her own degradation, but in another and deeper sense, not intended by the harlot, her utterance is a blasting anathema on all the institutions of love—or rather, on what has been made of love, the basic fact of life, by human institutions. In other wards, the venereal disease that blights the "Marriage hearse" becomes a symbol for the spiritual corruption that blights society.

EXERCISES

1. In both Blake's poem and Wordsworth's poem we find expressed an indictment of society. In each case the idea may have been held with equal sincerity. What is the tone of Blake's poem and what that of Wordsworth's?

2. The two poets have dramatized the degradation of London in different ways. Wordsworth says that "altar, sword, and pen" have all alike "forfeited their ancient English dower." Blake uses utterances; he says that the cry of the infant and of the chimney sweeper and the sigh of the soldier and the curse of the harlot—all of them testify to London's degradation. In which poem do we find the greater sense of concreteness?

3. Wordsworth says that Milton, though he is

associated with the grand and elemental qualities of nature and had a soul that "dwelt apart," was willing to lay the "lowliest duties" upon his heart. Is this a startling contrast? What is its relation to the basic theme of Wordsworth's sonnet? To its tone?

4. What comparisons between the two poems in connection with structure, metrics, or verbal quality do you think might be relevant to the question of tone?

ON THE LATE MASSACRE
IN PIEDMONT

John Milton (1608–1674)

Avenge, O Lord, thy slaughtered saints, whose
　bones
Lie scattered on the Alpine mountains cold;
Even them who kept thy truth so pure of old,
When all our fathers worshiped stocks and stones,
Forget not; in thy book record their groans　　5
Who were thy sheep, and in their ancient fold
Slain by the bloody Piemontese, that rolled
Mother with infant down the rocks. Their moans
The vales redoubled to the hills, and they
To heaven. Their martyred blood and ashes sow　10
O'er all th' Italian fields, where still doth sway
The triple tyrant,[1] that from these may grow
A hundredfold, who, having learnt thy way,
Early may fly the Babylonian[2] woe.

In 1655, in northern Italy, a number of the Protestant Waldensian sect, which had been enjoying freedom of worship, were massacred by Catholic troops quartered among them. Milton—who, as secretary to Cromwell, wrote an official letter of protest to the duke of Savoy—composed this sonnet as a direct expression of his sense of outrage. In its directness, his poem stands in contrast to the ironical attitude, and method, in some of the preceding poems. Even so we must not assume that the heinousness of the event and the sincerity of the author's sense of outrage are what gives the poem power. It is the realization—the imaginative projection—of those things that count. And here the basic power depends on the realization in image

and language; it is, to put the matter another way, stylistic.

　　Let us scan the first two lines:

Avenge, | O Lord, | thy slaugh- | tered saints, |
　whose bones
Lie scat- | tered on | the Al- | pine moun- |
　tains cold.*

In general, the massing of accents, primary and secondary, gives weightiness and force. More particularly, the grouping of four accents in the last foot of line 1 and the first of line 2 focuses the symbolic force of the passage on *bones,* and then the metrical accent on the word *on* (which is usually not rhetorically significant) gives the image of bones scattered in a desolate scene a vivid immediacy, an effect supported by the falling away into regular accentuation in the subsequent feet. But notice, too, how the isolation of the monosyllabic word *cold* after the previous polysyllables reinforces the desolation of the scene. This, in other words, is one instance of the way whereby style dramatizes what might otherwise be little more than bare statement.

EXERCISES

1. Characterize the tone of the sonnet. Is it a curse? A prayer? Or what? Is there a change of tone in line 12?
2. In lines 3–14, what metrical features seem worthy of comment, especially in relation to tone?
3. Is the tone of the poem affected by the presence of the numerous monosyllables? By the quality of the vowels?

IF WE MUST DIE

Claude McKay (1890–1948)

If we must die—let it not be like hogs
Hunted and penned in an inglorious spot,
While round us bark the mad and hungry dogs,
Making their mock at our accursed lot.

---

[1] The "triple tyrant" is the pope, who would claim authority in heaven and hell as well as upon the earth.　[2] Protestants of the time of the Reformation regarded the corruption of the papacy as described in *Revelation* 14:8, 17:5, and 18:2; 17:5 includes the phrase "Babylon the Great, the Mother of Harlots and Abominations of the Earth."

　　* Some readers might quarrel with the markings of *thy* in line 1 and *-pine* in line 2, preferring to read *thy* with a secondary accent and *-pine* as an unaccented syllable.

If we must die—oh, let us nobly die,   5
So that our precious blood may not be shed
In vain; then even the monsters we defy
Shall be constrained to honor us though dead!
Oh, Kinsmen! We must meet the common foe;
Though far outnumbered, let us show us brave.   10
And for their thousand blows deal one death-
    blow!
What though before us lies the open grave?
Like men we'll face the murderous, cowardly pack,
Pressed to the wall, dying, but fighting back!

EXERCISE

This poem, like the three before, is a response to
evil in the world. All three of the preceding
poems, however, present a specific evil; this sonnet
refers only to an unspecified "common foe." Try
to describe the tone here. How do you justify your
description?

A DIRGE
Percy Bysshe Shelley (1792–1822)

> Rough wind, that moanest loud
>   Grief too sad for song;
> Wild wind, when sullen cloud
>   Knells all the night long;
> Sad storm, whose tears are vain,   5
> Bare woods, whose branches strain,
> Deep caves and dreary main,—
>   Wail, for the world's wrong!

EXERCISE

Shelley's dirge is even less specific than McKay's
sonnet, for McKay was black; it deals with the
"world's wrong"—with evil in the abstract. For
all its brevity, it is a powerful poem. How does
Shelley's cry of what we may term world pain
achieve the dramatic power of poetry?

GROUP 2: GOD AND THE WORLD

THE DAY OF JUDGEMENT
Jonathan Swift (1667–1745)

> With a whirl of thought oppressed,
> I sunk from reverie to rest.
> An horrid vision seized my head,
> I saw the graves give up their dead.

Jove, armed with terrors, burst the skies,   5
And thunder roars, and lightning flies!
Amazed, confused, its fate unknown,
The world stands trembling at his throne.
While each pale sinner hung his head,
Jove, nodding, shook the Heavens, and said,   10
'Offending race of human kind,
By nature, reason, learning, blind;
You who through frailty stepped aside;
And you who never fell—through pride;
You who in different sects have shammed,   15
And come to see each other damned
(So some folks told you, but they knew
No more of Jove's designs than you):
—The world's mad business now is o'er,
And I resent these pranks no more.   20
—I to such blockheads set my wit!
I damn such fools!—Go, go, you're bit.'

EXERCISE

1. Jonathan Swift was himself a parson. Does this
poem suggest that he was too skeptical to be a
good parson? Or is this the kind of poem that a
serious man of God might on occasion feel the
need to write?
2. What is the effect on the tone of the poem of
the suggestion (l. 14) that it was only pride that
prevented some of the souls from falling? And
(l. 15) that many of them are expectantly waiting
to see the others damned?
3. The eighteenth-century expression "you're bit"
meant something like the present-day expression
"you've been had." Why is this last line of the
poem such an effective "punch line"? How would
you define the tone of this poem?
4. Is this the only kind of God that these "sinners"
would understand?
5. Why do you think that Swift uses the word
Jove instead of *God*?

CHANNEL FIRING
Thomas Hardy (1840–1928)

> That night your great guns, unawares,
> Shook all our coffins as we lay,
> And broke the chancel window-squares,
> We thought it was the Judgment-day
>
> And sat upright. While drearisome   5
> Arose the howl of wakened hounds:
> The mouse let fall the altar-crumb,
> The worms drew back into the mounds,

The glebe cow drooled. Till God called, "No;
It's gunnery practice out at sea   10
Just as before you went below;
The world is as it used to be:

"All nations striving strong to make
Red war yet redder. Mad as hatters
They do no more for Christés sake   15
Than you who are helpless in such matters.

"That this is not the judgment-hour
For some of them's a blessed thing,
For if it were they'd have to scour
Hell's floor for so much threatening. . . .   20

"Ha, ha. It will be warmer when
I blow the trumpet (if indeed
I ever do; for you are men,
And rest eternal sorely need)."

So down we lay again. "I wonder,   25
Will the world ever saner be,"
Said one, "than when He sent us under
In our indifferent century!"

And many a skeleton shook his head.
"Instead of preaching forty year,"   30
My neighbour Parson Thirdly said,
"I wish I had stuck to pipes and beer."

Again the guns disturbed the hour,
Roaring their readiness to avenge,
As far inland as Stourton Tower,   35
And Camelot, and starlit Stonehenge.

Hardy's poem, like so many before it, comments on the irony and pity in man's continuing propensity for the massive bloodletting that war is. In ancient Greece Mars was considered a stupid and blundering god, and ever since the blind stupidity of war has remained a theme in literature.

How does Hardy make his poem fresh and interesting? By a fresh dramatization, we should probably answer, and the freshness of the dramatization is here associated with rather complex shifts and contrasts of tone.

To begin with, the speaker is a skeleton of a man who has, we gather, been comfortably dead in his coffin for a century or so, and to whom gunnery practice out at sea is of little more significance than a nocturnal racket that disturbs his long repose. Certainly, he does not speak in moral outrage, as the theme conventionally demands.

Another, and associated, contrast is between the expected atmosphere of horror in a graveyard scene and the comic, Halloween sort of scene that Hardy describes here. If the hound's howl is drearisome, the little mouse letting fall the altar crumb when the great guns boom is simply cute. And the skeletons seem merely peevish at the disturbance. After all, they are well accustomed to their way of life—or rather, way of death. It is God who speaks in outrage at man's murderous stupidity, but even he sees the situation with an ironic detachment, merging, now and then, into sarcasm. In the end all that the skeletons feel is a mild wonderment that things go on in the same old way, or, in the case of the dead parson, a regret that he had spent time trying to make the world better and not looked out more for his little personal pleasures.

After these incidental contrasts in the tone presented and the tone expected, or in incidental shifts of tone along the way, there comes, with the last stanza, a fundamental shift of tone. The gunnery becomes terrifyingly immediate, and in the last two lines—with the echoes of gunfire dying inland past Stourton Tower, Camelot, and Stonehenge—we have the evocation of mankind's blood-drenched history, not now ironically regarded, or with only the irony of its incorrigibility. With the last stanza the poem leaps into life.

EXERCISES

1. Point out the various comic effects in the poem.
2. What metrical qualities are involved in the shift of tone in the last stanza? In what way can it be said that the first two lines of the last stanza echo the first line of the poem? What significance, in structure or idea, do you attribute to this fact?
3. Is God's way of speaking (including vocabulary and attitude) consistent throughout? If not, what is the effect here? What kind of personality do you assume this God to have?
4. Stourton Tower marks the site of King Alfred's victory over the Danes in 890. Camelot is the fabled capital of the fifth-century King Arthur. Stonehenge, on Salisbury Plain, is a prehistoric monument, the purpose of which has been variously interpreted, but which some experts think

was constructed to observe the apparent movements of the sun, moon, and stars. Since all these places are in the southwest of England they are spots to which the sound of naval guns would penetrate. Do these places have any other kind of significance for the meaning of the poem?

5. Scan lines 35–36. What effect results from the massing of accents here, especially at the end of line 36?

THE FURY OF AERIAL BOMBARDMENT

Richard Eberhart (b. 1904)

You would think the fury of aerial bombardment
Would rouse God to relent; the infinite spaces
Are still silent. He looks on shock-pried faces.
History, even, does not know what is meant.

You would feel that after so many centuries　　　5
God would give man to repent; yet he can kill
As Cain could, but with multitudinous will.
No farther advanced than in his ancient furies.

Was man made stupid to see his own stupidity?
Is God by definition indifferent, beyond us all?　10
Is the eternal truth man's fighting soul
Wherein the Beast ravens in his own avidity?

Of Van Wettering I speak, and Averill,
Names on a list, whose faces I do not recall
But they are gone to early death, who late in
　　school　　　15
Distinguished the belt feed lever from the belt
　　holding pawl.

EXERCISES

1. Compare this poem in tone and method with Hardy's "Channel Firing."
2. What difference in tone do you notice between the first three stanzas and the last stanza of the poem? What do you think is the reason for this difference?
3. Both these poems deal with the horror of war. What similarities in idea—that is, in theme—do they exhibit?

Time

Turn to subsections 19.5 and 19.6 and read our discussions of the effect of word breaks and rhetorical pauses on poetic meter. Note especially our examples and explanations of how the timing of rhetorical units—

words and phrases—may affect the tone of a poem. Perform the exercises suggested there in addition to those that follow here.

EXERCISES

1. Comment on the relation of monosyllabic and polysyllabic words in Wordsworth's "London, 1802."
2. Mark the caesuras in Milton's "On the Late Massacre in Piedmont." In general, do you notice any difference in the position of caesuras in the first ten lines and in the last four lines? With what other technical difference does this seem to be associated? Can you connect this difference with a change of tone toward the end of the sonnet? Locate the run-on lines. With what metrical and rhetorical effects are these associated? That is, with what tone? Notice in lines 2 and 14 that the last foot begins with the final syllable (unaccented) of a divided word, and that this tends to isolate the final word (the accented syllable). Notice, too, that in each case here the line is end-stopped. What is the dramatic effect? Why is the effect more positive in line 14 than in line 2?
3. Scan the first three quatrains of "Channel Firing," by Hardy. Notice that line 1 exhibits a massing of accents:

That night your great guns unawares

and that the three following lines are generally regular and uninsistent. But notice, too, that line 5, the first line of the next stanza, opens, again, with the same general situation as line 1:

And sat upright. While drearisome

Is the rest of the general pattern repeated into line 9? What do you make of this? Is some contrast being set up metrically and rhetorically that is significant for the poem? In this connection it may be remarked that, in stanzas 1 and 2, the last line runs on into the succeeding stanza, with the run-on, in each case, breaking three lines of quite regular and almost pattering meter. The run-on, too, comes to a full stop, and involves, as we have seen, the massing of accents on monosyllables:

In line 5, stanza 2: And sat upright.

In line 9, stanza 3: The glebe cow drooled.

Do you observe other instances of a tension between the formality of stanza and line on the one hand and the tendency to disintegrate them on the other?

GROUP 3: TENDERNESS TOWARD CHILDREN

TO IANTHE

Percy Bysshe Shelley (1792–1822)

I love thee, Baby! for thine own sweet sake;
  Those azure eyes, that faintly dimpled cheek,
  Thy tender frame, so eloquently weak,
Love in the sternest heart of hate might wake;
But more when o'er thy fitfull slumber bending   5
  Thy mother folds thee to her wakeful heart,
  While love and pity, in her glances blending,
All that thy passive eyes can feel impart:
More, when some feeble lineaments of her,
  Who bore thy weight beneath her spotless bosom   10
  As with deep love I read thy face, recur,—
More dear art thou, O fair and fragile blossom;
  Dearest when thy tender traits express
  The image of thy mother's loveliness.

With this poem we turn to a group involving tender feeling for a child. In such poems the danger is that the tenderness will lead to mere sentimentality—that is, to the statement of emotion that does not seem dramatically justified in the work. Looking back on the poems in group 1, we may say that in them, with their "big" subjects, the temptation for the poet was to indulge in grandiloquence or empty rhetoric. Similarly, in poems with more intimate subjects, tone is a potential problem; the poet must achieve tone that seems sincere because justified dramatically in the poem. Notice that here we say "seems sincere," for the intensity of feeling in actual life does not necessarily mean that a subject will be dramatically realized in a poem.

    The present poem has for its subject the love of a father for his child. The father says that he loves the child because the innocence and weakness of the child would provoke love in even the hardest heart; and that he loves it even more because its tender traits express something of the tenderness and appeal of the mother. That is what the poem "says," and the feeling that is the subject of the poem must be a fairly usual one. But a poem is not good merely because it states a usual feeling, no matter how admirable that feeling may be. It must bring renewed strength to the subject, if the poem is to be better than a mere prose statement of the subject. As Wordsworth said, the poem must strip off "the veil of familiarity" from the subject.

EXERCISES

1. Here is a version of Shelley's poem in which descriptive words have been replaced. Compare it to the original version and underscore the words that have been replaced. Do you feel that much has been lost by the rewriting? If you find that little has been lost, do you agree that in this poem Shelley used easy stereotypes of sentimentality and did not really try to dramatize the subject?

I love thee, Baby, for thine own dear sake;
  Those bluest eyes, that gently dimpled cheek,
  Thy budding frame, so eloquently weak,
Love in the cruelest heart of hate might wake;
But more when o'er thy troubled slumber bending
  Thy mother folds thee to her watchful heart,
  While love and pity, in her glances blending,
All thy receptive eyes can feel impart:
More, when some weakest lineaments of her,
  Who bore thy weight beneath her fairest bosom,
  As with great love I read thy face, recur,—
More dear art thou, O white and tender blossom;
  Dearest when most thy fragile traits express
  The image of thy mother's loveliness.

2. Turn back to Shelley's "Ode to the West Wind" (sec. 13) and try to rewrite section III, IV, or V of the poem, as we have done with "To Ianthe." Remember that you must consider meter and verbal quality. How easy do you find the rewriting?

3. Try to rewrite "On the Late Massacre in Piedmont," by Milton, in group 1 of this section, or "God's Grandeur," by Hopkins, in group 6 of section 16.

4. If you feel that you are unable to rewrite such big, powerful poems, try to rewrite "O Western Wind" in group 4 of this section.

BELLS FOR JOHN WHITESIDE'S DAUGHTER

John Crowe Ransom (1888–1974)

  There was such speed in her little body,
  And such lightness in her footfall,

It is no wonder that her brown study
Astonishes us all.

Her wars were bruited in our high window.   5
We looked among orchard trees and beyond,
Where she took arms against her shadow,
Or harried unto the pond

The lazy geese, like a snow cloud
Dripping their snow on the green grass,   10
Tricking and stopping, sleepy and proud,
Who cried in goose, Alas,

For the tireless heart within the little
Lady with rod that made them rise
From their noon apple dreams, and scuttle   15
Goose-fashion under the skies!

But now go the bells, and we are ready;
In one house we are sternly stopped
To say we are vexed at her brown study,
Lying so primly propped.   20

This poem is one of tenderness toward a child who has just died. It is spoken, presumably, just before the funeral service, for the speaker is among those who gathered together "in one house." Furthermore, the speaker is a person—perhaps even a father—who has known the child well, who, it seems from the poem, has lived either in the same house or in one nearby, for the noise the child made had been under the speaker's "high window," perhaps disturbing his work or meditation. If the poem is about such a sad occasion, and one in which the speaker, we assume, is deeply involved, then why does the poem make such a minimal declaration of grief? What kind of man is this? Is he hardhearted? Indifferent? Self-absorbed? Read the poem with close attention. Read it aloud several times, for perhaps the rhythms will tell you something about the nature of the man and of his attitude toward the occasion.

Certain significant words are the keys to the tone, and to the meaning, of "Bells for John Whiteside's Daughter." One key, perhaps *the* key, is the word *astonishes* in line 4. The child's "brown study"—this sudden moment of absorbed meditation—is what astonishes the speaker, because she had been, clearly, an active, even a somewhat naughty, child. The death of a child is, of course, astonishing; childhood is the age of vitality and growth. The word *astonishes*, however, is scarcely the one we would ordinarily use to describe the effect of unexpected death. By exploring the contrast involved, the poet makes the word signify profound grief—but a grief somehow mastered, as by a superhuman effort.

Lines 5 and 7 contain further keys to the tone of the poem. In line 7, the child's playing is described as taking "arms against her shadow," a phrase that seems somewhat odd. Similarly, the word *bruited* in line 5 is a strange, old-fashioned, even learned word. It puts some distance between the man in the high window and the little girl, and, in a way, prepares us for the comparison. At first, we may accept the phrase and the word as part of the speaker's rather high-flown way of talking, but by the end of the poem we sense that the comparison is exactly suitable to the situation. The shadow against which the child takes arms is, we now realize, the shadow of death; all her play had been a losing battle against it. The idea does not come as a set comparison; dramatically, it grows on up to the moment of our shocking realization —which we share with those gathered in the house—that the little girl could die, that she is, in fact, dead.

Still another key word is *vexed* in line 19. Suppose we changed it to *grieved, outraged, horrified, anguished, heartbroken,* or *desolated.* What would be lost or gained? In thinking this over, you may look back on the image of the little girl playing noisily and perhaps a little naughtily below the high window. Which of all the words seems to fit that image? Only *vexed* is precisely right. It is a way of simultaneously denying and declaring grief, an understatement that makes the reader more ready to believe in the speaker's grief because the reader has, in a sense, entered into the process of developing the poem. That is, the reader has had to seize and "feel" the implications. He has not been merely bludgeoned by assertion and declaration.

EXERCISES

1. Examine the main image of the poem (ll. 8–16), that of the little girl driving the geese out of the apple orchard and back to the pond. The scene is

one from a fairy tale, as it were, with the geese talking and complaining as they "scuttle goose-fashion" across a picture-book landscape. What does this fanciful description indicate about the speaker's attitude? Is this a scene that he casually happens to remember, or do we feel it is deeply important to him?

2. Look up the origin of the word *astonish* in a dictionary. Do you now find that the meaning of line 4 is even richer?

3. What do you make of the words *primly* and *propped* in line 20 to describe a little girl? When are little girls prim? With what in the poem is such primness a contrast? What does the primness here signify? And what kind of object has to be propped? How effective is the word *propped* here? How does it qualify *primly*? Waiving the matters of meter and rime, discuss the difference in meaning if line 20 were "Lying propped so primly." In other words, what is gained by the original placement of the word? What is the effect of the rime with *stopped* in line 18? Suppose we rewrote that line to reverse the order of *sternly* and *stopped*. What would be the effect? Suppose we changed *sternly* to *grimly*, *sharply*, *unexpectedly*, *mercilessly*, *sadly*, or *painfully*. What then?

4. What is the tone of this poem?

SPRING AND FALL

To a Young Child

Gerard Manley Hopkins (1844–1889)

> Márgarét, are you grieving
> Over Goldengrove unleaving?
> Leáves, líke the things of man, you
> With your fresh thoughts care for, can you?
> Áh! ás the heart grows older   5
> It will come to such sights colder
> By and by, nor spare a sigh
> Though worlds of wanwood leafmeal lie;
> And yet you wíll weep and know why,
> Now no matter, child, the name: 10
> Sórrow's spríngs áre the same.
> Nor mouth had, no nor mind, expressed
> What heart heard of, ghost guessed:
> It ís the blight man was born for,
> It is Margaret you mourn for.   15

EXERCISES

1. What is the situation implied by the poem? Who is speaking to Margaret? What is implied as to the character of the speaker?

2. The child is sorrowful at the falling of the leaves. But what do the leaves come to stand for that justifies the speaker's question? How can you say that you merely think you are weeping for the loss of the leaves, when actually you are mourning for yourself?

3. What is meant by "fresh" thoughts—particularly in this context? *Wanwood* suggests a leafless wood that is pale and gray. What else does it suggest? *Leafmeal* is a word made up presumably on the analogy of words like *piecemeal*. What else does it imply? The word *ghost* in line 13 is apparently used in the sense of "spirit" or "soul." Compare it in meaning to "Holy Ghost," that is, "Holy Spirit."

4. Compare the subject and tone of this poem with those of "Bells for John Whiteside's Daughter." How close are they?

THE CHANGELING

James Russell Lowell (1819–1891)

> I had a little daughter,
> And she was given to me
> To lead me gently backward
> To the Heavenly Father's knee,
> That I, by the force of nature,   5
> Might in some dim wise divine
> The depth of his infinite patience
> To this wayward soul of mine.
>
> I know not how others saw her,
> But to me she was wholly fair,   10
> And the light of the heaven she came from
> Still lingered and gleamed in her hair;
> For it was as wavy and golden,
> And as many changes took,
> As the shadows of sun-gilt ripples   15
> On the yellow bed of a brook.
>
> To what can I liken her smiling
> Upon me, her kneeling lover,
> How it leaped from her lips to her eyelids,
> And dimpled her wholly over,   20
> Till her outstretched hands smiled also,
> And I almost seemed to see
> The very heart of her mother
> Sending sun through her veins to me!
>
> She had been with us scarce a twelve-month   25
> And it hardly seemed a day,
> When a troop of wandering angels
> Stole my little daughter away;
> Or perhaps those heavenly Zingari
> But loosed the hampering strings,   30
> And when they had opened her cage-door,
> My little bird used her wings.
>
> But they left in her stead a changeling,
> A little angel child,

That seems like her bud in full blossom,   35
  And smiles as she never smiled:
When I wake in the morning, I see it
  Where she always used to lie,
And I feel as weak as a violet
  Alone 'neath the awful sky.   40

As weak, yet as trustful also;
  For the whole year long I see
All the wonders of faithful Nature
  Still worked for the love of me;
Winds wander, and dews drip earthward,   45
  Rain falls, suns rise and set,
Earth whirls, and all but to prosper
  A poor little violet.

This child is not mine as the first was,
  I cannot sing it to rest,   50
I cannot lift it up fatherly
  And bless it upon my breast;
Yet it lies in my little one's cradle
  And sits in my little one's chair,
And the light of the heaven she's gone to   55
  Transfigures its golden hair.

EXERCISES

1. Lowell suffered great grief over the death of a little daughter. Does his poem seem better to you because of this fact?
2. Study the rhythm of stanza 1. How do you respond to it?
3. Examine the imagery of stanza 3. Can "smiling" really leap from lips to eyelids? What, in fact, have eyelids to do with smiling? One might say *eyes*, but not *eyelids*. Did the poet just tack on the word *lids* for rhythm? And how could smiling dimple a baby's body all over? Can the poet have really visualized what he was saying? Can hands smile? Can sunshine run down veins from a heart and come out in a hand? Has the poet really considered anything he was saying, or was he merely satisfied if an image or idea sounded vaguely poetical?

ON SOLOMON PAVY

A child of Queen Elizabeth's Chapel

Ben Jonson (1573–1637)

Weep with me, all you that read
  This little story:
And know for whom a tear you shed
  Death's self is sorry.
'Twas a child that so did thrive   5

  In grace and feature,
As Heaven and Nature seem'd to strive
  Which own'd the creature.
Years he number'd scarce thirteen
  When Fates turn'd cruel,   10
Yet three full zodiacs had he been
  The stage's jewel;
And did act (what now we moan)
  Old men so duly,
As sooth the Parcae thought him one,   15
  He play'd so truly.
So, by error, to his fate
  They all consented;
But, viewing him since, alas, too late!
  They have repented;   20
And have sought, to give new birth,
  In baths to steep him;
But, being so much too good for earth,
  Heaven vows to keep him.

Style in poetry, and conventions, change from age to age. In this early seventeenth-century poem on the death of a child, the summons to the reader to weep is, for instance, a convention of the period, and we do not have to give it a realistic criticism in our own terms. Elaborately turned, polite compliments characterize certain kinds of poetry in the seventeenth century, and, too, wit was then more common in serious poetry than is now the practice.

EXERCISE

Considering its period of origin, characterize the tone of this poem. How does it compare to the tone of "Bells for John Whiteside's Daughter"? Or to that of "To Ianthe"? How does the tone here relate to the specified age of Pavy? To his usual roles on the stage? What does the tone indicate about the intimacy of the relation of Jonson to the child?

A REFUSAL TO MOURN THE DEATH, BY FIRE, OF A CHILD IN LONDON

Dylan Thomas (1914–1953)

Never until the mankind making
Bird beast and flower
Fathering and all humbling darkness
Tells with silence the last light breaking
And the still hour   5
Is come of the sea tumbling in harness

And I must enter again the round
Zion of the water bead
And the synagogue of the ear of corn
Shall I let pray the shadow of a sound   10
Or sow my salt seed
In the least valley of sackcloth to mourn

The majesty and burning of the child's death.
I shall not murder
The mankind of her going with a grave truth   15
Nor blaspheme down the stations of the breath
With any further
Elegy of innocence and youth.

Deep with the first dead lies London's daughter,
Robed in the long friends,   20
The grains beyond age, the dark veins of her
    mother
Secret by the unmourning water
Of the riding Thames.
After the first death, there is no other.

      The child here referred to is one killed
in a firebombing of London in the early days
of World War II. This fact may give a special
poignancy to the poem in that the child may
stand, in a way, for all such victims in a time
of terror and brutality. The death of the
child is significant, it might be said, beyond
any particularity of grief—as a mark of the
tragedy of the human lot.

      In our study of earlier poems in this
group we have seen how poets by understatement, irony, or playful wit may write effective poems of grief. Here the poet declares
that he refuses to "mourn," but his refusal is,
we may say, based on the fact that the subject
is too big for mere mourning. Certainly, it
is not treated with an irony of understatement. The method is direct and aims at high
eloquence.

EXERCISES

1. The phrase "stations of the breath" is obviously modeled upon "stations of the cross."
What are some of the other religious terms that
occur in this poem? For what purpose does the
poet use them?
2. What is the tone of this poem?
3. What difference, if any, derives from the fact
that the child was killed in a war now fading into
history? Do you think that a reader of the 1940s

might have responded more immediately than is
now possible?

AT THE SLACKENING OF THE TIDE
James Wright (b. 1927)

Today I saw a woman wrapped in rags
Leaping along the beach to curse the sea.
Her child lay floating in the oil, away
From oarlock, gunwale, and the blades of oars.
The skinny lifeguard, raging at the sky,   5
Vomited sea, and fainted on the sand.

The cold simplicity of evening falls
Dead on my mind.
And underneath the piles the water
Leaps up, leaps up, and sags down slowly,
    farther   10
Than seagulls disembodied in the drag
Of oil and foam.

Plucking among the oyster shells a man
Stares at the sea, that stretches on its side.
Now far along the beach, a hungry dog   15
Announces everything I knew before:
Obliterate naiads weeping underground,
Where Homer's tongue thickens with human
    howls.

I would do anything to drag myself
Out of this place: 20
Root up a seaweed from the water,
To stuff it in my mouth, or deafen me,
Free me from all the force of human speech;
Go drown, almost.

Warm in the pleasure of the dawn I came   25
To sing my song
And look for mollusks in the shallows,
The whorl and coil that pretty up the earth,
While far below us, flaring in the dark,
The stars go out.   30

What did I do to kill my time today,
After the woman ranted in the cold,
The mellow sea, the sound blown dark as wine?
After the lifeguard rose up from the waves
Like a sea-lizard with the scales washed off?   35
Sit there, admiring sunlight on a shell?

Abstract with terror of the shell, I stared
Over the waters where
God brooded for the living all one day.
Lonely for weeping, starved for a sound of
    mourning.   40
I bowed my head, and heard the sea far off
Washing its hands.

The dead child here, like the child in Dylan Thomas's poem, is unknown to the poet, but in this case, at least, the speaker has been a witness to the drowning of the child; he has seen the nausea and despair of the exhausted lifeguard and the raging grief of the distracted mother. He does not "refuse to mourn" but admits to the full response he feels: the beauty and peace of the day—and of the world—is ruined, and he suddenly becomes aware of the brute suffering and irrational tragedy of the world. Although he does not know the child, the event has struck at his very sense of life. Even so, even as he announces in the fourth stanza the extent of his emotional involvement, he qualifies it by some streak of honesty and realism. To escape, he says, he would drown—"almost." And with the word *almost* we are prepared to accept the extravagance of the declaration of emotion in the preceding lines. In Ransom's "Bells for John Whiteside's Daughter," the speaker's tone is one of ironic understatement, indicating that he has stoically mastered his emotion (and thus powerfully appealing to our own). In Wright's poem, on the other hand, the speaker's tone is directly emotional; he utters the poem while he is still trying to master his emotional shock at the child's death. But notice that in Wright's poem, the shock is finally mastered.

EXERCISES

1. In stanza 3 what is the "everything" that the speaker had "known before" but, presumably, had not known so poignantly? In other words, explain the last two lines of the stanza.
2. In stanza 7, why is the speaker "lonely for weeping"? How does this statement lead to the final statement that he "heard the sea far off / Washing its hands"? If you cannot answer this last question, hunt up Matthew 27:18–24 in the Bible.
3. What do you make of the phrase "terror of the shell" in line 37?
4. What is the tone of stanza 7? Try putting yourself in the role of the speaker and reading the stanza aloud until it feels right to you.

COME UP FROM THE FIELDS, FATHER

Walt Whitman (1819–1892)

Come up from the fields, father, here's a letter
    from our Pete,
And come to the front door, mother, here's a letter
    from thy dear son.

Lo, 'tis autumn,
Lo, where the trees, deeper green, yellower and
    redder,
Cool and sweeten Ohio's villages with leaves
    fluttering in the moderate wind,   5
Where apples ripe in the orchards hang and
    grapes on the trellised vines,
(Smell you the smell of the grapes on the vines?
Smell you the buckwheat where the bees were
    lately buzzing?)
Above all, lo, the sky so calm, so transparent after
    the rain, and with wondrous clouds,
Below too, all calm, all vital and beautiful, and
    the farm prospers well.   10

Down in the fields all prospers well,
But now from the fields come, father, come at the
    daughter's call,
And come to the entry, mother, to the front door
    come right away.

Fast as she can she hurries, something ominous,
    her steps trembling,
She does not tarry to smooth her hair nor adjust
    her cap.   15

Open the envelope quickly,
O this is not our son's writing, yet his name is
    signed,
O a strange hand writes for our dear son, O
    stricken mother's soul!
All swims before her eyes, flashes with black, she
    catches the main words only.
Sentences broken, *gunshot wound in the breast,*
    cavalry skirmish, taken to hospital,   20
At present low, but will soon be better.

Ah, now the single figure to me,
Amid all teeming and wealthy Ohio with all its
    cities and farms,
Sickly white in the face and dull in the head, very
    faint,
By the jamb of a door leans.   25

Grieve not so, dear mother (the just-grown
    daughter speaks through her sobs,

The little sisters huddle around speechless and
    dismayed),
*See, dearest mother, the letter says Pete will soon
be better.*

Alas, poor boy, he will never be better (nor maybe
    needs to be better, that brave and simple soul),
While they stand at home at the door he is dead
    already,   30
The only son is dead.

But the mother needs to be better,
She with thin form presently drest in black,
By day her meals untouched, then at night fitfully
    sleeping, often waking,
In the midnight waking, weeping, longing with
    one deep longing,   35

O that she might withdraw unnoticed, silent from
    life escape and withdraw,
To follow, to seek, to be with her dear dead son.

Although this poem was written during
the American Civil War, the episode it describes might essentially belong to any war.
It is typical of war poems in general, and the
emotion it provokes is typical, too. Because
the poet actually stresses its typicality, we
may assume that what he found most moving
about the subject was, in fact, its common-
ness. But the typical, to be effective in literature, must be also vivid and immediate.
How, we must ask ourselves, did Whitman
manage to stress the typicality and, at the
same time, achieve the dramatic force of the
particular?

EXERCISES

1. Who speaks the first two lines of the poem? The
father is addressed directly as "father," the mother
as "mother," and the absent son is referred to as
"our Pete." In line 12 it is said that the father
comes to the "daughter's call," but we notice that
in lines 26 and 28, when the daughter speaks, a
direct quotation is indicated by italics. Would the
daughter, addressing her mother, have referred to
Pete as "thy dear son"? The mother is to become
the central character of the poem, certainly, but
would the daughter thus single her out with the
word *thy*? Can we say that the poet somehow

merges his voice with the daughter's, by a kind of
ventriloquism, as it were, identifying himself with
her?
2. But who speaks lines 3–15? Who is the "you"
of lines 7 and 8? Why this personal and intimate
question? What does it do for the poem?
3. Notice the complications in lines 16–18. This
passage is all one sentence, broken only by com-
mas; but line 16 is addressed to the mother (by
whom?), line 17 and most of 18 apparently are
uttered by the mother as she fumbles with the
paper, and the phrase "O stricken mother's soul" is
a pitying exclamation not addressed to her. What
does this complication of reference imply about
the poet's attitude toward the material?
4. In line 22, the mother is specified as the "single
figure," and with the word *me* the poet enters,
specifically and officially, the poem. The poet is
shown looking at the mother, singling her out not
only from the family but from the whole world. In
lines 22–25, how is this indicated? How does the
very structure of the sentence (it is all one sentence) dramatize the intent?
5. With line 28 what new role does the speaker
assume? For instance, he knows things that the
family do not know. Notice, too, how he makes
the wordplay with *better*. Would the mother accept his version of "better"? And in line 32, what
is the meaning of *better*? What are we to make
of the last two lines? Is this merely a paraphrase,
in indirect discourse, of the mother's longing? Or
is it the poet's notion of what would be "better"
for the mother, so that the last two lines (separated from the previous section, though in the
same sentence) might be an exclamation of desire
uttered by the poet? Or is it a fusion of both?
6. In what way is the shock of grief "mastered" in
this poem? On what tone does it end?

LITTLE BOY BLUE

Eugene Field (1850–1895)

The little toy dog is covered with dust,
    But sturdy and staunch he stands;
And the little toy soldier is red with rust,
    And his musket molds in his hands.
Time was when the little toy dog was new   5
    And the soldier was passing fair,
And that was the time when our Little Boy Blue
    Kissed them and put them there.

"Now, don't you go till I come," he said,
    "And don't you make any noise!"   10

So toddling off to his trundle-bed
  He dreamed of the pretty toys.
And as he was dreaming, an angel song
  Awakened our Little Boy Blue.—
Oh, the years are many, the years are long,   15
  But the little toy friends are true.

Ay, faithful to Little Boy Blue they stand,
  Each in the same old place,
Awaiting the touch of a little hand,
  The smile of a little face.   20
And they wonder, as waiting these long years
    through,
  In the dust of that little chair,
What has become of our Little Boy Blue
  Since he kissed them and put them there.

EXERCISES

1. Does this poem more resemble Lowell's "The Changeling" or Thomas's "A Refusal to Mourn"? Explain your choice.
2. Of all the poems in group 3, which do you prefer? Why?

GROUP 4: LOVE

O WESTERN WIND

Anonymous

  O Western wind, when wilt thou blow
    That the small rain down can rain?
  Christ, that my love were in my arms,
    And I in my bed again!

EXERCISES

1. At first glance this anonymous poem of the sixteenth century seems to be about as simple as a poem might be—a lover's cry of longing to have his beloved again in his arms. But the mere cry—which constitutes the last two lines of the poem—would not, taken in itself, be poetry. The poetry depends on the relationship between the first two lines and the last two. Try to explain this relationship. How does it help determine the tone of the poem?
2. Suppose the last line were revised to "And she smiled at me again." Would the poem be better or worse? Why?

A RED, RED ROSE
Robert Burns (1759–1796)

  Oh, my Luve is like a red, red rose,
    That's newly sprung in June:
  Oh, my Luve is like the melodie
    That's sweetly play'd in tune.

  As fair art thou, my bonnie lass,   5
    So deep in luve am I;
  And I will luve thee still, my Dear,
    Till a' the seas gang dry.

  Till a' the seas gang dry, my Dear,
    And the rocks melt wi' the sun: 10
  And I will luve thee still, my Dear,
    While the sands o' life shall run.

  And fare thee weel, my only Luve!
    And fare thee weel, awhile!
  And I will come again, my Luve,   15
    Tho' it were ten thousand mile!

Burns's poem is a celebration of love, spontaneous and untroubled by doubts or difficulties or by any sense of the complexities of life. The images are conventional, even hackneyed: the sweetheart is like a rose; the lover will love her till the seas go dry; and he would travel ten thousand miles to rejoin her. We accept the poem only insofar as we find the imagery naively charming, an indication, we might say, of the speaker's innocent sincerity, and of the simplicity of a folk society. But that impression might not be enough, taken alone, to recommend the piece. What has made it durable is the musicality. The tone is that of a song, a youthful, simple, innocent utterance.

EXERCISES

1. The poem is in Scots dialect. Copy it out in standard English. How do you feel about it now? If it impresses you differently now, can you relate the difference to anything said above?
2. Let us revise the first stanza:

  My Love is like a blushing rose
    That is newly sprung now in June.
  My Love is like a melodie
    That's being played sweetly in tune.

How do you like this?

3. Can you make any specific comment on the phonetic quality in relation to the musicality?

4. Suppose the last stanza did not exist. How much would this affect the poem? Why?

EMPTY BED BLUES

Bessie Smith (1895–1937)

I woke up this morning with an awful aching
   head,
I woke up this morning with an awful aching
   head,
My new man had left me just a room and an
   empty bed.

Bought me a coffee grinder, got the best one I
   could find,
Bought me a coffee grinder, got the best one I
   could find,   5
So he could grind me coffee, cause he had a brand
   new grind.

He's a deep-sea diver with a stroke that can't go
   wrong,
He's a deep-sea diver with a stroke that can't go
   wrong,
He can touch the bottom, and his wind holds out
   so long.

He knows how to thrill me, and he thrills me
   night and day,   10
He knows how to thrill me, and he thrills me
   night and day,
He's got a new way of loving, almost takes my
   breath away.

He's got that sweet something, and I told my gal-
   friend Lou,
He's got that sweet something, and I told my gal-
   friend Lou,
'Cause the way she's raving, she must have gone
   and tried.it too.   15

When my bed gets empty, makes me feel awful
   mean and blue,
When my bed gets empty, makes me feel awful
   mean and blue,
Cause my springs getting rusty, sleepin' single the
   way I do.

Bought him a blanket, pillow for his head at
   night,
Bought him a blanket, pillow for his head at
   night,   20

Then I bought him a mattress so he could lay just
   right.

He came home one evening with his fair head way
   up high,
He came home one evening with his fair head way
   up high,
What he had to give me made me wring my hands
   and cry.

He give me a lesson that I never had before,   25
He give me a lesson that I never had before,
When he got through teaching me, from my
   elbows down was sore.

He boiled my first cabbage, and he made it awful
   hot,
He boiled my first cabbage, and he made it awful
   hot,
Then he put in the bacon and it overflowed the
   pot.   30

When you get good lovin' never go and spread
   the news,
When you get good lovin' never go and spread
   the news,
They'll double-cross you and leave you with them
   empty bed blues.

EXERCISE

Compare the tone of this poem to that of "A Red, Red Rose."

THE PARTING

Michael Drayton (1563–1631)

Since there's no help, come let us kiss and part—
Nay, I have done, you get no more of me;
And I am glad, yea, glad with all my heart,
That thus so cleanly I myself can free.
Shake hands for ever, cancel all our vows,   5
And when we meet at any time again,
Be it not seen in either of our brows
That we one jot of former love retain.
Now at the last gasp of Love's latest breath,
When, his pulse failing, Passion speechless lies,   10
When Faith is kneeling by his bed of death,
And Innocence is closing up his eyes,
   —Now if thou wouldst, when all have given
      him over,
   From death to life thou might'st him yet
      recover.

EXERCISES

1. What is the attitude of the speaker toward his mistress? What shifts are observable here? Indicate the stages.
2. Drayton lived and wrote in the Elizabethan age, a period when poetry, especially love sonnets, was sometimes characterized by elaborate, artificial imagery, used either playfully or seriously, of the sort we find in lines 9–12 of this poem. How seriously do you think the speaker intends it here?
3. Considering the conventions of Elizabethan poetry, do you think that the closing couplet is merely a polite compliment to the lady? Or is it a serious (and somewhat self-abasing) statement? Or is it delicately poised? In relation to this, again examine the shift of tone between the lines 1–8 and lines 9–12.

SONNET 55

William Shakespeare (1564–1616)

Not marble, nor the gilded monuments
Of princes, shall outlive this powerful rhyme;
But you shall shine more bright in these contents
Than unswept stone besmeared with sluttish time.
When wasteful war shall statues overturn,   5
And broils root out the work of masonry,
Nor Mars his sword nor war's quick fire shall burn
The living record of your memory.
'Gainst death and all-oblivious enmity
Shall you pace forth; your praise shall still find
    room   10
Even in the eyes of all posterity
That wear this world out to the ending doom.
    So, till the judgment that yourself arise,
    You live in this, and dwell in lover's eyes.

EXERCISES

1. The idea stated in this poem is a common one. Does the poet succeed in giving it dignity and seriousness? Consider meter and phonetic quality in this connection.
2. Analyze too the imagery used here in the light of this purpose. Note that, although the poet is asserting the endurance of his praise of the friend, he has a vivid realization of the forces calculated to obliterate that praise.
3. Note that "the judgment" in line 13 refers to Judgment Day, when his friend will rise from the dead. How does the phrase "pace forth" give concreteness to the idea of his friend's posthumous life? How does it qualify "this powerful rhyme" (1. 2)? Does it focus attention upon the poet's prowess or on the friend's greatness?

4. Describe the shift in tone that comes with the closing couplet.

SONG

John Donne (1571/2–1631)

Go, and catch a falling star,
   Get with child a mandrake root,
Tell me where all past years are,
   Or who cleft the devil's foot,
Teach me to hear mermaids singing,   5
Or to keep off envy's stinging,
      And find
      What wind
Serves to advance an honest mind.

If thou be'est born to strange sights,   10
   Things invisible to see,
Ride ten thousand days and nights
   Till age snow white hairs on thee:
Thou, when thou return'st, will tell me
All strange wonders that befell thee,   15
      And swear
      No where
Lives a woman true, and fair.

If thou find'st one, let me know;
   Such a pilgrimage were sweet;   20
Yet, do not, I would not go,
   Though at next door we might meet.
Though she were true when you met her,
And last, till you write your letter,
      Yet she   25
      Will be
False, ere I come, to two, or three.

EXERCISES

1. Characterize the speaker. Is he shocked or pained that women are fickle? What attitude does he take? Can you imagine why? Is the poem gay, sad, matter-of-fact, ironical, self-pitying, or what?
2. Can you make any technical comments that bear on the tone of the poem? What about the stanza structure?

THEY FLEE FROM ME

Sir Thomas Wyatt (1503?–1542)

They flee from me that sometime did me seek
   With naked foot, stalking in my chamber.
I have seen them gentle, tame, and meek,
   That now are wild, and do not remember
   That sometime they did put themselves in
     danger   5

To take bread at my hand; and now they range
Busily seeking with a continual change.

Thankèd be fortune, it hath been otherwise
   Twenty times better; but once in special,
In thin array, after a pleasant guise,   10
   When her loose gown from her shoulders did
      fall
   And she me caught in her arms long and small
Therewith all sweetly did me kiss
And softly said, 'Dear heart, how like you this?'

It was no dream; I lay broad waking;   15
   But all is turnèd, through my gentleness,
Into a strange fashion of forsaking;
   And I have leave to go of her goodness,
   And she also to use newfangleness.
But since that I so kindly am served,   20
I would fain know what she hath deserved.

This poem, on the same theme as Donne's "Song," is in almost direct contrast in treatment and tone.

EXERCISES

1. To what does the word *they* refer in line 1? It seems to refer to birds (or to any wild, shy, timorous creatures), but it seems also in view of stanza 2 to refer to women and to one woman in particular. How does the first stanza in its description of the actions of those that "flee from me" prepare for the specific reference to a woman in stanza 2?

2. What is the tone of the first two stanzas? It seems to be relatively objective—not excited, not bitter, though the situation is evidently now, in the cold and altered present, so very different. What does line 15 do for the tone? Is the speaker saying in effect that "I have to pinch myself to believe that it was once otherwise, but I did not dream it. I was wide awake. I remember vividly that it actually happened"?

3. Try to characterize the tone of the last stanza. It evidently involves irony, but what kind of irony? Is it an irony primarily at the expense of the woman for whom love is merely a fashion—a mode of dress to be altered capriciously? Or does the irony also involve the speaker—as if he were intimating "how foolish of me to have expected anything else"? The word *kindly* in line 20, in addition to its present meaning, could mean in Wyatt's time "in accordance with nature," for the old original meaning of *kind* was "nature." One does not blame a bird for not coming up to the speaker's hand now that there is no bread to be

offered. Is one to blame the woman for acting likewise in terms of her "nature"?

4. If this poem does involve a deeply sardonic account of inconstancy how has the poet kept it from seeming passionately bitter or glibly cynical? Does it become a more moving and powerful poem for having been kept free of a more superficial and obvious bitterness?

THE CONSTANT LOVER
Sir John Suckling (1609–1642)

   Out upon it! I have loved
      Three whole days together;
   And am like to love three more,
      If it prove fair weather.

   Time shall moult away his wings,   5
      Ere he shall discover
   In the whole wide world again
      Such a constant lover.

   But the spite on 't is, no praise
      Is due at all to me: 10
   Love with me had made no stays
      Had it any been but she.

   Had it any been but she,
      And that very face,
   There had been at least ere this   15
      A dozen dozen in her place.

EXERCISE

Donne and Wyatt, in their differing tones of voice, wrote the two preceding poems commenting on the inconstancy of women, but here Suckling inverts that old theme, which had long since become a convention, and deplores his own constancy. What is the real point of the speaker's irony here? Is he poking fun at a literary convention? At sentimental self-abasement of men in love? At himself for not proving quite the free-spirited blade he had thought himself? Or at several things at once? Is, perhaps, the poem really aiming at something else? Experiment with reading the poem aloud to find the right "tone." Could it be that this is after all, a sincere love poem?

Let us now look at two poems that express the same basic idea, that have the same basic theme. The theme is an old one: *carpe diem,* as the Roman poet put it, "seize the day." Both Robert Herrick and Edmund Waller, English poets of the seventeenth century, here treat the theme, and both, we observe, use the fleeting beauty of the rose as an image for the fragility and transience of beauty and youth.

TO THE VIRGINS, TO MAKE MUCH OF TIME
Robert Herrick (1591–1674)

Gather ye rosebuds while ye may,
   Old Time is still a-flying:
And this same flower that smiles today
   Tomorrow will be dying.

The glorious lamp of heaven, the sun,   5
   The higher he's a-getting,
The sooner will his race be run,
   And nearer he's to setting.

That age is best which is the first,
   When youth and blood are warmer;   10
But being spent, the worse, and worst
   Times will succeed the former.

Then be not coy, but use your time,
   And while ye may, go marry:
For having lost but once your prime,   15
   You may for ever tarry.

SONG
Edmund Waller (1606–1687)

Go, lovely Rose,
Tell her that wastes her time and me,
   That now she knows,
When I resemble her to thee,
How sweet and fair she seems to be.   5

Tell her that's young,
And shuns to have her graces spied,
   That hadst thou sprung
In deserts where no men abide,
Thou must have uncommended died.   10

Small is the worth
Of beauty from the light retired:
   Bid her come forth,
Suffer herself to be desired,
And not blush so to be admired.   15

Then die, that she
The common fate of all things rare
   May read in thee,
How small a part of time they share,
That are so wondrous sweet and fair.   20

Both poems are charming and graceful examples of *vers de société* (see Glossary), poetry taken as an ornament of social life, an artistic adjunct to cultivated manners. Both poets, too, argue that the beautiful young maiden is in the natural trap of time, and, like the fading rosebud or rose, runs through a foreordained cycle. The difference between the poems is basically one of tone. Herrick hints only delicately at the threat of mortality in stanzas 1 and 2. In stanza 1, rosebuds are merely rosebuds;* in stanza 2, the sun is an index of the passing of time in general. In stanza 3 the idea of decay and failing powers is stated, but only in a general way. In stanza 4 the threat to the young ladies is not, actually, that of death but that of being left as old maids. The poet implies that the virgins should submit themselves to the course of nature, bear children, and after such affirmation of their natural destiny, die,—presumably fulfilled—but this opinion, though hinted at in several ways, is never directly stated.† Even at the end of the poem the threat is that if the virgins do not make use of their time, and their natural charms, they will "for ever tarry." The threat is merely that they will forever tarry as old maids— *forever* being interpreted as "for the rest of their lives." But the more dire interpretation that they will literally die, and die unfulfilled, only lurks in the background in the secondary meaning of *forever* as "for eternity."

The general feeling of gaiety and gallantry that characterizes the poem is emphatically supported by the briskness of the rhythm. The rhythm is strongly marked, with few secondary accents, and generally weak accentuation on the unaccented syllables. There are only two run-on lines in

---

* The virgins are urged to gather rosebuds, literal and figurative (pleasure), and there is only a hint, in the word *smiles* (l. 3), that the virgins are to be identified with the "flowers" that "tomorrow will be dying."

† The word *virgins*, rather than *maidens* or *girls*, is significant here. The word emphasizes the fact that the young women addressed are holding themselves outside natural process as though they might conquer time.

the whole poem (ll. 3 and 11), and this fact contributes to the brisk effect. In general, there is, then, little tension between the meter and the rhetoric.

When we turn to Waller's poem, we find, beneath the charmingly turned compliment of the suitor (for that is the speaker's role here), a deep seriousness. As for the content, we may start with the word *wastes* in line 2. If we change one word in the line we get a very different meaning. If the suitor says that the lady "wastes her time and mine," the meaning becomes rather trivial: the affair is a mere flirtation that will come to nothing and had better be broken off. But in the real text, the word takes on an additional and much deeper meaning, the meaning we find in such phrases as "a wasting disease," "wasting away," and "waste places." In stanzas 2 and 3 the poet toys, but toys seriously, with the idea that beauty does not exist except in the eye of the beholder, using this idea as a step in the logical argument that the lady must "come forth" if she wishes to exist at all. In this connection we remark that the word *suffer* has a significant depth of meaning. One meaning, and here the most obvious one, is that of "permitting," of "tolerating." But when the word appears in the context of "desired" it takes on a sexual charge, the actual surrender of the body, with a hint of the physical "suffering" in the violation of the virgin.

With stanza 4, in contrast to the tone of Herrick's poem, we find the first line beginning "Then die." Notice how sudden and abrupt this logical injunction comes. The word *Then*, for all practical purposes, says that to die is the logical consequence of what has previously been stated: if the rose is to fulfill its errand to the lady, it must die. It must remind the lady that she will die and that seeing the death of the rose, she should take heed and at once seek the fulfillment of life. The rose, we should now recall, is not only a reminder for the lady; in lines 4 and 5 there is also, as in Herrick's poem, a metaphorical identification of rose and lady; and in this connection, it may be pointed out that the verb *to die* had as one meaning, in Wal-

ler's time, to reach climax in the sexual act. The lady is, thus, exhorted to fulfill herself in nature—but the literal meaning is also absorbed into the poem.

The last stanza is in emphatic contrast to that of Herrick's poem. Herrick merely abjures the "virgins" to make thrifty use of their fleeting charms or they may "for ever tarry" as old maids. Waller shifts the meaning of the poem from the exhortation to make haste, or to seize the day, or to surrender to the suitor's plea, and concludes on a note of pathos at the fact that all things, no matter how "wondrous sweet and fair" are caught in the "common fate." The tone at the end is not of lament, a sentimental cry; it is a simple, objective statement, a grave but controlled recognition of the general condition of man in nature.

Waller's poem, like Herrick's, is on the surface a charming piece of *vers de société*, but unlike Herrick's, there is here a tension between the surface commitment of the gallant, complimentary poem to a lady, and the depth of meaning not stated but implied in the elements that we have been discussing. We have, however, omitted one of the most significant elements contributing to the tone, that of the rhythm and verbal "feel." The most obvious difference between this poem and Herrick's is, in fact, in the rhythm. Against Herrick's brisk, clipped movement, we find here a number of secondary accents, especially in stanza 3:

> / // /
> Small is the worth
> / / / /
> Of beauty from the light retired:
> / // // / // /
> Bid her (Bid her?) come forth,
> / / / /
> Suffer herself to be desired,
> / / / /
> And not blush so to be admired.

Lines 3 and 5 are especially significant. In line 3 the emphatic spondaic movement announces the long-expected coming forth, and the same effect in the first two feet of line 5 hints at the complex significance of the blushing that prepares for the injunction "Then die." *

* But notice how in stanza 4, after the sudden turn of the poem with the injunction "Then die," the rhythm sinks to a calm, almost matter-of-fact movement, especially in the last summarizing couplet.

The contrast in the use of run-on lines in the two poems also has some relevance. In Herrick's poem the relative fewness of run-on lines significantly contributes to the characteristic clipped movement, to the emphasis of the metrical rhythm. In Waller's poem, however, run-on lines occur in stanzas 2, 3, and 4. In stanzas 2 and 3 we get a sharp sense of the pull of the rhetorical structure from the metrical, and stanzaic, structure, the very opposite effect from that in Herrick. In stanza 4 there are two run-on lines, with a remarkable result. The climactic injunction "Then die" is set off by a comma, and that line and the next are run on, so that we get a rhetorical result something like this:

> Then die!—[in order] that she the common
> fate of all things rare may read
> in thee

Then, after this shocking breaking up of the general structure,* we return, of course, to the cleanly accented meter of the rimed couplet that concludes the poem.

EXERCISE

Scan stanzas 1 and 2 of Waller's "Song."

LAY YOUR SLEEPING HEAD
W. H. Auden (1907–1973)

> Lay your sleeping head, my love,
> Human on my faithless arm;
> Time and fevers burn away
> Individual beauty from
> Thoughtful children, and the grave   5
> Proves the child ephemeral:
> But in my arms till break of day
> Let the living creature lie,
> Mortal, guilty, but to me
> The entirely beautiful.   10
>
> Soul and body have no bounds:
> To lovers as they lie upon
> Her tolerant enchanted slope
> In their ordinary swoon,
> Grave the vision Venus sends   15

> Of supernatural sympathy,
> Universal love and hope;
> While an abstract insight wakes
> Among the glaciers and the rocks
> The hermit's sensual ecstasy.   20
>
> Certainty, fidelity
> On the stroke of midnight pass
> Like vibrations of a bell
> And fashionable madmen raise
> Their pedantic boring cry: 25
> Every farthing of the cost,
> All the dreaded cards foretell,
> Shall be paid, but from this night
> Not a whisper, not a thought,
> Not a kiss nor look be lost.   30
>
> Beauty, midnight, vision dies:
> Let the winds of dawn that blow
> Softly round your dreaming head
> Such a day of sweetness show
> Eye and knocking heart may bless   35
> Find the mortal world enough;
> Noons of dryness see you fed
> By the involuntary powers,
> Nights of insult let you pass
> Watched by every human love.   40

Auden's poem involves several of the ideas that have appeared in previous poems about love in group 4, for instance, constancy and inconstancy, the transience of beauty, the joy of love, love as illusion. But the basic idea here is the contrast between the fact of love and the context in which it occurs. Let us paraphrase the poem in general terms:

> Stanza 1: Though you are merely human (as I am) with human faults, and though your beauty is fleeting, you are "entirely beautiful" to me.
>
> Stanza 2: The soul and the body are not really to be separated; man is a unit. The love-making of the ordinary, physical sort may lead to "universal love and hope," just as an "abstract insight" (an idea or spiritual intuition) may prove physically stimulating.
>
> Stanza 3: In this world, in spite of all the learned debate about man and love, we know that fidelity may pass after the act of love; but even though we know this, and

---

* When the stanza and line pattern are so drastically weakened the metrical accents tend to dissolve into simple rhetorical stress. We may observe, too, that the stanza Waller uses is much more complicated than that of Herrick, and that the difference in lengths of line (two feet against four instead of the regular alternation of four and three) contrasts with the brisk effect in "To the Virgins."

that pain may follow, we, nevertheless, find fulfillment in love.

Stanza 4: Given the human condition, we must try to "find the mortal world enough." After all, soul and body are not separate.

From this paraphrase, a reader would not know whether the speaker were bitter, ironical, resigned, challenged, self-pitying, gay and bantering, satisfied, or what. In other words, the attitude, the feeling, that the speaker has about the condition he describes is what is significant about the poem. Indeed, it may be said to create the poem. In the following exercises we invite you to dwell on some of the aspects of the poem that contribute to the tone, that dramatize the attitude and feeling of the speaker.

EXERCISES

1 "Lay Your Sleeping Head" is very musical, and musical in a lyrical way. How does this fact affect our sense of the speaker's attitude toward the subject—and toward the beloved? Is the musicality here more complex than that of, say, Burns's "A Red, Red Rose," or Herrick's "To the Virgins"? Do you think it a little odd to find this musicality in the treatment of such a complex, and even intellectually difficult, subject? If so, what do you make of the fact?
2. Specify certain factors that create the musicality here. Examine, for instance, lines 15–20. What sets the tune, as it were, of lines 15–17? Do you find any change in effect in lines 18 and 19? From what verbal circumstances? Do you find this change expressive? In lines 21–23 can there be said to be an onomatopoeic effect? If so, explain.
3. Suppose, in lines 5 and 6, we replace "Thoughtful children" with "Even lovers," and *child* with "loved one." What is the difference in tone—and meaning? Suppose, in line 8, we replace *creature* with "loved one," and in line 10, *entirely* with *perfectly*. Then what? How does the word *entirely* prepare for the next stanza. In line 18, comment on the word *abstract*. Exactly what does it mean here? Relate it to the general context. In lines 24 and 25, do you find that "fashionable madmen" and "pedantic boring cry" come as a sort of shock? Now that you are better acquainted with the poem, how do you explain those phrases?
4. What is the relation of line 31 to the stanza it introduces? If it is saying that love and all the values associated with it ("vision") are illusory,

what does the colon at the end of the line signify? What does this final stanza contribute to the poem as a whole? Is there a change of tone here? Might it be said that the tone of this stanza is that of a prayer? The stanza just preceding has ended with an affirmation. How would a prayer modify the affirmation? What does this imply about the speaker's attitude?
5. What is the implication of the word *human* in the last line? If irony is here, what is the tone?

NEUTRAL TONES

Thomas Hardy (1840–1928)

We stood by a pond that winter day,
And the sun was white, as though chidden of God,
And a few leaves lay on the starving sod;
   —They had fallen from an ash, and were gray.

Your eyes on me were as eyes that rove   5
Over tedious riddles solved years ago;
And some words played between us to and fro
   On which lost the more by our love.

The smile on your mouth was the deadest thing
Alive enough to have strength to die;   10
And a grin of bitterness swept thereby
   Like an ominous bird a-wing. . . .

Since then, keen lessons that love deceives,
And wrings with wrong, have shaped to me
Your face, and the God-curst sun, and a tree,   15
   And a pond edged with grayish leaves.

The situation in the poem is a simple one: a man recalls the occasion of a quarrel with his beloved, on a winter day, beside a pond where the gray leaves of an ash tree lay on the dead grass. This recollection is put in the form of a direct address, even though the woman, apparently, is absent and perhaps has been parted from him for many years; and this device of direct address gives a dramatic quality and force to a commonplace situation. But what really lifts the poem above the commonplace attempt to render the pathos of defeated love, and what defines the real theme of the poem, is the last stanza. The theme depends on the answer to the question implied in the last stanza: Why have the "keen lessons that love deceives" always shaped for the speaker the face of the first beloved in that particular background, "the God-curst sun, and a tree, and a pond edged with grayish leaves"? The answer may run something like this: early, and perhaps first, disappointment in love has become a symbol for all the later disappointments and frustrations of life, and the "God-curst" landscape has become a symbol of all the curse of evil that hangs over man and nature—a curse the speaker has, we sense, managed to endure with fortitude.

Therefore, this poem does in a very clear and apparently simple and direct way what all poetry tries to do: it takes a single incident, fact, or observation (the quarrel) and manages to link it with, or fuse it with, other things out of experience (the "starving sod," the dead leaves, the misty sun), to make a new kind of experience and perception of some kind of coordination or ordering of separate things. That is to say, the poet creates a symbolic experience, which means more than the mere experience of the incident originally chosen for the subject. It gives a meaning to the incident.

The symbolism here, the meaning, arises largely from the speaker's tone, which is embodied in his choice of words and in the rhythms of his utterance. For instance, take the first line: "We stood by a pond that winter day." Then think what the difference in tone would be if the poet had said *pool* or *lake* instead of *pond*. Yet a pond is after all a pool or a little lake. But *pond* is a more usual and homely word, a more realistic word, a less romantic word, a less "poetical" word. It implies a less formal tone, a less set and rhetorical tone, than would *lake* or *pool*.

This conversational tone of word choice is reinforced by the rhythms of the poem. The movement of the lines is more like that of ordinary conversation than of regular verse, such as we find in another poem by the same poet:

> I squared the broad foundations in
> Of ashlared masonry;
> I moulded mullions thick and thin,
>   Hewed fillet and agee;
>   I circleted
>   Each sculptured head
> With nimb and canopy.

The rhythm of stanza 1 of "Neutral Tones" continues the conversational tone and slows the movement as if the speaker were trying to recollect every detail of the scene by the pond. This is made specific by the last line, "They had fallen from an ash, and were gray," which is put on as though a kind of afterthought in the process of recollection. The sentence structure, too, is such that the loose groping movement of the mind trying to repicture a scene is perceived by the reader; for the whole sentence is not constructed with the proper subordination of detail to a main thought—the structure of a logical, planned sentence—but is constructed by the accumulation of detail, after a general statement, strung together by *and*s and then followed by a dash and an afterthought. The structure of the sentence by its very logical crudity implies that groping movement, the mind trying to recollect something that has already been mentioned. The tone here is informal and meditative.

Stanzas 2 and 3, less emphatically, continue this tone of the attempt to re-create the scene of the past. But with the opening of stanza 4, an entirely different rhythm appears, at the moment, that is, when the summarizing general and objective meaning of the particular scene of memory emerges. The rhythm here is that of a strongly defined and formal metrical beat, made more marked by the alliterative reinforcement. Then, with line 15, a shift in rhythm occurs as the mind of the speaker reverts to the scene of the past, reviewing it item by item, lingering not lovingly or nostalgically but, as it were, with stoic determination. In these lines, the speaker returns to the sentence structure characteristic of the first stanza, items strung together by *and*s. But here the sequence is made more weighty by forced pauses. For instance, the syllabic transitions in the phrase "God-curst sun" are hard to make, and some pause is forced between the syllables; the same is true of "pond edged" and "grayish leaves." The poem comes to rest here on the itemized list of remembered details: the loved one's face, the sun, a tree, a pond, and, climactically, the grayish leaves, the same detail on which the first stanza had ended. The focus, the emphasis, creates the symbolism, which, in fact, might have been ineffective, too obvious, if stated.

And it is the slow, steady look at the image that defines the underlying attitude of the speaker, his fatalism, his fortitude.

EXERCISE

Compare the tone of "Neutral Tones" with that of James Joyce's story "Araby" (sec. 7).

ROSE AYLMER

Walter Savage Landor (1775–1864)

> Ah, what avails the sceptred race!
>   Ah, what the form divine!
> What every virtue, every grace!
>   Rose Aylmer, all were thine.
>
> Rose Aylmer, whom these wakeful eyes   5
>   May weep, but never see,
> A night of memories and of sighs
>   I consecrate to thee.

EXERCISES

1. Rose Aylmer, the speaker's lost love, is, presumably, dead. Stanza 1 of the poem does not state the fact of her death or the speaker's reaction. It asks a rhetorical question. What is the nature of the question? Can it be said that it depersonalizes the loss, and puts it as part of the common human lot? If you accept this idea, explain how it can be justified. In this connection, it may be useful to ask how long before the time of the poem the death had occurred.
2. As the question is in a sense formal and objective so is the structure of stanza 1. Explain this statement.
3. In stanza 2 we find "wakeful eyes" and "memories and sighs," both clichés of bereavement. In contrast to these conventional and overt statements of emotion we find the word *consecrate*. How can it be said that this is the key word of the poem, the word that defines the speaker's attitude?
4. Notice that in stanza 2, in contrast to the end-stopped lines throughout stanza 1, we find two run-on lines. Can you associate this fact with the overtness of emotion in the beginning of the stanza? What does the metrical accentuation do to lift and emphasize the word *consecrate*? What is the thematic significance of this fact?

MIDWINTER BLUES

Langston Hughes (1902–1967)

> In the middle of the winter,
> Snow all over the ground.
> In the middle of the winter,
> Snow all over the ground—

> 'Twas the night befo' Christmas   5
> My good man turned me down.
>
> Don't know's I'd mind his goin'
> But he left me when the coal was low.
> Don't know's I'd mind his goin'
> But he left me when the coal was low.   10
> Now, if a man loves a woman
> That ain't no time to go.
>
> He told me that he loved me
> But he must a been tellin' a lie.
> He told me that he loved me.   15
> He must a been tellin' a lie.
> But he's the only man I'll
> Love till the day I die.
>
> I'm gonna buy me a rose bud
> An' plant it at my back door,   20
> Buy me a rose bud,
> Plant it at my back door,
> So when I'm dead they won't need
> No flowers from the store.

As the title states, this poem is a "blues," and it has the emotional overtness of that type of lamentory song. It gains its great force and immediacy, however, by the playing off of overt emotion against cold, hard facts. In stanza 2, the speaker's greater grief at the loss of her lover is set against the fact that her coal supply is low, a lesser grief but one that for the very poor is real enough. Here the worry about the coal works somehow to validate the sincerity of the woman's grief for her lost love. The loss of love is taking place in a real world, where people get, literally, cold. Stanza 4 also works, but in a very different way, to validate the speaker's sincerity. We find here a subtle use of the imagery of the rose—in contrast with the overtness of the declaration of lost love.

EXERCISES

1. Why is the woman going to buy her own "rose bud" to plant at her own back door? Why doesn't she want "flowers from the store"?
2. Is this poem more like "O Western Wind" or "A Red, Red Rose"? Explain your choice.
3. "Midwinter Blues" is, of course, similar in many ways to Bessie Smith's "Empty Bed Blues." How do the two poems differ?

AT HER WINDOW
Frederick Locker Lampson (1821–1895)

Beating Heart!
  Where my Love reposes:
This is Mabel's window-pane;
  These are Mabel's roses.

Is she nested? Does she kneel   5
  In the twilight stilly,
Lily clad from throat to heel,
  She, my virgin Lily?

Soon the wan, the wistful stars,
  Fading, will forsake her;   10
Elves of light, on beamy bars,
  Whisper then, and wake her.

Let this friendly pebble plead
  At her flowery grating;
If she hear me will she heed?   15
  Mabel, I am waiting.

Mabel will be deck'd anon,
  Zoned in bride's apparel;
Happy zone! O hark to yon
  Passion-shaken carol!   20

Sing thy song, thou trancèd thrush,
  Pipe thy best, thy clearest;—
Hush, her lattice moves, O hush—
  Dearest Mabel!—dearest. . . .

EXERCISE

What do you think of this poem?

Syllabic Time and Rime

Like word breaks and rhetorical pauses, the
length of time required to pronounce certain
syllables may affect the tone of a poem. Turn
to subsection 19.7 and continue your study
of the qualities of time inherent in language.
Also read subsection 19.8 for a brief explanation of the kinds of rime and some other possibilities of language related to it.

EXERCISES

1. Find a line more or less parallel to each of the
lines given at the beginning of subsection 19.7.
Such lines may be drawn from any section of this
book, whether or not previously assigned.
2. Choose five lines from any source illustrating
marked variation in the positioning of lips and
tongue.
3. Find five lines or passages in which, in a run of
at least three examples, alliteration serves as a
binder. Find three lines or passages in which, in a
run of at least two examples, alliteration serves as
emphasis. (Lines 13–14 of Milton's "On the Late
Massacre in Piedmont" comprise one such passage;
the alliteration of the terminal words *way* and
woe emphasizes the meaning.)
4. Examine the rimes in "Bells for John Whiteside's Daughter" by John Crowe Ransom. Has the
poet been careless, or do you feel that the slant
rimes and approximate rimes contribute something to the effect of the poem?

Section 15

IMAGERY

In the poems already studied we have called
attention, especially in section 13, to the importance of imagery. Visual and auditory
images (but also evocations of touch, taste,
and smell) provide us with a vivid appreciation of "the world's body"—to use the phrase
of a fine modern poet. Poetic images, however, do much more. They awaken certain

emotional responses; they imply attitudes
and suggest moods. They may even come to
suggest concepts.

To take an obvious instance of emotional response: the descriptions of a gray
November landscape on which a chill rain is
falling and that of a sunlit April meadow
with field flowers in bloom suggest quite dif-

ferent moods. The first is somber; the second joyful. The reader of this book is, of course, already acquainted with images used to develop and support much more complicated effects. Compare, for example, the landscape described by Tennyson in "The Lotos-Eaters" with that described by Yeats in "The Wild Swans at Coole." The emotional atmosphere of the former is one of languor, worldweariness, and listless enervation. The mood is that of a settled and dreamy hopelessness. In Yeats's poem the mood is one of melancholy too, but the melancholy is of a very different kind. The atmosphere is chill and bracing; the anguish, keen and piercing, not quietly hopeless. In Tennyson's poem, time stands still ("seemed always afternoon"), but in Yeats's, time flies inexorably and the past cannot be recovered.

Some of the poems in section 13—and elsewhere in this book—show a further stage: the images have attained the status of symbols. That is, the images have come to stand for concepts and ideas. See, for example, Blake's "The Lamb" and "The Tyger," or Shelley's "Ode to the West Wind." Shelley uses images that suggest the power of the wind and what it does to leaf, cloud, and wave. Such images body forth its tremendous, sweeping power. But as the poem develops, the destructive force is also associated with vitality and life. The old must be destroyed so that the new life may come into being. Such symbolism comes to a head in the final stanza. If leaf, cloud, and wave represent three of the four elements in nature (earth, air, and water), the fourth element, fire, is used to clinch the association of destructiveness with vital power. For the wind is to blow the dead ashes into flame, bringing forth life out of death.

How would one spell out this idea, putting it in more general and abstract terms? One might say that in this poem the west wind signifies the primal revolutionary force, a part of nature but also of human nature. The work of destruction is necessary and

finally benevolent. But it is important to note that Shelley does *not* spell out his idea. He does not seek to make an abstract statement, but to present a complex of idea and emotion, a dramatic instance of a principle, a concrete embodiment of a concept.

How does a poet convert images into symbols? By making use of the associations with which various images are endowed and by putting them into a context that will bring out the qualities that he wishes to emphasize.* Not only his choice of images, but his control of the context is all-important here. A skillful poet sometimes can even reverse the usual associations of images by shaping the context in which the image appears. Thus, though God is traditionally associated with light, Henry Vaughan, in a poem entitled "The Night," makes the very darkness the proper time of Christian prayer and religious devotion.

Images, then, can be built up into symbols, but the images used in poetry also function in other ways. They occur, for example, in the various forms of figurative language (see Glossary), as, for example, in metaphors and similes. What is the difference between a symbol and a metaphor? Perhaps the best way to proceed is to look at concrete examples. The four short poems that immediately follow will furnish us with plenty of instances, after which we will venture some definitions.

GROUP 1: FROM IMAGE TO SYMBOL

ARS POETICA
Archibald MacLeish (b. 1892)

A poem should be palpable and mute
As a globed fruit

Dumb
As old medallions to the thumb

Silent as the sleeve-worn stone   5
Of casement ledges where the moss has grown—

---

* We would argue that the use that a poet makes of conventional or arbitrary symbolism—for example, the cross as a symbol of Christianity or the Stars and Stripes as a symbol of the United States—is only incidental to his creative power. He has a perfect right to use such fixed symbols—they are part of his emotional and intellectual heritage—but he does not show his special poetic gift in merely pointing to established symbolisms. In fact, one finds that the poet characteristically enforces or enriches or extends such emblems, converting mere *signs* into rich symbolisms.

A poem should be wordless
As the flight of birds

A poem should be motionless in time
As the moon climbs   10

Leaving, as the moon releases
Twig by twig the night-entangled trees,

Leaving, as the moon behind the winter leaves,
Memory by memory the mind—

A poem should be motionless in time   15
As the moon climbs

A poem should be equal to:
Not true

For all the history of grief
An empty doorway and a maple leaf   20

For love
The leaning grasses and two lights above the sea—

A poem should not mean
But be.

A reader may well say that this poem is a self-contradiction. It is not merely "being," it is also "meaning," but what it means is that a poem should not mean but be. Certainly we talk about the "meaning" of poems, but we must remember that the logically paraphrasable meaning is not the poem. A poem is concerned with experiential meaning as well as with abstract meaning—that is, meaning that can be logically stated. In this sense a poem means *the experience of that poem,* but we must keep in mind that the experience of the poem involves ideas, references to events in the actual world, objective facts in that world, and human feelings in that world, as well as the poet's own reactions as dramatized and expressed in the poem. This may seem very complex and ungraspable, but how do we abstractly express the meaning of an experience such as love or grief? We find ourselves groping toward comparisons and images—groping toward poetry, in fact. What MacLeish's poem "means," then, is that a poem must undertake to embody, dramatize, express what would otherwise be inexpressible, the "mean-ing" that would be unavailable to us without the "being" of the poem.

EXERCISES

1. Although this poem can be said to involve a self-contradiction, in what way can it also be said to embody its own meaning and therefore not be self-contradictory?
2. In what sense is the language of a poem, metaphorically at least, "palpable and mute"? How does the image of "globed fruit" apply? In what sense are rhythm and tone aspects of the imagery of a poem?
3. Why should a poem "be equal to" and not "true"?

VERY LIKE A WHALE
Ogden Nash (1902–1971)

One thing that literature would be greatly the
    better for
Would be a more restricted employment by
    authors of simile and metaphor.
Authors of all races, be they Greeks, Romans,
    Teutons or Celts,
Can't seem just to say that anything is the thing
    it is but have to go out of their way to say that
    it is like something else.
What does it mean when we are told   5
That the Assyrian came down like a wolf on the
    fold?
In the first place, George Gordon Byron had had
    enough experience
To know that it probably wasn't just one Assyrian,
    it was a lot of Assyrians.
However, as too many arguments are apt to induce
    apoplexy and thus hinder longevity,
We'll let it pass as one Assyrian for the sake of
    brevity.   10
Now then, this particular Assyrian, the one whose
    cohorts were gleaming in purple and gold,
Just what does the poet mean when he says he
    came down like a wolf on the fold?
In heaven and earth more than is dreamed of in
    our philosophy there are a great many things,
But I don't imagine that among them there is a
    wolf with purple and gold cohorts or purple
    and gold anythings.
No, no, Lord Byron, before I'll believe that this
    Assyrian was actually like a wolf I must have
    some kind of proof;   15
Did he run on all fours and did he have a hairy
    tail and a big red mouth and big white teeth
    and did he say Woof woof woof?

Frankly I think it very unlikely, and all you were
  entitled to say, at the very most,
Was that the Assyrian cohorts came down like a
  lot of Assyrian cohorts about to destroy the
  Hebrew host.
But that wasn't fancy enough for Lord Byron, oh
  dear me no, he had to invent a lot of figures of
  speech and then interpolate them,
With the result that whenever you mention Old
  Testament soldiers to people they say Oh yes,
  they're the ones that a lot of wolves dressed up
  in gold and purple ate them.   20
That's the kind of thing that's being done all the
  time by poets, from Homer to Tennyson;
They're always comparing ladies to lilies and veal
  to venison.
How about the man who wrote,
Her little feet stole in and out like mice beneath
  her petticoat?
Wouldn't anybody but a poet think twice   25
Before stating that his girl's feet were mice?
Then they always say things like that after a
  winter storm
The snow is a white blanket. Oh it is, is it, all
  right then, you sleep under a six-inch blanket of
  snow and I'll sleep under a half-inch blanket of
  unpoetical blanket material and we'll see which
  one keeps warm,
And after that maybe you'll begin to comprehend
  dimly
What I mean by too much metaphor and simile. 30

EXERCISES

1. Why do you think the editors have used this
poem?
2. The first lines of Lord Byron's "Destruction of
Sennacherib" are:

> The Assyrian came down like the wolf on
>   the fold,
> And his cohorts were gleaming in purple
>   and gold. . . .

What about Nash's literalistic and commonsense
objections?
3. In line 22 Nash says that poets are "always
comparing ladies to lilies." One poem in this text,
"At Her Window" (sec. 14), makes use of this comparison. Is it well used in your opinion? Waller's
"Song" (sec. 14) compares a lady to a rose. Is this
comparison well used in your opinion?
4. Line 24 refers to Sir John Suckling's "Ballad
upon a Wedding": "Her feet beneath her petticoat like little mice stole in and out." Why did the
poet make this comparison? Is it an apt comparison? What does it tell us about the poet's
attitude?

5. What is the tone of Nash's poem? How is the
tone indicated?
6. The title of the poem is taken from *Hamlet*,
Act 3, scene 2. What is the significance of the title?
7. Comment on any technical features that help
to establish the tone of the poem.

I STROVE WITH NONE
Walter Savage Landor (1775–1864)

I strove with none, for none was worth my strife,
  Nature I loved, and, next to Nature, Art;
I warmed both hands before the fire of life,
  It sinks, and I am ready to depart.

EXERCISE

Here is another version of the same poem:

I strove with none, for none was worth my strife,
  Nature I loved, and, next to Nature, Art;
I sought to have all pleasure from my life;
  But now I am old and ready to depart.

What is the difference here? Is the poem better
or worse?

A SLUMBER DID MY SPIRIT SEAL
William Wordsworth (1770–1850)

> A slumber did my spirit seal;
>   I had no human fears—
> She seemed a thing that could not feel
>   The touch of earthly years.
>
> No motion has she now, no force;   5
>   She neither hears nor sees;
> Rolled round in earth's diurnal course,
>   With rocks, and stones, and trees.

EXERCISES

1. This poem, like Landor's "I Strove with None,"
depends for its effect on a single image. Let us
rewrite the second stanza to change the image:

> No motion has she now, no strength;
>   She neither sees nor hears,
> But sweetly sleeps the long night's length
>   Careless of smiles or tears.

What is the difference?
2. The poem is based on a reversal. When the
beloved was alive the lover's spirit was sealed in a
"slumber"—was dead to some reality; but now

that the beloved, who had seemed so vital, is dead, the lover has been awakened. Awakened to what? Does the last line of the poem indicate an answer?

Before we pursue the distinctions among simile, metaphor, and symbol, we should remark that a poem does not necessarily confine itself to one such device. For instance, in "Ars Poetica," we find several similes (see Glossary)—"As a globed fruit" and "as the sleeveworn stones," and so on. But we also find two instances of symbolism: lines 19–20 and lines 21–22. In the first the two lights readily suggest two lovers glowing with their love. As for the second example, some readers may want to ask how a doorway and a maple leaf can stand for "all the history of grief." Perhaps in this way. Time goes on. The maple tree has once more renewed its leaf (or perhaps its last leaf in autumn has fallen), but the doorway is still empty. The person mourned does not appear in the doorway still held open to receive him or her.

To return to the matter of distinctions, we understand that both simile and metaphor involve comparison, announced or implied. With Ogden Nash's mock-vehement diatribe against poetic gaudiness and problematic comparisons, we get a criticism of two full-blown similes and of at least one metaphor. We are not much concerned here with Nash's criticism of specific comparisons: Byron wrote much better poems than "The Destruction of Sennacherib," and Nash's blasting of the wolf-sheepfold simile would, if accepted, involve no serious loss to poetry. But Nash makes what is, for our present purpose, a very useful observation: he stresses the fact that you can't take metaphors and similes literally. A purple and gold wolf would be an incredible freak, and a "blanket" of snow would indeed give the human being cold comfort. In human terms it wouldn't be a "blanket" at all.

This leads us to the crucial distinction that images used symbolically *can* be taken literally, though of course this is not to say that they do not have significance far beyond that literal meaning.

Is "fire of life" in line 3 of "I Strove with None" a metaphor? If we apply the test of nonliterality, yes. For though the comparison of life to a fire is familiar and almost trite, it can't be taken literally—and least of all in the form in which the fire is presented here: a fire burning on a hearth or in a grate, before which a man may warm his hands. Look at the rewritten version of the poem in the exercise following it. The metaphorical action in Landor's poem has been obliterated. What replaces it is something that can be taken literally, but the force and richness of the original have been lost.

The term *replaces* in our last sentence is worth noting. Christine Brooke-Rose, in her *Grammar of Metaphor* (London, 1958), defines metaphor as "any replacement of one word by another, or any identification of one thing, concept, or person with another." (Another authority moves toward the same point in defining a metaphor as "a new naming.") One ought to remark, incidentally, that the tendency to use metaphor is deeply rooted in human nature. A still respected theory is that language began as metaphor. Modern slang, such of it as is still fresh and new, is basically metaphoric. Men for a long time have been extending terms to cover new meanings: inspection of any unabridged dictionary will abundantly confirm this observation.

What are the metaphors in Wordsworth's "A Slumber Did My Spirit Seal"? We may begin with line 1. The "slumber" is not some literal sleep. The speaker says that he was "asleep" to the possibility that his loved one might die, though he walked around with his eyes wide open. When the late President Kennedy wrote his book on Britain's fatal lack of preparation for the coming clash with Hitler, he entitled it *While England Slept*. Such a use of *slumber* and *sleep* is thus quite familiar, but, nonetheless, metaphorical. (The "sealing" of one's "spirit" probably has to be taken metaphorically too, but let's move on here to the metaphor clearly indicated in lines 3–4.)

What is the "touch of earthly years"? Scarcely a literal contact, a pressure that a human body could "feel." Of course, we know what the poet means—at least, part of what he means. But though the lines burst with meaning, we cannot take them literally.

What does "feel/The touch of earthly years" replace? There are several possible replacements, though none of them as rich and massive as the meaning conveyed by the metaphor; but clearly something like the following is conveyed: the touch of earthly years is the pressure exerted on all mortals by time. It brings wrinkles and graying hair and finally death itself.

The second quatrain, however, contains no metaphors. Every assertion can be taken literally. But the stanza does not thereby lack force. Indeed, the images are beautifully chosen and the context so managed as to render impressively the shock of the girl's unforeseen death and the numbed grief of the lover at the stunning metamorphosis of a vibrant and responsive being into a mere lump, caught up in the insensate whirl of the earth that makes up the succession of the days by which human beings measure time. In the context of the whole poem, the metaphor "touch of earthly years" is still active and powerful. The dead girl feels the "touch" of those years indeed. She is held fast by the earth itself as it measures the years by moving around the sun in its annual cycle.

We have remarked earlier that the poet develops the symbolism that is potential in his images by organizing his poem into a verbal context that will achieve this end. But, as "A Slumber Did My Spirit Seal" shows, the poet's control over the context is an overall condition of his achieving meaning for the poem as a whole—not merely that of developing particular images into incidental symbolizations. It involves his use of metaphor too, figurative language in general, and even rhythmic and metrical factors. In a very important sense, then, the whole poem—if it is truly unified and achieves coherent meaning—is a symbolic structure. This symbolic structure may depend very heavily on the poet's use of metaphors and other kinds of figurative language—as in much of Marvell and Donne. We must keep in mind, therefore, that the symbolic process as such is not confined to the production of incidental symbolizations like "An empty doorway and a maple leaf," but must see that it is the very principle of poetry itself.

There is a sense, then, in which one can speak of the poem itself as a symbol. A particularly clear example would be Keats's "To Autumn," which is our next poem. Keats makes use in the poem of metaphors, similes, personifications, and incidental symbolizations, but he uses them to build up a highly unified poem in which the season of autumn itself is endowed with human meaning. Someone has said that everything in the poem speaks of autumn—says over and over, autumn, autumn, autumn. This is true. But the poem also says something very massive and rich about life itself—about growth, fulfillment, the meaning of maturity, and a sense of triumph as well as quiet resignation before the fact of death.

TO AUTUMN

John Keats (1795–1821)

I

Season of mists and mellow fruitfulness,
　　Close bosom-friend of the maturing sun;
Conspiring with him how to load and bless
　　With fruit the vines that round the thatch-eves run;
To bend with apples the moss'd cottage-trees, 　5
　　And fill all fruit with ripeness to the core;
　　　To swell the gourd, and plump the hazel shells
　　With a sweet kernel; to set budding more,
And still more, later flowers for the bees,
Until they think warm days will never cease, 　10
　　　For Summer has o'er-brimm'd their clammy cells.

II

Who hath not seen thee oft amid thy store?
　　Sometimes whoever seeks abroad may find
Thee sitting careless on a granary floor,
　　Thy hair soft-lifted by the winnowing wind; 　15
Or on a half-reap'd furrow sound asleep,
　　Drows'd with the fume of poppies, while thy hook
　　　Spares the next swath and all its twined flowers:
And sometimes like a gleaner thou dost keep
　　Steady thy laden head across a brook; 　20
　　Or by a cider-press, with patient look,
　　　Thou watchest the last oozings hours by hours.

III

Where are the songs of Spring? Ay, where are
      they?
   Think not of them, thou hast thy music too,—
While barréd clouds bloom the soft-dying day,   25
   And touch the stubble-plains with rosy hue;
Then in a wailful choir the small gnats mourn
      Among the river sallows, borne aloft
      Or sinking as the light wind lives or dies;
And full-grown lambs loud bleat from hilly
      bourn;   30
Hedge-crickets sing; and now with treble soft
The red-breast whistles from a garden-croft;
   And gathering swallows twitter in the skies.

In this poem of thirty-three lines almost all are descriptive, that is, they are devoted to the objective presentation of imagery. All the imagery is related to "autumn-
ness," enriching our sense of the fall season.
But does the season carry one exclusive sense,
association, or connotation? Autumn, on the
one hand, implies fruition, fulfillment, peace.
On the other, it implies endings, death, the
end of hope.

Stanza I is clearly devoted to the first
set of associations. Mellowness, fruitfulness,
ripeness, fullness, heaviness, sweetness,
warmth, drowsiness—these are the qualities
constantly insisted upon. Furthermore, in
this stanza, though we have the fulfilled end
of a process of maturation, the sense of time
involved in the process has been abolished, or
lulled to rest. The season is the "bosom-
friend of the maturing sun," but the hint—
the quite illogical hint—is that the sun would
not desert a "bosom-friend" and let cruel
winter come. The season and the sun are, indeed, fellow conspirators. At the end of the
stanza, though it is implied that the bees
deceive themselves, the whole force of lines
9–11 is to make us deceive ourselves too—
more and more later flowers keep coming for
us too, and warm days will never cease.

At this point we may notice that, though
we have had the commonsense warning in
connection with the self-deception of the
bees, stanza II resumes the series of images
involving a rich, timeless fulfillment. Think
what the difference of effect would be if stanza
II were canceled and we jumped from line 11
directly to line 23, with its question emphasizing the inevitable passing of time: "Where
are the songs of Spring? Ay, where are they?"

The imagery of stanza II shifts the emphasis. The poet continues to stress a sense
of ripeness, fruition, fullness, even heaviness,
but he allows the qualities of sweet drowsiness, bemusement, and hypnotic blankness to
emerge, too. The stanza is addressed to
Autumn, the season as personified by a
woman who tends the granary, the field, and
the cider press, overseeing the gathering of
the bounty of the harvest. All the richness,
sweetness, and fruition of the season are embodied in her. Delicious languor and somno-
lence are the basic feelings of the stanza. In
this stanza, too, the idea of finality specifically appears. In stanza I we feel that warm
days will never cease, but here Autumn drow-
sily watches the drop-by-drop oozing of the
cider press "hours by hours"—as though
watching the trickling of sand in an hourglass. And her sleep, her repose, implies the
idea of ending—delicious, satisfying, but
nevertheless an ending.

This introduction of the idea of time,
though time in a casual and beneficent mood,
prepares the way for the nostalgia and pain
of the question that introduces stanza III:
"Where are the songs of Spring?" In other
words, in the midst of the sense of fulfillment
and peace, the fear of time and death has
suddenly, though with very subtle poetic preparation, intruded. Line 24 is the generalized
answer to the question in line 23: You
(Autumn) must not think of what songs have
been left behind, for you have your own
appropriate music. With line 25 the poem
resumes the catalogue of images that are related to the appropriate music, but since the
comforting answer refers to songs and music
the basic images now are auditory: the choir
of gnats, the bleating of lambs, the song of
crickets, the whistle of the red-breast, the
twitter of swallows. In these images the idea
of time and death becomes more specific; the
words *dying* and *dies* appear; the cut-over
stubble, not the rich sheaf, is mentioned; the
gnats "mourn"; and the swallows gather for
an escape from the land of winter. Even so,
these images are set in contrast with positive
elements: the day dies, but it is "soft-dying,"
with the adverb *soft* giving a hint of the pleasant drowsiness of stanza II; the "stubble-
plains" are not drab but of "rosy hue"; the
lambs that bleat are "full-grown," as they

would be in the fall; the red-breast's whistle is, again, "soft," with an echo from *soft-dying;* the swallows that prepare to migrate will be back.

    The poem, to sum up, moves from the static sense of fruition to the nostalgia of loss and the melancholy of endings to a resolution in the acceptance of cyclic process, birth and growth and death, as constituting the reality in which man must find his happiness. We must qualify this general statement, however, by remembering that the basic tone of the poem is one of rich repose and fulfillment, that the nostalgia and melancholy in the world ruled by time never break into a cry of protest or tragic intensity. The thematic resolution of the poem is implicit in the beginning.

    A REMINDER. In this section we are concerned with the special function of imagery. In "To Autumn" the burden of meaning, the thematic development, is carried by the imagery. Statement is minimal. The poem is very close in method to the work of the Imagists, to whom we have referred in section 13, but with one difference: here the theme is given a complex development, with numerous tonal shifts.

EXERCISES

1. Return to Shelley's "Ode to the West Wind" (sec. 13). What similarities of general theme do you observe? What differences in tone? How do differences in tone alter meanings here?
2. What other poems read thus far would provide fruitful comparison with Keats's "To Autumn"?
3. Clearly, there is a sharp difference in the way imagery is used in Keats's poem and in Landor's "I Strove with None." Describe this difference.
4. Return to "The Gulls" by John Gould Fletcher and to "The Red Wheelbarrow" by William Carlos Williams (both, sec. 13). Compare "To Autumn" with these poems in method.

GHOSTLY TREE
Léonie Adams (b. 1899)

O Beech, unbind your yellow leaf, for deep
The honeyed time lies sleeping, and lead shade
Seals up the eyelids of its golden sleep.

Long are your flutes, chimes, little bells, at rest,
And here is only the cold scream of the fox,   5
Only the hunter following on the hound;
While your quaint-plumaged,
The bird that your green summer boughs lapped
   round,
Bends south its soft bright breast.

Before the winter and the terror break,   10
Scatter the leaf that broadened with the rose
Not for a tempest, but a sigh, to take.
Four nights to exorcise the thing that stood
Bound by these frail which dangle at your branch,
They ran a frosty dagger to its heart;   15
And it, wan substance,
No more remembered it might cry or start
Or stain a point with blood.

EXERCISE

Here is another poem to autumn. Compare it with Keats's poem in regard to both meaning and method.

SPRING
William Shakespeare (1564–1616)

    When daisies pied and violets blue
      And lady-smocks all silver-white
    And cuckoo-buds of yellow hue
      Do paint the meadows with delight,
    The cuckoo then, on every tree,   5
    Mocks married men; for thus sings he,
                "Cuckoo!
    Cuckoo, cuckoo!" Oh word of fear,
    Unpleasing to a married ear! [1]

    When shepherds pipe on oaten straws,   10
      And merry larks are plowmen's clocks,
    When turtles[2] tread,[3] and rooks, and daws,
      And maidens bleach their summer smocks,
    The cuckoo then, on every tree,
    Mocks married men; for thus sings he,   15
                "Cuckoo!
    Cuckoo, cuckoo!" Oh word of fear,
    Unpleasing to a married ear!

WINTER
William Shakespeare (1564–1616)

    When icicles hang by the wall,
      And Dick the shepherd blows his nail,[4]
    And Tom bears logs into the hall

---

[1] The cuckoo lays its eggs in the nests of other birds; it has thus been traditionally associated with cuckolded husbands
[2] turtledoves [3] couple, mate [4] fingernails, i.e., hands

And milk comes frozen home in pail,
When blood is nipp'd, and ways be foul,   5
Then nightly sings the staring owl,
                    "Tu-whit, tu-who!"
A merry note,
While greasy Joan doth keel[1] the pot.

When all aloud the wind doth blow,
And coughing drowns the parson's saw,   10
And birds sit brooding in the snow,
    And Marian's nose looks red and raw,
When roasted crabs[2] hiss in the bowl,
Then nightly sings the staring owl,
                    "Tu-whit, tu-who!"
A merry note,   15
While greasy Joan doth keel the pot.

Like "To Autumn" by Keats, these two
songs by Shakespeare (from his play *Love's
Labour's Lost*) assemble sets of images characteristic of seasons. Like stanza III of Keats's
poem, both "Spring" and "Winter" offer
some images that are pleasant and some that
are unpleasant. There is one significant difference, however, between Shakespeare's
poems and that of Keats. In "To Autumn,"
the theme, or meaning, is overtly presented,
although it is compressed into only two lines
(lines 23 and 24); in "Spring" and "Winter"
the themes are not overtly stated. Does this
mean that in Shakespeare's poems the speakers have no basic attitude toward the subjects? That is, that there is no "meaning"?
We may answer this general question by asking some particular ones.

EXERCISES

1. In "Spring," what is the attitude of the speaker
toward the husbands whose wives take a fling in
the bright spring weather? What is his attitude toward the wives?
2. In "Winter," how unpleasant are the unpleasant images? Can you think of grimmer images
that, factually, might have been inserted to change
the tone of the poem? Do you think that the
scullery maid Joan and the serving men doing
their chores about the manor are presented as
resentful and bitter?
3. Comment on the relation of rhythms and meaning in these two poems.

---

[1] skim   [2] crab apples

ANECDOTE OF THE JAR
Wallace Stevens (1879–1955)

I placed a jar in Tennessee,
And round it was, upon a hill.
It made the slovenly wilderness
Surround that hill.

The wilderness rose up to it,   5
And sprawled around, no longer wild.
The jar was round upon the ground
And tall and of a port in air.

It took dominion everywhere.
The jar was gray and bare.   10
It did not give of bird or bush,
Like nothing else in Tennessee.

The image of the jar is at the center of
the poem. The jar seems to be very ordinary,
"gray and bare," a crock perhaps. But the
poem is rather odd, and the oddness begins
with the first line. One may say, "In Tennessee, one time, on a hill, I set a jar down on the
ground." Factually, this is what the speaker
here does say, but in a very twisted way that
distorts meaning. If he had said, "I placed
a jar on the second shelf" or "on the table"
or "on the doorstep," we would infer from
his statement a matter of reasonable choice.
But the speaker says, "I placed a jar in Tennessee," and we have no idea of what kind of
choice is being made—only a vague notion of
a disembodied hand holding a jar moving
across Kentucky, or Virginia perhaps, as
though across a map, and then placing the
jar on a hill. Placing a jar on a hill is, however, an odd idea. A jar is small; you set it
on the ground or on a stump or rock; you
don't "place" it "upon a hill." The stump or
rock may be on a hill, but that is another
question. This jar somehow looms up like a
tree, or a great boulder, or a monument. The
jar has some mysterious quality.

EXERCISES

1. The jar is in contrast to the wilderness. What is
the basis of the contrast? Why is the wilderness
"slovenly"? Then, why is it "no longer wild"?

2. If the speaker of the poem had planted a flowering bush on the hill instead of setting a jar there, would there still be a poem?

3. What does the word *port* mean here? Consult an unabridged dictionary. Is the word a common word in this sense? Why would Stevens use this word in this connection? How "tall" would a jar have to be to have a "port," do you think? What kind of image are we actually seeing here? Has the jar changed size before our eyes? What about the word *dominion*? Is this an unexpected word here? Can you justify it in relation to the poem?

4. Interpret the last two lines.

5. If the poem can be said to be about man in contrast to nature, what is implied in the image of the jar? How does the wrenching of language and imagery connect with the meaning?

6. Do the red wheelbarrow in William Carlos Williams's poem (sec. 13) and the jar in Stevens's poem have similar significance? If not, why not?

7. Is the jar a symbol? If so, of what? If not, why not?

DESERT PLACES

Robert Frost (1874–1963)

Snow falling and night falling fast, oh, fast
In a field I looked into going past,
And the ground almost covered smooth in snow,
But a few weeds and stubble showing last.

The woods around it have it—it is theirs.   5
All animals are smothered in their lairs.
I am too absent-spirited to count;
The loneliness includes me unawares.

And lonely as it is, that loneliness
Will be more lonely ere it will be less—   10
A blanker whiteness of benighted snow
With no expression, nothing to express.

They cannot scare me with their empty spaces
Between stars—on stars where no human race is.
I have it in me so much nearer home   15
To scare myself with my own desert places.

EXERCISES

1. If the poem consisted of only stanzas 1–3, what would it mean? What would be the import of the image of the snowy field?

2. If stanza 4 did not exist, how would you compare the idea of nature with that in Stevens's "Anecdote of the Jar"? How would you compare the attitude of the speaker with that of the speaker in Keats's "To Autumn"?

3. Taking the poem whole, all four stanzas, what is the attitude of the speaker?

4. Turn back to Ransom's "Bells for John Whiteside's Daughter" (sec. 14). Compare the crucial effect of the word *vexed* in stanza 4 with the effect of the word *scared* in stanza 4 here. What difference in meaning would follow if we replaced *scare* by *appall*?

5. Compare the meaning of "Desert Places" with that of "The Tree of Man" by A. E. Housman (sec. 13). What is the difference in tone?

THE HEAVY BEAR

Delmore Schwartz (1913–1966)

The heavy bear who goes with me,
A manifold honey to smear his face,
Clumsy and lumbering here and there,
The central ton of every place,
The hungry beating brutish one   5
In love with candy, anger, and sleep,
Crazy factotum, dishevelling all,
Climbs the building, kicks the football,
Boxes his brother in the hate-ridden city.

Breathing at my side, that heavy animal,   10
That heavy bear who sleeps with me,
Howls in his sleep for a world of sugar,
A sweetness intimate as the water's clasp,
Howls in his sleep because the tight rope
Trembles and shows the darkness beneath.   15
—The strutting show-off is terrified,
Dressed in his dress suit, bulging his pants,
Trembles to think that his quivering meat
Must finally wince to nothing at all.

That inescapable animal walks with me,   20
Has followed me since the black womb held,
Moves when I move, distoring my gesture,
A caricature, a swollen shadow,
A stupid clown of the spirit's motive,
Perplexes and affronts with his own darkness,   25
The secret life of belly and bone,
Opaque, too near, my private, yet unknown,
Stretches to embrace the very dear
With whom I would walk without him near,
Touches her grossly, although a word   30
Would bare my heart and make me clear,
Stumbles, flounders, and strives to be fed
Dragging me with him in his mouthing care,
Amid the hundred million of his kind,
The scrimmage of appetite everywhere.   35

EXERCISES

1. In the early pages to this section, in discussing metaphor and symbol as types of imagery, we have said that images used symbolically can be taken literally, whereas images used metaphorically cannot. We have also noted that the symbol tends to have a broader and deeper range of reference than the metaphor, and to be more central in its use. Do you regard the bear in this poem as a symbol? Explain your view. To make such an explanation you must, of course, interpret the role of the bear as fully as possible.

2. What is the theme of this poem?

THE CAMEO

Edna St. Vincent Millay (1892–1950)

Forever over now, forever, forever gone
That day. Clear and diminished like a scene
Carven in cameo, the lighthouse, and the cove between
The sandy cliffs, and the boat drawn up on the beach;
And the long skirt of a lady innocent and young,   5
Her hand resting on her bosom, her head hung;
And the figure of a man in earnest speech.

Clear and diminished like a scene cut in cameo
The lighthouse, and the boat on the beach, and the two shapes
Of the woman and the man; lost like the lost day   10
Are the words that passed, and the pain,—discarded, cut away
From the stone, as from memory the heat of the tears escapes.

O troubled forms, O early love unfortunate and hard,
Time has estranged you into a jewel cold and pure;
From the action of the waves and from the action of sorrow forever secure,   15
White against a ruddy cliff you stand, chalcedony on sard.

EXERCISES

1. Can you justify our placing this poem in the group entitled "Image to Symbol"?

2. Look up the words *chalcedony* and *sard*. What have you gained by doing so?

3. Compare this poem with "Neutral Tones," by Hardy.

COMMEMORATIVE OF A NAVAL VICTORY

Herman Melville (1819–1891)

Sailors there are of gentlest breed,
  Yet strong, like every goodly thing;
The discipline of arms refines,
  And the wave gives tempering.
  The damasked blade its beam can fling;   5
It lends the last grave grace:
The hawk, the hound, and sworded nobleman
  In Titian's picture for a king,
Are of hunter or warrior race.

In social halls a favored guest   10
  In years that follow victory won,
How sweet to feel your festal fame
  In woman's glance instinctive thrown:
  Repose is yours—your deed is known,
It musks the amber wine;   15
It lives, and sheds a light from storied days
  Rich as October sunsets brown,
Which make the barren place to shine.

But seldom the laurel wreath is seen
  Unmixed with pensive pansies dark;   20
There's a light and a shadow on every man
  Who at last attains his lifted mark—
  Nursing through night the ethereal spark.
Elate he never can be;
He feels that spirits which glad had hailed his worth,   25
  Sleep in oblivion.—The shark
Glides white through the phosphorous sea.

Each stanza of this poem represents a stage in the development of the theme. In the first stanza, against the background of an unspecified naval victory in the American Civil War, there is the comment on the gentleness mixed with strength in the "sailors." They are, the poet says, like a well-tempered steel blade that gives off a gleam and illuminates the place where it lies. In the last three lines of the stanza the description of the painting by Titian serves as another image for the sailor; the rich lordliness of the Renaissance figure is absorbed, as it were, into the modern hero. We realize that the organization of this stanza is not very clear, the logical continuity is faulty. But do we make the leaps necessary to follow Melville despite his poor organization? Or can we say that the poor organization and loose syntax have a virtue of their own in this instance? In any case, we follow the drift of the stanza, and understand the kind of praise that Melville would give his sailors.

The second stanza is addressed, we learn, to the hero himself, the "you," who now, long after his great moment, still enjoys his "festal fame," the respect of men and the glances of women as a tribute to his now storied bravery that shines over his later life like rich October light. The hero deserves his fame. Melville is paying an honest compliment to the hero. There is no hint of irony, even if the hero seems to bask somewhat complacently in the old glory. His is an earned "repose."

But, as the last stanza puts it, the hero cannot enjoy his fame fully and easily. There is an irony after all. Even success has a shadow on it. The last three lines explain the nature of this shadow. Those who generously would best have appreciated his bravery are dead. Not only are they dead, but they died, we suddenly realize, in the naval battle for which the "you" now enjoys the fame. How do we know this? There is the image of the white shark that suddenly appears like a shocking vision across the scene of "festal fame," the savage creature drawn to the bleeding bodies of the wounded and dying in the sea, the image of evil.

There is one more step to take, one more question to ask. Does Melville mean the poem to apply merely to the naval hero? Or is he writing, finally, about all success, and the shadow over all success? Does he mean to imply that any successful man, if he is honest and has humanity, will understand that others as worthy as he have failed and sleep in oblivion? That, in a way, he lives off of their virtue and their generosity, for they would "glad" have "hailed his worth," and perhaps even by their death or failure have prepared the way for his success?

EXERCISES

1. In each stanza of the poem we find an image of light. In the first, the finely tempered blade gives off a beam. In the second, the October light makes a barren landscape shine. In the third, there is light and shadow on every man, even in success. Interpret these three images as closely as possible. Is there any continuity of meaning among them? What do they imply about heroism and fame?

2. What is the meaning of the word *elate*? How does it apply here?

3. In the last two lines, we notice that "The shark" ends a line and is set off from the rest of the sentence to which it belongs and which composes the last line: "Glides white through the phosphorous sea." Is this arrangement effective?

4. Clearly, there is contrast between the scene of festivity and the human cost. But can it be said that those who now celebrate the victory and the hero's fame are, themselves, somehow like the shark, drawn to the taint of blood? How much irony is there in the last image?

5. What would the poem mean without the shark?

6. Does the shark become a symbol?

GROUP 2: DISCOURSE AND COMPLEXITY OF METAPHOR

In this group of poems the use of imagery differs radically from that in many poems earlier in this section. In "The Heavy Bear," for example, the image of the bear *is* the poem. The representation of his qualities and behavior contains the poem; it is coterminous with the poem. In the following poems, the images are themselves contained; they are attached to the discourse to develop and interpret it. The fundamental meaning may, indeed, come through the imagery and not by generalized statements, but the frame contains the images.

A PRAYER FOR MY DAUGHTER
W. B. Yeats (1865–1939)

Once more the storm is howling, and half hid
Under this cradle-hood and coverlid
My child sleeps on. There is no obstacle
But Gregory's wood and one bare hill
Whereby the haystack- and roof-leveling wind,   5
Bred on the Atlantic, can be stayed;
And for an hour I have walked and prayed
Because of the great gloom that is in my mind.

I have walked and prayed for this young child an hour
And heard the sea-wind scream upon the tower,   10
And under the arches of the bridge, and scream

In the elms above the flooded stream;
Imagining in excited reverie
That the future years had come,
Dancing to a frenzied drum,   15
Out of the murderous innocence of the sea.

May she be granted beauty, and yet not
Beauty to make a stranger's eye distraught,
Or hers before a looking-glass, for such,
Being made beautiful overmuch,   20
Consider beauty a sufficient end,
Lose natural kindness and maybe
The heart-revealing intimacy
That chooses right, and never find a friend.

Helen being chosen found life flat and dull   25
And later had much trouble from a fool,
While that great Queen, that rose out of the spray,
Being fatherless could have her way
Yet chose a bandy-leggèd smith for man.
It's certain that fine women eat   30
A crazy salad with their meat
Whereby the Horn of Plenty is undone.

In courtesy I'd have her chiefly learned;
Hearts are not had as a gift but hearts are earned
By those that are not entirely beautiful;   35
Yet many, that have played the fool
For beauty's very self, has charm made wise,
And many a poor man that has roved,
Loved and thought himself beloved,
From a glad kindness cannot take his eyes.   40

May she become a flourishing hidden tree
That all her thoughts may like the linnet be,
And have no business but dispensing round
Their magnanimities of sound,
Nor but in merriment begin a chase,   45
Nor but in merriment begin a quarrel.
Oh, may she live like some green laurel
Rooted in one dear perpetual place.

My mind, because the minds that I have loved,
The sort of beauty that I have approved,   50
Prosper but little, has dried up of late,
Yet knows that to be choked with hate
May well be of all evil chances chief.
If there's no hatred in a mind
Assault and battery of the wind   55
Can never tear the linnet from the leaf.

An intellectual hatred is the worst,
So let her think opinions are accursed.
Have I not seen the loveliest woman born
Out of the mouth of Plenty's horn,   60
Because of her opinionated mind
Barter that horn and every good

By quiet natures understood
For an old bellows full of angry wind?

Considering that, all hatred driven hence,   65
The soul recovers radical innocence
And learns at last that it is self-delighting,
Self-appeasing, self-affrighting,
And that its own sweet will is Heaven's will;
She can, though every face should scowl   70
And every windy quarter howl
Or every bellows burst, be happy still.

And may her bride-groom bring her to a house
Where all's accustomed, ceremonious;
For arrogance and hatred are the wares   75
Peddled in the thoroughfares.
How but in custom and in ceremony
Are innocence and beauty born?
Ceremony's a name for the rich horn,
And custom for the spreading laurel tree.   80

    In this poem a father prays for his in-
fant daughter. The father's state of mind
and the occasion that prompts his prayer are
significant: they help us to understand the
meaning of the prayer. The poet begins by
presenting the circumstances vividly and
dramatically.

    It is night, and a storm is howling in
from the Atlantic as the child sleeps. (Yeats
actually lived at this time in an old tower
near the west coast of Ireland, and details of
the setting—"Gregory's wood" and the bridge
spanning the stream near which the tower
stands—are mentioned in the description.)
The child is safely asleep. Though the prayer
is not for physical protection, the storm presumably does have something to do with the
"great gloom" that fills the father's mind.
For him, the storm typifies the violence and
uncertainty of the future—the violent and
perhaps bloody future in which his daughter
is to live.

    The poem was written in 1919 and the
years that have followed since then have indeed been confused and bloody years. One
points this out, not to claim the gift of prophecy for the poet, but a realization of this
fact may make it easier for present-day readers to feel that the insight that dictated the
poem was no mere "excited reverie," in spite
of the speaker's disclaimer, but rather a serious and realistic consideration of what sort
of world probably lay before the child.

The phrase "murderous innocence of the sea" (l. 16) is sharp and arresting. Why has the poet used it? A natural force cannot literally be *murderous*. A lion, for instance, cannot commit murder, for it has no sense of right and wrong. And, by the same token, no natural force can be "innocent." And yet the phrase is justified, for it describes vividly a kind of aimless violence—not vindictive, not consciously evil, indeed without any purpose at all. Even a consciously malignant violence is somehow less ominous than this uncomprehending and unpitying force. We shall have to read further into the poem, however, before we see the full implications of the phrase.

After such an account of the father's sense of foreboding, the prayer itself (which begins with stanza 3) may seem rather anticlimactic. The father prays for rather simple and rather ordinary things. He prays that the girl may be granted beauty, though not great beauty; that she may be learned chiefly "in courtesy"; that she may "think opinions are accursed"; and that she may find a husband who will bring her into a house "where all's accustomed, ceremonious." But how can such gifts as these protect the girl in the kind of future that looms ahead of her?

The prayer may seem open to even more serious objections. Is the father simply asking that his daughter may find a sheltered and pleasant life, presumably by attracting a wealthy husband? Is he not praying that—the better to achieve this end—she may be "sweet" and pliant rather than thoughtful and forceful? The prayer, read in this fashion, may well seem shallow and cynical—even vulgarly snobbish.

To paraphrase the poem in this fashion is to distort it. For one thing, this paraphrase neglects entirely the images that run through the poem and that, as we shall see, are much more than bits of ornamentation. It is only through the dominant images that we may possess the poem and actually understand for what the father prays.

Why does the father hope that his child will not be granted "beauty to make a stranger's eye distraught" or to dazzle her own eyes? Because such beauty is a disruptive force. Helen of Troy (l. 25) brought on the Trojan War and the destruction of a great city because her beauty made distraught the eyes of Paris, the Trojan prince. The "great Queen" of line 27 is Aphrodite, the Greek goddess of beauty, who, according to the myth, rose from the sea foam and was thus "fatherless." But she married the lame smith-god Hephaestus (Vulcan)—presumably because her beauty made her own eye distraught, so that, though free to choose, she could not choose well.

The "Horn of Plenty" (l. 32) is also from Greek legend: it is the cornucopia, the fabulous horn that poured out to the recipient anything for which he could ask. Those, however, who are granted all that they could want—perhaps just because they are sated with good things—seem to crave as a perverse relish "a crazy salad" that maddens them and cancels the gifts of abundance. The paradox of full abundance undoing the recipient is thus worked out primarily through this image of eating. But the sea image of the earlier stanzas is also echoed. Aphrodite rose out of the sea foam, out of the sea, the character of which is a "murderous innocence."

Helen of Troy bears a special relation to Aphrodite. Helen was the prize that the goddess held out to Paris in order to persuade him to proclaim her most beautiful; but the prize was in a special way "murderously innocent." Through Helen, though she was innocent of any intent to destroy the Trojan state, Troy was destroyed, for the Greeks attacked Troy and finally burned it to avenge the honor of Helen's husband, the Greek prince Menelaus.

If the last comment seems to read too much into the phrase "Heaven's will," it need not be pressed. Suffice it to say that the contrast between angry self-assertion and joyful self-realization has been defined and developed through the imagery of the poem. But the imagery has done more: it has associated with these two views of self, contrasted views of innocence and of nature. The "murderous innocence" that is amoral is set against a "radical innocence" out of which all that is good grows; nature as capricious and cruel, mere brute force, is set against a nature that yields norms and archetypes of order, that indeed reflects the divine order.

The concluding stanza treats all these matters in their social aspect. Man lives in the society of his fellows. What, in terms of his life in human society, is the horn of plenty? What the "spreading laurel tree"? Ceremony and custom, the poet boldly answers. The true dowering of gifts comes from ceremony—it is not a gift of nature; the true organic stability comes from custom, not from some inborn virtue.

The answer is bold and somewhat surprising. We usually think of innocence and beauty as the gift of nature; and we oppose them to custom and ceremony, for we think of custom and ceremony as tending to sophisticate and perhaps corrupt the person who subjects himself to them. The last lines of the poem invert these relations; for they maintain that innocence and beauty are not the products of nature but of a disciplined life. They spring from order—they grow out of something—they are not the casual gifts of a blind and capricious force.

Does the poet make these assertions convincing? The student will have to decide for himself. But if they are rendered convincing, it is because "innocence" and "beauty" as used in this last stanza have been carefully defined. They have been defined in large part, however, through imagery—and so indeed it is with the whole argument of the poem: the poem is a "thinking out" in terms of images.

EXERCISES

1. Are lines 49–52 related to the tree imagery? How?
2. How, if at all, are the images of lines 75–76 related to the field of imagery used earlier? Is the "old bellows" (l. 64) the sort of "ware" a peddler would hawk through the streets? How are "thoroughfares" related to "One dear perpetual place" (l. 48)? What do the horn of plenty and the bellows have in common, if anything?
3. What is the tone of the first two stanzas? Of stanzas three through six? What shift in tone marks the beginning of the seventh stanza? What is the tone of the final stanza? How is the imagery used to modify and control the tone?
4. Notice how many expressions in the poem echo homely and colloquial phrases: "a crazy salad,"

"played the fool," "assault and battery," "own sweet will." Notice too that some of the images suggest the images that underlie modern slang expressions: compare lines 59–60 with "a nice dish" or "a peach" and line 64 with "an old windbag." Is this echoing of the colloquial and slangy a fault in this poem or a virtue? How does it affect the tone?

THE GOOD-MORROW
John Donne (1571/2–1631)

I wonder by my troth, what thou, and I
Did, till we loved? Were we not weaned till then,
But sucked on country pleasures, childishly?
Or snorted we in the seven sleepers' den?
'Twas so; but this, all pleasures fancies be.   5
If ever any beauty I did see,
Which I desired, and got, 'twas but a dream of
      thee.

And now good morrow to our waking souls,
Which watch not one another out of fear;
For love all love of other sights controls,   10
And makes one little room, an every where.
Let sea-discoverers to new worlds have gone,
Let maps to other, worlds on worlds have shown,
Let us possess one world, each hath one, and is
      one.

My face in thine eye, thine in mine appears,   15
And true plain hearts do in the faces rest;
Where can we find two better hemispheres
Without sharp north, without declining west?
Whatever dies was not mixed equally;
If our two loves be one, or thou and I   20
Love so alike, that none do slacken, none can die.

The poem begins with an expression of wonder. What, says the lover, to his loved one—what could they have done—how did they spend their time before this? In the light of this intensity, all previous experience pales into something drab and meaningless.

But the poet does not use a metaphor of light (*intensity, pales, drab*) as we have done in the preceding sentence. He has his own metaphor, and it is an important one for defining the full and precise meaning of the poem. His metaphor involves a contrast between the life of an infant (feeding and sleeping) and the full consciousness of adult life.

The lovers, until they found each other, were "not weaned." They "sucked on" their pleasures "childishly." They did not possess desirable things—they merely dreamed of them. The dominant metaphor is, of course, complicated by other references. The pleasures on which they sucked were "country" pleasures—the sort that would appeal to naive rustics who do not know the great world. Their sleeping reminds the speaker of the legend of the Seven Sleepers of Ephesus, seven adults who drank enchanted wine and in their cave snored away for centuries. The implication that the delights of their earlier life were mere dreams receives special development and emphasis.

Except for this present delight into which they have come, all pleasure is a mere figment of the imagination. The lover appeals to his own personal experience: whatever beauty heretofore attracted him was only a dream, a foreshadowing, of the loved one—not only all his previous dreams of beauty, but even that beauty he came to possess turns out to be, in the light of this experience, unsubstantial, shadowy, and dreamlike.

Yet, in spite of the complications it receives, the dominant figure is sustained; it is reaffirmed in the first line of the second stanza. Their two souls are waking up. Their long nonage—the long sleep of their previous dreamlike experience—is over. They open their eyes and say "good morning" to each other.

The act of opening their eyes—implied in the preceding line—is seized upon and emphasized in the lines that immediately follow. The intensity of their gaze as they look at each other is underscored in line 9, by the mention of the only other instance of the absolutely fixed intensity of watching—that of the person or animal watching in wariness for the first hostile movement. The lovers' gaze embodies that riveted attention—but it is directed not "out of fear," but out of loving wonder.

The intensity of the gaze is developed further in lines 10–11: it is able to *see* in one little place the whole world, making "one little room, an every where." Let the explorers find the new world of the Americas, and go on to explore that new world. The lovers have found their new world in themselves. They have not only found it: they

possess it, for each is such a world (in the eyes of the loved one) and possesses such a world (in the person of the other loved one).

The grammar of lines 12–13 may be puzzling to the student. The sentences are not only highly condensed, but they embody a structure now archaic. Although we can still say: "Let discoverers *go* to new worlds," we should now have to say: "Grant that discoverers have gone to new worlds; well, let them," and so on.

Stanza 3 carries forward the metaphor of the lovers as constituting a new world, discovered and possessed. But it also sustains the picture of the lovers watching each other with rapt attention (l. 9). For as the lovers look into each other's eyes, each sees his own face reflected in the other's eyes—two "hemispheres," two half globes, which contain himself. We may note that here Donne has taken a time-worn image, that of the soul of an honest person sitting in the face (l. 16) and has intensified it by the elaborate image in line 15, which revivifies, as it were, the old conventional idea. Now the image suggests, not only candor and trust, but the total communion of the lovers.

The technical word *hemispheres,* with its special association with maps and globes, ties the image used here firmly to the earlier allusion to the "sea-discoverers" in line 12. And the poet goes on to argue that the world the lovers have discovered and possess is a better world than the one the voyagers have found. The lovers' world (which is themselves) has no north (with its implications of storm and cold) and no west (with its implications of sunset, evening, decline, and death).

Indeed, the last three lines of the poem go on to assert that the world discovered by the lovers carries the promise of immortality. The poet's argument rests upon the medieval belief that things that were completely one thing could not lose their perfection or that things "mixt equally," things possessing a perfect internal harmony, could not suffer change. If the love of each for the other has become merged in a love that is itself one and undivided, or if their loves completely balance each other, neither more nor less than the other, neither can die.

It is important to notice, however, that the speaker does not claim that their love will indeed last forever. The promise of immortality is conditioned by an *if*. The poet here does not prophesy. He is content to keep the whole poem focused upon the scene of waking, the fact of sudden initiation, the joyful but awed sense of discovery that the lovers experience in coming into possession of the new world that they did not know existed.

The images are abundant, and some of them may seem fantastic and bizarre. But it ought to be apparent that they are really tightly linked together. The "psychological line" through them is remarkably firm. The imagery is constantly shifted and extended, but the reader who grasps the dramatic situation will find that the shifts do not confuse.

One might make a further argument for the essential unity of the imagery. It could be claimed that all the images are simply variations on one dominant image, that implied in the title of the poem. For coming of age is itself a kind of waking up to the fullness of life, and Europe's discovery of the new world of the Americas can be regarded as a kind of coming of age, a kind of waking up to the fullness of the world. At least, one can argue that all three experiences have in common the sense of illumination and discovery, in the light of which the past experience becomes a sort of half-life—whether the life of dream or of childhood or (as Donne and other men of the Renaissance must have felt it) the more limited and confined life of the medieval world.

The last paragraph is not intended to imply that the poet consciously worked out variations and extensions of the metaphor of waking as a kind of preliminary blueprint for his poem, or that he was even conscious of all the interconnections among the images when he had completed the poem. Poets do not usually work by blueprint and formula. The process of writing a poem may be on the poet's part a work of exploration and discovery of "what he wants to say"—which he may come to know only *after* he has completed his poem. But the poet who possesses a disciplined sensibility may be able to accomplish quite intricate patternings of imagery "naturally" and without the self-consciousness which subsequent analysis of the imagery would imply.

Furthermore, we do not mean to imply that the relationship among the images that we have argued for is the only way of seeing them, *the* way in which they necessarily appear. But an examination of the imagery of this poem may suggest two things of some importance to the student: (1) that the imagery of a good poem may be studied with profit by the student, and that his further readings may result in his enriching his experience of the poem; and (2) that when the order of images seems somehow "right" in spite of apparently sharp and rapid shifts, the images may actually be aspects of a larger submerged image that gives a deeper coherence to the images than can be accounted for in examining merely their superficial relationships. And all this implies that the imagery of a poem may to a considerable extent be affecting us even before we have consciously explored it.

John Donne is probably the most famous member of what is known as the metaphysical school of poetry, which developed in the early seventeenth century in England. This poem, in its complicated, fantastic, and sometimes even bizarre imagery, is a splendid example of the work of that school. Observe that in this poem, as in all the best work of the metaphysicals, the imagery that at first may appear strained and recondite is made to justify itself on a logical and psychological basis. The tension that is at the root of all metaphor is simply pushed to an extreme, a typical feature of metaphysical practice.

EXERCISES

1. In our discussion of this poem we have properly stressed imagery and the way in which the argument of the poem is worked out through the images, but this poem also provides a very fine example of the poet's ability to manage the complications of tone. What is the tone of the first stanza? What is the tone with which the poem ends? How does it differ from the tone with which it begins?

2. How does the metrical situation of the closing

lines serve to develop and support the tone with which the poem ends?

3. Compare this poem with Auden's "Lay Your Sleeping Head" (sec. 14). That poem begins with the lovers' going to sleep in each other's arms. "The Good-Morrow" begins with the lovers' waking up together. Compare and contrast these two poems in tone, theme, and in the characteristic kind of imagery that each employs.

A VALEDICTION: FORBIDDING MOURNING

John Donne (1571/2–1631)

As virtuous men pass mildly away,
  And whisper to their souls, to go,
Whilst some of their sad friends do say,
  "The breath goes now," and some say, "No":

So let us melt, and make no noise,   5
  No tear-floods nor sigh-tempests move;
'Twere profanation of our joys
  To tell the laity our love.

Moving of the earth brings harms and fears;
  Men reckon what it did, and meant;   10
But trepidation of the spheres,
  Though greater far, is innocent.

Dull sublunary lovers' love
  —Whose soul is sense—cannot admit
Absence, because it doth remove   15
  Those things which elemented it.

But we by a love so much refined
  That ourselves know not what it is,
Inter-assurèd of the mind,
  Care less eyes, lips, and hands to miss.   20

Our two souls therefore, which are one,
  Though I must go, endure not yet
A breach, but an expansïon,
  Like gold to airy thinness beat.

If they be two, they are two so   25
  As stiff twin compasses are two;
Thy soul, the fixed foot, makes no show
  To move, but doth, if the other do.

And though it in the center sit,
  Yet, when the other far doth roam,   30
It leans, and hearkens after it,
  And grows erect, as that comes home.

Such wilt thou be to me, who must,
  Like the other foot, obliquely run.

Thy firmness draws my circle just,   35
  And makes me end, where I begun.

A poem of the English Renaissance such as this one may require a few notes if it is fully to be understood.

  Lines 7–8. The reference to the "laity" suggests that the two lovers are initiates in a cult or religion—they are priest and priestess as compared to the mere laity.

  Line 9. "Moving of the earth" signifies an earthquake. In the older astronomy the earth was at the center of the universe; around it revolved the various spheres that held the moon, the planets, the sun, and the stars.

  Line 11. "Trepidation of the spheres" is a quivering movement, more specifically the "libration" or oscillating movement attributed in the late Middle Ages to the ninth or crystalline sphere. The basic contrast in lines 9 and 11 is that between the harmful shaking of the little, corruptible earth and the harmless and unnoticed, vastly greater movement of the incorruptible heavens.

  Line 13. *Sublunary* (literally, "beneath the moon") means "earthly." The sphere of the moon was thought to be the first sphere, that nearest the earth.

  Line 16. "Which elemented it" means "which constituted its essential nature." Since the "love" of the sublunary lovers is grounded in the senses, for such lovers "out of sight" means indeed "out of mind."

  Line 24. Gold leaf is made by beating a small pellet of gold (placed between gold beater's skin) into thinner and thinner tissue. Baser metals would break up under this process.

  Line 26. The compass referred to is, of course, not a mariner's compass but the compass that we use to draw circles.

EXERCISES

Draw up a set of questions concerning the images in this poem and their effect on the tone. Then write an account of the poem.

THE GRASSHOPPER

To my Noble Friend Charles Cotton

Richard Lovelace (1618–1658)

Oh thou that swings't upon the waving hair
  Of some well-filled oaten beard,
Drunk ev'ry night with a delicious tear
    Dropped thee from Heav'n, where now th'art
    reared.

The joys of earth and air are thine entire,   5
  That with thy feet and wings dost hop and fly;
And when thy poppy works thou dost retire
  To thy carved acorn-bed to lie.

Up with the day, the sun thou welcom'st then,
  Sport'st in the gilt-plats of his beams,   10
And all these merry days mak'st merry men,
  Thy self, and melancholy streams.

But ah the sickle! Golden ears are cropped;
  Ceres and Bacchus bid goodnight;
Sharp frosty fingers all your flowers have
    topped,   15
  And what scythes spared, winds shave off quite.

Poor verdant fool! and now green ice! thy joys
  Large and as lasting as thy perch of grass,
Bid us lay in 'gainst winter, rain, and poise
  Their floods, with an o'erflowing glass.   20

Thou best of men and friends! we will create
  A genuine summer in each other's breast;
And spite of this cold time and frozen fate
  Thaw us a warm seat to our rest.

Our sacred hearths shall burn eternally   25
  As vestal flames; the North-wind, he
Shall strike his frost stretched wings, dissolve and
    fly
This Etna in epitome.

Dropping December shall come weeping in,
  Bewail th' usurping of his reign;   30
But when in showers of old Greek we begin,
  Shall cry, he hath his crown again!

Night as clear as Hesper shall our tapers whip
  From the light casements where we play,
And the dark Hag from her black mantle strip,   35
  And stick there everlasting day.

Thus richer than untempted kings are we,
  That asking nothing, nothing need:
Though lord of all what seas embrace, yet he
  That wants himself, is poor indeed.   40

EXERCISES

1. What is the speaker's attitude toward the grasshopper? Note that it is *not* the attitude taken in the fable of the ant and the grasshopper. The poet is not blaming the grasshopper for being a wastrel and a happy-go-lucky time-killer.
2. What part does the imagery play in depicting the grasshopper's joys? How much of it has a human reference? The grasshopper is "drunk ev'ry night" (l. 3), has a "carved acorn-bed" (l. 8); what other human references do you find?
3. What shift of tone occurs in line 17? How does the phrase "green ice" epitomize the grasshopper's innocent gullibility? Does the image have a realistic basis? What are the associations of "green"? How are the associations of "green" played off against those of "golden"? [Note that *gilt-plats* (l. 10) means "golden spots or platelets."]
4. On what basis does the poet shift from the grasshopper to a tribute to his friend? Is the poet arguing that the grasshopper enjoys only a spurious summer? That the only genuine summer is that which man can find within himself? In discussing the imagery, the student will probably require the following notes:

    In classic mythology, Ceres was the goddess of grain; Bacchus, the god of wine. *Poise* (l. 19) means "to balance". *Dropping* (l. 29) means "dripping." The "old Greek" (l. 31) probably refers to Greek wine. The "crown" of December (l. 32) is apparently a reference to the Christmas festivities that in 1642 had been banned by the Puritan regime in England.

From HAMLET

(Act 3, scene 1)

William Shakespeare (1564–1616)

  To be, or not to be: that is the question:
Whether 'tis nobler in the mind to suffer
The slings and arrows of outrageous fortune,
Or to take arms against a sea of troubles,
And by opposing end them? To die: to sleep;   5
No more; and by a sleep to say we end
The heart-ache and the thousand natural shocks
That flesh is heir to, 'tis a consummation
Devoutly to be wished. To die, to sleep;
To sleep; perchance to dream: ay, there's the
    rub;   10

For in that sleep of death what dreams may come
When we have shuffled off this mortal coil,
Must give us pause: there's the respect
That makes calamity of so long life;
For who would bear the whips and scorns of
    time,
The oppressor's wrong, the proud man's con-
    tumely,
The pangs of despised love, the law's delay,
The insolence of office, and the spurns
That patient merit of the unworthy takes,
When he himself might his quietus make   20
With a bare bodkin? who would fardels bear,
To grunt and sweat under a weary life,
But that the dread of something after death,
The undiscovered country from whose bourn
No traveler returns, puzzles the will,   25
And makes us rather bear those ills we have
Than fly to others that we know not of?
Thus conscience does make cowards of us all;
And thus the native hue of resolution
Is sicklied o'er with the pale cast of thought.   30

With this famous soliloquy of Hamlet, we find an extension of the method in the two poems by John Donne we have just read. In the Donne poems a series of images develops the discourse, but in Hamlet's soliloquy there is very little discourse. At this point in the play, Hamlet is debating suicide. His general theme is "To be or not to be?" The debate that goes on in his mind is conducted, not through a series of statements, but through a series of images with the force of metaphor. Earlier we have of course encountered poems with a series of images, for instance Keats's "To Autumn," but in many of those poems the images may have, as in "To Autumn," certain qualities that bind them together: all the images in Keats's poem are aspects of autumn. In Hamlet's speech the unity is not to be found in the sense of any overall image, but in the psychological thrust and emotional shifts of the speech; the speaker's motivation and feeling are the binding elements. Let us examine the passage with that idea in mind.

EXERCISES

1. Isolate and note down the separate metaphors that occur in this passage.
2. Are the metaphors consistent with each other? Are there any instances of mixed metaphor? If so, does such a mixture seem merely haphazard and confusing, or can you detect an underlying psychological connection?
3. One can conceive of troubles as missiles (slings and arrows); and the sea with its waves, rank on rank, pouring upon a beach may suggest an enormous army. But how can one take arms against a sea of troubles? Is the comparison absurd, or can you justify it in this context?
4. What image underlies line 12? (*Rub* in line 10 means "obstacle" or "hindrance.") What image underlies lines 29–30?

From *MACBETH*

(Act 1, scene 7)

William Shakespeare (1564–1616)

If it were done when 'tis done, then 'twere well
It were done quickly: if the assassination
Could trammel up the consequence, and catch
With his surcease success; that but this blow
Might be the be-all and the end-all here,   5
But here, upon this bank and shoal of time,
We'd jump the life to come. But in these cases
We still have judgment here; that we but teach
Bloody instructions, which, being taught, return
To plague the inventor: this even-handed
    justice   10
Commends the ingredients of our poisoned
    chalice
To our own lips. He's here in double trust;
First, as I am his kinsman and his subject
Strong both against the deed; then, as his host,
Who should against his murderer shut the door, 15
Not bear the knife myself. Besides, this Duncan
Hath borne his faculties so meek, hath been
So clear in his great office that his virtues
Will plead like angels, trumpet-tongued, against
The deep damnation of his taking-off;   20
And pity, like a naked new-born babe,
Striding the blast, or heaven's cherubim, horsed
Upon the sightless couriers of the air,
Shall blow the horrid deed in every eye,
That tears shall drown the wind. I have no spur 25
To prick the sides of my intent, but only
Vaulting ambition, which o'erleaps itself
And falls on the other.

In this speech, Macbeth contemplates the murder of Duncan, the king, who is his kinsman, and who has just that day bestowed honors upon him. The king is spending the night in Macbeth's castle. There is opportunity; and Lady Macbeth has urged her husband to murder the king and seize the crown for himself.

EXERCISES

1. Do lines 1–4 convey the sense of excitement and conspiratorial whispering? How?

2. What is the meanings of lines 2–7? What is the proviso that appeals to Macbeth—that would decide him if he could but be sure of it? (*Trammel* in line 3 means "to entangle as in a kind of net." *cf.* modern *trammel net. Jump* in line 7 is interpreted by *A Shakespeare Glossary* to mean "risk," "hazard.") What image or images are to be found in these lines?

3. Pick out the various images that occur in the rest of the passage. How are the images related to each other? Do you find any mixed metaphors? Can you or can you not justify them?

4. Consider in particular the metaphors that occur in lines 21–28. References to babes, angels, horses, tears, and the wind occur in a remarkable mixture in these lines. What does the passage mean? How are the images interrelated? Is the poet confused? Or does the passage constitute great poetry?

THE FORCE THAT THROUGH THE GREEN FUSE DRIVES THE FLOWER
Dylan Thomas (1914–1953)

The force that through the green fuse drives the
    flower
Drives my green age; that blasts the roots of trees
Is my destroyer.
And I am dumb to tell the crooked rose
My youth is bent by the same wintry fever.   5

The force that drives the water through the rocks
Drives my red blood; that dries the mouthing
    streams
Turns mine to wax.
And I am dumb to mouth unto my veins
How at the mountain spring the same mouth
    sucks.   10

The hand that whirls the water in the pool
Stirs the quicksand; that ropes the blowing wind
Hauls my shroud sail.
And I am dumb to tell the hanging man
How of my clay is made the hangman's lime.   15

The lips of time leech to the fountain head;
Love drips and gathers, but the fallen blood
Shall calm her sores.
And I am dumb to tell a weather's wind
How time has ticked a heaven round the stars.   20

And I am dumb to tell the lover's tomb
How at my sheet goes the same crooked worm.

EXERCISE

The imagery in this poem is bold and violent. Frame a set of questions that will allow you to explore the poet's specific use of these images and write, on the basis of these, an interpretation of this poem.

ODE ON MELANCHOLY
John Keats (1795–1821)

I

No, no! go not to Lethe, neither twist
    Wolf's-bane, tight-rooted, for its poisonous
      wine;
Nor suffer thy pale forehead to be kist
    By nightshade, ruby grape of Proserpine;
Make not your rosary of yew-berries,   5
    Nor let the beetle, nor the death-moth be
      Your mournful Psyche, nor the downy owl
A partner in your sorrow's mysteries;
    For shade to shade will come too drowsily,
      And drown the wakeful anguish of the soul. 10

II

But when the melancholy fit shall fall
    Sudden from heaven like a weeping cloud,
That fosters the droop-headed flowers all,
    And hides the green hill in an April shroud:
Then glut thy sorrow on a morning rose,   15
    Or on the rainbow of a salt sand-wave,
      Or on the wealth of globèd peonies;
Or if thy mistress some rich anger shows,
    Imprison her soft hand, and let her rave,
      And feed deep, deep upon her peerless eyes. 20

III

She dwells with Beauty—Beauty that must die;
    And Joy, whose hand is ever at his lips
Bidding adieu; and aching Pleasure nigh,
    Turning to poison while the bee-mouth sips;
Ay, in the very temple of Delight   25
    Veiled Melancholy has her sovran shrine,
      Though seen of none save him whose
        strenuous tongue
Can burst Joy's grape against his palate fine;
    His soul shall taste the sadness of her might,
      And be among her cloudy trophies hung. 30

    The poem begins with a rather simple statement: the intensity of sorrow is not to be found in the usual places in which one has been taught to expect it. On the contrary, melancholy haunts scenes of the greatest beauty; for beauty fades, it cannot endure. Logically, the structure of the poem is the development of this paradox, but psychologically—and in its depth of meaning as experience—the structure of the poem is in the relation among the images. The poet makes his reader to feel, as well as to understand, what he is saying, and one function of the imagery in this poem is to ensure the reader's experiencing the insight rather than merely noting it as an abstraction. In writing this poem, Keats thought *through* his images, which the reader must also do.

The speaker is ordering someone *not* to do certain things. As the developing context makes clear, the person addressed wants to have the experience of melancholy, but the poet thinks that he is about to seek it in the wrong way. Thus the poem begins with a rather abrupt and dramatic dismissal of the conventional appurtenances of melancholy —death moths, the mournful owl, the berries of the yew, the tree so often seen in European graveyards, and so on. The poet's reason is this: a person who is really concerned with "sorrow's mysteries" will find that wolf's-bane and the grapes associated with Proserpine, the Greek death goddess, will simply dull his anguish rather than enable him to experience its intensity. The man who wants to savor the essence of melancholy is counseled to seek out the fresh but evanescent objects of beauty like the morning rose or the rainbow that hangs for a moment over the breaking wave.

The poet's advice is evidently addressed to someone who does not wish to *drown* his sorrow but rather wishes to explore it and come to understand what it means. This advice, it also becomes clear, is not given by a sentimentalist, nor is it advice suited to a sentimentalist, that is, to the kind of person who would like to enjoy a good cry—to indulge himself in a sweet sadness. For the man who speaks the advice in this poem, a love of melancholy is much more than a kind of self-indulgence. The procedure that he recommends is designed to relate the melancholy mood to some constant truths about human life, and it will turn the morbidly obsessive mood into insight and understanding.

In accomplishing this transformation, the poet (or the person through whom the poet speaks) depends heavily upon imagery. The first figure of the second stanza at once tends to mark off the melancholy mood from mere sentimentality, for the mood is identified with the inevitability of the processes of nature: not consciously sought, but allowed to come of itself. So the speaker describes the melancholy fit's falling "Sudden from heaven like a weeping cloud."

The fact that the cloud is a "weeping cloud" may seem to the reader to be the obvious point of the comparison, and it is this mournful note that seems to be carried forward in the figure of the shroud, two lines further on. But the shroud figure is much richer than a casual reader might think, and the poet is not content to depend merely upon its usual associations. Indeed the phrase "April shroud" is startling, for the word *April* brings in associations—the joyfulness and fruitfulness of spring—that seem to run counter to death and sorrow. The cloud is an emblem of mournfulness, but the poet is reminding the reader that it is also an emblem of fruitfulness, and the implication would seem to be that, like the cloud, melancholy has a fruitfulness of its own. Such a mood may help one see more clearly the meaning of life—to see the close connection of joy with sorrow, and to find in their contrast a kind of paradoxical unity. To sum up: the "weeping cloud" figure is not simple and "easy"; and in its own complication and richness it moves us away from the stock response and the sentimental effect.

With line 15 the speaker's positive recommendations begin. When the melancholy "fit shall fall," one ought to "glut" his "sorrow on a morning rose." Why *morning*? Because the rose at evening may not bear quite the exquisite bloom it had at the beginning of the day. Or, he is to contemplate "the rainbow of a salt sand-wave." The rainbow made by the sunlight's falling on the spray of an ocean wave breaking on the sandy beach is another example of beauty perishing almost as quickly as seen.

The third instance, "the wealth of globéd peonies," does not stress the fleetingness of beauty, but perhaps the poet wanted here a less striking—a more desultory—image before he reached his climactic image, that of the woman in the fullness of her beauty, a woman agitated, filled with emotion, seen for a moment in all her pride of life.

The woman is treated like another object rather than like an equal human being. The imagined scene presents us with the rather Byronic young man, a connoisseur of beauty, treating the loved one as another and highest instance of his connoisseurship. When she shows some "rich anger" he is to seize her soft hand "and let her rave," paying no attention to what she says but looking deep into her matchless eyes.

The lady's anger is evidently not thought of here as a very serious matter but perhaps as a conscious pose that the lady knows will set off her beauty to better advantage. The connoisseur of melancholy, at any rate, is to savor her beauty as he would a particularly fine wine.

What is the poet's attitude here? Is it identical with that he counsels his friend to adopt? Is he teasing the ladies here? Or is he teasing his friend? Or is he simply saying to the man who aspires to a knowledge of melancholy: the woman whom you adore, considered simply as a beautiful *object,* considered as a more precious morning rose, as a speaking flower, is a supreme instance of beauty that is fleeting and doomed to pass away?

Whatever we consider the tone of this second stanza to be, the tone of the third stanza modulates into the deepest kind of seriousness. The lady is the supreme instance of "Beauty that must die," beauty heightened by the very fact that it is not lasting. In stanza III, Keats rather boldly associates the lady with personifications like Delight, Pleasure, Beauty, Joy, and Melancholy herself. How does he manage to do so and yet render the scene without a sense of artificiality or affectation? The answer may lie in the fact that the woman is considered to be a sort of priestess of Melancholy, though she resides in the "temple of Delight," where Joy and Pleasure abide, for in this temple "veiled Melancholy has her sovran shrine. . . ." The temple figure has been quietly prepared for in the first stanza. There the poet refers to one possessed by melancholy as a person indulging in a religious rite; he describes him as one seeking "a partner in your sorrow's mysteries." (*Mysteries* has among its meanings "the rites of certain religions, specially secret and esoteric religions.") Indeed, in stanza I, the whole assemblage of conventional objects associated with melancholy such as the "ruby grape of Proserpine" and the "rosary of yew-berries" finds its proper counterpart and contrast in this last stanza. For the "poisonous wine" of the temple of Melancholy is something so intensely pleasant that it makes the senses ache for it, but it turns "to poison while the bee-mouth sips" it. So with the other furnishings of the temple: there are no death-moths or downy owls but objects of joy and delight. The discerning person sees that melancholy is to be worshiped in no other temple than that of pleasure itself.

Throughout the poem, then, there is a thinking through images. We have yet to mention, however, the most forceful image of the poem. It occurs in lines 27–28 in the last stanza: "Though seen of none save him whose strenuous tongue/Can burst Joy's grape against his palate fine." The image is not a sentimentally pretty one. The poet has not chosen the image for its superficial attractiveness, but because he needs the image for what he has to say. What does it say? It says that the requisites for feeling the full force of melancholy are sensitiveness on the part of the observer (the "palate fine") but also force and penetration of insight (the "strenuous tongue") which will allow the observer to taste the essence of joy, an act that will necessitate destroying it. The figure of the bursting of Joy's grape is given dramatically: only the *strenuous* tongue can burst that grape. The word *burst* gathers up into itself both elements of the comparison: a flood of rich sweetness tasted at the instant of bursting but also the necessity of bursting—the necessary destruction—of joy.

Even this account does not fully explain why the figure is so successful as it is. Though it has a dramatic element and comes with a hint of surprise, it has actually been prepared for very carefully from the earliest stanzas. One may go back and notice how many images of taste appear in the poem, images that prepare for this last great figure of tasting. Stanza I gives us two instances: the water of the river Lethe and the "poisonous wine." In stanza II, the admonition to "glut" and to "feed" imply tasting. In the third stanza itself there is a tasting image in line 24. Pleasure turns to "poison while the bee-mouth sips." These and the great taste image of lines 27 and 28 are what supply the power for line 29: "His soul shall *taste* the sadness of her might" (italics ours). As a matter of fact, images of tasting and images of temple rites bind the poem together. The poem has been developed very subtly around these two basic images. They are central to the psychological —and eventually, the thematic—structure of the poem.

EXERCISE

What questions can you propose to lead to a fuller appreciation of this poem?

VOYAGES (II)

Hart Crane (1899–1932)

—And yet this great wink of eternity,
Of rimless floods, unfettered leewardings,
Samite sheeted and processioned where
Her undinal vast belly moonward bends,
Laughing the wrapt inflections of our love;   5

Take this Sea, whose diapason knells
On scrolls of silver snowy sentences,
The sceptered terror of whose sessions rends
As her demeanors motion well or ill,
All but the pieties of lovers' hands.   10

And onward, as bells off San Salvador
Salute the crocus lustres of the stars,
In these poinsettia meadows of her tides,—
Adagios of islands, O my Prodigal,
Complete the dark confessions her veins spell.   15

Mark how her turning shoulders wind the hours,
And hasten while her penniless rich palms
Pass superscription of bent foam and wave,—
Hasten, while they are true,—sleep, death, desire,
Close round one instant in one floating flower.   20

Bind us in time, O Seasons clear, and awe.
O minstrel galleons of Carib fire,
Bequeath us to no earthly shore until

Is answered in the vortex of our grave
The seal's wide spindrift gaze toward paradise.   25

This poem is little more than a series of images punctuated by certain exhortations: "Take this Sea" (l. 6), "Mark how her turning shoulders" (l. 16), and "Bind us in time" (l. 21). Those exhortations constitute the nearest thing to a discourse that the poem offers. But the images all relate to the sea— they assert its complex "sea-ness." Or rather, they develop what the speaker takes to be a mystical reality with which he wishes to be united in a deep fulfillment.

EXERCISE

Try to interpret the images, remembering that the basic unity is an emotional and tonal one.

THE ABYSS

Theodore Roethke (1908–1963)

I

Is the stair here?
Where's the stair?
"The stair's right there,
But it goes nowhere."

And the abyss? the abyss?   5
"The abyss you can't miss:
It's right where you are—
A step down the stair."

  Each time ever
  There always is   10
  Noon of failure,
  Part of a house.

  In the middle of,
  Around a cloud,
  On top a thistle   15
  The wind's slowing.

II

I have been spoken to variously
But heard little.
My inward witness is dismayed
By my unguarded mouth.   20
I have taken, too often, the dangerous path,
The vague, the arid,
Neither in nor out of this life.

Among us, who is holy?
What speech abides?   25
I hear the noise of the wall.
They have declared themselves,
Those who despise the dove.

Be with me, Whitman, maker of catalogues:
For the world invades me again,   30
And once more the tongues begin babbling.
And the terrible hunger for objects quails me:
The sill trembles.
And there on the blind
A furred caterpillar crawls down a string.   35
My symbol!
For I have moved closer to death, lived with
    death;
Like a nurse he sat with me for weeks, a sly surly
    attendant,
Watching my hands, wary.
Who sent him away?   40
I'm no longer a bird dipping a beak into rippling
    water
But a mole winding through earth,
A night-fishing otter.

III

Too much reality can be a dazzle, a surfeit;
Too close immediacy an exhaustion: 45
As when the door swings open in a florist's store-
    room—
The rush of smells strikes like a cold fire, the
    throat freezes,
And we turn back to the heat of August,
Chastened.

So the abyss—   50
The slippery cold heights,
After the blinding misery,
The climbing, the endless turning,
Strike like a fire,
A terrible violence of creation,   55
A flash into the burning heart of the abominable;
Yet if we wait, unafraid, beyond the fearful
    instant,
The burning lake turns into a forest pool,
The fire subsides into rings of water,
A sunlit silence.   60

IV

How can I dream except beyond this life?
Can I outleap the sea—
The edge of all the land, the final sea?
I envy the tendrils, their eyeless seeking,
The child's hand reaching into the coiled
    smilax,   65

And I obey the wind at my back
Bringing me home from the twilight fishing.

    In this, my half-rest,
    Knowing slows for a moment,
    And not-knowing enters, silent,   70
    Bearing being itself,
    And the fire dances
    To the stream's
    Flowing.

Do we move toward God, or merely another
    condition?   75
By the salt waves I hear a river's undersong,
In a place of mottled clouds, a thin mist morning
    and evening.
I rock between dark and dark,
My soul nearly my own,
My dead selves singing.   80
And I embrace this calm—
Such quiet under the small leaves!—
Near the stem, whiter at root,
A luminous stillness.

    The shade speaks slowly: 85
    'Adore and draw near.
    Who knows this—
    Knows all.'

V

I thirst by day. I watch by night.
I receive! I have been received!   90
I hear the flowers drinking in their light,
I have taken counsel of the crab and the sea-
    urchin,
I recall the falling of small waters,
The stream slipping beneath the mossy logs,
Winding down to the stretch of irregular sand, 95
The great logs piled like matchsticks.

I am most immoderately married:
The Lord God has taken my heaviness away;
I have merged, like the bird, with the bright air,
And my thought flies to the place by the
    bo-tree.   100

Being, not doing, is my first joy.

This poem obviously dramatizes a bout
with madness. The speaker says that "Too
much reality can be a dazzle, a surfeit." He
observes that his "inward witness is dis-
mayed/By [his] unguarded mouth." He cries
out that "the world invades me again/And
once more the tongues begin babbling."

EXERCISES

1. What is "the abyss"?
2. Can you find any principle that seems to govern the poet's selection and deployment of the images in this poem?
3. Does the last line of the poem signal a recovery from madness, or a relapse into madness, or what?
4. Though the poem is concerned with a lapse into madness, is it merely a sort of case history, a clinical note? Or does it concern an experience of general relevance and an assessment of values?

YOU, ANDREW MARVELL
Archibald MacLeish (b. 1892)

And here face down beneath the sun
And here upon earth's noonward height
To feel the always coming on
The always rising of the night:

To feel creep up the curving east   5
The earthly chill of dusk and slow
Upon those under lands the vast
And ever climbing shadow grow

And strange at Ecbatan the trees
Take leaf by leaf the evening strange   10
The flooding dark about their knees
The mountains over Persia change

And now at Kermanshah the gate
Dark empty and the withered grass
And through the twilight now the late   15
Few travelers in the westward pass

And Baghdad darken and the bridge
Across the silent river gone
And through Arabia the edge
Of evening widen and steal on   20

And deepen on Palmyra's street
The wheel rut in the ruined stone
And Lebanon fade out and Crete
High through the clouds and overblown

And over Sicily the air   25
Still flashing with the landward gulls
And loom and slowly disappear
The sails above the shadowy hulls

And Spain go under and the shore
Of Africa the gilded sand   30
And evening vanish and no more
The low pale light across that land

Nor now the long light on the sea:

And here face downward in the sun
To feel how swift how secretly   35
The shadow of the night comes on . . .

EXERCISES

1. The title alludes to a couplet in Marvell's poem "To His Coy Mistress":
     And at my back I always hear
     Time's winged chariot hurrying near.
Is the title appropriate?
2. Locate on a globe the places named. Does their location bear on the meaning of the poem?
3. This poem traces the creeping shadow of night as the globe of the earth turns from west to east. Are the descriptive details well chosen? What do the details suggest?
4. The phrase "rising of the night" suggests the rising of flood waters. Is this hint developed as the poem goes on?
5. The poet uses the word *and* twenty-two times in this poem. Can you justify his insistence upon this word?
6. The rhythm changes in the last lines of the poem. Scan the last stanza. Try to define the nature of the change in rhythm. Is it justified?
7. What attitude toward the coming on of night does the speaker take? How do you know? Compare the attitude here to that in Keats's "To Autumn." To that in Ransom's "Bells for John Whiteside's Daughter."

THE CONVERGENCE OF THE TWAIN
Lines on the Loss of the Titanic
Thomas Hardy (1840–1928)

I

In a solitude of the sea
Deep from human vanity,
And the Pride of Life that planned her, stilly couches she.

II

Steel chambers, late the pyres
Of her salamandrine fires,   5
Cold currents thrid, and turn to rhythmic tidal lyres.

III

Over the mirrors meant
To glass the opulent
The sea-worm crawls—grotesque, slimed, dumb, indifferent.

IV

Jewels in joy designed   10
To ravish the sensuous mind
Lie lightless, all their sparkles bleared and black and blind.

V

Dim moon-eyed fishes near
Gaze at the gilded gear
And query: "What does this vaingloriousness
down here?" . . .   15

VI

Well: while was fashioning
This creature of cleaving wing,
The Immanent Will that stirs and urges everything

VII

Prepared a sinister mate
For her—so gaily great—   20
A Shape of Ice, for the time far and dissociate.

VIII

And as the smart ship grew
In stature, grace, and hue,
In shadowy silent distance grew the Iceberg too.

IX

Alien they seemed to be: 25
No mortal eye could see
The intimate welding of their later history,

X

Or sign that they were bent
By paths coincident
On being anon twin halves of one august event,   30

XI

Till the Spinner of the Years
Said "Now!" And each one hears,
And consummation comes, and jars two hemispheres.

The subtitle of the poem tells us that it was written upon the loss of the *Titanic*, which plowed into an iceberg on her maiden voyage. Many different kinds of poems might have been written upon such a subject: this particular poem, however, is not a narra-tive, nor is it an objective description. It very frankly tries to read a meaning or an interpretation into the event. The meaning is, in part, the "vanity of human wishes." The great ship, which represented the peak of man's ambition and attainment in his attempt to conquer nature, does not conquer, but is conquered by, nature.

The poem begins, indeed, with the interpretation. The ship, planned by "the Pride of Life," finds its place of rest in the loneliness of the sea, "Deep from human vanity." The reader expects the more usual phrase, "*far* from human vanity." But *deep* is correct. The ship is on the seafloor, and the phrase is important for two considerations: it helps prevent the interpretation from falling into a conventional moralization—the poet twists the conventional phrase into a more subtle and accurate one; and it directs our view to the seafloor where the ship reposes.

The first two lines in each tercet give a sense of rapidity that contrasts sharply with the slow and heavy march of the long last line. Notice that Hardy, in stanzas II–V, specifically associates this rapidity with a sense of frail instability. He uses the first two lines in each case to describe some detail of the ship, and then the last line for his ironical comment on that detail, thus associating the long roll of the line with the sea and with the dark irony of fate itself.

This is in general the plan of rhythmic effects in the poem: the contrast between the rhythms supports the ironical contrasts in the poem. But Hardy does not allow the rhythm to become monotonous. For example, in stanza II there is a competition between *cold* and *current* for the accent. To take another example, in stanza III it is impossible to read the last line without giving a heavy and separate emphasis to each of the adjectives: *grotesque, slimed, dumb, indifferent.*

Not the least of the ironical effects that Hardy employs in the earlier stanzas of the poem is that of putting in the mouths of the fishes, with a kind of grim comedy, a question that in phrasing and rhythm might have come out of Ecclesiastes: "What does this vaingloriousness down here?"

So much for the poet's comment on the vanity of human wishes. Up to this point the poem has occupied itself with the large, sardonic handling of a conventional theme. But Hardy does not risk tiring the reader. He has another theme to state that is a matter for irony no less than the theme just mentioned and that forces the poem out of sardonic comment into ironic interpretation—an interpretation not narrowed to one event but valid for the whole wider implications of life.

The transition from the first section of the poem to the second is afforded by the question asked by the fishes. Hardy decides to answer their question. The colloquial word *Well* is tremendously important. It is as if Hardy had said, "I shall put a period to my sardonic play with the idea. If you really want to know what happened, this is what happened." And the rhythm supports this also. There is a heavy pause on the word *Well,* and the pause effectively contrasts with, and breaks the rhythm of, what has gone before, and introduces the new section.

The reader should be warned here, that the foregoing sentences do not mean that Hardy has broken his poem in two. Far from it. The irony built up in the preceding stanzas between the vanity of man's frail works and the elemental strength of nature is employed in the stanzas that follow. Fate, Hardy says, unknown to man, had planned all along the meeting of the iceberg and the *Titanic.* He proceeds then to prove it, with irony again; this time, however, there is not only the ironical contrast between man's works and nature's, there is another contrast between the foreknowledge of man and that of fate. Stanzas VIII, IX, and X develop the contrast between the iceberg and the ship, contrasting them in extremes, but each time, in the last lines, tying them together again. Our acceptance of the paradox is in large part the result of Hardy's figures in these stanzas. For example, "intimate welding": the image is that of the most stable form of union possible, where one piece of metal becomes an integral part of another. And the further we explore the image, the more appropriate it becomes. The ship and iceberg fuse into trag-edy when they meet. The image in stanza X is drawn from mathematics, and gives to the meeting of the two objects the inevitability of mathematics. The paths the two travel are in the purposes of fate, lines that are *coincident.* The phrase "august event" in this stanza also deserves notice. *August* means "imperial in splendor," "impressive," "commanding dignity." We are now far from the more conventional contrasts of the first part of the poem. The sinking of the great vessel is an *august* event, and Hardy, having fully established the power and inevitability of fate, is prepared now to let man have his due to this extent at least.

The climax of the poem comes, of course, in the last stanza. Both man and nature are in the grip of a master power that uses the works of both indiscriminately. When fate, the Spinner of the Years, gives the command, they leap to their places. Here the rhythm of the lines rises to the situation. There is a pause after the heavy *Now* of command and the rest of the second line leaps forward with the first part of the last line to come to a momentary pause on *comes,* with another pause on *jars.* If one asks how the poet manages this, one can point out the effect of alliteration in the last line, and the fact that there can be only a partially heavy accent on the third syllable of *consummation.* *Comes* is the first word in the line that can be stressed heavily.

The whole poem is a splendid study in the variations of meter a poet may use, as it is also a fine study in the effective use of contrasts of varying degree and of varying effect.

The ground plan of the poem is a system of contrasts and fusions of opposites—a ground plan used in many of the greatest poems. In the case of this poem, the welding of the ship and the iceberg into "one august event" is a sort of parable of the internal structure of the poem, so that the story of the poem itself reflects what the poet is doing beneath the surface.

EXERCISE

Write a brief treatment of this as a symbolic poem.

Musicality

Thus far in discussing the technical aspects of poetry we have dwelt primarily on the dramatic aspects of meter, rhythm, and tone—that is, on the aspects we generally associate with speech. But poetry is often thought of as musical—as giving a pleasure in the mere sequence of sounds as such. Turn to subsection 19.9 and give it very careful attention, for this is a subject that invites many misconceptions.

EXERCISES

1. Thumb over the poems read thus far and locate the three that have pleased you most by their verbal quality.
2. Discuss the factors contributing to the musicality of stanza I of Keats's "To Autumn." Stanza III may be said to be equally musical, but can you detect a difference in the emotional effect of the two stanzas? Can you relate this to specific phonetic differences?
3. Write a metrical and phonetic analysis of "Ghostly Tree."
4. Wordsworth's "A Slumber Did My Spirit Seal" is not so obviously musical as Keats's "To Autumn" or Adams's "Ghostly Tree." But it is musical. What factors are involved?
5. In "Desert Places," by Frost, do you notice any difference in musicality between the last stanza and the rest of the poem? Be specific. How would a difference here be dramatically related to the meaning of the poem?
6. Turn to Melville's "Commemorative of a Naval Victory." Upon rereading it, do you feel that a versification approximating that of "To Autumn" or even "A Slumber Did My Spirit Seal" would have improved it? Inspect line 26. Do you think that the first three feet of the line give a musical effect? What about the last foot? What effect does it give? Do you have any comment here?
7. Examine "A Glass of Beer" by James Stephens (sec. 14). Comment on the verbal effects. What instances of cacophony do you find?
8. Return to Waller's "Song" (sec. 14) and examine the rhythmic and phonetic factors in the last stanza. What bearing do you think they have on the tone?

9. Consider the rhythmic and the phonetic qualities of the last two lines of Auden's "Lay Your Sleeping Head" (sec. 14) in contrast to the body of the poem. What do you make of this?

GROUP 3: IMAGES—OR SYMBOLS— TO EXPLORE

EXPERIENCE OF THE WEST*
John Peale Bishop (1892–1944)

They followed the course of heaven, as before
Trojan in smoky armor westward fled
Disastrous walls and on his shoulders bore
A dotard recollection had made mad,

Depraved by years, Anchises: on the strong   5
Tall bronze upborne, small sack of impotence;
Yet still he wore that look of one who young
Had closed with Love in cloudy radiance.

So the discoverers when they wading came
From shallow ships and climbed the wooded
    shores;   10
They saw the west: a sky of falling flame
And by the streams savage ambassadors.

O happy, brave and vast adventure! Where
Each day the sun beat rivers of new gold;
The wild grape ripened; springs reflected fear;   15
The wild deer fled; the bright snake danger
    coiled.

They too, the stalwart conquerors of space,
Each on his shoulders wore a wise delirium
Of memory and age; ghostly embrace
Of fathers slanting toward a western tomb.   20

A hundred and a hundred years they stayed
Aloft, until they were as light as autumn
Shells of locusts. Where then were they laid?
And in what wilderness oblivion?

SONNET 97

William Shakespeare (1564–1616)

How like a winter hath my absence been
From thee, the pleasure of the fleeting year!
What freezing have I felt, what dark days seen!

---

* According to Virgil's poem, the Trojan hero Aeneas, son of Anchises and Aphrodite, the Greek goddess of love, escaped from Troy when it was captured by the Greeks and sailed westward to found the new city of Rome. He carried his aged father on his back through the burning city, though Anchises was to die in Sicily before the new homeland was reached.

What old December's bareness everywhere!
And yet this time removed was summer's time;   5
The teeming autumn, big with rich increase,
Bearing the wanton burden of the prime,
Like widowed wombs after their lord's decease:
Yet this abundant issue seem'd to me

But hope of orphans, and unfathered fruit;   10
For summer and his pleasures wait on thee,
And, thou away, the very birds are mute;
    Or if they sing, 'tis with so dull a cheer,
    That leaves look pale, dreading the winter's
    near.

A PASSER-BY

Robert Bridges (1844–1930)

Whither, O splendid ship, thy white sails crowding,
    Leaning across the bosom of the urgent West,
That fearest nor sea rising, nor sky clouding,
    Whither away, fair rover, and what thy quest?
    Ah! soon, when Winter has all our vales opprest,   5
When skies are cold and misty, and hail is hurling,
    Wilt thou glide on the blue Pacific, or rest
In a summer haven asleep, thy white sails furling.

I there before thee, in the country that well thou knowest,
    Already arrived am inhaling the odorous air: 10
I watch thee enter unerringly where thou goest,
    And anchor queen of the strange shipping there,
    Thy sails for awnings spread, thy masts bare;
Nor is aught from the foaming reef to the snow-capp'd, grandest
    Peak, that is over the feathery palms more fair.   15
Than thou, so upright, so stately, and still thou standest.

And yet, O splendid ship, unhailed and nameless,
    I know not if, aiming a fancy, I rightly divine
That thou hast a purpose joyful, a courage blameless,
    Thy port assured in a happier land than mine.   20
    But for all I have given thee, beauty enough is thine,
As thou, aslant with trim tackle, and shrouding,
    From the proud nostril curve of a prow's line
    In the offing scatterest foam, thy white sails crowding.

DEATH OF LITTLE BOYS

Allen Tate (b. 1899)

When little boys grow patient at last, weary,
Surrender their eyes immeasurably to the night,
The event will rage terrific as the sea;
Their bodies fill a crumbling room with light.

Then you will touch at the bedside, torn in two,   5
Gold curls now deftly intricate with gray
As the windowpane extends a fear to you
From one peeled aster drenched with the wind all
    day.

And over his chest the covers in the ultimate
    dream,

Will mount to the teeth, ascend the eyes, press
    back   10
The locks—while round his sturdy belly gleam
The suspended breaths, white spars above the
    wreck:

Till all the guests, come in to look, turn down
Their palms; and delirium assails the cliff
Of Norway where you ponder, and your little
    town   15
Reels like a sailor drunk in a rotten skiff. . . .

The bleak sunshine shrieks its chipped music then
Out to the milkweed amid the fields of wheat.
There is a calm for you where men and women
Unroll the chill precision of moving feet.   20

TEARS, IDLE TEARS
Alfred, Lord Tennyson (1809–1892)

Tears, idle tears, I know not what they mean,
Tears from the depth of some divine despair
Rise in the heart, and gather to the eyes,
In looking on the happy Autumn-fields,
And thinking of the days that are no more.   5

Fresh as the first beam glittering on a sail,
That brings our friends up from the underworld,
Sad as the last which reddens over one
That sinks with all we love below the verge;
So sad, so fresh, the days that are no more.   10

Ah, sad and strange as in dark summer dawns
The earliest pipe of half-awaken'd birds
To dying ears, when unto dying eyes
The casement slowly grows a glimmering square;
So sad, so strange, the days that are no more.   15

Dear as remember'd kisses after death,
And sweet as those by hopeless fancy feign'd
On lips that are for others; deep as love,
Deep as first love, and wild with all regret;
O Death in Life, the days that are no more.   20

DEATH THE LEVELER
James Shirley (1596–1666)

The glories of our blood and state
    Are shadows, not substantial things;
There is no armour against Fate;
    Death lays his icy hand on kings:
        Sceptre and Crown   5
        Must tumble down,
And in the dust be equal made
With the poor crookèd scythe and spade.

Some men with swords may reap the field,
    And plant fresh laurels where they kill: 10
But their strong nerves at last must yield;
    They tame but one another still:
        Early or late
        They stoop to fate,
And must give up their murmuring breath   15
When they, pale captives, creep to death.

The garlands wither on your brow;
    Then boast no more your mighty deeds!
Upon Death's purple altar now
    See where the victor-victim bleeds.   20
        Your heads must come
        To the cold tomb:
Only the actions of the just
Smell sweet and blossom in their dust.

RHAPSODY ON A WINDY NIGHT
T. S. Eliot (1888–1965)

Twelve o'clock.
Along the reaches of the street
Held in a lunar synthesis,
Whispering lunar incantations
Dissolve the floors of memory   5
And all its clear relations
Its divisions and precisions.
Every street lamp that I pass
Beats like a fatalistic drum,
And through the spaces of the dark   10
Midnight shakes the memory
As a madman shakes a dead geranium.

    Half-past one,
The street-lamp sputtered,
The street-lamp muttered,   15
The street-lamp said, "Regard that woman
Who hesitates toward you in the light of the door
Which opens on her like a grin.
You see the border of her dress
Is torn and stained with sand,   20
And you see the corner of her eye
Twists like a crooked pin."

    The memory throws up high and dry
A crowd of twisted things;
A twisted branch upon the beach   25
Eaten smooth, and polished
As if the world gave up
The secret of its skeleton,
Stiff and white,
A broken spring in a factory yard,   30
Rust that clings to the form that the strength has
        left
Hard and curled and ready to snap.

    Half-past two,
The street-lamp said,
"Remark the cat which flattens itself in the
        gutter,   35
Slips out its tongue
And devours a morsel of rancid butter."
So the hand of the child, automatic,
Slipped out and pocketed a toy that was running
        along the quay.
I could see nothing behind that child's eye.   40
I have seen eyes in the street
Trying to peer through lighted shutters,
And a crab one afternoon in a pool,
An old crab with barnacles on his back,
Gripped the end of a stick which I held him.   45

    Half-past three,
The lamp sputtered,

The lamp muttered in the dark.
The lamp hummed:
"Regard the moon,   50
La lune ne garde aucune rancune,
She winks a feeble eye,
She smiles into corners.
She smooths the hair of the grass.
The moon has lost her memory.   55
A washed-out smallpox cracks her face,
Her hand twists a paper rose,
That smells of dust and eau de Cologne,
She is alone
With all the old nocturnal smells   60
That cross and cross across her brain."
The reminiscence comes
Of sunless dry geraniums
And dust in crevices,
Smells of chestnuts in the streets,   65
And female smells in shuttered rooms,
And cigarettes in corridors
And cocktail smells in bars.

   The lamp said,
"Four o'clock,   70
Here is the number on the door.
Memory!
You have the key,
The little lamp spreads a ring on the stair.
Mount.   75
The bed is open; the tooth-brush hangs on the
    wall,
Put your shoes at the door, sleep, prepare for life."

   The last twist of the knife.

LITTLE EXERCISE

For Thomas Edwards Wanning

Elizabeth Bishop (b. 1911)

Think of the storm roaming the sky uneasily
like a dog looking for a place to sleep in,
listen to it growling.

Think how they must look now, the mangrove
    keys
lying out there unresponsive to the lightning   5
in dark, coarse-fibred families,

where occasionally a heron may undo his head,
shake up his feathers, make an uncertain comment
when the surrounding water shines.

Think of the boulevard and the little palm trees [10]
all stuck in rows, suddenly revealed
as fistfuls of limp fish-skeletons.

It is raining there. The boulevard
and its broken sidewalks with weeds in every
    crack
are relieved to be wet, the sea to be freshened.   15

Now the storm goes away again in a series
of small, badly lit battle-scenes,
each in "Another part of the field."

Think of someone sleeping in the bottom of a
    row-boat
tied to a mangrove root or the pile of a bridge;   20
think of him as uninjured, barely disturbed.

SNOWFLAKES

Henry Wadsworth Longfellow (1807–1882)

Out of the bosom of the Air,
   Out of the cloud-folds of her garment shaken,
Over the woodlands brown and bare,
    Over the harvest-fields forsaken
      Silent and soft and slow
      Descends the snow.

Even as our cloudy fancies take
   Suddenly shape in some divine expression,
Even as the troubled heart doth make
    In white countenance confession,
      The troubled sky reveals
      The grief it feels.

This is the poem of the Air,
   Slowly in silent syllables recorded;
This is the secret of despair,
    Long in its cloudy bosom hoarded.
      Now whispered and revealed
      To wood and field.

Onomatopoeia

To continue the study of factors that
make for verbal richness and expressiveness,
turn to subsection 19.10.

EXERCISES

1. Return to "Meeting at Night" by Robert
Browning (sec. 12), and discuss the instances of
onomatopoeia you find there.
2. Reread Macbeth's soliloquy ("If it were done
when 'tis done"). If you do not remember the
exact circumstances of the speech, go back to the
play and get your bearings. After getting well
soaked in the passage, actually stand up and move

around and try to act out the part as on a stage, saying the words out loud. Through what range of emotion and attitude does Macbeth pass? What basis does the text give for saying that lines 1–5 have a sense of suppressed excitement and conspiratorial whispering—as though the very walls had ears? What is the basic attitude in lines 6–18? Of what is Macbeth now trying to persuade himself? What phonic qualities, including rhythm, indicate a shift in feeling in lines 19–25? What change occurs in line 25? To answer these questions you will probably have to go back and scan the text and study its other aspects.

3. In the first and last stanzas of Thomas Hardy's "Channel Firing" (sec. 14), what instances of onomatopoeia do you find?

Section 16

THEME

Over and over again, in discussing poems we have had to deal with the question of theme. We have necessarily distinguished subject from theme, though, of course, the two are intimately related. For instance, the subject of the ballad "Sir Patrick Spens" (sec. 12) may possibly be an episode in history and legend, an ill-advised voyage undertaken to bring a Norwegian princess to Scotland for marriage* But the theme is a celebration of fidelity and courage, and in the end it includes the notion that true nobility depends on such qualities rather than on birth and rank. Or in Keats's "To Autumn" (sec. 15), the subject is a series of aspects of that season, but the theme concerns an attitude toward time and the notion that true fulfillment and happiness come in the acceptance of the life process in time.

With the distinction between subject and theme in mind, we realize that the same subject—or kind of subject—may lead to many different themes, and conversely, that the same theme, or similar themes, may develop from many different subjects. For instance, Suckling's "The Constant Lover," Wyatt's "They Flee from Me," and Auden's "Lay Your Sleeping Head" (all, sec. 14) have a common subject—the instability of love—but we immediately recognize, even if we do not easily define, basic differences in the way the several poets view the subject. Wyatt looks back with a satiric bitterness on love betrayed. Suckling advertises himself as the inconsistent one trapped into an at least provisional constancy by the surpassing charms of his lady, asserting this with gay, self-deprecating humor. Auden admits the pathos of the instability of love but considers that love is redeemed by the nature of the illusion it springs from, implying that, though all human values are in one sense illusory, since they are created by man, they are, nevertheless, necessary, since they give life what significance and happiness it does have. These differences among the views of the individual poets are thematic differences—and even though we find it hard to label them, we see them as basic differences in the way of looking at life in general.

In discussing such differences of theme, we have often returned to the idea that, though a poem may make general statements—may, that is, present its theme more or less overtly—a poem must always dramatize, embody, its meaning. This idea implies the basic significance of imagery, rhythm, and tone as aspects of meaning, as elements in

---

* This was Sir Walter Scott's notion of the ballad, as he indicates in his *Minstrelsy of the Scottish Border* (1802–1803). But the earlier (and simpler) version of the poem, published in 1765, gives no hint of any particular mission that Sir Patrick was to perform.

establishing theme. In discussing the theme of a poem, we must always remind ourselves that the *direct statement* of the theme is never adequate to the full meaning of a poem. We must constantly try to see how the poem is the experiential embodiment of meaning, how any statement that we may make must be qualified by the actual "being" of the poem. The rhythms of "To Autumn," for instance, are aspects of the poet's attitude toward time and all human experience.

Poems embody their themes, and the way of the embodiment is, ultimately, an aspect of the theme. The vigor and subtlety of the embodiment, the immediacy and brilliance of realization in a poem, are what first draw us to it. These qualities are what enrich our sense of the world and enlarge our experience. But by their fullness of embodiment, poems not only excite our imagination, directly or indirectly, they make evaluations of experience. What Keats finds valuable in life is not precisely what Blake or T. S. Eliot finds valuable. So each reader, early on, finds one poet more congenial than another, in terms of his basic values, attitudes, emotional appeals. We are human beings living in a world of such concerns, and inevitably we are affected by them in poetry; these concerns are as much a part of experience as the sight of the sea or the joys of love. But we should not make these concerns our first consideration as we approach a poem. The simple fact of the intensity, immediacy, or subtlety of the poem as an embodiment and an expression has its own value in heightening our sense of life. Let us start there.

GROUP 1: THE CONDUCT OF LIFE

A PSALM OF LIFE

What the Heart of the Young Man
Said to the Psalmist

Henry Wadsworth Longfellow (1807–1882)

Tell me not in mournful numbers,
    Life is but an empty dream!—
For the soul is dead that slumbers,
    And things are not what they seem.

Life is real! Life is earnest!   5
    And the grave is not its goal;

Dust thou art, to dust returnest,
    Was not spoken of the soul.

Not enjoyment, and not sorrow,
    Is our destined end or way;   10
But to act, that each tomorrow
    Find us farther than today.

Art is long, and Time is fleeting,
    And our hearts, though stout and brave,
Still, like muffled drums, are beating   15
    Funeral marches to the grave.

In the world's broad field of battle,
    In the bivouac of Life,
Be not like dumb, driven cattle!
    Be a hero in the strife!   20

Trust no Future, howe'er pleasant!
    Let the dead Past bury its dead!
Act,—act in the living Present!
    Heart within, and God o'erhead!

Lives of great men all remind us   25
    We can make our lives sublime,
And, departing leave behind us
    Footprints on the sands of time;

Footprints, that perhaps another,
    Sailing o'er life's solemn main,   30
A forlorn and shipwrecked brother,
    Seeing, shall take heart again.

Let us, then, be up and doing,
    With a heart for any fate;
Still achieving, still pursuing,   35
    Learn to labor and to wait.

When "A Psalm of Life" first appeared, in 1839, in Longfellow's first book of poems, it fitted perfectly the spirit of enterprise and energy that a new expanding nation needed in the face of the challenge of the western spaces of the continent and the promise of the future. It fitted so perfectly the optimism and expansionism of the age that nobody looked very closely at the poem.

Let us take a close look at it now, beginning with its thematic structure. First, take stanza 2, in which the notion that life is real seems to be a consequence of the idea that man is immortal and that life is a preparation for eternity. In this connection stanza 3 affirms that the basic purpose of life is to get "farther" along. But to what end? Presumably eternity and our reward? When we get to stanzas 5 and 6, however, action in "the living present" seems to be the important thing—with some passing reference, of course, to "God o'erhead." Then comes another switch. In stanzas 7 and 8, we are told that anybody can be "great" and can make his life "sublime." How? By winning, or simply by having the satisfaction of trying very hard? Presumably the latter, for in stanza 9 we are told that we had better have a "heart for any fate"—including failure, no doubt. But the implied notion of the possibility of failure is canceled by the ideas of "achieving" and "pursuing" in the next line. But what, then, of the bypassed idea that sublimity may be in the encouraging footprints we leave on the sands of time?

Since the thematic structure seems not very coherent, perhaps the imagery will pull the ideas together. Let us look at some of the implications. In stanza 4, the drums are "muffled" as for a funeral, and the drums are "our hearts"—a metaphor for man's natural condition, we assume. But in stanza 5, on the battlefield, what drums are urging us to be heroes? Those same old hearts? And another confusion has set in. One can be a hero on the field, but how in the "bivouac"? Nobody "drives" anybody in a bivouac, like cattle or otherwise. Then in stanza 7 we find the "sands of time." The normal expectation for such sands would be the sands of an hourglass, in which, of course, no footprints can be left. And after the hero has been shipwrecked and has left his footprint, where has he gone? Did somebody come and pick him up? The imagery seems not only to be no help in resolving our questions about theme but to pose still more questions. What, we well may ask, *has* "the heart of the young man said to the psalmist"?

EXERCISES

1. Because the poem fitted the spirit of enterprise and energy of the times when it was published it was widely popular. No doubt enterprise and energy are always needed, but how effective do you find the poem now? Effective as a poem? Effective as an inspiration to action? Or are you inclined to relate the two questions?

2. Is the poem more than a series of more or less detached pieces of encouraging advice? That is, does it have a thematic structure? Do you think our questions about the poem's thematic structure are fair? If they are, what effect does the poem's slap-dash incoherence have on the advice it offers? And on the poem in general?

3. How effective is the imagery here? Is it too complicated in the wrong way? That is, does it demand too much second-guessing and too much mechanical explanation? The questions it raises are logically confusing. Do such questions present themselves in the complicated metaphors of, say, Sonnet 73 by Shakespeare or "The Tyger" by Blake (both, sec. 13), or "A Valediction: Forbidding Mourning" by Donne, "Voyages (II)" by Crane, or "Rhapsody on a Windy Night" by Eliot (all, sec. 15)? Or, even, Hamlet's or Macbeth's soliloquy (both, sec. 15)?

4. What is the tone of this poem? Are there any variations? Can you relate the tone to any technical features?

From *KING HENRY IV, PART 1*

(Act 5, scene 2)

William Shakespeare (1564–1616)

> O gentlemen, the time of life is short!
> To spend that shortness basely were too long,
> If life did ride upon a dial's point,
> Still ending at the arrival of an hour.
> An if we live, we live to tread on kings;
> If die, brave death, when princes die with us!

EXERCISE

This speech is made by Sir Henry Percy, called Hotspur, just before the Battle of Shrewsbury, in which the rebellion of the Percys was put down by the king's victory and Hotspur himself killed. From this speech, what kind of young man do you think Hotspur was? Valiant? Reckless? Or what? Aside from his character, do you accept the idea he states here?

SAY NOT, THE STRUGGLE NOUGHT AVAILETH

Arthur Hugh Clough (1819–1861)

> Say not, the struggle nought availeth,
>   The labour and the wounds are vain,
> The enemy faints not, nor faileth,
>   And as things have been they remain.
>
> If hopes were dupes, fears may be liars;   5
>   It may be, in yon smoke concealed,

Your comrades chase e'en now the fliers,
   And, but for you, possess the field.

For while the tired waves, vainly breaking,
   Seem here no painful inch to gain,   10
Far back, through creeks and inlets making,
   Comes silent, flooding in, the main.

And not by eastern windows only,
   When daylight comes, comes in the light,
In front, the sun climbs slow, how slowly,   15
   But westward, look, the land is bright.

EXERCISES

1. If the last stanza were omitted, would the poem have a different meaning for you? Explain your answer.
2. In terms of thematic structure, how does this poem compare with "A Psalm of Life"? In the use of imagery?

THE LAST WORD

Matthew Arnold (1822–1888)

Creep into thy narrow bed,
Creep, and let no more be said!
Vain thy onset! all stands fast;
Thou thyself must break at last.

Let the long contention cease!   5
Geese are swans and swans are geese.
Let them have it how they will!
Thou art tired; best be still!

They out-talk'd thee, hiss'd thee, tore thee.
Better men fared thus before thee;   10
Fired their ringing shot and pass'd,
Hotly charged—and broke at last.

Charge once more, then, and be dumb!
Let the victors, when they come,
When the forts of folly fall,   15
Find thy body by the wall.

EXERCISES

1. Does the tone of this poem more clearly resemble that of Hotspur's speech from *King Henry IV, Part 1* or that of "Say Not, the Struggle Nought Availeth"? Explain.
2. Both this poem and "Say Not, the Struggle Nought Availeth" are in tetrameter, but there are differences in rhythm. Analyze these differences.

How do your findings relate to the question above?
3. In content the image in stanzas 7 and 8 of "A Psalm of Life" has some similarity to the image in the last stanza of "The Last Word." Explain the similarity. Which is the more effective image? Why? Relate your answers to the first question above.
4. Explain the title of this poem.

EPITAPH ON AN ARMY OF MERCENARIES

A. E. Housman (1859–1936)

These, in the day when heaven was falling,
   The hour when earth's foundations fled,
Followed their mercenary calling
   And took their wages and are dead.

Their shoulders held the sky suspended;   5
   They stood, and earth's foundations stay;
What God abandoned, these defended,
   And saved the sum of things for pay.

EXERCISES

1. It is sometimes suggested that Housman had in mind, in this poem, the small British professional army that held off the first thrust of the German army in World War I. Do you think that this idea, if justified by fact, has any fundamental importance for the meaning of the poem? Would it make any difference if Housman had been thinking of the Praetorian Guard of a Roman emperor (professional soldiers and "mercenaries," too), who died holding a palace gate (as is a matter of record)? If such specific instances are not fundamentally important, what is the poem about?
2. Following the line of thought above, we may ask what the distinguishing characteristics of mercenaries are. They fight for pay, yes. But are they necessarily bad fighters? If a man fights not for patriotism, religious belief, moral conviction, or some other ideal commitment, but for money, what could make him willing to die? Does anyone ever die merely for pay?
3. In interpreting the theme of this poem, it may be argued that the phrase "What God abandoned" is the key. God has abandoned the "sum of things" (the whole world, shall we say?) and the "mercenaries" hold things together, their "pay" being simply the "sum of things." Does this interpretation make the poem a commentary on the modern, naturalistic view of the universe and man's place in it? Defend your view.

IF

Rudyard Kipling (1865–1936)

If you can keep your head when all about you
    Are losing theirs and blaming it on you,
If you can trust yourself when all men doubt you,
    But make allowance for their doubting too;
If you can wait and not be tired by waiting,   5
    Or being lied about don't deal in lies,
Or being hated don't give way to hating,
    And yet don't look too good, nor talk too wise:

If you can dream—and not make dreams your
    master;
    If you can think—and not make thoughts your
    aim,   10
If you can meet with Triumph and Disaster
    And treat those two impostors just the same;
If you can bear to hear the truth you've spoken
    Twisted by knaves to make a trap for fools,
Or watch the things you gave your life to,
    broken,   15
    And stoop and build 'em up with worn-out
    tools;

If you can make one heap of all your winnings
    And risk it on one turn of pitch-and-toss,
And lose, and start again at your beginnings
    And never breathe a word about your loss: 20
If you can force your heart and nerve and sinew
    To serve your turn long after they are gone,
And so hold on when there is nothing in you
    Except the Will which says to them: 'Hold on!'

If you can talk with crowds and keep your
    virtue,   25
    Or walk with Kings—nor lose the common
    touch,
If neither foes nor loving friends can hurt you,
    If all men count with you, but none too much;
If you can fill the unforgiving minute
    With sixty seconds' worth of distance run,   30
Yours is the Earth and everything that's in it,
    And—which is more—you'll be a Man, my son!

EXERCISES

1. Does the idea of "If" more nearly resemble that of "Epitaph on an Army of Mercenaries," "The Last Word," or "A Psalm of Life"?
2. Which does it most resemble in tone?
3. How does it compare with the other poems as a "dramatization" or "embodiment" of its theme?
4. Specify five similes and metaphors in the poem. How effective do you find them?

ODE TO DUTY

William Wordsworth (1770–1850)

Stern Daughter of the Voice of God!
O Duty! if that name thou love
Who art a light to guide, a rod
To check the erring, and reprove;
Thou, who art victory and law   5
When empty terrors overawe;
From vain temptations dost set free;
And calm'st the weary strife of frail humanity!

There are who ask not if thine eye
Be on them; who, in love and truth,   10
Where no misgiving is, rely
Upon the genial sense of youth:
Glad Hearts! without reproach or blot
Who do thy work, and know it not:
Oh! if through confidence misplaced   15
They fail, thy saving arms, dread Power! around
    them cast.

Serene will be our days and bright,
And happy will our nature be,
When love is an unerring light,
And joy its own security.   20
And they a blissful course may hold
Even now, who, not unwisely bold,
Live in the spirit of this creed;
Yet seek thy firm support, according to their need.

I, loving freedom, and untried;   25
No sport of every random gust,
Yet being to myself a guide,
Too blindly have reposed my trust:
And oft, when in my heart was heard
Thy timely mandate, I deferred   30
The task, in smoother walks to stray;
But thee I now would serve more strictly, if I may.

Through no disturbance of my soul,
Or strong compunction in me wrought,
I supplicate for thy control;   35
But in the quietness of thought:
Me this unchartered freedom tires;
I feel the weight of chance-desires:
My hopes no more must change their name,
I long for a repose that ever is the same.   40

Stern Lawgiver! yet thou dost wear
The Godhead's most benignant grace;
Nor know we anything so fair
As is the smile upon thy face:
Flowers laugh before thee on their beds   45
And fragrance in thy footing treads;
Thou dost preserve the stars from wrong;

And the most ancient heavens, through Thee, are
    fresh and strong.

To humbler functions, awful Power!
I call thee: I myself commend   50
Unto thy guidance from this hour;
Oh, let my weakness have an end!
Give unto me, made lowly wise,
The spirit of self-sacrifice;
The confidence of reason give;   55
And in the light of truth thy Bondman let me live!

EXERCISES

1. Does this poem more resemble Kipling's "If" or Hotspur's speech from *King Henry IV*? Explain your opinion.
2. Turn to "Kind of an Ode to Duty," by Ogden Nash, which immediately follows. Do you find it funny? If so, what qualities in Wordsworth's poem make it open to parody? What view of human nature does Nash oppose to Wordsworth's? Does Wordsworth merely oversimplify his subject? How might his method of treatment in the poem be related to oversimplification? Is the method of "Epitaph on an Army of Mercenaries" less vulnerable to parody than Wordsworth's method here? If so, why?

KIND OF AN ODE TO DUTY

Ogden Nash (1902–1971)

O Duty,
Why hast thou not the visage of a sweetie or a
    cutie?
Why displayest thou the countenance of the kind
    of conscientious organizing spinster
That the minute you see her you are aginster?
Why glitter thy spectacles so ominously?   5
Why art thou clad so abominously?
Why art thou so different from Venus
And why do thou and I have so few interests
    mutually in common between us?
Why art thou fifty per cent martyr
And fifty-one per cent Tartar?   10
Why is it thy unfortunate wont
To try to attract people by calling on them either
    to leave undone the deeds they like, or to do the
    deeds they don't?
Why art thou so like an April post mortem
On something that died in the autumn?
Above all, why dost thou continue to hound me? 15
Why art thou always albatrossly hanging around
    me?
Thou so ubiquitous,

And I so iniquitous.
I seem to be the one person in the world thou art
    perpetually preaching at who or to who;
Whatever looks like fun, there art thou standing
    between me and it, calling yoo-hoo.   20
O Duty, Duty!
How noble a man should I be hadst thou the
    visage of a sweetie or a cutie!
Wert thou but houri instead of hag
Then would my halo indeed be in the bag!
But as it is thou art so much forbiddinger than
    a Wodehouse hero's forbiddingest aunt 25
That in the words of the poet, When Duty
    whispers low, Thou must, this erstwhile youth
    replies, I just can't.

EXERCISES

1. Is Nash here implying that a sense of duty is stupid? If he isn't saying that, then what is he saying? Relate your answer to the questions in exercise 2 on Wordsworth's "Ode to Duty."
2. Describe the tone of this poem.

Stanza

Perhaps some explanation is due for the postponement until this point of the treatment of stanza. Stanza, indeed, is one of the structural units in poetry, and is often of great significance. But the line (and the foot in relation to line in accentual-syllabic verse) is the basic unit in that it involves more immediately and particularly all the problems of rhythm, verbal texture, and rhetoric. The line is the unit in the stanza, and unless we have a familiarity with what is entailed in the line, any discussion of stanza must rest at the purely formal level. Now turn to section 19.11.

EXERCISES

1. What is the stanza form of "Sir Patrick Spens" (sec. 12) called? Scan stanzas 1, 2, 6, and 11. In these stanzas (or elsewhere in the poem) do you notice any effects that you think are particularly expressive? In the last stanza do you find any remarkable phonetic effects?
2. Scan the first stanza of "Edward" (sec. 12) and describe the stanza. How can it be said that this stanza form is basically the ballad stanza with certain fixed additions?

3. In the last stanza of A. E. Housman's "Bredon Hill" (sec. 12), what tensions are set up against the stanza form? What effect do they have?

4. Describe the stanza form of "Mama and Daughter" by Langston Hughes (sec. 12).

5. By what system can "The Farmer's Bride" by Charlotte Mew (sec. 12) be scanned? Describe the stanza form—or forms. Do you see any justification for the meter and stanza?

6. In D. H. Lawrence's "Love on the Farm" (sec. 12), what effect do we get from the rather random use of rime as contrasted with a fixed rime and stanza scheme? What sense do you make of the remark that language in this poem is used with greater intensity of effect than in Charlotte Mew's poem on a similar subject? Support your position by a series of examples, and comment on particular effects.

7. What is the verse form of Robert Browning's "My Last Duchess" (sec. 12)?

8. Analyze the divisions of Shakespeare's Sonnet 18 (sec. 13). How strictly does it conform to the general description?

9. Remembering that it is not the abstract stanza form itself that is significant, but the use made of it in a particular poem, comment on the stanza form of Shelley's "Ode to the West Wind" (sec. 13).

10. Comment on the use of stanza in Ransom's "Bells for John Whiteside's Daughter," Thomas's "A Refusal to Mourn," and Waller's "Song" (all, sec. 14).

GROUP 2: WAR

From KING HENRY V
(Act 4, scene 3)
William Shakespeare (1564–1616)

This day is call'd the feast of Crispian.
He that outlives this day and comes safe home,
Will stand a tip-toe when this day is nam'd,
And rouse him at the name of Crispian.
He that shall live this day, and see old age, 5
Will yearly on the vigil feast his neighbors
And say, "Tomorrow is Saint Crispian."
Then he will strip his sleeve and show his scars,
And say, "These wounds I had on Crispin's day."
Old men forget; yet all shall be forgot, 10
But he'll remember with advantages
What feats he did that day. Then shall our names,
Familiar in his mouth as household words,
Harry the King, Bedford and Exeter,
Warwick and Talbot, Salisbury and Gloucester, 15
Be in their flowing cups freshly remember'd.

This story shall the good man teach his son;
And Crispin Crispian shall ne'er go by,
From this day to the ending of the world,
But we in it shall be remember'd, 20
We few, we happy few, we band of brothers;
For he today that sheds his blood with me
Shall be my brother; be he ne'er so vile,
This day shall gentle his condition;
And gentlemen in England now a-bed 25
Shall think themselves accurs'd they were not here,
And hold their manhoods cheap whiles any speaks
That fought with us upon Saint Crispin's day.

EXERCISES

1. In the poems in group 1 war is several times used metaphorically to embody a common theme. In the poems in this group war is the general subject used to embody or dramatize various attitudes—various themes. This speech is made by King Henry before the Battle of Agincourt. What is his attitude toward war? Might this poem also fit easily in group 1?

2. Evaluate King Henry's appeal to his army. What human qualities does he appeal to? Do you find any of them admirable?

RECESSIONAL
June 22, 1897
Rudyard Kipling (1865–1936)

God of our fathers, known of old—
 Lord of our far-flung battle-line—
Beneath whose awful Hand we hold
 Dominion over palm and pine—
Lord God of Hosts, be with us yet, 5
Lest we forget, lest we forget!

The tumult and the shouting dies—
 The captains and the kings depart—
Still stands Thine ancient sacrifice,
 An humble and a contrite heart. 10
Lord God of Hosts, be with us yet,
Lest we forget, lest we forget!

Far-call'd our navies melt away—
 On dune and headland sinks the fire—
Lo, all our pomp of yesterday 15
 Is one with Nineveh and Tyre!
Judge of the Nations, spare us yet,
Lest we forget, lest we forget!

If, drunk with sight of power we loose
 Wild tongues that have not Thee
  in awe— 20

Such boastings as the Gentiles use
  Or lesser breeds without the Law—
Lord God of Hosts, be with us yet,
  Lest we forget, lest we forget!

For heathen heart that puts her trust   25
  In reeking tube and iron shard—
All valiant dust that builds on dust,
  And guarding calls not Thee to guard—
For frantic boast and foolish word,
  Thy Mercy on Thy people, Lord!   30

Kipling wrote this poem to celebrate the sixtieth anniversary of Queen Victoria's reign, and he seems to have conceived of the Jubilee as a great religious service in which sacrifices to God have been (or ought to have been) offered. After composing the poem, Kipling threw it away; only by accident was it recovered and published—to become instantly famous.

EXERCISES

1. Consult a dictionary for the meaning of *recessional*.
2. As a general background for this poem, you might find it interesting to read Psalms 2, 20, and 51. What relevance, if any, do they have to this poem?
3. What qualities, technical and other, does "Recessional" have that make it appropriate for the celebration of a great public occasion?
4. This poem recommends the virtue of humility. For what reason? Before what power? In fear of what?
5. On the basis of this poem, what general view of history do you think Kipling held? Of war?

1887

A. E. Housman (1859–1936)

From Clee to heaven the beacon burns,
  The shires have seen it plain,
From north and south the sign returns
  And beacons burn again.

Look left, look right, the hills are bright,   5
  The dales are light between,
Because 'tis fifty years to-night
  That God has saved the Queen.

Now, when the flame they watch not towers
  About the soil they trod,   10
Lads, we'll remember friends of ours
  Who shared the work with God.

To skies that knit their heartstrings right,
  To fields that bred them brave,
The saviours come not home to-night: 15
  Themselves they could not save.

It dawns in Asia, tombstones show
  And Shropshire names are read;
And the Nile spills his overflow
  Beside the Severn's dead.   20

We pledge in peace by farm and town
  The Queen they served in war,
And fire the beacons up and down
  The land they perished for.

'God save the Queen' we living sing,   25
  From height to height 'tis heard;
And with the rest your voices ring,
  Lads of the Fifty-third.

Oh, God will save her, fear you not:
  Be you the men you've been,   30
Get you the sons your fathers got,
  And God will save the Queen.

This poem was inspired by Queen Victoria's Golden Jubilee of 1887, celebrating the fiftieth year of her reign. The first two stanzas do not imply a great ceremonial occasion, but are the description of the whole countryside of England—a sweeping night scene—with beacon fires seen from shire to shire, in celebration of the Jubilee, with people all over the darkening countryside singing the words of "God Save the Queen." Ordinarily these were, and still are, ritual words; the tune is struck up at the beginning of any public occasion and the words are scarcely attended to. On the night of the nation-wide Jubilee, however, the words of the national anthem undoubtedly took on a little more meaning than usual: God had, quite literally, "saved the queen" for fifty years. So much for the introductory two stanzas. The rest of the poem amounts to an investigation of what is really to be understood by the fact "That God has saved the Queen."

EXERCISES

1. What does this investigation, in stanzas 3–8, consist of?
2. Do you think that Housman's poem would

generally be regarded as appropriate to the occasion for which it was written? To begin an answer, ask to whom Kipling's "Recessional" is addressed. To whom is "1887" addressed? Who is the speaker in Kipling's poem? Who in Housman's poem? Who are "the friends of ours" in line 11? Who is meant by the "we" of line 21? Do you feel any difference between this "we" and the "we" of "Recessional"? In other words, what is the difference in tone between the two poems?

3. What irony lies in the poem? Is the poem the satirical outburst of a pacifist? Is it antiimperialistic? Does it say that great institutions such as a nation forget the individual? This poem is by the same author as "Epitaph on an Army of Mercenaries." Does this fact help you in describing the irony here?

EIGHTH AIR FORCE
Randall Jarrell (1914–1965)

If, in an odd angle of the hutment,
A puppy laps the water from a can
Of flowers, and the drunk sergeant shaving
Whistles *O Paradiso!*—shall I say that man
Is not as men have said: a wolf to man?   5

The other murderers troop in yawning;
Three of them play Pitch, one sleeps, and one
Lies counting missions, lies there sweating
Till even his heart beats: One; One; One.
O murderers! . . . Still, this is how it's done: 10

This is a war. . . . But since these play, before
   they die,
Like puppies with their puppy; since, a man,
I did as these have done, but did not die—
I will content the people as I can
And give up these to them: Behold the man!   15

I have suffered, in a dream, because of him,
Many things; for this last saviour, man,
I have lied as I lie now. But what is lying?
Men wash their hands, in blood, as best they can:
I find no fault in this just man.   20

This poem provides a very interesting example of how a poem makes its "statement" and how the method of the presentation qualifies and defines what is presented. This poem is, we may say, "about" modern war. It is also about the individual's sense of guilt and responsibility. It is also about the nature of man—especially as man's nature is revealed by participation in modern war.

But what does the poem "say" about war, about guilt, about man's essential nature?

To answer this question adequately, we shall have to examine, not only what is literally said by the speaker but the implied character of the speaker, the circumstances under which he speaks, and the tone in which what he says is uttered. That is to say: we shall have to consider the speaker, not merely to be the mouthpiece of the poet—he may very well be that—but also as a dramatic character whose actions and utterances are rooted in a dramatic context. Let us consider this poem therefore as we would consider a play.

The scene is evidently an air base in England during World War II. The airmen in their hutment are casual enough and honest enough to be convincing. The raw building is domesticated: there are the flowers in water from which the mascot, a puppy, laps. There is the drunken sergeant, whistling an opera aria as he shaves. These "murderers," as the speaker is casually to call the airmen in the next stanza, display a touching regard for the human values. How, then, can one say that man is a wolf to man (*cf.* Benjamin Franklin's statement: "O that . . . men would cease to be as wolves to one another . . .") since these young soldiers "play before they die, / Like puppies with their puppy." But the casual presence of the puppy in the hutment allows us to take the stanza both ways, for the dog is a kind of tamed and domesticated wolf, and his presence may suggest that the hutment is a wolf den. After all, the timber wolf plays with its puppies.

The second stanza takes the theme to a perfectly explicit conclusion. If three of the men play pitch, and one is asleep, at least one man is awake and counts himself and his companions murderers. But his unvoiced cry "O murderers" is met, countered, and dismissed with the next two lines: ". . . Still, this is how it is done: / This is a war. . . ."

The note of casuistry and cynical apology prepares for a brilliant and rich resolving image, the image of Pontius Pilate, which is announced specifically in the third stanza:

I will content the people as I can
And give up these to them: Behold the man!

Yet if Pilate as he is first presented is a jesting Pilate, who asks "What is truth?" it is a bitter and grieving Pilate who speaks the conclusion of the poem. It is the integrity of man himself that is at stake. Is man a cruel animal, a wolf, or is he the last saviour, the Christ of our modern religion of humanity?

The Pontius Pilate metaphor, as the poet uses it, becomes a device for tremendous concentration. For the speaker (presumably the young airman who cried "O murderers") is himself the confessed murderer under judgment, and also the Pilate who judges, and he is, at least as a representative of man, the saviour whom the mob would condemn. He is even Pilate's better nature, his wife, for the lines "I have suffered, in a dream, because of him, / Many things" is merely a rearrangement of Matthew 27:19, the speech of Pilate's wife to her husband. But this last item is more than a reminiscence of the scriptural scene. It reinforces the speaker's present dilemma. The modern has had high hopes for mankind: are the hopes merely a dream? The speaker's present torture springs from the hope and from his reluctance to dismiss it as an empty dream. This Pilate is even harder pressed than was the Roman magistrate. For he must convince himself of this last saviour's innocence. But he has lied for him before. He will lie for him now.

Men wash their hands, in blood, as best they can:
I find no fault in this just man.

Here we recall that Pilate publicly washed his hands (in water) to show that he was "innocent of the blood of this just person"—of Jesus. What, however, may we take the last two lines of the poem to mean? The speaker may mean "since my own hands are bloody, I have no right to condemn the rest." It can mean "I know that man can love justice even though his hands are bloody, for there is blood on mine." It can mean "men are essentially decent; they try to keep their hands clean even if they have only blood in which to wash them." None of these meanings cancels the others. All are relevant.

Does the poem say that man is not a beast but essentially good? Yes, but the affirmation is qualified—qualified by the whole context of the situation—qualified by the fact that it is spoken by a Pilate who contents the people as he washes his own hands in blood. The sense of self-guilt, the yearning to believe in man's goodness, the knowledge of the difficulty in maintaining such a belief—all work to render accurately and sensitively the whole situation.

But the last paragraph may be misleading. To some students it may lead to a misapprehension of the function of irony; that is, the student may feel that the function of the irony in the poem is to pare the theme of man's goodness down to acceptable dimensions. We can accept it because the poet has indicated that he does not really believe in it himself. Such an account is, however, not what the editors intend to say.

A better way of stating the matter would be something like this: we do not ask the poet—in this or any other case—to bring his poem into line with our personal beliefs; still less ought we demand that he flatter our personal beliefs, whatever they may be. What we do ask is that the poet dramatize the situation so sensitively, so honestly, and with such fidelity to the total situation that it is no longer a question of our beliefs, but of our participation in the poetic experience. In "Eighth Air Force," the poet manages to bring us, by an act of imagination, to the most penetrating insight. Participating in that insight, we doubtless become better citizens. (One of the "uses" of poetry is to make us better citizens.) But poetry is not the eloquent rendition of the good citizen's creed. Poetry must carry us beyond the abstract creed into the very matrix from which our creeds come and from which they are abstracted.

For the theme in a genuine poem does not confront us as abstraction—that is, as one man's generalization from the relevant particulars. Finding its proper symbol, defined and refined by the participating metaphors, the theme becomes a part of the reality in which we live—an insight, rooted in and growing out of concrete experience, many-sided, three-dimensional. Even the resistance to generalization has its part in this process—even the drag of the particulars away from the universal—even the tension of opposing themes—play their parts.

EXERCISE

On what basis does Jarrell organize his stanzas in this poem?

THE COLLEGE COLONEL
Herman Melville (1819–1891)

He rides at their head;
  A crutch by his saddle just slants in view,
One slung arm is in splints, you see,
  Yet he guides his strong steed—how coldly too.

He brings his regiment home—   5
  Not as they filed two years before,
But a remnant half-tattered, and battered, and
    worn,
Like castaway sailors, who—stunned
      By the surf's loud roar,
  Their mates dragged back and seen no
    more—   10
Again and again breast the surge,
  And at last crawl, spent, to shore.

A still rigidity and pale—
  An Indian aloofness lones his brow;
He has lived a thousand years   15
Compressed in battle's pains and prayers,
  Marches and watches slow.

There are welcoming shouts, and flags;
  Old men off hat to the Boy,
Wreaths from gay balconies fall at his feet,   20
But to *him*—there comes alloy.

It is not that a leg is lost,
  It is not that an arm is maimed,
It is not that the fever has racked—
  Self he has long disclaimed.   25

But all through the Seven Days' Fight,
  And deep in the Wilderness grim,
And in the field-hospital tent,
  And Petersburg crater, and dim
Lean brooding in Libby, there came—   30
  Ah Heaven!—what *truth* to him.

In August 1863, in Pittsfield, Massachusetts, Melville witnessed a certain William F. Bartlett leading a group of Civil War veterans in a parade. Bartlett was then still little more than a boy, having enlisted in the Union army while a student at Harvard. Despite his youth, he had seen considerable action in several battles and had been seriously wounded. One leg had been amputated and

one arm was in splints from a recent wound. Later, when he had returned to the fighting, Bartlett was captured and confined in Libby Prison in Richmond, Virginia, where, in the general starvation in the Confederacy toward the end of the war, rations were very short. The "Seven Days' Fight," the Wilderness, and Petersburg are battles in Bartlett's career; he lost his leg during the Seven Days, and was captured at Petersburg. Notice that in his poem Melville has shifted the date of the parade from 1863 to some time after the end of the war (after Bartlett had been in Libby), and that the parade is presumably a victory parade.

EXERCISES

1. Do you feel it important for the poem to know that a real "college colonel" gave Melville the idea? If so, do you feel that Melville was justified in shifting the occasion from 1863 to, say, late 1865? Explain your answer.
2. Would a tough, brave, career officer of middle age have done as well for the character in this poem? What differences might have been involved?
3. Reread Melville's "Commemorative of a Naval Victory" (sec. 15). What general similarities do you find in the situations presented? What similarities in the attitude of the characters in the two poems? In the attitude of the poet? Do you accept the notion that the image of the shark in "Commemorative of a Naval Victory" and the unspecified "truth" at the end of "The College Colonel" have, generally speaking, the same thematic significance? Explain.
4. Consider the statement that the image of the shark in "Commemorative of a Naval Victory" and the "truth" mentioned in "The College Colonel" do not refer to a single, simple idea or fact, but to a complex of ideas and feelings, in some respects contradictory, brought to focus in a symbol. Do you accept this statement? Explain your answer by making a thematic analysis of the poems.
5. Melville was a Northerner, a strong Unionist, an emancipationist, and a supporter of the war. Do "Commemorative of a Naval Victory" and "The College Colonel" tend to contradict that statement? Less than a year after the Civil War ended at Appomattox, Melville had this to say: "Let us pray that the terrible historic tragedy of our time may not have been enacted without in-

structing our whole beloved country through terror and pity. . . ." Can you relate this view to the poems?

6. Consider the statement that the most obvious ironic contrast in Housman's "1887" is the same as that in the two poems by Melville. What do you think this statement means? Do you think it true?

7. Compare Melville's "The College Colonel" with Jarrell's "Eighth Air Force."

WAR IS KIND
Stephen Crane (1871–1900)

Do not weep, maiden, for war is kind.
Because your lover threw wild hands towards the
    sky
And the affrighted steed ran on alone,
Do not weep.
War is kind.   5

    Hoarse, booming drums of the regiment,
    Little souls who thirst for fight,
    These men were born to drill and die.
    The unexplained glory flies above them,
    Great is the battle-god, great, and his king-
        dom—   10
    A field where a thousand corpses lie.

Do not weep, babe, for war is kind.
Because your father tumbled in the yellow
    trenches,
Raged at his breast, gulped, and died,
Do not weep.   15
War is kind.

    Swift, blazing flag of the regiment,
    Eagle with crest of red and gold,
    These men were born to drill and die.
    Point for them the virtue of slaughter,   20
    Make plain to them the excellence of killing
    And a field where a thousand corpses lie.

Mother whose heart hung humble as a button
On the bright, splendid shroud of your son,
Do not weep.   25
War is kind.

EXERCISES

1. Compare this poem, thematically, with Melville's "The College Colonel."
2. Clearly, the injunction to maiden, babe, and

mother not to weep, for "war is kind," is ironical. War has deprived them all, so how can war be kind? The main question of the poem is how to establish a relation between the addresses to maiden, babe, and mother, and the two inset commentaries. Are the commentaries simple irony, merely continuing the irony in the three addresses? Or is there some nonironical element involved too? Here we are immediately concerned with the single poem, but if we turn to Stephen Crane's famous novel *The Red Badge of Courage* we find a treatment of war that may shed some light on the poem. If you have read the novel, try to see the relation.

3. What is the basis for the organization of stanzas here? Why, for instance, are stanzas 2 and 4 indented?

COLONEL SHAW AND THE MASSACHUSETTS' 54th
Robert Lowell (b. 1917)

"Relinquunt omnia servare rem publicam." [1]

The old South Boston Aquarium stands
in a Sahara of snow now. Its broken windows are
    boarded.
The bronze weathervane cod has lost half its
    scales.
The air tanks are dry.

Once my nose crawled like a snail on the glass;   5
my hand tingled
to burst the bubbles
drifting from the noses of the cowed, compliant
    fish.

My hand draws back. I often sigh still
for the dark downward and vegetating kingdom 10
of the fish and reptile. One morning last March,
I pressed against the new barbed and galvanized

fence on the Boston Common. Behind their cage,
yellow dinosaur steamshovels were grunting
as they cropped up tons of mush and grass   15
to gouge their underworld garage.

Parking-spaces luxuriate like civic
sandpiles in the heart of Boston.
A girdle of orange, Puritan-pumpkin colored
    girders
braces the tingling Statehouse,   20
shaking over the excavations, as it faces Colonel
    Shaw

[1] "They left all to serve the public good."

and his bell-cheeked Negro infantry
on St. Gaudens' shaking Civil War relief,
propped by a plank splint against the garage's
    earthquake.

Two months after marching through Boston,   25
half the regiment was dead;
at the dedication,
William Jones could almost hear the bronze
    Negroes breathe.
Their monument sticks like a fishbone
in the City's throat.   30
Its Colonel is as lean
as a compass-needle.

He has an angry wrenlike vigilance,
a greyhound's gentle tautness;
he seems to wince at pleasure,   35
and suffocate for privacy.

He is out of bounds now. He rejoices in man's
    lovely,
peculiar power to choose life and die—
when he leads his black soldiers to death,
he cannot bend his back.   40

On a thousand small town New England greens,
the old white churches hold their air
of sparse, sincere rebellion; frayed flags
quilt the graveyards of the Grand Army of the
    Republic.

The stone statues of the abstract Union Soldier   45
grow slimmer and younger each year—
wasp-waisted, they doze over muskets
and muse through their sideburns . . .

Shaw's father wanted no monument
except the ditch,   50
where his son's body was thrown
and lost with his "niggers."

The ditch is nearer.
There are no statues for the last war here;
on Boyleston Street, a commercial photograph   55
shows Hiroshima boiling
over a Mosler Safe, the "Rock of Ages"
that survived the blast. Space is nearer.
When I crouch to my television set,
the drained faces of Negro children rise like
    balloons.   60

Colonel Shaw
is riding on his bubble,
he waits
for the blessed break.

The Aquarium is gone. Everywhere,   65
giant finned cars nose forward like fish;
a savage servility
slides by on grease.

During the Civil War, Colonel Robert Shaw left his friends and classmates of the Harvard regiment to take command of a Negro regiment, which he led through heavy fighting. After his death in the war, a monument sculpted by Augustus St. Gaudens was erected in Boston to his memory. William James, the celebrated psychologist and brother of the novelist, spoke at the dedication of the monument. This poem is from Robert Lowell's collection entitled *For the Union Dead* (1964) and it contains details of styles and references to events current in the early 1960s. (The violence associated with racial integration of schools was then at its height; hence, on the television screen "the drained faces of Negro children rise like balloons.") Lowell, who has spent much of his life in Boston, reflects in the poem that Colonel Shaw is now "out of bounds." His monument faces a new world—of bulldozers, television sets, atomic bombs, and fin-tailed automobiles.

EXERCISES

1. In what sense is Colonel Shaw now "out of bounds"?
2. Why the contrast between the poet as boy looking at the fish in the aquarium and the poet as man watching the "dinosaur steamshovels"? Why the contrast between the "cowed, compliant fish" and the "finned cars" that "nose forward like fish"? What principle determined the choice of images in this poem?
3. Colonel Shaw is said to be like a wren and like a greyhound. How does he—according to this poem—define himself as a man and not a thing or an animal?
4. What are we to make of lines 41–48?
5. The idealism that led Shaw to his service with the Massachusetts' 54th and death is contrasted with what has since happened to the descendants of the slaves Shaw fought to free. What do you think is the point of the contrast? To awaken society to its unfulfilled duties and promises? Or more?
6. The poem contains references to World War

II (Hiroshima and the first atomic bomb). Are we to understand that the Civil War was a "good war" and World War II a bad one?

7. Is the poem, in its contrast of modernity and the Civil War, making an attack in general on our age? Have we lost "man's lovely, / peculiar power to choose life and die"?

8. What is the meaning of the last two lines of the poem? How do these lines relate to the heroism of Shaw and his men?

9. Are we to assume that the poet thinks that Shaw was typical of an age? What is the role of Shaw in the poem, generally considered? Answering this question will not be easy, no easier than explaining the image of the shark or the "truth" in Melville's poems.

10. Since this poem actually raises the question of the "just war"—whether wars of the past or of the present—do you think that the author might accept a poem written in praise of a young, non-Jewish Harvard graduate who, outraged by Hitler's treatment of the Jews, volunteered for the U.S. Army in 1942 and died gallantly leading an attack? Or do you think this question irrelevant?

DULCE ET DECORUM EST
Wilfred Owen (1893–1918)

Bent double, like old beggars under sacks,
Knock-kneed, coughing like hags, we cursed
    through sludge,
Till on the haunting flares we turned our backs,
And toward our distant rest began to trudge.
Men marched asleep. Many had lost their boots, 5
But limped on, blood-shod. All went lame, all
    blind;
Drunk with fatigue; deaf even to the hoots
Of gas-shells dropping softly behind

Gas! GAS! Quick, boys!—An ecstasy of fumbling,
Fitting the clumsy helmets just in time,   10
But someone still was yelling out and stumbling
And flound'ring like a man in fire or lime.—
Dim through the misty panes and thick green
    light,
As under a green sea, I saw him drowning.

In all my dreams, before my helpless sight,   15
He plunges at me, guttering, choking, drowning.

If in some smothering dreams, you too could pace
Behind the wagon that we flung him in,
And watch the white eyes writhing in his face,
His hanging head, like a devil's sick of sin,   20
If you could hear, at every jolt, the blood
Come gargling from the froth-corrupted lungs
Bitter as the cud

Of vile, incurable sores on innocent tongues,—
My friend, you would not tell with such high
    zest   25
To children ardent for some desperate glory,
The old lie: *Dulce et decorum est*
Pro patria mori.

EXERCISES

1. Wilfred Owen was a talented poet killed in World War I. What do you think that he thought of the speeches of Hotspur and Harry that we have included in this section? Remember that Owen was a poet and that the speeches represent famous moments in Shakespeare's plays.

2. Compare Owen's attitude toward war with that of Melville, Jarrell, and Lowell.

3. Compare, carefully, the style of this poem by Owen and those preceding by Melville, Jarrell, and Lowell. Does your comparison tell you anything beyond facts about style?

Stressed Meters

The student will have noticed that up to this point almost all our discussions of meter and other technical questions have dealt with poems in accentual-syllabic verse. Our reason has been simple: without some grasp of the basis of that verse it is hard to realize what is at stake in the distinction between it and the two other general types, *stressed meter* and *free verse*. Furthermore, unless the relation of certain verbal factors, such as alliteration, assonance, and onomatopoeia, to formal verse is understood, it is hard to realize their importance in the other types. But now let us turn to stressed meters in subsection 19.12.

EXERCISES

1. Reread "Frankie and Johnny" (sec. 12). Examine the rhythm of the refrain, in its several variations. They can be resolved in four accents:

      /   /   /   /
He was her man, but he done her wrong.

It can be argued, of course, that the accents on *man* and *wrong* are secondary, and that the line can be thought of as two dipodic feet. Nonetheless, the main point is that the four accents here, however we choose to regard them, indicate the pattern in each stanza, for the three long, loose preceding lines. With this notion in mind, scan stanzas 1, 2, 3, and 13.

2. Reexamine Kipling's "Danny Deever" (sec. 12), and try to scan it as accentual-syllabic verse. You will no doubt find that iambic heptameter seems to be the prevailing meter, but that the first, third, and eighth lines of each stanza cause trouble. The first and third lines may, however, with some wrenching, be made to fit the pattern:

> 'What are | the bu- | gles blow- | in' for?' |
> said Files- | ᴧon- | Parade.

But the eighth line is more difficult. In stanza 1, it readily resolves as pentameter, but in other stanzas the first syllable may be taken as an imperfect foot:

> ᴧWhile | they're hang- | in' . . . .

But this still does not yield heptameter. Try, however, to resolve the poem as dipodic verse. Line 1, for instance, seems to be:

> 'What are the bu- | gles blowin' for?' | said
> Files-on- | Parade.ᴧ

And this is supported by the next line:

> 'To turn you out, | to turn you out,' | the
> Colour-Ser- | geant said.ᴧ

Scan the rest of stanza 1 and all of stanza 4. What effect do you find in this counterpoint of the two systems of meter?

3. Discuss the rhythm of Langston Hughes's "Mama and Daughter" (sec. 12).

4. Discuss the rhythm of Bessie Smith's "Empty Bed Blues" (sec. 14).

5. It is sometimes said that in much blank verse the shadow of stressed meter is perceptible. Examine "The Parting" by Michael Drayton (sec. 14). Do you find any evidence for this view?

6. In Thomas Hardy's "Neutral Tones" (sec. 14), in terms of the accentual-syllabic system, it can be said that the first three lines of each stanza are prevailing iambic tetrameter and the last line

anapestic trimeter. But do you detect a shadow of the old stressed meter? Explain your view.

7. Is it possible to think of Hughes's "Midwinter Blues" (sec. 14) in terms of dipodic feet?

8. Think of Wilfred Owen's "Dulce et Decorum Est" in terms of stressed meter. How does it turn out?

GROUP 3: LOVE

TO HIS COY MISTRESS
Andrew Marvell (1621–1678)

> Had we but world enough, and time,
> This coyness, Lady, were no crime.
> We would sit down and think which way
> To walk and pass our long love's day.
> Thou by the Indian Ganges' side   5
> Shouldst rubies find; I by the tide
> Of Humber would complain. I would
> Love you ten years before the Flood,
> And you should, if you please, refuse
> Till the conversion of the Jews.   10
> My vegetable love would grow
> Vaster than empires, and more slow;
> An hundred years would go to praise
> Thine eyes and on thy forehead gaze;
> Two hundred to adore each breast,   15
> But thirty thousand to the rest;
> An age at least to every part,
> And the last age should show your heart.
> For, Lady, you deserve this state,
> Nor would I love at lower rate.   20
>
> But at my back I always hear
> Time's wingèd chariot hurrying near;
> And yonder all before us lie
> Deserts of vast eternity.
> Thy beauty shall no more be found,   25
> Nor, in thy marble vault, shall sound
> My echoing song; then worms shall try
> That long preserved virginity,
> And your quaint honor turn to dust,
> And into ashes all my lust: 30
> The grave's a fine and private place,
> But none, I think, do there embrace.
>
> Now therefore, while the youthful hue
> Sits on thy skin like morning dew,[1]
> And while thy willing soul transpires   35
> At every pore with instant fires,

---

[1] The first edition of the poem reads *glew* instead of *dew*. The present reading is a conjecture but is generally accepted.

Now let us sport us while we may,
And now, like amorous birds of prey,
Rather at once our time devour
Than languish in his slow-chapped power.   40
Let us roll all our strength and all
Our sweetness up into one ball,
And tear our pleasures with rough strife
Through the iron gate of life:
Thus, though we cannot make our sun   45
Stand still, yet we will make him run.

The situation of the poem is this: a lover is trying to persuade his mistress to accept his suit. The three parts of the poem are really the three steps in his argument: (1) If life were not so short, the delays of your coyness would be appropriate, and I should be willing to gratify it by praising you for thousands of years before you eventually accepted my love. (2) But life is short, and in death both love and honor are meaningless. (3) Therefore, accept what pleasure there is in love while there is yet youth and time. That is the bare outline of the argument, and is all of the poem that comes out in a direct and general statement.

The question is, what use does the poet make of such an outline of argument? In other words, how does the meaning of the poem differ, in the end, from the meaning of the argument?

It is a question that cannot be answered explicitly and at once. It can only be answered by investigating various aspects of the poem.

First, one may notice how the tone of the poem changes from section to section. The poem starts with the tone of almost playful conversation, the tone of polite and not-too-serious verse, usually called *vers de société*, introducing certain exaggerations so tremendous that they become a kind of playful and witty absurdity. While the lady picked up rubies by the Ganges in India, the lover, in England by the side of the Humber, would perform some of the polite preliminaries of his courtship by "complaining" on the subject of his love. All history, from before the Flood to the "conversion of the Jews," an event so remote as to be inconceivable, would be but the history of their courtship. But the phrase "vegetable love" introduces an exaggeration of another kind: why

would such a kind of love be *vegetable*? The poet means *vegetable* in the sense of belonging to the vegetable kingdom, simply some great plant, like a sequoia, the life span of which would be greater than that of any other living thing. But vegetable growth is a kind of blind, aimless, and undirected growth, further removed from the direction of the intelligence and will found in man than any form of animal life whatever. So the phrase serves as a kind of commentary, and a serious one, on the imagined courtship described. It implies the idea of an almost endless time, and as well the idea of the lack of intelligent direction in such a courtship. But on the surface, by the superficial absurdity of the phrase, the playful attitude is reinforced. The last two lines of the section give a kind of summarizing couplet that is a compliment to the lady.

The first section of the poem is playful, conversational, and absurd, but thereafter is a sharp and dramatic contrast. Observe the sudden and shocking turn to the serious in the first couplet of the second section. The lover is haunted by the brevity of life. And observe the different kind of imagery used, imagery no longer absurd or playful but grand: "Time's winged chariot," "Deserts of vast eternity," and the stillness of the "marble vault" of the tomb. But then the poet again changes the tone, and the approach to his subject, by establishing another contrast. From the grand imagery of the marble vault, the chariot, and the desert, he turns to the worm, presenting, with a kind of suppressed sarcasm, the idea of the grave worm as a lover. The implied question to the lady is this: which lover does she prefer, the speaker or the worm—for the worm will later have the freedom of her body no matter how vigilantly she maintains her virtue in life? Then, as in the first section, the poet closes with a kind of summarizing couplet:

> The grave's a fine and private place,
> But none, I think, do there embrace.

The couplet is all the more effective because it says less than could be said. The poet even pretends that he does not know, that he has only heard it reported, that there is no love in the grave. Furthermore, it is ironical, because the poet says that the grave has the very finest quality of a place for love, for it is "private." In the last six lines of the second section the poet repeats the playful and politely ironical manner of the first section, but now the subject matter, death and physical decay, is one of terrifying seriousness. But the poet refuses to surrender to that, and so treats it indirectly. The ironical overstatement, or exaggeration, of the first section is contrasted with the ironical understatement of the second section. The contrast gives an added point to each section after the reader is acquainted with the poem.

The third section, which gives the conclusion of the argument, also gives a resolution of the ironical contrasts built up in the preceding parts of the poem, just as a chord may resolve a musical composition. Observe the exciting quality of the imagery—"instant fires," "amorous birds of prey," "at once our time devour," "tear our pleasures"—and the faster rhythm. All the imagery is directed, without irony or reservation on the part of the poet in the immediate statement, toward giving the effect of swiftness and exuberant vitality. But observe how the last couplet changes the effect from one of sheer exuberance and uncontrolled vitality by bringing the last section into a more complicated relation with the preceding sections. The last couplet is a kind of epigram, a paradox, a summary of the whole poem. It says: if we are not strong enough to conquer time and make ourselves immortal, we at least can be strong enough to make time pass faster. This connects the last section with the other two by emphasizing again the ideas of time and death. Furthermore, it makes the connection, by the very tone of the statement, for the couplet is again ironical and conversational, in contrast to the tone of the preceding ten lines; therefore, it echoes effects found earlier in the poem.

This discussion began with one question stated in two different ways. What use does the poet make of the outline of his argument? How does the meaning of the poem differ, in the end, from the meaning of the argument? It may now be easier to give some answer.

The poet merely uses the argument as a framework for the poem, for the situation of a lover speaking to his mistress is a fiction adopted by the poet to give a dramatic form to his theme. This theme may be stated in the form of a question: what should man's attitude be in the face of death and his ignorance of any life after death? He proposes this question, through the lips of the lover, to the mistress, and then gives the answer; man cannot master death, but he can attempt, by an exercise of his will, to master life by living as intensely as possible.

To indicate that his theme was important and his subject complicated and difficult, the poet used variations of tone, contrasted overstatement and understatement, and employed irony. He did not want the reader to feel that any one part of the poem was, as it were, ignorant of the rest of the poem. He did not want the poem to appear too glib and easy, for he believed that that would insult the underlying seriousness of his subject. He wanted the poem to appear controlled, and self-possessed; to give this effect he used overstatement only for the witty and playful part of the poem, and understatement for the most serious parts. He did not want to give an impression of simple pathos over the fact that beauty must fade and love must pass. He wanted to give a more mature impression, one mixed with intelligence and will.

After this examination, one may see that the prose paraphrase of the poem—the attempt to say the thing directly in so many words—will result in a forced and didactic effect. That is, the idea of the poem has to be communicated through the operation of many factors: tone, attitude, imagery, rhythm, and so on. The paraphrase is not a true paraphrase, and can never be, because it must remain too simple; it omits most of the things that make the poem what it is—an experience in itself.

Other matters necessarily omitted in the foregoing account have to do with the relation of the poem to its historical and cultural background, the special literary conventions that it embodies and certain traditional themes that it echoes. Let us point out briefly some of the conventional and traditional material that forms the special literary setting of this poem.

We might begin with Petrarchan imagery, which is named for the Italian poet Petrarch (1304–1374). His sonnets to his mistress Laura greatly influenced Renaissance poetry, including the poetry of the English Renaissance. The typical Petrarchan mistress is beautiful and virtuous but cold-hearted and disdainful of love. Petrarchan imagery is usually extravagant: the mistress has teeth of pearl, lips of coral, hair of gold, cheeks in which roses bloom, but her breast is as cold and hard as marble. By Elizabethan times, the extravagance had gone so far and the images had become so trite that a poet like Shakespeare sometimes mocked the imagery. In Sonnet 130 he tells us that *his* mistress' eyes "are nothing like the sun" and that if hairs are wires, then black, not gold, wires grow upon his mistress' head.

Michael Drayton's sonnet "The Parting" (sec. 14) shows another aspect of Petrarchan imagery, the use of the adventures of Cupid as a device for complimenting the lady. Though the little god of love is mortally sick and lies on his death bed, the poet's mistress is such that she could work the miracle of making him recover if she but would. Donne's "The Good-Morrow" (sec. 15) represents still another strategy for revivifying the Petrarchan mode. He uses its bloodless abstractions and trite absurdities as a foil for his own realism, cynicism, and gay wit. But in doing so he does not forego the ingenuity with which Petrarchan imagery was often so elaborately wrought.

Marvell's "To His Coy Mistress" exhibits a related method for turning to account the Petrarchan conventions of compliment. Notice, for example, the first twenty lines. The compliments to the lady are as extravagant as any Petrarchan sonneteer ever devised. But their very absurdity allows the poet to topple them over into an irony that perfectly fits his purpose.

We have already remarked that the lady of the Petrarchan convention, though beautiful and exciting ardent love, is herself cold and disdainful. Her diffidence calls to mind another convention, that was very popular in the poetry of the Renaissance. Many poems —though not necessarily worked out in Petrarchan imagery—plead with the mistress to put off coyness and accept love while the lovers are still young. For examples of this *carpe diem* theme, refer to Herrick's "To the Virgins, to Make Much of Time" and Waller's "Song" (both, sec. 14).

SONNET 129
William Shakespeare (1564–1616)

Th' expense of Spirit in a waste of shame
Is lust in action; and till action, lust
Is perjured, murderous, bloody, full of blame,
Savage, extreme, rude, cruel, not to trust;
Enjoyed no sooner but despisèd straight;   5
Past reason hunted; and, no sooner had,
Past reason hated, as a swallow'd bait
On purpose laid to make the taker mad:
Mad in pursuit, and in possession so;
Had, having, and in quest to have, extreme;   10
A bliss in proof, and proved, a very woe;
Before, a joy proposed; behind, a dream.
  All this the world well knows; yet none knows well
  To shun the heaven that leads men to this hell.

EXERCISES

1. What is the theme of this sonnet? What does the imagery contribute to the theme?
2. Does the speaker merely make a series of "statements" about the nature of lust? Does he give a sense of dramatic force to his utterance? If so, how?
3. How complex is the idea expressed in this sonnet? Is the complexity justified?
4. What is the purpose of the frequent repetitions of particular words?

THE FUNERAL
John Donne (1571/2–1631)

Whoever comes to shroud me, do not harm
  Nor question much
That subtle wreath of hair, which crowns my arm;
The mystery, the sign you must not touch,
  For 'tis my outward soul,   5
Viceroy to that, which unto heaven being gone,
  Will leave this to control
And keep these limbs, her provinces, from dissolution.

For if the sinewy thread my brain lets fall
  Through every part,   10
Can tie those parts, and make me one of all;
Those hairs which upward grew, and strength
    and art
  Have from a better brain,
Can better do 't; except she meant that I
  By this should know my pain,   15
As prisoners then are manacled, when they're
    condemned to die.

Whate'er she meant by 't, bury it with me,
  For since I am
Love's martyr, it might breed idolatry
If into other's hands these reliques came;   20
  As 'twas humility
To afford to it all that a soul can do,
  So, 'tis some bravery,
That since you would have none of me, I
    bury some of you.

    The poet's mistress has given him a
bracelet woven out of her own hair. He wears
it about his arm, and asks that it be left upon
his arm when his body is buried. The motive
for such an act is one that most of us can take
for granted: even in death one wishes to cling
to a precious memento of the beloved. But it
is precisely the motive (or the various motives)
that the speaker here undertakes to discuss.

EXERCISES

1. The bracelet of hair is to be his "outward
soul" and is thus to serve to preserve his body.
How are the various analogies between nerves
and hairs, kings and viceroys, etc., worked out in
lines 1–14? What is the tone of the passage? How
does the elaborate (and even fantastic) analogy
qualify the tone?
2. What shift of tone occurs with "except she
meant" (l. 14)? Had it just occurred to him that
she may have given him the bracelet for purposes
quite different from those envisaged in lines 1–
14? What is the speaker's attitude toward his
mistress?
3. What is the tone of lines 17ff.? How does his
new justification for burying the bracelet with
him grow out of the preceding lines? What is implied by his calling himself "Love's martyr" (l. 19)?
4. Is his final gesture one of adoration or of
arrogance? What is the tone of lines 21–24? Is he
teasing his mistress? Persisting in his love for her
in spite of the fact that she will "have none of"
him? Or what?
5. What is the poet's final attitude toward his

mistress? What is the effect of the complex reasoning on the tone of the poem ?

FOR RHODA
Delmore Schwartz (1913–1966)

Calmly we walk through this April's day,
Metropolitan poetry here and there,
In the park sit pauper and rentier,
The screaming children, the motor car
Fugitive about us, running away,   5
Between the worker and the millionaire
Number provides all distances,
It is Nineteen Thirty-Seven now,
Many great dears are taken away,
What will become of you and me   10
(This is the school in which we learn . . .)
Besides the photo and the memory?
(. . . that time is the fire in which we burn.)

(This is the school in which we learn . . .)
What is the self amid this blaze?   15
What am I now that I was then
Which I shall suffer and act again,
The theodicy I wrote in my high school days
Restored all life from infancy,
The children shouting are bright as they run   20
(This is the school in which they learn . . .)
Ravished entirely in their passing play!
(. . . . that time is the fire in which they burn.)

Avid its rush, that reeling blaze!
Where is my father and Eleanor?   25
Not where are they now, dead seven years,
But what they were then?
                          No more? No more?
From Nineteen-Fourteen to the present day,
Bert Spira and Rhoda consume, consume
Not where they are now (where are they now?)   30
But what they were then, both beautiful;
Each minute bursts in the burning room,
The great globe reels in the solar fire,
Spinning the trivial and unique away.
(How all things flash! How all things flare!)   35
What am I now that I was then ?
May memory restore again and again
The smallest color of the smallest day:
Time is the school in which we learn,
Time is the fire in which we burn.   40

EXERCISES

1. Several people are mentioned in this poem by
name. Does it matter that we do not know who
Eleanor is, or Bert Spira, or Rhoda? What is the

advantage of using particular names even if the reader cannot be expected to know who the people are?

2. The speaker of this poem is conscious of time; in fact, the poem is about the nature of love in time. He looks back toward his childhood and forward to imagine what he and Rhoda and the others will some day become. It is easy to see why he regards time as a kind of school. How is time also a kind of fire? Look carefully at the fire imagery from line 24 to the end. What does the poet mean by "the burning room"? What does he mean when he exclaims "How all things flash!"? How can the great globe of earth be said to reel "in the solar fire"?

3. Does the rest of the poem serve to indicate how we are to take the imagery of fire and burning? Or is the meaning of the poem as a whole heavily dependent upon this imagery of fire and burning?

4. Compare this poem thematically with "To His Coy Mistress." Be sure to comment on the differences in tone, and on the effect such differences have on overall meaning.

5. On what basis would you scan this poem?

GROUP 4: THE CITY AND HUMAN LIFE

WEST LONDON

Matthew Arnold (1822–1888)

Crouched on the pavement close by Belgrave
   Square,
A tramp I saw, ill, moody, and tongue-tied;
A babe was in her arms, and at her side
A girl; their clothes were rags, their feet were bare.
Some labouring men, whose work lay somewhere
   there,   5
Passed opposite; she touched her girl, who hied
Across and begged, and came back satisfied.
The rich she had let pass with frozen stare.
Thought I: Above her state this spirit towers;
She will not ask of aliens, but of friends,   10
Of sharers in a common human fate.
She turns from that cold succor, which attends
The unknown little from the unknowing great,
And points us to a better time than ours.

EXERCISES

1. This poem embodies a simple anecdote, followed by a clearly stated thought provoked by it. In a number of poems discussed earlier we have commented on the subtlety and suggestiveness by which an idea may be dramatized. Has Arnold here been too direct, too obvious? Or has the extreme boldness and directness of the presentation, and the speaker's own reaction as part of the dramatization ("Thought I"), made this poem effective?

2. Return to William Blake's "London" and Wordsworth's "London, 1802" (both, sec. 14) and compare Arnold's method with Blake's and Wordsworth's.

3. Examine line 9. What about the statement "Above her state this spirit towers"? What "spirit"? Why the grandiloquent, or apparently grandiloquent word, *towers*? Doesn't this line seem in rather absurd contrast to the hard factuality of the preceding part of the poem—and of the part following? Or is this difference in style—and tone—significant and justifiable?

COMPOSED UPON WESTMINSTER BRIDGE

September 3, 1802

William Wordsworth (1770–1850)

Earth has not anything to show more fair:
Dull would he be of soul who could pass by
A sight so touching in its majesty:
This City now doth, like a garment, wear
The beauty of the morning; silent, bare,   5
Ships, towers, domes, theatres, and temples lie
Open unto the fields, and to the sky;
All bright and glittering in the smokeless air.
Never did sun more beautifully steep
In his first splendour, valley, rock, or hill;   10
Ne'er saw I, never felt, a calm so deep!
The river glideth at his own sweet will:
Dear God! the very houses seem asleep;
And all that mighty heart is lying still!

EXERCISES

1. Again return to Wordsworth's "London, 1802" (sec. 14). If in that poem there is, as we have hinted in our comment, some question about the effectiveness of the imagery, there can scarcely be, in our opinion, any question about the power of the imagery here in dramatizing the idea. What is that idea? Observe the fact that here, though a city is generally assumed to be antithetical to nature, the imagery is drawn from nature.

2. If here the speaker describes a delighted surprise at the aspect of London in early morning, what accounts for his surprise?

3. Could it be that London has to become almost as quiet as death for the observer to notice that it is, in a peculiar way, astir with life?

4. Contrast the idea of this poem with that of "London, 1802." Does one poem cancel the other? Can both be accepted as serious comments on London? On life in general? Here we may be facing one of the questions that often recurs in literature. Great works often seem to contradict each other at the level of idea, as we have earlier commented. How do you now feel about this question?

AN ELEMENTARY SCHOOL CLASSROOM IN A SLUM

Stephen Spender (b. 1909)

Far far from gusty waves, these children's faces,
Like rootless weeds the torn hair round their paleness.
The tall girl with her weighed-down head. The paper-
seeming boy with rat's eyes. The stunted unlucky heir
Of twisted bones, reciting a father's gnarled disease, 5
His lesson from his desk. At back of the dim class
One unnoted, mild and young: his eyes live in a dream
Of squirrels' game, in tree room, other than this.

On sour cream walls, donations. Shakespeare's head
Cloudless at dawn, civilized dome riding all cities. 10
Belled, flowery, Tyrolese valley. Open-handed map
Awarding the world its world. And yet, for these
Children, these windows, not this world, are world,
Where all their future's painted with a fog,
A narrow street sealed in with a lead sky, 15
Far far from rivers, capes, and stars of words.

Surely Shakespeare is wicked, the map a bad example
With ships and sun and love tempting them to steal—
For lives that slyly turn in their cramped holes
From fog to endless night? On their slag heap, these children 20
Wear skins peeped through by bones, and spectacles of steel
With mended glass, like bottle bits in slag.
Tyrol is wicked; map's promising a fable:
All of their time and space are foggy slum,
So blot their maps with slums as big as doom. 25

Unless, governor, teacher, inspector, visitor,
This map becomes their window and these windows
That open on their lives like crouching tombs
Break, O break open, till they break the town
And show the children to the fields and all their world 30
Azure on their sands, to let their tongues
Run naked into books, the white and green leaves open
The history theirs whose language is the sun.

EXERCISES

1. Why does the poet say that "Surely Shakespeare is wicked" (l. 17)? Is he saying that unless some better life is offered to them, teaching these children that there is a better life is worse than meaningless?

2. How effective is the imagery in this poem? In what sense can the boy be said to be "reciting a father's gnarled disease" (l. 5)? How are the windows of the classroom related to the pictures and maps on the classroom wall? Examine the imagery of the slag heap in stanza 3.

3. How is the last stanza related to the rest of the poem? Is it a preachment, direct and explicit?

4. Compare the theme of this poem with that of "West London" and with that of Blake's "London." All three poems (not to mention Wordsworth's "London, 1802") deal with one city, though in different ages, and involve the same or closely related themes. But what of Wordsworth's "Composed upon Westminster Bridge," in which the city is seen as continuous with nature and sharing in its spirit? Do you think that Spender could accept that poem, and not feel it as contradicting his own?

PRELUDES

T. S. Eliot (1888–1965)

I

The winter evening settles down
With smell of steaks in passageways.
Six o'clock.
The burnt-out ends of smoky days.
And now a gusty shower wraps 5
The grimy scraps
Of withered leaves about your feet
And newspapers from vacant lots;
The showers beat
On broken blinds and chimney-pots 10
And at the corner of the street
A lonely cab-horse steams and stamps.
And then the lighting of the lamps.

II

The morning comes to consciousness
Of faint stale smells of beer   15
From the sawdust-trampled street
With all its muddy feet that press
To early coffee-stands.
With the other masquerades
That time resumes,   20
One thinks of all the hands
That are raising dingy shades
In a thousand furnished rooms.

III

You tossed a blanket from the bed,
You lay upon your back, and waited;   25
You dozed, and watched the night revealing
The thousand sordid images
Of which your soul was constituted;
They flickered against the ceiling.
And when all the world came back   30
And the light crept up between the shutters
And you heard the sparrows in the gutters,
You had such a vision of the street
As the street hardly understands;
Sitting along the bed's edge, where   35
You curled the papers from your hair,
Or clasped the yellow soles of feet
In the palms of both soiled hands.

IV

His soul stretched tight across the skies
That fade behind a city block,   40
Or trampled by insistent feet
At four and five and six o'clock;
And short square fingers stuffing pipes,
And evening newspapers, and eyes
Assured of certain certainties,   45
The conscience of a blackened street
Impatient to assume the world.

I am moved by fancies that are curled
Around these images, and cling:
The notion of some infinitely gentle   50
Infinitely suffering thing.

Wipe your hand across your mouth, and
    laugh;
The worlds revolve like ancient women
Gathering fuel in vacant lots.

Like Blake's "The Chimney Sweeper"
and "London" and Wordsworth's "London,
1802," Eliot's "Preludes" is about a great
modern city. Like them, too, it is concerned
with the dehumanizing effect of the city, but
its method is more imagistic, with less reli-

ance on statement. Furthermore, this poem,
somewhat longer than the others, has several
quite distinct parts. Sections I and II are
generalized impressions of evening and morning in a great city, with no individual indicated. Section III involves a "you"—a
woman, we gather (the "you" has curl papers
in her hair)—who wakes to face the world.
Section IV, opens with a "he"—an unidentified man—and his implied reactions to the
city. But then an "I" appears—the speaker of
the poem, who addresses another "you," presumably the reader. These facts about the
poem suggest certain questions that bear on
its meaning.

EXERCISES

1. Sections I and II provide a view of urban life
very different from that described by Wordsworth
in "Composed upon Westminster Bridge." Do you
think the poet plays fair here?
2. We have said that Sections I and II give a
generalized impression of the city. What is that
impression? In what way does the speaker imply
personal significance in the "generalized" impression? What do you make of the image of the cab-
horse? Would a taxi do as well? Suppose the taxi
driver had gone into a restaurant for a cup of
coffee and was seen chatting with a waitress. Then
what? What about the word *masquerades* in line
19? A mask conceals, but behind the mask there is,
presumably, some reality, some real person. What
is thematically being suggested here? What is suggested by the fact that in the "thousand furnished
rooms" (l. 23) only hands are visible?
3. Examine lines 27–28. They imply that a soul is
composed of images. Don't you have the general
notion that a soul has identity and continuity?
(Substitute the word *self* for *soul* if you like.)
What does the poet here imply about the state of
this inhabitant of the modern world?
4. What are the "certain certainties" in line 45?
Has the answer already been given in the poem,
in sections I and II and particularly in the preceding part of section IV? In what sense can these
physical "certainties" be said to be the "conscience" of the "street"? Notice that in sections II
and III we have seen "consciousness" and "soul"
played off against the images of "certain certainties." Does this suggest a thematic progression in
the poem?
5. If the theme of the poem involves a contrast
between "consciousness-soul-conscience" and the
"certain certainties," what is the final attitude of

the poet toward this blank world? Why do we use the word *blank* here?

HOLLYWOOD
Karl Shapiro (b. 1913)

Farthest from any war, unique in time
Like Athens or Baghdad, this city lies
Between dry purple mountains and the sea.
The air is clear and famous, every day
Bright as a postcard, bringing bungalows　　　5
　　And sights. The broad nights advertise
For love and music and astronomy.

Heart of a continent, the hearts converge
On open boulevards where palms are nursed
With flare-pots like a grove, on villa roads　　10
Where castles cultivated like a style
Breed fabulous metaphors in foreign stone,
　　And on enormous movie lots
Where history repeats its vivid blunders.

Alice and Cinderella are most real.　　　　15
Here may the tourist, quite sincere at last,
Rest from his dream of travels. All is new,
No ruins claim his awe, and permanence,
Despised like customs, fails at every turn.
　　Here where the eccentric thrives,　　　20
Laughter and love are leading industries.

Luck is another. Here the body-guard,
The parasite, the scholar are well paid,
The quack erects his alabaster office,
The moron and the genius are enshrined,　　25
And the mystic makes a fortune quietly;
　　Here all superlatives come true
And beauty is marketed like a basic food.

O can we understand it? Is it ours,
A crude whim of a beginning people,　　　30
A private orgy in a secluded spot?
Or alien like the word *harem*, or true
Like hideous Pittsburgh or depraved Atlanta?
　　Is adolescence just as vile
As this its architecture and its talk?　　　35

Or are they parvenus, like boys and girls?
Or ours and happy, cleverest of all?
Yes, Yes. Though glamorous to the ignorant
This is the simplest city, a new school.
What is more nearly ours? If soul can mean　　40
　　The civilization of the brain,
This is a soul, a possibly proud Florence.

EXERCISE

How ironical do you think the end of the poem is?

GROUP 5: MORTALITY

ON THE TOMBS IN WESTMINSTER ABBEY
Francis Beaumont (1584–1616)

Mortality, behold and fear!
What a change of flesh is here!
Think how many royal bones
Sleep within this heap of stones:
Here they lie had realms and lands,　　　5
Who now want strength to stir their hands:
Where from their pulpits seal'd with dust
They preach, "In greatness is no trust."
Here's an acre sowed indeed
With the richest, royal'st seed　　　　10
That the earth did e'er suck in
Since the first man died for sin:
Here the bones of birth have cried—
"Though gods they were, as men they died."
Here are sands, ignoble things,　　　　15
Dropt from the ruin'd sides of kings;
Here's a world of pomp and state,
Buried in dust, once dead by fate.

EXERCISES

1. Suppose we rewrite line 4 to read "Sleep beneath these carven stones." What would be gained or lost?
2. Would the poem be improved by dropping the last couplet?

ELEGY
Written in a Country Churchyard
Thomas Gray (1716–1771)

The Curfew tolls the knell of parting day,
　　The lowing herd wind slowly o'er the lea,
The plowman homeward plods his weary way,
　　And leaves the world to darkness and to me.

Now fades the glimmering landscape on the sight,　　　5
　　And all the air a solemn stillness holds,
Save where the beetle wheels his droning flight,
　　And drowsy tinglings lull the distant folds;

Save that from yonder ivy-mantled tower
　　The moping owl does to the moon complain　　10
Of such, as wandering near her secret bower,
　　Molest her ancient solitary reign.

Beneath those rugged elms, that yew-tree's shade,
　　Where heaves the turf in many a mouldering heap,

Each in his narrow cell for ever laid,　　　　　15
  The rude Forefathers of the hamlet sleep.

The breezy call of incense-breathing Morn,
  The swallow twittering from the straw-built
    shed,
The cock's shrill clarion, or the echoing horn,
  No more shall rouse them from their lowly
    bed.　　　　　20

For them no more the blazing hearth shall burn,
  Or busy housewife ply her evening care;
No children run to lisp their sire's return,
  Or climb his knees the envied kiss to share.

Oft did the harvest to their sickle yield,　　　　　25
  Their furrow oft the stubborn glebe has broke;
How jocund did they drive their team afield!
  How bowed the woods beneath their sturdy
    stroke!

Let not Ambition mock their useful toil,
  Their homely joys, and density obscure;　　　　　30
Nor Grandeur hear with a disdainful smile
  The short and simple annals of the poor.

The boast of heraldry, the pomp of power,
  And all that beauty, all that wealth e'er gave,
Awaits alike the inevitable hour.　　　　　35
  The paths of glory lead but to the grave.

Nor you, ye Proud, impute to These the fault,
  If Memory o'er their Tomb no Trophies raise,
Where through the long-drawn aisle and fretted
    vault
  The pealing anthem swells the note of praise.　40

Can storied urn or animated bust
  Back to its mansion call the fleeting breath?
Can Honor's voice provoke the silent dust,
  Or Flattery sooth the dull cold ear of Death?

Perhaps in this neglected spot is laid　　　　　45
  Some heart once pregnant with celestial fire;
Hands, that the rod of empire might have swayed,
  Or waked to ecstasy the living lyre.

But Knowledge to their eyes her ample page
  Rich with the spoils of time did ne'er unroll;　50
Chill Penury repressed their noble rage,
  And froze the genial current of the soul.

Full many a gem of purest ray serene,
  The dark unfathomed caves of ocean bear:
Full many a flower is born to blush unseen,　　　　　55
  And waste its sweetness on the desert air.

Some village Hampden, that with dauntless breast
  The little tyrant of his fields withstood;

Some mute inglorious Milton here may rest,
  Some Cromwell guiltless of his country's
    blood.　　　　　60

The applause of listening senates to command,
  The threats of pain and ruin to despise,
To scatter plenty o'er a smiling land,
  And read their history in a nation's eyes,

Their lot forbade: nor circumscribed alone　　　　　65
  Their growing virtues, but their crimes confin'd;
Forbade to wade through slaughter to a throne,
  And shut the gates of mercy on mankind,

The struggling pangs of conscious truth to hide,
  To quench the blushes of ingenuous shame,　　70
Or heap the shrine of Luxury and Pride
  With incense kindled at the Muses's flame.

Far from the madding crowd's ignoble strife,
  Their sober wishes never learned to stray;
Along the cool sequestered vale of life　　　　　75
  They kept the noiseless tenor of their way.

Yet even these bones from insult to protect,
  Some frail memorial still erected nigh,
With uncouth rhymes and shapeless sculpture
    decked,
  Implores the passing tribute of a sigh.　　　　　80

Their names, their years, spelt by the unlettered
    muse,
  The place of fame and elegy supply:
And many a holy text around she strews,
  That teach the rustic moralist to die.

For who to dumb Forgetfulness a prey,　　　　　85
  This pleasing anxious being e'er resigned,
Left the warm precincts of the cheerful day,
  Nor cast one longing lingering look behind?

On some fond breast the parting soul relies,
  Some pious drops the closing eye requires;　　90
Ev'n from the tomb the voice of Nature cries,
  Ev'n in our Ashes live their wonted Fires.

For thee, who mindful of the unhonoured Dead
  Dost in these lines their artless tale relate,
If chance, by lonely contemplation led,　　　　　95
  Some kindred Spirit shall inquire thy fate,

Haply some hoary-headed Swain may say,
  "Oft have we seen him at the peep of dawn
Brushing with hasty steps the dews away
  To meet the sun upon the upland lawn.　　　　　100

"There at the foot of yonder nodding beech
  That wreathes its old fantastic roots so high,

His listless length at noontide would he stretch,
　　And pore upon the brook that babbles by.

"Hard by yon wood, now smiling as in scorn,　105
　　Muttering his wayward fancies he would rove,
Now drooping, woeful wan, like one forlorn,
　　Or crazed with care, or crossed in hopeless love.

"One morn I missed him on the customed hill,
　　Along the heath and near his favorite tree;　110
Another came; nor yet beside the rill,
　　Nor up the lawn, nor at the wood was he;

"The next with dirges due in sad array
　　Slow through the church-way path we saw him
　　　borne.
Approach and read (for thou can'st read) the
　　lay,　　　　　　　　　　　　　　　　115
　　Graved on the stone beneath yon agèd thorn."

The Epitaph

Here rests his head upon the lap of earth
　　A youth to fortune and to fame unknown.
Fair Science frowned not on his humble birth,
　　And Melancholy marked him for her own.　120

Large was his bounty, and his soul sincere,
　　Heav'n did a recompense as largely send:
He gave to Misery all he had, a tear,
　　He gained from Heaven ('twas all he wished)
　　a friend.

No farther seek his merits to disclose,　125
　　Or draw his frailties from their dread abode,
(There they alike in trembling hope repose),
　　The bosom of his Father and his God.

EXERCISE

Prepare a set of questions calculated to further
your understanding of this poem. Some of your
questions will have to do, of course, with such
matters as the development of the theme and the
use of imagery, but you may need to ask also who
such people as Hampton and Cromwell were.
Look up these names in the library. You may also
want to find in the library some account of the
poet Gray and even of the "graveyard school" of
English poets of the eighteenth century. A good
starting point for your questions would be to consider what the differences are between Gray's
"Elegy" and Beaumont's "On the Tombs in Westminster Abbey," which is concerned with the most
obvious irony of the contrast between human
pride and the common lot of mortals. What over-

tones—emotional, philosophical, and social—does
Gray's "Elegy" have?

I WALKED OUT TO THE GRAVEYARD
TO SEE THE DEAD
Richard Eberhart (b. 1904)

I walked out to the graveyard to see the dead
The iron gates were locked, I couldn't get in,
A golden pheasant on the dark fir boughs
Looked with fearful method at the sunset,

Said I, Sir bird, wink no more at me　　　　　5
I have had enough of my dark eye-smarting,
I cannot adore you, nor do I praise you,
But assign you to the rafters of Montaigne.

Who talks with the Absolute salutes a Shadow,
Who seeks himself shall lose himself;　　　　10
And the golden pheasants are no help
And action must be learned from love of man.

EXERCISES

1. Hunt up Montaigne in a biographical dictionary. Perhaps he is referred to here because of
his association with speculations on man and
nature carried out in a skeptical spirit. (His motto
was *Que sais-je?*, "What do I know?")
2. Compare and contrast the mood of this poem
with that of Gray's "Elegy."
3. Presumably the fact that the speaker encountered the pheasant was an accident, but the poet
turns this fact to account in the poem. What does
the bird symbolize?
4. Is this poem about the dead? Or about the way
in which man is related to nature? Or what?

FIDELE'S DIRGE
William Shakespeare (1564–1616)

Fear no more the heat o' the sun,
　　Nor the furious winter's rages;
Thou thy worldly task hast done,
　　Home art gone, and ta'en thy wages;
Golden lads and girls all must,　　　　　　5
As chimney-sweepers, come to dust.

Fear no more the frown o' the great,
　　Thou art past the tyrant's stroke;
Care no more to clothe and eat;
　　To thee the reed is as the oak;　　　　　10
The sceptre, learning, physic, must
All follow this, and come to dust.

Fear no more the lightning-flash,
   Nor the all-dreaded thunder-stone;
Fear not slander, censure rash;   15
   Thou hast finished joy and moan;
All lovers young, all lovers must
Consign to thee, and come to dust.

No exorciser harm thee!
Nor no witchcraft charm thee!   20
Ghost unlaid forbear thee!
Nothing ill come near thee!
Quiet consummation have;
And renownèd be thy grave!

EXERCISES

1. This song, from the play *Cymbeline*, is sung by Imogen while disguised as a boy; Fidele is the name she assumes. What is the attitude toward death established in this poem?
2. What is the effect on the tone of the poem of the reiteration of the words "Fear no more"? On what basis has the poet selected the particular items that are no longer to be feared?
3. Does the poem succeed in making death seem a consolation and the grave a place of quiet and repose?
4. What is the effect of the emphasis upon the coming "to dust" of all things high and low, weak or powerful?
5. Can you account for the shift in style and tone in the last stanza? Is it meant to be a kind of charm against whatever might trouble the grave? Does it have the quality of a ritual? Does it make an effective ending for the dirge?
6. Scan stanzas 2 and 3. Can you justify the substitutions and variations of the metrical pattern?
7. Turn back to "At the Slackening of the Tide" by James Wright (sec. 14). If that is a good poem, how can this be?

GROUP 6: RELIGION

SONNET 146

William Shakespeare (1564–1616)

Poor soul, the center of my sinful earth,
Thrall to these rebel powers that thee array
Why dost thou pine within and suffer dearth,
Painting thy outward walls so costly gay?
Why so large cost, having so short a lease,   5
Dost thou upon thy fading mansion spend?
Shall worms, inheritors of this excess,

Eat up thy charge? is this thy body's end?
Then, soul, live thou upon thy servant's loss,
And let that pine to aggravate thy store;   10
Buy terms divine in selling hours of dross;
Within be fed, without be rich no more:
   So shall thou feed on Death, that feeds on men,
   And Death once dead, there's no more dying then.

This sonnet is obviously based upon Christian theology. To say so is not, however, to imply that the sonnet is simply a bit of versified theology, that it does not have its own dramatic organization, or that it has nothing to say to people who are unable to accept its theology. As a work of art it has its own structure through which its meaning is presented. But it may be interesting—and useful—to see how this poem is related to the culture out of which it came, a culture shot through and through with theological concepts.

In the orthodox Christian conception, God created the world and what he created was good, including man's senses and his appetites. But though man was created good and sinless, he "fell," through pride, followed his own will rather than God's, and in so doing, cut himself off from the fountain of life. Hence the wages of sin was indeed death. (Milton was to put it thus in his *Paradise Lost:* Adam's sin of pride "Brought Death into the World, and all our woe.") In the Christian scheme, however, man is given a second chance when God, taking on human flesh in the person of Christ, becomes "the second Adam" and through his sacrificial death, promises to redeem man from the death that in his now corrupted nature he is doomed to suffer.

The notion that the flesh is in itself evil runs counter to the Hebraic-Christian conception of its originally divine origin; even so, the tendency to regard all matters as evil did appear early in the Christian era, and though vigorously condemned as heretical, is still to be met with. The reference to "my sinful earth" may suggest that Shakespeare's sonnet partakes of this heresy. But one must take into account the stress upon the "rebel powers" that hold the soul in thrall: in the general context, the rebellion is not merely against the soul but against God. Indeed, it can be argued that the emphasis here is not upon the essential wickedness of the flesh but upon the subversion that the rebel powers have effected, a subversion in which the master is being ruled by his own servant. In these terms the body can become a distraction and worse. At best, it is no permanent abiding place but "now to Death devote." Hence, the admonition given in this poem echoes Matthew 6:19–20: "Lay not up for yourselves treasures upon earth, where moth and rust does corrupt, and where thieves break through and steal: but lay up for yourselves treasures in heaven, where neither moth nor rust does corrupt, and where thieves do not break through nor steal."

So much for the general doctrinal basis. Consider now how the poem manages to state and dramatize the theological position on which it rests.

EXERCISES

1. Paraphrase the argument of the poem. What does even a careful paraphrase leave out?
2. The dominant metaphor is drawn from business life—investment in a house. Is this metaphor out of keeping with the solemnity of the theme? Or is it well chosen? How does it affect the tone of the poem?
3. How is the dominant metaphor related to the subsidiary imagery of the poem?

DOVER BEACH
Matthew Arnold (1822–1888)

The sea is calm to-night,
The tide is full, the moon lies fair
Upon the straits;—on the French coast, the light
Gleams and is gone; the cliffs of England stand,
Glimmering and vast, out in the tranquil bay.   5
Come to the window, sweet is the night air!
Only, from the lone line of spray
Where the sea meets the moon-blanch'd land,
Listen! you hear the grating roar
Of pebbles which the waves draw back, and
    fling,   10
At their return, up the high strand,
Begin, and cease, and then again begin,
With tremulous cadence slow, and bring
The eternal note of sadness in.

Sophocles long ago   15
Heard it on the Aegean, and it brought
Into his mind the turbid ebb and flow

Of human misery; we
Find also in the sound a thought,
Hearing it by this distant northern sea.   20

The Sea of Faith
Was once, too, at the full, and round earth's shore
Lay like the folds of a bright girdle furl'd.
But now I only hear
Its melancholy, long, withdrawing roar,   25
Retreating, to the breath
Of the night-wind, down the vast edges drear
And naked shingles of the world.

Ah, love, let us be true
To one another! for the world, which seems   30
To lie before us like a land of dreams,
So various, so beautiful, so new,
Hath really neither joy, nor love, nor light,
Nor certitude, nor peace, nor help for pain;
And we are here as on a darkling plain   35
Swept with confused alarms of struggle and flight,
Where ignorant armies clash by night.

EXERCISES

1. "Dover Beach" is a very famous expression of the shock felt by many thoughtful people in the nineteenth century when modern scientific developments, most notably the work of Charles Darwin, began to undermine traditional Christianity. How effective do you think the poet's symbol of the ebbing tide is for the decline of faith? Does the poem suggest that faith will sometime in the future return like an incoming tide? If it doesn't, then doesn't the fact that the literal tide withdraws only to come again impair the effectiveness of the symbol? Or, to take another view of the matter, does Arnold manage to focus our attention and interest in such a way that the question does not necessarily arise? On this point you might turn to poems by John Donne and Andrew Marvell and compare their method with that of Arnold.
2. What does Arnold gain by opening the poem with the description of the actual sea, and with the sense of a room from which he and his companion look out? After all, the descriptive section occupies more than a third of the poem.
3. What is the function of lines 15–20? Why not simply proceed from line 14 to line 21? For Sophocles the sea had a significance quite different from that Arnold gives it here. Or is there a relation intended between the feeling of Sophocles and that of the speaker? What, if anything, is gained by withholding the "Sea of Faith" comparison until line 21, well past the midpoint of the poem?

4. To whom is the phrase "Ah, love" in line 29 addressed? Does the address give an immediate and literal dramatic effect to the poem? What has provoked this address? What difference, if any, would there be in the nature of human love in an age of Christian faith and in one of scientific naturalism? What difference in regard to any kind of experience?

5. On the basis of "Say Not, the Struggle Nought Availeth," "Epitaph on an Army of Mercenaries," "If," "Ode to Duty," "The College Colonel," and "Dulce et Decorum Est," can you imagine Clough, Housman, Kipling, Wordsworth, Melville, or Owen writing "Dover Beach"? If so, why? If not, why not?

6. Are the assumptions about life underlying Arnold's "The Last Word" the same as those underlying "Dover Beach"? Explain.

7. Do you find the rhythm of lines 24–28 especially effective? Explain.

8. What is the significance of the word *naked* in line 28?

9. In the first three sections of the poem rime is used but is extremely recessive. In the last section, however, it becomes more and more marked. What is the logic of this, if any?

10. Turn to "The Dover Bitch" by Anthony Hecht (sec. 18). What is the "point" of that poem in relation to this?

BATTER MY HEART, THREE-PERSONED GOD

John Donne (1571/2–1631)

Batter my heart, three-personed God; for, you
As yet but knock, breathe, shine, and seek to mend;
That I may rise and stand, o'erthrow me, and bend
Your force, to break, blow, burn, and make me new.
I, like an usurped town to another due,　　　　5
Labour to admit you, but Oh, to no end;
Reason your viceroy in me, me should defend,
But is captived, and proves weak or untrue,
Yet dearly I love you, and would be loved fain
But am betrothed unto your enemy;　　　　10
Divorce me, untie or break that knot again;
Take me to you, imprison me, for I,
Except you enthrall me, never shall be free,
Not ever chaste, except you ravish me.

EXERCISES

1. Compare the tone of Donne's "Batter My Heart" with that of Shakespeare's Sonnet 146 ("Poor soul, the center of my sinful earth"). Which poem dramatizes an urgent spiritual crisis? Which apparently appeals to reason and which is an anguished emotional cry? Base your answers on rhythm and imagery.

2. Throughout Donne's poem the images are of assault, but an assault for which the would-be victim pleads. In the last line the image is specifically sexual, which suddenly lends a different connotation to all the earlier images. How can it be argued that the rhythm of the line, in contrast to the prevailing rhythm of the poem, dramatizes the content?

3. If this is a poem of urgent emotional excitement, how do you account for the presence of rather complicated and paradoxical metaphors? Is this fact dramatically out of keeping or dramatically in keeping with the basic quality of the poem?

GOD'S GRANDEUR

Gerard Manley Hopkins (1844–1889)

The world is charged with the grandeur of God.
　　It will flame out, like shining from shook foil;
　　It gathers to a greatness, like the ooze of oil
Crushed. Why do men then now not reck his rod?
Generations have trod, have trod, have trod;　　　5
　　And all is seared with trade; bleared, smeared with toil;
　　And wears man's smudge and shares man's smell: the soil
Is bare now, nor can foot feel, being shod.

And for all this, nature is never spent;
　　There lives the dearest freshness deep down things;　　　10
And though the last lights off the black West went
　　Oh, morning, at the brown brink eastward, springs—
Because the Holy Ghost over the bent
　　World broods with warm breast and with ah! bright wings.

What this sonnet "says" is quite explicitly put in lines 1, 4, 9, and 13–14. These lines give the "argument"—to use the old-fashioned term—that the poem develops:

1. The world is charged with the grandeur of God.

4. Why do men then now not reck his rod?

9. And for all this, nature is never spent;

13. Because the Holy Ghost over the bent

14. World broods. . . .

The body of the poem fleshes out—realizes, dramatizes—this rather abstract argument. Our concern here is to see and understand—and therefore feel more fully—how this occurs. First, however, we should try to give ourselves as fully as possible to the experience of the poem. Read it aloud a number of times; try *really* to hear it, its rhythms and verbal qualities.

Much of the power of this poem derives from its rhythmical and verbal effects. Let us consider lines 5–8. In line 5, the onomatopoeic effect of the repetion of *have trod* is obvious, but somewhat less obvious, and very important, is the effect associated with the word *generations*. The meaning—the indeterminate millions of men over the ages—is, of course, clear, but the rhythm deserves comment. In the four syllables of *generations* the two metrical accents cause an effect of lengthening that opens up into the emphatic mounting repetition of *have trod*. Lines 6 and 7 also have a very powerful expressive effect. The most obvious device is the vowel run (emphasized by rime) in the series *seared, bleared, smeared*, which pile up the suggestion of ruin and dirtiness. It is not merely that the words have such denotations; if that were true, we should get an equivalent effect by substituting another series—say, *seared, blotched, fouled*.* But we get nothing. In the original version, the verbal quality itself provides intensification. As one aspect of this, we find, as we have said, internal rime, but there is also alliteration: the befouling indicated by the word *smeared* in line 6 is intensified by *smudge* and *smell* in line 7—an intensification that makes "man's smell" foul indeed.

EXERCISES

1. What is the general tone of the poem?
2. Lines 2 and 3 present, each in a vivid image, two opposing ways in which the "grandeur of God" manifests itself, one an image of expansion, one of contraction. In what other ways are they opposed? What do these images, and the paradox they embody, do for the statement in line 1? How do they relate to the subsequent development of the argument?
3. Lines 5–8 illustrate the ways in which man has not recked God's rod. What is the basic way in which man has disobeyed God, or been ungrateful for the world? How does this lead to the statement in line 9? What rhythmical and verbal effects other than those discussed above do you find in lines 5–8?
4. Lines 9–12 develop the image of nature as being constantly renewed. But is it self-renewing? The word *because* becomes the key word here, and lines 13 and 14 return us structurally to the opening statement of the poem. But how—in what spirit and attitude—does God renew the world and manifest his "grandeur"?
5. Scan lines 1–8. Comment on the meter as related to the tone, and variations of tone.
6. Discuss the dramatic force of the last six lines, 9–14, with reference to meter and rhetorical variation.
7. To what poem earlier in this section is "God's Grandeur" closest in method? Compare the tone of the two poems.

THE PULLEY

George Herbert (1593–1633)

When God at first made man,
Having a glass of blessings standing by;
Let us (said he) pour on him all we can:
Let the world's riches, which dispersed lie,
  Contract into a span.   5

So strength first made a way,
Then beauty flow'd, then wisdom, honour, pleasure:
When almost all was out, God made a stay,
Perceiving that alone of all his treasure
  Rest in the bottom lay.   10

For if I should (said he)
Bestow this jewel also on my creature,
He would adore my gifts instead of me,
And rest in Nature, not the God of Nature:
  So both should losers be.   15

Yet let him keep the rest,
But keep them with repining restlessness:
Let him be rich and weary, that at least,
Of goodness lead him not, yet weariness
  May toss him to my breast.   20

---

* We may now reverse the process and set up a new series to see what effect we get. For instance with the line "And all is botched with trade; blotched, smutched with toil."

EXERCISE

On the basis of "Dover Beach" and "Batter My Heart," can you more easily imagine Arnold or Donne as the author of "The Pulley"? In what way do considerations of style, including rhythm and imagery, help you to arrive at an answer to this question?

SONNETS AT CHRISTMAS

1934

Allen Tate (b. 1899)

I

This is the day His hour of life draws near,
Let me get ready from head to foot for it
Most handily with eyes to pick the year
For small feed to reward a feathered wit.
Some men would see it an epiphany   5
At ease, at food and drink, others at chase
Yet I, stung lassitude, with ecstasy
Unspent argue with the season's difficult case
So: Man dull critter of enormous head,
What would he look at in the coiling sky?   10
But I must kneel again unto the Dead
While Christmas bells of paper white and red,
Figured with boys and girls spilt from a sled,
Ring out the silence I am nourished by.

II

Ah, Christ, I love you rings to the wild sky
And I must think a little of the past:
When I was ten I told a stinking lie
That got a black boy whipped; but now at last
The going years, caught in an accurate glow,   5
Reverse like balls, englished upon green baize—
Let them return, let the round trumpets blow
The ancient crackle of the Christ's deep gaze.
Deafened and blind, with senses yet unfound,
Am I, untutored to the after-wit   10
Of knowledge, knowing a nightmare has no
     sound;
Therefore with idle hands and head I sit
In late December before the fire's daze
Punished by crimes of which I would be quit.

EXERCISES

1. What is the situation portrayed in these sonnets? What sort of person is the speaker? If the Christmas season stirs him neither to simple holiday gaiety nor to fervent devotion, in what way does it affect him?
2. How has the poet used the circumstantial detail of the Christmas season? Consider, for example, this detail: Christmas bells have become holiday decoration of gaily colored paper; they "ring" out only silence.
3. What is the season's "difficult case"? In what sense has the speaker argued it? Why is modern man said to be a creature of "enormous head"? Does the enormity of his head have anything to do with his plight? What light does the Christmas season shed upon his characteristic plight?
4. Thematically, do these sonnets more resemble "Dover Beach" or "Batter My Heart"?
5. It is sometimes pointed out that in method Tate has derived much from Donne and other metaphysical poets. Can you find any basis for that notion in the present poems?

CHRISTMAS EVE UNDER HOOKER'S STATUE

Robert Lowell (b. 1917)

Tonight in a blackout. Twenty years ago
I hung my stocking on the tree, and hell's
Serpent entwined the apple in the toe
To sting the child with knowledge. Hooker's heels
Kicking at nothing in the shifting snow,   5
A cannon and a cairn of cannon balls
Rusting before the blackened Statehouse, know
How the long horn of plenty broke like glass
In Hooker's gauntlets. Once I came from Mass;
Now storm-clouds shelter Christmas, once again   10
Mars meets his fruitless star with open arms,
His heavy sabre flashes with the rime,
The war-god's bronzed and empty forehead forms
Anonymous machinery from raw men;
The cannon on the Common cannot stun   15
The blundering butcher as he rides on Time—
The barrel clinks with holly. I am cold:
I ask for bread, my father gives me mould;

His stocking is full of stones. Santa in red
Is crowned with wizened berries. Man of war,   20
Where is the summer's garden? In its bed
The ancient speckled serpent will appear,
And black-eyed susan with her frizzled head.
When Chancellorsville mowed down the volun-
     teer,
"All wars are boyish," Herman Melville said;   25
But we are old, our fields are running wild:
Till Christ again turn wanderer and child.

The scene is Boston ("the cannon on the Common"), the time 1944. Hooker, whose statue is alluded to, commanded the Army of the Potomac in its defeat at Chancellorsville.

EXERCISES

1. Compare the situation presented here with that presented in the preceding sonnets by Tate. Compare and contrast the attitudes characterizing the speakers in these poems.

2. What comment does this poem make upon our civilization? How is this comment made? What part is played by the imagery and other devices of indirection? May it be said that in this poem references to childhood (the Christmas stocking, Santa Claus) are played off against images of brutality and war (Hooker's gauntlets, Mars)? To what effect?

3. The comparisons seem almost studiedly violent (for example, "The barrel clinks with holly," line 17). Is the violence justified?

4. What is the meaning of the last line of the poem? Does it summarize what the poem "says"? Does it depend for its precise meaning upon the rest of the poem?

5. What similarities does this poem have to the author's "Colonel Shaw and the Massachusetts' 54th" in group 2 of this section?

MASTER OF BEAUTY*

John Berryman (1914–1972)

Master of beauty, craftsman of the snowflake,
inimitable contriver,
endower of Earth so gorgeous & different from the
    boring Moon,
thank you for such as it is my gift.

I have made up a morning prayer to you   5
containing with precision everything that most
    matters.
'According to Thy will,' the thing begins.
It took me off & on two days. It does not aim at
    eloquence.

You have come to my rescue again & again
In my impassable, sometimes despairing years.   10
You have allowed my brilliant friends to destroy
    themselves
and I am still here, severely damaged, but func-
    tioning.

Unknowable, as I am unknown to my guinea pigs:
how can I 'love' you?
I only as far as gratitude & awe   15
confidently and absolutely go.

I have no idea whether we live again.
It doesn't seem likely
from either the scientific or the philosophical
    point of view
but certainly all things are possible to you,   20

and I believe as fixedly in the Resurrection-
    appearances to Peter & to Paul
as I believe I sit in this blue chair.
Only that may have been a special case
to establish their initiatory faith.

Whatever your end may be, accept my amaze-
    ment.   25
May I stand until death forever at attention
for any your least instruction or enlightenment.
I even feel sure you will assist me again, Master of
    insight & beauty.

EXERCISES

1. Compare the "belief" of Berryman to that of Donne, Arnold, Tate, and Lowell.

2. Compare the general style of this poem with that of the poets named above. What is the tone of this poem? What is the difference in style between stanza 1 and stanza 5? Why is the color of the chair in stanza 6 specified? Does "blue chair" seem to fit with the phrase "initiatory faith"?

GROUP 7: THE NATURE OF POETRY

KUBLA KHAN
OR, A VISION IN A DREAM

Samuel Taylor Coleridge (1772–1834)

  In Xanadu did Kubla Khan
A stately pleasure-dome decree:
Where Alph, the sacred river, ran
Through caverns measureless to man
    Down to a sunless sea.   5

So twice five miles of fertile ground
With walls and towers were girdled round:
And here were gardens bright with sinuous rills,
Where blossomed many an incense-bearing tree;
And here were forests ancient as the hills   10
Enfolding sunny spots of greenery.

---

* This poem is number 1 in a series called "Eleven Addresses to the Lord." The present title has been inserted by the editors.

But oh! that deep romantic chasm which slanted
Down the green hill athwart a cedarn cover!
A savage place! as holy and enchanted
As e'er beneath a waning moon was haunted   15
By woman wailing for her demon-lover!
And from this chasm, with ceaseless turmoil
     seething,
As if this earth in fast thick pants were breathing
A mighty fountain momently was forced:
Amid whose swift half-intermitted burst   20
Huge fragments vaulted like rebounding hail,
Or chaffy grain beneath the thresher's flail:
And 'mid these dancing rocks at once and ever
It flung up momently the sacred river.
Five miles meandering with a mazy motion   25
Through wood and dale the sacred river ran,
Then reached the caverns measureless to man,
And sank in tumult to a lifeless ocean:
And 'mid this tumult Kubla heard from far
Ancestral voices prophesying war!   30

    The shadow of the dome of pleasure
    Floated midway on the waves;
    Where was heard the mingled measure
    From the fountain and the caves.
It was a miracle of rare device,   35
A sunny pleasure-dome with caves of ice!

    A damsel with a dulcimer
    In a vision once I saw:
    It was an Abyssinian maid,
    And on her dulcimer she played,   40
    Singing of Mount Abora.
    Could I revive within me
    Her symphony and song,
    To such a deep delight 'twould win me,
That with music loud and long,   45
I would build that dome in air,
That sunny dome! those caves of ice!
And all who heard should see them there,
And all should cry, Beware! Beware!
His flashing eyes, his floating hair!   50
Weave a circle round him thrice,
And close your eyes with holy dread,
For he on honey-dew hath fed,
And drunk the milk of Paradise.

"Kubla Khan" raises in a most acute form the whole question of meaning in a poem and the poet's intention. We have already touched on this, but now let us examine the matter a little more closely. We have Coleridge's account of how the poem was composed:

> In the summer of the year 1797 [1798], the Author, then in ill health, had retired to a lonely farm-house between Porlock and Linton, on the Exmoor confines of Somerset and Devonshire. In consequence of a slight indisposition, an anodyne had been prescribed, from the effects of which he fell asleep in his chair at the moment that he was reading the following sentence, or words of the same substance, in 'Purchas's Pilgrimage': 'Here the Khan Kubla commanded a palace to be built, and a stately garden thereunto. And thus ten miles of fertile ground were inclosed within a wall.' The Author continued for about three hours in a profound sleep, at least of the external senses, during which time he has the most vivid confidence, that he could not have composed less than from two to three hundred lines; if that indeed can be called composition in which all the images rose up before him as *things*, with a parallel production of the correspondent expressions, without any sensation or consciousness of effort. On awaking he appeared to himself to have a distinct recollection of the whole, and taking his pen, ink, and paper, instantly and eagerly wrote down the lines that are here preserved. At this moment he was unfortunately called out by a person on business from Porlock, and detained by him above an hour, and on his return to his room, found, to his no small surprise and mortification, that though he still retained some vague and dim recollection of the general purport of the vision, yet, with the exception of some eight or ten scattered lines and images, all the rest has passed away like the images on the surface of a stream into which a stone has been cast, but, alas! without the after restoration of the latter!

Can a poem dreamed up in this fashion be said to have a meaning? Can it be the expression of some idea held by the poet? Suppose, however, that what was dreamed up was not a poem but a mathematical discovery or chemical formula. Would either of these have less validity because dreamed up? We should have to say no, for the validity of the formula does not depend upon how it came to the scientist but upon its own nature. There are, in fact, many accounts of how important scientific discoveries did come in some flash of intuition or in dream. For instance, the great German chemist Kekulé dreamed up two of his most important discoveries. But whether it is a poem or a chemical formula that is dreamed up, this important fact must be remembered: only poets dream up poems and only scientists dream up scientific discoveries. The dream, or the moment of inspiration, really sums up a long period of hard conscious work.

Wordsworth, in the preface to the second edition of *Lyrical Ballads*, has a very important remark on how meaning gets into poetry. Having just said that he hopes his poems to be distinguished by a "worthy purpose," he continues:

> Not that I always began to write with a distinct purpose formally conceived: but habits of meditation have, I trust, so prompted and regulated my feelings, that my descriptions of such objects as strongly excite those feelings, will be found to carry along with them a *purpose*. If this opinion be erroneous, I can have little right to the name of a Poet. For all good poetry is the spontaneous overflow of powerful feelings: and though this be true, Poems to which any value can be attached were never produced on any variety of subjects but by a man who, being possessed of more than usual organic sensibility, had also thought long and deeply.

The important point is that Wordsworth takes a poem that happens to come in a flash as embodying the ideas carefully developed over a long period of time.

Sometimes, of course, a poet does start with a pretty clear notion of what he wants his poem to be and works systematically. Sometimes he starts with only the vaguest feeling and with no defined theme. Sometimes he may simply have a line or a phrase as a kind of germ. But no matter how he starts, he is working toward a conception of the poem that will hold all the parts in significant relation to each other. Therefore, as his general conception becomes clearer, he may find more and more need for going back and changing parts already composed. The process is a process of exploration and development. The poet is busy finding out his own full meanings, for the meanings themselves do not exist until they are composed.

The poem isn't a way of saying something that could be said equally well another way. Its "saying" is the whole poem, the quality of the imagery, the feel of the rhythm, the dramatic force, the ideas, and the meaning does not exist until the words are all in their order.

It does not matter, then, whether the composition is slow and painful or easy and fast. We do not have two kinds of poetry, one spontaneous and one calculated. Without reference to the origin, we consider the quality of the poem, for the poem must deliver its own meaning. Some of those meanings may have entered in a flash, out of the poet's unconscious, but once they are absorbed into the poem they are part of the poem; they are ours and not the poet's.

It is possible that "Kubla Khan" was not dreamed up quite as literally as Coleridge said it was. In 1934 there came to light another note by Coleridge telling how he wrote the poem. The note reads as follows: "This fragment with a good deal more, not recoverable, composed in a sort of Reverie brought on by two grains of Opium, taken to check a dysentry, at a Farm House between Porlock & Linton, a quarter of a mile from Culbone Church, in the fall of the year, 1797." Miss Elizabeth Schneider believes that this is the earlier of the two accounts and probably the more accurate. In *Coleridge, Opium, and Kubla Khan** she has argued quite persuasively against the idea that "Kubla Khan" was a "literal opium dream or any other extremely remarkable kind of automatic composition. . . ." But whether Miss Schneider is right or wrong on this point, "Kubla Khan" is the product of Coleridge's special experience, closely resembling his other poems. As a comparison with his "The Ancient Mariner" and his famous unfinished work "Christabel" will show, "Kubla Khan" is very similar to these poems in tone and method.

We know the origin of almost every image and of many phrases in "Kubla Khan," for John Livingston Lowes has tracked them down in Coleridge's reading.† The materials

---

* Elizabeth Schneider, *Coleridge, Opium, and Kubla Khan* (Chicago: University of Chicago Press, 1953), p. 81.

†John L. Lowes, *The Road to Xanadu* (Boston: Houghton Mifflin Co., 1930), p. 356–413.

from Coleridge's reading do not give us the meaning of the poem any more than the fact of the composition under the influence of opium necessarily renders it meaningless. We have to look at the poem itself. The poem falls into two main sections. The first describes the dome of pleasure, the garden, the chasm, the great fountain and the ancestral voices prophesying war. The second, beginning with the line, "A damsel with a dulcimer," says that music might rebuild the world of Xanadu—or rather, that the special music of the Abyssinian maid might rebuild that world—and if the poet could recapture that music all who saw him would recognize his strange power as both beautiful and terrible. In other words, without treating the poem as an allegory and trying to make each detail equate with some notion, we can still take it to be a poem about creative imagination: "song," the imaginative power, the poetic power, could "build that dome in air" and re-create the enchanted and ominous world of Xanadu.

Does the fact that Coleridge called his poem a fragment argue against this interpretation? Probably not. Even though we can imagine that Coleridge might have planned to take the poem on through this or that line of development, we possess, nevertheless, a poem that is in itself coherent and that comes to a significant climax. Even though these fifty-four lines might have been envisaged as a section within a larger work the section can, in default of that larger work, stand alone.

How do we know that Coleridge "intended" the poem to mean what we have just suggested it means? Now we are back to our starting point. We do not know that he "intended" anything. He simply had a dream or perhaps it was a kind of waking reverie. But it is a product of the Coleridgean imagination. It embodies a meaningful structure. And for this meaning, the poem is its own best warrant.

EXERCISE

1. This poem is celebrated for its suggestiveness —that is, its power to stimulate the imagination. Notice that a very large part of this power resides in the imagery. Examine the aura of association and suggestion that emanates from phrases such as "forests ancient as the hills," "deep romantic chasm," "holy and enchanted," "waning moon," and so on.

2. Does the series of contrasts, stated or implied, help indicate what the poem is about: that is, "sunny" and "caves of ice," the tumultuous river and the "lifeless ocean" and so forth?

3. The khan seems to have chosen the site of his pleasure dome with great care. The spot exhibits a special kind of nature, rich, varied, and above all, numinous. May this poem be said to represent a kind of union of art and nature? Or to hint that a special relation to nature must obtain if the artist, either as builder of pleasure dome or of poem, is to succeed?

PHILOMELA

Matthew Arnold (1822–1888)

Hark! ah, the Nightingale!
The tawny-throated!
Hark, from that moonlit cedar what a burst!
What triumph! hark!—what pain!

O wanderer from a Grecian shore,   5
Still, after many years, in distant lands,
Still nourishing in thy bewilder'd brain
That wild, unquench'd, deep-sunken, old-world
     pain—
Say, will it never heal?
And can this fragrant lawn   10
With its cool trees, and night,
And the sweet, tranquil Thames,
And moonshine, and the dew,
To thy rack'd heart and brain
Afford no balm?   15

Dost thou to-night behold,
Here, through the moonlight on this English
     grass,
The unfriendly palace in the Thracian wild?
Dost thou again peruse
With hot cheeks and sear'd eyes   20
The too clear web, and thy dumb Sister's shame?
Dost thou once more assay
Thy flight, and feel come over thee,
Poor fugitive, the feathery change
Once more, and once more seem to make re-
     sound   25
Lone Daulis, and the high Cephissian vale?
Listen, Eugenia—
How thick the bursts come crowding through the
     leaves!
Again—thou hearest!
Eternal passion!   30
Eternal pain!

The basis of this poem is a Greek myth about a woman who was turned into a nightingale. Philomela was the sister of Procne, wife of King Tereus of Thrace. While Tereus was escorting Philomela to visit her sister, he raped her, and then cut out her tongue that she might not report his dishonor. He told Procne that Philomela was dead, but Philomela wove a tapestry depicting her rape and sent it to her sister. Procne revenged Philomela by killing her son, Itylus, and serving his flesh to his father, Tereus, as food. Upon discovering this, Tereus pursued his wife, who fled to Philomela. At this point the gods intervened and turned all three of them into birds: Philomela into a nightingale, Procne into a swallow, and Tereus into the hawk that pursues them.

EXERCISE

What interpretation does Arnold make of the myth in his poem?

PHILOMELA

John Crowe Ransom (1888–1974)

Procne, Philomela, and Itylus,
Your names are liquid, your improbable tale
Is recited in the classic numbers of the nightingale.
Ah, but our numbers are not felicitous,
It goes not liquidly for us.   5

Perched on a Roman ilex, and duly apostrophized,
The nightingale descanted unto Ovid;
She has even appeared to the Teutons, the swilled
    and gravid;
At Fontainebleau it may be the bird was gallicized;
Never was she baptized.   10

To England came Philomela with her pain,
Fleeing the hawk her husband; querulous ghost,
She wanders when he sits heavy on his roost,
Utters herself in the original again,
The untranslatable refrain.   15

Not to these shores she came! this other Thrace,
Environ barbarous to the royal Attic;
How could her delicate dirge run democratic,
Delivered in a cloudless boundless public place
To an inordinate race?   20

I pernoctated with the Oxford students once,
And in the quadrangles, in the cloisters, on the
    Cher,
Precociously knocked at antique doors ajar,
Fatuously touched the hems of the hierophants,
Sick of my dissonance.   25

I went out to Bagley Wood, I climbed the hill;
Even the moon had slanted off in a twinkling,
I heard the sepulchral owl and a few bells tinkling,
There was no more villainous day to unfulfil,
The diuturnity was still.   30

Up from the darkest wood where Philomela sat,
Her fairy numbers issued. What then ailed me?
My ears are called capacious but they failed me,
Her classics registered a little flat!
I rose, and venomously spat.   35

Philomela, Philomela, lover of song,
I am in despair if we may make us worthy,
A bantering breed sophistical and swarthy;
Unto more beautiful, persistently more young
Thy fabulous provinces belong.   40

EXERCISES

1. What is the attitude of the speaker in the first three stanzas? What is the effect of the witty expressions in such lines as 5 and 10? What is the effect of the homely word *roost* in line 13?
2. What is the poet's attitude toward his own country? What is his attitude toward himself?
3. Is the poet mocking the pursuit of "culture"? Is he debunking the Greek myth? Or is he after all in some sense serious and quite in earnest?
4. Try to define the shifts of tone occurring at line 16, line 21, and line 36. On what note does the poem end? Try to state the theme. Many philosophers have considered the possibility that poetry (and the other arts) cannot survive in a world dominated by science and technology. Does this idea seem to lie behind the poem? Do the details of the poem fit this idea?

THE IDEA OF ORDER AT KEY WEST

Wallace Stevens (1879–1955)

She sang beyond the genius of the sea.
The water never formed to mind or voice,
Like a body wholly body, fluttering
Its empty sleeves; and yet its mimic motion
Made constant cry, caused constantly a cry,   5
That was not ours although we understood,
Inhuman, of the veritable ocean.

The sea was not a mask. No more was she.
The song and water were not medleyed sound
Even if what she sang was what she heard,   10
Since what she sang was uttered word by word.
It may be that in all her phrases stirred
The grinding water and the gasping wind;
But it was she and not the sea we heard.

For she was the maker of the song she sang.   15
The ever-hooded, tragic-gestured sea
Was merely a place by which she walked to sing.
Whose spirit is this? we said, because we knew
It was the spirit that we sought and knew
That we should ask this often as she sang.   20

If it was only the dark voice of the sea
That rose, or even colored by many waves;
If it was only the outer voice of sky
And cloud, of the sunken coral water-walled,
However clear, it would have been deep air,   25
The heaving speech of air, a summer sound
Repeated in a summer without end
And sound alone. But it was more than that,
More even than her voice, and ours, among
The meaningless plungings of water and the
    wind,   30
Theatrical distances, bronze shadows heaped
On high horizons, mountainous atmospheres
Of sky and sea.
            It was her voice that made
The sky acutest at its vanishing.   35
She measured to the hour its solitude.
She was the single artificer of the world
In which she sang. And when she sang, the sea,
Whatever self it had, became the self
That was her song, for she was the maker. Then
    we,   40
As we beheld her striding there alone,
Knew that there never was a world for her
Except the one she sang and, singing, made.

Ramon Fernandez, tell me, if you know,
Why, when the singing ended and we turned   45

Toward the town, tell why the glassy lights,
The lights in the fishing boats at anchor there,
As the night descended, tilting in the air,
Mastered the night and portioned out the sea,
Fixing emblazoned zones and fiery poles,   50
Arranging, deepening, enchanting night.

Oh! Blessed rage for order, pale Ramon,
The maker's rage to order words of the sea,
Words of the fragrant portals, dimly-starred,
And of ourselves and our origins,   55
In ghostlier demarcations, keener sounds.

EXERCISES

1. Notice that the poet very carefully specifies the relation of the singing girl to the sea by which she sings. He is not content to have it that she imitates the sea or expresses its spirit in her song, though he does not deny that she is perhaps inspired by the sea, and that something of the sea is in her song. Is he pedantic in insisting on his discriminations? What is the relation of the girl to the sea?

2. The older word for poet in English was *maker*, and so when the singing girl is called "the maker" we are being told that she is a type of poet. Would you say that this poem is about, among things, the relation of the poet to nature?

3. Wallace Stevens has said that when he wrote "Ramon Fernandez," he was simply choosing a name, not referring to any particular person. (But it is a nice accident that there is a Ramon Fernandez who is an aesthetician and philosopher of art.) In any case, is not the question put to Fernandez a question that has to do with the function of art and the meaning of the imagination?

4. In what sense, if any, do lights seen at night —whether of a fishing boat or of something else— "arrange" and "deepen" night? Would their ability to do this be heightened in the mind of one who had been listening to the girl's song and reflecting upon the poet's "rage for order"?

From *SONG OF MYSELF*
Walt Whitman (1819–1892)

The wild gander leads his flock through the cool night.
Ya-honk he says, and sounds it down to me like an invitation,
The pert may suppose it meaningless, but I listening close,
Find its purpose and place up there toward the wintry sky.
The sharp-hoof'd moose of the north, the cat on the house-sill, the chickadee, the
    prairie-dog,   5
The litter of the grunting sow as they tug at her teats,
The brood of the turkey-hen and she with her half-spread wings,
I see in them and myself the same old law.

The press of my foot to the earth springs a hundred affections,
They scorn the best I can do to relate them.   10
I am enamour'd of growing out-doors,
Of men that live among cattle or taste of the ocean or woods,
Of the builders and steerers of ships and the wielders of axes and mauls, and the
    drivers of horses,
I can eat and sleep with them week in and week out.

What is commonest, cheapest, nearest, easiest, is Me,   15
Me going in for my chances, spending for vast returns,
Adorning myself to bestow myself on the first that will take me,
Not asking the sky to come down to my good will,
Scattering it freely forever.
The pure contralto sings in the organ loft,   20
The carpenter dresses his plank, the tongue of his foreplane whistles its wild
    ascending lisp,
The married and unmarried children ride home to their Thanksgiving dinner,
The pilot seizes the king-pin, he heaves down with a strong arm,
The mate stands braced in the whale-boat, lance and harpoon are ready,
The duck-shooter walks by silent and cautious stretches,   25
The deacons are ordain'd with cross'd hands at the altar,
The spinning-girl retreats and advances to the hum of the big wheel,
The farmer stops by the bars as he walks on a First-day loafe and looks at the oats
    and rye,
The lunatic is carried at last to the asylum a confirm'd case,
(He will never sleep any more as he did in the cot in his mother's bedroom;)   30
The jour printer with gray head and gaunt jaws works at his case,
He turns his quid of tobacco while his eyes blurr with the manuscript;
The malform'd limbs are tied to the surgeon's table,
What is removed drops horribly in a pail;
The quadroon girl is sold at the auction-stand, the drunkard nods by the bar-room
    stove,   35
The machinist rolls up his sleeves, the policeman travels his beat, the gate-keeper
    marks who pass,
The young fellow drives the express-wagon, (I love him, though I do not know
    him;)
The half-breed straps on his light boots to compete in the race,
The western turkey-shooting draws old and young, some lean on their rifles, some sit
    on logs,
Out from the crowd steps the marksman, takes his position, levels his piece;   40
The groups of newly-come immigrants cover the wharf or levee,
As the woolly-pates hoe in the sugar-field, the overseer views them from his saddle,
The bugle calls in the ball-room, the gentlemen run for their partners, the dancers
    bow to each other,
The youth lies awake in the cedar-roof'd garret and harks to the musical rain,
The Wolverine sets traps on the creek that helps fill the Huron,   45
The squaw wrapt in her yellow-hemm'd cloth is offering moccasins and bead-bags for
    sale,
The connoisseur peers along the exhibition-gallery with half-shut eyes bent sideways,
As the deck-hands make fast the steamboat the plank is thrown for the shore-going
    passengers,
The young sister holds out the skein while the elder sister winds it off in a ball, and
    stops now and then for the knots,
The one-year wife is recovering and happy having a week ago borne her first child. 50
The clean-hair'd Yankee girl works with her sewing-machine or in the factory or mill,

The paving-man leans on his two-handed rammer, the reporter's lead flies swiftly over the note-book, the sign-painter is lettering with blue and gold,
The canal boy trots on the tow-path, the bookkeeper counts at his desk, the shoe-maker waxes his thread,
The conductor beats time for the band and all the performers follow him,
The child is baptized, the convert is making his first professions,   55
The regatta is spread on the bay, the race is begun, (how the white sails sparkle!)
The drover watching his drove sings out to them that would stray,
The pedler sweats with his pack on his back, (the purchaser higgling about the odd cent;)
The bride unrumples her white dress, the minute-hand of the clock moves slowly,
The opium-eater reclines with rigid head and just-open'd lips,   60
The prostitute draggles her shawl, her bonnet bobs on her tipsy and pimpled neck,
The crowd laugh at her blackguard oaths, the men jeer and wink to each other,
(Miserable! I do not laugh at your oaths nor jeer at you;)
The President holding a cabinet council is surrounded by the great Secretaries,
On the piazza walk three matrons stately and friendly with twined arms,   65
The crew of the fish-smack pack repeated layers of halibut in the hold,
The Missourian crosses the plains toting his wares and his cattle,
As the fare-collector goes through the train he gives notice by the jingling of loose change,
The floor-men are laying the floor, the tinners are tinning the roof, the masons are calling for mortar,
In single file each shouldering his hod pass onward the laborers;   70
Seasons pursuing each other the indescribable crowd is gather'd, it is the fourth of Seventh-month, (what salutes of cannon and small arms!)
Seasons pursuing each other the plougher ploughs, the mower mows, and the winter-grain falls in the ground;
Off on the lakes the pike-fisher watches and waits by the hole in the frozen surface,
The stumps stand thick round the clearing, the squatter strikes deep with his axe,
Flatboatmen make fast towards dusk near the cotton-wood or pecan-trees,   75
Coon-seekers go through the regions of the Red River or through those drain'd by the Tennessee, or through those of the Arkansas,
Torches shine in the dark that hangs on the Chattahooche or Altamahaw,
Patriarchs sit at supper with sons and grandsons and great-grandsons around them,
In walls of adobie, in canvas tents, rest hunters and trappers after their day's sport,
The city sleeps and the country sleeps,   80
The living sleep for their time, the dead sleep for their time,
The old husband sleeps by his wife and the young husband sleeps by his wife;
And these tend inward to me, and I tend outward to them,
And such as it is to be of these more or less I am,
And of these one and all I weave the song of myself. . . .   85

I resist any thing better than my own diversity,
Breathe the air but leave plenty after me,
And am not stuck up, and am in my place.
(The moth and the fish-eggs are in their place,
The bright suns I see and the dark suns I cannot see are in their place,   90
The palpable is in its place and the impalpable is in its place.)

These are really the thoughts of all men in all ages and lands, they are not original with me,
If they are not yours as much as mine they are nothing, or next to nothing,
If they are not the riddle and the untying of the riddle they are nothing,
If they are not just as close as they are distant they are nothing.   95

This is the grass that grows wherever the land is and the water is,
This is the common air that bathes the globe. . . .

Who goes there? hankering, gross, mystical, nude;
How is it I extract strength from the beef I eat?
What is a man anyhow? what am I? what are you?   100
All I mark as my own you shall offset it with your own,
Else it were time lost listening to me.
I do not snivel that snivel the world over,
That months are vacuums and the ground but wallow and filth.
Whimpering and truckling fold with powders for invalids, conformity goes to the
    fourth-remov'd,   105
I wear my hat as I please indoors or out.
Why should I pray? why should I venerate and be ceremonious?
Having pried through the strata, analyzed to a hair, counsel'd with doctors and
    calculated close,
I find no sweeter fat than sticks to my own bones.
In all people I see myself, none more and not one a barley-corn less,   110
And the good or bad I say of myself I say of them.
I know I am solid and sound,
To me the converging objects of the universe perpetually flow,
All are written to me, and I must get what the writing means.
I know I am deathless,   115
I know this orbit of mine cannot be swept by a carpenter's compass,
I know I shall not pass like a child's carlacue cut with a burnt stick at night.
I know I am august,
I do not trouble my spirit to vindicate itself or be understood,
I see that the elementary laws never apologize,   120
(I reckon I behave no prouder than the level I plant my house by, after all.)
I exist as I am, that is enough,
If no other in the world be aware I sit content,
And if each and all be aware I sit content.
One world is aware and by far the largest to me, and that is myself,   125
And whether I come to my own to-day or in ten thousand or ten million years,
I can cheerfully take it now, or with equal cheerfulness I can wait.
My foothold is tenon'd and mortis'd in granite,
I laugh at what you call dissolution,
And I know the amplitude of time. . . .   130

Walt Whitman, a kosmos, of Manhattan the son,
Turbulent, fleshy, sensual, eating, drinking and breeding,
No sentimentalist, no stander above men and women or apart from them,
No more modest than immodest.
Unscrew the locks from the doors!   135
Unscrew the doors themselves from their jambs!
Whoever degrades another degrades me,
And whatever is done or said returns at last to me.
Through me the afflatus surging and surging, through me the current and index.
I speak the pass-word primevel, I give the sign of democracy,   140
By God! I will accept nothing which all cannot have their counterpart of on the
    same terms.
Through me many long dumb voices,
Voices of the interminable generations of prisoners and slaves,
Voices of the diseas'd and despairing and of thieves and dwarfs,
Voices of cycles of preparation and accretion,   145
And of the threads that connect the stars, and of wombs and of the father-stuff,

And of the rights of them the others are down upon,
Of the deform'd, trivial, flat, foolish, despised,
Fog in the air, beetles rolling balls of dung.
To behold the day-break!   150
The little light fades the immense and diaphanous shadows,
The air tastes good to my palate.
Hefts of the moving world at innocent gambols silently rising, freshly exuding,
Scooting obliquely high and low.
Something I cannot see puts upward libidinous prongs,   155
Seas of bright juice suffuse heaven.
The earth by the sky staid with, the daily close of their junction,
The heav'd challenge from the east that moment over my head,
The mocking taunt, See then whether you shall be master!

Dazzling and tremendous how quick the sunrise would kill me,   160
If I could not now and always send sun-rise out of me.
We also ascend dazzling and tremendous as the sun,
We found our own O my soul in the calm and cool of the daybreak.
My voice goes after what my eyes cannot reach,
With the twirl of my tongue I encompass worlds and volumes of worlds.   165
Speech is the twin of my vision, it is unequal to measure itself,
It provokes me forever, it says sarcastically,
Walt you contain enough, why don't you let it out then?
Come now I will not be tantalized, you conceive too much of articulation,
Do you not know O speech how the buds beneath you are folded?   170
Waiting in gloom, protected by frost,
The dirt receding before my prophetical screams,
I underlying causes to balance them at last,
My knowledge my live parts, it keeping tally with the meaning of all things,
Happiness, (which whoever hears me let him or her set out in search of this day.)   175
My final merit I refuse you, I refuse putting from me what I really am,
Encompass worlds, but never try to encompass me,
I crowd your sleekest and best by simply looking toward you.

Writing and talk do not prove me,
I carry the plenum of proof and every thing else in my face,   180
With the hush of my lips I wholly confound the skeptic. . . .

Space and Time! now I see it is true, what I guess'd at,
What I guess'd when I loaf'd on the grass,
What I guess'd while I lay alone in my bed,
And again as I walk'd the beach under the paling stars of the morning.   185
My ties and ballasts leave me, my elbows rest in sea-gaps,
I skirt sierras, my palms cover continents,
I am afoot with my vision.
By the city's quadrangular houses—in log huts, camping with lumbermen,
Along the ruts of the turnpike, along the dry gulch and rivulet bed,   190
Weeding my onion-patch or hoeing rows of carrots and parsnips, crossing savannas,
    trailing in forests,
Prospecting, gold-digging, girdling the trees of a new purchase,
Scorch'd ankle-deep by the hot sand, hauling my boat down the shallow river,
Where the panther walks to and fro on a limb overhead, where the buck turns
    furiously at the hunter,
Where the rattlesnake suns his flabby length on a rock, where the otter is feeding
    on fish,   195
Where the alligator in his tough pimples sleeps by the bayou,

Where the black bear is searching for roots or honey, where the beaver pats the mud
    with his paddle-shaped tail;
Over the growing sugar, over the yellow-flower'd cotton plant, over the rice in its
    low moist field,
Over the sharp-peak'd farmhouse, with its scallop'd scum and slender shoots from
    the gutters,
Over the western persimmon, over the long-leav'd corn, over the delicate blue-flower
    flax,   200
Over the white and brown buckwheat, a hummer and buzzer there with the rest,
Over the dusky green of the rye as it ripples and shades in the breeze;

Scaling mountains, pulling myself cautiously up, holding on by low scragged limbs,
Walking the path worn in the grass and beat through the leaves of the brush,
Where the quail is whistling betwixt the woods and the wheat-lot,   205
Where the bat flies in the Seventh-month eve, where the great gold-bug drops
    through the dark,
Where the brook puts out of the roots of the old tree and flows to the meadow,
Where cattle stand and shake away flies with the tremulous shuddering of their hides,
Where the cheese-cloth hangs in the kitchen, where andirons straddle the hearth-slab,
    where cobwebs fall in festoons from the rafters;
Where trip-hammers crash, where the press is whirling its cylinders,   210
Where the human heart beats with terrible throes under its ribs,
Where the pear-shaped balloon is floating aloft, (floating in it myself and looking
    composedly down,)
Where the life-car is drawn on the slip-noose, where the heat hatches pale-green eggs
    in the dented sand,
Where the she-whale swims with her calf and never forsakes it,
Where the steam-ship trails hind-ways its long pennant of smoke,   215
Where the fin of the shark cuts like a black chip out of the water,
Where the half-burn'd brig is riding on unknown currents,
Where shells grow to her slimy deck, where the dead are corrupting below;
Where the dense-starr'd flag is borne at the head of the regiments,
Approaching Manhattan up by the long-stretching island,   220
Under Niagara, the cataract falling like a veil over my countenance,
Upon a door-step, upon the horse-block of hard wood outside,
Upon the race-course, or enjoying picnics or jigs or a good game of base-ball,
At he-festivals, with blackguard gibes, ironical license, bull-dances, drinking, laughter,
At the cider-mill tasting the sweets of the brown mash, sucking the juice through a
    straw,   225
At apple-peelings wanting kisses for all the red fruit I find,
At musters, beach-parties, friendly bees, huskings, house-raisings;
Where the mocking-bird sounds his delicious gurgles, cackles, screams, weeps,
Where the hay-rick stands in the barn-yard, where the dry-stalks are scatter'd, where
    the brood-cow waits in the hovel,
Where the bull advances to do his masculine work, where the stud to the mare, where
    the cock is treading the hen,   230
Where the heifers browse, where geese nip their food with short jerks,
Where sun-down shadows lengthen over the limitless and lonesome prairie,
Where herds of buffalo make a crawling spread of the square miles far and near,
Where the humming-bird shimmers, where the neck of the long-lived swan is curving
    and winding,
Where the laughing-gull scoots by the shore, where she laughs her near-human
    laugh,   235
Where bee-hives range on a gray bench in the garden half hid by the high weeds,
Where band-neck'd partridges roost in a ring on the ground with their heads out,
Where burial coaches enter the arch'd gates of a cemetery,

Where winter wolves bark amid wastes of snow and icicled trees,
Where the yellow-crown'd heron comes to the edge of the marsh at night and feeds
    upon small crabs,   240
Where the splash of swimmers and divers cools the warm noon,
Where the katy-did works her chromatic reed on the walnut-tree over the well,
Through patches of citrons and cucumbers with silver-wired leaves,
Through the salt-lick or orange glade, or under conical firs,
Through the gymnasium, through the curtain'd saloon, through the office or public
    hall;   245
Pleas'd with the native and pleas'd with the foreign, pleas'd with the new and old,
Pleas'd with the homely woman as well as the handsome,
Pleas'd with the quakeress as she puts off her bonnet and talks melodiously,
Pleas'd with the tune of the choir of the whitewash'd church,
Pleas'd with the earnest words of the sweating Methodist preacher, impress'd
    seriously at the camp-meeting;   250
Looking in at the shop-windows of Broadway the whole forenoon, flatting the flesh of
    my nose on the thick plate glass,
Wandering the same afternoon with my face turn'd up to the clouds, or down a lane
    or along the beach,
My right and left arms round the sides of two friends, and I in the middle;
Coming home with the silent and dark-cheek'd bush-boy, (behind me he rides at the
    drape of the day,)
Far from the settlements studying the print of animals' feet, or the moccasin print, 255
By the cot in the hospital reaching lemonade to a feverish patient,
Nigh the coffin'd corpse when all is still, examining with a candle;
Voyaging to every port to dicker and adventure,
Hurrying with the modern crowd as eager and fickle as any,
Hot toward one I hate, ready in my madness to knife him,   260
Solitary at midnight in my back yard, my thoughts gone from me a long while,
Walking the old hills of Judæa with the beautiful gentle God by my side,
Speeding through space, speeding through heaven and the stars,
Speeding amid the seven satellites and the broad ring, and the diameter of eighty
    thousand miles,
Speeding with tail'd meteors, throwing fire-balls like the rest,   265
Carrying the crescent child that carries its own full mother in its belly,
Storming, enjoying, planning, loving, cautioning,
Backing and filling, appearing and disappearing,
I tread day and night such roads.

I visit the orchards of spheres and look at the product,   270
And look at quintillions ripen'd and look at quintillions green.
I fly those flights of a fluid and swallowing soul,
My course runs below the soundings of plummets.
I help myself to material and immaterial,
No guard can shut me off, no law prevent me.
I anchor my ship for a little while only,   275
My messengers continually cruise away or bring their returns to me.

I go hunting polar furs and the seal, leaping chasms with a pike-pointed staff,
    clinging to topples of brittle and blue.

I ascend to the foretruck,
I take my place late at night in the crow's-nest,
We sail the arctic sea, it is plenty light enough,   280
Through the clear atmosphere I stretch around on the wonderful beauty,

The enormous masses of ice pass me and I pass them, the scenery is plain in all
     directions,
The white-topt mountains show in the distance, I fling out my fancies toward them,
We are approaching some great battle-field in which we are soon to be engaged,   285
We pass the colossal outposts of the encampment, we pass with still feet and caution,
Or we are entering by the suburbs some vast and ruin'd city,
The blocks and fallen architecture more than all the living cities of the globe.
I am a free companion, I bivouac by invading watchfires,
I turn the bridegroom out of bed and stay with the bride myself,   290
I tighten her all night to my thighs and lips.
My voice is the wife's voice, the screech by the rail of the stairs,
They fetch my man's body up dripping and drown'd.

I understand the large hearts of heroes,
The courage of present times and all times,
How the skipper saw the crowded and rudderless wreck of the steamship, and Death
     chasing it up and down the storm,   295
How he knuckled tight and gave not back an inch, and was faithful of days and
     faithful of nights,
And chalk'd in large letters on a board, *Be of good cheer, we will not desert you*;
How he follow'd with them and tack'd with them three days and would not give it
     up,
How he saved the drifting company at last,
How the lank loose-gown'd women look'd when boated from the side of their
     prepared graves,   300
How the silent old-faced infants and the lifted sick, and the sharp-lipp'd unshaven
     men;
All this I swallow, it tastes good, I like it well, it becomes mine,
I am the man, I suffer'd, I was there.

EXERCISES

1. Here, Whitman, in giving a self-portrait, is really giving his portrait of a poet. In lines 3 and 4 he says that the wild gander leading his flock may be supposed meaningless by many people but that he, the poet, finds a purpose in the event. What might Frost have said about this? Or Wordsworth? Or Hopkins?
2. With line 5 Whitman begins a long catalogue of human types, and nature recedes from the discussion. Elsewhere in his work Whitman does show a deep responsiveness to nature, but on the basis of what is at hand, how would you compare his view of poetry with that of Wordsworth? Of Stevens? Of Hopkins?

Free Verse

Thus far no poems in free verse have been discussed in their technical aspects. Turn to subsection 19.13 and read it thoughtfully. Notice particularly the different kinds of "freedom" illustrated by the various examples

EXERCISES

1. Discuss the basis of the form of each of the following poems: Masters' "Lucinda Matlock," Mew's "The Farmer's Bride," Lawrence's "Love on the Farm" (all, sec. 12), H.D.'s "Pear Tree" (sec. 13), Nash's "A Visit from Dr. Fell" (sec. 14), and Crane's "War Is Kind" (sec. 16).
2. Turn ahead to section 18, and choose two free verse poems that you think effective. Try to explain your choices.
3. Restudy John Donne's sonnet "Batter My Heart" in group 6 of this section. Be sure to read it aloud several times. Then try to reline it as free verse. Do not be arbitrary about this. Ponder what you are doing, line by line. Do not hesitate to go back and change an arrangement if it feels wrong in the light of a new development in your work. When you are satisfied, try to define the basis on which you have acted.

THE INDIVIDUAL POET

In earlier sections, even though we have often compared and contrasted poems in regard to both method and meaning, we have, necessarily, been concerned with the individual poem. A reader soon realizes, however, that behind the poem always stands the poet, and that the poem is his, that it comes from his life and his imagination. The reader also realizes that the poems of the individual poet, since they have a common origin, must have, in idea, feeling, and style, various internal relationships, and that the stronger a poet is, the deeper, the more fascinating, and the more instructive are the interrelationships among his poems. Thus, the poems of any one poet may be taken as constituting, in one sense, one long poem. And the significance of the interrelationships among the particular poems that make up the "long poem" is an essential dimension of poetry.

Here we take three strongly individualized poets—John Keats, Emily Dickinson, and Robert Frost—and try, within our present limits, to indicate the nature of the individuality of each.

A GROUP OF POEMS BY
JOHN KEATS (1795–1821)

In section 15, we read and discussed Keats's "Ode on Melancholy" primarily as an example of the poet's handling of images. We noticed how rich the imagery is, and how this richness gives the theme of the poem solidity and depth. But we also noticed how many of the images worked at several different levels, not only enriching the poem but tying the parts of it together. For example, when the melancholy fit was compared to a weeping cloud and the cloud itself to a kind of April shroud hiding the springtime hill, the metaphor associated the cloud not only with tears but with fruitfulness, implying that melancholy can feed the soul just as the rain can bring greenness to the springtime landscape. To mention another point: we noticed how the great image having to do with the bursting of Joy's grape gathered up in itself the allusions to tasting that occur throughout the poem.

Yet, as we have indicated earlier, the "Ode to Melancholy" has to be looked at in other ways than as an exercise in imagery. Indeed, the theme that dominates the "Ode to Melancholy" is one that runs through a great many poems by Keats. One way to study a poet is to see how his poems can help interpret each other and how the whole mass of poems sometimes has a unity of mood and even of technique, how, in fact, the body of a poet's work is a personal projection, an elaboration of some central and perhaps obsessive concern of the poet.

The theme of melancholy, though present in many of Keats's poems, is treated in different ways in such poems as "To Autumn" (sec. 15), "Ode on a Grecian Urn," and "Ode to a Nightingale."

ODE TO A NIGHTINGALE

I

My heart aches, and a drowsy numbness pains
  My sense, as though of hemlock I had drunk,
Or emptied some dull opiate to the drains
  One minute past, and Lethe-wards had sunk:
'Tis not through envy of thy happy lot,   5
  But being too happy in thine happiness,—
    That thou, light-winged Dryad of the trees,
      In some melodious plot

Of beechen green, and shadows numberless,
  Singest of summer in full-throated ease.   10

II

O, for a draught of vintage! that hath been
  Cool'd a long age in the deep-delved earth,
Tasting of Flora and the country green,
  Dance, and Provençal song, and sunburnt mirth!
O for a beaker full of the warm South,   15
  Full of the true, the blushful Hippocrene,
    With beaded bubbles winking at the brim,
      And purple-stained mouth;
  That I might drink, and leave the world unseen,
  And with thee fade away into the forest
    dim: 20

III

Fade far away, dissolve, and quite forget
  What thou among the leaves hast never known,
The weariness, the fever, and the fret
  Here, where men sit and hear each other groan;
Where palsy shakes a few, sad, last grey hairs,   25
  Where youth grows pale, and spectre-thin, and
    dies;
    Where but to think is to be full of sorrow
      And leaden-ey'd despairs,
  Where Beauty cannot keep her lustrous eyes,
    Or new Love pine at them beyond to-
    morrow.   30

IV

Away! away! for I will fly to thee,
  Not charioted by Bacchus and his pards,
But on the viewless wings of Poesy,
  Though the dull brain perplexes and retards:
Already with thee! tender is the night,   35
  And haply the Queen-Moon is on her throne,
    Cluster'd around by all her starry Fays;
      But here there is no light,
Save what from heaven is with the breezes
    blown
    Through verdurous glooms and winding
    mossy ways.   40

V

I cannot see what flowers are at my feet,
  Nor what soft incense hangs upon the boughs,
But, in embalmed darkness, guess each sweet
  Wherewith the seasonable month endows
The grass, the thicket, and the fruit-tree wild;   45
  White hawthorn, and the pastoral eglantine;
    Fast fading violets cover'd up in leaves;
      And mid-May's eldest child,
The coming musk-rose, full of dewy wine,

The murmurous haunt of flies on summer
  eves.   50

VI

Darkling I listen; and, for many a time
  I have been half in love with easeful Death,
Call'd him soft names in many a mused rhyme,
  To take into the air my quiet breath;
Now more than ever seems it rich to die,   55
  To cease upon the midnight with no pain,
    While thou art pouring forth thy soul abroad
      In such an ecstacy!
  Still wouldst thou sing, and I have ears in vain—
  To thy high requiem become a sod.   60

VII

Thou wast not born for death, immortal Bird!
  No hungry generations tread thee down;
The voice I hear this passing night was heard
  In ancient days by emperor and clown:
Perhaps the self-same song that found a path   65
  Through the sad heart of Ruth, when, sick for
    home,
    She stood in tears amid the alien corn;
      The same that oft-times hath
  Charm'd magic casements, opening on the foam
    Of perilous seas, in faery lands forlorn.   70

VIII

Forlorn! the very word is like a bell
  To toll me back from thee to my sole self!
Adieu! the fancy cannot cheat so well
  As she is fam'd to do, deceiving elf.
Adieu! adieu! thy plaintive anthem fades   75
  Past the near meadows, over the still stream,
    Up the hill-side; and now 'tis buried deep
      In the next valley-glades:
  Was it a vision, or a waking dream?
    Fled is that music:—Do I wake or sleep?   80

The person who speaks this poem begins by saying that his heart aches, but the heartache in this instance is not simply a matter of sadness, and not so much a piercing ache as a sort of "drowsy numbness." It comes, the poet tells us, not from being sad but from being too happy—too happy in the bird's happiness as he hears it sing "of summer in full-throated ease." How a sense of pain that is also a sense of half-drugged torpor—a sense of forgetfulness and yet withal a sense of piercing joy in contemplating another creature's joy—how all of these are related (if indeed they are related) are matters that the student will have to determine after he has mastered the poem.

At this time it is enough to point out that the poet, charmed by the bird's song and delighting in the world of which it seems to speak, indulges in the fancy of flying away from the human world, with its disappointments, to the different world expressed through the bird's song. That world is so harmonious and so little haunted by anxiety that it might seem to be a world of pure imagination, though the speaker, under the influence of the nightingale's song, seems to identify it with the world of nature itself.

The means that the poet would use to reach the world of the nightingale are wine and the imagination. The first is contemplated and then rejected in favor of the second. The obstructing force that has to be overcome is not the poet's body but his brain. He writes (l. 34) that "the dull brain perplexes and retards." That the poet names the brain as the barrier to be overcome is significant: the wine would tend to release him from the inhibitions and discriminations made by the brain; the imagination would tend to transcend these discriminations.

The human world, the poem suggests, classified and categorized as it is by the analytic brain, is inimical to the rich, warm, undifferentiated world of nature. At this point the student may very well ask whether the poem really says anything like this, and his question will be well put, for the poem does not say this in so many words. But it can be argued that the poem does embody some such conception. Notice, for example, that the nightingale sings in darkness, that when the poet has imagined himself into the thicket in which the nightingale is singing, he cannot "see what flowers" are at his feet (l. 41), and that though the moon is shining and dominating the night, in the nightingale's thicket there is "no light, / Save what from heaven is by the breezes blown," and that the very heart of the nightingale's world is a place of "verdurous glooms" (l. 40) and of "embalmed darkness" (l. 43). Notice too that the poet, yearning to escape from the world of human anxiety and disappointment, wishes to "fade away" into this "forest dim" (l. 20) —into this place of "shadows numberless" (l. 9).

There is a pattern of related contrasts, the human being isolated and cut off from nature, in contrast to the nightingale, singing happily of nature; the world dominated by the dull brain—and analytic intellect— "where but to think is to be full of sorrow" (l. 27)—in contrast to the world of feeling and the imagination; the world of clear demarcations and sharp boundaries, in contrast to a world of rich warm darkness in which no boundaries exist. One must not, however, suppose that Keats, in his concern for a life of feelings and intense sensations, was celebrating mere brainlessness. By implication the poem, in repudiating a narrow notion of reason, affirms the deep unity of the human personality in which ideas and sensations flow together and the past, present, and future modify each other. The "Ode to a Nightingale" is, in fact, a thoughful poem, for it concerns itself with the realms opened up to man by his consciousness and with the penalties imposed by consciousness.

At this point, let us consider another poem by Keats, a kind of blank-verse sonnet on knowledge and on what a bird's song may mean to a thoughtful man.

WHAT THE THRUSH SAID

O thou whose face hath felt the Winter's wind,
    Whose eye has seen the snow-clouds hung in
        mist,
    And the black elm tops 'mong the freezing
        stars,
    To thee the spring will be a harvest-time.
O thou whose only book has been the light   5
    Of supreme darkness, which thou feedest on
    Night after night, when Phoebus was away!
    To thee the Spring shall be a triple morn.
O fret not after knowledge—I have none,
    And yet my song comes native with the
        warmth.   10
O fret not after knowledge—I have none,
    And yet the Evening listens. He who saddens
At thought of idleness cannot be idle,
And he's awake who thinks himself asleep.

This little poem was addressed to a friend of Keats and forms part of a letter to him written on February 19, 1818. The bird is speaking to a young man who is wearied with the winter and longs for springtime. Since this young man is John Keats, we know that he too has been wearied with the waiting for his own talent as a poet to blossom and that he now hopes that his springtime as a writer will soon come. [The student might remember that Phoebus (l. 7) is not only the Greek god of the sun, for which the poet longs, but the god of poetry too.]

In stanza III of "Ode to a Nightingale," Keats describes the ills of life that he would happily forget: sickness, weariness, and age. These ills are all finally summed up in death. Yet one notes that the world out of which the nightingale sings is also touched by change and death. "The seasonable month" (l. 44), "Fast fading violets" (l. 47), "Mid-May's eldest child" (l. 48), and "The coming musk-rose" (l. 49) point to the passage of time. The nightingale's is not a world of ideal and unchanging forms, but a world of process; yet in the harmony of nature, death itself seems rid of its horror, and the poet, now listening to the voice of the nightingale, actually finds death attractive. He has, he tells us (l. 52), "been half in love with easeful Death, / Called him soft names in many a mused rhyme. . . ." The adjective *easeful* suggests why in the past death has seemed attractive: it offered a way out of the world of human fret and anxiety. But now death takes on a positive quality as if it were a sort of fulfillment. The poet says "Now more than ever seems it rich to die, . . . / While thou art pouring forth thy soul abroad / In such an ecstasy!" (ll. 55, 57–58).

Keats elsewhere expressed this notion of death as a fulfillment. In a sonnet written about two months before he wrote "Ode to a Nightingale," he intimated that death, because it was more intense than any other human experience, was the most significant and even the most rewarding. Death, he wrote, "is Life's high meed," that is, high reward.

SONNET

March 1819

Why did I laugh to-night? No voice will tell:
  No God, no Demon of severe response,
Designs to reply from Heaven or from Hell.
  Then to my human heart I turn at once.
Heart! Thou and I are here sad and alone;   5
  Say, wherefore did I laugh? O mortal pain!

O Darkness! Darkness! ever must I moan,
  To question Heaven and Hell and Heart in vain.
Why did I laugh? I know this Being's lease,
  My fancy to its utmost blisses spreads;   10
Yet would I on this very midnight cease,
  And the world's gaudy ensigns see in shreds;
Verse, Fame, and Beauty are intense indeed,
  But Death intenser—Death is Life's high meed.

The meaning attached to death in this sonnet is not *necessarily*, of course, the same as that in "Ode to a Nightingale," but a general parallelism is obvious and the student will do well to examine with some care the attitude toward death exhibited in the two poems.

EXERCISES

1. Does the poem suggest the quality of the poet's laugh? Merry? Thoughtless? Sardonic?
2. What is the relation of the last four lines to the preceding ten?

The nightingale's song (see stanza VI) renders even death attractive, but the listener, though tempted to "cease upon the midnight" to the bird's "high requiem," is fully aware of what death will mean to him: he will become oblivious to the requiem, being a mere senseless lump, "a sod." Though he yearns to attain the nightingale's world, he is inextricably linked to death as the nightingale is not. For the nightingale was "not born for death" and is an "immortal Bird."

What can be meant? Keats certainly knew that the small creature to whose song he listened had a shorter life span than his own. He addresses here, not a particular bird, but a representative of the species, whose "self-same song" through the ages may have been heard, for example, by the biblical character Ruth, or by ladies in some fabled castle of the Middle Ages.

Why does the bird seem to be deathless? The answer lies in its harmonious rapport with nature. The human being's bitter conflict with time does not trouble the nightingale: "No hungry generations tread thee down" (l. 62). Earlier, the poet had expressed the desire to "forget / What thou among the leaves hast never known. . . ." What the bird has never known is the passage of time, which leaves man, at the end, to shake "a few, sad, last grey hairs." The nightingale's immortality springs from the fact that it was "not born for death" (l. 61). Man, unfortunately, is born for death and speedily learns that fact. The shadow of death lies over all his activities, but the nightingale "among the leaves" truly has never known anything about death. He is so completely merged with nature that the life of nature seems to flow harmoniously through him and to find voice in his song.

We have seen in stanza VI that the speaker makes a pointed contrast between the bird's continuing to sing and his own death-stopped ears, and at the beginning of stanza VIII he sharpens the contrast between the bird and himself. *Forlorn*, the last word in stanza VII, conjures up the romantic world in which the nightingale sings, but the poet suddenly realizes that the word also applies to himself, for if *forlorn* means "romantically remote," it also literally means "lost, alienated," and describes his own dejected state—separated from nature and indeed born for death. With the clang of the word *forlorn*, the poet abandons the attempt to join the nightingale through an effort of the imagination. He realizes that he is irrevocably barred out of the world of the nightingale, and with this realization, what had been the nightingale's "high requiem" becomes a "plaintive anthem" (l. 75). Earlier, in response to the nightingale's song, the man had hoped to fade back into the world of nature; now (l. 75) it is the nightingale's song that *fades*, "Past the near meadows, over the still stream," and is finally "buried deep / In the next valley-glades. . . ." The song of the nightingale that the sad listener hoped might confer immortality upon him, now itself seems to sink into a grave. The listener is left questioning: "Was it a vision, or a waking dream? / Fled is that music:—Do I wake or sleep?"

What is the relevance of waking and sleeping to the meaning of this poem? Here, the student might profitably look back to "What the Thrush Said," with its last line: "And he's awake who thinks himself asleep." In both poems, Keats seems to be preoccupied with an experience that holds man in the trancelike state of dream and yet renders him

peculiarly sensitive and receptive. (Compare Coleridge's account of the composition of "Kubla Khan" in section 16.) Clearly, both poems turn upon the problem of consciousness and both celebrate a kind of knowledge that in its wholeness transcends the ordinary analytical procedures of the "dull brain." In the "Ode" of course, the insight into the nature of consciousness is more profound: the bird's harmony with nature and its happiness stem from the fact that it has practically no consciousness—very little memory of the past and almost no prevision of the future. Yet if self-consciousness is the source of man's anxiety and his disappointments, the world described in stanza II—or in stanza VII—is a world that is available only to man's consciousness. One might go further: the joy that the man takes in the nightingale's song is a joy peculiar to man and different from the thoughtless happiness of any merely natural creature.

EXERCISES

1. What is the relation of the imagery in stanza II to the theme of the poem as a whole? Are the associations summoned up by the idea of wine simply so much embroidery, charmingly rich, but presented for their own sake? Or are they also important for the theme of the poem? If so, how?

2. We have argued that in "Ode to a Nightingale" the sense of sight is played down in favor of that of sound—that is, the song of the nightingale wells up out of a warm and engulfing darkness. In this connection, what about the sight imagery in stanza III—"leaden-eyed despair" and beauty not able to keep her "lustrous eyes"? Do these visual references violate or substantiate the general pattern we have suggested?

3. In stanza V, Keats uses the phrase "embalmed darkness." The adjective *embalmed* will, for many readers, suggest death. If so, is the notion necessarily inappropriate here? Do you think that Keats intended the association? Or if he did not, would he have been happy nevertheless if someone had later pointed it out to him?

4. In stanza VII what is the force of the phrase "alien corn"? Why is this more moving, if it is so, than "alien sky" or "alien fields"?

The human situation in which joy is so intimately related to melancholy is also the theme of "Ode on a Grecian Urn."

ODE ON A GRECIAN URN

I

Thou still unravish'd bride of quietness,
  Thou foster-child of silence and slow time,
Sylvan historian, who canst thus express
  A flowery tale more sweetly than our rhyme:
What leaf-fring'd legend haunts about thy shape 5
  Of deities or mortals, or of both,
    In Tempe or the dales of Arcady?
What men or gods are these? What maidens loth?
  What mad pursuit? What struggle to escape?
    What   pipes   and   timbrels?   What   wild
      ecstasy?   10

II

Heard melodies are sweet, but those unheard
  Are sweeter; therefore, ye soft pipes, play on;
Not to the sensual ear, but, more endear'd,
  Pipe to the spirit ditties of no tone:
Fair youth, beneath the trees, thou canst not
      leave   15
  Thy song, nor ever can those trees be bare;
    Bold Lover, never, never canst thou kiss,
Though winning near the goal—yet, do not
      grieve;
  She cannot fade, though thou hast not thy
      bliss,
    For ever wilt thou love, and she be fair!   20

III

Ah, happy, happy boughs! that cannot shed
  Your leaves, nor ever bid the Spring adieu;
And happy melodist, unwearied,
  For ever piping songs for ever new;
More happy love! more happy, happy love!   25
  For ever warm and still to be enjoy'd,
    For ever panting, and for ever young;
All breathing human passion far above,
  That leaves a heart high-sorrowful and cloy'd,
    A burning forehead, and a parching
      tongue.   30

IV

Who are these coming to the sacrifice?
  To what green altar, O mysterious priest,
Lead'st thou that heifer lowing at the skies,
  And all her silken flanks with garlands drest?
What little town by river or sea shore,   35
  Or mountain-built with peaceful citadel,
    Is emptied of this folk, this pious morn?
And, little town, thy streets for evermore
  Will silent be; and not a soul to tell
    Why thou art desolate, can e'er return.   40

V

O Attic shape! Fair attitude! with brede
  Of marble men and maidens overwrought,
With forest branches and the trodden weed;
  Thou, silent form, dost tease us out of thought
As doth eternity: Cold Pastoral!   45
  When old age shall this generation waste,
    Thou shalt remain, in midst of other woe
Than ours, a friend to man, to whom thou say'st,
"Beauty is truth, truth beauty,"—that is all
    Ye know on earth, and all ye need to know.   50

In "Ode to a Nightingale," the speaker sought to achieve wholeness by merging himself into the rich, always changing, but ultimately unchanged world of natural process. In "Ode on a Grecian Urn," Keats sets our human world, with its frustrations and disappointments, against the world of art, which is immortal, not through unending process, but through stasis: a moment out of the flux of becoming has been frozen and perpetuated for our contemplation.

This ode begins with an imaginative exploration of the world depicted upon the urn; but our human world lies in the background and remains a constant point of reference. Notice for example lines 19–20 or lines 26–30. The world of "breathing human passion" leaves the heart "high-sorrowful and cloy'd," and it leaves too often a "burning forehead, and a parching tongue." In the actual human world within which we live, attainment of joy brings listlessness and satiety. Better the situation of the young lover figured on the urn who will never attain his love and therefore will never risk knowing the disappointment of a love that has lost its savor.

This general thesis dominates stanzas II and III. The unattainable is better than the attained; the imagined melody is sweeter than the one that actually strikes the eardrums. The implications of these stanzas are realistic and also pessimistic. (Line 30 comes close to being a description of a hangover on the morning after!) But the pessimistic note is not to the fore: the poet keeps our attention on the figures sculptured upon the urn. What we see there is recognizably human life, but life raised to an ideal plane, and, because it cannot change, not threatened by mortality. The scenes described in the first three stanzas are dynamic; there is "mad pursuit"; maidens "struggle to escape." The dominant theme is that of romantic love—that of gods or men attempting to embrace the maidens or, as in the scene dwelt upon in stanzas II and III that of the "fair youth, beneath the trees" who attempts to bestow a kiss.

Stanza IV presents another aspect of human activity. It is a religious rite. The population of some little Greek town has turned out to sacrifice to one of the gods. The urn does not, through some inscription or insignia, tell us the name of the town or to what god the altar is erected. In fact, the poet makes a point of this indefiniteness. The priest is a "mysterious" priest: that is, he could be a priest of Apollo or of Zeus or of some other god. The little town whose inhabitants we see in the procession might be "mountain-built" (l. 36) or else situated "by river or sea shore" (l. 35), and none of the figures that take part in the procession can move his marble lips to tell us the town's name.

The artist who sculptured the urn has captured for the imagination a vision of human life in some of its most significant and universal aspects, and the urn, which Keats calls a "sylvan historian" (l. 3), can silently relate a "flowery tale" more effectively, the poet modestly says, than his own rime can do. The urn presents human love and human worship, the individual assertion and the communal ceremony—and presents them with a fullness and vividness that stir our imagination.

By surviving the erosion of time, the urn has preserved the spirit of an older civilization. Two thousand and more years later, men can participate in the scenes depicted on it and feel the continuity of the human spirit. (It does not matter that we cannot locate on a map the town whose houses have been "emptied of this folk," or that we do not know whether the revelers in stanza I are divine beings or mere mortals.) Yet time has been conquered only at a certain price: if the love celebrated in stanza III, unlike mortal and human love, remains "forever warm and still to be enjoyed," it remains so only because it has been reduced to cold marble. This is the point that the poet is willing to

recognize quite realistically in stanza V, where he calls the urn a "Cold Pastoral." (A cold pastoral is something of a contradiction in terms, for *pastoral* suggests what is warm and simple—the elementary concerns of a pastoral society.)

Though it is a "silent form," the urn is capable of teasing "us out of thought." The phrase is rich and even ambiguous: it teases us, the poet says, "as doth eternity"—and the implication is that, through having conquered time, the urn partakes of the mystery of eternity. Perhaps the poet also implies that the urn provokes in us some deeper musing than is usually comprehended by the term *thought*. Yet the urn, even if it "teases us," is regarded by the poet as friendly to man, to whom it has something comforting to say. What is the special revelation that the urn has to make? Something that has impressed some readers as a kind of high-flown nonsense: "Beauty is truth, truth beauty."

Much ink has been shed in the past over the meaning of this statement, and some commentators have regarded this explicit statement as a blemish on the poem. Yet the thoughtful reader will perceive that the urn has been presented all along as a speaker. It was called a "historian" (l. 3), and its ability to express a flowery tale more sweetly than the poet can is explicitly stated in lines 4 and 5. Stanzas II, III, and IV are filled with the tales that the urn can tell, and the poet has indeed demonstrated how vividly and movingly the urn, for all its silence, can express them. There is really no break in the continuity of the poem in this last stanza when the speaker, stepping back, as it were, from the urn, and viewing it as an object ("O Attic shape") declares that it says, and will continue to say, something that man ought to hear.

In trying to determine the meaning of what the urn says, scholars have appealed to the letters of Keats—for example, to Keats's letter to his friend Bailey: "I am certain of nothing but the holiness of the Heart's affections and the truth of Imagination—what the imagination seizes as Beauty must be truth . . ."; or, to Keats's statement that he "never can feel certain of any truth but for a clear perception of its beauty." The truth with which Keats is concerned in these letters is obviously not scientific truth or historical truth, but the truth of man's nature and his relation to reality. Truth of that order might very well seem to a poet to possess the inevitability, harmony, and rightness of shape with which he associates beauty. But we do not need to go beyond the "Ode" itself in order to understand what Keats means in equating beauty with truth and truth with beauty. The visions of mankind as embodied in the sculptured form on the urn are beautiful in their harmony and clarity and ordered significance, but they are also "true." They do not give us "facts"—names, dates, and locations—but they do give us the essential dignity and pathos of man, the knowledge of himself that it suffices man to know.

Keats's "Ode on a Grecian Urn" differs so much in emphasis and in tone from his "Ode to a Nightingale" that the student may feel that the two poems have little in common. Yet a little reflection will indicate that in both poems the sadness and perplexity of human life is put in a special perspective. In the "Nightingale" it is contrasted with the fullness and harmony of nature as exhibited in a happy unconscious creature like the bird; in the "Urn," with the enduring but cold stasis of art. Both odes are also clearly related to "Ode to Melancholy," for both imply that the man who is most aware of the threat of mortality and the frailty of beauty is the man who is most sensitive to the beauty of nature or of art. This is not to say that "Melancholy" or the "Urn" or the "Nightingale" is in the least sentimental; the poet does not whine or complain. He is very much aware of the intense beauty of both nature and art, but he is a realist too. Neither nature nor art is really a refuge for man. Neither will save man from old age, sickness, or sorrow, though they will give him something very precious. Moreover, man feels the power of nature and art as intensely as he does just because their immortality stands in contrast to his own mortality.

EXERCISES

1. What is the appropriateness of "still unravish'd bride of quietness" as a description of the urn?

2. What has the poet gained by calling the urn the "foster-child of silence and slow time"?

3. What are some of the ways in which the poet has emphasized the advantages of the moment before enjoyment over the moment itself? Has the poet been fair in acknowledging the disadvantages? Give concrete instances here.

4. In stanza IV, the poet suggests that the little town whose inhabitants have all gone forth to take part in the sacrificial rite will forever be silent and empty; that is, caught in their frozen stasis on the urn, they are always about to move forward and will never be able to go back into their town. Notice too that the poet has suggested that for this reason any person coming upon the silent little town will not be able to know why its inhabitants have left it. Is this last observation too fanciful? Too far-fetched? Someone carping at the poem would object that nobody will ever know that the little town is empty or indeed that it existed at all, except by inferring it from the urn. How would you reply to this objection?

5. In the preceding stanzas we have been close up to the scenes depicted on the urn, examining them and imaginatively participating in them. What is the stance of the observer in the last stanza? How is the change of stance marked?

6. Another question having to do with the last two lines of the poem has provoked a good deal of discussion. Does the urn speak all of the last two lines, or is only the statement "Beauty is truth, truth beauty" spoken by the urn, the rest spoken by the poet himself? Some commentators have argued that the poet, in the last line and a half, is telling the figures on the urn ("ye") that *they* know that beauty is truth and truth is beauty and that is all that *they* need to know, but that living, breathing human beings need to know something besides this. (In our reading of the poem, we take the last two lines to be spoken by the urn.)

For a discussion of the reading and punctuation of the text as it survives in the manuscript copies, the student might look up Alvin Whitley's "The Message of the Grecian Urn," *Keats-Shelley Memorial Bulletin*, vol. 5 (London, 1953), pp. 1–3. The student may well want to take into account the evidence of the manuscript copies as he tries to determine whether the last lines are divided between urn and poet, or are all spoken by the urn.

7. Mr. Whitley's essay has been reprinted in the volume entitled *Keats' Well-Read Urn*, edited by Harvey T. Lyon (New York: Holt, Rinehart and Winston, Inc., 1958). The student may want to consult this little book in order to see how many different interpretations of "Ode on a Grecian Urn" have been proposed and try to decide for himself what an acceptable interpretation is.

Man's journey from childhood to maturity and then on to old age and death is part of the natural process. In spite of the pain with which the young poet contemplates old age and death, he has never blenched from the fact that they are inevitable, and as we have seen, he accepts the fact in both the "Nightingale" and the "Urn." In another of his great odes, "To Autumn" (sec. 14), Keats treats the cycle of birth, growth, and death with full acceptance.

In this poem, Keats's emphasis is not upon loss or decay but upon maturation and fulfillment. The mood is one of warmth and brightness: heavy with its fruitfulness, the season is suffused with drowsiness, but it is a drowsiness that is not so much dullness as the weight of plentitude.

Stanza II personifies autumn, turning her into a goddess. Rarely has a goddess ever been made to emerge from the landscape with more authority and authentic power. She is placid, sleepy, subdued by the very richness she has produced and over which she reigns. She is even "careless" of the wealth surrounding her simply because it is overpowering in its abundance. The whole tone is one of quiet fulfillment—there is nothing of nervous or anxious foreboding with reference to the cold winds and frost that are to descend upon the landscape. Time is made here to stand still, or to seem to stand still, because complete fulfillment makes one indifferent to time and what it can bring.

The last stanza does not, however, try to out-face approaching winter and death with a false optimism. The key of the stanza is definitely minor. It is evening now, and the stanza is full of hints—though they are no more than hints—of approaching death. There is clearly a touch of chill in the air, and the sense that something is over. The poet faces this fact, but he does so by finding the beauty and the charm that is in the season and exulting in it. He recognizes that the songs of spring are gone, but he exhorts Autumn to disregard them, for "thou hast thy music too. . . ." The rest of the stanza evokes that music, and if the music is in part "wailful," it is nevertheless appropriate, has its own beauty, and is to be accepted on the assumption that all experience is good and that autumn too has in it something uniquely precious. None of this is said in so many words, nor need it be, but the relevance of the seasonal description to the human season will be perfectly plain to any sensitive reader.

EXERCISES

1. Note that stanzas I and II are filled with visual imagery but that auditory imagery dominates the last stanza. Is there any significance in this shift from sight to sound?

2. In stanza I, autumn is associated with the sun—it is the "close bosom-friend" of the sun. How is the association actually reinforced by the imagery of stanza I? Does the sun-association manage to give to autumn a special quality—linking it, not to the waning of the year, and rain, and cold winds, but to the ripe culmination of the year?

3. What is the force of such words as *load, bend, swell,* and *plump* in stanza I?

4. In stanza II, Autumn is portrayed as a laborer in the harvest, on the granary floor: as a reaper with sickle, carrying a sheaf of grain, or watching the cider press. Does this labor seem to be one of weariness, languor, repletion, or what?

5. What is the mood of stanza III? Is it implied that Autumn needs consolation (see line 24)? Is the character of the music to which the speaker alludes unhappy? Is it *all* mournful and minor in key?

6. What is the tone of "To Autumn"? Remember that tone, which has to do with the author's attitude toward his material and toward his reader, is different from mood, which has to do with the more general quality of feeling. To be specific: what is the poet's attitude toward the process of maturing? Toward the fulfillment of the period of growth and the onset of the period of decay? Does he dread it? Rejoice in it? Understand and accept it? Does he find—perhaps to his own surprise—a special beauty in it?

7. Are there any connections between this poem and Keats's "Ode on Melancholy"? How do the poems resemble each other? How do they differ?

In the discussion thus far we have been primarily concerned with linking one poem with another by way of comparison and contrast so that the student will have a better chance to see how the body of Keats's poetry forms a larger whole with its own unity and coherence. To this end, the student may want to explore further. He might look up, for example, Keats's sonnet "On the Grasshopper and the Cricket" as a slight but charming foreshadowing of one of the elements in "To Autumn." He might also enjoy looking into Keats's letters for passages that throw light upon the poems and consulting other poems of Keats to see their connection with the poems already examined. For example, remembering the first lines of "Ode on Melancholy," he might find it interesting that Keats's sonnet "On Seeing the Elgin Marbles" uses the phrase "dizzy pain," or that line 275 of "The Eve of Saint Agnes" combines the idea of drowsing and aching: "Or I shall drowse beside thee, so my soul doth ache." With reference to "Ode on a Grecian Urn," he might read Keats's "Sleep and Poetry."

The student might profitably go on to relate this group of poems not only to the rest of Keats but to the other Romantic poets, such as Shelley, Byron, Wordsworth, and Coleridge. These poets shared a world view, characteristic attitudes toward nature, and, for all their differences, similar poetic methods. A recent and authoritative account of Romanticism sees it as constituting "a closely coherent body of thought and feeling," not only in England, but in Germany and France as well." * The fundamental characteristic is described as the endeavor "to overcome the split between subject and object, the self and the world, the conscious and the unconscious." In this connection, the student might recall what was said above with regard to Keats's "Ode to a Nightingale," a poem in which the relation of the self and the world is of primary importance and which can be regarded as a dramatization of the whole problem of consciousness.

The literature dealing with Romanticism is immense. A handy guidebook is *The English Romantic Poets*, edited by T. M. Raysor (New York: Modern Language Association, 1956). During the last twenty-five years the Romantic poets have received renewed attention and their work has been reassessed. A sampling of recent discussion of these poets may be found in *English Romantic Poets*, edited by M. H. Abrams (New York: Oxford University Press, Inc., 1960).

A GROUP OF POEMS BY EMILY DICKINSON (1830–1886)

The ten poems that follow are rather typical of the themes, methods, and metrical patterns used by this poet. A quality of sensibility—a special insight, a peculiar vision—is stamped upon nearly everything that Emily Dickinson ever wrote. Whether she is describing the weather, or a landscape, or the aspirations of human life and the disappointments to which it is subject, the poems bear her special signature. The student should examine them and try to see for himself how much unity this group of poems has.

If the student wishes, however, to go beyond a few very general observations, he will find it useful to frame some more particular questions and to reexamine the poem in the light of them. (The comments made and the questions put with reference to reading the Keats poems earlier in this section will provide suggestions for the student.) For a start, here are two concrete observations, the first on the poet's themes, the other on her imagery. (1) Death informs a great deal of Emily Dickinson's poetry and constitutes the background of many of her poems that ostensibly have nothing at all to do with it. (2) The concrete images for much of her poetry—even that dealing with exalted and profound themes—is provided by matter-of-fact domestic life: household activities and the sights and smells of the yards and fields about the house. Test these comments against the poems themselves and see if you can frame others that will bring into focus the essential unity to be found in these poems.

Because Emily Dickinson's life and work were intimately connected, it may be useful to gain some acquaintance with the poet's biography. The student may do well to examine such studies as George F. Whicher's *This Was a Poet* (New York: Charles Scribner's Sons, 1939); Richard Chase's *Emily Dickinson* (New York: William Morrow and Co., Inc., 1951); Thomas H. Johnson's *Emily Dickinson: An Interpretive Biography* (Cambridge, Mass:

---

* René Wellek, "Romanticism Re-examined," *Concepts of Criticism* (New Haven, Conn.: Yale University Press, 1963), p. 220.

Harvard University Press, 1955); and Jay
Leyda, *The Years and Hours of Emily Dickin-
son* (New Haven, Conn: Yale University
Press, 1960).

THESE ARE THE DAYS
WHEN BIRDS COME BACK

These are the days when Birds come back—
A very few—a Bird or two—
To take a backward look.

These are the days when skies resume
The old—old sophistries of June—   5
A blue and gold mistake.

Oh fraud that cannot cheat the Bee—
Almost thy plausibility
Induces my belief.

Till ranks of seeds their witness bear—   10
And softly thro' the altered air
Hurries a timid leaf.

Oh Sacrament of summer days,
Oh Last Communion in the Haze—
Permit a child to join.   15

Thy sacred emblems to partake—
Thy consecrated bread to take
And thine immortal wine!

THE SKY IS LOW—
THE CLOUDS ARE MEAN

The Sky is low—the Clouds are mean.
A Travelling Flake of Snow
Across a Barn or through a Rut
Debates if it will go—

A Narrow Wind complains all Day   5
How some one treated him.
Nature, like Us is sometimes caught
Without her Diadem.

THE MOUNTAINS STOOD IN HAZE

The Mountains stood in Haze—
The Valleys stopped below
And went or waited as they liked
The River and the Sky.

At leisure was the Sun—   5
His interests of Fire
A little from remark withdrawn—
The Twilight spoke the Spire,

So soft upon the Scene
The Act of evening fell   10
We felt how neighborly a Thing
Was the Invisible.

I COULD NOT PROVE
THE YEARS HAD FEET

I could not prove the Years had feet—
Yet confident they run
Am I, from symptoms that are past
And Series that are done—

I find my feet have further Goals—   5
I smile upon the Aims
That felt so ample—Yesterday—
Today's—have vaster claims—

I do not doubt the self I was
Was competent to me—   10
But something awkward in the fit—
Proves that—outgrown—I see—

"HOPE" IS THE THING
WITH FEATHERS

"Hope" is the thing with feathers—
That perches in the soul—
And sings the tune without the words—
And never stops—at all—

And sweetest—in the Gale—is heard—   5
And sore must be the storm—
That could abash the little Bird
That kept so many warm—

I've heard it in the chillest land—
And on the strangest Sea—   10
Yet, never, in Extremity,
It asked a crumb—of Me.

SUCCESS IS COUNTED SWEETEST

Success is counted sweetest
By those who ne'er succeed.
To comprehend a nectar
Requires sorest need.

Not one of all the purple Host   5
Who took the Flag today
Can tell the definition
So clear of Victory

As he defeated—dying—
On whose forbidden ear   10
The distant strains of triumph
Burst agonized and clear!

OUR JOURNEY HAD ADVANCED

Our journey had advanced—
Our feet were almost come
To that odd Fork in Being's Road—
Eternity—by Term—

Our pace took sudden awe—   5
Our feet—reluctant—led—
Before—were Cities—but Between—
The Forest of the Dead—

Retreat—was out of Hope—
Behind—a Sealed Route—   10
Eternity's White Flag—Before—
And God—at every Gate—

HER FINAL SUMMER WAS IT

Her final Summer was it—
And yet We guessed it not—
If tenderer industriousness
Pervaded Her, We thought

A further force of life   5
Developed from within—
When Death lit all the shortness up
It made the hurry plain—

We wondered at our blindness
When nothing was to see   10
But Her Carrara Guide post—
At Our Stupidity—

When duller than our dullness
The Busy Darling lay—
So busy was she—finishing—   15
So Leisurely—were We—

BECAUSE I COULD NOT STOP
FOR DEATH

Because I could not stop for Death—
He kindly stopped for me—
The Carriage held but just Ourselves—
And Immortality.

We slowly drove—He knew no haste   5
And I had put away
My labor and my leisure too,
For His Civility—

We passed the School, where Children strove
At Recess—in the Ring—   10
We passed the Fields of Gazing Grain—
We passed the Setting Sun—

Or rather—He passed Us—
The Dews drew quivering and chill—
For only Gossamer, my Gown—   15
My Tippet—only Tulle—

We paused before a House that seemed
A Swelling of the Ground—
The Roof was scarcely visible—
The Cornice—in the Ground—   20

Since then—'tis Centuries—and yet
Feels shorter than the Day
I first surmised the Horses' Heads
Were toward Eternity—

I HEARD A FLY BUZZ—
WHEN I DIED

I heard a Fly buzz—when I died—
The Stillness in the Room
Was like the Stillness in the Air—
Between the Heaves of Storm—

The Eyes around—had wrung them dry—   5
And Breaths were gathering firm
For that last Onset—when the King
Be witnessed—in the Room—

I willed my Keepsakes—Signed away
What portion of me be   10
Assignable—and then it was
There interposed a Fly—

With Blue—uncertain stumbling Buzz—
Between the light—and me—
And then the Windows failed—and then   15
I could not see to see—

A GROUP OF POEMS BY
ROBERT FROST (1874–1963)

In section 12 we examined Frost's "The Star-Splitter" as a narrative poem, remarking by the way that Frost is well known for his ability to capture in verse the accents of ordinary speech. We might have further remarked that the speech in question was the vernacular of his neighbors in rural New England. In fact, Frost's acquaintance with rural life provided not only the basis of a style, but also the characteristic theme of man's relation to nature. Consider the following:

THE WOOD-PILE

Out walking in the frozen swamp one gray day,
I paused and said, 'I will turn back from here.
No, I will go on farther—and we shall see.'
The hard snow held me, save where now and then
One foot went through. The view was all in lines 5
Straight up and down of tall slim trees
Too much alike to mark or name a place by
So as to say for certain I was here
Or somewhere else: I was just far from home.
A small bird flew before me. He was careful   10
To put a tree between us when he lighted,
And say no word to tell me who he was
Who was so foolish as to think what *he* thought.
He thought that I was after him for a feather—
The white one in his tail; like one who takes   15
Everything said as personal to himself.
One flight out sideways would have undeceived
     him.
And then there was a pile of wood for which
I forgot him and let his little fear
Carry him off the way I might have gone,   20
Without so much as wishing him good-night.
He went behind it to make his last stand.
It was a cord of maple, cut and split
And piled—and measured, four by four by eight
And not another like it could I see.   25
No runner tracks in this year's snow looped near
     it.
And it was older sure than this year's cutting,
Or even last year's or the year's before.
The wood was gray and the bark warping off it
And the pile somewhat sunken. Clematis   30
Had wound strings round and round it like a
     bundle.
What held it though on one side was a tree
Still growing, and on one a stake and prop,
These latter about to fall. I thought that only
Someone who lived in turning to fresh tasks   35
Could so forget his handiwork on which
He spent himself, the labor of his axe,
And leave it there far from a useful fireplace
To warm the frozen swamp as best it could
With the slow smokeless burning of decay.   40

This poem seems to describe a rather aimless walk. Nothing very much happens. The speaker tells how the frozen swamp looks on a gray winter day. He has no special place to go; he is simply taking a walk.

The bird that kept flitting in front of him and putting a tree between them is amusingly like certain human beings who, as the poet says, take "everything said as personal" to themselves. But the little incident is treated casually and is of no special importance. Finally the speaker comes upon the woodpile, and here his walk terminates, or at least all that the poet has chosen to tell us about it.

What is the significance of the woodpile? The cord is described with a countryman's eye: it is of maple wood; the wood is weathered gray, and the bark is warping off. The cord is held up, on one side by a growing tree and on the other by a stake and prop, though these last are about ready to fall.

What seems curious to the observer is that anyone would have taken the trouble to cut and split and pile a cord of wood and then abandon it, leaving it there in the swamp to rot away. The poem ends with this bit of speculation about the man who split and piled the wood: he must have been a man who kept irons in a good many fires—the sort of person who is always turning from one task to another. And with this observation the poem comes to an end. To some readers the poem will seem as aimless and inconsequential as the walk that ended with the discovery of the abandoned woodpile.

Yet the reader may very well feel that the poem does have a point and that the pretense of a story, the account of the walk, and the description of the woodpile all work together to maintain the interest of the reader as the poem goes along, but that none of them actually makes the point of the poem, a point that is given much less directly—almost glancingly—in the last three lines:

> . . . leave it there far from a useful fireplace
> To warm the frozen swamp as best it could
> With the slow smokeless burning of decay.

Having in mind what we learned about Frost's concern with nature in "The Need of Being Versed in Country Things," one might try to see what happens if we read these lines as a commentary on man's relation to nature. The abandoned woodpile is presented with just a hint of pathos, the sort of pathos provoked by abandoned and forgotten objects that remain as evidence of the lives of nameless and unknown people. But we notice that the poet is not willing to leave the matter at that. The last two lines in particular take the concern one stage further. The woodpile is, after all, on a fireplace, though it is not "a useful fireplace," and the wood is being burned, even though in the frozen swamp.

Thus the woodpile, a common and homely object, is, for the purpose of this poem, something more than a woodpile; it gains symbolic force and becomes a commentary, not only on the personality and temperament of the unknown man who set it up, but on the activities of all men. The implication is that if man drops one activity in favor of another and forgets one accomplishment in his fever to get on with some other, nature, which never works in a hurry and never forgets anything, goes right on to take care of the tasks that man, in his forgetfulness, abandons.

This general point has already been hinted at earlier. The poet says of the woodpile that "Clematis / Had wound strings round and round it like a bundle." The primary purpose of the comparison is to make us see the woodpile more vividly and to emphasize the length of time that has elapsed since the cutting of the wood. But the comparison also suggests that nature is doing what the man had failed to do. Nature, in its own way, is man's collaborator and assistant. Nature seems to be tying the pile together and keeping it from falling. Or perhaps nature is claiming the woodpile again for its own, taking possession of what man had tried to remove for his own purposes. Both of these meanings may seem to be involved in the comparison, and both meanings may be relevant. The implication that nature is both man's friend and man's enemy—and that it may finally be indifferent to him altogether—in the light of the whole poem, makes good sense.

Consider too the final comparison with which the poem closes. "The slow smokeless burning of decay" is actually an extremely accurate way of putting matters, for the decay of wood amounts to a slow oxidation. The difference between the wood's rotting in the swamp or burning on a useful fireplace is primarily a difference in the speed of the process. In fact, we have already suggested that the swamp is really a kind of fireplace and that nature will in its own way burn the wood that man forgot to burn.

If the point of the poem, then, has to do with man's relation to nature, it has been put subtly—so subtly that the attempt to phrase it

briefly may appear to overstate it. Certainly we shall do well to go back and reread the poem carefully, letting the poem dramatize its point in its own way. But we must not make the mistake of thinking that the poem is without a point. Frost's method of approaching the true subject of "The Wood-Pile" is very cunning. This definition of the factual theme of the poem is delayed until the very end, with the result that the reader seems to stumble upon it unexpectedly just as the man discovered the woodpile. Yet when the end of the poem is reached, one can see that the arrangement of materials in the poem, at first glance so casual, has actually been disposed to culminate in the final effect.

EXERCISES

1. What is implied about the character of the man who takes this walk? How do you know that he is more than usually observant? How do you know that he has a sense of humor? *Philosophy* means literally "love of truth." What is the evidence that the observer in this poem is a "philosopher"?
2. Could one argue that the poem's trailing off into inconsequence at the end is only apparent—that is, the trailing off is in reality a dramatic device to help make the essential point of the poem?
3. Can you see any relation in theme between this poem and "To Autumn" by Keats?

The theme of man's relation to nature comes in for a characteristic statement in the following poem:

A LEAF TREADER

I have been treading on leaves all day until I am autumn-tired.
God knows all the color and form of leaves I have trodden on and mired.
Perhaps I have put forth too much strength and been too fierce from fear.
I have safely trodden underfoot the leaves of another year.

All summer long they were over head, more lifted up than I.   5
To come to their final place in earth they had to pass me by.
All summer long I thought I heard them threatening under their breath.
And when they came it seemed with a will to carry me with them to death.

They spoke to the fugitive in my heart as if it
were leaf to leaf.
They tapped at my eyelids and touched my lips
with an invitation to grief.   10
But it was no reason I had to go because they had
to go.
Now up, my knee, to keep on top of another year
of snow.

The poem begins almost as casually as "The Wood-Pile." It is an autumn day and the speaker, going about his chores on the farm, is conscious of having trodden leaves into the mud, golden, orange, crimson. Yet even as early as the second line of the poem, we get a hint that his experience had some deeper meaning for him. The hint is developed in lines 3 and 4. Why does the speaker hazard the guess that perhaps he has put forth "too much strength"? And why does he remark that he has been "too fierce from fear"? Fear of what, if all he has done has been merely to tramp leaves down into the mud?

The adverb *safely* in line 4 supplies the answer: to the casual glance, he was simply a man treading upon the autumn leaves, but to the man himself the action had a deeper meaning. He had just concluded a contest with nature as to whether he should be on top of the leaves at the end of this autumn or whether the leaves should be on top of him.

In stanza 2 the summer leaves are made to take on an ominous quality. All summer long he thought he heard them threatening him "under their breath," and now as they fall past him on this autumn day, he imagines they wish to carry him with them to death. The threat in the seasonal change—the suggestion that man too is a leaf who has his season and finally must come to rest in the earth along with the other leaves—runs on into the third stanza, though there it takes on a rather different tone. In this stanza, the leaves do not so much threaten as cajole. A Freudian might find in this passage the death wish in man, but whether or not we use the term "death wish," most of us do feel, at some time or other, the attraction of subsiding into nature, of ceasing to strive against it.

In stanza 3 the poet puts the point very well indeed. He says that the leaves spoke "to the fugitive in my heart as if it were leaf to leaf." The point is made graphically and concretely with the statement that the leaves "tapped at my eyelids and touched my lips with an invitation to grief." But one notices that even in this line the poet has not lost his hold on the concrete details of the situation. On a gusty autumn day some of the flying leaves would blow against one's eyelids or against one's lips.

The poem has moved a good long way from its rather casual opening. The term *autumn-tired* in the first line has been developed into a wistfulness attuned to the autumn, a season in which man is inclined to feel a kind of resignation knowing that he is doomed to pass from the scene even as the leaves do. But man, though a part of nature, is no mere leaf. The speaker asserts as much when suddenly (l. 11) there is a change of mood and a change of tone. He says "But it was no reason I had to go because they had to go." What is the tone? Well, it resembles as nearly as anything else the tone of one little boy taunting another little boy who had been called into the house by his mother: "It's no reason I've got to go in just because you've got to go in." But the student may prefer to supply his own, and perhaps better, analogy for the tone here. Perhaps the tone is not really taunting; but it is certainly colloquial, common-sensical, and sharp—sharp enough at least to break the somber mood into which the poem has gravitated.

The fact that the leaves have come to their dying time does not mean that the speaker has arrived at his. Yet if there is a slight note of cockiness here, the speaker is not carelessly overconfident. After all, he faces another season: soon the snowflakes will be flying and he will have to try to keep on top of them. As he says wryly in the last line, "Now up my knee to keep on top of another year of snow."

This little poem is a brilliant exercise in the use of imagery: the image of the falling leaves provides the speaker with all that he needs or wants to say. The poem is also a brilliant exercise in tone: if the tone were inept or oversimple, the poem would become something mawkishly sentimental or laboriously trivial. The manipulation of tone, and particularly the shift in tone in the last lines, keeps the poem nimble and graceful.

Does "A Leaf Treader" embody the

same attitude toward nature and man's partial alienation from nature as that found in "The Wood-Pile"? The student ought to determine this for himself, but there can be no doubt that both poems deal with the theme of man's relation to nature.

EXERCISES

1. Is the man who recounts "A Leaf Treader" essentially the same man who took the walk in "The Wood-Pile"? If it is the same man, is his mood quite the same in the two poems? Look back at Housman's poem entitled "The Tree of Man" (sec. 13) and compare the way in which the two poets have treated the analogy between man and leaf. How do the two poems differ in tone?

2. Compare "A Leaf Treader" with "Bells for John Whiteside's Daughter" by John Crowe Ransom (sec. 14) with regard to a fundamental attitude toward life.

COME IN

As I came to the edge of the woods,
Thrush music—hark!
Now if it was dusk outside,
Inside it was dark.

Too dark in the woods for a bird   5
By sleight of wing
To better its perch for the night,
Though it still could sing.

The last of the light of the sun
That had died in the west   10
Still lived for one song more
In a thrush's breast.

Far in the pillared dark
Thrush music went—
Almost like a call to come in   15
To the dark and lament.

But no, I was out for stars:
I would not come in.
I meant not even if asked,
And I hadn't been.   20

Out for a walk at evening, the speaker hears a thrush's music and thinks of the bird singing out of the now dark woods. With the fourth stanza he comes to a position very close to that reached in lines 9 and 10 of "A Leaf Treader." The thrush's music seems melancholy, the voice of nature itself, calling for man to join the lament rising out of the gathering darkness, the darkness that will eventually claim him and that, though frightening, exerts a positive attraction.

But the man out for the walk is one indeed versed in country things. He knows that the thrush is not really lamenting and phrases his comment very carefully. He says "*Almost like a call to come in / To the dark and lament.*" The last stanza—like that of "A Leaf Treader"—changes tone sharply and effectively. The speaker reminds himself that he did not come out for thrush music anyway, but to look at the stars. He refuses the invitation; he says "I would not come in." But then he remembers his manners, and with a further shift in tone adds "I meant not even if asked, / And I hadn't been." He takes care not to presume upon an invitation that may not have been intended, for he knows that indeed no invitation has been given. Nature is supremely indifferent to man. Her thrush is not lamenting, and Nature does not care whether man himself laments or rejoices.

EXERCISES

1. The description in this poem is not vague but quite detailed and exact. For example, notice such phrases as "By sleight of wing (l. 6) or "To better its perch" (l. 7). Notice too that the observer is aware of the exact shades of light at this moment: "The last light of the sun," the dusk outside the wood, and the complete darkness within the wood. What is the effect on the poem of this sense of precise statement?

2. In line 15, what is the sense of "the pillared dark"?

3. How would you characterize the tone of this poem? What shifts of tone occur in the poem?

4. Do you gain any sense of the speaker's personality? How does it compare with that of the man who narrates "The Wood-Pile"? "The Star-Splitter" (sec. 12)? Why is the speaker "out for stars"?

THE OVEN BIRD

There is a singer everyone has heard,
Loud, a mid-summer and a mid-wood bird,
Who makes the solid tree trunks sound again.
He says that leaves are old and that for flowers
Mid-summer is to spring as one to ten.   5

He says the early petal-fall is past,
When pear and cherry bloom went down in
 showers
On sunny days a moment overcast;
And comes that other fall we name the fall.
He says the highway dust is over all.   10
The bird would cease and be as other birds
But that he knows in singing not to sing.
The question that he frames in all but words
Is what to make of a diminished thing.

As this sonnet implies, the oven bird's song is not particularly musical, and since the oven bird really has very little to sing about, this fact is appropriate. His world is a world in which the spring flowers are gone, in which the leaves have lost their freshness, and "the highway dust is over all." What matters is that this bird still manages to sing when the other birds, under such conditions, have given over. It may be amusing to compare Frost's account of the bird with that given in a technical bird guide. *A Guide to Birdsongs* by Aretas A. Saunders (Garden City, N. Y.: Doubleday & Co., Inc., 1951) states that

> the Ovenbird is common in summer practically throughout the northeastern United States. . . . It sings from its arrival, the last of April, till the third week in July. . . . The common song of this bird is very distinctive and not easily mistaken for any other. It is a series of two-note phrases repeated to the end usually without variation in pitch or time, but increasing in loudness to the end of the song. The quality is not particularly musical, but the song is loud and one of the commonest sounds of the forest in early summer.

EXERCISES

1. Frost's account is evidently accurate enough, even by technical standards. What does his poem give us that the prose exposition cannot give?
2. What does the poet mean in line 12 in saying that the oven bird "knows in singing not to sing"? What is the meaning of *singing* in this context?
3. What is the tone of this poem? What is the poet's attitude toward the bird? Amusement? Admiration? He apparently cannot give the oven bird high marks for singing. Does he award him an E for effort? Is it stupidity or intelligent taste that the bird displays in knowing "not to sing"?
4. Compare this poem to Keats's "To Autumn."

Is the season described by Keats a "diminished thing"? Or not? What is the relation of Keats's "wailful choir" of gnats and the no-song of the oven bird?
5. Is there any hint in this poem of Frost's attitude toward nature? Does the human being in this instance feel perhaps a little closer to the oven bird than to some of the finer songsters? If you feel that this is hinted, why should he feel closer?

THE NEED OF BEING VERSED
IN COUNTRY THINGS

The house had gone to bring again
To the midnight sky a sunset glow.
Now the chimney was all of the house that stood,
Like a pistil after the petals go.

The barn opposed across the way,   5
That would have joined the house in flame
Had it been the will of the wind, was left
To bear forsaken the place's name.

No more it opened with all one end
For teams that came by the stony road   10
To drum on the floor with scurrying hoofs
And brush the mow with the summer load.

The birds that came to it through the air
At broken windows flew out and in,
Their murmur more like the sigh we sigh   15
From too much dwelling on what has been.

Yet for them the lilac renewed its leaf,
And the agèd elm, though touched with fire;
And the dry pump flung up an awkward arm;
And the fence post carried a strand of wire.   20

For them there was really nothing sad.
But though they rejoiced in the nest they kept,
One had to be versed in country things
Not to believe the phoebes wept.

This poem seems to confine itself largely to description: a rural scene in which the chimney of a burned farmhouse still stands, the barn, untouched by the fire, but with some of its windows broken, an old elm, one side of which had been scorched by the fire, a fence from which all but one strand of wire has fallen away, the now unused pump.

The details are well chosen, and their concrete vividness has been enforced by appropriate comparisons. The lone chimney, for example, stands like a pistil (the upright spike of certain flowers) after the cup-shaped part of the blossom has withered and fallen away. The arm of the pump has been left standing at an awkward angle—like a human arm thrown up in a clumsy gesture of protest and then arrested there.

The poem emphasizes the present scene, but there are several references to the past: there is a reference to the fire itself, which caused a glow like that of sunset unseasonably at midnight; and there is a picture of the barn as it used to be when the hayloads were coming in at the end of summer. The sense of life and bustling, purposeful activity contrasts sharply with the present sense of deadness and desolation in the present scene. (The same contrast is unobtrusively implied in the fifth stanza: the pump is "dry"—the fence is in human practical terms now hardly a "fence" at all.)

Although the poem seems to confine itself to description—admirably detailed, objective description—the mention of phoebes suggests an interpretation. For the scene is not completely desolate: the observer shares it with the birds, which have taken over the abandoned barn for their nesting place. The scene spells melancholy desolation, and the mournful cry of the birds seems to voice appropriately the quality of the scene.

Suppose that the poem ended with this fourth stanza. What sort of poem would it be? We should still have much of the descriptive detail (though we should sorely miss that of the fifth stanza); but the poem would seem a little predictable and trite in its interpretation of the scene, and might not entirely escape a certain hint of sentimentality.

But the poet does not stop with the fourth stanza. The speaker's realistic grasp on the situation is not relaxed; nor is his hold on the essential difference between man and nature. The phoebes are not weeping. Presumably, they are happy. And why should they not be? However desolate the setting in *human* terms, it is admirably accommodated to them. As a place to perch, *one* strand of wire is just as good as three or four. Nature, like the fire-damaged elm, has been only momentarily deflected by man's fortunes and misfortunes. Its flood of vitality perennially renews itself. What man abandons, nature casually repossesses.

Even the lines that may seem to tilt most dangerously toward the sentimental (ll. 15–16) actually enforce the distinction between man and nature. If the "murmur" of the phoebes resembles a human sigh over the vanished past, it is like "the sigh *we* [that is, human beings] sigh," and will seem so only to human beings.

The observer who speaks the poem is, then, tough-minded. He knows nature too well to attribute to it human concerns and human values. Nature does not weep over the abandoned home: it does not even know that the house is a house or that it has been abandoned. The mournful—to human ears—cry of the birds is only accidentally appropriate. But if the speaker is tough-minded and realistic, he is also sensitive; and he acknowledges the poignant sense of melancholy in the most powerful way possible: unless, he says, you really were "versed in country things," you would have been taken in—you might have believed that "the phoebes wept."

What is the advantage of having the scene reported through the lips of an observer who is, as this one is, evidently "versed in country things"? There is a great advantage. We properly discount the outburst of someone whose emotions are on hair-trigger—who responds easily and glibly to slight occasions—who has no sense of proportion, who is more concerned with the pleasure of emotional release than with the occasion that provokes it. Conversely, we are impressed by the expression of emotion when it comes from a tough-grained sensibility, not prone to easy outbursts.

In this poem, we may say that the poet succeeds in "having it both ways"—in doing justice to the hard realities of life and yet acknowledging the melancholy implicit in that life. But the use of the phrase "having it both ways" may smack of trickery, as if the poet were skillfully but coldly manipulating our feelings—palming off on us a trite and worn theme. Perhaps, then, we had better state in other terms what the poet accomplishes. The accomplishment may be put in this way: the poet has refused to make a vague and general appeal to our feelings by sketching in a conventionally melancholy scene in the hope that certain clichés of sentiment— the sadness of the past, of man's broken hopes, of simple rural life—will work. Instead he has defined for us in the poem quite precisely the quality and degree of melancholy that such a scene ought to elicit. In doing so, he has moreover refused to exploit this sentiment of regret as something to be dwelt upon for its own sake and in isolation from the hard facts of our world or from the hardest thinking that man can give to those facts. Last of all, he has merely implied his own attitude to the scene—not urging us to adopt it, but doing his reader the compliment of allowing him to apprehend it for himself.

EXERCISES

1. Reread Richard Eberhart's "I Walked Out to the Graveyard to See the Dead" (sec. 16). How does his attitude toward the pheasant in that poem compare with Frost's attitude toward the phoebes in this one? In what sense can it be said that both poets have the same notion of man's relation to nature?
2. Compare the theme of this poem to that of "The Wood-Pile." How is the contrast between man and nature handled in each poem?
3. Compare the theme of this poem to that of Yeats's "The Wild Swans at Coole" (sec 13). What differences in tone do you note?

STOPPING BY WOODS ON
A SNOWY EVENING

Whose woods these are I think I know.
His house is in the village though;
He will not see me stopping here
To watch his woods fill up with snow.

My little horse must think it queer   5
To stop without a farmhouse near

Between the woods and frozen lake
The darkest evening of the year.

He gives his harness bells a shake
To ask if there is some mistake.   10
The only other sound's the sweep
Of easy wind and downy flake.

The woods are lovely, dark and deep.

But I have promises to keep,
And miles to go before I sleep,   15
And miles to go before I sleep.

EXERCISES

1. Here, as in "Desert Places" (sec. 15), a snowy scene viewed by the speaker as he moves past at night is the basic image of the poem. But in the two poems the speakers' attitudes toward the scene are very different. In the first poem the speaker finds only blankness, and his mind leaps to the blankness of interstellar space. In the second poem the scene makes some deep appeal to the wayfarer. What is the nature of that appeal? What, in other words, is the significance of the image?
2. Why would the owner of the land think it queer of the speaker to stop here? What about the horse? What do the owner and the horse have in common in contrast with the speaker? With the last stanza does the speaker accept the values of the owner and the horse? Or is it more complicated than that? Let us revise the last stanza:

The woods are lovely, dark and deep.
But I have promises to keep,
And chores to do before I sleep,
Then a good warm supper before I sleep.

What now is the difference in meaning?
3. Comment on the rhythms and phonetic quality here in contrast to those of "Desert Places."

Section 18

SOME POEMS OF THIS TIME

In the poems thus far offered we have undertaken to give some sense of both the continuity and the interplay between poetry of the past and that of the modern age. We have exhibited and considered among the moderns the work, for example, of Robert Frost, T. S.

Eliot, John Crowe Ransom, Allen Tate, Robert Lowell, James Wright, Louise Bogan, W. B. Yeats, Léonie Adams, and John Berryman. Some of these poets are still active, but, by and large, they stand for the older generation.

We have, therefore, thought that the student might find it exciting to plunge into a body of recent work by poets much younger than these moderns—and to plunge into it without commentary or questions, to savor it, find their own way in it, and make their own terms with it.

These poets have been chosen not with the idea of showing the "best" poems or the "best" poets of the period. There are fine poems and fine poets not included here. What we have tried to do is to give representative poems and representative poets, to offer a kind of spectrum of the time. It is a spectrum of high interest.

The poets included here are arranged in alphabetical order.

THE QUINCE BUSH

A. R. Ammons (b. 1926)

The flowering quince bush
on the back hedge has been
run through by a morning
glory vine

and this morning three blooms
are open as if for all light,
sound, and motion: their adjustment
to light is

pink, though they reach for
stellar reds and core violets:
they listen as if for racket's
inner silence

and focus, as if to starve, all motion:
patterns of escaped sea
they tip the defeated, hostile,
oceanic wind:

elsewhere young men scratch and fire:
a troubled child shudders to a freeze:
an old man bursts finally and
rattles down

clacking slats: the caterpillar pierced
by a wasp egg blooms inside with
the tender worm: wailing
walls float

luminous with the charge of grief:
a day pours through a morning glory
dayblossom's adequate, poised,
available center.

YEARS OF INDISCRETION

John Ashbery (b. 1927)

Whatever your eye alights on this morning is
    yours:
Dotted rhythms of colors as they fade to the color,
A gray agate, translucent and firm, with nothing
Beyond its purifying reach. It's all there.
These are things offered to your participation.

These pebbles in a row are the seasons.
This is a house in which you may wish to live.
There are more than any of us to choose from
But each must live its own time.

And with the urging of the year each hastens
    onward separately
In strange sensations of emptiness, anguish,
    romantic
Outbursts, visions and wraiths. One meeting
Cancels another. "The seven-league boot
Gliding hither and thither of its own accord"
Salutes these forms for what they now are:

Fables that time invents
To explain its passing. They entertain
The very young and the very old, and not
One's standing up in them to shoulder
Task and vision, vision in the form of a task
So that the present seems like yesterday
And yesterday the place where we left off a little
    while ago.

POEM FOR HALFWHITE
COLLEGE STUDENTS

Imamu Amiri Baraka* (b. 1934)

Who are you, listening to me, who are you
listening to yourself? Are you white or
black, or does that have anything to do
with it? Can you pop your fingers to no
music, except those wild monkies go on

---

* The name adopted by LeRoi Jones when he identified himself with the cause of black nationalism.

in your head, can you jerk, to no melody,
except finger poppers get it together
when you turn from starchecking to checking
yourself. How do you sound, your words, are they
yours? The ghost you see in the mirror, is it really
you, can you swear you are not an imitation grey-
    boy,
can you look right next to you in that chair, and
    swear,
that the sister you have your hand on is not really
so full of Elizabeth Taylor, Richard Burton is
coming out of her ears. You may even have to be
    Richard
with a white shirt and face, and four million
    negroes
think you cute, you may have to be Elizabeth
    Taylor, old lady,
if you want to sit up in your crazy spot dreaming
    about dresses,
and the sway of certain porters' hips. Check your-
    self, learn who it is
speaking, when you make some ultrasophisticated
    point, check yourself,
when you find yourself gesturing like Steve
    McQueen, check it out, ask
in your black heart who it is you are, and is that
    image black or white,

you might be surprised right out the window,
    whistling dixie on the way in.

THE PLEADERS

Peter Davison (b. 1928)

What are you going to do with us, who have
No edges, no talents, no discriminations,
Who hear no inner voices, who perceive
No visions of the future, no horizons?
We are among you; we are going to stay.

We crush, we drag, we heave, we draw the water
For you to spill. We gather together to listen
To your speeches, though your tongues run on so
    fast
We cannot follow, and your jokes dart in and out
Too quickly for our laughter to form itself. •
We are your children, whom you treat like horses.

When crowds surge out into the streets
You have invited them; we run with them.
You give us order, speak on our behalf,
For we speak up too slowly to interrupt you.
We are the numbers ranked on your computers.
We are among you; we are going to stay.

If we knew how to pray to you, we'd pray
That you could listen long enough to listen
To what it is we think we want. We know
That what you think we want lies far away
From anything that has occurred to us.
We are your children, whom you treat like horses.

We are the eyes your eyes have never met.
We are the voice you will not wait to hear.
We are the part of you you have forgotten,
Or trampled out, or lost and wept to lose.
We are your children, whom you treat like horses.
We are among you; we are going to stay.

ADULTERY

James Dickey (b. 1923)

We have all been in rooms
We cannot die in, and they are odd places, and
    sad.
Often Indians are standing eagle-armed on hills

In the sunrise   open wide to the Great Spirit
Or gliding in canoes   or cattle are browsing on
    the walls
Far away   gazing down with the eyes of our
    children

Not far away   or there are men driving
The last railspike, which has turned
Gold in their hands. Gigantic forepleasure lives

Among such scenes, and we are alone with it
At last. There is always some weeping
Between us   and someone is always checking

A wrist watch by the bed to see how much
Longer we have left. Nothing can come
Of this   nothing can come

Of us: of me with my grim techniques
Or you who have sealed your womb
With a ring of convulsive rubber:

Although we come together,
Nothing will come of us. But we would not give
It up, for death is beaten

By praying Indians   by distant cows   historical
Hammers   by hazardous meetings that bridge
A continent. One could never die here

Never die   never die
While crying. My lover, my dear one
I will see you next week

When I'm in town. I will call you
If I can. Please get hold of   please don't
Oh God, Please don't any more I can't bear . . .
    Listen:

We have done it again   we are
Still living. Sit up and smile,
God bless you. Guilt is magical.

A SUPERMARKET IN CALIFORNIA
Allen Ginsberg (b. 1926)

What thought I have of you tonight, Walt Whitman, for I walked down the sidestreets under the trees with a headache self-conscious looking at the full moon.

In my hungry fatigue, and shopping for images, I went into the neon fruit supermarket, dreaming of your enumerations!

What peaches and what penumbras! Whole families shopping at night! Aisles full of husbands! Wives in the avocados, babies in the tomatoes!—and you, Garcia Lorca, what were you doing down by the watermelons?

I saw you, Walt Whitman, childless, lonely old grubber, poking among the meats in the refrigerator and eyeing the grocery boys.

I heard you asking questions of each: Who killed the pork chops? What price bananas? Are you my Angel?

I wandered in and out of the brilliant stacks of cans following you, and followed in my imagination by the store detective.

We strode down the open corridors together in our solitary fancy tasting artichokes, possessing every frozen delicacy, and never passing the cashier.

Where are we going, Walt Whitman? The doors close in an hour. Which way does your beard point tonight?

(I touch your book and dream of our odyssey in the supermarket and feel absurd.)

Will we walk all night through solitary streets? The trees add shade to shade, lights out in the houses, we'll both be lonely.

Will we stroll dreaming of the lost America of love past blue automobiles in driveways, home to our silent cottage?

Ah, dear father, graybeard, lonely old courage-teacher, what America did you have when Charon quit poling his ferry and you got out on a smoking bank and stood watching the boat disappear on the black waters of Lethe?

THE ONLY SONG I'M SINGING
Nikki Giovanni (b. 1943)

they tell me that i'm beautiful i know
i'm Black and proud
the people ask for autographs
i sometimes draw a crowd
i've written lots of poetry and other
kinds of books
i've heard that white men crumble
from one of my mean looks
i study hard and know my facts
in fact the truth is true
the only song i'm singing now is my song
of you
        and i'm asking you baby please
        please somehow show me what i need
        to know so i can love you right
        now

i've had great opportunities to move
the world around
whenever they need love and truth they call
me to their town
the president he called me up and asked
me to come down
but if you think you want me home i think
i'll stick around
        and i'm asking you baby please baby baby
          show me
        right now most of the things i need to know
        so i can love you somehow

BLACK JACKETS
Thom Gunn (b. 1929)

In the silence that prolongs the span
Rawly of music when the record ends,

The red-haired boy who drove a van
In weekday overalls but, like his friends,

Wore cycle boots and jacket here
To suit the Sunday hangout he was in,
  Heard, as he stretched back from his beer,
Leather creak softly round his neck and chin.

  Before him, on a coal-black sleeve
Remote exertion had lined, scratched, and burned
  Insignia that could not revive
The heroic fall or climb where they were earned.

  On the other drinkers bent together,
Concocting selves for their impervious kit,
  He saw it as no more than leather
Which, taut across the shoulders grown to it,

  Sent through the dimness of a bar
As sudden and anonymous hints of light
  As those that shipping give, that are
Now flickers in the Bay, now lost in night.

  He stretched out like a cat, and rolled
The bitterish taste of beer upon his tongue,
  And listened to a joke being told:
The present was the things he stayed among.

  If it was only loss he wore,
He wore it to assert, with fierce devotion,
  Complicity and nothing more.
He recollected his initiation,

  And one especially of the rites.
For on his shoulders they had put tattoos:
  The group's name on the left, The Knights,
And on the right the slogan Born To Lose.

THE DOVER BITCH*

A Criticism of Life

Anthony Hecht (b. 1922)

So there stood Matthew Arnold and this girl
With the cliffs of England crumbling away behind
  them,
And he said to her, "Try to be true to me,
And I'll do the same for you, for things are bad
All over, etc., etc."
Well now, I knew this girl. It's true she had read
Sophocles in a fairly good translation
And caught that bitter allusion to the sea,
But all the time he was talking she had in mind
The notion of what his whiskers would feel like
On the back of her neck. She told me later on
That after a while she got to looking out
At the lights across the channel, and really felt sad,

Thinking of all the wine and enormous beds
And blandishments in French and the perfumes.
And then she got really angry. To have been
  brought
All the way down from London, and then be
  addressed
As sort of a mournful cosmic last resort
Is really tough on a girl, and she was pretty.
Anyway, she watched him pace the room
And finger his watch-chain and seem to sweat a
  bit,
And then she said one or two unprintable things.
But you mustn't judge her by that. What I mean
  to say is,
She's really all right. I still see her once in a while
And she always treats me right. We have a drink
And I give her a good time, and perhaps it's a year
Before I see her again, but there she is,
Running to fat, but dependable as they come,
And sometimes I bring her a bottle of *Nuit
  d'Amour.*

ALASKA BROWN BEAR

John Hollander (b. 1929)

O my Best Bear who stands
And, not by reason of light
But by fiat of fur, commands
The height, the essential shore, the mere,
The dryness outreaching into an icy, rich sea.

The lord of our landless pole
Is white, is white, and he hides
On stretches of chlorous ice; the pale aurora,
Rising behind him, thunders across the night.
But I am too wise now and fat
To acknowledge a lesser one, here, than His
  Blackness.

Teddy, the squeaky ginger,
The umptieth Marquis of Mumph,
He of the weepings: absorbent and not unfrayed
Master of childhood, midnight was in his care
In the tropic of bedroom. Then it came that I
  said:
I know thee not, old bear.

But He, Thou, the Big Brown, the soft turret,
Thrust by the dead earth at the sky,
Quickening yet this buff of twilight,
His she nearby—
O, downstream from Him a small
Something blurred and dark, something of baser
  fur
Slinks off, leaving a half-torn salmon
Before the Regent of the barest lands,

---

* See "Dover Beech," by Matthew Arnold, p. 458.

The Lord of no hall.
He stands
Among the regions of wind beyond winds. Behold!
At his own call
He has crashed through from behind the horizon
Where the great bells of summit ring with cold.

FURTHER INSTRUCTIONS TO THE ARCHITECT
Richard Howard (b. 1929)

Now about the attic: please allow
    For easy access to the roof
So Cousin Agnes can get out there.
    Fall, did you say? Remember all
    The servants' bedrooms must include
A dream book in the dresser, and there was
    Always a gate across the stairs:
Our pantry sibyl walked in her sleep,
    Read tea leaves, knew what "horses" meant.

    Make sure the smell of apple peel
    Lingers in the master bedroom,
Keep lewd prints for the *Decameron*
Locked in the library, and repair
    The stained glass over the landing:
If the Lorelei's hair is still clear
The amber can always be replaced.
    I hear one ilex has fallen
Across the pond. Better plant rushes
    So the frogs will come back, evenings,
And sing their songs; restore the *allée*
Of Lombardy poplars where the doves
    Nested: we need all our mourners.

    See that the four black junipers
Don't overgrow the lawn: after dark
    The silver grass is luminous
Around them. There should be a wheezing
French bulldog on my grandmother's lap,
    Of course, and the sound of grape seeds
    Being flicked onto the porch floor
Where Ernestine is reading. Even

The corridor back to whatever
    Surprise you have in store must be
Merely the ones between the (witch's)
    Kitchen and the dim hall closet
Where velveteen hangers may have turned
By now to something else unlikely.

You can't help getting it right if you
    Listen to me. Recognition
Is not to be suppressed. Why the whole
Place seems just the way it was, I tell you
    I was there last night: in dreams
We are always under house arrest.

BED
Judith Kroll (b. 1943)

The lights are off.
Across the room
it sweats
out of the walls,

its breath warms up
like a cold motor. I lie
and watch its body
thicken and swarm:
I am
as irresistible as food.

This must be a dream,
or else I am falling asleep.

It moves.

Unbelievable,
like really seeing
a wine-dark sea.

It has no mouth.
It says:

You fooled around enough.
Flirted
and tempted. Jeered. No one
can pull my leg: I

am the daddy whose name
is death, and come
to tuck you in

& in
& in

THE OLD ADAM
Denise Levertov (b. 1923)

A photo of someone else's childhood,
a garden in another country—world
he had no part in and has no power to imagine:

yet the old man who has failed his memory
keens over the picture—'Them happy days—
gone—gone for ever!'—glad for a moment to
    suppose

a focus for unspent grieving, his floating
sense of loss.
He wanders

asking the day of the week, the time,
over and over the wrong questions.
Missing his way in the streets

he acts out
the bent of his life,
the lost way

never looked for, life
unlived, of which he is dying
very slowly.

'A man,'
says his son, 'who never
made a right move in all his life.' A man

who thought the dollar was sweet and
couldn't make a buck, riding the subway
year after year to untasted sweetness,

loving his sons obscurely, incurious
who they were, these men, his sons—
a shadow of love, for love longs

to know the beloved, and a light goes with it
into the dark mineshafts of feeling . . . A man
who now, without knowing,

in endless concern for the smallest certainties,
looking again and again at a paid bill,
inquiring again and again, 'When was I here last?'

asks what it's too late to ask:
'Where is my life? Where is my life?
What have I done with my life?'

A TIMEPIECE
James Merrill (b. 1926)

Of a pendulum's mildness, with her feet up
My sister lay expecting her third child.
Over the hammock's crescent spilled
Her flushed face, grazing clover and buttercup.

Her legs were troubling her, a vein had burst.
Even so, among partial fullness she lay
Of pecked damson, of daughters at play
Who in the shadow of the house rehearsed

Her gait, her gesture, unnatural to them,
But they would master it soon enough, grown tall
Trusting that out of themselves came all
That full grace, while she out of whom these came

Shall have thrust fullness from her, like a death.
Already, seeing the little girls listless
She righted herself in a new awkwardness.
It was not *her* life she was heavy with.

Let us each have some milk, my sister smiled
Meaning to muffle with the taste

Of unbuilt bone a striking in her breast,
For soon by what it tells the clock is stilled.

LONG ISLAND SPRINGS
Howard Moss (b. 1922)

Long Island springs not much went on,
Except the small plots gave their all
In weeds and good grass; the mowers mowed
Up to the half-moon gardens crammed
With anything that grew. Our colored maid

Lived downstairs in a room too small
To keep a bird in, or so she claimed;
She liked her drinks, sloe-gin, gin-and . . .
When she was fired, my grandma said,
"Give them a finger, they'll take your hand."

So much for the maid. My grandma lived
In a room almost as small. She gave
Bread to the birds, saved bits of string,
Paper, buttons, old shoelaces, thread . . .
Not peasant stock but peasant—the real thing.

What stuff we farmed in our backyard!
Horseradish that my grandma stained beet-red—
Hot rouge for fish—her cosmos plants
With feathery-fine carrot leaves, and my
Poor vegetables, no first class restaurant's

Idea of France. "Your radishes are good,"
My sister said, who wouldn't touch the soil.
My mother wouldn't either. "Dirt, that's all."
Those afternoons of bridge and mah-jongg games,
Those tournaments! Click-click went forty nails

That stopped their racket for the candy dish.
"Coffee, girls?" came floating up the stairs.
Our house was "French Provincial." Chinese
mirrors
Warred against the provinces. The breakfast nook
Had a kind of style. But it wasn't ours.

I'd walk down to the bay and sit alone
And listen to the tide chew gum. There was
An airport on the other shore. Toy-like,
It blew toy moths into the air. At night,
We'd hear the distant thunder of New York.

Grandpa, forgive me. When you called for me
At school in a sudden rain or snow, I was
Ashamed that anyone would see your beard
Or hear you talk in broken English. You
Would bring a black umbrella, battle-scarred,

And walk me home beneath it through the lots,
Where seasonal wild roses took a spill

And blew their cups, and sumac bushes grew
Up from the sand, attached to secret springs,
As I was secretly attached to you.

Friday night. The Bible. The smell of soup,
Fresh bread in the oven, the mumbling from
The kitchen where my grandma said her prayers.
Reading the Bible, she kept one finger under
Every line she read. Alone, upstairs,

The timelessness of swamps came over me,
A perpetual passing of no time, it seemed,
Waiting for dinner, waiting to get up
From dinner, waiting, waiting all the time.
For what? For love, as longed-for as a trip

A shut-in never takes. It came to me.
But what Proust said is true: If you get
What you want in life, by the time you do,
You no longer want it. But that's another
Story, or stories, I should say, much too

Pointless to go into now. For what
Matters to me are those lifelong two
Transplanted figures in a suburb who
Loved me without saying, "I love you."
Grandpa, tonight, I think of you

Envoi:
Grandma, your bones lie out in Queens.
The black funeral parlor limousines
Just make it up the narrow aisles.
When flowers on your headstone turn to moss,
Russian cossack horses leap across
The stone, the stone parentheses of years.

THE LAST ONE
W. S. Merwin (b. 1927)

Well they'd made up their minds to be everywhere
  because why not.
Everywhere was theirs because they thought so.
They with two leaves they whom the birds despise.
In the middle of stones they made up their minds.
They started to cut.

Well they cut everything because why not.
Everything was theirs because they thought so.
It fell into its shadows and they took both away.
Some to have some for burning.

Well cutting everything they came to the water.
They came to the end of the day there was one
  left standing.
They would cut it tomorrow they went away.
The night gathered in the last branches.
The shadow of the night gathered in the shadow
  on the water.

The night and the shadow put on the same head.
And it said Now.

Well in the morning they cut the last one.
Like the others the last one fell into its shadow.
It fell into its shadow on the water.
They took it away its shadow stayed on the water.

Well they shrugged they started trying to get the
  shadow away.
They cut right to the ground the shadow stayed
  whole.
They laid boards on it the shadow came out on
  top.
They shone lights on it the shadow got blacker
  and clearer.
They exploded the water the shadow rocked.
They built a huge fire on the roots.
They sent up black smoke between the shadow
  and the sun.
The new shadow flowed without changing the
  old one.
They shrugged they went away to get stones.

They came back the shadow was growing.
They started setting up stones it was growing.
They looked the other way it went on growing.
They decided they would make a stone out of it.
They took stones to the water they poured them
  into the shadow.
They poured them in they poured them in the
  stones vanished.
The shadow was not filled it went on growing.
That was one day.

The next day was just the same it went on
  growing.
They did all the same things it was just the same.
They decided to take its water from under it.
They took away water they took it away the water
  went down.
The shadow stayed where it was before.
It went on growing it grew onto the land.
They started to scrape the shadow with machines.
When it touched the machines it stayed on them.
They started to beat the shadow with sticks.
Where it touched the sticks it stayed on them.
They started to beat the shadow with hands.
Where it touched the hands it stayed on them.
That was another day.

Well the next day started about the same it went
  on growing.
They pushed lights into the shadow.
Where the shadow got onto them they went out.
They began to stomp on the edge it got their feet.

And when it got their feet they fell down.
It got into the eyes the eyes went blind.

The ones that fell down it grew over and they
  vanished.
The ones that went blind and walked into it
  vanished.
The ones that could see and stood still
It swallowed their shadows.
Then it swallowed them too and they vanished.
Well the others ran.

The ones that were left went away to live if it
  would let them.
They went as far as they could.
The lucky ones with their shadows.

COLOR
Ned O'Gorman (b. 1929)

Blue is the stammerer's color.
Yellow is the color of the lion tamer.
Red, the signum of the clown.
White is the flag the hawk flies.
Orange, the kingdom's staff.
Green, the water bug's legs on the bank.
Black is the father's dream.
Rose, the candle-maker's, the purple the jeweler's
  colors.
Ochre, the potter's wrist.
Lapis for the seated knight.
Opal, the bear.
Burnt sienna, the plowman's hood.
Cobalt, the color of the horse asleep.

Peridot is the color of the steeple jack.
Olive is the wind over the steeple.
Wasp green, what the steeple jack sees sprout
  from the timber of his fall.

Dun is what the rain turns over in the grave.
Turquoise the color of a toad's death.

The garnet is the color of the trumpeter.

The color of blood is no color for in the ground
it runs like a bullet toward the root of wheat
and drives through snakes and seed
to rise up like breath in the simple grass.

THE APRICOT SEASON
Frank O'Hara (1926–1966)

There comes a moment in anxiety
when a run in the ceiling spreads
its ladders across the orange sunset
and the clock tower shows no monkeys.

Swooping through dazed eyes the blood
couples go by like years of sadness,
that sadness which signs itself "together"
and is not of the slit-skirt air or airs.

No distance appears at the head of the stairs
to provoke the next partner to move
and pull out his pencil, no lattices
break. Losing a brooch is like losing
a fleet. A fingernail's worth a loaf
of meat. The girl in the grey wool suit
turns on the bar stool and looks brightly
where the effeminate men in trench coats
pick their noses and suck their glasses' rims.
She can't keep her eyes off them nor can
they keep her eyes off them. It's all over

when it's over, and again a suited figure
stands in the spacious panes of twilight
waiting for the clock's lights to go on
so it will sweat its wrist band across the sky
downtown. His white shirt and black pants
are heaped with lavender pyramids, are crowded
like a view of Venice. There's the plaza where
St Mark was found and summoned to be someone
not much better in the world of painting.

The tires mourn onto the edge of the error
and as they vote they spread an odor of glass
over the brown drape which has dropped from,
like an evening handkerchief, the Milky Way,
so poorly conceived and so inconvenient. Let
him wave to the growing grass as he goes up, green
which cupped his open mouth ignorantly for years
while his tears burnt its roots and weakened him.

THE APPLICANT
Sylvia Plath (1932–1963)

First, are you our sort of person?
Do you wear
A glass eye, false teeth or a crutch,
A brace or a hook,
Rubber breasts or a rubber crotch,

Stitches to show something's missing? No, no?
  Then
How can we give you a thing?
Stop crying.
Open your hand.
Empty? Empty. Here is a hand

To fill it and willing
To bring teacups and roll away headaches
And do whatever you tell it.
Will you marry it?
It is guaranteed

To thumb shut your eyes at the end
And dissolve of sorrow.
We make new stock from the salt.
I notice you are stark naked.
How about this suit—

Black and stiff, but not a bad fit.
Will you marry it?
It is waterproof, shatterproof, proof
Against fire and bombs through the roof.
Believe me, they'll bury you in it.

Now your head, excuse me, is empty.
I have the ticket for that.
Come here, sweetie, out of the closet.
Well, what do you think of *that*?
Naked as paper to start

But in twenty-five years she'll be silver,
In fifty, gold.
A living doll, everywhere you look.
It can sew, it can cook,
It can talk, talk, talk.

It works, there is nothing wrong with it.
You have a hole, it's a poultice.
You have an eye, it's an image.
My boy, it's your last resort.
Will you marry it, marry it, **marry it.**

THE BLACK COCK

For Jim Hendrix, HooDoo from his natural born

Ishmael Reed (b. 1938)

He frightens all the witches and the dragons in
their lair
He cues the clear blue daylight and He gives the
night its dare
He flaps his wings for warning and He struts atop
a mare
for when He crows they quiver and when He
comes they flee

In His coal black plummage and His bright red
crown
and His golden beaked fury and His calculated
frown
in His webbed footed glory He sends Jehovah
down
for when He crows they quiver and when He
comes they flee

O they dance around the fire and they boil the
gall of wolves

and they sing their strange crude melodies and
play their
weirder tunes and the villagers close their windows
and the grave-
yard starts to heave and the cross wont help their
victims and
the screaming fills the night and the young girls
die with
open eyes and the skies are lavender light
but when He crows they quiver and when He
comes they flee

Well the sheriff is getting desperate as they go
their nature's way
killing cattle smothering infants slaughtering
those who block their way
and the countryside swarms with numbness as
their magic circle grows
but when He crows they tremble and when He
comes they flee

Posting hex-signs on their wagons simple worried
farmers pray
passing laws and faking justice only feed the
witches brew
violet stones are rendered helpless drunken priests
are helpless too
but when He crows they quiver and when He
comes they flee

We have seen them in their ritual we have
catalogued their crimes
we are weary of their torture but we cannot bring
them down
their ancient hoodoo enemy who does the work,
the trick,
strikes peril in their dead fiend's hearts and pecks
their flesh to quick
love Him feed Him He will never let you down
for when He crows they quiver and when He
comes they frown

LIVING IN SIN

Adrienne Rich (b. 1931)

She had thought the studio would keep itself;
no dust upon the furniture of love.
Half heresy, to wish the taps less vocal,
the panes relieved of grime. A plate of pears,
a piano with a Persian shawl, a cat
stalking the picturesque amusing mouse
had risen at his urging.
Not that at five each separate stair would writhe
under the milkman's tramp; that morning light
so coldly would delineate the scraps
of last night's cheese and three sepulchral bottles;

that on the kitchen shelf among the saucers
a pair of beetle-eyes would fix her own—
envoy from some black village in the mouldings
   . . .
Meanwhile, he, with a yawn,
sounded a dozen notes upon the keyboard,
declared it out of tune, shrugged at the mirror,
rubbed at his beard, went out for cigarettes;
while she, jeered by the minor demons,
pulled back the sheets and made the bed and
    found
a towel to dust the table-top,
and let the coffee-pot boil over on the stove.
By evening she was back in love again,
though not so wholly but throughout the night
she woke sometimes to feel the daylight coming
like a relentless milkman up the stairs.

THE DAYS : CYCLE
Hugh Seidman (b. 1940)

Black Saturday bubbles up &
Peace Eye Bookstore is closed.
In the park mammas & kids
pass time at the benches.
Flat-chested copper-haired girl
consoles her son. For a second
I think she's speaking to me.
No wedding ring. Kids & ex-husband
stare thru her face & dare me.
I go back to Avenue A.
Peace Eye is still shut tight.

A woman consults me concerning
her misfortune in FORTRAN.
Her long glazed fingernail
is polished pink & glides over
the 132 character per line
printer output. We examine
her logic & sources of error.
A scale factor is incorrect.
Her face registers the desire
I have awakened in her.
The jargon of acronyms & chance
encounters. Later we make it.

Boredom, revolutions, money,
& love. Human dignity.
The stars wheel overhead.
Newton believed them fixed
altho now we are wiser.
A woman put me down & Freud
smoked twenty cigars a day.
My friend spoke of prophets
& profit. The air conditioner
makes the only living sound.

If the flowers blacken & the sun
is unending? Delicate pastels & perfume.
Letters on the thinnest papers.
To the watcher: This is to inform you
I am alive & content amid the acreage
& private ruins. The mirrors
contrive to enamour me of distance.
The gold millimeter encircles my finger.
I have feared that pain would pass
& have known that endurance would robe me.
Perforce & perforce.

Her lingering finger smell &
Saturday afternoon I walk,
buy a cigar, & read in the bar.
We lie & the wind blows in
from the garden she asks of
& and if the maple & the oak
are beautiful in the fall.
The ageless stars that hold us
by the force which is our own.
The laws of God & those
who are beyond the forms.
Hilarious to see my face
in the face I try not to see.

FOR MY LOVER, RETURNING
TO HIS WIFE
Anne Sexton (1928–1974)

She is all there.
She was melted carefully down for you
and cast up from your childhood,
cast up from your one hundred favorite aggies.

She has always been there, my darling.
She is, in fact, exquisite.
Fireworks in the dull middle of February
and as real as a cast-iron pot.

Let's face it. I have been momentary.
A luxury. A bright red sloop in the harbor.
My hair rising like smoke from the car window.
Littleneck clams out of season.

She is more than that. She is your have to have,
has grown you your practical your tropical growth.
This is not an experiment. She is all harmony.
She sees to oars and oarlocks for the dinghy,

has placed wild flowers at the window at breakfast,
sat by the potter's wheel at midday,
set forth three children under the moon,
three cherubs drawn by Michelangelo,

done this with her legs spread out
in the terrible months in the chapel.
If you glance up, the children are there
like delicate balloons resting on the ceiling.

She has also carried each one down the hall
after supper, their heads privately bent,
two legs protesting, person to person,
her face flushed with song and their little sleep.

I give you back your heart.
I give you permission—

for the fuse inside her, throbbing
angrily in the dirt, for the bitch in her
and the burying of her wound—
for the burying of her small red wound alive—

for the pale flickering flare under her ribs,
for the drunken sailor who waits in her left pulse,
for the mother's knee, for the stockings,
for the garter belt, for the call—

the curious call
when you will burrow in arms and breasts
and tug at the orange ribbon in her hair
and answer the call, the curious call.

She is so naked and singular.
She is the sum of yourself and your dream.
Climb her like a monument, step after step.
She is solid.

As for me, I am a watercolor.
I wash off.

DOUBTING

Louis Simpson (b. 1923)

I remember the day I arrived.
In the dawn the land seemed clear
and green and mysterious.

I could see the children of Adam
walking among the haystacks;
then, over the bay, a million sparkling windows.

Make room, let me see too!
Let me see how the counters are served
and move with the crowd's excitement the way it
   goes.

Since then so much has changed;
as though Washington, Jefferson, Lincoln
were only money and we didn't have it.

As though the terrible saying of Toqueville
were true: 'There is nothing so sordid . . .
as the life of a man in the States.'

I would like to destroy myself, or failing that, my
   neighbors;
to run in the streets, shouting 'To the wall!'
I would like to kill a hundred, two hundred, a
   thousand.

I would like to march, to conquer foreign capitals.

And there's no end, it seems, to the wars of
   democracy.
What would Washington, what would Jefferson
   say
of the troops so heavily armed?

They would think they were Hessians,
and ride back into the hills
to find the people that they knew.

I remember another saying:
'It is not the earth, it is not America who is so
   great . . .'
but 'to form individuals.'

Every day the soul arrives,
and the light on the mental shore
is still as clear, and still it is mysterious.

I can see each tree distinctly.
I could almost reach out
and touch each house, and the hill blossoming
   with lilacs.

I myself am the union of these states,
offering liberty and equality to all.
I share the land equally, I support the arts,

I am developing backward areas.
I look on the negro as myself, I accuse myself
of sociopathic tendencies, I accuse my accusers.

I write encyclopedias and I revise the encyclopedias.
Inside myself there is a record-breaking shot-
   putter and a track team in training.

I send up rockets to the stars.

Then once more, suddenly, I'm depressed.
Seeming conscious, falling back,
I sway with the soul's convulsion the way it goes;

and learn to be patient with the soul,
breathe in, breathe out,
and to sit by the bed and watch.

WHAT WE SAID
W. D. Snodgrass (b. 1926)

Stunned in that first estrangement,
We went through the turning woods
Where inflamed leaves sick as words
Spun, wondering what the change meant.

Half gone, our road led onwards
By barbed wire, past the ravine
Where a lost couch, snarled in vines,
Spilled its soiled, gray innards

Into a garbage mound.
We came, then, to a yard
Where tarpaper, bottles and charred
Boards lay on the trampled ground.

This had been someone's lawn.
And, closing up like a wound,
The cluttered hole in the ground
A life has been built upon.

In the high grass, cars had been.
On the leafless branches, rags
And condoms fluttered like the flags
Of new orders moving in.

We talked of the last war, when
Houses, cathedral towns, shacks—
Whole continents went into wreckage.
What fools could do that again?

Ruin on every side—
We would set our loves in order,

Surely, we told each other.
Surely. That's what we said.

FOR THE BOY WHO WAS DODGER POINT LOOKOUT FIFTEEN YEARS AGO
Gary Snyder (b. 1930)

[*On a backpacking trip with my first wife in the Olympic mountains, having crossed over from the Dosewallips drainage, descended to and forded the Elwha and the Goldie, and climbed again to the high country. Hiking alone down the Elwha from Queets basin, these years later, brings it back.*]

The thin blue smoke of our campfire
down in the grassy, flowery,
heather meadow
two miles from your perch.
The snowmelt pond, and Alison,
half-stoopt bathing like
Swan Maiden, lovely naked,
ringed with Alpine fir and
gleaming snowy peaks. We
had come miles without trails,
you had been long alone.
We talked for half an hour up
there above the foaming creeks
and forest valleys, in our
world of snow and flowers.

I don't know where she is now;
I never asked your name.
In this burning, muddy, lying,
blood-drenched world
that quiet meeting in the mountains
cool and gentle as the muzzles of
three elk, helps keep me sane.

FROM A LITANY
Mark Strand (b. 1934)

There is an open field I lie down in a hole I once dug and I praise the sky.
I praise the clouds that are like lungs of light.
I praise the owl that wants to inhabit me and the hawk that does not.
I praise the mouse's fury, the wolf's consideration.
I praise the dog that lives in the household of people and shall never be one of them.
I praise the whale that lives under the cold blankets of salt.
I praise the formations of squid, the domes of meandra.
I praise the secrecy of doors, the openness of windows.
I praise the depth of closets.
I praise the wind, the rising generations of air.
I praise the trees on whose branches shall sit the Cock of Portugal and the Polish
     Cock.

I praise the palm trees of Rio and those that shall grow in London.
I praise the gardeners, the worms and the small plants that praise each other.
I praise the sweet berries of Georgetown, Maine and the song of the white-throated
    sparrow.
I praise the poets of Waverly Place and Eleventh Street, and the one whose bones
    turn to dark emeralds when he stands upright in the wind.
I praise the clocks for which I grow old in a day and young in a day.
I praise all manner of shade, that which I see and that which I do not.
I praise all roofs from the watery roof of the pond to the slate roof of the customs
    house.
I praise those who have made of their bodies final embassies of flesh.
I praise the failure of those with ambition, the authors of leaflets and notebooks of
    nothing.
I praise the moon for suffering men.
I praise the sun its tributes.
I praise the pain of revival and the bliss of decline.
I praise all for nothing because there is no price.
I praise myself for the way I have with a shovel and I praise the shovel.
I praise the motive of praise by which I shall be reborn.
I praise the morning whose sun is upon me.
I praise the evening whose son I am.

I LAY NEXT TO YOU ALL NIGHT, TRYING, AWAKE, TO UNDERSTAND THE WATERING PLACES OF THE MOON

Diane Wakoski (b. 1937)

I lay next to you
all night,
trying,
awake,
to understand the watering places
of the moon,
          how my own body
dry and restless
like rootless tumbleweed
moves through the night,
through my eyes,
staying awake in bed
while you sleep
allowing my presence
but not wanting to touch,
allowing my presence
in the way
the earth
tolerates the moon,
allowing its restless pull.

I lay next to you
all night,
trying,
awake,
to understand what dead moon
I am,
why I shine in the sky at all.

But it is a physical function
of presence.
The moon
never complains.
The moon knows
it shines
at night
moving relentlessly
awake
through the sky
while everyone else sleeps,
while you're away.
                  The metaphor fatigues me.
I am less patient from my sleepless night.
I could carry the moon
across this room,
across the lawn,
telling them to ignore the lack of love in their
    lives,
telling them to smile and walk past telescopes
photographing their dissatisfactions
like craters on the moon,
out through the wet morning streets
through this whole town
and make
references
that would make you
as impatient with my life
as I am.

          But my sharp tongue
gleams at me
out of its drawer,
a sharpened knife,
and reminds me of the people I've been chiding
for the past few weeks,

telling them to burn
like the sun,
telling them to name them and find
new landscapes,
while I lie awake
next to you
all night
trying
to understand why
the sun's rays leave me so hot and thirsty,
why I am lonely and chilly at night,
why I,
the avid astronomer,
allow myself to be confused
and look out of the wrong end of the telescope.

Forgive me
for my restlessness
and my expectations.
I am the moon. Diane.
Poets have speculated about me too long.
At last I am circled,
photographed,
and soon to be explored.
A dry dusty shell

of something that once lived.
My literary content
is a vanishing species,
like sea otters.
Forgive me if I dive into the desert every night
and call out for water.
Forgive me if I dive into the moon, myself,
and cannot escape the pull of your gravity.
Forgive me if I expect you to love me. I mistake
    you
for a poet.
I lay next to you
all night,
trying,
awake,
to understand the watering places
of the moon,
knowing there are no Li Pos left
to drunkenly fall into a river
attempting to hold its radiant face
all night.
My dry arms
try to gather
water.

Section 19

METRICS

19.1 General Remarks

The study of metrics seems to many people a deadly distraction from the enjoyment of poetry. But when we remember two facts, things begin to feel different. First, rhythm, as we have said in our introduction to poetry (sec. 11), is constant in all life, and its presence in poetry is simply an inevitable aspect of that fact; to be more specific, rhythm is an aspect of language, and poetry is a form of language. Second, rhythm, being an essential aspect of poetry, represents an aspect of its significance. The first of these statements is obvious. The

second, though it follows from the first, may not be obvious, and it concerns us, directly and indirectly, throughout this book.

Once we accept these two notions, we know that if we do not *really hear* the rhythm of a poem we cannot fully respond to it: we cannot feel or understand it.* And this leads to the notion that the study of metrics is simply a way of learning to *hear*.

It may be objected that a reader, without study, naturally hears the rhythm of a poem. In a limited way this is indeed true. As a parallel with music, it is true that a child naturally hears the sounds of a symphony.

---

* It may be worth stopping here to insist that feeling and understanding are, in a deep sense, aspects of the process of engaging a poem; each involves the other, and, ultimately, neither is achieved without the other.

But does a child hear the sounds of a symphony in their complex structural relations that endow it with its final significance as music? The inexperienced reader of poetry does hear the words of a poem and does hear something of its rhythm, but it can scarcely be held that he naturally hears the more or less complex relations as a continuing structure that is also in relation to all the other aspects of the poem.

We must grant, of course, that different people have different degrees of aptitude in such matters and that some, by the mere immersion in poetry (or in any of the arts), achieve a wonderful awareness of its nature. The great poet W. B. Yeats once confessed that he did not even know the names of the English metrical feet. But why should he? He had been immersed in poetry for decades; he had a wonderful natural ear and a passionate concern for poetry; and he, like many poets, composed out loud, letting a poem grow in terms of its sound.

Why, one may ask, can't a person who is interested in poetry, and has some natural sensitivity, simply immerse himself in poetry and bypass the forbidding study of metrics? Of course, he can—and furthermore, he must immerse himself, in some degree at least, if he really wants to enjoy poetry. But the study of metrics, taken in conjunction with immersion, provides a short cut. And for some readers, even interested and sensitive readers, it may provide more than a short cut; it may lead to awarenesses that mere immersion might never give.

"But how much study of metrics?" you ask. "Enough," we answer. Enough, that is, for any given moment. It would obviously be folly to settle down to master a handbook of metrics, with the notion that afterward one might begin to read poetry. But there is some point where one can profitably study metrical structure and acquire a vocabulary that will permit him to think about it systematically and to talk about it. But after that the study of metrics may become a gradually broadening and deepening process that is naturally associated with the reading of poetry.

In section 11, our general introduction to poetry, we have touched on rhythm and certain other elements of language as natural to common speech and grounded in our physical makeup. Now we may extend that idea and point out that in poetry, in the sense that we use the word here, such natural elements develop a special formality and a special intensification that lead to a special expressiveness. In this section we undertake to explore what is meant by that statement.

Let us begin with rhythm. The basic fact about rhythm is, as we have said, that it is a pattern of recurrence. There is, of course, a mechanical rhythm, as that of a metronome or a clock. On the other hand, there are vital rhythms that emerge more or less insistently from a context of variation, the rhythm we find in the beat of the waves of the sea or the pulse of the blood.

The rhythm we are concerned with in poetry is a rhythm emerging in a context of variation. Rhythm in English depends, as we shall see, upon more than one factor, but the basic factor is what is called *stress*. English is a *stressed language*—in contrast with certain other languages. By this is meant that in any group of syllables, from the single word of two syllables up to the most elaborate sentence, a certain syllable (or syllables, as the case may be) receives special emphasis. As a corollary, among the stressed syllables, some will receive more emphasis than others.

Considering individual words, we realize that every word of two syllables has a stress on one of them and that words of several syllables may have a secondary stress as well.* (In this book, main stresses are marked ′ and secondary stresses are marked ″.) We realize, too, that the placement of stresses is not arbitrary, but is determined by usage that is recorded in dictionaries:

alum	al- um
aluminum	al- um- i- num
category	cat- e- go- ry

---

* Some words of two syllables may have secondary stresses. For example: *midnight, hardhead*, and *headlong*.

Consider the following prose sentence:

>   /   /   //
> Out walking in the frozen swamp one
> /   //   /
> gray day, I lost my bearings.

We realize that the stresses (though literally each falls on a syllable) indicate the key words —and the key ideas—of the sentence. In such instances, the stresses depend on the meaning: in a prose sentence the stress is *rhetorical*. That the meaning is the basis of stress in a prose sentence is clearly demonstrated by the fact that the same group of words placed in sentences of different meanings may demand a different placement of stress.

For instance, consider this bit of dialogue:

> FIRST LADY: Whenever I go down-
> /   /   /
> town, I drop by for an ice cream soda at the
> /
> drugstore.

>   /
> SECOND LADY: Whenever I go down-
> /   /   /
> town, I drop by to see how poor old Mr.
> /
> Smith is getting along.

The second lady, we notice, shifts the stress to herself—the first *I* in her sentence—to insist on the flattering contrast to the first lady. She is emphasizing her virtue in visiting Mr. Smith instead of going to enjoy a soda.

So much for the factor of stress in determining the rhythm of prose sentences. If we turn to poetry, we find another and different principle involved in rhythm. This principle is called *meter*, and a metrical line is called a *verse*.*

A passage of verse, however, is more than arbitrarily lined-up prose. Let us line up the prose sentence spoken above by the First Lady:

> Whenever I go downtown I drop by
> For an ice cream soda at the drugstore.

It so happens that each line here has ten syllables, and at first glance, one might suppose these lines to be verse. But the stresses here are the same as in the original sentence, and do not make a pattern. We sense this fact immediately if we contrast the First Lady's lines with two that are in verse:

> Whenever Richard Cory went down town
> We people on the pavement looked at him.

These lines, like those above, are of ten syllables each, but we become immediately aware that there is a pattern in the distribution of the stresses (which in verse are called *accents*) in relation to the syllable count, five to each line. In other words, these lines are metrical.

EXERCISE

Turn back to "Richard Cory" (sec. 12), and read it aloud several times. Then mark the metrical accents in these lines. After you have proceeded a little further in your study of metrics, come back and check what you have done.

19.2 Meter: The General Consideration

The word *meter* means "a measure," and not infrequently we hear it said that a poem is written in a certain measure, the word *measure* being employed as a synonym for *meter*. But what, we ask, is measured? A line—a verse, as we have said before—is measured.

By what unit is a verse measured? By the *foot*. And for present purposes we may describe a foot as a unit composed of two or three syllables, one of which is accented

The metrical system to which we now refer is called *accentual syllabic*, and is standard for most English verse.† We may, for convenient reference, set up a summary of the types of foot and line as defined in this system.

FOOT. As we have just said, the foot is the unit of measure for verse, that is, it is the smallest combination of accented (/) and unaccented (‿) syllables occurring in verse. The regular recurrence of this arrangement of syllables basically determines the rhythm of a

---

* This discussion does not apply, of course, to what is called "free" verse, which is considered separately in subsection 19.13.

† There are other kinds of verse written in English—for instance, free verse—and there are, too, other theories of versification than that presented here.

verse. The five kinds of foot are iambs, anapests, trochees, dactyls, and spondees.

An *iamb* consists of one unaccented and
one accented syllable. A line of *iambic* feet
is:

Whenev- | er Rich- | ard Cor- | y came |
　1　　　　2　　　　3　　　　4

down town.
　5

An *anapest* consists of two unaccented
syllables and one accented syllable. A line of
anapestic feet is:

For I'm sick | at the heart, | and I fain |
　1　　　　　2　　　　　　3

wald lie down.
　4

A *trochee* consists of one accented and
one unaccented syllable. A line of *trochaic*
feet is:

Like a | rose em- | bowered.
　1　　　2　　　　3

A *dactyl* consists of one accented and
two unaccented syllables. A line of *dactylic*
feet is:

Where is my | lovely one, | where is my |
　1　　　　　2　　　　　3

loveliest?
　4

A *spondee* consists of two accented syllables. Some theorists hold that, strictly
speaking, the spondee does not exist in English, and certainly a *spondaic* line is hard to
find. But the term is, in any case, sometimes
useful to describe limited metrical situations.
The following line, from Milton's *Paradise
Lost*, is sometimes taken as spondaic in the
first three feet:

Rocks, caves, | lakes, fens, | bogs, dens, |
　1　　　　　2　　　　　3

and shades | of death.
　4　　　　　5

LINE. Meter as we have indicated, marks
off the basic rhythm of a poem by the verse
(the single line) It defines the *abstract pattern of the line*, giving a principle of regularity and order distinct from considerations
of meaning and feeling. (Exactly what is at
stake here will appear later.) According to
number of feet, lines may be defined as follows:

monometer—one foot

dimeter—two feet

trimeter—three feet

tetrameter—four feet

pentameter—five feet

hexameter—six feet

heptameter—seven feet

For a full description of the metrical structure
of a line, the kind of foot must also be indicated. For example:

iambic pentameter—five iambic feet

trochaic trimeter—three trochaic feet

Lines longer than five feet are difficult
to handle with grace and effectiveness. A line
is really a unit of attention, and must therefore be short enough for the reader to grasp
unconsciously the pattern as a unit of composition. The six-foot line is, however, not
too uncommon. The heptameter tends to
break up into two units, one of four and one
of three feet, so that it is not felt readily as a
unit in itself

In a broad, general way, we find two
basic rhythmic movements, *rising* and *falling*.
Iambic and anapestic lines are in rising meter,
trochaic and dactylic, in falling meter. But
other distinctions are possible. Different
rhythms (and therefore different meters) give
different effects and are often associated with
different ranges of feeling. On this matter of
the appropriateness of various meters for
various effects, the poet Coleridge offers a
clever little composition:

Trochee | trips from | long to | short,

From long | to long | in sol- | emn sort

Slow Spon- | dee stalks; | strong foot | yet ill
able
Ever to | come up with | Dactyl tri- | syllable.
Iam- | bics march | from short | to long:—
With a leap | and a bound | the swift An- |
apests throng.

To put the matter negatively, in the following lines from Shelley's "Death," the choice of meter would seem, at best, ill advised:

> Death is here and death is there,
> Death is busy everywhere.

But let us take some positive examples. "How They Brought the Good News from Ghent to Aix," by Robert Browning, is an account of a stirring ride on a mission of great urgency, and the rhythm in the following stanza is clearly that of a steadily galloping horse, with the pounding beat of the rhythm echoing the pounding beat of not one, but three, horses, as specified in the second line.

> I sprang to the stirrup, and Joris, and he;
> I galloped, Dirck galloped, we galloped all three;
> 'Good speed!' cried the watch, as the gate-bolts undrew;
> 'Speed!' echoed the wall to us galloping through;
> Behind shut the postern, the lights sank to rest,
> And into the midnight we galloped abreast.

EXERCISE

Scan the stanza (that is, mark the metrical feet and accents). The first foot of each line, except line 4, is an iamb:

I sprang

I gal-

'Good speed!'

'Speed!' ech-

Behind

And in-

But what of the other feet?

In the following stanza, from a poem entitled "Boadicea," by Tennyson, note that the meter, though somewhat less specifically than in Browning's poem, works to support the general effect of the subject. Boadicea was a queen of the Britons while the country was actually held by Roman garrisons; even so, she was regarded as an ally of Rome. On a pretext she was seized and flogged, and her daughters raped. The poem is, presumably, the speech by which she raised her countrymen to a bloody revolt against the Romans. It is described by Gilbert Highet as composed of "long racing trochaic lines, one two, one two, one two, kill them, kill them, kill them, kill them—which, instead of pausing at the end of each measure, dash off into a frenzy of excitements."

> Burst the gates and burn the palaces, break the
>   works of the statuary,
> Take the hoary Roman head and shatter it, hold
>   it abominable,
> Cut the Roman boy to pieces in his lust and
>   voluptuousness,
> Lash the maiden into swooning, me they lashed
>   and humiliated,
> Chop the breast off the mother, dash the brains of
>   the little one out,
> Up my Britons, on my chariot, on my chargers,
>   trample them under us.

EXERCISE

Scan the passage, being careful to observe Highet's comment on the metrical situation at the end of each line.

Tennyson's poem, like Browning's, represents the obvious kind of relation between rhythm and subject, something approaching the direct imitation of a rhythm specified in the subject. Such a situation is, however, rare in poetry. Certainly, the fact that there may occasionally be such relations between rhythm and subject does not automatically suggest that a given subject demands a certain meter. The relations of meter and subject are, in general, more subtle and complex, and a major concern of this book is to explore at least some of them. There may even occur ironic reversals of expectation regarding subject and meter, as in the first stanza of a famous poem by Emily Dickinson (sec. 18):

> Because I could not stop for Death—
> He kindly stopped for me—
> The Carriage held but just Ourselves—
> And Immortality.

We must observe, however, that the handling of the particular meter, as well as the particular meter itself, is involved here. Notice that the weak syllables of the iambics are unusually weak, thus making for a brisk, clipped pace, and that the same effect comes from the fact that in the last line all three accents are in the one word *Immortality*. (See subsection 19.5 for further comment on this poem.)

It is very easy to attribute an effect to a meter in itself that is, in fact, the result of handling of the meter or of other factors, and a good deal of our comment on particular poems from this point on will be in connection with such matters. For instance, it is often said that anapests give a rushing, bounding effect (see the stanza from "How They Brought the Good News," by Browning, and the last line of the quotation from Coleridge, just above). But the illustration that we gave for the definition of *anapest* is anything but rushing and bounding:

For I'm sick at the heart, and I fain wald lie down.

A WARNING FOR SCANSION. Here we should isolate and emphasize certain things that have already been said but must be held firmly in mind.

1. A metrical foot may or may not correspond to a word or words. In the quatrain just quoted from Emily Dickinson, the first word, *Because*, does coincide with an iambic foot, but the first foot of the second line is composed of one word and part of the next:

Hĕ kínd-. In the last line, the word *Immortality* is spread over three feet: Ănd Ím- | mŏrtal- | ĭty. This is a way of saying that the foot, like meter in general, is *abstract*.

2. Meter (and therefore scansion) is concerned with sound, not spelling. A dipthong is treated as if it were a single syllable (*howl,*

coil); but there are exceptions, not merely from word to word but from poet to poet. When in doubt about pronunciation, consult a good dictionary. But it must be remembered that over the years pronunciation of words may change; thus, in dealing with traditional poetry we cannot always be sure of our ground.

3. To determine the basic meter of a poem, the inspection of a line or two may not be enough. The whole poem should be investigated to determine what is basic and what is variation. Sometimes, for instance, we find stanzas with lines of different lengths, and sometimes lines with metrical complications that are completely atypical.

19.3 Metrical Variation

A line of verse represents a *metrical order*, but only a very inexperienced reader of poetry will praise a composition for metrical regularity as such. Here is an example of impeccable regularity:

> I put my hat upon my head
> And walked into the Strand;
> And there I met another man
> Whose hat was in his hand.

Indeed, the meter here is so impeccable—so emphatic—that it eats up the sense of language; the fact that the utterance itself is nonsense merely tends to isolate the jabber of the meter even more. The meter here determines a mechanical rhythm, like that of a clock or metronome, not a rhythm of vital speech. The relation of meter to the rhythm of speech is to be one of our basic concerns in this book, but for the moment let us simply distinguish certain types of variation in meter.

The most obvious kind of variation occurs when another type of foot is *substituted* for the type characteristic of a line (or poem). For example, in stanza 1 of "The Eagle" by Tennyson (sec. 13):

Hĕ clasps | thĕ crág | wĭth crook- | ĕd hánds;

Clóse tŏ | thĕ sún | ĭn lóne- | lў lánds,

Rínged wĭth | thĕ az- | ŭre wórld, | hĕ stánds.

If you scan the stanza you will find that the normal line is iambic tetrameter, but clearly the opening of lines 2 and 3 are not iambic. Both *Close* and *Ringed* must be accented, and so we have the *substitution* of a trochee for an iamb.

In theory, any type of foot may be substituted for another, but the substitution of the trochee for the iamb, as in the example just offered, and of the anapest for the iamb are most common. For examples of both such substitutions, examine the opening lines of Tennyson's "The Lotos-Easters" (sec. 13):

'Courage!' he said, and pointed toward the land,
'This mounting wave will roll us shoreward soon.'
In the afternoon they came unto a land
In which it seemed always afternoon.

The meter is prevailingly iambic pentameter, but line 1 opens with a trochaic substitution ('Courage!'), and line 3 with an anapestic substitution (In the aft-).

More violent and less common forms of substitution are those involving the *imperfect foot* and the *secondary accent*. For an extreme example of two imperfect feet in one line, let us examine the concluding lines of a short poem by Yeats.

THAT THE NIGHT COME

W. B. Yeats (1865–1939)

> She lived in storm and strife,
> Her soul had such desire
> For what proud death may bring
> That it could not endure
> The common good of life,   5
> But lived as 'twere a king
> That packed his marriage day
> With banneret and pennon,
> Trumpet and kettledrum,
> And the outrageous cannon,   10
> To bundle time away
> That the night come.

Lines 7 and 8 are in the basic meter of the poem, iambic trimeter. Line 9 opens with a trochaic substitution (*Trumpet*), as does line 10 (*And the*).* Line 11 is regular. The last line, however, has only four instead of the required six syllables, and these four syllables must accommodate three metrical accents. We find the following scansion, with two imperfect feet:

$$_\wedge \text{That} \mid \text{the night} \mid _\wedge \text{come.}$$

An imperfect foot occurs whenever an accented syllable lacks the normally accompanying unaccented syllable (or syllables). The deficiency, however, is compensated by the fact that our ear, once accustomed to the metrical pattern, assumes a time interval in place of the missing unaccented syllable. In marking the scansion in such a situation we use a caret ($_\wedge$) placed as above.

To take a more complicated example, let us examine the first stanza of Tennyson's "Break, Break, Break":

> Break, break, break,
>   On thy cold gray stones, O Sea!
> And I would that my tongue could utter
>   The thoughts that arise in me.

We recognize line 1 as trimeter, even before we read the rest of the stanza with its strongly marked anapests and iambs. Instinctively, too, before moving into the body of the poem, we have taken the pauses in line 1, which we scan as three imperfect feet:

$$_\wedge \text{Break,} \mid _\wedge \text{break,} \mid _\wedge \text{break,}$$

It may well be asked why we mark the first foot with the caret. The answer might be given that this is merely conventional, a way of recognizing the theory, we may say, of the line. But actually, once we sense the metrical nature of the line (and the poem), we sense, too—retroactively, as it were—that a syllable is missing.

---

* The preceding line, opening with the trochee *Trumpet,* tends to dictate this scansion. But see the discussion of the "annunciatory conjunction" in connection with *Paradise Lost* in subsection 19.4, Rhetorical Variation.

So, in the following lines from "A Leaf Treader" by Robert Frost (sec. 17), we mark the initial foot of the poem as imperfect:

I | have been tread- | ing on leaves | all day | until | I am au- | tumn-tired.

God knows | all the col- | or and form | of leaves | I have trod- | den on | and mired.

If asked why we do not take the initial foot as a trochee (*I have*), we reply that, although some feet are iambic, anapestic movement strongly dominates the first line, and, as we shall see later, the whole poem.

These lines from "A Leaf Treader" lead us naturally to the question of *secondary accents*. A reader may well feel that in line 1, in the fourth foot, the syllable (and word) *all* is very important, perhaps the most important in the line, and that the syllable *God* at the beginning of the next line presents a similar situation. Such a reader would be right. Not infrequently, by reason of the sense, strong accents do intrude themselves into an established metrical pattern and demand recognition. As we have already suggested in discussing the spondee, it would be possible to treat our examples here as comprising two accented syllables: *all day* and *God knows*. It is true that sometimes the weights of accents seem so nearly balanced that we cannot readily choose between them; but usually such situations are more or less isolated, and the prevailing meter tends to modify our feeling so that one accent does seem, however slightly, dominant. If we accept this line of reasoning, we may call the weaker accent *secondary* and indicate it as follows: *all day* and *God knows*.

Even if we take such an extreme example as that from Milton given to demonstrate the spondee (subsec. 19.2), the tendency, certainly in a context of iambic pentameter, will be to scan it as follows:

Rocks, caves, | lakes, fens, | bogs, dens, | and shades | of death.*

And here we may notice that the rime between the words *fens* and *dens*, which encourages emphasis on them, works against the simple spondee as a metrical interpretation. Furthermore, there are many instances in which an extra accent is certainly strong enough to demand recognition but not strong enough to balance the main accent; such situations cannot be read as spondees, though the effect may be said to be spondaic because of the heaviness and retardation. For instance, in this passage from Milton's sonnet "On the Late Massacre in Piedmont" (sec. 14):

Avenge, | O Lord, | thy slaugh- | tered saints, | whose bones Lie scat- | tered on | the Al- | pine moun- | tains cold.

Thus, far, in this subsection, we have been merely describing the metrical situations of imperfect feet and secondary accents. But let us pause to inspect, in a few examples, the effect of meaning and feeling—that is, the dramatic effect—of such variations.

Here is the whole of a poem we have earlier looked at in part:

BREAK, BREAK, BREAK

Alfred, Lord Tennyson (1809–1892)

Break, break, break,
  On thy cold gray stones, O Sea!
And I would that my tongue could utter
  The thoughts that arise in me.

O well for the fisherman's boy,   5
  That he shouts with his sister at play!
O well for the sailor lad,
  That he sings in his boat on the bay!

And the stately ships go on
  To their haven under the hill;   10

---

* This reading is not universally accepted.

> But O for the touch of a vanish'd hand,
>   And the sound of a voice that is still!
>
> Break, break, break,
>   At the foot of thy crags, O Sea!
> But the tender grace of a day that is dead   15
>   Will never come back to me.

The poem is clearly trimeter, and prevailingly anapestic, even though there are two lines composed of imperfect feet, and a number of secondary accents, which echo, as it were, the effect established in lines 1 and 13 of the heavy, monotonous beat of the surf at the base of the cliff. The whole poem, we may say, depends on the contrast between the vigorous, ongoing life of the world around, and the deadened, stoic melancholy of the speaker who looks back on his bereavement. This contrast is supported—and dramatized—by the contrast between the heavy retarded effect of lines 1 and 13, along with the secondary accents, and the energetic, rising rhythm of the anapests. We may add that the secondary accents occur in the iambs interspersed among the anapests, and that in some of such iambs it is very difficult to resolve the difference between the primary and the secondary accents. This, of course, emphasizes the sense of weight and retardation.

Thus far we have not remarked that secondary accents may well occur in feet other than iambic. In the following poem, however, secondary accents are employed in a prevailingly anapestic meter, and employed to brilliant poetic effect.

AH, SUN-FLOWER

William Blake (1757–1827)

> Ah, Sun-flower! weary of time,
>   Who countest the steps of the Sun,
> Seeking after that sweet golden clime
>   Where the traveller's journey is done;
>
> Where the Youth pined away with desire,   5
>   And the pale Virgin shrouded in snow,
> Arise from their graves and aspire
>   Where my Sun-flower wishes to go.

The poem concerns a world, or state of being, somehow beyond time, a realm of peace and fulfillment that all being yearns after. But earthly creatures are, like the sunflower, rooted in the world of time, and the tension of their existence is between the fact of this condition and the aspiration that they cherish. This thematic tension is reflected in the metrical variation of the poem, which is based on an anapestic line. We have earlier remarked that the characteristic effect of the anapest is swiftness; Coleridge, you remember, said that anapests moved "with a leap and a bound." That, however, is scarcely the effect here. In this poem Blake frequently weights the anapest (and the iamb too) with a secondary accent (on the first syllable of the anapest), and this metrical situation gives a rhythmic base for the tension of the theme. *It does not specify that theme, but it is supportively consistent with it.*

To document what we have said, let us scan the poem:

Ah, Sun- | flower! wea- | ry of time,
    Who count- | est the steps | of the Sun,
Seeking af- | ter that sweet | golden clime
    Where the trav- | eller's jour- | ney is done;

Where the Youth | pined away | with desire,   5
    And the pale | Virgin shroud- | ed in snow,
Arise | from their graves | and aspire
    Where my Sun- | flower wish- | es to go.

19.4 Rhetorical Variation

Meter, as we have said, is, in one sense, abstract. But in discussing secondary accents we have said that the *sense*, the meaning, of a line or passage may force an extra accent to be recognized. In other words, what would be a prose stress—a *rhetorical* stress—would violate the abstract metrical pattern we hold in our mind. We do not, in fact, ever hear the abstract pattern of meter, except from a metronome or clock. Language is infinitely various and fluid, and the actual rhythm we do hear in verse is never that of the meter as such. When we do hear something approximating the mere pattern of the meter—as in our quatrain about the man who took his hat into his hand—we get a mechanical jingle, and the effect is usually boring, comic, or ironic. What we hear in ordinary verse is something that results from an interplay of the metrical pattern we hold in mind and the rhetorical thrust of what is being said.

Let us take a sentence and try to chart the various degrees of rhetorical emphasis in the most obvious prose reading:

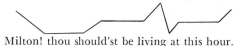

Milton! thou should'st be living at this hour.

But this sentence is not prose; it happens to be the first line of a famous sonnet by Wordsworth (sec. 14). If we scan it as a *strictly* metrical line we get:

Milton! | thou should'st | be liv- | ing at | this hour.*

We do not, however, hear the metrical line as such. What we hear is something like this:

Milton! thou should'st be living at this hour.

As the reading we have suggested implies, meter and rhetoric are not necessarily at loggerheads. They may coincide, or indeed the meter may suggest a particular and significant interpretation. For instance, in the line from Wordsworth just quoted, the meter insists on the accent on *should'st*, which in the ordinary prose reading is recessive. This accent suggests the urgency of the need for a man like Milton to set the times aright; and we see that the metrical accent on *at* supports the same idea. In this connection, it should be noticed that the word (and syllable) *this* in the last foot is charted at almost the same level as the preceding *at*, even though in the strict metrical sense it would be unaccented. But the sense suggests that *this* be accented to

give, again, the sense of urgency: "at this very hour."

Let us review what we have just said. In this particular line, the meter has emphasized *should'st* and *at* to dramatic effect. But it is the rhetoric that emphasizes *this*, to disrupt the strictly metrical pattern by the intrusion of a secondary accent. So here we see an example of one kind of interplay between meter and rhetoric. There are, however, innumerable shadings of such interplay between pattern and vital thrust—between, that is, meter and rhetoric.

Let us take another example of such interplay. The first line of Milton's *Paradise Lost* is scanned as follows:

Ŏf man's | fírst dis- | ŏbe- | dĭence and | thĕ fruit
Of that forbidden tree, whose mortal taste
Brought death into the world, and all our woe . . .

The passage is, on the whole, very regular iambic pentameter, but in the first line several features demand attention. The sense has intruded a secondary accent. A casual prose interpretation might make little of the word *first*, but here Milton speaks of the Fall of Man, the act from which all human history flows. Furthermore, the word *disobedience* is lifted and spread for our attention by the meter. It has five syllables, with a secondary verbal stress on *dis-*, but in ordinary pronunciation the main stress, on *-be-*, is so strong that the one on *dis-* is almost lost. But once the word is set in the metrical pattern the syllable *dis-* is insisted on, carrying a metrical accent, which, in fact, is forced into additional prominence by the presence of the secondary accent in the same foot. The word receives an entirely new force. The meter dramatizes the meaning.

In the fourth foot, with the metrical accent on the word *and*, we find another dramatization of meaning. Ordinarily, in prose, the conjunction *and* rarely receives emphasis. If the first line here were to be

---

* In an ordinary scansion we should indicate the last foot with a secondary accent: *thìs hóur*. But, as we have said, the secondary accent is actually a rhetorical intrusion, and so for present purposes we do not mark it.

charted as prose, by an uninstructed reader, one who knew nothing of the general context, he would probably come up with something like this:

Of man's first disobedience and the fruit

But sometimes the word *and* may receive strong emphasis, as what we may call the "annunciatory conjunction." For example, if Mrs. Smith and Mrs. Jones have had a spat, and you encounter Mrs. Jones at one of Mrs. Smith's parties, you may, in telling a friend about the event, say: "Mrs. Tupper was there, and Mr. Tupper, and Mrs. Huggins, and— would you believe it!—Mrs. Jones." You might omit the interjected exclamation "would you believe it!" and simply give the word *and* exaggerated emphasis, with, perhaps, a pause after it. This would amount to the same thing; it would be a signal for special attention to something very important coming up. And that is what the metrical accent on *and* does in Milton's line; the accent announces the terrible importance of Adam's fall, the introduction of death and all woe, soon to be specified as the consequence.*

We have been examining examples of the interplay of meter and rhetoric in which the meter has been rather clear. But there are poems in which the meter is very recessive, is obscure because variations are numerous, or is overwhelmed by rhetorical considerations. In such cases, the rhythm of meaning almost absorbs the meter.

Robert Frost's "The Wood-Pile" (sec. 17) is one such poem. It can be resolved into iambic pentameter, but the pull of natural, conversational rhythms is constantly present. The first three lines may be scanned as follows:

Out walk- | ing in | the froz- | en swamp | one
gray day,
I paused | and said, | 'I will | turn back | from
here†
ᴧNo, | I will go | on far- | ther—and we | shall
see.'

The first line is very much like prose. The prose stresses on *walk-* and *froz-* are very strong, and then there appears another prose stress on *grey*; but this is very little above the level of *swamp one* before and *day* just after, so that the second half of the line is very flattened. In the second line, if we scan mechanically we get a perfectly regular iambic line, with a metrical accent on *will*. But this would imply that the poet is announcing a considered decision, against odds, emphasizing *will*, and clearly this violates the natural sense. In the next line the decision, if it was one, is reversed, and then, since little is at stake, the poet says what amounts to "Oh, well, we'll see." Notice, too, how in lines 2 and 3 the two main prose stresses are very strong:

I paused and said, 'I will turn back from here.

No, I will go on farther—and we shall see.'

Let us take another passage from the same poem :

The wood | was gray | and the bark | was warp- |
ing off it.

---

* In subsection 19.3, Metrical Variation, in our discussion of "That the Night Come," by W. B. Yeats, we have treated such an annunciatory conjunction merely with reference to its metrical situation. Line 10 reads:

And the outrageous cannon

Here the cannon is the climactic item in a series—banneret, pennon, trumpet, kettledrum, and cannon —and demands emphasis.

† The line might—and perhaps should—be scanned as follows:

I paused | and said, | ᴧ'I | will turn back | from here.

‸And | the pile some- | what sunk- | en. Cle- |
  matis*
Had wound | strings round | and round | it like |
  a bundle.

Compare line 1 with this regularized version:

The wood | was grey, | the bark | was warp- |
ing off | it.

In the original the anapestic substitution in the third foot and the feminine ending of the line, coupled with the very strong prose stresses on *grey* and *warp-*, practically absorb the meter. Notice, too, how the weak syllable *it* at the end of line 1 tends to throw the metrical accent on *And* at the beginning of line 2, even though the *And* is not an annunciatory support here; and how, lacking this rhetorical support, the metrical accent on *And* feels indecisive. Furthermore, in this line the massing of secondary and primary accents in *pile somewhat sunk-* undercuts the meter. The same kind of massing in line 3, with the feminine ending, has the same effect.

By and large the effect of the interplay of metrical and rhetorical variation in "The Wood-Pile" is, as we have said, a sense of common speech, even conversation. But in the opening quatrain of one of John Donne's "Holy Sonnets" (sec. 16) the effect is very different, as the poet here calls upon God to cease his kind beseeching and shock him into an awareness of sin that he may be saved:

Batter | my heart, | three-per- | soned God; | for,
  you
As yet | but knock, | breathe, shine, | and seek |
  to mend;
That I | may rise, | and stand, | o'erthrow | me,
  and bend
Your force, | to break, | blow, burn | and make |
  me new.

Iambic pentameter is the basic meter here, but the number of strongly emphasized accents almost overwhelms that pattern, with an effect of violent, demanding excitement. In fact, some of the syllables that we have marked as secondary might be taken to require full weight, which would give spondees, as in line 2 with *breathe, shine,* and in line 4 with *blow, burn.* We find a somewhat different situation in the last foot of line 1. Here, the meter naturally demands a strong accent on the last syllable, not only because the prevailing pattern is iambic, but also because the end of a line normally constitutes an emphatic position that reinforces metrical accent. The rhetoric, however, demands an accent on *for,* which we have marked with a secondary accent. So with the last foot of line 4. In any case, what we find in every line is the juxtaposition of several strong accents (however marked) to create a sense of strain, explosive emphasis, and unresolved tension.

An even more dramatic example of the interplay of metrical and rhetorical variation appears in the following passage from *Paradise Lost,* at the climax of the battle between the faithful angels and the rebels against God led by the Archangel Lucifer. When the rebels are, apparently, on the point of victory, the Son of God appears and drives them to the precipitous verge of Heaven, over which they finally hurl themselves. Here the accents are marked, with no indication of division into feet:

The monstrous sight
Struck them with horror backward; but far worse

* It may well be argued that this line could be scanned:

And the pile | somewhat | ‸sunk- | en. Cle- | matis

In any case, the meter tends to be overwhelmed by the rhetorical pull toward:

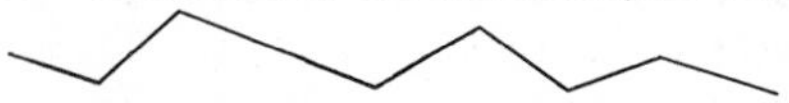

And the pile somewhat sunken. Clematis

Urged them behind; headlong themselves they threw

Down from the verge of heaven; eternal wrath

Burnt after them to the bottomless pit.

    We start, in line 1 (and the preceding context) with the general rising movement of iambic pentameter, but in lines 2, 3, and 4 a tension is created between the rising movement of the iambs and the falling movement of the trochees that open each line. One might take the second foot of line 2 as an iamb (*with hor-*), but the word *horror* picks up the falling movement of the first foot; and similarly, though the third foot might metrically be described as another iamb (*-ror back-*), the falling movement of the word *backward* (emphasized by the strong pause after it) pulls against the meter. The same general situation persists in lines 3 and 4, as we have said. But with line 5, after the first foot with its strong secondary accent,* the tension is released into the full, free movement of the final anapest. As the rebel angels struggle between a "horror" before them and one behind, until the struggle is resolved in their plunge over the precipice of Heaven— so the rhythm is a struggle between meter and rhetoric until it is released into a full, free movement.

    The examples above, from Donne and Milton, involve violent tensions, but we may remember that Blake's "Ah, Sunflower," is, in spite of numerous secondary accents, extremely musical. Or Frost's "The Wood-Pile," with its conversational tone. In other words, the interplay of meter and rhetoric may work significantly toward many different ends.

EXERCISE

The renowned passage below comes at the end of Shakespeare's tragedy *King Lear*. Here the old king holds in his arms the dead body of his beloved daughter Cordelia, who has just been hanged on the order of one of her evil sisters. The old man cries out in his grief:

And my poor fool† is hanged! No, no, no life!
Why should a dog, a horse, a rat, have life,
And thou no breath at all? Thou'lt come no more,
Never, never, never, never, never!

Scan this, and comment on the effect of the rhythm.

19.5 *Time: Word Length*

Meter, as we have said, is abstract. It is a measure of the line by the kind of foot and the count of feet, and though the nature of the content does affect the literal rhythm, it is not relevant to the meter as such. Metrical time is clearly a mathematical time, with each foot like every other, schematically considered; but the content of a verse line introduces a literal time that enters into the rhythm as actually experienced.

    That the length of words affects the time of rhythm can readily be seen if we examine a couple of lines (nonconsecutive) from Emily Dickinson's "Because I Could Not Stop for Death" (sec. 18). The meter is iambic, in alternating lines of tetrameter and trimeter. Consider the second line of the second stanza:

And I | had put | away

Here, with one exception, every word is monosyllabic; each accent falls on a different word; and no word is split between two feet. We therefore get a strongly marked pause between feet, and a sense of retardation in the line. Contrast this with the fourth line of the first stanza:

And Im- | mortal- | ity.

In ordinary speech (and as marked in dictionaries) the accentuation of the word *immor-*

---

    * The first foot might, in isolation, be taken with the secondary accent on *Burnt*, but the preceding lines have set up a disposition to the trochaic movement. In any case, the difficulty of resolving this foot is in itself significant.

    † In Elizabethan times a term of endearment

tality is as indicated here, with *-tal-* strongly stressed. Since all three metrical accents of the line fall in this single word, the word is "stretched" beyond its normal accentuation—that is, it is lifted up and emphasized.* But, at the same time—and here is our present point—we get the sense of a shorter rhythmic time than in the line that is largely monosyllabic.

To take a more extreme example of the principle, compare the two following ten-syllable lines:

1. Rocks, caves, lakes, fens, bogs, dens, and shades of death (Milton, *Paradise Lost*)

2. Between the worker and the millionaire (Schwartz, "For Rhoda")

We have already remarked on the effect of the clustering of secondary accents in the first example, but here we must also notice the heavy, retarding effect of the numerous word breaks, and, conversely, the absorption and relative diminution of accent in the second example, with a consequent acceleration of the line.

The interaction of short and long words in relation to the frame of the meter is one of the rhythmic resources of verse. This interaction does, of course, involve the relation of words of more than one syllable to the feet in a line; the basic question here is whether words are divided by feet and whether word ends coincide with foot ends. In so far, that is, as the structure of words coincides with the structure of feet, the rhetoric supports the meter, and conversely, insofar as they do not coincide, the rhetoric and the meter are in tension.

To take a simple instance, let us return to "Lord Randall" (sec. 12). As we shall see, ordinary accentual-syllabic scansion breaks down in the poem, but there is a prevailing anapestic movement, especially in the first two lines of each stanza. With the third line this rising rhythm is lost, and there is a portentous change of tone. For example, in stanza 1. As for scansion, we expect four stresses after the first two lines, in fact, the continuing pattern of four anapests. What we find is this:

I hae been | to the wild wood; | mother, make | my bed soon

Clearly, the second foot is a nameless anomaly, but what we are getting at is the fact that the rising rhythm has been profoundly altered. The phrase *wild wood* has a falling rhythm. Even if we take *mother make* as an anapest, the falling rhythm of *mother* modifies the movement, especially since the phrase *make my bed* tends to draw off the stress from *make* to *bed*. Furthermore, insofar as the phrasal stress on *bed* is felt, *soon* does not come with a rising rhythm—at the best with a delayed spondaic effect, perhaps even with a falling movement.

As for the last line of the stanza, we see how a more regular anapestic movement is modified by the fact that the falling movement of the words *weary* and *hunting* (each with the first syllable providing the accent of an anapest) tends to modify drastically the rising movement.

And we note, too, how in the last foot (if we scan in these terms) the tendency is toward a massing of accents, and the emphasis on *lie* in the phrase *lie down* (when not as a command) gives a falling movement:

For I'm wea- | ry with hunt- | ing, and fain | wald lie down.

It may be remarked here that the last line of the poem, a variant of the refrain of the earlier stanzas, though it exhibits no such word placement, has much the same effect.

For I'm sick | at the heart, | and I fain | wald lie down.

The general point here is that the placement of words of more than one syllable,

---

* This is a fine dramatic stroke in the poem, for the point here is that in the discovery of death is also the discovery of "Immortality"—the paradoxical discovery of the true and enduring life. The accentuation that lengthens the word—the slowing down, as it were—supports the impression of dawning wonderment and recognition.

which necessarily introduce their own movement, modifies the rhythm of a line; and further that phrasal units, even when composed on monosyllables, introduce their rhythms which in turn modify the rhythm of a line (*make my bed, lie down*).*

EXERCISES

1. Examine the relation of long and short words to the metrical structure of the following passages. Notice, too, the use of secondary accents in connection with the pace.

A. Here, in a passage from "Epistle to Dr. Arbuthnot" by Alexander Pope, the speaker calls on his servant John to shut the door against all the rimers and pretentious poetasters who intrude upon him, the great poet, and exploit him:

Shut, shut the door, good John! fatigued, I said,
Tie up the knocker, say I'm sick, I'm dead
The Dog Star rages! nay 'tis past a doubt,
All Bedlam, or Parnassus, is let out:
Fire in each eye, and papers in each hand,
They rave, recite, and madden round the land.

B. This is a stanza from Yeats's "Sailing to Byzantium":

An aged man is but a paltry thing,
A tattered coat upon a stick, unless
Soul clap its hands and sing, and louder sing
For every tatter in its mortal dress,
Nor is there singing school but studying
Monuments of its own magnificence;
And therefore I have sailed the seas and come
To the holy city of Byzantium.

C. These are the opening lines of Macbeth's soliloquy as he considers the murder of King Duncan:

If it were done when 'tis done, then 'twere well
It were done quickly: if the assassination
Could trammel up the consequence, and catch
With his surcease success; that but this blow
Might be the be-all and the end-all here,
But here upon this bank and shoal of time,
We'd jump the life to come.

2. From poems that you have already studied in this book, or in parts not yet assigned, select at least five examples in which the placement of words in relation to the metrical structure is significant. Explain your choices.

19.6 *Time: Pauses*

Pauses associated with larger rhetorical units play more obviously than word breaks against the abstract pattern of meter. In ordinary speech a sentence of any length naturally tends to break up into word groups, units of clause or phrase, with pauses of different value between—with or without punctuation. A sentence that enters verse retains this characteristic. The pauses may not fit the verse pause (the end of a line), but if a sense pause does fall there, the unity of the metrical pattern of the line is strengthened If it falls within a line, particularly within a foot, the rhythm of the metrical pattern is modified. The constantly shifting relation of pauses to metrical pattern gives variety and vitality to verse, and sometimes specific dramatic effects of the sort that we have discussed above.

Let us inspect first a passage in iambic pentameter from Hamlet's most famous soliloquy (sec. 15), a metrical line that, by reason of length, permits a great variety in the effect of pauses. Every line in this passage (as always in pentameter) is interrupted by at least one pause, however slight (called the *caesura*), and often by more than one. A line end—the completion of a metrical unit—inevitably suggests a pause, *even if it interrupts a rhetorical unit*; but here we indicate this minimal pause only if there is a rhetorical occasion for it. In general here, a light pause is marked by a bar (/), a heavy pause by a double bar (//), and the caesura by a bar (double or single as the case requires) plus an asterisk (*/):

To be, / or not to be: *// that / is the question: //
Whether 'tis nobler */ in the mind to suffer
The slings and arrows */ of outrageous fortune, /
Or to take arms */ against a sea of troubles, /
And by opposing / end them? *// To die: // to sleep; // 　　　　　　　　　　　　　　5
No more; *// and by a sleep / to say we end
The heart-ache */ and the thousand natural shocks
That flesh is heir to; *// 'tis a consummation /
Devoutly to be wished. *// To die, // to sleep; //

---

* In connection with this poem refer to the scansion of "Ah, Sun-flower," by Blake (subsec. 19.3).

To sleep: / perchance to dream: */ / ay, / there's
  the rub; / /   10
For / in that sleep of death */ what dreams may
  come /
When we have shuffled off */ this mortal coil, /
Must give us pause.

    In verse, there is no fixed place where
a pause is expected to fall. Furthermore, the
actual value of pauses certainly cannot be
regarded as merely light or heavy, and the
scale of possibilities is too subtle to indicate
schematically. When there is a definite pause
at the end of a line, the line is said to be *end-
stopped*, but here, too, we must recognize a
scaling of possibilities in the stop. When
there is no pause, that is, when the *sense
group* spills over into the next line, we have
what is called a *run-on line* or *enjambement*.
But there are shadowy instances. In the
soliloquy from *Hamlet,* all lines except 2, 6,
and 7 are marked as endstopped; but line 8
might be regarded as run-on.

    The general principle we have been dis-
cussing for iambic pentameter applies, of
course, to other verse; for, after all, the sentence, with its parts, is always present. For
example, the first stanza of "Death the
Leveler," by James Shirley (sec. 15):

The glories of our blood / and state
  Are shadows, / not substantial things; / /
There is no armour / against Fate; / /
  Death / lays his icy hand / on kings: / /
    Sceptre and Crown   5
      Must tumble down, /
And in the dust / be equal made
With the poor crookèd scythe / and spade.

As we have suggested above, there are often
borderline instances. Here, for instance, one
might argue that no pause should be marked
after the word *death* in line 4.

EXERCISES

1. Turn back to section 15 and mark the pauses
in the rest of Hamlet's soliloquy.
2. Turn back to section 15 and mark the pauses
in the last stanza of "Death the Leveler."
3. Turn back to section 12 and mark the pauses
in lines 1–10 of "The Star-Splitter," by Robert
Frost.
4. Return to Donne's sonnet "Batter My Heart"

(sec. 16) and mark caesuras and other pauses. How
do the pauses relate to other technical factors in
giving the characteristic effect here?

19.7 Syllabic Time

Like word length and pauses, syllabic time is
a factor in determining literal rhythm. Some
syllables literally require more time to pronounce than do others. As examples, take the
following lines:

    1. I sit with sad civility, I read (Pope,
       "Epistle to Dr. Arbuthnot")

    2. And wretches hang that jurymen may
       dine (Pope, *The Rape of the Lock*)

    3. Cool'd a long age in the deep-delved
       earth (Keats, "Ode to a Nightingale")

    4. Shield-breakings, and the clash of
       brands, the crash (Tennyson, "The
       Passing of Arthur")

    5. Rocks, caves, lakes, fens, bogs, dens,
       and shades of death (Milton, *Par-
       adise Lost*)

A little inspection of these five lines reveals
that the time that it takes to utter a word or
a line of verse is related to the presence of
"short" or "long" vowels.

    Thus the vowel in *sit* (and in each of the
four syllables of *civility*) in example 1 is felt as
short as compared with the vowel in *Shield-*
in example 4, which is felt as long. The vowel
in *sit* and the vowel in *Shield-* are both
formed in nearly the same place in the mouth,
with the tongue in about the same position.
A phonetician, using his technical language,
would say that both are "high," "front" vowels, but that the vowel in *sit* is "lax" and that
in *Shield-* is "tense." In English we distinguish carefully between the so-called short
(lax) *i* and the long (tense) *ee* sound, for the
difference affects meaning: *bit* and *beat, rill*
and *reel,* are heard as different words.

    Many other linguistic factors, however,
are involved in making syllables short or long.
High (palatal) vowels are, in general, felt as
short. (But as we have seen, the tense, high
vowel in *Shields-* is felt as long). Consonants
have much to do with the length of a syllable.
Nasals, such as *m* and *n;* "continuants," such
as *s, z, sh, f, v,* and *th;* and, in general, conson-

antal clusters, tend to make a syllable sound long even if its vowel is naturally short.*

Thus, in example 1 above, six of the ten vowels are short (high, front, and lax) and a seventh (*sad*) is also front and lax though formed a little lower than the vowel of *sit*. The line moves rapidly. In example 2, seven of the ten vowels also tend to be short. They are front and lax, though most of them are formed somewhat lower than short *i*. This line too reads rapidly.

Examples 3, 4, and 5, on the other hand, include a large number of long vowels, such as those in *cool'd, long, age, earth, Shield-breakings, clash, brands, crash, caves, lakes,* and *shades.* Moreover, the consonantal factor in these lines tends to lengthen further many of these syllables and even to confer a degree of length on a word like *death*, in spite of its short vowel.

We have quoted the five lines of poetry above in order to make a pointed contrast between lines that seem to move rapidly and those that seem long drawn-out. But with much verse, there is a constant fluctuation within the line, and the fluctuation makes for a sense of vitality, as in:

1. Tricking and stopping, sleepy and proud (Ransom, "Bells for John Whiteside's Daughter")

2. And quick sensations skip from vein to vein (Pope, *The Dunciad*)

The sense of vitality of verse is closely related to the constant change in the physical positioning of the lips and tongue—from high to low or front to back—in forming the vowels and consonants—that is, the flow of muscle and sensation in the process of shifting from one position to another. This factor fuses with the other factors we have been discussing; for poetry, in this as in other ways, insists on the unity of experience: mind and body, idea and emotion.

19.8 Rime

Rime is of course a correspondence in sound between the last accented syllables of two or more words (*glow–blow, address–repress*). If riming words end in one or more unaccented syllables, these must also correspond in sound (*potato–Plato, pattering–scattering*). Rime depends on *sound*, not spelling (*buy–why, write–fight*). Observe, however, that words that correspond in spelling often do not correspond in sound (*stone–gone*); this relationship is called *sight rime* or *eye rime*. In the strict sense, however, when we use the word *rime* we refer to correspondences of sound, and we generally mean one of three kinds: so-called masculine, feminine (or double), and triple rime.

In *masculine rime*, the accented syllables that are rimed are the last (*address–repress*).

In *feminine* or *double rime*, the accented syllables that are rimed are each followed by one unaccented syllable, and these unaccented syllables are not rimed but identical (*lightly–brightly*).

In *triple rime*, the accented syllables that are rimed are each followed by *two* unaccented syllables, and these unaccented syllables are identical (*slenderly–tenderly*). This type of rime, like double rime, is sometimes called feminine, because the accented syllables do not conclude the word.

Along the way, we have occasionally referred to alliteration, assonance, and consonance. Like rime, these qualities of language represent linkings by sound, and they are thus frequently discussed along with rime.

Alliteration is the identity of initial sounds—usually consonants—in a group of words (*forest, farmer, furtive*). Sometimes called *initial rime*, it is ordinarily used casually and informally to link elements of a line, or even a passage, but it may sometimes be used as a basic and continuing structural principle of a poem.

Assonance may be regarded as *interior rime*, for it involves the identity of interior vowel sounds without the identity of the following consonants, as in the line "Upon the lonely moated grange." Ordinarily, assonance is used for the internal linking of lines

---

* We do not pretend to give here an exhaustive account of all the phonetic factors that influence our sense of the relative length of a syllable. Least of all do we mean to imply that a poet has to have his head stuffed full of phonetic terms. A good ear and a feeling for the language will enable him—if he is a poet of God's making—to slow down or speed up a rhythm and in general give expressive variation to his verse.

or passages and for enriching sound effects, but it may be used instead of conventional rime at the ends of lines.

Consonance differs from rime in that the consonants of the related syllables are identical, though the vowels are different (*spilled–spelled, star–stir, gone–gun*). Consonance may be used for linking and enriching, but it is sometimes used in place of rime. A variant of such riming appears when the initial consonants do not correspond (*study–lady, blight–taught*); this is classed as *half rime, tangential rime,* or *slant rime.*

The most obvious function of rime is, of course, to act as a binder. It is, as we clearly see in rimed stanzas, a structural element, with or without the conjunction of meter; but even when rime is not used in a pattern, it may still provide some sort of a structural element. Later we shall discuss the stanza (subsec. 19.11) and the structural function of rime, but more immediately our concern will be with rime as what we may call a qualitative rather than a structural factor. This leads us to the question of musicality in verse.

19.9 Musicality

The variety and range of syllabic relations are, obviously, involved in what we ordinarily think of as the *musicality* of verse. Certainly, meter, too, has some connection with musicality, but taken by itself—and meter is, strictly speaking, "abstract," as we have insisted—it is not a determining factor here. Perhaps the best way to approach this question is to submit ourselves as fully as possible to a passage that is generally regarded as "musical," the first stanza of the "Choric Song" from Tennyson's "The Lotos-Eaters":

There is sweet music here that softer falls
Than petals from blown roses on the grass,
Or night-dews on still waters between walls
Of shadowy granite, in a gleaming pass;

Music that gentlier on the spirit lies,
Than tir'd eyelids upon tir'd eyes;
Music that brings sweet sleep down from the
blissful skies.
Here are cool mosses deep,
And thro' the moss the ivies creep,
And in the stream the long-leaved flowers weep,
And from the craggy ledge the poppy hangs in
sleep.

In reading this passage one of the first features that we notice is the prominence of vowel sounds. Such prominence is characteristic of highly musical verse; the vowels, that is, are the musical tones. Furthermore, if we notice the muscular motions involved in pronouncing these lines, we recognize the ease, the fluidity, of the transition from one sound—and one word—to the next. In musical verse the consonants—which are, we may say, mere "noise" in contrast to the musical vowels—are set in fluent relation so that we make a natural transition when a consonant ends one word and another begins the next. In such situations we have *euphonious* verse.*

Another factor that importantly enters into the musicality of verse is the repetition of sounds—in rime, alliteration, assonance, and consonance. Obviously such repetition may give a pattern beyond the metrical pattern. This appears most clearly in rime, but the other kinds of repetition may also work to establish the sounds basic to the "music" of a passage. For example, in the passage from Tennyson above, we observe that in the first two lines, with the long vowel sounds in *sweet, music, softer, blown,* and *roses,* and the droning nasal consonants of *m* and *n* in *music, then,* and *blown,* effects are established that are basic for the stanza and are more fully developed as it proceeds.

Let us inspect, too, the following lines from Keats's "Ode to a Nightingale" (sec. 17):

Perhaps the self-same song that found a path
Through the sad heart of Ruth, when, sick for
home,

---

* Examine the line "And a pond edged with grayish leaves" from Hardy's "Neutral Tones" (sec. 14). Here the transition from *pond* to *edged* forces a pause; otherwise we get something like the nonsensical *pondedged.* Again, there is a pause forced between *grayish* and *leaves* if we are not to produce something like *gra-y-shleaves.* Notice how different are the transitions in the passage from Tennyson. For instance, *sweet* to *music* and *softer* to *falls* in line 1 or *than* to *petals* and *blown* to *roses* in line 2. Difficult transitions make for *cacophony* instead of *euphony.* (We shall see, however, when we later consider the forced pause—in subsection 19.10, Onomatopoeia—that such forced pauses may sometimes be rhetorically appropriate and meaningly significant in particular contexts.)

She stood in tears amid the alien corn;
The same that oft-times hath
Charm'd magic casements, opening on the foam
Of perilous seas, in faery lands forlorn.

Here we notice the general resemblance of the vowels in *self-same, path, sad, She, tears, al-, same, hath, mag-, case-, per-, seas, faer-,* and *lands*; and, moreover, that of the vowels found in *song, home, corn, oft-, op-, on, foam,* and *-lorn.** We note also the run of nasals from the syllable *same* in the first line on to *-lorn* in the last line. But we should notice, also, the two runs of alliteration: of *f* in *foam, faery* and *for-* and of *l* in *-lous, lands,* and *-lorn.* These runs give a sense of unifying structure to the passage, not only by the mechanical fact of repetition, but by establishing the basic musical tone and temper.

Musicality of verse does, in itself, give a pleasure, but it is a fundamental error to hold that this particular kind of pleasure (which, in itself, is minimal) is the end of poetry. Poetry is not music. It involves a special use of language, and insofar as musicality is one of the potentials of language it *may* be involved in poetry. The basic fact is, however, that language has a primary function quite distinct from musicality, and musicality in poetry becomes important only insofar as, directly or indirectly, it is related to, or better, fused with, the primary function of language. By language we create symbols embodying events, ideas, and emotions, and in poetry, by means of a special refinement of language, we may fuse the musicality with other dimensions of meaning.

Some very powerful poetry, we know, is quite unmusical, and may even seem ugly to some readers. However, expressiveness, not musicality, is the end of poetry. Even in highly lyrical poetry some relation between content and musicality is crucial. The expressive heightening of language is of the essence of poetry, and musicality is but one of the ways of heightening language.

Sometimes musicality may even be the enemy of poetry. Let us take a stanza from Edgar Allan Poe's most famous poem, "The Raven":

Ah, distinctly I remember it was in the bleak December;
And each separate dying ember wrought its ghost upon the floor.
Eagerly I wished the morrow;—vainly I had sought to borrow
From my books surcease from sorrow — sorrow for the lost Lenore —
For the rare and radiant maiden whom the angels name Lenore —
     Nameless *here* forever more.

Do these very obvious sound effects, including the very assertive meter and emphatic riming, overwhelm the other aspects of the poem? The image presented is of a man, bereaved of his beloved, sitting late at night and trying to forget his grief in study, but does the "feel" of such a situation survive the demanding "musicality"? Does the effect seem, in the end, a little ludicrous?

Poe was enormously skillful in certain kinds of technique and could, on occasion, create very haunting effects, but it may be instructive to turn to another poem, which Poe is supposed to have plagiarized in "The Raven." Here is one stanza:

> As an egg, when broken never
> Can be mended, but must ever
> Be the same crushed egg forever—
> So shall this dark heart of mine!
> Which though broken is still breaking,
> And shall never more cease aching
> For the sleep which has no waking—
> For the sleep which now is thine!

This poem, "To Allegra Florence in Heaven," has the same subject, grief, as "The Raven." Though lined differently, it also has the same metrical and rime scheme and aims at the same kind of verbal richness. Because the author, Thomas Holly Chivers, had no shred of Poe's talent, and because of the absurdity of the image of the egg, we can see more readily the split between the verbal assertiveness—the mistaken musicality—and the content.

We do not mean to imply, however, that there is some easily established norm for the relation of musicality to other elements in poetry. There is more than one kind of poetry, and the virtues of de la Mare's

---

* The vowels in the first series are all "palatal" vowels, formed toward the front of the mouth; those of the second series are all "velar" vowels, formed toward the back of the mouth. Palatal or front vowels tend to have an "acute" quality; velars, a "grave" quality—deeper and more sonorous.

"Silver" (sec. 12), or Tennyson's "Choric Song" from "The Lotos-Eaters," part of which we have just quoted, are not the virtues of Shakespeare's Sonnet 55 (sec. 14) or Donne's "Batter My Heart" (sec. 16), with their tight logicality of structure and dramatic density of language. What we must do is to try to sensitize ourselves to poetry, taking it poem by poem, giving each poem a chance to prove itself to us.

EXERCISES

1. Which of the following passages do you think most musical? Do you find any that seem exaggeratedly so? Explain your choice of the two you regard as most musical, and your rejection of the two you regard as least satisfying in that respect.

A. Ah, sad and strange as in dark summer dawns
The earliest pipe of half-awakened birds
To dying ears, when unto dying eyes
The casement slowly grows a glimmering square;
So sad, so strange, the days that are no more.

B. The blackbird has fled to another retreat
Where the hazels afford him a screen from the heat,
And the scene where his melody charm'd me before,
Resounds with his sweet-flowing ditty no more.

C. Or they loved their life through and then went whither?
And were one to the end—but what end who knows?
Love as deep as the sea as a rose must wither,
As the rose-red seaweed that mocks the rose.
Shall the dead take thought for the dead to love them?
What love was ever as deep as a grave?
They are loveless now as the grass above them
Or the wave.

D.   When I dwell on my childhood,
I find one constant theme:
The pleasures of reality
Are surpassed by those of dream.

E. Haf owre, haf owre to Aberdour,
It's fiftie fadom deip,

And thair lies guid Sir Patrick Spens,
Wi the Scots lords at his feit.

F.   With deep affection,
And recollection
I often think of
Those Shandon bells,
Those sounds so wild would,
In the days of childhood,
Fling around my cradle
Their magic spells.

G. Lay your sleeping head, my love
Human on my faithless arm;
Time and fever burn away
Individual beauty from
Thoughtful children, and the grave
Proves the child ephemeral:
But in my arms till break of day,
Let the living creature lie,
Mortal, guilty, but to me
The entirely beautiful.

2. Account as best you can for the musicality of this poem by Robert Herrick, "Upon Julia's Voice":

So smooth, so sweet, so silvery is thy voice,
As, could they hear, the Damned would make no noise,
But listen to thee (walking in thy chamber)
Melting melodious words to Lutes of Amber.

3. Here are two versions of the same passage (the original by Keats). Which do your prefer? Why?

A. The tunes you hear are sweet, but the ones unheard
Are sweeter; therefore, you gentle pipes play on;
Not to the physical ear, but more endeared
To the deep heart, make a music of no tone.

B. Heard melodies are sweet, but those unheard
Are sweeter; therefore, ye soft pipes, play on;
Not to the sensual ear, but more endear'd
Pipe to the spirit ditties of no tone.

19.10 Onomatopoeia

In discussing musicality we have referred to the fact that an expressive relation of musicality to content is crucial, and we have discussed expressiveness in meter. As Alexander Pope puts it in "An Essay on Criticism," the "sound should seem an echo to the sense."

The simplest and most obvious example of the relation of sound to sense is to be found in certain words that echo the sounds that they denote—words such as *bang, boom, crack, clatter, hiss, bark, shriek, stutter, moan,* and *rattle.* Such imitative words are *onomatopoeic.* But *onomatopoeia*—the imitation of sense by sound—is not confined to single words. It may be extended to lines or even passages. Here is an often quoted example, from Tennyson's "Come Down, O Maid":

> The moan of doves in immemorial elms,
> And murmuring of innumerable bees.

We notice that only two words here, *moan* and *murmuring,* are in themselves onomatopoeic (three words, if *bees,* with its hint of literal buzzing, may be taken in this way); but the onomatopoeic effect is extended and, more importantly, intensified by repetition of sound in normally nononomatopoeic words, most obviously in *immemorial, elms,* and *innumerable,* but also in *doves,* with its vowel echoing but not repeating that of *moan.* We may note, too, how the sibilance at the end of *doves* and *elms* also reinforces the onomatopoeic force of *bees.*

Strictly speaking, the word *onomatopoeia* refers to the direct imitation of sound by the sound of a word, but it is not uncommonly extended to other kinds of imitation—for instance, to effects gained not by literal imitation but, perhaps, by association with sounds. Look, for instance, at this group of words: *gleam, glow, glint, gloss, glimmer, glister, glitter,* and *glare.** These all suggest light, as does *glory.* (The Latin *gloria,* from which it derives, means "a brightness, a shining.") What we find in common here is the initial consonantal *gl.* And we may even observe that the words *gloaming†* and *gloom* are also associated with the idea of light, though light by diminution. Another associational group of words—*groan, gloom, doom, woe,* and *forlorn*—which have a common association of sadness, is based on one of the series of "back" vowels (*oo* as in *moot, o* as in *note, aw* as in *awe*). With one exception, they end with a nasal consonant. The word *gloaming,* with the same structure, literally means "twilight," but *twilight* has acquired—at least in present usage—secondary association with dimness, sadness, and diminution.

Let us sort out some of the other "light" words listed above. Take *glint, glitter, glimmer,* and *glister.* These are words in which the characteristic vowel is the *i,* with its "short" quality of sound, a sound strongly associated with smallness, quickness, and sharpness, as found in *little, tittle, wink, thin, bit, slit, chink, sliver, twit, twitter, snip, twinkle, flicker, kitten.* So with this particular cluster of *gl-* words the idea of light is connected with smallness, quickness, sharpness.

Many other such groups exist. For example, the terminal *er* (not here as indicative of an agent, as in *kill-er*) and terminal *le* suggest a continuous and repetitive process: *twitter, twinkle, ripple, flicker, clatter, whisper, mutter, bubble* (verb), *shimmer, glitter, flutter, jangle.* And notice that with *glitter,* we have the combination of three associational groups: *gl* (light), *i* (small, quick, sharp), and *er* (continuing process).

In all discussion of such groups we must remember that we are definitely *not* dealing with a sort of fixed code. If the word *gloom* is sad and "gloomy," the word *groom* with the same vowel and nasal consonant, and a very similar initial sound, is not at all sad and gloomy—certainly not when it indicates a bridegroom. There are almost always negative cases in relation to such groups.

As another caution, one should remember that, though in special verbal groups there may well be a certain broad, general correlation between mood or stance of feeling and the muscular experience of a sound, we are eventually dealing, for all practical purposes, with *associations of meaning.* This fact is, of course, consistent with the way poetry works in general; in imagery and rhythm, for instance, it works by association, too.

EXERCISES

1. From the following list of words select those that are, strictly speaking, onomatopoeic. What

---

* All these words, as a matter of fact, derive from the same root in the hypothetical Indo-European language that is the remote ancestor of the language family to which English belongs. See *The American Heritage Dictionary,* which defines these words from the Indo-European root *ghel* 2, meaning "to shine."
† *Gloaming* also derives from the same primitive root as do *gleam* and *glow.*

other association groups can you select from the list?

chatter	whisper	bum
bingo	skimmer	whimper
chittering	skitter	slime
flame	rumble	slash
flute	ramble	slither
yammer	glare	slip
murmur	glaze	mutter
rattle	clatter	slide
bound	clash	slump
leap	mellow	slick
lissome	bosom	slobber
linger	bulge	slap
boulder	bump	slop
bold	bumptious	clap
flare	bountiful	rattle
flash	blunt	prattle

2. In the list below do you see any words that do not seem to belong to a basic group involved here? How would you describe the basis for such a group?

mare	stare	glare
blare	flare	dare
pair	fare	wear

3. In the following poem, "All Day I Hear," by James Joyce, comment on any verbal elements that may heighten meaning. Use all of your resources, including your knowledge of metrics.

All day I hear the noise of waters
    Making moan,
Sad as the sea-bird is, when going
    Forth alone
He hears the winds cry to the waters'
    Monotone.

The gray winds, the cold winds are blowing
    Where I go.
I hear the noise of many waters
    Far below.
All day, all night, I hear them flowing
    To and fro.

Let us turn to a more complicated example of the relation of sound and sense, a famous passage from Tennyson's "The Passing of Arthur." After King Arthur's disastrous last battle, one of his knights, Sir Bedivere, carries the wounded king, through a rugged, icy landscape, down to a lake where a magic barge, with three queens, receives him:

He [Sir Bedivere] heard the deep behind him and a cry
Before. His own thought drove him like a goad.
Dry clashed his harness in the icy caves
And barren chasms, and all to left and right
The bare black cliffs clanged round him, as he based
His feet on juts of slippery crag that rang
Sharp-smitten with the dint of armed heels—
And on a sudden, lo! the level lake,
And the long glories of the winter moon.

Here the language gives the feel of the straining effort of the knight clambering over the rocks with the burden of the wounded king. Some of the effects come from strictly onomatopoeic words (*clashed, clanged, rang*), which serve, we may say, as "governors" for the passage. But notice how the vowels of those words are seeded into the long run of related sounds in *barren, chasms, bare, black, crag.* A subsidiary run begins with *behind* and *cry* (which serve as governors) and continues with *Dry* and *icy.* Some readers will sense a third run with the repetition of the short *i* in *his* (twice), *in, him, cliffs, slippery, smitten, with, dint.* Notice, too, how the nasals (*m* and *n*), with their prolongation and resonance, support the echoing effect and also the frequent alliteration of the hard sound combinations with *c.*

As for the rhythm, the basic iambic pentameter is obviously modified by several factors. First, there is the great number of monosyllabic words. Second, there are a great number of secondary accents, with heavy spondaic effects Third, many of the transitions in *sound* are difficult, and *forced pauses* between words are common. In other words, we here have *cacophony* as opposed to euphony.

To illustrate, let us scan a few lines and also indicate forced pauses with an inverted caret (ˇ), and hard sounds* by underscoring:

The bāre black ˇcliffs clanged round him as he based

---

* "Hard" is admittedly a somewhat subjective characterization. What we have in mind are primarily monosyllables that begin and end with consonants *black* and *clanged.*

His feet on juts of slippery crag that rang

Sharp-smitten with the dint of armed heels

But another significant factor in the passage emerges in the last two lines: when Sir Bedivere has reached his goal, there is a "sudden" contrast in the phonic quality of the verse, with the fluent run of "lo! the level lake," marked by rather regular accentuation and the alliteration of the liquid *l* sound. The last line is particularly interesting. We may scan it:

And the long glories of the winter moon

It would be possible, of course, to take *And the long* as an anapest, but the scansion above seems more natural and effective with the "annunciatory" *and* introducing the summarizing and, it may be said, redemptive image of the glorious moon To return to the rhythm itself: As scanned above, there is only one anapest in the line, which ends with three quite regular iambs: *-ies of the winter moon.* But in this line the rhetorical thrust is so strong that the expected iambic accent on *of* is, for all practical purposes, annulled in this rhythm:

And the long glories of the winter moon

The rhythm here is based on three rhetorical accents (*And*, *glor-*, and *wint-*), and the tension with the meter gives it its characteristic vibrance and suggestiveness. The rhythm amounts to two wide anapestic swings, a release from the gnarled and tortuous movement of the preceding lines, with the swings stabilized in the muted iambs of the end. And note how the word *long* functions. It suggests the distance and openness offered by *level* in the preceding line, and with it, the sense of release: and this is supported by the sonorous (back) vowels in *long*, *glories*, and *moon*, and the three nasals, contrasted again, with the difficult verbal qualities preceding.

The relation between sound and sense in poetry (and in language in general) is infinitely various, complex, and subtle, and depends on many factors. Our discussion of metrics, rhetorical variations, onomatopoeia, and verse in general can give only a crude indication of the rich actuality of poetic language. If that is true, we may ask, why bother with such matters? Why not just hear the stuff and be done with it?

That question is reasonable. What we do want is to *hear*. But the conscious and systematic attempt to discriminate the elements of what we hear is the surest and quickest way to learn to *hear what is really there to be heard*. Poetry, as we have said, is not music, but it is like music in that, to learn to hear it, the best way is to give it studious attention. Not merely attention, but studious attention.

To go further, we are not merely hearing sounds, we must remind ourselves. We are hearing sounds that mean something, that mean a complex of things; the ultimate meaning inheres in the dramatic fusion of the sounds we hear with the complex of meanings, including our own emotional response. The phonic qualities of poetry are intimately interfused with tone, metaphor, symbolism, ideas, and all matters of human concern The interfusion is, in fact, a new meaning: the poem. That is, in an ultimate sense, a poem is coterminous with its meaning.

19.11 Stanza

The *stanza* is a pattern of lines that usually, though not necessarily, is repeated in a poem as a unit of composition. Traditional stanza patterns in English poetry are formed on the number of lines, the number and kind of metrical feet, and the *rime scheme*—which is usually described by repetition of letters, as a-b-a-b. Of the traditional stanzas that are more or less fixed in English, the most common are the couplet, the three-line stanza, the quatrain, the Spenserian stanza, and the sonnet.* The use of refrain is also a common feature of stanza construction.

---

* Many five- and six-line combinations appear in English poetry—see, for example, Housman's "Bredon Hill" (sec. 12), Waller's "Song" (sec. 14), and Tennyson's "The Bugle Song" (sec. 13)—but most of these have not been standardized and named. Similarly, unnamed stanzas of more than six lines are also often found.

COUPLET. The *couplet* consists of paired lines that may or may not be rimed. Whatever the length of the two lines, the term applies. The lines do not have to be of the same length.

The *heroic couplet* is composed of two rimed, iambic pentameter lines, such as these from Pope's "Windsor Forest":

See from the brake the whirring pheasant springs,
And mounts exultant on triumphant wings!

The *octosyllabic couplet* is composed of two rimed, iambic tetrameter lines, such as these from Marvell's "To His Coy Mistress";

Had we but world enough, and time,
This coyness, Lady, were no crime.

THREE-LINE STANZAS. Three kinds of stanza consisting of three lines are found in English poetry: the triplet, terza rima, and the tercet.

The *triplet* consists of three lines riming together; the length of the lines may vary. See, for example, Hardy's "The Convergence of the Twain" (sec. 16), which is made up of triplets riming a-a-a/b-b-b/c-c-c/ and so on.

Terza rima is a series of three-line stanzas linked by a rime scheme of a-b-a/ b-c-b/c-d-c/d-e-d/ and so on. Terza rima is not very common in English poetry. Shelley's "Ode to the West Wind" (sec. 13), the most famous English poem employing it, is in iambic pentameter, but the same rime scheme may be applied to lines of other length.

The *tercet* consists of three unrimed lines. In general usage the term refers to any stanza of three lines, whether rimed or not, but in technical usage it specifies a stanza of three unrimed lines.

QUATRAIN. The *quatrain* consists of four rimed or unrimed lines not necessarily of regular metrical length.

The *ballad stanza*, a popular form in English poetry, is a quatrain with alternating lines of iambic tetrameter and iambic trimeter, riming only in the second and fourth lines. Thus, its rime scheme is x-a-y-a. See, for example, "Sir Patrick Spens" (sec. 12).

The *heroic quatrain*, also very common, is iambic pentameter and rimes a-b-a-b. See, for example, Gray's "Elegy" (sec. 16).

SPENSERIAN STANZA. The *Spenserian stanza* is named for Edmund Spenser (1552?–1599), who invented it and made it famous in his *Faerie Queene*. It is composed of nine lines, of which the first eight are iambic pentameter and the ninth is iambic hexameter. (A line of iambic hexameter is sometimes called an *alexandrine*.) The rime scheme is a-b-a-b-b-c-b-c-c.

SONNET. The *sonnet* consists of fourteen lines and is one of the most important stanza forms in English poetry. There are several types, two of which are common.

The *Italian* or *legitimate sonnet* is composed of two parts: an *octet* of eight iambic pentameter lines riming a-b-b-a-a-b-b-a and a *sestet* of six lines riming usually c-d-c-d-c-d. In the sestet many variations of riming may occur.

The divisions of the sonnet are not purely artificial; they correspond to the treatment of the thought involved. It may be said that the octet presents the theme of the sonnet —a question, a situation, a reflection, a problem—and that the sestet gives a resolution or conclusion, sometimes merely an acceptance without further protests of the situation defined in the octet. There may or may not be a definite break between the octet and the sestet; when the break is not definite, not marked by a full pause, and when the thought spills over a little into the sestet, what is called *enjambement* occurs. See, for example, Milton's "On the Late Massacre in Piedmont" (sec. 14).

The *Shakespearian* or *English sonnet* is composed of three quatrains riming a-b-a-b-c-d-c-d-e-f-e-f and a couplet riming g-g. The lines are iambic pentameter.

The turn in thought mentioned above does not occur in the English sonnet with the regularity that appears in the legitimate sonnet. But the couplet almost always offers a kind of conclusion or resolution of the theme developed in the three preceding quatrains. Sometimes, however, that conclusion or resolution may begin earlier, in one of the quatrains; in such cases the psychological structure of the English sonnet approaches that of the legitimate.

REFRAIN. Technically, the *refrain* is distinguished from the stanza, although in some cases it may be a unit that can be called a stanza, such as a couplet. The refrain is a unit of poetic construction—usually a phrase or a single line—that is repeated at intervals throughout a poem. It is, of course, a device of emphasis, both for content and for structure. See, for example, "Edward," "Frankie and Johnny," or Kipling's "Danny Deever" (all, sec. 12).

Ordinarily, then, we think of a stanza as composed of metrical lines linked by rime into a fixed pattern. In fact, neither a metrical line nor a rime scheme is necessary to determine a stanza. Let us further explore the nature of stanza form by examining three diverse examples.

Here, from Tennyson's "The Lotos-Eaters" (sec. 13), is one of the best known stanza forms in English, the Spenserian:

1. They sat them down upon the yellow sand,   a
2. Between the sun and moon upon the shore;   b
3. And sweet it was to dream of Fatherland,   a
4. Of child, and wife, and slave; but evermore   b
5. Most weary seem'd the sea, weary the oar,   b
6. Weary the wandering fields of barren foam.   c
7. Then some one said, "We will return no more;"   b
8. And all at once they sang, "Our island home   c
9.   Is far beyond the wave; we will no longer roam."   c

The normal foot in this stanza is iambic, though there are some trochaic substitutions, notably in lines 5 and 6, and several normally unaccented syllables carry rather heavy secondary accents. Lines 1–8 are pentameter and line 9, the alexandrine, is hexameter.

The Spenserian stanza is, of course, bound by its fixed rime scheme of a-b-a-b-b-c-b-c-c. But here is a stanza without rime, from Karl Shapiro's "Hollywood" (sec. 16).

1. Alice and Cinderella are most real.
2. Here may the tourist, quite sincere at last,
3. Rest from his dream of travels. All is new,
4. No ruins claim his awe, and permanence,
5. Despised like customs, fails at every turn.
6.   Here where the eccentric thrives,
7. Laughter and love are leading industries.

Shapiro's stanza involves no pattern of rime, but it does depend on a metrical line: all

except line 6 are iambic pentameter. That line normally would be scanned as trimeter, but, to judge from parallels with all other stanzas of the poem, it should probably be taken as tetrameter, with both *here* and *where* constituting imperfect feet.

In the two stanzas above, both Tennyson and Shapiro were working in the tradition of the stanza as a unit having a fixed form, unlike John Berryman in his poem "Master of Beauty" (sec. 16), from which the following excerpt is drawn:

You have come to my rescue again & again
In my impassable, sometimes despairing years.
You have allowed my brilliant friends to destroy
   themselves
and I am still here, severely damaged, but functioning.
   tioning.

Unknowable, as I am unknown to my guinea pigs:
how can I 'love' you?
I only as far as gratitude & awe
confidently and absolutely go.

The only dependable factor determining a stanza in this whole poem is the line count. Four lines, without other considerations, constitute a stanza. And with some other modern poets, even the line count disappears, and the "stanza" is simply a unit of discourse, each one self-determining.

The stanza, of course, serves as structural unit in an obvious and mechanical way, as does the metrical line. But, like the metrical line, it may function in a much more complex and subtle fashion. We have seen, for instance, how meter may support meaning, or how it may pull against meaning, and how the interplay of stresses makes for expressive vibrance. In a like manner, the interplay of line and stanza generates a further principle of vibrance, and through both the fixed forms of line and stanza the discourse, with all its rhetorical considerations, must thread its way. Infinite variety is possible here, but we may at least look at a few samples.

To take one of the simplest instances, let us set side by side two samples of the heroic couplet. The first is from Pope's *Essay on Criticism*:

Hear how learned Greece her useful rules indites,
When to repress, and when indulge our flights:
High on Parnassus' top her sons she showed,
And pointed out those arduous paths they trod;
Held from afar, aloft, th' immortal prize,
And urged the rest by equal steps to rise.

Here the poet neatly packages each idea in a single couplet, an effective practice when a poet is dealing with a sequence of ideas rather than a sequence of actions or feelings.

The following passage is from Browning's "My Last Duchess" (sec. 12):

That's my last Duchess painted on the wall
Looking as if she were alive. I call
That piece a wonder, now: Frà Pandolf's hands
Worked busily a day, and there she stands.
Will't please you sit and look at her? I said
"Frà Pandolf" by design, for never read
Strangers like you that pictured countenance,
The depth and passion of its earnest glance,
But to myself they turned. . . .

Here the poet is creating one side of a conversation, a dramatic monologue. Notice how the rimes are almost lost in the run-on lines, and how the lines as units almost disappear in the sense of the movement of speech.

A somewhat different effect is involved in the following stanza from Longfellow's "Snowflakes" (sec. 15):

Out of the bosom of the Air,
    Out of the cloud-folds of her garment shaken,
Over the woodlands brown and bare,
    Over the harvest-fields forsaken
        Silent and soft and slow
        Descends the snow.

Let us observe, first, that the stanza falls into two structural sections: the first four lines are a quatrain riming a-b-a-b and the last two lines are a couplet riming c-c. How has the poet used this form in relation to the content?

In the quatrain the basic movement of the attention is downward. In lines 1 and 2 we are, as it were, looking upward into the sky, a vague, generalized sky that is merely implied rather than mentioned. In lines 3 and 4, our gaze moves down to the earth, specifically to the woodlands and fields, although the landscape is still generalized; it is "spread out," still not quite in focus. These four lines are, as we have said, bound together

by rime into a unit; and bound, we may add, by the long, swinging rhythm of the whole stanza. The shorter lines of the couplet shift the focus to a particular downward movement, the actual descent of snowflakes. Through the tighter rhythm of the couplet, the general qualities of snowflakes (silent, soft, slow) in line 5 lead finally to the last word of line 6, the first specific mention of the topic of the poem. The heavier stress that falls on the word *snow*—caused partly by the end stop—associates itself with the moment when falling flakes touch the earth. Thus, the focus of the content is gradually sharpened throughout the poem by the interplay of metrical line and stanza form until we reach the final word, *snow*, the climax, as it were, of the whole complicated rhythmic and syntactic structure.

If we turn to the whole poem, we see that Longfellow used the stanza form throughout in a similar way. The pattern of the downward movement of snowflakes and the pattern of moving from the general to the specific are repeated in all three stanzas, and each stanza, we see, is a single sentence. This is not to say, of course, that this particular stanza form is *necessarily* connected with such a subject or rhetorical structure or emotional effect. What we observe is, simply, that this poet used this stanza form in this way.

For two excellent examples of how a poet may achieve varying effects in the same stanza form, the student should turn back to "The Man He Killed" by Thomas Hardy (sec. 12) and to "Song" by Edmund Waller (sec. 14). After reading the exercises that follow Hardy's poem, the student should notice how in lines 8–16 the stanza form is almost lost—or at least given reduced emphasis—and that this occurs in the section where the reader gets the impression of the speaker puzzling over the moral problem that is the center of the poem. As for Waller's "Song," the student should carefully read the commentary on it and on Herrick's "To the Virgins, to Make Much of Time" (sec. 14).

The fundamental problem is always the interplay of the stanza with other factors, most obviously the line (and meter, if the line is metrical) and the rhetoric. Each case must be considered on its merits.

19.12 Stressed Meters

The accentual-syllabic type of meter that we have thus far been discussing came late into English, and was not firmly established until the latter part of the sixteenth century. The native meter had not involved the foot based on a count of syllables and an accent, but was an accentual meter—or, as it is more commonly called, a stressed meter.

The earliest form of the stressed meter, in Anglo-Saxon poetry, such as the epic *Beowulf*, involved, in fact, a combination of stress and alliteration in a line divided by a strong caesura. A line ordinarily exhibits four stresses with three syllables linked by alliteration; the unstressed syllables, which vary in number and placement, have no part in the definition of the meter. In the following lines, even if we cannot translate the Old English, we can detect the metrical pattern; here the stresses are marked and the alliteration is underscored:

> Waes sē grimma gæst   Grendel hāten
>
> mǣre mearcstape   sē þe mōras hēold*

What we have here is a line divided into halves, with two of the alliterated and stressed syllables in the first half, and the third of the alliterated and stressed syllables in the second half, plus a fourth stressed syllable, which, however, is not alliterated. The number of loose syllables, to repeat, is not relevant to the scansion. (This was the standard form, but there were variations from it.)

The following passage is from a modern adaptation, by Ezra Pound, of an Anglo-Saxon poem, "The Sea-Farer," in which we can see an approximation of the scheme:

> Chill its [frost's] chains are; chafing sighs
> Hew my heart round and hunger begot
> Mere-weary mood. Lest man know not
> That he on dry land loveliest liveth,
> List how I, care-wretched, on ice-cold sea,
> Weathered the winter, wretched outcast. . . .

And here is an original passage by another modern poet, W. H. Auden, using the same basic meter in a poem, "The Age of Anxiety," about a contemporary subject:

> . . . wondered our Bert, our
> Greenhouse gunner, forgot our answer,
> Then was not with us. We watched others
> Drop into death; dully we mourned each . . .

EXERCISE

Scan the excerpts by Pound and Auden.

Such exact adaptation of the Anglo-Saxon meter is relatively rare, but the native tradition of stressed meter, in various forms, from folk poetry such as ballads and nursery rimes on to sophisticated "literary" poetry, has vigorously flourished until the present day, usually without the alliterative pattern. Let us take some random samples.

Here, with the accents marked, are the two last stanzas from "Sir Patrick Spens" (sec. 12):

> O lang, lang may thair ladies stand,
>   Wi thair gold kems in their hair,
> Waiting for thair ain deir lords,
>   For they'll se thame na mair.
>
> Haf owre, haf owre to Aberdour,
>   It's fiftie fadom deip
> And thair lies guid Sir Patrick Spens,
>   Wi the Scots lords at his feit.

Here the stanza pattern of accents is 4, 3, 4, 3. We may, accordingly, be tempted to regard these stanzas as made up of alternate iambic tetrameter and iambic trimeter lines. The first three lines of the second stanza, for example, fit neatly into this pattern, but the occurrence of iambic feet in these lines is really no more than a happen-so, for if we

---

* D. H. Crawford has translated these lines thus:
    Grendel his name was—a savage spirit,
      great stalker of marches, he that held the moors.

look back at the previous stanza, scansion by an accentual syllabic system is, without ridiculous wrenching, impossible. (To support this notion, look at the whole poem.) The point is that what counts here is the number of stresses, without reference to the number or distribution of the weak syllables.

The following medieval poem (from the thirteenth century) has the same spirit as that we find in Shakespeare's "Spring" (sec. 15), and the same cuckoo:

CUCKOO SONG
Anonymous

Sumer is icumen[1] in,
Lhudè[2] sing cuccu;
Groweth sed[3] and bloweth med[4]
And springth the wudè[5] nu.[6]
Sing cuccu!　　　　　　　5
Awè[7] bleteth[8] after lomb,
Lhouth[9] after calvè cu;[10]
Belluc sterteth,[11] buckè verteth;[12]
Murie[13] sing cuccu.
Cuccu, cuccu,　　　　　　10
Wel singès thu, cuccu,
Ne swik[14] thu naver nu.
Sing cuccu nu! Sing cuccu!
Sing cuccu! Sing cuccu nu!

Here, as in the ballad above, but with a very different distribution of unaccented syllables and a different rhythm, the pattern is of 4, 3, 4, 3 stresses.

Now a nursery rime:

WHEN I WAS A LITTLE BOY
Anonymous

When I was a little boy I lived by myself,
And all the bread and cheese I got I laid upon a
shelf;
The rats and mice, they made such strife,
I had to go to London-town and buy me a wife.

The streets were so broad and the lanes were so
narrow,
I was forced to bring my wife home in a
wheelbarrow.
The wheelbarrow broke and my wife had a fall.
Farewell wheelbarrow, little wife and all.

This poem introduces a new metrical consideration. Here the basic rhythm is of four stresses; but there are not only unstressed syllables in the line but certain secondary stressed syllables as well (not marked above). These secondary stressed syllables are generally demanding, and set up a counterpoint rhythm.

EXERCISE

Reread "When I Was a Little Boy" until you feel that you have become thoroughly acquainted with the counterpoint rhythm. Then mark the secondary stresses.

More subtly controlled than "When I Was a Little Boy," but still modified by the native tradition is this passage from Ezra Pound's "Canto VII":

We also made ghostly visits, and the stair
That knew us, found us again on the turn of it,
Knocking at empty rooms, seeking for buried
beauty;
And the sun-tanned, gracious, and well-formed
fingers
Lift no latch of bent bronze, no Empire handle
Twists for the knocker's fall; no voice to answer.
A strange concierge in place of the gouty-footed.

The native tradition also emerges in

---

[1] come　[2] loudly　[3] seed　[4] meadow　[5] wood　[6] now　[7] ewe　[8] bleats　[9] lows　[10] cow　[11] leaps　[12] breaks wind
[13] merry　[14] stop

"Captain Carpenter" by John Crowe Ransom. Here is the first stanza:

Captain Carpenter mounted up one day

And rode straightway into a stranger rogue

That looked unchristian but be that as may

The Captain did not wait upon prologue.

In part at least, the peculiar rhythmical effect of Ransom's stanza comes from the fact that the sense of the native meter is now and then brought into collision with certain lines that may be scanned as accentual-syllabic. For instance, lines 2, 3, and 4, especially 3 and 4, could, taken in isolation, be treated as iambic pentameter. But the four-stress movement has been so firmly established that this is not acceptable, and we get a special tension, or vibration.

We can, as we have seen in some of the foregoing examples, isolate native meter, but there are often no clear-cut lines between it and mere modifications of standard accentual-syllabic practice. Also, as we shall soon see, native meter is one of the forces at work in free verse; that is, its presence makes for release from the accentual-syllabic mold.

Our point here, however, is not to make analyses of native meter as distinguished from accentual-syllabic meter. It is to sharpen our capacity to hear variation and subtleties in rhythm and to become aware of the rich complexities that may be introduced by the simultaneous operation of different principles. Indeed, the persistence of the native meter, however recessive it has been, sometimes for generations at a time, accounts for much of the richness of poetry written in English.

Let us look a little more closely at the structure of verse in the native tradition. As we have seen, it is readily apparent in a familiar source, nursery rimes. For example, consider the metrics of a rime almost everyone knows:

HICKORY, DICKORY, DOCK

Anonymous

Hickory, dickory, dock,
The mouse ran up the clock.
The clock struck one,
The mouse ran down,
Hickory, dickory, dock.

It would seem that lines 1, 2, and 5 could be taken as having three stresses, and lines 3 and 4 as having two. But let us try a preliminary scansion on a couple of stanzas of another famous rime:

Sing a song of sixpence,
A pocket full of rye;
Four-and-twenty blackbirds
Baked in a pie!

When the pie was opened
The birds began to sing;
Wasn't that a dainty dish
To set before the king?

Clearly, we have difficulty with lines 4 and 7. If we try another scheme, say of making lines 1, 3, 5, and 7 carry four stresses instead of three:

Sing a song of sixpence

we get in trouble in line 5, which would demand violent wrenching. Violent wrenchings do occur in verse, as we have seen, but here the solution is to recognize that another principle, that of folk practice, is operating. Here we have, simply, two basic stresses and one or two secondary stresses in each line:

Sing a song of sixpence,
A pocket full of rye;
Four-and-twenty blackbirds
Baked in a pie!

When the pie was opened
The birds began to sing;
Wasn't that a dainty dish
To set before the king?

EXERCISE

Scan "Hickory, Dickory, Dock" according to the pattern given above. The scansion may require some secondary stresses, as does that of "Sing a Song of Sixpence."

We can take into account the importance of secondary stresses in stress verse of the native tradition, such as "Sing a Song of Sixpence," by measuring its verse in terms of the *dipodic* foot. A *dipod* is a foot consisting of one primary stress and one secondary

stress: *a dáinty dísh, síxpénce,* and *bláckbírds* are all dipodic feet. The number of unstressed syllables is irrelevant to the definition: *a dainty dish* has two, but *sixpence* has none. Note further that a positive pause—a *metrical pause,* as we have seen in connection with the imperfect foot (subsec. 19.2)—may take the place of a secondary stress. For ex-

ample, in the line "Báked in a|píe∧" the single syllable *pie* functions as a dipodic foot: *viz.,* a primary stress plus a metrical pause.*

Dipodic verse occurs when there is a regular alternation between basic and secondary stresses. For example, consider this metrically sophisticated excerpt from "The Barrel-Organ," by Alfred Noyes:

Gó dówn to Kéw | in lílac-tíme, | in lílac-tíme, |

in lílac-tíme;

Gó dówn to Kéw | in lílac-tíme | (it ísn't fár |

from Lóndon!)——

And yóu shall wán- | der hánd in hánd | with

lóve in súm- | mer's wónderlánd;

Gó dówn to Kéw | in lílac-tíme | (it ísn't fár |

from Lóndon!)——

Notice that in lines 2 and 4 we find that the last foot, if taken as dipodic, is imperfect and that we tend to "feel," since we are accustomed to the pattern, another stress coming up—that is, we have here instances of a metrical pause. In general, we must remember that in dipodic verse, every foot need not be a dipod. For instance, from the same poem:

And thén the tróu- | badour begíns | to thríll |

the gólden | stréet.∧

Here the third foot is, taken in isolation, an iamb. We have, however, indicated with a carat that a metrical pause occurs, and in the "felt" rhythm compensates for the missing secondary accent. What is always important is the general rhythm, which determines the value of any pauses that occur.†

EXERCISES

1. Scan the following nursery rimes:

A.   I had a little husband,
      No bigger than my thumb;
   I put him in a pint-pot
      And there I bade him drum.
   I bought a little horse
      That galloped up and down;
   I bridled him, and saddled him
      And sent him out of town.
   I gave him some garters
      To garter up his hose,
   And a little silk handkerchief
      To wipe his pretty nose.

---

* Clearly, we get a spondaic effect in such a dipodic foot as *blackbirds,* but the dipod, we must remember, may have a number of unstressed syllables, as in *a dainty dish.* The distinction appears when we consider the *prevailing* rhythm of a poem.

† For a fuller discussion of dipodic verse, see Joseph Malof, *A Manual of English Meters* (Bloomington: Indiana Press, 1970). Incidentally, we may point out here that in Noyes's poem we can feel the old folk beat underlying the poem. We can, for instance, line it up as follows:

        Go down to Kew in lilac-time,
        In lilac-time, in lilac-time;
        Go down to Kew in lilac-time,
        (It isn't far from London!)

Here we notice that the two dipods in the first three lines are perfectly clear, but that the situation in

the last line is more complicated: (It ísn't fár from|Lóndon!)∧.

B.   Three blind mice!
     See how they run!
     They all ran after the farmer's wife,
     Who cut off their tails with the carving knife,
     Did you ever see such a sight in your life
       As three blind mice?

2. Turn back a few pages and renew your work on the exercise following the nursery rime "When I Was a Little Boy." In the light of our recent discussion, do you think it can be interpreted as dipodic verse?

19.13 Free Verse

What is *free verse* free from?

Clearly it is not free from rhythm, for even if it were merely prose set in irregular lengths of line (as some incompetent free verse winds up being), there would still be some rhythm—assuming, of course, that the prose was decent prose in the first place. Some free verse, too, is not free from meter as such; for instance, one may be able to scan any individual line, even though the length of line may constantly, and unpredictably, vary. But when no line can be expected to scan, and when length of line varies according to no predictable scheme, we still expect some principle of organization. To sum up, even though free verse may be free from meter or any predictable length of line, it still involves rhythm and *some* principle of organization.

In ordinary verse we work with certain expectations, though expectations may vary from instance to instance. In blank verse we expect unrimed iambic pentameter; in the sonnet we expect fourteen lines of rimed iambic pentameter; and in various traditional stanzas we expect various specific patterns of meter and length of line. The content of the poem—not only the meaning of the language but the emotional implications and the rhythms—is played off against the fixed structure, whatever that may, in a specific instance, be. This sense of interplay of content and a fixed structure is of the essence of traditional poetry, and some poets, even among the moderns—Robert Frost, for instance—maintain that free verse is a contradiction in terms: it can't be verse unless it has a measure, a fixed form. As Frost has put it, writing poetry without meter·is like playing tennis without a net. That is, Frost would have maintained that the fixed structures of traditional verse allow, in fact, a maximum of expressiveness.

Other poets, however, have preferred freedom from such fixed structures, and have written verse in nontraditional forms. The basic difference between traditional, or formal, verse and free verse is that in the first the verbal form is fixed, is predictable (as verse), and that the expressive development of the content must proceed within that form; while in the second, the verbal form is *emergent* with the development of the content. We are dealing then with two different conceptions of form; the fixed and the emergent.*

As we have observed, what we now think of as formal, traditional verse (the accentual-syllabic system) did not become dominant until well into the sixteenth century; and it had scarcely been perfected before tensions built up within the system, not merely as a continuing sense of the old stressed meter but in a more general loosening. It is reasonable to expect that the most notable tension of this latter sort occurred in verse written for the stage, for on the stage the pull of the natural rhythms of speech against formal verse would be most marked. The late verse of Shakespeare, along with that of other Jacobean† dramatists, gives the most useful examples.

---

* For convenience, we are making here a drastic and even misleading oversimplification, one that violates the basic assumptions of this book. In the final sense, the form of a poem, even of the most traditional type, is always emergent: the poem itself does not exist until the concrete, nonpredictable elements have fulfilled themselves in the context of the abstract and predictable (that is, meter, stanza, and so forth). When that occurs, the abstract predictable elements have, insofar as the poem is successful, entered into an expressive fusion with the concrete and nonpredictable to create an expressive form. But with this warning, the oversimplification above may be useful.

† Called Jacobean because their work falls in the period of the reign of James I. The best-known names are Webster, Beaumont, and Fletcher.

If we turn back to the soliloquies of Macbeth and Hamlet (sec. 15), we see examples of Shakespeare's blank verse written in his prime. Though varied and subtle in their rhythms, they clearly scan in the iambic pentameter of blank verse. But later, in *The Tempest* (act 2, scene 1), he was to write something quite different:

Whiles we stood here securing your repose,
Even now, we heard a hollow burst of bellowing
Like bulls, or rather lions: did't not wake you?

The first line is a standard blank-verse line of five feet, but the second line by ordinary scansion would give us six feet, with the last accent on the *-ing* of *bellowing*. The rhetorical thrust, however, is very strong toward this:

Éven nŏw, wĕ heárd ă hóllŏw búrst ŏf béllŏwĭng

or even this:

Ĕvĕn nŏw, wĕ heárd ă hŏllŏw búrst ŏf bĕllŏwĭng.

As for the third line, it can be scanned as iambic pentameter:

Líke búlls, ŏr ráthĕr líŏns: dĭd't nŏt wáke yŏu?

even though the pattern can scarcely survive the powerful rhetorical thrust toward a line in which only *bulls, li-*, and *wake* would be accented. As we know, there is always some degree of tension between meter and rhetoric, and in pentameter lines three (or sometimes two) of the accents are played against the five of the metrical pattern. But the matter of degree is important, and here the degree is so great that the lines move toward free verse.

EXERCISE

The following quotation from *The Tempest* (act 5, scene 1) is even more irregular. Scan it and comment on the tensions between meter and rhetorical thrust.

A solemn air and the best comforter
To an unsettled fancy cure thy brains,
Now useless, boil within thy skull! There stand,
For you are spell-stopp'd.
Holy Gonzalo, honorable man,
Mine eyes, ev'n sociable to the show of thine,
Fall fellowly drops. The charm dissolves apace . . .

Milton made even more positive departures from an iambic pentameter norm than did Shakespeare. In this passage from *Samson Agonistes*, the chorus sees the hero, blind and prisoner of the Philistines, brooding alone:

This, this is he; softly a while
Let us not break in upon him;
O change beyond report, thought, or belief!
See how he lies at random, carelessly diffus'd,
With languish'd head unpropt,   5
As one past hope, abandon'd
And by himself given over;
In slavish habit, ill-fitted weeds
O'er worn and soild;
Or do my eyes misrepresent? Can this be he,   10
That heroic, that renown'd
Irresistible Samson? who unarm'd
No strength of man, or fiercest wild beast could
    withstand;
Who tore the lion, as the lion tears the kid,
Ran on embattled armies clad in iron,   15
And weaponless himself,
Made arms ridiculous, useless the forgery
Of brazen shield and spear, the hammer'd
    cuirass,
Chalybean temper'd steel, and frock of mail
Adamantean proof. . . .   20

Some lines here are, with reasonable variation, standard blank verse (lines 1,* 3, 15, 17, 18, and 19), and some others, though not pentameter, can be regarded as iambic. But some, even in the light of Milton's rather violent and personal practice, simply cannot be felt in the pattern of blank verse. We recognize, of course, that when a pattern has been firmly established, our expectation creates a pull toward acceptance, but even so, the problem remains in some instances here. There are powerful, driving rhythms in this passage overriding the expectations of blank

* Line 1, for all its complication, can be accommodated as blank verse: the first two feet are defective, with compensatory pauses; the fourth foot can be read as a trochee (sóftlў) or as a defective foot with a compensatory pause, as indicated here; the fifth foot then becomes an anapest:

ˌThís, | ˌthís | ĭs hé; | ˌsóft- | lў ă whíle

verse, but at the same time, the rhythms are being played off against some shadow of blank verse.

If we jump from the seventeenth century to our own, we find free verse very similar to our samples from Shakespeare and Milton. For instance, this passage from T. S. Eliot's "Burnt Norton":

The inner freedom from the practical desire,
The release from action and suffering, release
    from the inner
And the outer compulsion, yet surrounded
By a grace of sense, a white light still and mov-
    ing. . . .

and this one from his "Gerontion":

Here I am, an old man in a dry month,
Being read to by a boy, waiting for rain.
I was neither at the hot gates
Nor fought in the warm rain
Nor knee deep in the salt marsh, heaving a cutlass,
Bitten by flies, fought.

and these opening stanzas of John Berryman's "Eleven Addresses to the Lord":

Master of beauty, craftsman of the snowflake,
    inimitable contriver,
endower of Earth so gorgeous & different from the
    boring Moon,
thank you for such as it is my gift.

I have made up a morning prayer to you
containing with precision everything that most
    matters.
'According to Thy will,' the thing begins.
It took me off & on two days. It does not aim at
    eloquence.

Modern free verse, however, finds its first great practitioner in Walt Whitman. If we look back to the long selection from "Song of Myself" (sec. 16), we see that the shadowy norm of blank verse is not generally to be felt. What Whitman's verse most reminds us of is, in fact, the King James Version of the Psalms and the Song of Solomon, which are translations of Hebrew poetry. Here the line unit is, generally speaking, a rhythmical unit determined by one or more natural syntactical groupings—a phrase, clause, or even a sentence. So it is with Whitman:

I speak the pass-word primeval, I give the sign
    of democracy,
By God! I will accept nothing which all cannot
    have their counterpart of on the same terms.
Through me many long dumb voices,
Voices of the interminable generations of
    prisoners and slaves,
Voices of the diseas'd and despairing and of
    thieves and dwarfs,   5
Voices of cycles of preparation and accretion,
And of the threads that connect the stars, and
    of wombs and of the father-stuff,
And of the rights of them the others are down
    upon,
Of the deform'd, trivial, flat, foolish, despised,
Fog in the air, beetles rolling balls of dung.   10
To behold the day-break!

Concerning traditional verse, we may say, speaking metaphorically, that the metrical form (and stanzaic form, if any) "contains" the material of the form, which develops within that form. In the same fashion, we may say that here the development of the material "contains" the development of the rhythms.*

To be specific, in this poem the most obvious form is the rhetorical one. In the first two lines, Whitman makes a statement about democracy and his general attitude in relation to it. In the next seven lines he develops his role as a "voice"—this by a series of parallel constructions, each of which determines a line unit. (Notice how the series of "Voices" in lines 4–6 slips into a set of parallels based on "And of.") In lines 10 and 11, in a very strange, and poetically exciting, juxtaposition of items Whitman sums up his feeling. As we have said, within this rhetorical structure the rhythms are developed, most obviously in the long, swinging series of parallels. But observe how in the last two lines, the rhythm draws in toward an effect approaching metrical control. We might scan it as follows:

Fog in the air, beetles rolling balls of dung.

To behold the day-break!

Since Whitman, there have been many developments and refinements of free verse. If we turn back to "The Gulls" by John

---

* When rhythm develops from rhetorical structure we have what is commonly referred to as *organic rhythm.* It grows with the "organism" of the poem.

Gould Fletcher or to "Pear Tree" by H.D. (both, sec. 13), we find something very different from Whitman's swinging, expanding rhythms, a verse aiming at more subtle and immediate effects. Such an impulse has been more fully exploited by Ezra Pound, as in this passage from his "Canto XVII":

    . . . cliff green-gray in the far,
    In the near, the gate-cliffs of amber,
    And the wave
            green clear and blue clear,
    And the cave salt-white, and glare-purple,   5
            cool, porphyry smooth,
            the rock sea-worn.
    No gull cry, no sound of porpoise,
    Sands as of malachite, and no cold there,
            the light not of the sun.   10

In this passage, Pound is working from the base of a trimeter line, as we clearly see if we reline the passage:

In the near, the gate-cliffs of amber,

And the wave green clear and blue clear,

And the cave salt-white, and glare-purple,
. . . .
No gull cry, no sound of porpoise

And we see, too, that lines 4, 6, and 7 are dimeter:

        green clear and blue clear
. . . .
        cool, porphyry smooth,
        the rock sea-worn.

Though here Pound uses something approximating a metrical base (as is not always his custom), he moves from the base, breaking his lines into smaller units, presumably to sharpen the reader's awareness, and even visual perception, of certain items—for instance, the wave (line 3) and the various details in lines 4, 6, and 7. The breaking of the basic line naturally modifies the overall rhythm.

Let us turn to an extreme instance of the repudiation of any hint of a metrical base.

NINE BIRDS

E. E. Cummings (1894–1962)

        nine birds(rising

        through a gold moment)climb:
        ing i

        -nto
        wintry
        twi-

        light
        (all together a
        manying
        one

        -ness)nine
        souls
        only alive with a single mys-

        tery(liftingly
        caught upon falling)silent!

        ly living the dying of glory

Not only is metrical base repudiated in this poem; the very unity of words is disowned. But the process of fracturing (which Cummings took far beyond anything in the practice of Pound or almost any other poet) is not merely whimsical. The fracturing sometimes creates a kind of rhythm of its own, an "organic" rhythm that grows out of, and dramatizes, the idea and emotion of the poem.

In this century, poets have experimented with many kinds of free verse, and some of the finest poetry of the age has emerged in that process. Here we have not undertaken to give samples of the various possibilities that have found success. We have merely presented some of the more obvious illustrations.

The main point that we have been trying to make is that the meaning of *free* in the term *free verse* is variable. In any of its senses and applications, however, it definitely does not mean to be free from the obligation of form. It means to be free to try to create a form different from that characteristic of traditional verse. It certainly does not mean a license to be arbitrary, whimsical, or slovenly. There is a moral to the fact that relatively few people have succeeded in writing really effective free verse, and almost all of those have had a keen awareness of the nature of traditional verse.

DRAMA

The dramatic method of presenting a fictional experience is to let the characters speak for themselves and perform their various actions before our eyes. If we sit down to read a play, we find the speeches of the various characters with directions telling what they do and, often, how they are to speak their lines, plus descriptions (usually fairly brief) of the stage setting, the background against which they perform.

Dramas are written to be performed, of course, and it may be argued that the appreciation of a play gained from reading it is not quite the same thing as that gained from seeing it on the stage. This is true. But the actors who through their performance help the dramatist to interpret his action for us had to shape their interpretation of the play from their reading of it. Good direction and excellent acting can indeed make the play richer and more meaningful for us. But if we have imagination, the lack of proper stage sets and the gestures and voices of the actors should not be a crippling handicap—that is, if we make, as we read, a serious effort to visualize the action and to hear the lines as spoken.

The dramatic mode, since it is merely one of the several modes possible to a writer, has certain strong points and certain limitations; that is, through drama the writer can present certain things more vividly and intensely than through other literary forms, but on the other hand, drama has certain limitations within which a skillful writer will develop his action. The great problem of the artist, of course, remains the same in drama as in poetry and fiction, the problem of creating for the reader an experience with intensity and meaning. The dramatic method of organizing his material is properly only one of a number of means to this end.

The general problems that the dramatist shares with writers of fiction have been dealt with in the early sections of this book. It is assumed that the reader will have worked through that material when he comes to read the plays that follow, and that he will bring to his reading of the verse plays whatever he has learned from his study of the preceding sections on poetry. Nevertheless, he might do well at this point to turn back to section 1 and recall what was said about such topics as conflict, action and plot, point of view, exposition, and so on. The dramatist shares with the writer of fiction the problem, to begin with a very general one, of building up characters in whom we can believe, and relating them to each other and to the story so that we can feel that their conduct is properly motivated and reveals its own logic. Common to both drama and fiction is the problem of choosing a beginning point, and the problem of exposition—the problem of telling the audience who the characters are and what the original situation is. There is the problem of movement, that of deciding how the various stages of the action are to be presented to the reader, and the problem of complicating the action. Above all, there is the general problem of making the play express the theme that the author wishes to present to his audience.

It ought to be observed that problems allowing a number of choices to the writer of fiction admit only one type of solution in drama. For example, the point of view for the dramatist is always the same—the objective view. We must see the events before our eyes, by and large, and, by and large, infer their meaning. Furthermore, for the dramatist, certain problems rather easily solved in fiction present additional complications.

Among the limitations of the dramatic form, four are especially notable: description, narrative progression, comment, and direct penetration into the character's mind.

Description

The author who depends a great deal upon descriptive writing for securing his effects will probably choose some other form, though some writers, Eugene O'Neill, for example, describe the setting in the detail usually reserved for prose fiction. Although we may often read such stage directions with enjoyment, they remain, however, *stage directions* —directions on how the stage is to be arranged for a performance or, if we are merely reading the play, hints to us of the setting—something, after all, outside the play proper.

Narrative Progression

The dramatist gives up his right to use a number of narrative methods at the disposal of the writer of fiction, particularly matters of scale and pace. He is forced to treat his narrative as a series of segments, that is to say, as individual scenes.* Such fictional devices as flashbacks or interior monologues, though not necessarily excluded, are made more difficult to achieve, and the general fluidity of movement possible to a novelist is constrained. Notice what happens when a movie is made out of a stage play: the camera usually enlarges the setting, gives some suggestion, or even a detailed presentation, of the world beyond the strictly limited scene. For instance, it may take us out of doors—though such added exterior shots often have little to do with the immediate business of the play. For example, the Ascot scene in *My Fair Lady*, the movie version of the musical based on *Pygmalion*, gives an effect impossible to the dramatic form—and an effect that might even be distracting in that medium.

Comment

The dramatist in writing a play gives up the right to comment on the characters and events. The interpretation otherwise given by such comment must be *implied* by the speeches of the various characters or by their actions. The dramatist gives up his identity, as it were, and speaks only in the person of his characters. But the dramatist's inability to comment on the action directly is not a disadvantage. Even in fiction, as we have seen in "Another Country," by Hemingway (sec.

8), the author's refusal to comment on action and the dependence on implication may give very powerful effects. The lack of direct comment does, of course, eliminate certain types of material from dramatic treatment.

Direct Penetration into the Character's Mind

Perhaps most important of all, the dramatist gives up his right to tell us directly what his characters are thinking or feeling. He limits himself to one means of revelation: the knowledge of their thoughts and feelings that we can draw from what they say and do. There are exceptions, of course: one character may confide in another character what he thinks and feels. And there is the soliloquy in which the character speaks aloud to himself, exposing thus directly to the audience his thoughts. But the confession and the soliloquy are the exception, not the rule. The essence of the dramatic method is to reveal to the audience the feelings of the character not explicitly but by implication—through his conversation with the other characters and through his behavior.

If the dramatist must limit himself rather severely by his methods, are there any corresponding compensations? Where does he really come into his own? What is the characteristic virtue of his method?

The most obvious effect of the dramatic form involves immediacy and intensity and such immediacy and intensity spring from the essential nature of drama. The basis of drama is conflict. In our discussions of fiction, we have noted the importance of conflict even in what are apparently rather slight stories, stories in which a careless reader might conclude that nothing really happens. See, for example, our discussions of the first two stories in this text: Williams's "The Use of Force" and Crane's "An Episode of War" (both, sec. 2). One is indeed justified in saying, "No conflict, no story." But if all fiction requires conflict, in drama the requirement is paramount. The most obvious feature of a good drama is the clash of wills as the various characters come into conflict with each other's purposes and desires. *Melodrama* (which

---

* Plays are usually also divided into *acts,* which may consist of one or more *scenes.* For the difference between an act and a scene, see the Glossary.

corresponds in drama to the crude action story in fiction) will clearly illustrate the point: the wicked villain attempts to win the beautiful heroine, and the handsome hero struggles in the face of tremendous odds to circumvent him, succeeding only in the nick of time. In tragedy, though problems of character and of human fate are explored, the struggle may be as violent as that of melodrama. Modes other than melodrama and tragedy may involve less violent conflict, but the dramatic effect—even in light comedy—derives, ultimately, from conflict.

This quality of tension and conflict is to be found to some degree in all forms of literature. Hence it is that one finds critics speaking of a "dramatic situation" or a "dramatic story" or even a "dramatic lyric." But obviously the dramatic form allows the author to display most directly and forcibly such a struggle, for he can represent it, not as one might meditate about it long after, but with all the immediacy, intensity, and vividness of the present. He can make the conflict develop and come to its climax, literally before our eyes. Obviously, one can put the most undramatic tale into the *form* of a play; but this is very different from using the dramatic form as the appropriate vehicle for dramatic material. And if we realize that struggle and conflict lie at the basis of drama, we shall better realize why the great tragedies deal so often with violence and why the great comedies move with such swiftness.

Tragedy and Comedy

The two great traditional classifications of drama are tragedy and comedy. It is true that we almost never find them in a pure state. Of the plays printed in this book, *Oedipus Rex* probably comes closest to an unmixed tragedy. The other plays contained in this text are, as we shall see, mixtures of tragedy and comedy. Yet the very fact that tragedy and comedy are best thought of as opposed limiting points, at the ends of a wide scale, renders them useful for our purposes here. It is important to define the concepts, for the terms are frequently very imprecisely used. What the newspapers often call a tragic death is simply a violent death through accident or misadventure. Moreover, more than the needs of drama are at stake in this matter of definition, for the terms are frequently applied to nondramatic forms of literature. Thus, we speak of a "comic story" or a "tragic ballad."

Tragedy and comedy, though at so many points antithetical, may involve actions that are fundamentally very much alike. Indeed, the same general circumstance may be interpreted as comedy or as tragedy. A commonplace example will illustrate. Suppose someone slips on a banana peeling and falls into a puddle of mud. We laugh. We laugh all the more if the person who slips into the puddle is dressed in evening clothes. The situation is incongruous. People dressed in evening clothes have nothing in common with mud puddles. If the person who slipped into the puddle wears patched overalls, the matter is not nearly so funny, perhaps because not nearly so incongruous.

But more than incongruity is involved in our reaction. Our sympathy or lack of sympathy for the person and the seriousness of the consequences his fall entails have a great deal to do with our reaction. The student might contemplate such variations as these. The person who slips is a feeble old man; or the person who slips, though not feeble but hearty and cocky, suffers a serious injury; or the person who slips is a little girl on crutches.

There are also instances in which we have conflicting and even alternating attitudes. The person who slips is a good friend of ours. He is wearing a fresh linen suit. We laugh when we see the surprise and chagrin on his face, but we happen to know that his errand is really an important one, and we are genuinely sorry for him. We tell him so, and hurry to render help, but as we observe him gazing woefully on his muddy suit, his plight becomes very funny again and once more we laugh until a realization that he has been put to really serious trouble silences our laughter.

If this particular example of an incongruous situation seems too farfetched to provide a useful illustration of the differences between tragedy and comedy, suppose we apply the same principles to a play.

Othello, Shakespeare's story of how a good man is so moved to jealousy by a scoundrel as to kill his wife whom he dearly loves, is surely an example of tragedy. Here a great and finely endowed man, who seems to deserve a good life, comes to a sorry and miserable end. The incongruity is shocking in the extreme, so shocking, in fact, that only a monster of heartlessness could consider the event funny.

Othello is not really a special case. Consider another Shakespearean tragedy, *Macbeth.* If we confine ourselves to the basic facts of the plot, Macbeth's story is that of a man duped. The Weird Sisters, playing upon his vanity and ambition, have taken him in. This is not to say, of course, that we apprehend Macbeth's downfall as comic. It is simply to say that if the "emotional lighting" of the play were altered, the tragic quality would disappear. Reconsider, at this point, our discussion of Thurber's story "The Catbird Seat" (sec. 6).

How might one go about changing *Othello* into a comedy? How might we change the "emotional lighting"? Let us consider the two principles mentioned earlier. First, we make our audience less sympathetic with Othello. He is somewhat pompous and a braggart after all. He does not really love his wife with a fine and sincere love. Second, we make the consequences of his fall less serious. He does not kill his wife. He is simply badly enough fooled to have his ego thoroughly deflated. But the essential situation we need not change. We need to change only our treatment of it in order to have a comedy. And as a matter of fact the jealous husband who is duped is one of the stock themes of comedy.

So much for the kinship of tragedy and comedy. They both spring from some fundamental incongruity—some shocking discrepancy between what we think should be and what has actually come to pass. And they become tragic or comic in proportion as we sympathize with the protagonist (the dominant character) or fail to sympathize—in proportion as the consequences are serious or trivial. It is not, then, the bare situation that makes a play tragic or comic—*it is largely the interpretation and treatment of the situation*

by the dramatist himself. To put matters a little differently, the difference between tragedy and comedy depends on what is stipulated as being at stake.

If the examples given make this point, they have served their purpose. One feature that the examples lack, however, is this: they do not take into account the fact that in drama the characters are not static but dynamic; they are not merely acted on or have things happen to them; they act. As we have already said, the essence of drama is a struggle, a conflict.

It is especially necessary to make this point in order to see the very important distinction that exists between *tragedy* and *pathos.* It is a distinction that critics who handle these terms do not make often enough, and yet it is a distinction vital to the whole conception of tragedy. The difference between the pathetic and the tragic may be stated briefly as follows: in the pathetic there is no emphasis on struggle. The protagonist suffers almost passively or struggles so ineffectually that the reader's attitude is one of pity. In the tragic action there is a definite emphasis on the struggle. The protagonist fights back, and fights so effectively, that at times the issue of the conflict seems in doubt. He may win, we feel, after all. True tragedy can never be, therefore, merely a matter of pity. The death of a child, for instance, may be pathetic; it cannot be tragic.

From this general principle a number of conclusions may be drawn.

1. The tragic character must not be spineless. Weaknesses he may have, as all human beings do, but he must be able to put up a fight.

2. The protagonist must not be set against overpowering odds. We must feel that he has a chance to win. For this reason, the struggle of a man against a disease, or a machine, or a completely overpowering environment is hardly tragic. The tragic character is not a worm ground under the heel of fate; he is a man. A modern critic, Bonamy Dobrée, defines tragedy as the trial of a man's individual strength.

3. The fate of the protagonist must flow from his character. One must not feel that it is merely the result of accident. The drama-

tist may make use of accident, but as we have observed in our study of fiction, there must be some "logic" of character. In Shakespeare's tragedies we often speak of the "tragic fault," the one grave defect of character responsible for the protagonist's ruin. Whether or not we call it the "tragic fault," the dramatist, no less than the writer of fiction, must relate the characters of his drama to the events that take place in the drama. To sum up, the tragic character is in some deep sense responsible for his own fate. For example, he cannot be merely a sick man. He cannot be an insane man. We must be able to recognize, in his plight, the problem of moral awareness.

4. The dramatist cannot afford to rest in mere character analysis. Tragedy often involves a great deal of psychological study, but it is always more than mere psychological analysis. For example, in *The Emperor Jones,* by Eugene O'Neill, the dramatist offers us a very interesting psychological case study of the distintegration of a man under certain powerful influences. The psychology involved is sound enough and the process of disintegration has its own interest. But we never imaginatively identify ourselves with the basic character. There is an air of clinical detachment. We stand aside, as it were, and consequently, *The Emperor Jones* is hardly a tragedy for us. Recall what was said in our discussion of Collier's story "Wet Saturday" (sec. 5). If the author had allowed us to feel much sympathy for the murdered man or for Mr. Sampson who, through Mr. Princey's machinations, is going to be convicted for a murder he didn't commit, the story would have a very different effect.

This identification of ourselves with the tragic protagonist so that he stands for universal human traits—stands indeed for us—brings us back to one of the primary differences between the tragic attitude and the comic—namely, our sympathy for the hero. If in tragedy we stand side by side with the protagonist, even with a protagonist like Macbeth, in comedy we stand in our sympathies with society itself, the laws or customs which the primary figure in the comedy is breaking. And this fact explains why many of the critics who have written on comedy in

the past have described the function of comedy as that of a social corrective. In comedy we make vivid and dramatic the breaking of the laws of society, but we stand by the laws, by the average good sense of mankind, and we laugh at the individual who breaks them—laugh at his clumsiness, or his egotism, or his ridiculous vanity. In tragedy, when the protagonist violates the principles on which human society is based, we find our interests sharply divided, for we realize the necessity of the principles but sympathize with the protagonist. In tragedy, then, the defeat of the protagonist produces tragic irony; in comedy, the defeat of the protagonist provokes us to satiric mirth.

To set off tragedy and comedy in such neat antithetical fashion is, of course, to oversimplify matters. We began this discussion of tragedy and comedy by pointing out that we meant to use these terms as opposed end points on a scale, and that few, if any, actual plays were absolutely one or the other. Shaw's *Pygmalion* and his *Saint Joan* will illustrate. *Pygmalion* is basically a comedy, but it is a very thoughtful comedy, with elements of seriousness and pathos. *Saint Joan,* most readers would say, is a tragedy, and yet it is filled with comic episodes and witty criticisms of society, past and present.

Or consider some particular dramatic characters. Shakespeare's Falstaff, for example, is a comic character so very human and in his own way so magnificent, and we sympathize with him so much that our laughter in his case is anything but satiric. Moreover, much of the time the satire is double-edged. We laugh not merely at Falstaff as he breaks the conventions of society; we often laugh with him at the conventions of society. Furthermore, we are moved to a feeling of pathos at his fall—so close he stands to the great figures of tragedy.

But what has been said is sufficiently true to indicate that in comedy, a vivid sense of the laws, the conventions, the rules of conduct in a society, is present. It is no accident, therefore, that the most brilliant comedy has usually come out of an urbane, sophisticated society like that of the Restoration period in England. Nor is it an accident, in view of what we have said about the relative lack of sympathy with the protagonist in comedy, that comedy is usually thought of as a more intellectual, less emotional mode than is tragedy. In the main this is true, subject always of course to the reservations any student of literature must be prepared to make: the constant realization that definitions and schemes of literary modes are only *tools* to help the reader in exploring literature and are not exact blueprints of literature itself. And we must remember that tragedy and comedy are ways of looking at life—ways of interpreting it.

We have pointed out earlier that the special virtue of the dramatic method is that it allows the author to throw conflict into very sharp focus, and have commented on some of the ways in which this fact influences the various aspects of drama. One further general aspect of the dramatic method should be mentioned. The emphasis on conflict in drama tends to force the dramatist to bring us to the scene when the problem is well advanced and near its culmination in *direct* conflict. Since he is interested in the actual conflict, he tends to open his play just early enough before the actual clash to allow time for the exposition of the characters, the primary situation of the characters, and the nature of the problem. This tendency toward compression may account for much of the discussion of the *unities of time and place* (see Glossary) that is frequently found in

criticism of drama. Problems *are* settled and decisions *are* made in a particular place and at a particular time, and if we take up the action near enough to its climax, the action of the play will *tend* to occur in a particular place and within a short time. This much truth resides, then, in the doctrine of the unities, and only this much. There is obviously nothing sacrosanct about observing the unity of place or of time as such.

To state that dramatic plots tend toward a high degree of unity and compression is not to say, however, that there are not many exceptions. Furthermore, it is not to say that there may be no development of character in drama, or that a dramatist, like Shakespeare, for example, may not often give us glimpses of characters over a period of months and even years. Moreover, whereas dramatic plots do tend to be relatively tightly unified, the plots of some plays are very complex, sometimes having in addition to the main plot a *subplot,* a secondary plot which is linked to the main action. But the tendency of drama is toward compression, and even Shakespeare's plays which seem most to violate this tendency give an effect of far greater compression than a narrative treatment of the same actions would give. *Oedipus Rex,* which represents a rather highly unified and compact plot, is typical of the dramatic method of organization in that it represents this tendency toward compression.

Section 21

EIGHT PLAYS

OEDIPUS REX
Sophocles (496?–406 B.C.)

An English Version by Dudley Fitts and Robert Fitzgerald

Characters

OEDIPUS	TEIRESIAS	SHEPHERD OF LAIOS
A PRIEST	IOCASTE	SECOND MESSENGER
CREON	MESSENGER	CHORUS OF THEBAN ELDERS

SCENE: *Before the palace of Oedipus, King of Thebes. A central door and two lateral doors open onto a platform which runs the length* *of the façade. On the platform, right and left, are altars; and three steps lead down into the "orchestra," or chorus-ground. At the be-*

*ginning of the action these steps are crowded
by suppliants who have brought branches and
chaplets of olive leaves and who lie in various
attitudes of despair.* OEDIPUS *enters.*

Prologue
OEDIPUS.
My children, generations of the living
In the line of Kadmos, nursed at his ancient
    hearth:
Why have you strewn yourselves before these
    altars
In supplication, with your boughs and
    garlands?
The breath of incense rises from the city
With a sound of prayer and lamentation.
                        Children,
I would not have you speak through
    messengers,
And therefore I have come myself to hear
    you—
I, Oedipus, who bear the famous name.
                    (*To a* PRIEST)
You, there, since you are eldest in the
    company
Speak for them all, tell me what preys upon
    you,
Whether you come in dread, or crave some
    blessing:
Tell me, and never doubt that I will help you
In every way I can; I should be heartless
Were I not moved to find you suppliant here.

PRIEST.
Great Oedipus, O powerful King of Thebes!
You see how all the ages of our people
Cling to your altar steps: here are boys
Who can barely stand alone, and here are
    priests
By weight of age, as I am a priest of God,
And young men chosen from those yet
    unmarried:
As for the others, all that multitude,
They wait with olive chaplets in the squares,
At the two shrines of Pallas, and where
    Apollo
Speaks in the glowing embers.
                    Your own eyes
Must tell you: Thebes is tossed on a
                    murdering sea
And can not lift her head from the death
    surge.

A rust consumes the buds and fruits of the
    earth;
The herds are sick; children die unborn,
And labor is vain. The god of plague and
    pyre
Raids like detestable lightning through the
    city,
And all the house of Kadmos is laid waste,
All emptied, and all darkened: Death alone
Battens upon the misery of Thebes.

You are not one of the immortal gods, we
    know;
Yet we have come to you to make our prayer
As to the man surest in mortal ways
And wisest in the ways of God. You saved us
From the Sphinx, that flinty singer, and the
    tribute
We paid to her so long; yet you were never
Better informed than we, nor could we teach
    you:
It was some god breathed in you to set us free.

Therefore, O mighty King, we turn to you:
Find us our safety, find us a remedy,
Whether by counsel of the gods or men.
A king of wisdom tested in the past
Can act in a time of troubles, and act well.
Noblest of men, restore
Life to your city! Think how all men call you
Liberator for your triumph long ago;
Ah, when your years of kingship are
    remembered,
Let them not say *We rose, but later fell*—
Keep the State from going down in the storm!
Once, years ago, with happy augury,
You brought us fortune; be the same again!
No man questions your power to rule the
    land:
But rule over men, not over a dead city!
Ships are only hulls, citadels are nothing,
When no life moves in the empty
    passageways.

OEDIPUS.
Poor children! You may be sure I know
All that you longed for in your coming here.
I know that you are deathly sick; and yet,
Sick as you are, not one is as sick as I.
Each of you suffers in himself alone
His anguish, not another's; but my spirit
Groans for the city, for myself, for you.

I was not sleeping, you are not waking me.
No, I have been in tears for a long while
And in my restless thought walked many
    ways.
In all my search, I found one helpful course,
And that I have taken: I have sent Creon,
Son of Menoikeus, brother of the Queen,
To Delphi, Apollo's place of revelation,
To learn there, if he can,
What act or pledge of mine may save the city.
I have counted the days, and now, this very
    day,
I am troubled, for he has overstayed his time.
What is he doing? He has been gone too long.
Yet whenever he comes back, I should do ill
To scant whatever duty God reveals.

PRIEST.
It is a timely promise. At this instant
They tell me Creon is here.

OEDIPUS.
                              O Lord Apollo!
May his news be fair as his face is radiant!

PRIEST.
It could not be otherwise: he is crowned with
    bay,
The chaplet is thick with berries.

OEDIPUS.
                              We shall soon know;
He is near enough to hear us now.
                              (Enter CREON)
                    O Prince:
Brother: son of Menoikeus:
What answer do you bring us from the god?

CREON.
A strong one. I can tell you, great afflictions
Will turn out well, if they are taken well.

OEDIPUS.
What was the oracle? These vague words
Leave me still hanging between hope and
    fear.

CREON.
Is it your pleasure to hear me with all these
Gathered around us? I am prepared to speak.
But should we not go in?

OEDIPUS.
                              Let them all hear it.
It is for them I suffer, more than for myself.

CREON.
Then I will tell you what I heard at Delphi.

In plain words
The god commands us to expel from the land
    of Thebes
An old defilement we are sheltering.
It is a deathly thing, beyond cure;
We must not let it feed upon us longer.

OEDIPUS.
What defilement? How shall we rid ourselves
    of it?

CREON.
By exile or death, blood for blood. It was
Murder that brought the plague-wind on the
    city.

OEDIPUS.
Murder of whom? Surely the god has named
    him?

CREON.
My lord: long ago Laïos was our king,
Before you came to govern us.

OEDIPUS.
                              I know;
I learned of him from others; I never saw
    him.

CREON.
He was murdered; and Apollo commands us
    now
To take revenge upon whoever killed him.

OEDIPUS.
Upon whom? Where are they? Where shall
    we find a clue
To solve that crime, after so many years?

CREON.
Here in this land, he said.
                              If we make enquiry,
We may touch things that otherwise escape
    us.

OEDIPUS.
Tell me: Was Laïos murdered in his house,
Or in the fields, or in some foreign country?

CREON.
He said he planned to make a pilgrimage.
He did not come home again.

OEDIPUS.
                    And was there no one,
No witness, no companion, to tell what
    happened?

CREON.
They were all killed but one, and he got away
So frightened that he could remember one
    thing only.

OEDIPUS.
What was that one thing? One may be the
    key
To everything, if we resolve to use it.

CREON.
He said that a band of highwaymen attacked
    them,
Outnumbered them, and overwhelmed the
    King.

OEDIPUS.
Strange, that a highwayman should be so
    daring—
Unless some faction here bribed him to do it.

CREON.
We thought of that. But after Laïos' death
New troubles arose and we had no avenger.

OEDIPUS.
What troubles could prevent your hunting
    down the killers?

CREON.
The riddling Sphinx's song
Made us deaf to all mysteries but her own.

OEDIPUS.
Then once more I must bring what is dark to
    light.
It is most fitting that Apollo shows,
As you do, this compunction for the dead.
You shall see how I stand by you, as I should,
To avenge the city and the city's god,
And not as though it were for some distant
    friend,
But for my own sake, to be rid of evil.
Whoever killed King Laïos might—who
    knows?—
Decide at any moment to kill me as well.
By avenging the murdered king I protect
    myself.

Come, then, my children: leave the altar
    steps,

Lift up your olive boughs!
                    One of you go
And summon the people of Kadmos to gather
    here.
I will do all that I can; you may tell them
    that.   (*Exit a* PAGE)
So, with the help of God,
We shall be saved—or else indeed we are lost.

PRIEST.
Let us rise, children. It was for this we came,
And now the King has promised it himself.
Phoibos has sent us an oracle; may he descend
Himself to save us and drive out the plague.

(*Exeunt* OEDIPUS *and* CREON *into the
    palace by the central door. The* PRIEST
    and the SUPPLIANTS *disperse R and L.
    After a short pause the* CHORUS *enters
    the* orchestra.)

Párodos
CHORUS.
                            (STROPHE 1)
What is God singing in his profound
Delphi of gold and shadow?
What oracle for Thebes, the sunwhipped
    city?

Fear unjoints me, the roots of my heart
    tremble.

Now I remember, O Healer, your power, and
    wonder:
Will you send doom like a sudden cloud, or
    weave it
Like nightfall of the past?

Speak, speak to us, issue of holy sound:
Dearest to our expectancy: be tender!

                            (ANTISTROPHE 1)
Let me pray to Athenê, the immortal
    daughter of Zeus,
And to Artemis her sister
Who keeps her famous throne in the market
    ring,
And to Apollo, bowman at the far butts of
    heaven—

O gods, descend! Like three streams leap
    against
The fires of our grief, the fires of darkness;
Be swift to bring us rest!

As in the old time from the brilliant house
Of air you stepped to save us, come again!

(STROPHE 2)

Now our afflictions have no end,
Now all our stricken host lies down
And no man fights off death with his mind;

The noble plowland bears no grain,
And groaning mothers can not bear—

See, how our lives like birds take wing,
Like sparks that fly when a fire soars,
To the shore of the god of evening.

(ANTISTROPHE 2)

The plague burns on, it is pitiless,
Though pallid children laden with death
Lie unwept in the stony ways,
And old gray women by every path
Flock to the strand about the altars

There to strike their breasts and cry
Worship of Phoibos in wailing prayers:
Be kind, God's golden child!

(STROPHE 3)

There are no swords in this attack by fire,
No shields, but we are ringed with cries.

Send the besieger plunging from our homes
Into the vast sea-room of the Atlantic
Or into the waves that foam eastward of
    Thrace—

For the day ravages what the night spares—

Destroy our enemy, lord of the thunder!
Let him be riven by lightning from heaven!

(ANTISTROPHE 3)

Phoibos Apollo, stretch the sun's bowstring,
That golden cord, until it sing for us,
Flashing arrows in heaven!
                            Artemis, Huntress,
Race with flaring lights upon our mountains!

O scarlet god, O golden-banded brow,
O Theban Bacchos in a storm of Maenads,
                    (*Enter* OEDIPUS, *C.*)
Whirl upon Death, that all the Undying
    hate!
Come with blinding torches, come in joy!

Scene 1

OEDIPUS.
Is this your prayer? It may be answered.
    Come,
Listen to me, act as the crisis demands,
And you shall have relief from all these evils.

Until now I was a stranger to this tale,
As I had been a stranger to the crime.
Could I track down the murderer without a
    clue?
But now, friends,
As one who became a citizen after the
    murder,
I make this proclamation to all Thebans:

If any man knows by whose hand Laïos, son
    of Labdakos,
Met his death, I direct that man to tell me
    everything,
No matter what he fears for having so long
    withheld it.
Let it stand as promised that no further
    trouble
Will come to him, but he may leave the land
    in safety.

Moreover: If anyone knows the murderer to
    be foreign,
Let him not keep silent: he shall have his
    reward from me.
However, if he does conceal it; if any man
Fearing for his friend or for himself disobeys
    this edict,
Hear what I propose to do:

I solemnly forbid the people of this country,
Where power and throne are mine, ever to
    receive that man
Or speak to him, no matter who he is, or let
    him
Join in sacrifice, lustration, or in prayer.
I decree that he be driven from every house,
Being, as he is, corruption itself to us: the
    Delphic
Voice of Zeus has pronounced this revelation.
Thus I associate myself with the oracle
And take the side of the murdered king.

As for the criminal, I pray to God—
Whether it be a lurking thief, or one of a
    number—

I pray that that man's life be consumed in evil
and wretchedness.
And as for me, this curse applies no less
If it should turn out that the culprit is my
guest here,
Sharing my hearth.
                    You have heard the penalty.

I lay it on you now to attend to this
For my sake, for Apollo's, for the sick
Sterile city that heaven has abandoned.
Suppose the oracle had given you no com-
mand:
Should this defilement go uncleansed for
ever?
You should have found the murderer: your
king,
A noble king, had been destroyed!
                                Now I,
Having the power that he held before me,
Having his bed, begetting children there
Upon his wife, as he would have, had he
lived—
Their son would have been my children's
brother,
If Laïos had had luck in fatherhood!
(But surely ill luck rushed upon his reign)—
I say I take the son's part, just as though
I were his son, to press the fight for him
And see it won! I'll find the hand that
brought
Death to Labdakos' and Polydoros' child,
Heir of Kadmos' and Agenor's line.
And as for those who fail me,
May the gods deny them the fruit of the earth,
Fruit of the womb, and may they rot utterly!
Let them be wretched as we are wretched,
and worse!

For you, for loyal Thebans, and for all
Who find my actions right, I pray the favor
Of justice, and of all the immortal gods.

CHORAGOS.
Since I am under oath, my lord, I swear
I did not do the murder, I can not name
The murderer. Might not the oracle
That has ordained the search tell where to
find him?

OEDIPUS.
An honest question. But no man in the world

Can make the gods do more than the gods
will.

CHORAGOS.
There is one last expedient—

OEDIPUS.
                              Tell me what it is.
Though it seem slight, you must not hold it
back.

CHORAGOS.
A lord clairvoyant to the lord Apollo,
As we all know, is the skilled Teiresias.
One might learn much about this from him,
Oedipus.

OEDIPUS.
I am not wasting time:
Creon spoke of this, and I have sent for him—
Twice, in fact; it is strange that he is not
here.

CHORAGOS.
The other matter—that old report—seems
useless.

OEDIPUS.
Tell me. I am interested in all reports.

CHORAGOS.
The King was said to have been killed by
highwaymen.

OEDIPUS.
I know. But we have no witnesses to that.

CHORAGOS.
If the killer can feel a particle of dread,
Your curse will bring him out of hiding!

OEDIPUS.
                                        No.
The man who dared that act will fear no
curse.
        (*Enter the blind seer* TEIRESIAS, *led by a*
        PAGE)

CHORAGOS.
But there is one man who may detect the
criminal.
This is Teiresias, this is the holy prophet
In whom, alone of all men, truth was born.

OEDIPUS.
Teiresias: seer: student of mysteries,
Of all that's taught and all that no man tells,
Secrets of Heaven and secrets of the earth:

Blind though you are, you know the city lies
Sick with plague; and from this plague, my
   lord,
We find that you alone can guard or save us.

Possibly you did not hear the messengers?
Apollo, when we sent to him,
Sent us back word that this great pestilence
Would lift, but only if we established clearly
The identity of those who murdered Laïos.
They must be killed or exiled.
                              Can you use
Birdflight or any art of divination
To purify yourself, and Thebes, and me
From this contagion? We are in your hands.
There is no fairer duty
Than that of helping others in distress.

TEIRESIAS.
How dreadful knowledge of the truth can be
When there's no help in truth! I knew this
   well,
But made myself forget. I should not have
   come.

OEDIPUS.
What is troubling you? Why are your eyes
   so cold?

TEIRESIAS.
Let me go home. Bear your own fate, and I'll
Bear mine. It is better so: trust what I say.

OEDIPUS.
What you say is ungracious and unhelpful
To your native country. Do not refuse to
   speak.

TEIRESIAS.
When it comes to speech, your own is neither
   temperate
Nor opportune. I wish to be more prudent.

OEDIPUS.
In God's name, we all beg you—

TEIRESIAS.
                              You are all ignorant.
No; I will never tell you what I know.
Now it is my misery; then, it would be yours.

OEDIPUS.
What! You do know something, and will not
   tell us?
You would betray us all and wreck the State?

TEIRESIAS.
I do not intend to torture myself, or you.
Why persist in asking? You will not persuade
   me.

OEDIPUS.
What a wicked old man you are! You'd try a
   stone's
Patience! Out with it! Have you no feeling
   at all?

TEIRESIAS.
You call me unfeeling. If you could only see
The nature of your own feelings . . .

OEDIPUS.
                              Why,
Who would not feel as I do? Who could
   endure
Your arrogance toward the city?

TEIRESIAS.
                    What does it matter!
Whether I speak or not, it is bound to come.

OEDIPUS.
Then, if "it" is bound to come, you are bound
   to tell me.

TEIRESIAS.
No, I will not go on. Rage as you please.

OEDIPUS.
Rage? Why not!
                    And I'll tell you what I think:
You planned it, you had it done, you all but
Killed him with your own hands: if you had
   eyes,
I'd say the crime was yours, and yours alone.

TEIRESIAS.
So? I charge you, then,
Abide by the proclamation you have made:
From this day forth
Never speak again to these men or to me;
You yourself are the pollution of this country.

OEDIPUS.
You dare say that! Can you possibly think
   you have
Some way of going free, after such insolence?

TEIRESIAS.
I have gone free. It is the truth sustains me.

OEDIPUS.
Who taught you shamelessness? It was not
   your craft.

TEIRESIAS.
You did. You made me speak. I did not want
    to.

OEDIPUS.
Speak what? Let me hear it again more
    clearly.

TEIRESIAS.
Was it not clear before? Are you tempting
    me?

OEDIPUS.
I did not understand it. Say it again.

TEIRESIAS.
I say that you are the murderer whom you
    seek.

OEDIPUS.
Now twice you have spat out infamy. You'll
    pay for it!

TEIRESIAS.
Would you care for more? Do you wish to be
    really angry?

OEDIPUS.
Say what you will. Whatever you say is
    worthless.

TEIRESIAS.
I say you live in hideous shame with those
Most dear to you. You can not see the evil.

OEDIPUS.
It seems you can go on mouthing like this for
    ever.

TEIRESIAS.
I can, if there is power in truth.

OEDIPUS.
                      There is:
But not for you, not for you,
You sightless, witless, senseless, mad old man!

TEIRESIAS.
You are the madman. There is no one here
Who will not curse you soon, as you curse me.

OEDIPUS.
You child of endless night! You can not hurt
    me
Or any other man who sees the sun.

TEIRESIAS.
True: it is not from me your fate will come.

That lies within Apollo's competence,
As it is his concern.

OEDIPUS.
                Tell me:
Are you speaking for Creon, or for yourself?

TEIRESIAS.
Creon is no threat. You weave your own
    doom.

OEDIPUS.
Wealth, power, craft or statesmanship!
Kingly position, everywhere admired!
What savage envy is stored up against these,
If Creon, whom I trusted, Creon my friend,
For this great office which the city once
Put in my hands unsought—if for this power
Creon desires in secret to destroy me!

He has bought this decrepit fortune-teller,
    this
Collector of dirty pennies, this prophet
    fraud—
Why, he is no more clairvoyant than I am!
                      Tell us:
Has your mystic mummery ever approached
    the truth?
When that hellcat the Sphinx was performing
    here,
What help were you to these people?
Her magic was not for the first man who
    came along:
It demanded a real exorcist. Your birds—
What good were they? or the gods, for the
    matter of that?
But I came by,
Oedipus, the simple man, who knows
    nothing—
I thought it out for myself, no birds helped
    me!
And this is the man you think you can
    destroy,
That you may be close to Creon when he's
    king!
Well, you and your friend Creon, it seems to
    me,
Will suffer most. If you were not an old man,
You would have paid already for your plot.

CHORAGOS.
We can not see that his words or yours
Have been spoken except in anger, Oedipus,

And of anger we have no need. How can
   God's will
Be accomplished best? That is what most
   concerns us.

TEIRESIAS.
You are a king. But where argument's
   concerned
I am your man, as much a king as you.
I am not your servant, but Apollo's.
I have no need of Creon to speak for me.

Listen to me. You mock my blindness, do
   you?
But I say that you, with both your eyes, are
   blind:
You can not see the wretchedness of your life,
Nor in whose house you live, no, nor with
   whom.
Who are your father and mother? Can you
   tell me?
You do not even know the blind wrongs
That you have done them, on earth and in
   the world below.
But the double lash of your parents' curse
   will whip you
Out of this land some day, with only night
Upon your precious eyes.
Your cries then—where will they not be
   heard?
What fastness of Kithairon will not echo
   them?
And that bridal-descant of yours—you'll
   know it then,
The song they sang when you came here to
   Thebes
And found your misguided berthing.
All this, and more, that you can not guess at
   now,
Will bring you to yourself among your
   children.

Be angry, then. Curse Creon. Curse my
   words.
I tell you, no man that walks upon the earth
Shall be rooted out more horribly than you.

OEDIPUS.
Am I to bear this from him?—Damnation
Take you! Out of this place! Out of my
   sight!

TEIRESIAS.
I would not have come at all if you had not
   asked me.

OEDIPUS.
Could I have told that you'd talk nonsense,
   that
You'd come here to make a fool of yourself,
   and of me?

TEIRESIAS.
A fool? Your parents thought me sane
   enough.

OEDIPUS.
My parents again!—Wait: who were my
   parents?

TEIRESIAS.
This day will give you a father, and break
   your heart.

OEDIPUS.
Your infantile riddles! Your damned
   abracadabra!

TEIRESIAS.
You were a great man once at solving riddles.

OEDIPUS.
Mock me with that if you like; you will find it
   true.

TEIRESIAS.
It was true enough. It brought about your
   ruin.

OEDIPUS.
But if it saved this town?

TEIRESIAS.
                      (*To the* PAGE)
          Boy, give me your hand.

OEDIPUS.
Yes, boy; lead him away.
                  —While you are here
We can do nothing. Go; leave us in peace.

TEIRESIAS.
I will go when I have said what I have to say.
How can you hurt me? And I tell you again:
The man you have been looking for all this
   time,
The damned man, the murderer of Laïos,

That man is in Thebes. To your mind he is
  foreign-born,
But it will soon be shown that he is a Theban,
A revelation that will fail to please.
                                    A blind man,
Who has his eyes now; a penniless man, who
  is rich now;
And he will go tapping the strange earth with
  his staff
To the children with whom he lives now he
  will be
Brother and father—the very same; to her
Who bore him, son and husband—the very
  same
Who came to his father's bed, wet with his
  father's blood.

Enough. Go think that over.
If later you find error in what I have said,
You may say that I have no skill in prophecy.
  (*Exit* TEIRESIAS, *led by his* PAGE. OEDIPUS
  goes into the palace)

Ode 1

CHORUS.   (STROPHE 1)
The Delphic stone of prophecies
Remembers ancient regicide
And a still bloody hand.
That killer's hour of flight has come.
He must be stronger than riderless
Coursers of untiring wind,
For the son of Zeus armed with his father's
  thunder
Leaps in lightning after him;
And the Furies follow him, the sad Furies.

                                    (ANTISTROPHE 1)
Holy Parnassos' peak of snow
Flashes and blinds that secret man,
That all shall hunt him down:
Though he may roam the forest shade
Like a bull gone wild from pasture
To rage through glooms of stone.
Doom comes down on him; flight will not
  avail him;
For the world's heart calls him desolate,
And the immortal Furies follow, for ever
  follow.

                                    (STROPHE 2)
But now a wilder thing is heard

From the old man skilled at hearing Fate in
  the wing-beat of a bird.
Bewildered as a blown bird, my soul hovers
  and can not find
Foothold in this debate, or any reason or rest
  of mind.
But no man ever brought—none can bring
Proof of strife between Thebes' royal house,
Labdakos' line, and the son of Polybos;
And never until now has any man brought
  word
Of Laïos' dark death staining Oedipus the
  King.

Divine Zeus and Apollo hold (ANTISTROPHE 2)
Perfect intelligence alone of all tales ever
  told;
And well though this diviner works, he works
  in his own night;
No man can judge that rough unknown or
  trust in second sight,
For wisdom changes hands among the wise.
Shall I believe my great lord criminal
At a raging word that a blind old man let
  fall?
I saw him, when the carrion woman faced
  him of old,
Prove his heroic mind! These evil words are
  lies.

Scene 2

CREON.
Men of Thebes:
I am told that heavy accusations
Have been brought against me by King
  Oedipus.

I am not the kind of man to bear this tamely.

If in these present difficulties
He holds me accountable for any harm to him
Through anything I have said or done—why,
  then,
I do not value life in this dishonor.

It is not as though this rumor touched upon
Some private indiscretion. The matter is
  grave.
The fact is that I am being called disloyal
To the State, to my fellow citizens, to my
  friends.

CHORAGOS.
He may have spoken in anger, not from his
  mind.

CREON.
But did you not hear him say I was the one
Who seduced the old prophet into lying?

CHORAGOS.
The thing was said; I do not know how
  seriously.

CREON.
But you were watching him! Were his eyes
  steady?
Did he look like a man in his right mind?

CHORAGOS.
                              I do not know.
I can not judge the behavior of great men.
But here is the King himself.

                              (*Enter* OEDIPUS)

OEDIPUS.
                    So you dared come back.
Why? How brazen of you to come to my
  house,
You murderer!
                    Do you think I do not know
That you plotted to kill me, plotted to steal
  my throne?
Tell me, in God's name: am I coward, a fool,
That you should dream you could accomplish
  this?
A fool who could not see your slippery game?
A coward, not to fight back when I saw it?
You are the fool, Creon, are you not? hoping
Without support or friends to get a throne?
Thrones may be won or bought: you could
  do neither.

CREON.
Now listen to me. You have talked; let me
  talk, too.
You can not judge unless you know the facts.

OEDIPUS.
You speak well: there is one fact; but I find it
  hard
To learn from the deadliest enemy I have.

CREON.
That above all I must dispute with you.

OEDIPUS.
That above all I will not hear you deny.

CREON.
If you think there is anything good in being
  stubborn
Against all reason, then I say you are wrong.

OEDIPUS.
If you think a man can sin against his own
  kind
And not be punished for it, I say you are mad.

CREON.
I agree. But tell me: what have I done to
  you?

OEDIPUS.
You advised me to send for that wizard, did
  you not?

CREON.
I did. I should do it again.

OEDIPUS.
                    Very well. Now tell me:
How long has it been since Laïos—

CREON.
                              What of Laïos?

OEDIPUS.
Since he vanished in that onset by the road?

CREON.
It was long ago, a long time.

OEDIPUS.
                    And this prophet,
Was he practicing here then?

CREON.
                    He was; and with honor, as now.

OEDIPUS.
Did he speak of me at that time?

CREON.
                                    He never did;
At least, not when I was present.

OEDIPUS.
                              But . . . the enquiry?
I suppose you held one?

CREON.
                    We did, but we learned nothing.

OEDIPUS.
Why did the prophet not speak against me
  then?

CREON.
I do not know; and I am the kind of man
Who holds his tongue when he has no facts
  to go on.

OEDIPUS.
There's one fact that you know, and you
  could tell it.

CREON.
What fact is that? If I know it, you shall
  have it.

OEDIPUS.
If he were not involved with you, he could
  not say
That it was I who murdered Laïos.

CREON.
If he says that, you are the one that knows
  it!—
But now it is my turn to question you.

OEDIPUS.
Put your questions. I am no murderer.

CREON.
First, then: You married my sister?

OEDIPUS.
                            I married your sister.

CREON.
And you rule the kingdom equally with her?

OEDIPUS.
Everything that she wants she has from me.

CREON.
And I am the third, equal to both of you?

OEDIPUS.
That is why I call you a bad friend.

CREON.
No. Reason it out, as I have done.
Think of this first: Would any sane man
  prefer
Power, with all a king's anxieties,
To that same power and the grace of sleep?
Certainly not I.
I have never longed for the king's power—
  only his rights.
Would any wise man differ from me in this?
As matters stand, I have my way in everything
With your consent, and no responsibilities.
If I were king, I should be a slave to policy.

How could I desire a scepter more
Than what is now mine—untroubled
  influence?
No, I have not gone mad; I need no honors,
Except those with the perquisites I have now.
I am welcome everywhere; every man salutes
  me,
And those who want your favor seek my ear,
Since I know how to manage what they ask.
Should I exchange this ease for that anxiety?
Besides, no sober mind is treasonable.
I hate anarchy
And never would deal with any man who
  likes it.

Test what I have said. Go to the priestess
At Delphi, ask if I quoted her correctly.
And as for this other thing: if I am found
Guilty of treason with Teiresias,
Then sentence me to death! You have my
  word
It is a sentence I should cast my vote for—
But not without evidence!
                              You do wrong
When you take good men for bad, bad men
  for good.
A true friend thrown aside—why, life itself
Is not more precious!
                          In time you will know this well:
For time, and time alone, will show the just
  man,
Though scoundrels are discovered in a day.

CHORAGOS.
This is well said, and a prudent man would
  ponder it.
Judgments too quickly formed are dangerous.

OEDIPUS.
But is he not quick in his duplicity?
And shall I not be quick to parry him?
Would you have me stand still, hold my
  peace, and let
This man win everything, through my
  inaction?

CREON.
And you want—what is it, then? To banish
  me?

OEDIPUS.
No, not exile. It is your death I want,
So that all the world may see what treason
  means.

CREON.
You will persist, then? You will not believe
  me?

OEDIPUS.
How can I believe you?

CREON.
                    Then you are a fool.

OEDIPUS.
To save myself?

CREON.
                In justice, think of me.

OEDIPUS.
You are evil incarnate.

CREON.
                    But suppose that you are wrong?

OEDIPUS.
Still I must rule.

CREON.
                    But not if you rule badly.

OEDIPUS.
O city, city!

CREON.
            It is my city, too!

CHORAGOS.
Now, my lords, be still. I see the Queen,
Iocastê, coming from her palace chambers;
And it is time she came, for the sake of you
  both.
This dreadful quarrel can be resolved
  through her.
                            (*Enter* IOCASTE)

IOCASTE.
Poor foolish men, what wicked din is this?
With Thebes sick to death, is it not shameful
That you should rake some private quarrel
  up?
                            (*To* OEDIPUS)
Come into the house.

            —And you, Creon, go now:
Let us have no more of this tumult over
  nothing.

CREON.
Nothing? No, sister: what your husband
  plans for me
Is one of two great evils: exile or death.

OEDIPUS.
He is right.
      Why, woman I have caught him squarely
Plotting against my life.

CREON.
                    No! Let me die
Accurst if ever I have wished you harm!

IOCASTE.
Ah, believe it, Oedipus!
In the name of the gods, respect this oath of
  his
For my sake, for the sake of these people here!

CHORAGOS.   (STROPHE 1)
Open your mind to her, my lord. Be ruled
  by her, I beg you!

OEDIPUS.
What would you have me do?

CHORAGOS.
Respect Creon's word. He has never spoken
  like a fool,
And now he has sworn an oath.

OEDIPUS.
                    You know what you ask?

CHORAGOS.
                                            I do.

OEDIPUS.
                                Speak on, then.

CHORAGOS.
A friend so sworn should not be baited so,
In blind malice, and without final proof.

OEDIPUS.
You are aware, I hope, that what you say
Means death for me, or exile at the least.

CHORAGOS.   (STROPHE 2)
No, I swear by Helios, first in Heaven!
    May I die friendless and accurst,
The worst of deaths, if ever I meant that!
        It is the withering fields
            That hurt my sick heart:
        Must we bear all these ills,
            And now your bad blood as well?

OEDIPUS.
Then let him go. And let me die, if I must,
Or be driven by him in shame from the land
  of Thebes.

It is your unhappiness, and not his talk,
That touches me.
                              As for him—
Wherever he goes, hatred will follow him.

CREON.
Ugly in yielding, as you were ugly in rage!
Natures like yours chiefly torment themselves.

OEDIPUS.
Can you not go? Can you not leave me?

CREON.
                                                    I can.
You do not know me; but the city knows me,
And in its eyes I am just, if not in yours.
                              (*Exit* CREON)

CHORAGOS.   (ANTISTROPHE 1)
Lady Iocastê, did you not ask the King to go
    to his chambers?

IOCASTE.
First tell me what has happened.

CHORAGOS.
There was suspicion without evidence; yet it
    rankled
As even false charges will.

IOCASTE.
                              On both sides?

CHORAGOS.
                                        On both.

IOCASTE.
                              But what was said?

CHORAGOS.
Oh let it rest, let it be done with!
Have we not suffered enough?

OEDIPUS.
You see to what your decency has brought
    you:
You have made difficulties where my heart
    saw none.

CHORAGOS.   (ANTISTROPHE 2)
Oedipus, it is not once only I have told you—
    You must know I should count myself
        unwise
To the point of madness, should I now
        forsake you—
        You, under whose hand,
            In the storm of another time,

Our dear land sailed out free.
        But now stand fast at the helm!

IOCASTE.
In God's name, Oedipus, inform your wife as
    well:
Why are you so set in this hard anger?

OEDIPUS.
I will tell you, for none of these men deserves
My confidence as you do. It is Creon's work,
His treachery, his plotting against me.

IOCASTE.
Go on, if you can make this clear to me.

OEDIPUS.
He charges me with the murder of Laïos.

IOCASTE.
Has he some knowledge? Or does he speak
    from hearsay?

OEDIPUS.
He would not commit himself to such a
    charge,
But he has brought in that damnable
    soothsayer
To tell his story.

IOCASTE.
                              Set your mind at rest.
If it is a question of soothsayers, I tell you
That you will find no man whose craft gives
    knowledge
Of the unknowable.

                              Here is my proof:

An oracle was reported to Laïos once
(I will not say from Phoibos himself, but from
His appointed ministers, at any rate)
That his doom would be death at the hands
    of his own son—
His son, born of his flesh and of mine!

Now, you remember the story: Laïos was
    killed
By marauding strangers where three
    highways meet;
But his child had not been three days in this
    world
Before the King had pierced the baby's ankles
And left him to die on a lonely mountainside.

Thus, Apollo never caused that child
To kill his father, and it was not Laïos' fate
To die at the hands of his son, as he had
    feared.
This is what prophets and prophecies are
    worth!
Have no dread of them.
                    It is God himself
Who can show us what he wills, in his own
    way.

OEDIPUS.
How strange a shadowy memory crossed my
    mind,
Just now while you were speaking; it chilled
    my heart.

IOCASTE.
What do you mean? What memory do you
    speak of?

OEDIPUS.
If I understand you, Laïos was killed
At a place where three roads meet.

IOCASTE.
                    So it was said;
We have no later story.

OEDIPUS.
                    Where did it happen?

IOCASTE.
Phokis, it is called: at a place where the
    Theban Way
Divides into the roads toward Delphi and
    Daulia.

OEDIPUS.
When?

IOCASTE.
    We had the news not long before you came
And proved the right to your succession here.

OEDIPUS.
Ah, what net has God been weaving for me?

IOCASTE.
Oedipus! Why does this trouble you?

OEDIPUS.
                    Do not ask me yet.
First, tell me how Laïos looked, and tell me
How old he was.

IOCASTE.
                    He was tall, his hair just touched
With white; his form was not unlike your
    own.

OEDIPUS.
I think that I myself may be accurst
By my own ignorant edict.

IOCASTE.
                    You speak strangely.
It makes me tremble to look at you, my King.

OEDIPUS.
I am not sure that the blind man can not see.
But I should know better if you were to tell
    me—

IOCASTE.
Anything—though I dread to hear you ask
    it.

OEDIPUS.
Was the King lightly escorted, or did he ride
With a large company, as a ruler should?

IOCASTE.
There were five men with him in all: one was
    a herald,
And a single chariot, which he was driving.

OEDIPUS.
Alas, that makes it plain enough!
                    But who—
Who told you how it happened?

IOCASTE.
                    A household servant,
The only one to escape.

OEDIPUS.
                    And is he still
A servant of ours?

IOCASTE.
                    No; for when he came back at last
And found you enthroned in the place of the
    dead king,
He came to me, touched my hand with his,
    and begged
That I would send him away to the frontier
    district
Where only the shepherds go—
As far away from the city as I could send him.
I granted his prayer; for although the man
    was a slave,

He had earned more than this favor at my hands.

OEDIPUS.
Can he be called back quickly?

IOCASTE.

Easily.

But why?

OEDIPUS.
I have taken too much upon myself
Without enquiry; therefore I wish to consult him.

IOCASTE.
Then he shall come.
But am I not one also
To whom you might confide these fears of yours?

OEDIPUS.
That is your right; it will not be denied you,
Now least of all; for I have reached a pitch
Of wild foreboding. Is there anyone
To whom I should sooner speak?

Polybos of Corinth is my father.
My mother is a Dorian: Meropê.
I grew up chief among the men of Corinth
Until a strange thing happened—
Not worth my passion, it may be, but strange.

At a feast, a drunken man maundering in his cups
Cries out that I am not my father's son!

I contained myself that night, though I felt anger
And a sinking heart. The next day I visited
My father and mother, and questioned them. They stormed,
Calling it all the slanderous rant of a fool;
And this relieved me. Yet the suspicion
Remained always aching in my mind;
I knew there was talk; I could not rest;
And finally, saying nothing to my parents,
I went to the shrine at Delphi.
The god dismissed my question without reply;
He spoke of other things.
Some were clear,
Full of wretchedness, dreadful, unbearable:
As, that I should lie with my own mother, breed

Children from whom all men would turn their eyes;
And that I should be my father's murderer.

I heard all this, and fled. And from that day
Corinth to me was only in the stars
Descending in that quarter of the sky,
As I wandered farther and farther on my way
To a land where I should never see the evil
Sung by the oracle. And I came to this country
Where, so you say, King Laïos was killed.

I will tell you all that happened there, my lady.

There were three highways
Coming together at a place I passed;
And there a herald came towards me, and a chariot
Drawn by horses, with a man such as you describe
Seated in it. The groom leading the horses
Forced me off the road at his lord's command;
But as this charioteer lurched over towards me
I struck him in my rage. The old man saw me
And brought his double goad down upon my head
As I came abreast.
He was paid back, and more!
Swinging my club in this right hand I knocked him
Out of his car, and he rolled on the ground.
I killed him.

I killed them all.
Now if that stranger and Laïos were—kin,
Where is a man more miserable than I?
More hated by the gods? Citizen and alien alike
Must never shelter me or speak to me—
I must be shunned by all.
And I myself
Pronounced this malediction upon myself!

Think of it: I have touched you with these hands,
These hands that killed your husband. What defilement!

Am I all evil, then? It must be so,
Since I must flee from Thebes, yet never again
See my own countrymen, my own country,
For fear of joining my mother in marriage
And killing Polybos, my father.
                              Ah,
If I was created so, born to this fate,
Who could deny the savagery of God?

O holy majesty of heavenly powers!
May I never see that day! Never!
Rather let me vanish from the race of men
Than know the abomination destined me!

CHORAGOS.
We too, my lord, have felt dismay at this.
But there is hope: you have yet to hear the
  shepherd.

OEDIPUS.
Indeed, I fear no other hope is left me.

IOCASTE.
What do you hope from him when he comes?

OEDIPUS.
                              This much:
If his account of the murder tallies with
  yours,
Then I am cleared.

IOCASTE.
                    What was it that I said
Of such importance?

OEDIPUS.
                    Why, "marauders," you said,
Killed the King, according to this man's story.
If he maintains that still, if there were several,
Clearly the guilt is not mine: I was alone.
But if he says one man, singlehanded, did it,
Then the evidence all points to me.

IOCASTE.
You may be sure that he said there were
  several;
And can he call back that story now? He can
  not.
The whole city heard it as plainly as I.
But suppose he alters some detail of it:
He can not ever show that Laïos' death
Fulfilled the oracle: for Apollo said
My child was doomed to kill him; and my
  child—
Poor baby!—it was my child that died first.

No. From now on, where oracles are
  concerned,
I would not waste a second thought on any.

OEDIPUS.
You may be right.
                    But come: let someone go
For the shepherd at once. This matter must
  be settled.

IOCASTE.
I will send for him.
I would not wish to cross you in anything,
And surely not in this.—Let us go in.
                    (Exeunt into the palace)

Ode 2

CHORUS.   (STROPHE 1)
Let me be reverent in the ways of right,
Lowly the paths I journey on;
Let all my words and actions keep
The laws of the pure universe
From highest Heaven handed down.
For Heaven is their bright nurse,
Those generations of the realms of light;
Ah, never of mortal kind were they begot,
Nor are they slaves of memory, lost in sleep:
Their Father is greater than Time, and ages
  not.

                              (ANTISTROPHE 1)
The tyrant is a child of Pride
Who drinks from his great sickening cup
Recklessness and vanity,
Until from his high crest headlong
He plummets to the dust of hope.
That strong man is not strong.
But let no fair ambition be denied;
May God protect the wrestler for the State
In government, in comely policy,
Who will fear God, and on His ordinance
  wait.

                              (STROPHE 2)
Haughtiness and the high hand of disdain
Tempt and outrage God's holy law;
And any mortal who dares hold
No immortal Power in awe
Will be caught up in a net of pain:
The price for which his levity is sold.
Let each man take due earnings, then,
And keep his hands from holy things,
And from blasphemy stand apart—
Else the crackling blast of heaven

Blows on his head, and on his desperate
    heart;
Though fools will honor impious men,
In their cities no tragic poet sings.

            (ANTISTROPHE 2)

Shall we lose faith in Delphi's obscurities,
We who have heard the world's core
Discredited, and the sacred wood
Of Zeus at Elis praised no more?
The deeds and the strange prophecies
Must make a pattern yet to be understood.
Zeus, if indeed you are lord of all,
Throned in light over night and day,
Mirror this in your endless mind:
Our masters call the oracle
Words on the wind, and the Delphic vision
    blind!
Their hearts no longer know Apollo,
And reverence for the gods has died away.

        Scene 3

           (*Enter* IOCASTE)

IOCASTE.

Prince of Thebes, it has occurred to me
To visit the altars of the gods, bearing
These branches as a suppliant, and this
    incense
Our King is not himself: his noble soul
Is overwrought with fantasies of dread,
Else he would consider
The new prophecies in the light of the old.
He will listen to any voice that speaks
    disaster,
And my advice goes for nothing.

        (*She approaches the altar, R.*)
          To you, then, Apollo,

Lycean lord, since you are nearest, I turn in
    prayer.
Receive these offerings, and grant us
    deliverance
From defilement. Our hearts are heavy with
    fear
When we see our leader distracted, as helpless
    sailors
Are terrified by the confusion of their
    helmsman.

        (*Enter* MESSENGER)

MESSENGER.

Friends, no doubt you can direct me:
Where shall I find the house of Oedipus,
Or, better still, where is the King himself?

CHORAGOS.

It is this very place, stranger; he is inside.
This is his wife and mother of his children.

MESSENGER.

I wish her happiness in a happy house,
Blest in all the fulfillment of her marriage.

IOCASTE.

I wish as much for you: your courtesy
Deserves a like good fortune. But now, tell
    me:
Why have you come? What have you to say
    to us?

MESSENGER.

Good news, my lady, for your house and your
    husband.

IOCASTE.

What news? Who sent you here?

MESSENGER.

           I am from Corinth.
The news I bring ought to mean joy for you,
Though it may be you will find some grief in
    it.

IOCASTE.

What is it? How can it touch us in both ways?

MESSENGER.

The word is that the people of the Isthmus
Intend to call Oedipus to be their king.

IOCASTE.

But old King Polybos—is he not reigning
    still?

MESSENGER.

No. Death holds him in his sepulchre.

IOCASTE.

What are you saying? Polybos is dead?

MESSENGER.

If I am not telling the truth, may I die myself.

IOCASTE.   (*To a* MAIDSERVANT)
Go in, go quickly; tell this to your master.

O riddlers of God's will, where are you now!
This was the man whom Oedipus, long ago,
Feared so, fled so, in dread of destroying
    him—
But it was another fate by which he died.

        (*Enter* OEDIPUS, *C.*)

OEDIPUS.
Dearest Iocastê, why have you sent for me?

IOCASTE.
Listen to what this man says, and then tell me
What has become of the solemn prophecies.

OEDIPUS.
Who is this man? What is his news for me?

IOCASTE.
He has come from Corinth to announce your
    father's death!

OEDIPUS.
Is it true, stranger? Tell me in your own
    words.

MESSENGER.
I can not say it more clearly: the King is dead.

OEDIPUS.
Was it by treason? Or by an attack of illness?

MESSENGER.
A little thing brings old men to their rest.

OEDIPUS.
It was sickness, then?

MESSENGER.
                            Yes, and his many years.

OEDIPUS.
Ah!
Why should a man respect the Pythian
    hearth, or
Give heed to the birds that jangle above his
    head?
They prophesied that I should kill Polybos,
Kill my own father; but he is dead and
    buried,
And I am here—I never touched him, never,
Unless he died of grief for my departure,
And thus, in a sense, through me. No.
    Polybos
Has packed the oracles off with him
    underground.
They are empty words.

IOCASTE.
                            Had I not told you so?

OEDIPUS.
You had; it was my faint heart that betrayed
    me.

IOCASTE.
From now on never think of those things
    again.

OEDIPUS.
And yet—must I not fear my mother's bed?

IOCASTE.
Why should anyone in this world be afraid,
Since Fate rules us and nothing can be
    foreseen?
A man should live only for the present day.

Have no more fear of sleeping with your
    mother:
How many men, in dreams, have lain with
    their mothers!
No reasonable man is troubled by such things.

OEDIPUS.
That is true; only—
If only my mother were not still alive!
But she is alive. I can not help my dread.

IOCASTE.
Yet this news of your father's death is
    wonderful.

OEDIPUS.
Wonderful. But I fear the living woman.

MESSENGER.
Tell me, who is this woman that you fear?

OEDIPUS.
It is Meropê, man; the wife of King Polybos.

MESSENGER.
Meropê? Why should you be afraid of her?

OEDIPUS.
An oracle of the gods, a dreadful saying.

MESSENGER.
Can you tell me about it or are you sworn to
    silence?

OEDIPUS.
I can tell you, and I will.
Apollo said through his prophet that I was
    the man
Who should marry his own mother, shed his
    father's blood
With his own hands. And so, for all these
    years

I have kept clear of Corinth, and no harm has
come—
Though it would have been sweet to see my
parents again.

MESSENGER.
And is this the fear that drove you out of
Corinth?

OEDIPUS.
Would you have me kill my father?

MESSENGER.
As for that
You must be reassured by the news I gave
you.

OEDIPUS.
If you could reassure me, I would reward you.

MESSENGER.
I had that in mind, I will confess: I thought
I could count on you when you returned to
Corinth.

OEDIPUS.
No: I will never go near my parents again.

MESSENGER.
Ah, son, you still do not know what you are
doing—

OEDIPUS.
What do you mean? In the name of God tell
me!

MESSENGER.
—If these are your reasons for not going
home.

OEDIPUS.
I tell you, I fear the oracle may come true.

MESSENGER.
And guilt may come upon you through your
parents?

OEDIPUS.
That is the dread that is always in my heart.

MESSENGER.
Can you not see that all your fears are
groundless?

OEDIPUS.
How can you say that? They are my parents,
surely?

MESSENGER.
Polybos was not your father.

OEDIPUS.
Not my father?

MESSENGER.
No more your father than the man speaking
to you.

OEDIPUS.
But you are nothing to me!

MESSENGER.
Neither was he.

OEDIPUS.
Then why did he call me son?

MESSENGER.
I will tell you:
Long ago he had you from my hands, as a gift.

OEDIPUS.
Then how could he love me so, if I was not
his?

MESSENGER.
He had no children, and his heart turned to
you.

OEDIPUS.
What of you? Did you buy me? Did you find
me by chance?

MESSENGER.
I came upon you in the crooked pass of
Kithairon.

OEDIPUS.
And what were you doing there?

MESSENGER.
Tending my flocks.

OEDIPUS.
A wandering shepherd?

MESSENGER.
But your savior, son, that day.

OEDIPUS.
From what did you save me?

MESSENGER.
Your ankles should tell you that.

OEDIPUS.
Ah, stranger, why do you speak of that
childhood pain?

MESSENGER.
I cut the bonds that tied your ankles together.

OEDIPUS.
I have had the mark as long as I can
    remember.

MESSENGER.
That was why you were given the name you
    bear.

OEDIPUS.
God! Was it my father or my mother who
    did it?
Tell me!

MESSENGER.
I do not know. The man who gave you to me
Can tell you better than I.

OEDIPUS.
It was not you that found me, but another?

MESSENGER.
It was another shepherd gave you to me.

OEDIPUS.
Who was he? Can you tell me who he was?

MESSENGER.
I think he was said to be one of Laïos' people.

OEDIPUS.
You mean the Laïos who was king here years
    ago?

MESSENGER.
Yes; King Laïos; and the man was one of his
    herdsmen.

OEDIPUS.
Is he still alive? Can I see him?

MESSENGER.
                              These men here
Know best about such things.

OEDIPUS.
                        Does anyone here
Know this shepherd that he is talking about?
Have you seen him in the fields, or in the
    town?
If you have, tell me. It is time things were
    made plain.

CHORAGOS.
I think the man he means is that same
    shepherd
You have already asked to see. Iocastê
    perhaps
Could tell you something.

OEDIPUS.
                            Do you know anything
About him, Lady? Is he the man we have
    summoned?
Is that the man this shepherd means?

IOCASTE.
                            Why think of him?
Forget this herdsman. Forget it all.
This talk is a waste of time.

OEDIPUS.
                            How can you say that,
When the clues to my true birth are in my
    hands?

IOCASTE.
For God's love, let us have no more
    questioning!
Is your life nothing to you?
My own is pain enough for me to bear.

OEDIPUS.
You need not worry. Suppose my mother a
    slave,
And born of slaves: no baseness can touch
    you.

IOCASTE.
Listen to me, I beg you: do not do this thing!

OEDIPUS.
I will not listen; the truth must be made
    known.

IOCASTE.
Everything that I say is for you own good!

OEDIPUS.
                            My own good
Snaps my patience, then; I want none of it.

IOCASTE.
You are fatally wrong! May you never learn
    who you are!

OEDIPUS.
Go, one of you, and bring the shepherd here.
Let us leave this woman to brag of her royal
    name.

IOCASTE.
Ah, miserable!
That is the only word I have for you now.
That is the only word I can ever have.
                            (Exit into the palace)

CHORAGOS.
Why has she left us, Oedipus? Why has she gone
In such a passion of sorrow? I fear this silence:
Something dreadful may come of it.

OEDIPUS.
                     Let it come!
However base my birth, I must know about it.
The Queen, like a woman, is perhaps ashamed
To think of my low origin. But I
Am a child of Luck; I can not be dishonored.
Luck is my mother; the passing months, my brothers,
Have seen me rich and poor.
                   If this is so,
How could I wish that I were someone else?
How could I not be glad to know my birth?

Ode 3

CHORUS.
If ever the coming time were known (STROPHE)
To my heart's pondering,
Kithairon, now by Heaven I see the torches
At the festival of the next full moon,
And see the dance, and hear the choir sing
A grace to your gentle shade:
Mountain where Oedipus was found,
O mountain guard of a noble race!
May the god who heals us lend his aid,
And let that glory come to pass
For our king's cradling-ground.

                   (ANTISTROPHE)
Of the nymphs that flower beyond the years,
Who bore you, royal child,
To Pan of the hills or the timberline Apollo,
Cold in delight where the upland clears,
Or Hermês for whom Kyllenê's heights are piled?
Or flushed as evening cloud,
Great Dionysos, roamer of mountains,
He—was it he who found you there,
And caught you up in his own proud
Arms from the sweet god-ravisher
Who laughed by the Muses' fountains?

Scene 4

OEDIPUS.
Sirs: though I do not know the man,

I think I see him coming, this shepherd we want:
He is old, like our friend here, and the men
Bringing him seem to be servants of my house.
But you can tell, if you have ever seen him.
           (*Enter* SHEPHERD *escorted by Servants*)

CHORAGOS.
I know him, he was Laïos' man. You can trust him.

OEDIPUS.
Tell me first, you from Corinth: is this the shepherd
We were discussing?

MESSENGER.
                 This is the very man.

OEDIPUS.   (*To* SHEPHERD)
Come here. No, look at me. You must answer
Everything I ask.—You belonged to Laïos?

SHEPHERD.
Yes: born his slave, brought up in his house.

OEDIPUS.
Tell me: what kind of work did you do for him?

SHEPHERD.
I was a shepherd of his, most of my life.

OEDIPUS.
Where mainly did you go for pasturage?

SHEPHERD.
Sometimes Kithairon, sometimes the hills near-by.

OEDIPUS.
Do you remember ever seeing this man out there?

SHEPHERD.
What would he be doing there? This man?

OEDIPUS.
This man standing here. Have you ever seen him before?

SHEPHERD.
No. At least, not to my recollection.

MESSENGER.
And that is not strange, my lord. But I'll refresh

His memory: he must remember, when we
  two
Spent three whole seasons together, March to
  September.
On Kithairon or thereabouts. He had two
  flocks;
I had one. Each autumn I'd drive mine home
And he would go back with his to Laïos'
  sheepfold.—
Is this not true, just as I have described it?

SHEPHERD.
True, yes; but it was all so long ago.

MESSENGER.
Well, then: do you remember, back in those
  days,
That you gave me a baby boy to bring up as
  my own?

SHEPHERD.
What if I did? What are you trying to say?

MESSENGER.
King Oedipus was once that little child.

SHEPHERD.
Damn you, hold your tongue!

OEDIPUS.
                          No more of that!
It is your tongue needs watching, not this
  man's.

SHEPHERD.
My King, my Master, what is it I have done
  wrong?

OEDIPUS.
You have not answered his question about
  the boy.

SHEPHERD.
He does not know . . . He is only making
  trouble . . .

OEDIPUS.
Come, speak plainly, or it will go hard with
  you.

SHEPHERD.
In God's name, do not torture an old man!

OEDIPUS.
Come here, one of you; bind his arms behind
  him.

SHEPHERD.
Unhappy king! What more do you wish to
  learn?

OEDIPUS.
Did you give this man the child he speaks of?

SHEPHERD.
                                        I did.
And I would to God I had died that very day.

OEDIPUS.
You will die now unless you speak the truth.

SHEPHERD.
Yet if I speak the truth, I am worse than dead.

OEDIPUS.
Very well; since you insist upon delaying—

SHEPHERD.
No! I have told you already that I gave him
  the boy.

OEDIPUS.
Where did you get him? From your house?
  From somewhere else?

SHEPHERD.
Not from mine, no. A man gave him to me.

OEDIPUS.
Is that man here? Do you know whose slave
  he was?

SHEPHERD.
For God's love, my King, do not ask me any
  more!

OEDIPUS.
You are a dead man if I have to ask you again.

SHEPHERD.
Then . . . Then the child was from the palace
  of Laïos.

OEDIPUS.
A slave child? or a child of his own line?

SHEPHERD.
Ah, I am on the brink of dreadful speech!

OEDIPUS.
And I of dreadful hearing. Yet I must hear.

SHEPHERD.
If you must be told, then . . .
                          They said it was Laïos' child;
But it is your wife who can tell you about
  that.

OEDIPUS.
My wife!—Did she give it to you?

SHEPHERD.

My lord, she did.

OEDIPUS.
Do you know why?

SHEPHERD.

I was told to get rid of it.

OEDIPUS.
An unspeakable mother!

SHEPHERD.

There had been prophecies . . .

OEDIPUS.
Tell me.

SHEPHERD.
It was said that the boy would kill his own
father.

OEDIPUS.
Then why did you give him over to this old
man?

SHEPHERD.
I pitied the baby, my King,
And I thought that this man would take him
far away
To his own country.
He saved him—but for what a fate!
For if you are what this man says you are,
No man living is more wretched than
Oedipus.

OEDIPUS.
Ah God!
It was true!
All the prophecies!
—Now,
O Light, may I look on you for the last time!
I, Oedipus,
Oedipus, damned in his birth, in his marriage
damned,
Damned in the blood he shed with his own
hand!

(*He rushes into the palace*)

Ode 4

CHORUS. (STROPHE 1)
Alas for the seed of men.
What measure shall I give these generations

That breathe on the void and are void
And exist and do not exist?

Who bears more weight of joy
Than mass of sunlight shifting in images,
Or who shall make his thought stay on
That down time drifts away?

Your splendor is all fallen.

O naked brow of wrath and tears,
O change of Oedipus!
I who saw your days call no man blest—
Your great days like ghósts góne.

(ANTISTROPHE 1)
That mind was a strong bow.

Deep, how deep you drew it then, hard
archer,
At a dim fearful range,
And brought dear glory down!

You overcame the stranger—
The virgin with her hooking lion claws—
And though death sang, stood like a tower
To make pale Thebes take heart.

Fortress against our sorrow!

True king, giver of laws,
Majestic Oedipus!
No prince in Thebes had ever such renown,
No prince won such grace of power.

(STROPHE 2)
And now of all men ever known
Most pitiful is this man's story:
His fortunes are most changed, his state
Fallen to a low slave's
Ground under bitter fate.

O Oedipus, most royal one!
The great door that expelled you to the light
Gave at night—ah, gave night to your glory:
As to the father, to the fathering son.

All understood too late.

How could that queen whom Laïos won,
The garden that he harrowed at his height,
Be silent when that act was done?

(ANTISTROPHE 2)
But all eyes fail before time's eye,

All actions come to justice there.
Though never willed, though far down the deep past,
Your bed, your dread sirings,
Are brought to book at last.

Child by Laïos doomed to die,
Then doomed to lose that fortunate little death,
Would God you never took breath in this air
That with my wailing lips I take to cry:

For I weep the world's outcast.

I was blind, and now I can tell why:
Asleep, for you had given ease of breath
To Thebes, while the false years went by.

Éxodos

(Enter, from the palace, SECOND MESSENGER)

SECOND MESSENGER.
Elders of Thebes, most honored in this land,
What horrors are yours to see and hear, what weight
Of sorrow to be endured, if, true to your birth,
You venerate the line of Labdakos!
I think neither Istros nor Phasis, those great rivers,
Could purify this place of the corruption
It shelters now, or soon must bring to light—
Evil not done unconsciously, but willed.

The greatest griefs are those we cause our-selves.

CHORAGOS.
Surely, friend, we have grief enough already;
What new sorrow do you mean?

SECOND MESSENGER.
                    The Queen is dead.

CHORAGOS.
Iocastê? Dead? But at whose hand?

SECOND MESSENGER.
                              Her own.
The full horror of what happened you can not know,
For you did not see it; but I, who did, will tell you
As clearly as I can how she met her death.

When she had left us,
In passionate silence, passing through the court,
She ran to her apartment in the house,
Her hair clutched by the fingers of both hands.
She closed the doors behind her; then, by that bed
Where long ago the fatal son was conceived—
That son who should bring about his father's death—
We heard her call upon Laïos, dead so many years,
And heard her wail for the double fruit of her marriage,
A husband by her husband, children by her child.

Exactly how she died I do not know:
For Oedipus burst in moaning and would not let us
Keep vigil to the end: it was by him
As he stormed about the room that our eyes were caught.
From one to another of us he went, begging a sword,
Cursing the wife who was not his wife, the mother
Whose womb had carried his own children and himself.
I do not know: it was none of us aided him,
But surely one of the gods was in control!
For with a dreadful cry
He hurled his weight, as though wrenched out of himself,
At the twin doors: the bolts gave, and he rushed in.
And there we saw her hanging, her body swaying
From the cruel cord she had noosed about her neck.
A great sob broke from him, heartbreaking to hear,
As he loosed the rope and lowered her to the ground.

I would blot out from my mind what happened next!
For the King ripped from her gown the golden brooches
That were her ornament, and raised them, and plunged them down

Straight into his own eyeballs, crying, "No more,
No more shall you look on the misery about me,
The horrors of my own doing! Too long you have known
The faces of those whom I should never have seen,
Too long been blind to those for whom I was searching!
From this hour, go in darkness!" And as he spoke,
He struck at his eyes—not once, but many times;
And the blood spattered his beard,
Bursting from his ruined sockets like red hail.

So from the unhappiness of two this evil has sprung,
A curse on the man and woman alike. The old
Happiness of the house of Labdakos
Was happiness enough: where is it today?
It is all wailing and ruin, disgrace, death—all
The misery of mankind that has a name—
And it is wholly and for ever theirs.

CHORAGOS.
Is he in agony still? Is there no rest for him?

SECOND MESSENGER.
He is calling for someone to lead him to the gates
So that all the children of Kadmos may look upon
His father's murderer, his mother's—no,
I can not say it!
                    And then he will leave Thebes,
Self-exiled, in order that the curse
Which he himself pronounced may depart from the house.
He is weak, and there is none to lead him,
So terrible is his suffering.
                    But you will see:
Look, the doors are opening; in a moment
You will see a thing that would crush a heart of stone.

> (*The central door is opened;* OEDIPUS, *blinded, is led in*)

CHORAGOS.
Dreadful indeed for men to see.
Never have my own eyes

Looked on a sight so full of fear.
Oedipus!
What madness came upon you, what daemon
Leaped on your life with heavier
Punishment than a mortal man can bear?
No: I can not even
Look at you, poor ruined one.
And I would speak, question, ponder,
If I were able. No.
You make me shudder.

OEDIPUS.
God.   God.
Is there a sorrow greater?
Where shall I find harbor in this world?
My voice is hurled far on a dark wind.
What has God done to me?

CHORAGOS.
Too terrible to think of, or to see.

OEDIPUS.
O cloud of night,   (STROPHE 1)
Never to be turned away: night coming on,
I can not tell how: night like a shroud!

My fair winds brought me here.
                    O God. Again
The pain of the spikes where I had sight,
The flooding pain
Of memory, never to be gouged out.

CHORAGOS.
This is not strange.
You suffer it all twice over, remorse in pain,
Pain in remorse.

OEDIPUS.
Ah dear friend   (ANTISTROPHE 1)
Are you faithful even yet, you alone?
Are you still standing near me, will you stay here,
Patient, to care for the blind?
                    The blind man!
Yet even blind I know who it is attends me,
By the voice's tone—
Though my new darkness hide the comforter.

CHORAGOS.
Oh fearful act!
What god was it drove you to rake black
Night across your eyes?

OEDIPUS.   (STROPHE 2)
Apollo. Apollo. Dear

Children, the god was Apollo.
He brought my sick, sick fate upon me.
But the blinding hand was my own!
How could I bear to see
When all my sight was horror everywhere?

CHORAGOS.
Everywhere; that is true.

OEDIPUS.
And now what is left?
Images? Love? A greeting even,
Sweet to the senses? Is there anything?
Ah, no, friends: lead me away.
Lead me away from Thebes.
                              Lead the great wreck
And hell of Oedipus, whom the gods hate.

CHORAGOS.
Your fate is clear, you are not blind to that.
Would God you had never found it out!

OEDIPUS.   (ANTISTROPHE 2)
Death take the man who unbound
My feet on that hillside
And delivered me from death to life! What
    life?
If only I had died,
This weight of monstrous doom
Could not have dragged me and my darlings
    down.

CHORAGOS.
I would have wished the same.

OEDIPUS.
Oh never to have come here
With my father's blood upon me! Never
To have been the man they call his mother's
    husband!
Oh accurst! Oh child of evil,
To have entered that wretched bed—
                              the selfsame one!
More primal than sin itself, this fell to me.

CHORAGOS.
I do not know how I can answer you.
You were better dead than alive and blind.

OEDIPUS.
Do not counsel me any more. This
    punishment
That I have laid upon myself is just.
If I had eyes,
I do not know how I could bear the sight

Of my father, when I came to the house of
    Death,
Or my mother: for I have sinned against them
    both
So vilely that I could not make my peace
By strangling my own life.
                        Or do you think my children,
Born as they were born, would be sweet to
    my eyes?
Ah never, never! Nor this town with its high
    walls,
Nor the holy images of the gods.
                              For I,
Thrice miserable!—Oedipus, noblest of all
    the line
Of Kadmos, have condemned myself to enjoy
These things no more, by my own
    malediction
Expelling that man whom the gods declared
To be a defilement in the house of Laïos.
After exposing the rankness of my own guilt,
How could I look men frankly in the eyes?
No, I swear it,
If I could have stifled my hearing at its source,
I would have done it and made all this body
A tight cell of misery, blank to light and
    sound:
So I should have been safe in a dark agony
Beyond all recollection.
                        Ah Kithairon!
Why did you shelter me? When I was cast
    upon you,
Why did I not die? Then I should never
Have shown the world my execrable birth.

Ah Polybos! Corinth, city that I believed
The ancient seat of my ancestors: how fair
I seemed, your child! And all the while this
    evil
Was cancerous within me!
                              For I am sick
In my daily life, sick in my origin.

O three roads, dark ravine, woodland and
    way
Where three roads met: you, drinking my
    father's blood,
My own blood, spilled by my own hand: can
    you remember
The unspeakable things I did there, and the
    things

I went on from there to do?

          O marriage, marriage!
The act that engendered me, and again the act
Performed by the son in the same bed—

                   Ah, the net
Of incest, mingling fathers, brothers, sons,
With brides, wives, mothers: the last evil
That can be known by men: no tongue can say
How evil!

        No. For the love of God, conceal me
Somewhere far from Thebes; or kill me; or hurl me
Into the sea, away from men's eyes for ever.

Come, lead me. You need not fear to touch me.
Of all men, I alone can bear this guilt.

                (*Enter* CREON)

CHORAGOS.
We are not the ones to decide; but Creon here
May fitly judge of what you ask. He only
Is left to protect the city in your place.

OEDIPUS.
Alas, how can I speak to him? What right have I
To beg his courtesy whom I have deeply wronged?

CREON.
I have not come to mock you, Oedipus,
Or to reproach you, either.

              (*To* ATTENDANTS)
        —You, standing there:
If you have lost all respect for man's dignity
At least respect the flame of Lord Helios:
Do not allow this pollution to show itself
Openly here, an affront to the earth
And Heaven's rain and the light of day. No, take him
Into the house as quickly as you can.
For it is proper
That only the close kindred see his grief.

OEDIPUS.
I pray you in God's name, since your courtesy
Ignores my dark expectation, visiting
With mercy this man of all men most execrable:

Give me what I ask—for your good, not for mine.

CREON.
And what is it that you would have me do?

OEDIPUS.
Drive me out of this country as quickly as may be
To a place where no human voice can ever greet me.

CREON.
I should have done that before now—only,
God's will had not been wholly revealed to me.

OEDIPUS.
But his command is plain: the parricide
Must be destroyed. I am that evil man.

CREON.
That is the sense of it, yes; but as things are,
We had best discover clearly what is to be done.

OEDIPUS.
You would learn more about a man like me?

CREON.
You are ready now to listen to the god.

OEDIPUS.
I will listen. But it is to you
That I must turn for help. I beg you, hear me.

The woman in there—
Give her whatever funeral you think proper:
She is your sister.

          —But let me go, Creon!
Let me purge my father's Thebes of the pollution
Of my living here, and go out to the wild hills,
To Kithairon, that has won such fame with me,
The tomb my mother and father appointed for me,
And let me die there, as they willed I should.
And yet I know
Death will not ever come to me through sickness
Or in any natural way: I have been preserved
For some unthinkable fate. But let that be.

As for my sons, you need not care for them.
They are men, they will find some way to live.
But my poor daughters, who have shared my
　table,
Who never before have been parted from
　their father—
Take care of them, Creon; do this for me.
And will you let me touch them with my
　hands
A last time, and let us weep together?
Be kind, my lord,
Great prince, be kind!
　　　　　　　　　　Could I but touch them,
They would be mine again, as when I had my
　eyes.
　　　(*Enter* ANTIGONE *and* ISMENE, *attended*)
Ah, God!
Is it my dearest children I hear weeping?
Has Creon pitied me and sent my daughters?

CREON.
Yes, Oedipus: I knew that they were dear to
　you
In the old days, and know you must love them
　still.

OEDIPUS.
May God bless you for this—and be a
　friendlier
Guardian to you than he has been to me!

Children, where are you?
Come quickly to my hands: they are your
　brother's—
Hands that have brought your father's once
　clear eyes
To this way of seeing—
　　　　　　　　　　Ah dearest ones,
I had neither sight nor knowledge then, your
　father
By the woman who was the source of his own
　life!
And I weep for you—having no strength to
　see you—,
I weep for you when I think of the bitterness
That men will visit upon you all your lives.
What homes, what festivals can you attend
Without being forced to depart again in
　tears?
And when you come to marriageable age,
Where is the man, my daughters, who would
　dare
Risk the bane that lies on all my children?

Is there any evil wanting? Your father killed
His father; sowed the womb of her who bore
　him;
Engendered you at the fount of his own
　existence!
That is what they will say of you.

　　　　　　　　　　　　　Then, whom
Can you ever marry? There are no
　bridegrooms for you,
And your lives must wither away in sterile
　dreaming.
O Creon, son of Menoikeus!
You are the only father my daughters have,
Since we, their parents, are both of us gone
　for ever.
They are your own blood: you will not let
　them
Fall into beggary and loneliness;
You will keep them from the miseries that are
　mine!
Take pity on them; see, they are only
　children,
Friendless except for you. Promise me this,
Great Prince, and give me your hand in token
　of it.
　　　　　　(CREON *clasps his right hand*)

Children:
I could say much, if you could understand me,
But as it is, I have only this prayer for you:
Live where you can, be as happy as you can—
Happier, please **God**, than **God** has made
　your father!

CREON.
Enough. You have wept enough. Now go
　within.

OEDIPUS.
I must; but it is hard.

CREON.
　　　　　　　　　Time eases all things.

OEDIPUS.
But you must promise—

CREON.
　　　　　　　　　Say what you desire.

OEDIPUS.
Send me from Thebes!

CREON.
　　　　　　　　　God grant that I may!

OEDIPUS.
But since God hates me . . .

CREON.
           No, he will grant your wish.

OEDIPUS.
You promise?

CREON.
     I can not speak beyond my knowledge.

OEDIPUS.
Then lead me in.

CREON.
       Come now, and leave your children.

OEDIPUS.
No! Do not take them from me!

CREON.
          Think no longer
That you are in command here, but rather think
How, when you were, you served your own destruction.

(Exeunt into the house all but the CHORUS; *the* CHORAGOS *chants directly to the audience)*

CHORAGOS.
Men of Thebes: look upon Oedipus.

This is the king who solved the famous riddle
And towered up, most powerful of men.
No mortal eyes but looked on him with envy,
Yet in the end ruin swept over him.

Let every man in mankind's frailty
Consider his last day; and let none
Presume on his good fortune until he find
Life, at his death, a memory without pain.

———◆·◄►·◆———

Oedipus Rex by Sophocles was produced at Athens sometime between 430 and 411 B.C. It has for long been regarded as one of the great masterpieces of Greek tragedy, and Aristotle, in his *Poetics,* seems to have regarded it as a sort of touchstone for tragedy. Through the centuries *Oedipus Rex* has drawn special praise for the brilliance of its plotting.

In an earlier page we observed that if the dramatist begins his play at a point not far removed from the climax of the action—near the finish line of the race, as it were—the total action need not involve any long span of time. This play begins at a point quite close to the revelation that will bring down Oedipus from his proud position as ruler of his city to the plight of a miserable, blinded man, begging to be exiled.

Yet there are problems and difficulties in beginning a play so close to its climactic point—for example, the difficulty of providing adequate exposition and complication. The disaster that befalls Oedipus has its beginnings in events that go far back in time, to a period before his very birth. Since all of this material must be marshalled and deployed in what had to be a relatively short play, the problem of plotting becomes most important.

The way in which the exposition is handled in this play is worth remarking. Before the play can go forward, the audience must know that a curse has fallen on the land of Thebes. Not only are human beings sick and dying, but the very cattle are sick too, and even the crops in the fields are blighted. As the play opens, the Thebans have come to the palace to appeal for help to Oedipus, their king. They have faith that he can discover the cause of the plague and find a means to remove it, for, years earlier, Oedipus had saved them from a like curse—the depredations of the monstrous Sphinx. The Sphinx put her riddle to every passer-by, and if the person accosted could not solve the riddle, she promptly devoured him. Oedipus had found the answer to the riddle, and the Sphinx, in furious despair, leaped from the rock on which she had stationed herself and dashed out her life.

Oedipus tells his people that he has all along been aware of the troubles from which they have been suffering and that he has considered what to do. He has resolved to send his brother-in-law, Creon, to consult the oracle at Delphi in the hope that the god Apollo will vouchsafe counsel. Creon's return is already past due, and Oedipus is now anxiously awaiting his arrival.

Just as Oedipus says this, Creon comes in sight. Now, having received the oracle's answer, Oedipus can begin to act in behalf of his people and the play goes forward. At this point, the exposition proper ends, for we now have come to know something of the principal characters; the playwright has set forth the vexing situation that will precipitate the action to follow; and we have been given at least a hint of the difficulties that this action may entail.

It should be added, however, that in this play the treatment of exposition is somewhat special. It is accomplished much more succinctly than in most other plays. The exposition required by *Hedda Gabler,* for example, is more elaborate; and so is that required for *Saint Joan.*

Sophocles, it is true, had some special advantages in the matter of plotting. Like most Greek tragedies, *Oedipus Rex* was founded on an ancient Greek myth, and the Athenian audience could be counted on to be thoroughly familiar with it. Even so, one notices that Sophocles has taken care to weave every bit of information relevant to the plot into the fabric of the play.

The real advantage of writing for an audience that knew the story of Oedipus comes out in a rather different way. From the beginning, the audience knows what will be the outcome of Oedipus's attempt to discover the murderer of Laïos. The situation is one, therefore, that legitimately allows for all sorts of ironies, and especially for what has come to be called "Sophoclean irony," where a speech that has one import for the character in the play carries a very different meaning to the ears of the audience. When Oedipus curses the murderer of Laïos, whoever that murderer may be, the audience is aware that he is cursing himself. Or when Iocaste, trying to describe Laïos, her former husband, to Oedipus, tells him that Laïos was tall, his hair just touched with white, and that his form "was not unlike your own," the audience knows exactly why the two men resembled each other.

Yet granted a brilliant compression of the plot of the play, and granted the stunning effect of some of the ironic reversals, what did this play have to say to a Greek audience of the fifth century B.C.? And what does it have to say to us?

As for the meaning that the play had for the Greeks: we must remember that the Greek gods do not correspond to our modern notion of divinity. They are immanent rather than transcendent, and they are closer to impersonal forces than to beings like the God of Abraham or the Christian God. H. B. F. Kitto, in his *Sophocles: Dramatist and Philosopher* (Oxford University Press, 1958), points out that the Greek gods, "the *theoi* individually or collectively, were never intended as a pattern of what *ought* to be; they are a statement of what *is.* . . . [Greek tragedy] is continually saying: '*These* are the permanent conditions of human life; these are the gods.'"

It behooves the modern reader, therefore, to be cautious in reading into this play his own ideas and valuations, for if he does so, he may very well misconstrue the meaning. Is the modern reader, then, barred out from the play? Is the play so tightly tied to the value assumptions of the civilization out of which it comes that it has little to say to us in the twentieth century? The modern reader, for instance, does not believe in oracles; yet in this play Sophocles—so it has been argued—is pounding home to his Athenian audience the necessity for such belief. Sophocles may in fact have believed in oracles; many intelligent Greeks did, though others did not. But the modern reader certainly does not.

An even greater obstacle for the modern reader may be the nature of the justice or injustice meted out to Oedipus. The modern reader may feel that Oedipus is punished quite savagely and beyond any crime that can be conceivably attributed to him. How are we to relate the ironic fall of Oedipus to the general human situation or see it as having meaning and relevance for our own time?

Here again Professor Kitto is helpful: the matter of importance, as he makes plain, is not the detail of Greek religion or the special nature of the warning sign—whether dreams, oracles, or portents—but the kind of universe that the poetry reveals, and it is a universe that has some relevance to twentieth-century man. It is a universe ordered by law and the man who breaks its laws, though in ignorance, will suffer the consequences.

When Oedipus, by killing his father and marrying his mother, offends against the *theoi* who guard the purity of the race, he incurs the penalty even though his offense is unwitting. To use Kitto's words: "If, in all innocence, a man eats potassium cyanide, thinking that it is sugar, his innocence and ignorance will not save him." Seen in such terms as these, the fall of Oedipus does have meaning for a man of the twentieth century, perhaps a most significant meaning for twentieth-century man, who lives under the threat of world disaster and may very well be vaporized through a wrong triggering of machinery he is just learning to manipulate to his potential benefit, but also at great potential peril to himself and his fellows.

One way to view the play, then, is as a commentary on knowledge—on man's splendid aspiration to knowledge, his inability ever to achieve full knowledge, and the perils of all partial knowledge. The prophecies of the Delphic oracle concerning Laïos and Iocaste and Oedipus present themselves as full knowledge, knowledge as of the gods who know all things and cannot be mistaken. The oracles do not compel the people concerned to act in a particular way: they simply foretell what the people concerned are in fact going to do. Naturally, Laïos and Iocaste and Oedipus try to avoid what is foretold of them, but their knowledge, because human, is necessarily imperfect and partial. Ironically, their very attempts to avoid the prophecies result in fulfilling them. If the consequences are terrible, and go beyond our notion of just deserts, the basic pattern nevertheless is grounded in human experience. As we know, human beings, in their very anxiety to avoid certain happenings, sometimes bring them about.

Though the parents of Oedipus were cruel in their attempt to avoid the prophecy, they were not cruel enough: they did not ensure the death of their baby son by having him killed before their eyes. In his attempt to avoid the prophecy, Oedipus, too, acted drastically and perhaps cruelly, for he deserted his parents (really, of course, his foster parents). But that action was not sufficiently drastic either. A more careful and prudent man would have tried to avoid killing any

man and marrying any woman. Yet even if the human characters had taken every precaution, the dread oracles might have fulfilled themselves, nevertheless. Who knows?

It was not Oedipus's fault that he was the child of Laïos and Iocaste, or that his parents sent him out to die, or that he was adopted by foster parents who did not tell him the secret of his birth. Oedipus is blameworthy only in his pride and in his confidence that he does know who he is and that with his human knowledge he can outwit the prophecies and manipulate the future. The tragic flaw of the Greek protagonist is overweening pride, or, to give it its Greek name, *hybris*. The man guilty of *hybris* forgets his humanity and thinks of himself as a man of unlimited—that is, godlike—powers. If we regard *Oedipus Rex* as a commentary on knowledge, Oedipus's presumption is in thinking that his own knowledge is as full and deep as that of the gods.

There are reasons—and they are perfectly natural human reasons—for Oedipus's taking pride in his powers. By solving the riddle of the Sphinx, the answer to which no one else had been able to discover, he had saved the city of Thebes. Now the people of Thebes are appealing to their ruler to save them once more. As Oedipus speedily learns, the salvation of Thebes will turn again on the solution of an intellectual problem: the plague can be ended only by discovering the murderer of Laïos. This is a problem after Oedipus's own heart. His past success gives him confidence, but more than that, Oedipus is a man who honestly values the truth. His faults and his virtues are all of a piece: he craves knowledge, and later in the play will prove that he is willing to suffer in order to gain it.

Another reason for Oedipus's pride in his own abilities lies in the way in which he had attained kingly power. The play should actually not be called *Oedipus Rex,* but ought to be given its proper Greek title, *Oedipus Tyrannos,* for the word *tyrannos* had a special significance for the ancient Athenians that the Latin *rex* (the king) does not convey to us. The *tyrannos* was the man who held power not because he had inherited it but because he had won it through sheer ability and skill. Ignorant that he possesses princely blood, or that he has any claim through inheritance to the throne of Thebes, Oedipus thinks of himself as indeed a self-made man.

Because he is a *tyrannos,* Oedipus tends to suspect that other people might like to seize power too, and speedily becomes suspicious of Creon, his brother-in-law. His conduct may be in part accounted for by his impetuousness and his hot temper, traits that revealed themselves long before this, when he killed the man and his servants at the crossroads. But now his temperamental edginess is heightened by his being aware that his position as ruler is not secured by claims of blood and "legitimacy."

It is important, however, to emphasize the point made earlier. Oedipus does not come to grief, merely because he has a high temper and thus gets into trouble in situations out of which a more prudent and less touchy man might come unscathed. Nor does he come to grief simply because he is suspicious of Creon. The choleric impatience that he manifests toward Teiresias and his quickness to suspect that Creon has designs on his throne may exhibit traits of character that account for his violent altercation with Laïos at the crossroads. It is entirely reasonable to associate high temper with violence and even a propensity to homicide, but homicide is not the same thing as parricide, and incest is a crime still more remote.

If the terrible things that befall Oedipus are to be related to some defect in his own character, we had best look for that defect where the ancient Greeks probably looked for it: in Oedipus' overweening confidence in his own powers and his presumptuous belief that he can attain to full knowledge such as only a god possesses. To the Greeks, this was presumption indeed. They believed that even the wisest human being could not foresee the future or know all the consequences of his acts. Worse still, and fraught with a greater potential for disaster, was the fact that even the wisest mortal could not be sure that he fully knew himself.

There is something pathetic in watching this great towering figure, so confident in his own good intentions and in his own abilities,

reassuring his people by telling them that he is going to find out who the murderer of Laïos is, and woe be to that person when he finds him; or pronouncing a curse upon the murderer who has brought the taint upon the city, and, in his ignorance, cursing himself. Though the spectacle is pitiable, it also has an aspect of heroism, particularly when Oedipus refuses to give up the search even when it has begun to take a darker and more personal direction, and attention has shifted to the problem of finding out who he himself is and where he came from. But the spectacle is also terrifying inasmuch as we can see in the action of Oedipus something of our own limitations and blindness, for we too, though we do not really know ourselves, are constantly forced to try to settle the affairs of ourselves and others.

Aristotle in his *Poetics* says that tragedy excites pity and terror, and whatever he meant by these terms (and whether or not he would apply them in just this fashion to Oedipus) he clearly regarded the case of Oedipus as providing "the spectacle of a virtuous man brought from prosperity to adversity," and not at all as the spectacle of "a bad man" suffering misfortune, or of the downfall of an "utter villain." As Aristotle put it, the proper tragic hero is "a man who is not eminently good and just, yet whose misfortune is brought about not by vice or depravity, but by some error or frailty. . . ."

Kitto, in summing up this play, remarks that "the gods can see the whole pattern of this Universe; Man cannot. . . . We should [therefore] remember how blind we are, avoiding *hybris,* arrogance, cocksureness." But Kitto, of course, does not mean to imply that the play is a moral tract presenting this "message" to its Athenian audience and to ourselves. The meaning of the play is much more massive than this, and not only more massive but richer and more complicated in the ramifications of its meanings. It does not preach a moral but rather dramatizes a very important aspect of man's fate: man finds himself in a universe that imposes terrible penalties upon those who break its laws though these are laws that no human being can fully understand.

EXERCISES

1. Notice that rather early in the play Teiresias, though he would avoid saying anything if he could, tells Oedipus the truth about himself. Is this an inartistic, because too early, divulging of the mystery? If not, why not? Why does Oedipus not believe the truth here told to him?

2. Three people try very hard during the course of the play to persuade Oedipus to desist from his inquiry. The first is Teiresias, the second is Iocaste. Who is the third?

3. Observe that not once but twice people trying to reassure Oedipus actually involve him in greater doubts. Iocaste, to assuage Oedipus's fears about soothsayers, tells him that a prophecy concerning the death of her first husband failed to come true, but some of the details of this pronouncement of the oracle disturb Oedipus greatly—not at the thought that Laïos is his father, but that it might have been he who killed Iocaste's first husband. What is the second instance of an attempt to reassure Oedipus that actually disturbs him the more? These reversals of expectation (Aristotle's term is *peripeteia*) have what effect upon the general theme of the play? What is their function in terms of the plot?

4. A modern commentator writes that Oedipus has some warrant for being suspicious of Creon, since Oedipus has felt "from the beginning that the death of Laïos is attributable to treachery and bribery at work within the state—and in his mind lies also the thought that he himself may be the victim of a similar plot. These are the natural suspicions of any tyrannos. . . ." Does this comment help to account for the promptness with which Oedipus expects the worst of Creon?

5. Is not Oedipus's act of blinding himself symbolically appropriate? Remember that the oracles have been pronounced by Apollo the god of light.

6. Note how many of the speeches in this play have to do with the matter of seeing and of blindness. For example, Oedipus says to Creon: "Then once more I must bring what is dark to light." Teiresias says to Oedipus: "You mock my blindness, do you? / I say that you, with both your eyes, are blind: / You cannot see the wretchedness of your life. . . ." Oedipus says to Iocaste: "I am not sure that the blind man [that is, Teiresias] cannot see," and this is the first hint on Oedipus's part that the man with good eyes may not be able to discern what the man without eyes can discern. The chorus sings: "But all eyes fail before time's eye." Notice particularly the comments on blindness and seeing in the last scene of the play.

7. Early in the play, someone suggests that the oracle that "ordained the search" for the murderer of Laïos might be appealed to to tell where the murderer now is. Oedipus replies that this solution is too easy, for "No man in the world / Can make the gods do more than the gods will." Yet Oedipus's whole adult life has been based upon the supposition that a mortal man can evade what the gods have foretold will happen. Notice how this double attitude toward the knowledge of the gods runs through the play, so that we have at one point the attempt to prove an oracle false, then reliance upon an oracle, then confidence that oracles do not tell truth, and finally the awesome knowledge that they do. Trace the pattern of attitudes toward oracular pronouncements and give special attention to the statements of the chorus and to the speeches of Iocaste and Oedipus.

8. One of the more interesting ironies in the play is that which contrasts the role of king (that is, the man who inherits rule) and *tyrannos* (the man who wins it by his own achievements). More than once Oedipus boasts of the fact that he is a self-made man who has won the rulership of Thebes through his own accomplishment. Yet Oedipus is to find that he is indeed the true king of Thebes, the child of Laïos and Iocaste. What is the bearing, if there is any, of this ironic reversal upon the conduct of Oedipus? Upon the theme of the tragedy? In pondering your answer, take into account Scene 3 of the play in which Oedipus mistakes the reason for Iocaste's dread of any revelation about his ancestry.

9. The horrible truth about Oedipus dawns on Iocaste before it becomes clear to Oedipus. When she first becomes sure that Oedipus is her son, can it be said that from this point onward she tries with—ironically—something of a mother's concern to save her child?

10. Consider carefully the Second Messenger's speech. What do you make of Oedipus's attitude toward Iocaste? Why does he beg for a sword? What is his attitude toward his children?

11. Oedipus wishes to leave Thebes. What motives does he give for wanting to go? Are these his only motives?

12. Creon says to Oedipus, "You are ready now to listen to the god," and Oedipus replies that he is ready. What is the bearing of this exchange upon Oedipus's attitude toward the gods? Upon his attitude toward his new-found knowledge? Upon the theme of the play? Note that Creon, though he would like to grant Oedipus's wish, and hopes that he will be able to do so, refuses to grant it until he has consulted the oracle once more.

13. Would you say from a review of this play that

Sophocles is an "anti-intellectual"? Would he discourage the active pursuit of the truth that Oedipus exemplifies? Or would the implied attitude toward man's pursuit of knowledge be better put in other terms? Is it implied, for example, that though truth is precious, it cannot always be won simply by confident seeking? That truth is more mysterious and intractable than we are wont to think? That the hardest truth to come by is the truth about ourselves?

The following are some recommended publications on Greek tragedy and the work of Sophocles: S. M. Adams, *Sophocles the Playwright* (Univ. of Toronto Press, 1957); H. D. F. Kitto, *Greek Tragedy* (New York:

Anchor Books, 1954); C. H. Whitman, *Sophocles: A Study of Heroic Humanism* (Cambridge, Mass.: Harvard University Press, 1951); and Bernard M. W. Knox, *Oedipus at Thebes* (New Haven: Yale University Press, 1957). Knox's work in particular will be interesting to the student who would like to see how the very diction and imagery of the Greek play are used to develop the many ironies that attach to the search for truth that Oedipus so heroically makes. Some of this material is included in Knox's "Sophocles' *Oedipus*," one of the essays in *Tragic Themes in Western Literature*, ed. Cleanth Brooks (New Haven: Yale University Press, 1955).

ANTONY AND CLEOPATRA
William Shakespeare (1564–1616)

Characters

MARK ANTONY,
OCTAVIOUS CAESAR, } *triumvirs*
M. AEMILIUS LEPIDUS,
SEXTUS POMPEIUS.

DOMITIUS ENOBARBUS,
VENTIDIUS,
EROS,
SCARUS, } *friends to Antony*
DERCETAS,
DEMETRIUS,
PHILO,

MECAENAS,
AGRIPPA,
DOLABELLA, } *friends to Caesar*
PROCULEIUS,
THYREUS,
GALLUS,

MENAS,
MENECRATES, } *friends to Pompey*
VARRIUS,

TAURUS, *Lieutenant-General to Caesar*
CANIDIUS, *Lieutenant-General to Antony*
SILIUS, *an officer under Ventidius*
EUPHRONIUS, *Ambassador from Antony to Caesar*
ALEXAS,
MARDIAN, } *attendants on Cleopatra*
SELEUCUS,
DIOMEDES,

A SOOTHSAYER
A Clown
CLEOPATRA, *Queen of Egypt*
OCTAVIA, *sister to Caesar, and wife to Antony*
CHARMIAN, } *attendants on Cleopatra*
IRAS,

Officers, Soldiers, Messengers, and other Attendants

SCENE: *In several parts of the Roman Empire.*

ACT 1

SCENE 1. *Alexandria. A room in* CLEOPATRA'S *palace.*

(*Enter* DEMETRIUS *and* PHILO)

PHILO. Nay, but this dotage of our general's
O'erflows the measure; those his goodly eyes,

That o'er the files and musters of the war
Have glowed like plated[1] Mars, now bend,
now turn
The office and devotion of their view   5
Upon a tawny front; his captain's heart,

[1] armored

Which in the scuffles of great fights hath burst
The buckles on his breast, reneges all tem-
per.[2]
And is become the bellows and the fan
To cool a gypsy's lust.

    (*Flourish. Enter* ANTONY *and* CLEOPATRA,
    with their trains; eunuchs fanning her.)
               Look! where they come.   10
Take but good note, and you shall see in him
The triple pillar of the world transformed
Into a strumpet's fool; behold and see.

CLEOPATRA. If it be love indeed, tell me how
much.

ANTONY. There's beggary in the love that can
be reckoned.   15

CLEOPATRA. I'll set a bourn[3] how far to be
beloved.

ANTONY. Then must thou needs find out new
heaven, new earth.

        (*Enter an* ATTENDANT)

ATTENDANT. News, my good lord, from Rome.

ANTONY.   Grates me; the sum.

CLEOPATRA. Nay, hear them, Antony.
Fulvia perchance is angry; or, who knows   20
If the scarce-bearded Caesar have not sent
His powerful mandate to you, "Do this, or
this;
Take in that kingdom, and enfranchise that;
Perform't, or else we damn thee."

ANTONY.   How, my love!

CLEOPATRA. Perchance! nay, and most like; 25
You must not stay here longer; your dismis-
sion
Is come from Caesar; therefore hear it, Antony.
Where's Fulvia's process?[4] Caesar's I would
say? both?
Call in the messengers. As I am Egypt's
queen,
Thou blushest, Antony, and that blood of
thine,   30
Is Caesar's homager; else so thy cheek pays
shame

When shrill-tongued Fulvia scolds. The mes-
sengers!
ANTONY. Let Rome in Tiber melt, and the
wide arch
Of the ranged empire fall! Here is my space.
Kingdoms are clay; our dungy earth alike   35
Feeds beast as man; the nobleness of life
Is to do thus; when such a mutual pair
    (*Embracing*)
And such a twain can do 't, in which I bind,
On pain of punishment, the world to weet[5]
We stand up peerless.

CLEOPATRA.   Excellent falsehood! 40
Why did he marry Fulvia, and not love her?
I'll seem the fool I am not; Antony
Will be himself.

ANTONY.   But stirred by Cleopatra.
Now, for the love of Love and her soft hours,
Let's not confound the time with conference
harsh: 45
There's not a minute of our lives should
stretch
Without some pleasure now. What sport to-
night?

CLEOPATRA. Hear the ambassadors.

ANTONY.   Fie, wrangling queen!
Whom every thing becomes, to chide, to
laugh,
To weep; whose every passion fully strives 50
To make itself, in thee, fair and admired.
No messenger, but thine; and all alone,
Tonight we'll wander through the streets and
note
The qualities of people. Come, my queen;
Last night you did desire it; speak not to us. 55
    (*Exeunt* ANTONY *and* CLEOPATRA,
             with their train)

DEMETRIUS. Is Caesar with Antonius prized
so slight?

PHILO. Sir, sometimes, when he is not Antony,
He comes too short of that great property
Which still should go with Antony.

DEMETRIUS.   I am full sorry
That he approves[6] the common liar, who 60
Thus speaks of him at Rome; but I will hope
Of better deeds tomorrow. Rest you happy!
              (*Exeunt*)

---

[2] renounces all self-restraint [3] boundary [4] command   [5] know [6] justifies

SCENE 2. *The same. Another room.*

(*Enter* CHARMIAN, IRAS, ALEXAS, *and a* SOOTHSAYER)

CHARMIAN. Lord Alexas, sweet Alexas, most any thing, Alexas, almost most absolute Alexas, where's the soothsayer that you praised so to the queen? O! that I knew this husband, which, you say, must charge his horns with garlands!   5

ALEXAS. Soothsayer!

SOOTHSAYER. Your will?

CHARMIAN. Is this the man? Is't you, sir, that know things?

SOOTHSAYER. In nature's infinite book of secrecy
A little I can read.

ALEXAS.   Show him your hand.   10

(*Enter* ENOBARBUS)

ENOBARBUS. Bring in the banquet quickly; wine enough
Cleopatra's health to drink.

CHARMIAN. Good sir, give me good fortune.

SOOTHSAYER. I make not, but foresee.

CHARMIAN. Pray then, forsee me one.   15

SOOTHSAYER. You shall be yet far fairer than you are.

CHARMIAN. He means in flesh.

IRAS. No, you shall paint when you are old.

CHARMIAN. Wrinkles forbid!

ALEXAS. Vex not his prescience; be attentive.

CHARMIAN. Hush!   21

SOOTHSAYER. You shall be more beloving than beloved.

CHARMIAN. I had rather heat my liver with drinking.

ALEXAS. Nay, hear him.   24

CHARMIAN. Good now, some excellent fortune! Let me be married to three kings in a forenoon, and widow them all; let me have a child at fifty, to whom Herod of Jewry may do

homage; find me to marry me with Octavius Caesar, and companion me with my mistress.

SOOTHSAYER. You shall outlive the lady whom you serve.   31

CHARMIAN. O excellent! I love long life better than figs.

SOOTHSAYER. You have seen and proved a fairer former fortune
Than that which is to approach.   34

CHARMIAN. Then, belike, my children shall have no names; prithee, how many boys and wenches must I have?

SOOTHSAYER. If every of your wishes had a womb,
And fertile every wish, a million.

CHARMIAN. Out, fool! I forgive thee for a witch.   40

ALEXAS. You think none but your sheets are privy to your wishes.

CHARMIAN. Nay, come, tell Iras hers.

ALEXAS. We'll know all our fortunes.

ENOBARBUS. Mine, and most of our fortunes, tonight, shall be,—drunk to bed.   46

IRAS. There's a palm presages chastity, if nothing else.

CHARMIAN. E'en as the overflowing Nilus presageth famine.   50

IRAS. Go, you wild bedfellow, you cannot soothsay.

CHARMIAN. Nay, if an oily palm be not a fruitful prognostication, I cannot scratch mine ear. Prithee, tell her but a worky-day[1] fortune.   55

SOOTHSAYER. Your fortunes are alike.

IRAS. But how? but how? give me particulars.

SOOTHSAYER. I have said.

IRAS. Am I not an inch of fortune better than she?   60

CHARMIAN. Well, if you were but an inch of

[1] everyday, ordinary

fortune better than I, where would you choose it?

IRAS. Not in my husband's nose.

CHARMIAN. Our worser thoughts Heavens mend! Alexas,—come, his fortune, his fortune. O! let him marry a woman that cannot go, sweet Isis, I beseech thee; and let her die too, and give him a worse; and let worse follow worse, till the worst of all follow him laughing to his grave, fiftyfold a cuckold! Good Isis, hear me this prayer, though thou deny me a matter of more weight; good Isis, I beseech thee!   73

IRAS. Amen. Dear goddess, hear that prayer of the people! for, as it is a heart-breaking to see a handsome man loose-wived, so it is a deadly sorrow to behold a foul knave uncuckolded: therefore, dear Isis, deep decorum, and fortune him accordingly;

CHARMIAN. Amen.   80

ALEXAS. Lo, now! if it lay in their hands to make me a cuckold, they would make themselves whores, but they'd do't.

(*Enter* CLEOPATRA)

ENOBARBUS. Hush! here comes Antony.

CHARMIAN.   Not he; the queen.

CLEOPATRA. Saw you my lord?   86

ENOBARBUS.   No, lady.

CLEOPATRA.   Was he not here?

CHARMIAN. No, madam.

CLEOPATRA. He was disposed to mirth; but on the sudden   90
A Roman thought hath struck him. Enobarbus!

ENOBARBUS. Madam!

CLEOPATRA. Seek him, and bring him hither. Where's Alexas?

ALEXAS. Here, at your service. My lord   95 approaches.

(*Enter* ANTONY, *with a* MESSENGER *and* ATTENDANTS)

CLEOPATRA. We will not look upon him; go with us.

(*Exeunt* CLEOPATRA, ENOBARBUS, ALEXAS, IRAS, CHARMIAN, SOOTHSAYER, *and* ATTENDANTS)

MESSENGER. Fulvia thy wife first came into the field.

ANTONY. Against my brother Lucius?

MESSENGER. Ay:
But soon that war had end, and the time's state   101
Made friends of them, jointing their force 'gainst Caesar,
Whose better issue[2] in the war, from Italy
Upon the first encounter drave them.

ANTONY.   Well, what worst?   105

MESSENGER. The nature of bad news infects the teller.

ANTONY. When it concerns the fool, or coward. On;
Things that are past are done with me. 'Tis thus:
Who tells me true, though in his tale lay death,
I hear him as[3] he flattered.

MESSENGER.   Labienus—   111
This is stiff news—hath, with his Parthian force
Extended Asia; from Euphrates
His conquering banner shook from Syria
To Lydia and to Ionia: whilst—   115

ANTONY. Antony, thou wouldst say,—

MESSENGER.   O! my lord.

ANTONY. Speak to me home, mince not the general tongue;
Name Cleopatra as she is called in Rome;
Rail thou in Fulvia's phrase; and taunt my faults   120
With such full licence as both truth and malice
Have power to utter. O! then we bring forth weeds
When our quick minds lie still; and our ills told us
Is as our earing.[4] Fare thee well awhile.   124

MESSENGER. At your noble pleasure.   (*Exit*)

---

[2] fortune   [3] as though   [4] plowing

ANTONY. From Sicyon, ho, the news! Speak there!

FIRST ATTENDANT. The man from Sicyon, is there such an one?

SECOND ATTENDANT. He stays upon your will.

ANTONY.   Let him appear.
These strong Egyptian fetters I must break,
Or lose myself in dotage.   131

(Enter another MESSENGER)

What are you?

SECOND MESSENGER. Fulvia thy wife is dead.

ANTONY.   Where died she?

SECOND MESSENGER. In Sicyon: 135
Her length of sickness, with what else more serious
Importeth thee to know, this bears.
(Giving a letter)

ANTONY.   Forbear me.
(Exit SECOND MESSENGER)
There's a great spirit gone! Thus did I desire it:
What our contempts do often hurl from us 140
We wish it ours again; the present pleasure,
By revolution lowering, does become
The opposite of itself: she's good, being gone;
The hand could pluck her back that shoved her on.
I must from this enchanting queen break off;   145
Ten thousand harms, more than the ills I know,
My idleness doth hatch. How now! Enobarbus!

(Re-enter ENOBARBUS)

ENOBARBUS. What's your pleasure, sir?

ANTONY. I must with haste from hence.   149

ENOBARBUS. Why, then, we kill all our women. We see how mortal an unkindness is to them; if they suffer our departure, death's the word.

ANTONY. I must be gone.

ENOBARBUS. Under a compelling occasion let women die; it were pity to cast them away for nothing; though between them and a great cause they should be esteemed nothing. Cleopatra, catching but the least noise of this, dies instantly; I have seen her die twenty times upon far poorer moment. I do think there is mettle in death which commits some loving act upon her, she hath such a celerity in dying.   163

ANTONY. She is cunning past man's thought.

ENOBARBUS. Alack! sir, no; her passions are made of nothing but the finest part of pure love. We cannot call her winds and waters sighs and tears; they are greater storms and tempests than almanacs can report: this cannot be cunning in her; if it be, she makes a shower of rain as well as Jove.   171

ANTONY. Would I had never seen her!

ENOBARBUS. Oh, sir! you had then left unseen a wonderful piece of work which not to have been blessed withal would have discredited your travel.   176

ANTONY. Fulvia is dead.

ENOBARBUS. Sir?

ANTONY. Fulvia is dead.

ENOBARBUS. Fulvia!   180

ANTONY. Dead.

ENOBARBUS. Why, sir, give the gods a thankful sacrifice. When it pleaseth their deities to take the wife of a man from him, it shows to man the tailors of the earth; comforting therein, that when old robes are worn out, there are members to make new. If there were no more women but Fulvia, then had you indeed a cut, and the case to be lamented: this grief is crowned with consolation; your old smock brings forth a new petticoat; and indeed the tears live in an onion that should water this sorrow.   193

ANTONY. The business she hath broached[5] in the state
Cannot endure my absence.

ENOBARBUS. And the business you have broached here cannot be without you; espe-

5 begun

cially that of Cleopatra's, which wholly depends on your abode.   199

ANTONY. No more light answers. Let our
   officers
Have notice what we purpose. I shall break
The cause of our expedience[6] to the queen,
And get her leave to part. For not alone
The death of Fulvia, with more urgent
   touches,
Do strongly speak to us, but the letters too   206
Of many our contriving friends in Rome
Petition us at home. Sextus Pompeius
Hath given the dare to Caesar, and commands
The empire of the sea; our slippery people—
Whose love is never linked to the deserver
Till his deserts are past—begin to throw
Pompey the Great and all his dignities
Upon his son; who, high in name and power,
Higher than both in blood and life, stands up
For the main soldier, whose quality, going on,
The side o' the world may danger. Much is
   breeding,
Which, like the courser's hair,[7] hath yet but
   life,
And not a serpent's poison. Say, our pleasure,
To such whose place is under us, requires   220
Our quick remove from hence .

ENOBARBUS. I shall do it.   (*Exeunt*)

SCENE 3. *The same. Another room.*

(*Enter* CLEOPATRA, CHARMIAN, IRAS,
     and ALEXAS)

CLEOPATRA. Where is he?

CHARMIAN.   I did not see him since.

CLEOPATRA. See where he is, who's with him,
   what he does;
I did not send you: if you find him sad,
Say I am dancing; if in mirth, report
That I am sudden sick: quick, and return.   5

                 (*Exit* ALEXAS)

CHARMIAN. Madam, methinks, if you did love
   him dearly,
You do not hold the method to enforce
The like from him.

---

[6] enterprise   [7] horse's hair, with a reference to the old
superstition that a horse hair dropped into a pond turned
into a serpent.

CLEOPATRA.   What should I do I do not?

CHARMIAN. In each thing give him way, cross
   him in nothing.

CLEOPATRA. Thou teachest like a fool; the
   way to lose him.   10

CHARMIAN. Tempt him not so too far; I wish,
   forbear:
In time we hate that which we often fear.
But here comes Antony.

             (*Enter* ANTONY)

CLEOPATRA.   I am sick and sullen.

ANTONY. I am sorry to give breathing to my
   purpose,—

CLEOPATRA. Help me away, dear Charmian,
   I shall fall: 15
It cannot be thus long, the sides of nature
Will not sustain it.

ANTONY.   Now, my dearest queen,—

CLEOPATRA. Pray you, stand further from me.

ANTONY.   What's the matter?

CLEOPATRA. I know, by that same eye, there's
   some good news.
What says the married woman? You may
   go: 20
Would she had never given you leave to
   come!
Let her not say 'tis I that keep you here;
I have no power upon you; hers you are.

ANTONY. The gods best know,—

CLEOPATRA.   O! never was there queen
So mightily betrayed yet at the first   25
I saw the treasons planted.

ANTONY.   Cleopatra,—

CLEOPATRA. Why should I think you can be
   mine and true,
Though you in swearing shake the thronèd
   gods,
Who have been false to Fulvia? Riotous madness,   29
To be entangled with those mouth-made
   vows,
Which break themselves in swearing!

ANTONY.   Most sweet queen,—

CLEOPATRA. Nay, pray you, seek no colour for
   your going,
But bid farewell, and go: when you sued stay-
   ing[1]
Then was the time for words; no going then:
Eternity was in our lips and eyes,   35
Bliss in our brows bent; none our parts so
   poor
But was a race of heaven; they are so still,
Or thou, the greatest soldier of the world,
Art turned the greatest liar.

ANTONY.   How now, lady!

CLEOPATRA. I would I had thy inches; thou
   shouldst know   40
There were a heart in Egypt.

ANTONY.   Hear, me, queen:
The strong necessity of time commands
Our services a while, but my full heart
Remains in use with you. Our Italy
Shines o'er with civil swords; Sextus Pompeius
Makes his approaches to the port of Rome;   46
Equality of two domestic powers
Breeds scrupulous faction. The hated, grown
   to strength,
Are newly grown to love; the condemned
   Pompey,
Rich in his father's honour, creeps apace   50
Into the hearts of such as have not thrived
Upon the present state, whose numbers
   threaten;
And quietness, grown sick of rest, would
   purge[2]
By any desperate change. My more particular,
And that which most with you should safe[3]
   my going,   55
Is Fulvia's death.

CLEOPATRA. Though age from folly could not
   give me freedom.
It does from childishness: can Fulvia die?

ANTONY. She's dead my queen:
Look here, and at thy sovereign leisure read [60]
The garboils[4] she awaked; at the last, best,
See when and where she died.

CLEOPATRA.   O most false love!
Where be the sacred vials thou shouldst fill
With sorrowful water? Now I see, I see,
In Fulvia's death, how mine received shall be.

ANTONY. Quarrel no more, but be prepared
   to know   66
The purposes I bear, which are or cease
As you shall give the advice. By the fire
That quickens Nilus' slime, I go from hence
Thy soldier, servant, making peace or war   70
As thou affect'st[5]

CLEOPATRA.   Cut my lace, Charmian, come;
But let it be: I am quickly ill, and well;
So Antony loves.

ANTONY.   My precious queen, forbear,
And give true evidence to his love which
   stands
An honourable trial.

CLEOPATRA.   So Fulvia told me,   75
I prithee, turn aside and weep for her;
Then bid adieu to me, and say the tears
Belong to Egypt: good now, play one scene
Of excellent dissembling, and let it look
Like perfect honour.

ANTONY.   You'll heat my blood; no more.

CLEOPATRA. You can do better yet, but this is
   meetly.   81

ANTONY. Now, by my sword,—

CLEOPATRA.   And target. Still he mends;
But this is not the best. Look, prithee, Char-
   mian,
How this Herculean Roman does become
The carriage of his chafe.   85

ANTONY. I'll leave you, lady.

CLEOPATRA.   Courteous lord, one word.
Sir, you and I must part, but that's not it:
Sir, you and I have loved, but there's not it;
That you know well: something it is I
   would,—
O! my oblivion is a very Antony,   90
And I am all forgotten.

ANTONY.   But that your royalty
Holds idleness your subject, I should take you
For idleness itself.

CLEOPATRA.   'Tis sweating labour
To bear such idleness so near the heart
As Cleopatra this. But, sir, forgive me;   95
Since my becomings[6] kill me when they do
   not

---

[1] begged to stay   [2] restore itself to healthy activity   [3] make
safe   [4] commotions

[5] art inclined   [6] graces

Eye[7] well to you: your honour calls you
   hence;
Therefore be deaf to my unpitied folly,
And all the gods go with you! Upon your
   sword
Sit laurel victory! and smooth success   100
Be strewed before your feet!

ANTONY.   Let us go. Come;
Our separation so abides, and flies,
That thou, residing here, go'st yet with me,
And I, hence fleeting, here remain with thee.
Away!   (*Exeunt*)   105

SCENE 4: *Rome. A room in Caesar's house.*

(*Enter* OCTAVIOUS CAESAR, LEPIDUS,
and ATTENDANTS)

CAESAR. You may see, Lepidus, and hence-
   forth know,
It is not Caesar's natural vice to hate
Our great competitor. From Alexandria
This is the news: he fishes, drinks, and wastes
The lamps of night in revel; is not more
   manlike   5
Than Cleopatra, nor the queen of Ptolemy
More womanly than he; hardly gave audi-
   ence, or
Vouchsafed to think he had partners: you
   shall find there
A man who is the abstract of all faults
That all men follow.

LEPIDUS.   I must not think there are
Evils enow to darken all his goodness;   11
His faults in him seem as the spots of heaven,
More fiery by night's blackness; hereditary
Rather than purchased; what he cannot
   change
Than what he chooses.   15

CAESAR. You are too indulgent. Let us grant
   it is not
Amiss to tumble on the bed of Ptolemy,
To give a kingdom for a mirth, to sit
And keep the turn of tippling with a slave,
To reel the streets at noon, and stand the
   buffet
With knaves that smell of sweat; say this be-
   comes him,—   21
As his composure[1] must be rare indeed

Whom these things cannot blemish,—yet
   must Antony
No way excuse his foils, when we do bear
So great weight in his lightness. If he filled   25
His vacancy with his voluptuousness,
Full surfeits and the dryness of his bones
Call on him for 't; but to confound such time
That drums him from his sport, and speaks as
   loud
As his own state and ours, 'tis to be chid   30
As we rate[2] boys, who, being mature in knowl-
   edge,
Pawn their experience to their present plea-
   sure,
And so rebel to judgment.

(*Enter a* MESSENGER)

LEPIDUS.   Here's more news.

MESSENGER. Thy biddings have been done,
   and every hour,
Most noble Caesar, shalt thou have report   35
How 'tis abroad. Pompey is strong at sea,
And it appears he is beloved of those
That only have feared Caesar; to the ports
The discontents repair, and men's reports
Give him much wronged.

CAESAR.   I should have known no less.   40
It hath been taught us from the primal state,
That he which is was wished until he were;
And the ebbed man, ne'er loved till ne'er
   worth love,
Comes deared[3] by being lacked. This com-
   mon body,
Like a vagabond flag upon the stream,   45
Goes to and back, lackeying the varying tide,
To rot itself with motion.

MESSENGER.   Caesar, I bring thee word,
Menecrates and Menas famous pirates,
Make the sea serve them, which they ear and
   wound
With keels of every kind: many hot inroads
They make in Italy; the borders maritime   51
Lack blood to think on 't, and flush[4] youth
   revolt;
No vessel can peep forth, but 'tis as soon
Taken as seen; for Pompey's name strikes
   more
Than could his war resisted.

---

[7] appear   [1] disposition

[2] berate, scold   [3] becomes endeared, valued   [4] lusty

CAESAR.   Antony,   55
Leave thy lascivious wassails. When thou once
Wast beaten from Modena, where thou slew'st
Hirtius and Pansa, consuls, at thy heel
Did famine follow, whom thou fought'st
    against,
Though daintily brought up, with patience
    more   60
Than savages could suffer; thou didst drink
The stale of horses and the gilded puddle
Which beast would cough at; thy palate then
    did deign
The roughest berry on the rudest hedge;
Yea, like the stag, when snow the pasture
    sheets,   65
The barks of trees thou browsed'st; on the
    Alps
It is reported thou didst eat strange flesh,
Which some did die to look on; and all this—
It wounds thy honour that I speak it now—
Was borne so like a soldier, that they cheek 70
So much as lanked⁵ not.

LEPIDUS.   'Tis pity of him.

CAESAR. Let his shames quickly
Drive him to Rome. 'Tis time we twain
Did show ourselves i' the field; and to that
    end
Assemble we immediate council; Pompey   75
Thrives in our idleness.

LEPIDUS.   Tomorrow, Caesar,
I shall be furnished to inform you rightly
Both what by sea and land I can be able
To front this present time.

CAESAR.   Till which encounter,
It is my business too. Farewell.   80

LEPIDUS. Farewell, my lord. What you shall
    know meantime
Of stirs abroad, I shall beseech you, sir,
To let me be partaker

CAESAR.   Doubt not, sir;
I knew it for my bond.   (Exeunt)

SCENE 5. *Alexandria. A room in the palace.*

(*Enter* CLEOPATRA, CHARMIAN, IRAS
    and MARDIAN)

CLEOPATRA. Charmian!

CHARMIAN. Madam!

CLEOPATRA. Ha, ha!
Give me to drink mandragora.¹

CHARMIAN.   Why, madam?

CLEOPATRA. That I might sleep out this great
    gap of time   5
My Antony is away.

CHARMIAN.   You think of him too much.

CLEOPATRA. O! 'tis treason.

CHARMIAN.   Madam, I trust, not so.

CLEOPATRA. Thou, eunuch Mardian!

MARDIAN.   What's your highness' pleasure?

CLEOPATRA. Not now to hear thee sing; I take
    no pleasure
In aught a eunuch has. 'Tis well for thee,   10
That, being unseminared,² thy freer thoughts
May not fly forth of Egypt. Hast thou affec-
    tions?

MARDIAN. Yes, gracious madam.

CLEOPATRA. Indeed!

MARDIAN. Not in deed, madam: for I can do
    nothing   15
But what indeed is honest to be done;
Yet have I fierce affections, and think
What Venus did with Mars.

CLEOPATRA.   O Charmian!
Where think'st thou he is now? Stands he, or
    sits he?
Or does he walk? or is he on his horse?   20
O happy horse, to bear the weight of Antony!
Do bravely, horse, for wot'st³ thou whom thou
    mov'st?
The demi-Atlas of this earth, the arm
And burgonet of men. He's speaking now,
Or murmuring 'Where's my serpent of old
    Nile?'   25
For so he calls me. Now I feed myself
With most delicious poison. Think on me,
That am with Phoebus' amorous pinches
    black,
And wrinkled deep in time? Broad-fronted
    Caesar,   29
When thou wast here above the ground I was
A morsel for a monarch, and great Pompey
Would stand and make his eyes grow in my
    brow;

⁵ did not become shrunken

¹ a narcotic   ² destitute of seed   ³ knowest

There would he anchor his aspect[4] and die
With looking on his life.

(*Enter* ALEXAS)

ALEXAS. Sovereign of Egypt, hail!

CLEOPATRA. How much unlike art thou Mark
Antony! 35
Yet, coming from him, that great medicine
hath
With his tinct gilded thee.
How goes it with my brave Mark Antony?

ALEXAS. Last thing he did, dear queen,
He kissed, the last of many doubled kisses, 40
This orient pearl. His speech sticks in my
heart.

CLEOPATRA. Mine ear must pluck it thence.

ALEXAS. "Good friend," quoth he,
"Say, the firm Roman to great Egypt sends
This treasure of an oyster; at whose foot,
To mend the petty present, I will piece 45
Her opulent throne with kingdoms; all the
east,
Say thou, shall call her mistress." So he
nodded,
And soberly did mount an arm-gaunt[5] steed,
Who neighed so high that what I would have
spoke
Was beastly dumbed by him.

CLEOPATRA. What! was he sad or merry?

ALEXAS. Like to the time o' the year between
the extremes 51
Of hot and cold; he was nor sad nor merry.

CLEOPATRA. O well-divided disposition! Note
him,
Note him, good Charmian, 'tis the man; but
note him:

He was not sad, for he would shine on those 55
That make their looks by his; he was not
merry,
Which seemed to tell them his remembrance
lay
In Egypt with his joy; but between both:
O heavenly mingle! Be'st thou sad or merry.
The violence of either thee becomes, 60
So does it no man else. Mett'st thou my posts?

ALEXAS. Ay, madam, twenty several messengers.
Why do you send so thick?

CLEOPATRA. Who's born that day
When I forget to send to Antony, 64
Shall die a beggar. Ink and paper, Charmian.
Welcome, my good Alexas. Did I, Charmian,
Ever love Caesar so?

CHARMIAN. O! that brave Caesar.

CLEOPATRA. Be choked with such another
emphasis!
Say the brave Antony.

CHARMIAN. The valiant Caesar!

CLEOPATRA. By Isis, I will give thee bloody
teeth, 70
If thou with Caesar paragon[6] again
My man of men.

CHARMIAN. By your most gracious pardon, I
sing but after you.

CLEOPATRA. My salad days,
When I was green in judgment, cold in blood,
To say as I said then! But come, away; 75
Get me ink and paper:
He shall have every day a several greeting,
Or I'll unpeople Egypt. (*Exeunt*)

ACT 2

SCENE 1. *Messina. A room in* POMPEY's *house.*

(*Enter* POMPEY, MENECRATES, *and* MENAS)

POMPEY. If the great gods be just, they shall
assist
The deeds of justest men.

MENECRATES. Know, worthy Pompey,
That what they do delay, they not deny.

POMPEY. Whiles we are suitors to their
throne, decays
The thing we sue for.

MENECRATES. We, ignorant of ourselves,
Beg often our own harms, which the wise
powers 6
Deny us for our good; so find we profit
By losing of our prayers.

---

[4] gaze   [5] lean from bearing arms (?)   [6] compare

POMPEY.   I shall do well:
The people love me, and the sea is mine;
My powers are crescent,[1] and my auguring
   hope
Says it will come to the full. Mark Antony   11
In Egypt sits at dinner, and will make
No wars without doors; Caesar gets money
   where
He loses hearts; Lepidus flatters both,
Of both is flattered; but he neither loves,   15
Nor either cares for him.

MENECRATES.   Caesar and Lepidus
Are in the field, a mighty strength they carry.

POMPEY. Where have you this? 'tis false.

MENECRATES.   From Silvius, sir.

POMPEY. He dreams; I know they are in
   Rome together,
Looking for Antony. But all the charms of
   love,
Salt[2] Cleopatra, soften thy wanèd[3] lip!   21
Let witchcraft join with beauty, lust with
   both!
Tie up the libertine in a field of feasts,
Keep his brain fuming; Epicurean cooks
Sharpen with cloyless sauce his appetite,   25
That sleep and feeding may prorogue his
   honour
Even till a Lethe'd dulness!

(*Enter* VARRIUS)

How now, Varrius!

VARRIUS. This is most certain that I shall
   deliver:
Mark Antony is every hour in Rome
Expected; since he went from Egypt 'tis   30
A space for further travel.

POMPEY.   I could have given less matter
A better ear, Menas, I did not think
This amorous surfeiter would have donned
   his helm
For such a petty war; his soldiership
Is twice the other twain. But let us rear   35
The higher our opinion,[4] that our stirring
Can from the lap of Egypt's widow pluck
The ne'er-lust-wearied Antony.

MENECRATES.   I cannot hope
Caesar and Antony shall well greet together;

His wife that's dead did trespasses to Caesar,   40
His brother warred upon him, although I
   think
Not moved by Antony.

POMPEY.   I know not, Menas,
How lesser enmities may give way to greater.
Were 't not that we stand up against them all
'Twere pregnant they should square between
   themselves,   45
For they have entertained cause enough
To draw their swords; but how the fear of us
May cement their divisions and bind up
The petty difference, we yet not know.
Be it as our gods have 't! It only stands   50
Our lives upon, to use our strongest hands
Come, Menas.   (*Exeunt*)

SCENE 2. *Rome. A room in* LEPIDUS' *house.*

(*Enter* ENOBARBUS *and* LEPIDUS)

LEPIDUS. Good Enobarbus, 'tis a worthy deed,
And shall become you well, to entreat your
   captain
To soft and gentle speech.

ENOBARBUS.   I shall entreat him
To answer like himself: if Caesar move him,
Let Antony look over Caesar's head,   5
And speak as loud as Mars. By Jupiter,
Were I the wearer of Antonius' beard,
I would not shave 't to-day.

LEPIDUS.   'Tis not a time
For private stomaching.[1]

ENOBARBUS.   Every time
Serves for the matter that is then born in 't.

LEPIDUS. But small to greater matters must
   give way.   11

ENOBARBUS. Not if the small come first.

LEPIDUS.   Your speech is passion;
But, pray you, stir no embers up. Here comes
The noble Antony.

(*Enter* ANTONY *and* VENTIDIUS)

ENOBARBUS.   And yonder, Caesar.

(*Enter* CAESAR, MECAENAS, *and* AGRIPPA)

ANTONY. If we compose[2] well here, to Parthia:
Hark ye, Ventidius.   16

---

[1] in the ascendant   [2] lecherous   [3] withered   [4] self-confidence   [1] resenting   [2] agree

CAESAR.   I do not know,
Mecaenas; ask Agrippa.

LEPIDUS.   Noble friends,
That which combined us was most great, and let not
A leaner action rend us. What's amiss,
May it be gently heard; when we debate   20
Our trivial difference loud, we do commit
Murder in healing wounds; then, noble partners,—
The rather, for I earnestly beseech,—
Touch you the sourest points with sweetest terms,
Nor curstness³ grow to the matter.

ANTONY.   'Tis spoken well.
Were we before our armies, and to fight,   26
I should do thus. (ANTONY *embraces* CAESAR)

CAESAR. Welcome to Rome.

ANTONY.   Thank you.

CAESAR.   Sit,

ANTONY.   Sit, sir.

CAESAR.   Nay, then.

ANTONY. I learn, you take things ill which are not so,
Or being, concern you not.

CAESAR.   I must be laughed at
If, or for nothing or a little, I   31
Should say myself offended, and with you
Chiefly i' the world; more laughed at that I should
Once name you derogately, when to sound your name
It not concerned me.

ANTONY.   My being in Egypt, Caesar,
What was 't to you?   36

CAESAR. No more than my residing here at Rome
Might be to you in Egypt; yet, if you there
Did practice on my state,⁴ your being in Egypt
Might be my question.

ANTONY.   How intend⁵ you, practiced?

CAESAR. You may be pleased to catch at mine intent   41
By what did here befall me. Your wife and brother
Made wars upon me, and their contestation
Was theme for you, you were the word of war.

ANTONY. You do mistake your business; my brother never   45
Did urge me in his act: I did inquire it;
And have my learning from some true reports,
That drew their swords with you. Did he not rather
Discredit my authority with yours,   49
And make the wars alike against my stomach,⁶
Having alike your cause? Of this my letters
Before did satisfy you. If you'll patch a quarrel,
As matter whole you have not to make it with,
It must not be with this.

CAESAR.   You praise yourself
By laying defects of judgment to me, but   55
You patched up your excuses.

ANTONY.   Not so, not so;
I know you could not lack, I am certain on 't,
Very necessity of this thought, that I,
Your partner in the cause 'gainst which he fought,   59
Could not with graceful eyes attend those wars
Which fronted mine own peace. As for my wife,
I would you had her spirit in such another:
The third o' the world is yours, which with a snaffle
You may pace easy, but not such a wife.

ENOBARBUS. Would we had all such wives, that the men might go to wars with the women!   66

ANTONY. So much uncurbable, her garboils, Caesar,
Made out of her impatience,—which not wanted
Shrewdness of policy too,—I grieving grant
Did you too much disquiet; for that you must
But say I could not help it.

CAESAR.   I wrote to you   71
When rioting in Alexandria; you
Did pocket up my letters, and with taunts
Did gibe my missive⁷ out of audience.

---

³ bad humor   ⁴ plot against my government   ⁵ mean   ⁶ disposition   ⁷ messenger

ANTONY.   Sir,
He fell upon me, ere admitted: then   75
Three kings I had newly feasted, and did
    want
Of what I was i' the morning; but next day
I told him of myself, which was as much
As to have asked him pardon. Let this fellow
Be nothing of our strife; if we contend,   80
Out of our question wipe him.

CAESAR.   You have broken
The article of your oath, which you·shall
    never
Have tongue to charge me with.

LEPIDUS.   Soft, Caesar!

ANTONY   No,
Lepidus, let him speak:
The honour's sacred which he talks on now, 85
Supposing that I lacked it. But on, Caesar;
The article of my oath.

CAESAR. To lend me arms and aid when I re-
    quired them,
The which you both denied.

ANTONY.   Neglected, rather;
And then, when poisoned hours had bound
    me up   90
From mine own knowledge. As nearly as I
    may,
I'll play the penitent to you; but mine
    honesty
Shall not make poor my greatness, nor my
    power
Work without it. Truth is, that Fulvia,
To have me out of Egypt, made wars here; 95
For which myself, the ignorant motive, do
So far ask pardon as befits mine honour
To stoop in such a case.

LEPIDUS.   'Tis noble spoken.

MECAENUS. If it might please you, to enforce
    no further
The griefs between ye: to forget them quite
Were to remember that the present need   101
Speaks to atone[8] you.

LEPIDUS.   Worthily spoken, Mecaenas.

ENOBARBUS. Or, if you borrow one another's
love for the instant, you may, when you hear

no more words of Pompey, return it again:
you shall have time to wrangle in when you
have nothing else to do.   107

ANTONY. Thou art a soldier only; speak no
    more.

ENOBARBUS. That truth should be silent I had
    almost forgot.

ANTONY. You wrong this presence; therefore
    speak no more.

ENOBARBUS. Go to, then; your considerate
    stone.

CAESAR. I do not much dislike the matter, but
The manner of his speech; for it cannot be
We shall remain in friendship, our condi-
    tions[9]
So differing in their acts. Yet, if I knew   116
What hoop should hold us stanch,[10] from
    edge to edge
O' the world I would pursue it.

AGRIPPA.   Give me leave, Caesar.

CAESAR. Speak Agrippa.

AGRIPPA. Thou hast a sister by the mother's
    side,   120
Admired Octavia; great Mark Antony
Is now a widower.

CAESAR.   Say not so, Agrippa:
If Cleopatra heard you, your reproof
Were well deserved of rashness.

ANTONY. I am not married, Caesar; let me
    hear Agrippa further speak.   126

AGRIPPA. To hold you in perpetual amity,
To make you brothers, and to knit your
    hearts
With an unslipping knot, take Antony
Octavia to his wife; whose beauty claims   130
No worse a husband than the best of men,
Whose virtue and whose general graces speak
That which none else can utter. By this mar-
    riage,
All little jealousies which now seem great,
And all great fears which now import[11] their
    dangers,   135
Would then be nothing; truths would be but
    tales

---

[8] reconcile   [9] characters [10] firm [11] bring with them

Where now half tales be truths; her love to
both
Would each to other and all loves to both
Draw after her. Pardon what I have spoke,
For 'tis a studied, not a present thought 140
By duty ruminated.

ANTONY.   Will Caesar speak?

CAESAR. Not till he hears how Antony is
touched
With what is spoke already.

ANTONY.   What power is in Agrippa,
If I would say, "Agrippa, be it so,"
To make this good?

CAESAR.   The power of Caesar, and
His power unto Octavia.

ANTONY.   May I never 146
To this good purpose, that so fairly shows,
Dream of impediment! Let me have thy
hand;
Further this act of grace, and from this hour
The heart of brothers govern in our loves
And sway our great designs!

CAESAR   There is my hand. 151
A sister I bequeath you, whom no brother
Did ever love so dearly; let her live
To join our kingdoms and our hearts, and
never
Fly off our loves again!

LEPIDUS.   Happily, amen! 155

ANTONY. I did not think to draw my sword
'gainst Pompey.
For he hath laid strange courtesies and great
Of late upon me; I must thank him only,
Lest my remembrance suffer ill report;
At heel of that, defy him.

LEPIDUS.   Time calls upon 's:
Of us must Pompey presently be sought, 161
Or else he seeks out us.

ANTONY.   Where lies he?

CAESAR. About the Mount Misenum.

ANTONY. What's his strength by land?

CAESAR. Great and increasing; but by sea 165
He is an absolute master.

ANTONY.   So is the fame.[12]
Would we had spoke[13] together! Haste we for
it;
Yet, ere we put ourselves in arms, dispatch we
The business we have talked of.

CAESAR.   With most gladness;
And do invite you to my sister's view, 170
Whither straight I'll lead you.

ANTONY.   Let us, Lepidus,
Not lack your company.

LEPIDUS.   Noble Antony,
Not sickness should detain me.

    (*Flourish. Exeunt* CAESAR, ANTONY,
        and LEPIDUS.)

MECAENAS. Welcome from Egypt, sir.

ENOBARBUS. Half the heart of Caesar, worthy
Mecaenas! 175
My honourable friend, Agrippa!

AGRIPPA. Good Enobarbus!

MECAENUS. We have cause to be glad that
matters are so well digested. You stayed well
by 't in Egypt. 180

ENOBARBUS. Ay, sir; we did sleep day out of
countenance, and made the night light with
drinking.

MECAENAS. Eight wild boars roasted whole at
a breakfast, and but twelve persons there; is
this true? 185

ENOBARBUS. This was but as a fly by an eagle;
we had much more monstrous matter of feast,
which worthily deserved noting.

MECAENAS. She's a most triumphant lady, if
report be square to her. 190

ENOBARBUS. When she first met Mark Antony
she pursed[14] up his heart, upon the river of
Cydnus.

AGRIPPA. There she appeared indeed, or my
reporter devised well for her.

ENOBARBUS. I will tell you. 195
The barge she sat in, like a burnished throne,
Burned on the water; the poop was beaten
gold,

---

[12] report [13] fought [14] pocketed

Purple the sails, and so perfumed, that
The winds were love-sick with them, the oars
  were silver,
Which to the tune of flutes kept stroke, and
  made   200
The water which they beat to follow faster,
As amorous of their strokes. For her own
  person,
It beggared all description; she did lie
In her pavilion,—cloth-of-gold of tissue,—
O'er-picturing that Venus where we see   205
The fancy outwork nature; on each side her
Stood pretty-dimpled boys, like smiling
  Cupids,
With divers-coloured fans, whose wind did
  seem
To glow the delicate cheeks which they did
  cool,   209
And what they undid did.

AGRIPPA.   O! rare for Antony.

ENOBARBUS. Her gentlewomen, like the Ne-
  reides,
So many mermaids, tended her 'i the eyes,
And made their bends adornings; at the helm
A seeming mermaid steers; the silken tackle
Swell with the touches of those flower-soft
  hands,   215
That yarely[15] frame the office. From the barge
A strange invisible perfume hits the sense
Of the adjacent wharfs. The city cast
Her people out upon her, and Antony,   219
Enthroned i' the market-place, did sit alone,
Whistling to the air; which, but for vacancy,
Had gone to gaze on Cleopatra too
And made a gap in nature.

AGRIPPA.   Rare Egyptian!

ENOBARBUS. Upon her landing, Antony sent to
  her,
Invited her to supper; she replied   225
It should be better he became her guest,
Which she entreated. Our courteous Antony,
Whom ne'er the word of "No" woman heard
  speak,
Being barbered ten times o'er, goes to the
  feast,
And, for his ordinary[16] pays his heart   230
For what his eyes eat only.

AGRIPPA.   Royal wench!

She made great Caesar lay his sword to bed.
He ploughed her, and she cropped.

ENOBARBUS.   I saw her once
Hop forty paces through the public street;
And having lost her breath, she spoke, and
  panted   235
That[17] she did make defect perfection,
And, breathless, power breathe forth.

MECAENAS. Now Antony must leave her utterly.

ENOBARBUS. Never; he will not:
Age cannot wither her, nor custom stale   240
Her infinite variety; other women cloy
The appetites they feed, but she makes
  hungry
Where most she satisfies; for vilest things
Become themselves[18] in her, that the holy
  priests
Bless her when she is riggish.[19]   245

MECAENAS. If beauty, wisdom, modesty, can
  settle
The heart of Antony, Octavia is
A blessed lottery to him.

AGRIPPA.   Let us go.
Good Enobarbus, make yourself my guest
Whilst you abide here.

ENOBARBUS.   Humbly, sir, I thank you.   250
                                      (Exeunt)

SCENE 3. The same. A room in CAESAR's house.

(Enter CAESAR, ANTONY, OCTAVIA
  between them; ATTENDANTS)

ANTONY. The world and my great office will
  sometimes
Divide me from your bosom.

OCTAVIA.   All which time
Before the gods my knee shall bow my prayers
To them for you.

ANTONY.   Good night, sir, My Octavia,
Read not my blemishes in the world's re-
  port;   5
I have not kept my square,[1] but that to come
Shall all be done by the rule. Good night,
  dear lady.

---

[15] nimbly   [16] dinner

[17] so that   [18] are becoming, delightful   [19] wanton   [1] due
proportion in conduct

OCTAVIA. Good night, sir.

CAESAR. Good night; (*Exeunt* CAESAR *and* OCTAVIA)

(*Enter* SOOTHSAYER)

ANTONY. Now, sirrah; you do wish yourself in Egypt? 10

SOOTHSAYER. Would I had never come from thence, nor you
Thither!

ANTONY. If you can, your reason?

SOOTHSAYER. I see it in
My motion,[2] have it not in my tongue: but yet
Hie you to Egypt again.

ANTONY. Say to me, 15
Whose fortunes shall rise higher, Caesar's or mine?

SOOTHSAYER. Caesar's.
Therefore, O Antony! stay not by his side;
Thy demon—that's thy spirit which keeps thee—is
Noble, courageous, high, unmatchable, 20
Where Caesar's is not; but near him thy angel
Becomes a fear, as being o'erpowered; therefore
Make space enough between you.

ANTONY. Speak this no more.

SOOTHSAYER. To none but thee; no more but when to thee.
If thou dost play with him at any game 25
Thou art sure to lose, and, of that natural luck,
He beats thee 'gainst the odds; thy lustre thickens[3]
When he shines by. I say again, thy spirit
Is all afraid to govern thee near him,
But he away, 'tis noble.

ANTONY. Get thee gone: 30
Say to Ventidius I would speak with him.

(*Exit* SOOTHSAYER)

He shall to Parthia. Be it art or hap[4]
He hath spoken true; the very dice obey him.
And in our sports my better cunning faints
Under his chance; if we draw lots he speeds,[5]
His cocks do win the battle still of mine 36

When it is to nought, and his quails ever
Beat mine, inhooped,[6] at odds. I will to Egypt;
And though I make this marriage for my peace,
I' the East my pleasure lies.

(*Enter Ventidius*)

O! come, Ventidius, 40
You must to Parthia; your commission's ready;
Follow me, and receive 't. (*Exeunt*)

SCENE 4. *The same. A street.*

(*Enter* LEPIDUS, MECAENAS, *and* AGRIPPA)

LEPIDUS. Trouble yourselves no further; pray you hasten
Your generals after.

AGRIPPA. Sir, Mark Antony
Will e'en but kiss Octavia, and we'll follow.

LEPIDUS. Till I shall see you in your soldier's dress,
Which will become you both, farewell.

MECAENAS. We shall, 6
As I conceive the journey, be at the Mount
Before you, Lepidus.

LEPIDUS. Your way is shorter;
My purposes do draw me much about:
You'll win two days upon me.

MECAENAS. ⎫
  ⎬ Sir, good success!
AGRIPPA. ⎭

LEPIDUS. Farewell. (*Exeunt*) 10

SCENE 5. *Alexandria. A room in the palace.*

(*Enter* CLEOPATRA, CHARMIAN, IRAS, ALEXAS, *and* ATTENDANT)

CLEOPATRA. Give me some music; music, moody food
Of us that trade in love.

ATTENDANT. The music, ho!..

(*Enter* MARDIAN)

CLEOPATRA. Let it alone; let's to billiards: come, Charmian.

---

[2] intuitively [3] dims [4] chance [5] wins

[6] pitted against each other in a hoop or ring

CHARMIAN. My arm is sore; best play with
    Mardian.

CLEOPATRA. As well a woman with a eunuch
    played   5
As with a woman. Come, you'll play with me,
    sir?

MARDIAN. As well as I can, madam.

CLEOPATRA. As when good will is showed,
    though 't come too short,
The actor may plead pardon. I'll none now.
Give me mine angle; we'll to the river;
    there—
My music playing far off—I will betray   11
Tawny-finned fishes; my bended hook shall
    pierce
Their slimy jaws; and, as I draw them up,
I'll think them every one an Antony,
And say, "Ah, ha!" you're caught.

CHARMIAN.   'Twas merry when
You wagered on your angling; when your
    diver
Did hang a salt-fish on his hook, which he   17
With fervency drew up.

CLEOPATRA.   That time—O times!—
I laughed him out of patience; and that night
I laughed him into patience: and next morn,
Ere the ninth hour, I drunk him to his bed; 21
Then put my tires[1] and mantles on him whilst
I wore his sword Philippan.[2]

              (*Enter a* MESSENGER)

                    O! from Italy;
Ram thou thy fruitful tidings in mine ears,
That long time have been barren.

MESSENGER.   Madam, madam—

CLEOPATRA. Antony's dead! if you say so, vil-
    lain,   26
Thou kill'st thy mistress; but well and free,
If thou so yield him, there is gold, and here
My bluest veins to kiss; a hand that kings
Have lipped, and trembled kissing.   30

MESSENGER. First, madam, he is well.

CLEOPATRA.   Why, there's more gold.
But, sirrah, mark, we use
To say the dead are well: bring it to that,

The gold I give thee will I melt, and pour
Down thy ill-uttering throat.   35

MESSENGER. Good madam, hear me.

CLEOPATRA.   Well, go to, I will;
But there's no goodness in thy face; if Antony
Be free and healthful, so tart a favour[3]
To trumpet such good tidings! if not well,
Thou shouldst come like a Fury crowned
    with snakes,   40
Not like a formal man.[4]

MESSENGER.   Will 't please you hear me?

CLEOPATRA. I have a mind to strike thee ere
    thou speak'st:
Yet, if thou say Antony lives, is well,
Or friends with Caesar, or not captive to him,
I'll set thee in a shower of gold, and hail   45
Rich pearls upon thee.

MESSENGER.   Madam, he's well.

CLEOPATRA.   Well said.

MESSENGER. And friends with Caesar.

CLEOPATRA.   Thou'rt an honest man.

MESSENGER. Caesar and he are greater friends
    than ever.

CLEOPATRA. Make thee a fortune from me.

MESSENGER.   But yet, madam,—

CLEOPATRA. I do not like "but yet," it does
    allay   51
The good precedence;[5] fie upon "but yet!"
"But yet" is as a gaoler to bring forth
Some monstrous malefactor. Prithee, friend,
Pour out the pack of matter to mine ear,
The good and bad together. He's friends
    with Caesar;   55
In state of health, thou sayst; and thou sayst,
    free.

MESSENGER. Free, madam! no; I made no such
    report;
He's bound unto Octavia.

CLEOPATRA.   For what good turn?

MESSENGER. For the best turn i' the bed.

CLEOPATRA.   I am pale, Charmian.

---

[1] head-dresses   [2] the sword Antony had wielded at his victory at Philippi

[3] sour an aspect   [4] man in form   [5] thing said before

MESSENGER. Madam, he's married to Octavia.

CLEOPATRA. The most infectious pestilence upon thee! 61

(*Strikes him down*)

MESSENGER. Good madam, patience.

CLEOPATRA.　　　　　What say you? Hence,

(*Strikes him again*)

Horrible villain! or I'll spurn thine eyes
Like balls before me; I'll unhair thy head:

(*She hales him up and down*)

Thou shalt be whipped with wire, and stewed in brine, 65
Smarting in lingering pickle.

MESSENGER.　　　　　Gracious madam,
I, that do bring the news made not the match.

CLEOPATRA. Say 'tis not so, a province I will give thee,
And make thy fortunes proud; the blow thou hadst 69
Shall make thy peace for moving me to rage,
And I will boot[6] thee with what gift beside
Thy modesty can beg.

MESSENGER.　　　　　He's married, madam.

CLEOPATRA. Rogue! thou has lived too long.

(*Draws a knife*)

MESSENGER.　　　　　Nay, then I'll run.
What mean you, madam? I have made no fault.　　　　　(*Exit*)

CHARMIAN. Good madam, keep yourself within yourself; 75
The man is innocent.

CLEOPATRA. Some innocents 'scape not the thunder-bolt.
Melt Egypt into Nile! and kindly creatures
Turn all to serpents! Call the slave again: 79
Though I am mad, I will not bite him. Call.

CHARMIAN. He is afeared to come.

CLEOPATRA.　　　　　I will not hurt him.

(*Exit* CHARMIAN)

These hands do lack nobility, that they strike
A meaner than myself; since I myself
Have given myself the cause.

(*Re-enter* CHARMIAN, *and* MESSENGER)

　　　　　　　　　Come hither, sir.
Though it be honest, it is never good 85
To bring bad news; give to a gracious message
A host of tongues, but let ill tidings tell
Themselves when they be felt.

MESSENGER.　　　　　I have my duty.

CLEOPATRA. Is he married?
I cannot hate thee worser than I do 90
If thou again say "Yes."

MESSENGER.　　　　　He's married, madam.

CLEOPATRA. The gods confound thee! dost thou hold there still?

MESSENGER. Should I lie, madam?

CLEOPATRA.　　　　　O! I would thou didst,
So[7] half my Egypt were submerged and made
A cistern for scaled snakes. Go, get thee hence;
Hadst thou Narcissus in thy face, to me 96
Thou wouldst appear most ugly. He is married?

MESSENGER. I crave your highness' pardon.

CLEOPATRA.　　　　　He is married?

MESSENGER. Take no offence that I would not offend you;
To punish me for what you make me do 100
Seems much unequal; he's married to Octavia.

CLEOPATRA. O! that his fault should make a knave of thee,
That art not what thou 'rt sure of. Get thee hence;
The merchandise which thou hast brought from Rome
Are all too dear for me; lie they upon thy hand 105
And be undone by 'em!　　(*Exit* MESSENGER)

CHARMIAN.　　Good your highness, patience.

CLEOPATRA. In praising Antony I have dispraised Caesar.

CHARMIAN. Many times, madam.

---

[6] enrich in addition

[7] even though

CLEOPATRA.   I am paid for 't now.
Lead me from hence;   109
I faint. O Iras! Charmian! 'Tis no matter.
Go to the fellow, good Alexas; bid him
Report the feature of Octavia, her years,
Her inclination,[8] let him not leave out
The colour of her hair; bring me word
    quickly   (*Exit* ALEXAS)
Let him for ever go:—let him not—Char-
    mian!—
Though he be painted one way like a Gorgon,
The other way's a Mars. (*To* MARDIAN) Bid
    you Alexas   117
Bring me word how tall she is. Pity me, Char-
    mian,
But do not speak to me. Lead me to my
    chamber.   (*Exeunt*)

SCENE 6. *Near Misenum.*

(*Flourish. Enter* POMPEY *and* MENAS, *at
one side, with drum and trumpet; at the
other,* CAESAR, ANTONY, LEPIDUS, ENO-
BARBUS, MECAENAS, *with* SOLDIERS *marching.*)

POMPEY. Your hostages I have, so have you
    mine;
And we shall talk before we fight.

CAESAR.   Most meet
That first we come to words, and therefore
    have we
Our written purposes before us sent;
Which if thou hast considered, let us know   5
If 'twill tie up thy discontented sword,
And carry back to Sicily much tall youth
That else must perish here.

POMPEY.   To you all three,
The senators alone of this great world,
Chief factors[1] for the gods I do not know   10
Wherefore my father should revengers want,
Having a son and friends; since Julius Caesar,
Who at Philippi the good Brutus ghosted,
There saw you labouring for him. What
    was 't
That moved pale Cassius to conspire? and
    what   15
Made the all-honoured, honest Roman,
    Brutus,

With the armed rest, courtiers of beauteous
    freedom,
To drench the Capitol, but that they would
Have one man but a man? And that is it   19
Hath made me rig my navy, at whose burden
The angered ocean foams, with which I
    meant
To scourge the ingratitude that despiteful
    Rome
Cast on my noble father.

CAESAR.   Take your time.

ANTONY. Thou canst not fear[2] us, Pompey,
    with thy sails;
We'll speak with thee at sea: at land, thou
    know'st   25
How much we do o'er-count[3] thee.

POMPEY.   At land, indeed,
Thou dost o'er-count me of my father's house;
But, since the cuckoo builds not for himself,
Remain in't as thou mayst.

LEPIDUS.   Be pleased to tell us—
For this is from the present—how you take 30
The offers we have sent you.

CAESAR.   There's the point.

ANTONY. Which do not be entreated to, but
    weigh
What it is worth embraced.

CAESAR.   And what may follow.
To try a larger fortune.

POMPEY.   You have made me offer
Of Sicily, Sardinia; and I must   35
Rid all the sea of pirates; then, to send
Measures of wheat to Rome; this 'greed upon,
To part with unhacked edges, and bear back
Our targets undinted.

CAESAR.
ANTONY.   } That's our offer.
LEPIDUS.

POMPEY.   Know, then,
I came before you here a man prepared   41
To take this offer; but Mark Antony
Put me to some impatience. Though I lose
The praise of it by telling, you must know,
When Caesar and your brother were at blows,

---

[8] disposition   [1] agents   [2] frighten   [3] over-reach

Your mother came to Sicily and did find   46
Her welcome friendly.

ANTONY.   I have heard it, Pompey;
And am well studied for a liberal thanks
Which I do owe you.

POMPEY.   Let me have your hand:
I did not think, sir, to have met you here.   50

ANTONY. The beds i' the East are soft; and
     thanks to you,
That called me timelier than my purpose
     hither,
For I have gained by 't.

CAESAR.   Since I saw you last,
There is a change upon you.

POMPEY.   Well, I know not
What counts[4] harsh Fortune casts upon my
     face,   55
But in my bosom shall she never come
To make my heart her vassal.

LEPIDUS.   Well met here.

POMPEY. I hope so, Lepidus. Thus we are
     agreed.
I crave our composition may be written
And sealed between us.

CAESAR.   That's the next to do.

POMPEY. We'll feast each other ere we part;
     and let's   61
Draw lots who shall begin.

ANTONY.   That will I, Pompey.

POMPEY. No, Antony, take the lot:
But, first or last, your fine Egyptian cookery
Shall have the fame. I have heard that Julius
     Caesar   65
Grew fat with feasting there.

ANTONY.   You have heard much.

POMPEY. I have fair meanings, sir.

ANTONY.   And fair words to them.

POMPEY. Then, so much have I heard;
And I have heard Apollodorus carried—

ENOBARBUS. No more of that: he did so.

POMPEY.   What I pray you?

ENOBARBUS. A certain queen to Caesar in a
     mattress.   71

POMPEY. I know thee now, how far'st thou,
     soldier?

ENOBARBUS.   Well;
And well am like to do; for I perceive
Four feasts are toward.

POMPEY.   Let me shake thy hand;
I never hated thee. I have seen thee fight,   76
When I have envied thy behaviour.

ENOBARBUS.   Sir,
I never loved you much, but I ha' praised ye
When you have well deserved ten times as
     much
As I have said you did.

POMPEY.   Enjoy thy plainness,   80
It nothing ill becomes thee.
Aboard my galley I invite you all:
Will you lead, lords?

CAESAR. ⎫
ANTONY. ⎬ Show us the way, sir.
LEPIDUS. ⎭

POMPEY.   Come.

(Exeunt all except MENAS *and* ENOBARBUS)

MENAS. Thy father, Pompey, would ne'er
have made this treaty. You and I have
known, sir.   86

ENOBARBUS. At sea, I think.

MENAS. We have, sir.

ENOBARBUS. You have done well by water.

MENAS. And you by land.   90

ENOBARBUS. I will praise any man that will
praise me: though it cannot be denied what I
have done by land.

MENAS. Nor what I have done by water.   94

ENOBARBUS. Yes, something you can deny for
your own safety; you have been a great thief
by sea.

MENAS. And you by land.

ENOBARBUS. There I deny my land service.
But give me your hand, Menas; if our eyes

---

[4] reckonings

had authority,[5] here they might take two thieves kissing.   101

MENAS. All men's faces are true, whatsoe'er their hands are.

ENOBARBUS. But there is never a fair woman has a true face.   105

MENAS. No slander; they steal hearts.

ENOBARBUS. We came hither to fight with you.

MENAS. For my part, I am sorry it is turned to a drinking. Pompey doth this day laugh away his fortune.   110

ENOBARBUS. If he do, sure, he cannot weep it back again.

MENAS. You have said, sir. We looked not for Mark Antony here: pray you, is he married to Cleopatra?   115

ENOBARBUS. Caesar's sister is called Octavia.

MENAS. True, sir; she was the wife of Caius Marcellus.

ENOBARBUS. But she is now the wife of Marcus Antonius.

MENAS. Pray ye, sir?   120

ENOBARBUS. 'Tis true.

MENAS. Then is Caesar and he for ever knit together.

ENOBARBUS. If I were bound to divine of this unity, I would not prophesy so.   125

MENAS. I think the policy of that purpose made more in the marriage than the love of the parties.

ENOBARBUS. I think so too; but you shall find the band that seems to tie their friendship together will be the very strangler of their amity. Octavia is of a holy, cold, and still conversation.[6]   131

MENAS. Who would not have his wife so?

ENOBARBUS. Not he that himself is not so; which is Mark Antony. He will to his Egyptian dish again; then, shall the sighs of Octavia blow the fire up in Caesar, and, as I said before, that which is the strength of their

amity shall prove the immediate author of their variance. Antony will use his affection where it is; he married but his occasion[7] here.

MENAS. And thus it may be. Come sir, will you aboard? I have a health for you.   142

ENOBARBUS. I shall take it, sir: we have used our throats in Egypt.

MENAS. Come; let's away.   (*Exeunt*) 145

SCENE 7. *On board* POMPEY's *galley off Misenum.*

    (*Music. Enter two or three* SERVANTS, *with a banquet.*)

FIRST SERVANT. Here they'll be, man. Some o' their plants are ill-rooted already; the least wind i' the world will blow them down.

SECOND SERVANT. Lepidus is high-coloured.

FIRST SERVANT. They have made him drink alms-drink.[1]   6

SECOND SERVANT. As they pinch[2] one another by the disposition, he cries out, "No more;" reconciles them to his entreaty, and himself to the drink.

FIRST SERVANT. But it raises the greater war between him and his discretion.   11

SECOND SERVANT. Why, this it is to have a name in great men's fellowship; I had as lief have a reed that will do me no service as a partisan I could not heave.[3]   15

FIRST SERVANT. To be called into a huge sphere, and not to be seen to move in 't, are the holes where eyes should be, which pitifully disaster[4] the cheeks.

    (*A sennet sounded. Enter* CAESAR, ANTONY, LEPIDUS, POMPEY, AGRIPPA, MECAENAS, ENOBARBUS, MENAS, *with other* CAPTAINS.)

ANTONY. Thus do they, sir. They take the flow o' the Nile   20
By certain scales i' the pyramid; they know
By the height, the lowness, or the mean, if dearth
or foison[5] follow. The higher Nilus swells

---

[5] legal power to arrest [6] quiet behavior

[7] opportunity [1] leavings [2] irritate [3] weapon I could not lift [4] ruin [5] scarcity or abundance

The more it promises; as it ebbs, the seeds-
   man
Upon the slime and ooze scatters his grain,   25
And shortly comes to harvest.

LEPIDUS. You've strange serpents there.

ANTONY. Ay, Lepidus.

LEPIDUS. Your serpent of Egypt is bred now of
your mud by the operation of your sun; so is
your crocodile.   31

ANTONY. They are so.

POMPEY. Sit,—and some wine! A health to
Lepidus!

LEPIDUS. I am not so well as I should be, but
I'll ne'er out.   36

ENOBARBUS. Not till you have slept; I fear me
you'll be in till then.

LEPIDUS. Nay, certainly, I have heard the
Ptolemies' pyramises are very goodly things;
without contradiction, I have heard that.   41

MENAS. Pompey, a word.

POMPEY. Say in mine ear; what is 't?

MENAS. Forsake thy seat, I do beseech thee,
  captain,
And hear me speak a word.

POMPEY.   Forbear me till anon.
This wine for Lepidus!   45

LEPIDUS. What manner o' thing is your crocodile?

ANTONY. It is shaped, sir, like itself, and it is
as broad as it hath breadth; it is just so high
as it is, and moves with it own organs; it lives
by that which nourisheth it; and the elements
once out of it, it transmigrates.   51

LEPIDUS. What colour is it of?

ANTONY. Of it own colour too.

LEPIDUS. 'Tis a strange serpent.

ANTONY. 'Tis so; and the tears of it are wet.

CAESAR. Will this description satisfy him?   56

ANTONY. With the health that Pompey gives
him, else he is a very epicure.

POMPEY. Go hang, sir, hang! Tell me of that?
  Away!

Do as I bid you. Where's this cup I called
  for?

MENAS. If for the sake of merit thou wilt hear
  me,   61
Rise from thy stool.

POMPEY. I think thou 'rt mad. The matter?

    (Walks aside)

MENAS. I have ever held my cap off to thy
  fortunes.

POMPEY. Thou hast served me with much
  faith. What's else to say?
Be jolly, lords.

ANTONY. These quick-sands, Lepidus,   65
Keep off them, for you sink.

MENAS. Wilt thou be lord of all the world?

POMPEY.   What sayst thou?

MENAS. Wilt thou be lord of the whole
  world? That's twice.

POMPEY. How should that be?

MENAS.   But entertain it,
And though thou think me poor, I am the
  man
Will give thee all the world.   71

POMPEY.   Hast thou drunk well?

MENAS. No, Pompey, I have kept me from the
  cup.
Thou art, if thou dar'st be, the earthly Jove:
Whate'er the ocean pales,[6] or sky inclips,[7]
Is thine, if thou wilt ha't.

POMPEY.   Show me which way.

MENAS. These three world-sharers, these com-
  petitors,   76
Are in thy vessel: let me cut the cable;
And, when we are put off, fall to their throats:
All there is thine.

POMPEY. Ah! this thou shouldst have done,
And not have spoke on't. In me 'tis villany;
In thee't had been good service. Thou must
  know   81
'Tis not my profit that does lead mine
  honour;
Mine honour, it. Repent that e'er thy tongue

---

[6] encloses   [7] embraces

Hath so betrayed thine act; being done un-
known,   84
I should have found it afterwards well done,
But must condemn it now. Desist, and drink.

MENAS (*aside*). For this,
I'll never follow thy palled fortunes more.
Who seeks, and will not take when once 'tis
offered,
Shall never find it more.

POMPEY.   This health to Lepidus!

ANTONY. Bear him ashore. I'll pledge it for
him, Pompey.   91

ENOBARBUS. Here's to thee, Menas!

MENAS.   Enobarbus, welcome!

POMPEY. Fill till the cup be hid.

ENOBARBUS. There's a strong fellow, Menas.

(*Pointing to the* Attendant *who carries
off* LEPIDUS)   95

MENAS. Why?

ENOBARBUS. A'[8] bears the third part of the
world, man; see'st not?

MENAS. The third part then is drunk; would
it were all,
That it might go on wheels!

ENOBARBUS Drink thou; increase the reels.

MENAS. Come.   101

POMPEY. This is not yet an Alexandrian feast.

ANTONY. It ripens towards it. Strike the vessels, ho!
Here is to Caesar!

CAESAR.   I could well forbear 't.
It's monstrous labour, when I wash my brain,
And it grows fouler.

ANTONY.   Be a child o' the time

CAESAR. Possess it, I'll make answer;   107
But I had rather fast from all four days
Than drink so much in one.

ENOBARBUS (*to* ANTONY). Ha! my brave em-
peror;   110
Shall we dance now the Egyptian Bacchanals,
And celebrate our drink?

POMPEY.   Let's ha't, good soldier.

ANTONY. Come, let's all take hands,
Till that the conquering wine hath steeped
our sense
In soft and delicate Lethe.

ENOBARBUS.   All take hands.   115
Make battery to our ears with the loud music;
The while I'll place you: then the boy shall
sing,
The holding[9] every man shall bear as loud
As his strong sides can volley.

(*Music plays.* ENOBARBUS *places them
hand in hand.*)

SONG.

Come, thou monarch of the vine,
Plumpy Bacchus, with pink eyne![10]   120
In thy fats[11] our cares be drowned,
With thy grapes our hairs be crowned:
      Cup us, till the world go round,
      Cup us, till the world go round!   125

CAESAR. What would you more? Pompey,
good night. Good brother,
Let me request you off; our graver business
Frowns at this levity. Gentle lords, let's part;
You see we have burnt our cheeks; strong
Enobarb
Is weaker than the wine, and mine own
tongue
Splits what it speaks; the wild disguise hath
almost   131
Anticked[12] us all. What needs more words?
Good night.
Good Antony, your hand.

POMPEY.   I'll try you on the shore.

ANTONY. And shall, sir. Give's your hand

POMPEY.   O, Antony!
You have my father's house,—But, what? we
are friends.   135
Come down into the boat.

ENOBARBUS.   Take heed you fall not.

(*Exeunt* POMPEY, CAESAR, ANTONY,
                    and Attendants)

Menas, I'll not on shore.

---

[8] he

[9] chorus   [10] half-shut eyes   [11] vats   [12] made us all like buf-
foons

MENAS.   No, to my cabin.
These drums! these trumpets, flutes! what!
Let Neptune hear we bid a loud farewell
To these great fellows: sound and be hanged!
   sound out!   140

(A flourish of trumpets with drums)

ENOBARBUS. Hoo! says a'. There's my cap.

MENAS. Hoo! noble captain! come.   *(Exeunt)*

ACT 3

SCENE 1. *A plain in Syria.*

> *(Enter* VENTIDIUS, *in triumph, with* SILIUS
> *and other* Romans, Officers, *and* Soldiers;
> *the dead body of* PACORUS *borne before
> him)*

VENTIDIUS. Now, darting Parthia, art thou
   struck; and now
Pleased fortune does of Marcus Crassus' death
Make me revenger. Bear the king's son's body
Before our army. Thy Pacorus, Orodes,
Pays this for Marcus Crassus.

SILIUS.   Noble Ventidius,
Whilst yet with Parthian blood thy sword is
   warm,   6
The fugitive Parthians follow; spur through
   Media,
Mesopotamia, and the shelters whither
The routed fly; so thy grand captain Antony
Shall set thee on triumphant chariots and   10
Put garlands on thy head.

VENTIDIUS.   O Silius, Silius!
I have done enough; a lower place, note well,
May make too great an act; for learn this,
   Silius,
Better to leave undone than by our deed
Acquire too high a fame when him we serve's
   away.   15
Caesar and Antony have ever won
More in their officer than person; Sossius,
One of my place in Syria, his lieutenant,
For quick accumulation of renown,
Which he achieved by the minute,[1] lost his
   favour.   20
Who does i' the wars more than his captain
   can
Becomes his captain's captain; and ambition,
The soldier's virtue, rather makes choice of
   loss
Than gain which darkens him.
I could do more to do Antonius good,   25

But 'twould offend him; and in his offence
Should my performance perish.

SILIUS.   Thou hast, Ventidius, that
Without the which a soldier, and his sword,
Grants scarce distinction. Thou wilt write to
   Antony?

VENTIDIUS. I'll humbly signify what in his
   name,   30
That magical word of war, we have effected;
How, with his banners and his well-paid
   ranks,
The ne'er-yet-beaten horse of Parthia
We have jaded[2] out o' the field.

SILIUS.   Where is he now?

VENTIDIUS. He purposeth to Athens; whither,
   with what haste   35
The weight we must convey with's will permit,
We shall appear before him. On, there; pass
   along   *(Exeunt)*

SCENE 2. *Rome. A room in* CAESAR's *house.*

(Enter AGRIPPA *and* ENOBARBUS, *meeting)*

AGRIPPA. What! are the brothers parted?

ENOBARBUS. They have dispatched with Pom-
   pey; he is gone;
The other three are sealing.[1] Octavia weeps
To part from Rome; Caesar is sad; and
   Lepidus,
Since Pompey's feast, as Menas says, is
   troubled
With the green sickness.   5

AGRIPPA.   'Tis a noble Lepidus.

ENOBARBUS. A very fine one. O! how he loves
   Caesar.

AGRIPPA. Nay, but how dearly he adores Mark
   Antony!

---

[1] every moment   [2] driven, exhausted   [1] setting seals to an argument

ENOBARBUS. Caesar? Why, he's the Jupiter of men.

AGRIPPA. What's Antony? The god of Jupiter.

ENOBARBUS. Spake you of Caesar? Hoo! the nonpareil!   11

AGRIPPA. O, Antony! O thou Arabian bird!

ENOBARBUS. Would you praise Caesar, say "Caesar," go no further.

AGRIPPA. Indeed, he plied them both with excellent praises.

ENOBARBUS. But he loves Caesar best; yet he loves Antony.   15
Hoo! hearts, tongues, figures, scribes, bards, poets, cannot
Think, speak, cast,² write, sing, number; hoo!
His love to Antony. But as for Caesar,
Kneel down, kneel down, and wonder.

AGRIPPA.   Both he loves.

ENOBARBUS.   They are his shards, and he
their beetle. (*Trumpets within*) So;   20
This is to horse. Adieu, noble Agrippa.

AGRIPPA. Good fortune, worthy soldier, and farewell.

(*Enter* CAESAR, ANTONY, LEPIDUS,
and OCTAVIA)

ANTONY. No further, sir.

CAESAR. You take from me a great part of myself;
Use me well in 't. Sister, prove such a wife   25
As my thoughts make thee, and as my furthest band
Shall pass on thy approof. Most noble Antony,
Let not the piece of virtue, which is set
Betwixt us as the cement of our love
To keep it builded, be the ram to batter   30
The fortress of it; for better might we
Have loved without this mean, if on both parts
This be not cherished.

ANTONY.   Make me not offended
In your distrust.

CAESAR.   I have said.

ANTONY.   You shall not find,
Though you be therein curious,³ the least cause
For what you seem to fear. So, the gods keep you,   36
And make the hearts of Romans serve your ends!
We will here part.

CAESAR. Farewell, my dearest sister, fare thee well:
The elements be kind to thee, and make   40
Thy spirits all of comfort; fare thee well.

OCTAVIA. My noble brother!

ANTONY. The April's in her eyes; it is love's spring,
And these the showers to bring it on. Be cheerful.

OCTAVIA. Sir, look well to my husband's house; and—

CAESAR.   What,   45
Octavia.

OCTAVIA. I'll tell you in your ear.

ANTONY. Her tongue will not obey her heart, nor can
Her heart inform her tongue; the swan's down-feather,
That stands upon the swell at full of tide,
And neither way inclines.   49

ENOBARBUS (*aside to* AGRIPPA). Will Caesar weep?

AGRIPPA. He has a cloud in 's face.

ENOBARBUS. He were the worse for that were he a horse;
So is he, being a man.

AGRIPPA.   Why, Enobarbus,
When Antony found Julius Caesar dead
He cried almost to roaring; and he wept   55
When at Philippi he found Brutus slain.

ENOBARBUS. That year, indeed, he was troubled with a rheum,⁴
What willingly he did confound⁵ he wailed,
Believ't, till I wept too.

---

² calculate

³ particular   ⁴ cold   ⁵ ruin

CAESAR.   No, sweet Octavia,
You shall hear from me still; the time shall
  not   60
Out-go my thinking on you.

ANTONY.   Come, sir, come;
I'll wrestle with you in my strength of love:
Look, here I have you; thus I let you go,
And give you to the gods.

CAESAR.   Adieu; be happy!

LEPIDUS. Let all the number of the stars give
  light   65
To thy fair way!

CAESAR.   Farewell, farewell! (*Kisses*
OCTAVIA)

ANTONY.   Farewell!

      (*Trumpets sound. Exeunt.*)

SCENE 3. *Alexandria. A room in the palace.*

      (*Enter* CLEOPATRA, CHARMIAN, IRAS,
            and ALEXAS)

CLEOPATRA. Where is the fellow?

ALEXAS   Half afeared to come.

CLEOPATRA. Go to, go to.

      (*Enter a* MESSENGER)

             Come hither, sir.

ALEXAS.   Good majesty,
Herod of Jewry dare not look upon you
But when you are well pleased.

CLEOPATRA.   That Herod's head
I'll have; but how, when Antony is gone   5
Through whom I might command it? Come
  thou near.

MESSENGER. Most gracious majesty!

CLEOPATRA. Didst thou behold Octavia?

MESSENGER. Ay, dread queen.

CLEOPATRA. Where?   10

MESSENGER. Madam, in Rome;
I looked her in the face, and saw her led
Between her brother and Mark Antony.

CLEOPATRA. Is she as tall as me?

MESSENGER.   She is not, madam.

CLEOPATRA. Didst hear her speak? is she shrill-
  tongued, or low?   15

MESSENGER. Madam, I heard her speak; she
  is low-voiced.

CLEOPATRA. That's not so good. He cannot
  like her long.

CHARMIAN. Like her! O Isis! 'tis impossible.

CLEOPATRA. I think so, Charmian: dull of
  tongue, and dwarfish!
What majesty is in her gait? Remember,   20
If e'er thou look'dst on majesty.

MESSENGER.   She creeps;
Her motion and her station[1] are as one;
She shows a body rather than a life,
A statue than a breather.

CLEOPATRA.   Is this certain?   24

MESSENGER. Or I have no observance.

CHARMIAN.   Three in Egypt
Cannot make better note.

CLEOPATRA.   He's very knowing,
I do perceive 't. There's nothing in her yet.
The fellow has good judgment.

CHARMIAN.   Excellent.

CLEOPATRA. Guess at her years, I prithee.

MESSENGER.   Madam,
She was a widow,—

CLEOPATRA.   Widow! Charmian, hark.

MESSENGER. And I do think she's thirty.   31

CLEOPATRA. Bear'st thou her face in mind? is
  't long or round?

MESSENGER. Round even to faultiness.

CLEOPATRA. For the most part, too, they are
  foolish that are so.
Her hair, what colour?   35

MESSENGER. Brown, madam; and her forehead
As low as she would wish it.

CLEOPATRA.   There's gold for thee:
Thou must not take my former sharpness ill.
I will employ thee back again; I find thee

---
[1] manner of standing

Most fit for business. Go, make thee ready; 40
Our letters are prepared.   (*Exit* MESSENGER)

CHARMIAN.   A proper man.

CLEOPATRA. Indeed, he is so; I repent me
    much
That so I harried him. Why, methinks, by
    him,
This creature's no such thing.

CHARMIAN.   Nothing, madam.

CLEOPATRA. The man hath seen some majesty,
    and should know.   45

CHARMIAN. Hath he seen majesty? Isis else
    defend,
And serving you so long!

CLEOPATRA. I have one thing more to ask him
    yet, good Charmian:
But 'tis no matter; thou shalt bring him to me
Where I will write. All may be well enough. 50

CHARMIAN. I warrant you, madam.
                              (*Exeunt*)

SCENE 4. *Athens. A room in* ANTONY'S *house.*

(*Enter* ANTONY *and* OCTAVIA)

ANTONY. Nay, nay, Octavia, not only that,
That were excusable, that, and thousands
    more
Of semblable import,[1] but he hath waged
New wars 'gainst Pompey; made his will, and
    read it
To public ear: 5
Spoke scantly of me; when perforce he could
    not
But pay me terms of honour, cold and sickly
He vented them; most narrow measure lent
    me;[2]
When the best hint was given him, he not
    took 't,
Or did it from his teeth.[3]

OCTAVIA.   O my good lord! 10
Believe not all; or, if you must believe,
Stomach[4] not all. A more unhappy lady,
If this division chance, ne'er stood between,
Praying for both parts:
The good gods will mock me presently,   15

When I shall pray, "O! bless my lord and
    husband;"
Undo that prayer, by crying out as loud,
"O! bless my brother!" Husband win, win
    brother,
Prays, and destroys the prayer; no midway
'Twixt these extremes at all.

ANTONY.   Gentle Octavia,
Let your best love draw to that point which
    seeks   21
Best to preserve it. If I lose mine honour
I lose myself; better I were not yours
Than yours so branchless. But, as you re-
    quested,
Yourself shall go between 's; the mean time,
    lady,   25
I'll raise the preparation of a war
Shall stain your brother; make your soonest
    haste,
So your desires are yours

OCTAVIA.   Thanks to my lord.
The Jove of power make me most weak, most
    weak,
Your reconciler! Wars 'twixt you twain would
    be   30
As if the world should cleave, and that slain
    men
Should solder up the rift.

ANTONY. When it appears to you where this
    begins,
Turn your displeasure that way; for our
    faults
Can never be so equal that your love   35
Can equally move with them. Provide[5] your
    going;
Choose your own company, and command
    what cost
Your heart has mind to.   (*Exeunt*)

SCENE 5. *The same. Another room.*

(*Enter* ENOBARBUS *and* EROS, *meeting*)

ENOBARBUS. How now, friend Eros!

EROS. There's strange news come, sir.

ENOBARBUS. What, man?

EROS. Caesar and Lepidus have made wars
    upon Pompey.   5

---

[1] like meaning   [2] gave as little credit as possible to me
[3] grudgingly   [4] resent

[5] make provision for

ENOBARBUS. This is old; what is the success?[1]

EROS. Caesar, having made use of him in the wars 'gainst Pompey, presently denied him rivality,[2] would not let him partake in the glory of the action; and not resting here, accuses him of letters he had formerly wrote to Pompey; upon his own appeal, seizes him: so the poor third is up, till death enlarge his confine.

ENOBARBUS. Then, world, thou hast a pair of chaps,[3] no more;   14
And throw between them all the food thou hast,
They'll grind the one the other. Where's Antony?

EROS. He's walking in the garden—thus: and spurns
The rush that lies before him; cries, "Fool, Lepidus!"
And threats the throat of that his officer
That murdered Pompey.

ENOBARBUS.   Our great navy's rigged.

EROS. For Italy and Caesar. More, Domitius;
My lord desires you presently:[4] my news   22
I might have told hereafter.

ENOBARBUS.   'Twill be naught;
But let it be. Bring me to Antony.

EROS. Come, sir.   (*Exeunt*)   25

SCENE 6. *Rome. A room in* CAESAR'S *house.*

(*Enter* CAESAR, AGRIPPA, *and* MECAENAS)

CAESAR. Contemning Rome, he has done all this and more
In Alexandria; here's the manner of 't;
I' the market-place, on a tribunal[1] silvered,
Cleopatra and himself in chairs of gold
Were publicly enthroned; at the feet sat   5
Caesarion, whom they call my father's son,
And all the unlawful issue that their lust
Since then hath made between them. Unto her
He gave the 'stablishment[2] of Egypt; made her
Of Lower Syria, Cyprus, Lydia,   10
Absolute queen.

MECAENAS.   This in the public eye?

CAESAR. I' the common show-place, where they exercise.
His sons he there proclaimed the kings of kings;
Great Media, Parthia, and Armenia
He gave to Alexander; to Ptolemy he assigned
Syria, Cilicia, and Phoenicia. She   16
In the habiliments of the goddess Isis
That day appeared; and oft before gave audience,
As 'tis reported, so.

MECAENAS.   Let Rome be thus Informed.

AGRIPPA. Who, queasy[3] with his insolence   20
Already, will their good thoughts call from him.

CAESAR. The people know it; and have now received.
His accusations.

AGRIPPA.   Whom does he accuse?

CAESAR. Caesar; and that, having in Sicily
Sextus Pompeius spoiled, we had not rated[4] him   25
His part o' the isle; then does he say, he lent me
Some shipping unrestored; lastly, he frets
That Lepidus of the triumvirate
Should be deposed; and, being, that we detain
All his revenue.

AGRIPPA.   Sir, this should be answered. 30

CAESAR. 'Tis done already, and the messenger gone.
I have told him, Lepidus was grown too cruel;
That he his high authority abused,
And did deserve his change: for what I have conquered,
I grant his part; but then, in his Armenia,   35
And other of his conquered kingdoms, I
Demand the like.

MECAENAS.   He'll never yield to that.

CAESAR. Nor must not then be yielded to in this.

(*Enter* OCTAVIA, *with her train*)

---

[1] outcome [2] partnership [3] jaws [4] at once [1] dais [2] settled possession of

[3] nauseated [4] allotted

OCTAVIA. Hail, Caesar, and my lord! hail, most dear Caesar!

CAESAR. That ever I should call thee castaway!   40

OCTAVIA. You have not called me so, nor have you cause.

CAESAR. Why have you stol'n upon us thus? You come not
Like Caesar's sister; the wife of Antony
Should have an army for an usher, and
The neighs of horse to tell of her approach   45
Long ere she did appear; the trees by the way
Should have borne men; and expectation fainted,
Longing for what it had not; nay, the dust
Should have ascended to the roof of heaven,
Raised by your populous troops. But you are come   50
A market-maid to Rome, and have prevented[5]
The ostentation[6] of our love, which, left, unshown,
Is often left unloved: we should have met you
By sea and land, supplying every stage
With an augmented greeting.

OCTAVIA.   Good my lord,   55
To come thus was I not constrained, but did it
On my free-will. My lord, Mark Antony,
Hearing that you prepared for war, acquainted
My grieved ear withal; whereon, I begged
His pardon for return.

CAESAR.   Which soon he granted,
Being an obstruct 'tween his list and him.   61

OCTAVIA. Do not say so, my lord.

CAESAR.   I have eyes upon him,
And his affairs come to me on the wind.
Where is he now?

OCTAVIA.   My lord, in Athens.

CAESAR. No, my most wronged sister; Cleopatra   65
Hath nodded him to her. He hath given his empire
Up to a whore; who now are levying

The kings o' the earth for war. He hath assembled
Bocchus, the King of Libya; Archelaus,
Of Cappadocia; Philadelphos, King   70
Of Paphlagonia; the Thracian king, Adallas;
King Malchus of Arabia; King of Pont;
Herod of Jewry; Mithridates, King
Of Comagene; Polemon and Amyntas,
The Kings of Mede and Lycaonia,   75
With a more larger list of sceptres.

OCTAVIA.   Ay me, most wretched.
That have my heart parted betwixt two friends
That do afflict each other!

CAESAR.   Welcome hither:
Your letters did withhold our breaking forth,
Till we perceived both how you were wrong led   80
And we in negligent danger. Cheer your heart;
Be you not troubled with the time, which drives
O'er your content these strong necessities,
But let determined things to destiny
Hold unbewailed their way. Welcome to Rome;
Nothing more dear to me. You are abused   86
Beyond the mark of thought, and the high gods,
To do you justice, make them ministers
Of us and those that love you. Best of comfort,
And ever welcome to us.

AGRIPPA.   Welcome, lady.   90

MECAENAS. Welcome dear madam.
Each heart in Rome does love and pity you;
Only the adulterous Antony, most large[7]
In his abominations, turns you off,
And gives his potent regiment to a trull,[8]   95
That noises it against us.

OCTAVIA.   Is it so, sir?

CAESAR Most certain. Sister, welcome; pray you,
Be ever known to patience; my dearest sister!
(*Exeunt*)

---

[5] anticipated   [6] display   [7] gross   [8] powerful rule of a wanton

SCENE 7. ANTONY'S *camp, near to the promontory of Actium.*

(*Enter* CLEOPATRA *and* ENOBARBUS)

CLEOPATRA. I will be even with thee, doubt it not.

ENOBARBUS. But why, why, why?

CLEOPATRA. Thou hast forspoke[1] my being in these wars,
And sayst it is not fit.

ENOBARBUS.   Well, is it, is it?

CLEOPATRA. If not denounced[2] against us, why should not we   5
Be there in person?

ENOBARBUS (*aside*). Well, I could reply.
If we should serve with horse and mares together
The horse were merely lost; the mares would bear
A soldier and his horse.

CLEOPATRA. What is 't you say?

ENOBARBUS. Your presence needs must puzzle Antony;   10
Take from his heart, take from his brain, from 's time,
What should not then be spared. He is already
Traduced for levity, and 'tis said in Rome
That Photinus a eunuch and your maids
Manage this war.   15

CLEOPATRA. Sink Rome, and their tongues rot
That speak against us! A charge[3] we bear i' the war,
And, as president of my kingdom, will
Appear there for a man. Speak not against it;
I will not stay behind.

ENOBARBUS.   Nay, I have done.
Here comes the emperor.   20

(*Enter* ANTONY *and* CANIDIUS)

ANTONY   Is it not strange, Canidius,
That from Tarentum and Brundusium
He could so quickly cut the Ionian sea,
And take in Toryne? You have heard on 't, sweet?

CLEOPATRA. Celerity is never more admired
Than by the negligent.

ANTONY.   A good rebuke,   26
Which might have well becomed the best of men,
To taunt at slackness. Canidius, we
Will fight with him by sea.

CLEOPATRA.   By sea! What else?

CANIDIUS. Why will my lord do so?

ANTONY.   For that he dares us to 't.   30

ENOBARBUS. So hath my lord dared him to single fight.

CANIDIUS. Ay, and to wage his battle at Pharsalia,
Where Caesar fought with Pompey; but these offers,
Which serve not for his vantage, he shakes off;
And so should you.

ENOBARBUS.   Your ships are not well manned;   35
Your mariners are muleters, reapers, people
Ingrossed by swift impress,[4] in Caesar's fleet
Are those that often have 'gainst Pompey fought:
Their ships are yare,[5] yours, heavy. No disgrace
Shall fall[6] you for refusing him at sea,   40
Being prepared for land.

ANTONY.   By sea, by sea.

ENOBARBUS. Most worthy sir, you therein throw away
The absolute soldiership you have by land;
Distract your army, which doth most consist
Of war-marked footmen; leave unexecuted   45
Your own renowned knowledge; quite forego
The way which promises assurance; and
Give up yourself merely to chance and hazard
From firm security.

ANTONY.   I'll fight at sea.

---

[1] spoken against   [2] proclaimed   [3] military command

[4] collected by sudden conscription   [5] easily handled   [6] befall

CLEOPATRA I have sixty sails, Caesar none better.

ANTONY. Our overplus of shipping will we burn;
And with the rest, full-manned, from the head of Actium
Beat the approaching Caesar. But if we fail,
We then can do 't at land.

(*Enter a* MESSENGER)

Thy business,

MESSENGER. The news is true, my lord; he is descried;   55
Caesar has taken Toryne.

ANTONY. Can he be there in person? 'tis impossible;
Strange that his power should be. Canidius,
Our nineteen legions thou shalt hold by land,
And our twelve thousand horse. We'll to our ship: 60
Away, my Thetis!

(*Enter a* SOLDIER)

How now, worthy soldier!

SOLDIER. O noble emperor! do not fight by sea;
Trust not to rotten planks: do you misdoubt
This sword and these my wounds? Let the Egyptians
And the Phoenicians go a-ducking; we   65
Have used to conquer, standing on the earth,
And fighting foot to foot.

ANTONY.   Well, well: away!

(*Exeunt* ANTONY, CLEOPATRA,
and ENOBARBUS)

SOLDIER. By Hercules, I think I am i' the right.

CANIDIUS. Soldier, thou art; but his whole action grows
Not in the power on 't: so our leader's led,   70
And we are women's men.

SOLDIER.   You keep by land
The legions and the horse whole, do you not?

CANIDIUS. Marcus Octavius, Marcus Justeius,
Publicola, and Caelius, are for sea;

But we keep whole by land. This speed of Caesar's   75
Carries beyond belief.

SOLDIER.   While he was yet in Rome
His power went out in such distractions[7] as
Beguiled all spies.

CANIDIUS.   Who's his lieutenant, hear you?

SOLDIER. They say, one Taurus.

CANIDIUS.   Well I know the man.

(*Enter a* MESSENGER)

MESSENGER. The emperor calls Canidius.   80

CANIDIUS. With news the time's with labour, and throes forth
Each minute some.   (*Exeunt*)

SCENE 8. *A plain near Actium.*

(*Enter* CAESAR, TAURUS, Officers, *and others*)

CAESAR. Taurus!

TAURUS. My lord?

CAESAR. Strike not by land; keep whole: provoke not battle,
Till we have done at sea. Do not exceed
The prescript of this scroll: our fortune lies   5
Upon this jump.[1]   (*Exeunt*)

(*Enter* ANTONY *and* ENOBARBUS)

ANTONY. Set we our squadrons on yond side o' the hill,
In eye of Caesar's battle; from which place
We may the number of the ships behold,
And so proceed accordingly.   (*Exeunt*)   10

(*Enter* CANIDIUS, *marching with his land army one way over the stage; and* TAURUS, *the lieutenant of* CAESAR, *the other way. After their going in is heard the noise of a sea-fight*)

(*Alarum. Re-enter* ENOBARBUS.)

ENOBARBUS. Naught, naught, all naught! I can behold no longer.
The Antoniad, the Egyptian admiral,[2]

---

[7] detachments   [1] hazard   [2] flagship

With all their sixty, fly, and turn the rudder;
To see 't mine eyes are blasted.

(*Enter* SCARUS)

SCARUS. Gods and Goddesses,
All the whole synod of them!

ENOBARBUS. What's thy passion?

SCARUS. The greater cantle[3] of the world is
lost   16
With very ignorance; we have kissed away
Kingdoms and provinces.

ENOBARBUS. How appears the fight?

SCARUS. On our side like the tokened pesti-
lence,[4]
Where death is sure. Yon ribaudred[5] nag of
Egypt,   20
Whom leprosy o'ertake! i' the midst o' the
fight,
When vantage like a pair of twins appeared,
Both as the same, or rather ours the elder,
The breese[6] upon her, like a cow in June,
Hoists sails and flies.

ENOBARBUS. That I beheld: 25
Mine eyes did sicken at the sight, and could
not
Endure a further view.

SCARUS. She once being loofed,[7]
The noble ruin of her magic, Antony,
Claps on his sea-wing, and like a doting mal-
lard,
Leaving the fight in height, flies after her.   30
I never saw an action of such shame;
Experience, manhood, honour, ne'er before
Did violate so itself.

ENOBARBUS. Alack, alack!

(*Enter* CANIDIUS)

CANIDIUS. Our fortune on the sea is out of
breath,
And sinks most lamentably. Had our gen-
eral   35
Been what he knew himself, it had gone well:
O! he has given example for our flight
Most grossly by his own.

ENOBARBUS. Ay, are you thereabouts?
Why, then, good night, indeed.

CANIDIUS. Toward Peloponnesus are they
fled.

SCARUS. 'Tis easy to 't; and there I will attend
What further comes.

CANIDIUS. To Caesar will I render
My legions and my horse; six kings already
Show me the way of yielding.

ENOBARBUS. I'll yet follow
The wounded chance of Antony, though my
reason   45
Sits in the wind against me.   (*Exeunt*)

SCENE 9. *Alexandria. A room in the palace.*

(*Enter* ANTONY *and* ATTENDANTS)

ANTONY. Hark! the land bids me tread no
more upon 't;
It is ashamed to bear me. Friends, come
hither:
I am so lated[1] in the world that I
Have lost my way for ever. I have a ship
Laden with gold; take that, divide it; fly,   5
And make your peace with Caesar.

ATTENDANTS. Fly! not we.

ANTONY. I have fled myself, and have in-
structed cowards
To run and show their shoulders. Friends, be
gone;
I have myself resolved upon a course
Which has no need of you; be gone: 10
My treasure's in the harbour, take it. O!
I followed that I blush to look upon:
My very hairs do mutiny, for the white
Reprove the brown for rashness, and they
them
For fear and doting. Friends, be gone; you
shall   15
Have letters from me to some friends that will
Sweep your way for you. Pray you, look not
sad,
Nor make replies of loathness; take the hint
Which my despair proclaims; let that be left
Which leaves itself; to the sea-side straight-
way;   20
I will possess you of that ship and treasure.
Leave me, I pray, a little; pray you now:

---

[3] portion   [4] the plague   [5] lewd   [6] goadfly   [7] luffed   [1] belated

Nay, do so; for, indeed, I have lost command,
Therefore I pray you I'll see you by and by.

   (*Sits down*)

   (*Enter* EROS *following* CLEOPATRA, *led by*
   CHARMIAN *and* IRAS)

EROS. Nay, gentle madam, to him, comfort
   him.   25

IRAS. Do, most dear queen.

CHARMIAN. Do! Why, what else?

CLEOPATRA. Let me sit down. O Juno!

ANTONY. No, no, no, no, no.

EROS. See you here, sir?   30

ANTONY. O fie, fie, fie!

CHARMIAN. Madam!

IRAS. Madam; O good empress!

EROS. Sir, sir!

ANTONY. Yes, my lord, yes. He, at Philippi
   kept   35
His sword e'en like a dancer, while I struck
The lean and wrinkled Cassius; and 'twas I
That the mad Brutus ended: he alone
Dealt on lieutenantry,[2] and no practice had
In the brave squares of war: yet now—No
   matter.

CLEOPATRA. Ah! stand by.

EROS. The queen, my lord, the queen.

IRAS. Go to him, madam, speak to him;
He is unqualitied[3] with very shame.

CLEOPATRA. Well then, sustain me: O!   45

EROS. Most noble sir, arise; the queen approaches:
Her head's declined, and death will seize her,
   but
Your comfort makes the rescue.

ANTONY. I have offended reputation,
A most unnoble swerving.

EROS.   Sir, the queen.   50

ANTONY. O! whither hast thou led me, Egypt?
   See,

How I convey my shame out of thine eyes
By looking back what I have left behind
'Stroyed in dishonour.

CLEOPATRA.   O my lord, my lord!
Forgive my fearful sails: I little thought   55
You would have followed.

ANTONY.   Egypt, thou knew'st too well
My heart was to thy rudder tied by the strings,
And thou shouldst tow me after; o'er my
   spirit
Thy full supremacy thou knew'st, and that
Thy beck might from the bidding of the
   gods   60
Command me.

CLEOPATRA. O! my pardon.

ANTONY.   Now I must
To the young man send humble treaties,
   dodge
And palter[4] in the shifts of lowness, who
With half the bulk o' the world played as I
   pleased,   64
Making and marring fortunes. You did know
How much you were my conqueror, and that
My sword, made weak by my affection, would
Obey it on all cause.

CLEOPATRA.   Pardon, pardon!

ANTONY. Fall not a tear, I say; one of them
   rates[5]
All that is won and lost. Give me a kiss;   70
Even this repays me. We sent our school-
   master;
Is he come back? Love, I am full of lead.
Some wine, within there, and our viands!
   Fortune knows,
We scorn her most when most she offers
   blows.   (*Exeunt*)

SCENE 10. *Egypt.* CAESAR's *camp.*

   (*Enter* CAESAR, DOLABELLA, THYREUS,
        and others)

CAESAR. Let him appear that's come from
   Antony.
Know you him?

DOLABELLA. Caesar, 'tis his schoolmaster:
An argument that he is plucked, when hither

---

[2] acted by proxy   [3] divested of his character   [4] use tricks   [5] is worth

He sends so poor a pinion of his wing,
Which had superfluous kings for messengers 5
Not many moons gone by.

(Enter EUPHRONIUS*)*

CAESAR.   Approach, and speak.

EUPHRONIUS. Such as I am, I come from
   Antony:
I was of late as petty to his ends
As is the morn-dew on the myrtle-leaf
To his grand sea.

CAESAR.   Be't so. Declare thine office.   10

EUPHRONIUS. Lord of his fortunes he salutes
   thee, and
Requires to live in Egypt; which not granted,
He lessens his requests, and to thee sues
To let him breathe between the heavens and
   earth,
A private man in Athens; this for him.   15
Next, Cleopatra does confess thy greatness,
Submits her to thy might, and of thee craves
The circle[1] of the Ptolemies for her heirs,
Now hazarded to thy grace.

CAESAR.   For Antony,
I have no ears to his request. The queen   20
Of audience nor desire shall fail, so she
From Egypt drive her all-disgracèd friend,
Or take his lfe there; this if she perform,
She shall not sue unheard. So to them both.

EUPHRONIUS. Fortune pursue thee!

CAESAR.   Bring him through the bands.

(Exit EUPHRONIUS*)*

(To THYREUS*)*   To try thy eloquence, now
   'tis time; dispatch.   26
From Antony win Cleopatra; promise,
And in our name, what she requires; add
   more,
From thine invention, offers. Women are not
In their best fortunes strong, but want will
   perjure   30
The ne'er-touched vestral. Try thy cunning,
   Thyreus;
Make thine own edict for thy pains, which we
Will answer as a law.

THYREUS.   Caesar, I go.

CAESAR. Observe how Antony becomes his
   flaw,[2]   34
And what thou think'st his very action speaks
In every power that moves.

THYREUS.   Caesar, I shall.
                               (Exeunt)

SCENE 11. *Alexandria. A room in the palace.*

(Enter CLEOPATRA, ENOBARBUS,
CHARMIAN, *and* IRAS*)*

CLEOPATRA. What shall we do, Enobarbus?

ENOBARBUS.   Think and die.

CLEOPATRA. Is Antony or we, in fault for this?

ENOBARBUS. Antony only, that would make
   his will
Lord of his reason. What though you fled
From that great face of war, whose several
   ranges   5
Frighted each other, why should he follow?
The itch of his affection should not then
Have nicked[1] his captainship; at such a point,
When half to half the world opposed, he
   being
The mered question.[2] 'Twas a shame no less 10
Than was his loss, to course[3] your flying flags,
And leave his navy gazing.

CLEOPATRA.   Prithee, peace.

(Enter ANTONY, *with* EUPHRONIUS*)*

ANTONY. Is that his answer?

EUPHRONIUS. Ay, my lord.

ANTONY. The queen shall then have courtesy,
   so she   15
Will yield us up?

EUPHRONIUS.   He says so.

ANTONY.   Let her know 't.
To the boy Caesar send this grizzled head,
And he will fill thy wishes to the brim
With principalities.

CLEOPATRA.   That head, my lord?

ANTONY. To him again. Tell him he wears the
   rose   20

---

[1] crown

[2] crack in his fortunes, ruin   [1] cut off   [2] the matter to which
the dispute is limited   [3] chase

Of youth upon him, from which the world
should note
Something particular; his coin, ships, legions,
May be a coward's, whose ministers would
prevail
Under the service of a child as soon
As i' the command of Caesar: I dare him
therefore   25
To lay his gay comparisons[4] apart,
And answer me declined,[5] sword against
sword,
Ourselves alone. I'll write it: follow me.

    (Exeunt ANTONY *and* EUPHRONIUS)

ENOBARBUS *(aside).* Yes, like enough, high-
battled Caesar will
Unstate[6] his happiness, and be staged to the
show   30
Against a sworder! I see men's judgments are
A parcel[7] of their fortunes, and things out-
ward
Do draw the inward quality after them,
To suffer all alike. That he should dream,
Knowing all measures, the full Caesar will 35
Answer his emptiness! Caesar, thou hast sub-
dued
His judgment too.

    (Enter an ATTENDANT)

ATTENDANT.   A messenger from Caesar.

CLEOPATRA. What! no more ceremony? See!
my women;
Against the blown rose may they stop their
nose,
That kneeled unto the buds. Admit him, sir.

    (Exit ATTENDANT)

ENOBARBUS *(aside).* Mine honesty and I begin
to square.   41
The loyalty well held to fools does make
Our faith mere folly; yet he that can endure
To follow with allegiance a fall'n lord,
Does conquer him that did his master con-
quer,
And earns a place i' the story.   46

    (Enter THYREUS)

CLEOPATRA.   Caesar's will?

THYREUS. Hear it apart.

CLEOPATRA. None but friends; say boldly.

THYREUS. So, haply,[8] are they friends to
Antony.

ENOBARBUS. He needs as many, sir, as Caesar
has,
Or needs not us. If Caesar please, our
master   50
Will leap to be his friend; for us, you know
Whose he is we are, and that is Caesar's.

THYREUS.   So.
Thus then, thou most renowned: Caesar en-
treats,
Not to consider in what case thou stand'st,
Further than he is Caesar.

CLEOPATRA.   Go on; right royal.

THYREUS. He knows that you embrace not
Antony   56
As you did love, but as you feared him.

CLEOPATRA.   O!

THYREUS. The scars upon your honour there-
fore he
Does pity, as constrained blemishes,
Not as deserved.

CLEOPATRA. He is a god and knows   60
What is most right. Mine honour was not
yielded,
But conquered merely.

ENOBARBUS *(aside).* To be sure of that,
I will ask Antony. Sir, sir, thou'rt so leaky,
That we must leave thee to thy sinking, for
Thy dearest quit thee.   *(Exit)*

THYREUS.   Shall I say to Caesar 65
What you require of him? for he partly begs
To be desired to give. It much would please
him,
That of his fortunes you should make a staff
To lean upon; but it would warm his spirits
To hear from me you had left Antony,   70
And put yourself under his shroud,[9]
The universal landlord.

CLEOPATRA.   What's your name?

THYREUS. My name is Thyreus.

CLEOPATRA.   Most kind messenger,

---

[4] advantages   [5] weakened   [6] deprive of dignity   [7] part   [8] perhaps   [9] shelter, protecion

Say to great Caesar this: in deputation[10]
I kiss his conqu'ring hand; tell him, I am prompt   75
To lay my crown at 's feet, and there to kneel;
Tell him, from his all-obeying breath I hear
The doom of Egypt.

THYREUS.   'Tis your noblest course.
Wisdom and fortune combating together,
If that the former dare but what it can,   80
No chance may shake it. Give me grace to lay
My duty on your hand.

CLEOPATRA.   Your Caesar's father oft,
When he hath mused of taking kingdoms in,
Bestowed his lips on that unworthy place,
As it rained kisses.   84

(*Re-enter* ANTONY *and* ENOBARBUS)

ANTONY.   Favours, by Jove that thunders!
What art thou, fellow?

THYREUS.   One that but performs
The bidding of the fullest man, and worthiest
To have command obeyed.

ENOBARBUS (*aside*). You will be whipped.

ANTONY. Approach there! Ah, you kite! Now,
     gods and devils!
Authority melts from me: of late, when I
     cried "Ho!"   90
Like boys unto a muss,[11] kings would start
     forth,
And cry, "Your will?" Have you no ears? I am
Antony yet.
          (*Enter* ATTENDANTS)
     Take hence this Jack and whip him.

ENOBARBUS (*aside*). 'Tis better playing with a
     lion's whelp
Than with an old one dying.

ANTONY.   Moon and stars!
Whip him. Were 't twenty of the greatest
     tributaries   96
That do acknowledge Caesar, should I find
     them
So saucy with the hand of—she here, what's
     her name,
Since she was Cleopatra? Whip him, fellows,
Till, like a boy, you see him cringe his face   100
And whine aloud for mercy; take him hence.

THYREUS. Mark Antony,—

ANTONY.   Tug him away; being whipped,
Bring him again; this Jack of Caesar's shall
Bear us an errand to him.

          (*Exeunt* ATTENDANTS *with* THYREUS)

You were half blasted ere I knew you: ha!   105
Have I my pillow left unpressed in Rome,
Forborne the getting of a lawful race,
And by a gem of women, to be abused
By one that looks on feeders?

CLEOPATRA.   Good my lord,—

ANTONY. You have been a boggler ever: 110
But when we in our viciousness grow hard,—
O misery on 't!—the wise gods seel our eyes;
In our own filth drop our clear judgments;
     make us
Adore our errors; laugh at 's while we strut
To our confusion.

CLEOPATRA.   O! is 't come to this?   115

ANTONY. I found you as a morsel, cold upon
Dear Caesar's trencher; nay, you were a frag-
     ment
     Of Gneius Pompey's; besides what hotter
     hours,
Unregistered in vulgar fame, you have
Luxuriously picked out; for, I am sure,   120
Though you can guess what temperance
     should be,
You know not what it is.

CLEOPATRA.   Wherefore is this?

ANTONY. To let a fellow that will take re-
     wards
And say "God quit[12] you!" be familiar with
My playfellow, your hand; this kingly seal   125
And plighter of high hearts. O! that I were
Upon the hill of Basan,[13] to outroar
The hornèd[14] herd; for I have savage cause;
And to proclaim it civilly were like
A haltered neck, which does the hangman
     thank
For being yare about him.

          (*Re-enter* ATTENDANTS, *with* THYREUS)

                    Is he whipped?   131

---

[10] by proxy   [11] scramble

[12] reward   [13] see Psalms 22:12   [14] the cuckold was fabled to have horns

FIRST ATTENDANT. Soundly, my lord.

ANTONY.   Cried he? and begged a' pardon?

FIRST ATTENDANT. He did ask favour.

ANTONY. If that thy father live, let him repent
Thou wast not made his daughter; and be
  thou sorry   135
To follow Caesar in his triumph, since
Thou hast been whipped for following him:
  henceforth,
The white hand of a lady fever thee,
Shake thou to look on 't. Get thee back to
  Caesar,   139
Tell him thy entertainment; look, thou say
He makes me angry with him; for he seems
Proud and disdainful, harping on what I am,
Not what he knew I was: he makes me angry;
And at this time most easy 'tis to do 't,
When my good stars, that were my former
  guides,   145
Have empty left their orbs, and shot their
  fires
Into the abysm of hell. If he mislike
My speech and what is done, tell him he has
Hipparchus,   my   enfranched[15]   bondman,
  whom
He may at pleasure whip, or hang, or torture,
As he shall like, to quit[16] me: urge it thou: 151
Hence with thy stripes; be gone!

                        (*Exit* THYREUS)

CLEOPATRA. Have you done yet?

ANTONY.   Alack! our terrene moon
Is now eclipsed; and it portends alone
The fall of Antony.

CLEOPATRA. I must stay his time.   157

ANTONY. To flatter Caesar, would you mingle
  eyes
With one that ties his points? [17]

CLEOPATRA.   Not know me yet?

ANTONY. Cold-hearted toward me?

CLEOPATRA.   Ah! dear, if I be so,
From my cold heart let heaven engender hail,
And poison it in the source; and the first stone
Drop in my neck: as it determines,[18] so   161

Dissolve my life. The next Caesarion smite,
Till by degrees the memory of my womb,
Together with my brave Egyptians all,
By the discandying[19] of this pelleted storm, 165
Lie graveless, till the flies and gnats of Nile
Have buried them for prey!

ANTONY.   I am satisfied.
Caesar sits down in Alexandria, where
I will oppose his fate. Our force by land
Hath nobly held; our severed navy too   170
Have knit again, and fleet,[20] threat'ning most
  sea-like.
Where hast thou been, my heart? Dost thou
  hear, lady?
If from the field I shall return once more
To kiss these lips, I will appear in blood;
I and my sword will earn our chronicle: 175
There's hope in 't yet.

CLEOPATRA.   That's my brave lord!

ANTONY. I will be treble-sinewed, hearted,
  breathed,
And fight maliciously; for when mine hours
Were nice and lucky, men did ransom lives 180
Of me for jests; but now I'll set my teeth,
And send to darkness all that stop me. Come,
Let's have one other gaudy night: call to me
All my sad captains; fill our bowls once more;
Let's mock the midnight bell.

CLEOPATRA.   It is my birthday.
I had thought to have held it poor; but, since
  my lord   186
Is Antony again, I will be Cleopatra.

ANTONY. We will yet do well.

CLEOPATRA. Call all his noble captains to my
  lord.

ANTONY. Do so, we'll speak to them; and to-
  night I'll force.   190
The wine peep through their scars. Come on,
  my queen;
There's sap in 't yet. The next time I do fight
I'll make death love me, for I will contend
Even with his pestilent scythe.

                    (*Exeunt all but* ENOBARBUS)

ENOBARBUS. Now he'll outstare the lightning.
  To be furious   195

---

[15] freed   [16] be even with me   [17] laces   [18] comes to an end   [19] melting   [20] floats

Is to be frighted out of fear, and in that mood
The dove will peck the estridge,[21] and I see still,
A diminution in our captain's brain

Restores his heart. When valour preys on reason
It eats the sword it fights with. I will seek 200
Some way to leave him. (*Exit*)

ACT 4

SCENE 1. *Before Alexandria.* CAESAR's *camp.*

(*Enter* CAESAR, *reading a letter;* AGRIPPA, MECAENAS, *and others*)

CAESAR. He calls me boy, and chides as he had power
To beat me out of Egypt; my messenger
He hath whipped with rods; dares me to personal combat,
Caesar to Antony. Let the old ruffian know
I have many other ways to die; meantime 5
Laugh at his challenge.

MECAENAS. Caesar must think,
When one so great begins to rage, he's hunted
Even to falling. Give him no breath, but now
Make boot[1] of his distraction: never anger 9
Made good guard for itself.

CAESAR. Let our best heads
Know that tomorrow the last of many battles
We mean to fight. Within our files there are,
Of those that served Mark Antony but late,
Enough to fetch him in. See it done;
And feast the army; we have store to do 't, 15
And they have earned the waste. Poor Antony! (*Exeunt*)

SCENE 2. *Alexandria. A room in the palace.*

(*Enter* ANTONY, CLEOPATRA, ENOBARBUS, CHARMIAN, IRAS, ALEXAS, *and others*)

ANTONY. He will not fight with me, Domitius.

ENOBARBUS. No.

ANTONY. Why should he not?

ENOBARBUS. He thinks, being twenty times of better fortune,
He is twenty men to one.

ANTONY. Tomorrow, soldier,
By sea and land I'll fight: or I will live, 5
Or bathe my dying honour in the blood
Shall make it live again. Woo 't thou fight well?

ENOBARBUS. I'll strike, and cry, "Take all."

ANTONY. Well said; come on.
Call forth my household servants; let's tonight
Be bounteous at our meal.

(*Enter three of four* SERVITORS)

Give me thy hand, 10
Thou hast been rightly honest; so hast thou;
Thou; and thou, and thou: you have served me well,
And kings have been your fellows.

CLEOPATRA. What means this?

ENOBARBUS (*aside to* CLEOPATRA). 'Tis one of those odd tricks which sorrow shoots
Out of the mind.

ANTONY. And thou art honest too. 15
I wish I could be made so many men,
And all of you clapped up together in
An Antony, that I might do you service
So good as you have done.

SERVANTS. The gods forbid!

ANTONY. Well, my good fellows, wait on me tonight, 20
Scant not my cups, and make as much of me
As when mine empire was your fellow too,
And suffered my command.

CLEOPATRA (*aside to* ENOBARBUS). What does he mean?

ENOBARBUS (*aside to* CLEOPATRA). To make his followers weep.

[21] ostrich [1] profit

ANTONY.   Tend me tonight;
May be it is the period[1] of your duty: 25
Haply, you shall not see me more; or if,
A mangled shadow: perchance tomorrow
You'll serve another master. I look on you
As one that takes his leave. Mine honest
    friends,
I turn you not away; but, like a master   30
Married to your good service, stay till death.
Tend me tonight two hours, I ask no more,
And the gods yield[2] you for 't!

ENOBARBUS.   What mean you, sir,
To give them this discomfort? Look, they
    weep;
And I, an ass, am onion-eyed: for shame,   35
Transform us not to women.

ANTONY.   Ho, ho, ho!
Now, the witch take me, if I meant it thus!
Grace grow where those drops fall! My hearty
    friends,
You take me in too dolorous a sense,
For I spake to you for your comfort; did
    desire you   40
To burn this night with torches. Know, my
    hearts,
I hope well of tomorrow; and will lead you
Where rather I'll expect victorious life
Than death and honour. Let 's to supper,
    come,
And drown consideration.   (Exeunt) 45

SCENE 3. *The same. Before the palace.*

(*Enter two* SOLDIERS *to their guard*)

FIRST SOLDIER. Brother, good night; tomorrow
    is the day.

SECOND SOLDIER. It will determine one way;
    fare you well.
Heard you of nothing strange about the
    streets?

FIRST SOLDIER. Nothing. What news?

SECOND SOLDIER. Belike, 'tis but a rumour.
    Good night, to you.   5

FIRST SOLDIER. Well, sir, good night.

(*Enter two other* SOLDIERS)

SECOND SOLDIER. Soldiers, have careful watch.

THIRD SOLDIER. And you. Good night, good
    night.

(*The first two place themselves at their
    posts*)

FOURTH SOLDIER. Here we: (*They take their
    posts*)
                            And if tomorrow
Our navy thrive, I have an absolute hope   10
Our landmen will stand up.

THIRD SOLDIER.   'Tis a brave army,
And full of purpose. (*Music of hautboys
    under the stage*)

FOURTH SOLDIER. Peace! what noise?

FIRST SOLDIER.   List, list!

SECOND SOLDIER. Hark!

FIRST SOLDIER.   Music i' the air.

THIRD SOLDIER.   Under the earth.

FOURTH SOLDIER. It signs well, does it not?

THIRD SOLDIER.   No.

FIRST SOLDIER.   Peace, I say!
What should this mean?   15

SECOND SOLDIER. 'Tis the god Hercules, whom
    Antony loved,
Now leaves him.

FIRST SOLDIER. Walk; let's see if other watch-
    men
Do hear what we do. (*They advance to an-
    other post*)

SECOND SOLDIER. How now, master?

SOLDIERS.   How now!—
How now!—do you hear this?

FIRST SOLDIER.   Ay; is 't not strange?

THIRD SOLDIER. Do you hear, masters? do you
    hear?   21

FIRST SOLDIER. Follow the noise so far as we
    have quarter;[1]
Let's see how 't will give off.

SOLDIERS (*speaking together*). Content.—'Tis
    strange.   (*Exeunt*)

---

[1] termination [2] reward   [1] occupy positions

SCENE 4. *The same. A room in the palace.*

(*Enter* ANTONY *and* CLEOPATRA; CHARMIAN, *and others, attending*)

ANTONY. Eros! mine armour, Eros!

CLEOPATRA. Sleep a little.

ANTONY. No, my chuck. Eros, come; mine armour, Eros!

(*Enter* EROS, *with armour*)

Come, good fellow, put mine iron on:
If Fortune be not ours today, it is
Because we brave her. Come.   4

CLEOPATRA. Nay, I'll help too.
What's this for?

ANTONY. Ah! let be, let be; thou art
The armourer of my heart: false, false; this, this.

CLEOPATRA. Sooth, la! I'll help: thus it must be.

ANTONY. Well, well;
We shall thrive now. Seest thou, my good fellow?
Go put on thy defences.

EROS. Briefly, sir.   10

CLEOPATRA. Is not this buckled well?

ANTONY. Rarely, rarely:
He that unbuckles this, till we do please
To daff 't[1] for our repose, shall hear a storm.
Thou fumblest, Eros; and my queen's a squire
More tight[2] at this than thou: dispatch. O love!
That thou couldst see my wars today, and knew'st   16
The royal occupation, thou shouldst see
A workman in 't.

(*Enter an armed* SOLDIER)

Good morrow to thee; welcome;
Thou look'st like him that knows a war-like charge:
To business that we love we rise betime,   20
And go to 't with delight.

SOLDIER. A thousand, sir,
Early though 't be, have on their riveted trim,

And at the port[3] expect you.

(*Shout. Trumpets flourish.*)

(*Enter* CAPTAINS *and* SOLDIERS)

CAPTAIN. The morn is fair. Good morrow, general.

ALL. Good morrow, general.

ANTONY. 'Tis well blown, lads.
This morning, like the spirit of a youth   26
That means to be of note, begins betimes.
So, so; come, give me that: this way; well said.
Fare thee well, dame, whate'er becomes of me;
This is a soldier's kiss. Rebukable (*Kisses her*)   30
And worthy shameful check it were, to stand
On more mechanic compliment I'll leave thee
Now, like a man of steel. You that will fight,
Follow me close; I'll bring you to 't. Adieu.

(*Exeunt* ANTONY, EROS, CAPTAINS, *and* SOLDIERS)

CHARMIAN. Please you, retire to your chamber.

CLEOPATRA. Lead me.
He goes forth gallantly. That he and Caesar might   36
Determine this great war in single fight!
Then, Antony,—but now.—well, on.

(*Exeunt*)

SCENE 5. *Alexandria.* ANTONY'S *camp.*

(*Trumpets sound. Enter* ANTONY *and* EROS; *a* SOLDIER *meeting them.*)

SOLDIER. The gods make this a happy day to Antony!

ANTONY. Would thou and those thy scars had once prevailed
To make me fight at land!

SOLDIER. Hadst thou done so,
The kings that have revolted, and the soldier
That has this morning left thee, would have still   5
Followed thy heels.

ANTONY. Who's gone this morning?

---

[1] doff, put off   [2] deft   [3] gate

SOLDIER.   Who!
One ever near thee: call for Enobarbus,
He shall not hear thee; or from Caesar's camp
Say, "I am none of thine."

ANTONY.   What sayst thou?

SOLDIER.   Sir,
He is with Caesar.

EROS.   Sir, his chests and treasure [10]
He has not with him.

ANTONY.   Is he gone?

SOLDIER.   Most certain.

ANTONY. Go, Eros, send his treasure after; do
  it;
Detain no jot, I charge thee. Write to him—
I will subscribe—gentle adieus and greetings;
Say that I wish he never find more cause   [15]
To change a master. O! my fortunes have
Corrupted honest men. Dispatch. Enobar-
bus!   (*Exeunt*)

SCENE 6. *Before Alexandria.* CAESAR'S *camp.*

(*Flourish. Enter* CAESAR, *with* AGRIPPA,
  ENOBARBUS, *and others.*)

CAESAR. Go forth, Agrippa, and begin the
  fight:
Our will is Antony be took alive;
Make it so known.

AGRIPPA. Caesar, I shall.   (*Exit*)

CAESAR. The time of universal peace is near:
Prove this a prosperous day, the three-nook'd[1]
  world   [6]
Shall bear the olive freely.

(*Enter a* MESSENGER)

MESSENGER.   Antony
Is come into the field.

CAESAR.   Go charge Agrippa
Plant those that have revolted in the van,
That Antony may seem to spend his fury   [10]
Upon himself. (*Exeunt* CAESAR *and his* Train)

ENOBARBUS. Alexas did revolt, and went to
  Jewry on
Affairs of Antony; there did persuade

Great Herod to incline himself to Caesar,   [14]
And leave his master Antony: for this pains
Caesar hath hanged him. Canidius and the
  rest
That fell away have entertainment, but
No honourable trust. I have done ill,
Of which I do accuse myself so sorely
That I will joy no more.

(*Enter a* SOLDIER *of* CAESAR'S)

SOLDIER.   Enobarbus, Antony
Hath after thee sent all thy treasure, with   [21]
His bounty overplus: the messenger
Came on my guard; and at thy tent is now
Unloading of his mules.

ENOBARBUS.   I give it you.

SOLDIER. Mock not, Enobarbus.   [25]
I tell you true: best you safed[2] the bringer
Out of the host; I must attend mine office
Or would have done 't myself. Your emperor
Continues still a Jove.   (*Exit*)

ENOBARBUS. I am alone the villain of the
  earth,   [30]
And feel I am so most. O Antony!
Thou mine of bounty, how wouldst thou
  have paid
My better service, when my turpitude
Thou dost so crown with gold! This blows[3]
  my heart:
If swift thought break it not, a swifter mean
Shall outstrike thought; but thought will do
  't, I feel.   [36]
I fight against thee? No: I will go seek
Some ditch, wherein to die; the foul'st best fits
My latter part of life.   (*Exit*)

SCENE 7. *Field of battle between the camps.*

(*Alarum. Drums and trumpets. Enter*
  AGRIPPA *and others.*)

AGRIPPA. Retire, we have engaged ourselves
  too far.
Caesar himself has work, and our oppression[1]
Exceeds what we expected.   (*Exeunt*)

(*Alarum. Enter* ANTONY, *and* SCARUS
  wounded.)

---

[1] three-cornered   [2] conducted safely   [3] swells   [1] force opposed to us

SCARUS. O my brave emperor, this is fought
  indeed!
Had we done so at first, we had droven them
  home   5
With clouts about their heads.

ANTONY.   Thou bleed'st apace.

SCARUS. I had a wound here that was like a T,
But now 'tis made an H.

ANTONY.   They do retire.

SCARUS. We'll beat 'em into bench-holes:[2] I
  have yet
Room for six scotches[3] more.   10

      (*Enter* EROS)

EROS. They are beaten, sir; and our advantage
  serves
For a fair victory.

SCARUS.   Let us score their backs,
And snatch 'em up, as we take hares, behind:
'Tis sport to maul a runner.

ANTONY.   I will reward thee
Once for thy sprightly comfort, and ten-fold [15]
For thy good valour. Come thee on.

SCARUS.   I'll halt[4] after   (*Exeunt*)

SCENE 8. *Under the walls of Alexandria.*

      (*Alarum. Enter* ANTONY, *marching;*
      SCARUS *and forces*)

ANTONY. We have beat him to his camp; run
  one before
And let the queen know of our gests.[1] To-
  morrow,
Before the sun shall see 's, we'll spill the blood
That has today escaped. I thank you all;   4
For dougty-handed are you, and have fought
Not as you served the cause, but as 't had been
Each man's like mine; you have shown all
  Hectors.
Enter the city, clip[2] your wives, your friends,
Tell them your feats; whilst they with joyful
  tears
Wash the congealment from your wounds,
  and kiss   10
The honoured gashes whole. (*To* SCARUS)
Give me thy hand:

      (*Enter* CLEOPATRA, *attended*)

To this great fairy[3] I commend thy acts,
Make her thanks bless thee. O thou day o' the
  world!
Chain mine armed neck; leap thou, attire and
  all,
Through proof of harness[4] to my heart, and
  there   15
Ride on the pants triumphing.

CLEOPATRA.   Lord of lords!
O infinite virtue! com'st thou smiling from
The world's great snare uncaught?

ANTONY.   My nightingale,
We have beat them to their beds. What, girl!
  though grey
Do something mingle with our younger
  brown, yet ha' we   20
A brain that nourishes our nerves, and can
Get goal for goal of youth. Behold this man;
Commend unto his lips thy favouring hand:
Kiss it, my warrior: he hath fought today
As if a god, in hate of mankind, had   25
Destroyed in such a shape.

CLEOPATRA.   I'll give thee, friend,
An armour all of gold; it was a king's.

ANTONY. He had deserved it, were it car-
  buncled
Like holy Phoebus' car. Give me thy hand:
Through Alexandria make a jolly march;   30
Bear our hacked targets like the men that
  owe[5] them:
Had our great palace the capacity
To camp this host, we all would sup together
And drink carouses to the next day's fate,
Which promises royal peril. Trumpeters,   35
With brazen din blast you the city's ear,
Make mingle with our rattling tabourines,
That heaven and earth may strike their
  sounds together,
Applauding our approach.   (*Exeunt*)

SCENE 9. CAESAR'S *camp.*

      (SENTINELS *on their post*)

FIRST SOLDIER. If we be not relieved within
  this hour,
We must return to the court of guard:[1] the
  night

---

[2] privy holes   [3] gashes   [4] limp   [1] deeds   [2] embrace

[3] enchantress   [4] impenetrability of armour   [5] own   [1] guard
house

Is shiny, and they say we shall embattle
By the second hour i' the morn.

SECOND SOLDIER.   This last day was
A shrewd one to 's.

(*Enter* ENOBARBUS)

ENOBARBUS.   O! bear me witness, night,—5

THIRD SOLDIER. What man is this?

SECOND SOLDIER. Stand close and list him.

ENOBARBUS. Be witness to me, O thou blessed
    moon,
When men revolted shall upon record
Bear hateful memory, poor Enobarbus did
Before thy face repent!

FIRST SOLDIER.   Enobarbus!

THIRD SOLDIER.   Peace!   10
Hark further.

ENOBARBUS. O sovereign mistress of true mel-
    ancholy,
The poisonous damp of night disponge² upon
    me,
That life, a very rebel to my will,   14
May hang no longer on me; throw my heart
Against the flint and hardness of my fault,
Which, being dried with grief, will break to
    powder,
And finish all foul thoughts. O Antony!
Nobler than my revolt is infamous,
Forgive me in thine own particular;³   20
But let the world rank me in register
A master-leaver and a fugitive.
O Antony! O Antony! (*Dies*)

SECOND SOLDIER. Let's speak to him.

FIRST SOLDIER. Let's hear him, for the things
    he speaks.   25
May concern Caesar.

THIRD SOLDIER. Let's do so. But he sleeps.

FIRST SOLDIER. Swounds rather; for so bad a
    prayer as his
Was never yet for sleep.

SECOND SOLDIER.   Go we to him.

THIRD SOLDIER. Awake sir, awake! speak to us.

SECOND SOLDIER.   Hear you, sir?

FIRST SOLDIER. The hand of death hath
    raught⁴ him.

(*Drums afar off*)

        Hark! the drums   30
Demurely⁵ wake the sleepers. Let us bear him
To the court of guard; he is of note: our hour
Is fully out.

THIRD SOLDIER. Come on, then;
He may recover yet.   (*Exeunt with the body*)

SCENE 10. *Between the two camps.*

(*Enter* ANTONY *and* SCARUS,
        with forces, marching)

ANTONY. Their preparation is today by sea;
We please them not by land.

SCARUS.   For both, my lord.

ANTONY. I would they'd fight i' the fire or i'
    the air;
We'd fight there too. But this it is; our foot
Upon the hills adjoining to the city   5
Shall stay with us; order for sea is given,
They have put forth the haven,
Where their appointment we may best dis-
cover
And look on their endeavour.   (*Exeunt*)

(*Enter* CAESAR, *and his forces, marching*)

CAESAR. But being charged, we will be still by
    land,   10
Which, as I take 't, we shall; for his best force
Is forth to man his galleys. To the vales,
And hold our best advantage!   (*Exeunt*)

(*Re-enter* ANTONY *and* SCARUS)

ANTONY. Yet they are not joined. Where
    yond pine does stand
I shall discover all; I'll bring thee word   15
Straight how 'tis like to go.   (*Exit*)

SCARUS.   Swallows have built
In Cleopatra's sails their nests; the augurers
Say they know not, they cannot tell; look
    grimly,
And dare not speak their knowledge. Antony
Is valiant, and dejected; and, by starts,   20

---

² squeeze out   ³ as far as you are concerned   ⁴ seized   ⁵ with subdued sound

His fretted fortunes give him hope and fear
Of what he has and has not.

(Alarum afar off, as at a sea-fight)

(Re-enter ANTONY)

ANTONY. All is lost!
This foul Egyptian hath betrayed me;
My fleet hath yielded to the foe, and yonder 25
They cast their caps up and carouse together
Like friends long lost. Triple-turned whore, thou
Hast sold me to this novice, and my heart
Makes only wars on thee. Bid them all fly;
For when I am revenged upon my charm,[1] 30
I have done all. Bid them all fly; be gone.

(Exit SCARUS)

O sun! thy uprise shall I see no more;
Fortune and Antony part here; even here
Do we shake hands. All come to this? The hearts
That spanieled me at heels, to whom I gave 35
Their wishes, do discandy, melt their sweets
On blossoming Caesar; and this pine is barked,
That overtopped them all. Betrayed I am.
O this false soul of Egypt; this grave charm,
Whose eyes becked forth my wars, and called them home, 40
Whose bosom was my crownet,[2] my chief end,
Like a right[3] gipsy, hath, at fast and loose,
Beguiled me to the very heart of loss.
What, Eros! Eros!

(Enter CLEOPATRA)

Ah! thou spell. Avaunt!

CLEOPATRA. Why is my lord enraged against his love? 45

ANTONY. Vanish, or I shall give thee thy deserving,
And blemish Caesar's triumph. Let him take thee,
And hoist thee up to the shouting plebeians;
Follow his chariot, like the greatest spot
Of all thy sex; most monster-like, be shown
For poor'st diminutives,[4] for doits; and let 51
Patient Octavia plough thy visage up
With her prepared nails. *(Exit* CLEOPATRA)
'Tis well thou'rt gone,

If it be well to live; but better 'twere
Thou fell'st into my fury, for one death
Might have prevented many. Eros, ho! 56
The shirt of Nessus is upon me; teach me,
Alcides, thou mine ancestor, thy rage;
Let me lodge Lichas on the horns o' the moon;
And with those hands, that grasped the heaviest club, 60
Subdue my worthiest self. The witch shall die:
To the young Roman boy she hath sold me, and I fall
Under this plot; she dies for 't. Eros, ho!

(Exit)

SCENE 11. *Alexandria. A room in the palace.*

(Enter CLEOPATRA, CHARMIAN, IRAS, *and* MARDIAN)

CLEOPATRA. Help me, my women! O! he is more mad
Than Telamon for his shield; the boar of Thessaly
Was never so embossed.

CHARMIAN. To the monument!
There lock yourself, and send him word you are dead.
The soul and body rive[1] not more in parting
Than greatness going off. 5

CLEOPATRA. To the monument!
Mardian, go tell him I have slain myself;
Say that the last I spoke was "Antony,"
And word it, prithee, piteously. Hence,
Mardian, and bring me how he takes my death.
To the monument! *(Exeunt)* 10

SCENE 12. *The same. Another room.*

(Enter ANTONY *and* EROS)

ANTONY. Eros, thou yet behold'st me?

EROS. Ay, noble lord.

ANTONY. Sometimes we see a cloud that's dragonish;
A vapour sometime like a bear or lion,
A towered citadel, a pendant rock,

---

[1] charmer [2] coronet [3] true [4] insignificant persons   [1] are torn

A forked mountain, or blue promontory   5
With trees upon 't, that nod unto the world
And mock our eyes with air: thou hast seen
these signs;
They are black vesper's pageants.

EROS.   Ay, my lord.

ANTONY. That which is now a horse, even
with a thought
The rack dislimns,[1] and makes it indistinct. 10
As water is in water.

EROS.   It does, my lord.

ANTONY. My good knave, Eros, now thy cap-
tain is
Even such a body: here I am, Antony;
Yet cannot hold this visible shape, my knave.
I made these wars for Egypt; and the queen, 15
Whose heart I thought I had, for she had
mine,
Which whilst it was mine had annexed unto 't
A million more, now lost; she, Eros, has
Packed cards with Caesar, and false-played my
glory
Unto an enemy's triumph.   20
Nay, weep not, gentle Eros; there is left us
Ourselves to end ourselves.

                (*Enter* MARDIAN)

                    O! the vile lady;
She has robbed me of my sword.

MARDIAN.   No, Antony;
My mistress loved thee, and her fortunes
mingled   24
With thine entirely.

ANTONY.   Hence, saucy eunuch; peace!
She hath betrayed me and shall die the death.

MARDIAN. Death of one person can be paid
but once,
And that she has discharged. What thou
wouldst do
Is done unto thy hand; the last she spake
Was, "Antony! most noble Antony!"   30
Then in the midst a tearing groan did break
The name of Antony; it was divided
Between her heart and lips. She rendered life,
Thy name so buried in her.

ANTONY.   Dead, then?

MARDIAN.   Dead.

ANTONY. Unarm, Eros; the long day's task is
done,   35
And we must sleep. (*To* MARDIAN) That thou
depart'st hence safe,
Does pay thy labour richly; go.

                        (*Exit* MARDIAN)

                        Off, pluck off:
The seven-fold shield of Ajax cannot keep
The battery[2] from my heart. O! cleave, my
sides;
Heart, once be stronger than thy continent,[3] 40
Crack thy frail case! Apace, Eros, apace.
No more a soldier; bruised pieces, go;
You have been nobly borne. From me awhile.

                        (*Exit* EROS)

I will o'ertake thee, Cleopatra, and
Weep for my pardon. So it must be, for now 45
All length is torture; since the torch is out,
Lie down, and stray no further. Now all
labour
Mars what it does; yea, very force entangles
Itself with strength; seal[4] then, and all is done
Eros!—I come, my queen.—Eros!—Stay for
me: 50
Where souls do couch on flowers, we'll hand
in hand,
And with our sprightly port[5] make the ghosts
gaze;
Dido and her Aeneas shall want troops,
And all the haunt be ours. Come, Eros! Eros!

                (*Re-enter* EROS)

EROS. What would my lord?

ANTONY.   Since Cleopatra died, 55
I have lived in such dishonour, that the gods
Detest my baseness. I, that with my sword
Quartered the world, and o'er green Nep-
tune's back
With ships made cities, condemn myself to
lack
The courage of a woman; less noble mind 60
Than she, which by her death our Caesar tells
"I am conqueror of myself." Thou art sworn,
Eros,
That, when the exigent[6] should come,—
which now

---

[1] cloud loses its outlines

[2] assault [3] container [4] bring to completion [5] demeanor
[6] emergency

Is come indeed,—when I should see behind me
The inevitable prosecution of   65
Disgrace and horror, that, on my command,
Thou then wouldst kill me: do 't; the time is come
Thou strik'st not me, 'tis Caesar thou defeat'st.
Put colour in thy cheek.

EROS.   The gods withhold me!
Shall I do that which all the Parthian darts, 70
Though enemy, lost aim and could not?

ANTONY.   Eros,
Wouldst thou be windowed in great Rome, and see
Thy master thus with pleached[7] arms, bending down
His corrigible[8] neck, his face subdued   74
To penetrative shame, whilst the wheeled seat
Of fortunate Caesar, drawn before him, branded
His baseness that ensued?

EROS.   I would not see 't.

ANTONY. Come, then; for with a wound I must be cured.
Draw that thy honest sword, which thou hast worn
Most useful for thy country.

EROS.   O, sir! pardon me.

ANTONY. When I did make thee free, swor'st thou not then   81
To do this when I bade thee? Do it at once,
Or thy precedent services are all
But accidents unpurposed. Draw, and come.

EROS. Turn from me then that noble countenance,   85
Wherein the worship[9] of the whole world lies.

ANTONY. Lo thee! (*Turning from him*)

EROS. My sword is drawn.

ANTONY.   Then let it do at once
The thing why thou hast drawn it.

EROS.   My dear master,
My captain, and my emperor, let me say, 90
Before I strike this bloody stroke, farewell.

---

[7] folded   [8] submissive   [9] dignity

ANTONY. 'Tis said, man; and farewell.

EROS. Farewell, great chief. Shall I strike now?

ANTONY. Now, Eros.

EROS. Why, there then; thus do I escape the sorrow
Of Antony's death. (*Kills himself*)

ANTONY.   Thrice-nobler than myself! 95
Thou teachest me, O valiant Eros, what
I should, and thou couldst not. My queen and Eros
Have by their brave instruction got upon me
A nobleness in record; but I will be
A bridegroom in my death, and run into 't 100
As to a lover's bed. Come, then; and, Eros,
Thy master dies thy scholar: to do thus (*Falls on his sword*)
I learned of thee. How! not dead? not dead?
The guard, ho! O! dispatch me.

(*Enter* DERCETAS *and* GUARD)

FIRST GUARD.   What's the noise?

ANTONY. I have done my work ill, friends:
O! make an end   105
Of what I have begun.

SECOND GUARD.   The star is fallen.

FIRST GUARD. And time is at his period.

ALL.   Alas, and woe!

ANTONY. Let him that loves me strike me dead.

FIRST GUARD. Not I.

SECOND GUARD. Nor I.   109

THIRD GUARD.   Nor any one.

(*Exeunt* GUARD)

DERCETAS. Thy death and fortunes bid thy followers fly.
This sword but shown to Caesar, with this tidings,
Shall enter me with him.

(*Enter* DIOMEDES)

DIOMEDES. Where's Antony?

DERCETAS.   There, Diomed, there,

DIOMEDES.   Lives he?

Wilt thou not answer, man?   115

(*Exit* DERCETAS)

ANTONY. Art thou there, Diomed? Draw thy
  sword, and give me
Sufficing strokes for death.

DIOMEDES.   Most absolute lord,
My mistress Cleopatra sent me to thee.

ANTONY. When did she send thee?

DIOMEDES.   Now, my lord.

ANTONY.   Where is she?

DIOMEDES. Locked in her monument. She
  had a prophesying fear   120
Of what hath come to pass; for when she
  saw—
Which never shall be found—you did suspect
She had disposed[10] with Caesar, and that your
  rage
Would not be purged,[11] she sent you word she
  was dead:
But, fearing since how it might work, hath
  sent   125
Me to proclaim the truth; and I am come,
I dread, too late.

ANTONY. Too late, good Diomed. Call my
  guard, I prithee.

DIOMEDES. What, ho! the emperor's guard!
  The guard, what, ho!
Come, your lord calls!   130

(*Enter four or five of the* GUARD *of* ANTONY)

ANTONY. Bear me, good friends, where Cleopatra bides;
'Tis the last service that I shall command you.

FIRST GUARD. Woe, woe are we, sir, you may
  not live to wear
All your true followers out.

ALL.   Most heavy day!

ANTONY. Nay, good my fellows, do not please
  sharp fate   135
To grace it with your sorrows; bid that welcome
Which comes to punish us, and we punish it

Seemingly to bear it lightly. Take me up;
I have led you oft; carry me now, good
  friends,
And have my thanks for all.   140

(*Exeunt, bearing* ANTONY)

SCENE 13. *The same. A monument.*

(*Enter* CLEOPATRA *and her maids aloft,*
  with CHARMIAN *and* IRAS)

CLEOPATRA. O Charmian! I will never go
from hence.

CHARMIAN. Be comforted, dear madam.

CLEOPATRA.   No, I will not.
All strange and terrible events are welcome,
But comforts we despise; our size of sorrow,
Proportioned to our cause, must be as great 5
As that which makes it.

(*Enter, below,* DIOMEDES)

                          How now! is he dead?

DIOMEDES. His death 's upon him, but not
  dead.
Look out o' the other side your monument;
His guard have brought him thither.

(*Enter, below,* ANTONY, *borne by the Guard*)

CLEOPATRA.   O sun!
Burn the great sphere thou mov'st in; dark-
  ling stand   10
The varying shore o' the world. O Antony,
Antony, Antony! Help, Charmian, help, Iras,
  help;
Help, friends below! let's draw him hither.

ANTONY.   Peace!
Not Caesar's valour hath o'erthrown Antony,
But Antony's hath triumphed on itself.   15

CLEOPATRA. So it should be, that none but
  Antony.
Should conquer Antony; but woe 'tis so!

ANTONY. I am dying, Egypt, dying; only
I here importune death awhile, until
Of many thousand kisses the poor last   20
I lay upon thy lips.

CLEOPATRA.   I dare not, dear,—
Dear my lord, pardon,—I dare not,
Lest I be taken: not the imperious show

---

[10] come to terms   [11] cleared away

Of the full-fortuned Caesar ever shall
Be brooched[1] with me; if knife, drugs, ser-
  pents, have   25
Edge, sting, or operation, I am safe:
Your wife Octavia, with her modest eyes
And still conclusion,[2] shall acquire no honour
Demuring[3] upon me. But come, come, An-
  tony,—   29
Help me, my women,—we must draw thee up.
Assist, good friends.

ANTONY.   O! quick, or I am gone.

CLEOPATRA. Here's sport indeed! How heavy
  weighs my lord!
Our strength is all gone into heaviness,
That makes the weight. Had I great Juno's
  power,
The strong-winged Mercury should fetch thee
  up,   35
And set thee by Jove's side. Yet come a little,
Wishers were ever fools. O! come, come,
  come;

(*They heave* ANTONY *aloft to* CLEOPATRA)

And welcome, welcome! die where thou hast
  lived;
Quicken with kissing; had my lips that power,
Thus would I wear them out.

ALL.   A heavy sight! 40

ANTONY. I am dying, Egypt, dying:
Give me some wine, and let me speak a little.

CLEOPATRA. No, let me speak and let me rail
  so high,
That the false housewife[4] Fortune break her
  wheel,
Provoked by my offence.

ANTONY.   One word, sweet queen. 45
Of Caesar seek your honour with your safety.
  O!

CLEOPATRA. They do not go together.

ANTONY.   Gentle, hear me:
None about Caesar trust, but Proculeius.

CLEOPATRA. My resolution and my hands I'll
  trust;
None about Caesar.   50

ANTONY. The miserable change now at my
  end
Lament nor sorrow at; but please your
  thoughts
In feeding them with those my former for-
  tunes
Wherein I lived, the greatest prince o' the
  world,
The noblest; and do now not basely die,   55
Not cowardly put off my helmet to
My countryman; a Roman by a Roman
Valiantly vanquished. Now my spirit is going;
I can no more.

CLEOPATRA. Noblest of men, woo 't die?
Hast thou no care of me? shall I abide   60
In this dull world, which in thy absence is
No better than a sty? O! see my women,

     (ANTONY *dies*)

The crown o' the earth doth melt. My lord!
O! withered is the garland of the war,
The soldier's pole[5] is fall'n; young boys and
  girls   65
Are level now with men; the odds[6] is gone,
And there is nothing left remarkable
Beneath the visiting moon.   (*Swoons*)

CHARMIAN.   O, quietness, lady!

IRAS. She is dead too, our sovereign.

CHARMIAN.   Lady!

IRAS.   Madam!

CHARMIAN. O madam, madam, madam!

IRAS.   Royal Egypt!
Empress!   71

CHARMIAN. Peace, peace, Iras!

CLEOPATRA. No more, but e'en a woman, and
  commanded
By such poor passion as the maid that milks 74
And does the meanest chares.[7] It were for me
To throw my sceptre at the injurious gods;
To tell them that this world did equal theirs
Till they had stol'n our jewel. All's but
  naught;
Patience is sottish, and impatience does
Become a dog that's mad; then is it sin   80

---

[1] adorned   [2] quiet inference   [3] looking   soberly   [4] hussy, slattern   [5] polestar, guiding star   [6] superiority, gradation   [7] chores, tasks

To rush into the secret house of death,
Ere death dare come to us? How do you,
women?
What, what! good cheer! Why, how now,
Charmian!
My noble girls! Ah, women, women, look!
Our lamp is spent, it's out. Good sirs, take
heart;—   85
We'll bury him; and then, what's brave,
what's noble,

Let's do it after the high Roman fashion,
And make death proud to take us. Come,
away;
This case of that huge spirit now is cold;
Ah! women, women! Come; we have no
friend
But resolution, and the briefest end.   91

(Exeunt; those above bearing off
Antony's *body)*

ACT 5

Scene 1. *Alexandria.* Caesar's *camp.*

(Enter Caesar, Agrippa, Dolabella,
Mecaenas, Gallus, Proculeius, *and
others)*

Caesar. Go to him, Dolabella, bid him yield;
Being so frustrate, tell him he mocks
The pauses that he makes.

Dolabella.   Caesar, I shall. *(Exit)*

(Enter Dercetas, *with the sword of* Antony)

Caesar. Wherefore is that? and what art thou
that dar'st
Appear thus to us?

Dercetas.   I am called Dercetas;   5
Mark Antony I served, who best was worthy
Best to be served; whilst he stood up and
spoke
He was my master, and I wore my life
To spend upon his haters. If thou please
To take me to thee, as I was to him   10
I'll be to Caesar; if thou pleasest not,
I yield thee up my life.

Caesar.   What is 't thou sayst?

Dercetas. I say, O Caesar, Antony is dead.

Caesar. The breaking of so great a thing
should make
A greater crack; the round world   15
Should have shook lions into civil[1] streets,
And citizens to their dens. The death of
Antony
Is not a single doom; in the name lay
A moiety[2] of the world.

Dercetas.   He is dead, Caesar;
Not by a public minister of justice,   20
Nor by a hired knife; but that self hand,
Which writ his honour in the acts it did,
Hath, with the courage which the heart did
lend it,
Splitted the heart. This is his sword;
I robbed his wound of it; behold it stained 25
With his most noble blood.

Caesar.   Look you sad, friends?
The gods rebuke me, but it is tidings
To wash the eyes of kings.

Agrippa.   And strange it is,
That nature must compel us to lament
Our most persisted deeds.

Mecaenas.   His taints and honours
Waged equal with him.

Agrippa.   A rarer spirit never   31
Did steer humanity; but you, gods, will give
us
Some faults to make us men. Caesar is
touched.

Mecaenas. When such a spacious mirror's set
before him,
He needs must see himself.

Caesar.   O Antony!   35
I have followed thee to this; but we do lance
Disease in our bodies: I must perforce
Have shown to thee such a declining day,
Or look on thine; we could not stall together
In the whole world. But yet let me lament, 40
With tears as sovereign as the blood of hearts,
That thou, my brother, my competitor
In top of all design,[3] my mate in empire,

---

[1] well-governed   [2] half   [3] in the supreme conception of enterprise

Friend and companion in the front of war,
The arm of mine own body, and the heart   45
Where mine his thoughts did kindle, that our stars,
Unreconciliable, should divide
Our equalness to this. Hear me, good friends,—

(Enter an EGYPTIAN*)*

But I will tell you at some meeter season:
The business of this man looks out of him;   50
We'll hear him what he says. Whence are you?

EGYPTIAN. A poor Egyptian yet. The queen my mistress,
Confined in all she has, her monument,
Of thy intents desires instruction,
That she preparedly may frame herself   55
To the way she's forced to.

CAESAR.   Bid her have good heart;
She soon shall know of us, by some of ours,
How honourable and how kindly we
Determine for her; for Caesar cannot live
To be ungentle.

EGYPTIAN.   So the gods preserve thee! 60
(Exit)

CAESAR. Come hither, Proculeius. Go and say,
We purpose her no shame; give her what comforts
The quality of her passion shall require,
Lest, in her greatness, by some mortal stroke
She do defeat us; for her life in Rome   65
Would be eternal in our triumph. Go,
And with your speediest bring us what she says,
And how you find of her.

PROCULEIUS.   Caesar, I shall.
(Exit)

CAESAR. Gallus, go you along.
(Exit GALLUS*)*

                    Where's Dolabella.
To second Proculeius?

AGRIPPA. ⎫
         ⎬   Dollabella!   70
MECAENAS. ⎭

CAESAR. Let him alone, for I remember now
How he's employed, he shall in time be ready.
Go with me to my tent; where you shall see

How hardly I was drawn into this war;
How calm and gentle I proceeded still   75
In all my writings. Go with me, and see
What I can show in this.   *(Exeunt)*

SCENE 2. *The same. The monument.*

(Enter aloft, CLEOPATRA, CHARMIAN,
and IRAS*)*

CLEOPATRA. My desolation does begin to make
A better life. 'Tis paltry to be Caesar;
Not being Fortune, he's but Fortune's knave,
A minister of her will; and it is great
To do that thing that ends all other deeds. 5
Which shackles accidents, and bolts up change,
Which sleeps, and never palates more the dung,
The beggar's nurse and Caesar's.

(Enter, below, PROCULEIUS, GALLUS,
and SOLDIERS*)*

PROCULEIUS. Caesar sends greeting to the Queen of Egypt;
And bids thee study on what fair demands   10
Thou mean'st to have him grant thee.

CLEOPATRA.   What's thy name?

PROCULEIUS. My name is Proculeius.

CLEOPATRA.   Antony
Did tell me of you, bade me trust you; but
I do not greatly care to be deceived,
That have no use for trusting. If your master
Would have a queen his beggar, you must tell him,   16
That majesty, to keep decorum, must
No less beg than a kingdom: if he please
To give me conquered Egypt for my son,
He gives me so much of mine own as I   20
Will kneel to him with thanks.

PROCULEIUS.   Be of good cheer;
You're fall'n into a princely hand, fear nothing,
Make your full reference[1] freely to my lord,
Who is so full of grace, that it flows over
On all that need; let me report to him   25
Your sweet dependancy, and you shall find

[1] refer the whole matter

A conqueror that will pray in aid for kindness
Where he for grace is kneeled to.

CLEOPATRA.   Pray you, tell him
I am his fortune's vassal, and I send him
The greatness he has got. I hourly learn   30
A doctrine of obedience, and would gladly
Look him i' the face.

PROCULEIUS.   This I'll report, dear lady:
Have comfort, for I know your plight is pitied
Of him that caused it.

GALLUS. You see how easily she may be sur-
    prised.   35

> (PROCULEIUS *and two of the* Guard
> *ascend the monument by a ladder, and*
> *come behind* CLEOPATRA. *Some of the*
> *Guard unbar and open the gates, discov-*
> *ering the lower room of the mon-*
> *ument.*)

> (*To* PROCULEIUS *and the Guard*) Guard
> her till Caesar come.   (*Exit*)

IRAS. Royal queen!

CHARMIAN. O Cleopatra! thou art taken,
    queen.

CLEOPATRA. Quick, quick, good hands.

> (*Drawing a dagger*)

PROCULEIUS.   Hold, worthy lady, hold!

> (*Seizes and disarms her*)

Do not yourself such wrong, who are in this 40
Relieved, but not betrayed.

CLEOPATRA.   What, of death too,
That rids our dogs of languish?

PROCULEIUS.   Cleopatra,
Do not abuse my master's bounty by
The undoing of yourself; let the world see
His nobleness well acted, which your death 45
Will never let come forth.

CLEOPATRA.   Where art thou, death?
Come hither, come! come, come, and take a
    queen
Worth many babes and beggars!

PROCULEIUS.   O! temperance, lady.

CLEOPATRA. Sir, I will eat no meat, I'll not
    drink sir;
If idle talk will once be necessary,   50

I'll not sleep neither. This mortal house I'll
    ruin,
Do Caesar what he can. Know, sir, that I
Will not wait pinioned at your master's court,
Nor once be chastised with the sober eye
Of dull Octavia. Shall they hoist me up   55
And show me to the shouting varletry
Of censuring Rome? Rather a ditch in Egypt
Be gentle grave unto me! rather on Nilus'
    mud
Lay me stark naked, and let the water flies
Blow me into abhorring! rather make   60
My country's high pyramides my gibbet,
And hang me up in chains!

PROCULEIUS.   You do extend
These thoughts of horror further than you
    shall
Find cause in Caesar.

> (*Enter* DOLABELLA)

DOLABELLA.   Proculeius,
What thou has done thy master Caesar knows,
And he hath sent for thee; as for the queen, 66
I'll take her to my guard.

PROCULEIUS.   So, Dolabella,
It shall content me best; be gentle to her.

(*To* CLEOPATRA) To Caesar I will speak what
you shall please,
If you'll employ me to him.

CLEOPATRA.   Say, I would die.

> (*Exeunt* PROCULEIUS *and* SOLDIERS)

DOLABELLA. Most noble empress, you have
    heard of me?   71

CLEOPATRA. I cannot tell.

DOLABELLA.   Assuredly you know me.

CLEOPATRA. No matter, sir, what I have heard
    or known.
You laugh when boys or women tell their
    dreams;
Is 't not your trick?

DOLABELLA.   I understand not, madam.

CLEOPATRA. I dreamed there was an Emperor
    Antony: 76
O! such another sleep, that I might see
But such another man.

DOLABELLA.   If it might please ye,—

CLEOPATRA. His face was as the heavens, and therein stuck
A sun and moon, which kept their course, and lighted,   80
The little O, the earth.

DOLABELLA.   Most sovereign creature,—

CLEOPATRA. His legs bestrid the ocean; his reared arm
*Crested the world; his voice was propertied
As all the tunèd spheres, and that to friends;
But when he meant to quail[2] and shake the orb,
He was as rattling thunder. For his bounty, 86
There was no winter in 't, an autumn 'twas
That grew the more by reaping; his delights
Were dolphin-like, they showed his back above
The element they lived in; in his livery   90
Walked crowns and crownets, realms and islands were
As plates[3] dropped from his pocket.

DOLABELLA.   Cleopatra,—

CLEOPATRA. Think you there was, or might be, such a man
As this I dreamed of?

DOLABELLA.   Gentle madam, no.

CLEOPATRA. You lie, up to the hearing of the gods!   95
But, if there be, or ever were, one such,
It's past the size of dreaming; nature wants stuff
To vie strange forms with fancy; yet to imagine
An Antony were nature's piece 'gainst fancy,
Condemning shadows quite.

DOLABELLA.   Hear me, good madam. 100
Your loss is as yourself, great; and you bear it
As answering to the weight: would I might never
O'ertake pursued success, but I do feel,
By the rebound of yours, a grief that smites
My very heart at root.

CLEOPATRA.   I thank you, sir.   105
Know you what Caesar means to do with me?

DOLABELLA. I am loath to tell you what I would you knew.

CLEOPATRA. Nay, pray you, sir,—

DOLABELLA.   Though he be honourable,—

CLEOPATRA. He'll lead me then in triumph?

DOLABELLA. Madam, he will; I know 't.   110

     (*Within,* "Make way there!—Caesar!")

     (*Enter* CAESAR, GALLUS, PROCULEIUS, MECAENAS, SELEUCUS, *and* ATTENDANTS)

CAESAR. Which is the Queen of Egypt?

DOLABELLA. It is the emperor, madam.

       (CLEOPATRA *kneels*)

CAESAR. Arise, you shall not kneel.
I pray you, rise; rise, Egypt.

CLEOPATRA.   Sir, the gods   115
Will have it thus; my master and my lord
I must obey.

CAESAR.   Take to you no hard thoughts;
The record of what injuries you did us,
Though written in our flesh, we shall remember
As things but done by chance.

CLEOPATRA.   Sole sir o' the world,
I cannot project[4] mine own cause so well   121
To make it clear; but do confess I have
Been laden with like frailties which before
Have often shamed our sex.

CAESAR.   Cleopatra, know,
We will extenuate rather than enforce: 125
If you apply yourself to our intents,—
Which towards you are most gentle,—you shall find
A benefit in this change; but if you seek
To lay on me a cruelty, by taking   129
Antony's course, you shall bereave yourself
Of my good purposes, and put your children
To that destruction which I'll guard them from,
If thereon you rely. I'll take my leave.

CLEOPATRA. And may through all the world: 'tis yours; and we,
Your scutcheons, and your signs of conquest, shall   135
Hang in what place you please. Here, my good lord.

---

[2] overpower   [3] coins   [4] put forth

CAESAR. You shall advise me in all for Cleopatra.

CLEOPATRA (*giving a scroll*). This is the brief of money, plate, and jewels,   139
I am possessed of: 'tis exactly valued;
Not petty things admitted. Where's Seleucus?

SELEUCUS. Here, madam.

CLEOPATRA. This is my treasurer; let him speak, my lord,
Upon his peril, that I have reserved
To myself nothing. Speak the truth, Seleucus.

SELEUCUS. Madam,   145
I had rather seal my lips, than, to my peril,
Speak that which is not.

CLEOPATRA.   What have I kept back?

SELEUCUS. Enough to purchase what you have made known.

CAESAR. Nay, blush not, Cleopatra; I approve
Your wisdom in the deed.

CLEOPATRA.   See! Caesar! O, behold,
How pomp is followed; mine will now be yours;   151
And, should we shift estates, yours would be mine.
The ingratitude of this Seleucus does
Even make me wild. O slave! of no more trust
Than love that's hired. What! goest thou back? thou shalt   155
Go back, I warrant thee; but I'll catch thine eyes,
Though they had wings: slave, soulless villain, dog!
O rarely base!

CAESAR.   Good queen, let us entreat you.

CLEOPATRA. O Caesar! what a wounding shame is this,
That thou, vouchsafing here to visit me,   160
Doing the honour of thy lordliness
To one so meek, that mine own servant should
Parcel the sum[5] of my disgraces by
Addition of his envy. Say, good Caesar,
That I some lady trifles have reserved,   165
Immoment toys,[6] things of such dignity

As we greet modern[7] friends withal; and say,
Some nobler token I have kept apart
For Livia and Octavia, to induce
Their mediation; must I be unfolded   170
With[8] one that I have bred? The gods! it smites me
Beneath the fall I have. (*To* SELEUCUS)
    Prithee, go hence;
Or I shall show the cinders of my sprits
Through the ashes of my chance.[9] Wert thou a man,
Thou wouldst have mercy on me.

CAESAR.   Forbear, Seleucus.

(*Exit* SELEUCUS)

CLEOPATRA. Be it known that we, the greatest, are misthought   176
For things that others do; and, when we fall,
We answer others' merits in our name,
Are therefore to be pitied.

CAESAR.   Cleopatra,
Not what you have reserved, nor what acknowledged,   180
Put we i' the roll of conquest: still be 't yours,
Bestow it at your pleasure; and believe,
Caesar's no merchant, to make prize[10] with you
Of things that merchants sold. Therefore be cheered;
Make not your thoughts your prisons: no, dear queen;   185
For we intend so to dispose you as
Yourself shall give us counsel. Feed, and sleep:
Our care and pity is so much upon you,
That we remain your friend; and so, adieu. 189

CLEOPATRA. My master, and my lord!

CAESAR.   Not so. Adieu.

(*Flourish. Exeunt* CAESAR *and his train*)

CLEOPATRA. He words me, girls, he words me, that I should not
Be noble to myself: but, hark thee, Charmian.

(*Whispers* CHARMIAN)

IRAS. Finish, good lady; the bright day is done,
And we are for the dark.

---

[5] sum up   [6] unimportant trifles   [7] ordinary   [8] by   [9] fortune   [10] appraisal

CLEOPATRA.   Hie thee again:
I have spoke already, and it is provided;   195
Go, put it to the haste

CHARMIAN.   Madam, I will.

(Re-enter DOLABELLA*)*

DOLABELLA. Where is the queen?

CHARMIAN.   Behold, sir.
(Exit)

CLEOPATRA.   Dolabella!

DOLABELLA. Madam, as thereto sworn by
your command.
Which my love makes religion to obey,
I tell you this: Caesar through Syria   200
Intends his journey; and within three days
You with your children will he send before.
Make your best use of this; I have performed
Your pleasure and my promise.

CLEOPATRA.   Dolabella,
I shall remain your debtor.

DOLABELLA.   I your servant.   205
Adieu, good queen; I must attend on Caesar.

CLEOPATRA. Farewell, and thanks.

(Exit DOLABELLA*)*

          Now, Iras, what think'st thou?
Thou, an Egyptian puppet, shall be shown
In Rome, as well as I; mechanic slaves
With greasy aprons, rules and hammers, shall
Uplift us to the view; in their thick breaths,
Rank of gross diet, shall we be enclouded,   212
And forced to drink their vapour.

IRAS.   The gods forbid!

CLEOPATRA. Nay, 'tis most certain, Iras. Saucy
lictors
Will catch at us, like strumpets, and scald[11]
rimers   215
Ballad us out o' tune; the quick comedians
Extemporally will stage us, and present
Our Alexandrian revels. Antony
Shall be brought drunken forth, and I shall
see
Some squeaking Cleopatra boy my greatness
I' the posture of a whore.

IRAS.   O, the good gods!   221

CLEOPATRA. Nay, that's certain.

IRAS. I'll never see it; for, I am sure my nails
Are stronger than mine eyes.

CLEOPATRA.   Why, that's the way
To fool their preparation, and to conquer   225
Their most absurd intents.

(Re-enter CHARMIAN*)*

          Now, Charmian,
Show me, my women, like a queen; go fetch
My best attires; I am again for Cydnus,
To meet Mark Antony. Sirrah Iras, go.
Now, noble Charmian, we'll dispatch indeed;
And, when thou hast done this chare, I'll give
thee leave   231
To play till doomsday. Bring our crown and
all.

(Exit IRAS. *A noise heard)*

Wherefore's this noise?

(Enter one of the GUARD*)*

GUARD.   Here is a rural fellow
That will not be denied your highness'
presence:
He brings you figs.   235

CLEOPATRA. Let him come in.   *(Exit* GUARD*)*
          What poor an instrument
May do a noble deed! he brings me liberty.
My resolution's placed, and I have nothing
Of woman in me; now from head to foot
I am marble-constant, now the fleeting moon
No planet is of mine.

(Re-enter GUARD, *with a* CLOWN *bringing
in a basket)*

GUARD.   This is the man.   241

CLEOPATRA. Avoid,[12] and leave him.

(Exit GUARD*)*

Hast thou the pretty worm of Nilus there,
That kills and pains not?   244

CLOWN. Truly, I have him; but I would not
be the party that should desire you to touch
him, for his biting is immortal; those that do
die of it do seldom or never recover.

CLEOPATRA. Remember'st thou any that have
died on 't?   249

---

[11] scurvy, base   [12] withdraw

CLOWN. Very many, men and women too. I heard of one of them no longer than yesterday; a very honest woman, but something given to lie, as a woman should not do but in the way of honesty, how she died of the biting of it, what pain she felt. Truly, she makes a very good report o' the worm; but he that will believe all that they say shall never be saved by half that they do. But this is most fallible, the worm's an odd worm.

CLEOPATRA. Get thee hence; farewell.   260

CLOWN. I wish you all joy of the worm.

(*Sets down the basket*)

CLEOPATRA. Farewell.

CLOWN. You must think this, look you, that the worm will do his kind.[13]

CLEOPATRA. Ay, ay; farewell   265

CLOWN. Look you, the worm is not to be trusted but in the keeping of wise people; for indeed there is no goodness in the worm.

CLEOPATRA. Take thou no care; it shall be heeded.

CLOWN. Very good. Give it nothing, I pray you, for it is not worth the feeding.   271

CLEOPATRA. Will it eat me?

CLOWN. You must not think I am so simple but I know the devil himself will not eat a woman; I know that a woman is a dish for the gods, if the devil dress her not. But, truly, these same whoreson devils do the gods great harm in their women, for in every ten that they make, the devils mar five.

CLEOPATRA. Well, get thee gone; farewell.   280

CLOWN. Yes, forsooth; I wish you joy of the worm.   (*Exit*)

(*Re-enter* IRAS, *with a robe, crown, &c.*)

CLEOPATRA. Give me my robe, put on my crown; I have
Immortal longings in me; now no more
The juice of Egypt's grape shall moist this lip.
Yare,[14] yare, good Iras; quick. Methinks I hear   285
Antony call; I see him rouse himself

To praise my noble act; I hear him mock
The luck of Caesar, which the gods give men
To excuse their after wrath: husband, I come: 289
Now to that name my courage prove my title!
I am fire, and air; my other elements
I give to baser life. So; have you done?
Come then, and take the last warmth of my lips.
Farewell, kind Charmian; Iras, long farewell.

(*Kisses them.* IRAS *falls and dies*)

Have I the aspic[15] in my lips? Dost fall?   295
If thou and nature can so gently part,
The stroke of death is as a lover's pinch,
Which hurts, and is desired. Dost thou lie still?
If thus thou vanishest, thou tell'st the world
It is not worth leave-taking   300

CHARMIAN. Dissolve, thick cloud, and rain; that I may say,
The gods themselves do weep.

CLEOPATRA.   This proves me base:
If she first meet the curled Antony,
He'll make demand of her, and spend that kiss   305
Which is my heaven to have. Come, thou mortal wretch,

(*To the asp, which she applies to her breast*)

With thy sharp teeth this knot intrinsicate
Of life at once untie; poor venomous fool,
Be angry, and dispatch. O! couldst thou speak,
That I might hear thee call great Caesar ass   310
Unpolicied.

CHARMIAN. O eastern star!

CLEOPATRA.   Peace, peace!
Dost thou not see my baby at my breast,
That sucks the nurse asleep?

CHARMIAN.   O, break! O, break!

CLEOPATRA. As sweet as balm, as soft as air, as gentle,—
O Antony!—Nay, I will take thee too.   315

(*Applying another asp to her arm*)

What should I stay— (*Dies*)

---

[13] act according to his nature   [14] briskly   [15] asp

CHARMIAN. In this vile world? So, fare thee
  well.
Now boast thee, death, in thy possession lies
A lass unparalleled. Downy windows, close;
And golden Phoebus never be beheld   320
Of eyes again so royal! Your crown's awry;
I'll mend it, and then play.

(*Enter the* GUARD, *rushing in*)

FIRST GUARD. Where is the queen?

CHARMIAN.   Speak softly, wake her not.

FIRST GUARD. Caesar hath sent—

CHARMIAN.   Too slow a messenger.

(*Applies an asp*)

O! come apace, dispatch; I partly feel thee. 325

FIRST GUARD. Approach, ho! All's not well;
  Caesar's beguiled.

SECOND GUARD. There's Dolabella sent from
  Caesar; call him.

FIRST GUARD. What work is here! Charmian,
  is this well done?

CHARMIAN. It is well done, and fitting for a
  princess
Descended of so many royal kings.   330
Ah! soldier. (*Dies*)

(*Re-enter* DOLABELLA)

DOLABELLA. How goes it here?

SECOND GUARD.   All dead.

DOLABELLA.   Caesar, thy thoughts
Touch their effects[16] in this; thyself art com-
  ing
To see performed the dreaded act which thou
So sought'st to hinder.   335

(*Within.* "A way there!—a way for
  Caesar!")

(*Re-enter* CAESAR *and all his train*)

DOLABELLA. O! sir, you are too sure an
  augurer;
That you did fear is done.

CAESAR.   Bravest at the last,
She levelled[17] at our purposes, and, being
  royal,

Took her own way. The manner of their
  deaths?   340
I do not see them bleed.

DOLABELLA.   Who was last with them?

FIRST GUARD. A simple countryman that
  brought her figs:
This was his basket.

CAESAR.   Poisoned then.

FIRST GUARD.   O Caesar!
This Charmian lived but now; she stood, and
  spake:
I found her trimming up the diadem   345
On her dead mistress; tremblingly she stood,
And on the sudden dropped.

CAESAR.   O noble weakness!
If they had swallowed poison 'twould appear
By external swelling; but she looks like sleep,
As she would catch another Antony   350
In her strong toil[18] of grace.

DOLABELLA.   Here, on her breast,
There is a vent of blood, and something
  blown;[19]
The like is on her arm.

FIRST GUARD. This is an aspic's trail; and these
  fig-leaves
Have slime upon them, such as the aspic
  leaves
Upon the caves of Nile.

CAESAR.   Most probable   356
That so she died; for her physician tells me
She hath pursued conclusions[20] infinite
Of easy ways to die. Take up her bed;
And bear her women from the monument.   360
She shall be buried by her Antony:
No grave upon the earth shall clip[21] in it
A pair so famous. High events as these
Strike those that make them; and their story
  is
No less in pity than his glory which   365
Brought them to be lamented. Our army
  shall,
In solemn show, attend this funeral,
And then to Rome. Come, Dolabella, see
High order in this great solemnity.   (*Exeunt*)

---

[16] fulfilment   [17] guessed   [18] net   [19] swollen   [20] experiments   [21] enfold

The obvious conflict in this play, emphasized by all commentators, lies between love and honor, or love and ambition, between Antony's "Roman thought" and the attraction of the "Egyptian spirit." But there are other complications, an exploration of which may help to illuminate the characters of the two central figures. Antony is a man with vast natural capacities for many different activities: politics, generalship, love, friendship, pleasure. Indeed, his very versatility prevents his finding any meaningful center for his life, and his problem, in one sense, is to find some basic principle by which he may realize his essential self.

More than Antony's versatility, of course, is involved in his failure to realize his essential self. He is a man who, as the play opens, is confused and who is flagrantly derelict. Demetrius and Philo in the first scene comment upon what has happened to Antony. In their opinion he has become "a strumpet's fool." And though Antony in the same scene exclaims "Let Rome in Tiber melt . . . the nobleness of life / Is to do thus," still Antony himself has a bad conscience about his conduct. In the next scene he exclaims "I must from this enchanting queen break off" (1, 2, 145). He is ashamed of his dissipation in Egypt and sees his indulgence in it as a betrayal of his Roman character.

Cleopatra also sees Rome and Egypt as diametrically opposed. When Antony suddenly becomes serious, she remarks, "A Roman thought hath struck him" (1, 2, 91). Thus, the first act shows Rome and Egypt as opposed principles competing for Antony's spirit. Our sympathies are probably—and Antony's better conscience is certainly—on the side of Rome.

Before the play is over we shall find the two principles no longer in opposition: Antony and Cleopatra unite the best that is in the Roman principle with the best in the Egyptian principle—or perhaps it would be more accurate to say that they transcend the conflict between Roman and Egyptian. But

Shakespeare has not represented the process of unification as an easy one. The Antony we see early in the play is delinquent, and Cleopatra, for all her charm, is pleasure-loving and more than half interested in the love game merely as an exhibition of her own skill. Shakespeare did not simplify his characters and he was relentlessly honest in his statement of the moral problem.

In the scenes that follow, Anthony, for all his charm, continues to conduct himself as the skillful and cynical politician. He enters into marriage with Octavia, the sister of Octavius Caesar, because it is to his political advantage. In Act 3, scene 1, Antony's general, Ventidius, comments upon the fact that "Caesar and Antony have ever won / More in their officer than person" (ll. 16–17). He hints that Antony will jealously resent one of his subordinates' winning more than moderate glory. Even Enobarbus, Antony's staunch follower, comments upon Antony's ability to make an effective display of weeping when it is to his advantage ("What willingly he did confound he wailed,") (3, 2, 58).

Antony, in the end, comes closest to finding a meaningful center for his life in his love for Cleopatra; but ironically enough, this discovery is in a sense forced upon him by the collapse of everything else in his life. A superficial reader might even find that his love for Cleopatra was no real center at all, since his failure as a politician and as a practical man leaves only this as a meaning—a meaning upon which he seizes in desperation for want of something better.

A more careful reading of the play will, however, indicate that Antony at the end has made a discovery about himself and the world, and has thus won to something positive. But in order to see this we shall have to consider the nature of the world in which the story of Antony and Cleopatra occurs, and the nature of Octavius, Antony's great rival before whom Antony's power goes down. The world in which Antony lives is a world fallen into almost complete disorder. The Roman virtues and the Roman social and personal discipline have decayed. It has become a world in which the strong compete with each other for mastery without reference to any social ideal—such as the Roman patriotism that had subordinated the individual to the general good. If Antony had lived in the great days of the Roman Republic, the social values dictated by the Republic might have directed his vast talents and energies according to some principle, and he would, in that case, not have been the brilliant but purposeless man who appears in the play. Indeed, it may be said that Antony epitomizes his world.

In the light of this interpretation, such an incident as that on Pompey's galley (2, 7) reveals itself as having a fundamental relationship to the central fact of the play. The scene on the galley gives us a glimpse of the condition of this world; it is a piece of exposition, but exposition presented in terms of action. Pompey is a pirate, a freebooter, but we see that he is in reality no different from the triumvirs. (In effect, they acknowledge this by their dealing with him.) Pompey owes no obligations to anyone except himself; yet he cannot bring himself to become the pure opportunist and murder the triumvirs while they are in his power. In other words, in this world in which all general values have collapsed, Pompey clings to a rag of personal honour, an ideal beyond mere practical success.

Menas, as we learn from his advice to Pompey, has thoroughly accepted his world and is a pure opportunist. When Pompey refuses his advice to cut the cable that holds the barge at anchor and then to cut the triumvirs' throats, Menas decides at once to desert Pompey's service. We learn something further about the nature of Antony's world when we hear what price Pompey pays for his clinging to personal honor. Octavius Caesar breaks the truce and makes war on Pompey, and Pompey is murdered.

Pompey's situation thus foreshadows that of Antony and Cleopatra—the attempt to achieve some ideal interpretation of their own lives as opposed to the possession of mere power. Pompey's situation foreshadows quite literally the situation of Enobarbus, who late in the play tries to act in accord with Menas's opportunism and deserts his master, Antony, for service with Octavius, but who finds, grizzled old warrior though he is, that he cannot really follow such a course and so, in remorse, dies of a broken heart.

What is the character of Octavius Caesar, and what is his relation to this world in which honor has become a quixotic gesture? Octavius is all cool efficiency. He is the pure politician who is unhampered by the distractions of passion or the claims of honor. This is not to say that Octavius is a flagrantly wicked person. He is "moral" as the world goes, and respectable. He is probably on the side of conventional virtue, but he is coldly and ruthlessly efficient. Doubtless he found his justification for making war on Pompey and perhaps he convinced himself quite sincerely that the inefficient Lepidus had to be crushed. But his justification that "Lepidus was grown too cruel" (3, 6, 32) is almost amusing in view of the impression of Lepidus given us earlier (2, 7): that of a fatuous, ineffectual man, though of course even fatuous men can be cruel. The point is that the charge rings oddly coming from the lips of this completely ruthless and efficient organizer. Doubtless the Roman world of the time needed such efficiency, and Octavius, whom history knows as the great Roman emperor Augustus, did give the Mediterranean world efficient government and peace.

These are not matters that come directly into our play, and Shakespeare does not deny, even by implication, that Octavius was superior to Antony as a potential organizer and ruler. But if humanity is to have any meaning other than ruthless efficiency, then some of the qualities of Antony are of intrinsic value, even though they are conjoined with glaring and heinous faults and even though those very qualities fatally handicap Antony in his contest with the cold-blooded Octavius. For Cleopatra at least, Antony is the greater man, and whereas she recognizes Octavius's power, it is Antony who is godlike—not only in her personal affections but in her judgment of him as a character.

With Cleopatra, however, as with Antony, Shakespeare was thoroughly honest. She is vain and irresponsible. She is proud and wayward. She can be almost savagely brutal.

Antony himself sees her, in spite of his infatuation for her, as a destructive force. Indeed, almost to the end, he feels that she has destroyed him—though he is manly enough to put the final responsibility not upon her but upon himself. Antony's soldiers, particularly Enobarbus, certainly see her as a destructive force. It is made quite plain that, in their opinion, it is she who was responsible for Antony's downfall: what happened at Actium simply represented the dramatic culmination of a long and general process of degradation under her influence.

Yet even Enobarbus testifies to something more in the relationship than mere sensuality. Qualities of mind and spirit inform it; and Shakespeare gives us some sense of these qualities early in the play—even in the scenes in which Antony thinks of his conduct as sensual dissipation and in which Cleopatra's mood is basically pride in her power for conquest. The regeneration of the pair, if one may call it that, is not an incredible transformation, totally unprepared for.

It is the defeat at Actium, however, that brings out the best in Antony—and, as we shall find, in Cleopatra. He advises his friends to leave him: he would not pull them down in his own ruin. He does not waste time in reproaches to Cleopatra: he takes the responsibility for his following her ship out of the engagement, and fully forgives her for her action.

He sues to Caesar for peace, asking to be allowed to live "A private man in Athens" (3, 10, 15). He touches his nadir here. But when he is stung by the insolence of Caesar's emissary, he is once more aroused, and when he is convinced that Cleopatra is not selling him out to Caesar (cf. Cleopatra's "Not know me yet?" 3, 11, 157), the recovery begins. With the world well lost, he becomes the old Antony again—or rather a new Antony who is freed from politic compromises and who can live now—the short time allowed him—for honor and for love. For him, love and honor are no longer forces opposed to each other. The speeches of Cleopatra and Enobarbus serve to underline the situation for us: Cleopatra says, ". . . but, since my lord / Is Antony again, I will be Cleopatra" (3, 11, 185); Enobarbus remarks: "I will seek / Some

way to leave him" (3, 11, 199–200). The return to a fine and ardent magnanimity coincides with the abandonment of "reasonable" actions calculated to gain worldly success. Caesar can refer to his opponent as "Poor Antony" (4, 1, 16); but Cleopatra sees him in these hours as at his greatest and noblest self.

This is not to say that Shakespeare has made the relationship between the lovers now calm and untroubled. Antony does not yet "know" Cleopatra. There are further doubtings and recriminations. But Cleopatra speaks over the dead Antony what she truly feels about his greatness of spirit (4, 13, 63–67), and she plainly associates this insight into true greatness with a contempt for worldly success. She can say, " 'Tis paltry to be Caesar" (5, 2, 2). She chooses "honor" too—chooses not to dishonor herself or Antony by gracing Caesar's triumph, but to die instead. Cleopatra becomes "Roman": she says to her women, "Let's do it after the high Roman fashion, / And make death proud to take us" (4, 13, 87–88).

The uniting of the Roman and Egyptian principles or of the themes of honor and love can be suggested in still another way. Both Antony and Cleopatra have flouted the idea of conventional wedded love. We remember Antony's marriage of convenience and Cleopatra's scornful taunt: "What says the married woman?" (1, 3, 20). But at the end of the play, Antony and Cleopatra are "wedded" and Cleopatra claims the name proudly: "husband, I come: / Now to that name my courage prove my title!" (5, 2, 289–90).

EXERCISES

1. In this play, Shakespeare drew heavily on Sir Thomas North's translation (1579) of Plutarch's *Lives*. The student might find it interesting and illuminating to note what passages Shakespeare chose to take and how he reworked them. The Arden edition of *Antony and Cleopatra* (Harvard University Press, 1951) prints the relevant passages from North's Plutarch in an appendix.
2. Define the character of Enobarbus. What is his relation to Antony? To Cleopatra? What is his general function in the play?
3. What forces does Octavius represent in the

play? How does he differ from Menas in his attitude toward the world? Why does Octavius refuse Antony's challenge to personal combat? How do you relate this refusal to the general theme of the play?

4. Note the various ways in which Cleopatra's death is led up to: the death of Enobarbus; false report of her death sent to Antony as a ruse; the death of Eros; the death of Antony himself. All of these deaths are (or purport to be) deaths for honor, and all are in some sense suicides. How do they prepare the audience for Cleopatra's death? How do they bear upon her own resolution to die?

5. Anthony says (1, 1, 33), "Let Rome in Tiber melt. . . ." Cleopatra says (2, 5, 78) "Melt Egypt into Nile!" Discuss this echo. Is it a meaningful one?

6. Antony reproaches Caesar with having waged "New wars 'gainst Pompey" (3, 4, 4). How serious is he here? If he is, why should this act affect him especially?

7. In Act 5, what is the meaning of Cleopatra's speeches and messages to Caesar? Is she still playing a double game? Has she already resolved to do away with herself? Or does she still hope to escape with her life and some remnants of power? It has been argued that her attempt to withhold part of her wealth from Caesar was a ruse (perhaps entered into with Seleucus) to make Caesar think that she did not mean to kill herself. Reread Act 2, scene 5, and see whether you agree with this argument.

8. How important a character is Charmian? Compare her function with that of Enobarbus.

9. Cleopatra is several times compared to the goddess Venus; Antony, to Mars, and to his reputed ancestor, the demigod Hercules. What is the function of these references? Are they used to build up the suggestions of the godlike nobility of the lovers?

10. How is Cleopatra's "husband, I come" prefigured in the speeches of Antony in the latter scenes of Act 4?

11. Do the speeches of the Clown in Act 5, scene 2, conflict with the mood of heroic dignity and tragic exaltation? If you feel that they do not, how would you justify them?

12. Discuss the imagery of 4, 13, 63–68 and 5, 2, 82–92.

13. Note the number of references to food in the imagery of this play (1, 5, 29–31; 2, 1, 23–27; 2, 2, 241–43). Find others. What is the function of this imagery?

14. Caroline Spurgeon, a renowned Shakespearean scholar, remarks upon "images of the world, the firmament, the ocean, and vastness generally" in this play. Locate some of the passages in which such images occur. How important is this imagery? For what specific purposes does Shakespeare use it?

15. Discuss some of the various kinds of irony to be found in this play.

16. What is Antony's "tragic flaw"?

HEDDA GABLER

Henrik Ibsen (1828–1906)

Characters

GEORGE TESMAN
HEDDA TESMAN, *his wife*
MISS JULIANA TESMAN, *his aunt*
MRS. ELVSTED

JUDGE BRACK
EILERT LÖVBORG
BERTA, *servant at the Tesmans'*.

The scene of the action is Tesman's villa, in the west end of Christiania.

ACT 1

SCENE: *A spacious, handsome, and tastefully furnished drawing-room, decorated in dark colors. In the back, a wide doorway with curtains drawn back, leading into a smaller room decorated in the same style as the drawing-room. In the right-hand wall of the front room, a folding door leading out to the hall. In the opposite wall, on the left, a glass door, also with curtains drawn back. Through the panes can be seen part of a veranda outside, and trees covered with autumn foliage. An oval table, with a cover on it, and surrounded* by chairs, stands well forward. In front, by the wall on the right, a wide stove of dark porcelain, a high-backed arm-chair, a cushioned foot-rest, and two footstools. A settee, with a small round table in front of it, fills the upper right-hand corner. In front, on the left, a little way from the wall, a sofa. Farther back than the glass door, a piano. On either side of the doorway at the back a whatnot with terra-cotta and majolica ornaments. —Against the back wall of the inner room a sofa, with a table, and one or two chairs. Over the sofa hangs the portrait of a handsome elderly man in a general's uniform. Over the table a hanging lamp, with an opal glass shade.—A number of bouquets are arranged about the drawing-room, in vases and glasses. Others lie upon the tables. The floors in both rooms are covered with thick carpets.—Morning light. The sun shines in through the glass door.

(MISS JULIANA TESMAN, with her bonnet on and carrying a parasol, comes in from the hall, followed by BERTA, who carries a bouquet wrapped in paper. MISS TESMAN is a comely and pleasant-looking lady of about sixty-five. She is nicely but simply dressed in a gray walking-costume. BERTA is a middle-aged woman of plain and rather countrified appearance.)

MISS TESMAN (stops close to the door, listens, and says softly). Upon my word, I don't believe they are stirring yet!

BERTA (also softly). I told you so, Miss. Remember how late the steamboat got in last night. And then, when they got home!—good Lord, what a lot the young mistress had to unpack before she could get to bed.

MISS TESMAN. Well, well—let them have their sleep out. But let us see that they get a good breath of the fresh morning air when they do appear. (She goes to the glass door and throws it open)

BERTA (beside the table, at a loss what to do with the bouquet in her hand). I declare there isn't a bit of room left. I think I'll put it down here, Miss. (She places it on the piano)

MISS TESMAN. So you've got a new mistress now, my dear Berta. Heaven knows it was a wrench to me to part with you.

BERTA (on the point of weeping). And do you think it wasn't hard for me too, Miss? After all the blessed years I've been with you and Miss Rina.

MISS TESMAN. We must make the best of it, Berta. There was nothing else to be done. George can't do without you, you see—he absolutely can't. He has had you to look after him ever since he was a little boy.

BERTA. Ah, but, Miss Julia, I can't help thinking of Miss Rina lying helpless at home there, poor thing. And with only that new girl, too! She'll never learn to take proper care of an invalid.

MISS TESMAN. Oh, I shall manage to train her. And of course, you know, I shall take most of it upon myself. You needn't be uneasy about my poor sister, my dear Berta.

BERTA. Well, but there's another thing, Miss. I'm so mortally afraid I shan't be able to suit the young mistress.

MISS TESMAN. Oh, well—just at first there may be one or two things—

BERTA. Most like she'll be terrible grand in her ways.

MISS TESMAN. Well, you can't wonder at that —General Gabler's daughter! Think of the sort of life she was accustomed to in her father's time. Don't you remember how we used to see her riding down the road along with the General? In that long black habit —and with feathers in her hat?

BERTA. Yes, indeed—I remember well enough—! But good Lord, I should never have dreamt in those days that she and Master George would make a match of it.

MISS TESMAN. Nor I.—But, by-the-bye, Berta —while I think of it: in future you mustn't say Master George. You must say Dr. Tesman.

BERTA. Yes, the young mistress spoke of that too—last night—the moment they set foot in the house. Is it true, then, Miss?

MISS TESMAN. Yes, indeed it is. Only think, Berta—some foreign university has made him a doctor—while he has been abroad, you understand. I hadn't heard a word about it, until he told me himself upon the pier.

BERTA. Well, well, he's clever enough for anything, he is. But I didn't think he'd have gone in for doctoring people too.

MISS TESMAN. No, no, it's not that sort of doctor he is. (*Nods significantly*) But let me tell you, we may have to call him something still grander before long.

BERTA. You don't say so! What can that be, Miss?

MISS TESMAN (*smiling*). H'm—wouldn't you like to know! (*With emotion*) Ah, dear, dear —if my poor brother could only look up from his grave now, and see what his little boy has grown into! (*Looks around*) But bless me, Berta—why have you done this? Taken the chintz covers off all the furniture?

BERTA. The mistress told me to. She can't abide covers on the chairs, she says.

MISS TESMAN. Are they going to make this their everyday sitting-room then?

BERTA. Yes, that's what I understood—from the mistress. Master George—the doctor—he said nothing.

(GEORGE TESMAN *comes from the right into the inner room, humming to himself, and carrying an unstrapped empty portmanteau. He is a middle-sized, young-looking man of thirty-three, rather stout, with a round, open, cheerful face, fair hair and beard. He wears spectacles, and is somewhat carelessly dressed in comfortable indoor clothes.*)

MISS TESMAN. Good morning, good morning, George.

TESMAN (*in the doorway between the rooms*). Aunt Julia! Dear Aunt Julia! (*Goes up to her and shakes hands warmly*) Come all this way —so early! Eh?

MISS TESMAN. Why of course I had to come and see how you were getting on.

TESMAN. In spite of your having had no proper night's rest?

MISS TESMAN. Oh, that makes no difference to me.

TESMAN. Well, I suppose you got home all right from the pier? Eh?

MISS TESMAN. Yes, quite safely, thank goodness. Judge Brack was good enough to see me right to my door.

TESMAN. We were so sorry we couldn't give you a seat in the carriage. But you saw what a pile of boxes Hedda had to bring with her.

MISS TESMAN. Yes, she had certainly plenty of boxes.

BERTA (*to* TESMAN). Shall I go in and see if there's anything I can do for the mistress?

TESMAN. No, thank you, Berta—you needn't. She said she would ring if she wanted anything.

BERTA (*going towards the right*). Very well.

TESMAN. But look here—take this portmanteau with you.

BERTA (*taking it*). I'll put it in the attic.

(*She goes out by the hall door*)

TESMAN. Fancy, Aunty—I had the whole of that portmanteau chock full of copies of documents. You wouldn't believe how much I have picked up from all the archives I have been examining—curious old details that no one has had any idea of—

MISS TESMAN. Yes, you don't seem to have wasted your time on your wedding trip, George.

TESMAN. No, that I haven't. But do take off your bonnet, Aunty. Look here! Let me untie the strings—eh?

MISS TESMAN (*while he does so*). Well, well —this is just as if you were still at home with us.

TESMAN (*with the bonnet in his hand, looks at it from all sides*). Why, what a gorgeous bonnet you've been investing in!

MISS TESMAN. I bought it on Hedda's account.

TESMAN. On Hedda's account? Eh?

MISS TESMAN. Yes, so that Hedda needn't be ashamed of me if we happened to go out together.

TESMAN (*patting her cheek*). You always think of everything, Aunt Julia. (*Lays the bonnet on a chair beside the table*) And now, look here—suppose we sit comfortably on the sofa and have a little chat, till Hedda comes.

(*They seat themselves. She places her parasol in the corner of the sofa*)

MISS TESMAN (*takes both his hands and looks at him*). What a delight it is to have you again, as large as life, before my very eyes, George! My George—my poor brother's own boy!

TESMAN. And it's a delight for me, too, to see you again, Aunt Julia! You, who have been father and mother in one to me.

MISS TESMAN. Oh, yes, I know you will always keep a place in your heart for your old aunts.

TESMAN. And what about Aunt Rina? No improvement—eh?

MISS TESMAN. Oh, no—we can scarcely look for any improvement in her case, poor thing. There she lies, helpless, as she has lain for all these years. But heaven grant I may not lose her yet awhile! For if I did, I don't know what I should make of my life, George—especially now that I haven't you to look after any more.

TESMAN (*patting her back*). There, there, there—!

MISS TESMAN (*suddenly changing her tone*). And to think that here you a married man, George!—And that you should be the one to carry off Hedda Gabler—the beautiful Hedda Gabler! Only think of it—she, that was so beset with admirers!

TESMAN (*hums a little and smiles complacently*). Yes, I fancy I have several good friends about town who would like to stand in my shoes—eh?

MISS TESMAN. And then this fine long wedding-tour you have had! More than five—nearly six months—

TESMAN. Well, for me it has been a sort of tour of research as well. I have had to do so much grubbing among old records—and to read no end of books too, Auntie.

MISS TESMAN. Oh, yes, I suppose so. (*More confidentially, and lowering her voice a little*) But listen now, George—have you nothing—nothing special to tell me?

TESMAN. As to our journey?

MISS TESMAN. Yes.

TESMAN. No, I don't know of anything except what I have told you in my letters. I had a doctor's degree conferred on me—but that I told you yesterday.

MISS TESMAN. Yes, yes, you did. But what I mean is—haven't you any—any—expectations—?

TESMAN. Expectations?

MISS TESMAN. Why, you know, George—I'm your old auntie!

TESMAN. Why, of course I have expectations.

MISS TESMAN. Ah!

TESMAN. I have every expectation of being a professor one of these days.

MISS TESMAN. Oh, yes, a professor—

TESMAN. Indeed, I may say I am certain of it. But my dear Auntie—you know all about that already!

MISS TESMAN (*laughing to herself*). Yes, of course I do. You are quite right there. (*Changing the subject*) But we were talking about your journey. It must have cost a great deal of money, George?

TESMAN. Well, you see—my handsome traveling-scholarship went a good way.

MISS TESMAN. But I can't understand how you can have made it go far enough for two.

TESMAN. No, that's not so easy to understand—eh?

MISS TESMAN. And especially traveling with a lady—they tell me that makes it ever so much more expensive.

TESMAN. Yes, of course—it makes it a little more expensive. But Hedda had to have this trip, Auntie! She really had to. Nothing else would have done.

MISS TESMAN. No, no, I suppose not. A wedding-tour seems to be quite indispensable nowadays.—But tell me now—have you gone thoroughly over the house yet?

TESMAN. Yes, you may be sure I have. I have been afoot ever since daylight.

MISS TESMAN. And what do you think of it all?

TESMAN. I'm delighted! Quite delighted! Only I can't think what we are to do with the two empty rooms between this inner parlor and Hedda's bedroom.

MISS TESMAN (*laughing*). Oh, my dear George, I dare say you may find some use for them—in the course of time.

TESMAN. Why of course you are quite right, Aunt Julia! You mean as my library increases —eh?

MISS TESMAN. Yes, quite so, my dear boy. It was your library I was thinking of.

TESMAN. I am specially pleased on Hedda's account. Often and often, before we were engaged, she said that she would never care to live anywhere but in Secretary Falk's villa.

MISS TESMAN. Yes, it was lucky that this very house should come into the market, just after you had started.

TESMAN. Yes, Aunt Julia, the luck was on our side, wasn't it—eh?

MISS TESMAN. But the expense, my dear George! You will find it very expensive, all this.

TESMAN (*looks at her, a little cast down*). Yes, I suppose I shall, Aunt!

MISS TESMAN. Oh, frightfully!

TESMAN. How much do you think? In round numbers?—Eh?

MISS TESMAN. Oh, I can't even guess until all the accounts come in.

TESMAN. Well, fortunately, Judge Brack has secured the most favorable terms for me,—so he said in a letter to Hedda.

MISS TESMAN. Yes, don't be uneasy, my dear boy.—Besides, I have given security for the furniture and all the carpets.

TESMAN. Security? You? My dear Aunt Julia—what sort of security could you give?

MISS TESMAN. I have given a mortgage on our annuity.

TESMAN (*jumps up*). What! On your—and Aunt Rina's annuity!

MISS TESMAN. Yes, I knew of no other plan, you see.

TESMAN (*placing himself before her*). Have you gone out of your senses, Auntie! Your annuity—it's all that you and Aunt Rina have to live upon.

MISS TESMAN. Well, well, don't get so excited about it. It's only a matter of form you know—Judge Brack assured me of that. It was he that was kind enough to arrange the whole affair for me. A mere matter of form, he said.

TESMAN. Yes, that may be all very well. But nevertheless—

MISS TESMAN. You will have your own salary to depend upon now. And, good heavens, even if we did have to pay up a little—! To eke things out a bit at the start—! Why, it would be nothing but a pleasure to us.

TESMAN. Oh, Auntie—will you never be tired of making sacrifices for me!

MISS TESMAN (*rises and lays her hands on his shoulders*). Have I had any other happiness in this world except to smooth your way for you, my dear boy? You, who have had neither father nor mother to depend on. And now we have reached the goal, George! Things have looked black enough for us, sometimes; but, thank heaven, now you have nothing to fear.

TESMAN. Yes, it is really marvelous how everything has turned out for the best.

MISS TESMAN. And the people who opposed you—who wanted to bar the way for you—now you have them at your feet. They have fallen, George. Your most dangerous rival—his fall was the worst.—And now he has to lie on the bed he has made for himself—poor misguided creature.

TESMAN. Have you heard anything of Eilert? Since I went away, I mean.

MISS TESMAN. Only that he is said to have published a new book.

TESMAN. What! Eilert Lövborg! Recently —eh?

MISS TESMAN. Yes, so they say. Heaven knows whether it can be worth anything! Ah, when your new book appears—that will be another story, George! What is it to be about?

TESMAN. It will deal with the domestic industries of Brabant during the Middle Ages.

MISS TESMAN. Fancy—to be able to write on such a subject as that!

TESMAN. However, it may be some time before the book is ready. I have all these collections to arrange first, you see.

MISS TESMAN. Yes, collecting and arranging —no one can beat you at that. There you are my poor brother's own son.

TESMAN. I am looking forward eagerly to setting to work at it; especially now that I have my own delightful home to work in.

MISS TESMAN. And, most of all, now that you have got the wife of your heart, my dear George.

TESMAN (*embracing her*). Oh, yes, yes, Aunt Julia. Hedda—she is the best part of all! (*Looks toward the doorway*) I believe I hear her coming—eh?

(HEDDA *enters from the left through the inner room. She is a woman of nine-and-twenty. Her face and figure show refinement and distinction. Her complexion is pale and opaque. Her steel-gray eyes express a cold, unruffled repose. Her hair is of an agreeable*

medium brown, but not particularly abundant. She is dressed in a tasteful, somewhat loose-fitting morning-gown.)

MISS TESMAN (*going to meet* HEDDA). Good morning, my dear Hedda! Good morning, and a hearty welcome.

HEDDA (*holds out her hand*). Good morning, dear Miss Tesman! So early a call! That is kind of you.

MISS TESMAN (*with some embarrassment*). Well—has the bride slept well in her new home?

HEDDA. Oh yes, thanks. Passably.

TESMAN (*laughing*). Passably! Come, that's good, Hedda! You were sleeping like a stone when I got up.

HEDDA. Fortunately. Of course one has always to accustom one's self to new surroundings, Miss Tesman—little by little. (*Looking towards the left*) Oh—there the servant has gone and opened the veranda door, and let in a whole flood of sunshine.

MISS TESMAN (*going towards the door*). Well, then, we will shut it.

HEDDA. No, no, not that! Tesman, please draw the curtains. That will give a softer light.

TESMAN (*at the door*). All right—all right. There now, Hedda, now you have both shade and fresh air.

HEDDA. Yes, fresh air we certainly must have, with all these stacks of flowers— But—won't you sit down, Miss Tesman?

MISS TESMAN. No, thank you. Now that I have seen that everything is all right here— thank heaven!—I must be getting home again. My sister is lying longing for me, poor thing.

TESMAN. Give her my very best love, Auntie; and say I shall look in and see her later in the day.

MISS TESMAN. Yes, yes, I'll be sure to tell her. But by-the-bye, George—(*feeling in her dress pocket*)—I have almost forgotten—I have something for you here.

TESMAN. What is it, Auntie? Eh?

MISS TESMAN (*produces a flat parcel wrapped in newspaper and hands it to him*). Look here, my dear boy.

TESMAN (*opening the parcel*). Well, I declare!—Have you really saved them for me, Aunt Julia! Hedda! Isn't this touching—eh?

HEDDA (*beside the whatnot on the right*). Well, what is it?

TESMAN. My old morning-shoes! My slippers.

HEDDA. Indeed. I remember you often spoke of them while we were abroad.

TESMAN. Yes, I missed them terribly. (*Goes up to her*) Now you shall see them, Hedda!

HEDDA (*going towards the stove*). Thanks, I really don't care about it.

TESMAN (*following her*). Only think—ill as she was, Aunt Rina embroidered these for me. Oh you can't think how many associations cling to them.

HEDDA (*at the table*). Scarcely for me.

MISS TESMAN. Of course not for Hedda, George.

TESMAN. Well, but now that she belongs to the family; I thought—

HEDDA (*interrupting*). We shall never get on with this servant, Tesman.

MISS TESMAN. Not get on with Berta?

TESMAN. Why, dear, what puts that in your head? Eh?

HEDDA (*pointing*). Look there! She has left her old bonnet lying about on a chair.

TESMAN (*in consternation, drops the slippers on the floor*). Why, Hedda—

HEDDA. Just fancy, if any one should come in and see it!

TESMAN. But Hedda—that's Aunt Julia's bonnet.

HEDDA. Is it!

MISS TESMAN (*taking up the bonnet*). Yes, indeed it's mine. And, what's more, it's not old, Madame Hedda.

HEDDA. I really did not look closely at it, Miss Tesman.

MISS TESMAN (*trying on the bonnet*). Let me tell you it's the first time I have worn it—the very first time.

TESMAN. And a very nice bonnet it is too—quite a beauty!

MISS TESMAN. Oh, it's no such great thing, George. (*Looks around her*) My parasol—? Ah, here. (*Takes it*) For this is mine too—(*mutters*)—not Berta's.

TESMAN. A new bonnet and a new parasol! Only think, Hedda!

HEDDA. Very handsome indeed.

TESMAN. Yes, isn't it? But Auntie, take a good look at Hedda before you go! See how handsome she is!

MISS TESMAN. Oh, my dear boy, there's nothing new in that. Hedda was always lovely. (*She nods and goes towards the right*)

TESMAN (*following*). Yes, but have you noticed what splendid condition she is in? How she has filled out on the journey?

HEDDA (*crossing the room*). Oh, do be quiet—!

MISS TESMAN (*who has stopped and turned*). Filled out?

TESMAN. Of course you don't notice it so much now that she has that dress on. But I, who can see—

HEDDA (*at the glass door, impatiently*). Oh, you can't see anything.

TESMAN. It must be the mountain air in the Tyrol—

HEDDA (*curtly, interrupting*). I am exactly as I was when I started.

TESMAN. So you insist; but I'm quite certain you are not. Don't you agree with me, Auntie?

MISS TESMAN (*who has been gazing at her with folded hands*). Hedda is lovely—lovely

—lovely. (*Goes up to her, takes her head between both hands, draws it downwards, and kisses her hair*) God bless and preserve Hedda Tesman—for George's sake.

HEDDA (*gently freeing herself*). Oh—! Let me go.

MISS TESMAN (*in quiet emotion*). I shall not let a day pass without coming to see you.

TESMAN. No you won't, will you, Auntie? Eh?

MISS TESMAN. Good-bye—good-bye!

> (*She goes out by the hall door. TESMAN accompanies her. The door remains half open. TESMAN can be heard repeating his message to Aunt Rina and his thanks for the slippers.*
> *In the meantime,* HEDDA *walks about the room raising her arms and clenching her hands as if in desperation. Then she flings back the curtains from the glass door, and stands there looking out.*
> *Presently* TESMAN *returns and closes the door behind him.*)

TESMAN (*picks up the slippers from the floor*). What are you looking at, Hedda?

HEDDA (*once more calm and mistress of herself*). I am only looking at the leaves. They are so yellow—so withered.

TESMAN (*wraps up the slippers and lays them on the table*). Well you see, we are well into September now.

HEDDA (*again restless*). Yes, to think of it!—Already in—in September.

TESMAN. Don't you think Aunt Julia's manner was strange, dear? Almost solemn? Can you imagine what was the matter with her? Eh?

HEDDA. I scarcely know her, you see. Is she often like that?

TESMAN. No, not as she was today.

HEDDA (*leaving the glass door*). Do you think she was annoyed about the bonnet?

TESMAN. Oh, scarcely at all. Perhaps a little, just at the moment—

HEDDA. But what an idea, to pitch her bonnet about in the drawing-room! No one does that sort of thing.

TESMAN. Well you may be sure Aunt Julia won't do it again.

HEDDA. In any case, I shall manage to make my peace with her.

TESMAN. Yes, my dear, good Hedda, if you only would.

HEDDA. When you call this afternoon, you might invite her to spend the evening here.

TESMAN. Yes, that I will. And there's one thing more you can do that would delight her heart.

HEDDA. What is it?

TESMAN. If you could only prevail on yourself to say *du*[1] to her. For my sake, Hedda? Eh?

HEDDA. No, no, Tesman—you really mustn't ask that of me. I have told you so already. I shall try to call her "Aunt"; and you must be satisfied with that.

TESMAN. Well, well. Only I think now that you belong to the family, you—

HEDDA. H'm—I can't in the least see why—

(*She goes up towards the middle doorway*)

TESMAN (*after a pause*). Is there anything the matter with you, Hedda? Eh?

HEDDA. I'm only looking at my old piano. It doesn't go at all well with all the other things.

TESMAN. The first time I draw my salary, we'll see about exchanging it.

HEDDA. No, no—no exchanging. I don't want to part with it. Suppose we put it there in the inner room, and then get another here in its place. When it's convenient, I mean.

TESMAN (*a little taken aback*). Yes—of course we could do that.

HEDDA (*takes up the bouquet from the piano*). These flowers were not here last night when we arrived.

[1] *Du* = thou, the familiar form of *you*, employed in conversation with close relatives and intimate friends.

TESMAN. Aunt Julia must have brought them for you.

HEDDA (*examining the bouquet*). A visiting-card. (*Takes it out and reads*) "Shall return later in the day." Can you guess whose card it is?

TESMAN. No. Whose? Eh?

HEDDA. The name is "Mrs. Elvsted."

TESMAN. Is it really? Sheriff Elvsted's wife? Miss Rysing that was.

HEDDA. Exactly. The girl with the irritating hair, that she was always showing off. An old flame of yours, I've been told.

TESMAN (*laughing*). Oh, that didn't last long; and it was before I knew you, Hedda. But fancy her being in town!

HEDDA. It's odd that she should call upon us. I have scarcely seen her since we left school.

TESMAN. I haven't seen her either for—heaven knows how long. I wonder how she can endure to live in such an out-of-the-way hole —eh?

HEDDA (*after a moment's thought says suddenly*). Tell me, Tesman—isn't it somewhere near there that he—that—Eilert Lövborg is living?

TESMAN. Yes, he is somewhere in that part of the country.

(BERTA *enters by the hall door*)

BERTA. That lady, ma'am, that brought some flowers a little while ago, is here again. (*Pointing*) The flowers you have in your hand, ma'am.

HEDDA. Ah, is she? Well, please show her in.

(BERTA *opens the door for* MRS. ELVSTED, *and goes out herself.—*MRS. ELVSTED *is a woman of fragile figure, with pretty, soft features. Her eyes are light blue, large, round, and somewhat prominent, with a startled, inquiring expression. Her hair is remarkably light, almost flaxen, and unusually abundant and wavy. She is a couple of years younger than* HEDDA. *She wears a dark visiting dress, tasteful, but not quite in the latest fashion.*)

HEDDA (*receives her warmly*). How do you do, my dear Mrs. Elvsted? It's delightful to see you again.

MRS. ELVSTED (*nervously, struggling for self-control*). Yes, it's a very long time since we met.

TESMAN (*gives her his hand*). And we too— eh?

HEDDA. Thanks for your lovely flowers—

MRS. ELVSTED. Oh, not at all— I would have come straight here yesterday afternoon; but I heard that you were away—

TESMAN. Have you just come to town? Eh?

MRS. ELVSTED. I arrived yesterday, about midday. Oh, I was quite in despair when I heard that you were not at home.

HEDDA. In despair! How so?

TESMAN. Why, my dear Mrs. Rysing—I mean Mrs. Elvsted—

HEDDA. I hope that you are not in any trouble?

MRS. ELVSTED. Yes, I am. And I don't know another living creature here that I can turn to.

HEDDA (*laying the bouquet on the table*). Come—let us sit here on the sofa—

MRS. ELVSTED. Oh, I am too restless to sit down.

HEDDA. Oh no, you're not. Come here. (*She draws* MRS. ELVSTED *down upon the sofa and sits at her side*)

TESMAN. Well? What is it, Mrs. Elvsted?

HEDDA. Has anything particular happened to you at home?

MRS. ELVSTED. Yes—and no. Oh—I am so anxious you should not misunderstand me—

HEDDA. Then your best plan is to tell us the whole story, Mrs. Elvsted.

TESMAN. I suppose that's what you have come for—eh?

MRS. ELVSTED. Yes, yes—of course it is. Well then, I must tell you—if you don't already know—that Eilert Lövborg is in town, too.

HEDDA. Lövborg—!

TESMAN. What! Has Eilert Lövborg come back? Fancy that, Hedda!

HEDDA. Well, well—I hear it.

MRS. ELVSTED. He has been here a week already. Just fancy—a whole week! In this terrible town, alone! With so many temptations on all sides.

HEDDA. But my dear Mrs. Elvsted—how does he concern you so much?

MRS. ELVSTED (*looks at her with a startled air, and says rapidly*). He was the children's tutor.

HEDDA. Your children's?

MRS. ELVSTED. My husband's. I have none.

HEDDA. Your step-children's, then?

MRS. ELVSTED. Yes.

TESMAN (*somewhat hesitatingly*). Then was he—I don't know how to express it—was he—regular enough in his habits to be fit for the post? Eh?

MRS. ELVSTED. For the last two years his conduct has been irreproachable.

TESMAN. Has it indeed? Fancy that, Hedda!

HEDDA. I hear it.

MRS. ELVSTED. Perfectly irreproachable. I assure you! In every respect. But all the same—now that I know he is here—in this great town—and with a large sum of money in his hands—I can't help being in mortal fear for him.

TESMAN. Why did he not remain where he was? With you and your husband? Eh?

MRS. ELVSTED. After his book was published he was too restless and unsettled to remain with us.

TESMAN. Yes, by-the-bye, Aunt Julia told me he had published a new book.

MRS. ELVSTED. Yes, a big book, dealing with the march of civilization—in broad outline, as it were. It came out about a fortnight ago. And since it has sold so well, and been so much read—and made such a sensation—

TESMAN. Has it indeed? It must be something he has had lying by since his better days.

MRS. ELVSTED. Long ago, you mean?

TESMAN. Yes.

MRS. ELVSTED. No, he has written it all since he has been with us—within the last year.

TESMAN. Isn't that good news, Hedda? Think of that.

MRS. ELVSTED. Ah, yes, if only it would last!

HEDDA. Have you seen him here in town?

MRS. ELVSTED. No, not yet. I have had the greatest difficulty in finding out his address. But this morning I discovered it at last.

HEDDA (*looks searchingly at her*). Do you know, it seems to me a little odd of your husband—h'm—

MRS. ELVSTED (*starting nervously*). Of my husband. What?

HEDDA. That he should send you to town on such an errand—that he does not come himself and look after his friend.

MRS. ELVSTED. Oh no, no—my husband has no time. And besides, I—I had some shopping to do.

HEDDA (*with a slight smile*). Ah, that is a different matter.

MRS. ELVSTED (*rising quickly and uneasily*). And now I beg and implore you, Mr. Tesman—receive Eilert Lövborg kindly if he comes to you! And that he is sure to do. You see you were such great friends in the old days. And then you are interested in the same studies—the same branch of science—so far as I can understand.

TESMAN. We used to be, at any rate.

MRS. ELVSTED. That is why I beg so earnestly that you—you too—will keep a sharp eye upon him. Oh, you will promise me that, Mr. Tesman—won't you?

TESMAN. With the greatest of pleasure, Mrs. Rysing—

HEDDA. Elvsted.

TESMAN. I assure you I shall do all I possibly can for Eilert. You may rely upon me.

MRS. ELVSTED. Oh, how very, very kind of you! (*Presses his hands*) Thanks, thanks, thanks! (*Frightened*) You see, my husband is very fond of him!

HEDDA (*rising*). You ought to write to him, Tesman. Perhaps he may not care to come to you of his own accord.

TESMAN. Well, perhaps it would be the right thing to do, Hedda? Eh?

HEDDA. And the sooner the better. Why not at once?

MRS. ELVSTED (*imploringly*). Oh, if you only would!

TESMAN. I'll write this moment. Have you his address, Mrs.—Mrs. Elvsted?

MRS. ELVSTED. Yes. (*Takes a slip of paper from her pocket, and hands it to him*) Here it is.

TESMAN. Good, good. Then I'll go in— (*Looks about him*) By-the-bye,—my slippers? Oh, here. (*Takes the packet, and is about to go*)

HEDDA. Be sure you write him a cordial, friendly letter. And a good long one too.

TESMAN. Yes, I will.

MRS. ELVSTED. But please, please don't say a word to show that I have suggested it.

TESMAN. No, how could you think I would? Eh?

   (*He goes out to the right, through the inner room*)

HEDDA (*goes up to* MRS. ELVSTED, *smiles, and says in a low voice*). There. We have killed two birds with one stone.

MRS. ELVSTED. What do you mean?

HEDDA. Could you not see that I wanted him to go?

MRS. ELVSTED. Yes, to write the letter—

HEDDA. And that I might speak to you alone.

MRS. ELVSTED (*confused*). About the same thing?

HEDDA. Precisely.

MRS. ELVSTED (*apprehensively*). But there is nothing more, Mrs. Tesman! Absolutely nothing!

HEDDA. Oh, yes, but there is. There is a great deal more—I can see that. Sit here— and we'll have a cozy, confidential chat. (*She forces* MRS. ELVSTED *to sit in the easy-chair beside the stove, and seats herself on one of the footstools*)

MRS. ELVSTED (*anxiously, looking at her watch*). But, my dear Mrs. Tesman—I was really on the point of going.

HEDDA. Oh, you can't be in such a hurry.— Well? Now tell me something about your life at home.

MRS. ELVSTED. Oh, that is just what I care least to speak about.

HEDDA. But to me, dear—? Why, weren't we schoolfellows?

MRS. ELVSTED. Yes, but you were in the class above me. Oh, how dreadfully afraid of you I was then!

HEDDA. Afraid of me?

MRS. ELVSTED. *Yes,* dreadfully. For when we met on the stairs you used always to pull my hair.

HEDDA. Did I, really?

MRS. ELVSTED. Yes, and once you said you would burn it off my head.

HEDDA. Oh, that was all nonsense, of course.

MRS. ELVSTED. Yes, but I was so silly in those days.—And since then, too—we have drifted so far—far apart from each other. Our circles have been so entirely different.

HEDDA. Well then, we must try to drift together again. Now listen! At school we said *du* to each other; and we called each other by our Christian names—

MRS. ELVSTED. No, I am sure you must be mistaken.

HEDDA. No, not at all! I can remember quite distinctly. So now we are going to renew our old friendship. (*Draws the footstool closer to* MRS. ELVSTED) There now! (*Kisses her cheek*) You must say *du* to me and call me Hedda.

MRS. ELVSTED (*presses and pats her hands*). Oh, how good and kind you are! I am not used to such kindness.

HEDDA. There, there, there! And I shall say *du* to you, as in the old days, and call you my dear Thora.

MRS. ELVSTED. My name is Thea.

HEDDA. Why, of course! I meant Thea. (*Looks at her compassionately*) So you are not accustomed to goodness and kindness, Thea? Not in your own home?

MRS. ELVSTED. Oh, if I only had a home! But I haven't any; I have never had a home.

HEDDA (*looks at her for a moment*). I almost suspected as much.

MRS. ELVSTED (*gazing helplessly before her*). Yes—yes—yes.

HEDDA. I don't quite remember—was it not as housekeeper that you first went to Mr. Elvsted's?

MRS. ELVSTED. I really went as governess. But his wife—his late wife—was an invalid, —and rarely left her room. So I had to look after the housekeeping as well.

HEDDA. And then—at last—you became mistress of the house.

MRS. ELVSTED (*sadly*). Yes, I did.

HEDDA. Let me see—about how long ago was that?

MRS. ELVSTED. My marriage?

HEDDA. Yes.

MRS. ELVSTED. Five years ago.

HEDDA. To be sure; it must be that.

MRS. ELVSTED. Oh, those five years—! Or at all events the last two or three of them! Oh, if you[2] could only imagine—

HEDDA (*giving her a little slap on the hand*). De? Fie, Thea!

MRS. ELVSTED. Yes, yes, I will try— Well if— you could only imagine and understand—

HEDDA (*lightly*). Eilert Lövborg has been in your neighborhood about three years, hasn't he?

MRS. ELVSTED (*looks at her doubtfully*). Eilert Lövborg? Yes—he has.

HEDDA. Had you known him before, in town here?

MRS. ELVSTED. Scarcely at all. I mean—I knew him by name of course.

HEDDA. But you saw a good deal of him in the country?

MRS. ELVSTED. Yes, he came to us every day. You see, he gave the children lessons; for in the long run I couldn't manage it all myself.

HEDDA. No, that's clear.—And your husband—? I suppose he is often away from home?

MRS. ELVSTED. Yes. Being sheriff, you know, he has to travel about a good deal in his district.

HEDDA (*leaning against the arm of the chair*). Thea—my poor, sweet Thea—now you must tell me everything—exactly as it stands.

MRS. ELVSTED. Well, then, you must question me.

HEDDA. What sort of a man is your husband, Thea? I mean—you know—in everyday life. Is he kind to you?

MRS. ELVSTED (*evasively*). I am sure he means well in everything.

HEDDA. I should think he must be altogether too old for you. There is at least twenty years' difference between you, is there not?

---

[2] Mrs. Elvsted here uses the formal pronoun *De*, whereupon Hedda rebukes her. In her next speech Mrs. Elvsted says *du*.

Mrs. Elvsted (*irritably*). Yes, that is true, too. Everything about him is repellent to me! We have not a thought in common. We have no single point of sympathy—he and I.

Hedda. But is he not fond of you all the same? In his own way?

Mrs. Elvsted. Oh, I really don't know. I think he regards me simply as a useful property. And then it doesn't cost much to keep me. I am not expensive.

Hedda. That is stupid of you.

Mrs. Elvsted (*shakes her head*). It cannot be otherwise—not with him. I don't think he really cares for any one but himself—and perhaps a little for the children.

Hedda. And for Eilert Lövborg, Thea.

Mrs. Elvstad (*looking at her*). For Eilert Lövborg? What puts that into your head?

Hedda. Well, my dear—I should say, when he sends you after him all the way to town— (*Smiling almost imperceptibly*) And besides, you said so yourself, to Tesman.

Mrs. Elvsted (*with a little nervous twitch*). Did I? Yes, I suppose I did. (*Vehemently, but not loudly*) No—I may just as well make a clean breast of it at once! For it must all come out in any case.

Hedda. Why, my dear Thea—?

Mrs. Elvsted. Well, to make a long story short: My husband did not know that I was coming.

Hedda. What! Your husband didn't know it!

Mrs. Elvsted. No, of course not. For that matter, he was away from home himself—he was traveling. Oh, I could bear it no longer, Hedda! I couldn't indeed—so utterly alone as I should have been in future.

Hedda. Well? And then?

Mrs. Elvsted. So I put together some of my things—what I needed most—as quietly as possible. And then I left the house.

Hedda. Without a word?

Mrs. Elvsted. Yes—and took the train straight to town.

Hedda. Why, my dear, good Thea—to think of you daring to do it!

Mrs. Elvsted (*rises and moves about the room*). What else could I possibly do?

Hedda. But what do you think your husband will say when you go home again?

Mrs. Elvsted (*at the table, looks at her*). Back to him?

Hedda. Of course.

Mrs. Elvsted. I shall never go back to him again.

Hedda (*rising and going towards her*). Then you have left your home—for good and all?

Mrs. Elvsted. Yes. There was nothing else to be done.

Hedda. But then—to take flight so openly.

Mrs. Elvsted. Oh, it's impossible to keep things of that sort secret.

Hedda. But what do you think people will say of you, Thea?

Mrs. Elvsted. They may say what they like for aught *I* care. (*Seats herself wearily and sadly on the sofa*) I have done nothing but what I had to do.

Hedda (*after a short silence*). And what are your plans now? What do you think of doing?

Mrs. Elvsted. I don't know yet. I only know this, that I must live here, where Eilert Lövborg is—if I am to live at all.

Hedda (*takes a chair from the table, seats herself beside her, and strokes her hands*). My dear Thea—how did this—this friendship —between you and Eilert Lövborg come about?

Mrs. Elvsted. Oh, it grew up gradually. I gained a sort of influence over him.

Hedda. Indeed?

Mrs. Elvsted. He gave up his old habits. Not because I asked him to, for I never dared do that. But of course he saw how repulsive they were to me; and so he dropped them.

HEDDA (*concealing an involuntary smile of scorn*). Then you have reclaimed him—as the saying goes—my little Thea.

MRS. ELVSTED. So he says himself, at any rate. And he, on his side, has made a real human being of me—taught me to think, and to understand so many things.

HEDDA. Did he give you lessons too, then?

MRS. ELVSTED. No, not exactly lessons. But he talked to me—talked about such an infinity of things. And then came the lovely, happy time when I began to share in his work—when he allowed me to help him!

HEDDA. Oh, he did, did he?

MRS. ELVSTED. Yes! He never wrote anything without my assistance.

HEDDA. You were two good comrades, in fact?

MRS. ELVSTED (*eagerly*). Comrades! Yes, fancy, Hedda—that is the very word he used! —Oh, I ought to feel perfectly happy; and yet I cannot; for I don't know how long it will last.

HEDDA. Are you no surer of him than that?

MRS. ELVSTED (*gloomily*). A woman's shadow stands between Eilert Lövborg and me.

HEDDA (*looks at her anxiously*). Who can that be?

MRS. ELVSTED. I don't know. Some one he knew in his—in his past. Some one he has never been able wholly to forget.

HEDDA. What has he told you—about this?

MRS. ELVSTED. He has only once—quite vaguely—alluded to it.

HEDDA. Well! And what did he say?

MRS. ELVSTED. He said that when they parted, she threatened to shoot him with a pistol.

HEDDA (*with cold composure*). Oh, nonsense! No one does that sort of thing here.

MRS. ELVSTED. No. And that is why I think it must have been that red-haired singing woman whom he once—

HEDDA. Yes, very likely.

MRS. ELVSTED. For I remember they used to say of her that she carried loaded firearms.

HEDDA. Oh—then of course it must have been she.

MRS. ELVSTED (*wringing her hands*). And now just fancy, Hedda—I hear that this singing-woman—that she is in town again! Oh, I don't know what to do—

HEDDA (*glancing towards the inner room*). Hush! Here comes Tesman. (*Rises and whispers*) Thea—all this must remain between you and me.

MRS. ELVSTED (*springing up*). Oh, yes, yes! for heaven's sake—!

(GEORGE TESMAN, *with a letter in his hand, comes from the right through the inner room.*)

TESMAN. There now—the epistle is finished.

HEDDA. That's right. And now Mrs. Elvsted is just going. Wait a moment—I'll go with you to the garden gate.

TESMAN. Do you think Berta could post the letter, Hedda dear?

HEDDA (*takes it*). I will tell her to.

(BERTA *enters from the hall*)

BERTA. Judge Brack wishes to know if Mrs. Tesman will receive him.

HEDDA. Yes, ask Judge Brack to come in. And look here—put this letter in the post.

(BERTA *taking the letter. Yes, ma'am. She opens the door for* JUDGE BRACK *and goes out herself.* BRACK *is a man of forty-five; thick-set, but well-built and elastic in his movements. His face is roundish with an aristocratic profile. His hair is short, still almost black, and carefully dressed. His eyes are lively and sparkling. His eyebrows thick. His moustaches are also thick, with short-cut ends. He wears a well-cut walking-suit, a little too youthful for his age. He uses an eye-glass, which he now and then lets drop.*)

JUDGE BRACK (*with his hat in his hand, bowing*). May one venture to call so early in the day?

HEDDA. Of course one may.

TESMAN (*presses his hand*). You are welcome at any time. (*Introducing him*) Judge Brack —Miss Rysing—

HEDDA. Oh—!

BRACK (*bowing*). Ah—delighted—

HEDDA (*looks at him and laughs*). It's nice to have a look at you by daylight, Judge!

BRACK. Do you find me—altered?

HEDDA. A little younger, I think.

BRACK. Thank you so much.

TESMAN. But what do you think of Hedda—eh? Doesn't she look flourishing? She has actually—

HEDDA. Oh, do leave me alone. You haven't thanked Judge Brack for all the trouble he has taken—

BRACK. Oh, nonsense—it was a pleasure to me—

HEDDA. Yes, you are a friend indeed. But here stands Thea all impatience to be off—so *au revoir* Judge. I shall be back again presently.

(*Mutual salutations.* MRS. ELVSTED *and* HEDDA *go out by the hall door*)

BRACK. Well,—is your wife tolerably satisfied—

TESMAN. Yes, we can't thank you sufficiently. Of course she talks a little re-arrangement here and there; and one or two things are still wanting. We shall have to buy some additional trifles.

BRACK. Indeed!

TESMAN. But we won't trouble you about these things. Hedda says she herself will look after what is wanting.—Shan't we sit down? Eh?

BRACK. Thanks, for a moment. (*Seats himself beside the table*) There is something I

wanted to speak to you about, my dear Tesman.

TESMAN. Indeed? Ah, I understand! (*Seating himself*) I suppose it's the serious part of the frolic that is coming now. Eh?

BRACK. Oh, the money question is not so very pressing; though, for that matter, I wish we had gone a little more economically to work.

TESMAN. But that would never have done, you know! Think of Hedda, my dear fellow! You, who know her so well—. I couldn't possibly ask her to put up with a shabby style of living!

BRACK. No, no—that is just the difficulty.

TESMAN. And then—fortunately—it can't be long before I receive my appointment.

BRACK. Well, you see—such things are often apt to hang fire for a time.

TESMAN. Have you heard anything definite? Eh?

BRACK. Nothing exactly definite— (*Interrupting himself*) But, by-the-bye—I have one piece of news for you.

TESMAN. Well?

BRACK. Your old friend, Eilert Lövborg, has returned to town.

TESMAN. I know that already.

BRACK. Indeed! How did you learn it?

TESMAN. From that lady who went out with Hedda.

BRACK. Really? What was her name? I didn't quite catch it.

TESMAN. Mrs. Elvsted.

BRACK. Aha—Sheriff Elvsted's wife? Of course—he has been living up in their regions.

TESMAN. And fancy—I'm delighted to hear that he is quite a reformed character!

BRACK. So they say.

TESMAN. And then he has published a new book—eh?

BRACK. Yes, indeed he has.

TESMAN. And I hear it has made some sensation!

BRACK. Quite an unusual sensation.

TESMAN. Fancy—isn't that good news! A man of such extraordinary talents— I felt so grieved to think that he had gone irretrievably to ruin.

BRACK. That was what everybody thought.

TESMAN. But I cannot imagine what he will take to now! How in the world will he be able to make his living? Eh?

(*During the last words,* HEDDA *has entered by the hall door*)

HEDDA (*to* BRACK, *laughing with a touch of scorn*). Tesman is forever worrying about how people are to make their living.

TESMAN. Well, you see, dear—we were talking about poor Eilert Lövborg.

HEDDA (*glancing at him rapidly*). Oh, indeed? (*Seats herself in the arm-chair beside the stove and asks indifferently*) What is the matter with him?

TESMAN. Well—no doubt he has run through all his property long ago; and he can scarcely write a new book every year—eh? So I really can't see what is to become of him.

BRACK. Perhaps I can give you some information on that point.

TESMAN. Indeed!

BRACK. You must remember that his relations have a good deal of influence.

TESMAN. Oh, his relations, unfortunately, have entirely washed their hands of him.

BRACK. At one time they called him the hope of the family.

TESMAN. At one time, yes! But he has put an end to all that.

HEDDA. Who knows? (*With a slight smile*) I hear they have reclaimed him up at Sheriff Elvsted's—

BRACK. And then this book that he has published—

TESMAN. Well, well, I hope to goodness they may find something for him to do. I have just written to him. I asked him to come and see us this evening, Hedda dear.

BRACK. But, my dear fellow, you are booked for my bachelors' party this evening. You promised on the pier last night.

HEDDA. Had you forgotten, Tesman?

TESMAN. Yes, I had utterly forgotten.

BRACK. But it doesn't matter, for you may be sure he won't come.

TESMAN. What makes you think that? Eh?

BRACK (*with a little hesitation, rising and resting his hands on the back of his chair*). My dear Tesman—and you too, Mrs. Tesman —I think I ought not to keep you in the dark about something that—that—

TESMAN. That concerns Eilert—?

BRACK. Both you and him.

TESMAN. Well, my dear Judge, out with it.

BRACK. You must be prepared to find your appointment deferred longer than you desired or expected.

TESMAN (*jumping up uneasily*). Is there some hitch about it? Eh?

BRACK. The nomination may perhaps be made conditional on the result of a competition—

TESMAN. Competition! Think of that, Hedda!

HEDDA (*leans farther back in the chair*). Aha —aha!

TESMAN. But who can my competitor be? Surely not—?

BRACK. Yes, precisely—Eilert Lövborg.

TESMAN (*clasping his hands*). No, no—it's quite inconceivable! Quite impossible! Eh?

BRACK. H'm—that is what it may come to, all the same.

TESMAN. Well but, Judge Brack—it would show the most incredible lack of consideration for me. (*Gesticulates with his arms*) For

—just think—I'm a married man. We have been married on the strength of these prospects, Hedda and I; and run deep into debt; and borrowed money from Aunt Julia too. Good heavens, they had as good as promised me the appointment. Eh?

BRACK. Well, well, well—no doubt you will get it in the end; only after a contest.

HEDDA (*immovable in her arm-chair*). Fancy, Tesman, there will be a sort of sporting interest in that.

TESMAN. Why, my dearest Hedda, how can you be so indifferent about it.

HEDDA (*as before*). I am not at all indifferent. I am most eager to see who wins.

BRACK. In any case, Mrs. Tesman, it is best that you should know how matters stand. I mean—before you set about the little purchases I hear you are threatening.

HEDDA. This can make no difference.

BRACK. Indeed! Then I have no more to say. Good-bye! (*To* TESMAN) I shall look in on my way back from my afternoon walk, and take you home with me.

TESMAN. Oh, yes, yes—your news has quite upset me.

HEDDA (*reclining, holds out her hand*). Good-bye, Judge; and be sure you call in the afternoon.

BRACK. Many thanks. Good-bye, good-bye!

TESMAN (*accompanying him to the door*). Good-bye, my dear Judge! You must really excuse me— (JUDGE BRACK *goes out by the hall door*)

TESMAN (*crosses the room*). Oh, Hedda—one should never rush into adventures. Eh?

HEDDA (*looks at him, smiling*). Do you do that?

TESMAN. Yes, dear—there is no denying—it was adventurous to go and marry and set up house upon mere expectations.

HEDDA. Perhaps you are right there.

TESMAN. Well—at all events, we have our delightful home, Hedda! Fancy, the home we both dreamed of—the home we were in love with, I may almost say. Eh?

HEDDA (*rising slowly and wearily*). It was part of our compact that we were to go into society —to keep open house.

TESMAN. Yes, if you only knew how I had been looking forward to it! Fancy—to see you as hostess—in a select circle? Eh? Well, well, well—for the present we shall have to get on without society, Hedda—only to invite Aunt Julia now and then.—Oh, I intended you to lead such an utterly different life, dear—!

HEDDA. Of course I cannot have my man in livery just yet.

TESMAN. Oh no, unfortunately. It would be out of the question for us to keep a footman, you know.

HEDDA. And the saddle-horse I was to have had—

TESMAN (*aghast*). The saddle-horse!

HEDDA. —I suppose I must not think of that now.

TESMAN. Good heavens, no!—that's as clear as daylight.

HEDDA (*goes up the room*). Well, I shall have one thing at least to kill time with in the meanwhile.

TESMAN (*beaming*). Oh, thank heaven for that! What is it, Hedda? Eh?

HEDDA (*in the middle doorway, looks at him with covert scorn*). My pistols, George.

TESMAN (*in alarm*). Your pistols!

HEDDA (*with cold eyes*). General Gabler's pistols. (*She goes out through the inner room, to the left*)

TESMAN (*rushes up to the middle doorway and calls after her*). No, for heaven's sake, Hedda darling—don't touch those dangerous things! For my sake, Hedda! Eh?

ACT 2

SCENE: *The room at the* TESMANS' *as in the first act, except that the piano has been removed, and an elegant little writing-table with book-shelves put in its place. A smaller table stands near the sofa at the left. Most of the bouquets have been taken away.* MRS. ELVSTED'S *bouquet is upon the large table in front.—It is afternoon.*

(HEDDA, *dressed to receive callers, is alone in the room. She stands by the open glass door, loading a revolver. The fellow to it lies in an open pistol-case on the writing-table.*)

HEDDA (*looks down the garden, and calls*). So you are here again, Judge!

BRACK (*is heard calling from a distance*). As you see, Mrs. Tesman!

HEDDA (*raises the pistol and points*). Now I'll shoot you, Judge Brack!

BRACK (*calling unseen*). No, no, no! Don't stand aiming at me!

HEDDA. This is what comes of sneaking in by the back way.[1] (*She fires*)

BRACK (*nearer*). Are you out of your senses—!

HEDDA. Dear me—did I happen to hit you?

BRACK (*still outside*). I wish you would let these pranks alone!

HEDDA. Come in then, Judge.

(JUDGE BRACK, *dressed as though for a men's party, enters by the glass door. He carries a light overcoat over his arm.*)

BRACK. What the deuce—haven't you tired of that sport, yet? What are you shooting at?

HEDDA. Oh, I am only firing in the air.

BRACK (*gently takes the pistol out of her hand*). Allow me, madam! (*Looks at it*) Ah —I know this pistol well! (*Looks around*)

[1] *Bagueje* means both "back ways" and "underhand courses."

Where is the case? Ah, here it is. (*Lays the pistol in it, and shuts it*) Now we won't play at that game any more today.

HEDDA. Then what in heaven's name would you have me do with myself?

BRACK. Have you had no visitors?

HEDDA (*closing the glass door*). Not one. I suppose all our set are still out of town.

BRACK. And is Tesman not at home either?

HEDDA (*at the writing-table, putting the pistol-case in a drawer which she shuts*). No. He rushed off to his aunt's directly after lunch; he didn't expect you so early.

BRACK. H'm—how stupid of me not to have thought of that!

HEDDA (*turning her head to look at him*). Why stupid?

BRACK. Because if I had thought of it I should have come a little—earlier.

HEDDA (*crossing the room*). Then you would have found no one to receive you; for I have been in my room changing my dress ever since lunch.

BRACK. And is there no sort of little chink that we could hold a parley through?

HEDDA. You have forgotten to arrange one.

BRACK. That was another piece of stupidity.

HEDDA. Well, we must just settle down here —and wait. Tesman is not likely to be back for some time yet.

BRACK. Never mind; I shall not be impatient.

(HEDDA *seats herself in the corner of the sofa.* BRACK *lays his overcoat over the back of the nearest chair, and sits down, but keeps his hat in his hand. A short silence. They look at each other.*)

HEDDA. Well?

BRACK (*in the same tone*). Well?

HEDDA. I spoke first.

BRACK (*bending a little forward*). Come, let us have a cozy little chat, Mrs. Hedda.

HEDDA (*leaning further back in the sofa*). Does it not seem like a whole eternity since our last talk? Of course I don't count those few words yesterday evening and this morning.

BRACK. You mean since our last confidential talk? Our last tête-à-tête?

HEDDA. Well, yes—since you put it so.

BRACK. Not a day has passed but I have wished that you were home again.

HEDDA. And I have done nothing but wish the same thing.

BRACK. You? Really, Mrs. Hedda? And I thought you had been enjoying your tour so much!

HEDDA. Oh, yes, you may be sure of that!

BRACK. But Tesman's letters spoke of nothing but happiness.

HEDDA. Oh, Tesman! You see, he thinks nothing so delightful as grubbing in libraries and making copies of old parchments, or whatever you call them.

BRACK (*with a spice of malice*). Well, that is his vocation in life—or part of it at any rate.

HEDDA. Yes, of course; and no doubt when it's your vocation— But I! Oh, my dear Mr. Brack, how mortally bored I have been.

BRACK (*sympathetically*). Do you really say so? In downright earnest?

HEDDA. Yes, you can surely understand it—! To go for six whole months without meeting a soul that knew anything of our circle, or could talk about the things we are interested in.

BRACK. Yes, yes—I too should feel that a deprivation.

HEDDA. And then, what I found most intolerable of all—

BRACK. Well?

HEDDA. —was being everlastingly in the company of—one and the same person—

BRACK (*with a nod of assent*). Morning, noon, and night, yes—at all possible times and seasons.

HEDDA. I said "everlastingly."

BRACK. Just so. But I should have thought, with our excellent Tesman, one could—

HEDDA. Tesman is—a specialist, my dear Judge.

BRACK. Undeniably.

HEDDA. And specialists are not at all amusing to travel with. Not in the long run at any rate.

BRACK. Not even—the specialist one happens to love?

HEDDA. Faugh—don't use that sickening word!

BRACK (*taken aback*). What do you say, Mrs. Hedda?

HEDDA (*half laughing, half irritated*). You should just try it! To hear of nothing but the history of civilization, morning, noon, and night—

BRACK. Everlastingly.

HEDDA. Yes, yes, yes! And then all this about the domestic industry of the Middle Ages—! That's the most disgusting part of it!

BRACK (*looks searchingly at her*). But tell me —in that case, how am I to understand your —? H'm—

HEDDA. My accepting George Tesman, you mean?

BRACK. Well, let us put it so.

HEDDA. Good heavens, do you see anything so wonderful in that?

BRACK. Yes and no—Mrs. Hedda.

HEDDA. I had positively danced myself tired, my dear Judge. My day was done— (*With a slight shudder*) Oh no—I won't say that; nor think it either!

BRACK. You have assuredly no reason to.

HEDDA. Oh, reasons— (*Watching him closely*) And George Tesman—after all, you must admit that he is correctness itself.

BRACK. His correctness and respectability are beyond all question.

HEDDA. And I don't see anything absolutely ridiculous about him.—Do you?

BRACK. Ridiculous? N—no—I shouldn't exactly say so—

HEDDA. Well—and his powers of research, at all events, are untiring.—I see no reason why he should not one day come to the front, after all.

BRACK (*looks at her hesitatingly*). I thought that you, like every one else, expected him to attain the highest distinction.

HEDDA (*with an expression of fatigue*). Yes, so I did.—And then, since he was bent, at all hazards, on being allowed to provide for me —I really don't know why I should not have accepted his offer?

BRACK. No—if you look at it in that light—

HEDDA. It was more than my other adorers were prepared to do for me, my dear Judge.

BRACK (*laughing*). Well, I can't answer for all the rest; but as for myself, you know quite well that I have always entertained a—a certain respect for the marriage tie—for marriage as an institution, Mrs. Hedda.

HEDDA (*jestingly*). Oh, I assure you I have never cherished any hopes with respect to you.

BRACK. All I require is a pleasant and intimate interior, where I can make myself useful in every way, and am free to come and go as—as a trusted friend—

HEDDA. Of the master of the house, do you mean?

BRACK (*bowing*). Frankly—of the mistress first of all; but of course of the master, too, in the second place. Such a triangular friendship—if I may call it so—is really a great convenience for all parties, let me tell you.

HEDDA. Yes, I have many a time longed for some one to make a third on our travels. Oh —those railway-carriage tête-à-têtes—!

BRACK. Fortunately your wedding journey is over now.

HEDDA (*shaking her head*). Not by a long— long way. I have only arrived at a station on the line.

BRACK. Well, then the passengers jump out and move about a little, Mrs. Hedda.

HEDDA. I never jump out.

BRACK. Really?

HEDDA. No—because there is always some one standing by to—

BRACK (*laughing*). To look at your ankles, do you mean?

HEDDA. Precisely.

BRACK. Well but, dear me—

HEDDA (*with a gesture of repulsion*). I won't have it. I would rather keep my seat where I happen to be—and continue the tête-à-tête.

BRACK. But suppose a third person were to jump in and join the couple.

HEDDA. Ah—that is quite another matter!

BRACK. A trusted, sympathetic friend—

HEDDA. —with a fund of conversation on all sorts of lively topics—

BRACK. —and not the least bit of a specialist!

HEDDA (*with an audible sigh*). Yes, that would be a relief indeed.

BRACK (*hears the front door open, and glances in that direction*). The triangle is completed.

HEDDA (*half aloud*). And on goes the train.

(GEORGE TESMAN, *in a gray walking-suit, with a soft felt hat, enters from the hall. He has a number of unbound books under his arm and in his pockets.*)

TESMAN (*goes up to the table beside the corner settee*). Ouf—what a load for a warm day—all these books. (*Lays them on the table*) I'm positively perspiring, Hedda. Hallo—are you there already, my dear Judge? Eh? Berta didn't tell me.

BRACK (*rising*). I came in through the garden.

HEDDA. What books have you got there?

TESMAN (*stands looking them through*). Some new books on my special subjects— quite indispensable to me.

HEDDA. Your special subjects?

BRACK. Yes, books on his special subjects, Mrs. Tesman. (BRACK *and* HEDDA *exchange a confidential smile*)

HEDDA. Do you need still more books on your special subjects?

TESMAN. Yes, my dear Hedda, one can never have too many of them. Of course one must keep up with all that is written and published.

HEDDA. Yes, I suppose one must.

TESMAN (*searching among his books*). And look here—I have got hold of Eilert Lövborg's new book too. (*Offering it to her*) Perhaps you would like to glance through it, Hedda? Eh?

HEDDA. No, thank you. Or rather—afterwards perhaps.

TESMAN. I looked into it a little on the way home.

BRACK. Well, what do you think of it—as a specialist?

TESMAN. I think it shows quite remarkable soundness of judgment. He never wrote like that before. (*Putting the books together*) Now I shall take all these into my study. I'm longing to cut the leaves—! And then I must change my clothes. (*To* BRACK) I suppose we needn't start just yet? Eh?

BRACK. Oh, dear no—there is not the slightest hurry.

TESMAN. Well then, I will take my time. (*Is going with his books, but stops in the doorway and turns*) By-the-bye, Hedda—Aunt Julia is not coming this evening.

HEDDA. Not coming? Is it that affair of the bonnet that keeps her away?

TESMAN. Oh, not at all. How could you think such a thing of Aunt Julia? Just fancy —! The fact is, Aunt Rina is very ill.

HEDDA. She always is.

TESMAN. Yes, but today she is much worse than usual, poor dear.

HEDDA. Oh, then it's only natural that her sister should remain with her. I must bear my disappointment.

TESMAN. And you can't imagine, dear, how delighted Aunt Julia seemed to be—because you had come home looking so flourishing!

HEDDA (*half aloud, rising*). Oh, those everlasting aunts!

TESMAN. What?

HEDDA (*going to the glass door*). Nothing.

TESMAN. Oh, all right. (*He goes through the inner room, out to the right*)

BRACK. What bonnet were you talking about?

HEDDA. Oh, it was a little episode with Miss Tesman this morning. She had laid down her bonnet on the chair there—(*Looks at him and smiles*)—and I pretended to think it was the servant's.

BRACK (*shaking his head*). Now my dear Mrs. Hedda, how could you do such a thing? To that excellent old lady, too!

HEDDA (*nervously crossing the room*). Well, you see—these impulses come over me all of a sudden; and I cannot resist them. (*Throws herself down in the easy-chair by the stove*) Oh, I don't know how to explain it.

BRACK (*behind the easy-chair*). You are not really happy—that is at the bottom of it.

HEDDA (*looking straight before her*). I know of no reason why I should be—happy. Perhaps you can give me one?

BRACK. Well—amongst other things, because you have got exactly the home you had set your heart on.

HEDDA (*looks up at him and laughs*). Do you too believe in that legend?

BRACK. Is there nothing in it, then?

HEDDA. Oh, yes, there is something in it.

BRACK. Well?

HEDDA. There is this in it, that I made use of Tesman to see me home from evening parties last summer—

BRACK. I, unfortunately, had to go quite a different way.

HEDDA. That's true. I know you were going a different way last summer.

BRACK (*laughing*). Oh fie, Mrs. Hedda! Well, then—you and Tesman—?

HEDDA. Well, we happened to pass here one evening; Tesman, poor fellow, was writhing in the agony of having to find conversation; so I took pity on the learned man—

BRACK (*smiles doubtfully*). You took pity? H'm—

HEDDA. Yes, I really did. And so—to help him out of his torment—I happened to say, in pure thoughtlessness, that I should like to live in this villa.

BRACK. No more than that?

HEDDA. Not that evening.

BRACK. But afterwards?

HEDDA. Yes, my thoughtlessness had consequences, my dear Judge.

BRACK. Unfortunately that too often happens, Mrs. Hedda.

HEDDA. Thanks! So you see it was this enthusiasm for Secretary Falk's villa that first constituted a bond of sympathy between George Tesman and me. From that came our engagement and our marriage, and our wedding journey, and all the rest of it. Well, well, my dear Judge—as you make your bed so you must lie, I could almost say.

BRACK. This is exquisite! And you really cared not a rap about it all the time.

HEDDA. No, heaven knows I didn't.

BRACK. But now? Now that we have made it so homelike for you?

HEDDA. Ugh—the rooms all seem to smell of lavender and dried love-leaves.—But perhaps it's Aunt Julia that has brought that scent with her.

BRACK (*laughingly*). No, I think it must be a legacy from the late Mrs. Secretary Falk.

HEDDA. Yes, there is an odor of mortality about it. It reminds me of a bouquet—the day after the ball. (*Clasps her hands behind her head, leans back in her chair and looks at him*) Oh, my dear Judge—you cannot imagine how horribly I shall bore myself here.

BRACK. Why should not you, too, find some sort of vocation in life, Mrs. Hedda?

HEDDA. A vocation—that should attract me?

BRACK. If possible, of course.

HEDDA. Heaven knows what sort of a vocation that could be. I often wonder whether— (*Breaking off*) But that would never do either.

BRACK. Who can tell? Let me hear what it is.

HEDDA. Whether I might not get Tesman to go into politics, I mean.

BRACK (*laughing*). Tesman? No, really now, political life is not the thing for him—not at all in his line.

HEDDA. No, I daresay not.—But if I could get him into it all the same?

BRACK. Why—what satisfaction could you find in that? If he is not fitted for that sort of thing, why should you want to drive him into it?

HEDDA. Because I am bored, I tell you! (*After a pause*) So you think it quite out of the question that Tesman should ever get into the ministry?

BRACK. H'm—you see, my dear Mrs. Hedda —to get into the ministry, he would have to be a tolerably rich man.

HEDDA (*rising impatiently*). Yes, there we have it! It is this genteel poverty I have managed to drop into—! (*Crosses the room*) That is what makes life so pitiable! So utterly ludicrous!—For that's what it is.

BRACK. Now *I* should say the fault lay elsewhere.

HEDDA. Where, then?

BRACK. You have never gone through any really stimulating experience.

HEDDA. Anything serious, you mean?

BRACK. Yes, you may call it so. But now you may perhaps have one in store.

HEDDA (*tossing her head*). Oh, you're thinking of the annoyances about this wretched professorship! But that must be Tesman's own affair. I assure you I shall not waste a thought upon it.

BRACK. No, no, I daresay not. But suppose now that what people call—in elegant language—a solemn responsibility were to come upon you? (*Smiling*) A new responsibility, Mrs. Hedda?

HEDDA (*angrily*). Be quiet! Nothing of that sort will ever happen!

BRACK (*warily*). We will speak of this again a year hence—at the very outside.

HEDDA (*curtly*). I have no turn for anything of the sort, Judge Brack. No responsibilities for me!

BRACK. Are you so unlike the generality of women as to have no turn for duties which—?

HEDDA (*beside the glass door*). Oh, be quiet, I tell you!—I often think there is only one thing in the world I have any turn for.

BRACK (*drawing near to her*). And what is that, if I may ask?

HEDDA (*stands looking out*). Boring myself to death. Now you know it. (*Turns, looks towards the inner room, and laughs*) Yes, as I thought! Here comes the Professor.

BRACK (*softly, in a tone of warning*). Come, come, come, Mrs. Hedda!

(GEORGE TESMAN, *dressed for the party, with his gloves and hat in his hand, enters from the right through the inner room*)

TESMAN. Hedda, has no message come from Eilert Lövborg? Eh?

HEDDA. No.

TESMAN. Then you'll see he'll be here presently.

BRACK. Do you really think he will come?

TESMAN. Yes, I am almost sure of it. For what you were telling us this morning must have been a mere floating rumor.

BRACK. You think so?

TESMAN. At any rate, Aunt Julia said she did not believe for a moment that he would ever stand in my way again. Fancy that!

BRACK. Well then, that's all right.

TESMAN (*placing his hat and gloves on a chair on the right*). Yes, but you must really let me wait for him as long as possible.

BRACK. We have plenty of time yet. None of my guests will arrive before seven or half-past.

TESMAN. Then meanwhile we can keep Hedda company, and see what happens. Eh?

HEDDA (*placing* BRACK's *hat and overcoat upon the corner settee*). And at the worst Mr. Lövborg can remain here with me.

BRACK (*offering to take his things*). Oh, allow me, Mrs. Tesman!—What do you mean by "At the worst"?

HEDDA. If he won't go with you and Tesman.

TESMAN (*looks dubiously at her*). But, Hedda dear—do you think it would quite do for him to remain with you? Eh? Remember, Aunt Julia can't come.

HEDDA. No, but Mrs. Elvsted is coming. We three can have a cup of tea together.

TESMAN. Oh, yes, that will be all right.

BRACK (*smiling*). And that would perhaps be the safest plan for him.

HEDDA. Why so?

BRACK. Well, you know, Mrs. Tesman, how you used to gird at my little bachelor parties. You declared they were adapted only for men of the strictest principles.

HEDDA. But no doubt Mr. Lövborg's principles are strict enough now. A converted sinner— (BERTA *appears at the hall door*)

BERTA. There's a gentleman asking if you are at home, ma'am—

HEDDA. Well, show him in.

TESMAN (*softly*). I'm sure it is he! Fancy that!

(EILERT LÖVBORG *enters from the hall. He is slim and lean; of the same age as* TESMAN, *but looks older and somewhat worn-out. His hair and beard are of a blackish brown, his face long and pale, but with patches of color on the cheekbones. He is dressed in a well-cut black visiting suit, quite new. He has dark gloves and a silk hat. He stops near the door, and makes a rapid bow, seeming somewhat embarrassed.*)

TESMAN (*goes up to him and shakes him warmly by the hand*). Well, my dear Eilert —so at last we meet again!

EILERT LÖVBORG (*speaks in a subdued voice*). Thanks for your letter, Tesman. (*Approaching* HEDDA) Will you too shake hands with me, Mrs. Tesman?

HEDDA (*taking his hand*). I am glad to see you, Mr. Lövborg. (*With a motion of her hand*) I don't know whether you two gentlemen—?

LÖVBORG (*bowing slightly*). Judge Brack, I think.

BRACK (*doing likewise*). Oh, yes,—in the old days—

TESMAN (*to* LÖVBORG, *with his hands on his shoulders*). And now you must make yourself entirely at home, Eilert! Mustn't he, Hedda?—For I hear you are going to settle in town again? Eh?

LÖVBORG. Yes, I am.

TESMAN. Quite right, quite right. Let me tell you, I have got hold of your new book; but I haven't had time to read it yet.

LÖVBORG. You may spare yourself the trouble.

TESMAN. Why so?

LÖVBORG. Because there is very little in it.

TESMAN. Just fancy—how can you say so?

BRACK. But it has been much praised, I hear.

LÖVBORG. That was what I wanted; so I put nothing into the book but what everyone would agree with.

BRACK. Very wise of you.

TESMAN. Well but, my dear Eilert—!

LÖVBORG. For now I mean to win myself a position again—to make a fresh start.

TESMAN (*a little embarrassed*). Ah, that is what you wish to do? Eh?

LÖVBORG (*smiling, lays down his hat, and draws a packet, wrapped in paper, from his coat pocket*). But when this one appears, George Tesman, you will have to read it. For this is the real book—the book I have put my true self into.

TESMAN. Indeed? And what is it?

LÖVBORG. It is the continuation.

TESMAN. The continuation? Of what?

LÖVBORG. Of the book.

TESMAN. Of the new book?

LÖVBORG. Of course.

TESMAN. Why, my dear Eilert—does it not come down to our own days?

LÖVBORG. Yes, it does; and this one deals with the future.

TESMAN. With the future! But, good heavens, we know nothing of the future!

LÖVBORG. No; but there is a thing or two to be said about it all the same. (*Opens the packet*) Look here—

TESMAN. Why, that's not your handwriting.

LÖVBORG. I dictated it. (*Turning over the pages*) It falls into two sections. The first deals with the civilizing forces of the future. And here is the second—(*running through the pages towards the end*)—forecasting the probable line of development.

TESMAN. How odd now! I should never have thought of writing anything of that sort.

HEDDA (*at the glass door, drumming on the pane*). H'm—I daresay not.

LÖVBORG (*replacing the manuscript in its paper and laying the packet on the table*). I brought it, thinking I might read you a little of it this evening.

TESMAN. That was very good of you, Eilert. But this evening—? (*Looking at* BRACK) I don't quite see how we can manage it—

LÖVBORG. Well then, some other time. There is no hurry.

BRACK. I must tell you, Mr. Lövborg—there is a little gathering at my house this evening —mainly in honor of Tesman, you know—

LÖVBORG (*looking for his hat*). Oh—then I won't detain you—

BRACK. No, but listen—will you not do me the favor of joining us?

LÖVBORG (*curtly and decidedly*). No, I can't —thank you very much.

BRACK. Oh, nonsense—do! We shall be quite a select little circle. And I assure you we shall have a "lively time" as Mrs. Hed—as Mrs. Tesman says.

LÖVBORG. I have no doubt of it. But nevertheless—

BRACK. And then you might bring your manuscript with you, and read it to Tesman at my house. I could give you a room to yourselves.

TESMAN. Yes, think of that, Eilert,—why shouldn't you? Eh?

HEDDA (*interposing*). But, Tesman, if Mr. Lövborg would really rather not! I am sure Mr. Lövborg is much more inclined to remain here and have supper with me.

LÖVBORG (*looking at her*). With you, Mrs. Tesman?

HEDDA. And with Mrs. Elvsted.

LÖVBORG. Ah— (*Lightly*) I saw her for a moment this morning.

HEDDA. Did you? Well, she is coming this evening. So you see you are almost bound to remain, Mr. Lövborg, or she will have no one to see her home.

LÖVBORG. That's true. Many thanks, Mrs. Tesman—in that case I will remain.

HEDDA. Then I have one or two orders to give the servant—

> (*She goes to the hall door and rings.* BERTA *enters.* HEDDA *talks to her in a whisper, and points towards the inner room.* BERTA *nods and goes out again.*)

TESMAN (*at the same time, to* LÖVBORG). Tell me, Eilert—is it this new subject—the future —that you are going to lecture about?

LÖVBORG. Yes.

TESMAN. They told me at the bookseller's, that you are going to deliver a course of lectures this autumn.

LÖVBORG. That is my intention. I hope you won't take it ill, Tesman.

TESMAN. Oh no, not in the least! But—?

LÖVBORG. I can quite understand that it must be disagreeable to you.

TESMAN (*cast down*). Oh, I can't expect you, out of consideration for me, to—

LÖVBORG. But I shall wait till you have received your appointment.

TESMAN. Will you wait? Yes, but—yes, but —are you not going to compete with me? Eh?

LÖVBORG. No; it is only the moral victory I care for.

TESMAN. Why, bless me—then Aunt Julia was right after all! Oh yes—I knew it! Hedda! Just fancy—Eilert Lövborg is not going to stand in our way!

HEDDA (*curtly*). Our way? Pray leave me out of the question.

(*She goes up towards the inner room, where* BERTA *is placing a tray with decanters and glasses on the table.* HEDDA *nods approval, and comes forward again.* BERTA *goes out.*)

TESMAN (*at the same time*). And you, Judge Brack—what do you say to this? Eh?

BRACK. Well, I say that a moral victory— h'm—may be all very fine—

TESMAN. Yes, certainly. But all the same—

HEDDA (*looking at* TESMAN *with a cold smile*). You stand there looking as if you were thunderstruck—

TESMAN. Yes—so I am—I almost think—

BRACK. Don't you see, Mrs. Tesman, a thunderstorm has just passed over?

HEDDA (*pointing towards the inner room*) Will you not take a glass of cold punch, gentlemen?

BRACK (*looking at his watch*). A stirrup-cup? Yes, it wouldn't come amiss.

TESMAN. A capital idea, Hedda! Just the thing! Now that the weight has been taken off my mind—

HEDDA. Will you not join them, Mr. Lövborg?

LÖVBORG (*with a gesture of refusal*). No, thank you. Nothing for me.

BRACK. Why, bless me—cold punch is surely not poison.

LÖVBORG. Perhaps not for everyone.

HEDDA. I will keep Mr. Lövborg company in the meantime.

TESMAN. Yes, yes, Hedda dear, do.

(*He and* BRACK *go into the inner room, seat themselves, drink punch, smoke cigarettes, and carry on a lively conversation during what follows.* EILERT LÖVBORG *remains beside the stove.* HEDDA *goes to the writing-table.*)

HEDDA (*raising her voice a little*). Do you care to look at some photographs, Mr. Lövborg? You know Tesman and I made a tour in the Tyrol on our way home?

(*She takes up an album, and places it on the table beside the sofa, in the farther corner of which she seats herself.* EILERT LÖVBORG *approaches, stops, and looks at her. Then he takes a chair and seats himself at her left, with his back towards the inner room.*)

HEDDA (*opening the album*). Do you see this range of mountains, Mr. Lövborg? It's the Ortler group. Tesman has written the name underneath. Here it is: "The Ortler group near Meran."

LÖVBORG (*who has never taken his eyes off her, says softly and slowly*). Hedda—Gabler!

HEDDA (*glancing hastily at him*). Ah, hush!

LÖVBORG (*repeats softly*). Hedda Gabler!

HEDDA (*looking at the album*). That was my name in the old days—when we two knew each other.

LÖVBORG. And I must teach myself never to say Hedda Gabler again—never, as long as I live.

HEDDA (*still turning over the pages*). Yes, you must. And I think you ought to practice in time. The sooner the better, I should say.

LÖVBORG (*in a tone of indignation*). Hedda Gabler married? And married to—George Tesman!

HEDDA. Yes—so the world goes.

LÖVBORG. Oh, Hedda, Hedda—how could you[2] throw yourself away!

HEDDA (*looks sharply at him*). What? I can't allow this!

LÖVBORG. What do you mean? (TESMAN *comes into the room and goes towards the sofa*)

HEDDA (*hears him coming and says in an indifferent tone*). And this is a view from the Val d'Ampezzo, Mr. Lövborg. Just look at

[2] He uses the familiar *du*.

these peaks! (*Looks affectionately up at* TES-MAN) What's the name of these curious peaks, dear?

TESMAN. Let me see? Oh, those are the Dolomites.

HEDDA. Yes, that's it!—Those are the Dolomites, Mr. Lövborg.

TESMAN. Hedda dear,—I only wanted to ask whether I shouldn't bring you a little punch after all? For yourself at any rate—eh?

HEDDA. Yes, do, please; and perhaps a few biscuits.

TESMAN. No cigarettes?

HEDDA. No.

TESMAN. Very well.

(*He goes into the inner room and out to the right.* BRACK *sits in the inner room, and keeps an eye from time to time on* HEDDA *and* LÖVBORG.)

LÖVBORG (*softly, as before*). Answer me, Hedda—how could you go and do this?

HEDDA (*apparently absorbed in the album*). If you continue to say *du* to me I won't talk to you.

LÖVBORG. May I not say *du* when we are alone?

HEDDA. No. You may think it; but you mustn't say it.

LÖVBORG. Ah, I understand. It is an offense against George Tesman, whom you[3]—love.

HEDDA (*glances at him and smiles*). Love? What an idea!

LÖVBORG. You don't love him then!

HEDDA. But I won't hear of any sort of unfaithfulness! Remember that.

LÖVBORG. Hedda—answer me one thing—

HEDDA. Hush!

(TESMAN *enters with a small tray from the inner room*)

TESMAN. Here you are! Isn't this tempting? (*He puts the tray on the table*)

HEDDA. Why do you bring it yourself?

TESMAN (*filling the glasses*). Because I think it's such fun to wait upon you, Hedda.

HEDDA. But you have poured out two glasses. Mr. Lövborg said he wouldn't have any—

TESMAN. No, but Mrs. Elvsted will soon be here, won't she?

HEDDA. Yes, by-the-bye—Mrs. Elvsted—

TESMAN. Had you forgotten her? Eh?

HEDDA. We were so absorbed in these photographs. (*Shows him a picture*) Do you remember this little village?

TESMAN. Oh, it's that one just below the Brenner Pass. It was there we passed the night—

HEDDA. —and met that lively party of tourists.

TESMAN. Yes, that was the place. Fancy—if we could only have had you with us, Eilert! Eh? (*He returns to the inner room and sits beside* BRACK)

LÖVBORG. Answer me this one thing, Hedda—

HEDDA. Well?

LÖVBORG. Was there no love in your friendship for me either? Not a spark—not a tinge of love in it?

HEDDA. I wonder if there was? To me it seems as though we were two good comrades —two thoroughly intimate friends. (*Smilingly*) You especially were frankness itself.

LÖVBORG. It was you that made me so.

HEDDA. As I look back upon it all, I think there was really something beautiful, something fascinating—something daring—in—in that secret intimacy—that comradeship which no living creature so much as dreamed of.

LÖVBORG. Yes, yes, Hedda! Was there not? —When I used to come to your father's in the

---

[3] From this point onward Lövborg uses the formal *De*.

afternoon—and the General sat over at the window reading his papers—with his back towards us—

HEDDA. And we two on the corner sofa—

LÖVBORG. Always with the same illustrated paper before us—

HEDDA. For want of an album, yes.

LÖVBORG. Yes, Hedda, and when I made my confessions to you—told you about myself, things that at that time no one else knew! There I would sit and tell you of my escapades—my days and nights of devilment. Oh, Hedda—what was the power in you that forced me to confess these things?

HEDDA. Do you think it was any power in me?

LÖVBORG. How else can I explain it? And all those—those roundabout questions you used to put to me—

HEDDA. Which you understood so particularly well—

LÖVBORG. How could you sit and question me like that? Question me quite frankly—

HEDDA. In roundabout terms, please observe.

LÖVBORG. Yes, but frankly nevertheless. Cross-question me about—all that sort of thing?

HEDDA. And how could you answer, Mr. Lövborg?

LÖVBORG. Yes, that is just what I can't understand—in looking back upon it. But tell me now, Hedda—was there not love at the bottom of our friendship? On your side, did you not feel as though you might purge my stains away if I made you my confessor? Was it not so?

HEDDA. No, not quite.

LÖVBORG. What was your motive, then?

HEDDA. Do you think it quite incomprehensible that a young girl—when it can be done—without any one knowing—

LÖVBORG. Well?

HEDDA. —should be glad to have a peep, now and then, into a world which—

LÖVBORG. Which—?

HEDDA. —which she is forbidden to know anything about?

LÖVBORG. So that was it?

HEDDA. Partly. Partly—I almost think.

LÖVBORG. Comradeship in the thirst for life. But why should not that, at any rate, have continued?

HEDDA. The fault was yours.

LÖVBORG. It was you that broke with me.

HEDDA. Yes, when our friendship threatened to develop into something more serious. Shame upon you, Eilert Lövborg! How could you think of wronging your—your frank comrade?

LÖVBORG (*clenching his hands*). Oh, why did you not carry out your threat? Why did you not shoot me down?

HEDDA. Because I have such a dread of scandal.

LÖVBORG. Yes, Hedda, you are a coward at heart.

HEDDA. A terrible coward. (*Changing her tone*) But it was a lucky thing for you. And now you have found ample consolation at the Elvsteds'.

LÖVBORG. I know what Thea has confided to you.

HEDDA. And perhaps you have confided to her something about us?

LÖVBORG. Not a word. She is too stupid to understand anything of that sort.

HEDDA. Stupid?

LÖVBORG. She is stupid about matters of that sort.

HEDDA. And I am cowardly. (*Bends over towards him, without looking him in the face, and says more softly*) But now I will confide something to you.

LÖVBORG (*eagerly*). Well?

HEDDA. The fact that I dared not shoot you down—

LÖVBORG. Yes!

HEDDA. —that was not my most arrant cowardice—that evening.

LÖVBORG (*looks at her a moment, understands, and whispers passionately*). Oh, Hedda! Hedda Gabler! Now I begin to see a hidden reason beneath our comradeship! You[4] and I—! After all, then, it was your craving for life—

HEDDA (*softly, with a sharp glance*). Take care! Believe nothing of the sort!

(*Twilight has begun to fall. The hall door is opened from without by* BERTA.)

HEDDA (*closes the album with a bang and calls smilingly*). Ah, at last! My darling Thea,—come along!

(MRS. ELVSTED *enters from the hall. She is in evening dress. The door is closed behind her.*)

HEDDA (*on the sofa, stretches out her arms towards her*). My sweet Thea—you can't think how I have been longing for you!

(MRS. ELVSTED, *in passing, exchanges slight salutations with the gentlemen in the inner room, then goes up to the table and gives* HEDDA *her hands.* EILERT LÖVBORG *has risen. He and* MRS. ELVSTED *greet each other with a silent nod.*)

MRS. ELVSTED. Ought I to go in and talk to your husband for a moment?

HEDDA. Oh, not at all. Leave those two alone. They will soon be going.

MRS. ELVSTED. Are they going out?

HEDDA. Yes, to a supper-party.

MRS. ELVSTED (*quickly, to* LÖVBORG). Not you?

LÖVBORG. No.

[4] In this speech he once more says *du*. Hedda addresses him throughout as *De*.

HEDDA. Mr. Lövborg remains with us.

MRS. ELVSTED (*takes a chair and is about to seat herself at his side*). Oh, how nice it is here!

HEDDA. No, thank you, my little Thea! Not there! You'll be good enough to come over here to me. I will sit between you.

MRS. ELVSTED. Yes, just as you please.

(*She goes around the table and seats herself on the sofa on* HEDDA'S *right.* LÖVBORG *reseats himself on his chair.*)

LÖVBORG (*after a short pause, to* HEDDA). Is not she lovely to look at?

HEDDA (*lightly stroking her hair*). Only to look at?

LÖVBORG. Yes. For we two—she and I—we are two real comrades. We have absolute faith in each other; so we can sit and talk with perfect frankness—

HEDDA. Not roundabout, Mr. Lövborg?

LÖVBORG. Well—

MRS. ELVSTED (*softly clinging close to* HEDDA). Oh, how happy I am, Hedda; for, only think, he says I have inspired him too.

HEDDA (*looks at her with a smile*). Ah! Does he say that, dear?

LÖVBORG. And then she is so brave, Mrs. Tesman!

MRS. ELVSTED. Good heavens—am I brave?

LÖVBORG. Exceedingly—where your comrade is concerned.

HEDDA. Ah, yes—courage! If one only had that!

LÖVBORG. What then? What do you mean?

HEDDA. Then life would perhaps be livable, after all. (*With a sudden change of tone*) But now, my dearest Thea, you really must have a glass of cold punch.

MRS. ELVSTED. No, thanks—I never take anything of that kind.

HEDDA. Well then, you, Mr. Lövborg.

LÖVBORG. Nor I, thank you.

MRS. ELVSTED. No, he doesn't either.

HEDDA (*looks fixedly at him*). But if I say you shall?

LÖVBORG. It would be no use.

HEDDA (*laughing*). Then I, poor creature, have no sort of power over you?

LÖVBORG. Not in that respect.

HEDDA. But seriously, I think you ought to —for your own sake.

MRS. ELVSTED. Why, Hedda—!

LÖVBORG. How so?

HEDDA. Or rather on account of other people.

LÖVBORG. Indeed?

HEDDA. Otherwise people might be apt to suspect that—in your heart of hearts—you did not feel quite secure—quite confident of yourself.

MRS. ELVSTED (*softly*). Oh please, Hedda—

LÖVBORG. People may suspect what they like —for the present.

MRS. ELVSTED (*joyfully*). Yes, let them!

HEDDA. I saw it plainly in Judge Brack's face a moment ago.

LÖVBORG. What did you see?

HEDDA. His contemptuous smile, when you dared not go with them into the inner room.

LÖVBORG. Dared not? Of course I preferred to stop here and talk to you.

MRS. ELVSTED. What could be more natural, Hedda?

HEDDA. But the Judge could not guess that. And I saw, too, the way he smiled and glanced at Tesman when you dared not accept his invitation to this wretched little supper-party of his.

LÖVBORG. Dared not! Do you say I dared not?

HEDDA. *I* don't say so. But that was how Judge Brack understood it.

LÖVBORG. Well, let him.

HEDDA. Then you are not going with them?

LÖVBORG. I will stay here with you and Thea.

MRS. ELVSTED. Yes, Hedda—how can you doubt that?

HEDDA (*smiles and nods approvingly to* LÖVBORG). Firm as a rock! Faithful to your principles, now and forever! Ah, that is how a man should be! (*Turns to* MRS. ELVSTED *and caresses her*) Well now, what did I tell you, when you came to us this morning in such a state of distraction—

LÖVBORG (*surprised*). Distraction!

MRS. ELVSTED (*terrified*). Hedda—oh Hedda—!

HEDDA. You can see for yourself; you haven't the slightest reason to be in such mortal terror— (*Interrupting herself*) There! Now we can all three enjoy ourselves!

LÖVBORG (*who has given a start*). Ah—what is all this, Mrs. Tesman?

MRS. ELVSTED. Oh my God, Hedda! What are you saying? What are you doing?

HEDDA. Don't get excited! That horrid Judge Brack is sitting watching you.

LÖVBORG. So she was in mortal terror! On my account!

MRS. ELVSTED (*softly and piteously*). Oh, Hedda—now you have ruined everything!

LÖVBORG (*looks fixedly at her for a moment. His face is distorted.*). So that was my comrade's frank confidence in me?

MRS. ELVSTED (*imploringly*). Oh, my dearest friend—only let me tell you—

LÖVBORG (*takes one of the glasses of punch, raises it to his lips, and says in a low, husky voice*). Your health, Thea!

(*He empties the glass, puts it down, and takes the second*)

MRS. ELVSTED (*softly*). Oh, Hedda, Hedda— how could you do this?

HEDDA. *I* do it? Are you crazy?

LÖVBORG. Here's to your health too, Mrs. Tesman. Thanks for the truth. Hurrah for the truth!

> (*He empties the glass and is about to re-fill it*)

HEDDA (*lays her hand on his arm*). Come, come—no more for the present. Remember you are going out to supper.

MRS. ELVSTED. No, no, no!

HEDDA. Hush! They are sitting watching you.

LÖVBORG (*putting down the glass*). Now, Thea—tell me the truth—

MRS. ELVSTED. Yes.

LÖVBORG. Did your husband know that you had come after me?

MRS. ELVSTED (*wringing her hands*). Oh, Hedda—do you hear what he is asking?

LÖVBORG. Was it arranged between you and him that you were to come to town and look after me? Perhaps it was the Sheriff himself that urged you to come? Aha, my dear—no doubt he wanted my help in his office! Or was it at the card-table that he missed me?

MRS. ELVSTED (*softly, in agony*). Oh, Löv-borg, Lövborg—!

LÖVBORG (*seizes a glass and is on the point of filling it*). Here's a glass for the old Sheriff too!

HEDDA (*preventing him*). No more just now. Remember you have to read your manuscript to Tesman.

LÖVBORG (*calmly, putting down the glass*). It was stupid of me—all this, Thea—to take it in this way, I mean. Don't be angry with me, my dear, dear comrade. You shall see—both you and the others—that if I was fallen once —now I have risen again! Thanks to you, Thea.

MRS. ELVSTED (*radiant with joy*). Oh, heaven be praised—!

> (BRACK *has in the meantime looked at his watch. He and* TESMAN *rise and come into the drawing-room.*)

BRACK (*takes his hat and overcoat*). Well, Mrs. Tesman, our time has come.

HEDDA. I suppose it has.

LÖVBORG (*rising*). Mine too, Judge Brack.

MRS. ELVSTED (*softly and imploringly*). Oh, Lövborg, don't do it!

HEDDA (*pinching her arm*). They can hear you!

MRS. ELVSTED (*with a suppressed shriek*). Ow!

LÖVBORG (*to* BRACK). You were good enough to invite me.

BRACK. Well, are you coming after all?

LÖVBORG. Yes, many thanks.

BRACK. I'm delighted—

LÖVBORG (*to* TESMAN, *putting the parcel of MS. in his pocket*). I should like to show you one or two things before I send it to the printers.

TESMAN. Fancy—that will be delightful. But, Hedda dear, how is Mrs. Elvsted to get home? Eh?

HEDDA. Oh, that can be managed somehow.

LÖVBORG (*looking towards the ladies*). Mrs. Elvsted? Of course, I'll come again and fetch her. (*Approaching*) At ten or thereabouts, Mrs. Tesman? Will that do?

HEDDA. Certainly. That will do capitally.

TESMAN. Well, then, that's all right. But you must not expect me so early, Hedda.

HEDDA. Oh, you may stop as long—as long as ever you please.

MRS. ELVSTED (*trying to conceal her anxiety*). Well then, Mr. Lövborg—I shall remain here until you come.

LÖVBORG (*with his hat in his hand*). Pray do, Mrs. Elvsted.

BRACK. And now off goes the excursion train, gentlemen! I hope we shall have a lively time, as a certain fair lady puts it.

HEDDA. Ah, if only the fair lady could be present unseen—!

BRACK. Why unseen?

HEDDA. In order to hear a little of your liveliness at first hand, Judge Brack.

BRACK (*laughingly*). I should not advise the fair lady to try it.

TESMAN (*also laughing*). Come, you're a nice one Hedda! Fancy that!

BRACK. Well, good-bye, good-bye, ladies.

LÖVBORG (*bowing*). About ten o'clock, then.

(BRACK, LÖVBORG, *and* TESMAN *go out by the hall door. At the same time* BERTA *enters from the inner room with a lighted lamp, which she places on the dining-room table; she goes out by the way she came.*)

MRS. ELVSTED (*who has risen and is wandering restlessly about the room*). Hedda—Hedda—what will come of all this?

HEDDA. At ten o'clock—he will be here. I can see him already—with vine-leaves in his hair—flushed and fearless—

MRS. ELVSTED. Oh, I hope he may.

HEDDA. And then, you see—then he will have regained control over himself. Then he will be a free man for all his days.

MRS. ELVSTED. Oh God!—if he would only come as you see him now!

HEDDA. He will come as I see him—so, and not otherwise! (*Rises and approaches* THEA)

You may doubt him as long as you please; I believe in him. And now we will try—

MRS. ELVSTED. You have some hidden motive in this, Hedda!

HEDDA. Yes, I have. I want for once in my life to have power to mold a human destiny.

MRS. ELVSTED. Have you not the power?

HEDDA. I have not—and have never had it.

MRS. ELVSTED. Not your husband's?

HEDDA. Do you think that is worth the trouble? Oh, if you could only understand how poor I am. And fate has made you so rich! (*Clasps her passionately in her arms*) I think I must burn your hair off, after all.

MRS. ELVSTED. Let me go! Let me go! I am afraid of you, Hedda!

BERTA (*in the middle doorway*). Tea is laid in the dining room, ma'am.

HEDDA. Very well. We are coming.

MRS. ELVSTED. No, no, no! I would rather go home alone! At once!

HEDDA. Nonsense? First you shall have a cup of tea, you little stupid. And then—at ten o'clock—Eilert Lövborg will be here—with vine-leaves in his hair.

(*She drags* MRS. ELVSTED *almost by force towards the middle doorway.*)

ACT 3

SCENE: *The room at the* TESMANS'. *The curtains are drawn over the middle doorway, and also over the glass door. The lamp, half turned down, and with a shade over it, is burning on the table. In the stove, the door of which stands open, there has been a fire, which is now nearly burnt out.*

(MRS. ELVSTED, *wrapped in a large shawl, and with her feet upon a foot-rest, sits close to the stove, sunk back in the arm-chair.* HEDDA, *fully dressed, lies sleeping upon the sofa, with a sofa-blanket over her.*)

MRS. ELVSTED (*after a pause, suddenly sits up in her chair, and listens eagerly. Then she sinks back again wearily, moaning to herself.*). Not yet!—Oh God—oh God—not yet!

(BERTA *slips in by the hall door. She has a letter in her hand.*)

MRS. ELVSTED (*turns and whispers eagerly*). Well—has anyone come?

BERTA (*softly*). Yes, a girl has brought this letter.

MRS. ELVSTED (*quickly, holding out her hand*). A letter! Give it to me!

BERTA. No, it's for Dr. Tesman, ma'am.

MRS. ELVSTED. Oh, indeed.

BERTA. It was Miss Tesman's servant that brought it. I'll lay it here on the table.

MRS. ELVSTED. Yes, do.

BERTA (*laying down the letter*). I think I had better put out the lamp. It's smoking.

MRS. ELVSTED. Yes, put it out. It must soon be daylight now.

BERTA (*putting out the lamp*). It is daylight already, ma'am.

MRS. ELVSTED. Yes, broad day! And no one come back yet—!

BERTA. Lord bless you, ma'am! I guessed how it would be.

MRS. ELVSTED. You guessed?

BERTA. Yes, when I saw that a certain person had come back to town—and that he went off with them. For we've heard enough about that gentleman before now.

MRS. ELVSTED. Don't speak so loud. You will waken Mrs. Tesman.

BERTA (*looks towards the sofa and sighs*). No, no—let her sleep, poor thing. Shan't I put some wood on the fire?

MRS. ELVSTED. Thanks, not for me.

BERTA. Oh, very well. (*She goes softly out by the hall door*)

HEDDA (*is awakened by the shutting of the door, and looks up*). What's that—?

MRS. ELVSTED. It was only the servant—

HEDDA (*looking about her*). Oh, we're here—! Yes now I remember. (*Sits erect upon the sofa, stretches herself, and rubs her eyes*) What o'clock is it, Thea?

MRS. ELVSTED (*looks at her watch*). It's past seven.

HEDDA. When did Tesman come home?

MRS. ELVSTED. He has not come.

HEDDA. Not come home yet?

MRS. ELVSTED (*rising*). No one has come.

HEDDA. Think of our watching and waiting here till four in the morning—

MRS. ELVSTED (*wringing her hands*). And how I watched and waited for him!

HEDDA (*yawns, and says with her hand before her mouth*). Well, well—we might have spared ourselves the trouble.

MRS. ELVSTED. Did you get a little sleep?

HEDDA. Oh yes; I believe I have slept pretty well. Have you not?

MRS. ELVSTED. Not for a moment. I couldn't, Hedda!—not to save my life.

HEDDA (*rises and goes towards her*). There, there, there! There's nothing to be so alarmed about. I understand quite well what has happened.

MRS. ELVSTED. Well, what do you think? Won't you tell me?

HEDDA. Why, of course it has been a very late affair at Judge Brack's—

MRS. ELVSTED. Yes, yes, that is clear enough. But all the same—

HEDDA. And then, you see, Tesman hasn't cared to come home and ring us up in the middle of the night. (*Laughing*) Perhaps he wasn't inclined to show himself either—immediately after a jollification.

MRS. ELVSTED. But in that case—where can he have gone?

HEDDA. Of course he has gone to his aunts' and slept there. They have his old room ready for him.

MRS. ELVSTED. No, he can't be with them; for a letter has just come for him from Miss Tesman. There it lies.

HEDDA. Indeed? (*Looks at the address*) Why yes, it's addressed in Aunt Julia's own hand. Well then, he has remained at Judge Brack's. And as for Eilert Lövborg—he is sitting, with vine-leaves in his hair, reading his manuscript.

MRS. ELVSTED. Oh Hedda, you are just saying things you don't believe a bit.

HEDDA. You really are a little blockhead, Thea.

MRS. ELVSTED. Oh yes, I suppose I am.

HEDDA. And how mortally tired you look.

MRS. ELVSTED. Yes, I am mortally tired.

HEDDA. Well then, you must do as I tell you. You must go into my room and lie down for a little while.

MRS. ELVSTED. Oh no, no—I shouldn't be able to sleep.

HEDDA. I am sure you would.

MRS. ELVSTED. Well, but your husband is certain to come soon now; and then I want to know at once—

HEDDA. I shall take care to let you know when he comes.

MRS. ELVSTED. Do you promise me, Hedda?

HEDDA. Yes, rely upon me. Just you go in and have a sleep in the meantime.

MRS. ELVSTED. Thanks; then I'll try to. (*She goes off through the inner room*)

(HEDDA *goes up to the glass door and draws back the curtains. The broad daylight streams into the room. Then she takes a little hand-glass from the writing-table, looks at herself in it, and arranges her hair. Next she goes to the hall door and presses the bell-button.*

BERTA *presently appears at the hall door.*)

BERTA. Did you want anything, ma'am?

HEDDA. Yes; you must put some more wood in the stove. I am shivering.

BERTA. Bless me—I'll make up the fire at once. (*She rakes the embers together and lays a piece of wood upon them; then stops and listens*) That was a ring at the front door, ma'am.

HEDDA. Then go to the door. I will look after the fire.

BERTA. It'll soon burn up. (*She goes out by the hall door*)

(HEDDA *kneels on the foot-rest and lays some more pieces of wood in the stove. After a short pause,* GEORGE TESMAN *enters from the hall. He looks tired and rather serious. He steals on tiptoe towards the middle doorway and is about to slip through the curtains.*)

HEDDA (*at the stove, without looking up*). Good morning.

TESMAN (*turns*). Hedda! (*Approaching her*) Good heavens—are you up so early? Eh?

HEDDA. Yes, I am up very early this morning.

TESMAN. And I never doubted you were still sound asleep! Fancy that, Hedda!

HEDDA. Don't speak so loud. Mrs. Elvsted is resting in my room.

TESMAN. Has Mrs. Elvsted been here all night?

HEDDA. Yes, since no one came to fetch her.

TESMAN. Ah, to be sure.

HEDDA (*closes the door of the stove and rises*). Well, did you enjoy yourself at Judge Brack's?

TESMAN. Have you been anxious about me? Eh?

HEDDA. No, I should never think of being anxious. But I asked if you had enjoyed yourself.

TESMAN. Oh yes,—for once in a way. Especially the beginning of the evening; for then Eilert read me part of his book. We arrived more than an hour too early—fancy that! And Brack had all sorts of arrangements to make—so Eilert read to me.

HEDDA (*seating herself by the table on the right*). Well? Tell me, then—

TESMAN (*sitting on a footstool near the stove*). Oh Hedda, you can't conceive what a book that is going to be! I believe it is one of the most remarkable things that have ever been written. Fancy that!

HEDDA. Yes, yes; I don't care about that—

TESMAN. I must make a confession to you, Hedda. When he had finished reading—a horrid feeling came over me.

HEDDA. A horrid feeling?

TESMAN. I felt jealous of Eilert for having had it in him to write such a book. Only think, Hedda!

HEDDA. Yes, yes, I am thinking!

TESMAN. And then how pitiful to think that he—with all his gifts—should be irreclaimable after all.

HEDDA. I suppose you mean that he has more courage than the rest?

TESMAN. No, not at all—I mean that he is incapable of taking his pleasures in moderation.

HEDDA. And what came of it all—in the end?

TESMAN. Well, to tell the truth, I think it might best be described as an orgy, Hedda.

HEDDA. Had he vine-leaves in his hair?

TESMAN. Vine-leaves? No, I saw nothing of the sort. But he made a long, rambling speech in honor of the woman who had inspired him in his work—that was the phrase he used.

HEDDA. Did he name her?

TESMAN. No, he didn't; but I can't help thinking he meant Mrs. Elvsted. You may be sure he did.

HEDDA. Well—where did you part from him?

TESMAN. On the way to town. We broke up —the last of us at any rate—all together; and Brack came with us to get a breath of fresh air. And then, you see, we agreed to take Eilert home; for he had had far more than was good for him.

HEDDA. I daresay.

TESMAN. But now comes the strange part of it, Hedda; or, I should rather say, the melancholy part of it. I declare I am almost ashamed—on Eilert's account—to tell you—

HEDDA. Oh, go on—

TESMAN. Well, as we were getting near town, you see, I happened to drop a little behind the others. Only for a minute or two—fancy that!

HEDDA. Yes, yes, yes, but—?

TESMAN. And then, as I hurried after them —what do you think I found by the wayside? Eh?

HEDDA. Oh, how should I know!

TESMAN. You mustn't speak of it to a soul, Hedda! Do you hear! Promise me, for Eilert's sake. (*Draws a parcel, wrapped in paper, from his coat pocket*) Fancy, dear—I found this.

HEDDA. Is not that the parcel he had with him yesterday?

TESMAN. Yes, it is the whole of his precious, irreplaceable manuscript! And he had gone and lost it, and knew nothing about it. Only fancy, Hedda! So deplorably—

HEDDA. But why did you not give him back the parcel at once?

TESMAN. I didn't dare to—in the state he was then in—

HEDDA. Did you not tell any of the others that you had found it?

TESMAN. Oh, far from it. You can surely understand that, for Eilert's sake, I wouldn't do that.

HEDDA. So no one knows that Eilert Lövborg's manuscript is in your possession?

TESMAN. No. And no one must know it.

HEDDA. Then what did you say to him afterwards?

TESMAN. I didn't talk to him again at all; for when we got in among the streets, he and two or three of the others gave us the slip and disappeared. Fancy that!

HEDDA. Indeed! They must have taken him home then.

TESMAN. Yes, so it would appear. And Brack, too, left us.

HEDDA. And what have you been doing with yourself since?

TESMAN. Well, I and some of the others went home with one of the party, a jolly fellow, and took our morning coffee with him; or perhaps I should rather call it our night coffee—eh? But now, when I have rested a little, and given Eilert, poor fellow, time to have his sleep out, I must take this back to him.

HEDDA (*holds out her hand for the packet*). No—don't give it to him! Not in such a hurry, I mean. Let me read it first.

TESMAN. No, my dearest Hedda, I mustn't, I really mustn't.

HEDDA. You must not?

TESMAN. No—for you can imagine what a state of despair he will be in when he awakens and misses the manuscript. He has no copy of it, you know! He told me so.

HEDDA (*looking searchingly at him*). Can such a thing not be reproduced? Written over again?

TESMAN. No, I don't think that would be possible. For the inspiration, you see—

HEDDA. Yes, yes—I suppose it depends on that. (*Lightly*) But, by-the-bye—here is a letter for you.

TESMAN. Fancy—!

HEDDA (*handing it to him*). It came early this morning.

TESMAN. It's from Aunt Julia! What can it be? (*He lays the packet on the other footstool, opens the letter, runs his eye through it, and jumps up*) Oh, Hedda—she says that poor Aunt Rina is dying!

HEDDA. Well, we were prepared for that.

TESMAN. And that if I want to see her again, I must make haste. I'll run in to them at once.

HEDDA (*suppressing a smile*). Will you run?

TESMAN. Oh, dearest Hedda—if you could only make up your mind to come with me! Just think!

HEDDA (*rises and says wearily, repelling the idea*). No, no, don't ask me. I will not look upon sickness and death. I loathe all sorts of ugliness.

TESMAN. Well, well, then—! (*Bustling around*) My hat—My overcoat—? Oh, in the hall—I do hope I mayn't come too late, Hedda! Eh?

HEDDA. Oh, if you run—

BERTA. Judge Brack is at the door, and wishes to know if he may come in.

TESMAN. At this time! No, I can't possibly see him.

HEDDA. But I can. (*To* BERTA) Ask Judge Brack to come in. (BERTA *goes out*)

HEDDA (*quickly whispering*). The parcel, Tesman! (*She snatches it up from the stool*)

TESMAN. Yes, give it to me!

HEDDA. No, no, I will keep it till you come back.

> (*She goes to the writing-table and places it in the bookcase.* TESMAN *stands in a flurry of haste, and cannot get his gloves on.*
> JUDGE BRACK *enters from the hall.*)

HEDDA (*nodding to him*). You are an early bird, I must say.

BRACK. Yes, don't you think so? (*To* TESMAN) Are you on the move, too?

TESMAN. Yes, I must rush off to my aunts'. Fancy—the invalid one is lying at death's door, poor creature.

BRACK. Dear me, is she indeed? Then on no account let me detain you. At such a critical moment—

TESMAN. Yes, I must really rush—Good-bye! Good-bye! (*He hastens out by the hall door*)

HEDDA (*approaching*). You seem to have made a particularly lively night of it at your rooms, Judge Brack.

BRACK. I assure you I have not had my clothes off, Mrs. Hedda.

HEDDA. Not you, either?

BRACK. No, as you may see. But what has Tesman been telling you of the night's adventures?

HEDDA. Oh, some tiresome story. Only that they went and had coffee somewhere or other.

BRACK. I have heard about that coffee-party already. Eilert Lövborg was not with them, I fancy?

HEDDA. No, they had taken him home before that.

BRACK. Tesman, too?

HEDDA. No, but some of the others, he said.

BRACK (*smiling*). George Tesman is really an ingenuous creature, Mrs. Hedda.

HEDDA. Yes, heaven knows he is. Then is there something behind all this?

BRACK. Yes, perhaps there may be.

HEDDA. Well then, sit down, my dear Judge, and tell your story in comfort.

(*She seats herself to the left of the table.* BRACK *sits near her, at the long side of the table.*)

HEDDA. Now then?

BRACK. I had special reasons for keeping track of my guests—or rather of some of my guests—last night.

HEDDA. Of Eilert Lövborg among the rest, perhaps?

BRACK. Frankly, yes.

HEDDA. Now you make me really curious—

BRACK. Do you know where he and one or two of the others finished the night, Mrs. Hedda?

HEDDA. If it is not quite unmentionable, tell me.

BRACK. Oh no, it's not at all unmentionable. Well, they put in an appearance at a particularly animated soirée.

HEDDA. Of the lively kind?

BRACK. Of the very liveliest—

HEDDA. Tell me more of this, Judge Brack—

BRACK. Lövborg, as well as the others, had been invited in advance. I knew all about it. But he had declined the invitation; for now, as you know, he has become a new man.

HEDDA. Up at the Elvsteds', yes. But he went after all, then?

BRACK. Well, you see, Mrs. Hedda—unhappily the spirit moved him at my rooms last evening—

HEDDA. Yes, I hear he found inspiration.

BRACK. Pretty violent inspiration. Well, I fancy that altered his purpose; for we men folk are unfortunately not always so firm in our principles as we ought to be.

HEDDA. Oh, I am sure you are an exception, Judge Brack. But as to Lövborg—?

BRACK. To make a long story short—he landed at last in Mademoiselle Diana's rooms.

HEDDA. Mademoiselle Diana's?

BRACK. It was Mademoiselle Diana that was giving the soirée, to a select circle of her admirers and her lady friends.

HEDDA. Is she a red-haired woman?

BRACK. Precisely.

HEDDA. A sort of a—singer?

BRACK. Oh yes—in her leisure moments. And moreover a mighty huntress—of men— Mrs. Hedda. You have no doubt heard of her. Eilert Lövborg was one of her most enthusiastic protectors—in the days of his glory.

HEDDA. And how did all this end?

BRACK. Far from amicably, it appears. After a most tender meeting, they seem to have come to blows—

HEDDA. Lövborg and she?

BRACK. Yes. He accused her or her friends of having robbed him. He declared that his pocket-book had disappeared—and other things as well. In short, he seems to have made a furious disturbance.

HEDDA. And what came of it all?

BRACK. It came to a general scrimmage, in which the ladies as well as the gentlemen took part. Fortunately the police at last appeared on the scene.

HEDDA. The police too?

BRACK. Yes. I fancy it will prove a costly frolic for Eilert Lövborg, crazy being that he is.

HEDDA. How so?

BRACK. He seems to have made a violent resistance—to have hit one of the constables on the head and torn the coat off his back. So they had to march him off to the police station with the rest.

HEDDA. How have you learnt all this?

BRACK. From the police themselves.

HEDDA (gazing straight before her). So that is what happened. Then he had no vine-leaves in his hair.

BRACK. Vine-leaves, Mrs. Hedda?

HEDDA (changing her tone). But tell me now, Judge—what is your real reason for tracking out Eilert Lövborg's movements so carefully?

BRACK. In the first place, it could not be entirely indifferent to me if it should appear in the police-court that he came straight from my house.

HEDDA. Will the matter come into court, then?

BRACK. Of course. However, I should scarcely have troubled so much about that. But I thought that, as a friend of the family, it was my duty to supply you and Tesman with a full account of his nocturnal exploits.

HEDDA. Why so, Judge Brack?

BRACK. Why, because I have a shrewd suspicion that he intends to use you as a sort of blind.

HEDDA. Oh, how can you think such a thing!

BRACK. Good heavens, Mrs. Hedda—we have eyes in our head. Mark my words! This Mrs. Elvsted will be in no hurry to leave town again.

HEDDA. Well, even if there should be anything between them, I suppose there are plenty of other places where they could meet.

BRACK. Not a single home. Henceforth, as before, every respectable house will be closed against Eilert Lövborg.

HEDDA. And so ought mine to be, you mean?

BRACK. Yes. I confess it would be more than painful to me if this personage were to be made free of your house. How superfluous, how intrusive, he would be, if he were to force his way into—

HEDDA. —into the triangle?

BRACK. Precisely. It would simply mean that I should find myself homeless.

HEDDA (looks at him with a smile). So you want to be the one cock in the basket—that is your aim.

BRACK (nods slowly and lowers his voice). Yes, that is my aim. And for that I will fight —with every weapon I can command.

HEDDA (her smile vanishing). I see you are a dangerous person—when it comes to the point.

BRACK. Do you think so?

HEDDA. I am beginning to think so. And I am exceedingly glad to think—that you have no sort of hold over me.

BRACK (laughing equivocally). Well, well, Mrs. Hedda—perhaps you are right there. If I had, who knows what I might be capable of?

HEDDA. Come, come now, Judge Brack. That sounds almost like a threat.

BRACK (rising). Oh, not at all! The triangle, you know, ought, if possible, to be spontaneously constructed.

HEDDA. There I agree with you.

BRACK. Well, now I have said all I had to say; and I had better be getting back to town. Goodbye, Mrs. Hedda. (He goes towards the glass door)

HEDDA (rising). Are you going through the garden?

BRACK. Yes, it's a short cut for me.

HEDDA. And then it is the back way, too.

BRACK. Quite so. I have no objection to back ways. They may be piquant enough at times.

HEDDA. When there is ball practice going on, you mean?

BRACK (*in the doorway, laughing to her*). Oh, people don't shoot their tame poultry, I fancy.

HEDDA (*also laughing*). Oh no, when there is only one cock in the basket—

> (*They exchange laughing nods of farewell. He goes. She closes the door behind him.*
> HEDDA, *who has become quite serious, stands for a moment looking out. Presently she goes and peeps through the curtain over the middle doorway. Then she goes to the writing-table, takes* LÖVBORG'S *packet out of the bookcase, and is on the point of looking through its contents.* BERTA *is heard speaking loudly in the hall.* HEDDA *turns and listens. Then she hastily locks up the packet in the drawer, and lays the key on the inkstand.*
> EILERT LÖVBORG, *with his great coat on and his hat in his hand, tears open the hall door. He looks somewhat confused and irritated.*)

LÖVBORG (*looking towards the hall*). And I tell you I must and will come in! There!

> (*He closes the door, turns and sees* HEDDA, *at once regains his self-control, and bows*)

HEDDA (*at the writing table*). Well, Mr. Lövborg, this is rather a late hour to call for Thea.

LÖVBORG. You mean rather an early hour to call on you. Pray pardon me.

HEDDA. How do you know that she is still here?

LÖVBORG. They told me at her lodgings that she had been out all night.

HEDDA (*going to the oval table*). Did you notice anything about the people of the house when they said that?

LÖVBORG (*looks inquiringly at her*). Notice anything about them?

HEDDA. I mean, did they seem to think it odd?

LÖVBORG (*suddenly understanding*). Oh yes, of course! I am dragging her down with me! However, I didn't notice anything.—I suppose Tesman is not up yet?

HEDDA. No—I think not—

LÖVBORG. When did he come home?

HEDDA. Very late.

LÖVBORG. Did he tell you anything?

HEDDA. Yes, I gathered that you had had an exceedingly jolly evening at Judge Brack's.

LÖVBORG. Nothing more?

HEDDA. I don't think so. However, I was so dreadfully sleepy—

> (MRS. ELVSTED *enters through the curtains of the middle doorway*)

MRS. ELVSTED (*going towards him*). Ah, Lövborg! At last—!

LÖVBORG. Yes, at last. And too late!

MRS. ELVSTED (*looks anxiously at him*). What is too late?

LÖVBORG. Everything is too late now. It is all over with me.

MRS. ELVSTED. Oh no, no—don't say that.

LÖVBORG. You will say the same when you hear—

MRS. ELVSTED. I won't hear anything!

HEDDA. Perhaps you would prefer to talk to her alone! If so, I will leave you.

LÖVBORG. No, stay—you too. I beg you to stay.

MRS. ELVSTED. Yes, but I won't hear anything, I tell you.

LÖVBORG. It is not last night's adventures that I want to talk about.

MRS. ELVSTED. What is it then—?

LÖVBORG. I want to say that now our ways must part.

MRS. ELVSTED. Part!

HEDDA (*involuntarily*). I knew it!

LÖVBORG. You can be of no more service to me, Thea.

MRS. ELVSTED. How can you stand there and say that! No more service to you! Am I not to help you now, as before? Are we not to go on working together?

LÖVBORG. Henceforward I shall do no work.

MRS. ELVSTED (*despairingly*). Then what am I to do with my life?

LÖVBORG. You must try to live your life as if you had never known me.

MRS. ELVSTED. But you know I cannot do that!

LÖVBORG. Try if you cannot, Thea. You must go home again—

MRS. ELVSTED (*in vehement protest*). Never in this world! Where you are, there will I be also! I will not let myself be driven away like this! I will remain here! I will be with you when the book appears.

HEDDA (*half aloud, in suspense*). Ah yes—the book!

LÖVBORG (*looks at her*). My book and Thea's; for that is what it is.

MRS. ELVSTED. Yes, I feel that it is. And that is why I have a right to be with you when it appears! I will see with my own eyes how respect and honor pour in upon you afresh. And the happiness—the happiness—oh, I must share it with you!

LÖVBORG. Thea—our book will never appear.

HEDDA. Ah!

MRS. ELVSTED. Never appear!

LÖVBORG. Can never appear.

MRS. ELVSTED (*in agonized foreboding*). Lövborg—what have you done with the manuscript?

HEDDA (*looks anxiously at him*). Yes, the manuscript—?

MRS. ELVSTED. Where is it?

LÖVBORG. Oh Thea—don't ask me about it!

MRS. ELVSTED. Yes, yes, I will know. I demand to be told at once.

LÖVBORG. The manuscript— Well then—I have torn the manuscript into a thousand pieces.

MRS. ELVSTED (*shrieks*). Oh no, no—!

HEDDA (*involuntarily*). But that's not—

LÖVBORG (*looks at her*). Not true, you think?

HEDDA (*collecting herself*). Oh well, of course —since you say so. But it sounded so improbable—

LÖVBORG. It is true, all the same.

MRS. ELVSTED (*wringing her hands*). Oh God —oh God, Hedda—torn his own work to pieces!

LÖVBORG. I have torn my own life to pieces. So why should I not tear my life-work too—?

MRS. ELVSTED. And you did this last night?

LÖVBORG. Yes, I tell you! Tore it into a thousand pieces and scattered them on the fiord —far out. There there is cool sea-water at any rate—let them drift upon it—drift with the current and the wind. And then presently they will sink—deeper and deeper—as I shall, Thea.

MRS. ELVSTED. Do you know, Lövborg, that what you have done with the book—I shall think of it to my dying day as though you had killed a little child.

LÖVBORG. Yes, you are right. It is a sort of child-murder.

MRS. ELVSTED. How could you, then—! Did not the child belong to me too?

HEDDA (*almost inaudibly*). Ah, the child—

MRS. ELVSTED (*breathing heavily*). It is all over then. Well, well, now I will go, Hedda.

HEDDA. But you are not going away from town?

MRS. ELVSTED. Oh, I don't know what I shall do. I see nothing but darkness before me. (*She goes out by the hall door*)

HEDDA (*stands waiting for a moment*). So you are not going to see her home, Mr. Lövborg?

LÖVBORG. I? Through the streets? Would you have people see her walking with me?

HEDDA. Of course I don't know what else may have happened last night. But is it so utterly irretrievable?

LÖVBORG. It will not end with last night—I know that perfectly well. And the thing is that now I have no taste for that sort of life either. I won't begin it anew. She has broken my courage and my power of braving life out.

HEDDA (*looking straight before her*). So that pretty little fool has had her fingers in a man's destiny. (*Looks at him*) But all the same, how could you treat her so heartlessly?

LÖVBORG. Oh, don't say that it was heartless!

HEDDA. To go and destroy what has filled her whole soul for months and years! You do not call that heartless!

LÖVBORG. To you I can tell the truth, Hedda.

HEDDA. The truth?

LÖVBORG. First promise me—give me your word—that what I now confide to you Thea shall never know.

HEDDA. I give you my word.

LÖVBORG. Good. Then let me tell you that what I said just now was untrue.

HEDDA. About the manuscript?

LÖVBORG. Yes. I have not torn it to pieces—nor thrown it into the fiord.

HEDDA. No, n— But—where is it then?

LÖVBORG. I have destroyed it none the less—utterly destroyed it, Hedda!

HEDDA. I don't understand.

LÖVBORG. Thea said that what I had done seemed to her like a child-murder.

HEDDA. Yes, so she said.

LÖVBORG. But to kill his child—that is not the worst thing a father can do to it.

HEDDA. Not the worst?

LÖVBORG. No. I wanted to spare Thea from hearing the worst.

HEDDA. Then what is the worst?

LÖVBORG. Suppose now, Hedda, that a man—in the small hours of the morning—came home to his child's mother after a night of riot and debauchery, and said: "Listen—I have been here and there—in this place and in that. And I have taken our child with me —to this place and to that. And I have lost the child—utterly lost it. The devil knows into what hands it may have fallen—who may have had their clutches on it."

HEDDA. Well—but when all is said and done, you know—that was only a book—

LÖVBORG. Thea's pure soul was in that book.

HEDDA. Yes, so I understand.

LÖVBORG. And you can understand, too, that for her and me together no future is possible.

HEDDA. What path do you mean to take then?

LÖVBORG. None. I will only try to make an end of it all—the sooner the better.

HEDDA (*a step nearer to him*). Eilert Lövborg—listen to me. Will you not try to—to do it beautifully?

LÖVBORG. Beautifully? (*Smiling*) With vine-leaves in my hair, as you used to dream in the old days—?

HEDDA. No, no. I have lost my faith in the vine-leaves. But beautifully, nevertheless! For once in a way!—Good-bye! You must go now—and do not come here any more.

LÖVBORG. Good-bye, Mrs. Tesman. And give George Tesman my love. (*He is on the point of going*)

HEDDA. No, wait! I must give you a memento to take with you.

(*She goes to the writing-table and opens the drawer and the pistol-case; then returns to* LÖVBORG *with one of the pistols*)

LÖVBORG (*looks at her*). This? Is this the memento?

HEDDA (*nodding slowly*). Do you recognize it? It was aimed at you once.

LÖVBORG. You should have used it then.

HEDDA. Take it—and do you use it now.

LÖVBORG (*puts the pistol in his breast pocket*). Thanks!

HEDDA. And beautifully, Eilert Lövborg. Promise me that!

LÖVBORG. Good-bye, Hedda Gabler. (*He goes out by the hall door*)

(HEDDA *listens for a moment at the door. Then she goes up to the writing-table, takes out the packet of manuscript, peeps under the cover, draws a few of the sheets half out, and looks at them. Next she goes over and seats herself in the armchair beside the stove, with the packet in her lap. Presently she opens the stove door, and then the packet.*)

HEDDA (*throws one of the quires into the fire and whispers to herself*). Now I am burning your child, Thea!—Burning it, curly-locks! (*Throwing one or two more quires into the stove*) Your child and Eilert Lövborg's. (*Throws the rest in*) I am burning—I am burning your child.

ACT 4

SCENE: *The same rooms at the* TESMANS'. *It is evening. The drawing-room is in darkness. The back room is lighted by the hanging lamp over the table. The curtains over the glass door are drawn close.*

(HEDDA, *dressed in black, walks to and fro in the dark room. Then she goes into the back room and disappears for a moment to the left. She is heard to strike a few chords on the piano. Presently she comes in sight again, and returns to the drawing-room.*

BERTA *enters from the right, through the inner room, with a lighted lamp, which she places on the table in front of the corner settee in the drawing-room. Her eyes are red with weeping, and she has black ribbons in her cap. She goes quietly and circumspectly out to the right.*

HEDDA *goes up to the glass door, lifts the curtain a little aside, and looks out into the darkness.*

Shortly afterwards, MISS TESMAN, *in mourning, with a bonnet and veil on, comes in from the hall.* HEDDA *goes towards her and holds out her hand.*)

MISS TESMAN. Yes, Hedda, here I am, in mourning and forlorn; for now my poor sister has at last found peace.

HEDDA. I have heard the news already, as you see. Tesman sent me a card.

MISS TESMAN. Yes, he promised me he would. But nevertheless I thought that to Hedda—here in the house of life—I ought myself to bring the tidings of death.

HEDDA. That was very kind of you.

MISS TESMAN. Ah, Rina ought not to have left us just now. This is not the time for Hedda's house to be a house of mourning.

HEDDA (*changing the subject*). She died quite peacefully, did she not, Miss Tesman?

MISS TESMAN. Oh, her end was so calm, so beautiful. And then she had the unspeakable happiness of seeing George once more—and bidding him good-bye.—Has he come home yet?

HEDDA. No. He wrote that he might be detained. But won't you sit down?

MISS TESMAN. No thank you, my dear, dear Hedda. I should like to, but I have so much to do. I must prepare my dear one for her rest as well as I can. She shall go to her grave looking her best.

HEDDA. Can I not help you in any way?

MISS TESMAN. Oh, you must not think of it! Hedda Tesman must have no hand in such mournful work. Nor let her thoughts dwell on it either—not at this time.

HEDDA. One is not always mistress of one's thoughts—

MISS TESMAN (*continuing*). Ah yes, it is the way of the world. At home we shall be sewing a shroud; and here there will soon be sewing too, I suppose—but of another sort, thank God!

(GEORGE TESMAN *enters by the hall door*)

HEDDA. Ah, you have come at last!

TESMAN. You here, Aunt Julia? With Hedda? Fancy that!

MISS TESMAN. I was just going, my dear boy. Well, have you done all you promised?

TESMAN. No; I'm really afraid I have forgotten half of it. I must come to you again tomorrow. Today my brain is all in a whirl. I can't keep my thoughts together.

MISS TESMAN. Why, my dear George, you mustn't take it in this way.

TESMAN. Mustn't—? How do you mean?

MISS TESMAN. Even in your sorrow you must rejoice, as I do—rejoice that she is at rest.

TESMAN. Oh yes, yes—you are thinking of Aunt Rina.

HEDDA. You will feel lonely now, Miss Tesman.

MISS TESMAN. Just at first, yes. But that will not last very long, I hope. I daresay I shall soon find an occupant for poor Rina's little room.

TESMAN. Indeed? Who do you think will take it? Eh?

MISS TESMAN. Oh, there's always some poor invalid or other in want of nursing, unfortunately.

HEDDA. Would you really take such a burden upon you again?

MISS TESMAN. A burden! Heaven forgive you, child—it has been no burden to me.

HEDDA. But suppose you had a total stranger on your hands—

MISS TESMAN. Oh, one soon makes friends with sick folk; and it's such an absolute necessity for me to have some one to live for. Well, heaven be praised, there may soon be something in this house, too, to keep an old aunt busy.

HEDDA. Oh, don't trouble about anything here.

TESMAN. Yes, just fancy what a nice time we three might have together, if—?

HEDDA. If—?

TESMAN (*uneasily*). Oh, nothing. It will all come right. Let us hope so—eh?

MISS TESMAN. Well, well, I daresay you two want to talk to each other. (*Smiling*) And perhaps Hedda may have something to tell you too, George. Good-bye! I must go home to Rina. (*Turning at the door*) How strange it is to think that now Rina is with me and with my poor brother as well!

TESMAN. Yes, fancy that, Aunt Julia! Eh?

(MISS TESMAN *goes out by the hall door*)

HEDDA (*follows* TESMAN *coldly and searchingly with her eyes*). I almost believe your Aunt Rina's death affects you more than it does your Aunt Julia.

TESMAN. Oh, it's not that alone. It's Eilert I am so terribly uneasy about.

HEDDA (*quickly*). Is there anything new about him?

TESMAN. I looked in at his rooms this afternoon, intending to tell him the manuscript was in safe keeping.

HEDDA. Well, did you not find him?

TESMAN. No. He wasn't at home. But afterwards I met Mrs. Elvsted, and she told me that he had been here early this morning.

HEDDA. Yes, directly after you had gone.

TESMAN. And he said that he had torn his manuscript to pieces—eh?

HEDDA. Yes, so he declared.

TESMAN. Why, good heavens, he must have been completely out of his mind! And I suppose you thought it best not to give it back to him, Hedda?

HEDDA. No, he did not get it.

TESMAN. But of course you told him that we had it?

HEDDA. No. (*Quickly*) Did you tell Mrs. Elvsted?

TESMAN. No; I thought I had better not. But you ought to have told him. Fancy, if, in desperation, he should go and do himself some injury! Let me have the manuscript, Hedda! I will take it to him at once. Where is it?

HEDDA (*cold and immovable, leaning on the armchair*). I have not got it.

TESMAN. Have not got it? What in the world do you mean?

HEDDA. I have burnt it—every line of it.

TESMAN (*with a violent movement of terror*). Burnt! Burnt Eilert's manuscript!

HEDDA. Don't scream so. The servant might hear you.

TESMAN. Burnt! Why, good God—! No, no, no! It's impossible!

HEDDA. It is so, nevertheless.

TESMAN. Do you know what you have done, Hedda? It's unlawful appropriation of lost property. Fancy that! Just ask Judge Brack, and he'll tell you what it is.

HEDDA. I advise you not to speak of it—either to Judge Brack, or to any one else.

TESMAN. But how could you do anything so unheard-of? What put it into your head? What possessed you? Answer me that—eh?

HEDDA (*suppressing an almost imperceptible smile*). I did it for your sake, George.

TESMAN. For my sake!

HEDDA. This morning, when you told me about what he had read to you—

TESMAN. Yes, yes—what then?

HEDDA. You acknowledged that you envied him his work.

TESMAN. Oh, of course I didn't mean that literally.

HEDDA. No matter—I could not bear the idea that any one should throw you into the shade.

TESMAN (*in an outburst of mingled doubt and joy*). Hedda! Oh, is this true? But—but—I never knew you to show your love like that before. Fancy that!

HEDDA. Well, I may as well tell you that—just at this time— (*Impatiently, breaking off*) No, no; you can ask Aunt Julia. She will tell you, fast enough.

TESMAN. Oh, I almost think I understand you, Hedda! (*Clasps his hands together*) Great heavens! do you really mean it! Eh?

HEDDA. Don't shout so. The servant might hear.

TESMAN (*laughing in irrepressible glee*). The servant! Why, how absurd you are, Hedda. It's only my old Berta! Why, I'll tell Berta myself.

HEDDA (*clenching her hands together in desperation*). Oh, it is killing me,—it is killing me, all this!

TESMAN. What is, Hedda? Eh?

HEDDA (*coldly, controlling herself*). All this—absurdity—George.

TESMAN. Absurdity! Do you see anything absurd in my being overjoyed at the news! But after all perhaps I had better not say anything to Berta.

HEDDA. Oh—why not that too?

TESMAN. No, no, not yet! But I must certainly tell Aunt Julia. And then that you have begun to call me George too! Fancy that! Oh, Aunt Julia will be so happy—so happy.

HEDDA. When she hears that I have burnt Eilert Lövborg's manuscript—for your sake?

TESMAN. No, by-the-bye—that affair of the manuscript—of course nobody must know about that. But that you love me so much, Hedda—Aunt Julia must really share my joy in that! I wonder, now, whether this sort of thing is usual in young wives? Eh?

HEDDA. I think you had better ask Aunt Julia that question too.

TESMAN. I will indeed, some time or other. (*Looks uneasy and downcast again*) And yet the manuscript—the manuscript! Good God! it is terrible to think what will become of poor Eilert now.

> (MRS. ELVSTED, *dressed as in the first act, with hat and cloak, enters by the hall door*)

MRS. ELVSTED (*greets them hurriedly, and says in evident agitation*). Oh, dear Hedda, forgive my coming again.

HEDDA. What is the matter with you, Thea?

TESMAN. Something about Eilert Lövborg again—eh?

MRS. ELVSTED. Yes! I am dreadfully afraid some misfortune has happened to him.

HEDDA (*seizes her arm*). Ah,—do you think so?

TESMAN. Why, good Lord—what makes you think that, Mrs. Elvsted?

MRS. ELVSTED. I heard them talking of him at my boarding-house—just as I came in. Oh, the most incredible rumors are afloat about him to-day.

TESMAN. Yes, fancy, so I heard too! And I can bear witness that he went straight home to bed last night. Fancy that!

HEDDA. Well, what did they say at the boarding-house?

MRS. ELVSTED. Oh, I couldn't make out anything clearly. Either they knew nothing definite, or else— They stopped talking when they saw me; and I did not dare to ask.

TESMAN (*moving about uneasily*). We must hope—we must hope that you misunderstood them, Mrs. Elvsted.

MRS. ELVSTED. No, no; I am sure it was of him they were talking. And I heard something about the hospital or—

TESMAN. The hospital?

HEDDA. No—surely that cannot be!

MRS. ELVSTED. Oh, I was in such mortal terror! I went to his lodgings and asked for him there.

HEDDA. You could make up your mind to that, Thea!

MRS. ELVSTED. What else could I do? I really could bear the suspense no longer.

TESMAN. But you didn't find him either—eh?

MRS. ELVSTED. No. And the people knew nothing about him. He hadn't been home since yesterday afternoon, they said.

TESMAN. Yesterday! Fancy, how could they say that?

MRS. ELVSTED. Oh, I am sure something terrible must have happened to him.

TESMAN. Hedda dear—how would it be if I were to go and make inquiries—?

HEDDA. No, no—don't you mix yourself up in this affair.

> (JUDGE BRACK, *with his hat in his hand, enters by the hall door, which* BERTA *opens, and closes behind him. He looks grave and bows in silence.*)

TESMAN. Oh, is that you, my dear Judge? Eh?

BRACK. Yes. It was imperative I should see you this evening.

TESMAN. I can see you have heard the news about Aunt Rina.

BRACK. Yes, that among other things.

TESMAN. Isn't it sad—eh?

BRACK. Well, my dear Tesman, that depends on how you look at it.

TESMAN (*looks doubtfully at him*). Has anything else happened?

BRACK. Yes.

HEDDA (*in suspense*). Anything sad, Judge Brack?

BRACK. That, too, depends on how you look at it, Mrs. Tesman.

MRS. ELVSTED (*unable to restrain her anxiety*). Oh! it is something about Eilert Lövborg!

BRACK (*with a glance at her*). What makes you think that, Madam? Perhaps you have already heard something—?

MRS. ELVSTED (*in confusion*). No, nothing at all, but—

TESMAN. Oh, for heaven's sake, tell us!

BRACK (*shrugging his shoulders*). Well, I regret to say Eilert Lövborg has been taken to the hospital. He is lying at the point of death.

MRS. ELVSTED (*shrieks*). Oh God! Oh God—

TESMAN. To the hospital! And at the point of death.

HEDDA (*involuntarily*). So soon then—

MRS. ELVSTED (*wailing*). And we parted in anger, Hedda!

HEDDA (*whispers*). Thea—Thea—be careful!

MRS. ELVSTED (*not heeding her*). I must go to him! I must see him alive!

BRACK. It is useless, Madam. No one will be admitted.

MRS. ELVSTED. Oh, at least tell me what has happened to him? What is it?

TESMAN. You don't mean to say that he has himself— Eh?

HEDDA. Yes, I am sure he has.

TESMAN. Hedda, how can you—?

BRACK (*keeping his eyes fixed upon her*). Unfortunately you have guessed quite correctly, Mrs. Tesman.

MRS. ELVSTED. Oh, how horrible!

TESMAN. Himself, then! Fancy that!

HEDDA. Shot himself!

BRACK. Rightly guessed again, Mrs. Tesman.

MRS. ELVSTED (*with an effort at self-control*). When did it happen, Mr. Brack?

BRACK. This afternoon—between three and four.

TESMAN. But, good Lord, where did he do it? Eh?

BRACK (*with some hesitation*). Where? Well —I suppose at his lodgings.

MRS. ELVSTED. No, that cannot be; for I was there between six and seven.

BRACK. Well, then, somewhere else. I don't know exactly. I only know that he was found—. He had shot himself—in the breast.

MRS. ELVSTED. Oh, how terrible! That he should die like that!

HEDDA (*to* BRACK). Was it in the breast?

BRACK. Yes—as I told you.

HEDDA. Not in the temple?

BRACK. In the breast, Mrs. Tesman.

HEDDA. Well, well—the breast is a good place, too.

BRACK. How do you mean, Mrs. Tesman?

HEDDA (*evasively*). Oh, nothing—nothing.

TESMAN. And the wound is dangerous, you say—eh?

BRACK. Absolutely mortal. The end has probably come by this time.

MRS. ELVSTED. Yes, yes, I feel it. The end! The end! Oh, Hedda—!

TESMAN. But tell me, how have you learnt all this?

BRACK (*curtly*). Through one of the police. A man I had some business with.

HEDDA (*in a clear voice*). At last a deed worth doing!

TESMAN (*terrified*). Good heavens, Hedda; what are you saying?

HEDDA. I say there is beauty in this.

BRACK. H'm, Mrs. Tesman—

TESMAN. Beauty! Fancy that!

MRS. ELVSTED. Oh, Hedda, how can you talk of beauty in such an act!

HEDDA. Eilert Lövborg has himself made up his account with life. He has had the courage to do—the one right thing.

MRS. ELVSTED. No, you must never think that was how it happened! It must have been in delirium that he did it.

TESMAN. In despair!

HEDDA. That he did not. I am certain of that.

MRS. ELVSTED. Yes, yes! In delirium! Just as when he tore up our manuscript.

BRACK (*starting*). The manuscript? Has he torn that up?

MRS. ELVSTED. Yes, last night.

TESMAN (*whispers softly*). Oh, Hedda, we shall never get over this.

BRACK. H'm, very extraordinary.

TESMAN (*moving about the room*). To think of Eilert going out of the world in this way! And not leaving behind him the book that would have immortalized his name—

MRS. ELVSTED. Oh, if only it could be put together again!

TESMAN. Yes, if it only could! I don't know what I would not give—

MRS. ELVSTED. Perhaps it can, Mr. Tesman.

TESMAN. What do you mean?

MRS. ELVSTED (*searches in the pocket of her dress*). Look here. I have kept all the loose notes he used to dictate from.

HEDDA (*a step forward*). Ah—!

TESMAN. You have kept them, Mrs. Elvsted! Eh?

MRS. ELVSTED. Yes, I have them here. I put them in my pocket when I left home. Here they still are—

TESMAN. Oh, do let me see them!

MRS. ELVSTED (*hands him a bundle of papers*). But they are in such disorder—all mixed up.

TESMAN. Fancy, if we could make something out of them, after all! Perhaps if we two put our heads together—

MRS. ELVSTED. Oh, yes, at least let us try—

TESMAN. We will manage it! We must! I will dedicate my life to this task.

HEDDA. You, George! Your life?

TESMAN. Yes, or rather all the time I can spare. My own collections must wait in the meantime. Hedda—you understand, eh? I owe this to Eilert's memory.

HEDDA. Perhaps.

TESMAN. And so, my dear Mrs. Elvsted, we will give our whole minds to it. There is no use in brooding over what can't be undone —eh? We must try to control our grief as much as possible, and—

MRS. ELVSTED. Yes, yes, Mr. Tesman, I will do the best I can.

TESMAN. Well then, come here. I can't rest until we have looked through the notes. Where shall we sit? Here? No, in there, in the back room. Excuse me, my dear Judge. Come with me, Mrs. Elvsted.

MRS. ELVSTED. Oh, if only it were possible!

> (TESMAN and MRS. ELVSTED *go into the back room. She takes off her hat and cloak. They both sit at the table under the hanging lamp, and are soon deep in an eager examination of the papers.* HEDDA *crosses to the stove and sits in the armchair. Presently* BRACK *goes up to her.*)

HEDDA (*in a low voice*). Oh, what a sense of freedom it gives one, this act of Eilert Lövborg's.

BRACK. Freedom, Mrs. Hedda? Well, of course, it is a release for him—

HEDDA. I mean for me. It gives me a sense of freedom to know that a deed of deliberate courage is still possible in this world,—a deed of spontaneous beauty.

BRACK (*smiling*). H'm—my dear Mrs. Hedda—

HEDDA. Oh, I know what you are going to say. For you are a kind of a specialist too, like—you know!

BRACK (*looking hard at her*). Eilert Lövborg was more to you than perhaps you are willing to admit to yourself. Am I wrong?

HEDDA. I don't answer such questions. I only know Eilert Lövborg has had the courage to live his life after his own fashion. And then—the last great act, with its beauty! Ah! that he should have the will and the strength to turn away from the banquet of life—so early.

BRACK. I am sorry, Mrs. Hedda,—but I fear I must dispel an amiable illusion.

HEDDA. Illusion.

BRACK. Which could not have lasted long in any case.

HEDDA. What do you mean?

BRACK. Eilert Lövborg did not shoot himself voluntarily.

HEDDA. Not voluntarily?

BRACK. No. The thing did not happen exactly as I told it.

HEDDA (in suspense). Have you concealed something? What is it?

BRACK. For poor Mrs. Elvsted's sake I idealized the facts a little.

HEDDA. What are the facts?

BRACK. First, that he is already dead.

HEDDA. At the hospital?

BRACK. Yes—without regaining consciousness.

HEDDA. What more have you concealed?

BRACK. This—the event did not happen at his lodgings.

HEDDA. Oh, that can make no difference.

BRACK. Perhaps it may. For I must tell you—Eilert Lövborg was found shot in—in Mademoiselle Diana's boudoir.

HEDDA (makes a motion as if to rise, but sinks back again). That is impossible, Judge Brack! He cannot have been there again to-day.

BRACK. He was there this afternoon. He went there, he said, to demand the return of something which they had taken from him. Talked wildly about a lost child—

HEDDA. Ah—so that was why—

BRACK. I thought probably he meant his manuscript; but now I hear he destroyed that himself. So I suppose it must have been his pocketbook.

HEDDA. Yes, no doubt. And there—there he was found?

BRACK. Yes, there. With a pistol in his breastpocket, discharged. The ball had lodged in a vital part.

HEDDA. In the breast—yes.

BRACK. No—in the bowels.

HEDDA (looks up at him with an expression of loathing). That too! Oh, what curse is it that makes everything I touch turn ludicrous and mean?

BRACK. There is one point more, Mrs. Hedda —another disagreeable feature in the affair.

HEDDA. And what is that?

BRACK. The pistol he carried—

HEDDA (breathless). Well? What of it?

BRACK. He must have stolen it.

HEDDA (leaps up). Stolen it! That is not true! He did not steal it!

BRACK. No other explanation is possible. He must have stolen it— Hush!

(TESMAN and MRS. ELVSTED have risen from the table in the back room, and come into the drawing room)

TESMAN (with the papers in both his hands). Hedda dear, it is almost impossible to see under that lamp. Think of that!

HEDDA. Yes, I am thinking.

TESMAN. Would you mind our sitting at your writing-table—eh?

HEDDA. If you like. (Quickly) No, wait! Let me clear it first!

TESMAN. Oh, you needn't trouble, Hedda. There is plenty of room.

HEDDA. No, no; let me clear it, I say! I will take these things in and put them on the piano. There!

(*She has drawn out an object, covered with sheet music, from under the bookcase, places several other pieces of music upon it, and carries the whole into the inner room, to the left.* TESMAN *lays the scraps of paper on the writing-table, and moves the lamp there from the corner table.* HEDDA *returns.*)

HEDDA (*behind* MRS. ELVSTED's *chair, gently ruffling her hair*). Well, my sweet Thea,— how goes it with Eilert Lövborg's monument?

MRS. ELVSTED (*looks dispiritedly up at her*). Oh, it will be terribly hard to put in order.

TESMAN. We must manage it. I am determined. And arranging other people's papers is just the work for me.

(HEDDA *goes over to the stove, and seats herself on one of the foot-stools.* BRACK *stands over her, leaning on the armchair.*)

HEDDA (*whispers*). What did you say about the pistol?

BRACK (*softly*). That he must have stolen it.

HEDDA. Why stolen it?

BRACK. Because every other explanation ought to be impossible, Mrs. Hedda.

HEDDA. Indeed?

BRACK (*glances at her*). Of course Eilert Lövborg was here this morning. Was he not?

HEDDA. Yes.

BRACK. Were you alone with him?

HEDDA. Part of the time.

BRACK. Did you not leave the room whilst he was here?

HEDDA. No.

BRACK. Try to recollect. Were you not out of the room a moment?

HEDDA. Yes, perhaps just a moment—out in the hall.

BRACK. And where was your pistol-case during that time?

HEDDA. I had it locked up in—

BRACK. Well, Mrs. Hedda?

HEDDA. The case stood there on the writing-table.

BRACK. Have you looked since, to see whether both the pistols are there?

HEDDA. No.

BRACK. Well, you need not. I saw the pistol found in Lövborg's pocket, and I knew it at once as the one I had seen yesterday—and before, too.

HEDDA. Have you it with you?

BRACK. No; the police have it.

HEDDA. What will the police do with it?

BRACK. Search till they find the owner.

HEDDA. Do you think they will succeed?

BRACK (*bends over her and whispers*). No, Hedda Gabler—not so long as I say nothing.

HEDDA (*looks frightened at him*). And if you do not say nothing,—what then?

BRACK (*shrugs his shoulders*). There is always the possibility that the pistol was stolen.

HEDDA (*firmly*). Death rather than that.

BRACK (*smiling*). People say such things—but they don't do them.

HEDDA (*without replying*). And supposing the pistol was stolen, and the owner is discovered? What then?

BRACK. Well, Hedda—then comes the scandal.

HEDDA. The scandal!

BRACK. Yes, the scandal—of which you are mortally afraid. You will, of course, be brought before the court—both you and Mademoiselle Diana. She will have to explain how the thing happened—whether it was an accidental shot or murder. Did the pistol go off as he was trying to take it out of his pocket, to threaten her with? Or did she tear the pistol out of his hand, shoot him, and push it back into his pocket? That would be quite like her; for she is an able-bodied young person, this same Mademoiselle Diana.

HEDDA. But *I* have nothing to do with all this repulsive business.

BRACK. No. But you will have to answer the question: Why did you give Eilert Lövborg the pistol? And what conclusions will people draw from the fact that you did give it to him?

HEDDA (*lets her head sink*). That is true. I did not think of that.

BRACK. Well, fortunately, there is no danger, so long as I say nothing.

HEDDA (*looks up at him*). So I am in your power, Judge Brack. You have me at your beck and call, from this time forward.

BRACK (*whispers softly*). Dearest Hedda—believe me—I shall not abuse my advantage.

HEDDA. I am in your power none the less. Subject to your will and your demands. A slave, a slave then! (*Rises impetuously*) No, I cannot endure the thought of that! Never!

BRACK (*looks half-mockingly at her*). People generally get used to the inevitable.

HEDDA (*returns his look*). Yes, perhaps. (*She crosses to the writing-table. Suppressing an involuntary smile, she imitates* TESMAN'S *intonations.*) Well? Are you getting on, George? Eh?

TESMAN. Heaven knows, dear. In any case it will be the work of months.

HEDDA (*as before*). Fancy that! (*Passes her hands softly through* MRS. ELVSTED'S *hair*) Doesn't it seem strange to you, Thea? Here are you sitting with Tesman—just as you used to sit with Eilert Lövborg?

MRS. ELVSTED. Ah, if I could only inspire your husband in the same way.

HEDDA. Oh, that will come too—in time.

TESMAN. Yes, do you know, Hedda—I really think I begin to feel something of the sort. But won't you go and sit with Brack again?

HEDDA. Is there nothing I can do to help you two?

TESMAN. No, nothing in the world. (*Turning his head*) I trust to you to keep Hedda company, my dear Brack.

BRACK (*with a glance at* HEDDA). With the very greatest of pleasure.

HEDDA. Thanks. But I am tired this evening. I will go in and lie down a little on the sofa.

TESMAN. Yes, do dear—eh?

(HEDDA *goes into the back room and draws the curtains. A short pause. Suddenly she is heard playing a wild dance on the piano.*)

MRS. ELVSTED (*starts from her chair*). Oh—what is that?

TESMAN (*runs to the doorway*). Why, my dearest Hedda—don't play dance music to-night! Just think of Aunt Rina! And of Eilert too!

HEDDA (*puts her head out between the curtains*). And of Aunt Julia. And of all the rest of them.—After this, I will be quiet. (*Closes the curtains again*)

TESMAN (*at the writing-table*). It's not good for her to see us at this distressing work. I'll tell you what, Mrs. Elvsted,—you shall take the empty room at Aunt Julia's, and then I will come over in the evenings, and we can sit and work there—eh?

HEDDA (*in the inner room*). I hear what you are saying, Tesman. But how am *I* to get through the evenings out here?

TESMAN (*turning over the papers*). Oh, I daresay Judge Brack will be so kind as to look in now and then, even though I am out.

BRACK (*in the armchair, calls out gaily*). Every blessed evening, with all the pleasure in life, Mrs. Tesman! We shall get on capitally together, we two!

HEDDA (*speaking loud and clear*). Yes, don't you flatter yourself we will, Judge Brack? Now that you are the one cock in the basket—

(*A shot is heard within.* TESMAN, MRS. ELVSTED, *and* BRACK *leap to their feet.*)

TESMAN. Oh, now she is playing with those pistols again.

(*He throws back the curtains and runs in, followed by* MRS. ELVSTED. HEDDA *lies stretched on the sofa, lifeless. Confusion and cries.* BERTA *enters in alarm from the right.*)

TESMAN (*shrieks to* BRACK). Shot herself! Shot herself in the temple! Fancy that!

BRACK (*half-fainting in the armchair*). Good God!—people don't do such things.

Hedda is the main character, and a consideration of what Ibsen would have us make of her may suggest what he would have us make of the play. Almost at once we become conscious of Hedda's pride and independence and her dissatisfaction with the dull life that seems to be closing around her. We can have some sympathy with her dissatisfaction. Tesman is an amiable dullard, an academic grubber without ideas, a cautious careerist. His attachment to Hedda seems to be primarily—or at least in part—vanity in her aristocratic background as a kind of mark of his own success: he would like to see her, his wife, the center of a "select" little circle. Ibsen has been careful to give us the full value of Tesman's conventionality of mind, his fussy "Eh's," his constantly reiterated fatuous bafflement in his "Fancy that now," his triviality of feeling. His knitted morning shoes, which he had so much missed all during the long honeymoon trip, sum up, at the very beginning of the play, the husband of Hedda. We shall come back to Tesman, but for the moment we are concerned with the general picture of the husband and the kind of life he will probably make for Hedda.

Hedda rebels at the thought of life with Tesman, and we can scarcely blame her. But on second thought we realize, remembering her talk with Judge Brack, that the situation is one of her own creating. She had danced herself tired, as she tells Judge Brack, had become bored with life, had found no man to excite her, and in full awareness of Tesman's qualities had married him, just because he wanted, as she puts it, to provide for her. Thus cynically and somewhat desperately she has made her bargain. But she does not keep

it. She lacks sportsmanship and honor, the very virtues we would assume to be the virtues of her aristocratic heritage.

Not that she is overtly unfaithful to Tesman. She is far too afraid of social pressures for that. We see that it is not virtue but conventionality of mind that makes her a faithful wife. In a sense she is just as conventional in mind and as trivial in feeling as her husband. Notice, for example, how astonished and even envious she is that Thea, seemingly a much more timid creature than she, has been willing to make a bold decision and follow Lövborg. We know from Hedda's early relations with Lövborg that she had been drawn to him, partly at least, by her curiosity about his dissipations, a kind of dishonest curiosity, for she had wanted vicarious satisfactions from his wild life without the risks. And we know that when Judge Brack, in the end, pushes himself forward as her lover, he does so by a blackmail based on her fear of breaking the conventions. He is clever enough to sense this fear in her character, and to guess that if anything would make her take the risk of an illicit affair with him it would be, ironically enough, the threat of scandal.

Yet Hedda, with all this timorousness and conventionality of mind, longs for some moment of noble and fulfilling freedom. She has thought of Lövborg as a person who, by his very dissipations, his willingness to throw away respectability and his career, might achieve freedom: the free pagan with vine leaves in his hair. But for Hedda, freedom is a negative thing, for she has found no positive value of any kind in life. She cannot conceive of Lövborg's redemption and his fulfillment through his work as an achievement of freedom. So she drives Lövborg to his ruin and to death to gratify her notion of freedom, to make him affirm by his death that at least one kind of freedom is possible.

But we may notice here that her attitude toward Lövborg's suicide as she drives him toward it is very much like her earlier attitude toward his dissipations: she would get a vicarious satisfaction out of his experience at no risk to herself. This vicarious satisfaction, however, fails her too. Instead of dying with a noble gesture, the pistol ball through his head or heart, Lövborg falls with a wound in the bowels, and not even with the dignity of suicide. The noble gesture that Hedda had planned—at somebody else's expense, of course—has, as she puts it, turned, "ludicrous and mean." Her faith in the possibility of significance in life is destroyed. We must emphasize the phrase "her faith," for we are not to equate her view with the dramatist's view. Her faith comes to nothing. Even her own suicide, though the ball is in her head, is scarcely a free act: she is driven to it by desperation, by the closing in of the world on her. Her faith comes to nothing, because her whole approach to the question of freedom and significance had been negative, merely destructive.

Thinking along this line, let us turn back to earlier elements in the play. For one thing, Ibsen's first presentation of Hedda describes her hair as "not particularly abundant." This at first may strike us as a peculiarly irrelevant detail, but its apparent irrelevance may point to a deeper relevance. Then we find Thea, who is played off as the opposite (the ordinary word is *foil*) of Hedda, given hair that is "unusually abundant and wavy." Later on we learn how, back in school, Hedda had tortured the little Thea by pulling her hair, as though driven by an unconscious envy, and how she had threatened to burn it off her head. In Act 2, in the episode with Hedda, Thea, and Lövborg, Hedda strokes Thea's hair (as she will do at the very end of the play as she goes into the next room to her own death). At the end of Act 2, when Hedda has won the victory over Thea and sent Lövborg off to the party at Judge Brack's establishment, we find the following passage:

MRS. ELVSTED. You have some hidden motive in this, Hedda!

HEDDA. Yes, I have. I want for once in my life to have power to mold a human destiny.

MRS. ELVSTED. Have you not the power?

HEDDA. I have not—and have never had it.

MRS. ELVSTED. Not your husband's?

HEDDA. Do you think that is worth the trouble? Oh, if you could only understand how poor I am. And fate has made you so rich! (*Clasps her passionately in her arms*) I think I must burn your hair off, after all.

Here Hedda, in her first moment of triumph over Thea, cries out in envy of Thea, whom fate has made "rich." But rich in what sense? At first thought, it may seem that Hedda is saying that she herself is poor because she has only George Tesman while Thea has Lövborg. But at this moment Hedda has control of Lövborg, and if she were courageous enough, as courageous as Thea, might have him as a lover. But it is not merely the possession of Lövborg that is in question. It is the particular kind of relation to Lövborg. Hedda's relation is sterile, destructive. Thea's has been fruitful, creative. In this connection we remember that the book on which Thea had worked with Lövborg is called their "child," and that much is made of the fact. At the very end of Act 3, when Hedda seems to have scored her greatest triumph, she has sent Lövborg out to shoot himself "beautifully." Now that he is, as it seems, completely hers and Thea is vanquished, Hedda burns the manuscript:

HEDDA. Now I am burning your child, Thea!—Burning it, curly-locks! (*Throwing one or two more quires into the stove*) Your child and Eilert Lövborg's. (*Throws the rest in*) I am burning—I am burning your child.

The last mark of Hedda's moment of triumph is to destroy the "child," the sign of Thea's creative relation with Lövborg. But we see that here, too, Hedda comes back to the subject of Thea's hair, and we see how closely it is associated with the subject of Thea's creativity. The women's hair functions as a symbol for creativity, for fertility, the mark of the power that Thea has and Hedda lacks. Ibsen, of course, did not "make up" this symbol: woman's hair has, for thousands of years, had this symbolic significance, the mark of the fully and fruitfully feminine. Hedda, whose hair is "not particularly abundant," lacks, as it were, something of the specially feminine quality, and in the end she refuses her natural feminine role as mother.

In Hedda's first private conversation with Judge Brack, in Act 2, she says that she does not want children: "no responsibilities for me!" Yet we are given to understand that she is pregnant, as she implies to her husband significantly in the same breath when she tells him that she has destroyed the manuscript, the "child" of Thea and Lövborg. So with this fact, another motive enters into Hedda's suicide. After she has found that Lövborg's beautiful gesture is nothing but a ludicrous and mean accident, she can find no significance in life. Her own unwanted burden of creativity is something she cannot bear, and in one sense her suicide is a flight from it.

General Gabler's pistols may be seen to have a symbolic function. In fact they suggest several different levels of meaning. For one thing, they are reminders of Hedda's aristocratic background, a mark of her pride. For another, they imply the dangerous, destructive quality inherent in her. But for a third thing, the pistols carry some symbolic implication of masculinity. And in this connection we can see that three times in the play the pistols are used to indicate a relation between Hedda and a man. Tesman is afraid of them. Hedda fires at Judge Brack to make him jump, to scare him. She had once threatened Lövborg with a pistol, at the time when he was trying to pass from the role of comrade to that of lover.

The symbolism of pistols and hair thus implies that because of some unnatural masculine quality, some defect in femininity, in creativity, Hedda rejects love. And if we take this line of reasoning, her suicide is also a rejection of Judge Brack. It is a declaration of her independence, a refusal to accept the role of the "molded" instead of the "molder," a desperate gesture to affirm significance— but all this does not prevent the act from being a last and characteristic rejection of love. It does not matter that Judge Brack's love is of a rather debasing and tawdry order; it is still a kind of love, and Hedda rejects it.

Obviously Thea is a natural foil to Hedda. Of the various conflicts in the play (between Judge Brack and Hedda, between Tesman and Hedda, between Lövborg and Tesman), the main conflict is between Hedda and Thea for the possession of Lövborg.

What is Thea like? We have already learned that she is "curly-locks," and in the first presentation of her we find the adjectives *fragile, pretty,* and *soft,* adjectives carrying implications of the feminine. With these qualities, with her feminine devotion, she has, to a degree, regenerated and gained possession of Lövborg. At least she has possession of him until he comes again into Hedda's orbit, where Hedda can play upon the old attraction between them and can challenge his manhood by taunting him about his cowardice in not going to the party and in being, in a way, under the thumb of Thea. But, as Lövborg says to Hedda, Thea is "stupid" about certain things, for instance, about the hidden significance, of the relation that had existed between Hedda and Lövborg and about the streak of desperation in Lövborg's character and his wild appetite for experience. She does not fully understand Lövborg, and therefore fails to regenerate or possess him fully.

Thea seems to be the very image of feminine devotion and self-abnegation, but is she quite that simple? Let us remember her own situation, an unloved wife, childless, on a lonely country estate. Lövborg brings to her the single possibility of fulfilment. It is not merely selfless devotion to him that spurs her to her act of courage; it is also her only chance for life. She says to Hedda: "I only know this, that I must live here, where Eilert Lövborg is—if I am to live at all." But we must ask ourselves if Thea's desertion of Lövborg when he tells her that he has destroyed the manuscript is a mark of selfless love and devotion. Instead of taking his act as an indication of his desperate condition and realizing that now is his moment of greatest need for her, she says: "Do you know, Lövborg, that what you have done with the book —I shall think of it to my dying day as though you had killed a little child." And then, after his reply, she says: "How could you, then—! Did not the child belong to me too?" With that she leaves him. Here her devotion has changed to resentment, perhaps to a sense of outraged egotism. One might properly speculate that Thea is not really interested in ideas and books, and the work done with Lövborg is a kind of substitute for the real children of which she has been deprived.

We recall that when Thea parts from Lövborg she says, "I see nothing but darkness before me." She goes out, we assume at that moment, to her own tragedy. But later when she returns to the Tesman house and learns of Lövborg's death and hears Tesman say that Lövborg has gone without leaving the book to immortalize his name, she produces the notes and she and Tesman fall to work to reconstruct Lövborg's book. Both do this in memory of Lövborg. Tesman has his bad conscience about the destruction of the manuscript, which, in a way, he had been party to. But also he is fulfilling his natural function: "arranging other people's papers is just the work for me," he says happily. As for Thea, her work is done in memory of Lövborg, but we know that as soon as Hedda and Lövborg are well cold underground, the common work of Thea and Tesman will lead to a match. How do we know this? Hedda implies as much as she goes out of the room to her death, but the little tableau of the two with their heads together under the lamp speaks louder than words. Thea will get her home and family, after all, and Lövborg's book about the future will have done it for her. Tesman will suit her perfectly. She will never know what Hedda had known with such desperate clarity, that Tesman is a fatuous dullard. Tesman will serve her purpose, and that is all, in the end, that she will ask. Poor Lövborg, whom she had not understood, will be forgotten.

Is this a way of saying that Thea's virtues are not real virtues? No, her virtues remain virtues. She had been devoted to Lövborg; she had performed acts of great courage for him. But this is a way of saying that people are complicated, and that we do not have in this play merely the "good" Thea set against the "bad" Hedda. Thea, in her own fashion, had used Lövborg.

This brings us to another, and more general, consideration. How are the characters to be "grouped" in the play? What kind of pattern do they make in relation to the central idea of the play? We can say, from one standpoint, that Hedda is the central character, and that we are to see other characters in relation to her. She is a study in a certain kind of neurotic frustration, a certain kind of destructiveness masquerading under a romantic idealism, under her passion for the noble and beautiful gesture. The pattern of characters may be taken in terms of the effect of her destructiveness upon each. But is the play to be taken, then, just as a case history, a psychiatric history cleverly dramatized?

The play is considerably more than that. Hedda's story is a comment on our human capacity for self-deception and destructiveness. It makes a judgment, implicitly of course, on conduct and values. But we can go beyond that. If we take Lövborg as the central figure, we arrive at a broader conception of the meaning of the play. Lövborg is the creative force, the creative personality, in the world of the play. This world is so bound by convention, so barren of ideas, and so lacking in courage, that a man like Lövborg is out of place. In a blind rebellion —and in his own weakness, we may add—he throws away his talents, the force that would shape the "future." But everybody around him, aware of barrenness and lack of creativity, preys on Lövborg in one way or another. Hedda, in the old days, had sought experience vicariously through him, and finally drives him to his death to affirm her dream of the noble gesture. Thea had used him to fill up her childless life, had made his book her "child." Tesman, with Lövborg's death, gets his own proper occupation, "arranging other people's papers," mechanical scholarship devoid of ideas. In this perspective the play becomes a comment on the frustration of creativity of various kinds in the modern world. Lövborg's work, the vision of the future, will survive, but it will survive, ironically enough, through Tesman and Thea, two decent, dull people who do not really grasp the meaning of the work they are reconstructing from Lövborg's notes.

Is *Hedda Gabler* a tragedy? Certainly, it is a serious play, and it is a play involving violence and death. But seriousness of meaning and violence of action are not enough to constitute what we ordinarily think of as tragedy. To take things at the simplest level, we expect to give the tragic character some sympathy or admiration. It is easy to see why we sympathize with a tragic character like

Romeo in Shakespeare's play. He is an attractive personality. It is only a little less easy to see why we admire him. He is willing to take great risks, to pay the highest price for what he values most, the love of Juliet. There is some largeness in his character. It is more difficult to see how we sympathize with a tragic character like Richard III of Shakespeare's play by that name, when Richard is bloodthirsty, and ambitious, and cunning. But in Shakespeare's play he is set in a world largely populated by vicious, confused, or self-deceiving weaklings, and he at least has the strength of mind and honesty to see his own position quite clearly and not to flinch or apologize to himself or for himself. So he draws, against our will and our ultimate moral judgment, our sympathy and admiration.

But how does Ibsen first present Hedda? It is in the performance of a mean-spirited act. First, she complains about the scent of the flowers, the very flowers that are there as a tribute to her. Second, and quite deliberately as we later learn, she hurts old Aunt Juliana's feelings about her new bonnet. Ibsen poisons us against Hedda from the very start. It will be difficult to see any largeness of mind or spirit after this. All Hedda's talk about nobility and beauty comes to us against this recollection. And when she complains that all she touches turns "mean and ludicrous," we already know why: the meanness of spirit is in her.

The only character here who might serve as the central figure of a tragedy is Lövborg himself. He has some largeness, and we can sympathize with him. But the step to his ruin is a step forced on him by Hedda, and forced on him by her playing on a weak and mean streak in his character. He is, we are tempted to say, too much the victim to be a tragic hero. Yet when he discovers the loss of his manuscript the lie he tells Thea has something of the tragic quality—even if it is a lie. In the end, however, he dies with the pistol ball in his bowels, not in his head or heart, and he dies by accident in a sordid house. It is as though Ibsen were saying "This is the only kind of end possible in this kind of world." The play, then, instead of being a tragedy, is a kind of parody, an intended parody, of tragedy, almost an anti-

tragedy, a way of indicating that the tragic scale is not possible in a world that has forfeited, or lost, its sense of mission, its creativity.

EXERCISES

1. Aunt Juliana is a good woman, we grant that. But can you discover anything in her makeup to lead you to sympathize with Hedda's distaste for her? Can it be said that she has more than a trace of George Tesman's fatuousness? What is her attitude toward Lövborg? Does this make us modify our notion of her goodness?

2. Very early in the first act Tesman says to his aunt, "We were so sorry we couldn't give you a seat in the carriage. But you saw what a pile of boxes Hedda had to bring with her." What is the purpose of this little episode in the play?

3. In Act 1, after Juliana goes, Hedda looks out at the yellowing leaves and comments on them. What is the meaning of this?

4. In the first act, before Hedda appears, Tesman and his aunt have discussed Lövborg. Later, with no prompting from anyone, Hedda mentions him. The reference to the home of the Elvsteds suggests him to her. She says: "Tell me, Tesman—isn't it somewhere near there that he—that—Eilert Lövborg is living?" What is the significance of the fact that she says "he" before she mentions Lövborg's name, or before it has been mentioned in her presence? What lies behind her unprovoked question?

5. What is the significance of the fact that everyone who comes to the Tesman house the first morning mentions Lövborg?

6. What are we to make of the fact that Hedda, when she hears that there may be a competition for the post that Tesman seeks, says, "Fancy, Tesman, there will be a sort of sporting interest in that"?

7. Define the dramatic intention of the last few speeches in Act 1.

8. Interpret the fact that Lövborg has put into his current book about the present nothing but "what everyone would agree with," and into the book about the future has put his "true self."

9. In Act 2, when Hedda is showing Lövborg the photographs taken during the honeymoon trip, she looks up once at Tesman "affectionately." How does Ibsen mean this stage direction to be understood? If this is only simulated affection, why does Hedda simulate it at this particular moment?

10. More than one impulse is involved in Lövborg's taking his glass of punch in Act 2. What are these several impulses?

11. The end of Act 2 is a triumphant statement by Hedda; she sees Lövborg returning with "vine-leaves in his hair." What is the tone of the opening of Act 3? What is the value of this shift of tone?

12. What is Tesman's attitude toward Lövborg's new book, the book still in manuscript? When he tells Hedda, in Act 3, that he has picked up the manuscript and intends to take it back to Lövborg, is he entirely sincere in the statement of intention? Or does he really hope, in some obscure and unadmitted way, that Hedda will prevent him? Hedda tempts him in this scene. Compare the scene with the scene in Shakespeare's *Macbeth* where Lady Macbeth tempts her husband to kill Duncan (act I, scene 7).

13. In Act 3, about two-thirds of the way into the act, Hedda and Judge Brack have had a quiet conversation about their relationship. Just after Brack has left, Lövborg suddenly bursts into the room. What dramatic contrasts are involved here?

14. When Tesman, in Act 4, asks for Lövborg's manuscript from Hedda and she tells him that she has burnt it, he cries out, "Burnt! Burnt Eilert's manuscript!" The stage direction indicates that this is accompanied by a "violent movement of terror." Of what is Tesman terrified? A little later Tesman says to Hedda: "Do you know what you have done, Hedda? It's unlawful appropriation of lost property." Is "unlawful appropriation of lost property" an accurate description of the content of Hedda's act in destroying the manuscript? If it is not, why does Ibsen put this in the mouth of Tesman? What does it tell us about Tesman? What does it imply about the nature

and depth of his shock when he discovers the manuscript to be destroyed? On the same point, what does his sudden joy tell us when he thinks that Hedda has done the deed for love of him? How fundamental had been his moral distress? Later, when Tesman finds that Thea has the notes of Lövborg's book he undertakes to reconstruct the work, and says: "I owe this to Eilert's memory." Why does he "owe" something to Lövborg's memory? Are his motives mixed in undertaking this project?

15. At the very end of the play we see Thea and Tesman together with the notes, hear Tesman suggesting that he and Thea work at Aunt Juliana's house, and note Judge Brack's confidence that he at last has the upper hand with Hedda. Does all this suggest a kind of new sympathy and justification for Hedda?

16. When the death shot is heard, Tesman says: "Oh, now she is playing with those pistols again." What ironical elements are involved in the word *playing*?

17. What ironical elements are involved in Judge Brack's final words: "Good God!—people don't do such things"?

18. If you have read Gustave Flaubert's novel *Madame Bovary*, how would you compare Emma Bovary and Hedda Gabler?

19. The theme of *Hedda Gabler* contrasts with that of *Antony and Cleopatra*. Hedda, surrounded by a world "ordered" to the point of dull routine, wishes for something dashing and heroic. She asks that Lövborg come from the banquet "with vine-leaves in his hair"—somewhat, perhaps, like Antony in the scene on Pompey's galley. How far may the contrast between the two plays be carried?

*PYGMALION**

George Bernard Shaw (1856–1950)

ACT 1

Covent Garden at 11.15 p.m. Torrents of heavy summer rain. Cab whistles blowing frantically in all directions. Pedestrians running for shelter into the market and under the portico of St Paul's Church, where there are already several people, among them a lady and her daughter in evening dress. They are all peering out gloomily at the rain, except

one man with his back turned to the rest, who seems wholly preoccupied with a notebook in which he is writing busily.

The church clock strikes the first quarter.

THE DAUGHTER [*in the space between the central pillars, close to the one on her left*]

---

* Shaw's somewhat eccentric ideas on language included the occasional use of spaced-out lettering to indicate emphasis where most writers would use italics. Notice, too, Shaw's frequent omission of apostrophes.

I'm getting chilled to the bone. What can Freddy be doing all this time? He's been gone twenty minutes.

THE MOTHER [*on her daughter's right*] Not so long. But he ought to have got us a cab by this.

A BYSTANDER [*on the lady's right*] He wont get no cab not until half-past eleven, missus, when they come back after dropping their theatre fares.

THE MOTHER. But we must have a cab. We cant stand here until half-past eleven. It's too bad.

THE BYSTANDER. Well, it aint my fault, missus.

THE DAUGHTER. If Freddy had a bit of gumption, he would have got one at the theatre door.

THE MOTHER. What could he have done, poor boy?

THE DAUGHTER. Other people got cabs. Why couldnt he?

> *Freddy rushes in out of the rain from the Southampton Street side, and comes between them closing a dripping umbrella. He is a young man of twenty, in evening dress, very wet round the ankles.*

THE DAUGHTER. Well, havnt you got a cab?

FREDDY. Theres not one to be had for love or money.

THE MOTHER. Oh, Freddy, there must be one. You cant have tried.

THE DAUGHTER. It's too tiresome. Do you expect us to go and get one ourselves?

FREDDY. I tell you theyre all engaged. The rain was so sudden: nobody was prepared; and everybody had to take a cab. Ive been to Charing Cross one way and nearly to Ludgate Circus the other; and they were all engaged.

THE MOTHER. Did you try Trafalgar Square?

FREDDY. There wasnt one at Trafalgar Square.

THE DAUGHTER. Did you try?

FREDDY. I tried as far as Charing Cross Station. Did you expect me to walk to Hammersmith?

THE DAUGHTER. You havnt tried at all.

THE MOTHER. You really are very helpless, Freddy. Go again; and dont come back until you have found a cab.

FREDDY. I shall simply get soaked for nothing.

THE DAUGHTER. And what about us? Are we to stay here all night in this draught, with next to nothing on? You selfish pig—

FREDDY. Oh, very well: I'll go, I'll go. [*He opens his umbrella and dashes off Strandwards, but comes into collision with a flower girl, who is hurrying in for shelter, knocking her basket out of her hands. A blinding flash of lightning, followed instantly by a rattling peal of thunder, orchestrates the incident*].

THE FLOWER GIRL. Nah then, Freddy: look wh' y' gowin, deah.

FREDDY. Sorry [*he rushes off*].

THE FLOWER GIRL [*picking up her scattered flowers and replacing them in the basket*] Theres menners f' yer! Te-oo banches of voylets trod into the mad. [*She sits down on the plinth of the column, sorting her flowers, on the lady's right. She is not at all an attractive person. She is perhaps eighteen, perhaps twenty, hardly older. She wears a little sailor hat of black straw that has long been exposed to the dust and soot of London and has seldom if ever been brushed. Her hair needs washing rather badly: its mousy color can hardly be natural. She wears a shoddy black coat that reaches nearly to her knees and is shaped to her waist. She has a brown skirt with a coarse apron. Her boots are much the worse for wear. She is no doubt as clean as she can afford to be; but compared to the ladies she is very dirty. Her features are no worse than theirs; but their condition leaves something to be desired; and she needs the services of a dentist*].

THE MOTHER. How do you know that my son's name is Freddy, pray?

THE FLOWER GIRL. Ow, eez ye-ooa san, is e? Wal, fewd dan y' de-ooty bawmz a mather should, eed now bettern to spawl a pore gel's flahrzn than ran awy athaht pyin. Will ye-oo py me f'them? [*Here, with apologies, this desperate attempt to represent her dialect without a phonetic alphabet must be abandoned as unintelligible outside London*].

THE DAUGHTER. Do nothing of the sort, mother. The idea!

THE MOTHER. Please allow me, Clara. Have you any pennies?

THE DAUGHTER. No. Ive nothing smaller than sixpence.

THE FLOWER GIRL [*hopefully*] I can give you change for a tanner, kind lady.

THE MOTHER [*to Clara*] Give it to me. [*Clara parts reluctantly*]. Now [*to the girl*] this is for your flowers.

THE FLOWER GIRL. Thank you kindly, lady.

THE DAUGHTER. Make her give you the change. These things are only a penny a bunch.

THE MOTHER. Do hold your tongue, Clara. [*To the girl*] You can keep the change.

THE FLOWER GIRL. Oh, thank you, lady.

THE MOTHER. Now tell me how you know that young gentleman's name.

THE FLOWER GIRL. I didnt.

THE MOTHER. I heard you call him by it. Dont try to deceive me.

THE FLOWER GIRL [*protesting*] Who's trying to deceive you? I called him Freddy or Charlie same as you might yourself if you was talking to a stranger and wished to be pleasant. [*She sits down beside her basket*].

THE DAUGHTER. Sixpence thrown away! Really, mamma, you might have spared Freddy that. [*She retreats in disgust behind the pillar*].

An elderly gentleman of an amiable military type rushes into the shelter, and closes a dripping umbrella. He is in the same plight as Freddy, very wet about the ankles. He is in evening dress, with a light overcoat. He takes the place left vacant by the daughter's retirement.

THE GENTLEMAN. Phew!

THE MOTHER [*to the gentleman*] Oh, sir, is there any sign of its stopping?

THE GENTLEMAN. I'm afraid not. It started worse than ever about two minutes ago [*he goes to the plinth beside the flower girl; puts up his foot on it; and stoops to turn down his trouser ends*].

THE MOTHER. Oh dear! [*She retires sadly and joins her daughter*].

THE FLOWER GIRL [*taking advantage of the military gentleman's proximity to establish friendly relations with him*] If it's worse, it's a sign it's nearly over. So cheer up, Captain; and buy a flower off a poor girl.

THE GENTLEMAN. I'm sorry. I havnt any change.

THE FLOWER GIRL. I can give you change, Captain.

THE GENTLEMAN. For a sovereign? Ive nothing less.

THE FLOWER GIRL. Garn! Oh do buy a flower off me, Captain. I can change half-a-crown. Take this for tuppence.

THE GENTLEMAN. Now dont be troublesome: theres a good girl. [*Trying his pockets*] I really havnt any change—Stop: heres three hapence, if thats any use to you [*he retreats to the other pillar*].

THE FLOWER GIRL [*disappointed, but thinking three halfpence better than nothing*] Thank you, sir.

THE BYSTANDER [*to the girl*] You be careful: give him a flower for it. Theres a bloke here behind taking down every blessed word youre saying. [*All turn to the man who is taking notes*].

THE FLOWER GIRL [*springing up terrified*] I aint done nothing wrong by speaking to the gentleman. Ive a right to sell flowers if I keep off the kerb. [*Hysterically*] I'm a respectable girl: so help me, I never spoke to him except to ask him to buy a flower off me. [*General hubbub, most sympathetic to the flower girl, but deprecating her excessive sensibility. Cries of* Dont start hollerin. Who's hurting you? Nobody's going to touch you. Whats the good of fussing? Steady on. Easy easy, etc., *come from the elderly staid spectators, who pat her comfortingly. Less patient ones bid her shut her head, or ask her roughly what is wrong with her. A remoter group, not knowing what the matter is, crowd in and increase the noise with question and answer:* Whats the row? Whatshe do? Where is he? A tec taking her down. What! him? Yes: him over there: Took money off the gentleman, etc. *The flower girl, distraught and mobbed, breaks through them to the gentleman, crying wildly*] Oh, sir, dont let him charge me. You dunno what it means to me. Theyll take away my character and drive me on the streets for speaking to gentlemen. They—

THE NOTE TAKER [*coming forward on her right, the rest crowding after him*] There, there, there, there! who's hurting you, you silly girl? What do you take me for?

THE BYSTANDER. It's all right: he's a gentleman: look at his boots. [*Explaining to the note taker*] She thought you was a copper's nark, sir.

THE NOTE TAKER [*with quick interest*] Whats a copper's nark?

THE BYSTANDER [*inapt at definition*] It's a— well, it's a copper's nark, as you might say. What else would you call it? A sort of informer.

THE FLOWER GIRL [*still hysterical*] I take my Bible oath I never said a word—

THE NOTE TAKER [*overbearing but good-humored*] Oh, shut up, shut up. Do I look like a policeman?

THE FLOWER GIRL [*far from reassured*] Then what did you take down my words for? How do I know whether you took me down right? You just shew me what youve wrote about me. [*The note taker opens his book and holds it steadily under her nose, though the pressure of the mob trying to read it over his shoulders would upset a weaker man*]. Whats that? That aint proper writing. I cant read that.

THE NOTE TAKER. I can. [*Reads, reproducing her pronunciation exactly*] "Cheer ap, Keptin; n' baw ya flahr orf a pore gel."

THE FLOWER GIRL [*much distressed*] It's because I called him Captain. I meant no harm. [*To the gentleman*] Oh, sir, dont let him lay a charge agen me for a word like that. You—

THE GENTLEMAN. Charge! I make no charge. [*To the note taker*] Really, sir, if you are a detective, you need not begin protecting me against molestation by young women until I ask you. Anybody could see that the girl meant no harm.

THE BYSTANDERS GENERALLY [*demonstrating against police espionage*] Course they could. What business is it of yours? You mind your own affairs. He wants promotion, he does. Taking down people's words. Girl never said a word to him. What harm if she did? Nice thing a girl cant shelter from the rain without being insulted, etc., etc., etc. [*She is conducted by the more sympathetic demonstrators back to her plinth, where she resumes her seat and struggles with her emotion*].

THE BYSTANDER. He aint a tec. He's a blooming busybody: thats what he is. I tell you, look at his boots.

THE NOTE TAKER [*turning on him genially*] And how are all your people down at Selsey?

THE BYSTANDER [*suspiciously*] Who told you my people come from Selsey?

THE NOTE TAKER. Never you mind. They did. [*To the girl*] How do you come to be so far east? You were born in Lisson Grove.

THE FLOWER GIRL [*appalled*] Oh, what harm is there in my leaving Lisson Grove? It wasnt fit for a pig to live in; and I had to pay four-and-six a week. [*In tears*] Oh, boo—hoo—oo—

THE NOTE TAKER. Live where you like; but stop that noise.

THE GENTLEMAN [*to the girl*] Come, come! he cant touch you: you have a right to live where you please.

A SARCASTIC BYSTANDER [*thrusting himself between the note taker and the gentleman*] Park Lane, for instance. I'd like to go into the Housing Question with you, I would.

THE FLOWER GIRL [*subsiding into a brooding melancholy over her basket, and talking very low-spiritedly to herself*] I'm a good girl, I am.

THE SARCASTIC BYSTANDER [*not attending to her*] Do you know where *I* come from?

THE NOTE TAKER [*promptly*] Hoxton.

> *Titterings. Popular interest in the note taker's performance increases.*

THE SARCASTIC ONE [*amazed*] Well, who said I didnt? Bly me! You know everything, you do.

THE FLOWER GIRL [*still nursing her sense of injury*] Aint no call to meddle with me, he aint.

THE BYSTANDER [*to her*] Of course he aint. Dont you stand it from him. [*To the note taker*] See here: what call have you to know about people what never offered to meddle with you? Wheres your warrant?

SEVERAL BYSTANDERS [*encouraged by this seeming point of law*] Yes: wheres your warrant?

THE FLOWER GIRL. Let him say what he likes. I dont want to have no truck with him.

THE BYSTANDER. You take us for dirt under your feet, dont you? Catch you taking liberties with a gentleman!

THE SARCASTIC BYSTANDER. Yes: tell him where he come from if you want to go fortune-telling.

THE NOTE TAKER. Cheltenham, Harrow, Cambridge, and India.

THE GENTLEMAN. Quite right. [*Great laughter. Reaction in the note taker's favor. Exclamations of* He knows all about it. Told him proper. Hear him tell the toff where he come from? *etc.*]. May I ask, sir, do you do this for your living at a music hall?

THE NOTE TAKER. Ive thought of that. Perhaps I shall some day.

> *The rain has stopped; and the persons on the outside of the crowd begin to drop off.*

THE FLOWER GIRL [*resenting the reaction*] He's no gentleman, he aint, to interfere with a poor girl.

THE DAUGHTER [*out of patience, pushing her way rudely to the front and displacing the gentleman, who politely retires to the other side of the pillar*] What on earth is Freddy doing? I shall get pneumonia if I stay in this draught any longer.

THE NOTE TAKER [*to himself, hastily making a note of her pronunciation of "monia"*] Earlscourt.

THE DAUGHTER [*violently*] Will you please keep your impertinent remarks to yourself.

THE NOTE TAKER. Did I say that out loud? I didnt mean to. I beg your pardon. Your mother's Epsom, unmistakeably.

THE MOTHER [*advancing between her daughter and the note taker*] How very curious! I was brought up in Largelady Park, near Epsom.

THE NOTE TAKER [*uproariously amused*] Ha! ha! What a devil of a name! Excuse me. [*To the daughter*] You want a cab, do you?

THE DAUGHTER. Dont dare speak to me.

THE MOTHER. O please, please Clara. [*Her daughter repudiates her with an angry shrug and retires haughtily*]. We should be so grateful to you, sir, if you found us a cab. [*The note taker produces a whistle*]. Oh, thank you. [*She joins her daughter*].

> *The note taker blows a piercing blast.*

THE SARCASTIC BYSTANDER. There! I knowed he was a plain-clothes copper.

THE BYSTANDER. That aint a police whistle: thats a sporting whistle

THE FLOWER GIRL [*still preoccupied with her wounded feelings*] He's no right to take away my character. My character is the same to me as any lady's.

THE NOTE TAKER. I dont know whether youve noticed it; but the rain stopped about two minutes ago.

THE BYSTANDER. So it has. Why didnt you say so before? and us losing our time listening to your silliness! [*He walks off towards the Strand*].

THE SARCASTIC BYSTANDER. I can tell where y o u come from. You come from Anwell. Go back there.

THE NOTE TAKER [*helpfully*] *H*anwell.

THE SARCASTIC BYSTANDER [*affecting great distinction of speech*] Thenk you, teacher. Haw haw! So long [*he touches his hat with mock respect and strolls off*].

THE FLOWER GIRL. Frightening people like that! How would he like it himself?

THE MOTHER. It's quite fine now, Clara. We can walk to a motor bus. Come. [*She gathers her skirts above her ankles and hurries off towards the Strand*].

THE DAUGHTER. But the cab—[*her mother is out of hearing*]. Oh, how tiresome! [*She follows angrily*].

All the rest have gone except the note taker, the gentleman, and the flower girl, who sits arranging her basket and still pitying herself in murmurs.

THE FLOWER GIRL. Poor girl! Hard enough for her to live without being worrited and chivied.

THE GENTLEMAN [*returning to his former place on the note taker's left*] How do you do it, if I may ask?

THE NOTE TAKER. Simply phonetics. The science of speech. Thats my profession: also my hobby. Happy is the man who can make a living by his hobby! You can spot an Irishman or a Yorkshireman by his brogue. *I* can place any man within six miles. I can place him within two miles in London. Sometimes within two streets.

THE FLOWER GIRL. Ought to be ashamed of himself, unmanly coward!

THE GENTLEMAN. But is there a living in that?

THE NOTE TAKER. Oh yes. Quite a fat one. This is an age of upstarts. Men begin in Kentish Town with £80 a year, and end in Park Lane with a hundred thousand. They want to drop Kentish Town; but they give themselves away every time they open their mouths. Now I can teach them—

THE FLOWER GIRL. Let him mind his own business and leave a poor girl—

THE NOTE TAKER [*explosively*] Woman: cease this detestable boohooing instantly; or else seek the shelter of some other place of worship.

THE FLOWER GIRL [*with feeble defiance*] Ive a right to be here if I like, same as you.

THE NOTE TAKER. A woman who utters such depressing and disgusting sounds has no right to be anywhere—no right to live. Remember that you are a human being with a soul and the divine gift of articulate speech: that your native language is the language of Shakespear and Milton and The Bible: and dont sit there crooning like a bilious pigeon.

THE FLOWER GIRL [*quite overwhelmed, looking up at him in mingled wonder and deprecation without daring to raise her head*] Ah-ah-ah-ow-ow-ow-oo!

THE NOTE TAKER [*whipping out his book*] Heavens! what a sound! [*He writes; then holds out the book and reads, reproducing her vowels exactly*] Ah-ah-ah-ow-ow-ow-oo!

THE FLOWER GIRL [*tickled by the performance, and laughing in spite of herself*] Garn!

THE NOTE TAKER. You see this creature with her kerbstone English: the English that will keep her in the gutter to the end of her days. Well, sir, in three months I could pass that girl off as a duchess at an ambassador's garden party. I could even get her a place as lady's maid or shop assistant, which requires better English. Thats the sort of thing I do for commercial millionaires. And on the profits of it I do genuine scientific work in phonetics, and a little as a poet on Miltonic lines.

THE GENTLEMAN. I am myself a student of Indian dialects; and—

THE NOTE TAKER [*eagerly*] Are you? Do you know Colonel Pickering, the author of Spoken Sanscrit?

THE GENTLEMAN. I a m Colonel Pickering. Who are you?

THE NOTE TAKER. Henry Higgins, author of Higgins's Universal Alphabet.

PICKERING [*with enthusiasm*] I came from India to meet you.

HIGGINS. I was going to India to meet you.

PICKERING. Where do you live?

HIGGINS. 27A Wimpole Street. Come and see me tomorrow.

PICKERING. I'm at the Carlton. Come with me now and lets have a jaw over some supper.

HIGGINS. Right you are.

THE FLOWER GIRL [*to Pickering, as he passes her*] Buy a flower, kind gentleman. I'm short for my lodging.

PICKERING. I really havnt any change. I'm sorry [*he goes away*].

HIGGINS [*shocked at the girl's mendacity*] Liar. You said you could change half-a-crown.

THE FLOWER GIRL [*rising in desperation*] You ought to be stuffed with nails, you ought. [*Flinging the basket at his feet*] Take the whole blooming basket for sixpence.

The church clock strikes the second quarter.

HIGGINS [*hearing in it the voice of God, rebuking him for his Pharisaic want of charity to the poor girl*] A reminder. [*He raises his hat solemnly; then throws a handful of money into the basket and follows Pickering*].

THE FLOWER GIRL [*picking up a half-crown*] Ah-ow-ooh! [*Picking up a couple of florins*] Aaah-ow-ooh! [*Picking up several coins*] Aaaaaah-ow-ooh! [*Picking up a half-sovereign*] Aaaaaaaaaaaah-ow-ooh!!!

FREDDY [*springing out of a taxicab*] Got one at last. Hallo! [*To the girl*] Where are the two ladies that were here?

THE FLOWER GIRL. They walked to the bus when the rain stopped.

FREDDY. And left me with a cab on my hands! Damnation!

THE FLOWER GIRL [*with grandeur*] Never mind, young man. *I'm going home in a taxi.* [*She sails off to the cab. The driver puts his hand behind him and holds the door firmly shut against her. Quite understanding his mistrust, she shews him her handful of money*]. Eightpence aint no object to me, Charlie. [*He grins and opens the door*]. Angel court, Drury Lane, round the corner of Micklejohn's oil shop. Lets see how fast you can make her hop it. [*She gets in and pulls the door to with a slam as the taxicab starts*].

FREDDY. Well, I'm dashed!

ACT 2

Next day at 11 a.m. Higgins's laboratory in Wimpole Street. It is a room on the first floor, looking on the street, and was meant for the drawing room. The double doors are in the middle of the back wall; and persons entering find in the corner to their right two tall file cabinets at right angles to one another against the walls. In this corner stands a flat writing-table, on which are a phonograph, a laryngoscope, a row of tiny organ pipes with bellows, a set of lamp chimneys for singing flames with burners attached to a gas plug in the wall by an indiarubber tube, several tuning-forks of different sizes, a life-size image of half a human head, shewing in section the vocal organs, and a box containing a supply of wax cylinders for the phonograph.

Further down the room, on the same side, is a fireplace, with a comfortable leather-covered easy-chair at the side of the hearth nearest the door, and a coal-scuttle. There is a clock on the mantelpiece. Between the fireplace and the phonograph table is a stand for newspapers.

On the other side of the central door, to the left of the visitor, is a cabinet of shallow drawers. On it is a telephone and the telephone directory. The corner beyond, and most of the side wall, is occupied by a grand piano, with the keyboard at the end furthest from the door, and a bench for the player extending the full length of the keyboard. On the piano is a dessert dish heaped with fruit and sweets, mostly chocolates.

The middle of the room is clear. Besides the easy-chair, the piano bench, and two chairs at the phonograph table, there is one stray chair. It stands near the fireplace. On the walls, engravings: mostly Piranesis and mezzotint portraits. No paintings.

Pickering is seated at the table, putting down some cards and a tuning-fork which he has been using. Higgins is standing up near him, closing two or three file drawers which are hanging out. He appears in the morning light as a robust, vital, appetizing sort of man of forty or thereabouts, dressed in a professional-looking black frock-coat with a white linen collar and black silk tie. He is of the energetic, scientific type, heartily, even violently interested in everything that can be studied as a scientific subject, and careless about himself and other people, including their feelings. He is, in fact, but for his years and size, rather like a very impetuous baby "taking notice" eagerly and loudly, and requiring almost as much watching to keep him out of unintended mischief. His manner varies from genial bullying when he is in a good humor to stormy petulance when anything goes wrong; but he is so entirely frank and void of malice that he remains likeable even in his least reasonable moments.

HIGGINS [*as he shuts the last drawer*] Well, I think thats the whole show.

PICKERING. It's really amazing. I havnt taken half of it in, you know.

HIGGINS. Would you like to go over any of it again?

PICKERING [*rising and coming to the fireplace, where he plants himself with his back to the fire*] No, thank you; not now. I'm quite done up for this morning.

HIGGINS [*following him, and standing beside him on his left*] Tired of listening to sounds?

PICKERING. Yes. It's a fearful strain. I rather fancied myself because I can pronounce twenty-four distinct vowel sounds; but your

hundred and thirty beat me. I cant hear a bit of difference between most of them.

HIGGINS [*chuckling, and going over to the piano to eat sweets*] Oh, that comes with practice. You hear no difference at first; but you keep on listening, and presently you find theyre all as different as A from B. [*Mrs Pearce looks in: she is Higgins's housekeeper*]. Whats the matter?

MRS PEARCE [*hesitating, evidently perplexed*] A young woman wants to see you sir.

HIGGINS. A young woman! What does she want?

MRS PEARCE. Well, sir, she says youll be glad to see her when you know what she's come about. She's quite a common girl, sir. Very common indeed. I should have sent her away, only I thought perhaps you wanted her to talk into your machines. I hope Ive not done wrong; but really you see such queer people sometimes—youll excuse me, I'm sure, sir—

HIGGINS. Oh, thats all right, Mrs. Pearce. Has she an interesting accent?

MRS PEARCE. Oh, something dreadful, sir, really. I dont know how you can take an interest in it.

HIGGINS [*to Pickering*] Lets have her up. Shew her up, Mrs Pearce [*he rushes across to his working table and picks out a cylinder to use on the phonograph*].

MRS PEARCE [*only half resigned to it*] Very well, sir. It's for you to say. [*she goes downstairs*].

HIGGINS. This is rather a bit of luck. I'll shew you how I make records. We'll set her talking; and I'll take it down first in Bell's visible Speech; then in broad Romic; and then we'll get her on the phonograph so that you can turn her on as often as you like with the written transcript before you.

MRS PEARCE [*returning*] This is the young woman, sir.

The flower girl enters in state. She has a hat with three ostrich feathers, orange, sky-blue, and red. She has a nearly clean apron, and the shoddy coat has been tidied a little. The pathos of this deplorable figure, with its innocent vanity and consequential air, touches Pickering, who has already straightened himself in the presence of Mrs Pearce. But as to Higgins, the only distinction he makes between men and women is that when he is neither bullying nor exclaiming to the heavens against some feather-weight cross, he coaxes women as a child coaxes its nurse when it wants to get anything out of her.

HIGGINS [*brusquely, recognizing her with unconcealed disappointment, and at once, babylike, making an intolerable grievance of it*] Why, this is the girl I jotted down last night. She's no use: Ive got all the records I want of the Lisson Grove lingo; and I'm not going to waste another cylinder on it. [*To the girl*] Be off with you: I dont want you.

THE FLOWER GIRL. Dont you be so saucy. You aint heard what I come for yet. [*To Mrs Pearce, who is waiting at the door for further instructions*] Did you tell him I come in a taxi?

MRS PEARCE. Nonsense, girl! what do you think a gentleman like Mr Higgins cares what you came in?

THE FLOWER GIRL. Oh, we a r e proud! He aint above giving lessons, not him: I heard him say so. Well, I aint come here to ask for any compliment; and if my money's not good enough I can go elsewhere.

HIGGINS. Good enough for what?

THE FLOWER GIRL. Good enough for ye-oo. Now you know, dont you? I'm come to have lessons, I am. And to pay for em too: make no mistake.

HIGGINS [*stupent*] Well!!! [*Recovering his breath with a gasp*] What do you expect me to say to you?

THE FLOWER GIRL. Well, if you was a gentleman, you might ask me to sit down, I think. Dont I tell you I'm bringing you business?

HIGGINS. Pickering: shall we ask this baggage to sit down, or shall we throw her out of the window?

THE FLOWER GIRL [*running away in terror to the piano, where she turns at bay*] Ah-ah-oh-ow-ow-ow-oo! [*Wounded and whimpering*] I wont be called a baggage when Ive offered to pay like any lady.

Motionless, the two men stare at her from the other side of the room, amazed.

PICKERING [*gently*] What is it you want, my girl?

THE FLOWER GIRL. I want to be a lady in a flower shop stead of selling at the corner of Tottenham Court Road. But they wont take me unless I can talk more genteel. He said he could teach me. Well, here I am ready to pay him—not asking any favor—and he treats me as if I was dirt.

MRS PEARCE. How can you be such a foolish ignorant girl as to think you could afford to pay Mr Higgins?

THE FLOWER GIRL. Why shouldnt I? I know what lessons cost as well as you do; and I'm ready to pay.

HIGGINS. How much?

THE FLOWER GIRL [*coming back to him, triumphant*] Now youre talking! I thought youd come off it when you saw a chance of getting back a bit of what you chucked at me last night. [*Confidentially*] Youd had a drop in, hadnt you?

HIGGINS [*peremptorily*] Sit down.

THE FLOWER GIRL. Oh, if youre going to make a compliment of it—

HIGGINS [*thundering at her*] Sit down.

MRS PEARCE [*severely*] Sit down, girl. Do as youre told. [*She places the stray chair near the hearthrug between Higgins and Pickering, and stands behind it waiting for the girl to sit down*].

THE FLOWER GIRL. Ah-ah-ah-ow-ow-oo! [*She stands, half rebellious, half bewildered*].

PICKERING [*very courteous*] Wont you sit down?

THE FLOWER GIRL [*coyly*] Dont mind if I do. [*She sits down. Pickering returns to the hearthrug*].

HIGGINS. Whats your name?

THE FLOWER GIRL. Liza Doolittle.

HIGGINS [*declaiming gravely*]
Eliza, Elizabeth, Betsy and Bess,
They went to the woods to get a bird's nes':

PICKERING. They found a nest with four eggs in it:

HIGGINS. They took one apiece, and left three in it.

They laugh heartily at their own wit.

LIZA. Oh, dont be silly.

MRS PEARCE. You mustnt speak to the gentleman like that.

LIZA. Well, why wont he speak sensible to me?

HIGGINS. Come back to business. How much do you propose to pay me for the lessons?

LIZA. Oh, I know whats right. A lady friend of mine gets French lessons for eighteenpence an hour from a real French gentleman. Well, you wouldnt have the face to ask me the same for teaching me my own language as you would for French; so I wont give more than a shilling. Take it or leave it.

HIGGINS [*walking up and down the room, rattling his keys and his cash in his pockets*] You know, Pickering, if you consider a shilling, not as a simple shilling, but as a percentage of this girl's income, it works out as fully equivalent to sixty or seventy guineas from a millionaire.

PICKERING. How so?

HIGGINS. Figure it out. A millionaire has about £150 a day. She earns about half-a-crown.

LIZA [*haughtily*] Who told you I only—

HIGGINS [*continuing*] She offers me two-fifths of her day's income for a lesson. Two-fifths of a millionaire's income for a day would be somewhere about £60. It's handsome. By George, it's enormous! it's the biggest offer I ever had.

LIZA [*rising, terrified*] Sixty pounds! What are you talking about? I never offered you sixty pounds. Where would I get—

HIGGINS. Hold your tongue.

LIZA [*weeping*] But I aint got sixty pounds. Oh—

MRS PEARCE. Dont cry, you silly girl. Sit down. Nobody is going to touch your money.

HIGGINS. Somebody is going to touch you, with a broomstick, if you dont stop snivelling. Sit down.

LIZA [*obeying slowly*] Ah-ah-ah-ow-oo-o! One would think you was my father.

HIGGINS. If I decide to teach you, I'll be worse than two fathers to you. Here [*he offers her his silk handkerchief*]!

LIZA. Whats this for?

HIGGINS. To wipe your eyes. To wipe any part of your face that feels moist. Remember: thats your handkerchief; and thats your sleeve. Dont mistake the one for the other if you wish to become a lady in a shop.

Liza, utterly bewildered, stares helplessly at him.

MRS PEARCE. It's no use talking to her like that, Mr Higgins: she doesnt understand you. Besides, youre quite wrong: she doesnt do it that way at all [*she takes the handkerchief*].

LIZA [*snatching it*] Here! You give me that handkerchief. He give it to me, not to you.

PICKERING [*laughing*] He did. I think it must be regarded as her property, Mrs Pearce.

MRS PEARCE [*resigning herself*] Serve you right, Mr Higgins.

PICKERING. Higgins: I'm interested. What about the ambassador's garden party? I'll say youre the greatest teacher alive if you make that good. I'll bet you all the expenses of the experiment you cant do it. And I'll pay for the lessons.

LIZA. Oh, you are real good. Thank you, Captain.

HIGGINS [*tempted, looking at her*] It's almost irresistible. She's so deliciously low—so horribly dirty—

LIZA [*protesting extremely*] Ah-ah-ah-ah-ow-ow-oo-oo!!! I aint dirty: I washed my face and hands afore I come, I did.

PICKERING. Youre certainly not going to turn her head with flattery, Higgins.

MRS PEARCE [*uneasy*] Oh, dont say that, sir: theres more ways than one of turning a girl's head; and nobody can do it better than Mr Higgins, though he may not always mean it. I do hope, sir, you wont encourage him to do anything foolish.

HIGGINS [*becoming excited as the idea grows on him*] What is life but a series of inspired follies? The difficulty is to find them to do. Never lose a chance: it doesnt come every day. I shall make a duchess of this draggletailed guttersnipe.

LIZA [*strongly deprecating this view of her*] Ah-ah-ah-ow-ow-oo!

HIGGINS [*carried away*] Yes: in six months—in three if she has a good ear and a quick tongue—I'll take her anywhere and pass her off as anything. We'll start today: now! this moment! Take her away and clean her, Mrs Pearce. Monkey Brand, if it wont come off any other way. Is there a good fire in the kitchen?

MRS PEARCE [*protesting*] Yes; but—

HIGGINS [*storming on*] Take all her clothes off and burn them. Ring up Whiteley or somebody for new ones. Wrap her up in brown paper til they come.

LIZA. Youre no gentleman, youre not, to talk of such things. I'm a good girl, I am; and I know what the like of you are, I do.

HIGGINS. We want none of your Lisson Grove prudery here, young woman. Youve got to learn to behave like a duchess. Take her away, Mrs Pearce. If she gives you any trouble, wallop her.

LIZA [*springing up and running between Pickering and Mrs Pearce for protection*] No! I'll call the police, I will.

MRS PEARCE. But Ive no place to put her.

HIGGINS. Put her in the dustbin.

LIZA. Ah-ah-ah-ow-ow-oo!

PICKERING. Oh come, Higgins! be reasonable.

MRS PEARCE [*resolutely*] You m u s t be reasonable, Mr Higgins: really you must. You cant walk over everybody like this.

Higgins, thus scolded, subsides. The hurricane is succeeded by a zephyr of amiable surprise.

HIGGINS [*with professional exquisiteness of modulation*] I walk over everybody! My dear Mrs Pearce, my dear Pickering, I never had the slightest intention of walking over anyone. All I propose is that we should be kind to this poor girl. We must help her to prepare and fit herself for her new station in life. If I did not express myself clearly it was because I did not wish to hurt her delicacy, or yours.

Liza, reassured, steals back to her chair.

MRS PEARCE [*to Pickering*] Well, did you ever hear anything like that, sir?

PICKERING [*laughing heartily*] Never, Mrs Pearce: never.

HIGGINS [*patiently*] Whats the matter?

MRS PEARCE. Well, the matter is, sir, that you cant take a girl up like that as if you were picking up a pebble on the beach.

HIGGINS. Why not?

MRS PEARCE. Why not! But you dont know anything about her. What about her parents? She may be married.

LIZA. Garn!

HIGGINS. There! As the girl very properly says, Garn! Married indeed! Dont you know that a woman of that class looks a worn out drudge of fifty a year after she's married?

LIZA. Whood marry me?

HIGGINS [*suddenly resorting to the most thrillingly beautiful low tones in his best elocutionary style*] By George, Eliza, the streets will be strewn with the bodies of men shooting themselves for your sake before Ive done with you.

MRS PEARCE. Nonsense, sir. You mustnt talk like that to her.

LIZA [*rising and squaring herself determinedly*] I'm going away. He's off his chump, he is. I dont want no balmies teaching me.

HIGGINS [*wounded in his tenderest point by her insensibility to his elocution*] Oh, indeed! I'm mad, am I? Very well, Mrs Pearce: you neednt order the new clothes for her. Throw her out.

LIZA [*whimpering*] Nah-ow. You got no right to touch me.

MRS PEARCE. You see now what comes of being saucy. [*Indicating the door*] This way, please.

LIZA [*almost in tears*] I didnt want no clothes. I wouldnt have taken them [*she throws away the handkerchief*]. I can buy my own clothes.

HIGGINS [*deftly retrieving the handkerchief and intercepting her on her reluctant way to the door*] Youre an ungrateful wicked girl. This is my return for offering to take you out of the gutter and dress you beautifully and make a lady of you.

MRS PEARCE. Stop, Mr Higgins. I wont allow it. It's you that are wicked. Go home to your parents, girl; and tell them to take better care of you.

LIZA. I aint got no parents. They told me I was big enough to earn my own living and turned me out.

MRS PEARCE. Wheres your mother?

LIZA. I aint got no mother. Her that turned me out was my sixth stepmother. But I done without them. And I'm a good girl, I am.

HIGGINS. Very well, then, what on earth is all this fuss about? The girl doesnt belong to anybody—is no use to anybody but me. [*He goes to Mrs Pearce and begins coaxing*]. You can adopt her, Mrs Pearce: I'm sure a daughter would be a great amusement to you. Now dont make any more fuss. Take her downstairs; and—

MRS PEARCE. But whats to become of her? Is she to be paid anything? Do be sensible, sir.

HIGGINS. Oh, pay her whatever is necessary: put it down in the housekeeping book. [*Impatiently*] What on earth will she want with money? She'll have her food and her clothes. She'll only drink if you give her money.

LIZA [*turning on him*] Oh you a r e a brute. It's a lie: nobody ever saw the sign of liquor on me. [*She goes back to her chair and plants herself there defiantly*].

PICKERING [*in good-humored remonstrance*] Does it occur to you, Higgins, that the girl has some feelings?

HIGGINS [*looking critically at her*] Oh no, I dont think so. Not any feelings that we need bother about. [*Cheerily*] Have you, Eliza?

LIZA. I got my feelings same as anyone else.

HIGGINS [*to Pickering, reflectively*] You see the difficulty?

PICKERING. Eh? What difficulty?

HIGGINS. To get her to talk grammar. The mere pronunciation is easy enough.

LIZA. I dont want to talk grammar. I want to talk like a lady.

MRS PEARCE. Will you please keep to the point, Mr. Higgins? I want to know on what terms the girl is to be here. Is she to have any wages? And what is to become of her when youve finished your teaching? You must look ahead a little.

HIGGINS [*impatiently*] Whats to become of her if I leave her in the gutter? Tell me that, Mrs Pearce.

MRS PEARCE. Thats her own business, not yours, Mr Higgins.

HIGGINS. Well, when Ive done with her, we can throw her back into the gutter; and then it will be her own business again; so thats all right.

LIZA. Oh, youve no feeling heart in you: you dont care for nothing but yourself [*she rises and takes the floor resolutely*]. Here! Ive had enough of this. I'm going [*making for the door*]. You ought to be ashamed of yourself, you ought.

HIGGINS [*snatching a chocolate cream from the piano, his eyes suddenly beginning to twinkle with mischief*] Have some chocolates, Eliza.

LIZA [*halting, tempted*] How do I know what might be in them? Ive heard of girls being drugged by the like of you.

> *Higgins whips out his penknife; cuts a chocolate in two; puts one half into his mouth and bolts it; and offers her the other half.*

HIGGINS. Pledge of good faith, Eliza. I eat one half: you eat the other. [*Liza opens her mouth to retort: he pops the half chocolate into it*]. You shall have boxes of them, barrels of them, every day. You shall live on them. Eh?

LIZA [*who has disposed of the chocolate after being nearly choked by it*] I wouldnt have ate it, only I'm too ladylike to take it out of my mouth.

HIGGINS. Listen, Eliza. I think you said you came in a taxi.

LIZA. Well, what if I did? Ive as good a right to take a taxi as anyone else.

HIGGINS. You have, Eliza; and in future you shall have as many taxis as you want. You shall go up and down and round the town in a taxi every day. Think of that, Eliza

MRS PEARCE. Mr Higgins: youre tempting the girl. It's not right. She should think of the future.

HIGGINS. At her age! Nonsense! Time enough to think of the future when you havnt any future to think of. No, Eliza: do as this lady does: think of other people's futures; but never think of your own. Think of chocolates, and taxis, and gold, and diamonds.

LIZA. No: I dont want no gold and no diamonds. I'm a good girl, I am. [*She sits down again, with an attempt at dignity*].

HIGGINS. You shall remain so, Eliza, under the care of Mrs Pearce. And you shall marry an officer in the Guards, with a beautiful moustache: the son of a marquis, who will disinherit him for marrying you, but will relent when he sees your beauty and goodness—

PICKERING. Excuse me, Higgins; but I really must interfere. Mrs Pearce is quite right. If this girl is to put herself in your hands for six months for an experiment in teaching, she must understand thoroughly what she's doing.

HIGGINS. How can she? She's incapable of understanding anything. Besides, do any of us understand what we are doing? If we did, would we ever do it?

PICKERING. Very clever, Higgins; but not sound sense. [*To Eliza*] Miss Doolittle—

LIZA [*overwhelmed*] Ah-ah-ow-oo!

HIGGINS. There! Thats all youll get out of Eliza. Ah-ah-ow-oo! No use explaining. As a military man you ought to know that. Give her her orders: thats what she wants. Eliza: you are to live here for the next six months, learning how to speak beautifully, like a lady in a florist's shop. If youre good and do whatever youre told, you shall sleep in a proper bedroom, and have lots to eat, and money to buy chocolates and take rides in taxis. If youre naughty and idle you will sleep in the back kitchen among the black beetles, and be walloped by Mrs Pearce with a broomstick. At the end of six months you shall go to Buckingham Palace in a carriage, beautifully dressed. If the King finds out youre not a lady, you will be taken by the police to the Tower of London, where your head will be cut off as a warning to other presumptuous flower girls. If you are not found out, you shall have a present of seven-and-sixpence to start life with as a lady in a shop. If you refuse this offer you will be a most ungrateful and wicked girl; and the angels will weep for you. [*To Pickering*] Now are you satisfied, Pickering? [*To Mrs Pearce*] Can I put it more plainly and fairly, Mrs Pearce?

MRS PEARCE [*patiently*] I think youd better let me speak to the girl properly in private. I dont know that I can take charge of her or consent to the arrangement at all. Of course I know you dont mean her any harm; but when you get what you call interested in people's accents, you never think or care what may happen to them or you. Come with me, Eliza.

HIGGINS Thats all right. Thank you, Mrs Pearce. Bundle her off to the bath-room.

LIZA [*rising reluctantly and suspiciously*] Youre a great bully, you are. I wont stay here if I dont like. I wont let nobody wallop me. I never asked to go to Bucknam Palace, I didnt. I was never in trouble with the police, not me. I'm a good girl—

MRS PEARCE. Dont answer back, girl. You dont understand the gentleman. Come with me. [*She leads the way to the door, and holds it open for Eliza*].

LIZA [*as she goes out*] Well, what I say is right. I wont go near the King, not if I'm going to have my head cut off. If I'd known what I was letting myself in for, I wouldnt have come here. I always been a good girl; and I never offered to say a word to him; and I dont owe him nothing; and I dont care; and I wont be put upon; and I have my feelings the same as anyone else—

Mrs Pearce shuts the door and Eliza's plaints are no longer audible. Pickering comes from the hearth to the chair and sits astride it with his arms on the back.

PICKERING. Excuse the straight question, Higgins. Are you a man of good character where women are concerned?

HIGGINS [*moodily*] Have you ever met a man of good character where women are concerned?

PICKERING. Yes: very frequently.

HIGGINS [*dogmatically, lifting himself on his hands to the level of the piano, and sitting on it with a bounce*] Well, I havnt. I find that the moment I let a woman make friends with me, she becomes jealous, exacting, suspicious, and a damned nuisance. I find that the moment I let myself make friends with a woman, I become selfish and tyrannical. Women upset everything. When you let them into your life, you find that the woman is driving at one thing and youre driving at another.

PICKERING. At what, for example?

HIGGINS [*coming off the piano restlessly*] Oh, Lord knows! I suppose the woman wants to live her own life; and the man wants to live his; and each tries to drag the other on to the wrong track. One wants to go north and the other south; and the result is that both have to go east, though they both hate the east wind. [*He sits down on the bench at the keyboard*]. So here I am, a confirmed old bachelor, and likely to remain so.

PICKERING [*rising and standing over him gravely*] Come, Higgins! You know what I mean. If I'm to be in this business I shall feel responsible for that girl. I hope it's understood that no advantage is to be taken of her position.

HIGGINS. What! That thing! Sacred, I assure you. [*Rising to explain*] You see, she'll be a pupil; and teaching would be impossible unless pupils were sacred. Ive taught scores of American millionairesses how to speak English: the best looking women in the world. I'm seasoned. They might as well be blocks of wood. *I* might as well be a block of wood. It's—

Mrs Pearce opens the door. She has Eliza's hat in her hand. Pickering retires to the easy-chair at the hearth and sits down.

HIGGINS [*eagerly*] Well, Mrs Pearce: is it all right?

MRS PEARCE [*at the door*] I just wish to trouble you with a word, if I may, Mr Higgins.

HIGGINS. Yes, certainly. Come in. [*She comes forward*]. Dont burn that, Mrs Pearce. I'll keep it as a curiosity. [*He takes the hat*].

MRS PEARCE. Handle it carefully, sir, please. I had to promise her not to burn it; but I had better put it in the oven for a while.

HIGGINS [*putting it down hastily on the piano*] Oh! thank you. Well, what have you to say to me?

PICKERING. Am I in the way?

MRS PEARCE. Not at all, sir. Mr Higgins: will you please be very particular what you say before the girl?

HIGGINS [*sternly*] Of course. I'm always particular about what I say. Why do you say this to me?

Mrs Pearce [*unmoved*] No, sir: youre not at all particular when youve mislaid anything or when you get a little impatient. Now it doesnt matter before me: I'm used to it. But you really must not swear before the girl.

Higgins [*indignantly*] I swear! [*Most emphatically*] I never swear. I detest the habit. What the devil do you mean?

Mrs Pearce [*stolidly*] Thats what I mean, sir. You swear a great deal too much. I dont mind your damning and blasting, and w h a t the devil and w h e r e the devil and w h o the devil—

Higgins. Mrs Pearce: this language from your lips! Really!

Mrs Pearce [*not to be put off*]—but there is a certain word I must ask you not to use. The girl has just used it herself because the bath was too hot. It begins with the same letter as bath. She knows no better: she learnt it at her mother's knee. But she must not hear it from y o u r lips.

Higgins [*loftily*] I cannot charge myself with having ever uttered it, Mrs Pearce. [*She looks at him steadfastly. He adds, hiding an uneasy conscience with a judicial air*] Except perhaps in a moment of extreme and justifiable excitement.

Mrs Pearce. Only this morning, sir, you applied it to your boots, to the butter, and to the brown bread.

Higgins. Oh, that! Mere alliteration, Mrs Pearce, natural to a poet.

Mrs Pearce. Well, sir, whatever you choose to call it, I beg you not to let the girl hear you repeat it.

Higgins. Oh, very well, very well. Is that all?

Mrs Pearce. No, sir. We shall have to be very particular with this girl as to personal cleanliness.

Higgins. Certainly. Quite right. Most important.

Mrs Pearce. I mean not to be slovenly about her dress or untidy in leaving things about.

Higgins [*going to her solemnly*] Just so. I intended to call your attention to that. [*He passes on to Pickering, who is enjoying the conversation immensely*]. It is these little things that matter, Pickering. Take care of the pence and the pounds will take care of themselves is as true of personal habits as of money. [*He comes to anchor on the hearthrug, with the air of a man in an unassailable position*].

Mrs Pearce. Yes, sir. Then might I ask you not to come down to breakfast in your dressing-gown, or at any rate not to use it as a napkin to the extent you do, sir. And if you would be so good as not to eat everything off the same plate, and to remember not to put the porridge saucepan out of your hand on the clean tablecloth, it would be a better example to the girl. You know you nearly choked yourself with a fishbone in the jam only last week.

Higgins [*routed from the hearthrug and drifting back to the piano*] I may do these things sometimes in absence of mind; but surely I dont do them habitually. [*Angrily*] By the way: my dressing-gown smells most damnably of benzine.

Mrs Pearce. No doubt it does, Mr Higgins. But if you will wipe your fingers—

Higgins [*yelling*] Oh very well, very well: I'll wipe them in my hair in future.

Mrs Pearce. I hope youre not offended, Mr Higgins.

Higgins [*shocked at finding himself thought capable of an unamiable sentiment*] Not at all, not at all. Youre quite right, Mrs Pearce: I shall be particularly careful before the girl. Is that all?

Mrs Pearce. No, sir. Might she use some of those Japanese dresses you brought from abroad? I really cant put her back into her old things.

Higgins. Certainly. Anything you like. Is t h a t all?

Mrs Pearce. Thank you, sir. Thats all. [*She goes out*].

HIGGINS. You know, Pickering, that woman has the most extraordinary ideas about me. Here I am, a shy, diffident sort of man. Ive never been able to feel really grown-up and tremendous, like other chaps. And yet she's firmly persuaded that I'm an arbitrary over-bearing bossing kind of person. I cant account for it.

Mrs Pearce returns.

MRS PEARCE. If you please, sir, the trouble's beginning already. Theres a dustman downstairs, Alfred Doolittle, wants to see you. He says you have his daughter here.

PICKERING [*rising*] Phew! I say! [*He retreats to the hearthrug*].

HIGGINS [*promptly*] Send the blackguard up.

MRS PEARCE. Oh, very well, sir. [*She goes out*].

PICKERING. He may not be a blackguard, Higgins.

HIGGINS. Nonsense. Of course he's a blackguard.

PICKERING. Whether he is or not, I'm afraid we shall have some trouble with him.

HIGGINS [*confidently*] Oh no: I think not. If theres any trouble he shall have it with me, not I with him. And we are sure to get something interesting out of him.

PICKERING. About the girl?

HIGGINS. No. I mean his dialect.

PICKERING. Oh!

MRS PEARCE [*at the door*] Doolittle, sir. [*She admits Doolittle and retires*].

> *Alfred Doolittle is an elderly but vigorous dustman, clad in the costume of his profession, including a hat with a back brim covering his neck and shoulders. He has well marked and rather interesting features, and seems equally free from fear and conscience. He has a remarkably expressive voice, the result of a habit of giving vent to his feelings without reserve. His present pose is that of wounded honor and stern resolution.*

DOOLITTLE [*at the door, uncertain which of the two gentlemen is his man*] Professor Higgins?

HIGGINS. Here. Good morning. Sit down.

DOOLITTLE. Morning, Governor. [*He sits down magisterially*] I come about a very serious matter, Governor.

HIGGINS [*to Pickering*] Brought up in Hounslow. Mother Welsh, I should think. [*Doolittle opens his mouth, amazed. Higgins continues*] What do you want, Doolittle?

DOOLITTLE [*menacingly*] I want my daughter: thats what I want. See?

HIGGINS. Of course you do. Youre her father, arnt you? You dont suppose anyone else wants her, do you? I'm glad to see you have some spark of family feeling left. She's upstairs. Take her away at once.

DOOLITTLE [*rising, fearfully taken aback*] What!

HIGGINS. Take her away. Do you suppose I'm going to keep your daughter for you?

DOOLITTLE [*remonstrating*] Now, now, look here, Governor. Is this reasonable? Is it fairity to take advantage of a man like this? The girl belongs to me. You got her. Where do I come in? [*He sits down again*].

HIGGINS. Your daughter had the audacity to come to my house and ask me to teach her how to speak properly so that she could get a place in a flower-shop. This gentleman and my housekeeper have been here all the time. [*Bullying him*] How dare you come here and attempt to blackmail me? You sent her here on purpose.

DOOLITTLE [*protesting*] No, Governor.

HIGGINS. You must have. How else could you possibly know that she is here?

DOOLITTLE. Dont take a man up like that, Governor.

HIGGINS. The police shall take you up. This is a plant—a plot to extort money by threats. I shall telephone for the police. [*He goes resolutely to the telephone and opens the directory*].

DOOLITTLE. Have I asked you for a brass farthing? I leave it to the gentleman here: have I said a word about money?

HIGGINS [*throwing the book aside and marching down on Doolittle with a poser*] What else did you come for?

DOOLITTLE [*sweetly*] Well what w o u l d a man come for? Be human, Governor.

HIGGINS [*disarmed*] Alfred: did you put her up to it?

DOOLITTLE. So help me, Governor, I never did. I take my Bible oath I aint seen the girl these two months past.

HIGGINS. Then how did you know she was here?

DOOLITTLE [*"most musical, most melancholy"*] I'll tell you, Governor, if youll only let me get a word in. I'm willing to tell you. I'm wanting to tell you. I'm waiting to tell you.

HIGGINS. Pickering: this chap has a certain natural gift of rhetoric. Observe the rhythm of his native woodnotes wild. "I'm willing to tell you: I'm wanting to tell you: I'm waiting to tell you." Sentimental rhetoric! thats the Welsh strain in him. It also accounts for his mendacity and dishonesty.

PICKERING. Oh, p l e a s e, Higgins: I'm west country myself. [*To Doolittle*] How did you know the girl was here if you didnt send her?

DOOLITTLE. It was like this, Governor. The girl took a boy in the taxi to give him a jaunt. Son of her landlady, he is. He hung about on the chance of her giving him another ride home. Well, she sent him back for her luggage when she heard you was willing for her to stop here. I met the boy at the corner of Long Acre and Endell Street.

HIGGINS. Public house. Yes?

DOOLITTLE. The poor man's club, Governor: why shouldnt I?

PICKERING. Do let him tell his story, Higgins.

DOOLITTLE. He told me what was up. And I ask you, what was my feelings and my duty as a father? I says to the boy, "You bring me the luggage," I says—

PICKERING. Why didnt you go for it yourself?

DOOLITTLE. Landlady wouldnt have trusted me with it, Governor. She's that kind of woman: you know. I had to give the boy a penny afore he trusted me with it, the little swine. I brought it to her just to oblige you like, and make myself agreeable. Thats all.

HIGGINS. How much luggage?

DOOLITTLE. Musical instrument, Governor. A few pictures, a trifle of jewlery, and a birdcage. She said she didnt want no clothes. What was I to think from that, Governor? I ask you as a parent what was I to think?

HIGGINS. So you came to rescue her from worse than death, eh?

DOOLITTLE [*appreciatively: relieved at being so well understood*] Just so, Governor. Thats right.

PICKERING. But why did you bring her luggage if you intended to take her away?

DOOLITTLE. Have I said a word about taking her away? Have I now?

HIGGINS [*determinedly*] Youre going to take her away, double quick. [*He crosses to the hearth and rings the bell*].

DOOLITTLE [*rising*] No, Governor. Dont say that. I'm not the man to stand in my girl's light. Heres a career opening for her, as you might say; and—

Mrs Pearce opens the door and awaits orders.

HIGGINS. Mrs Pearce: this is Eliza's father. He has come to take her away. Give her to him. [*He goes back to the piano, with an air of washing his hands of the whole affair*].

DOOLITTLE. No. This is a misunderstanding. Listen here—

MRS PEARCE. He cant take her away, Mr Higgins: how can he? You told me to burn her clothes.

DOOLITTLE. Thats right. I cant carry the girl through the streets like a blooming monkey, can I? I put it to you.

HIGGINS. You have put it to me that you want your daughter. Take your daughter. If she has no clothes go out and buy her some.

DOOLITTLE [*desperate*] Wheres the clothes she come in? Did I burn them or did your missus here?

MRS PEARCE. I am the housekeeper, if you please. I have sent for some clothes for the girl. When they come you can take her away. You can wait in the kitchen. This way, please.

Doolittle, much troubled, accompanies her to the door; then hesitates; finally turns confidentially to Higgins.

DOOLITTLE. Listen here, Governor. You and me is men of the world, aint we?

HIGGINS. Oh! Men of the world, are we? Youd better go, Mrs Pearce.

MRS PEARCE. I think so, indeed, sir. [*She goes, with dignity*].

PICKERING. The floor is yours, Mr Doolittle.

DOOLITTLE [*To Pickering*] I thank you, Governor. [*To Higgins, who takes refuge on the piano bench, a little overwhelmed by the proximity of his visitor; for Doolittle has a professional flavor of dust about him*]. Well, the truth is, Ive taken a sort of fancy to you, Governor; and if you want the girl, I'm not so set on having her back home again but what I might be open to an arrangement. Regarded in the light of a young woman, she's a fine handsome girl. As a daughter she's not worth her keep; and so I tell you straight. All I ask is my rights as a father; and youre the last man alive to expect me to let her go for nothing; for I can see youre one of the straight sort, Governor. Well, whats a five-pound note to you? And whats Eliza to me? [*He returns to his chair and sits down judicially*].

PICKERING. I think you ought to know, Doolittle, that Mr Higgins's intentions are entirely honorable.

DOOLITTLE. Course they are, Governor. If I thought they wasnt, I'd ask fifty.

HIGGINS [*revolted*] Do you mean to say, you callous rascal, that you would sell your daughter for £50?

DOOLITTLE. Not in a general way I wouldnt; but to oblige a gentleman like you I'd do a good deal, I do assure you.

PICKERING. Have you no morals, man?

DOOLITTLE [*unabashed*] Cant afford them, Governor. Neither could you if you was as poor as me. Not that I mean any harm, you know. But if Liza is going to have a bit out of this, why not me too?

HIGGINS [*troubled*] I dont know what to do, Pickering. There can be no question that as a matter of morals it's a positive crime to give this chap a farthing. And yet I feel a sort of rough justice in his claim.

DOOLITTLE. Thats it, Governor. Thats all I say. A father's heart, as it were.

PICKERING. Well, I know the feeling; but really it seems hardly right—

DOOLITTLE. Dont say that, Governor. Dont look at it that way. What am I, Governors both? I ask you, what am I? I'm one of the undeserving poor: thats what I am. Think of what that means to a man. It means that he's up agen middle class morality all the time. If theres anything going, and I put in for a bit of it, it's always the same story: "Youre undeserving; so you cant have it." But my needs is as great as the most deserving widow's that ever got money out of six different charities in one week for the death of the same husband. I dont need less than a deserving man: I need more. I dont eat less hearty than him; and I drink a lot more. I want a bit of amusement, cause I'm a thinking man. I want cheerfulness and a song and a band when I feel low. Well, they charge me just the same for everything as they charge the deserving. What is middle class morality? Just an excuse for never giving me anything. Therefore, I ask you, as two gentlemen, not to play that game on me. I'm playing straight with you. I aint pretending to be deserving. I'm undeserving; and I mean to go on being undeserving. I like it; and that the truth. Will you take advantage of a man's nature to do him out of the price of his own daughter what he's brought up and fed and clothed by the sweat of his brow until she's growed big enough to be interesting to you two gentlemen? Is five pounds unreasonable? I put it to you; and I leave it to you.

HIGGINS [*rising, and going over to Pickering*] Pickering: if we were to take this man in hand for three months, he could choose between a seat in the Cabinet and a popular pulpit in Wales.

PICKERING. What do you say to that, Doolittle?

DOOLITTLE. Not me, Governor, thank you kindly. Ive heard all the preachers and all the prime ministers—for I'm a thinking man and game for politics or religion or social reform same as all the other amusements—and I tell you it's a dog's life any way you look at it. Undeserving poverty is my line. Taking one station in society with another, it's—it's—well, it's the only one that has any ginger in it, to my taste.

HIGGINS. I suppose we must give him a fiver.

PICKERING. He'll make a bad use of it, I'm afraid.

DOOLITTLE. Not me, Governor, so help me I wont. Dont you be afraid that I'll save it and spare it and live idle on it. There wont be a penny of it left by Monday: I'll have to go to work same as if I'd never had it. It wont pauperize me, you bet. Just one good spree for myself and the missus, giving pleasure to ourselves and employment to others, and satisfaction to you to think it's not been throwed away. You couldnt spent it better.

HIGGINS [*taking out his pocket book and coming between Doolittle and the piano*] This is irresistible. Lets give him ten. [*He offers two notes to the dustman*].

DOOLITTLE. No, Governor. She wouldnt have the heart to spend ten; and perhaps I shouldnt neither. Ten pounds is a lot of money: it makes a man feel prudent like; and then goodbye to happiness. You give me what I ask you, Governor: not a penny more, and not a penny less.

PICKERING. Why dont you marry that missus of yours? I rather draw the line at encouraging that sort of immorality.

DOOLITTLE. Tell her so, Governor: tell her so. *I'm* willing. It's me that suffers by it. Ive no hold on her. I got to be agreeable to her. I got to give her presents. I got to buy her clothes something sinful. I'm a slave to that woman, Governor, just because I'm not her lawful husband. And she knows it too. Catch her marrying me! Take my advice, Governor: marry Eliza while she's young and dont know no better. If you dont youll be sorry for it after. If you do, she'll be sorry for it after; but better her than you, because youre a man, and she's only a woman and dont know how to be happy anyhow.

HIGGINS. Pickering: if we listen to this man another minute, we shall have no convictions left. [*To Doolittle*] Five pounds I think you said.

DOOLITTLE. Thank you kindly, Governor.

HIGGINS. Youre sure you wont take ten?

DOOLITTLE. Not now. Another time, Governor.

HIGGINS [*handing him a five-pound note*] Here you are.

DOOLITTLE. Thank you, Governor. Good morning. [*He hurries to the door, anxious to get away with his booty. When he opens it he is confronted with a dainty and exquisitely clean young Japanese lady in a simple blue cotton kimono printed cunningly with small white jasmine blossoms. Mrs Pearce is with her. He gets out of her way deferentially and apologizes*]. Beg pardon, miss.

THE JAPANESE LADY. Garn! Dont you know your own daughter?

DOOLITTLE		Bly me! it's Eliza!
HIGGINS	*exclaiming simultaneously*	Whats that! This!
PICKERING		By Jove!

LIZA. Dont I look silly?

HIGGINS. Silly?

MRS PEARCE [*at the door*] Now, Mr. Higgins, please dont say anything to make the girl conceited about herself.

HIGGINS [*conscientiously*] Oh! Quite right, Mrs Pearce. [*To Eliza*] Yes: damned silly.

MRS PEARCE. Please, sir.

HIGGINS [*correcting himself*] I mean extremely silly.

LIZA. I should look all right with my hat on. [*She takes up her hat; puts it on; and walks across the room to the fireplace with a fashionable air*].

HIGGINS. A new fashion, by George! And it ought to look horrible!

DOOLITTLE [*with fatherly pride*] Well, I never thought she'd clean up as good looking as that, Governor. She's a credit to me, aint she?

LIZA. I tell you, it's easy to clean up here. Hot and cold water on tap, just as much as you like, there is. Woolly towels, there is; and a towel horse so hot, it burns your fingers. Soft brushes to scrub yourself, and a wooden bowl of soap smelling like primroses. Now I know why ladies is so clean. Washing's a treat for them. Wish they saw what it is for the like of me!

HIGGINS. I'm glad the bathroom met with your approval.

LIZA. It didn't: not all of it; and I dont care who hears me say it. Mrs Pearce knows.

HIGGINS. What was wrong, Mrs Pearce?

MRS PEARCE [*blandly*] Oh, nothing, sir. It doesnt matter.

LIZA. I had a good mind to break it. I didn't know which way to look. But I hung a towel over it, I did.

HIGGINS. Over what?

MRS PEARCE. Over the looking-glass, sir.

HIGGINS. Doolittle: you have brought your daughter up too strictly.

DOOLITTLE. Me! I never brought her up at all, except to give her a lick of a strap now and again. Dont put it on me, Governor. She aint accustomed to it, you see: thats all. But she'll soon pick up your free-and-easy ways.

LIZA. I'm a good girl, I am; and I wont pick up no free-and-easy ways.

HIGGINS. Eliza: if you say again that youre a good girl, your father shall take you home.

LIZA. Not him. You dont know my father. All he come here for was to touch you for some money to get drunk on.

DOOLITTLE. Well, what else would I want money for? To put into the plate in church, I suppose. [*She puts out her tongue at him. He is so incensed by this that Pickering presently finds it necessary to step between them*]. Dont you give me none of your lip; and dont let me hear you giving this gentleman any of it neither, or youll hear from me about it. See?

HIGGINS. Have you any further advice to give her before you go, Doolittle? Your blessing, for instance.

DOOLITTLE. No, Governor: I aint such a mug as to put up my children to all I know myself. Hard enough to hold them in without that. If you want Eliza's mind improved, Governor, you do it yourself with a strap. So long, gentlemen. [*He turns to go*].

HIGGINS [*impressively*] Stop. Youll come regularly to see your daughter. It's your duty, you know. My brother is a clergyman; and he could help you in your talks with her.

DOOLITTLE [*evasively*] Certainly. I'll come, Governor. Not just this week, because I have a job at a distance. But later on you may depend on me. Afternoon, gentlemen. Afternoon, maam. [*He takes off his hat to Mrs Pearce, who disdains the salutation and goes out. He winks at Higgins, thinking him probably a fellow-sufferer from Mrs Pearce's difficult disposition, and follows her*].

LIZA. Dont you believe the old liar. He'd as soon you set a bull-dog on him as a clergyman. You wont see him again in a hurry.

HIGGINS. I dont want to, Eliza. Do you?

LIZA. Not me. I dont want never to see him again, I dont. He's a disgrace to me, he is, collecting dust, instead of working at his trade.

PICKERING. What is his trade, Eliza?

LIZA. Taking money out of other people's pockets into his own. His proper trade's a navvy; and he works at it sometimes too—for exercise—and earns good money at it. Aint you going to call me Miss Doolittle any more?

PICKERING. I beg your pardon, Miss Doolittle. It was a slip of the tongue.

LIZA. Oh, I dont mind; only it sounded so genteel. I should just like to take a taxi to the corner of Tottenham Court Road and get out there and tell it to wait for me, just to put the girls in their place a bit. I wouldnt speak to them, you know.

PICKERING. Better wait til we get you something really fashionable.

HIGGINS. Besides, you shouldnt cut your old friends now that you have risen in the world. Thats what we call snobbery.

LIZA. You dont call the like of them my friends now, I should hope. Theyve took it out of me often enough with their ridicule when they had the chance; and now I mean to get a bit of my own back. But if I'm to have fashionable clothes, I'll wait. I should like to have some. Mrs Pearce says youre going to give me some to wear in bed at night different to what I wear in the daytime; but it do seem a waste of money when you could get something to shew. Besides, I never could fancy changing into cold things on a winter night.

MRS PEARCE [coming back] Now, Eliza. The new things have come for you to try on.

LIZA. Ah-ow-oo-ooh! [She rushes out].

MRS PEARCE [following her] Oh, dont rush about like that, girl. [She shuts the door behind her].

HIGGINS. Pickering: we have taken on a stiff job.

PICKERING [with conviction] Higgins: we have.

ACT 3

It is Mrs Higgins's at-home day. Nobody has yet arrived. Her drawing room, in a flat on Chelsea Embankment, has three windows looking on the river; and the ceiling is not so lofty as it would be in an older house of the same pretension. The windows are open, giving access to a balcony with flowers in pots. If you stand with your face to the windows, you have the fireplace on your left and the door in the right-hand wall close to the corner nearest the windows.

Mrs. Higgins was brought up on Morris and Burne Jones; and her room, which is very unlike her son's room in Wimpole Street, is not crowded with furniture and little tables and nicknacks. In the middle of the room there is a big ottoman; and this, with the carpet, the Morris wall-papers, and the Morris chintz window curtains and brocade covers of the ottoman and its cushions, supply all the ornament, and are much too handsome to be hidden by odds and ends of useless things. A few good oil-paintings from the exhibitions in the Grosvenor Gallery thirty years ago (the Burne Jones, not the Whistler side of them) are on the walls. The only landscape is a Cecil Lawson on the scale of a Rubens. There is a portrait of Mrs Higgins as she was when she defied fashion in her youth in one of the beautiful Rossettian costumes which, when caricatured by people who did not understand, led to the absurdities of popular esthetticism in the eighteen-seventies.

In the corner diagonally opposite the door Mrs Higgins, now over sixty and long past taking the trouble to dress out of the fashion, sits writing at an elegantly simple writing-table with a bell button within reach of her hand. There is a Chippendale chair further back in the room between her and the window nearest her side. At the other side of the room, further forward, is an Elizabethan chair roughly carved in the taste of Inigo Jones. On the same side a piano in a dec-

orated case. The corner between the fireplace and the window is occupied by a divan cushioned in Morris chintz.

It is between four and five in the afternoon.

The door is opened violently; and Higgins enters with his hat on.

MRS HIGGINS [*dismayed*] Henry [*scolding him*]! What are you doing here to-day? It is my at-home day: you promised not to come. [*As he bends to kiss her, she takes his hat off, and presents it to him*].

HIGGINS. Oh bother! [*He throws the hat down on the table*].

MRS HIGGINS. Go home at once.

HIGGINS [*kissing her*] I know, mother. I came on purpose.

MRS HIGGINS. But you mustnt. I'm serious, Henry. You offend all my friends: they stop coming whenever they meet you.

HIGGINS. Nonsense! I know I have no small talk; but people dont mind. [*He sits on the settee*].

MRS HIGGINS. Oh! dont they? Small talk indeed! What about your large talk? Really, dear, you mustnt stay.

HIGGINS. I must. Ive a job for you. A phonetic job.

MRS HIGGINS. No use, dear. I'm sorry; but I cant get round your vowels; and though I like to get pretty postcards in your patent shorthand, I always have to read the copies in ordinary writing you so thoughtfully send me.

HIGGINS. Well, this isnt a phonetic job.

MRS HIGGINS. You said it was.

HIGGINS. Not your part of it. Ive picked up a girl.

MRS HIGGINS. Does that mean that some girl has picked you up?

HIGGINS. Not at all. I dont mean a love affair.

MRS HIGGINS. What a pity!

HIGGINS. Why?

MRS HIGGINS. Well, you never fall in love with anyone under forty-five. When will you discover that there are some rather nice looking young women about?

HIGGINS. Oh, I cant be bothered with young women. My idea of a lovable woman is something as like you as possible. I shall never get into the way of seriously liking young women: some habits lie too deep to be changed. [*Rising abruptly and walking about, jingling his money and his keys in his trouser pockets*] Besides, theyre all idiots.

MRS HIGGINS. Do you know what you would do if you really loved me, Henry?

HIGGINS. Oh bother! What? Marry, I suppose?

MRS HIGGINS. No. Stop fidgeting and take your hands out of your pockets. [*With a gesture of despair, he obeys and sits down again.*] Thats a good boy. Now tell me about the girl.

HIGGINS. She's coming to see you.

MRS HIGGINS. I dont remember asking her.

HIGGINS. You didnt. *I* asked her. If youd known her you wouldnt have asked her.

MRS HIGGINS. Indeed! Why?

HIGGINS. Well, it's like this. She's a common flower girl. I picked her off the kerbstone.

MRS HIGGINS. And invited her to my at-home!

HIGGINS [*rising and coming to her to coax her*] Oh, thatll be all right. Ive taught her to speak properly; and she has strict orders as to her behavior. She's to keep to two subjects: the weather and everybody's health—Fine day and How do you do, you know—and not to let herself go on things in general. That will be safe.

MRS. HIGGINS. Safe! To talk about our health! about our insides! perhaps about our outsides! How could you be so silly, Henry?

HIGGINS [*impatiently*] Well, she must talk about something. [*He controls himself and sits down again*]. Oh, she'll be all right: dont you fuss. Pickering is in it with me. Ive a sort of bet on that I'll pass her off as a duchess in six months. I started on her some months ago; and she's getting on like a house on fire. I shall win my bet. She has a quick ear; and she's been easier to teach than my middle class pupils because she's had to learn a complete new language. She talks English almost as you talk French.

MRS HIGGINS. Thats satisfactory, at all events.

HIGGINS. Well, it is and it isnt.

MRS HIGGINS. What does that mean?

HIGGINS. You see, Ive got her pronunciation all right; but you have to consider not only h o w a girl pronounces, but w h a t she pronounces; and thats where—

They are interrupted by the parlor-maid, announcing guests.

THE PARLOR-MAID. Mrs and Miss Eynsford Hill. [*She withdraws*].

HIGGINS. Oh Lord! [*He rises; snatches his hat from the table; and makes for the door; but before he reaches it his mother introduces him*].

Mrs and Miss Eynsford Hill are the mother and daughter who sheltered from the rain in Covent Garden. The mother is well bred, quiet, and has the habitual anxiety of straitened means. The daughter has acquired a gay air of being very much at home in society: the bravado of genteel poverty.

MRS EYNSFORD HILL [*to Mrs Higgins*] How do you do? [*They shake hands*].

MISS EYNSFORD HILL. How d'you do? [*She shakes*].

MRS HIGGINS [*introducing*] My son Henry.

MRS EYNSFORD HILL. Your celebrated son! I have so longed to meet you, Professor Higgins.

HIGGINS [*glumly, making no movement in her direction*] Delighted. [*He backs against the piano and bows brusquely*].

MISS EYNSFORD HILL [*going to him with confident familiarity*] How do you do?

HIGGINS [*staring at her*] Ive seen you before somewhere. I havnt the ghost of a notion where but Ive heard your voice. [*Drearily*] It doesnt matter. Youd better sit down.

MRS HIGGINS. I'm sorry to say that my celebrated son has no manners. You mustnt mind him.

MISS EYNSFORD HILL [*gaily*] I dont. [*She sits in the Elizabethan chair*].

MRS EYNSFORD HILL [*a little bewildered*] Not at all. [*She sits on the ottoman between her daughter and Mrs Higgins, who has turned her chair away from the writing-table*].

HIGGINS. Oh, have I been rude? I didn't mean to be.

He goes to the central window, through which, with his back to the company, he contemplates the river and the flowers in Battersea Park on the opposite bank as if they were a frozen desert.
The parlor-maid returns, ushering in Pickering.

THE PARLOR-MAID. Colonel Pickering. [*She withdraws*].

PICKERING. How do you do, Mrs Higgins?

MRS HIGGINS. So glad youve come. Do you know Mrs Eynsford Hill—Miss Eynsford Hill? [*Exchange of bows. The Colonel brings the Chippendale chair a little forward between Mrs Hill and Mrs Higgins, and sits down*].

PICKERING. Has Henry told you what weve come for?

HIGGINS [*over his shoulder*] We were interrupted: damn it!

MRS HIGGINS. Oh Henry, Henry, really!

MRS EYNSFORD HILL [*half rising*] Are we in the way?

MRS HIGGINS [*rising and making her sit down again*] No, no. You couldnt have come more fortunately: we want you to meet a friend of ours.

HIGGINS [*turning hopefully*] Yes, by George! We want two or three people. Youll do as well as anybody else.

The parlor-maid returns, ushering Freddy.

THE PARLOR-MAID. Mr Eynsford Hill.

HIGGINS [*almost audibly, past endurance*] God of Heaven! another of them.

FREDDY [*shaking hands with Mrs Higgins*] Ahdedo?

MRS HIGGINS. Very good of you to come. [*Introducing*] Colonel Pickering.

FREDDY [*bowing*] Ahdedo?

MRS HIGGINS. I don't think you know my son, Professor Higgins.

FREDDY [*going to Higgins*] Ahdedo?

HIGGINS [*looking at him much as if he were a pickpocket*] I'll take my oath Ive met y o u before somewhere. Where was it?

FREDDY. I dont think so.

HIGGINS [*resignedly*] It dont matter, anyhow. Sit down.

He shakes Freddy's hand, and almost slings him on to the ottoman with his face to the windows; then comes round to the other side of it.

HIGGINS. Well, here we are, anyhow! [*He sits down on the ottoman next Mrs Eynsford Hill, on her left*]. And now, what the devil are we going to talk about until Eliza comes?

MRS HIGGINS. Henry: you are the life and soul of the Royal Society's soirées; but really youre rather trying on more commonplace occasions.

HIGGINS. Am I? Very sorry. [*Beaming suddenly*] I suppose I am, you know. [*Uproariously*] Ha, ha!

MISS EYNSFORD HILL [*who considers Higgins quite eligible matrimonially*] I sympathize. I havnt any small talk. If people would only be frank and say what they really think!

HIGGINS [*relapsing into gloom*] Lord forbid!

MRS EYNSFORD HILL [*taking up her daughter's cue*] But why?

HIGGINS. What they think they ought to think is bad enough, Lord knows; but what they really think would break up the whole show. Do you suppose it would be really agreeable if I were to come out now with what *I* really think?

MISS EYNSFORD HILL [*gaily*] Is it so very cynical?

HIGGINS. Cynical! Who the dickens said it was cynical? I mean it wouldnt be decent.

MRS EYNSFORD HILL [*seriously*] Oh! I'm sure you dont mean that, Mr Higgins.

HIGGINS. You see, we're all savages, more or less. We're supposed to be civilized and cultured—to know all about poetry and philosophy and art and science, and so on; but how many of us know even the meanings of these names? [*To Miss Hill*] What do y o u know of poetry? [*To Mrs Hill*] What do y o u know of science? [*Indicating Freddy*] What does h e know of art or science or anything else? What the devil do you imagine I know of philosophy?

MRS HIGGINS [*warningly*] Or of manners, Henry?

THE PARLOR-MAID [*opening the door*] Miss Doolittle. [*She withdraws*].

HIGGINS [*rising hastily and running to Mrs Higgins*] Here she is, mother. [*He stands on tiptoe and makes signs over his mother's head to Eliza to indicate to her which lady is her hostess*].

Eliza, who is exquisitely dressed, produces an impression of such remarkable distinction and beauty as she enters that they all rise, quite fluttered. Guided by Higgins's signals, she comes to Mrs Higgins with studied grace.

LIZA [*speaking with pedantic correctness of pronunciation and great beauty of tone*] How do you do, Mrs Higgins? [*She gasps slightly in making sure of the H in Higgins, but is quite successful*]. Mr Higgins told me I might come.

MRS HIGGINS [*cordially*] Quite right: I'm very glad indeed to see you.

PICKERING. How do you do, Miss Doolittle?

LIZA [*shaking hands with him*] Colonel Pickering, is it not?

MRS EYNSFORD HILL. I feel sure we have met before, Miss Doolittle. I remember your eyes.

LIZA. How do you do? [*She sits down on the ottoman gracefully in the place just left vacant by Higgins*].

MRS EYNSFORD HILL [*introducing*] My daughter Clara.

LIZA. How do you do?

CLARA [*impulsively*] How do you do? [*She sits down on the ottoman beside Eliza, devouring her with her eyes*].

FREDDY [*coming to their side of the ottoman*] Ive certainly had the pleasure.

MRS EYNSFORD HILL [*introducing*] My son Freddy.

LIZA. How do you do?

Freddy bows and sits down in the Elizabethan chair, infatuated.

HIGGINS [*suddenly*] By George, yes: it all comes back to me! [*They stare at him*]. Covent Garden! [*Lamentably*] What a damned thing!

MRS HIGGINS. Henry, please! [*He is about to sit on the edge of the table*] Dont sit on my writing-table: youll break it.

HIGGINS [*sulkily*] Sorry.

He goes to the divan, stumbling into the fender and over the fire-irons on his way; extricating himself with muttered imprecations; and finishing his disastrous journey by throwing himself so impatiently on the divan that he almost breaks it. Mrs Higgins looks at him, but controls herself and says nothing.

A long and painful pause ensues.

MRS HIGGINS [*at last, conversationally*] Will it rain, do you think?

LIZA. The shallow depression in the west of these islands is likely to move slowly in an easterly direction. There are no indications of any great change in the barometrical situation.

FREDDY. Ha! ha! how awfully funny!

LIZA. What is wrong with that, young man? I bet I got it right.

FREDDY. Killing!

MRS EYNSFORD HILL. I'm sure I hope it wont turn cold. Theres so much influenza about. It runs right through our whole family regularly every spring.

LIZA [*darkly*] My aunt died of influenza: so they said.

MRS EYNSFORD HILL [*clicks her tongue sympathetically*] !!!

LIZA [*in the same tragic tone*] But it's my belief they done the old woman in.

MRS HIGGINS [*puzzled*] Done her in?

LIZA. Y-e-e-e-es, Lord love you! Why should she die of influenza? She come through diphtheria right enough the year before. I saw her with my own eyes. Fairly blue with it, she was. They all thought she was dead; but my father he kept ladling gin down her throat til she came to so sudden that she bit the bowl off the spoon.

MRS EYNSFORD HILL [*startled*] Dear me!

LIZA [*piling up the indictment*] What call would a woman with that strength in her have to die of influenza? What become of her new straw hat that should have come to me? Somebody pinched it; and what I say is, them as pinched it done her in.

MRS EYNSFORD HILL. What does doing her in mean?

HIGGINS [*hastily*] Oh, thats the new small talk. To do a person in means to kill them.

MRS EYNSFORD HILL [*to Eliza, horrified*] You surely dont believe that your aunt was killed?

LIZA. Do I not! Them she lived with would have killed her for a hat-pin, let alone a hat.

MRS EYNSFORD HILL. But it cant have been right for your father to pour spirits down her throat like that. It might have killed her.

LIZA. Not her. Gin was mother's milk to her. Besides, he'd poured so much down his own throat that he knew the good of it.

MRS EYNSFORD HILL. Do you mean that he drank?

LIZA. Drank! My word! Something chronic.

MRS EYNSFORD HILL. How dreadful for you!

LIZA. Not a bit. It never did him no harm what I could see. But then he did not keep it up regular. [*Cheerfully*] On the burst, as you might say, from time to time. And always more agreeable when he had a drop in. When he was out of work, my mother used to give him fourpence and tell him to go out and not come back until he'd drunk himself cheerful and loving-like. Theres lots of women has to make their husbands drunk to make them fit to live with. [*Now quite at her ease*] You see, it's like this. If a man has a bit of a conscience, it always takes him when he's sober; and then it makes him low-spirited. A drop of booze just takes that off and makes him happy. [*To Freddy, who is in convulsions of suppressed laughter*] Here! what are you sniggering at?

FREDDY. The new small talk. You do it so awfully well.

LIZA. If I was doing it proper, what was you laughing at? [*To Higgins*] Have I said anything I oughtnt?

MRS HIGGINS [*interposing*] Not at all, Miss Doolittle.

LIZA. Well, thats a mercy, anyhow. [*Expansively*] What I always say is—

HIGGINS [*rising and looking at his watch*] Ahem!

LIZA [*looking round at him; taking the hint; and rising*] Well: I must go. [*They all rise. Freddy goes to the door*]. So pleased to have met you. Goodbye. [*She shakes hands with Mrs Higgins*].

MRS HIGGINS. Goodbye.

LIZA. Goodbye, Colonel Pickering.

PICKERING. Goodbye, Miss Doolittle. [*They shake hands*].

LIZA [*nodding to the others*] Goodbye, all.

FREDDY [*opening the door for her*] Are you walking across the Park, Miss Doolittle? If so—

LIZA. Walk! Not bloody likely. [*Sensation*]. I am going in a taxi. [*She goes out*].

> *Pickering gasps and sits down. Freddy goes out on the balcony to catch another glimpse of Eliza.*

MRS EYNSFORD HILL [*suffering from shock*] Well, I really cant get used to the new ways.

CLARA [*throwing herself discontentedly into the Elizabethan chair*] Oh, it's all right, mamma, quite right. People will think we never go anywhere or see anybody if you are so old-fashioned.

MRS EYNSFORD HILL. I daresay I am very old-fashioned; but I do hope you wont begin using that expression, Clara. I have got accustomed to hear you talking about men as rotters, and calling everything filthy and beastly; though I do think it horrible and unladylike. But this last is really too much. Dont you think so, Colonel Pickering?

PICKERING. Dont ask me. Ive been away in India for several years; and manners have changed so much that I sometimes dont know whether I'm at a respectable dinner-table or in a ship's forecastle.

CLARA. It's all a matter of habit. Theres no right or wrong in it. Nobody means anything by it. And it's s o quaint, and gives such a smart emphasis to things that are not in themselves very witty. I find the new small talk delightful and quite innocent.

MRS EYNSFORD HILL [*rising*] Well, after that, I think its time for us to go.

> *Pickering and Higgins rise.*

CLARA [*rising*] Oh yes: we have three at-homes to go to still. Goodbye, Mrs Higgins. Goodbye, Colonel Pickering. Goodbye, Professor Higgins.

HIGGINS [*coming grimly at her from the divan, and accompanying her to the door*] Goodbye. Be sure you try on that small talk at the three at-homes. Dont be nervous about it. Pitch it in strong.

CLARA [*all smiles*] I will. Goodbye. Such nonsense, all this early Victorian prudery!

HIGGINS [*tempting her*] Such damned nonsense!

CLARA. Such bloody nonsense!

MRS EYNSFORD HILL [*convulsively*] Clara!

CLARA. Ha! ha! [*She goes out radiant, conscious of being thoroughly up to date, and is heard descending the stairs in a stream of silvery laughter*].

FREDDY [*to the heavens at large*] Well, I ask you— [*He gives it up, and comes to Mrs Higgins*]. Goodbye.

MRS HIGGINS [*shaking hands*] Goodbye. Would you like to meet Miss Doolittle again?

FREDDY [*eagerly*] Yes, I should, most awfully.

MRS HIGGINS. Well, you know my days.

FREDDY. Yes. Thanks awfully. Goodbye. [*He goes out*].

MRS EYNSFORD HILL. Goodbye, Mr Higgins.

HIGGINS. Goodbye, Goodbye.

MRS EYNSFORD HILL [*to Pickering*] It's no use. I shall never be able to bring myself to use that word.

PICKERING. Dont. It's not compulsory, you know. Youll get on quite well without it.

MRS EYNSFORD HILL. Only, Clara is so down on me if I am not positively reeking with the latest slang. Goodbye.

PICKERING. Goodbye [*They shake hands*].

MRS EYNSFORD HILL [*to Mrs Higgins*] You mustnt mind Clara. [*Pickering, catching from her lowered tone that this is not meant for him to hear, discreetly joins Higgins at the window*]. We're so poor! and she gets so few parties, poor child! She doesnt quite know. [*Mrs Higgins, seeing that her eyes are moist, takes her hand sympathetically and goes with her to the door*]. But the boy is nice. Dont you think so?

MRS HIGGINS. Oh, quite nice. I shall always be delighted to see him.

MRS EYNSFORD HILL. Thank you, dear. Goodbye. [*She goes out*].

HIGGINS [*eagerly*] Well? Is Eliza presentable? [*He swoops on his mother and drags her to the ottoman, where she sits down in Eliza's place with her son on her left*].

Pickering returns to his chair on her right.

MRS HIGGINS. You silly boy, of course she's not presentable. She's a triumph of your art and of her dressmaker's; but if you suppose for a moment that she doesnt give herself away in every sentence she utters, you must be perfectly cracked about her.

PICKERING. But dont you think something might be done? I mean something to eliminate the sanguinary element from her conversation.

MRS HIGGINS. Not as long as she is in Henry's hands.

HIGGINS [*aggrieved*] Do you mean that m y language is improper?

MRS HIGGINS. No, dearest: it would be quite proper—say on a canal barge; but it would not be proper for her at a garden party.

HIGGINS [*deeply injured*] Well I must say—

PICKERING [*interrupting him*] Come, Higgins: you must learn to know yourself. I havnt heard such language as yours since we used to review the volunteers in Hyde Park twenty years ago.

HIGGINS [*sulkily*] Oh well, if y o u say so, I suppose I dont always talk like a bishop.

MRS HIGGINS [*quieting Henry with a touch*] Colonel Pickering: will you tell me what is the exact state of things in Wimpole Street?

PICKERING [*cheerfully: as if this completely changed the subject*] Well, I have come to live there with Henry. We work together at my Indian Dialects; and we think it more convenient—

MRS HIGGINS. Quite so. I know all about that: it's an excellent arrangement. But where does this girl live?

HIGGINS. With us, of course. Where s h o u l d she live?

MRS HIGGINS. But on what terms? Is she a servant? If not, what is she?

PICKERING [*slowly*] I think I know what you mean, Mrs Higgins.

HIGGINS. Well, dash me if *I* do! Ive had to work at the girl every day for months to get her to her present pitch. Besides, she's useful. She knows where my things are, and remembers my appointments and so forth.

MRS HIGGINS. How does your housekeeper get on with her?

HIGGINS. Mrs Pearce? Oh, she's jolly glad to get so much taken off her hands; for before Eliza came, s h e used to have to find things and remind me of my appointments. But she's got some silly bee in her bonnet about Eliza. She keeps saying "You dont t h i n k, sir": doesnt she, Pick?

PICKERING. Yes: thats the formula. "You dont t h i n k, sir." Thats the end of every conversation about Eliza.

HIGGINS. As if I ever stop thinking about the girl and her confounded vowels and consonants. I'm worn out, thinking about her, and watching her lips and her teeth and her tongue, not to mention her soul, which is the quaintest of the lot.

MRS HIGGINS. You certainly are a pretty pair of babies, playing with your live doll.

HIGGINS. Playing! The hardest job I ever tackled: make no mistake about that, mother. But you have no idea how frightfully interesting it is to take a human being and change her into a quite different human being by creating a new speech for her. It's filling up the deepest gulf that separates class from class and soul from soul.

PICKERING [*drawing his chair closer to Mrs Higgins and bending over to her eagerly*] Yes: it's enormously interesting. I assure you, Mrs Higgins, we take Eliza very seriously. Every week—every day almost—there is some new change. [*Closer again*] We keep records of every stage—dozens of gramophone disks and photographs—

HIGGINS [*assailing her at the other ear*] Yes, by George: it's the most absorbing experiment I ever tackled. She regularly fills our lives up: doesnt she, Pick?

PICKERING. We're always talking Eliza.

HIGGINS. Teaching Eliza.

PICKERING. Dressing Eliza.

MRS HIGGINS. What!

HIGGINS. Inventing new Elizas.

	[*speaking together*]	
HIGGINS.		You know, she has the most extraordinary quickness of ear:
PICKERING.		I assure you, my dear Mrs Higgins, that girl
HIGGINS.		just like a parrot. Ive tried her with every
PICKERING.		is a genius. She can play the piano quite beautifully.
HIGGINS.		possible sort of sound that a human being can make—
PICKERING.		We have taken her to classical concerts and to music
HIGGINS.		Continental dialects, African dialects, Hottentot
PICKERING.		halls; and it's all the same to her: she plays everything
HIGGINS.		clicks, things it took me years to get hold of; and
PICKERING.		she hears right off when she comes home, whether it's
HIGGINS.		she picks them up like a shot, right away, as if she had
PICKERING.		Beethoven and Brahms or Lehar and Lionel Monckton;

HIGGINS. ⎫
PICKERING. ⎬

⎰ been at it all her life.

⎱ though six months ago, she'd never as much as touched a piano—

MRS HIGGINS [*putting her fingers in her ears, as they are by this time shouting one another down with an intolerable noise*] Sh-sh-sh—sh! [*They stop*].

PICKERING. I beg your pardon. [*He draws his chair back apologetically*].

HIGGINS. Sorry. When Pickering starts shouting nobody can get a word in edgeways.

MRS HIGGINS. Be quiet, Henry. Colonel Pickering: dont you realize that when Eliza walked into Wimpole Street, something walked in with her?

PICKERING. Her father did. But Henry soon got rid of him.

MRS HIGGINS. It would have been more to the point if her mother had. But as her mother didnt something else did.

PICKERING. But what?

MRS HIGGINS [*unconsciously dating herself by the word*] A problem.

PICKERING. Oh, I see. The problem of how to pass her off as a lady.

HIGGINS. I'll solve that problem. Ive half solved it already.

MRS. HIGGINS. No, you two infinitely stupid male creatures: the problem of what is to be done with her afterwards.

HIGGINS. I dont see anything in that. She can go her own way, with all the advantages I have given her.

MRS HIGGINS. The advantages of that poor woman who was here just now! The manners and habits that disqualify a fine lady from earning her own living without giving her a fine lady's income! Is that what you mean?

PICKERING [*indulgently, being rather bored*] Oh, that will be all right, Mrs Higgins. [*He rises to go*].

HIGGINS [*rising also*] We'll find her some light employment.

PICKERING. She's happy enough. Dont you worry about her. Goodbye. [*He shakes hands as if he were consoling a frightened child, and makes for the door*].

HIGGINS. Anyhow, theres no good bothering now. The thing's done. Goodbye, mother. [*He kisses her, and follows Pickering*].

PICKERING [*turning for a final consolation*] There are plenty of openings. We'll do whats right. Goodbye.

HIGGINS [*to Pickering as they go out together*] Let's take her to the Shakespeare exhibition at Earls Court.

PICKERING. Yes: lets. Her remarks will be delicious.

HIGGINS. She'll mimic all the people for us when we get home.

PICKERING. Ripping. [*Both are heard laughing as they go downstairs*].

MRS HIGGINS [*rises with an impatient bounce, and returns to her work at the writing-table. She sweeps a litter of disarranged papers out of her way; snatches a sheet of paper from her stationery case; and tries resolutely to write. At the third line she gives it up; flings down her pen; grips the table angrily and exclaims*] Oh, men! men!! men!!!

ACT 4

The Wimpole Street laboratory. Midnight. Nobody in the room. The clock on the mantelpiece strikes twelve. The fire is not alight: it is a summer night.

　　Presently Higgins and Pickering are heard on the stairs.

HIGGINS [*calling down to Pickering*] I say, Pick: lock up, will you? I shant be going out again.

PICKERING. Right. Can Mrs Pearce go to bed? We dont want anything more, do we?

HIGGINS. Lord, no!

Eliza opens the door and is seen on the lighted landing in opera cloak, brilliant evening dress, and diamonds, with fan, flowers, and all accessories. She comes to the hearth, and switches on the electric lights there. She is tired: her pallor contrasts strongly with her dark eyes and hair; and her expression is almost tragic. She takes off her cloak; puts her fan and flowers on the piano; and sits down on the bench, brooding and silent. Higgins, in evening dress, with overcoat and hat, comes in, carrying a smoking jacket which he has picked up downstairs. He takes off the hat and overcoat; throws them carelessly on the newspaper stand; disposes of his coat in the same way; puts on the smoking jacket; and throws himself wearily into the easy-chair at the hearth. Pickering, similarly attired, comes in. He also takes off his hat and overcoat, and is about to throw them on Higgins's when he hesitates.

PICKERING. I say: Mrs Pearce will row if we leave these things lying about in the drawing room.

HIGGINS. Oh, chuck them over the bannisters into the hall. She'll find them there in the morning and put them away all right. She'll think we were drunk.

PICKERING. We are, slightly. Are there any letters?

HIGGINS. I didnt look. [*Pickering takes the overcoats and hats and goes downstairs. Higgins begins half singing half yawning an air from La Fanciulla del Golden West. Suddenly he stops and exclaims*] I wonder where the devil my slippers are!

Eliza looks at him darkly; then rises suddenly and leaves the room.
Higgins yawns again, and resumes his song.
Pickering returns, with the contents of the letter-box in his hand

PICKERING. Only circulars, and this coroneted billet-doux for you. [*He throws the circulars into the fender, and posts himself on the hearthrug, with his back to the grate*].

HIGGINS [*glancing at the billet-doux*] Money-lender. [*He throws the letter after the circulars*].

Eilza returns with a pair of large down-at-heel slippers. She places them on the carpet before Higgins, and sits as before without a word.

HIGGINS [*yawning again*] Oh Lord! What an evening! What a crew! What a silly tom-foolery! [*He raises his shoe to unlace it, and catches sight of the slippers. He stops unlacing and looks at them as if they had appeared there of their own accord*]. Oh! theyre there, are they?

PICKERING [*stretching himself*] Well, I feel a bit tired. It's been a long day The garden party, a dinner party, and the opera! Rather too much of a good thing. But youve won your bet, Higgins. Eliza did the trick, and something to spare, eh?

HIGGINS [*fervently*] Thank God it's over!

Eliza flinches violently; but they take no notice of her; and she recovers herself and sits stonily as before.

PICKERING. Were you nervous at the garden party? *I* was. Eliza didnt seem a bit nervous.

HIGGINS. Oh, s h e wasnt nervous. I knew she'd be all right. No: it's the strain of putting the job through all these months that has told on me. It was interesting enough at first, while we were at the phonetics; but after that I got deadly sick of it. If I hadnt backed myself to do it I should have chucked the whole thing up two months ago. It was a silly notion: the whole thing has been a bore.

PICKERING. Oh come! the garden party was frightfully exciting. My heart began beating like anything.

HIGGINS. Yes, for the first three minutes. But when I saw we were going to win hands down, I felt like a bear in a cage, hanging about doing nothing. The dinner was worse: sitting gorging there for over an hour, with nobody but a damned fool of a fashionable woman to talk to! I tell you, Pickering, never again for me. No more artificial duchesses. The whole thing has been simple purgatory.

PICKERING. Youve never been broken in properly to the social routine. [*Strolling over to the piano*] I rather enjoy dipping into it occasionally myself: it makes me feel young again. Anyhow, it was a great success: an immense success. I was quite frightened once or twice because Eliza was doing it so well. You see, lots of the real people cant do it at all: theyre such fools that they think style comes by nature to people in their position; and so they never learn. Theres always something professional about doing a thing superlatively well.

HIGGINS. Yes: thats what drives me mad: the silly people dont know their own silly business. [*Rising*] However, it's over and done with; and now I can go to bed at last without dreading tomorrow.

Eliza's beauty becomes murderous.

PICKERING. I think I shall turn in too. Still, it's been a great occasion: a triumph for you. Goodnight [*He goes*].

HIGGINS [*following him*] Goodnight. [*Over his shoulder, at the door*] Put out the lights, Eliza; and tell Mrs Pearce not to make coffee for me in the morning: I'll take tea. [*He goes out*].

Eliza tries to control herself and feel indifferent as she rises and walks across to the hearth to switch off the lights. By the time she gets there she is on the point of screaming. She sits down in Higgins's chair and holds on hard to the arms. Finally she gives way and flings herself furiously on the floor, raging.

HIGGINS [*in despairing wrath outside*] What the devil have I done with my slippers? [*He appears at the door*]

LIZA [*snatching up the slippers, and hurling them at him one after the other with all her force*] There are your slippers. And there. Take your slippers; and may you never have a day's luck with them!

HIGGINS [*astounded*] What on earth—! [*He comes to her*]. Whats the matter? Get up. [*He pulls her up*]. Anything wrong?

LIZA [*breathless*] Nothing wrong—with y o u. Ive won your bet for your, havnt I? Thats enough for you. *I* dont matter, I suppose.

HIGGINS. Y o u won my bet! You! Presumptuous insect! *I* won it. What did you throw those slippers at me for?

LIZA. Because I wanted to smash your face. I'd like to kill you, you selfish brute. Why didnt you leave me where you picked me out of—in the gutter? You thank God it's all over, and that now you can throw me back again there, do you? [*She crisps her fingers frantically*].

HIGGINS [*looking at her in cool wonder*] The creature is nervous, after all.

LIZA [*gives a suffocated scream of fury, and instinctively darts her nails at his face*] ! !

HIGGINS [*catching her wrists*] Ah! would you? Claws in, you cat. How dare you shew your temper to me? Sit down and be quiet. [*He throws her roughly into the easy-chair*].

LIZA [*crushed by superior strength and weight*] Whats to become of me? Whats to become of me?

HIGGINS. How the devil do I know whats to become of you? What does it matter what becomes of you?

LIZA. You dont care. I know you dont care. You wouldnt care if I was dead. I'm nothing to you—not so much as them slippers.

HIGGINS [*thundering*] T h o s e slippers.

LIZA [*with bitter submission*] Those slippers. I didnt think it made any difference now.

A pause. Eliza hopeless and crushed. Higgins a little uneasy.

HIGGINS [*in his loftiest manner*] Why have you begun going on like this? May I ask whether you complain of your treatment here?

LIZA. No.

HIGGINS. Has anybody behaved badly to you? Colonel Pickering? Mrs Pearce? Any of the servants?

LIZA. No.

HIGGINS. I presume you dont pretend that *I* have treated you badly?

LIZA. No.

HIGGINS. I am glad to hear it. [*He moderates his tone*]. Perhaps youre tired after the strain of the day. Will you have a glass of champagne? [*He moves towards the door*].

LIZA. No. [*Recollecting her manners*] Thank you.

HIGGINS [*good-humored again*] This has been coming on you for some days. I suppose it was natural for you to be anxious about the garden party. But thats all over now. [*He pats her kindly on the shoulder. She writhes*]. Theres nothing more to worry about.

LIZA. Nothing more for y o u to worry about. [*She suddenly rises and gets away from him by going to the piano bench, where she sits and hides her face*]. Oh God! I wish I was dead.

HIGGINS [*staring after her in sincere surprise*] Why? In heaven's name, why? [*Reasonably, going to her*] Listen to me, Eliza. All this irritation is purely subjective.

LIZA. I dont understand. I'm too ignorant.

HIGGINS. It's only imagination. Low spirits and nothing else. Nobody's hurting you. Nothing's wrong. You go to bed like a good girl and sleep it off. Have a little cry and say your prayers: that will make you comfortable.

LIZA. I heard y o u r prayers. "Thank God it's all over!"

HIGGINS [*impatiently*] Well, d o n t you thank God it's all over? Now you are free and can do what you like.

LIZA [*pulling herself together in desperation*] What am I fit for? What have you left me fit for? Where am I to go? What am I to do? Whats to become of me

HIGGINS [*enlightened, but not at all impressed*] Oh t h a t s whats worrying you, is it? [*He thrusts his hands into his pockets, and walks about in his usual manner, rattling the contents of his pockets, as if condescending to a trivial subject out of pure kindness*]. I shouldnt bother about it if I were you. I should imagine you wont have much difficulty in settling yourself somewhere or other, though I hadnt quite realized that you were going away. [*She looks quickly at him: he does not look at her, but examines the dessert stand on the piano and decides that he will eat an apple*]. You might marry, you know. [*He bites a large piece out of the apple and munches it noisily*]. You see, Eliza, all men are not confirmed old bachelors like me and the Colonel. Most men are the marrying sort (poor devils!); and youre not bad-looking: it's quite a pleasure to look at you sometimes —not now, of course, because youre crying and looking as ugly as the very devil; but when youre all right and quite yourself, youre what I should call attractive. That is, to the people in the marrying line, you understand. You go to bed and have a good nice rest; and then get up and look at yourself in the glass; and you wont feel so cheap.

> *Eliza again looks at him, speechless, and does not stir.*
> *The look is quite lost on him: he eats his apple with a dreamy expression of happiness, as it is quite a good one.*

HIGGINS [*a genial afterthought occurring to him*] I daresay my mother could find some chap or other who would do very well.

LIZA. We were above that at the corner of Tottenham Court Road.

HIGGINS [*waking up*] What do you mean?

LIZA. I sold flowers. I didnt sell myself. Now youve made a lady of me I'm not fit to sell anything else. I wish youd left me where you found me.

HIGGINS [*slinging the core of the apple decisively into the grate*] Tosh, Eliza. Dont you insult human relations by dragging all this cant about buying and selling into it. You neednt marry the fellow if you dont like him.

LIZA. What else am I to do?

HIGGINS. Oh, lots of things. What about your old idea of a florist's shop? Pickering could set you up in one: he's lots of money. [*Chuckling*] He'll have to pay for all those togs you have been wearing today; and that, with the hire of the jewellery, will make a big hole in two hundred pounds. Why, six months ago you would have thought it the millennium to have a flower shop of your own. Come! youll be all right. I must clear off to bed: I'm devilish sleepy. By the way, I came down for something: I forget what it was.

LIZA. Your slippers.

HIGGINS. Oh yes, of course. You shied them at me. [*He picks them up, and is going out when she rises and speaks to him*].

LIZA. Before you go, sir—

HIGGINS [*dropping the slippers in his surprise at her calling him Sir*] Eh?

LIZA. Do my clothes belong to me or to Colonel Pickering?

HIGGINS [*coming back into the room as if her question were the very climax of unreason*] What the devil use would they be to Pickering?

LIZA. He might want them for the next girl you pick up to experiment on.

HIGGINS [*shocked and hurt*] Is t h a t the way you feel towards us?

LIZA. I dont want to hear anything more about that. All I want to know is whether anything belongs to me. My own clothes were burnt.

HIGGINS. But what does it matter? Why need you start bothering about that in the middle of the night?

LIZA. I want to know what I may take away with me. I dont want to be accused of stealing.

HIGGINS [*now deeply wounded*] Stealing! You shouldnt have said that, Eliza. That shews a want of feeling.

LIZA. I'm sorry. I'm only a common ignorant girl; and in my station I have to be careful.

There cant be any feelings between the like of you and the like of me. Please will you tell me what belongs to me and what doesnt?

HIGGINS [*very sulky*] You may take the whole damned houseful if you like. Except the jewels. Theyre hired. Will that satisfy you? [*He turns on his heel and is about to go in extreme dudgeon*].

LIZA [*drinking in his emotion like nectar, and nagging him to provoke a further supply*] Stop, please. [*She takes off her jewels*]. Will you take these to your room and keep them safe? I dont want to run the risk of their being missing.

HIGGINS [*furious*] Hand them over. [*She puts them into his hands*]. If these belonged to me instead of to the jeweller, I'd ram them down your ungrateful throat. [*He perfunctorily thrusts them into his pockets, unconsciously decorating himself with the protruding ends of the chains*].

LIZA [*taking a ring off*] This ring isnt the jeweller's: it's the one you bought me at Brighton. I dont want it now. [*Higgins dashes the ring violently into the fireplace, and turns on her so threateningly that she crouches over the piano with her hands over her face, and exclaims*] Dont you hit me.

HIGGINS. Hit you! You infamous creature, how dare you accuse me of such a thing? It is you who have hit me. You have wounded me to the heart.

LIZA [*thrilling with hidden joy*] I'm glad. Ive got a little of my own back, anyhow.

HIGGINS [*with dignity, in his finest professional style*] You have caused me to lose my temper: a thing that has hardly ever happened to me before. I prefer to say nothing more tonight. I am going to bed.

LIZA [*pertly*] Youd better leave a note for Mrs Pearce about the coffee; for she wont be told by me.

HIGGINS [*formally*] Damn Mrs Pearce; and damn the coffee; and damn you; and damn my own folly in having lavished hard-earned knowledge and the treasure of my regard and intimacy on a heartless guttersnipe. [*He goes out with impressive decorum, and spoils it by slamming the door savagely*].

Eliza smiles for the first time; expresses her feelings by a wild pantomime in which an imitation of Higgins's exit is confused with her own triumph; and finally goes down on her knees on the hearthrug to look for the ring.

ACT 5

Mrs Higgins's drawing room. She is at her writing-table as before. The parlor-maid comes in.

THE PARLOR-MAID [*at the door*] Mr Henry, maam, is downstairs with Colonel Pickering.

MRS HIGGINS. Well, shew them up.

THE PARLOR-MAID. Theyre using the telephone, maam. Telephoning to the police, I think.

MRS HIGGINS. What!

THE PARLOR-MAID [*coming further in and lowering her voice*] Mr Henry is in a state, maam. I thought I'd better tell you.

MRS HIGGINS. If you had told me that Mr Henry was not in a state it would have been more surprising. Tell them to come up when theyve finished with the police. I suppose he's lost something.

THE PARLOR-MAID. Yes, maam [*going*].

MRS HIGGINS. Go upstairs and tell Miss Doolittle that Mr Henry and the Colonel are here. Ask her not to come down til I send for her.

THE PARLOR-MAID. Yes, maam.

Higgins bursts in. He is, as the parlor-maid has said, in a state.

HIGGINS. Look here, mother: heres a confounded thing!

MRS HIGGINS. Yes, dear. Good morning. [*He checks his impatience and kisses her, whilst the parlor-maid goes out*]. What is it?

HIGGINS. Eliza's bolted.

MRS HIGGINS [*calmly continuing her writing*] You must have frightened her.

HIGGINS. Frightened her! nonsense! She was left last night, as usual, to turn out the lights and all that; and instead of going to bed she changed her clothes and went right off: her bed wasnt slept in. She came in a cab for her things before seven this morning; and that fool Mrs Pearce let her have them without telling me a word about it. What am I to do?

MRS HIGGINS. Do without, I'm afraid, Henry. The girl has a perfect right to leave if she chooses.

HIGGINS [*wandering distractedly across the room*] But I cant find anything. I dont know what appointments Ive got. I'm— [*Pickering comes in. Mrs Higgins puts down her pen and turns away from the writing-table*].

PICKERING [*shaking hands*] Good morning, Mrs Higgins. Has Henry told you? [*He sits down on the ottoman*].

HIGGINS. What does that ass of an inspector say? Have you offered a reward?

MRS HIGGINS [*rising in indignant amazement*] You dont mean to say you have set the police after Eliza.

HIGGINS. Of course. What are the police for? What else could we do? [*He sits in the Elizabethan chair*].

PICKERING. The inspector made a lot of difficulties. I really think he suspected us of some improper purpose.

MRS HIGGINS. Well, of course he did. What right have you to go to the police and give the girl's name as if she were a thief, or a lost umbrella, or something? Really! [*She sits down again, deeply vexed*].

HIGGINS. But we want to find her.

PICKERING. We cant let her go like this, you know, Mrs Higgins. What were we to do?

MRS HIGGINS. You have no more sense, either of you, than two children. Why—

The parlor-maid comes in and breaks off the conversation.

THE PARLOR-MAID. Mr Henry: a gentleman wants to see you very particular. He's been sent on from Wimpole Street.

HIGGINS. Oh, bother! I cant see anyone now. Who is it?

THE PARLOR-MAID. A Mr Doolittle, sir.

PICKERING. Doolittle! Do you mean the dustman?

THE PARLOR-MAID. Dustman! Oh no, sir: a gentleman.

HIGGINS [*springing up excitedly*] By George, Pick, it's some relative of hers that she's gone to. Somebody we know nothing about. [*To the parlor-maid*] Send him up, quick.

THE PARLOR-MAID. Yes, sir. [*She goes*].

HIGGINS [*eagerly, going to his mother*] Genteel relatives! now we shall hear something. [*He sits down in the Chippendale chair*].

MRS HIGGINS. Do you know any of her people?

PICKERING. Only her father: the fellow we told you about.

THE PARLOR-MAID [*announcing*] Mr Doolittle. [*She withdraws*].

> *Doolittle enters. He is brilliantly dressed in a new fashionable frock-coat, with white waistcoat and grey trousers. A flower in his buttonhole, a dazzling silk hat, and patent leather shoes complete the effect. He is too concerned with the business he has come on to notice Mrs Higgins. He walks straight to Higgins, and accosts him with vehement reproach.*

DOOLITTLE [*indicating his own person*] See here! Do you see this? Y o u done this.

HIGGINS. Done what, man?

DOOLITTLE. This, I tell you. Look at it. Look at this hat. Look at this coat.

PICKERING. Has Eliza been buying you clothes?

DOOLITTLE. Eliza! not she. Not half. Why would she buy me clothes?

MRS HIGGINS. Good morning, Mr Doolittle. Wont you sit down?

DOOLITTLE [*taken aback as he becomes conscious that he has forgotten his hostess*] Asking your pardon, maam. [*He approaches her and shakes her proffered hand*]. Thank you. [*He sits down on the ottoman, on Pickering's right*]. I am that full of what has happened to me that I cant think of anything else.

HIGGINS. What the dickens h a s happened to you?

DOOLITTLE. I shouldnt mind if it had only h a p p e n e d to me: anything might happen to anybody and nobody to blame but Providence, as you might say. But this is something that y o u done to me: yes, you, Henry Higgins.

HIGGINS. Have you found Eliza? Thats the point.

DOOLITTLE. Have you lost her?

HIGGINS. Yes.

DOOLITTLE. You have all the luck, you have. I aint found her; but she'll find me quick enough now after what you done to me.

MRS HIGGINS. But what has my son done to you, Mr Doolittle?

DOOLITTLE. Done to me! Ruined me. Destroyed my happiness. Tied me up and delivered me into the hands of middle class morality.

HIGGINS [*rising intolerantly and standing over Doolittle*] Youre raving. Youre drunk. Youre mad. I gave you five pounds. After that I had two conversations with you, at half-a-crown an hour. Ive never seen you since.

DOOLITTLE. Oh! Drunk! am I? Mad! am I? Tell me this. Did you or did you not write a letter to an old blighter in America that was giving five millions to found Moral Reform Societies all over the world, and that wanted you to invent a universal language for him?

HIGGINS. What! Ezra D. Wannafeller! He's dead. [*He sits down again carelessly*].

DOOLITTLE. Yes: he's dead; and I'm done for. Now did you or did you not write a letter to him to say that the most original moralist at present in England, to the best of your knowledge, was Alfred Doolittle, a common dustman.

HIGGINS. Oh, after your last visit I remember making some silly joke of the kind.

DOOLITTLE. Ah! you may well call it a silly joke. It put the lid on me right enough. Just give him the chance he wanted to shew that Americans is not like us: that they recognize and respect merit in every class of life, however humble. Them words is in his blooming will, in which, Henry Higgins, thanks to your silly joking, he leaves me a share in his Predigested Cheese Trust worth three thousand a year on condition that I lecture for his Wannafeller Moral Reform World League as often as they ask me up to six times a year.

HIGGINS. The devil he does! Whew! [*Brightening suddenly*] What a lark!

PICKERING. A safe thing for you, Doolittle. They wont ask you twice.

DOOLITTLE. It aint the lecturing I mind. I'll lecture them blue in the face, I will, and not turn a hair. It's making a gentleman of me that I object to. Who asked him to make a gentleman of me? I was happy. I was free. I touched pretty nigh everybody for money when I wanted it, same as I touched you, Henry Higgins. Now I am worrited; tied neck and heels; and everybody touches me for money. It's a fine thing for you, says my solicitor. Is it? says I. You mean it's a good thing for you, I says. When I was a poor man and had a solicitor once when they found a pram in the dust cart, he got me off, and got shut of me and got me shut of him as quick as he could. Same with the doctors: used to shove me out of the hospital before I could hardly stand on my legs, and nothing to pay. Now they finds out that I'm not a healthy man and cant live unless they looks after me twice a day. In the house I'm not let do a hand's turn for myself: somebody else must do it and touch me for it. A year ago I hadnt a relative in the world except two or three that wouldnt speak to me. Now Ive fifty, and not

a decent week's wages among the lot of them. I have to live for others and not for myself: thats middle class morality. Y o u talk of losing Eliza. Dont you be anxious: I bet she's on my doorstep by this: she that could support herself easy by selling flowers if I wasnt respectable. And the next one to touch me will be you, Henry Higgins. I'll have to learn to speak middle class language from you, instead of speaking proper English. Thats where y o u l l come in; and I daresay thats what you done it for.

MRS HIGGINS. But, my dear Mr Doolittle, you need not suffer all this if you are really in earnest. Nobody can force you to accept this bequest. You can repudiate it. Isnt that so, Colonel Pickering?

PICKERING. I believe so.

DOOLITTLE [*softening his manner in deference to her sex*] Thats the tragedy of it, maam. It's easy to say chuck it; but I havnt the nerve. Which of us has? We're all intimidated. Intimidated, maam: thats what we are. What is there for me if I chuck it but the workhouse in my old age? I have to dye my hair already to keep my job as a dustman. If I was one of the deserving poor, and had put by a bit, I could chuck it; but then why should I, acause the deserving poor might as well be millionaires for all the happiness they ever has. They dont know what happiness is. But I, as one of the undeserving poor, have nothing between me and the pauper's uniform but this here blasted three thousand a year that shoves me into the middle class. (Excuse the expression, maam: youd use it yourself if you had my provocation.) Theyve got you every way you turn: it's a choice between the Skilly of the workhouse and the Char Bydis of the middle class; and I havnt the nerve for the workhouse. Intimidated: thats what I am. Broke. Bought up. Happier men than me will call for my dust, and touch me for their tip; and I'll look on helpless, and envy them. And thats what your son has brought me to. [*He is overcome by emotion*].

MRS HIGGINS. Well, I'm very glad youre not going to do anything foolish, Mr Doolittle.

For this solves the problem of Eliza's future. You can provide for her now.

DOOLITTLE [*with melancholy resignation*] Yes, maam: I'm expected to provide for everyone now, out of three thousand a year.

HIGGINS [*jumping up*] Nonsense! he cant provide for her. He shant provide for her. She doesnt belong to him. I paid him five pounds for her. Doolittle: either youre an honest man or a rogue.

DOOLITTLE [*tolerantly*] A little of both, Henry, like the rest of us: a little of both.

HIGGINS. Well, you took that money for the girl; and you have no right to take her as well.

MRS HIGGINS. Henry: dont be absurd. If you want to know where Eliza is, she is upstairs.

HIGGINS [*amazed*] Upstairs!!! Then I shall jolly soon fetch her downstairs. [*He makes resolutely for the door*].

MRS HIGGINS [*rising and following him*] Be quiet, Henry. Sit down.

HIGGINS. I—

MRS HIGGINS. Sit down, dear; and listen to me.

HIGGINS. Oh very well, very well, very well. [*He throws himself ungraciously on the ottoman, with his face towards the windows*]. But I think you might have told us this half an hour ago.

MRS HIGGINS. Eliza came to me this morning. She passed the night partly walking about in a rage, partly trying to throw herself into the river and being afraid to, and partly in the Carlton Hotel. She told me of the brutal way you two treated her.

HIGGINS [*bounding up again*] What!

PICKERING [*rising also*] My dear Mrs Higgins, she's been telling you stories. We didnt treat her brutally. We hardly said a word to her; and we parted on particularly good terms. [*Turning on Higgins*]. Higgins: did you bully her after I went to bed?

HIGGINS. Just the other way about. She threw my slippers in my face. She behaved in the most outrageous way. I never gave her the slightest provocation. The slippers came bang into my face the moment I entered the room—before I had uttered a word. And used perfectly awful language.

PICKERING [*astonished*] But why? What did we do to her?

MRS HIGGINS. I think I know pretty well what you did. The girl is naturally rather affectionate, I think. Isnt she, Mr Doolittle?

DOOLITTLE. Very tender-hearted, maam. Takes after me.

MRS HIGGINS. Just so. She had become attached to you both. She worked very hard for you, Henry! I dont think you quite realize what anything in the nature of brain work means to a girl like that. Well, it seems that when the great day of trial came, and she did this wonderful thing for you without making a single mistake, you two sat there and never said a word to her, but talked together of how glad you were that it was all over and how you had been bored with the whole thing. And then you were surprised because she threw your slippers at you! *I* should have thrown the fire-irons at you.

HIGGINS. We said nothing except that we were tired and wanted to go to bed. Did we, Pick?

PICKERING [*shrugging his shoulders*] That was all.

MRS HIGGINS [*ironically*] Quite sure?

PICKERING. Absolutely. Really, that was all.

MRS HIGGINS. You didnt thank her, or pet her, or admire her, or tell her how splendid she'd been.

HIGGINS [*impatiently*] But she knew all about that. We didnt make speeches to her, if thats what you mean.

PICKERING [*conscience stricken*] Perhaps we were a little inconsiderate. Is she very angry?

MRS HIGGINS [*returning to her place at the writing-table*] Well, I'm afraid she wont go back to Wimpole Street, especially now that Mr Doolittle is able to keep up the position you have thrust on her; but she says she is quite. willing to meet you on friendly terms and to let bygones be bygones.

HIGGINS [*furious*] Is she, by George? Ho!

MRS HIGGINS. If you promise to behave yourself, Henry, I'll ask her to come down. If not, go home; for you have taken up quite enough of my time.

HIGGINS. Oh, all right. Very well. Pick: you behave yourself. Let us put on our best Sunday manners for this creature that we picked out of the mud. [*He flings himself sulkily into the Elizabethan chair*].

DOOLITTLE [*remonstrating*] Now, now, Henry Higgins! have some consideration for my feelings as a middle class man.

MRS HIGGINS. Remember your promise, Henry. [*She presses the bell-button on the writing-table*]. Mr Doolittle: will you be so good as to step out on the balcony for a moment. I dont want Eliza to have the shock of your news until she has made it up with these two gentlemen. Would you mind?

DOOLITTLE. As you wish, lady. Anything to help Henry to keep her off my hands. [*He disappears through the window*].

> *The parlor-maid answers the bell. Pickering sits down in Doolittle's place.*

MRS HIGGINS. Ask Miss Doolittle to come down, please.

THE PARLOR-MAID. Yes, maam. [*She goes out*].

MRS HIGGINS. Now, Henry: be good.

HIGGINS. I am behaving myself perfectly.

PICKERING. He is doing his best, Mrs Higgins.

> *A pause. Higgins throws back his head; stretches out his legs; and begins to whistle.*

MRS HIGGINS. Henry, dearest, you dont look at all nice in that attitude.

HIGGINS [*pulling himself together*] I was not trying to look nice, mother.

MRS HIGGINS. It doesnt matter, dear. I only wanted to make you speak.

HIGGINS. Why?

MRS HIGGINS. Because you cant speak and whistle at the same time.

> *Higgins groans. Another very trying pause.*

HIGGINS [*springing up, out of patience*] Where the devil is that girl? Are we to wait here all day?

> *Eliza enters, sunny, self-possessed, and giving a staggeringly convincing exhibition of ease of manner. She carries a little work-basket, and is very much at home. Pickering is too much taken aback to rise.*

LIZA. How do you do, Professor Higgins? Are you quite well?

HIGGINS [*choking*] Am I—[*He can say no more*].

LIZA. But of course you are: you are never ill. So glad to see you again, Colonel Pickering. [*He rises hastily; and they shake hands*]. Quite chilly this morning, isnt it? [*She sits down on his left. He sits beside her*].

HIGGINS. Dont you dare try this game on me. I taught it to you; and it doesnt take me in. Get up and come home; and dont be a fool.

> *Eliza takes a piece of needlework from her basket, and begins to stitch at it, without taking the least notice of this outburst.*

MRS HIGGINS. Very nicely put, indeed, Henry. No woman could resist such an invitation.

HIGGINS. You let her alone, mother. Let her speak for herself. You will jolly soon see whether she has an idea that I havnt put into her head or a word that I havnt put into her mouth. I tell you I have created this thing out of the squashed cabbage leaves of Covent Garden; and now she pretends to play the fine lady with me.

MRS HIGGINS [*placidly*] Yes, dear; but youll sit down, wont you?

> *Higgins sits down again, savagely.*

LIZA [*to Pickering, taking no apparent notice of Higgins, and working away deftly*] Will y o u drop me altogether now that the experiment is over, Colonel Pickering?

PICKERING. Oh dont. You mustnt think of it as an experiment. It shocks me, somehow.

LIZA. Oh, I'm only a squashed cabbage leaf—

PICKERING [*impulsively*] No.

LIZA [*continuing quietly*]— but I owe so much to you that I should be very unhappy if you forgot me.

PICKERING. It's very kind of you to say so, Miss Doolittle.

LIZA. It's not because you paid for my dresses. I know you are generous to everybody with money. But it was from you that I learnt really nice manners; and that is what makes one a lady, isnt it? You see it was so very difficult for me with the example of Professor Higgins always before me. I was brought up to be just like him, unable to control myself, and using bad language on the slightest provocation. And I should never have known that ladies and gentlemen didnt behave like that if you hadnt been there.

HIGGINS. Well!!

PICKERING. Oh, thats only his way, you know. He doesnt mean it.

LIZA. Oh, *I* didnt mean it either, when I was a flower girl. It was only my way. But you see I did it; and thats what makes the difference after all.

PICKERING. No doubt. Still, he taught you to speak; and I couldnt have done that, you know.

LIZA [*trivially*] Of course: that is his profession.

HIGGINS. Damnation!

LIZA [*continuing*] It was just like learning to dance in the fashionable way: there was nothing more than that in it. But do you know what began my real education?

PICKERING. What?

LIZA [*stopping her work for a moment*] Your calling me Miss Doolittle that day when I first came to Wimpole Street. That was the beginning of self-respect for me. [*She resumes her stitching*]. And there were a hundred little things you never noticed, because they came naturally to you. Things about standing up and taking off your hat and opening doors—

PICKERING. Oh, that was nothing.

LIZA. Yes: things that shewed you thought and felt about me as if I were something better than a scullery-maid; though of course I know you would have been just the same to a scullery-maid if she had been let into the drawing room. You never took off your boots in the dining room when I was there.

PICKERING. You mustnt mind that. Higgins takes off his boots all over the place.

LIZA. I know. I am not blaming him. It is his way, isnt it? But it made s u c h a difference to me that you didnt do it. You see, really and truly, apart from the things anyone can pick up (the dressing and the proper way of speaking and so on), the difference between a lady and a flower girl is not how she behaves, but how she's treated. I shall always be a flower girl to Professor Higgins, because he always treats me as a flower girl, and always will; but I know I can be a lady to you, because you always treat me as a lady, and always will.

MRS HIGGINS. Please dont grind your teeth, Henry.

PICKERING. Well, this is really very nice of you, Miss Doolittle.

LIZA. I should like you to call me Eliza, now, if you would.

PICKERING. Thank you. Eliza, of course.

LIZA. And I should like Professor Higgins to call me Miss Doolittle.

HIGGINS. I'll see you damned first.

MRS HIGGINS. Henry! Henry!

PICKERING [*laughing*] Why dont you slang back at him? Dont stand it. It would do him a lot of good.

LIZA. I cant. I could have done it once; but now I cant go back to it. Last night, when I was wandering about, a girl spoke to me; and I tried to get back into the old way with her; but it was no use. You told me, you know, that when a child is brought to a foreign country, it picks up the language in a few weeks, and forgets its own. Well, I am a child in your country. I have forgotten my own language, and can speak nothing but yours. Thats the real break-off with the corner of Tottenham Court Road. Leaving Wimpole Street finishes it.

PICKERING [*much alarmed*] Oh! but youre coming back to Wimpole Street, arnt you? Youll forgive Higgins?

HIGGINS [*rising*] Forgive! Will she, by George! Let her go. Let her find out how she can get on without us. She will relapse into the gutter in three weeks without me at her elbow.

> *Doolittle appears at the centre window. With a look of dignified reproach at Higgins, he comes slowly and silently to his daughter, who, with her back to the window, is unconscious of his approach.*

PICKERING. He's incorrigible, Eliza. You wont relapse, will you?

LIZA. No: not now. Never again. I have learnt my lesson. I dont believe I could utter one of the old sounds if I tried. [*Doolittle touches her on her left shoulder. She drops her work, losing her self-possession utterly at the spectacle of her father's splendor*] A-a-a-a-a-a-ah-ow-ooh!

HIGGINS [*with a crow of triumph*] Aha! Just so. A-a-a-a-ahowooh! A-a-a-a-ahowooh! A-a-a-a-ahowooh! Victory! Victory! [*He throws himself on the divan, folding his arms, and spraddling arrogantly*].

DOOLITTLE. Can you blame the girl? Dont look at me like that, Eliza. It aint my fault. Ive come into some money.

LIZA. You must have touched a millionaire this time, dad.

DOOLITTLE. I have. But I'm dressed something special today. I'm going to St. George's, Hanover Square. Your stepmother is going to marry me.

LIZA [*angrily*] Youre going to let yourself down to marry that low common woman!

PICKERING [*quietly*] He ought to, Eliza. [*To Doolittle*] Why has she changed her mind?

DOOLITTLE [*sadly*] Intimidated, Governor. Intimidated. Middle class morality claims its victim. Wont you put on your hat, Liza, and come and see me turned off?

LIZA. If the Colonel says I must, I—I'll [*almost sobbing*] I'll demean myself. And get insulted for my pains, like enough.

DOOLITTLE. Don't be afraid: she never comes to words with anyone now, poor woman! respectability has broke all the spirit out of her.

PICKERING [*squeezing Eliza's elbow gently*] Be kind to them, Eliza. Make the best of it.

LIZA [*forcing a little smile for him through her vexation*] Oh well, just to shew theres no ill feeling. I'll be back in a moment. [*She goes out*].

DOOLITTLE [*sitting down beside Pickering*] I feel uncommon nervous about the ceremony, Colonel. I wish youd come and see me through it.

PICKERING. But youve been through it before, man. You were married to Eliza's mother.

DOOLITTLE. Who told you that, Colonel?

PICKERING. Well, nobody told me. But I concluded—naturally—

DOOLITTLE. No: that aint the natural way, Colonel: it's only the middle class way. My way was always the undeserving way. But dont say nothing to Eliza. She dont know: I always had a delicacy about telling her.

PICKERING. Quite right. We'll leave it so, if you dont mind.

DOOLITTLE. And youll come to the church, Colonel, and put me through straight?

PICKERING. With pleasure. As far as a bachelor can.

MRS HIGGINS. May I come, Mr Doolittle? I should be very sorry to miss your wedding.

DOOLITTLE. I should indeed be honored by your condescension, maam; and my poor old woman would take it as a tremenjous compliment. She's been very low, thinking of the happy days that are no more.

MRS HIGGINS [*rising*] I'll order the carriage and get ready. [*The men rise, except Higgins*]. I shant be more than fifteen minutes. [*As she goes to the door Eliza comes in, hatted and buttoning her gloves*]. I'm going to the church to see your father married, Eliza. You had better come in the brougham with me. Colonel Pickering can go on with the bridegroom.

> *Mrs Higgins goes out. Eliza comes to the middle of the room between the centre window and the ottoman. Pickering joins her.*

DOOLITTLE. Bridegroom! What a word! It makes a man realize his position, somehow. [*He takes up his hat and goes towards the door*].

PICKERING. Before I go, Eliza, do forgive him and come back to us.

LIZA. I dont think papa would allow me. Would you, dad?

DOOLITTLE [*sad but magnanimous*] They played you off very cunning, Eliza, them two sportsmen. If it had been only one of them, you could have nailed him. But you see, there was two; and one of them chaperoned the other, as you might say. [*To Pickering*] It was artful of you, Colonel; but I bear no malice: I should have done the same myself. I been the victim of one woman after another all my life; and I dont grudge you two getting the better of Eliza. I shant interfere. It's time for us to go, Colonel. So long, Henry. See you in St George's, Eliza. [*He goes out*].

PICKERING [*coaxing*] Do stay with us, Eliza. [*He follows Doolittle*].

> *Eliza goes out on the balcony to avoid being alone with Higgins. He rises and joins her there. She immediately comes back into the room and makes for the door; but he goes along the balcony quickly and gets his back to the door before she reaches it.*

HIGGINS. Well, Eliza, youve had a bit of your own back, as you call it. Have you had enough? and are you going to be reasonable? Or do you want any more?

LIZA. You want me back only to pick up your slippers and put up with your tempers and fetch and carry for you.

HIGGINS. I havnt said I wanted you back at all.

LIZA. Oh, indeed. Then what are we talking about?

HIGGINS. About you, not about me. If you come back I shall treat you just as I have always treated you. I cant change my nature; and I dont intend to change my manners. My manners are exactly the same as Colonel Pickering's.

LIZA. Thats not true. He treats a flower girl as if she was a duchess.

HIGGINS. And I treat a duchess as if she was a flower girl.

LIZA. I see. [*She turns away composedly, and sits on the ottoman, facing the window*]. The same to everybody.

HIGGINS. Just so.

LIZA. Like father.

HIGGINS [*grinning, a little taken down*] Without accepting the comparison at all points, Eliza, it's quite true that your father is not a snob, and that he will be quite at home in any station of life to which his eccentric destiny may call him. [*Seriously*] The great secret, Eliza, is not having bad manners or good manners or any other particular sort of manners, but having the same manner for all human souls: in short, behaving as if you were in Heaven, where there are no third-class carriages, and one soul is as good as another.

LIZA. Amen. You are a born preacher.

HIGGINS [*irritated*] The question is not whether I treat you rudely, but whether you ever heard me treat anyone else better.

LIZA [*with sudden sincerity*] I dont care how you treat me. I dont mind your swearing at me. I dont mind a black eye: Ive had one before this. But [*standing up and facing him*] I wont be passed over.

HIGGINS. Then get out of my way; for I wont stop for you. You talk about me as if I were a motor bus.

LIZA. So you are a motor bus: all bounce and go, and no consideration for anyone. But I can do without you: dont think I cant.

HIGGINS. I know you can. I told you you could.

LIZA [*wounded, getting away from him to the other side of the ottoman with her face to the hearth*] I know you did, you brute. You wanted to get rid of me.

HIGGINS. Liar.

LIZA. Thank you. [*She sits down with dignity*].

HIGGINS. You never asked yourself, I suppose, whether *I* could do without you.

LIZA [*earnestly*] Dont you try to get round me. Youll h-a-v-e to do without me.

HIGGINS [*arrogant*] I can do without anybody. I have my own soul: my own spark of divine fire. But [*with sudden humility*] I shall miss you, Eliza. [*He sits down near her on the ottoman*]. I have learnt something from your idiotic notions: I confess that humbly and gratefully. And I have grown accustomed to your voice and appearance. I like them, rather.

LIZA. Well, you have both of them on your gramophone and in your book of photographs. When you feel lonely without me, you can turn the machine on. It's got no feelings to hurt.

HIGGINS. I cant turn your soul on. Leave me those feelings; and you can take away the voice and the face. They are not you.

LIZA. Oh, you a r e a devil. You can twist the heart in a girl as easy as some could twist her arms to hurt her. Mrs Pearce warned me. Time and again she has wanted to leave you; and you always got round her at the last minute. And you dont care a bit for her. And you dont care a bit for me.

HIGGINS. I care for life, for humanity; and you are a part of it that has come my way and been built into my house. What more can you or anyone ask?

LIZA. I wont care for anybody that doesnt care for me.

HIGGINS. Commercial principles, Eliza. Like [*reproducing her Covent Garden pronunciation with professional exactness*] s'yollin voylets [*selling violets*], isnt it?

LIZA. Dont sneer at me. It's mean to sneer at me.

HIGGINS. I have never sneered in my life. Sneering doesnt become either the human face or the human soul. I am expressing my righteous contempt for Commercialism. I dont and wont trade in affection. You call me a brute because you couldnt buy a claim on me by fetching my slippers and finding my spectacles. You were a fool: I think a woman fetching a man's slippers is a disgusting sight: did I ever fetch y o u r slippers? I think a good deal more of you for throwing them in my face. No use slaving for me and then saying you want to be cared for: who cares for a slave? If you come back, come back for the sake of good fellowship; for youll get nothing else. Youve had a thousand times as much out of me as I have out of you; and if you dare to set up your little dog's tricks of fetching and carrying slippers against my creation of a Duchess Eliza, I'll slam the door in your silly face.

LIZA. What did you do it for if you didnt care for me?

HIGGINS [*heartily*] Why, because it was my job.

LIZA. You never thought of the trouble it would make for me.

HIGGINS. Would the world ever have been made if its maker had been afraid of making trouble? Making life means making trouble. Theres only one way of escaping trouble; and thats killing things. Cowards, you notice, are always shrieking to have troublesome people killed.

LIZA. I'm no preacher: I dont notice things like that. I notice that you dont notice me.

HIGGINS [*jumping up and walking about intolerantly*] Eliza: youre an idiot. I waste the treasures of my Miltonic mind by spreading them before you. Once for all, understand that I go my way and do my work without caring twopence what happens to either of us. I am not intimidated, like your father and your stepmother. So you can come back or go to the devil: which you please.

LIZA. What am I to come back for?

HIGGINS [*bouncing up on his knees on the ottoman and leaning over it to her*] For the fun of it. Thats why I took you on.

LIZA [*with averted face*] And you may throw me out tomorrow if I dont do everything you want me to?

HIGGINS. Yes; and you may walk out tomorrow if I dont do everything you want me to.

LIZA. And live with my stepmother?

HIGGINS. Yes, or sell flowers.

LIZA. Oh! if I only c o u l d go back to my flower basket! I should be independent of both you and father and all the world! Why did you take my independence from me? Why did I give it up? I'm a slave now, for all my fine clothes.

HIGGINS. Not a bit. I'll adopt you as my daughter and settle money on you if you like. Or would you rather marry Pickering?

LIZA [*looking fiercely round at him*] I wouldnt marry y o u if you asked me; and youre nearer my age than what he is.

HIGGINS [*gently*] Than he is: not "than what he is."

LIZA [*losing her temper and rising*] I'll talk as I like. Youre not my teacher now.

HIGGINS [*reflectively*] I dont suppose Pickering would, though. He's as confirmed an old bachelor as I am.

LIZA. Thats not what I want; and dont you think it. Ive always had chaps enough wanting me that way. Freddy Hill writes to me twice and three times a day, sheets and sheets.

HIGGINS [*disagreeably surprised*] Damn his impudence! [*He recoils and finds himself sitting on his heels*].

LIZA. He has a right to if he likes, poor lad. And he does love me.

HIGGINS [*getting off the ottoman*] You have no right to encourage him.

LIZA. Every girl has a right to be loved.

HIGGINS. What! By fools like that?

LIZA. Freddy's not a fool. And if he's weak and poor and wants me, may be he'd make me happier than my betters that bully me and dont want me.

HIGGINS. Can he make anything of you? Thats the point.

LIZA. Perhaps I could make something of him. But I never thought of us making anything of one another; and you never think of anything else. I only want to be natural.

HIGGINS. In short, you want me to be as infatuated about you as Freddy? Is that it?

LIZA. No I dont. Thats not the sort of feeling I want from you. And dont you be too sure of yourself or of me. I could have been a bad girl if I'd liked. Ive seen more of some things than you, for all your learning. Girls like me can drag gentlemen down to make love to them easy enough. And they wish each other dead the next minute.

HIGGINS. Of course they do. Then what in thunder are we quarrelling about?

LIZA [*much troubled*] I want a little kindness. I know I'm a common ignorant girl, and you a book-learned gentleman; but I'm not dirt under your feet. What I done [*correcting herself*] what I did was not for the dresses and the taxis: I did it because we were pleasant together and I come—came—to care for you; not to want you to make love to me, and not forgetting the difference between us, but more friendly like.

HIGGINS. Well, of course. Thats just how I feel. And how Pickering feels. Eliza: youre a fool.

LIZA. Thats not a proper answer to give me [*she sinks on the chair at the writing-table in tears*].

HIGGINS. It's all youll get until you stop being a common idiot. If youre going to be a lady, youll have to give up feeling neglected if the men you know dont spend half their time snivelling over you and the other half giving you black eyes. If you cant stand the coldness of my sort of life, and the strain of it, go back to the gutter. Work til you are more a brute than a human being; and then cuddle and squabble and drink til you fall asleep. Oh, it's a fine life, the life of the gutter. It's real: it's warm: it's violent: you can feel it through the thickest skin: you can taste it and smell it without any training or any work. Not like Science and Literature and Classical Music and Philosophy and Art. You find me cold, unfeeling, selfish, dont you? Very well: be off with you to the sort of people you like. Marry some sentimental hog or other with lots of money, and a thick pair of lips to kiss you with and a thick pair of boots to kick you with. If you cant appreciate what youve got, youd better get what you can appreciate.

LIZA [*desperate*] Oh, you a r e a cruel tyrant. I cant talk to you: you turn everything against me: I'm always in the wrong. But you know very well all the time that youre nothing but a bully. You know I cant go back to the gutter, as you call it, and that I have no real friends in the world but you and the Colonel. You know well I couldnt bear to live with a low common man after you two; and it's wicked and cruel of you to insult me by pretending I could. You think I must go back to Wimpole Street because I have nowhere else to go but father's. But dont you be too sure that you have me under your feet to be trampled on and talked down. I'll marry Freddy, I will, as soon as he's able to support me.

HIGGINS [*sitting down beside her*] Rubbish! you shall marry an ambassador. You shall marry the Governor-General of India or the Lord-Lieutenant of Ireland, or somebody who wants a deputy-queen. I'm not going to have my masterpiece thrown away on Freddy.

LIZA. You think I like you to say that. But I havnt forgot what you said a minute ago; and I wont be coaxed round as if I was a baby or a puppy. If I cant have kindness, I'll have independence.

HIGGINS. Independence? Thats middle class blasphemy. We are all dependent on one another, every soul of us on earth.

LIZA [*rising determinedly*] I'll let you see whether I'm dependent on you. If you can preach, I can teach. I'll go and be a teacher.

HIGGINS. Whatll you teach, in heaven's name?

LIZA. What you taught me. I'll teach phonetics.

HIGGINS. Ha! ha! ha!

LIZA. I'll offer myself as an assistant to Professor Nepean.

HIGGINS [*rising in a fury*] What! That imposter! that humbug! that toadying ignoramus! Teach him m y methods! m y discoveries! You take one step in his direction and I'll wring your neck. [*He lays hands on her*]. Do you hear?

LIZA [*defiantly non-resistant*] Wring away. What do I care? I knew youd strike me some day. [*He lets her go, stamping with rage at having forgotten himself, and recoils so hastily that he stumbles back into his seat on the ottoman*]. Aha! Now I know how to deal with you. What a fool I was not to think of it before! You cant take away the knowledge you gave me. You said I had a finer ear than you. And I can be civil and kind to people, which is more than you can. Aha! Thats done you, Henry Higgins, it has. Now I dont care t h a t [*snapping her fingers*] for your bullying and your big talk. I'll advertize it in the papers that your duchess is only a flower girl that you taught, and that she'll teach anybody to be a duchess just the same in six months for a thousand guineas. Oh, when I think of myself crawling under your feet and being trampled on and called names, when all the time I had only to lift up my finger to be as good as you, I could just kick myself.

HIGGINS [*wondering at her*] You damned impudent slut, you! But it's better than snivelling; better than fetching slippers and finding spectacles, isnt it? [*Rising*] By George, Eliza, I said I'd make a woman of you; and I have. I like you like this.

LIZA. Yes: you turn round and make up to me now that I'm not afraid of you, and can do without you.

HIGGINS Of course I do, you little fool. Five minutes ago you were like a millstone round my neck. Now youre a tower of strength: a consort battleship. You and I and Pickering will be three old bachelors together instead of only two men and a silly girl.

> *Mrs. Higgins returns, dressed for the wedding. Eliza instantly becomes cool and elegant.*

MRS HIGGINS. The carriage is waiting, Eliza. Are you ready?

LIZA. Quite. Is the Professor coming?

MRS. HIGGINS. Certainly not. He cant behave himself in church. He makes remarks out loud all the time on the clergyman's pronunciation.

LIZA. Then I shall not see you again, Professor. Goodbye. [*She goes to the door*].

MRS HIGGINS [*coming to Higgins*] Goodbye, dear.

HIGGINS. Goodbye, mother. [*He is about to kiss her, when he recollects something*]. Oh, by the way, Eliza, order a ham and a Stilton cheese, will you? And buy me a pair of reindeer gloves, number eights, and a tie to match that new suit of mine, at Eale & Binman's. You can choose the color. [*His cheerful, careless, vigorous voice shows that he is incorrigible*].

LIZA [*disdainfully*] Buy them yourself. [*She sweeps out*].

MRS HIGGINS. I'm afraid youve spoiled that girl, Henry. But never mind, dear: I'll buy you the tie and gloves.

HIGGINS [*sunnily*] Oh, dont bother. She'll buy em all right enough. Goodbye.

> *They kiss. Mrs Higgins runs out. Higgins, left alone, rattles his cash in his pocket; chuckles; and disports himself in a highly self-satisfied manner.*

Like most of Shaw's plays, *Pygmalion* is concerned with ideas: about middle-class morality, about the proper attitude to take toward the lower classes, about what to do with the "undeserving poor," about the position of women in society, about the damaging effects of having a "substandard" accent, and about the science of phonetics.

Shaw was not very much interested in phonetics for its own sake. He doesn't seem to have had much grasp of the technical details of the science. For example, he transcribes Eliza's pronunciation of *dear* as *deah* apparently without realizing that this would also have to be his transcription of the way that Higgins himself pronounced the word. *Deah* is merely "eye dialect." Shaw was not a scientific phonetician but a humanist, a socialist, and a playwright. He realized that the inability of the lower classes in England to speak "received English" forced them to remain in the station, not to "which God had appointed them," but to which they had been condemned by their upbringing. Phonetic training might be a practical instrument for liberating them.

Accent as an index of social standing was much more powerful in the England of the nineteenth and early twentieth centuries than most Americans can understand. A recent writer on *Pygmalion* tells us that "the actual class barrier which Eliza overcomes" seems old-fashioned today. Perhaps so, but a proper accent is still very important in England, and parents who can afford it are careful to send their children to proper schools where they will get a sound education—and not least, a correct accent. But back to the England of 1914. Professor Higgins clearly speaks for Shaw himself when he says to Colonel Pickering (Act 1): "You see this creature with her kerbstone English: the English that will keep her in the gutter to the end of her days. Well, sir, in three months I could pass that girl off as a duchess at an ambassador's garden party."

In the preface to his play, Shaw tells his reader that in describing Henry Higgins he had in mind an actual person, Henry Sweet, a member of the Oxford English faculty, whom Shaw regarded as the most brilliant phonetician of the age. But Shaw was frank to say that "Pygmalion Higgins is not a portrait of Sweet" and that for Sweet "the adventure of Eliza Doolittle would have been impossible; still, as will be seen, there are touches of Sweet in the play." Shaw goes on to say in his preface that "the change wrought by Professor Higgins in the flower-girl is neither impossible nor uncommon." But Shaw makes it quite clear that Higgins had in him none of Shaw's own socialistic zeal, that he undertakes the transformation of Eliza Doolittle's English, not as a project in social engineering, but to demonstrate his own skill and the possibilities of the science he professed. Like Sweet, Higgins is a professional, and he cultivates a scientific detachment.

Why did Shaw choose *Pygmalion* for the title of his play? He picked up the name from one of the legends of classical antiquity. In his *Metamorphoses,* the poet Ovid tells the story of Pygmalion, an artist who lived on the island of Cyprus. Pygmalion carved a statue in which he embodied his ideal of the perfect woman. He became so enamoured of the figure that he prayed to the goddess Venus to turn it into a living woman, and the goddess granted him his prayer.

Pygmalion and his beloved Galatea married and presumably lived happily ever after. Shaw's play *Pygmalion* does not end in quite that fashion. We shall have more to say about that later. At the moment, it is sufficient to observe that Shaw used only so much of the Pygmalion story as fitted his purpose, just as he used only so much of the character of Henry Sweet as fitted his purpose.

Thus far we have dealt primarily with Shaw's reforming aims and his declared reason for writing the play. But *Pygmalion* amounts to much more than a political tract on the English class structure or a pamphlet

advertising the potentialities of phonetics. Strictly in terms of Shaw's avowed purpose, *Pygmalion* can hardly be termed a success. A great many of the people of England still do not speak the Queen's English, nor can one claim that the class system has been abolished. Some would say that it has not even been seriously shaken. But the play *Pygmalion* is still very much alive.

In 1938 a very popular film was made of the play. Later still, an extremely successful musical comedy, *My Fair Lady,* was based on the play, and of this too a film has been made. To what extent these various adaptations represent Shaw's original play is a matter to be discussed later. But the general vitality of Shaw's basic plot situation and the characters he created, as well as the brilliance of the dialogue, can scarcely be in question. Obviously *Pygmalion* is bigger than its ostensible thesis; it has survived the failure of its thesis and it could probably survive even the success of its thesis.

It may be useful, therefore, to look at certain aspects of Shaw's play that extend beyond his immediate didactic purpose—at least as he usually stated that purpose. What are these extra or peripheral qualities? Well, in the first place, Shaw has not simply set forth a few illustrations to point up an abstract thesis. Life is more complicated than any thesis. Professor Higgins himself is more than an expert in languages. Moreover, the problem that he set himself turns out to be more complex than he had imagined. Finally, Eliza is not merely a pupil but a woman, and her humanity complicates the problem still further.

Higgins begins by oversimplifying the problem. For it is not enough to teach Eliza the correct pronunciation of English. If he is really to succeed in passing her off as a duchess, he will have to take some care of her grammar too, and her vocabulary. But a new and enlarged vocabulary means new experiences and ideas, and thus involves education in the larger sense—the training of mind and sensibility, of character and personality.

Shaw makes the point very wittily in Act 3. Eliza gets carried away with the response of her audience and is soon expressing sentiments and ideas shocking to upper-class society, though she utters them "with pedantic correctness of pronunciation and great beauty of tone." She has no idea that she is being shocking and her listeners think that she is putting on an act.

Something more important still is involved. Suppose that Eliza, through the miracle of Higgins's devoted teaching and coaching, becomes a passable duchess. What then? How can a duchess live on a flower-girl's income? (Higgins estimates this to be in the neighborhood of about forty-five pounds a year—in 1914, $225.) Eliza herself is very much conscious of this matter. In Act 5, she finds that she has floated out of her social class and has been beached high and dry far above her economic station. It's all very well for Higgins—he obviously hasn't really thought about the matter—to tell her that a clever and pretty girl ought to have no trouble in getting married to a suitable husband. But Eliza refuses to accept such a solution. She had refused to sell herself when she was a poor flower-girl in Covent Garden, and she has no idea now of accepting marriage in terms of selling herself, in effect, though "respectably," of course, and of course for a better price.

Higgins, as he tells his mother in Act 2, has come to think of Eliza as a kind of fascinating toy. But Eliza is a woman, and as Eric Bentley, the critic, has put it, the play consists of two basic movements, both of them "Pygmalion myths." In the first, "a duchess is made out of a flower-girl. In the second, a woman is made out of a duchess." With this observation we come back once more to Shaw's real interest in the class situation, which is finally concerned with human beings. We come back also to his characteristic manner of presentation, a manner that is not dry argument but a presentation through dramatic clash and counterclash. Much of Shaw's wit, by the way, has to do with the irrationality of social convention, the absurdities implicit in a good many of our social generalizations, and, not least, with the foibles and foolishness that one finds in human nature itself.

In short, though *Pygmalion* is a play about "society," it is also about the human beings who partially create society and who are in large part created by it. Shaw himself once noted that "social questions are produced by the conflict of human institutions with human feeling." In his play, however, Shaw is not interested in human institutions apart from the individual with his feelings.

That Eliza has human feelings is something Henry Higgins comes to realize only rather late in the day, and even the essentially kindhearted Colonel Pickering is not at first sufficiently aware of them. Eliza is not an experimental guinea pig, interesting only insofar as her reactions confirm or refute a daring hypothesis. She is interesting in her own right, which means that she has a will of her own, and is no mere doll or puppet. If Eliza had remained to the end a mere puppet manipulated by Higgins, the play would lose all dramatic force and amount to little more than a rather improbable case history illustrating the positive effects of acquiring "good English." Thus, the transformation of the duchess (or simulacrum of a duchess) into a real live woman is an essential aspect of the play.

Does the play have a happy ending? Does Professor Henry Higgins marry the delightful creature whom he believes he has, like Pygmalion, "created"? Does the ending of the play hint of romance? Or does it remain thoroughly ambiguous? Eliza's last speech seems to be a brush-off. To Higgins's request (order?) that she buy certain things for him on her way home, she replies, "disdainfully," as the stage direction has it, "Buy them yourself," and she sweeps out of the room. But is her reply really a snub? Or is it a piece of coquetry? Does Eliza's bristling independence spring from her knowledge that she now has her mentor on a leash? After she has left the room, Higgins tells his mother, who offers to take care of the purchases, "Oh, don't bother. She'll buy em all right enough." Then his mother in turn leaves the room and the stage direction tells us that Higgins "rattles his cash in his pocket; chuckles; and disports himself in a highly self-satisfied manner."

Why is Higgins so self-satisfied? Because Eliza has become a true woman with a will of her own? Because she is no longer a doll but a real woman and therefore attractive? Has he discovered to his pleased surprise that he has fallen in love with his pupil?

The actor who played the role of Higgins in its first London production, in 1914, tried to suggest some such romantic ending. At the end of the play he threw flowers to Eliza. Shaw, however, didn't approve of this bit of stage business (or at least pretended not to like it—one is never completely sure about Shaw). At any rate, in 1915 he wrote to Mrs. Patrick Campbell, the actress who played Eliza, as follows:

> . . . I have passed Pygmalion for press among sheets of my new volume of plays; and it now has a sequel, not in dialogue, but in prose, which you will never be able to live up to. It describes in an absolutely convincing manner how Eliza married Freddy; how she realized her dream of a florist's shop; how neither of them knew how to keep the shop; how she had to beg from the Colonel again and again to avert bankruptcy; how the wretched pair had to go to shorthand and typewriting commercial schools to learn; how they went even to the London School of Economics and to Kew Gardens simultaneously to learn about business and flowers and combine the information; how Eliza wrote such a shameful hand that she had to abase herself to Higgins to be taught his wonderful Italian handwriting; how Clara was converted by H. G. Wells and Galsworthy and went into a shop herself and saved her soul alive; how the flowershop began to pay at last when they tried asparagus and Freddy became Mr. Hill, greengrocer; how Eliza never got out of the habit of nagging Higgins that she acquired in the fourth act, and, though deeply interested in him, did not quite like him any more than she liked her father, who was rejected by the middle classes and forced into the highest society, where he was a huge success but poorer than he had ever been in his life before on his four thousand a year. The publication of that sequel will be the end of the romance of Sir Herbert Tree [the actor who played Higgins]; and you will have to play Eliza properly and seriously for ever after[,] which is impossible.

EXERCISES

1. Is Shaw's account of what really happened "absolutely convincing" to you? The interested reader may want to go to the library and read Shaw's sequel in full. (In order to save space we have omitted it here. It is worth noting that in *My Fair Lady*, the Lerner-Loewe musical comedy that is based on *Pygmalion*, Higgins and Eliza do marry, and even the 1938 film of *Pygmalion* (the first film that Shaw ever allowed to be made of one of his plays) hints strongly at a romantic conclusion.

2. If you have ever seen *My Fair Lady* on the stage (or have seen the movie) do you feel that the ending is inevitable or at least plausible? Does Shaw's sequel settle the matter of what *really* happened to Eliza and Higgins? That is, does an author have a right to say what his play really means and what the authentic outcome has to be? Or is the reader necessarily compelled to choose between *Pygmalion* and *My Fair Lady*? Could they be regarded as two different plays, though based on the same general plot situation? If so, can both be considered comedies? Explain.

3. The first act of *Pygmalion* has been praised as a superb example of exposition. Do you agree? What are some of the things it does? The introduction of those who are to be the principal characters of the play, obviously. But what else? Matters of theme? The "problem" with which the play will concern itself? Give some instances.

4. Could the ordinary phonetician accomplish with an ordinary cockney girl what Higgins accomplishes with Eliza? How *ordinary* is Eliza? Does this line of inquiry have any real relevance to the enjoyment of this play? If not, why not?

5. It has been pointed out that Shaw's *Pygmalion* is really the story of Cinderella. One could also call it a retelling of the story of the ugly duckling that turned out to be a beautiful swan. Has Shaw tried to give a realistic basis to these fairy tales? In what ways? Has he succeeded? Or does the story of Eliza remain finally simply a fairy tale?

6. Is the character of Henry Higgins self-consistent? He is generally presented as the dedicated scholar, rather dry, intellectual, preoccupied with his own concerns, and unaware of, or indifferent to, the feelings of others. But what about his generous gesture at the end of Act 1, or what he tells his mother near the end of Act 3 about turning Eliza into a new human being, or his sudden confession to Eliza in Act 5 that he will miss her? Can you find other such passages? Do they represent contradictions in Higgins's character or are they merely instances of the complexity of his character? Explain.

7. What is the function in the play of Doolittle, Eliza's father? Eliza's attitude toward him is clear enough. What is the attitude of Higgins? Amusement, certainly. But does he show any element of sympathy? Of admiration even? Do you suppose, for example, that Higgins shared Doolittle's dislike of "middle-class morality"? What is your evidence?

8. To what class of society, by the way, does Higgins belong? He is an expert in pronunciation and dialects, and he knows how to teach Eliza received English. But is his own speech prim or pedantic? By the way, note that in Act 3 he says to Freddy: "It dont matter, anyhow"? Is this a slip on Higgins's part? Or on Shaw's? What do you make of it?

9. Notice how Shaw in various parts of the action plants comments that look forward to Eliza's anguished questions in Act 4 about what is to become of her. Mrs. Pearce has seen the problem earlier in Act 2, and Mrs. Higgins, in Act 3. Can you locate the specific passages? Are the women in this play generally much wiser than the men? Can it be said that Eliza, at the end of the play, is a "liberated woman"?

10. Jacques Barzun has remarked on "the tenseness generated as you read [Shaw's plays]. No need to remember the story or the background of the characters. Each person is fighting all the time, making drama as he goes: only recall the crowd at the opening of *Pygmalion*. . . ." Do you agree? If so, can you locate other such passages in this play in which—to quote Barzun further—"each speech . . . amount[s] to a twisting and turning over of the previous one—a rebuke or contradiction or misunderstanding of the interlocutor. . . ." Can you give instances from other parts of the play?

11. Shaw's wit is a hallmark of his work. It enlivens exchanges between characters with unexpected turns, frequent jumps in the logic—but meaningful ones—cross-questions that receive crazy answers that turn out not to be crazy at all. In general, Shaw's is a play of wit that disconcerts our normal expectations, knocks out of shape our comfortable worn clichés, and produces sparks of uncomfortable truth. A good example of this sort of thing occurs in Act 2 when Doolittle, obviously out to "sell" his daughter to Higgins, asks, "whats a five-pound note to you?" When Colonel Pickering, proper gentleman that he is, informs Doolittle that Mr. Higgins's intentions are "entirely honorable," Doolittle, not shamed or in the least at a loss for a reply, says: "Course they are, Governor. If I thought they wasnt, I'd ask fifty." Can you find other passages of this general order?

SAINT JOAN

George Bernard Shaw (1856–1950)

Characters

BERTRAND DE POULENGEY	DUNOIS' PAGE
STEWARD	RICHARD DE BEAUCHAMP, EARL OF WARWICK
JOAN	CHAPLAIN DE STOGUMBER
ROBERT DE BAUDRICOURT	PETER CAUCHON, BISHOP OF BEAUVAIS
THE ARCHBISHOP OF RHEIMS	WARWICK'S PAGE
MGR DE LA TRÉMOUILLE	THE INQUISITOR
COURT PAGE	D'ESTIVET
GILLES DE RAIS	DE COURCELLES
CAPTAIN LA HIRE	BROTHER MARTIN LADVENU
THE DAUPHIN (later CHARLES VII)	THE EXECUTIONER
DUCHESS DE LA TRÉMOUILLE	AN ENGLISH SOLDIER
DUNOIS, BASTARD OF ORLEANS	A GENTLEMAN OF 1920

SCENE 1

A fine spring morning on the river Meuse, between Lorraine and Champagne, in the year 1429 A.D., in the castle of Vaucouleurs.

Captain ROBERT DE BAUDRICOURT, *a military squire, handsome and physically ener-* *getic, but with no will of his own, is disguising that defect in his usual fashion by storming terribly at his* STEWARD, *a trodden worm, scanty of flesh, scanty of hair, who might be any age from 18 to 55, being the sort of man whom age cannot wither because he has never bloomed.*

The two are in a sunny stone chamber on the first floor of the castle. At a plain strong oak table, seated in chair to match, the captain presents his left profile. The STEWARD *stands facing him at the other side of the table, if so deprecatory a stance as his can be called standing. The mullioned thirteenth-century window is open behind him. Near it in the corner is a turret with a narrow arched doorway leading to a winding stair which descends to the courtyard. There is a stout fourlegged stool under the table, and a wooden chest under the window.*

ROBERT. No eggs! No eggs!! Thousand thunders, man, what do you mean by no eggs?

STEWARD. Sir: it is not my fault. It is the act of God.

ROBERT. Blasphemy. You tell me there are no eggs; and you blame your Maker for it.

STEWARD. Sir: what can I do? I cannot lay eggs.

ROBERT (*sarcastic*). Ha! You jest about it.

STEWARD. No, sir, God knows. We all have to go without eggs just as you have, sir. The hens will not lay.

ROBERT. Indeed! (*Rising*). Now listen to me, you.

STEWARD (*humbly*). Yes, sir.

ROBERT. What am I?

STEWARD. What are you, sir?

ROBERT (*coming at him*). Yes: what am I? Am I Robert, squire of Baudricourt and captain of this castle of Vaucouleurs; or am I a cowboy?

STEWARD. Oh, sir, you know you are a greater man here than the king himself.

ROBERT. Precisely. And now, do you know what you are?

STEWARD. I am nobody, sir, except that I have the honor to be your steward.

ROBERT (*driving him to the wall, adjective by adjective*). You have not only the honor of being my steward, but the privilege of being the worst, most incompetent, drivelling snivelling jibbering jabbering idiot of a steward in France. (*He strides back to the table*)

STEWARD (*cowering on the chest*). Yes, sir: to a great man like you I must seem like that.

ROBERT (*turning*). My fault, I suppose. Eh?

STEWARD (*coming to him deprecatingly*). Oh, sir: you always give my most innocent words such a turn!

ROBERT. I will give your neck a turn if you dare tell me when I ask you how many eggs there are that you cannot lay any.

STEWARD (*protesting*). Oh sir, oh sir—

ROBERT. No: not oh sir, oh sir, but no sir, no sir. My three Barbary hens and the black are the best layers in Champagne. And you come and tell me that there are no eggs! Who stole them? Tell me that, before I kick you out through the castle gate for a liar and a seller of my goods to thieves. The milk was short yesterday, too: do not forget that.

STEWARD (*desperate*). I know, sir. I know only too well. There is no milk: there are no eggs: tomorrow there will be nothing.

ROBERT. Nothing! You will steal the lot: eh?

STEWARD. No, sir: nobody will steal anything. But there is a spell on us: we are bewitched.

ROBERT. That story is not good enough for me. Robert de Baudricourt burns witches and hangs thieves. Go. Bring me four dozen eggs and two gallons of milk here in this room before noon, or Heaven have mercy on your bones! I will teach you to make a fool of me. (*He resumes his seat with an air of finality*)

STEWARD. Sir: I tell you there are no eggs. There will be none—not if you were to kill me for it—as long as The Maid is at the door.

ROBERT. The Maid! What maid? What are you talking about?

STEWARD. The girl from Lorraine, sir. From Domrémy.

ROBERT (*rising in fearful wrath*). Thirty thousand thunders! Fifty thousand devils! Do you mean to say that that girl, who had the impudence to ask to see me two days ago, and whom I told you to send back to her father with my orders that he was to give her a good hiding, is here still?

STEWARD. I have told her to go, sir. She wont.

ROBERT. I did not tell you to tell her to go: I told you to throw her out. You have fifty men-at-arms and a dozen lumps of able-bodied servants to carry out my orders. Are they afraid of her?

STEWARD. She is so positive, sir.

ROBERT (*seizing him by the scruff of the neck*). Positive! Now see here. I am going to throw you downstairs.

STEWARD. No, sir. Please.

ROBERT. Well, stop me by being positive. It's quite easy: any slut of a girl can do it.

STEWARD (*hanging limp in his hands*). Sir, sir: you cannot get rid of h e r by throwing m e out. (ROBERT *has to let him drop. He squats on his knees on the floor, contemplating his master resignedly.*) You see, sir, you are much more positive than I am. But so is she.

ROBERT. I am stronger than you are, you fool.

STEWARD. No, sir: it isnt that: it's your strong character, sir. She is weaker than we are: she is only a slip of a girl; but we cannot make her go.

ROBERT. You parcel of curs: you are afraid of her.

STEWARD (*rising cautiously*). No sir: we are afraid of you; but she puts courage into us. She really doesnt seem to be afraid of anything. Perhaps you could frighten her, sir.

ROBERT (*grimly*). Perhaps. Where is she now?

STEWARD. Down in the courtyard, sir, talking to the soldiers as usual. She is always talking to the soldiers except when she is praying.

ROBERT. Praying! Ha! You believe she prays, you idiot. I know the sort of girl that is al-ways talking to soldiers. She shall talk to me a bit. (*He goes to the window and shouts fiercely through it*) Hallo, you there!

A GIRL'S VOICE (*bright, strong and rough*). Is it me, sir?

ROBERT. Yes, you.

THE VOICE. Be you captain?

ROBERT. Yes, damn your impudence, I be captain. Come up here. (*To the soldiers in the yard*) Shew her the way, you. And shove her along quick. (*He leaves the window, and returns to his place at the table, where he sits magisterially*)

STEWARD (*whispering*). She wants to go and be a soldier herself. She wants you to give her soldier's clothes. Armor, sir! And a sword! Actually! (*He steals behind* ROBERT)

(JOAN *appears in the turret doorway. She is an ablebodied country girl of 17 or 18, respectably dressed in red, with an uncommon face; eyes very wide apart and bulging as they often do in very imaginative people, a long well-shaped nose with wide nostrils, a short upper lip, resolute but full-lipped mouth, and handsome fighting chin. She comes eagerly to the table, delighted at having penetrated to* BAUDRICOURT'S *presence at last, and full of hope as to the results. His scowl does not check or frighten her in the least. Her voice is normally a hearty coaxing voice, very confident, very appealing, very hard to resist.*)

JOAN (*bobbing a curtsey*). Good morning, captain squire. Captain: you are to give me a horse and armor and some soldiers, and send me to the Dauphin. Those are your orders from my Lord.

ROBERT (*outraged*). Orders from your lord! And who the devil may your lord be? Go back to him, and tell him that I am neither duke nor peer at his orders: I am squire of Baudricourt; and I take no orders except from the king.

JOAN (*reassuringly*). Yes, squire: that is all right. My Lord is the King of Heaven.

ROBERT. Why, the girl's mad. (*To the* STEWARD) Why didnt you tell me so, you blockhead?

STEWARD. Sir: do not anger her: give her what she wants.

JOAN (*impatient, but friendly*). They all say I am mad until I talk to them, squire. But you see that it is the will of God that you are to do what He has put into my mind.

ROBERT. It is the will of God that I shall send you back to your father with orders to put you under lock and key and thrash the madness out of you. What have you to say to that?

JOAN. You think you will, squire; but you will find it all coming quite different. You said you would not see me; but here I am.

STEWARD (*appealing*). Yes, sir. You see, sir.

ROBERT. Hold your tongue, you.

STEWARD (*abjectly*). Yes, sir.

ROBERT (*to* JOAN, *with a sour loss of confidence*). So you are presuming on my seeing you, are you?

JOAN (*sweetly*). Yes, squire.

ROBERT (*feeling that he has lost ground, brings down his two fists squarely on the table, and inflates his chest imposingly to cure the unwelcome and only too familiar sensation*). Now listen to me. I am going to assert myself.

JOAN (*busily*). Please do, squire. The horse will cost sixteen francs. It is a good deal of money: but I can save it on the armor. I can find a soldier's armor that will fit me well enough: I am very hardy; and I do not need beautiful armor made to my measure like you wear. I shall not want many soldiers: the Dauphin will give me all I need to raise the siege of Orleans.

ROBERT (*flabbergasted*). To raise the siege of Orleans!

JOAN (*simply*). Yes, squire: that is what God is sending me to do. Three men will be enough for you to send with me if they are good men and gentle to me. They have promised to come with me. Polly and Jack and—

ROBERT. Polly!! You impudent baggage, do you dare call squire Bertrand de Poulengey Polly to my face?

JOAN. His friends call him so, squire: I did not know he had any other name. Jack—

ROBERT. That is Monsieur John of Metz, I suppose?

JOAN. Yes, squire. Jack will come willingly: he is a very kind gentleman, and gives me money to give to the poor. I think John Godsave will come, and Dick the Archer, and their servants John of Honecourt and Julian. There will be no trouble for you, squire: I have arranged it all: you have only to give the order.

ROBERT (*contemplating her in a stupor of amazement*). Well, I am damned!

JOAN (*with unruffled sweetness*). No, squire: God is very merciful; and the blessed saints Catherine and Margaret, who speak to me every day (*he gapes*), will intercede for you. You will go to paradise; and your name will be remembered for ever as my first helper.

ROBERT (*to the* STEWARD, *still much bothered, but changing his tone as he pursues a new clue*). Is this true about Monsieur de Poulengey?

STEWARD (*eagerly*). Yes, sir, and about Monsieur de Metz too. They both want to go with her.

ROBERT (*thoughtful*). Mf! (*He goes to the window, and shouts into the courtyard*) Hallo! You there: send Monsieur de Poulengey to me, will you? (*He turns to* JOAN) Get out; and wait in the yard.

JOAN (*smiling brightly at him*). Right, squire. (*She goes out*)

ROBERT (*to the* STEWARD). Go with her, you, you dithering imbecile. Stay within call; and keep your eye on her. I shall have her up here again.

STEWARD. Do so in God's name, sir. Think of those hens, the best layers in Champagne; and—

ROBERT. Think of my boot; and take your backside out of reach of it.

(*The* STEWARD *retreats hastily and finds himself confronted in the doorway by* BERTRAND DE POULENGEY, *a lymphatic French gentleman-at-arms, aged 36 or thereabout, employed in the department of the provost-marshal, dreamily absent-minded, seldom speaking unless spoken to, and then slow and obstinate in reply; altogether in contrast to the self-assertive, loud-mouthed, superficially energetic, fundamentally will-less* ROBERT. *The* STEWARD *makes way for him, and vanishes.*
POULENGEY *salutes, and stands awaiting orders.*)

ROBERT (*genially*). It isnt service, Polly. A friendly talk. Sit down. (*He hooks the stool from under the table with his instep*)

(POULENGEY, *relaxing, comes into the room: places the stool between the table and the window: and sits down ruminatively.* ROBERT, *half sitting on the end of the table, begins the friendly talk.*)

ROBERT. Now listen to me, Polly. I must talk to you like a father.

(POULENGEY *looks up at him gravely for a moment, but says nothing.*)

ROBERT. It's about this girl you are interested in. Now, I have seen her. I have talked to her. First, she's mad. That doesnt matter. Second, she's not a farm wench. She's a bourgeoise. That matters a good deal. I know her class exactly. Her father came here last year to represent his village in a lawsuit: he is one of their notables. A farmer. Not a gentleman farmer: he makes money by it, and lives by it. Still, not a laborer. Not a mechanic. He might have a cousin a lawyer, or in the Church. People of this sort may be of no account socially; but they can give a lot of bother to the authorities. That is to say, to m e. Now no doubt it seems to you a very simple thing to take this girl away, humbugging her into the belief that you are taking her to the Dauphin. But if you get her

into trouble, you may get m e into no end of a mess, as I am her father's lord, and responsible for her protection. So friends or no friends, Polly, hands off her.

POULENGEY (*with deliberate impressiveness*). I should as soon think of the Blessed Virgin herself in that way, as of this girl.

ROBERT (*coming off the table*). But she says you and Jack and Dick have offered to go with her. What for? You are not going to tell me that you take her crazy notion of going to the Dauphin seriously, are you?

POULENGEY (*slowly*). There is something about her. They are pretty foulmouthed and foulminded down there in the guardroom, some of them. But there hasnt been a word that has anything to do with her being a woman. They have stopped swearing before her. There is something. Something. It may be worth trying.

ROBERT. Oh, come, Polly! pull yourself together. Commonsense was never your strong point; but this is a little too much. (*He retreats disgustedly*)

POULENGEY (*unmoved*). What is the good of commonsense? If we had any commonsense we should join the Duke of Burgundy and the English king. They hold half the country, right down to the Loire. They have Paris. They have this castle: you know very well that we had to surrender it to the Duke of Bedford, and that you are only holding it on parole. The Dauphin is in Chinon, like a rat in a corner, except that he wont fight. We dont even know that he i s the Dauphin: his mother says he isnt; and she ought to know. Think of that! the queen denying the legitimacy of her own son!

ROBERT. Well, she married her daughter to the English king. Can you blame the woman?

POULENGEY. I blame nobody. But thanks to her, the Dauphin is down and out; and we may as well face it. The English will take Orleans: the Bastard will not be able to stop them.

ROBERT. He beat the English the year before last at Montargis. I was with him.

POULENGEY. No matter: his men are cowed now; and he cant work miracles. And I tell you that nothing can save our side now but a miracle.

ROBERT. Miracles are all right, Polly. The only difficulty about them is that they dont happen nowadays.

POULENGEY. I used to think so. I am not so sure now. (*Rising, and moving ruminatively towards the window*) At all events this is not a time to leave any stone unturned. There is something about the girl.

ROBERT. Oh! You think the girl can work miracles, do you?

POULENGEY. I think the girl herself is a bit of a miracle. Anyhow, she is the last card left in our hand. Better play her than throw up the game. (*He wanders to the turret*)

ROBERT (*wavering*). You really think that?

POULENGEY (*turning*). Is there anything else left for us to think?

ROBERT (*going to him*). Look here, Polly. If you were in my place would you let a girl like that do you out of sixteen francs for a horse?

POULENGEY. I will pay for the horse.

ROBERT. You will!

POULENGEY. Yes: I will back my opinion.

ROBERT. You will really gamble on a forlorn hope to the tune of sixteen francs?

POULENGEY. It is not a gamble.

ROBERT. What else is it?

POULENGEY. It is a certainty. Her words and her ardent faith in God have put fire into me.

ROBERT (*giving him up*). Whew! You are as mad as she is.

POULENGEY (*obstinately*). We want a few mad people now. See where the sane ones have landed us!

ROBERT (*his irresoluteness now openly swamping his affected decisiveness*). I shall feel like a precious fool. Still, if you feel sure—?

POULENGEY. I feel sure enough to take her to Chinon—unless you stop me.

ROBERT. This is not fair. You are putting the responsibility on me.

POULENGEY. It is on you whichever way you decide.

ROBERT. Yes: thats just it. Which way am I to decide? You dont see how awkward this is for me. (*Snatching at a dilatory step with an unconscious hope that* JOAN *will make up his mind for him*) Do you think I ought to have another talk to her?

POULENGEY (*rising*). Yes. (*He goes to the window and calls*) Joan!

JOAN'S VOICE. Will he let us go, Polly?

POULENGEY. Come up. Come in. (*Turning to Robert*) Shall I leave you with her?

ROBERT. No: stay here; and back me up.

> (POULENGEY *sits down on the chest.* ROBERT *goes back to his magisterial chair, but remains standing to inflate himself more imposingly.* JOAN *comes in, full of good news.*)

JOAN. Jack will go halves for the horse.

ROBERT. Well!! (*He sits, deflated*)

POULENGEY (*gravely*). Sit down, Joan.

JOAN (*checked a little, and looking to* ROBERT). May I?

ROBERT. Do what you are told.

> (JOAN *curtsies and sits down on the stool between them.* ROBERT *outfaces his perplexity with his most peremptory air.*)

ROBERT. What is your name?

JOAN (*chattily*). They always call me Jenny in Lorraine. Here in France I am Joan. The soldiers call me The Maid.

ROBERT. What is your surname?

JOAN. Surname? What is that? My father sometimes calls himself d'Arc; but I know nothing about it. You met my father. He—

ROBERT. Yes, yes; I remember. You come from Domrémy in Lorraine, I think.

JOAN. Yes; but what does it matter? we all speak French.

ROBERT. Dont ask questions: answer them. How old are you?

JOAN. Seventeen: so they tell me. It might be nineteen. I dont remember.

ROBERT. What did you mean when you said that St Catherine and St Margaret talked to you every day?

JOAN. They do.

ROBERT. What are they like?

JOAN (*suddenly obstinate*). I will tell you nothing about that: they have not given me leave.

ROBERT. But you actually see them; and they talk to you just as I am talking to you?

JOAN. No: it is quite different. I cannot tell you: you must not talk to me about my voices.

ROBERT. How do you mean? voices?

JOAN. I hear voices telling me what to do. They come from God.

ROBERT. They come from your imagination.

JOAN. Of course. That is how the messages of God come to us.

POULENGEY. Checkmate.

ROBERT. No fear! (*To* JOAN) So God says you are to raise the siege of Orleans?

JOAN. And to crown the Dauphin in Rheims Cathedral.

ROBERT (*gasping*). Crown the D—! Gosh!

JOAN. And to make the English leave France.

ROBERT (*sarcastic*). Anything else?

JOAN (*charming*). Not just at present, thank you, squire.

ROBERT. I suppose you think raising a siege is as easy as chasing a cow out of a meadow. You think soldiering is anybody's job?

JOAN. I do not think it can be very difficult if God is on your side, and you are willing to put your life in His hand. But many soldiers are very simple.

ROBERT (*grimly*). Simple! Did you ever see English soldiers fighting?

JOAN. They are only men. God made them just like us; but He gave them their own country and their own language; and it is not His will that they should come into our country and try to speak our language.

ROBERT. Who has been putting such nonsense into your head? Dont you know that soldiers are subject to their feudal lord, and that it is nothing to them or to you whether he is the duke of Burgundy or the king of England or the king of France? What has their language to do with it?

JOAN. I do not understand that a bit. We are all subject to the King of Heaven; and He gave us our countries and our languages, and meant us to keep to them. If it were not so it would be murder to kill an Englishman in battle; and you, squire, would be in great danger of hell fire. You must not think about your duty to your feudal lord, but about your duty to God.

POULENGEY. It's no use, Robert: she can choke you like that every time.

ROBERT. Can she, by Saint Dennis! We shall see. (*To* JOAN) We are not talking about God: we are talking about practical affairs. I ask you again, girl, have you ever seen English soldiers fighting? Have you ever seen them plundering, burning, turning the countryside into a desert? Have you heard no tales of their Black Prince who was blacker than the devil himself, or of the English king's father?

JOAN. You must not be afraid, Robert—

ROBERT. Damn you, I am not afraid. And who gave you leave to call me Robert?

JOAN. You were called so in church in the name of our Lord. All the other names are your father's or your brother's or anybody's.

ROBERT. Tcha!

JOAN. Listen to me, squire. At Domrémy we had to fly to the next village to escape from the English soldiers. Three of them were left behind, wounded. I came to know these three poor goddams quite well. They had not half my strength.

ROBERT. Do you know why they are called goddams?

JOAN. No. Everyone calls them goddams.

ROBERT. It is because they are always calling on their God to condemn their souls to perdition. That is what goddam means in their language. How do you like it?

JOAN. God will be merciful to them; and they will act like His good children when they go back to the country He made for them, and made them for. I have heard the tales of the Black Prince. The moment he touched the soil of our country the devil entered into him, and made him a black fiend. But at home, in the place made for him by God, he was good. It is always so. If I went into England against the will of God to conquer England, and tried to live there and speak its language, the devil would enter into me; and when I was old I should shudder to remember the wickedness I did.

ROBERT. Perhaps. But the more devil you were the better you might fight. That is why the goddams will take Orleans. And you cannot stop them, nor ten thousand like you.

JOAN. O n e thousand like me can stop them. Ten like me can stop them with God on our side. (*She rises impetuously, and goes at him, unable to sit quiet any longer*) You do not understand, squire. Our soldiers are always beaten because they are fighting only to save their skins; and the shortest way to save your skin is to run away. Our knights are thinking only of the money they will make in ransoms: it is not kill or be killed with them, but pay or be paid. But I will teach them all to fight that the will of God may be done in France; and then they will drive the poor goddams before them like sheep. You and Polly will live to see the day when there will not be an English soldier on the soil of France; and there will be but one king there: not the feudal English king, but God's French one.

ROBERT (*to* POULENGEY). This may be all rot, Polly; but the troops might swallow it, though nothing that we can say seems able to put any fight into them. Even the Dauphin might swallow it. And if she can put fight into him, she can put it into anybody.

POULENGEY. I can see no harm in trying. Can you? And there is something about the girl—

ROBERT (*turning to* JOAN). Now listen you to me; and (*desperately*) dont cut in before I have time to think.

JOAN (*plumping down on the stool again, like an obedient schoolgirl*). Yes, squire.

ROBERT. Your orders are, that you are to go to Chinon under the escort of this gentleman and three of his friends.

JOAN (*radiant, clasping her hands*). Oh, squire! Your head is all circled with light, like a saint's.

POULENGEY. How is she to get into the royal presence?

ROBERT (*who has looked up for his halo rather apprehensively*). I dont know: how did she get into m y presence? If the Dauphin can keep her out he is a better man than I take him for. (*Rising*) I will send her to Chinon; and she can say I sent her. Then let come what may: I can do no more.

JOAN. And the dress? I may have a soldier's dress, maynt I, squire?

ROBERT. Have what you please. I wash my hands of it.

JOAN (*wildly excited by her success*). Come, Polly. (*She dashes out*)

ROBERT (*shaking* POULENGEY's *hand*). Goodbye, old man, I am taking a big chance. Few other men would have done it. But as you say, there is something about her.

POULENGEY. Yes: there is something about her. Goodbye. (*He goes out*)

(ROBERT, *still very doubtful whether he has not been made a fool of by a crazy female, and a social inferior to boot, scratches his head and slowly comes back from the door.*
The STEWARD *runs in with a basket.*)

STEWARD. Sir, sir—

ROBERT. What now?

STEWARD. The hens are laying like mad, sir. Five dozen eggs!

ROBERT (*stiffens convulsively: crosses himself: and forms with his pale lips the words*). Christ in heaven! (*Aloud but breathless*) She d i d come from God.

SCENE 2

Chinon, in Touraine. An end of the throne room in the castle, curtained off to make an antechamber. The ARCHBISHOP *of Rheims, close on 50, a full-fed prelate with nothing of the ecclesiastic about him except his imposing bearing, and the Lord Chamberlain,* MONSEIGNEUR DE LA TRÉMOUILLE, *a monstrous arrogant wineskin of a man, are waiting for the* DAUPHIN. *There is a door in the wall to the right of the two men. It is late in the afternoon on the 8th of March, 1429.* THE ARCHBISHOP *stands with dignity whilst the* CHAMBERLAIN, *on his left, fumes about in the worst of tempers.*

LA TRÉMOUILLE. What the devil does the Dauphin mean by keeping us waiting like this? I dont know how you have the patience to stand there like a stone idol.

THE ARCHBISHOP. You see, I am an archbishop; and an archbishop is a sort of idol. At any rate he has to learn to keep still and suffer fools patiently. Besides, my dear Lord Chamberlain, it is the Dauphin's royal privilege to keep you waiting, is it not?

LA TRÉMOUILLE. Dauphin be damned! saving your reverence. Do you know how much money he owes me?

THE ARCHBISHOP. Much more than he owes me, I have no doubt, because you are a much richer man. But I take it he owes you all you could afford to lend him. That is what he owes me.

LA TRÉMOUILLE. Twenty-seven thousand: that was his last haul. A cool twenty-seven thousand!

THE ARCHBISHOP. What becomes of it all? He never has a suit of clothes that I would throw to a curate.

LA TRÉMOUILLE. He dines on a chicken or a scrap of mutton. He borrows my last penny; and there is nothing to shew for it. (*A* PAGE *appears in the doorway*) At last!

THE PAGE. No, my lord: it is not His Majesty. Monsieur de Rais is approaching.

LA TRÉMOUILLE. Young Bluebeard! Why announce him?

THE PAGE. Captain La Hire is with him. Something has happened, I think.

(GILLES DE RAIS, *a young man of 25, very smart and self-possessed, and sporting the extravagance of a little curled beard dyed blue at a clean-shaven court, comes in. He is determined to make himself agreeable, but lacks natural joyousness, and is not really pleasant. In fact when he defies the Church some eleven years later he is accused of trying to extract pleasure from horrible cruelties, and hanged. So far, however, there is no shadow of the gallows on him. He advances gaily to the* ARCHBISHOP. THE PAGE *withdraws.*)

BLUEBEARD. Your faithful lamb, Archbishop. Good day, my lord. Do you know what has happened to La Hire?

LA TRÉMOUILLE. He has sworn himself into a fit, perhaps.

BLUEBEARD. No: just the opposite. Foul Mouthed Frank, the only man in Touraine who could beat him at swearing, was told by a soldier that he shouldnt use such language when he was at the point of death.

THE ARCHBISHOP. Nor at any other point. But w a s Foul Mouthed Frank on the point of death?

BLUEBEARD. Yes: he has just fallen into a well and been drowned. La Hire is frightened out of his wits.

(CAPTAIN LA HIRE *comes in: a war dog with no court manners and pronounced camp ones.*)

BLUEBEARD. I have been telling the Chamberlain and the Archbishop. The Archbishop says you are a lost man.

LA HIRE (*striding past* BLUEBEARD, *and planting himself between the* ARCHBISHOP *and* LA TRÉMOUILLE). This is nothing to joke about. It is worse than we thought. It was not a soldier, but an angel dressed as a soldier.

THE ARCHBISHOP
THE CHAMBERLAIN }(*exclaiming all together*). An Angel!
BLUEBEARD

LA HIRE. Yes, an angel. She has made her way from Champagne with half a dozen men through the thick of everything: Burgundians, Goddams, deserters, robbers, and Lord knows who; and they never met a soul except the country folk. I know one of them: de Poulengey. He says she's an angel. If ever I utter an oath again may my soul be blasted to eternal damnation!

THE ARCHBISHOP. A very pious beginning, Captain.

(BLUEBEARD *and* LA TRÉMOUILLE *laugh at him. The* PAGE *returns.*)

THE PAGE. His Majesty.

(*They stand perfunctorily at court attention. The* DAUPHIN, *aged 26, really King Charles the Seventh since the death of his father, but as yet uncrowned, comes in through the curtains with a paper in his hands. He is a poor creature physically; and the current fashion of shaving closely, and hiding every scrap of hair under the headcovering or headdress, both by women and men, makes the worst of his appearance. He has little narrow eyes, near together, a long pendulous nose that droops over his thick short upper lip, and the expression of a young dog accustomed to be kicked, yet incorrigible and irrepressible. But he is neither vulgar nor stupid; and he has a cheeky humor which enables him to hold his own in conversation. Just at present he is excited, like a child with a new toy. He comes to*

THE ARCHBISHOP's *left hand*. BLUEBEARD *and* LA HIRE *retire towards the curtains.*)

CHARLES. Oh, Archbishop, do you know what Robert de Baudricourt is sending me from Vaucouleurs?

THE ARCHBISHOP (*contemptuously*). I am not interested in the newest toys.

CHARLES (*indignantly*). It isnt a toy. (*Sulkily*) However, I can get on very well without your interest.

THE ARCHBISHOP. Your Highness is taking offence very unnecessarily.

CHARLES. Thank you. You are always ready with a lecture, arnt you?

LA TRÉMOUILLE (*roughly*). Enough grumbling. What have you got there?

CHARLES. What is that to you?

LA TRÉMOUILLE. It is my business to know what is passing between you and the garrison at Vaucouleurs. (*He snatches the paper from the* DAUPHIN's *hand, and begins reading it with some difficulty, following the words with his finger and spelling them out syllable by syllable*)

CHARLES (*mortified*). You all think you can treat me as you please because I owe you money, and because I am no good at fighting. But I have the blood royal in my veins.

THE ARCHBISHOP. Even that has been questioned, your Highness. One hardly recognizes in you the grandson of Charles the Wise.

CHARLES. I want to hear no more of my grandfather. He was so wise that he used up the whole family stock of wisdom for five generations, and left me the poor fool I am, bullied and insulted by all of you.

THE ARCHBISHOP. Control yourself, sir. These outbursts of petulance are not seemly.

CHARLES. Another lecture! Thank you. What a pity it is that though you are an archbishop saints and angels dont come to see y o u !

THE ARCHBISHOP. What do you mean?

CHARLES. Aha! Ask that bully there (*pointing to* LA TRÉMOUILLE).

LA TRÉMOUILLE (*furious*). Hold your tongue. Do you hear?

CHARLES. Oh, I hear. You neednt shout. The whole castle can hear. Why dont you go and shout at the English, and beat them for me?

LA TRÉMOUILLE (*raising his fist*). You young—

CHARLES (*running behind the* ARCHBISHOP). Dont you raise your hand to me. It's high treason.

LA HIRE. Steady, Duke! Steady!

THE ARCHBISHOP (*resolutely*). Come, come! this will not do. My Lord Chamberlain: please! please! we must keep some sort of order. (*To the* DAUPHIN) And you, sir: if you cannot rule your kingdom, at least try to rule yourself.

CHARLES. Another lecture! Thank you.

LA TRÉMOUILLE (*handing over the paper to the* ARCHBISHOP). Here: read the accursed thing for me. He has sent the blood boiling into my head: I cant distinguish the letters.

CHARLES (*coming back and peering round* LA TRÉMOUILLE'S *left shoulder*). I will read it for you if you like. I c a n read, you know.

LA TRÉMOUILLE (*with intense contempt, not at all stung by the taunt*). Yes: reading is about all you are fit for. Can you make it out, Archbishop?

THE ARCHBISHOP. I should have expected more commonsense from De Baudricourt. He is sending some cracked country lass here—

CHARLES (*interrupting*). No: he is sending a saint: an angel. And she is coming to me: to m e, the king, and not to you, Archbishop, holy as you are. She knows the blood royal if you dont. (*He struts up to the curtains between* BLUEBEARD *and* LA HIRE)

THE ARCHBISHOP. You cannot be allowed to see this crazy wench.

CHARLES (*turning*). But I am the king; and I will.

LA TRÉMOUILLE (*brutally*). Then she cannot be allowed to see y o u. Now!

CHARLES. I tell you I will. I am going to put my foot down—

BLUEBEARD (*laughing at him*). Naughty! What would your wise grandfather say?

CHARLES. That just shews your ignorance, Bluebeard. My grandfather had a saint who used to float in the air when she was praying, and told him everything he wanted to know. My poor father had two saints, Marie de Maillé and the Gasque of Avignon. It is in our family; and I dont care what you say: I will have my saint too.

THE ARCHBISHOP. This creature is not a saint. She is not even a respectable woman. She does not wear women's clothes. She is dressed like a soldier, and rides round the country with soldiers. Do you suppose such a person can be admitted to your Highness's court?

LA HIRE. Stop. (*Going to the* ARCHBISHOP) Did you say a girl in armor, like a soldier?

THE ARCHBISHOP. So De Baudricourt describes her.

LA HIRE. But by all the devils in hell—Oh, God forgive me, what am I saying?—by Our Lady and all the saints, this must be the angel that struck Foul Mouthed Frank dead for swearing.

CHARLES (*triumphant*). You see! A miracle!

LA HIRE. She may strike the lot of us dead if we cross her. For Heaven's sake, Archbishop, be careful what you are doing.

THE ARCHBISHOP (*severely*). Rubbish! Nobody has been struck dead. A drunken blackguard who has been rebuked a hundred times for swearing has fallen into a well, and been drowned. A mere coincidence.

LA HIRE. I do not know what a coincidence is. I do know that the man is dead, and that she told him he was going to die.

THE ARCHBISHOP. We are all going to die, Captain.

LA HIRE (*crossing himself*). I hope not. (*He backs out of the conversation*)

BLUEBEARD. We can easily find out whether she is an angel or not. Let us arrange when she comes that I shall be the Dauphin, and see whether she will find me out.

CHARLES. Yes: I agree to that. If she cannot find the blood royal I will have nothing to do with her.

THE ARCHBISHOP. It is for the Church to make saints: let De Baudricourt mind his own business, and not dare usurp the function of his priest. I say the girl shall not be admitted.

BLUEBEARD. But, Archbishop—

THE ARCHBISHOP (*sternly*). I speak in the Church's name. (*To the* DAUPHIN) Do you dare say she shall?

CHARLES (*intimidated but sulky*). Oh, if you make it an excommunication matter, I have nothing more to say, of course. But you havnt read the end of the letter. De Baudricourt says she will raise the siege of Orleans, and beat the English for us.

LA TRÉMOUILLE. Rot!

CHARLES. Well, will y o u save Orleans for us, with all your bullying?

LA TRÉMOUILLE (*savagely*). Do not throw that in my face again: do you hear? I have done more fighting than you ever did or ever will. But I cannot be everywhere.

THE DAUPHIN. Well, thats something.

BLUEBEARD (*coming between the* ARCHBISHOP *and* CHARLES). You have Jack Dunois at the head of your troops in Orleans: the brave Dunois, the handsome Dunois, the wonderful invincible Dunois, the darling of all the ladies, the beautiful bastard. Is it likely that the country lass can do what he cannot do?

CHARLES. Why doesnt he raise the siege, then?

LA HIRE. The wind is against him.

BLUEBEARD. How can the wind hurt him at Orleans? It is not on the Channel.

LA HIRE. It is on the river Loire; and the English hold the bridgehead. He must ship his men across the river and upstream, if he is to take them in the rear. Well, he cannot, because there is a devil of a wind blowing the

other way. He is tired of paying the priests to pray for a west wind. What he needs is a miracle. You tell me that what the girl did to Foul Mouthed Frank was no miracle. No matter: it finished Frank. If she changes the wind for Dunois, that may not be a miracle either; but it may finish the English. What harm is there in trying?

THE ARCHBISHOP (*who has read the end of the letter and become more thoughtful*). It is true that De Baudricourt seems extraordinarily impressed.

LA HIRE. De Baudricourt is a blazing ass; but he is a soldier; and if he thinks she can beat the English, all the rest of the army will think so too.

LA TRÉMOUILLE (*to the* ARCHBISHOP, *who is hesitating*). Oh, let them have their way. Dunois' men will give up the town in spite of him if somebody does not put some fresh spunk into them.

THE ARCHBISHOP. The Church must examine the girl before anything decisive is done about her. However, since his Highness desires it, let her attend the Court.

LA HIRE. I will find her and tell her. (*He goes out*)

CHARLES. Come with me, Bluebeard; and let us arrange so that she will not know who I am. You will pretend to be me. (*He goes out through the curtains*)

BLUEBEARD. Pretend to be that thing! Holy Michael! (*He follows the* DAUPHIN)

LA TRÉMOUILLE. I wonder will she pick him out!

THE ARCHBISHOP. Of course she will.

LA TRÉMOUILLE. Why? How is she to know?

THE ARCHBISHOP. She will know what everybody in Chinon knows: that the Dauphin is the meanest-looking and worst-dressed figure in the Court, and that the man with the blue beard is Gilles de Rais.

LA TRÉMOUILLE. I never thought of that.

THE ARCHBISHOP. You are not so accustomed to miracles as I am. It is part of my profession.

LA TRÉMOUILLE (*puzzled and a little scandalized*). But that would not be a miracle at all.

THE ARCHBISHOP (*calmly*). Why not?

LA TRÉMOUILLE. Well, come! what is a miracle?

THE ARCHBISHOP. A miracle, my friend, is an event which creates faith. That is the purpose and nature of miracles. They may seem very wonderful to the people who witness them, and very simple to those who perform them. That does not matter: if they confirm or create faith they are true miracles.

LA TRÉMOUILLE. Even when they are frauds, do you mean?

THE ARCHBISHOP. Frauds deceive. An event which creates faith does not deceive: therefore it is not a fraud, but a miracle.

LA TRÉMOUILLE (*scratching his neck in his perplexity*). Well, I suppose as you are an archbishop you must be right. It seems a bit fishy to me. But I am no churchman, and dont understand these matters.

THE ARCHBISHOP. You are not a churchman; but you are a diplomatist and a soldier. Could you make our citizens pay war taxes, or our soldiers sacrifice their lives, if they knew what is really happening instead of what seems to them to be happening?

LA TRÉMOUILLE. No, by Saint Dennis: the fat would be in the fire before sundown.

THE ARCHBISHOP. Would it not be quite easy to tell them the truth?

LA TRÉMOUILLE. Man alive, they wouldnt believe it.

THE ARCHBISHOP. Just so. Well, the Church has to rule men for the good of their souls as you have to rule them for the good of their bodies. To do that, the Church must do as you do: nourish their faith by poetry.

LA TRÉMOUILLE. Poetry! I should call it humbug.

THE ARCHBISHOP. You would be wrong, my friend. Parables are not lies because they describe events that have never happened. Miracles are not frauds because they are often —I do not say always—very simple and innocent contrivances by which the priest fortifies the faith of his flock. When this girl picks out the Dauphin among his courtiers, it will not be a miracle for me, because I shall know how it has been done, and my faith will not be increased. But as for the others, if they feel the thrill of the supernatural, and forget their sinful clay in a sudden sense of the glory of God, it will be a miracle and a blessed one. And you will find that the girl herself will be more affected than anyone else. She will forget how she really picked him out. So, perhaps, will you.

LA TRÉMOUILLE. Well, I wish I were clever enough to know how much of you is God's archbishop and how much the most artful fox in Touraine. Come on, or we shall be late for the fun; and I want to see it, miracle or no miracle.

THE ARCHBISHOP (*detaining him a moment*). Do not think that I am a lover of crooked ways. There is a new spirit rising in men: we are at the dawning of a wider epoch. If I were a simple monk, and had not to rule men, I should seek peace for my spirit with Aristotle and Pythagoras rather than with the saints and their miracles.

LA TRÉMOUILLE. And who the deuce was Pythagoras?

THE ARCHBISHOP. A sage who held that the earth is round, and that it moves round the sun.

LA TRÉMOUILLE. What an utter fool! Couldnt he use his eyes?

(*They go out together through the curtains, which are presently withdrawn, revealing the full depth of the throne room with the Court assembled. On the right are two Chairs of State on a dais. BLUEBEARD is standing theatrically on the dais, playing the king, and, like the courtiers, enjoying the joke rather obviously. There is a curtained arch in the wall behind the dais; but the main door, guarded by men-at-arms, is at the other side of the room; and a clear path across is kept and lined by the courtiers. CHARLES is in this path in the middle of the room. La Hire is on his right. The Archbishop, on his left, has taken his place by the dais: La Trémouille at the other side of it. The Duchess de la Trémouille, pretending to be the Queen, sits in the Consort's chair, with a group of ladies in waiting close by, behind the Archbishop.*

The chatter of the courtiers makes such a noise that nobody notices the appearance of the Page at the door.)

THE PAGE. The Duke of—(*Nobody listens*). The Duke of—(*The chatter continues. Indignant at his failure to command a hearing, he snatches the halberd of the nearest man-at-arms, and thumps the floor with it. The chatter ceases; and everybody looks at him in silence*). Attention! (*He restores the halberd to the man-at-arms*) The Duke of Vendôme presents Joan the Maid to his Majesty.

CHARLES (*putting his finger on his lip*). Ssh! (*He hides behind the nearest courtier, peering out to see what happens*)

BLUEBEARD (*majestically*). Let her approach the throne.

(*Joan, dressed as a soldier, with her hair bobbed and hanging thickly round her face, is led in by a bashful and speechless nobleman, from whom she detaches herself to stop and look round eagerly for the Dauphin.*)

THE DUCHESS (*to the nearest lady in waiting*). My dear! Her hair! (*All the ladies explode in uncontrollable laughter.*)

BLUEBEARD (*trying not to laugh, and waving his hand in deprecation of their merriment*). Ssh—ssh! Ladies! Ladies!

JOAN (*not at all embarrassed*). I wear it like this because I am a soldier. Where be Dauphin?

(*A titter runs through the Court as she walks to the dais.*)

BLUEBEARD (*condescendingly*). You are in the presence of the Dauphin.

(*Joan looks at him sceptically for a moment, scanning him hard up and*

down to make sure. Dead silence, all watching her. Fun dawns in her face.)

JOAN. Coom, Bluebeard! Thou canst not fool me. Where be Dauphin?

(*A roar of laughter breaks out as Gilles, with a gesture of surrender, joins in the laugh, and jumps down from the dais beside La Trémouille. Joan, also on the broad grin, turns back, searching along the row of courtiers, and presently makes a dive, and drags out Charles by the arm.*)

JOAN (*releasing him and bobbing him a little curtsey*). Gentle little Dauphin, I am sent to you to drive the English away from Orleans and from France, and to crown you king in the cathedral at Rheims, where all true kings of France are crowned.

CHARLES (*triumphant, to the Court*). You see, all of you: she knew the blood royal. Who dare say now that I am not my father's son? (*To Joan*) But if you want me to be crowned at Rheims you must talk to the Archbishop, not to me. There he is (*he is standing behind her*)!

JOAN (*turning quickly, overwhelmed with emotion*). Oh, my lord! (*She falls on both knees before him, with bowed head, not daring to look up*) My lord: I am only a poor country girl; and you are filled with the blessedness and glory of God Himself; but you will touch me with your hands, and give me your blessing, wont you?

BLUEBEARD (*whispering to La Trémouille*). The old fox blushes.

LA TRÉMOUILLE. Another miracle!

THE ARCHBISHOP (*touched, putting his hand on her head*). Child: you are in love with religion.

JOAN (*startled: looking up at him*). Am I? I never thought of that. Is there any harm in it?

THE ARCHBISHOP. There is no harm in it, my child. But there is danger.

JOAN (*rising, with a sunflush of reckless happiness irradiating her face*). There is always danger, except in heaven. Oh, my lord, you have given me such strength, such courage. It must be a most wonderful thing to be Archbishop.

(*The Court smiles broadly: even titters a little.*)

THE ARCHBISHOP (*drawing himself up sensitively*). Gentlemen: your levity is rebuked by this maid's faith. I am, God help me, all unworthy; but your mirth is a deadly sin.

(*Their faces fall. Dead silence.*)

BLUEBEARD. My lord: we were laughing at her, not at you.

THE ARCHBISHOP. What? Not at my unworthiness but at her faith! Gilles de Rais: this maid prophesied that the blasphemer should be drowned in his sin—

JOAN (*distressed*). No!

THE ARCHBISHOP (*silencing her by a gesture*). I prophesy now that you will be hanged in yours if you do not learn when to laugh and when to pray.

BLUEBEARD. My lord: I stand rebuked. I am sorry: I can say no more. But if you prophesy that I shall be hanged, I shall never be able to resist temptation, because I shall always be telling myself that I may as well be hanged for a sheep as a lamb.

(*The courtiers take heart at this. There is more tittering.*)

JOAN (*scandalized*). You are an idle fellow, Bluebeard; and you have great impudence to answer the Archbishop.

LA HIRE (*with a huge chuckle*). Well said, lass! Well said!

JOAN (*impatiently to the* ARCHBISHOP). Oh, my lord, will you send all these silly folks away so that I may speak to the Dauphin alone?

LA HIRE (*goodhumoredly*). I can take a hint. (*He salutes; turns on his heel; and goes out*)

THE ARCHBISHOP. Come, gentlemen. The Maid comes with God's blessing, and must be obeyed.

(*The courtiers withdraw, some through the arch, others at the opposite side. The* ARCHBISHOP *marches across to the door, followed by the* DUCHESS *and* LA TRÉMOUILLE. *As the* ARCHBISHOP *passes* JOAN, *she falls on her knees, and kisses the hem of his robe fervently. He shakes his head in instinctive remonstrance; gathers the robe from her; and goes out. She is left kneeling directly in the* DUCHESS'S *way.*)

THE DUCHESS (*coldly*). Will you allow me to pass, please?

JOAN (*hastily rising, and standing back*). Beg pardon, maam, I am sure.

(*The* DUCHESS *passes on.* JOAN *stares after her; then whispers to the* DAUPHIN.)

JOAN. Be that Queen?

CHARLES. No. She thinks she is.

JOAN (*again staring after the* DUCHESS). Oo-oo-ooh! (*Her awestruck amazement at the figure cut by the magnificently dressed lady is not wholly complimentary*)

LA TRÉMOUILLE (*very surly*). I'll trouble your Highness not to gibe at my wife. (*He goes out. The others have already gone*)

JOAN (*to the Dauphin*). Who be old Gruff-and-Grum?

CHARLES. He is the Duke de la Trémouille.

JOAN. What be his job?

CHARLES. He pretends to command the army. And whenever I find a friend I can care for, he kills him.

JOAN. Why dost let him?

CHARLES (*petulantly moving to the throne side of the room to escape from her magnetic field*). How can I prevent him? He bullies me. They all bully me.

JOAN. Art afraid?

CHARLES. Yes: I am afraid. It's no use preaching to me about it. It's all very well for these big men with their armor that is too heavy for me, and their swords that I can hardly lift, and their muscle and their shouting and their bad tempers. They like fighting: most of them are making fools of themselves all the time they are not fighting; but I am quiet and sensible; and I dont want to kill people: I only want to be left alone to enjoy myself in my own way. I never asked to be a king: it was pushed on me. So if you are going to say 'Son of St Louis: gird on the sword of your ancestors, and lead us to victory' you may spare your breath to cool your porridge; for I cannot do it. I am not built that way; and there is an end of it.

JOAN (*trenchant and masterful*). Blethers! We are all like that to begin with. I shall put courage into thee.

CHARLES. But I dont want to have courage put into me. I want to sleep in a comfortable bed, and not live in continual terror of being killed or wounded. Put courage into the others, and let them have their bellyful of fighting; but let me alone.

JOAN. It's no use, Charlie: thou must face what God puts on thee. If thou fail to make thyself king, thoult be a beggar: what else art fit for? Come! Let me see thee sitting on the throne. I have looked forward to that.

CHARLES. What is the good of sitting on the throne when the other fellows give all the orders? However! (*he sits enthroned, a piteous figure*) here is the king for you! Look your fill at the poor devil.

JOAN. Thou art not king yet, lad: thou art but Dauphin. Be not led away by them around thee. Dressing up dont fill empty noddle. I know the people: the real people that make thy bread for thee; and I tell thee they count no man king of France until the holy oil has been poured on his hair, and himself consecrated and crowned in Rheims Cathedral. And thou needs new clothes, Charlie. Why does not Queen look after thee properly?

CHARLES. We're too poor. She wants all the money we can spare to put on her own back. Besides, I like to see her beautifully dressed; and I dont care what I wear myself: I should look ugly anyhow.

JOAN. There is some good in thee, Charlie; but it is not yet a king's good.

CHARLES. We shall see. I am not such a fool as I look. I have my eyes open; and I can tell you that one good treaty is worth ten good fights. These fighting fellows lose all on the treaties that they gain on the fights. If we can only have a treaty, the English are sure to have the worst of it, because they are better at fighting than at thinking.

JOAN. If the English win, it is they that will make the treaty: and then God help poor France! Thou must fight, Charlie, whether thou will or no. I will go first to hearten thee. We must take our courage in both hands: aye, and pray for it with both hands too.

CHARLES (*descending from his throne and again crossing the room to escape from her dominating urgency*). Oh do stop talking about God and praying. I cant bear people who are always praying. Isnt it bad enough to have to do it at the proper times?

JOAN (*pitying him*). Thou poor child, thou hast never prayed in thy life. I must teach thee from the beginning.

CHARLES. I am not a child: I am a grown man and a father; and I will not be taught any more.

JOAN. Aye, you have a little son. He that will be Louis the Eleventh when you die. Would you not fight for him?

CHARLES. No: a horrid boy. He hates me. He hates everybody, selfish little beast! I dont want to be bothered with children. I dont want to be a father; and I dont want to be a son: especially a son of St Louis. I dont want to be any of these fine things you all have your heads full of: I want to be just what I am. Why cant you mind your own business, and let me mind mine?

JOAN (*again contemptuous*). Minding your own business is like minding your own body: it's the shortest way to make yourself sick. What is my business? Helping mother at home. What is thine? Petting lapdogs and sucking sugarsticks. I call that muck. I tell thee it is God's business we are here to do: not our own. I have a message to thee from God; and thou must listen to it, though thy heart break with the terror of it.

CHARLES. I dont want a message; but can you tell me any secrets? Can you do any cures? Can you turn lead into gold, or anything of that sort?

JOAN. I can turn thee into a king, in Rheims Cathedral; and that is a miracle that will take some doing, it seems.

CHARLES. If we go to Rheims, and have a coronation, Anne will want new dresses. We cant afford them. I am all right as I am.

JOAN. As you are! And what is that? Less than my father's poorest shepherd. Thourt not lawful owner of thy own land of France till thou be consecrated.

CHARLES. But I shall not be lawful owner of my own land anyhow. Will the consecration pay off my mortgages? I have pledged my last acre to the Archbishop and that fat bully. I owe money even to Bluebeard.

JOAN (earnestly). Charlie: I come from the land, and have gotten my strength working on the land; and I tell thee that the land is thine to rule righteously and keep God's peace in, and not to pledge at the pawnshop as a drunken woman pledges her children's clothes. And I come from God to tell thee to kneel in the cathedral and solemnly give thy kingdom to Him for ever and ever, and become the greatest king in the world as His steward and His bailiff, His soldier and His servant. The very clay of France will become holy: her soldiers will be the soldiers of God: the rebel dukes will be rebels against God: the English will fall on their knees and beg thee let them return to their lawful homes in peace. Wilt be a poor little Judas, and betray me and Him that sent me?

CHARLES (tempted at last). Oh, if I only dare!

JOAN. I shall dare, dare, and dare again, in God's name! Art for or against me?

CHARLES (excited). I'll risk it, I warn you I shant be able to keep it up; but I'll risk it. You shall see. (Running to the main door and shouting) Hallo! Come back, everybody. (To JOAN, as he runs back to the arch opposite) Mind you stand by and dont let me be bullied. (Through the arch) Come along, will you: the whole Court. (He sits down in the royal chair as they all hurry in to their former places, chattering and wondering) Now I'm in for it; but no matter: here goes! (To the PAGE) Call for silence, you little beast, will you?

THE PAGE (snatching a halberd as before and thumping with it repeatedly). Silence for His Majesty the King. The King speaks. (Peremptorily) Will you be silent there? (Silence)

CHARLES (rising). I have given the command of the army to The Maid. The Maid is to do as she likes with it. (He descends from the dais)

> (General amazement. LA HIRE, delighted, slaps his steel thigh-piece with his gauntlet.)

LA TRÉMOUILLE (turning threateningly towards Charles). What is this? I command the army.

> (JOAN quickly puts her hand on CHARLES's shoulder as he instinctively recoils. CHARLES, with a grotesque effort culminating in an extravagant gesture, snaps his fingers in the CHAMBERLAIN's face.)

JOAN. Thourt answered, old Gruff-and-Grum. (Suddenly flashing out her sword as she divines that her moment has come) Who is for God and His Maid? Who is for Orleans with me?

LA HIRE (carried away, drawing also). For God and His Maid. To Orleans!

ALL THE KNIGHTS (following his lead with enthusiasm). To Orleans!

> (JOAN, radiant, falls on her knees in thanksgiving to God. They all kneel, except the ARCHBISHOP, who gives his benediction with a sigh, and LA TRÉMOUILLE, who collapses, cursing.)

SCENE 3

Orleans, April 29th, 1429. DUNOIS, aged 26, is pacing up and down a patch of ground on the south bank of the silver Loire, command- *ing a long view of the river in both directions. He has had his lance stuck up with a pennon, which streams in a strong east wind.*

His shield with its bend sinister lies beside it. He has his commander's baton in his hand. He is well built, carrying his armor easily. His broad brow and pointed chin give him an equilaterally triangular face, already marked by active service and responsibility, with the expression of a good-natured and capable man who has no affectations and no foolish illusions. His PAGE *is sitting on the ground, elbows on knees, cheeks on fists, idly watching the water. It is evening; and both man and boy are affected by the loveliness of the Loire.*

DUNOIS (*halting for a moment to glance up at the streaming pennon and shake his head wearily before he resumes his pacing*). West wind, west wind, west wind. Strumpet: steadfast when you should be wanton, wanton when you should be steadfast. West wind on the silver Loire: what rhymes to Loire? (*He looks again at the pennon, and shakes his fist at it*) Change, curse you, change, English harlot of a wind, change. West, west, I tell you. (*With a growl he resumes his march in silence, but soon begins again*) West wind, wanton wind, wilful wind, womanish wind, false wind from over the water, will you never blow again?

THE PAGE (*bounding to his feet*). See! There! There she goes!

DUNOIS (*startled from his reverie: eagerly*). Where? Who? The Maid?

THE PAGE. No: the kingfisher. Like blue lightning. She went into that bush.

DUNOIS (*furiously disappointed*). Is that all? You infernal young idiot: I have a mind to pitch you into the river.

THE PAGE (*not afraid, knowing his man*). It looked frightfully jolly, that flash of blue. Look! There goes the other!

DUNOIS (*running eagerly to the river brim*). Where? Where?

THE PAGE (*pointing*). Passing the reeds.

DUNOIS (*delighted*). I see.

(*They follow the flight till the bird takes cover.*)

THE PAGE. You blew me up because you were not in time to see them yesterday.

DUNOIS. You knew I was expecting The Maid when you set up your yelping. I will give you something to yelp for next time.

THE PAGE. Arnt they lovely? I wish I could catch them.

DUNOIS. Let me catch you trying to trap them, and I will put you in the iron cage for a month to teach you what a cage feels like. You are an abominable boy.

THE PAGE (*laughs, and squats down as before*)!

DUNOIS (*pacing*). Blue bird, blue bird, since I am friend to thee, change thou the wind for me. No: it does not rhyme. He who has sinned for thee: thats better. No sense in it, though. (*He finds himself close to the* PAGE) You abominable boy! (*He turns away from him*) Mary in the blue snood, kingfisher color: will you grudge me a west wind?

A SENTRY'S VOICE WESTWARD. Halt! Who goes there?

JOAN'S VOICE. The Maid.

DUNOIS. Let her pass. Hither, Maid! To me!

(JOAN, *in splendid armor, rushes in in a blazing rage. The wind drops; and the pennon flaps idly down the lance; but* DUNOIS *is too much occupied with* JOAN *to notice it.*)

JOAN (*bluntly*). Be you Bastard of Orleans?

DUNOIS (*cool and stern, pointing to his shield*). You see the bend sinister. Are you Joan the Maid?

JOAN. Sure.

DUNOIS. Where are your troops?

JOAN. Miles behind. They have cheated me. They have brought me to the wrong side of the river.

DUNOIS. I told them to.

JOAN. Why did you? The English are on the other side!

DUNOIS. The English are on both sides.

JOAN. But Orleans is on the other side. We must fight the English there. How can we cross the river?

DUNOIS (*grimly*). There is a bridge.

JOAN. In God's name, then, let us cross the bridge, and fall on them.

DUNOIS. It seems simple; but it cannot be done.

JOAN. Who says so?

DUNOIS. I say so; and older and wiser heads than mine are of the same opinion.

JOAN (*roundly*). Then your older and wiser heads are fatheads: they have made a fool of you; and now they want to make a fool of me too, bringing me to the wrong side of the river. Do you not know that I bring you better help than ever came to any general or any town?

DUNOIS (*smiling patiently*). Your own?

JOAN. No: the help and counsel of the King of Heaven. Which is the way to the bridge?

DUNOIS. You are impatient, Maid.

JOAN. Is this a time for patience? Our enemy is at our gates; and here we stand doing nothing. Oh, why are you not fighting? Listen to me: I will deliver you from fear. I—

DUNOIS (*laughing heartily, and waving her off*). No, no, my girl: if you delivered me from fear I should be a good knight for a story book, but a very bad commander of the army. Come! let me begin to make a soldier of you. (*He takes her to the water's edge*). Do you see those two forts at this end of the bridge? the big ones?

JOAN. Yes. Are they ours or the goddams'?

DUNOIS. Be quiet, and listen to me. If I were in either of those forts with only ten men I could hold it against an army. The English have more than ten times ten goddams in those forts to hold them against us.

JOAN. They cannot hold them against God. God did not give them the land under those forts: they stole it from Him. He gave it to us. I will take those forts.

DUNOIS. Single-handed?

JOAN. Our men will take them. I will lead them.

DUNOIS. Not a man will follow you.

JOAN. I will not look back to see whether anyone is following me.

DUNOIS (*recognizing her mettle, and clapping her heartily on the shoulder*). Good. You have the makings of a soldier in you. You are in love with war.

JOAN (*startled*). Oh! And the Archbishop said I was in love with religion.

DUNOIS. I, God forgive me, am a little in love with war myself, the ugly devil! I am like a man with two wives. Do you want to be like a woman with two husbands?

JOAN (*matter-of-fact*). I will never take a husband. A man in Toul took an action against me for breach of promise; but I never promised him. I am a soldier: I do not want to be thought of as a woman. I will not dress as a woman. I do not care for the things women care for. They dream of lovers, and of money. I dream of leading a charge, and of placing the big guns. You soldiers do not know how to use the big guns: you think you can win battles with a great noise and smoke.

DUNOIS (*with a shrug*). True. Half the time the artillery is more trouble than it is worth.

JOAN. Aye, lad; but you cannot fight stone walls with horses: you must have guns, and much bigger guns too.

DUNOIS (*grinning at her familiarity, and echoing it*). Aye, lass; but a good heart and a stout ladder will get over the stoniest wall.

JOAN. I will be first up the ladder when we reach the fort, Bastard. I dare you to follow me.

DUNOIS. You must not dare a staff officer, Joan: only company officers are allowed to indulge in displays of personal courage. Besides, you must know that I welcome you as a saint, not as a soldier. I have daredevils enough at my call, if they could help me.

JOAN. I am not a daredevil: I am a servant of God. My sword is sacred: I found it behind the altar in the church of St Catherine, where God hid it for me; and I may not strike a blow with it. My heart is full of courage, not of anger. I will lead; and your men will follow: that is all I can do. But I must do it: you shall not stop me.

DUNOIS. All in good time. Our men cannot take those forts by a sally across the bridge. They must come by water, and take the English in the rear on this side.

JOAN (*her military sense asserting itself*). Then make rafts and put big guns on them; and let your men cross to us.

DUNOIS. The rafts are ready; and the men are embarked. But they must wait for God.

JOAN. What do you mean? God is waiting for them.

DUNOIS. Let Him send us a wind then. My boats are downstream: they cannot come up against both wind and current. We must wait until God changes the wind. Come: let me take you to the church.

JOAN. No. I love church; but the English will not yield to prayers: they understand nothing but hard knocks and slashes. I will not go to church until we have beaten them.

DUNOIS. You must: I have business for you there.

JOAN. What business?

DUNOIS. To pray for a west wind. I have prayed; and I have given two silver candlesticks; but my prayers are not answered. Yours may be: you are young and innocent.

JOAN. Oh yes: you are right. I will pray: I will tell St Catherine: she will make God give me a west wind. Quick: shew me the way to the church.

THE PAGE (*sneezes violently*). At-cha!!!

JOAN. God bless you, child! Coom, Bastard.

(*They go out. THE PAGE rises to follow. He picks up the shield, and is taking the spear as well when he notices the pennon, which is now streaming eastward.*)

THE PAGE (*dropping the shield and calling excitedly after them*). Seigneur! Seigneur! Mademoiselle!

DUNOIS (*running back*). What is it? The kingfisher? (*He looks eagerly for it up the river*)

JOAN (*joining them*). Oh, a kingfisher! Where?

THE PAGE. No: the wind, the wind, the wind (*pointing to the pennon*): that is what made me sneeze.

DUNOIS (*looking at the pennon*). The wind has changed. (*He crosses himself*) God has spoken. (*Kneeling and handing his baton to JOAN*) You command the king's army. I am your soldier.

THE PAGE (*looking down the river*). The boats have put off. They are ripping upstream like anything.

DUNOIS (*rising*). Now for the forts. You dared me to follow. Dare you lead?

JOAN (*bursting into tears and flinging her arms round Dunois, kissing him on both cheeks*). Dunois, dear comrade in arms, help me. My eyes are blinded with tears. Set my foot on the ladder, and say 'Up, Joan.'

DUNOIS (*dragging her out*). Never mind the tears: make for the flash of the guns.

JOAN (*in a blaze of courage*). Ah!

DUNOIS (*dragging her along with him*). For God and Saint Dennis!

THE PAGE (*shrilly*). The Maid! The Maid! God and The Maid! Hurray-ay-ay! (*He snatches up the shield and lance, and capers out after them, mad with excitement*)

SCENE 4

A tent in the English camp. A bullnecked English chaplain of 50 is sitting on a stool at a table, hard at work writing. At the other side of the table an imposing nobleman, aged 46, is seated in a handsome chair turning over the leaves of an illuminated Book of Hours. The nobleman is enjoying himself: the chaplain is struggling with suppressed wrath. There is an unoccupied leather stool on the nobleman's left. The table is on his right.

THE NOBLEMAN. Now this is what I call workmanship. There is nothing on earth more exquisite than a bonny book, with well-placed columns of rich black writing in beautiful borders, and illuminated pictures cunningly inset. But nowadays, instead of looking at books, people read them. A book might as well be one of those orders for bacon and bran that you are scribbling.

THE CHAPLAIN. I must say, my lord, you take our situation very coolly. Very coolly indeed.

THE NOBLEMAN (*supercilious*). What is the matter?

THE CHAPLAIN. The matter, my lord, is that we English have been defeated.

THE NOBLEMAN. That happens, you know. It is only in history books and ballads that the enemy is always defeated.

THE CHAPLAIN. But we are being defeated over and over again. First, Orleans—

THE NOBLEMAN (*poohpoohing*). Oh, Orleans!

THE CHAPLAIN. I know what you are going to say, my lord: that was a clear case of witch-craft and sorcery. But we are still being defeated. Jargeau, Meung, Beaugency, just like Orleans. And now we have been butchered at Patay, and Sir John Talbot taken prisoner. (*He throws down his pen, almost in tears*) I feel it, my lord: I feel it very deeply. I cannot bear to see my countrymen defeated by a parcel of foreigners.

THE NOBLEMAN. Oh! you are an Englishman, are you?

THE CHAPLAIN. Certainly not, my lord: I am a gentleman. Still, like your lordship, I was born in England; and it makes a difference.

THE NOBLEMAN. You are attached to the soil, eh?

THE CHAPLAIN. It pleases your lordship to be satirical at my expense: your greatness privileges you to be so with impunity. But your lordship knows very well that I am not attached to the soil in a vulgar manner, like a serf. Still, I have a feeling about it; (*with growing agitation*) and I am not ashamed of it; and (*rising wildly*) by God, if this goes on any longer I will fling my cassock to the devil, and take arms myself, and strangle the accursed witch with my own hands.

THE NOBLEMAN (*laughing at him good-naturedly*). So you shall, chaplain: so you shall, if we can do nothing better. But not yet, not quite yet.

(THE CHAPLAIN *resumes his seat very sulkily.*)

THE NOBLEMAN (*airily*). I should not care very much about the witch—you see, I have made my pilgrimage to the Holy Land; and the Heavenly Powers, for their own credit, can hardly allow me to be worsted by a village sorceress—but the Bastard of Orleans is a harder nut to crack; and as he has been to the Holy Land too, honors are easy between us as far as that goes.

THE CHAPLAIN. He is only a Frenchman, my lord.

THE NOBLEMAN. A Frenchman! Where did you pick up that expression? Are these Burgundians and Bretons and Picards and Gascons beginning to call themselves Frenchmen, just as our fellows are beginning to call themselves Englishmen? They actually talk of France and England as their countries. T h e i r s, if you please! What is to become of me and you if that way of thinking comes into fashion?

THE CHAPLAIN. Why, my lord? Can it hurt us?

THE NOBLEMAN. Men cannot serve two masters. If this cant of serving their country once takes hold of them, goodbye to the authority of their feudal lords, and goodbye to the authority of the Church. That is, goodbye to you and me.

THE CHAPLAIN. I hope I am a faithful servant of the Church; and there are only six cousins between me and the barony of Stogumber, which was created by the Conqueror.

But is that any reason why I should stand by and see Englishmen beaten by a French bastard and a witch from Lousy Champagne?

THE NOBLEMAN. Easy, man, easy: we shall burn the witch and beat the bastard all in good time. Indeed I am waiting at present for the Bishop of Beauvais, to arrange the burning with him. He has been turned out of his diocese by her faction.

THE CHAPLAIN. You have first to catch her, my lord.

THE NOBLEMAN. Or buy her. I will offer a king's ransom.

THE CHAPLAIN. A king's ransom! For that slut!

THE NOBLEMAN. One has to leave a margin. Some of Charles's people will sell her to the Burgundians; the Burgundians will sell her to us; and there will probably be three or four middlemen who will expect their little commissions.

THE CHAPLAIN. Monstrous. It is all those scoundrels of Jews: they get in every time money changes hands. I would not leave a Jew alive in Christendom if I had my way.

THE NOBLEMAN. Why not? The Jews generally give value. They make you pay; but they deliver the goods. In my experience the men who want something for nothing are invariably Christians.

(A PAGE *appears.*)

THE PAGE. The Right Reverend the Bishop of Beauvais: Monseigneur Cauchon.

(CAUCHON, *aged about 60, comes in.* THE PAGE *withdraws. The two Englishmen rise.*)

THE NOBLEMAN (*with effusive courtesy*). My dear Bishop, how good of you to come! Allow me to introduce myself: Richard de Beauchamp, Earl of Warwick, at your service.

CAUCHON. Your lordship's fame is well known to me.

WARWICK. This reverend cleric is Master John de Stogumber.

THE CHAPLAIN (*glibly*). John Bowyer Spenser Neville de Stogumber, at your service, my lord: Bachelor of Theology, and Keeper of the Private Seal to His Eminence the Cardinal of Winchester.

WARWICK (*to* CAUCHON). You call him the Cardinal of England, I believe. Our king's uncle.

CAUCHON. Messire John de Stogumber: I am always the very good friend of His Eminence. (*He extends his hand to* THE CHAPLAIN, *who kisses his ring*)

WARWICK. Do me the honor to be seated. (*He gives* CAUCHON *his chair, placing it at the head of the table*)

(CAUCHON *accepts the place of honor with a grave inclination.* WARWICK *fetches the leather stool carelessly, and sits in his former place.* THE CHAPLAIN *goes back to his chair.*

Though WARWICK *has taken second place in calculated deference to the Bishop, he assumes the lead in opening the proceedings as a matter of course. He is still cordial and expansive; but there is a new note in his voice which means that he is coming to business.*)

WARWICK. Well, my Lord Bishop, you find us in one of our unlucky moments. Charles is to be crowned at Rheims, practically by the young woman from Lorraine; and—I must not deceive you, nor flatter your hopes—we cannot prevent it. I suppose it will make a great difference to Charles's position.

CAUCHON. Undoubtedly. It is a masterstroke of The Maid's.

THE CHAPLAIN (*again agitated*). We were not fairly beaten, my lord. No Englishman is ever fairly beaten.

(CAUCHON *raises his eyebrow slightly, then quickly composes his face.*)

WARWICK. Our friend here takes the view that the young woman is a sorceress. It would, I presume, be the duty of your reverend lordship to denounce her to the Inquisition, and have her burnt for that offence.

CAUCHON. If she were captured in my diocese: yes.

WARWICK (*feeling that they are getting on capitally*). Just so. Now I suppose there can be no reasonable doubt that she is a sorceress.

THE CHAPLAIN. Not the least. An arrant witch.

WARWICK (*gently reproving the interruption*). We are asking for the Bishop's opinion, Messire John.

CAUCHON. We shall have to consider not merely our own opinions here, but the opinions—the prejudices, if you like—of a French court.

WARWICK (*correcting*). A Catholic court, my lord.

CAUCHON. Catholic courts are composed of mortal men, like other courts, however sacred their function and inspiration may be. And if the men are Frenchmen, as the modern fashion calls them, I am afraid the bare fact that an English army has been defeated by a French one will not convince them that there is any sorcery in the matter.

THE CHAPLAIN. What! Not when the famous Sir Talbot himself has been defeated and actually taken prisoner by a drab from the ditches of Lorraine!

CAUCHON. Sir John Talbot, we all know, is a fierce and formidable soldier, Messire; but I have yet to learn that he is an able general. And though it pleases you to say that he has been defeated by this girl, some of us may be disposed to give a little of the credit to Dunois.

THE CHAPLAIN (*contemptuously*). The Bastard of Orleans!

CAUCHON. Let me remind—

WARWICK (*interposing*). I know what you are going to say, my lord. Dunois defeated m e at Montargis.

CAUCHON (*bowing*). I take that as evidence that the Seigneur Dunois is a very able commander indeed.

WARWICK. Your lordship is the flower of courtesy. I admit, on our side, that Talbot is a mere fighting animal, and that it probably served him right to be taken at Patay.

THE CHAPLAIN (*chafing*). My lord: at Orleans this woman had her throat pierced by an English arrow, and was seen to cry like a child from the pain of it. It was a death wound; yet she fought all day; and when our men had repulsed all her attacks like true Englishmen, she walked alone to the wall of our fort with a white banner in her hand; and our men were paralyzed, and could neither shoot nor strike whilst the French fell on them and drove them on to the bridge, which immediately burst into flames and crumbled under them, letting them down into the river, where they were drowned in heaps. Was this your bastard's generalship? or were those flames of hell, conjured up by witchcraft?

WARWICK. You will forgive Messire John's vehemence, my lord; but he has put our case. Dunois is a great captain, we admit; but why could he do nothing until the witch came?

CAUCHON. I do not say that there were no supernatural powers on her side. But the names on that white banner were not the names of Satan and Beelzebub, but the blessed names of our Lord and His holy mother. And your commander who was drowned—Clahz-da I think you call him—

WARWICK. Glasdale. Sir William Glasdale.

CAUCHON. Glass-dell, thank you. He was no saint; and many of our people think that he was drowned for his blasphemies against The Maid.

WARWICK (*beginning to look very dubious*). Well, what are we to infer from all this, my lord? Has The Maid converted you?

CAUCHON. If she had, my lord, I should have known better than to have trusted myself here within your grasp.

WARWICK (*blandly deprecating*). Oh! oh! My lord!

CAUCHON. If the devil is making use of this girl—and I believe he is—

WARWICK (*reassured*). Ah! You hear, Messire John? I knew your lordship would not fail us. Pardon my interruption. Proceed.

CAUCHON. If it be so, the devil has longer views than you give him credit for.

WARWICK. Indeed? In what way? Listen to this, Messire John.

CAUCHON. If the devil wanted to damn a country girl, do you think so easy a task would cost him the winning of half a dozen battles? No, my lord: any trumpery imp could do that much if the girl could be damned at all. The Prince of Darkness does not condescend to such cheap drudgery. When he strikes, he strikes at the Catholic Church, whose realm is the whole spiritual world. When he damns, he damns the souls of the entire human race. Against that dreadful design The Church stands ever on guard. And it is as one of the instruments of that design that I see this girl. She is inspired, but diabolically inspired.

THE CHAPLAIN. I told you she was a witch.

CAUCHON (*fiercely*). She is not a witch. She is a heretic.

THE CHAPLAIN. What difference does that make?

CAUCHON. You, a priest, ask me that! You English are strangely blunt in the mind. All these things that you call witchcraft are capable of a natural explanation. The woman's miracles would not impose on a rabbit: she does not claim them as miracles herself. What do her victories prove but that she has a better head on her shoulders than your swearing Glass-dells and mad bull Talbots, and that the courage of faith, even though it be a false faith, will always outstay the courage of wrath?

THE CHAPLAIN (*hardly able to believe his ears*). Does your lordship compare Sir John Talbot, three times Governor of Ireland, to a mad bull?!!!

WARWICK. It would not be seemly for you to do so, Messire John, as you are still six removes from a barony. But as I am an earl, and Talbot is only a knight, I may make bold

to accept the comparison. (*To the* BISHOP) My lord: I wipe the slate as far as the witchcraft goes. None the less, we must burn the woman.

CAUCHON. I cannot burn her. The Church cannot take life. And my first duty is to seek this girl's salvation.

WARWICK. No doubt. But you do burn people occasionally.

CAUCHON. No. When The Church cuts off an obstinate heretic as a dead branch from the tree of life, the heretic is handed over to the secular arm. The Church has no part in what the secular arm may see fit to do.

WARWICK. Precisely. And I shall be the secular arm in this case. Well, my lord, hand over your dead branch; and I will see that the fire is ready for it. If you will answer for The Church's part, I will answer for the secular part.

CAUCHON (*with smouldering anger*). I can answer for nothing. You great lords are too prone to treat The Church as a mere political convenience.

WARWICK (*smiling and propitiatory*). Not in England, I assure you.

CAUCHON. In England more than anywhere else. No, my lord: the soul of this village girl is of equal value with yours or your king's before the throne of God; and my first duty is to save it. I will not suffer your lordship to smile at me as if I were repeating a meaningless form of words, and it were well understood between us that I should betray the girl to you. I am no mere political bishop: my faith is to me what your honor is to you; and if there be a loophole through which this baptized child of God can creep to her salvation, I shall guide her to it.

THE CHAPLAIN (*rising in a fury*). You are a traitor.

CAUCHON (*springing up*). You lie, priest. (*Trembling with rage*) If you dare do what this woman has done—set your country above the holy Catholic Church—you shall go to the fire with her.

THE CHAPLAIN. My lord: I—I went too far. I—(*he sits down with a submissive gesture*)

WARWICK (*who has risen apprehensively*). My lord: I apologize to you for the word used by Messire John de Stogumber. It does not mean in England what it does in France. In your language traitor means betrayer: one who is perfidious, treacherous, unfaithful, disloyal. In our country it means simply one who is not wholly devoted to our English interests.

CAUCHON. I am sorry: I did not understand. (*He subsides into his chair with dignity*)

WARWICK (*resuming his seat, much relieved*). I must apologize on my own account if I have seemed to take the burning of this poor girl too lightly. When one has seen whole countrysides burnt over and over again as mere items in military routine, one has to grow a very thick skin. Otherwise one might go mad: at all events, I should. May I venture to assume that your lordship also, having to see so many heretics burned from time to time, is compelled to take—shall I say a professional view of what would otherwise be a very horrible incident?

CAUCHON. Yes: it is a painful duty: even, as you say, a horrible one. But in comparison with the horror of heresy it is less than nothing. I am not thinking of this girl's body, which will suffer for a few moments only, and which must in any event die in some more or less painful manner, but of her soul, which may suffer to all eternity.

WARWICK. Just so; and God grant that her soul may be saved! But the practical problem would seem to be how to save her soul without saving her body. For we must face it, my lord: if this cult of The Maid goes on, our cause is lost.

THE CHAPLAIN (*his voice broken like that of a man who has been crying*). May I speak, my lord?

WARWICK. Really, Messire John, I had rather you did not, unless you can keep your temper.

THE CHAPLAIN. It is only this. I speak under correction; but The Maid is full of deceit: she pretends to be devout. Her prayers and confessions are endless. How can she be accused of heresy when she neglects no observance of a faithful daughter of The Church?

CAUCHON (*flaming up*). A faithful daughter of The Church! The Pope himself at his proudest dare not presume as this woman presumes. She acts as if she herself were The Church. She brings the message of God to Charles; and The Church must stand aside. She will crown him in the cathedral of Rheims: s h e, not The Church! She sends letters to the king of England giving him God's command through her to return to his island on pain of God's vengeance, which she will execute. Let me tell you that the writing of such letters was the practice of the accursed Mahomet, the anti-Christ. Has she ever in all her utterances said one word of The Church? Never. It is always God and herself.

WARWICK. What can you expect? A beggar on horseback! Her head is turned.

CAUCHON. Who has turned it? The devil. And for a mighty purpose. He is spreading this heresy everywhere. The man Hus, burnt only thirteen years ago at Constance, infected all Bohemia with it. A man named WcLeef, himself an anointed priest, spread the pestilence in England; and to your shame you let him die in his bed. We have such people here in France too: I know the breed. It is cancerous: if it be not cut out, stamped out, burnt out, it will not stop until it has brought the whole body of human society into sin and corruption, into waste and ruin. By it an Arab camel driver drove Christ and His Church out of Jerusalem, and ravaged his way west like a wild beast until at last there stood only the Pyrenees and God's mercy between France and damnation. Yet what did the camel driver do at the beginning more than this shepherd girl is doing? He had his voices from the angel Gabriel: s h e has her voices from St Catherine and St Margaret and the Blessed Michael. He declared himself the messenger of God, and wrote in God's name to the kings of the earth. Her letters to them are going forth daily. It is not the Mother of God now to whom we must look for intercession, but to Joan the Maid. What will the world be like when The Church's accumulated wisdom and knowledge and experience, its councils of learned, venerable pious men, are thrust into the kennel by every ignorant laborer or dairymaid whom the devil can puff up with the monstrous self-conceit of being directly inspired from heaven? It will be a world of blood, of fury, of devastation, of each man striving for his own hand: in the end a world wrecked back into barbarism. For now you have only Mahomet and his dupes, and the Maid and her dupes; but what will it be when every girl thinks herself a Joan and every man a Mahomet? I shudder to the very marrow of my bones when I think of it. I have fought it all my life; and I will fight it to the end. Let all this woman's sins be forgiven her except only this sin; for it is the sin against the Holy Ghost; and if she does not recant in the dust before the world, and submit herself to the last inch of her soul to her Church, to the fire she shall go if she once falls into my hand.

WARWICK (*unimpressed*). You feel strongly about it, naturally.

CAUCHON. Do not you?

WARWICK. I am a soldier, not a churchman. As a pilgrim I saw something of the Mahometans. They were not so ill-bred as I had been led to believe. In some respects their conduct compared favorably with ours.

CAUCHON (*displeased*). I have noticed this before. Men go to the East to convert the infidels. And the infidels pervert them. The Crusader comes back more than half a Saracen. Not to mention that all Englishmen are born heretics.

THE CHAPLAIN. Englishmen heretics!!! (*Appealing to* WARWICK) My lord: must we endure this? His lordship is beside himself. How can what an Englishman believes be heresy? It is a contradiction in terms.

CAUCHON. I absolve you, Messire de Stogumber, on the ground of invincible ignorance. The thick air of your country does not breed theologians.

WARWICK. You would not say so if you heard us quarrelling about religion, my lord! I am sorry you think I must be either a heretic or

a blockhead because, as a travelled man, I know that the followers of Mahomet profess great respect for our Lord, and are more ready to forgive St Peter for being a fisherman than your lordship is to forgive Mahomet for being a camel driver. But at least we can proceed in this matter without bigotry.

CAUCHON. When men call the zeal of the Christian Church bigotry I know what to think.

WARWICK. They are only east and west views of the same thing.

CAUCHON (*bitterly ironical*). Only east and west! Only!!

WARWICK. Oh, my Lord Bishop, I am not gain-saying you. You will carry The Church with you; but you have to carry the nobles also. To my mind there is a stronger case against The Maid than the one you have so forcibly put. Frankly, I am not afraid of this girl becoming another Mahomet, and superseding The Church by a great heresy. I think you exaggerate that risk. But have you noticed that in these letters of hers, she proposes to all the kings of Europe, as she has already pressed on Charles, a transaction which would wreck the whole social structure of Christendom?

CAUCHON. Wreck The Church. I tell you so.

WARWICK (*whose patience is wearing out*). My lord: pray get The Church out of your head for a moment; and remember that there are temporal institutions in the world as well as spiritual ones. I and my peers represent the feudal aristocracy as you represent The Church. We are the temporal power. Well, do you not see how this girl's idea strikes at us?

CAUCHON. How does her idea strike at you, except as it strikes at all of us, through The Church?

WARWICK. Her idea is that the kings should give their realms to God, and then reign as God's bailiffs.

CAUCHON (*not interested*). Quite sound theologically, my lord. But the king will hardly care, provided he reign. It is an abstract idea: a mere form of words.

WARWICK. By no means. It is a cunning device to supersede the aristocracy, and make the king sole and absolute autocrat. Instead of the king being merely the first among his peers, he becomes their master. That we cannot suffer: we call no man master. Nominally we hold our lands and dignities from the king, because there must be a keystone to the arch of human society; but we hold our lands in our own hands, and defend them with our own swords and those of our own tenants. Now by The Maid's doctrine the king will take our lands—o u r lands!—and make them a present to God; and God will then vest them wholly in the king.

CAUCHON. Need you fear that? You are the makers of kings after all. York or Lancaster in England, Lancaster or Valois in France: they reign according to your pleasure.

WARWICK. Yes; but only as long as the people follow their feudal lords, and know the king only as a travelling show, owning nothing but the highway that belongs to everybody. If the people's thoughts and hearts were turned to the king, and their lords became only the king's servants in their eyes, the king could break us across his knee one by one; and then what should we be but liveried courtiers in his halls?

CAUCHON. Still you need not fear, my lord. Some men are born kings; and some are born statesmen. The two are seldom the same. Where would the king find counsellors to plan and carry out such a policy for him?

WARWICK (with a not too friendly smile). Perhaps in the Church, my lord.

(CAUCHON, with an equally sour smile, shrugs his shoulders, and does not contradict him.)

WARWICK. Strike down the barons; and the cardinals will have it all their own way.

CAUCHON (conciliatory, dropping his polemical tone). My lord: we shall not defeat The Maid if we strive against one another. I know well that there is a Will to Power in the world. I know that while it lasts there will be a struggle between the Emperor and the Pope, between the dukes and the political cardinals, between the barons and the kings. The devil divides us and governs. I see you are no friend to The Church: you are an earl first and last, as I am a churchman first and last. But can we not sink our differences in the face of a common enemy? I see now that what is in your mind is not that this girl has never once mentioned The Church, and thinks only of God and herself, but that she has never once mentioned the peerage, and thinks only of the king and herself.

WARWICK. Quite so. These two ideas of hers are the same idea at bottom. It goes deep, my lord. It is the protest of the individual soul against the interference of priest or peer between the private man and his God. I should call it Protestantism if I had to find a name for it.

CAUCHON (looking hard at him). You understand it wonderfully well, my lord. Scratch an Englishman, and find a Protestant.

WARWICK (playing the pink of courtesy). I think you are not entirely void of sympathy with The Maid's secular heresy, my lord. I leave you to find a name for it.

CAUCHON. You mistake me, my lord. I have no sympathy with her political presumptions. But as a priest I have gained a knowledge of the minds of the common people; and there you will find yet another most dangerous idea. I can express it only by such phrases as France for the French, England for the English, Italy for the Italians, Spain for the Spanish, and so forth. It is sometimes so narrow and bitter in country folk that it surprises me that this country girl can rise above the idea of her village for its villagers. But she can. She does. When she threatens to drive the English from the soil of France she is undoubtedly thinking of the whole extent of country in which French is spoken. To her the French-speaking people are what the Holy Scriptures describe as a nation. Call this side of her heresy Nationalism if you will: I can find you no better name for it. I can only tell you that it is essentially anti-Catholic and anti-Christian; for the Catholic Church knows only one realm, and that is the realm of Christ's kingdom. Divide that kingdom into nations, and you dethrone Christ.

Dethrone Christ, and who will stand between our throats and the sword? The world will perish in a welter of war.

WARWICK. Well, if you will burn the Protestant, I will burn the Nationalist, though perhaps I shall not carry Messire John with me there. England for the English will appeal to him.

THE CHAPLAIN. Certainly England for the English goes without saying: it is the simple law of nature. But this woman denies to England her legitimate conquests, given her by God because of her peculiar fitness to rule over less civilized races for their own good. I do not understand what your lordships mean by Protestant and Nationalist: you are too learned and subtle for a poor clerk like myself. But I know as a matter of plain commonsense that the woman is a rebel; and that is enough for me. She rebels against Nature by wearing man's clothes, and fighting. She rebels against The Church by usurping the divine authority of the Pope. She rebels against God by her damnable league with Satan and his evil spirits against our army. And all these rebellions are only excuses for her great rebellion against England. That is not to be endured. Let her perish. Let her burn. Let her not infect the whole flock. It is expedient that one woman die for the people.

WARWICK (*rising*). My lord: we seem to be agreed.

CAUCHON (*rising also, but in protest*). I will not imperil my soul. I will uphold the justice of the Church. I will strive to the utmost for this woman's salvation.

WARWICK. I am sorry for the poor girl. I hate these severities. I will spare her if I can.

THE CHAPLAIN (*implacably*). I would burn her with my own hands.

CAUCHON (*blessing him*). Sancta simplicitas!

SCENE 5

The ambulatory in the cathedral of Rheims, near the door of the vestry. A pillar bears one of the stations of the cross. The organ is playing the people out of the nave after the coronation. JOAN *is kneeling in prayer before the station. She is beautifully dressed, but still in male attire. The organ ceases as* DUNOIS, *also splendidly arrayed, comes into the ambulatory from the vestry.*

DUNOIS. Come, Joan! you have had enough praying. After that fit of crying you will catch a chill if you stay here any longer. It is all over: the cathedral is empty; and the streets are full. They are calling for The Maid. We have told them you are staying here alone to pray; but they want to see you again.

JOAN. No: let the king have all the glory.

DUNOIS. He only spoils the show, poor devil. No, Joan: you have crowned him; and you must go through with it.

JOAN (*shakes her head reluctantly*).

DUNOIS (*raising her*). Come come! it will be over in a couple of hours. It's better than the bridge at Orleans: eh?

JOAN. Oh, dear Dunois, how I wish it were the bridge at Orleans again! We lived at that bridge.

DUNOIS. Yes, faith, and died too: some of us.

JOAN. Isnt it strange, Jack? I am such a coward: I am frightened beyond words before a battle; but it is so dull afterwards when there is no danger: oh, so dull! dull! dull!

DUNOIS. You must learn to be abstemious in war, just as you are in your food and drink, my little saint.

JOAN. Dear Jack: I think you like me as a soldier likes his comrade.

DUNOIS. You need it, poor innocent child of God. You have not many friends at court.

JOAN. Why do all these courtiers and knights and churchmen hate me? What have I done to them? I have asked nothing for myself except that my village shall not be taxed; for we cannot afford war taxes. I have brought them luck and victory: I have set them right when they were doing all sorts of stupid things: I have crowned Charles and made him a real king; and all the honors he is handing out have gone to them. Then why do they not love me?

DUNOIS (*rallying her*). Sim-ple-ton! Do you expect stupid people to love you for shewing them up? Do blundering old military dug-outs love the successful young captains who supersede them? Do ambitious politicians love the climbers who take the front seats from them? Do archbishops enjoy being played off their own altars, even by saints? Why, I should be jealous of you myself if I were ambitious enough.

JOAN. You are the pick of the basket here, Jack: the only friend I have among all these nobles. I'll wager your mother was from the country. I will go back to the farm when I have taken Paris.

DUNOIS. I am not so sure that they will let you take Paris.

JOAN (*startled*). What!

DUNOIS. I should have taken it myself before this if they had all been sound about it. Some of them would rather Paris took you, I think. So take care.

JOAN. Jack: the world is too wicked for me. If the goddams and the Burgundians do not make an end of me, the French will. Only for my voices I should lose all heart. That is why I had to steal away to pray here alone after the coronation. I'll tell you something, Jack. It is in the bells I hear my voices. Not to-day, when they all rang: that was nothing but jangling. But here in this corner, where the bells come down from heaven, and the echoes linger, or in the fields, where they come from a distance through the quiet of the country-side, my voices are in them. (*The cathedral clock chimes the quarter*) Hark! (*She becomes rapt*) Do you hear? 'Dear-child-of-God': just what you said. At the half-hour they will say 'Be-brave-go-on'. At the three-quarters they will say 'I-am-thy-Help'. But it is at the hour, when the great bell goes after

'God-will-save-France': it is then that St Margaret and St Catherine and sometimes even the blessed Michael will say things that I cannot tell beforehand. Then, oh then—

DUNOIS (*interrupting her kindly but not sympathetically*). Then, Joan, we shall hear whatever we fancy in the booming of the bell. You make me uneasy when you talk about your voices: I should think you were a bit cracked if I hadnt noticed that you give me very sensible reasons for what you do, though I hear you telling others you are only obeying Madame Saint Catherine.

JOAN (*crossly*). Well, I have to find reasons for you, because you do not believe in my voices. But the voices come first; and I find the reasons after: whatever you may choose to believe.

DUNOIS. Are you angry, Joan?

JOAN. Yes. (*Smiling*) No: not with you. I wish you were one of the village babies.

DUNOIS. Why?

JOAN. I could nurse you for awhile.

DUNOIS. You are a bit of a woman after all.

JOAN. No: not a bit: I am a soldier and nothing else. Soldiers always nurse children when they get a chance.

DUNOIS. That is true. (*He laughs*)

(KING CHARLES, *with* BLUEBEARD *on his left and* LA HIRE *on his right, comes from the vestry, where he has been disrobing.* JOAN *shrinks away behind the pillar.* DUNOIS *is left between* CHARLES *and* LA HIRE.)

DUNOIS. Well, your Majesty is an anointed king at last. How do you like it?

CHARLES. I would not go through it again to be emperor of the sun and moon. The weight of those robes! I thought I should have dropped when they loaded that crown on to me. And the famous holy oil they talked so much about was rancid: phew! The Archbishop must be nearly dead: his robes must have weighed a ton: they are stripping him still in the vestry.

DUNOIS (*drily*). Your majesty should wear armor oftener. That would accustom you to heavy dressing.

CHARLES. Yes: the old jibe! Well, I am not going to wear armor: fighting is not my job. Where is The Maid?

JOAN (*coming forward between* CHARLES *and* BLUEBEARD, *and falling on her knee*). Sire: I have made you king: my work is done. I am going back to my father's farm.

CHARLES (*surprised, but relieved*). Oh, are you? Well, that will be very nice.

(JOAN *rises, deeply discouraged*.)

CHARLES (*continuing heedlessly*). A healthy life, you know.

DUNOIS. But a dull one.

BLUEBEARD. You will find the petticoats tripping you up after leaving them off for so long.

LA HIRE. You will miss the fighting. It's a bad habit, but a grand one, and the hardest of all to break yourself of.

CHARLES (*anxiously*). Still, we dont want you to stay if you would really rather go home.

JOAN (*bitterly*). I know well that none of you will be sorry to see me go. (*She turns her shoulder to* CHARLES *and walks past him to the more congenial neighborhood of* DUNOIS *and* LA HIRE)

LA HIRE. Well, I shall be able to swear when I want to. But I shall miss you at times.

JOAN. La Hire: in spite of all your sins and swears we shall meet in heaven; for I love you as I love Pitou, my old sheep dog. Pitou could kill a wolf. You will kill the English wolves until they go back to their country and become good dogs of God, will you not?

LA HIRE. You and I together: yes.

JOAN. No: I shall last only a year from the beginning.

ALL THE OTHERS. What!

JOAN. I know it somehow.

DUNOIS. Nonsense!

JOAN. Jack: do you think you will be able to drive them out?

DUNOIS (*with quiet conviction*). Yes: I shall drive them out. They beat us because we thought battles were tournaments and ransom markets. We played the fool while the goddams took war seriously. But I have learnt my lesson, and taken their measure. They have no roots here. I have beaten them before; and I shall beat them again.

JOAN. You will not be cruel to them, Jack?

DUNOIS. The goddams will not yield to tender handling. We did not begin it.

JOAN (*suddenly*). Jack: before I go home, let us take Paris.

CHARLES (*terrified*). Oh no no. We shall lose everything we have gained. Oh dont let us have any more fighting. We can make a very good treaty with the Duke of Burgundy.

JOAN. Treaty! (*She stamps with impatience*)

CHARLES. Well, why not, now that I am crowned and anointed? Oh, that oil!

(THE ARCHBISHOP *comes from the vestry, and joins the group between* CHARLES *and* BLUEBEARD.)

CHARLES. Archbishop: The Maid wants to start fighting again.

THE ARCHBISHOP. Have we ceased fighting, then? Are we at peace?

CHARLES. No: I suppose not; but let us be content with what we have done. Let us make a treaty. Our luck is too good to last; and now is our chance to stop before it turns.

JOAN. Luck! God has fought for us; and you call it luck! And you would stop while there are still Englishmen on this holy earth of dear France!

THE ARCHBISHOP (*sternly*). Maid: the king addressed himself to me, not to you. You forget yourself. You very often forget yourself.

JOAN (*unabashed, and rather roughly*). Then speak, you; and tell him that it is not God's will that he should take his hand from the plough.

THE ARCHBISHOP. If I am not so glib with the name of God as you are, it is because I interpret His will with the authority of The Church and of my sacred office. When you first came you respected it, and would not have dared to speak as you are now speaking. You came clothed with the virtue of humility; and because God blessed your enterprises accordingly, you have stained yourself with the sin of pride. The old Greek tragedy is rising among us. It is the chastisement of hubris.

CHARLES. Yes: but she thinks she knows better than everyone else.

JOAN (*distressed, but naïvely incapable of seeing the effect she is producing*). But I do know better than any of you seem to. And I am not proud: I never speak unless I know I am right.

BLUEBEARD } (*exclaiming { Ha ha!
CHARLES }   together*) { Just so.

THE ARCHBISHOP. How do you know you are right?

JOAN. I always know. My voices—

CHARLES. Oh, your voices, your voices. Why dont the voices come to me? I am king, not you.

JOAN. They do come to you; but you do not hear them. You have not sat in the field in the evening listening for them. When the angelus rings you cross yourself and have done with it; but if you prayed from your heart, and listened to the thrilling of the bells in the air after they stop ringing, you would hear the voices as well as I do. (*Turning brusquely from him*) But what voices do you need to tell you what the blacksmith can tell you: that you must strike while the iron is hot? I tell you we must make a dash at Compiègne and relieve it as we relieved Orleans. Then Paris will open its gates; or if not, we will break through them. What is your crown worth without your capital?

LA HIRE. That is what I say too. We shall go through them like a red hot shot through a pound of butter. What do you say, Bastard?

DUNOIS. If our cannon balls were all as hot as your head, and we had enough of them, we should conquer the earth, no doubt. Pluck and impetuosity are good servants in war, but bad masters: they have delivered us into the hands of the English every time we have trusted to them. We never know when we are beaten: that is our great fault.

JOAN. You never know when you are victorious; that is a worse fault. I shall have to make you carry looking-glasses in battle to convince you that the English have not cut off all your noses. You would have been besieged in Orleans still, you and your councils of war, if I had not made you attack. You should always attack; and if you only hold on long enough the enemy will stop first. You dont know how to begin a battle; and you dont know how to use your cannons. And I do.

(*She squats down on the flags with crossed ankles, pouting.*)

DUNOIS. I know what you think of us, General Joan.

JOAN. Never mind that, Jack. Tell them what you think of me.

DUNOIS. I think that God was on your side; for I have not forgotten how the wind changed, and how our hearts changed when you came; and by my faith I shall never deny that it was in your sign that we conquered. But I tell you as a soldier that God is no man's daily drudge, and no maid's either. If you are worthy of it He will sometimes snatch you out of the jaws of death and set you on your feet again; but that is all: once on your feet you must fight with all your might and all your craft. For He has to be fair to your enemy too: dont forget that. Well, He set us on our feet through you at Orleans; and the glory of it has carried us through a few good battles here to the coronation. But if we presume on it further, and trust to God to do the work we should do ourselves, we shall be defeated; and serve us right!

JOAN. But—

DUNOIS. Sh! I have not finished. Do not think, any of you, that these victories of ours were won without generalship. King

Charles: you have said no word in your proclamations of my part in this campaign; and I make no complaint of that; for the people will run after The Maid and her miracles and not after the Bastard's hard work finding troops for her and feeding them. But I know exactly how much God did for us through The Maid, and how much He left me to do by my own wits; and I tell you that your little hour of miracles is over, and that from this time on he who plays the war game best will win—if the luck is on his side.

JOAN. Ah! if, if, if, if! If ifs and ans were pots and pans there'd be no need of tinkers. (*Rising impetuously*) I tell you, Bastard, your art of war is no use, because your knights are no good for real fighting. War is only a game to them, like tennis and all their other games: they make rules as to what is fair and what is not fair, and heap armor on themselves and on their poor horses to keep out the arrows; and when they fall they cant get up, and have to wait for their squires to come and lift them to arrange about the ransom with the man that has poked them off their horse. Cant you see that all the like of that is gone by and done with? What use is armor against gunpowder? And if it was, do you think men that are fighting for France and for God will stop to bargain about ransoms, as half your knights live by doing? No: they will fight to win; and they will give up their lives out of their own hand into the hand of God when they go into battle, as I do. Common folks understood this. They cannot afford armor and cannot pay ransoms; but they followed me half naked into the moat and up the ladder and over the wall. With them it is my life or thine, and God defend the right! You may shake your head, Jack; and Bluebeard may twirl his billygoat's beard and cock his nose at me; but remember the day your knights and captains refused to follow me to attack the English at Orleans! You locked the gates to keep me in; and it was the townsfolk and the common people that followed me, and forced the gate, and shewed you the way to fight in earnest.

BLUEBEARD (*offended*). Not content with being Pope Joan, you must be Caesar and Alexander as well.

THE ARCHBISHOP. Pride will have a fall, Joan.

JOAN. Oh, never mind whether it is pride or not: is it true? is it commonsense?

LA HIRE. It is true. Half of us are afraid of having our handsome noses broken; and the other half are out for paying off their mortgages. Let her have her way, Dunois: she does not know everything; but she has got hold of the right end of the stick. Fighting is not what it was; and those who know least about it often make the best job of it.

DUNOIS. I know all that. I do not fight in the old way: I have learnt the lesson of Agincourt, of Poitiers and Crecy. I know how many lives any move of mine will cost; and if the move is worth the cost I make it and pay the cost. But Joan never counts the cost at all: she goes ahead and trusts to God: she thinks she has God in her pocket. Up to now she has had the numbers on her side; and she has won. But I know Joan; and I see that some day she will go ahead when she has only ten men to do the work of a hundred. And then she will find that God is on the side of the big battalions. She will be taken by the enemy. And the lucky man that makes the capture will receive sixteen thousand pounds from the Earl of Ouareek.

JOAN (*flattered*). Sixteen thousand pounds! Eh, laddie, have they offered that for me? There cannot be so much money in the world.

DUNOIS. There is, in England. And now tell me, all of you, which of you will lift a finger to save Joan once the English have got her? I speak first, for the army. The day after she has been dragged from her horse by a goddam or a Burgundian, and he is not struck dead: the day after she is locked in a dungeon, and the bars and bolts do not fly open at the touch of St Peter's angel: the day when the enemy finds out that she is as vulnerable as I am and not a bit more invincible, she will not be worth the life of a single soldier to us; and I will not risk that life, much as I cherish her as a companion-in-arms.

JOAN. I dont blame you, Jack: you are right. I am not worth one soldier's life if God lets me be beaten; but France may think me worth my ransom after what God has done for her through me.

CHARLES. I tell you I have no money; and this coronation, which is all your fault, has cost me the last farthing I can borrow.

JOAN. The Church is richer than you. I put my trust in the Church.

THE ARCHBISHOP. Woman: they will drag you through the streets, and burn you as a witch.

JOAN (*running to him*). Oh, my lord, do not say that. It is impossible. I a witch!

THE ARCHBISHOP. Peter Cauchon knows his business. The University of Paris has burnt a woman for saying that what you have done was well done, and according to God.

JOAN (*bewildered*). But why? What sense is there in it? What I have done is according to God. They could not burn a woman for speaking the truth.

THE ARCHBISHOP. They did.

JOAN. But you know that she was speaking the truth. You would not let them burn me.

THE ARCHBISHOP. How could I prevent them?

JOAN. You would speak in the name of the Church. You are a great prince of the Church. I would go anywhere with your blessing to protect me.

THE ARCHBISHOP. I have no blessing for you while you are proud and disobedient.

JOAN. Oh, why will you go on saying things like that? I am not proud and disobedient. I am a poor girl, and so ignorant that I do not know A from B. How could I be proud? And how can you say that I am disobedient when I always obey my voices, because they come from God.

THE ARCHBISHOP. The voice of God on earth is the voice of the Church Militant; and all the voices that come to you are the echoes of your own wilfulness.

JOAN. It is not true.

THE ARCHBISHOP (*flushing angrily*). You tell the Archbishop in his cathedral that he lies; and yet you say you are not proud and disobedient.

JOAN. I never said you lied. It was you that as good as said my voices lied. When have they ever lied? If you will not believe in them: even if they are only the echoes of my own commonsense, are they not always right? and are not your earthly counsels always wrong?

THE ARCHBISHOP (*indignantly*). It is waste of time admonishing you.

CHARLES. It always comes back to the same thing. She is right; and everyone else is wrong.

THE ARCHBISHOP. Take this as your last warning. If you perish through setting your private judgment above the instructions of your spiritual directors, the Church disowns you, and leaves you to whatever fate your presumption may bring upon you. The Bastard has told you that if you persist in setting up your military conceit above the counsels of your commanders—

DUNOIS (*interposing*). To put it quite exactly, if you attempt to relieve the garrison in Compiègne without the same superiority in numbers you had at Orleans—

THE ARCHBISHOP. The army will disown you, and will not rescue you. And His Majesty the King has told you that the throne has not the means of ransoming you.

CHARLES. Not a penny.

THE ARCHBISHOP. You stand alone: absolutely alone, trusting to your own conceit, your own ignorance, your own headstrong presumption, your own impiety in hiding all these sins under the cloak of a trust in God. When you pass through these doors into the sunlight, the crowd will cheer you. They will bring you their little children and their invalids to heal: they will kiss your hands and feet, and do what they can, poor simple souls, to turn your head, and madden you with the self-confidence that is leading you to your destruction. But you will be none the less alone: they cannot save you. We and we only can stand between you and the stake at which our enemies have burnt that wretched woman in Paris.

JOAN (*her eyes skyward*). I have better friends and better counsel than yours.

THE ARCHBISHOP. I see that I am speaking in vain to a hardened heart. You reject our protection, and are determined to turn us all against you. In future, then, fend for yourself; and if you fail, God have mercy on your soul.

DUNOIS. That is the truth, Joan. Heed it.

JOAN. Where would you all have been now if I had heeded that sort of truth? There is no help, no counsel, in any of you. Yes: I am alone on earth: I have always been alone. My father told my brothers to drown me if I would not stay to mind his sheep while France was bleeding to death: France might perish if only our lambs were safe. I thought France would have friends at the court of the king of France; and I find only wolves fighting for pieces of her poor torn body. I thought God would have friends everywhere, because He is the friend of everyone; and in my innocence I believed that you who now cast me out would be like strong towers to keep harm from me. But I am wiser now; and nobody is any the worse for being wiser. Do not think you can frighten me by telling me that I am alone. France is alone; and God is alone; and what is my loneliness before the loneliness of my country and my God? I see now that the loneliness of God is His strength: what would He be if He listened to your jealous little counsels? Well, my loneliness shall be my strength too; it is better to be alone with God; His friendship will not fail me, nor His counsel, nor His love. In His strength I will dare, and dare, and dare, until I die. I will go out now to the common people, and let the love in their eyes comfort me for the hate in yours. You will all be glad to see me burnt; but if I go through the fire I shall go through it to their hearts for ever and ever. And so, God be with me!

(*She goes from them. They stare after her in glum silence for a moment. Then* GILLES DE RAIS *twirls his beard.*)

BLUEBEARD. You know, the woman is quite impossible. I dont dislike her, really; but what are you to do with such a character?

DUNOIS. As God is my judge, if she fell into the Loire I would jump in in full armor to fish her out. But if she plays the fool at Compiègne, and gets caught, I must leave her to her doom.

LA HIRE. Then you had better chain me up; for I could follow her to hell when the spirit rises in her like that.

THE ARCHBISHOP. She disturbs my judgment too: there is a dangerous power in her outbursts. But the pit is open at her feet; and for good or evil we cannot turn her from it.

CHARLES. If only she would keep quiet, or go home!

(*They follow her dispiritedly.*)

SCENE 6

Rouen, 30th May 1431. A great stone hall in the castle, arranged for a trial-at-law, but not a trial-by-jury, the court being the Bishop's court with the Inquisition participating: hence there are two raised chairs side by side for the Bishop and the Inquisitor as judges. Rows of chairs radiating from them at an obtuse angle are for the canons, the doctors of law and theology, and the Dominican monks, who act as assessors. In the angle is a table for the scribes, with stools. There is also a heavy rough wooden stool for the prisoner.

All these are at the inner end of the hall. The further end is open to the courtyard through a row of arches. The court is shielded from the weather by screens and curtains.

Looking down the great hall from the middle of the inner end, the judicial chairs and scribes' tables are to the right. The prisoner's stool is to the left. There are arched doors right and left. It is a fine sunshiny May morning.

WARWICK *comes in through the arched*

doorway on the judges' side, followed by his page.

THE PAGE (*pertly*). I suppose your lordship is aware that we have no business here. This is an ecclesiastical court; and we are only the secular arm.

WARWICK. I am aware of that fact. Will it please your impudence to find the Bishop of Beauvais for me, and give him a hint that he can have a word with me here before the trial, if he wishes?

THE PAGE (*going*). Yes, my lord.

WARWICK. And mind you behave yourself. Do not address him as Pious Peter.

THE PAGE. No, my lord. I shall be kind to him, because, when The Maid is brought in, Pious Peter will have to pick a peck of pickled pepper.

(CAUCHON *enters through the same door with a Dominican monk and a canon, the latter carrying a brief.*)

THE PAGE. The Right Reverend his lordship the Bishop of Beauvais. And two other reverend gentlemen.

WARWICK. Get out; and see that we are not interrupted.

THE PAGE. Right, my lord (*he vanishes airily*).

CAUCHON. I wish your lordship good-morrow.

WARWICK. Good-morrow to your lordship. Have I had the pleasure of meeting your friends before? I think not.

CAUCHON (*introducing the monk, who is on his right*). This, my lord, is Brother John Lemaître, of the order of St Dominic. He is acting as deputy for the Chief Inquisitor into the evil of heresy in France. Brother John: the Earl of Warwick.

WARWICK. Your Reverence is most welcome. We have no Inquisitor in England, unfortunately; though we miss him greatly, especially on occasions like the present.

(*The Inquisitor smiles patiently, and bows. He is a mild elderly gentleman,*

but has evident reserves of authority and firmness.)

CAUCHON (*introducing the Canon, who is on his left*). This gentleman is Canon John D'Estivet, of the Chapter of Bayeux. He is acting as Promoter.

WARWICK. Promoter?

CAUCHON. Prosecutor, you would call him in civil law.

WARWICK. Ah! prosecutor. Quite, quite. I am very glad to make your acquaintance, Canon D'Estivet.

(D'ESTIVET *bows. He is on the young side of the middle age, well mannered, but vulpine beneath his veneer.*)

WARWICK. May I ask what stage the proceedings have reached? It is now more than nine months since The Maid was captured at Compiègne by the Burgundians. It is fully four months since I bought her from the Burgundians for a very handsome sum, solely that she might be brought to justice. It is very nearly three months since I delivered her up to you, my Lord Bishop, as a person suspected of heresy. May I suggest that you are taking a rather unconscionable time to make up your minds about a very plain case? Is this trial never going to end?

THE INQUISITOR (*smiling*). It has not yet begun, my lord.

WARWICK. Not yet begun! Why, you have been at it eleven weeks!

CAUCHON. We have not been idle, my lord. We have held fifteen examinations of The Maid: six public and nine private.

THE INQUISITOR (*always patiently smiling*). You see, my lord, I have been present at only two of these examinations. They were proceedings of the Bishop's court solely, and not of the Holy Office. I have only just decided to associate myself—that is, to associate the Holy Inquisition—with the Bishop's court. I did not at first think that this was a case of heresy at all. I regarded it as a political case, and The Maid as a prisoner of war. But having now been present at two of the examinations, I must admit that this seems to be one of the gravest cases of heresy within my experience. Therefore everything is now in order, and we proceed to trial this morning. (*He moves towards the judicial chairs*)

CAUCHON. This moment, if your lordship's convenience allows.

WARWICK (*graciously*). Well, that is good news, gentlemen. I will not attempt to conceal from you that our patience was becoming strained.

CAUCHON. So I gathered from the threats of your soldiers to drown those of our people who favor The Maid.

WARWICK. Dear me! At all events their intentions were friendly to y o u, my lord.

CAUCHON (*sternly*). I hope not. I am determined that the woman shall have a fair hearing. The justice of The Church is not a mockery, my lord.

THE INQUISITOR (*returning*). Never has there been a fairer examination within my experience, my lord. The Maid needs no lawyers to take her part: she will be tried by her most faithful friends, all ardently desirous to save her soul from perdition.

D'ESTIVET. Sir: I am the Promoter; and it has been my painful duty to present the case against the girl; but believe me, I would throw up my case today and hasten to her defence if I did not know that men far my superiors in learning and piety, in eloquence and persuasiveness, have been sent to reason with her, to explain to her the danger she is running, and the ease with which she may avoid it. (*Suddenly bursting into forensic eloquence, to the disgust of* CAUCHON *and the Inquisitor, who have listened to him so far with patronizing approval*) Men have dared to say that we are acting from hate; but God is our witness that they lie. Have we tortured her? No. Have we ceased to exhort her; to implore her to have pity on herself; to come to the bosom of her Church as an erring but beloved child? Have we—

CAUCHON (*interrupting drily*). Take care, Canon. All that you say is true; but if you make his lordship believe it I will not answer for your life, and hardly for my own.

WARWICK (*deprecating, but by no means denying*). Oh, my lord, you are very hard on us poor English. But we certainly do not share your pious desire to save The Maid: in fact I tell you now plainly that her death is a political necessity which I regret but cannot help. If The Church lets her go—

CAUCHON (*with fierce and menacing pride*). If The Church lets her go, woe to the man, were he the Emperor himself, who dares lay a finger on her! The Church is not subject to political necessity, my lord.

THE INQUISITOR (*interposing smoothly*). You need have no anxiety about the result, my lord. You have an invincible ally in the matter: one who is far more determined than you that she shall burn.

WARWICK. And who is this very convenient partisan, may I ask?

THE INQUISITOR. The Maid herself. Unless you put a gag in her mouth you cannot prevent her from convicting herself ten times over every time she opens it.

D'ESTIVET. That is perfectly true, my lord. My hair bristles on my head when I hear so young a creature utter such blasphemies.

WARWICK. Well, by all means do your best for her if you are quite sure it will be of no avail. (*Looking hard at* CAUCHON) I should be sorry to have to act without the blessing of The Church.

CAUCHON (*with a mixture of cynical admiration and contempt*). And yet they say Englishmen are hypocrites! You play for your side, my lord, even at the peril of your soul. I cannot but admire such devotion; but I dare not go so far myself. I fear damnation.

WARWICK. If we feared anything we could never govern England, my lord. Shall I send your people in to you?

CAUCHON. Yes: it will be very good of your lordship to withdraw and allow the court to assemble.

(WARWICK *turns on his heel, and goes out through the courtyard.* CAUCHON *takes one of the judicial seats; and* D'ESTIVET *sits at the scribes' table, studying his brief.*)

CAUCHON (*casually, as he makes himself comfortable*). What scoundrels these English nobles are!

THE INQUISITOR (*taking the other judicial chair on* CAUCHON's *left*). All secular power makes men scoundrels. They are not trained for the work; and they have not the Apostolic Succession. Our own nobles are just as bad.

(*The* BISHOP's *assessors hurry into the hall, headed by* CHAPLAIN DE STOGUMBER *and* CANON DE COURCELLES, *a young priest of 30. The scribes sit at the table, leaving a chair vacant opposite* D'ESTIVET. *Some of the assessors take their seats: others stand chatting, waiting for the proceedings to begin formally.* DE STOGUMBER, *aggrieved and obstinate, will not take his seat: neither will the* CANON, *who stands on his right.*)

CAUCHON. Good morning, Master de Stogumber. (*To the* INQUISITOR) Chaplain to the Cardinal of England.

THE CHAPLAIN (*correcting him*). Of Winchester, my lord. I have to make a protest, my lord.

CAUCHON. You make a great many.

THE CHAPLAIN. I am not without support, my lord. Here is Master de Courcelles, Canon of Paris, who associates himself with me in my protest.

CAUCHON. Well, what is the matter?

THE CHAPLAIN (*sulkily*). Speak you, Master de Courcelles, since I do not seem to enjoy his lordship's confidence. (*He sits down in dudgeon next to* CAUCHON, *on his right*)

COURCELLES. My lord: we have been at great pains to draw up an indictment of The Maid on sixty-four counts. We are now told that they have been reduced, without consulting us.

THE INQUISITOR. Master de Courcelles: I am the culprit. I am overwhelmed with admiration for the zeal displayed in your sixty-four counts; but in accusing a heretic, as in other things, enough is enough. Also you must remember that all the members of the court are not so subtle and profound as you, and that some of your very great learning might appear to them to be very great nonsense. Therefore I have thought it well to have your sixty-four articles cut down to twelve—

COURCELLES (*thunderstruck*). Twelve!!!

THE INQUISITOR. Twelve will, believe me, be quite enough for your purpose.

THE CHAPLAIN. But some of the most important points have been reduced almost to nothing. For instance, The Maid has actually declared that the blessed saints Margaret and Catherine, and the holy Archangel Michael, spoke to her in French. That is a vital point.

THE INQUISITOR. You think, doubtless, that they should have spoken in Latin?

CAUCHON. No: he thinks they should have spoken in English.

THE CHAPLAIN. Naturally, my lord.

THE INQUISITOR. Well, as we are all here agreed, I think, that these voices of The Maid are the voices of evil spirits tempting her to her damnation, it would not be very courteous to you, Master de Stogumber, or to the King of England, to assume that English is the devil's native language. So let it pass. The matter is not wholly omitted from the twelve articles. Pray take your places, gentlemen; and let us proceed to business.

(*All who have not taken their seats, do so.*)

THE CHAPLAIN. Well, I protest. That is all.

COURCELLES. I think it hard that all our work should go for nothing. It is only another example of the diabolical influence which this woman exercises over the court. (*He takes his chair, which is on the* CHAPLAIN's *right*)

CAUCHON. Do you suggest that I am under diabolical influence?

COURCELLES. I suggest nothing, my lord. But it seems to me that there is a conspiracy here to hush up the fact that The Maid stole the Bishop of Senlis's horse.

CAUCHON (*keeping his temper with difficulty*). This is not a police court. Are we to waste our time on such rubbish?

COURCELLES (*rising, shocked*). My lord: do you call the Bishop's horse rubbish?

THE INQUISITOR (*blandly*). Master de Courcelles: The Maid alleges that she paid handsomely for the Bishop's horse, and that if he did not get the money the fault was not hers. As that may be true, the point is one on which The Maid may well be acquitted.

COURCELLES. Yes, if it were an ordinary horse. But the Bishop's horse! how can she be acquitted for that? (*He sits down again, bewildered and discouraged*)

THE INQUISITOR. I submit to you, with great respect, that if we persist in trying The Maid on trumpery issues on which we may have to declare her innocent, she may escape us on the great main issue of heresy, on which she seems so far to insist on her own guilt. I will ask you, therefore, to say nothing, when The Maid is brought before us, of these stealings of horses, and dancings round fairy trees with the village children, and prayings at haunted wells, and a dozen other things which you were diligently inquiring into until my arrival. There is not a village girl in France against whom you could not prove such things: they all dance round haunted trees, and pray at magic wells. Some of them would steal the Pope's horse if they got the chance. Heresy, gentlemen, heresy is the charge we have to try. The detection and suppression of heresy is my peculiar business: I am here as an inquisitor, not as an ordinary magistrate. Stick to the heresy, gentlemen; and leave the other matters alone.

CAUCHON. I may say that we have sent to the girl's village to make inquiries about her, and there is practically nothing serious against her.

THE CHAPLAIN

COURCELLES

(*rising and clamoring together*).

Nothing serious, my lord—

What! The fairy tree not—

CAUCHON (*out of patience*). Be silent, gentlemen; or speak one at a time.

(COURCELLES *collapses into his chair, intimidated.*)

THE CHAPLAIN (*sulkily resuming his seat*). That is what The Maid said to us last Friday.

CAUCHON. I wish you had followed her counsel, sir. When I say nothing serious, I mean nothing that men of sufficiently large mind to conduct an inquiry like this would consider serious. I agree with my colleague the Inquisitor that it is on the count of heresy that we must proceed.

LADVENU (*a young but ascetically fine-drawn Dominican who is sitting next* COURCELLES, *on his right*). But is there any great harm in the girl's heresy? Is it not merely her simplicity? Many saints have said as much as Joan.

THE INQUISITOR (*dropping his blandness and speaking very gravely*). Brother Martin: if you had seen what I have seen of heresy, you would not think it a light thing even in its most apparently harmless and even lovable and pious origins. Heresy begins with people who are to all appearance better than their neighbors. A gentle and pious girl, or a young man who has obeyed the command of our Lord by giving all his riches to the poor, and putting on the garb of poverty, the life of austerity, and the rule of humility and charity, may be the founder of a heresy that will wreck both Church and Empire if not ruthlessly stamped out in time. The records of the Holy Inquisition are full of histories we dare not give to the world, because they are beyond the belief of honest men and innocent women; yet they all began with saintly simpletons. I have seen this again and again. Mark what I say: the woman who quarrels with her clothes, and puts on the dress of a man, is like the man who throws off his fur gown and dresses like John the Baptist: they are followed, as surely as the night follows the day, by bands of wild women and men who refuse to wear any clothes at all. When maids will neither marry nor take regular vows, and men reject marriage and exalt their lusts into divine inspirations, then, as surely as the summer follows the spring, they begin with polygamy, and end by incest. Heresy at first seems innocent and even laudable; but it ends in such a monstrous horror of unnatural wickedness that the most tender-hearted among you, if you saw it at work as I have seen it, would clamor against the mercy of The Church in dealing with it. For two hundred years the Holy Office has striven with these diabolical madnesses; and it knows that they begin always by vain and ignorant persons setting up their own judgment against The Church, and taking it upon themselves to be the interpreters of God's will. You must not fall into the common error of mistaking these simpletons for liars and hypocrites. They believe honestly and sincerely that their diabolical inspiration is divine. Therefore you must be on your guard against your natural compassion. You are all, I hope, merciful men: how else could you have devoted your lives to the service of our gentle Savior? You are going to see before you a young girl, pious and chaste; for I must tell you, gentlemen, that the things said of her by our English friends are supported by no evidence, whilst there is abundant testimony that her excesses have been excesses of religion and charity and not of worldliness and wantonness. This girl is not one of those whose hard features are the sign of hard hearts, and whose brazen looks and lewd demeanor condemn them before they are accused. The devilish pride that has led her into her present peril has left no mark on her countenance. Strange as it may seem to you, it has even left no mark on her character outside those special matters in which she is proud; so that you will see a diabolical pride and a natural humility seated side by side in the self-same soul. Therefore be on your guard. God forbid that I should tell you to harden your hearts; for her punishment if we condemn her will be so cruel that we should forfeit our own hope of divine mercy were there one grain of malice against her in our hearts. But if you hate cruelty— and if any man here does not hate it I command him on his soul's salvation to quit this holy court—I say, if you hate cruelty, remember that nothing is so cruel in its consequences as the toleration of heresy. Remember also that no court of law can be so cruel as the common people are to those whom they suspect of heresy. The heretic in the hands of the Holy Office is safe from violence, is assured of a fair trial, and cannot suffer death, even when guilty, if repentance follows sin. Innumerable lives of heretics have been saved because the Holy Office has taken them out of the hands of the people, and because the people have yielded them up, knowing that the Holy Office would deal with them. Before the Holy Inquisition existed, and even now when its officers are not within reach, the unfortunate wretch suspected of heresy, perhaps quite ignorantly and injustly, is stoned, torn in pieces, drowned, burned in his house with all his innocent children, without a trial, unshriven, unburied save as a dog is buried: all of them deeds hateful to God and most cruel to man. Gentlemen: I am compassionate by nature as well as by my profession; and though the work I have to do may seem cruel to those who do not know how much more cruel it would be to leave it undone, I would go to the stake myself sooner than do it if I did not know its righteousness, its necessity, its essential mercy. I ask you to address yourself to this trial in that conviction. Anger is a bad counsellor: cast out anger. Pity is sometimes worse: cast out pity. But do not cast out mercy. Remember only that justice comes first. Have you anything to say, my lord, before we proceed to trial?

CAUCHON. You have spoken for me, and spoken better than I could. I do not see how any sane man could disagree with a word that has fallen from you. But this I will add. The crude heresies of which you have told us are horrible; but their horror is like that of the black death: they rage for a while and then die out, because sound and sensible men will not under any incitement be reconciled to nakedness and incest and polygamy and the like. But we are confronted today throughout Europe with a heresy that is spreading among men not weak in mind nor diseased in brain: nay, the stronger the mind, the more obstinate the heretic. It is neither discredited by fantastic extremes nor corrupted by the common lusts of the flesh; but it, too, sets up the private judgment of the single erring mortal against the considered wisdom and experience of The Church. The mighty structure of Catholic Christendom will never be shaken by naked madmen or by the sins of Moab and Ammon. But it may be betrayed from within, and brought to barbarous ruin and desolation, by this arch heresy which the English Commander calls Protestantism.

THE ASSESSORS (*whispering*). Protestantism! What was that? What does the Bishop mean? Is it a new heresy? The English Commander, he said. Did y o u ever hear of Protestantism? etc., etc.

CAUCHON (*continuing*). And that reminds me. What provision has the Earl of Warwick made for the defence of the secular arm should The Maid prove obdurate, and the people be moved to pity her?

THE CHAPLAIN. Have no fear on that score, my lord. The noble earl has eight hundred men-at-arms at the gates. She will not slip through our English fingers even if the whole city be on her side.

CAUCHON (*revolted*). Will you not add, God grant that she repent and purge her sin?

THE CHAPLAIN. That does not seem to me to be consistent; but of course I agree with your lordship.

CAUCHON (*giving him up with a shrug of contempt*). The court sits.

THE INQUISITOR. Let the accused be brought in.

LADVENU (*calling*). The accused. Let her be brought in.

(JOAN, *chained by the ankles, is brought in through the arched door behind the prisoner's stool by a guard of English soldiers. With them is the Executioner and his assistants. They lead her to the prisoner's stool, and place themselves behind it after taking off her chain. She wears a page's black suit. Her long imprisonment and the strain of the examinations which have preceded the trial have left their mark on her; but her vitality still holds; she confronts the court unabashed, without a trace of the awe which their formal solemnity seems to require for the complete success of its impressiveness.*)

THE INQUISITOR (*kindly*). Sit down, Joan. (*She sits on the prisoner's stool*) You look very pale today. Are you not well?

JOAN. Thank you kindly: I am well enough. But the Bishop sent me some carp; and it made me ill.

CAUCHON. I am sorry. I told them to see that it was fresh.

JOAN. You meant to be good to me, I know; but it is a fish that does not agree with me. The English thought you were trying to poison me—

CAUCHON $\left.\begin{array}{l} \\ \\ \end{array}\right\}$ (*together*). $\begin{array}{l}\text{What!}\\ \\ \text{No, my lord.}\end{array}$
THE CHAPLAIN

JOAN (*continuing*). They are determined that I shall be burnt as a witch; and they sent their doctor to cure me; but he was forbidden to bleed me because the silly people believe that a witch's witchery leaves her if she is bled; so he only called me filthy names. Why do you leave me in the hands of the English? I should be in the hands of The Church. And why must I be chained by the feet to a log of wood? Are you afraid I will fly away?

D'ESTIVET (*harshly*). Woman: it is not for you to question the court: it is for us to question you.

COURCELLES. When you were left unchained, did you not try to escape by jumping from a tower sixty feet high? If you cannot fly like a witch, how is it that you are still alive?

JOAN. I suppose because the tower was not so high then. It has grown higher every day since you began asking me questions about it.

D'ESTIVET. Why did you jump from the tower?

JOAN. How do you know that I jumped?

D'ESTIVET. You were found lying in the moat. Why did you leave the tower?

JOAN. Why would anybody leave a prison if they could get out?

D'ESTIVET. You tried to escape?

JOAN. Of course I did; and not for the first time either. If you leave the door of the cage open the bird will fly out.

D'ESTIVET (*rising*). That is a confession of heresy. I call the attention of the court to it.

JOAN. Heresy, he calls it! Am I a heretic because I try to escape from prison?

D'ESTIVET. Assuredly, if you are in the hands of the Church, and you wilfully take yourself out of its hands, you are deserting the Church; and that is heresy.

JOAN. It is great nonsense. Nobody could be such a fool as to think that.

D'ESTIVET. You hear, my lord, how I am reviled in the execution of my duty by this woman. (*He sits down indignantly*)

CAUCHON. I have warned you before, Joan, that you are doing yourself no good by these pert answers.

JOAN. But you will not talk sense to me. I am reasonable if you will be reasonable.

THE INQUISITOR (*interposing*). This is not yet in order. You forget, Master Promoter, that the proceedings have not been formally opened. The time for questions is after she has sworn on the Gospels to tell us the whole truth.

JOAN. You say this to me every time. I have said again and again that I will tell you all that concerns this trial. But I cannot tell you the whole truth: God does not allow the whole truth to be told. You do not understand it when I tell it. It is an old saying that he who tells too much truth is sure to be hanged. I am weary of this argument: we have been over it nine times already. I have sworn as much as I will swear; and I will swear no more.

COURCELLES. My lord: she should be put to the torture.

THE INQUISITOR. You hear, Joan? That is what happens to the obdurate. Think before you answer. Has she been shewn the instruments?

THE EXECUTIONER. They are ready, my lord. She has seen them.

JOAN. If you tear me limb from limb until you separate my soul from my body you will get nothing out of me beyond what I have told you. What more is there to tell that you could understand? Besides, I cannot bear to be hurt; and if you hurt me I will say anything you like to stop the pain. But I will take it all back afterwards; so what is the use of it?

LADVENU. There is much in that. We should proceed mercifully.

COURCELLES. But the torture is customary.

THE INQUISITOR. It must not be applied wantonly. If the accused will confess voluntarily, then its use cannot be justified.

COURCELLES. But this is unusual and irregular. She refuses to take the oath.

LADVENU (*disgusted*). Do you want to torture the girl for the mere pleasure of it?

COURCELLES (*bewildered*). But it is not a pleasure. It is the law. It is customary. It is always done.

THE INQUISITOR. That is not so, Master, except when the inquiries are carried on by people who do not know their legal business.

COURCELLES. But the woman is a heretic. I assure you it is always done.

CAUCHON (*decisively*). It will not be done today if it is not necessary. Let there be an end of this. I will not have it said that we proceeded on forced confessions. We have sent our best preachers and doctors to this woman to exhort and implore her to save her soul and body from the fire: we shall not now send the executioner to thrust her into it.

COURCELLES. Your lordship is merciful, of course. But it is a great responsibility to depart from the usual practice.

JOAN. Thou art a rare noodle, Master. Do what was done last time is thy rule, eh?

COURCELLES (*rising*). Thou wanton: dost thou dare call me noodle?

THE INQUISITOR. Patience, Master, patience: I fear you will soon be only too terribly avenged.

COURCELLES (*mutters*). Noodle indeed! (*He sits down, much discontented*)

THE INQUISITOR. Meanwhile, let us not be moved by the rough side of a shepherd lass's tongue.

JOAN. Nay: I am no shepherd lass, though I have helped with the sheep like anyone else. I will do a lady's work in the house—spin or weave—against any woman in Rouen.

THE INQUISITOR. This is not a time for vanity, Joan. You stand in great peril.

JOAN. I know it: have I not been punished for my vanity? If I had not worn my cloth of gold surcoat in battle like a fool, that Burgundian soldier would never have pulled me backwards off my horse; and I should not have been here.

THE CHAPLAIN. If you are so clever at woman's work why do you not stay at home and do it?

JOAN. There are plenty of other women to do it; but there is nobody to do my work.

CAUCHON. Come! we are wasting time on trifles. Joan: I am going to put a most solemn question to you. Take care how you answer; for your life and salvation are at stake on it. Will you for all you have said and done, be it good or bad, accept the judgment of God's Church on earth? More especially as to the acts and words that are imputed to you in this trial by the Promoter here, will you submit your case to the inspired interpretation of the Church Militant?

JOAN. I am faithful child of The Church. I will obey The Church—

CAUCHON (*hopefully leaning forward*). You will?

JOAN. —provided it does not command anything impossible.

(CAUCHON *sinks back in his chair with a heavy sigh. The* INQUISITOR *purses his lips and frowns.* LADVENU *shakes his head pitifully.*)

D'ESTIVET. She imputes to The Church the error and folly of commanding the impossible.

JOAN. If you command me to declare that all that I have done and said, and all the visions and revelations I have had, were not from God, then that is impossible: I will not declare it for anything in the world. What God made me do I will never go back on; and what He has commanded or shall command I will not fail to do in spite of any man alive. That is what I mean by impossible. And in case The Church should bid me do anything contrary to the command I have from God, I will not consent to it, no matter what it may be.

THE ASSESSORS (*shocked and indignant*). Oh! The Church contrary to God! What do you say now? Flat heresy. This is beyond everything, etc., etc.

D'ESTIVET (*throwing down his brief*). My lord: do you need anything more than this?

CAUCHON. Woman: you have said enough to burn ten heretics. Will you not be warned? Will you not understand?

THE INQUISITOR. If the Church Militant tells you that your revelations and visions are sent by the devil to tempt you to your damnation, will you not believe that The Church is wiser than you?

JOAN. I believe that God is wiser than I; and it is His commands that I will do. All the things that you call my crimes have come to me by the command of God. I say that I have done them by the order of God: it is impossible for me to say anything else. If any Churchman says the contrary I shall not mind him: I shall mind God alone, whose command I always follow.

LADVENU (*pleading with her urgently*). You do not know what you are saying, child. Do you want to kill yourself? Listen. Do you not believe that you are subject to The Church of God on earth?

JOAN. Yes. When have I ever denied it?

LADVENU. Good. That means, does it not, that you are subject to our Lord the Pope, to the cardinals, the archbishops, and the bishops for whom his lordship stands here today?

JOAN. God must be served first.

D'ESTIVET. Then your voices command you not to submit yourself to the Church Militant?

JOAN. My voices do not tell me to disobey The Church; but God must be served first.

CAUCHON. And you, and not the Church, are to be the judge?

JOAN. What other judgment can I judge by but my own?

THE ASSESSORS (*scandalized*). Oh! (*They cannot find words*)

CAUCHON. Out of your own mouth you have condemned yourself. We have striven for your salvation to the verge of sinning ourselves: we have opened the door to you again and again; and you have shut it in our faces and in the face of God. Dare you pretend, after what you have said, that you are in a state of grace?

JOAN. If I am not, may God bring me to it: if I am, may God keep me in it!

LADVENU. That is a very good reply, my lord.

COURCELLES. Were you in a state of grace when you stole the Bishop's horse?

CAUCHON (*rising in a fury*). Oh, devil take the Bishop's horse and you too! We are here to try a case of heresy; and no sooner do we come to the root of the matter than we are thrown back by idiots who understand nothing but horses. (*Trembling with rage, he forces himself to sit down*)

THE INQUISITOR. Gentlemen, gentlemen: in clinging to these small issues you are The Maid's best advocates. I am not surprised that his lordship has lost patience with you. What does the Promoter say? Does he press these trumpery matters?

D'ESTIVET. I am bound by my office to press everything; but when the woman confesses a heresy that must bring upon her the doom of excommunication, of what consequence is it that she has been guilty also of offences which expose her to minor penances? I share the impatience of his lordship as to these minor charges. Only, with great respect, I must emphasize the gravity of two very horrible and blasphemous crimes which she does not deny. First, she has intercourse with evil spirits, and is therefore a sorceress. Second, she wears men's clothes, which is indecent, unnatural, and abominable; and in spite of our most earnest remonstrances and entreaties, she will not change them even to receive the sacrament.

JOAN. Is the blessed St Catherine an evil spirit? Is St Margaret? Is Michael the Archangel?

COURCELLES. How do you know that the spirit which appears to you is an archangel? Does he not appear to you as a naked man?

JOAN. Do you think God cannot afford clothes for him?

(*The* ASSESSORS *cannot help smiling, especially as the joke is against* COURCELLES.)

LADVENU. Well answered, Joan.

THE INQUISITOR. It is, in effect, well answered. But no evil spirit would be so simple as to appear to a young girl in a guise that would scandalize her when he meant her to take him for a messenger from the Most High. Joan: The Church instructs you that these apparitions are demons seeking your soul's perdition. Do you accept the instruction of The Church?

JOAN. I accept the messenger of God. How could any faithful believer in The Church refuse him?

CAUCHON. Wretched woman: again I ask you, do you know what you are saying?

THE INQUISITOR. You wrestle in vain with the devil for her soul, my lord: she will not be saved. Now as to this matter of the man's dress. For the last time, will you put off that impudent attire, and dress as becomes your sex?

JOAN. I will not.

D'ESTIVET (*pouncing*). The sin of disobedience, my lord.

JOAN (*distressed*). But my voices tell me I must dress as a soldier.

LADVENU. Joan, Joan: does not that prove to you that the voices are the voices of evil spirits? Can you suggest to us one good reason why an angel of God should give you such shameless advice?

JOAN. Why, yes: what can be plainer commonsense? I was a soldier living among soldiers. I am a prisoner guarded by soldiers. If I were to dress as a woman they would think of me as a woman; and then what would become of me? If I dress as a soldier they think of me as a soldier, and I can live with them as I do at home with my brothers. That is why St Catherine tells me I must not dress as a woman until she gives me leave.

COURCELLES. When will she give you leave?

JOAN. When you take me out of the hands of the English soldiers. I have told you that I should be in the hands of The Church, and not left night and day with four soldiers of the Earl of Warwick. Do you want me to live with them in petticoats?

LADVENU. My lord: what she says is, God knows, very wrong and shocking; but there is a grain of worldly sense in it such as might impose on a simple village maiden.

JOAN. If we were as simple in the village as you are in your courts and places, there would soon be no wheat to make bread for you.

CAUCHON. That is the thanks you get for trying to save her, Brother Martin.

LADVENU. Joan: we are all trying to save you. His lordship is trying to save you. The Inquisitor could not be more just to you if you were his own daughter. But you are blinded by a terrible pride and self-sufficiency.

JOAN. Why do you say that? I have said nothing wrong. I cannot understand.

THE INQUISITOR. The blessed St Athanasius has laid it down in his creed that those who cannot understand are damned. It is not enough to be simple. It is not enough even to be what simple people call good. The simplicity of a darkened mind is no better than the simplicity of a beast.

JOAN. There is great wisdom in the simplicity of a beast, let me tell you; and sometimes great foolishness in the wisdom of scholars.

LADVENU. We know that, Joan: we are not so foolish as you think us. Try to resist the temptation to make pert replies to us. Do you see that man who stands behind you (*he indicates* THE EXECUTIONER)?

JOAN (*turning and looking at the man*). Your torturer? But the Bishop said I was not to be tortured.

LADVENU. You are not to be tortured because you have confessed everything that is necessary to your condemnation. That man is not only the torturer: he is also the Executioner. Executioner: let The Maid hear your answers to my questions. Are you prepared for the burning of a heretic this day?

THE EXECUTIONER. Yes, Master.

LADVENU. Is the stake ready?

THE EXECUTIONER. It is. In the market-place. The English have built it too high for me to get near her and make the death easier. It will be a cruel death.

JOAN (*horrified*). But you are not going to burn me now?

THE INQUISITOR. You realize it at last.

LADVENU. There are eight hundred English soldiers waiting to take you to the market-place the moment the sentence of excommunication has passed the lips of your judges. You are within a few short moments of that doom.

JOAN (*looking round desperately for rescue*). Oh God!

LADVENU. Do not despair, Joan. The Church is merciful. You can save yourself.

JOAN (*hopefully*). Yes: my voices promised me I should not be burnt. St Catherine bade me be bold.

CAUCHON. Woman: are you quite mad? Do you not yet see that your voices have deceived you?

JOAN. Oh no: that is impossible.

CAUCHON. Impossible! They have led you straight to your excommunication, and to the stake which is there waiting for you.

LADVENU (*pressing the point hard*). Have they kept a single promise to you since you were taken at Compiègne? The devil has betrayed you. The Church holds out its arms to you.

JOAN (*despairing*). Oh, it is true: it is true: my voices have deceived me. I have been mocked by devils: my faith is broken. I have dared and dared; but only a fool will walk into a fire: God, who gave me my common-sense, cannot will me to do that.

LADVENU. Now God be praised that He has saved you at the eleventh hour! (*He hurries to the vacant seat at the scribes' table, and snatches a sheet of paper, on which he sets to work writing eagerly*)

CAUCHON. Amen!

JOAN. What must I do?

CAUCHON. You must sign a solemn recantation of your heresy.

JOAN. Sign? That means to write my name. I cannot write.

CAUCHON. You have signed many letters before.

JOAN. Yes; but someone held my hand and guided the pen. I can make my mark.

THE CHAPLAIN (*who has been listening with growing alarm and indignation*). My lord: do you mean that you are going to allow this woman to escape us?

THE INQUISITOR. The law must take its course, Master de Stogumber. And you know the law.

THE CHAPLAIN (*rising, purple with fury*). I know that there is no faith in a Frenchman. (*Tumult, which he shouts down*) I know what my lord the Cardinal of Winchester will say when he hears of this. I know what the Earl of Warwick will do when he learns that you intend to betray him. There are eight hundred men at the gate who will see that this abominable witch is burnt in spite of your teeth.

THE ASSESSORS (*meanwhile*). What is this? What did he say? He accuses us of treachery! This is past bearing. No faith in a Frenchman! Did you hear that? This is an intolerable fellow. Who is he? Is this what English Churchmen are like? He must be mad or drunk, etc., etc.

THE INQUISITOR (*rising*). Silence, pray! Gentlemen: pray silence! Master Chaplain: bethink you a moment of your holy office: of what you are, and where you are. I direct you to sit down.

THE CHAPLAIN (*folding his arms doggedly, his face working convulsively*). I will NOT sit down.

CAUCHON. Master Inquisitor: this man has called me a traitor to my face before now.

THE CHAPLAIN. So you are a traitor. You are all traitors. You have been doing nothing but begging this damnable witch on your knees to recant all through this trial.

THE INQUISITOR (*placidly resuming his seat*). If you will not sit, you must stand: that is all.

THE CHAPLAIN. I will NOT stand (*he flings himself back into his chair*).

LADVENU (*rising with the paper in his hand*). My lord: here is the form of recantation for The Maid to sign.

CAUCHON. Read it to her.

JOAN. Do not trouble. I will sign it.

THE INQUISITOR. Woman: you must know what you are putting your hand to. Read it to her, Brother Martin. And let all be silent.

LADVENU (*reading quietly*). 'I, Joan, commonly called The Maid, a miserable sinner, do confess that I have most grievously sinned in the following articles. I have pretended to have revelations from God and the angels and the blessed saints, and perversely rejected The Church's warnings that these were temptations by demons. I have blasphemed abominably by wearing an immodest dress, contrary to the Holy Scripture and the canons of the Church. Also I have clipped my hair in the style of a man, and, against all the duties which have made my sex specially acceptable in heaven, have taken up the sword, even to the shedding of human blood, inciting men to slay each other, invoking evil spirits to delude them, and stubbornly and most blasphemously imputing these sins to Almighty God. I confess to the sin of sedition, to the sin of idolatry, to the sin of disobedience, to the sin of pride, and to the sin of heresy. All of which sins I now renounce and abjure and depart from, humbly thanking you Doctors and Masters who have brought me back to the truth and into the grace of our Lord. And I will never return to my errors, but will remain in communion with our Holy Church and in obedience to our Holy Father the Pope of Rome. All this I swear by God Almighty and the Holy Gospels, in witness whereto I sign my name to this recantation.'

THE INQUISITOR. You understand this, Joan?

JOAN (*listless*). It is plain enough, sir.

THE INQUISITOR. And it is true?

JOAN. It may be true. If it were not true, the fire would not be ready for me in the market-place.

LADVENU (*taking up his pen and a book, and going to her quickly lest she should compromise herself again*). Come, child: let me guide your hand. Take the pen. (*She does so; and they begin to write, using the book as a desk*) J.E.H.A.N.E. So. Now make your mark by yourself.

JOAN (*makes her mark, and gives him back the pen, tormented by the rebellion of her soil against her mind and body*). There!

LADVENU (*replacing the pen on the table, and handing the recantation to* CAUCHON *with a reverence*). Praise be to God, my brothers, the lamb has returned to the flock; and the shepherd rejoices in her more than in ninety and nine just persons. (*He returns to his seat*)

THE INQUISITOR (*taking the paper from* CAUCHON). We declare thee by this act set free from the danger of excommunication in which thou stoodest. (*He throws the paper down to the table*)

JOAN. I thank you.

THE INQUISITOR. But because thou has sinned most presumptuously against God and the Holy Church, and that thou mayst repent thy errors in solitary contemplation, and be shielded from all temptation to return to them, we, for the good of thy soul, and for a penance that may wipe out thy sins and bring thee finally unspotted to the throne of grace, do condemn thee to eat the bread of sorrow and drink the water of affliction to the end of thy earthly days in perpetual imprisonment.

JOAN (*rising in consternation and terrible anger*). Perpetual imprisonment! Am I not then to be set free?

LADVENU (*mildly shocked*). Set free, child, after such wickedness as yours! What are you dreaming of?

JOAN. Give me that writing. (*She rushes to the table; snatches up the paper; and tears it into fragments*) Light your fire: do you think I dread it as much as the life of a rat in a hole? My voices were right.

LADVENU. Joan! Joan!

JOAN. Yes: they told me you were fools (*the word gives great offence*), and that I was not to listen to your fine words nor trust to your charity. You promised me my life; but you lied (*indignant exclamations*). You think that life is nothing but not being stone dead. It is not the bread and water I fear: I can live on bread: when have I asked for more? It is no hardship to drink water if the water be clean. Bread has no sorrow for me, and water no affliction. But to shut me from the light of the sky and the sight of the fields and flowers; to chain my feet so that I can never again ride with the soldiers nor climb the hills; to make me breathe foul damp darkness, and keep from me everything that brings me back to the love of God when your wickedness and foolishness tempt me to hate Him: all this is worse than the furnace in the Bible that was heated seven times. I could do without my warhorse; I could drag about in a skirt; I could let the banners and the trumpets and the knights and soldiers pass me and leave me behind as they leave the other women, if only I could still hear the wind in the trees, the larks in the sunshine, the young lambs crying through the healthy frost, and the blessed blessed church bells that send my angel voices floating to me on the wind. But without these things I cannot live; and by your wanting to take them away from me, or from any human creature, I know that your counsel is of the devil, and that mine is of God.

THE ASSESSORS (*in great commotion*). Blasphemy! blasphemy! She is possessed. She said our counsel was of the devil. And hers of God. Monstrous! The devil is in our midst, etc., etc.

D'ESTIVET (*shouting above the din*). She is a relapsed heretic, obstinate, incorrigible, and altogether unworthy of the mercy we have shewn her. I call for her excommunication.

THE CHAPLAIN (*to* THE EXECUTIONER). Light your fire, man. To the stake with her.

(THE EXECUTIONER *and his assistants hurry out through the courtyard.*)

LADVENU. You wicked girl: if your counsel were of God would He not deliver you?

JOAN. His ways are not your ways. He wills that I go through the fire to His bosom; for I am His child, and you are not fit that I should live among you. That is my last word to you.

(*The soldiers seize her.*)

CAUCHON (*rising*). Not yet.

(*They wait. There is a dead silence.* CAUCHON *turns to* THE INQUISITOR *with an inquiring look.* THE INQUISITOR *nods affirmatively. They rise solemnly, and intone the sentence antiphonally.*)

CAUCHON. We decree that thou art a relapsed heretic.

THE INQUISITOR. Cast out from the unity of the Church.

CAUCHON. Sundered from her body.

THE INQUISITOR. Infected with the leprosy of heresy.

CAUCHON. A member of Satan.

THE INQUISITOR. We declare that thou must be excommunicate.

CAUCHON. And now we do cast thee out, segregate thee, and abandon thee to the secular power.

THE INQUISITOR. Admonishing the same secular power that it moderate its judgement of thee in respect of death and division of the limbs. (*He resumes his seat*)

CAUCHON. And if any true sign of penitence appear in thee, to permit our Brother Martin to administer to thee the sacrament of penance.

THE CHAPLAIN. Into the fire with the witch (*he rushes at her, and helps the soldiers to push her out*).

(JOAN *is taken away through the courtyard. The assessors rise in disorder, and follow the soldiers, except* LADVENU, *who has hidden his face in his hands.*)

CAUCHON (*rising again in the act of sitting down*). No, no: this is irregular. The representative of the secular arm should be here to receive her from us.

THE INQUISITOR (*also on his feet again*). That man is an incorrigible fool.

CAUCHON. Brother Martin: see that everything is done in order.

LADVENU. My place is at her side, my Lord. You must exercise your own authority. (*He hurries out*)

CAUCHON. These English are impossible: they will thrust her straight into the fire. Look!

(*He points to the courtyard, in which the glow and flicker of fire can now be seen reddening the May daylight. Only the* BISHOP *and the* INQUISITOR *are left in the court.*)

CAUCHON (*turning to go*). We must stop that.

THE INQUISITOR (*calmly*). Yes; but not too fast, my lord.

CAUCHON (*halting*). But there is not a moment to lose.

THE INQUISITOR. We have proceeded in perfect order. If the English choose to put themselves in the wrong, it is not our business to put them in the right. A flaw in the procedure may be useful later on: one never knows. And the sooner it is over, the better for that poor girl.

CAUCHON (*relaxing*). That is true. But I suppose we must see this dreadful thing through.

THE INQUISITOR. One gets used to it. Habit is everything. I am accustomed to the fire: it is soon over. But it is a terrible thing to see a young and innocent creature crushed between these mighty forces, The Church and the Law.

CAUCHON. You call her innocent!

THE INQUISITOR. Oh, quite innocent. What does she know of The Church and the Law? She did not understand a word we were saying. It is the ignorant who suffer. Come, or we shall be late for the end.

CAUCHON (*going with him*). I shall not be sorry if we are: I am not so accustomed as you.

(*They are going out when* WARWICK *comes in, meeting them.*)

WARWICK. Oh, I am intruding. I thought it was all over. (*He makes a feint of retiring*)

CAUCHON. Do not go, my lord. It is all over.

THE INQUISITOR. The execution is not in our hands, my lord; but it is desirable that we should witness the end. So by your leave— (*He bows, and goes out through the courtyard*).

CAUCHON. There is some doubt whether your people have observed the forms of law, my lord.

WARWICK. I am told that there is some doubt whether your authority runs in this city, my lord. It is not in your diocese. However, if you will answer for that I will answer for the rest.

CAUCHON. It is to God that we both must answer. Good morning, my lord.

WARWICK. My lord: good morning.

(*They look at one another for a moment with unconcealed hostility. Then* CAUCHON *follows* THE INQUISITOR *out.*)

WARWICK *looks round. Finding himself alone, he calls for attendance.*)

WARWICK. Hallo: some attendance here! (*Silence*) Hallo, there! (*Silence*) Hallo! Brian, you young blackguard, where are you? (*Silence*) Guard! (*Silence*) They have all gone to see the burning: even that child.

(*The silence is broken by someone frantically howling and sobbing.*)

WARWICK. What in the devil's name—?

(*The* CHAPLAIN *staggers in from the courtyard like a demented creature, his face streaming with tears, making the piteous sounds that* WARWICK *has heard. He stumbles to the prisoner's stool, and throws himself upon it with heartrending sobs.*)

WARWICK (*going to him and patting him on the shoulder*). What is it, Master John? What is the matter?

THE CHAPLAIN (*clutching at his hand*). My lord, my lord: for Christ's sake pray for my wretched guilty soul.

WARWICK (*soothing him*). Yes, yes: of course I will. Calmly, gently—

THE CHAPLAIN (*blubbering miserably*). I am not a bad man, my lord.

WARWICK. No, no: not at all.

THE CHAPLAIN. I meant no harm. I did not know what it would be like.

WARWICK (*hardening*). Oh! You saw it, then?

THE CHAPLAIN. I did not know what I was doing. I am a hotheaded fool; and I shall be damned to all eternity for it.

WARWICK. Nonsense! Very distressing, no doubt; but it was not your doing.

THE CHAPLAIN (*lamentably*). I let them do it. If I had known, I would have torn her from their hands. You dont know: you havnt seen: it is so easy to talk when you dont know. You madden yourself with words: you damn yourself because it feels grand to throw oil on the flaming hell of your own temper. But when it is brought home to you; when you see the thing you have done; when it is blinding your eyes, stifling your nostrils, tearing your heart, then—then— (*Falling on his knees*). O God, take away this sight from me! O Christ, deliver me from this fire that is consuming me! She cried to Thee in the midst of it: Jesus! Jesus! Jesus! She is in Thy bosom; and I am in hell for evermore.

WARWICK (*summarily hauling him to his feet*). Come come, man! you must pull yourself together. We shall have the whole town talking of this. (*He throws him not too gently into a chair at the table*) If you have not the nerve to see these things, why do you not do as I do, and stay away?

THE CHAPLAIN (*bewildered and submissive*). She asked for a cross. A soldier gave her two sticks tied together. Thank God he was an Englishman! I might have done it; but I did not: I am a coward, a mad dog, a fool. But he was an Englishman too.

WARWICK. The fool! they will burn him too if the priests get hold of him.

THE CHAPLAIN (*shaken with a convulsion*). Some of the people laughed at her. They would have laughed at Christ. They were French people, my lord: I know they were French.

WARWICK. Hush! someone is coming. Control yourself.

(LADVENU *comes back through the court-yard to* WARWICK's *right hand, carrying a bishop's cross which he has taken from a church. He is very grave and composed.*)

WARWICK. I am informed that it is all over, Brother Martin.

LADVENU (*enigmatically*). We do not know, my lord. It may have only just begun.

WARWICK. What does that mean, exactly?

LADVENU. I took this cross from the church for her that she might see it to the last: she had only two sticks that she put into her bosom. When the fire crept round us, and she saw that if I held the cross before her I should be burnt myself, she warned me to get down and save myself. My lord: a girl who could think of another's danger in such a moment

was not inspired by the devil. When I had to snatch the cross from her sight, she looked up to heaven. And I do not believe that the heavens were empty. I firmly believe that her Savior appeared to her then in His tenderest glory. She called to Him and died. This is not the end for her, but the beginning.

WARWICK. I am afraid it will have a bad effect on the people.

LADVENU. It had, my lord, on some of them. I heard laughter. Forgive me for saying that I hope and believe it was English laughter.

THE CHAPLAIN (*rising frantically*). No: it was not. There was only one Englishman there that disgraced his country; and that was the mad dog, de Stogumber. (*He rushes wildly out, shrieking*) Let them torture him. Let them burn him. I will go pray among her ashes. I am no better than Judas: I will hang myself.

WARWICK. Quick, Brother Martin: follow him: he will do himself some mischief. After him, quick.

(LADVENU *hurries out,* WARWICK *urging him.* THE EXECUTIONER *comes in by the door behind the judges' chairs; and* WARWICK, *returning, finds himself face to face with him.*)

WARWICK. Well, fellow: who are you?

THE EXECUTIONER (*with dignity*). I am not addressed as fellow, my lord. I am the Master Executioner of Rouen: it is a highly skilled mystery. I am come to tell your lordship that your orders have been obeyed.

WARWICK. I crave your pardon, Master Executioner; and I will see that you lose nothing by having no relics to sell. I have your word, have I, that nothing remains, not a bone, not a nail, not a hair?

THE EXECUTIONER. Her heart would not burn, my lord; but everything that was left is at the bottom of the river. You have heard the last of her.

WARWICK (*with a wry smile, thinking of what* LADVENU *said*). The last of her? Hm! I wonder!

EPILOGUE

A restless fitfully windy night in June 1456, full of summer lightning after many days of heat. King CHARLES *the Seventh of France, formerly* JOAN'S DAUPHIN, *now* CHARLES *the Victorious, aged 51, is in bed in one of his royal chateaux. The bed, raised on a dais of two steps, is towards the side of the room so as to avoid blocking a tall lancet window in the middle. Its canopy bears the royal arms in embroidery. Except for the canopy and the huge down pillows there is nothing to distinguish it from a broad settee with bedclothes and a valance. Thus its occupant is in full view from the foot.*

> CHARLES *is not asleep: he is reading in bed, or rather looking at the pictures in Fouquet's Boccaccio with his knees doubled up to make a reading-desk. Beside the bed on his left is a little table with a picture of the Virgin, lighted by candles of painted wax. The walls are hung from ceiling to floor with painted curtains which stir at times in the draughts. At first glance the prevailing yellow and red in these hanging pictures is somewhat flamelike when the folds breathe in the wind.*

> *The door is on* CHARLES'S *left, but in front of him close to the corner farthest from him. A large watchman's rattle, handsomely designed and gaily painted, is in the bed under his hand.*

> CHARLES *turns a leaf. A distant clock strikes the half-hour softly.* CHARLES *shuts the book with a clap; throws it aside; snatches up the rattle; and whirls it energetically, making a deafening clatter.* LADVENU *enters, 25 years older, strange and stark in bearing, and still carrying the cross from Rouen.* CHARLES *evidently does not expect him; for he springs out of bed on the farther side from the door.*

CHARLES. Who are you? Where is my gentleman of the bedchamber? What do you want?

LADVENU (*solemnly*). I bring you glad tidings of great joy. Rejoice, O king; for the taint is removed from your blood, and the stain from your crown. Justice, long delayed, is at last triumphant.

CHARLES. What are you talking about? Who are you?

LADVENU. I am Brother Martin.

CHARLES. And who, saving your reverence, may Brother Martin be?

LADVENU. I held this cross when The Maid perished in the fire. Twenty-five years have passed since then: nearly ten thousand days. And on every one of those days I have prayed to God to justify His daughter on earth as she is justified in heaven.

CHARLES (*reassured, sitting down on the foot of the bed*). Oh, I remember now. I have heard of you. You have a bee in your bonnet about The Maid. Have you been at the inquiry?

LADVENU. I have given my testimony.

CHARLES. Is it over?

LADVENU. It is over.

CHARLES. Satisfactorily?

LADVENU. The ways of God are very strange.

CHARLES. How so?

LADVENU. At the trial which sent a saint to the stake as a heretic and a sorceress, the truth was told; the law was upheld; mercy was shewn beyond all custom; no wrong was done but the final and dreadful wrong of the lying sentence and the pitiless fire. At this inquiry from which I have just come, there was shameless perjury, courtly corruption, calumny of the dead who did their duty according to their lights, cowardly evasion of the issue, testimony made of idle tales that could not impose on a ploughboy. Yet out of this insult to justice, this defamation of the Church, this orgy of lying and foolishness, the truth is set in the noonday sun on the hilltop; the white robe of innocence is cleansed from the smirch of the burning faggots; the holy life is sanctified; the true heart that lived through the flame is consecrated; a great lie is silenced for ever; and a great wrong is set right before all men.

CHARLES. My friend: provided they can no longer say that I was crowned by a witch and a heretic, I shall not fuss about how the trick has been done. Joan would not have fussed about it if it came all right in the end: she was not that sort: I knew her. Is her rehabilitation complete? I made it pretty clear that there was to be no nonsense about it.

LADVENU. It is solemnly declared that her judges were full of corruption, cozenage, fraud, and malice. Four falsehoods.

CHARLES. Never mind the falsehoods: her judges are dead.

LADVENU. The sentence on her is broken, annulled, annihilated, set aside as non-existent, without value or effect.

CHARLES. Good. Nobody can challenge my consecration now, can they?

LADVENU. Not Charlemagne nor King David himself was more sacredly crowned.

CHARLES (rising). Excellent. Think of what that means to me!

LADVENU. I think of what it means to her!

CHARLES. You cannot. None of us ever knew what anything meant to her. She was like nobody else; and she must take care of herself wherever she is; for I cannot take care of her; and neither can you, whatever you may think: you are not big enough. But I will tell you this about her. If you could bring her back to life, they would burn her again within six months, for all their present adoration of her. And you would hold up the cross, too, just the same. So (crossing himself) let her rest; and let you and I mind our own business, and not meddle with hers.

LADVENU. God forbid that I should have no share in her, nor she in me! (He turns and strides out as he came, saying) Henceforth my path will not lie through palaces, nor my conversation be with kings.

CHARLES (following him towards the door, and shouting after him). Much good may it do you, holy man! (He returns to the middle of the chamber, where he halts, and says quizzically to himself) That was a funny chap. How did he get in? Where are my people?

(He goes impatiently to the bed, and swings the rattle. A rush of wind through the open door sets the walls swaying agitatedly. The candles go out. He calls in the darkness) Hallo! Someone come and shut the windows: everything is being blown all over the place. (A flash of summer lightning shews up the lancet window. A figure is seen in silhouette against it.) Who is there? Who is that? Help! Murder! (Thunder. He jumps into bed, and hides under the clothes)

JOAN'S VOICE. Easy, Charlie, easy. What art making all that noise for? No one can hear thee. Thourt asleep. (She is dimly seen in a pallid greenish light by the bedside)

CHARLES (peeping out). Joan! Are you a ghost, Joan?

JOAN. Hardly even that, lad. Can a poor burnt-up lass have a ghost? I am but a dream that thourt dreaming. (The light increases: they become plainly visible as he sits up) Thou looks older, lad.

CHARLES. I am older. Am I really asleep?

JOAN. Fallen asleep over thy silly book.

CHARLES. That's funny.

JOAN. Not so funny as that I am dead, is it?

CHARLES. Are you really dead?

JOAN. As dead as anybody ever is, laddie. I am out of the body.

CHARLES. Just fancy! Did it hurt much?

JOAN. Did what hurt much?

CHARLES. Being burnt.

JOAN. Oh, that! I cannot remember very well. I think it did at first; but then it all got mixed up; and I was not in my right mind until I was free of the body. But do not thou go handling fire and thinking it will not hurt thee. How hast been ever since?

CHARLES. Oh, not so bad. Do you know, I actually lead my army out and win battles? Down into the moat up to my waist in mud and blood. Up the ladders with the stones and hot pitch raining down. Like you.

JOAN. No! Did I make a man of thee after all, Charlie?

CHARLES. I am Charles the Victorious now. I had to be brave because you were. Agnes put a little pluck into me too.

JOAN. Agnes! Who was Agnes?

CHARLES. Agnes Sorel. A woman I fell in love with. I dream of her often. I never dreamed of you before.

JOAN. Is she dead, like me?

CHARLES. Yes. But she was not like you. She was very beautiful.

JOAN (*laughing heartily*). Ha ha! I was no beauty: I was always a rough one: a regular soldier. I might almost as well have been a man. Pity I wasnt: I should not have bothered you all so much then. But my head was in the skies; and the glory of God was upon me; and, man or woman, I should have bothered you as long as your noses were in the mud. Now tell me what has happened since you wise men knew no better than to make a heap of cinders of me?

CHARLES. Your mother and brothers have sued the courts to have your case tried over again. And the courts have declared that your judges were full of corruption and cozenage, fraud and malice.

JOAN. Not they. They were as honest a lot of poor fools as ever burned their betters.

CHARLES. The sentence on you is broken, annihilated, annulled: null, non-existent, without value or effect.

JOAN. I was burned, all the same. Can they unburn me?

CHARLES. If they could, they would think twice before they did it. But they have decreed that a beautiful cross be placed where the stake stood, for your perpetual memory and for your salvation.

JOAN. It is the memory and the salvation that sanctify the cross, not the cross that sanctifies the memory and the salvation. (*She turns away, forgetting him*) I shall outlast that cross. I shall be remembered when men will have forgotten where Rouen stood.

CHARLES. There you go with your self-conceit, the same as ever! I think you might say a word of thanks to me for having had justice done at last.

CAUCHON (*appearing at the window between them*). Liar!

CHARLES. Thank you.

JOAN. Why, if it isnt Peter Cauchon! How are you, Peter? What luck have you had since you burned me?

CAUCHON. None. I arraign the justice of Man. It is not the justice of God.

JOAN. Still dreaming of justice, Peter? See what justice came to with me! But what has happened to thee? Art dead or alive?

CAUCHON. Dead. Dishonored. They pursued me beyond the grave. They excommunicated my dead body: they dug it up and flung it into the common sewer.

JOAN. Your dead body did not feel the spade and the sewer as my live body felt the fire.

CAUCHON. But this thing that they have done against me hurts justice; destroys faith; saps the foundation of the Church. The solid earth sways like the treacherous sea beneath the feet of men and spirits alike when the innocent are slain in the name of the law, and their wrongs are undone by slandering the pure of heart.

JOAN. Well, well, Peter, I hope men will be the better for remembering me; and they would not remember me so well if you had not burned me.

CAUCHON. They will be the worse for remembering me: they will see in me evil triumphing over good, falsehood over truth, cruelty over mercy, hell over heaven. Their courage will rise as they think of you, only to faint as they think of me. Yet God is my witness I was just: I was merciful: I was faithful to my light: I could do no other than I did.

CHARLES (*scrambling out of the sheets and enthroning himself on the side of the bed*). Yes: it is always you good men that do the big mischiefs. Look at me! I am not Charles the Good, nor Charles the Wise, nor Charles the Bold. Joan's worshippers may even call me Charles the Coward because I did not pull her out of the fire. But I have done less harm than any of you. You people with your heads in the sky spend all your time trying to turn the world upside down; but I take the world as it is, and say that top-side up is right-side-up; and I keep my nose pretty close to the ground. And I ask you, what king of France has done better, or been a better fellow in his little way?

JOAN. Art really king of France, Charlie? Be the English gone?

DUNOIS (*coming through the tapestry on* JOAN's *left, the candles relighting themselves at the same moment, and illuminating his armor and surcoat cheerfully*). I have kept my word: the English are gone.

JOAN. Praised be God! now is fair France a province in heaven. Tell me all about the fighting, Jack. Was it thou that led them? Wert thou God's captain to thy death?

DUNOIS. I am not dead. My body is very comfortably asleep in my bed at Chateaudun; but my spirit is called here by yours.

JOAN. And you fought them m y way, Jack: eh? Not the old way, chaffering for ransoms; but The Maid's way: staking life against death, with the heart high and humble and void of malice, and nothing counting under God but France free and French. Was it my way, Jack?

DUNOIS. Faith, it was any way that would win. But the way that won was always your way. I give you best, lassie. I wrote a fine letter to set you right at the new trial. Perhaps I should never have let the priests burn you; but I was busy fighting; and it was The Church's business, not mine. There was no use in both of us being burned, was there?

CAUCHON. Ay! put the blame on the priests. But I, who am beyond praise and blame, tell you that the world is saved neither by its priests nor its soldiers, but by God and His Saints. The Church Militant sent this woman to the fire; but even as she burned, the flames whitened into the radiance of the Church Triumphant.

(*The clock strikes the third quarter. A rough male voice is heard trolling an improvised tune.*)

Rum tum trumpledum,
Bacon fat and rumpledum,
Old Saint mumpledum,
Pull his tail and stumpledum
　　O my Ma–ry Ann!

(*A ruffianly English soldier comes through the curtains and marches between* DUNOIS *and* JOAN.)

DUNOIS. What villainous troubadour taught you that doggrel?

THE SOLDIER. No troubadour. We made it up ourselves as we marched. We were not gentlefolks and troubadours. Music straight out of the heart of the people, as you might say. Rum tum trumpledum, Bacon fat and rumpledum, Old Saint mumpledum, Pull his tail and stumpledum: that dont mean anything, you know; but it keeps you marching. Your servant, ladies and gentlemen. Who asked for a saint?

JOAN. Be you a saint?

THE SOLDIER. Yes, lady, straight from hell.

DUNOIS. A saint, and from hell!

THE SOLDIER. Yes, noble captain: I have a day off. Every year, you know. Thats my allowance for my one good action.

CAUCHON. Wretch! In all the years of your life did you do only one good action?

THE SOLDIER. I never thought about it: it came natural like. But they scored it up for me.

CHARLES. What was it?

THE SOLDIER. Why, the silliest thing you ever heard of. I—

JOAN (*interrupting him by strolling across to the bed, where she sits beside* CHARLES). He tied two sticks together, and gave them to a poor lass that was going to be burned.

THE SOLDIER. Right. Who told you that?

JOAN. Never mind. Would you know her if you saw her again?

THE SOLDIER. Not I. There are so many girls! and they all expect you to remember them as if there was only one in the world. This one must have been a prime sort; for I have a day off every year for her; and, so, until twelve o'clock punctually, I am a saint, at your service, noble lords and lovely ladies.

CHARLES. And after twelve?

THE SOLDIER. After twelve, back to the only place fit for the likes of me.

JOAN (*rising*). Back there! You! that gave the lass the cross!

THE SOLDIER (*excusing his unsoldierly conduct*). Well, she asked for it; and they were going to burn her. She had as good a right to a cross as they had; and they had dozens of them. It was her funeral, not theirs. Where was the harm in it?

JOAN. Man: I am not reproaching you. But I cannot bear to think of you in torment.

THE SOLDIER (*cheerfully*). No great torment, lady. You see I was used to worse.

CHARLES. What! worse than hell?

THE SOLDIER. Fifteen years' service in the French wars. Hell was a treat after that.

(JOAN *throws up her arms, and takes refuge from despair of humanity before the picture of the Virgin.*)

THE SOLDIER (*continuing*). —Suits me somehow. The day off was dull at first, like a wet Sunday. I dont mind it so much now. They tell me I can have as many as I like as soon as I want them.

CHARLES. What is hell like?

THE SOLDIER. You wont find it so bad, sir. Jolly. Like as if you were always drunk without the trouble and expense of drinking. Tip top company too: emperors and popes and kings and all sorts. They chip me about giving that young judy the cross; but I dont care: I stand up to them proper, and tell them that if she hadnt a better right to it

than they, she'd be where they are. That dumbfounds them, that does. All they can do is gnash their teeth, hell fashion; and I just laugh, and go off singing the old chanty: Rum tum trumple—Hullo! Who's that knocking at the door?

(*They listen. A long gentle knocking is heard.*)

CHARLES. Come in.

(*The door opens; and an old priest, white-haired, bent, with a silly but benevolent smile, comes in and trots over to* JOAN.)

THE NEWCOMER. Excuse me, gentle lords and ladies. Do not let me disturb you. Only a poor old harmless English rector. Formerly chaplain to the cardinal: to my lord of Winchester. John de Stogumber, at your service. (*He looks at them inquiringly*) Did you say anything? I am a little deaf, unfortunately. Also a little—well, not always in my right mind, perhaps; but still, it is a small village with a few simple people. I suffice: I suffice: they love me there; and I am able to do a little good. I am well connected, you see; and they indulge me.

JOAN. Poor old John! What brought thee to this state?

DE STOGUMBER. I tell my folks they must be very careful. I say to them, 'If you only saw what you think about you would think quite differently about it. It would give you a great shock. Oh, a great shock.' And they all say 'Yes, parson: we all know you are a kind man, and would not harm a fly.' That is a great comfort to me. For I am not cruel by nature, you know.

THE SOLDIER. Who said you were?

DE STOGUMBER. Well, you see, I did a very cruel thing once because I did not know what cruelty was like. I had not seen it, you know. That is the great thing: you must see it. And then you are redeemed and saved.

CAUCHON. Were not the sufferings of our Lord Christ enough for you?

DE STOGUMBER. No. Oh no: not at all. I had seen them in pictures, and read of them in books, and been greatly moved by them, as I thought. But it was no use: it was not our Lord that redeemed me, but a young woman whom I saw actually burned to death. It was dreadful: oh, most dreadful. But it saved me. I have been a different man ever since, though a little astray in my wits sometimes.

CAUCHON. Must then a Christ perish in torment in every age to save those that have no imagination?

JOAN. Well, if I saved all those he would have been cruel to if he had not been cruel to me, I was not burnt for nothing, was I?

DE STOGUMBER. Oh no; it was not you. My sight is bad: I cannot distinguish your features: but you are not she: oh no: she was burned to a cinder: dead and gone, dead and gone.

THE EXECUTIONER (*stepping from behind the bed curtains on* CHARLES's *right, the bed being between them*). She is more alive than you, old man. Her heart would not burn; and it would not drown. I was a master at my craft: better than the master of Paris, better than the master of Toulouse; but I could not kill The Maid. She is up and alive everywhere.

THE EARL OF WARWICK (*sallying from the bed curtains on the other side, and coming to* JOAN's *left hand*). Madam: my congratulations on your rehabilitation. I feel that I owe you an apology.

JOAN. Oh, please dont mention it.

WARWICK (*pleasantly*). The burning was purely political. There was no personal feeling against you, I assure you.

JOAN. I bear no malice, my lord.

WARWICK. Just so. Very kind of you to meet me in that way: a touch of true breeding. But I must insist on apologizing very amply. The truth is, these political necessities sometimes turn out to be political mistakes; and this one was a veritable howler; for your spirit conquered us, madam, in spite of our

faggots. History will remember me for your sake, though the incidents of the connection were perhaps a little unfortunate.

JOAN. Ay, perhaps just a little, you funny man.

WARWICK. Still, when they make you a saint, you will owe your halo to me, just as this lucky monarch owes his crown to you.

JOAN (*turning from him*). I shall owe nothing to any man: I owe everything to the spirit of God that was within me. But fancy me a saint! What would St Catherine and St Margaret say if the farm girl was cocked up beside them!

(*A clerical-looking gentleman in black frockcoat and trousers, and tall hat, in the fashion of the year 1920, suddenly appears before them in the corner on their right. They all stare at him. Then they burst into uncontrollable laughter.*)

THE GENTLEMAN. Why this mirth, gentlemen?

WARWICK. I congratulate you on having invented a most extraordinary comic dress.

THE GENTLEMAN. I do not understand. You are all in fancy dress: I am properly dressed.

DUNOIS. All dress is fancy dress, is it not, except our natural skins?

THE GENTLEMAN. Pardon me: I am here on serious business, and cannot engage in frivolous discussions. (*He takes out a paper, and assumes a dry official manner*). I am sent to announce to you that Joan of Arc, formerly known as The Maid, having been the subject of an inquiry instituted by the Bishop of Orleans—

JOAN (*interrupting*). Ah! They remember me still in Orleans.

THE GENTLEMAN (*emphatically, to mark his indignation at the interruption*). —by the Bishop of Orleans into the claim of the said Joan of Arc to be canonized as a saint—

JOAN (*again interrupting*). But I never made any such claim.

THE GENTLEMAN (*as before*). —The Church has examined the claim exhaustively in the usual course, and, having admitted the said Joan successively to the ranks of Venerable and Blessed,—

JOAN (*chuckling*). Me venerable!

THE GENTLEMAN. —has finally declared her to have been endowed with heroic virtues and favored with private revelations, and calls the said Venerable and Blessed Joan to the communion of the Church Triumphant as Saint Joan.

JOAN (*rapt*). Saint Joan!

THE GENTLEMAN. On every thirtieth day of May, being the anniversary of the death of the said most blessed daughter of God, there shall in every Catholic church to the end of time be celebrated a special office in commemoration of her; and it shall be lawful to dedicate a special chapel to her, and to place her image on its altar in every such church. And it shall be lawful and laudable for the faithful to kneel and address their prayers through her to the Mercy Seat.

JOAN. Oh no. It is for the saint to kneel. (*She falls on her knees, still rapt*)

THE GENTLEMAN (*putting up his paper, and retiring beside* THE EXECUTIONER). In Basilica Vaticana, the sixteenth day of May, nineteen hundred and twenty.

DUNOIS (*raising* JOAN). Half an hour to burn you, dear Saint, and four centuries to find out the truth about you!

DE STOGUMBER. Sir: I was chaplain to the Cardinal of Winchester once. They always would call him the Cardinal of England. It would be a great comfort to me and to my master to see a fair statue of The Maid in Winchester Cathedral. Will they put one there, do you think?

THE GENTLEMAN. As the building is temporarily in the hands of the Anglican heresy, I cannot answer for that.

(*A vision of the statue in Winchester Cathedral is seen through the window.*)

DE STOGUMBER. Oh look! look! that is Winchester.

JOAN. Is that meant to be me? I was stiffer on my feet.

(*The vision fades.*)

THE GENTLEMAN. I have been requested by the temporal authorities of France to mention that the multiplication of public statues to The Maid threatens to become an obstruction to traffic. I do so as a matter of courtesy to the said authorities, but must point out on behalf of The Church that The Maid's horse is no greater obstruction to traffic than any other horse.

JOAN. Eh! I am glad they have not forgotten my horse.

(*A vision of the statue before Rheims Cathedral appears.*)

JOAN. Is that funny little thing me too?

CHARLES. That is Rheims Cathedral where you had me crowned. It must be you.

JOAN. Who has broken my sword. My sword was never broken. It is the sword of France.

DUNOIS. Never mind. Swords can be mended. Your soul is unbroken; and you are the soul of France.

(*The vision fades.* THE ARCHBISHOP *and* THE INQUISITOR *are now seen on the right and left of* CAUCHON.)

JOAN. My sword shall conquer yet: the sword that never struck a blow. Though men destroyed my body, yet in my soul I have seen God.

CAUCHON (*kneeling to her*). The girls in the field praise thee; for thou hast raised their eyes; and they see that there is nothing between them and heaven.

DUNOIS (*kneeling to her*). The dying soldiers praise thee, because thou art a shield of glory between them and the judgment.

THE ARCHBISHOP (*kneeling to her*). The princes of The Church praise thee, because thou hast redeemed the faith their worldlinesses have dragged through the mire.

WARWICK (*kneeling to her*). The cunning counsellors praise thee, because thou hast cut the knots in which they have tied their own souls.

DE STOGUMBER (*kneeling to her*). The foolish old men on their deathbeds praise thee, because their sins against thee are turned into blessings.

THE INQUISITOR (*kneeling to her*). The judges in the blindness and bondage of the law praise thee, because thou hast vindicated the vision and the freedom of the living soul.

THE SOLDIER (*kneeling to her*). The wicked out of hell praise thee, because thou hast shewn them that the fire that is not quenched is a holy fire.

THE EXECUTIONER (*kneeling to her*). The tormentors and executioners praise thee, because thou hast shewn that their hands are guiltless of the death of the soul.

CHARLES (*kneeling to her*). The unpretending praise thee, because thou hast taken upon thyself the heroic burdens that are too heavy for them.

JOAN. Woe unto me when all men praise me! I bid you remember that I am a saint, and that saints can work miracles. And now tell me: shall I rise from the dead, and come back to you a living woman?

> (*A sudden darkness blots out the walls of the room as they all spring to their feet in consternation. Only the figures and the bed remain visible.*)

JOAN. What! Must I burn again? Are none of you ready to receive me?

CAUCHON. The heretic is always better dead. And mortal eyes cannot distinguish the saint from the heretic. Spare them. (*He goes out as he came*)

DUNOIS. Forgive us, Joan: we are not yet good enough for you. I shall go back to my bed. (*He also goes*)

WARWICK. We sincerely regret our little mistake; but political necessities, though occasionally erroneous, are still imperative; so if you will be good enough to excuse me— (*He steals discreetly away*)

THE ARCHBISHOP. Your return would not make me the man you once thought me. The utmost I can say is that though I dare not bless you, I hope I may one day enter into your blessedness. Meanwhile, however— (*He goes*)

THE INQUISITOR. I who am of the dead, testified that day that you were innocent. But I do not see how The Inquisition could possibly be dispensed with under existing circumstances. Therefore— (*He goes*)

DE STOGUMBER. Oh, do not come back: you must not come back. I must die in peace. Give us peace in our time, O Lord! (*He goes*)

THE GENTLEMAN. The possibility of your resurrection was not contemplated in the recent proceedings for your canonization. I must return to Rome for fresh instructions. (*He bows formally, and withdraws*)

THE EXECUTIONER. As a master in my profession I have to consider its interests. And, after all, my first duty is to my wife and children. I must have time to think over this. (*He goes*)

CHARLES. Poor old Joan! They have all run away from you except this blackguard who has to go back to hell at twelve o'clock. And what can I do but follow Jack Dunois' example, and go back to bed too? (*He does so*)

JOAN (*sadly*). Goodnight, Charlie.

CHARLES (*mumbling in his pillows*). Goo ni. (*He sleeps. The darkness envelops the bed.*)

JOAN (*to the soldier*). And you, my one faithful? What comfort have you for Saint Joan?

THE SOLDIER. Well, what do they all amount to, these kings and captains and bishops and lawyers and such like? They just leave you in the ditch to bleed to death; and the next thing is, you meet them down there, for all the airs they give themselves. What I say is, you have as good a right to your notions as they have to theirs, and perhaps better. (*Settling himself for a lecture on the subject*) You see, it's like this. If— (*the first stroke of midnight is heard softly from a distant bell*). Excuse me: a pressing appointment— (*He goes on tiptoe*).

(The last remaining rays of light gather into a white radiance descending on JOAN. *The hour continues to strike.)*

JOAN. O God that madest this beautiful earth, when will it be ready to receive Thy saints? How long, O Lord, how long?

In the long preface to this play, Bernard Shaw says of Joan that she is "the most notable Warrior Saint in the Christian calendar, and the queerest fish among the eccentric worthies of the Middle Ages. Though a professed and most pious Catholic, and the projector of a Crusade against the Husites, she was in fact one of the first Protestant martyrs. She was also one of the first apostles of Nationalism, and the first French practitioner of Napoleonic realism in warfare as distinguished from the sporting ransom-gambling chivalry of her time." Joan, by insisting that the English should go back to England and leave France for the French, helped to undermine the old feudal system in which a man owed his primary allegiance to his liege lord, and in which nations as such did not properly exist. By heeding the divine instructions that came to her through her "voices" and not relying on the mediation of a teaching church, Joan, according to Shaw, was a kind of Protestant before Protestantism was invented.

Shaw's double thesis about Joan is interesting, and may possibly be true, but the power of his play does not depend on our believing that it is true. Many readers who differ sharply with Shaw's interpretation of Joan find his play admirable, and proceed, at least within limits, to make their own interpretations of the character. It would be unfair to say that this play represents a narrow triumph of Shaw the artist over Shaw the propagandist, for in the play itself (as distinguished from the preface) the artist is consistently dominant. *Saint Joan* shows that Shaw, however wedded to his thesis and however eager to make the argument of his preface convincing, knew his business as a

playwright well enough to let the drama itself take over and qualify his thesis. The result is a play in which the heroine is no mere puppet, but has a life of her own, a life that carries conviction and that, though it may lend some support to Shaw's thesis, is much more than a mere illustration of that thesis.

The plotting of the play is interesting. It is, in some senses, a history play, and, like many history plays—for instance, those of Shakespeare—it takes in a good deal of terrain and spans a considerable period of time: two years—and if we add the epilogue, nearly five centuries. The play does not sprawl, however, and for its own purposes, is admirably plotted.

Since Shaw was concerned, not with the spectacle, but with the meaning of Joan's life as it impinged upon various people, he could dispense with what might seem to be the big inevitable scenes. As he says in his preface, he is not concerned with a theatrical presentation that would provide a river with real water and "a real bridge across it," the scene of a sham fight "for possession of it, with the victorious French led by Joan on a real horse." Nor is he interested in satisfying the taste of people who don't care "in the least why a woman is burned provided she is burned and people can see it done." We do not see Joan at the stake, for example: her ordeal is simply "reported" to us. The principle upon which Shaw selected the scenes by which he would explore the meaning of Joan's life is clear: the incidents depicted show why she succeeded and why she failed.

The first three scenes portray Joan's rise to power. The first shows Joan's conquest of the captain, whom she persuades to send her to the Dauphin; the second, her conquest of the Dauphin, who puts her in command of the army; the third, her conquest of Dunois, the general with whom she must work if she is to capture Orleans from the English. Scene 4, by presenting the forces arrayed against Joan, foreshadows the fate that is in store for her. Scene 5 shows Joan at the height of her power, just after the coronation ceremony, but this scene also reveals Joan's great weakness. Because of her candor and ardor, she cannot help making her friends uncomfortable, and thus, once she has served her purpose, they wish that she would go away. Scene 6 depicts Joan's trial, and here the combination of her avowed enemies and her friends—for as Shaw presents them, even some of the men who accuse her of heresy wish to reclaim her and would save her from herself if they could—ensures her conviction and death.

Joan's fate is, therefore, thoroughly prepared for and can come as no shock to anyone who intelligently views the play. What happens to her in the end is not an accident or a piece of bad luck or a mere caprice of fate. The development and presentation of Joan's character makes her defeat inevitable, for her defeat grows out of her character. In some sense this is what we find true of nearly all great tragedies: a tragic flaw in the hero's character ensures his defeat and death. So it is, as we have seen, with Oedipus and with Antony. But does Joan's defeat come through *hybris*, an excess of pride? In his preface, Shaw does speak of Joan's "overweening presumption, the superbity as they called it," that led her to the stake, but he evidently does not think that Joan was possessed by vicious pride. His phrase "as they called it" indicates his own view of the situation: human nature being what it is, a person like Joan will always prove hard to live with—a burden even to those whom she aids. Shaw's play develops this notion consistently, and his epilogue ends with Joan's cry: "Oh God that madest this beautiful earth, when will it be ready to receive Thy saints? How long, O Lord, how long?"

Joan's outcry provides a moving and climactic restatement of the thesis that runs through the play. But, as we have seen, the situation that Shaw has developed for us is too complex for Joan's cry to be taken as its summation, especially if we are tempted to regard her despairing question as a kind of moral tag.

All this has a bearing on whether or not we can regard *Saint Joan* as a tragedy. Do the traits that make Joan a "difficult" person to live with constitute a sufficient tragic flaw? And can one have an authentic tragedy unless the protagonist does have a tragic flaw? Conversely, can a saint have this kind of tragic flaw and still be a saint? Whether or not Shaw took very seriously Joan's status as a saint in the Church's sense of the term, there seems little doubt that, in his own terms, Shaw regarded Joan as saintlike—that is, as a person endowed with heroic virtues, who suffered because those very virtues were too much for frail mankind.

A revealing aspect of Shaw's treatment of the related problems of Joan's sainthood, her tragic fate, and her success as a force in history, comes out in his treatment of Joan's "miracles." (The topic of miracles recurs throughout the play, and Shaw evidently gave a good deal of attention to it.) In general, Shaw grounds the miraculous and awe-inspiring qualities of Joan firmly within her own character and personality. How did Joan, a raw country girl, persuade Captain Robert de Baudricourt to do the unheard of thing of sending her to the court of the Dauphin? This is the matter of Shaw's first scene, and it serves admirably to mirror Joan's salient traits as a person and to prepare us for the larger conquests she is to make later in the play.

Joan's talk with the captain shows why she impresses people. She is perfectly fearless, and, as the steward comments to his master, this trait tends to give people confidence in her mission and in themselves. Since she is confident that she is acting in God's behalf, she can make her requests positively, without feminine coquetry, without wheedling, and without any tinge of egotistical pride. Finally, she treats people as if they made sense, or at least were trying to make sense, in what they said. Most of us are not used to that, and may find it disconcerting, but it puts us on our mettle, too. Joan has the disarming quality of sheer integrity. The person involved with her at first refuses to believe his ears, or says that the girl is crazy, but he does not experience the normal reaction to another person's self-assertion, for Joan so clearly wants nothing for herself. People do not find such honesty easy to put up with, as Joan is later to find, but the initial effect may be tonic and bracing.

At the end of Scene 1, Shaw does allow Joan a miracle, a very modest miracle, to be sure: the steward rushes in to say that the hens are laying like mad. But the author has been clever enough to have the captain make his decision in favor of Joan *before* this "miracle" occurs, and the incident is actually used primarily for a kind of comic effect. Poor Captain de Baudricourt, who has not had time to recover from Joan's ardent importunity, and who is far from sure that he was wise to give in, is surprised, but perhaps reassured by this minor manifestion of supernatural power. He says to himself with awe, "She did come from God."

Though Joan's first success is grounded on no miracle other than her own radiant integrity, Shaw, by raising the issue of miracles here, has prepared for its appearance in more important contexts. In Scene 2, for example, Joan identifies the true Dauphin in spite of the attempt to deceive her, but no less a person than the archbishop plays down the miraculous aspect of the incident. This rather skeptical archbishop defines a miracle as "an event which creates faith." The archbishop is certain that this clever girl will be able to pass successfully the test of identifying the blood royal. Indeed, it is Joan's candor, integrity, and good sense that persuade the Dauphin to entrust his armies to her. Joan's only "miracle" in this scene— aside from stiffening the spine of the pusillanimous Dauphin—is one that La Trémouille slyly calls a miracle: Joan actually calls a blush to the worldly old archbishop's face by spontaneously falling at his feet and asking, with obviously intense sincerity, for his blessing, since she thinks that he is "filled with the blessedness and glory of God Himself."

This presentation of miracles that are simply events that create "faith" and that will seem miraculous only to a person insufficiently alive to Joan's sharp-eyed but passionate devotion may represent Shaw's attempt to "secularize" Joan by deliberately playing down the supernatural and turning all miracles into mere accidents that Joan exploits through her own human powers. But whatever Shaw's purpose, the effect is to focus attention on Joan's ardent good sense. She is no vulgar magician and wields no power except that of a keen intelligence completely in the service of selfless devotion.

What are we to say, then, when the adverse wind suddenly changes at the end of Scene 3, and, just as Joan comes to lead the attack on Orleans, the boats are at last able to move upstream and make the attack possible? Is this not an authentic miracle? Shaw makes no comment on it. Perhaps it was a miracle, but winds do change, and it was high time that, after blowing for weeks from the west, the wind should at last shift. The wind shift is the kind of good fortune that often attends the brave. It not only allows Joan to enter into her military career at once; it gives confidence to her soldiers that she is indeed heaven sent.

Later references to miraculous happenings are used to develop further the nature of the confidence that she begets in her friends and the fears she arouses in her enemies. In Scene 5 we find that Dunois, though he is very fond of Joan and has great confidence in her, cannot make very much sense of the voices that she tells him she obeys. Dunois tells her, "You make me uneasy when you talk about your voices: I should think you were a bit cracked if I hadn't noticed that you give me very sensible reasons for what you do, though I hear you telling others that you are only obeying Madame Saint Catherine." In Scene 4 Bishop Cauchon, the man who is alarmed at Joan's claims of direct divine guidance, and wants to have her tried as a heretic, scotches the notion that Joan is a sorceress or a witch. He sees Joan as a heretic, and he tells Warwick and his chaplain, "All these things that you call witchcraft are capable of a natural explanation. The woman's miracles would not impose on a rabbit: she does not claim them as miracles herself. What do her victories prove but that she has a better head on her shoulders than your swearing Glass-dells and mad bull Talbots, that the courage of faith, even though it be a false faith, will always outstay the courage of wrath?"

Shaw's conception of Joan's relation to the miraculous is thus central to his conception of the character and to his interpretation of the meaning of Joan's life and of her significance in history. Moreover, this theme of the miraculous provides for the intelligent auditor or reader of the play a kind of central spine by which he can achieve an articulation of the play. But Shaw's treatment of Joan's relation to the miraculous is only one aspect of a very rich and interesting play. Other aspects may be explored by the student as he attempts to answer the following questions.

EXERCISES

1. Why, on the basis of this play, are the voices that Joan hears important to her? It is her insistence on her belief in her voices that eventually takes her to the stake. As we have seen, Dunois believes in Joan, not because, but in spite, of the fact that she claims to hear her voices. Later the Dauphin petulantly remarks that the voices don't come to him even though "I am king, not you." What are these voices in Shaw's opinion?

2. Is Joan guilty of *hybris*, as the archbishop thinks she is? She tells Dunois, for example, "You may shake your head, Jack; and Bluebeard may twirl his billygoat's beard and cock his nose at me; but remember the day your knights and captains refused to follow me to attack the English at Orleans!" If Joan lacked the spirit to make these retorts, she might appear to the reader to be a doleful little plaster saint indeed, not the girl who had saved France. But what is the nature of Joan's pride? The kind that goes with a consciousness of having baked a fine cake, or having kept a clean house? Or is it an ambitious pride? It worries the archbishop and it is deeply disturbing to Cauchon. What does a churchman like Ladvenu say of it at Joan's trial? Twenty-five years later?

3. In reading *Antony and Cleopatra*, *Hedda Gabler*, and *Saint Joan* we have encountered three strongminded and determined women. Do Cleopatra, Hedda, and Joan have anything else in common except their determination? Are they all willful as well?

4. What do you think of Shaw's treatment of the character of Cauchon? Questions of history and biography quite aside, does not the conception of Cauchon as an honest man actually make for the strength of Shaw's thesis about Joan and the church? And Shaw's thesis aside, is not a Cauchon who is honest and dedicated a more interesting character and a worthier dramatic opponent of Joan than a vicious and corrupt man would be?

5. What is Shaw's attitude toward the Dauphin?

Does he make him a more sympathetic or a less sympathetic character as the play develops? What does Joan see in the Dauphin aside from the fact that he is in her opinion her true king? Is the Dauphin a stupid man? Or is he a man who is at once rather cowardly but yet knowing? Sensitive and perceptive and yet realistic—perhaps even cynical?

6. What is the value of Dunois as a character in this play? He is obviously important for the plot since he represents Joan's most direct link with the armies of France. But is he more than simply a blunt soldier? How shrewd is he in his perception of Joan's strengths and weaknesses? Does his relationship to Joan reveal a side of her that we need to know in order fully to appreciate her character?

7. Is the about-face done by Warwick's chaplain, John de Stogumber, made convincing? Passionate men of the sort who become bloodthirsty over ideas are indeed sometimes the people who, when forced to realize their ideas, turn in revulsion from them and from themselves. Is his revulsion sufficiently prepared for? Or do you feel that the character is strained and unconvincing?

8. Historically, some length of time elapsed between Joan's recantation from her so-called heresies and her relapse into them. In this play, Shaw has made the recantation and the relapse occur within a few minutes' time. Why has he done so? Is the compression that he has attempted successful?

9. Consider the ending of the play proper. Scene 6 ends with a conversation between the executioner and Warwick. The executioner is a competent professional who knows his job, but Joan's heart would not burn. He has disposed of that, however, by putting it at the bottom of the river, and he concludes with the statement to Warwick: "You have heard the last of her." Prophetically, Warwick remarks: "The last of her? Hm! I wonder!" Comment on this as an effective way of closing the account of Joan. Even if there were no epilogue, would this still be an effective conclusion for the play?

10. The epilogue is sometimes regarded as an undramatic appendage that allows the author an opportunity to chat over the meaning of the play with his audience. But what kind of curiosity is aroused by this play? Is it a curiosity that requires and justifies the kind of retrospective view the epilogue affords? Moreover, is the epilogue necessarily "undramatic"? Could it not be argued that, since Joan, though burned at Rouen twenty-five years before, is still very much alive and since the last has not been heard of her, least of all by those people whose lives she had touched in her earthly career, the epilogue is really an integral part of the drama?

11. What is the special appropriateness of Joan's appearing to King Charles on this particular night?

12. What of King Charles's attitude toward Joan, now twenty-five years after her death? Is he merely selfish? Cynical? Admiring? Perceptive?

13. When Joan appears to the king on this night, she tells him: "I am but a dream that thourt dreaming." This is perhaps Shaw's conscious rationalization of Joan's appearance after death. But if so, are the other figures who appear in the Epilogue simply more dreams in Charles's mind? What about Peter Cauchon, the English chaplain, or the "clerical-looking gentleman in black frock-coat and trousers . . . in the fashion of the year 1920"? Will Shaw's rationalization cover these? Or does it matter whether we have some kind of realistic justification for the appearance of these various figures?

14. The people who appear in the epilogue are all persons upon whom Joan has made a radiant impression. Most of them had known her in the flesh. Even those who had a part in burning Joan now state their admiration for her. The ghost of Cauchon, kneeling to her, says: "The girls in the field praise thee; for thou hast raised their eyes; and they see that there is nothing between them and heaven." But in one relation to her the ghostly spirits stand precisely where they stood when enclosed in the flesh: none of them would really like her back again. A saint in heaven is one thing, and the devotion they express to her is undoubtedly sincere: but a saint in the next room is something else again. Has Shaw been too insistent on this point? Or does the epilogue reemphasize it effectively?

15. What is Shaw's attitude toward Joan in the epilogue? Does he indeed think of her as only a thought in the mind of the sleeping king, part of his dream? Do you think that he conceives of her as now a blessed spirit? Or does he count her still alive only as a force in history? Or does it matter to us, as we read the epilogue, what answer Shaw would give to these questions?

16. Is *Saint Joan* a tragedy or is it a comedy? Or does it have aspects of both tragedy and comedy? There is a great deal of comedy in the play; there is also the pathos of undeserved suffering; and there is some sense of exultation at heroic virtue. How are these attitudes related, if they are related?

17. Like *Antony and Cleopatra, Saint Joan* deals with historical events that occur over a period of years and scenes of action often quite far distant from one another. Shakespeare's way of handling these problems of space and time differs very much from Shaw's. How successful is each dramatist in this matter? Compare and contrast the solutions of each dramatist.

18. Toward the end of the epilogue, Cauchon says to Joan: "The girls in the field praise thee"; Dunois says: "The dying soldiers praise thee." The *Te Deum* ("We praise thee, O Lord") has lines such as "The glorious company of the Apostles praise thee. / The goodly fellowship of the Prophets praise thee. / The noble army of Martyrs praise thee." How does Show use this reminiscence of the *Te Deum*? Does it add anything to the play at this point? If so, what?

Louis Martz has commented that we "need not be too greatly concerned with Shaw's bland assertions that he is letting us in on the truth about the Middle Ages, telling us in the play all we need to know about Joan. Books and articles have appeared—a whole cloudburst of them—devoted to proving that Shaw's methods of historical research in his play and in his preface are open to serious question." Martz goes on to say that there is, for example, "no historical basis for [Shaw's] highly favorable characterizations of Cauchon and the Inquisitor, upon which the power and point of the trial scene are founded." If the student, by further reading, does decide that Shaw had played rather fast and loose with history, how much difference would that make with regard to the *play*? It would make a great deal of difference, obviously, with regard to a student's notion of the historical Joan and her contemporaries. How far and at what level would it alter his sense of the soundness of the play?

Martz's essay is to be found in *Tragic Themes in Western Literature*, ed. Cleanth Brooks (New Haven: Yale University Press, 1955). It is entitled "The Saint as Tragic Hero: *Saint Joan* and *Murder in the Cathedral*." His discussion will prove useful not only for *Saint Joan,* but for the play that follows, *Murder in the Cathedral,* in which T. S. Eliot also deals with a historical event and with a tragic protagonist who has been canonized by the church.

MURDER IN THE CATHEDRAL

T. S. Eliot (1888–1965)

Characters

A Chorus of Women of Canterbury.	Archbishop Thomas Becket
Three Priests of the Cathedral	Four Tempters
A Messenger	Attendants

PART 1

The Scene is the Archbishop's Hall, on December 2nd, 1170

CHORUS. Here let us stand, close by the cathedral. Here let us wait.
Are we drawn by danger? Is it the knowledge of safety, that draws our feet
Towards the cathedral? What danger can be
For us, the poor, the poor women of Canterbury? what tribulation
With which we are not already familiar? There is no danger   5
For us, and there is no safety in the cathedral. Some presage of an act
Which our eyes are compelled to witness, has forced our feet
Towards the cathedral. We are forced to bear witness.

Since golden October declined into sombre November
And the apples were gathered and stored, and the land became brown sharp points of death in a waste of water and mud,   10
The New Year waits, breathes, waits, whispers in darkness.
While the labourer kicks off a muddy boot and stretches his hand to the fire,
The New Year waits, destiny waits for the coming.
Who has stretched out his hand to the fire and remembered the Saints at All Hallows,
Remembered the martyrs and saints who wait? and who shall   15
Stretch out his hand to the fire, and deny his master? who shall be warm
By the fire, and deny his master?
Seven years and the summer is over
Seven years since the Archbishop left us,

He who was always kind to his people.   20
But it would not be well if he should return.
King rules or barons rule;
We have suffered various oppression,
But mostly we are left to our own devices,
And we are content if we are left alone.   25
We try to keep our households in order;
The merchant, shy and cautious, tries to compile a little fortune,
And the labourer bends to his piece of earth, earth-colour, his own colour,
Preferring to pass unobserved.
Now I fear disturbance of the quiet seasons: 30
Winter shall come bringing death from the sea,
Ruinous spring shall beat at our doors,
Root and shoot shall eat our eyes and our ears,
Disastrous summer burn up the beds of our streams
And the poor shall wait for another decaying October.   35
Why should the summer bring consolation
For autumn fires and winter fogs?
What shall we do in the heat of summer
But wait in barren orchards for another October?
Some malady is coming upon us. We wait, we wait.   40
And the saints and martyrs wait, for those who shall be martyrs and saints.
Destiny waits in the hand of God, shaping the still unshapen:
I have seen these things in a shaft of sunlight.
Destiny waits in the hand of God, not in the hands of statesmen

Who do, some well, some ill, planning and
    guessing,   45
Having their aims which turn in their hands
    in the pattern of time.
Come, happy December, who shall observe
    you, who shall preserve you?
Shall the Son of Man be born again in the
    litter of scorn?
For us, the poor, there is no action,
But only to wait and to witness.   50

(Enter PRIESTS*)*

FIRST PRIEST. Seven years and the summer is
    over.
Seven years since the Archbishop left us.

SECOND PRIEST. What does the Archbishop do,
    and our Sovereign Lord the Pope
With the stubborn King and the French King
In ceaseless intrigue, combinations,   55
In conference, meetings accepted, meetings
    refused,
Meetings unended or endless
At one place or another in France?

THIRD PRIEST. I see nothing quite conclusive
    in the art of temporal government,
But violence, duplicity and frequent malver-
    sation.   60
King rules or barons rule:
The strong man strongly and the weak man
    by caprice.
They have but one law, to seize the power
    and keep it,
And the steadfast can manipulate the greed
    and lust of others,
The feeble is devoured by his own.   65

FIRST PRIEST. Shall these things not end
Until the poor at the gate
Have forgotten their friend, their Father in
    God, have forgotten
That they had a friend?

(Enter MESSENGER*)*

MESSENGER. Servants of God, and watchers of
    the temple,   70
I am here to inform you, without circumlocu-
    tion:
The Archbishop is in England, and is close
    outside the city.
I was sent before in haste

To give you notice of his coming, as much as
    was possible.
That you may prepare to meet him.   75

FIRST PRIEST. What, is the exile ended, is our
    Lord Archbishop
Reunited with the King? what reconciliation
Of two proud men?

THIRD PRIEST. What peace can be found
To grow between the hammer and the anvil?

SECOND PRIEST. Tell us
Are the old disputes at an end, is the wall of
    pride cast down   80
That divided them? Is it peace or war?

FIRST PRIEST. Does he come
In full assurance, or only secure
In the power of Rome, the spiritual rule,
The assurance of right, and the love of the
    people?   85

MESSENGER. You are right to express a certain
    incredulity.
He comes in pride and sorrow, affirming all
    his claims,
Assured, beyond doubt, of the devotion of the
    people,
Who receive him with scenes of frenzied en-
    thusiasm,
Lining the road and throwing down their
    capes,   90
Strewing the way with leaves and late flowers
    of the season.
The streets of the city will be packed to suf-
    focation,
And I think that his horse will be deprived of
    its tail,
A single hair of which becomes a precious
    relic.
He is at one with the Pope, and with the King
    of France,   95
Who indeed would have liked to detain him
    in his kingdom:
But as for our King, that is another matter.

FIRST PRIEST. But again, is it war or peace?

MESSENGER. Peace, but not the kiss of peace.
A patched up affair, if you ask my opinion.
And if you ask me, I think the Lord Arch-
    bishop   100
Is not the man to cherish any illusions,

Or yet to diminish the least of his preten-
sions.
If you ask my opinion, I think that this peace
Is nothing like an end, or like a beginning.
It is common knowledge that when the Arch-
bishop   105
Parted from the King, he said to the King,
My lord, he said, I leave you as a man
Whom in this life I shall not see again.
I have this, I assure you, on the highest au-
thority;
There are several opinions as to what he
meant   110
But no one considers it a happy prognostic.
                                        (*Exit*)

FIRST PRIEST. I fear for the Archbishop, I fear
for the Church,
I know that the pride bred of sudden pros-
perity
Was but confirmed by bitter adversity.
I saw him as Chancellor, flattered by the
King,   115
Liked or feared by courtiers, in their over-
bearing fashion,
Despised and despising, always isolated,
Never one among them, always insecure;
His pride always feeding upon his own vir-
tues,
Pride drawing sustenance from impartiality,
Pride drawing sustenance from generosity, 121
Loathing power given by temporal devolu-
tion,
Wishing subjection to God alone.
Had the King been greater, or had he been
weaker
Things had perhaps been different for
Thomas.   125

SECOND PRIEST. Yet our lord is returned. Our
lord has come back to his own again.
We have had enough of waiting, from December to dismal December.
The Archbishop shall be at our head, dispel-
ling dismay and doubt.
He will tell us what we are to do, he will give
us our orders, instruct us.
Our Lord is at one with the Pope, and also
the King of France.   130
We can lean on a rock, we can feel a firm
foothold
Against the perpetual wash of tides of balance
of forces of barons and landholders.

The rock of God is beneath our feet. Let us
meet the Archbishop with cordial thanksgiving:
Our lord, our Archbishop returns. And when
the Archbishop returns
Our doubts are dispelled. Let us therefore
rejoice,   135
I say rejoice, and show a glad face for his
welcome.
I am the Archbishop's man. Let us give the
Archbishop welcome!

THIRD PRIEST. For good or ill, let the wheel
turn.
The wheel has been still, these seven years,
and no good.
For ill or good, let the wheel turn.   140
For who knows the end of good or evil?
Until the grinders cease
And the door shall be shut in the street,
And all the daughters of music shall be
brought low.

CHORUS. Here is no continuing city, here is
no abiding stay.   145
Ill the wind, ill the time, uncertain the profit,
certain the danger.
O late late late, late is the time, late too late,
and rotten the year;
Evil the wind, and bitter the sea, and grey the
sky, grey grey grey.
O Thomas, return, Archbishop; return, return to France.
Return. Quickly. Quietly. Leave us to perish
in quiet.   150
You come with applause, you come with rejoicing, but you come bringing death into
Canterbury:
A doom on the house, a doom on yourself, a
doom on the world.

We do not wish anything to happen.
Seven years we have lived quietly,
Succeeded in avoiding notice,   155
Living and partly living.
There have been oppression and luxury,
There have been poverty and licence,
There has been minor injustice.
Yet we have gone on living,   160
Living and partly living.
Sometimes the corn has failed us,
Sometimes the harvest is good,
One year is a year of rain,

Another a year of dryness,   165
One year the apples are abundant,
Another year the plums are lacking.
Yet we have gone on living,
Living and partly living.
We have kept the feasts, heard the masses,   170
We have brewed beer and cyder,
Gathered wood against the winter,
Talked at the corner of the fire,
Talked at the corners of streets,
Talked not always in whispers,   175
Living and partly living.
We have seen births, deaths and marriages,
We have had various scandals,
We have been afflicted with taxes,
We have had laughter and gossip,   180
Several girls have disappeared
Unaccountably, and some not able to.
We have all had our private terrors,
Our particular shadows, our secret fears.

But now a great fear is upon us, a fear not of
    one but of many,   185
A fear like birth and death, when we see birth
    and death alone
In a void apart. We
Are afraid in a fear which we cannot know,
    which we cannot face, which none under-
    stands,
And our hearts are torn from us, our brains
    unskinned like the layers of an onion, our
    selves are lost lost
In a final fear which none understands. O
    Thomas Archbishop,   190
O Thomas our Lord, leave us and leave us be,
    in our humble and tarnished frame of
    existence, leave us; do not ask us
To stand to the doom on the house, the doom
    on the Archbishop, the doom on the world.
Archbishop, secure and assured of your fate,
    unaffrayed among the shades, do you re-
    alise what you ask, do you realise what it
    means
To the small folk drawn into the pattern of
    fate, the small folk who live among small
    things,
The strain on the brain of the small folk who
    stand to the doom of the house, the doom
    of their lord, the doom of the world?   195
O Thomas, Archbishop, leave us, leave us,
    leave sullen Dover, and set sail for France.
    Thomas our Archbishop still our Arch-

bishop even in France. Thomas Archbishop, set the white sail between the grey
sky and the bitter sea, leave us, leave us for
France.

SECOND PRIEST. What a way to talk at such a
    juncture!
You are foolish, immodest and babbling
    women.
Do you not know that the good Archbishop
Is likely to arrive at any moment?   200
The crowds in the streets will be cheering
    and cheering,
You go on croaking like frogs in the treetops:
But frogs at least can be cooked and eaten.
Whatever you are afraid of, in your craven
    apprehension,
Let me ask you at the least to put on pleasant
    faces,   205
And give a hearty welcome to our good Arch-
    bishop.

(*Enter* THOMAS)

THOMAS. Peace. And let them be, in their
    exaltation.
They speak better than they know, and
    beyond your understanding.
They know and do not know, what it is to act
    or suffer.
They know and do not know, that acting is
    suffering   210
And suffering is action. Neither does the
    agent suffer
Nor the patient act. But both are fixed
In an eternal action, an eternal patience
To which all must consent that it may be
    willed
And which all must suffer that they may will
    it,   215
That the pattern may subsist, for the pattern
    is the action
And the suffering, that the wheel may turn
    and still
Be forever still.

SECOND PRIEST. O my Lord, forgive me, I did
    not see you coming,
Engrossed by the chatter of these foolish
    women.   220
Forgive us, my Lord, you would have had a
    better welcome
If we had been sooner prepared for the event.

But your Lordship knows that seven years of
waiting,
Seven years of prayer, seven years of emptiness,
Have better prepared our hearts for your
coming,   225
Than seven days could make ready Canter-
bury.
However, I will have fires laid in all your
rooms
To take the chill off our English December,
Your Lordship now being used to a better
climate.
Your Lordship will find your rooms in order
as you left them.   230

THOMAS. And will try to leave them in order
as I find them.
I am more than grateful for all your kind
attentions.
These are small matters. Little rest in Can-
terbury
With eager enemies restless about us.
Rebellious bishops, York, London, Salisbury,
Would have intercepted our letters,   236
Filled the coast with spies and sent to meet
me
Some who hold me in bitterest hate.
By God's grace aware of their prevision
I sent my letters on another day,   240
Had fair crossing, found at Sandwich
Broc, Warenne, and the Sheriff of Kent,
Those who had sworn to have my head from
me.
Only John, the Dean of Salisbury,
Fearing for the King's name, warning against
treason,   245
Made them hold their hands. So for the time
We are unmolested.

FIRST PRIEST.   But do they follow after?

THOMAS. For a little time the hungry hawk
Will only soar and hover, circling lower,
Waiting excuse, pretence, opportunity.   250
End will be simple, sudden, God-given.
Meanwhile the substance of our first act
Will be shadows, and the strife with shadows.
Heavier the interval than the consummation.
All things prepare the event. Watch.   255

(Enter FIRST TEMPTER)

FIRST TEMPTER. You see, my Lord, I do not
wait upon ceremony:

Here I have come, forgetting all acrimony,
Hoping that your present gravity
Will find excuse for my humble levity
Remembering all the good time past.   260
Your Lordship won't despise an old friend
out of favour?
Old Tom, gay Tom, Becket of London,
Your Lordship won't forget that evening on
the river
When the King, and you and I were all
friends together?
Friendship should be more than biting Time
can sever.   265
What, my Lord, now that you recover
Favour with the King, shall we say that sum-
mer's over.
Or that the good time cannot last?
Fluting in the meadows, viols in the hall,
Laughter and apple blossom floating on the
water,   270
Singing at nightfall, whispering in chambers,
Fires devouring the winter season,
Eating up the darkness, with wit and wine
and wisdom!
Now that the King and you are in amity,
Clergy and laity may return to gaiety,   275
Mirth and sportfulness need not walk warily.

THOMAS. You talk of seasons that are past. I
remember
Not worth forgetting.

TEMPTER.   And of the new season.
Spring has come in winter. Snow in the
branches
Shall float as sweet as blossoms. Ice along the
ditches   280
Mirror the sunlight. Love in the orchard
Send the sap shooting. Mirth matches melan-
choly.

THOMAS. We do not know very much of the
future
Except that from generation to generation
The same things happen again and again.   285
Men learn little from others' experience.
But in the life of one man, never
The same time returns. Sever
The cord, shed the scale. Only
The fool, fixed in his folly, may think   290
He can turn the wheel on which he turns.

TEMPTER. My Lord, a nod is as good as a
wink.

A man will often love what he spurns.
For the good times past, that are come again
I am your man.

THOMAS.   Not in this train.   295
Look to your behavior. You were safer
Think of penitence and follow your master.

TEMPTER. Not at this gait!
If you go so fast, others may go faster.
Your Lordship is too proud!   300
The safest beast is not the one that roars most
   loud.
This was not the way of the King our master!
You were not used to be so hard upon sinners
When they were your friends. Be easy, man!
The easy man lives to eat the best dinners. 305
Take a friend's advice. Leave well alone,
Or your goose may be cooked and eaten to
   the bone.

THOMAS. You come twenty years too late.

TEMPTER. Then I leave you to your fate.
I leave you to the pleasures of your higher
   vices,   310
Which will have to be paid for at higher
   prices.
Farewell, my Lord, I do not wait upon cer-
   emony,
I leave as I came, forgetting all acrimony,
Hoping that your present gravity
Will find excuse for my humble levity.   315
If you will remember me, my Lord, at your
   prayers,
I'll remember you at kissing-time below the
   stairs.

THOMAS. Leave-well-alone, the springtime
   fancy,
So one thought goes whistling down the wind.
The impossible is still temptation.   320
The impossible, the undesirable,
Voices under sleep, waking a dead world,
So that the mind may not be whole in the
   present.

(Enter SECOND TEMPTER)

SECOND TEMPTER. Your Lordship has forgot-
   ten me, perhaps. I will remind you.
We met at Clarendon, at Northhampton, 325
And last at Montmirail, in Maine. Now that
   I have recalled them,
Let us but set these not too pleasant memories

In balance against other, earlier
And weightier ones: those of the Chancellorship.
See how the late ones rise! You, master of
   policy   330
Whom all acknowledged, should guide the
   state again.

THOMAS. Your meaning?

TEMPTER. The Chancellorship that you re-
   signed
When you were made Archbishop—that was
   a mistake
On your part—still may be regained. Think,
   my Lord,
Power obtained grows to glory,   335
Life lasting, a permanent possession,
A temped tomb, monument of marble.
Rule over men reckon no madness.

THOMAS. To the man of God what gladness?

TEMPTER.   Sadness
Only to those giving love to God alone.   340
Shall he who held the solid substance
Wander waking with deceitful shadows?
Power is present. Holiness hereafter.

THOMAS. Who then?

TEMPTER. The Chancellor. King and Chan-
   cellor.
King commands. Chancellor richly rules. 345
This is a sentence not taught in the schools.
To set down the great, protect the poor,
Beneath the throne of God can man do more?
Disarm the ruffian, strengthen the laws,
Rule for the good of the better cause,   350
Dispensing justice make all even,
Is thrive on earth, and perhaps in heaven.

THOMAS. What means?

TEMPTER.   Real power
Is purchased at price of a certain submis-
   sion.   355
Your spiritual power is earthly perdition.
Power is present, for him who will wield.

THOMAS. Who shall have it?

TEMPTER.   He who will come.

THOMAS. What shall be the month?   360

TEMPTER.   The last from the first.

THOMAS. What shall we give for it?

TEMPTER.   Pretence of priestly power.

THOMAS. Why should we give it?

TEMPTER.   For the power and the glory. 365

THOMAS. No!

TEMPTER.   Yes! Or bravery will be broken,
Cabined in Canterbury, realmless ruler,
Self-bound servant of a powerless Pope,
The old stag, circled with hounds.

THOMAS. No!

TEMPTER.   Yes, Men must manoeuvre.
    Monarchs, also,   370
Waging war abroad, need fast friends at
    home.
Private policy is public profit;
Dignity still shall be dressed with decorum.

THOMAS. You forget the bishops
Whom I have laid under excommunication.

TEMPTER. Hungry hatred   376
Will not strive against intelligent self-interest.

THOMAS. You forget the barons. Who will
    not forget
Constant curbing of petty privilege.

TEMPTER. Against the barons   380
Is King's cause, churl's cause, Chancellor's
    cause.

THOMAS. No! shall I, who keep the keys
Of heaven and hell, supreme alone in En-
    gland,
Who bind and loose, with power from the
    Pope,
Descend to desire a punier power?   385
Delegate to deal the door of damnation,
To condemn kings, not serve among their
    servants,
Is my open office. No! Go.

TEMPTER. Then I leave you to your fate.
Your sin soars sunward, covering kings' fal-
    cons.   390

THOMAS. Temporal power, to build a good
    world,
To keep order, as the world knows order.
Those who put their faith in worldly order
Not controlled by the order of God,

In confident ignorance, but arrest disorder, 395
Make it fast, breed fatal disease,
Degrade what they exalt. Power with the
    King—
I *was* the King, his arm, his better reason.
But what was once exaltation
Would now be only mean descent.   400

(*Enter* THIRD TEMPTER)

THIRD TEMPTER. I am an unexpected visitor.

THOMAS.   I expected you.

TEMPTER. But not in this guise, or for my
    present purpose.

THOMAS. No purpose brings surprise.

TEMPTER.   Well, my Lord,
I am no trifler, and no politician.   405
To idle or intrigue at court
I have no skill. I am no courtier.
I know a horse, a dog, a wench;
I know how to hold my estates in order,
A country-keeping lord who minds his own
    business.
It is we country lords who know the coun-
    try   410
And we who know what the country needs.
It is our country. We care for the country.
We are the backbone of the nation.
We, not the plotting parasites
About the King. Excuse my bluntness: 415
I am a rough straightforward Englishman.

THOMAS. Proceed straight forward.

TEMPTER.   Purpose is plain.
Endurance of friendship does not depend
Upon ourselves, but upon circumstance.
But circumstance is not undetermined.   420
Unreal friendship may turn to real
But real friendship, once ended, cannot be
    mended.
Sooner shall enmity turn to alliance.
The enmity that never knew friendship
Can sooner know accord.

THOMAS.   For a countryman 425
You wrap your meaning in as dark generality
As any courtier.

TEMPTER.   This is the simple fact!
You have no hope of reconciliation
With Henry the King. You look only
To blind assertion in isolation.   430
That is a mistake.

THOMAS.   O Henry, O my King!

TEMPTER.   Other friends
May be found in the present situation.
King in England is not all-powerful;
King is in France, squabbling in Anjou;
Round him waiting hungry sons.   435
We are for England. We are in England.
You and I, my Lord, are Normans.
England is a land for Norman
Sovereignty. Let the Angevin
Destroy himself, fighting in Anjou.   440
He does not understand us, the English
  barons.
We are the people.

THOMAS. To what does this lead?

TEMPTER.   To a happy coalition
Of intelligent interests.

THOMAS.   But what have you—
If you do speak for barons—

TEMPTER.   For a powerful party   445
Which has turned its eyes in your direction—
To gain from you, your Lordship asks.
For us, Church favour would be an advan-
  tage,
Blessing of Pope powerful protection
In the fight for liberty. You, my Lord,   450
In being with us, would fight a good stroke
At once, for England and for Rome,
Ending the tyrannous jurisdiction
Of king's court over bishop's court,
Of king's court over baron's court.   455

THOMAS. Which I helped to found.

TEMPTER.   Which you helped to found.
But time past is time forgotten.
We expect the rise of a new constellation.

THOMAS. And if the Archbishop cannot trust
  the King,   460
How can he trust those who work for King's
  undoing?

TEMPTER. Kings will allow no power but
  their own;
Church and people have good cause against
  the throne.

THOMAS. If the Archbishop cannot trust the
  Throne,
He has good cause to trust none but God
  alone.   465

I ruled once as Chancellor
And men like you were glad to wait at my
  door.
Not only in the court, but in the field
And in the tilt-yard I made many yield.
Shall I who ruled like an eagle over doves   470
Now take the shape of a wolf among wolves?
Pursue your treacheries as you have done be-
  fore:
No one shall say that I betrayed a king.

TEMPTER. Then, my Lord, I shall not wait at
  your door;
And I well hope, before another spring   475
The King will show his regard for your
  loyalty.

THOMAS. To make, then break, this thought
  has come before,
The desperate exercise of failing power.
Samson in Gaza did no more.
But if I break, I must break myself alone.   480

(Enter FOURTH TEMPTER*)*

FOURTH TEMPTER. Well done, Thomas, your
  will is hard to bend.
And with me beside you, you shall not lack a
  friend.

THOMAS. Who are you? I expected
Three visitors, not four.

TEMPTER. Do not be surprised to receive one
  more.   485
Had I been expected, I had been here before.
I always precede expectation.

THOMAS.   Who are you?

TEMPTER. As you do not know me, I do not
  need a name,
And, as you know me, that is why I come.   490
You know me, but have never seen my face.
To meet before was never time or place.

THOMAS. Say what you come to say.

TEMPTER.   It shall be said at last.
Hooks have been baited with morsels of the
  past.   495
Wantonness is weakness. As for the King,
His hardened hatred shall have no end.
You know truly, the King will never trust
Twice, the man who has been his friend.
Borrow use cautiously, employ   500
Your services as long as you have to lend.

You should wait for trap to snap
Having served your turn, broken and
   crushed.
As for barons, envy of lesser men
Is still more stubborn than king's anger.   505
Kings have public policy, barons private
   profit,
Jealousy raging possession of the fiend.
Barons are employable against each other;
Greater enemies must kings destroy.

THOMAS. What is your counsel?

TEMPTER.   Fare forward to the end. 510
All other ways are closed to you
Except the way already chosen.
But what is pleasure, kingly rule,
Or rule of men beneath a king,
With craft in corners, stealthy stratagem, 515
To general grasp of spiritual power?
Man oppressed by sin, since Adam fell—
You hold the keys of heaven and hell.
Power to bind and loose: bind, Thomas,
   bind,
King and bishop under your heel.   520
King, emperor, bishop, baron, king:
Uncertain mastery of melting armies,
War, plague, and revolution,
New conspiracies, broken pacts;
To be master or servant within an hour, 525
This is the course of temporal power.
The Old King shall know it, when at last
   breath,
No sons, no empire, he bites broken teeth.
You hold the skein: wind, Thomas, wind
The thread of eternal life and death.   530
You hold this power, hold it.

THOMAS.   Supreme, in this land?

TEMPTER. Supreme, but for one.

THOMAS.   That I do not understand.

TEMPTER. It is not for me to tell you how this
   may be so;
I am only here, Thomas, to tell you what you
   know.

THOMAS. How long shall this be?   535

TEMPTER. Save what you know already, ask
   nothing of me.
But think, Thomas, think of glory after
   death.

When king is dead, there's another king.
And one more king is another reign.
King is forgotten, when another shall come:
Saint and Martyr rule from the tomb.   541
Think, Thomas, think of enemies dismayed,
Creeping in penance, frightened of a shade;
Think of pilgrims, standing in line
Before the glittering jewelled shrine,   545
From generation to generation
Bending the knee in supplication
Think of the miracles, by God's grace,
And think of your enemies, in another place.

THOMAS. I have thought of these things.

TEMPTER.   That is why I tell you. 550
Your thoughts have more power than kings
   to compel you.
You have also thought, sometimes at your
   prayers,
Sometimes hesitating at the angles of stairs,
And between sleep and waking, early in the
   morning,
When the bird cries, have thought of further
   scorning.   555
That nothing lasts, but the wheel turns,
The nest is rifled, and the bird mourns;
That the shrine shall be pillaged, and the
   gold spent,
The jewels gone for light ladies' ornament,
The sanctuary broken, and its stores   560
Swept into the laps of parasites and whores.
When miracles cease, and the faithful desert
   you,
And men shall only do their best to forget
   you.
And later is worse, when men will not hate
   you
Enough to defame or to execrate you,   565
But pondering the qualities that you lacked
Will only try to find the historical fact.
When men shall declare that there was no
   mystery
About this man who played a certain part in
   history.

THOMAS. But what is there to do? what is left
   to be done?   570
Is there no enduring crown to be won?

TEMPTER. Yes, Thomas, yes; you have
   thought of that too.
What can compare with glory of Saints
Dwelling forever in presence of God?

What earthly glory, of king or emperor,   575
What earthly pride, that is not poverty
Compared with richness of heavenly grandeur?
Seek the way of martyrdom, make yourself the lowest
On earth, to be high in heaven.
And see far off below you, where the gulf is fixed,   580
Your persecutors, in timeless torment,
Parched passion, beyond expiation.

THOMAS.   No!
Who are you, tempting with my own desires?
Others have come, temporal tempters,
With pleasure and power at palpable price. 585
What do you offer? what do you ask?

TEMPTER. I offer what you desire. I ask
What you have to give. Is it too much
For such a vision of eternal grandeur?

THOMAS. Others offered real goods, worthless   590
But real. You only offer
Dreams to damnation.

TEMPTER.   You have often dreamt them.

THOMAS. Is there no way, in my soul's sickness,
Does not lead to damnation in pride?
I well know that these temptations   595
Mean present vanity and future torment.
Can sinful pride be driven out
Only by more sinful? Can I neither act nor suffer
Without perdition?

TEMPTER. You know and do not know, what it is to act or suffer.   600
You know and do not know, that action is suffering,
And suffering action. Neither does the agent suffer
Nor the patient act. But both are fixed
In an eternal action, an eternal patience
To which all must consent that it may be willed   605
And which all must suffer that they may will it,
That the pattern may subsist, that the wheel may turn and still
Be forever still.

CHORUS. There is no rest in the house. There is no rest in the street.
I hear restless movement of feet. And the air is heavy and thick.   610
Thick and heavy the sky. And the earth presses up against our feet.
What is the sickly smell, the vapour? the dark green light from a cloud on a withered tree? The earth is heaving to parturition of issue of hell. What is the sticky dew that forms on the back of my hand?

THE FOUR TEMPTERS. Man's life is a cheat and a disappointment;
All things are unreal,
Unreal or disappointing: 615
The Catherine wheel, the pantomime cat,
The prizes given at the children's party,
The prize awarded for the English Essay,
The scholar's degree, the statesman's decoration.
All things become less real, man passes   620
From unreality to unreality.
This man is obstinate, blind, intent
On self-destruction,
Passing from deception to deception,
From grandeur to grandeur to final illusion,   625
Lost in the wonder of his own greatness,
The enemy of society, enemy of himself.

THE THREE PRIESTS. O Thomas my Lord do not fight the intractable tide,
Do not sail the irresistible wind; in the storm,
Should we not wait for the sea to subside, in the night   630
Abide the coming of day, when the traveller may find his way,
The sailor lay course by the sun?

CHORUS, PRIESTS *and* TEMPTERS (*alternately*).
C. Is it the owl that calls, or a signal between the trees?
P. Is the window-bar made fast, is the door under lock and bolt?
T. Is it rain that taps at the window, is it wind that pokes at the door?   635
C. Does the torch flame in the hall, the candle in the room?
P. Does the watchman walk by the wall?
T. Does the mastiff prowl by the gate?
C. Death has a hundred hands and walks by a thousand ways.

DRAMA

P. He may come in the sight of all, he may pass unseen unheard. 640

T. Come whispering through the ear, or a sudden shock on the skull.

C. A man may walk with a lamp at night, and yet be drowned in a ditch.

P. A man may climb the stair in the day, and slip on a broken step.

T. A man may sit at meat, and feel the cold in his groin.

CHORUS. We have not been happy, my Lord, we have not been too happy. 645

We are not ignorant women, we know what we must expect and not expect.

We know of oppression and torture,

We know of extortion and violence,

Destitution, disease,

The old without fire in winter, 650

The child without milk in summer,

Our labour taken away from us,

Our sins made heavier upon us.

We have seen the young man mutilated,

The torn girl trembling by the mill-stream. 655

And meanwhile we have gone on living,

Living and partly living,

Picking together the pieces,

Gathering faggots at nightfall,

Building a partial shelter, 660

For sleeping, and eating and drinking and laughter.

God gave us always some reason, some hope; but now a new terror has soiled us, which none can avert, none can avoid, flowing under our feet and over the sky;

Under doors and down chimneys, flowing in at the ear and the mouth and the eye.

God is leaving us, God is leaving us, more pang, more pain, than birth or death.

Sweet and cloying through the dark air 665

Falls the stifling scent of despair;

The forms take shape in the dark air:

Puss-purr of leopard, footfall of padding bear,

Palm-pat of nodding ape, square hyaena waiting

For laughter, laughter, laughter. The Lords of Hell are here. 670

They curl round you, lie at your feet, swing and wing through the dark air.

O Thomas Archbishop, save us, save us, save yourself that we may be saved;

Destroy yourself and we are destroyed.

THOMAS. Now is my way clear, now is the meaning plain:

Temptation shall not come in this kind again. 675

The last temptation is the greatest treason:

To do the right deed for the wrong reason.

The natural vigour in the venial sin

Is the way in which our lives begin.

Thirty years ago, I searched all the ways 680

That lead to pleasure, advancement and praise.

Delight in sense, in learning and in thought,

Music and philosophy, curiosity,

The purple bullfinch in the lilac tree,

The tiltyard skill, the strategy of chess, 685

Love in the garden, singing to the instrument,

Were all things equally desirable.

Ambition comes when early force is spent

And when we find no longer all things possible.

Ambition comes behind and unobservable. 690

Sin grows with doing good. When I imposed the King's law

In England, and waged war with him against Toulouse,

I beat the barons at their own game. I

Could then despise the men who thought me most contemptible,

The raw nobility, whose manners matched their fingernails. 695

While I ate out of the King's dish

To become servant of God was never my wish.

Servant of God has chance of greater sin

And sorrow, than the man who serves a king.

For those who serve the greater cause may make the cause serve them, 700

Still doing right: and striving with political men

May make that cause political, not by what they do

But by what they are. I know

What yet remains to show you of my history

Will seem to most of you at best futility, 705

Senseless self-slaughter of a lunatic,

Arrogant passion of a fanatic.

I know that history at all times draws

The strangest consequence from remotest cause.

But for every evil, every sacrilege, 710

Crime, wrong, oppression and the axe's edge,

Indifference, exploitation, you, and you,

And you, must all be punished. So must you.
I shall no longer act or suffer, to the sword's
    end.

Now my good Angel, whom God appoints [715]
To be my guardian, hover over the swords'
    points.

INTERLUDE

THE ARCHBISHOP *preaches in the Cathedral on Christmas Morning*, 1170

    'Glory to God in the highest, and on earth peace, to men of good will.' *The fourteenth verse of the second chapter of the Gospel according to Saint Luke.* In the Name of the Father, and of the Son, and of the Holy Ghost. Amen.

Dear children of God, my sermon this Christmas morning will be a very short one. I wish only that you should meditate in your hearts the deep meaning and mystery of our masses of Christmas Day. For whenever Mass is said, we re-enact the Passion and Death of Our Lord; and on this Christmas Day we do this in celebration of His Birth. So that at the same moment we rejoice in His coming for the salvation of men, and offer again to God His Body and Blood in sacrifice, oblation and satisfaction for the sins of the whole world. It was in this same night that has just passed, that a multitude of the heavenly host appeared before the shepherds at Bethlehem, saying, 'Glory to God in the highest, and on earth peace to men of good will'; at this same time of all the year that we celebrate at once the Birth of Our Lord and His Passion and Death upon the Cross. Beloved, as the World sees, this is to behave in a strange fashion. For who in the World will both mourn and rejoice at once and for the same reason? For either joy will be overborne by mourning, or mourning will be cast out by joy; so it is only in these our Christian mysteries that we can rejoice and mourn at once for the same reason. But think for a while on the meaning of this word 'peace.' Does it seem strange to you that the angels should have announced Peace, when ceaselessly the world has been stricken with War and the fear of War? Does it seem to you that the angelic voices were mistaken, and that the promise was a disappointment and a cheat?

Reflect now, how Our Lord Himself spoke of Peace. He said to His disciples 'My peace I leave with you, my peace I give unto you.' Did He mean peace as we think of it: the kingdom of England at peace with its neighbours, the barons at peace with the King, the householder counting over his peaceful gains, the swept hearth, his best wine for a friend at the table, his wife singing to the children? Those men His disciples knew no such things: they went forth to journey afar, to suffer by land and sea, to know torture, imprisonment, disappointment, to suffer death by martyrdom. What then did He mean? If you ask that, remember then that He said also, 'Not as the world gives, give I unto you.' So then, He gave to His disciples peace, but not peace as the world gives.

Consider also one thing of which you have probably never thought. Not only do we at the feast of Christmas celebrate at once Our Lord's Birth and His Death: but on the next day we celebrate the martyrdom of His first martyr, the blessed Stephen. Is it an accident, do you think, that the day of the first martyr follows immediately the day of the Birth of Christ? By no means. Just as we rejoice and mourn at once, in the Birth and in the Passion of Our Lord; so also, in a smaller figure, we both rejoice and mourn in the death of martyrs. We mourn, for the sins of the world that has martyred them; we rejoice, that another soul is numbered among the Saints in Heaven, for the glory of God and for the salvation of men.

Beloved, we do not think of a martyr simply as a good Christian who has been killed because he is a Christian: for that would be solely to mourn. We do not think of him simply as a good Christian who has been elevated to the company of the Saints: for that would be simply to rejoice: and neither our mourning nor our rejoicing is as the world's is. A Christian martyrdom is never an accident, for Saints are not made by accident. Still less is a Christian martyrdom the effect of a man's will to become a Saint, as a man by willing and contriving may become a ruler of men. A martyrdom is always the design of God, for His love of men, to warn them and to lead them, to bring them back to His ways. It is never the design of man; for the true martyr is he who has become the instrument of God, who has lost his will in the will of God, and who no longer desires anything for himself, not even the glory of being a martyr. So thus as on earth the Church mourns and rejoices at once, in a fashion that the world cannot understand; so in Heaven the Saints are most high, having made themselves most low, seeing themselves not as we see them, but in the light of the Godhead from which they draw their being.

I have spoken to you today, dear children of God, of the martyrs of the past, asking you to remember especially our martyr of Canterbury, the blessed Archbishop Elphege; because it is fitting, on Christ's birth day, to remember what is that Peace which He brought; and because, dear children, I do not think I shall ever preach to you again; and because it is possible that in a short time you may have yet another martyr, and that one perhaps not the last. I would have you keep in your hearts these words that I say, and think of them at another time. In the Name of the Father, and of the Son, and of the Holy Ghost. Amen.

Characters

THREE PRIESTS
FOUR KNIGHTS
ARCHBISHOP THOMAS BECKET

CHORUS OF WOMEN OF CANTERBURY
ATTENDANTS.

PART 2

The first scene is in the Archbishop's Hall, the second scene is in the Cathedral, on December 29th, 1170

CHORUS. Does the bird sing in the South?
Only the sea-bird cries, driven inland by the storm.
What sign of the spring of the year?
Only the death of the old: not a stir, not a shoot, not a breath.
Do the days begin to lengthen?   5
Longer and darker the day, shorter and colder the night.
Still and stifling the air: but a wind is stored up in the East.
The starved crow sits in the field, attentive; and in the wood
The owl rehearses the hollow note of death.
What signs of a bitter spring?   10
The wind stored up in the East.
What, at the time of the birth of Our Lord, at Christmastide,
Is there not peace upon earth, goodwill among men?
The peace of this world is always uncertain, unless men keep the peace of God.
And war among men defiles this world, but death in the Lord renews it,   15
And the world must be cleaned in the winter, or we shall have only

A sour spring, a parched summer, an empty harvest.
Between Christmas and Easter what work shall be done?
The ploughman shall go out in March and turn the same earth
He has turned before, the bird shall sing the same song.   20
When the leaf is out on the tree, when the elder and may
Burst over the stream, and the air is clear and high,
And voices trill at windows, and children tumble in front of the door,
What work shall have been done, what wrong
Shall the bird's song cover, the green tree cover, what wrong   25
Shall the fresh earth cover? We wait, and the time is short
But waiting is long.

(*Enter the* FIRST PRIEST *with a banner of St. Stephen borne before him. The lines sung are in italics.*)

FIRST PRIEST. Since Christmas a day: and the day of St. Stephen, First Martyr.

Princes moreover did sit, and did witness falsely against me.

A day that was always most dear to the Archbishop Thomas.

And he kneeled down and cried with a loud voice: 30

Lord, lay not this sin to their charge.

Princes moreover did sit.

(Introit of St. Stephen is heard.)

(Enter the SECOND PRIEST, *with a banner of St. John the Apostle borne before him.)*

SECOND PRIEST. Since St. Stephen a day: and the day of St. John the Apostle.

In the midst of the congregation he opened his mouth.

That which was from the beginning, which we have heard,   35

Which we have seen with our eyes, and our hands have handled

Of the word of life; that which we have seen and heard

Declare we unto you.

In the midst of the congregation.

(Introit of St. John is heard.)

(Enter the THIRD PRIEST, *with a banner of the Holy Innocents borne before him.)*

THIRD PRIEST. Since St. John the Apostle a day: and the day of the Holy Innocents.   40

Out of the mouth of very babes, O God.

As the voice of many waters, of thunder, of harps,

They sung as it were a new song.

The blood of thy saints have they shed like water,

And there was no man to bury them. Avenge, O Lord,   45

The blood of thy saints. In Rama, a voice heard weeping.

Out of the mouths of very babes, O God!

*(*THE PRIESTS *stand together with the banners behind them.)*

FIRST PRIEST. Since the Holy Innocents a day: the fourth day from Christmas.

THE THREE PRIESTS. *Rejoice we all, keeping holy day.*

FIRST PRIEST. As for the people, so also for himself, he offereth for sins.   50

He lays down his life for the sheep.

THE THREE PRIESTS. *Rejoice we all, keeping holy day.*

FIRST PRIEST. To-day?

SECOND PRIEST. To-day, what is to-day? For the day is half gone.

FIRST PRIEST. To-day, what is to-day? But another day, the dusk of the year.   55

SECOND PRIEST. To-day, what is to-day? Another night and another dawn.

THIRD PRIEST. What day is the day that we know that we hope for or fear for?

Every day is the day we should fear from or hope from. One moment

Weighs like another. Only in retrospection, selection,

We say, that was the day. The critical moment   60

That is always now, and here. Even now, in sordid particulars

The eternal design may appear.

(Enter the FOUR KNIGHTS. *The banners disappear.)*

FIRST KNIGHT. Servants of the King.

FIRST PRIEST.   And known to us.

You are welcome. Have you ridden far?

FIRST KNIGHT. Not far today, but matters urgent   65

Have brought us from France. We rode hard,

Took ship yesterday, landed last night,

Having business with the Archbishop.

SECOND KNIGHT. Urgent business.

THIRD KNIGHT.   From the King.

SECOND KNIGHT. By the King's order.

FIRST KNIGHT.   Our men are outside. 70

FIRST PRIEST. You know the Archbishop's hospitality.

We are about to go to dinner.

The good Archbishop would be vexed

If we did not offer you entertainment

Before your business. Please dine with us. 75

Your men shall be looked after also.

Dinner before business. Do you like roast pork?

FIRST KNIGHT. Business before dinner. We
will roast your pork
First, and dine upon it after.

SECOND KNIGHT. We must see the Arch-
bishop.   80

THIRD KNIGHT. Go, tell the Archbishop
We have no need of his hospitality.
We will find our own dinner.

FIRST PRIEST (to attendant). Go, tell His Lordship.

FOURTH KNIGHT.   How much longer
will you keep us waiting?   85

(Enter THOMAS)

THOMAS (to PRIESTS). However certain our
expectation
The moment foreseen may be unexpected
When it arrives. It comes when we are
Engrossed with matters of other urgency.
On my table you will find   90
The papers in order, and the documents
signed. (To KNIGHTS)
You are welcome, whatever your business
may be.
You say, from the King?

FIRST KNIGHT.   Most surely from the King.
We must speak with you alone.

THOMAS (to PRIESTS). Leave us then alone.
Now what is the matter?

FIRST KNIGHT.   This is the matter. 95

THE THREE KNIGHTS. You are the Archbishop
in revolt against the King; in rebellion to
the King and the law of the land;
You are the Archbishop who was made by the
King; whom he set in your place to carry
out his command.
You are his servant, his tool, and his jack,
You wore his favours on your back,
You had your honours all from his hand;
from him you had the power, the seal and
the ring.   100
This is the man who was the tradesman's son:
the backstairs brat who was born in Cheap-
side;
This is the creature that crawled upon the
King; swollen with blood and swollen with
pride.
Creeping out of the London dirt,

Crawling up like a louse on your shirt,
The man who cheated, swindled, lied; broke
his oath and betrayed his King.   105

THOMAS. This is not true.
Both before and after I received the ring
I have been a loyal subject to the King.
Saving my order, I am at his command,
As his most faithful vassal in the land.   110

FIRST KNIGHT. Saving your order! let your
order save you—
As I do not think it is like to do.
Saving your ambition is what you mean,
Saving your pride, envy and spleen.

SECOND KNIGHT. Saving your insolence and
greed.   115
Won't you ask us to pray to God for you, in
your need?

THIRD KNIGHT. Yes, we'll pray for you!

FIRST KNIGHT.   Yes, we'll pray for you!

THE THREE KNIGHTS. Yes, we'll pray that
God may help you!

THOMAS. But, gentlemen, your business
Which you said so urgent, is it only   120
Scolding and blaspheming?

FIRST KNIGHT.   That was only
Our indignation, as loyal subjects.

THOMAS. Loyal? to whom?

FIRST KNIGHT.   To the King!

SECOND KNIGHT.   The King!

THIRD KNIGHT. The King!

THE THREE KNIGHTS.   God bless him!

THOMAS. Then let your new coat of loyalty
be worn
Carefully, so it get not soiled or torn.   125
Have you something to say?

FIRST KNIGHT.   By the King's command.
Shall we say it now?

SECOND KNIGHT.   Without delay,
Before the old fox is off and away.

THOMAS.   What you have to say
By the King's command—if it be the King's
command—
Should be said in public. If you make
charges,   130

Then in public I will refute them.

FIRST KNIGHT.　　　　　　　No! here and now!

(*They make to attack him, but the priests
and attendants return and quietly in-
terpose themselves*)

THOMAS. Now and here!

FIRST KNIGHT. Of your earlier misdeeds I shall
make no mention.
They are too well known. But after dissen-
sion
Had ended, in France, and you were en-
dued　　　　　　　　　　　　　　　135
With your former privilege, how did you
show your gratitude?
You had fled from England, not exiled
Or threatened, mind you; but in the hope
Of stirring up trouble in the French do-
minions.
You sowed strife abroad, you reviled　140
The King to the King of France, to the Pope,
Raising up against him false opinions.

SECOND KNIGHT. Yet the King, out of his
charity,
And urged by your friends, offered clemency,
Made a pact of peace, and all dispute
ended　　　　　　　　　　　　　145
Sent you back to your See as you demanded.

THIRD KNIGHT. And burying the memory of
your transgressions
Restored your honours and your possessions.
All was granted for which you sued:
Yet how, I repeat, did you show your grat-
itude?　　　　　　　　　　　150

FOURTH KNIGHT. Suspending those who had
crowned the young prince,
Denying the legality of his coronation;
Binding with the chains of anathema,
Using every means in your power to evince
The King's faithful servants, everyone who
transacts　　　　　　　　　　155
His business in his absence, the business of
the nation.

FIRST KNIGHT. These are the facts.
Say therefore if you will be content
To answer in the King's presence. Therefore
were we sent.

THOMAS. Never was it my wish　　160
To uncrown the King's son, or to diminish

His honour and power. Why should he wish
To deprive my people of me and keep me
from my own
And bid me sit in Canterbury, alone?
I would wish him three crowns rather than
one,　　　　　　　　　　　165
And as for the bishops, it is not my yoke
That is laid upon them, or mine to revoke.
Let them go to the Pope. It was he who con-
demned them.

FIRST KNIGHT. Through you they were suspended.

SECOND KNIGHT. By you be this amended.　170

THIRD KNIGHT. Absolve them.

FIRST KNIGHT.　　　　　　　Absolve them.

THOMAS.　　　　　　　　I do not deny
That this was done through me. But it is not
I
Who can loose whom the Pope has bound.
Let them go to him, upon whom redounds
Their contempt towards me, their contempt
towards the Church shown.

FIRST KNIGHT. Be that as it may, here is the
King's command:　　　　　　175
That you and your servants depart from this
land.

THOMAS. If that *is* the King's command, I will
be bold
To say: seven years were my people without
My presence; seven years of misery and pain.
Seven years a mendicant on foreign charity 180
I lingered abroad: seven years is no brevity.
I shall not get those seven years back again.
Never again, you must make no doubt,
Shall the sea run between the shepherd and
his fold.

FIRST KNIGHT. The King's justice, the King's
majesty,　　　　　　　　185
You insult with gross indignity;
Insolent madman, whom nothing deters
From attainting his servants and ministers.

THOMAS. It is not I who insult the King,
And there is higher than I or the King.　190
It is not I, Becket from Cheapside,
It is not against me, Becket, that you strive.
It is not Becket who pronounces doom,
But the Law of Christ's church, the judge-
ment of Rome.

FIRST KNIGHT. Priest, you have spoken in peril of your life. [195]

SECOND KNIGHT. Priest, you have spoken in danger of the knife.

THIRD KNIGHT. Priest, you have spoken treachery and treason.

THE THREE KNIGHTS. Priest! Traitor confirmed in malfeasance.

THOMAS. I submit my cause to the judgement of Rome.
But if you kill me, I shall rise from my tomb [200]
To submit my cause before God's throne.

(*Exit*)

FOURTH KNIGHT. Priest! monk! and servant! take, hold, detain,
Restrain this man, in the King's name.

FIRST KNIGHT. Or answer with your bodies.

SECOND KNIGHT. Enough of words.

THE FOUR KNIGHTS. We come for the King's justice, we come with swords. [205]

(*Exeunt.*)

CHORUS. I have smelt them, the death-bringers, senses are quickened
By subtile forebodings; I have heard
Fluting in the nighttime, fluting and owls, have seen at noon
Scaly wings slanting over, huge and ridiculous. I have tasted
The savour of putrid flesh in the spoon. I have felt [210]
The heaving of earth at nightfall, restless, absurd. I have heard
Laughter in the noises of beasts that make strange noises: jackal, jackass, jackdaw; the scurrying noise of mouse and jerboa; the laugh of the loon, the lunatic bird. I have seen
Grey necks twisting, rat tails twining, in the thick light of dawn. I have eaten
Smooth creatures still living, with the strong salt taste of living things under sea; I have tasted
The living lobster, the crab, the oyster, the whelk and the prawn; and they live and spawn in my bowels, and my bowels dissolve in the light of dawn. I have smelt [215]
Death in the rose, death in the hollyhock, sweet pea, hyacinth, primrose and cowslip. I have seen
Trunk and horn, tusk and hoof, in odd places;
I have lain on the floor of the sea and breathed with the breathing of the sea-anemone, swallowed with ingurgitation of the sponge. I have lain in the soil and criticised the worm. In the air
Flirted with the passage of the kite, I have plunged with the kite and cowered with the wren. I have felt
The horn of the beetle, the scale of the viper, the mobile hard insensitive skin of the elephant, the evasive flank of the fish. I have smelt [220]
Corruption in the dish, incense in the latrine, the sewer in the incense, the smell of sweet soap in the woodpath, a hellish sweet scent in the woodpath, while the ground heaved. I have seen
Rings of light coiling downwards, leading
To the horror of the ape. Have I not known, not known
What was coming to be? It was here, in the kitchen, in the passage,
In the mews in the barn in the byre in the market place [225]
In our veins our bowels our skulls as well
As well as in the plottings of potentates
As well as in the consultations of powers.
What is woven on the loom of fate
What is woven in the councils of princes [230]
Is woven also in our veins, our brains,
Is woven like a pattern of living worms
In the guts of the women of Canterbury.

I have smelt them, the death-bringers; now is too late
For action, too soon for contrition. [235]
Nothing is possible but the shamed swoon
Of those consenting to the last humiliation.
I have consented, Lord Archbishop, have consented.
Am torn away, subdued, violated,
United to the spiritual flesh of nature, [240]
Mastered by the animal powers of spirit,
Dominated by the lust of self-demolition,
By the final utter uttermost death of spirit,
By the final ecstasy of waste and shame,
O Lord Archbishop, O Thomas Archbishop,
forgive us, forgive us, pray for us that we

may pray for you, out of our shame.   245

(*Enter* THOMAS.)

THOMAS. Peace, and be at peace with your
thoughts and visions.
These things had to come to you and you to
accept them.
This is your share of the eternal burden,
The perpetual glory. This is one moment,
But know that another   250
Shall pierce you with a sudden painful joy
When the figure of God's purpose is made
complete.
You shall forget these things, toiling in the
household,
You shall remember them, droning by the
fire,
When age and forgetfulness sweeten mem-
ory   255
Only like a dream that has often been told
And often been changed in the telling. They
will seem unreal.
Human kind cannot bear very much reality.

PRIESTS (*severally*). My Lord, you must not
stop here. To the minster. Through the
cloister. No time to waste. They are coming
back, armed. To the altar, to the altar.

THOMAS. All my life they have been coming,
these feet. All my life   260
I have waited. Death will come only when I
am worthy,
And if I am worthy, there is no danger.
I have therefore only to make perfect my
will.

PRIESTS. My Lord, they are coming. They
will break through presently.
You will be killed. Come to the altar. Make
haste, my Lord. Don't stop here talking. 265
It is not right. What shall become of us, my
Lord, if you are killed;
What shall become of us?

THOMAS. Peace! be quiet! remember where
you are, and what is happening;
No life here is sought for but mine,
And I am not in danger: only near to
death.   270

PRIESTS. My Lord, to vespers! You must not
be absent from vespers. You must not be
absent from the divine office. To vespers.
Into the cathedral!

THOMAS. Go to vespers, remember me at your
prayers
They shall find the shepherd here; the flock
shall be spared.
I have had a tremor of bliss, a wink of heaven,
a whisper,
And I would no longer be denied; all
things   275
Proceed to a joyful consummation.

PRIESTS. Seize him! force him! drag him!

THOMAS. Keep your hands off!

PRIESTS. To vespers! Hurry.

(*They drag him off. While the* CHORUS
*speak, the scene is changed to the
Cathedral.*)

CHORUS (*while a* Dies Irae *is sung in Latin by
a choir in the distance*).

Numb the hand and dry the eyelid,   280
Still the horror, but more horror
Than when tearing in the belly.

Still the horror, but more horror
Than when twisting in the fingers,
Than when splitting in the skull.   285

More than footfall in the passage,
More than shadow in the doorway,
More than fury in the hall.

The agents of hell disappear, the human,
they shrink and dissolve
Into dust on the wind, forgotten, unmem-
orable; only is here   290
The white flat face of Death, God's silent
servant,
And behind the face of Death the Judgement
And behind the Judgement the Void, more
horrid than active shapes of hell;
Emptiness, absence, separation from God;
The horror of the effortless journey, to the
empty land   295
Which is no land, only emptiness, absence,
the Void,
Where those who were men can no longer
turn the mind
To distraction, delusion, escape into dream,
pretence,
Where the soul is no longer deceived, for
there are no objects, no tones,

No colours, no forms to distract, to divert the
    soul   300
From seeing itself, foully united forever,
    nothing with nothing,
Not what we call death, but what beyond
    death is not death,
We fear, we fear. Who shall then plead for
    me,
Who intercede for me, in my most need?

Dead upon the tree, my Saviour,   305
Let not be in vain Thy labour;
Help me, Lord, in my last fear.

Dust I am, to dust am bending,
From the final doom impending
Help me, Lord, for death is near.   310

    (*In the cathedral.* THOMAS *and* PRIESTS.)

PRIESTS. Bar the door. Bar the door.
The door is barred.
We are safe. We are safe.
They dare not break in.
They cannot break in. They have not the
    force.   315
We are safe. We are safe.

THOMAS. Unbar the doors! throw open the
    doors!
I will not have the house of prayer, the
    church of Christ,
The sanctuary, turned into a fortress.
The Church shall protect her own, in her
    own way, not   320
As oak and stone; stone and oak decay,
Give no stay, but the Church shall endure.
The church shall be open, even to our en-
    emies. Open the door!

PRIEST. My Lord! these are not men, these
    come not as men come, but   325
Like maddened beasts. They come not like
    men, who
Respect the sanctuary, who kneel to the Body
    of Christ,
But like beasts. You would bar the door
Against the lion, the lèopard, the wolf or the
    boar,
Why not more   330
Against beasts with the souls of damned men,
    against men
Who would damn themselves to beasts. My
    Lord! My Lord!

THOMAS. You think me reckless, desperate
    and mad.
You argue by results, as this world does,
To settle if an act be good or bad.   335
You defer to the fact. For every life and every
    act
Consequence of good and evil can be shown.
And as in time results of many deeds are
    blended
So good and evil in the end become con-
    founded.
It is not in time that my death shall be
    known;   340
It is out of time that my decision is taken
If you call that decision
To which my whole being gives entire con-
    sent.
I give my life
To the Law of God above the Law of Man.
    Unbar the door! unbar the door!   345
We are not here to triumph by fighting, by
    stratagem, or by resistance,
Not to fight with beasts as men. We have
    fought the beast
And have conquered. We have only to con-
    quer
Now, by suffering. This is the easier victory.
Now is the triumph of the Cross, now   350
Open the door! I command it. OPEN THE
    DOOR!

    (*The door is opened. The* KNIGHTS *enter,*
        slightly tipsy.)

PRIESTS. This way, my Lord! Quick. Up the
    stair. To the roof. To the crypt. Quick.
    Come. Force him.

KNIGHTS (*one line each*)

Where is Becket, the traitor to the King?
    Where is Becket, the meddling priest?
Come down Daniel to the lions' den,   355
    Come down Daniel for the mark of the
    beast.

Are you washed in the blood of the Lamb?
    Are you marked with the mark of the beast?
Come down Daniel to the lions' den,
    Come down Daniel and join in the feast. 360

Where is Becket the Cheapside brat?
    Where is Becket the faithless priest?
Come down Daniel to the lions' den,
    Come down Daniel and join in the feast.

THOMAS. It is the just man who   365
Like a bold lion, should be without fear.
I am here.
No traitor to the King. I am a priest
A Christian, saved by the blood of Christ,
Ready to suffer with my blood.   370
This is the sign of the Church always,
The sign of blood. Blood for blood.
His blood given to buy my life,
My blood given to pay for His death,
My death for His death.   375

FIRST KNIGHT. Absolve all those you have
    excommunicated.

SECOND KNIGHT. Resign the powers you have
    arrogated.

THIRD KNIGHT. Restore to the King the
    money you appropriated.

FIRST KNIGHT. Renew the obedience you have
    violated.

THOMAS. For my Lord I am now ready to
    die,   380
That His Church may have peace and liberty.
Do with me as you will, to your hurt and
    shame;
But none of my people, in God's name,
Whether layman or clerk, shall you touch.
This I forbid.   385

KNIGHTS. Traitor! traitor! traitor!

THOMAS. You, Reginald, three times traitor
    you:
Traitor to me as my temporal vassal,
Traitor to me as your spiritual lord,
Traitor to God in desecrating His Church. 390

FIRST KNIGHT. No faith do I owe to a ren-
    egade,
And what I owe shall now be paid.

THOMAS. Now to Almighty God, to the
Blessed Mary ever Virgin, to the blessed John
the Baptist, the holy apostles Peter and Paul,
to the blessed martyr Denys, and to all the
Saints, I commend my cause and that of the
Church.

    (*While the* KNIGHTS *kill him, we hear the*
    CHORUS)

Clear the air! clean the sky! wash the wind!
    take stone from stone and wash them.
The land is foul, the water is foul, our beasts
    and ourselves defiled with blood.   395

A rain of blood has blinded my eyes. Where
    is England? where is Kent? where is Can-
    terbury?
O far far far far in the past; and I wander in
    a land of barren boughs: if I break them,
    they bleed; I wander in a land of dry
    stones: if I touch them they bleed.
How how can I ever return, to the soft quiet
    seasons?
Night stay with us, stop sun, hold season, let
    the day not come, let the spring not come.
Can I look again at the day and its common
    things, and see them all smeared with
    blood, through a curtain of falling
    blood?   400
We did not wish anything to happen.
We understood the private catastrophe,
The personal loss, the general misery,
Living and partly living;
The terror by night that ends in daily ac-
    tion,   405
The terror by day that ends in sleep;
But the talk in the market-place, the hand on
    the broom,
The nighttime heaping of the ashes,
The fuel laid on the fire at daybreak,
These acts marked a limit to our suffering. 410
Every horror had its definition,
Every sorrow had a kind of end:
In life there is not time to grieve long.
But this, this is out of life, this is out of time,
An instant eternity of evil and wrong.   415
We are soiled by a filth that we cannot clean,
    united to supernatural vermin,
It is not we alone, it is not the house, it is not
    the city that is defiled,
But the world that is wholly foul.
Clear the air! clean the sky! wash the wind!
    take the stone from the stone, take the skin
    from the arm, take the muscle from the
    bone, and wash them. Wash the stone,
    wash the bone, wash the brain, wash the
    soul, wash them wash them!

    (*The* KNIGHTS, *having completed the*
    murder, advance to the front of the
    stage and address the audience)

FIRST KNIGHT. We beg you to give us your
attention for a few moments. We know that
you may be disposed to judge unfavourably
of our action. You are Englishmen, and therefore you believe in fair play: and when you
see one man being set upon by four, then your

sympathies are all with the under dog. I respect such feelings, I share them. Nevertheless, I appeal to your sense of honour. You are Englishmen, and therefore will not judge anybody without hearing both sides of the case. That is in accordance with our long established principle of Trial by Jury. I am not myself qualified to put our case to you. I am a man of action and not of words. For that reason I shall do no more than introduce the other speakers, who, with their various abilities, and different points of view, will be able to lay before you the merits of this extremely complex problem. I shall call upon our eldest member to speak first, my neighbour in the country: Baron William de Traci.

THIRD KNIGHT. I am afraid I am not anything like such an experienced speaker as my old friend Reginald Fitz Urse would lead you to believe. But there is one thing I should like to say, and I might as well say it at once. It is this: in what we have done, and whatever you may think of it, we have been perfectly disinterested. (*The other* KNIGHTS: 'Hear! hear!') *We* are not getting anything out of this. We have much more to lose than to gain. We are four plain Englishmen who put our country first. I dare say that we didn't make a very good impression when we came in just now. The fact is that we knew we had taken on a pretty stiff job; I'll only speak for myself, but I had drunk a good deal —I am not a drinking man ordinarily—to brace myself up for it. When you come to the point, it does go against the grain to kill an Archbishop, especially when you have been brought up in good Church traditions. So if we seemed a bit rowdy, you will understand why it was; and for my part I am awfully sorry about it. We realised that this was our duty, but all the same we had to work ourselves up to it. And, as I said, *we* are not getting a penny out of this. We know perfectly well how things will turn out. King Henry—God bless him—will have to say, for reasons of state, that he never meant this to happen; and there is going to be an awful row; and at the best we shall have to spend the rest of our lives abroad. And even when reasonable people come to see that the Archbishop *had* to be put out of the way—and

personally I had a tremendous admiration for him—you must have noticed what a good show he put up at the end—they won't give *us* any glory. No, we have done for ourselves, there's no mistake about that. So, as I said at the beginning, please give us at least the credit for being completely disinterested in this business. I think that is about all I have to say.

FIRST KNIGHT. I think we will all agree that William de Traci has spoken well and has made a very important point. The gist of his argument is this: that we have been completely disinterested. But our act itself needs more justification than that; and you must hear our other speakers. I shall next call upon Hugh de Morville, who has made a special study of statecraft and constitutional law. Sir Hugh de Morville.

SECOND KNIGHT. I should like first to recur to a point that was very well put by our leader, Reginald Fitz Urse: that you are Englishmen, and therefore your sympathies are always with the under dog. It is the English spirit of fair play. Now the worthy Archbishop, whose good qualities I very much admired, has throughout been presented as the under dog. But is this really the case? I am going to appeal not to your emotions but to your reason. You are hard-headed sensible people, as I can see, and not to be taken in by emotional clap-trap. I therefore ask you to consider soberly: what were the Archbishop's aims? and what are King Henry's aims? In the answer to these questions lies the key to the problem.

The King's aim has been perfectly consistent. During the reign of the late Queen Matilda and the irruption of the unhappy usurper Stephen, the kingdom was very much divided. Our King saw that the one thing needful was to restore order: to curb the excessive powers of local government, which were usually exercised for selfish and often for seditious ends, and to reform the legal system. He therefore intended that Becket, who had proved himself an extremely able administrator—no one denies that—should unite the offices of Chancellor and Archbishop. Had Becket concurred with the King's wishes, we should have had an almost ideal State: a union of spiritual and temporal administration, under the central government. I knew Becket well, in various official relations; and I may say that I have never known a man so well qualified for the highest rank of the Civil Service. And what happened? The moment that Becket, at the King's instance, had been made Archbishop, he resigned the office of Chancellor, he became more priestly than the priests, he ostentatiously and offensively adopted an ascetic manner of life, he affirmed immediately that there was a higher order than that which our King, and he as the King's servant, had for so many years striven to establish; and that— God knows why—the two orders were incompatible.

You will agree with me that such interference by an Archbishop offends the instincts of a people like ours. So far, I know that I have your approval: I read it in your faces. It is only with the measures we have had to adopt, in order to set matters to rights, that you take issue. No one regrets the necessity for violence more than we do. Unhappily, there are times when violence is the only way in which social justice can be secured. At another time, you would condemn an Archbishop by vote of Parliament and execute him formally as a traitor, and no one would have to bear the burden of being called murderer. And at a later time still, even such temperate measures as these would become unnecessary. But, if you have now arrived at a just subordination of the pretensions of the Church to the welfare of the State, remember that it is we who took the first step. We have been instrumental in bringing about the state of affairs that you approve. We have served your interests; we merit your applause; and if there is any guilt whatever in the matter, you must share it with us.

FIRST KNIGHT. Morville has given us a great deal to think about. It seems to me that he has said almost the last word, for those who have been able to follow his very subtle reasoning. We have, however, one more speaker, who has I think another point of view to express. If there are any who are still unconvinced, I think that Richard Brito, coming as he does of a family distinguished for its loyalty to the Church, will be able to convince them. Richard Brito.

FOURTH KNIGHT. The speakers who have preceded me, to say nothing of our leader, Reginald Fitz Urse, have all spoken very much to the point. I have nothing to add along their particular lines of argument. What I have to say may be put in the form of a question: *Who killed the Archbishop?* As you have been eye-witnesses of this lamentable scene, you may feel some surprise at my putting it in this way. But consider the course of events. I am obliged, very briefly, to go over the ground traversed by the last speaker. While the late Archbishop was Chancellor, no one, under the King, did more to weld the country together, to give it the unity, the stability, order, tranquillity, and justice that it so badly needed. From the moment he became Archbishop, he completely reversed his policy; he showed himself to be utterly indifferent to the fate of the country, to be, in fact, a monster of egotism. This egotism grew upon him, until it became at last an undoubted mania. I have unimpeachable evidence to the effect that before he left France he clearly prophesied, in the presence of numerous witnesses, that he had not long to live, and that he would be killed in England. He used every means of provocation; from his conduct, step by step, there can be no inference except that he had determined upon a death by martyrdom. Even at the last, he could have given us reason: you have seen how he evaded our questions. And when he had deliberately exasperated us beyond human endurance, he could still have easily escaped; he could have kept himself from us long enough to allow our righteous anger to cool. That was just what he did not wish to happen; he insisted, while we were still inflamed with wrath, that the doors should be opened. Need I say more? I think, with these facts before you, you will unhesitatingly render a verdict of Suicide while of Unsound Mind. It is the only charitable verdict you can give, upon one who was, after all, a great man.

FIRST KNIGHT. Thank you, Brito. I think that there is no more to be said; and I suggest that you now disperse quietly to your homes. Please be careful not to loiter in groups at

street corners, and do nothing that might provoke any public outbreak.

(*Exeunt* KNIGHTS)

FIRST PRIEST. O father, father, gone from us,
lost to us,   420
How shall we find you, from what far place
Do you look down on us? You now in
Heaven,
Who shall now guide us, protect us, direct us?
After what journey through what further
dread
Shall we recover your presence? when in-
herit   425
Your strength? The Church lies bereft,
Alone, desecrated, desolated, and the heathen
shall build on the ruins,
Their world without God. I see it I see it.

THIRD PRIEST. No. For the Church is stronger
for this action,
Triumphant in adversity. It is fortified   430
By persecution: supreme, so long as men will
die for it.
Go, weak sad men, lost erring souls, homeless
in earth or heaven.
Go where the sunset reddens the last grey
rock
Of Brittany, or the Gates of Hercules.
Go venture shipwreck on the sullen coasts   435
Where blackamoors make captive Christian
men;
Go to the northern seas confined with ice
Where the dead breath makes numb the
hand, makes dull the brain;
Find an oasis in the desert sun,
Go seek alliance with the heathen Saracen,   440
To share his filthy rites, and try to snatch
Forgetfulness in his libidinous courts,
Oblivion in the fountain by the date-tree;
Or sit and bite your nails in Aquitaine.
In the small circle of pain within the skull   445
You still shall tramp and tread one endless
round
Of thought, to justify your action to your-
selves,
Weaving a fiction which unravels as you
weave,
Pacing forever in the hell of make-believe
Which never is belief: this is your fate on
earth   450
And we must think no further of you.

FIRST PRIEST.   O my lord

The glory of whose new state is hidden from
us,
Pray for us of your charity.

SECOND PRIEST.   Now in the sight of God
Conjoined with all the saints and martyrs
gone before you,
Remember us.

THIRD PRIEST.   Let our thanks ascend   455
To God, who has given us another Saint in
Canterbury.

CHORUS (*while a* Te Deum *is sung in Latin by
a choir in the distance*).
We praise Thee, O God, for Thy glory displayed in all the creatures of the earth,
In the snow, in the rain, in the wind, in the
storm; in all of Thy creatures, both the
hunters and the hunted.
For all things exist only as seen by Thee, only
as known by Thee, all things exist
Only in Thy light, and Thy glory is declared
even in that which denies Thee; the darkness declares the glory of light.   460
Those who deny Thee could not deny, if
Thou didst not exist; and their denial is
never complete, for if it were so, they would
not exist.
They affirm Thee in living; all things affirm
Thee in living; the bird in the air, both the
hawk and the finch; the beast on the earth,
both the wolf and the lamb; the worm in
the soil and the worm in the belly.
Therefore man, whom Thou hast made to be
conscious of Thee, must consciously praise
Thee, in thought and in word and in deed.
Even with the hand to the broom, the back
bent in laying the fire, the knee bent in
cleaning the hearth, we, the scrubbers and
sweepers of Canterbury,
The back bent under toil, the knee bent under sin, the hands to the face under fear,
the head bent under grief,   465
Even in us the voices of seasons, the snuffle of
winter, the song of spring, the drone of
summer, the voices of beasts and of birds,
praise Thee.
We thank Thee for Thy mercies of blood, for
Thy redemption by blood. For the blood
of Thy martyrs and saints
Shall enrich the earth, shall create the holy
places.
For wherever a saint has dwelt, wherever a

martyr has given his blood for the blood of
Christ,
There is holy ground, and the sanctity shall
not depart from it   470
Though armies trample over it, though sight-
seers come with guide-books looking over
it;
From where the western seas gnaw at the
coast of Iona,
To the death in the desert, the prayer in
forgotten places by the broken imperial
column,
From such ground springs that which forever
renews the earth
Though it is forever denied. Therefore, O
God, we thank Thee   475
Who hast given such blessing to Canterbury.

Forgive us, O Lord, we acknowledge ourselves
as type of the common man,
Of the men and women who shut the door
and sit by the fire;
Who fear the blessing of God, the loneliness
of the night of God, the surrender required, the deprivation inflicted;
Who fear the injustice of men less than the
justice of God;   480
Who fear the hand at the window, the fire in
the thatch, the fist in the tavern, the push
into the canal,
Less than we fear the love of God.
We acknowledge our trespass, our weakness,
our fault; we acknowledge
That the sin of the world is upon our heads;
that the blood of the martyrs and the agony
of the saints
Is upon our heads.   485
Lord, have mercy upon us.
Christ, have mercy upon us.
Lord, have mercy upon us.
Blessed Thomas, pray for us.

———————◆·◆◆◆·◆———————

This play deals with a historical event, the
murder of Thomas à Becket, Archbishop of
Canterbury, in his cathedral on December 29,
1170. In earlier years, Becket had been a
great favorite of the king, Henry II, and
served as his chancellor. In 1162 Becket was
consecrated archbishop, and "forthwith," as
one of old chronicles puts it, "refused to
deale any more with matters of the Court, re-
nouncing the Chauncellorship etc." Quarrels
ensued between the king and his former
favorite and in 1164, the archbishop fled England and went to Rome. At the time that
our play opens, he has just returned to Canterbury after restoration to his see, though as
the Messenger comments (Part 1, 1. 99), the
restoration is merely "A patched up affair, if
you ask my opinion."

But though the play deals with history
and makes use of certain archaicisms in its
language and sentence structure, it will
quickly become obvious to the reader that the
play aims at something more than the recreation of a historical scene. It is aimed
quite steadily at a modern audience. For example, the Fourth Tempter (Part 1, ll. 564–
69) suddenly makes a reference to the world
that the modern reader knows and in which
he lives:

> And later is worse, when men will not hate
>   you
> Enough to defame or to execrate you,
> But pondering the qualities that you lacked
> Will only try to find the historical fact.
> When men shall declare that there was no
>   mystery
> About this man who played a certain part
>   in history.

This play is concerned with something more
than making a "historical" interpretation.
Indeed, it challenges throughout the state of
mind that the Fourth Tempter describes in
the passage just quoted.

Other references to the modern world
and modern man occur throughout the play.
Note the references made in the speech of the
four tempters (Part 1, ll. 613–27); note that
Thomas's speech that closes Part 1 (ll. 703–16)
is addressed directly to the audience; and
note that the speeches of the four knights
(after their murder of Thomas) are written
in modern journalistic prose. The manner as
well as the matter of the knights' justification
of their act thus brings us squarely up against
a "modern" account of the meaning of
Thomas's act: it is an account that challenges
the whole religious conception of martyrdom.

The issues just raised have everything

to do with the meaning of this play and with the strategies the author has devised in order to present that meaning. Is the "martyr" a passive victim, and is martyrdom thus an accident, to be fully accounted for in historical terms? Or, if the "martyr" is not passive, but actively wills his death, is Brito not right in his charge that Thomas has really committed suicide?

The author may here seem to be caught in a cleft stick: either he writes a play in which there is no essential struggle, no real conflict, since Thomas "suffers" but cannot "act," and thus ends with a piece of pageantry that is essentially undramatic, or else Thomas invites his own death—"acts" to get himself killed—under delusion or for hope of glory, in which case the note on which the play ends (see the last chorus) is contradicted by the action of the play itself.

We do not seek to impose our own view here as to the success or lack of success of the play. But we do feel it important that the student should see early in his study of the play what the problem is; and we point out that the dramatist himself is certainly thoroughly aware of the problem: consider the emphasis on acting as suffering and suffering as action (Part 1, ll. 210–18, ll. 600–608, and l. 714). Consider the various definitions of martyrdom (Thomas's sermon, Brito's speech of justification, etc.). Consider most of all Thomas's own concern with his motives.

The sin that Thomas fears most is an insidious kind of pride that will constitute the wrong motive for the right action. He probably does well to fear it. From the very beginning of the play we hear constant references to Thomas's pride. The First Priest refers to Thomas's "pride always feeding upon his own virtues" (Part 1, l. 119); the Second Tempter says to him, "Your sin soars sunward" (Part 1, l. 390); the Fourth Tempter, urging him on to martyrdom, can even quote back to him his own earlier words, not even needing to alter them in order to make them serve his argument of temptation. And the four Tempters in the speech that they recite together condemn Thomas as a man "Lost in the wonder of his own greatness" (Part 1, l. 626).

Does Thomas succeed in avoiding what he calls "the greatest treason: To do the right deed for the wrong reason" (Part 1, ll. 676–77)? And if so, how has the dramatist been able to make convincing to us Thomas's growth in self-knowledge and his "perfecting" of his own will? In this connection, a consideration of the function of the other characters is in order.

The four knights are given names though the dramatist has been content to leave them as rather flat types without much distinguishing personality. The priests are not even given names. (They do, however, exhibit some differences in temperament and attitude: the Third Priest obviously is closest to Thomas in his awareness of the situation.) The women of Canterbury by the very fact that they constitute the chorus are not meant to register upon the audience as individuals. As for the tempters, they achieve special traits of personality only insofar as they represent past or present aspects of Thomas himself.

In view of this very special focusing upon the one main character, we may be inclined to say that the other characters are of little importance, and that they contribute little to Thomas's struggle—merely witnessing it as spectators. (Even the knights, who contribute the only overt "action" to the play, may seem to have little more than a physical relation to the conflict centered in Thomas.) Yet the minor characters have most important functions; and as we come to understand the essential issue of the play, those functions become easier to apprehend.

They have, in the first place, a great deal to do with defining the nature of the conflict in the play. Before the murder, the priests, the tempters, and the chorus all unite in urging Thomas to abandon his position. Their motives for urging this differ; but all are in opposition to Thomas's course of action (or "inaction"). This fact is pointed up in lines 633–44, where the three groups speak alternately, and the voices of the priests and the tempters become part of the "chorus."

After the murder, the knights in their speeches of justification restate in modern terms and in a modern idiom the case to be made against Thomas. All the speeches made before the murder oppose Thomas's taking the martyr's path; the speeches of the knights after the murder would rob the event of its significance as a martyrdom. Even before the murder, the speeches of the tempters challenge the conception of martyrdom, and thus look forward to what the knights are to say later. And even the groups sympathetic to Thomas, the priests and the chorus, ultimately by implication deny the significance of martyrdom.

The essential conflict—external and internal—is thus sharply defined. Moreover, the external and internal conflicts have much in common. The priests are by function and sympathy close to Thomas. The tempters, as we have remarked, make appeals with which Thomas is intimately familiar. The First Tempter is almost a shade of the Thomas of the past. The Fourth Tempter is almost Thomas's present secular self. And even the chorus has a special relation to Thomas. Like him, they are passive and condemned to "suffer." Thomas says of them "They know and do not know, what it is to act or suffer." And a little later the Fourth Tempter says to Thomas, "You know and do not know, what it is to act or suffer."

Of course the passivity of the chorus—"the small folk drawn into the pattern of fate"—is vastly different from the passivity of Thomas; and the contrast between the members of the chorus and Thomas is another means of defining his passivity, which is not really "passive" at all.

One further very important function of the chorus deserves mention. The ancient Greek dramatists used the chorus to give expression to the changing emotions of the audience. The chorus voiced the growing feeling of suspense, the sense of foreboding, or the surge of joy the audience experienced as it viewed the changing fortunes of the protagonist. But the chorus not only expressed, in a measure it directed, the response of the audience. Something of this function pertains to the chorus as used in this play. The chorus of old women charges us with the peculiar horror that attends the approaching act of violence, but it also transmits the sense of cleansing and power that flows from Thomas's triumphant death, and it is a means for drawing the reader into the mood of high exaltation with which the play ends.

EXERCISES

1. How is the exposition accomplished in this play? Is it sufficient? How heavily does the play lean upon a knowledge of history?

2. Thomas says that he had expected the first three tempters. Why had he not expected the fourth? What does his encounter with the Fourth Tempter reveal to Thomas about himself?

3. The women of the chorus (Part 1, ll. 645–73) express their sense of despair. Is Thomas himself at this point close to despair? Note that it is immediately after this chorus that Thomas says, "Now is my way clear, now is the meaning plain." Why has the way suddenly become clear for him? Has the despair of the chorus actually served to make his way clear to him?

4. Does "The Interlude," Thomas's sermon, break the dramatic pattern? If not, what does it contribute to the pattern?

5. Why do the women of the chorus dread what they sense is about to happen? Their dread goes beyond their wish to save the archbishop. It evidently goes beyond any concern for their own safety. It goes beyond their revulsion from mere suffering. They are used to suffering. What is the special nature of the horror and foreboding they feel? Does the poetry they speak in the choruses in Part 1 and in the first three choruses of Part 2 (ll. 1–27, 206–45, and 280–310) define this for you? Consider especially lines like 25 in Part 1 and 302 in Part 2.

6. Consider carefully Thomas's speech in Part 2, lines 272–76. Does his statement "I have had a tremor of bliss" argue that Thomas is really eager for and inviting his martyrdom after all? Does it indicate that he has not yet "made perfect his will"? Or does it indicate that he has? Defend your answer.

7. How do Joan and Thomas differ in their kinds of pride? Shaw apparently does not regard Joan's pride as reprehensible. Does Eliot regard Becket's as such?

8. Eliot once remarked that in writing *Murder in the Cathedral* he might have been, for all he knew, "slightly under the influence of *Saint Joan*." Do you find any elements in *Murder in the Cathedral* that might point to that influence?

9. Through most of the play, the choruses have suggested the sense of topsy-turviness and instability in the world. How does the chorus in Part 2, lines 394–419, sum up this sense of confusion and unreality? What is the meaning of line 414? Is the poet saying that the women who constitute the chorus here encounter the sense of eternity? How does this bear upon the "meaning" of Thomas's martyrdom? How does this chorus prepare for the chorus with which the play ends?

10. Eliot has been criticized for breaking so violently the mood and idiom of the play by the speeches of justification spoken by the four knights. Do you agree? Or can you justify the violence of the contrast as necessary to the play?

11. Discuss the use of animal imagery in the last chorus of the play. How do the animals referred to differ from the animals referred to in the earlier choruses? Note that the difference is not that the animals are all gentle (note the hawk) or attractive and beautiful (note "the worm in the belly").

12. Compare and contrast the imagery (or lack of imagery) in the knights' speeches of justification with the imagery in lines 394–419 and 420–89 of Part 2. Is the contrast meaningful and effective? Note the clichés of the knights' speeches, the sleazy political journalism, the euphemisms and circumlocutions.

13. The speech of the Third Priest (Part 2, ll. 429–51) develops the theme of "homelessness." How is the theme developed in terms of imagery? Is there a dominant metaphor? What does the handling of the metrical pattern contribute? Examine with special care the system of pauses and run-on lines.

14. On closer reading, the student will discover that one of the basic themes in this play concerns the nature of reality. Certain actions seem unreal —nightmarish. But some of the things that seemed most fantastically unreal are revealed, in the developed perspective, to lie at the center of reality, and other things that had seemed most real, turn out to be illusory. (This theme engages the problem of martyrdom, of course, most importantly: Is true martyrdom possible, or are martyrs simply deluded men or else men in the grip of a perverse kind of pride?)

Note how often such terms as *real* and *unreal* occur in this play. The four tempters, for example, say that "All things are unreal" (Part 1, l. 614). Consider also in this connection the passage beginning "The agents of hell disappear, the human, they shrink and dissolve . . ." (Part 2, ll. 289–304). Review the poetry of the play as a means for presenting this theme.

15. Is the poetry in this play "laid on from the outside," a kind of rhetorical gilding? Or is it part and parcel of the play? Try to justify your answer.

Note: A great many of Eliot's central themes are to be found in this play, themes that receive treatment in his other plays and poems. The student might consult Leonard Unger's *T. S. Eliot* (New York: Rinehart, 1948) for critical articles on Eliot's themes and techniques. Other useful texts are E. Martin Browne's *The Making of T. S. Eliot's Plays* (Cambridge Univ. Press, 1969) and David R. Clark, ed., *Twentieth Century Interpretations of Murder in the Cathedral* (Englewood Cliffs, N. J., Prentice-Hall, Inc., 1971).

THE SKIN OF OUR TEETH

Thornton Wilder (b. 1897)

Characters

ANNOUNCER	USHER
SABINA	GIRL ⎫ *Drum Majorettes*
MR. FITZPATRICK	GIRL ⎭
MRS. ANTROBUS	FORTUNE TELLER
DINOSAUR	CHAIR PUSHER
MAMMOTH	CHAIR PUSHER
TELEGRAPH BOY	CONVEENER
GLADYS	CONVEENER
HENRY	CONVEENER
MR. ANTROBUS	CONVEENER
DOCTOR	CONVEENER
PROFESSOR	BROADCAST OFFICIAL
JUDGE	DEFEATED CANDIDATE
HOMER	MR. TREMAYNE
MISS E. MUSE	HESTER
MISS T. MUSE	IVY
MISS M. MUSE	FRED BAILEY
USHER	

ACT 1

SCENE: *Home, Excelsior, New Jersey.*

A projection screen in the middle of the curtain. The first lantern slide: the name of the theatre, and the words: NEWS EVENTS OF THE WORLD. An ANNOUNCER'S *voice is heard.*

ANNOUNCER. The management takes pleasure in bringing to you—The News Events of the World:

(*Slide of the sun appearing above the horizon.*)

Freeport, Long Island.

The sun rose this morning at 6:32 A.M. This gratifying event was first reported by Mrs. Dorothy Stetson of Freeport, Long Island, who promptly telephoned the Mayor.

The Society for Affirming the End of the World at once went into a special session and postponed the arrival of that event for TWENTY-FOUR HOURS. All honor to Mrs. Stetson for her public spirit.

New York City:

(*Slide of the front doors of the theatre in which this play is playing; three cleaning* WOMEN *with mops and pails.*)

The X Theatre. During the daily cleaning of this theatre a number of lost objects were collected as usual by Mesdames Simpson, Pateslewski, and Moriarty.

Among these objects found today was a wedding ring, inscribed: To Eva from Adam. Genesis II:18. The ring will be restored to the owner or owners, if their credentials are satisfactory.

Tippehatchee, Vermont:

(*Slide representing a glacier.*)

The unprecedented cold weather of this summer has produced a condition that has not yet been satisfactorily explained. There is a report that a wall of ice is moving southward across these counties. The disruption of communications by the cold wave now crossing the country has rendered exact information difficult, but little credence is given to the rumor that the ice had pushed the Cathedral of Montreal as far as St. Albans, Vermont.

For further information see your daily papers.

Excelsior, New Jersey:

(*Slide of a modest suburban home.*)

The home of Mr. George Antrobus, the inventor of the wheel. The discovery of the wheel, following so closely on the discovery of the lever, has centered the attention of the country on Mr. Antrobus of this attractive suburban residence district. This is his home, a commodious seven-room house, conveniently situated near a public school, a Methodist church, and a firehouse; it is right handy to an A. and P.

(*Slide of* MR. ANTROBUS *on his front steps, smiling and lifting his straw hat. He holds a wheel.*)

Mr. Antrobus, himself. He comes of very old stock and has made his way up from next to nothing.

It is reported that he was once a gardener, but left that situation under circumstances that have been variously reported.

Mr. Antrobus is a veteran of foreign wars, and bears a number of scars, front and back.

(*Slide of* MRS. ANTROBUS, *holding some roses.*)

This is Mrs. Antrobus, the charming and gracious president of the Excelsior Mothers' Club.

Mrs. Antrobus is an excellent needlewoman; it is she who invented the apron on which so many interesting changes have been rung since.

(*Slide of the* FAMILY *and* SABINA.)

Here we see the Antrobuses with their two children, Henry and Gladys, and friend. The friend in the rear is Lily Sabina, the maid. I know we all want to congratulate this typical American family on its enterprise. We all wish Mr. Antrobus a successful future. Now the management takes you to the interior of this home for a brief visit.

(*Curtain rises. Living room of a commuter's home.* SABINA—*straw-blonde, over-rouged—is standing by the window back center, a feather duster under her elbow.*)

SABINA. Oh, oh, oh! Six o'clock and the master not home yet.

Pray God nothing serious has happened to him crossing the Hudson River. If anything happened to him, we would certainly be inconsolable and have to move into a less desirable residence district.

The fact is I don't know what'll become of us. Here it is the middle of August and the coldest day of the year. It's simply freezing; the dogs are sticking to the sidewalks; can anybody explain that? No.

But I'm not surprised. The whole world's at sixes and sevens, and why the house hasn't fallen down about our ears long ago is a miracle to me.

(A fragment of the right wall leans precariously over the stage. SABINA looks at it nervously and it slowly rights itself.)

Every night this same anxiety as to whether the master will get home safely: whether he'll bring home anything to eat. In the midst of life we are in the midst of death, a truer word was never said.

(The fragment of scenery flies up into the lofts. SABINA is struck dumb with surprise, shrugs her shoulders and starts dusting MR. ANTROBUS' chair, including the under side.)

Of course, Mr. Antrobus is a very fine man, an excellent husband and father, a pillar of the church, and has all the best interests of the community at heart. Of course, every muscle goes tight every time he passes a policeman; but what I think is that there are certain charges that ought not to be made, and I think I may add, ought not to be allowed to be made; we're all human; who isn't?

(She dusts MRS. ANTROBUS' rocking chair.)

Mrs. Antrobus is as fine a woman as you could hope to see. She lives only for her children; and if it would be any benefit to her children she'd see the rest of us stretched out dead at her feet without turning a hair—that's the truth. If you want to know anything more about Mrs. Antrobus, just go and look at a tigress, and look hard. As to the children— Well, Henry Antrobus is a real, clean-cut

American boy. He'll graduate from High School one of these days, if they make the alphabet any easier.—Henry, when he has a stone in his hand, has a perfect aim; he can hit anything from a bird to an older brother —Oh! I didn't mean to say that!—but it certainly was an unfortunate accident, and it was very hard getting the police out of the house.

Mr. and Mrs. Antrobus' daughter is named Gladys. She'll make some good man a good wife some day, if he'll just come down off the movie screen and ask her.

So here we are!

We've managed to survive for some time now, catch as catch can, the fat and the lean, and if the dinosaurs don't trample us to death, and if the grasshoppers don't eat up our garden, we'll all live to see better days, knock on wood.

Each new child that's born to the Antrobuses seems to them to be sufficient reason for the whole universe's being set in motion; and each new child that dies seems to them to have been spared a whole world of sorrow, and what the end of it will be is still very much an open question.

We've rattled along, hot and cold, for some time now—

(A portion of the wall above the door, right, flies up into the air and disappears.)

—and my advice to you is not to inquire into why or whither, but just enjoy your ice cream while it's on your plate—that's my philosophy.

Don't forget that a few years ago we came through the depression by the skin of our teeth! One more tight squeeze like that and where will we be?

(This is a cue line. SABINA looks angrily at the kitchen door and repeats:)

. . . we came through the depression by the skin of our teeth; one more tight squeeze like that and where will we be?

(Flustered, she looks through the opening in the right wall; then goes to the window and reopens the Act.)

Oh, oh, oh! Six o'clock and the master not

home yet. Pray God nothing has happened to him crossing the Hudson. Here it is the middle of August and the coldest day of the year. It's simply freezing; the dogs are sticking. One more tight squeeze like that and where will we be?

VOICE (*off-stage*). Make up something! Invent something!

SABINA. Well . . . uh . . . this certainly is a fine American home . . . and—uh . . . everybody's very happy . . . and—uh . . .

(*Suddenly flings pretense to the winds and coming downstage says with indignation:*)

I can't invent any words for this play, and I'm glad I can't. I hate this play and every word in it.

As for me, I don't understand a single word of it, anyway—all about the troubles the human race has gone through, there's a subject for you.

Besides, the author hasn't made up his silly mind as to whether we're all living back in caves or in New Jersey today, and that's the way it is all the way through.

Oh—why can't we have plays like we used to have—*Peg o' My Heart,* and *Smilin' Thru,* and *The Bat*—good entertainment with a message you can take home with you?

I took this hateful job because I had to. For two years I've sat up in my room living on a sandwich and a cup of tea a day, waiting for better times in the theatre. And look at me now: I—I who've played *Rain* and *The Barretts of Wimpole Street* and *First Lady*—God in Heaven!

(*The STAGE MANAGER puts his head out from the hole in the scenery.*)

MR. FITZPATRICK. Miss Somerset!! Miss Somerset!

SABINA. Oh! Anyway!—nothing matters! It'll all be the same in a hundred years.

(*Loudly.*)

We came through the depression by the skin of our teeth,—that's true!—one more tight squeeze like that and where will we be?

(*Enter MRS. ANTROBUS, a mother.*)

MRS. ANTROBUS. Sabina, you've let the fire go out.

SABINA (*in a lather*). One-thing-and-another; don't-know-whether-my-wits-are-upside-or-down; might-as-well-be-dead-as-alive-in-a-house-all-sixes-and-sevens.

MRS. ANTROBUS. You've let the fire go out. Here it is the coldest day of the year right in the middle of August and you've let the fire go out.

SABINA. Mrs. Antrobus, I'd like to give my two weeks' notice, Mrs. Antrobus. A girl like I can get a situation in a home where they're rich enough to have a fire in every room, Mrs. Antrobus, and a girl don't have to carry the responsibility of the whole house on her two shoulders. And a home without children, Mrs. Antrobus, because children are a thing only a parent can stand, and a truer word was never said; and a home, Mrs. Antrobus, where the master of the house don't pinch decent, self-respecting girls when he meets them in a dark corridor. I mention no names and make no charges. So you have my notice, Mrs. Antrobus. I hope that's perfectly clear.

MRS. ANTROBUS. You've let the fire go out!— Have you milked the mammoth?

SABINA. I don't understand a word of this play.—Yes, I've milked the mammoth.

MRS. ANTROBUS. Until Mr. Antrobus comes home we have no food and we have no fire. You'd better go over to the neighbors and borrow some fire.

SABINA. Mrs. Antrobus! I can't! I'd die on the way, you know I would. It's worse than January. The dogs are sticking to the sidewalks. I'd die.

MRS. ANTROBUS. Very well, I'll go.

SABINA (*even more distraught, coming forward and sinking on her knees*). You'd never come back alive; we'd all perish; if you weren't here, we'd just perish. How do we know Mr. Antrobus'll be back? We don't know. If you go out, I'll just kill myself.

MRS. ANTROBUS. Get up, Sabina.

SABINA. Every night it's the same thing. Will he come back safe, or won't he? Will we starve to death, or freeze to death, or boil to death or will we be killed by burglars? I don't know why we go on living. I don't know why we go on living at all. It's easier being dead.

> (*She flings her arms on the table and buries her head in them. In each of the succeeding speeches she flings her head up—and sometimes her hands— then quickly buries her head again.*)

MRS. ANTROBUS. The same thing! Always throwing up the sponge, Sabina. Always announcing your own death. But give you a new hat—or a plate of ice cream—or a ticket to the movies, and you want to live forever.

SABINA. You don't care whether we live or die; all you care about is those children. If it would be any benefit to them you'd be glad to see us all stretched out dead.

MRS. ANTROBUS. Well, maybe I would.

SABINA. And what do they care about? Themselves—that's all they care about.

> (*Shrilly.*)

They make fun of you behind your back. Don't tell me: they're ashamed of you. Half the time, they pretend they're someone else's children. Little thanks you get from them.

MRS. ANTROBUS. I'm not asking for any thanks.

SABINA. And Mr. Antrobus—you don't understand *him.* All that work he does—trying to discover the alphabet and the multiplication table. Whenever he tries to learn anything you fight against it.

MRS. ANTROBUS. Oh, Sabina, I know you. When Mr. Antrobus raped you home from your Sabine hills, he did it to insult me. He did it for your pretty face, and to insult me. You were the new wife, weren't you? For a year or two you lay on your bed all day and polished the nails on your hands and feet: You made puff-balls of the combings of your hair and you blew them up to the ceiling. And I washed your underclothes and I made you chicken broths.

I bore children and between my very groans I stirred the cream that you'd put on your face. But I knew you wouldn't last. You didn't last.

SABINA. But it was I who encouraged Mr. Antrobus to make the alphabet. I'm sorry to say it, Mrs. Antrobus, but you're not a beautiful woman, and you can never know what a man could do if he tried. It's girls like I who inspire the multiplication table. I'm sorry to say it, but you're not a beautiful woman, Mrs. Antrobus, and that's the God's truth.

MRS. ANTROBUS. And you didn't last—you sank to the kitchen. And what do you do there? *You let the fire go out!* No wonder to you it seems easier being dead. Reading and writing and counting on your fingers is all very well in their way—but I keep the home going.

MRS. ANTROBUS. —There's that dinosaur on the front lawn again.—Shoo! Go away. Go away.

> (*The baby* DINOSAUR *puts his head in the window.*)

DINOSAUR. It's cold.

MRS. ANTROBUS. You go around to the back of the house where you belong.

DINOSAUR. It's cold.

> (*The* DINOSAUR *disappears.* MRS. ANTROBUS *goes calmly out.* SABINA *slowly raises her head and speaks to the audience. The central portion of the center wall rises, pauses, and disappears into the loft.*)

SABINA. Now that you audience are listening to this, too, I understand it a little better. I wish eleven o'clock were here; I don't want to be dragged through this whole play again.

> (*The* TELEGRAPH BOY *is seen entering along the back wall of the stage from the right. She catches sight of him and calls:*)

Mrs. Antrobus! Mrs. Antrobus! Help! There's a strange man coming to the house.

He's coming up the walk, help!

(*Enter* MRS. ANTROBUS *in alarm, but efficient.*)

MRS. ANTROBUS. Help me quick!

(*They barricade the door by piling the furniture against it.*)

Who is it? What do you want?

TELEGRAPH BOY. A telegram for Mrs. Antrobus from Mr. Antrobus in the city.

SABINA. Are you sure, are you sure? Maybe it's just a trap!

MRS. ANTROBUS. I know his voice, Sabina. We can open the door.

(*Enter the* TELEGRAPH BOY, *12 years old, in uniform. The* DINOSAUR *and* MAMMOTH *slip by him into the room and settle down front right.*)

I'm sorry we kept you waiting. We have to be careful, you know.

(*To the* ANIMALS.)

H'm . . . Will you be quiet?

(*They nod.*)

Have you had your supper?

(*They nod.*)

Are you *ready* to come in?

(*They nod.*)

Young man, have you any fire with you? Then light the grate, will you?

(*He nods, produces something like a briquet; and kneels by the imagined fireplace, footlights center. Pause.*)

What are people saying about this cold weather?

(*He makes a doubtful shrug with his shoulders.*)

Sabina, take this stick and go and light the stove.

SABINA. Like I told you, Mrs. Antrobus; two weeks. That's the law. I hope that's perfectly clear. (*Exit.*)

MRS. ANTROBUS. What about this cold weather?

TELEGRAPH BOY (*lowered eyes*). Of course, I don't know anything . . . but they say there's a wall of ice moving down from the North, that's what they say. We can't get Boston by telegraph, and they're burning pianos in Hartford.
. . . It moves everything in front of it, churches and post offices and city halls.
I live in Brooklyn myself.

MRS. ANTROBUS. What are people doing about it?

TELEGRAPH BOY. Well . . . uh . . . Talking, mostly.
Or just what you'd do a day in February.
There are some that are trying to go South and the roads are crowded; but you can't take old people and children very far in a cold like this.

MRS. ANTROBUS. —What's this telegram you have for me?

TELEGRAPH BOY (*fingertips to his forehead*). If you wait just a minute; I've got to remember it.

(*The* ANIMALS *have left their corner and are nosing him. Presently they take places on either side of him, leaning against his hips, like heraldic beasts.*)

This telegram was flashed from Murray Hill to University Heights! And then by puffs of smoke from University Heights to Staten Island.
And then by lantern from Staten Island to Plainfield, New Jersey. What hath God wrought!

(*He clears his throat.*)

"To Mrs. Antrobus, Excelsior, New Jersey:
"My dear wife, will be an hour late. Busy day at the office. Don't worry the children about the cold just keep them warm burn everything except Shakespeare."

(*Pause.*)

MRS. ANTROBUS. Men! —He knows I'd burn ten Shakespeares to prevent a child of mine from having one cold in the head. What does it say next?

(*Enter* SABINA.)

TELEGRAPH BOY. "Have made great discoveries today have separated em from en."

SABINA. I know what that is, that's the alphabet, yes it is. Mr. Antrobus is just the cleverest man. Why, when the alphabet's finished, we'll be able to tell the future and everything.

TELEGRAPH BOY. Then listen to this: "Ten tens make a hundred semi-colon consequences far-reaching." (*Watches for effect.*)

MRS. ANTROBUS. The earth's turning to ice, and all he can do is to make up new numbers.

TELEGRAPH BOY. Well, Mrs. Antrobus, like the head man at our office said: a few more discoveries like that and we'll be worth freezing.

MRS. ANTROBUS. What does he say next?

TELEGRAPH BOY. I . . . I can't do this last part very well.

(*He clears his throat and sings.*)

"Happy w'dding ann'vers'ry to you, Happy ann'-vers'ry to you—"

(*The* ANIMALS *begin to howl soulfully;* SABINA *screams with pleasure.*)

MRS. ANTROBUS. Dolly! Frederick! Be quiet.

TELEGRAPH BOY (*above the din*). "Happy w'dding ann'-vers'ry, dear Eva; happy w'dding ann'vers'ry to you."

MRS. ANTROBUS. Is that in the telegram? Are they singing telegrams now?

(*He nods.*)

The earth's getting so silly no wonder the sun turns cold.

SABINA. Mrs. Antrobus, I want to take back the notice I gave you. Mrs. Antrobus, I don't want to leave a house that gets such interesting telegrams and I'm sorry for anything I said. I really am.

MRS. ANTROBUS. Young man, I'd like to give you something for all this trouble; Mr. Antrobus isn't home yet and I have no money and no food in the house—

TELEGRAPH BOY. Mrs. Antrobus . . . I don't like to . . . appear to . . . ask for anything, but . . .

MRS. ANTROBUS. What is it you'd like?

TELEGRAPH BOY. Do you happen to have an old needle you could spare? My wife just sits home all day thinking about needles.

SABINA (*shrilly*). We only got two in the house. Mrs. Antrobus, you know we only got two in the house.

MRS. ANTROBUS (*after a look at* SABINA *taking a needle from her collar*). Why yes, I can spare this.

TELEGRAPH BOY (*lowered eyes*). Thank you, Mrs. Antrobus. Mrs. Antrobus, can I ask you something else? I have two sons of my own; if the cold gets worse, what should I do?

SABINA. I think we'll all perish, that's what I think. Cold like this in August is just the end of the whole world.

(*Silence.*)

MRS. ANTROBUS. I don't know. After all, what does one do about anything? Just keep as warm as you can. And don't let your wife and children see that you're worried.

TELEGRAPH BOY. Yes. . . . Thank you, Mrs. Antrobus. Well, I'd better be going.—Oh, I forgot! There's one more sentence in the telegram. "Three cheers have invented the wheel."

MRS. ANTROBUS. A wheel? What's a wheel?

TELEGRAPH BOY. I don't know. That's what it said. The sign for it is like this. Well, goodbye.

(*The* WOMEN *see him to the door, with goodbyes and injunctions to keep warm.*)

SARINA (*apron to her eyes, wailing*). Mrs. Antrobus, it looks to me like all the nice men in the world are already married; I don't know why that is. (*Exit.*)

MRS. ANTROBUS (*thoughtful; to the* ANIMALS). Do you remember hearing tell of any cold like this in August?

(*The* ANIMALS *shake their heads.*)

From your grandmothers or anyone?

(*They shake their heads.*)

Have you any suggestions?

(*They shake their heads. She pulls her shawl around, goes to the front door and opening it an inch calls:*)

HENRY. GLADYS. CHILDREN. Come right in and get warm. No, no, when mama says a thing she means it.
Henry! HENRY. Put down that stone. You know what happened last time.

(*Shriek.*)

HENRY! Put down that stone!
Gladys! Put down your dress!! Try and be a lady.

(*The* CHILDREN *bound in and dash to the fire. They take off their winter things and leave them in heaps on the floor.*)

GLADYS. Mama, I'm hungry. Mama, why is it so cold?

HENRY (*at the same time*). Mama, why doesn't it snow? Mama, when's supper ready? Maybe it'll snow and we can make snowballs.

GLADYS. Mama, it's so cold that in one more minute I just couldn't of stood it.

MRS. ANTROBUS. Settle down, both of you, I want to talk to you.

(*She draws up a hassock and sits front center over the orchestra pit before the imaginary fire. The* CHILDREN *stretch out on the floor, leaning against her lap. Tableau by Raphael. The* ANIMALS *edge up and complete the triangle.*)

It's just a cold spell of some kind. Now listen to what I'm saying:
When your father comes home I want you to be extra quiet.
He's had a hard day at the office and I don't know but what he may have one of his moods.

I just got a telegram from him very happy and excited, and you know what that means. Your father's temper's uneven; I guess you know that.

(*Shriek.*)

Henry! Henry!
Why—why can't you remember to keep your hair down over your forehead? You must keep that scar covered up. Don't you know that when your father sees it he loses all control over himself? He goes crazy. He wants to die.

(*After a moment's despair she collects herself decisively, wets the hem of her apron in her mouth and starts polishing his forehead vigorously.*)

Lift your head up. Stop squirming. Blessed me, sometimes I think that it's going away— and then there it is: just as red as ever.

HENRY. Mama, today at school two teachers forgot and called me by my old name. They forgot, Mama. You'd better write another letter to the principal, so that he'll tell them I've changed my name. Right out in class they called me: Cain.

MRS. ANTROBUS (*putting her hand on his mouth, too late; hoarsely*). Don't say it.

(*Polishing feverishly.*)

If you're good they'll forget it. Henry, you didn't hit anyone . . . today, did you?

HENRY. Oh . . . no-o-o!

MRS. ANTROBUS (*still working, not looking at Gladys*). And, Gladys, I want you to be especially nice to your father tonight. You know what he calls you when you're good— his little angel, his little star. Keep your dress down like a little lady. And keep your voice nice and low. Gladys Antrobus!! What's that red stuff you have on your face?

(*Slaps her.*)

You're a filthy detestable child!

(*Rises in real, though temporary, repudiation and despair.*)

Get away from me, both of you! I wish I'd never seen sight or sound of you. Let the cold come! I can't stand it. I don't want to go on. (*She walks away.*)

GLADYS (*weeping*). All the girls at school do, Mama.

MRS. ANTROBUS (*shrieking*). I'm through with you, that's all!—Sabina! Sabina!—Don't you know your father'd go crazy if he saw that paint on your face? Don't you know your father thinks you're perfect? Don't you know he couldn't live if he didn't think you were perfect?—Sabina!

(*Enter* SABINA.)

SABINA. Yes, Mrs. Antrobus!

MRS. ANTROBUS. Take this girl out into the kitchen and wash her face with the scrubbing brush.

MR. ANTROBUS (*outside, roaring*). "I've been working on the railroad, all the livelong day . . . etc."

(*The* ANIMALS *start running around in circles, bellowing.* SABINA *rushes to the window.*)

MRS. ANTROBUS. Sabina, what's that noise outside?

SABINA. Oh, it's a drunken tramp. It's a giant, Mrs. Antrobus. We'll all be killed in our beds, I know it!

MRS. ANTROBUS. Help me quick. Quick. Everybody.

(*Again they stack all the furniture against the door.* MR. ANTROBUS *pounds and bellows.*)

Who is it? What do you want?—Sabina, have you any boiling water ready?—Who is it?

MR. ANTROBUS. Broken-down camel of a pig's snout, open this door.

MRS. ANTROBUS. God be praised! It's your father.—Just a minute, George!—Sabina, clear the door, quick. Gladys, come here while I clean your nasty face!

MR. ANTROBUS. She-bitch of a goat's gizzard, I'll break every bone in your body. Let me in or I'll tear the whole house down.

MRS. ANTROBUS. Just a minute, George, something's the matter with the lock.

MR. ANTROBUS. Open the door or I'll tear your livers out. I'll smash your brains on the ceiling, and Devil take the hindmost.

MRS. ANTROBUS. Now, you can open the door, Sabina. I'm ready.

(*The door is flung open. Silence.* MR. ANTROBUS—*face of a Keystone Comedy Cop—stands there in fur cap and blanket. His arms are full of parcels, including a large stone wheel with a center in it. One hand carries a railroad man's lantern. Suddenly he bursts into joyous roar.*)

MR. ANTROBUS. Well, how's the whole crooked family?

(*Relief. Laughter. Tears. Jumping up and down.* ANIMALS *cavorting.* ANTROBUS *throws the parcels on the ground. Hurls his cap and blanket after them. Heroic embraces. Melee of* HUMANS *and* ANIMALS, SABINA *included.*)

I'll be scalded and tarred if a man can't get a little welcome when he comes home. Well, Maggie, you old gunny-sack, how's the broken down old weather hen?—Sabina, old fishbait, old skunkpot.—And the children—how've the little smellers been?

GLADYS. Papa, Papa, Papa, Papa, Papa.

MR. ANTROBUS. How've they been, Maggie?

MRS. ANTROBUS. Well, I must say, they've been as good as gold. I haven't had to raise my voice once. I don't know what's the matter with them.

ANTROBUS (*kneeling before* GLADYS). Papa's little weasel, eh?—Sabina, there's some food for you.—Papa's little gopher?

GLADYS (*her arm around his neck*). Papa, you're always teasing me.

ANTROBUS. And Henry? Nothing rash today, I hope. Nothing rash?

HENRY. No, Papa.

ANTROBUS (*roaring*). Well that's good, that's good—I'll bet Sabina let the fire go out.

SABINA. Mr. Antrobus, I've given my notice. I'm leaving two weeks from today. I'm sorry, but I'm leaving.

ANTROBUS (*roar*). Well, if you leave now you'll freeze to death, so go and cook the dinner.

SABINA. Two weeks, that's the law. (*Exit.*)

ANTROBUS. Did you get my telegram?

MRS. ANTROBUS. Yes.—What's a wheel?

(*He indicates the wheel with a glance. HENRY is rolling it around the floor. Rapid, hoarse interchange:* MRS. ANTROBUS: *What does this cold weather mean? It's below freezing.* ANTROBUS: *Not before the children!* MRS. ANTROBUS: *Shouldn't we do something about it—start off, move?* ANTROBUS: *Not before the children!!! He gives* HENRY *a sharp slap.*)

HENRY. Papa, you hit me!

ANTROBUS. Well, remember it. That's to make you remember today. Today. The day the alphabet's finished; and the day that we *saw* the hundred—the hundred, the hundred, the hundred, the hundred, the hundred—there's no end to 'em.
I've had a day at the office!
Take a look at that wheel, Maggie—when I've got that to rights: you'll see a sight.
There's a reward there for all the walking you've done.

MRS. ANTROBUS. How do you mean?

ANTROBUS (*on the hassock looking into the fire; with awe*). Maggie, we've reached the top of the wave. There's not much more to be done. We're there!

MRS. ANTROBUS (*cutting across his mood sharply*). And the ice?

ANTROBUS. The ice!

HENRY (*playing with the wheel*). Papa, you could put a chair on this.

ANTROBUS (*broodingly*). Ye-e-s, any booby can fool with it now—but I thought of it first.

MRS. ANTROBUS. Children, go out in the kitchen. I want to talk to your father alone.

(*The* CHILDREN *go out.* ANTROBUS *has moved to his chair up left. He takes the goldfish bowl on his lap; pulls the canary cage down to the level of his face. Both the* ANIMALS *put their paws up on the arm of his chair.* MRS. ANTROBUS *faces him across the room, like a judge.*)

MRS. ANTROBUS. Well?

ANTROBUS (*shortly*). It's cold.—How things been, eh? Keck, keck, keck.—And you, Millicent?

MRS. ANTROBUS. I know it's cold.

ANTROBUS (*to the canary*). No spilling of sunflower seed, eh? No singing after lights-out, y'know what I mean?

MRS. ANTROBUS. You can try and prevent us freezing to death, can't you? You can do something? We can start moving. Or we can go on the animals' backs?

ANTROBUS. The best thing about animals is that they don't talk much.

MAMMOTH. It's cold.

ANTROBUS. Eh, eh, eh! Watch that!—
—By midnight we'd turn to ice. The roads are full of people now who can scarcely lift a foot from the ground. The grass out in front is like iron—which reminds me, I have another needle for you.—The people up north—where are they? Frozen . . . crushed. . . .

MRS. ANTROBUS. Is that what's going to happen to us?—Will you answer me?

ANTROBUS. I don't know. I don't know anything. Some say that the ice is going slower. Some say that it's stopped. The sun's growing cold. What can I do about that? Nothing we can do but burn everything in the house, and the fenceposts and the barn. Keep the fire going. When we have no more fire, we die.

MRS. ANTROBUS. Well, why didn't you say so in the first place?

(MRS. ANTROBUS *is about to march off when she catches sight of two* REFU-GEES, *men, who have appeared against the back wall of the theatre and who are soon joined by others.*)

REFUGEES. Mr. Antrobus! Mr. Antrobus! Mr. An-nn-tro-bus!

MRS. ANTROBUS. Who's that? Who's that calling you?

ANTROBUS (*clearing his throat guiltily*). H'm —let me see.

(*Two* REFUGEES *come up to the window.*)

REFUGEE. Could we warm our hands for a moment, Mr. Antrobus. It's very cold, Mr. Antrobus.

ANOTHER REFUGEE. Mr. Antrobus, I wonder if you have a piece of bread or something that you could spare.

(*Silence. They wait humbly.* MRS. AN-TROBUS *stands rooted to the spot. Suddenly a knock at the door, then another hand knocking in short rapid blows.*)

MRS. ANTROBUS. Who are these people? Why, they're all over the front yard. What have they come *here* for?

(*Enter* SABINA.)

SABINA. Mrs. Antrobus! There are some tramps knocking at the back door.

MRS. ANTROBUS. George, tell these people to go away. Tell them to move right along. I'll go and send them away from the back door. Sabina, come with me. (*She goes out energetically.*)

ANTROBUS. Sabina! Stay here! I have something to say to you.

(*He goes to the door and opens it a crack and talks through it.*)

Ladies and gentlemen! I'll have to ask you to wait a few minutes longer. It'll be all right . . . while you're waiting you might each one pull up a stake of the fence. We'll need them all for the fireplace. There'll be coffee and sandwiches in a moment.

(SABINA *looks out door over his shoulder and suddenly extends her arm pointing, with a scream.*)

SABINA. Mr. Antrobus, what's that??—that big white thing? Mr. Antrobus, it's ICE. It's ICE!!

ANTROBUS. Sabina, I want you to go in the kitchen and make a lot of coffee. Make a whole pail full.

SABINA. Pail full!!

ANTROBUS (*with gesture*). And sandwiches . . . piles of them . . . like this.

SABINA. Mr. An . . . !!

(*Suddenly she drops the play, and says in her own person as* MISS SOMERSET, *with surprise.*)

Oh, *I* see what this part of the play means now! This means refugees.

(*She starts to cross to the proscenium.*)

Oh, I don't like it. I don't like it.

(*She leans against the proscenium and bursts into tears.*)

ANTROBUS. Miss Somerset!

STAGE MANAGER (*off-stage*). Miss Somerset!

SABINA (*energetically, to the audience*). Ladies and gentlemen! Don't take this play serious. The world's not coming to an end. You know it's not. People exaggerate! Most people really have enough to eat and a roof over their heads. Nobody actually starves— you can always eat grass or something. That ice business—why, it was a long, long time ago. Besides they were only savages. Savages don't love their families—not like we do.

ANTROBUS *and* STAGE MANAGER. Miss Somerset!!

(*There is renewed knocking at the door.*)

SABINA. All right. I'll say the lines, but I won't think about the play.

(*Enter* MRS. ANTROBUS.)

SABINA (*parting thrust at the audience*). And I advise *you* not to think about the play, either. (*Exit* SABINA.)

MRS. ANTROBUS. George, these tramps say that you asked them to come to the house. What does this mean?

(*Knocking at the door.*)

ANTROBUS. Just . . . uh . . . There are a few friends, Maggie, I met on the road. Real nice, real useful people. . . .

MRS. ANTROBUS. (*back to the door*). Now, don't you ask them in!
George Antrobus, not another soul comes in here over my dead body.

ANTROBUS. Maggie, there's a doctor there. Never hurts to have a good doctor in the house. We've lost a peck of children, one way and another. You can never tell when a child's throat will get stopped up. What you and I have seen—!!! (*He puts his fingers on his throat, and imitates diphtheria.*)

MRS. ANTROBUS. Well, just one person then, the Doctor. The others can go right along the road.

ANTROBUS. Maggie, there's an old man, particular friend of mine—

MRS. ANTROBUS. I won't listen to you—

ANTROBUS. It was he that really started off the A.B.C.'s.

MRS. ANTROBUS. I don't care if he perishes. We can do without reading or writing. We can't do without food.

ANTROBUS. Then let the ice come!! Drink your coffee!! I don't want any coffee if I can't drink it with some good people.

MRS. ANTROBUS. Stop shouting. Who else is there trying to push us off the cliff?

ANTROBUS. Well, there's the man . . . who makes all the laws. Judge Moses!

MRS. ANTROBUS. Judges can't help us now.

ANTROBUS. And if the ice melts? . . . and if we pull through? Have you and I been able to bring up Henry? What have we done?

MRS. ANTROBUS. Who are those old women?

ANTROBUS (*coughs*). Up in town there are nine sisters. There are three or four of them

here. They're sort of music teachers . . . and one of them recites and one of them—

MRS. ANTROBUS. That's the end. A singing troupe! Well, take your choice, live or die. Starve your own children before your face.

ANTROBUS (*gently*). These people don't take much.
They're used to starving.
They'll sleep on the floor.
Besides, Maggie, listen: no, listen:
Who've we got in the house, but Sabina? Sabina's always afraid the worst will happen. Whose spirits can she keep up?
Maggie, these people never give up. They think they'll live and work forever.

MRS. ANTROBUS (*walks slowly to the middle of the room*). All right, let them in. Let them in. You're master here.
(*Softly.*)
—But these animals must go. Enough's enough. They'll soon be big enough to push the walls down, anyway. Take them away.

ANTROBUS (*sadly*). All right. The dinosaur and mammoth—! Come on, baby, come on, Frederick. Come for a walk. That's a good little fellow.

DINOSAUR. It's cold.

ANTROBUS. Yes, nice cold fresh air. Bracing.

(*He holds the door open and the ANI-MALS go out. He beckons to his friends. The REFUGEES are typical elderly out-of-works from the streets of New York today. JUDGE MOSES wears a skull cap. HOMER is a blind beggar with a guitar. The seedy crowd shuffles in and waits humbly and expectantly. ANTROBUS introduces them to his wife who bows to each with a stately bend of her head.*)

Make yourself at home. Maggie, this is the doctor . . . m . . . Coffee'll be here in a minute. . . . Professor, this is my wife. . . . And . . . Judge . . . Maggie, you know the Judge.

(*An old blind man with a guitar.*)

Maggie, you know . . . you know Homer?— Come right in, Judge.—

Miss Muse—are some of your sisters here? Come right in. . . .

Miss E. Muse; Miss T. Muse, Miss M. Muse.

MRS. ANTROBUS. Pleased to meet you. Just . . . make yourself comfortable. Supper'll be ready in a minute. (*She goes out, abruptly.*)

ANTROBUS. Make yourself at home, friends. I'll be right back.

(*He goes out. The* REFUGEES *stare about them in awe. Presently several voices start whispering "Homer! Homer!" All take it up.* HOMER *strikes a chord or two on his guitar, then starts to speak:*)

HOMER.

> Μῆνιν ἄειδε, θεὰ, Πηληϊάδεω
> Ἀχιλῆος, οὐλομένην, ἡ μυρί'
> Ἀχαιοῖς ἄλγε' ἔθηκε πολλὰς
> δ' ἰφθίμους ψυχὰς—

(HOMER'S *face shows he is lost in thought and memory and the words die away on his lips. The* REFUGEES *likewise nod in dreamy recollection. Soon the whisper "Moses, Moses!" goes around. An aged Jew parts his beard and recites dramatically:*)

MOSES.

> בְּרֵאשִׁית בָּרָא אֱלֹהִים אֵת הַשָּׁמַיִם וְאֵת הָאָרֶץ: וְהָאָרֶץ הָיְתָה תֹהוּ
> וָבֹהוּ וְחֹשֶׁךְ עַל־פְּנֵי תְהוֹם וְרוּחַ אֱלֹהִים מְרַחֶפֶת עַל־פְּנֵי הַמָּיִם:

(*The same dying away of the words take place, and on the part of the* REFUGEES *the same retreat into recollection. Some of them murmur, "Yes, yes." The mood is broken by the abrupt entrance of* MR. *and* MRS. ANTROBUS *and* SABINA *bearing platters of sandwiches and a pail of coffee.* SABINA *stops and stares at the guests.*)

MR. ANTROBUS. Sabina, pass the sandwiches.

SABINA. I thought I was working in a respectable house that had respectable guests. I'm giving my notice, Mr. Antrobus: two weeks, that's the law.

MR. ANTROBUS. Sabina! Pass the sandwiches.

SABINA. Two weeks, that's the law.

MR. ANTROBUS. There's the law. That's Moses.

SABINA (*stares*). The Ten Commandments—

FAUGH!!—(*To audience.*) That's the worst line I've ever had to say on any stage.

ANTROBUS. I think the best thing to do is just not to stand on ceremony; but pass the sandwiches around from left to right.—Judge, help yourself to one of these.

MRS. ANTROBUS. The roads are crowded, I hear?

THE GUESTS (*all talking at once*). Oh, ma'am, you can't imagine. . . . You can hardly put one foot before you . . . people are trampling one another.

(*Sudden silence.*)

MRS. ANTROBUS. Well, you know what I think it is—I think it's sun-spots!

THE GUESTS (*discreet hubbub*). Oh, you're right, Mrs. Antrobus . . . that's what it is. . . . That's what I was saying the other day.

(*Sudden silence.*)

ANTROBUS. Well, I don't believe the whole world's going to turn to ice.

(*All eyes are fixed on him, waiting.*)

I can't believe it. Judge! Have we worked for nothing? Professor! Have we just failed in the whole thing?

MRS. ANTROBUS. It is certainly very strange —well, fortunately on both sides of the family we come of very hearty stock.—Doctor, I want you to meet my children. They're eating their supper now. And of course I want them to meet you.

MISS M. MUSE. How many children have you, Mrs. Antrobus?

MRS. ANTROBUS. I have two—a boy and a girl.

MOSES (*softly*). I understand you had two sons, Mrs. Antrobus.

(MRS. ANTROBUS *in blind suffering; she walks toward the footlights.*)

MRS. ANTROBUS (*in a low voice*). Abel, Abel, my son, my son, Abel, my son, Abel, Abel, my son.

(*The* REFUGEES *move with few steps toward her as though in comfort murmuring words in Greek, Hebrew, German, et cetera. A piercing shriek from the kitchen—*SABINA'S *voice. All heads turn.*)

ANTROBUS. What's that?

(SABINA *enters, bursting with indignation, pulling on her gloves.*)

SABINA. Mr. Antrobus—that son of yours, that boy Henry Antrobus—I don't stay in this house another moment!—He's not fit to live among respectable folks and that's a fact.

MRS. ANTROBUS. Don't say another word, Sabina. I'll be right back.

(*Without waiting for an answer she goes past her into the kitchen.*)

SABINA. Mr. Antrobus, Henry has thrown a stone again and if he hasn't killed the boy that lives next door, I'm very much mistaken. He finished his supper and went out to play; and I heard such a fight; and then I saw it. I saw it with my own eyes. And it looked to me like stark murder.

(MRS. ANTROBUS *appears at the kitchen door, shielding* HENRY *who follows her. When she steps aside, we see on* HENRY'S *forehead a large ochre and scarlet scar in the shape of a C.* MR. ANTROBUS *starts toward him. A pause.* HENRY *is heard saying under his breath:*)

HENRY. He was going to take the wheel away from me. He started to throw a stone at me first.

MRS. ANTROBUS. George, it was just a boyish impulse. Remember how young he is.

(*Louder, in an urgent wail.*)

George, he's only four thousand years old.

SABINA. And everything was going along so nicely!

(*Silence.* ANTROBUS *goes back to the fireplace.*)

ANTROBUS. Put out the fire! Put out all the fires.

(*Violently.*)

No wonder the sun grows cold.

(*He starts stamping on the fireplace.*)

MRS. ANTROBUS. Doctor! Judge! Help me!— George, have you lost your mind?

ANTROBUS. There is no mind. We'll not try to live.

(*To the guests.*)

Give it up. Give up trying.

(MRS. ANTROBUS *seizes him.*)

SABINA. Mr. Antrobus! I'm downright ashamed of you.

MRS. ANTROBUS. George, have some more coffee.—Gladys! Where's Gladys gone?

(GLADYS *steps in, frightened.*)

GLADYS. Here I am, mama.

MRS. ANTROBUS. Go upstairs and bring your father's slippers. How could you forget a thing like that, when you know how tired he is?

(ANTROBUS *sits in his chair. He covers his face with his hands.* MRS. ANTROBUS *turns to the* REFUGEES:)

Can't some of you sing? It's your business in life to sing, isn't it? Sabina!

(*Several of the women clear their throats tentatively, and with frightened faces gather around* HOMER'S *guitar. He establishes a few chords. Almost inaudibly they start singing, led by* SABINA: *"Jingle Bells."* MRS. ANTROBUS *continues to* ANTROBUS *in a low voice, while taking off his shoes:*)

George, remember all the other times. When the volcanoes came right up in the front yard. And the time the grasshoppers ate every single leaf and blade of grass, and all the grain and spinach you'd grown with your own hands. And the summer there were earthquakes every night.

ANTROBUS. Henry! Henry!

(*Puts his hand on his forehead.*)

Myself. All of us, we're covered with blood.

MRS. ANTROBUS. Then remember all the times you were pleased with him and when you were proud of yourself.—Henry! Henry! Come here and recite to your father the multiplication table that you do so nicely.

(HENRY *kneels on one knee beside his father and starts whispering the multiplication table.*)

HENRY (*finally*). Two times six is twelve; three times six is eighteen—I don't think I know the sixes.

(*Enter* GLADYS *with the slippers.* MRS. ANTROBUS *makes stern gestures to her: Go in there and do your best. The* GUESTS *are now singing "Tenting To-night.*")

GLADYS (*putting slippers on his feet*). Papa . . . papa . . . I was very good in school today. Miss Conover said right out in class that if all the girls had as good manners as Gladys Antrobus, that the world would be a very different place to live in.

MRS. ANTROBUS. You recited a piece at assembly, didn't you? Recite it to your father.

GLADYS. Papa, do you want to hear what I recited in class?

(*Fierce directorial glance from her mother.*)

"THE STAR" by Henry Wadsworth LONGFELLOW.

MRS. ANTROBUS. Wait!!! The fire's going out. There isn't enough wood! Henry, go upstairs and bring down the chairs and start breaking up the beds.

(*Exit* HENRY. *The singers return to "Jingle Bells," still very softly.*)

GLADYS. Look, Papa, here's my report card. Lookit. Conduct A! Look, Papa. Papa, do you want to hear the Star, by Henry Wadsworth Longfellow? Papa, you're not mad at

me, are you?—I know it'll get warmer. Soon it'll be just like spring, and we can go to a picnic at the Hibernian Picnic Grounds like you always like to do, don't you remember? Papa, just look at me once.

(*Enter* HENRY *with some chairs.*)

ANTROBUS. You recited in assembly, did you?

(*She nods eagerly.*)

You didn't forget it?

GLADYS. No!!! I was perfect.

(*Pause. Then* ANTROBUS *rises, goes to the front door and opens it. The* REFUGEES *draw back timidly; the song stops; he peers out of the door, then closes it.*)

ANTROBUS (*with decision, suddenly*). Build up the fire. It's cold. Build up the fire. We'll do what we can. Sabina, get some more wood. Come around the fire, everybody. At least the young ones may pull through. Henry, have you eaten something?

HENRY. Yes, papa.

ANTROBUS. Gladys, have you had some supper?

GLADYS. I ate in the kitchen, papa.

ANTROBUS. If you do come through this— what'll you be able to do? What do you know? Henry, did you take a good look at that wheel?

HENRY. Yes, papa.

ANTROBUS. (*sitting down in his chair*). Six times two are—

HENRY. —twelve; six times three are eighteen: six times four are—Papa, it's hot and cold. It makes my head feel funny. It makes me sleepy.

ANTROBUS (*gives him a cuff*). Wake up. I don't care if your head is sleepy. Six times four are twenty-four. Six times five are—

HENRY. Thirty. Papa!

ANTROBUS. Maggie, put something into Gladys's head on the chance she can use it.

MRS. ANTROBUS. What do you mean, George?

ANTROBUS. Six times six are thirty-six.
Teach her the beginning of the Bible.

GLADYS. But, Mama, it's so cold and close.

(HENRY *has all but drowsed off. His
father slaps him sharply and the lesson
goes on.*)

MRS. ANTROBUS. "In the beginning God created the heavens and the earth; and the earth
was waste and void; and the darkness was
upon the face of the deep—"

(*The singing starts up again louder.
SABINA has returned with wood.*)

SABINA (*after placing wood on the fireplace
comes down to the footlights and addresses
the audience*). Will you please start handing
up your chairs? We'll need everything for
this fire. Save the human race.—Ushers, will
you pass the chairs up here? Thank you.

HENRY. Six times nine are fifty-four; six
times ten are sixty.

(*In the back of the auditorium the sound
of chairs being ripped up can be heard.
USHERS rush down the aisles with
chairs and hand them over.*)

GLADYS. "And God called the light Day and
the darkness he called Night."

SABINA. Pass up your chairs, everybody. Save
the human race.

ACT 2

SCENE: *Atlantic City Boardwalk.*

(*Toward the end of the intermission,
though with the house lights still up, lantern
slide projections begin to appear on the curtain. Timetables for trains leaving Pennsylvania Station for Atlantic City. Advertisements of Atlantic City hotels, drugstores,
churches, rug merchants; fortune tellers,
Bingo parlors.*

*When the house lights go down, the voice
of an* ANNOUNCER *is heard.*)

ANNOUNCER. The Management now brings
you the News Events of the World. Atlantic
City, New Jersey:

(*Projection of a chrome postcard of the
waterfront, trimmed in mica with the
legend: FUN AT THE BEACH*)

This great convention city is playing host this
week to the anniversary convocation of that
great fraternal order—the Ancient and Honorable Order of Mammals, Subdivision Humans. This great fraternal, militant and
burial society is celebrating on the Boardwalk, ladies and gentlemen, its six hundred
thousandth Annual Convention.
It has just elected its president for the ensuing term—

(*Projection of* MR. *and* MRS. ANTROBUS
*posed as they will be shown a few
moments later*)

Mr. George Antrobus of Excelsior, New Jersey. We show you President Antrobus and
his gracious and charming wife, every inch
a mammal. Mr. Antrobus has had a long
and chequered career. Credit has been paid
to him for many useful enterprises including
the introduction of the lever, of the wheel
and the brewing of beer. Credit has been also
extended to President Antrobus's gracious
and charming wife for many practical suggestions, including the hem, the gore, and
the gusset; and the novelty of the year—frying in oil. Before we show you Mr. Antrobus
accepting the nomination, we have an important announcement to make. As many of
you know, this great celebration of the Order
of the Mammals has received delegations
from the other rival Orders—or shall we say:
esteemed concurrent Orders: the WINGS, the
FINS, the SHELLS, and so on. These Orders
are holding their conventions also, in various
parts of the world, and have sent representatives to our own, two of a kind.
Later in the day we will show you President
Antrobus broadcasting his words of greeting
and congratulation to the collected assem-
blies of the whole natural world.
Ladies and Gentlemen! We give you President Antrobus!

(*The screen becomes a transparency.
MR. ANTROBUS stands beside a pedes-
tal; MRS. ANTROBUS is seated wearing*

a corsage of orchids. ANTROBUS *wears an untidy Prince Albert; spats; from a red rosette in his buttonhole hangs a fine long purple ribbon of honor. He wears a gay lodge hat—something between a fez and a legionnaire's cap.*)

ANTROBUS. Fellow-mammals, fellow-vertebrates, fellow-humans, I thank you. Little did my dear parents think—when they told me to stand on my own two feet—that I'd arrive at this place.

My friends, we have come a long way.

During this week of happy celebration it is perhaps not fitting that we dwell on some of the difficult times we have been through. The dinosaur is extinct—

(*Applause.*)

—the ice has retreated; and the common cold is being pursued by every means within our power.

(MRS. ANTROBUS *sneezes, laughs prettily, and murmers: "I beg your pardon."*)

In our memorial service yesterday we did honor to all our friends and relatives who are no longer with us, by reason of cold, earthquakes, plagues and . . . and . . . (*Coughs*) differences of opinion.

As our Bishop so ably said . . . uh . . . so ably said. . . .

MRS. ANTROBUS (*closed lips*). Gone, but not forgotten.

ANTROBUS. "They are gone, but not forgotten."

I think I can say, I think I can prophesy with complete . . . uh . . . with complete . . .

MRS. ANTROBUS. Confidence.

ANTROBUS. Thank you, my dear— With complete lack of confidence, that a new day of security is about to dawn.

The watchword of the closing year was: Work. I give you the watchword of the future: Enjoy Yourselves.

MRS. ANTROBUS. George, sit down!

ANTROBUS. Before I close, however, I wish to answer one of those unjust and malicious accusations that were brought against me during this last electoral campaign.

Ladies and gentlemen, the charge was made that at various points in my career I leaned toward joining some of the rival orders— that's a lie.

As I told reporters of the *Atlantic City Herald,* I do not deny that a few months before my birth I hesitated between . . . uh . . . between pin-feathers and gill-breathing— and so did many of us here—but for the last million years I have been viviparous, hairy and diaphragmatic.

(*Applause. Cries of "Good old Antrobus," "The Prince chap!" "Georgie," etc.*)

ANNOUNCER. Thank you. Thank you very much, Mr. Antrobus.

Now I know that our visitors will wish to hear a word from that gracious and charming mammal, Mrs. Antrobus, wife and mother— Mrs. Antrobus!

(MRS. ANTROBUS *rises, lays her program on her chair, bows and says:*)

MRS. ANTROBUS. Dear friends, I don't really think I should say anything. After all, it was my husband who was elected and not I.

Perhaps, as president of the Women's Auxiliary Bed and Board Society—I had some notes here, oh, yes, here they are—I should give a short report from some of our committees that have been meeting in this beautiful city.

Perhaps it may interest you to know that it has at last been decided that the tomato is edible. Can you all hear me? The tomato *is* edible.

A delegate from across the sea reports that the thread woven by the silkworm gives a cloth . . . I have a sample of it here . . . can you see it? smooth, elastic. I should say that it's rather attractive—though personally I prefer less shiny surfaces. Should the windows of a sleeping apartment be open or shut? I know all mothers will follow our debates on this matter with close interest. I am sorry to say that the most expert authorities have not yet decided. It does seem to me that the night air would be bound to be unhealthy for our children, but there are many distinguished authorities on both sides. Well, I could go on talking forever—as Shakespeare says: a woman's work is seldom done; but I think I'd better join my husband in saying thank you, and sit down. Thank you. (*She sits down*)

ANNOUNCER. Oh, Mrs. Antrobus!

MRS. ANTROBUS. Yes?

ANNOUNCER. We understand that you are about to celebrate a wedding anniversary. I know our listeners would like to extend their felicitations and hear a few words from you on that subject.

MRS. ANTROBUS. I have been asked by this kind gentleman . . . yes, my friends, this spring Mr. Antrobus and I will be celebrating our five thousandth wedding anniversary. I don't know if I speak for my husband, but I can say that, as for me, I regret every moment of it.

(*Laughter of confusion*)

I beg your pardon. What I *mean* to say is that I do not regret one moment of it. I hope none of you catch my cold. We have had two children. We've always had two children, though it hasn't always been the same two. But as I say, we have two fine children, and we're very grateful for that. Yes, Mr. Antrobus and I have been married five thousand years. Each wedding anniversary reminds me of the times when there were no weddings. We had to crusade for marriage. Perhaps there are some women within the sound of my voice who remember that crusade and those struggles; we fought for it, didn't we? We chained ourselves to lampposts and we made disturbances in the Senate—anyway, at last we women got the ring.

A few men helped us, but I must say that most men blocked our way at every step: they said we were unfeminine.

I only bring up these unpleasant memories, because I see some signs of backsliding from that great victory.

Oh, my fellow mammals, keep hold of that.

My husband says that the watchword for the year is Enjoy Yourself. I think that's very open to misunderstanding. My watchword for the year is: Save the Family. It's held together for over five thousand years: Save it! Thank you.

ANNOUNCER. Thank you, Mrs. Antrobus.

(*The transparency disappears*)

We had hoped to show you the Beauty Contest that took place here today.

President Antrobus, an experienced judge of pretty girls, gave the title of Miss Atlantic City 1942, to Miss Lily-Sabina Fairweather, charming hostess of our Boardwalk Bingo Parlor.

Unfortunately, however, our time is up, and I must take you to some views of the Convention City and conveeners—enjoying themselves.

(*A Burst of music; the curtain rises.*
The Boardwalk. The audience is sitting in the ocean. A handrail of scarlet cord stretches across the front of the stage. A ramp—also with scarlet handrail—descends to the right corner of the orchestra pit where a great scarlet beach umbrella or a cabana stands. Front and right stage left are benches facing the sea; attached to each bench is a street-lamp.

The only scenery is two cardboard cutouts six feet high, representing shops at the back of the stage. Reading from left to right they are: SALT WATER TAFFY; FORTUNE TELLER; then the blank space; BINGO PARLOR; TURKISH BATH. They have practical doors, that of the Fortune Teller's being hung with bright gypsy curtains.

By the left proscenium and rising from the orchestra pit is the weather signal; it is like the mast of a ship with cross bars. From time to time black discs are hung on it to indicate the storm and hurricane warnings. Three roller chairs, pushed by melancholy NEGROES file by empty. Throughout the act they traverse the stage in both directions.

From time to time, CONVEENERS, dressed like MR. ANTROBUS, cross the stage. Some walk sedately by; others engage in inane horseplay. The old gypsy FORTUNE TELLER is seated at the door of her shop, smoking a corncob pipe.

From the Bingo Parlor comes the voice of the CALLER.)

BINGO CALLER. A—Nine; A—Nine. C—Twenty-six; C—Twenty-six. A—Four; A—Four. B—Twelve.

CHORUS (*back-stage*). Bingo!!!

(*The front of the Bingo Parlor shudders, rises a few feet in the air and returns to the ground trembling*)

FORTUNE TELLER (*mechanically, to the unconscious back of a passerby, pointing with her pipe*). Bright's disease! Your partner's deceiving you in that Kansas City deal. You'll have six grandchildren. Avoid high places.

(*She rises and shouts after another:*)

Cirrhosis of the liver!

(SABINA *appears at the door of the Bingo Parlor. She hugs about her a blue raincoat that almost conceals her red bathing suit. She tries to catch the* FORTUNE TELLER'S *attention.*)

SABINA. Sssssst! Esmeralda! Sssssst!

FORTUNE TELLER. Keck!

SABINA. Has President Antrobus come along yet?

FORTUNE TELLER. No, no, no. Get back there. Hide yourself.

SABINA. I'm afraid I'll miss him. Oh, Esmeralda, if I fail in this, I'll die; I know I'll die. President Antrobus!!! And I'll be his wife! If it's the last thing I'll do, I'll be Mrs. George Antrobus.—Esmeralda, tell me my future.

FORTUNE TELLER. Keck!

SABINA. All right, I'll tell *you* my future.

(*Laughing dreamily and tracing it out with one finger on the palm of her hand*)

I've won the Beauty Contest in Atlantic City —well, I'll win the Beauty Contest of the whole world. I'll take President Antrobus away from that wife of his. Then I'll take every man away from his wife. I'll turn the whole earth upside down.

FORTUNE TELLER. Keck!

SABINA. When all those husbands just think about me they'll get dizzy. They'll faint in the streets. They'll have to lean against lampposts.—Esmeralda, who was Helen of Troy?

FORTUNE TELLER (*furiously*). Shut your foolish mouth. When Mr. Antrobus comes along you can see what you can do. Until then—go away.

(SABINA *laughs. As she returns to the door of her Bingo Parlor a group of* CONVEENERS *rush over and smother her with attentions: "Oh, Miss Lily, you know me. You've known me for years."*)

SABINA. Go away, boys, go away. I'm after bigger fry than you are.—Why, Mr. Simpson!! How *dare* you!! I expect that even you nobodies must have girls to amuse you; but where you find them and what you do with them is of absolutely no interest to me.

(*Exit. The* CONVEENERS *squeal with pleasure and stumble in after her. The* FORTUNE TELLER *rises, puts her pipe down on the stool, unfurls her voluminous skirts, gives a sharp wrench to her bodice and strolls towards the audience, swinging her hips like a young woman.*)

FORTUNE TELLER. I tell the future. Keck. Nothing easier. Everybody's future is in their face. Nothing easier.
But who can tell your past—eh? Nobody!
Your youth—where did it go? It slipped away while you weren't looking. While you were alseep. While you were drunk? Puh! You're like our friends, Mr. and Mrs. Antrobus; you lie awake nights trying to know your past. What did it mean? What was it trying to say to you?
Think! Think! Split your heads. I can't tell the past and neither can you. If anybody tries to tell you the past, take my word for it, they're charlatans! Charlatans! But I can tell the future.

(*She suddenly barks at a passing chairpusher*)

Apoplexy!

(She returns to the audience)

Nobody listens.—Keck! I see a face among you now—I won't embarrass him by pointing him out, listen, it may be you: Next year the watchsprings inside you will crumple up. Death by regret—Type Y. It's in the corners of your mouth. You'll decide that you should have lived for pleasure, but that you missed it. Death by regret—Type Y. . . . Avoid mirrors. You'll try to be angry—but no!—no anger.

(Far forward, confidentially)

And now what's the immediate future of our friends, the Antrobuses? Oh, you've seen it as well as I have, keck—that dizziness of the head; that Great Man dizziness? The inventor of beer and gunpowder. The sudden fits of temper and then the long stretches of inertia? "I'm a sultan; let my slave girls fan me"? You know as well as I what's coming. Rain. Rain. Rain in floods. The deluge. But first you'll see shameful things—shameful things. Some of you will be saying: "Let him drown. He's not worth saving. Give the whole thing up." I can see it in your faces. But you're wrong. Keep your doubts and despairs to yourselves.
Again there'll be the narrow escape. The survival of a handful. From destruction—total destruction.

(She points, sweeping with her hand, to the stage)

Even of the animals, a few will be saved: two of a kind, male and female, two of a kind.

(The heads of CONVEENERS appear about the stage and in the orchestra pit, jeering at her)

CONVEENERS. Charlatan! Madam Kill-joy! Mrs. Jeremiah! Charlatan!

FORTUNE TELLER. And *you!* Mark my words before it's too late. Where'll *you* be?

CONVEENERS. The croaking raven. Old dust and ashes. Rags, bottles, sacks.

FORTUNE TELLER. Yes, stick out your tongues. You can't stick your tongues out far enough to lick the death-sweat from your foreheads. It's too late to work now—bail out the flood with your soup spoons. You've had your chance and you've lost.

CONVEENERS. Enjoy yourselves!!!

(They disappear. The FORTUNE TELLER looks off left and puts her finger on her lip.)

FORTUNE TELLER. They're coming—the Antrobuses. Keck. Your hope. Your despair. Yourselves.

(Enter from the left, MR. and MRS. ANTROBUS and GLADYS)

MRS. ANTROBUS. Gladys Antrobus, stick your stummick in.

GLADYS. But it's easier this way.

MRS. ANTROBUS. Well, it's too bad the new president has such a clumsy daughter, that's all I can say. Try and be a lady.

FORTUNE TELLER. Aijah! That's been said a hundred billion times.

MRS. ANTROBUS. Goodness! Where's Henry! He was here just a minute ago. Henry!

(Sudden violent stir. A roller-chair appears from the left. About it are dancing in great excitement HENRY and a NEGRO CHAIR-PUSHER.)

HENRY *(slingshot in hand)*. I'll put your eye out. I'll make you yell, like you never yelled before.

NEGRO *(at the same time)*. Now, I warns you. I warns you. If you make me mad, you'll get hurt.

ANTROBUS. Henry! What is this? Put down that slingshot.

MRS. ANTROBUS *(at the same time)*. Henry! HENRY! Behave yourself.

FORTUNE TELLER. That's right, young man. There are too many people in the world as it is. Everybody's in the way, except one's self.

HENRY. All I wanted to do was—have some fun.

NEGRO. Nobody can't touch my chair, nobody, without I allow 'em to. You get clean away from me and you get away fast. (*He pushes his chair off, muttering*)

ANTROBUS. What are you doing, Henry?

HENRY. Everybody's always getting mad. Everybody's always trying to push you around. I'll make him sorry for this; I'll make him sorry.

ANTROBUS. Give me that slingshot.

HENRY. I won't. I'm sorry I came to this place. I wish I weren't here. I wish I weren't anywhere.

MRS. ANTROBUS. Now, Henry, don't get so excited about nothing. I declare I don't know what we're going to do with you. Put your slingshot in your pocket, and don't try to take hold of things that don't belong to you.

ANTROBUS After this you can stay home. I wash my hands of you.

MRS. ANTROBUS. Come now, let's forget all about it. Everybody take a good breath of that sea air and calm down.

(*A passing* CONVEENER *bows to* ANTROBUS *who nods to him*)

Who was that you spoke to, George?

ANTROBUS. Nobody, Maggie. Just the candidate who ran against me in the election.

MRS ANTROBUS. The man who ran against you in the election!!

(*She turns and waves her umbrella after the disappearing* CONVEENER)

My husband didn't speak to you and he never will speak to you.

ANTROBUS. Now, Maggie.

MRS. ANTROBUS. After those lies you told about him in your speeches! Lies, that's what they were.

GLADYS *and* HENRY. Mama, everybody's looking at you. Everybody's laughing at you.

MRS. ANTROBUS. If you must know, my husband's a SAINT, a downright SAINT, and you're not fit to speak to him on the street.

ANTROBUS. Now, Maggie, now, Maggie, that's enough of that.

MRS. ANTROBUS. George Antrobus, you're a perfect worm. If you won't stand up for yourself, I will.

GLADYS. Mama, you just act awful in public.

MRS. ANTROBUS (*laughing*). Well, I must say I enjoyed it. I feel better. Wish his wife had been there to hear it. Children, what do you want to do?

GLADYS. Papa, can we ride in one of those chairs? Mama, I want to ride in one of those chairs.

MRS. ANTROBUS. No, sir. If you're tired you just sit where you are. We have no money to spend on foolishness.

ANTROBUS. I guess we have money enough for a thing like that. It's one of the things you do at Atlantic City.

MRS. ANTROBUS. Oh, we have? I tell you it's a miracle my children have shoes to stand up in. I didn't think I'd ever live to see them pushed around in chairs.

ANTROBUS. We're on a vacation, aren't we? We have a right to some treats, I guess. Maggie, some day you're going to drive me crazy.

MRS. ANTROBUS. All right, go. I'll just sit here and laugh at you. And you can give me my dollar right in my hand. Mark my words, a rainy day is coming. There's a rainy day ahead of us. I feel it in my bones. Go on, throw your money around. I can starve. I've starved before. I know how.

(*A* CONVEENER *puts his head through Turkish Bath window, and says with raised eyebrows:*)

CONVEENER. Hello, George. How are ya? I see where you brought the WHOLE family along.

MRS. ANTROBUS. And what do you mean by that?

(CONVEENER *withdraws head and closes window*)

ANTROBUS. Maggie, I tell you there's a limit to what I can stand. God's Heaven, haven't

I worked *enough*? Don't I get any vacation? Can't I even give my children so much as a ride in a roller-chair?

MRS. ANTROBUS (*putting out her hand for raindrops*). Anyway, it's going to rain very soon and you have your broadcast to make.

ANTROBUS. Now, Maggie, I warn you. A man can stand a family only just so long. I'm warning you.

> (*Enter* SABINA *from the Bingo Parlor. She wears a flounced red silk bathing suit, 1905. Red socks, shoes, parasol. She bows demurely to* ANTROBUS *and starts down the ramp.* ANTROBUS *and the* CHILDREN *stare at her.* ANTROBUS *bows gallantly.*)

MRS. ANTROBUS. Why, George Antrobus, how can you say such a thing! You have the best family in the world.

ANTROBUS. Good morning, Miss Fairweather.

> (SABINA *finally disappears behind the beach umbrella or in a cabana in the orchestra pit*)

MRS. ANTROBUS. Who on earth was that you spoke to George?

ANTROBUS (*complacent; mock-modest*). Hm . . . m . . . just a . . . solambaka keray.

MRS. ANTROBUS. What? I can't understand you.

GLADYS. Mama, wasn't she beautiful?

HENRY. Papa, introduce her to me.

MRS. ANTROBUS. Children, will you be quiet while I ask your father a simple question?— Who did you say it was, George?

ANTROBUS. Why—uh . . . a friend of mine. Very nice refined girl.

MRS ANTROBUS. I'm waiting.

ANTROBUS. Maggie, that's the girl I gave the prize to in the beauty contest—that's Miss Atlantic City, 1942.

MRS. ANTROBUS. Hm! She looked like Sabina to me.

HENRY (*at the railing*). Mama, the life-guard knows her, too. Mama, he knows her well.

ANTROBUS. Henry, come here.—She's a very nice girl in every way and the sole support of her aged mother.

MRS. ANTROBUS. So was Sabina, so was Sabina; and it took a wall of ice to open your eyes about Sabina.—Henry, come over and sit down on this bench.

ANTROBUS. She's a very different matter from Sabina. Miss Fairweather is a college graduate, Phi Beta Kappa.

MRS. ANTROBUS. Henry, you sit here by mama. Gladys—

ANTROBUS (*sitting*). Reduced circumstances have required her taking a position as hostess in a Bingo Parlor; but there isn't a girl with higher princples in the country.

MRS. ANTROBUS. Well, let's not talk about it. —Henry, I haven't seen a whale yet.

ANTROBUS. She speaks seven languages and has more culture in her little finger than you've acquired in a lifetime.

MRS. ANTROBUS (*assumed amiability*). All right, all right, George. I'm glad to know there are such superior girls in the Bingo Parlors.—Henry what's that? (*Pointing at the storm signal, which has one black disk*)

HENRY. What is it, Papa?

ANTROBUS. What? Oh, that's the storm signal. One of those black disks means bad weather; two means storm; three means hurricane; and four means the end of the world.

> (*As they watch it a second black disk rolls into place*)

MRS. ANTROBUS. Goodness! I'm going this very minute to buy you all some raincoats.

GLADYS (*putting her cheek against her father's shoulder*). Mama, don't go yet. I like sitting this way. And the ocean coming in and coming in. Papa, don't you like it?

MRS. ANTROBUS. Well, there's only one thing I lack to make me a perfectly happy woman: I'd like to see a whale.

HENRY. Mama, we saw two. Right out there. They're delegates to the convention. I'll find you one.

GLADYS. Papa, ask me something. Ask me a question.

ANTROBUS. Well . . . how big's the ocean?

GLADYS. Papa, you're teasing me. It's—three hundred and sixty million square miles—and — it — covers — three-fourths — of — the — earth's — surface — and — its — deepest-place — is — five — and — a — half — miles — deep — and — its — average — depth — is twelve-thousand — feet. No, Papa, ask me something hard, real hard.

MRS. ANTROBUS (*rising*). Now I'm going off to buy those raincoats. I think that bad weather's going to get worse and worse. I hope it doesn't come before your broadcast. I should think we have about an hour or so.

HENRY. I hope it comes and *zzzzz* everything before it. I hope it—

MRS. ANTROBUS. Henry!—George, I think . . . maybe, it's one of those storms that are just as bad on land as on the sea. When you're just as safe and safer in a good stout boat.

HENRY. There's a boat out at the end of the pier.

MRS. ANTROBUS. Well, keep your eye on it. George, you shut your eyes and get a good rest before the broadcast.

ANTROBUS. Thundering Judas, do I have to be told when to open and shut my eyes? Go and buy your raincoats.

MRS. ANTROBUS. Now, children, you have ten minutes to walk around. Ten minutes. And, Henry: control yourself. Gladys, stick by your brother and don't get lost.

(*They run off*)

MRS. ANTROBUS. Will you be all right, George?

(CONVEENERS *suddenly stick their heads out of the Bingo Parlor and Salt Water Taffy store, and voices rise from the orchestra pit*)

CONVEENERS. George. Geo-r-r-rge! George! Leave the old hen-coop at home, George. Do-mes-ticated Georgie!

MRS. ANTROBUS (*shaking her umbrella*). Low common oafs! That's what they are. Guess a man has a right to bring his wife to a convention, if he wants to.

(*She starts off*)

What's the matter with a family, I'd like to know. What else have they got to offer?

(*Exit.* ANTROBUS *has closed his eyes. The* FORTUNE TELLER *comes out of her shop and goes over to the left proscenium. She leans against it, watching* SABINA *quizzically.*)

FORTUNE TELLER. Heh! Here she comes!

SABINA (*loud whisper*). What's he doing?

FORTUNE TELLER. Oh, he's ready for you. Bite your lips, dear, take a long breath and come on up.

SABINA. I'm nervous. My whole future depends on this. I'm nervous.

FORTUNE TELLER. Don't be a fool. What more could you want? He's forty-five. His head's a little dizzy. He's just been elected president. He's never known any other woman than his wife. Whenever he looks at her he realizes that she knows every foolish thing he's ever done.

SABINA (*still whispering*). I don't know why it is, but every time I start one of these I'm nervous.

(*The* FORTUNE TELLER *stands in the center of the stage watching the following:*)

FORTUNE TELLER. You make me tired.

SABINA. First tell me my fortune.

(*The* FORTUNE TELLER *laughs drily and makes the gesture of brushing away a nonsensical question.* SABINA *coughs and says:*)

Oh, Mr. Antrobus—dare I speak to you for a moment?

ANTROBUS. What?—Oh, certainly, certainly, Miss Fairweather.

SABINA. Mr. Antrobus . . . I've been so unhappy. I've wanted . . . I've wanted to make sure that you don't think that I'm the kind of girl who goes out for beauty contests.

FORTUNE TELLER. That's the way!

ANTROBUS. Oh, I understand. I understand perfectly.

FORTUNE TELLER. Give it a little more. Lean on it.

SABINA. I knew you would. My mother said to me this morning: Lily, she said, that fine Mr. Antrobus gave you the prize because he saw at once that you weren't the kind of girl who'd go in for a thing like that. But, honestly, Mr. Antrobus, in this world, honestly, a good girl doesn't know where to turn.

FORTUNE TELLER. Now you've gone too far.

ANTROBUS. My dear Miss Fairweather!

SABINA. You wouldn't know how hard it is. With that lovely wife and daughter you have. Oh, I think Mrs. Antrobus is the finest woman I ever saw. I wish I were like her.

ANTROBUS. There, there. There's . . . uh . . . room for all kinds of people in the world, Miss Fairweather.

SABINA. How wonderful of you to say that. How generous!—Mr. Antrobus, have you a moment free? . . . I'm afraid I may be a little conspicuous here . . . could you come down, for just a moment, to my beach cabana . . . ?

ANTROBUS. Why—uh . . . yes, certainly . . . for a moment . . . just for a moment.

SABINA. There's a deck chair there. Because: you know you *do* look tired. Just this morning my mother said to me: Lily, she said, I hope Mr. Antrobus is getting a good rest. His fine strong face has deep deep lines in it. Now isn't it true, Mr. Antrobus: you work too hard?

FORTUNE TELLER. Bingo! (*She goes into her shop*)

SABINA. Now you will just stretch out. No, I shan't say a word, not a word. I shall just sit there—privileged. That's what I am.

ANTROBUS (*taking her hand*). Miss Fairweather . . . you'll . . . spoil me.

SABINA. Just a moment. I have something I wish to say to the audience.—Ladies and gentlemen. I'm not going to play this particular scene tonight. It's just a short scene and we're going to skip it. But I'll tell you what takes place and then we can continue the play from there on. Now in this scene—

ANTROBUS (*between his teeth*). But, Miss Somerset!

SABINA. I'm sorry. I'm sorry. But I have to skip it. In this scene, I talk to Mr. Antrobus, and at the end of it he decides to leave his wife, get a divorce at Reno and marry me. That's all.

ANTROBUS. Fitz!—Fitz!

SABINA. So that now I've told you we can jump to the end of it—where you say—

(*Enter in fury* MR. FITZPATRICK, *the stage manager*)

MR. FITZPATRICK. Miss Somerset, we insist on your playing this scene.

SABINA. I'm sorry, Mr. Fitzpatrick, but I can't and I won't. I've told the audience all they need to know and now we can go on.

(*Other* ACTORS *begin to appear on the stage, listening*)

MR. FITZPATRICK. And *why* can't you play it?

SABINA. Because there are some lines in that scene that would hurt some people's feelings and I don't think the theatre is a place where people's feelings ought to be hurt.

MR. FITZPATRICK. Miss Somerset, you can pack up your things and go home. I shall call the understudy and I shall report you to Equity.

SABINA. I sent the understudy up to the corner for a cup of coffee and if Equity tries to penalize me I'll drag the case right up to the Supreme Court. Now listen, everybody, there's no need to get excited.

MR. FITZPATRICK *and* ANTROBUS. Why can't you play it . . . what's the matter with the scene?

SABINA. Well, if you must know, I have a personal guest in the audience tonight. Her life hasn't been exactly a happy one. I wouldn't have my friend hear some of these lines for the whole world. I don't suppose it occurred to the author that some other women might have gone through the experience of losing their husbands like this. Wild horses wouldn't drag from me the details of my friend's life, but . . . well, they'd been married twenty years, and before he got rich, why, she'd done the washing and everything.

MR. FITZPATRICK. Miss Somerset, your friend will forgive you. We must play this scene.

SABINA. Nothing, nothing will make me say some of those lines . . . about "a man outgrows a wife every seven years" and . . . and that one about "the Mohammedans being the only people who looked the subject square in the face." Nothing.

MR. FITZPATRICK. Miss Somerset! Go to your dressing room. I'll *read* your lines.

SABINA. Now everybody's nerves are on edge.

MR. ANTROBUS. Skip the scene.

(MR. FITZPATRICK *and the other* ACTORS *go off*)

SABINA. Thank you. I knew you'd understand. We'll do just what I said. So Mr. Antrobus is going to divorce his wife and marry me. Mr. Antrobus, you say: "It won't be easy to lay all this before my wife."

(*The* ACTORS *withdraw.* ANTROBUS *walks about, his hand to his forehead muttering:*)

ANTROBUS. Wait a minute. I can't get back into it as easily as all that. "My wife is a very obstinate woman." Hm . . . then you say . . . hm . . . Miss Fairweather, I mean Lily, it won't be easy to lay all this before my wife. It'll hurt her feelings a little.

SABINA. Listen, George: *other* people haven't got feelings. Not in the same way that we have—we who are presidents like you and prizewinners like me. Listen, other people haven't got feelings; they just imagine they have. Within two weeks they go back to playing bridge and going to the movies.

Listen, dear: everybody in the world except a few people like you and me are just people of straw. Most people have no insides at all. Now that you're president you'll see that. Listen, darling, there's a kind of secret society at the top of the world—like you and me—that know this. The world was made for us. What's life anyway? Except for two things, pleasure and power, what is life? Boredom! Foolishness. You know it is. Except for those two things, life's nau-se-at-ing. So—come here!

(*She moves close. They kiss.*)

So.
Now when your wife comes, it's really very simple; just tell her.

ANTROBUS. Lily, Lily: you're a wonderful woman.

SABINA. Of course I am.

(*They enter the cabana and it hides them from view. Distant roll of thunder. A third black disk appears on the weather signal. Distant thunder is heard.* MRS. ANTROBUS *appears carrying parcels. She looks about, seats herself on the bench left, and fans herself with her handkerchief. Enter* GLADYS *right, followed by two* CONVEENERS. *She is wearing red stockings.*)

MRS. ANTROBUS. Gladys!

GLADYS. Mama, here I am.

MRS. ANTROBUS. Gladys Antrobus!!! Where did you get those dreadful things?

GLADYS. Wha-a-t? Papa liked the color.

MRS. ANTROBUS. You go back to the hotel this minute!

GLADYS. I won't. I won't. Papa liked the color.

MRS. ANTROBUS. All right. All right. You stay here. I've a good mind to let your father see you that way. You stay right here.

GLADYS. I . . . I don't want to stay if . . . if you don't think he'd like it.

MRS. ANTROBUS. Oh . . . it's all one to me. I don't care what happens. I don't care if the biggest storm in the whole world comes. Let it come.

> (*She folds her hands*)

Where's your brother?

GLADYS (*in a small voice*). He'll be here.

MRS. ANTROBUS. Will he? Well, let him get into trouble. I don't care. I don't know where your father is, I'm sure.

> (*Laughter from the cabana*)

GLADYS (*leaning over the rail*). I think he's . . . Mama, he's talking to the lady in the red dress.

MRS. ANTROBUS. Is that so?

> (*Pause*)

We'll wait till he's through. Sit down here beside me and stop fidgeting . . . what are you crying about?

> (*Distant thunder. She covers* GLADYS's *stockings with a raincoat.*)

GLADYS. You don't like my stockings.

> (*Two* CONVEENERS *rush in with a microphone on a standard and various paraphernalia. The* FORTUNE TELLER *appears at the door of her shop. Other characters gradually gather.*)

BROADCAST OFFICIAL. Mrs. Antrobus! Thank God we've found you at last. Where's Mr. Antrobus? We've been hunting everywhere for him. It's about time for the broadcast to the conventions of the world.

MRS. ANTROBUS (*calm*). I expect he'll be here in a minute.

BROADCAST OFFICIAL. Mrs. Antrobus, if he doesn't show up in time, I hope you will consent to broadcast in his place. It's the most important broadcast of the year.

> (SABINA *enters from cabana followed by* ANTROBUS)

MRS. ANTROBUS. No, I shan't. I haven't one single thing to say.

BROADCAST OFFICIAL. Then won't you help us find him, Mrs. Antrobus? A storm's coming up. A hurricane. A deluge!

SECOND CONVEENER (*who has sighted* ANTROBUS *over the rail*). Joe! Joe! Here he is.

BROADCAST OFFICIAL. In the name of God, Mr. Antrobus, you're on the air in five minutes. Will you kindly please come and test the instrument? That's all we ask. If you just please begin the alphabet slowly.

> (ANTROBUS, *with set face, comes ponderously up the ramp. He stops at the point where his waist is level with the stage and speaks authoritatively to the* OFFICIALS.)

ANTROBUS. I'll be ready when the time comes. Until then, move away. Go away. I have something I wish to say to my wife.

BROADCAST OFFICIAL (*whimpering*). Mr. Antrobus! This is the most important broadcast of the year.

> (*The* OFFICIALS *withdraw to the edge of the stage.* SABINA *glides up the ramp behind* ANTROBUS.)

SABINA (*whispering.*) Don't let her argue. Remember arguments have nothing to do with it.

ANTROBUS. Maggie, I'm moving out of the hotel. In fact, I'm moving out of everything. For good. I'm going to marry Miss Fairweather. I shall provide generously for you and the children In a few years you'll be able to see that it's all for the best. That's all I have to say.

BROADCAST OFFICIAL. Mr. Antrobus! I hope you'll be ready. This is the most important broadcast of the year.	BINGO ANNOUNCER. A—Nine; A—Nine. D—Forty-two; D—Forty-two. C—Thirty; C—Thirty.
GLADYS. What did Papa, say, Mama? I didn't hear what Papa said.	B—Seventeen; B—Seventeen. C—Forty; C—Forty. CHORUS. Bingo!!
BROADCAST OFFICIAL. Mr. Antrobus. All we want to do is test your voice with the alphabet.	

ANTROBUS. Go away.
Clear out.

MRS. ANTROBUS (*composedly with lowered eyes*). George, I can't talk to you until you wipe those silly red marks off your face.

ANTROBUS. I think there's nothing to talk about. I've said what I have to say.

SABINA. Splendid!

ANTROBUS. You're a fine woman, Maggie, but . . . but a man has his own life to lead in the world.

MRS. ANTROBUS. Well, after living with you for five thousand years I guess I have a right to a word or two, haven't I?

ANTROBUS (*to* SABINA). What can I answer to that?

SABINA. Tell her that conversation would only hurt her feelings. It's-kinder-in-the-long-run-to-do-it-short-and-quick.

ANTROBUS. I want to spare your feelings in every way I can, Maggie.

BROADCAST OFFICIAL. Mr. Antrobus, the hurricane signal's gone up. We could begin right now.

MRS. ANTROBUS (*calmly, almost dreamily*). I didn't marry you because you were perfect. I didn't even marry you because I loved you. I married you because you gave me a promise.

(*She takes off her ring and looks at it*)

That promise made up for your faults. And the promise I gave you made up for mine. Two imperfect people got married and it was the promise that made the marriage.

ANTROBUS. Maggie . . . I was only nineteen.

MRS. ANTROBUS (*she puts her ring back on her finger*). And when our children were growing up, it wasn't a house that protected them; and it wasn't our love, that protected them—it was that promise.
And when that promise is broken—this can happen!

(*With a sweep of the hand she removes the raincoat from* GLADYS's *stockings.*)

ANTROBUS (*stretches out his arm, apoplectic*). Gladys!! Have you gone crazy? Has everyone gone crazy?

(*Turning on* SABINA)

You did this. You gave them to her.

SABINA. I never said a word to her.

ANTROBUS (*to* GLADYS). You go back to the hotel and take those horrible things off.

GLADYS (*pert*). Before I go, I've got something to tell you—it's about Henry.

MRS. ANTROBUS (*claps her hands peremptorily*). Stop your noise—I'm taking her back to the hotel, George. Before I go I have a letter. . . . I have a message to throw into the ocean.

(*Fumbling in her handbag*)

Where is the plagued thing? Here it is.

(*She flings something—invisible to us—far over the heads of the audience to the back of the auditorium.*)

It's a bottle. And in the bottle's a letter. And in the letter is written all the things that a woman knows. It's never been told to any man and it's never been told to any woman, and if it finds its destination, a new time will come. We're not what books and plays say we are. Were not what advertisements say we are. We're not in the movies and we're not on the radio.
We're not what you're all told and what you think we are:
We're ourselves. And if any man can find one of us he'll learn why the whole universe was set in motion. And if any man harm any one of us, his soul—the only soul he's got—had better be at the bottom of that ocean—and that's the only way to put it. Gladys, come here. We're going back to the hotel.

(*She drags* GLADYS *firmly off by the hand, but* GLADYS *breaks away and comes down to speak to her father*)

SABINA. Such goings-on. Don't give it a minute's thought.

GLADYS. Anyway, I think you ought to know that Henry hit a man with a stone. He hit one of those colored men that push the chairs and the man's very sick. Henry ran away and hid and some policemen are looking for him very hard. And I don't care a bit if you don't want to have anything to do with Mama and me, because I'll never like you again and I hope nobody ever likes you again—so there!

(*She runs off.* ANTROBUS *starts after her.*)

ANTROBUS. I . . . I have to go and see what I can do about this.

SABINA. You stay right here. Don't you go now while you're excited. Gracious sakes, all these things will be forgotten in a hundred years. Come, now, you're on the air. Just say anything—it doesn't matter what. Just a lot of birds and fishes and things.

BROADCAST OFFICIAL. Thank you, Miss Fairweather. Thank you very much. Ready, Mr. Antrobus.

ANTROBUS (*touching the microphone*). What is it, what is it? Who am I talking to?

BROADCAST OFFICIAL. Why, Mr. Antrobus! To our order and to all the other orders.

ANTROBUS (*raising his head*). What are all those birds doing?

BROADCAST OFFICIAL. Those are just a few of the birds. Those are the delegates to our convention—two of a kind.

ANTROBUS (*pointing into the audience*). Look at the water. Look at them all. Those fishes jumping. The children should see this!—There's Maggie's whales!! Here are your whales, Maggie!!

BROADCAST OFFICIAL. I hope you're ready, Mr. Antrobus.

ANTROBUS. And look on the beach! You didn't tell me these would be here!

SABINA. Yes, George. Those are the animals.

BROADCAST OFFICIAL (*busy with the apparatus*). Yes, Mr. Antrobus, those are the vertebrates. We hope the lion will have a word to say when you're through. Step right up,

Mr. Antrobus, we're ready. We'll just have time before the storm.

(*Pause. In a hoarse whisper:*)

They're wait-ing.

(*It has grown dark. Soon after he speaks a high whistling noise begins. Strange veering lights start whirling about the stage. The other characters disappear from the stage.*)

ANTROBUS. Friends. Cousins. Four score and ten billion years ago our forefather brought forth upon this planet the spark of life,—

(*He is drowned out by thunder. When the thunder stops the* FORTUNE TELLER *is seen standing beside him.*)

FORTUNE TELLER. Antrobus, there's not a minute to be lost. Don't you see the four disks on the weather signal? Take your family into that boat at the end of the pier.

ANTROBUS. My family? I have no family. Maggie! Maggie! They won't come.

FORTUNE TELLER. They'll come.—Antrobus! Take these animals into that boat with you. All of them—two of each kind.

SABINA. George, what's the matter with you? This is just a storm like any other storm.

ANTROBUS. Maggie!

SABINA. Stay with me, we'll go . . .

(*Losing conviction*)

This is just another thunderstorm—isn't it? Isn't it?

ANTROBUS. Maggie!!!

(MRS. ANTROBUS *appears beside him with Gladys*)

MRS. ANTROBUS (*matter-of-fact*). Here I am and here's Gladys.

ANTROBUS. Where've you been? Where have you been? Quick, we're going into that boat out there.

MRS. ANTROBUS. I know we are. But I haven't found Henry.

(She wanders off into the darkness calling "Henry!")

SABINA *(low urgent babbling, only occasionally raising her voice).* I don't believe it. I don't believe it's anything at all. I've seen hundreds of storms like this.

FORTUNE TELLER. There's no time to lose. Go. Push the animals along before you. Start a new world. Begin again.

SABINA. Esmeralda! George! Tell me—is it really serious?

ANTROBUS *(suddenly very busy).* Elephants first. Gently, gently.—Look where you're going.

GLADYS *(leaning over the ramp and striking an animal on the back).* Stop it or you'll be left behind!

ANTROBUS. Is the Kangaroo there? *There* you are! Take those turtles in your pouch, will you?

(To some other animals, pointing to his shoulder)

Here! You jump up here. You'll be trampled on.

GLADYS *(to her father, pointing below).* Papa, look—the snakes!

MRS. ANTROBUS. I can't find Henry. Hen-ry!

ANTROBUS. Go along. Go along. Climb on their backs.—Wolves! Jackals—whatever you are—tend to your own business!

GLADYS *(pointing, tenderly).* Papa—look.

SABINA. Mr. Antrobus—take me with you. Don't leave me here. I'll work. I'll help. I'll do anything.

(Three CONVEENERS cross the stage, marching with a banner.)

CONVEENERS. George! What are you scared of?—George! Fellas, it looks like rain.—"Maggie, where's my umbrella?"—George, setting up for Barnum and Bailey.

ANTROBUS *(again catching his wife's hand).*

Come on now, Maggie—the pier's going to break any minute.

MRS. ANTROBUS. I'm not going a step without Henry. Henry!

GLADYS *(on the ramp).* Mama! Papa! Hurry. The pier's cracking, Mama. It's going to break.

MRS. ANTROBUS. Henry! Cain! CAIN!

(Henry dashes onto the stage and joins his mother.)

HENRY. Here I am, Mama.
MRS. ANTROBUS. Thank God!—now come quick.

HENRY. I didn't think you wanted me.

MRS. ANTROBUS. Quick! *(She pushes him down before her into the aisle)*

SABINA *(All the ANTROBUSES are now in the theatre aisle. SABINA stands at the top of the ramp).* Mrs. Antrobus, take me. Don't you remember me? I'll work. I'll help. Don't leave me here!

MRS. ANTROBUS *(impatiently, but as though it were of no importance).* Yes, yes. There's a lot of work to be done. Only hurry.

FORTUNE TELLER *(now dominating the stage. To SABINA with a grim smile).* Yes, go—back to the kitchen with you.

SABINA *(half-down the ramp. To FORTUNE TELLER).* I don't know why my life's always being interrupted—just when everything's going fine!!

(She dashes up the aisle. Now the CONVEENERS emerge doing a serpentine dance on the stage. They jeer at the FORTUNE TELLER.)

CONVEENERS. Get a canoe—there's not a minute to be lost! Tell me my future, Mrs. Croaker.

FORTUNE TELLER. Paddle in the water, boys—enjoy yourselves.

VOICE *from the Bingo Parlor.* A—Nine; A—Nine. C—Twenty-four. C—Twenty-four.

CONVEENERS. Rags, bottles, and sacks.

FORTUNE TELLER. Go back and climb on your roofs. Put rags in the cracks under your doors.—Nothing will keep out the flood. You've had your chance. You've had your day. You've failed. You've lost.

VOICE *from the Bingo Parlor.* B—Fifteen. B —Fifteen.

FORTUNE TELLER (*shading her eyes and looking out to sea*). They're safe. George Antrobus! Think it over! A new world to make.— Think it over!

ACT 3

SCENE: *Home, Excelsior, New Jersey.*

Just before the curtain rises, two sounds are heard from the stage: a cracked bugle call.

The curtain rises on almost total darkness. Almost all the flats composing the walls of MR. ANTROBUS's *house, as of Act 1, are up, but they lean helter-skelter against one another, leaving irregular gaps. Among the flats missing are two in the back wall, leaving the frames of the window and door crazily out of line.*

Off-stage, back right, some red Roman fire is burning. The bugle call is repeated Enter SABINA *through the tilted door. She is dressed as a Napoleonic camp follower, "la fille du regiment," in begrimed reds and blues.*

SABINA. Mrs. Antrobus! Gladys! Where are you!
The war's over. The war's over. You can come out
The peace treaty's been signed.
Where are they—Hmph! Are they dead, too?
Mrs. Annnntrobus! Glaaaadus! Mr. Antrobus'll be here this afternoon. I just saw him downtown. Huuuurry and put things in order. He says that now that the war's over we'll all have to settle down and be perfect.

(*Enter* MR. FITZPATRICK, *the stage manager, followed by the whole company, who stand waiting at the edges of the stage.* MR. FITZPATRICK *tries to interrupt* SABINA.)

MR. FITZPATRICK. Miss Somerset, we have to stop a moment.

SABINA. They may be hiding out in the back—

MR. FITZPATRICK. Miss Somerset! We have to stop a moment.

SABINA. What's the matter?

MR. FITZPATRICK. There's an explanation we have to make to the audience.—Lights, please.
(*To the actor who plays* MR. ANTROBUS.)
Will you explain the matter to the audience?

(*The lights go up. We now see that a balcony or elevated runway has been erected at the back of the stage, back of the wall of the Antrobus house. From its extreme right and left ends ladder-like steps descend to the floor of the stage.*)

ANTROBUS. Ladies and gentlemen, an unfortunate accident has taken place back stage. Perhaps I should say *another* unfortunate accident.

SABINA. I'm sorry. I'm sorry.

ANTROBUS. The management feels, in fact, we all feel that you are due an apology. And now we have to ask your indulgence for the most serious mishap of all. Seven of our actors have . . . have been taken ill. Apparently, it was something they ate. I'm not exactly clear what happened.

(*All the* ACTORS *start to talk at once.* ANTROBUS *raises his hand.*)

Now, now—not all at once. Fitz, do you know what it was?

MR. FITZPATRICK. Why, it's perfectly clear. These seven actors had dinner together, and they ate something that disagreed with them.

SABINA. Disagreed with them!!! They have ptomaine poisoning. They're in Bellevue Hospital this very minute in agony. They're having their stomachs pumped out this very minute, in perfect agony.

ANTROBUS. Fortunately, we've just heard they'll all recover.

SABINA. It'll be a miracle if they do, a downright miracle. It was the lemon meringue pie.

ACTORS. It was the fish . . . it was the canned tomatoes . . . it was the fish.

SABINA. It was the lemon meringue pie. I saw it with my own eyes; it had blue mold all over the bottom of it.

ANTROBUS. Whatever it was, they're in no condition to take part in this performance. Naturally, we haven't enough understudies to fill all those roles; but we do have a number of splendid volunteers who have kindly consented to help us out. These friends have watched our rehearsals, and they assure me that they know the lines and the business very well. Let me introduce them to you—my dresser, Mr. Tremayne—himself a distinguished Shakespearean actor for many years; our wardrobe mistress, Hester; Miss Somerset's maid, Ivy; and Fred Bailey, captain of the ushers in this theatre.

(*These persons bow modestly.* IVY *and* HESTER *are colored girls.*)

Now this scene takes place near the end of the act. And I'm sorry to say we'll need a short rehearsal, just a short run-through. And as some of it takes place in the auditorium, we'll have to keep the curtain up. Those of you who wish can go out in the lobby and smoke some more. The rest of you can listen to us, or . . . or just talk quietly among yourselves, as you choose. Thank you. Now will you take it over, Mr. Fitzpatrick?

MR. FITZPATRICK. Thank you.—Now for those of you who are listening perhaps I should explain that at the end of this act, the men have come back from the war and the family's settled down in the house. And the author wants to show the hours of the night passing by over their heads, and the planets crossing the sky . . . uh . . . over their heads.

And he says—this is hard to explain—that each of the hours of the night is a philosopher, or a great thinker. Eleven o'clock, for instance, is Aristotle. And nine o'clock is Spinoza. Like that. I don't suppose it means anything. It's just a kind of poetic effect.

SABINA. Not mean anything! Why, it certainly does. Twelve o'clock goes by saying those wonderful things. I think it means that when people are asleep they have all those lovely thoughts, much better than when they're awake.

IVY. Excuse me, I think it means—excuse me, Mr. Fitzpatrick—

SABINA. What were you going to say, Ivy?

IVY. Mr. Fitzpatrick, you let my father come to a rehearsal; and my father's a Baptist minister, and he said that the author meant that —just like the hours and stars go by over our heads at night, in the same way the ideas and thoughts of the great men are in the air around us all the time and they're working on us, even when we don't know it.

MR. FITZPATRICK. Well, well, maybe that's it. Thank you, Ivy. Anyway—the hours of the night are philosophers. My friends are you ready? Ivy, can you be eleven o'clock? "This good estate of the mind possessing its object in energy we call divine." Aristotle.

IVY. Yes, sir. I know that and I know twelve o'clock and I know nine o'clock.

MR. FITZPATRICK. Twelve o'clock? Mr. Tremayne, the Bible.

TREMAYNE. Yes.

MR. FITZPATRICK. Ten o'clock? Hester— Plato?

(*She nods eagerly*)

Nine o'clock, Spinoza—Fred?

BAILEY. Yes, Sir.

(FRED BAILEY *picks up a great gilded cardboard numeral IX and starts up the steps to the platform.* MR. FITZPATRICK *strikes his forehead.*)

MR. FITZPATRICK. The planets!! We forgot all about the planets.

SABINA. O my God! The planets! Are they sick too?

(ACTORS *nod*)

MR. FITZPATRICK. Ladies and gentlemen, the planets are singers. Of course, we can't replace them, so you'll have to imagine them singing in this scene. Saturn sings from the orchestra pit down here. The Moon is way up there. And Mars with a red lantern in his hand, stands in the aisle over there— Tz-tz-tz. It's too bad; it all makes a very fine effect. However! Ready—nine o'clock: Spinoza.

BAILEY (*walking slowly across the balcony, left to right*). "After experience had taught me that the common occurrences of daily life are vain and futile—"

FITZPATRICK. Louder, Fred. "And I saw that all the objects of my desire and fear—"

BAILEY. "And I saw that all the objects of my desire and fear were in themselves nothing good nor bad save insofar as the mind was affected by them—"

FITZPATRICK. Do you know the rest? All right. Ten o'clock. Hester. Plato.

HESTER. "Then tell me, O Critias, how will a man choose the ruler that shall rule over him? Will he not—"

FITZPATRICK. Thank you. Skip to the end, Hester.

HESTER. ". . . can be multiplied a thousand fold in its effects among the citizens."

FITZPATRICK. Thank you.—Aristotle, Ivy?

IVY. "This good estate of the mind possessing its object in energy we call divine. This we mortals have occasionally and it is this energy which is pleasantest and best. But God has it always. It is wonderful in us; but in Him how much more wonderful."

FITZPATRICK. Midnight. Midnight, Mr. Tremayne. That's right—you've done it before. —All right, everybody. You know what you have to do.—Lower the curtain. House lights up. Act Three of THE SKIN OF OUR TEETH.

(*As the curtain descends he is heard saying:*)

You volunteers, just wear what you have on. Don't try to put on the costumes today.

(*House lights go down. The Act begins again. The Bugle call. Curtain rises. Enter SABINA.*)

SABINA. Mrs. Antrobus! Gladys! Where are you?
The war's over.—You've heard all this—

(*She gabbles the main points*)

Where—are—they? Are—they—dead, too, et cetera.
I—just—saw—Mr.—Antrobus—downtown, et cetera.

(*Slowing up:*)

He says that now that the war's over we'll all have to settle down and be perfect. They may be hiding out in the back somewhere. Mrs. An-tro-bus.

(*She wanders off. It has grown lighter. A trapdoor is cautiously raised and MRS. ANTROBUS emerges waist-high and listens. She is disheveled and worn; she wears a tattered dress and a shawl half covers her head. She talks down through the trapdoor.*)

MRS. ANTROBUS. It's getting light. There's still something burning over there—Newark, or Jersey City. What? Yes, I could swear I heard someone moving about up here. But I can't see anybody. I say: I can't see anybody.

(*She starts to move about the stage. GLADYS's head appears at the trapdoor. She is holding a BABY.*)

GLADYS. Oh, Mama. Be careful.

MRS. ANTROBUS. Now, Gladys, you stay out of sight.

GLADYS. Well, let me stay here just a minute. I want the baby to get some of this fresh air.

MRS. ANTROBUS. All right, but keep your eyes open. I'll see what I can find. I'll have a good hot plate of soup for you before you can say Jack Robinson. Gladys Antrobus! Do you know what I think I see? There's old Mr. Hawkins sweeping the sidewalk in front of his A. and P. store. Sweeping it with a broom. Why, he must have gone crazy, like the others! I see some other people moving about, too.

GLADYS. Mama, come back, come back.

(MRS. ANTROBUS *returns to the trapdoor and listens*)

MRS. ANTROBUS. Gladys, there's something in the air. Everybody's movement's sort of different. I see some women walking right out in the middle of the street.

SABINA'S VOICE. Mrs. An-tro-bus!

MRS. ANTROBUS *and* GLADYS. What's that?!!

SABINA'S VOICE. Glaaaadys! Mrs. An-tro-bus!

(*Enter* SABINA)

MRS. ANTROBUS. Gladys, that's Sabina's voice as sure as I live.—Sabina! Sabina!—Are you *alive?!!*

SABINA. Of course, I'm alive. How've you girls been?—*Don't* try and kiss me. I never want to kiss another human being as long as I live. Sh-sh, there's nothing to get emotional about. Pull yourself together, the war's over. Take a deep breath—the war's over.

MRS. ANTROBUS. The war's over!! I don't believe you. I don't believe you. I can't believe you.

GLADYS. Mama!

SABINA. Who's that?

MRS. ANTROBUS. That's Gladys and her baby. I don't believe you. Gladys, Sabina says the war's over. Oh, Sabina.

SABINA (*leaning over the* BABY). Goodness! Are there any babies left in the world! Can it *see?* And can it cry and everything?

GLADYS. Yes, he can. He notices everything very well.

SABINA. Where on earth did you get it? Oh, I won't ask.—Lord, I've lived all these seven years around camp and I've forgotten how to behave.—Now we've got to think about the men coming home.—Mrs. Antrobus, go and wash your face, I'm ashamed of you. Put your

best clothes on. Mr. Antrobus'll be here this afternoon. I just saw him downtown.

MRS. ANTROBUS *and* GLADYS. He's alive!! He'll be here!! Sabina, you're not joking?

MRS. ANTROBUS. And Henry?

SABINA (*dryly*). Yes, Henry's alive, too, that's what they say. Now don't stop to talk. Get yourselves fixed up. Gladys, you look terrible. Have you any decent clothes?

(SABINA *has pushed them toward the trapdoor*)

MRS. ANTROBUS (*half down*). Yes, I've something to wear just for this very day. But, Sabina—who won the war?

SABINA. Don't stop now—just wash your face.

(*A whistle sounds in the distance*)

Oh, my God, what's that silly little noise?

MRS. ANTROBUS. Why, it sounds like . . . it sounds like what used to be the noon whistle at the shoe-polish factory. (*Exit*)

SABINA. That's what it is. Seems to me like peacetime's coming along pretty fast—shoe polish!

GLADYS (*half down*). Sabina, how soon after peacetime begins does the milkman start coming to the door?

SABINA. As soon as he catches a cow. Give him time to catch a cow, dear.

(*Exit* GLADYS. SABINA *walks about a moment, thinking.*)

Shoe polish! My, I'd forgotten what peacetime was like.

(*She shakes her head, then sits down by the trapdoor and starts talking down the hole*)

Mrs. Antrobus, guess what I saw Mr. Antrobus doing this morning at dawn. He was tacking up a piece of paper on the door of the Town Hall. You'll die when you hear: it was a recipe for grass soup, for a grass soup that doesn't give you the diarrhea. Mr. Antrobus is still thinking up new things.—He told me to give you his love. He's got all sorts of ideas for peacetime, he says. No more laziness and idiocy, he says. And oh, yes! Where are his books? What? Well, pass them up. The first thing he wants to see are his books. He says if you've burnt those books, or if the rats have eaten them, he says it isn't worthwhile starting over again. Everybody's going to be beautiful, he says, and diligent, and very intelligent.

(*A hand reaches up with two volumes*)

What language is that? Pu-u-gh—mold! And he's got such plans for you, Mrs. Antrobus. You're going to study history and algebra—and so are Glady's and I—and philosophy. You should hear him talk:

(*Taking two more volumes*)

Well, these are in English, anyway.—To hear him talk, seems like he expects you to be a combination, Mrs. Antrobus, of a saint and a college professor, and a dancehall hostess, if you know what I mean.

(*Two more volumes*)

Ugh. German!

(*She is lying on the floor; one elbow bent, her cheek on her hand, meditatively*)

Yes, peace will be here before we know it. In a week or two we'll be asking the Perkinses in for a quiet evening of bridge. We'll turn on the radio and hear how to be big successes with a new toothpaste. We'll trot down to the movies and see how girls with wax faces live—all *that* will begin again. Oh, Mrs. Antrobus, God forgive me but I enjoyed the war. Everybody's at their best in wartime. I'm sorry it's over. And, oh, I forgot! Mr. Antrobus sent you another message—can you hear me?—

(*Enter* HENRY, *blackened and sullen. He is wearing torn overalls, but has one gaudy admiral's epaulette hanging by a thread from his right shoulder, and there are vestiges of gold and scarlet braid running down his left trouser leg. He stands listening.*)

Listen! Henry's never to put foot in this house again, he says. He'll kill Henry on sight, if he sees him.

You don't know about Henry??? Well, where have you been? What? Well, Henry rose right to the top. Top of *what*? Listen, I'm telling you. Henry rose from corporal to captain, to major, to general.—I don't know how to say it, but the enemy is *Henry*; Henry *is* the enemy. Everybody knows that.

HENRY. He'll kill me, will he?

SABINA. Who are *you*? I'm not afraid of you. The war's over.

HENRY. I'll kill him so fast. I've spent seven years trying to find him; the others I killed were just substitutes.

SABINA. Goodness! It's Henry!—

(*He makes an angry gesture*)

Oh, I'm not afraid of you. The war's over, Henry Antrobus, and you're not any more important than any other unemployed. You go away and hide yourself, until we calm your father down.

HENRY. The first thing to do is to burn up those old books; it's the ideas he gets out of those old books that . . . that makes the whole world so you can't live in it.

(*He reels forward and starts kicking the books about, but suddenly falls down in a sitting position*)

SABINA. You leave those books alone!! Mr. Antrobus is looking forward to them a-special.—Gracious sakes, Henry, you're so tired you can't stand up. Your mother and sister'll be here in a minute and we'll think what to do about you.

HENRY. What did they ever care about me?

SABINA. There's that old whine again. All you people think you're not loved enough, nobody loves you. Well, you start being lovable and we'll love you.

HENRY (*outraged*). I don't want anybody to love me.

SABINA. Then stop talking about it all the time.

HENRY. I *never* talk about it. The last thing I want is anybody to pay any attention to me.

SABINA. I can hear it behind every word you say.

HENRY. I want everybody to hate me.

SABINA. Yes, you've decided that's second best, but it's still the same thing.—Mrs. Antrobus! Henry's here. He's so tired he can't stand up.

MRS. ANTROBUS *and* GLADYS, *with her* BABY, *emerge.*

> (*They are dressed as in Act I.* MRS. AN-TROBUS *carries some objects in her apron, and* GLADYS *has a blanket over her shoulder.*)

MRS. ANTROBUS *and* GLADYS. Henry! Henry! Henry!

HENRY (*glaring at them*). Have you anything to eat?

MRS. ANTROBUS. Yes, I have, Henry. I've been saving it for this very day—two good baked potatoes. No! Henry! one of them's for your father. Henry!! Give me that other potato back this minute.

> (SABINA *sidles up behind him and snatches the other potato away*)

SABINA. He's so dog-tired he doesn't know what he's doing.

MRS. ANTROBUS. Now you just rest there, Henry, until I can get your room ready. Eat that potato good and slow, so you can get all the nourishment out of it.

HENRY. You all might as well know right now that I haven't come back here to live.

MRS. ANTROBUS. Sh. . . . I'll put this coat over you. Your room's hardly damaged at all. Your football trophies are a little tarnished, but Sabina and I will polish them up to-morrow.

HENRY. Did you hear me? I don't live here. I don't belong to anybody.

MRS. ANTROBUS. Why, how can you say a thing like that? You certainly do belong right here. Where else would you want to go? Your forehead's feverish, Henry, seems to me. You'd better give me that gun, Henry. You won't need that any more.

GLADYS (*whispering*). Look, he's fallen asleep already, with his potato half-chewed.

SABINA. Puh! The terror of the world.

MRS. ANTROBUS. Sabina, you mind your own business, and start putting the room to rights.

> (HENRY *has turned his face to the back of the sofa.* MRS. ANTROBUS *gingerly puts the revolver in her apron pocket, then helps* SABINA. SABINA *has found a rope hanging from the ceiling. Grunting, she hangs all her weight on it, and as she pulls the walls begin to move into their right places.* MRS. ANTROBUS *brings the overturned tables, chairs and hassock into the positions of Act 1.*)

SABINA. That's all we do—always beginning again! Over and over again. Always beginning again.

> (*She pulls on the rope and a part of the wall moves into place. She stops. Meditatively:*)

How do we know that it'll be any better than before? Why do we go on pretending? Some day the whole earth's going to have to turn cold anyway, and until that time all these other things'll be happening again: it will be more wars and more walls of ice and floods and earthquakes.

MRS. ANTROBUS. Sabina!! Stop arguing and go on with your work.

SABINA. All right. I'll go on just out of *habit*, but I won't believe in it.

MRS. ANTROBUS (*aroused*). Now, Sabina. I've let you talk long enough. I don't want to hear any more of it. Do I have to explain to you what everybody knows—everybody who keeps a home going? Do I have to say to you what nobody should ever *have* to say, because they can read it in each other's eyes?
Now listen to me:

> (MRS. ANTROBUS *takes hold of the rope*)

I could live for seventy years in a cellar and make soup out of grass and bark, without ever doubting that this world has a work to do and will do it.
Do you hear me?

SABINA (*frightened*). Yes, Mrs. Antrobus.

MRS. ANTROBUS. Sabina, do you see this house —216 Cedar Street—do you see it?

SABINA. Yes, Mrs. Antrobus.

MRS. ANTROBUS. Well, just to have known this house is to have seen the idea of what we can do someday if we keep our wits about us. Too many people have suffered and died for my children for us to start reneging now. So we'll start putting this house to rights. Now, Sabina, go and see what you can do in the kitchen.

SABINA. Kitchen! Why is it that however far I go away, I always find myself back in the kitchen? (*Exit.*)

MRS. ANTROBUS (*still thinking over her last speech, relaxes and says with a reminiscent smile*): Goodness gracious, wouldn't you know that my father was a parson? It was just like I heard his own voice speaking and he's been dead five thousand years. There! I've gone and almost waked Henry up.

HENRY (*talking in his sleep, indistinctly*). Fellows . . . what have they done for us? . . . Blocked our way at every step. Kept everything in their own hands. And you've stood it. When are you going to wake up?

MRS. ANTROBUS. Sh, Henry. Go to sleep. Go to sleep. Go to sleep.—Well, that looks better. Now let's go and help Sabina.

GLADYS. Mama, I'm going out into the backyard and hold the baby right up in the air. And show him that we don't have to be afraid any more.

(*Exit* GLADYS *to the kitchen.* MRS. ANTROBUS *glances at* HENRY, *exits into kitchen.* HENRY *thrashes about in his sleep. Enter* ANTROBUS, *his arms full of bundles, chewing the end of a carrot. He has a slight limp. Over the suit of Act 1 he is wearing an overcoat too long for him, its skirts trailing on the ground. He lets his bundles fall and stands looking about. Presently his attention is fixed on* HENRY, *whose words grow clearer.*)

HENRY. All right! What have you got to lose? What have they done for us? That's right—nothing. Tear everything down. I don't care what you smash. We'll begin again and we'll show 'em.

(ANTROBUS *takes out his revolver and holds it pointing downwards. With his back toward the audience he moves toward the footlights.* HENRY's *voice grows louder and he wakes with a start. They stare at one another. Then* HENRY *sits up quickly. Throughout the following scene* HENRY *is played, not as a misunderstood or misguided young man, but as a representation of strong unreconciled evil.*)

All right! Do something.

(*Pause*)

Don't think I'm afraid of you, either. All right, do what you were going to do. Do it.

(*Furiously*)

Shoot me, I tell you. You don't have to think I'm any relation of yours. I haven't got any father or any mother, or brothers or sisters. And I don't want any. And what's more I haven't got anybody over me; and I never will have. I'm alone, and that's all I want to be: alone. So you can shoot me.

ANTROBUS. You're the last person I wanted to see. The sight of you dries up all my plans and hopes. I wish I were back at war still, because it's easier to fight you than to live with you. War's a pleasure—do you hear me?—War's a pleasure compared to what faces us now: trying to build up a peacetime with you in the middle of it.

(ANTROBUS *walks up to the window*)

HENRY. I'm not going to be a part of any peacetime of yours. I'm going a long way from here and make my own world that's fit for a man to live in. Where a man can be free, and have a chance, and do what he wants to do in his own way.

ANTROBUS (*his attention arrested; thoughtfully. He throws the gun out of the window and turns with hope*). . . . Henry, let's try again.

HENRY. Try what? Living *here*?—Speaking polite downtown to all the old men like you? Standing like a sheep at the street corner until the red light turns to green? Being a good boy and a good sheep, like all the stinking ideas you get out of your books? Oh, no. I'll make a world, and I'll show you.

ANTROBUS (*hard*). How can you make a world for people to live in, unless you've first put order in yourself? Mark my words: I shall continue fighting you until my last breath as long as you mix up your idea of liberty with your idea of hogging everything for yourself. I shall have no pity on you. I shall pursue you to the far corners of the earth. You and I want the same thing, but until you think of it as something that everyone has a right to, you are my deadly enemy and I will destroy you.—I hear your mother's voice in the kitchen. Have you seen her?

HENRY. I have no mother. Get it into your head. I don't belong here. I have nothing to do here. I have no home.

ANTROBUS. Then why did you come here? With the whole world to choose from, why did you come to this one place: 216 Cedar Street, Excelsior, New Jersey. . . . Well?

HENRY. What if I did? What if I wanted to look at it once more, to see if—

ANTROBUS. Oh, you're related, all right— When your mother comes in you must behave yourself. Do you hear me?

HENRY (*wildly*). What is this?—*must behave* yourself. Don't you say *must* to me.

ANTROBUS. Quiet!

(*Enter* MRS. ANTROBUS *and* SABINA)

HENRY. Nobody can say *must* to me. All my life everybody's been crossing me—everybody, everything, all of you. I'm going to be free, even if I have to kill half the world for it. Right now, too. Let me get my hands on his throat. I'll show him.

(*He advances toward* ANTROBUS. *Suddenly* SABINA *jumps between them and calls out in her own person:*)

SABINA. Stop! Stop! Don't play this scene. You know what happened last night. Stop the play.

(*The men fall back, panting.* HENRY *covers his face with his hands.*)

Last night you almost strangled him. You became a regular savage. Stop it!

HENRY. It's true. I'm sorry. I don't know what comes over me. I have nothing against him personally. I respect him very much . . . I . . . I admire him. But something comes over me. It's like I become fifteen years old again. I . . . I . . . listen: my own father used to whip me and lock me up every Saturday night. I never had enough to eat. He never let me have enough money to buy decent clothes. I was ashamed to go downtown. I never could go to the dances. My father and my uncle put rules in the way of everything I wanted to do. They tried to prevent my living at all.—I'm sorry. I'm sorry.

MRS. ANTROBUS (*quickly*). No, go on. Finish what you were saying. Say it all.

HENRY. In this scene it's as though I were back in High School again. It's like I had some big emptiness inside me—the emptiness of being hated and blocked at every turn. And the emptiness fills up with the one thought that you have to strike and fight and kill. Listen, it's as though you have to kill somebody else so as not to end up killing yourself.

SABINA. That's not true. I knew your father and your uncle and your mother. You imagined all that. Why, they did everything they could for you. How can you say things like that? They didn't lock you up.

HENRY. They did. They did. They wished I hadn't been born.

SABINA. That's not true.

ANTROBUS (*in his own person, with self-condemnation, but cold and proud*). Wait a minute. I have something to say, too. It's not wholly his fault that he wants to strangle me in this scene. It's my fault, too. He wouldn't feel that way unless there were something in me that reminded him of all that. He talks about an emptiness. Well, there's an emptiness in me, too. Yes—work, work, work—that's all I do. I've ceased to *live*. No wonder he feels that anger coming over him.

MRS. ANTROBUS. There! At least you've said it.

SABINA. We're all just as wicked as we can be, and that's the God's truth.

MRS. ANTROBUS (*nods a moment, then comes forward; quietly*). Come. Come and put your head under some cold water.

SABINA (*in a whisper*). I'll go with him. I've known him a long while. You have to go on with the play. Come with me.

(HENRY *starts out with* SABINA, *but turns at the exit and says to* ANTROBUS:)

HENRY. Thanks. Thanks for what you said. I'll be all right tomorrow. I won't lose control in that place. I promise.

(*Exeunt* HENRY *and* SABINA. ANTROBUS *starts toward the front door, fastens it.* MRS. ANTROBUS *goes up stage and places the chair close to table.*)

MRS. ANTROBUS. George, do I see you limping?

ANTROBUS. Yes, a little. My old wound from the other war started smarting again. I can manage.

MRS. ANTROBUS (*looking out of the window*). Some lights are coming on—the first in seven years. People are walking up and down looking at them. Over in Hawkins' open lot they've built a bonfire to celebrate the peace. They're dancing around it like scarecrows.

ANTROBUS. A bonfire! As though they hadn't seen enough things burning.—Maggie —the dog died?

MRS. ANTROBUS. Oh, yes. Long ago. There are no dogs left in Excelsior.—You're back again! All these years. I gave up counting on letters. The few that arrived were anywhere from six months to a year late.

ANTROBUS. Yes, the ocean's full of letters, along with the other things.

MRS. ANTROBUS. George, sit down, you're tired.

ANTROBUS. No, you sit down. I'm tired but I'm restless.

(*Suddenly, as she comes forward*)

Maggie! I've lost it. I've lost it.

MRS. ANTROBUS. What, George? What have you lost?

ANTROBUS. The most important thing of all: The desire to begin again, to start building.

MRS. ANTROBUS (*sitting in the chair right of the table*). Well, it will come back.

ANTROBUS (*at the window*). I've lost it. This minute I feel like all those people dancing around the bonfire—just relief. Just the desire to settle down; to slip into the old grooves and keep the neighbors from walking over my lawn.—Hm. But during the war—in the middle of all that blood and dirt and hot and cold—every day and night, I'd have moments, Maggie, when I *saw* the things that we could do when it was over. When you're at war you think about a better life; when you're at peace you think about a more comfortable one. I've lost it. I feel sick and tired.

MRS. ANTROBUS. Listen! The baby's crying. I hear Gladys talking. Probably she's quieting Henry again. George, while Gladys and I were living here—like moles, like rats, and when we were at our wits' end to save the baby's life—the only thought we clung to was that you were going to bring something good out of this suffering. In the night, in the dark, we'd whisper about it, starving and sick.—Oh, George, you'll have to get it back again. Think! What else kept us alive all these years? Even now, it's not comfort we want. We can suffer whatever's necessary; only give us back that promise.

(*Enter* SABINA *with a lighted lamp. She is dressed as in Act 1.*)

SABINA. Mrs. Antrobus...

MRS. ANTROBUS. Yes, Sabina?

SABINA. Will you need me?

MRS. ANTROBUS. No, Sabina, you can go to bed.

SABINA. Mrs. Antrobus, if it's all right with you, I'd like to go to the bonfire and celebrate seeing the war's over. And, Mrs. Antrobus, they've opened the Gem Movie Theatre and they're giving away a hand-painted soup tureen to every lady, and I thought one of us ought to go.

ANTROBUS. Well, Sabina, I haven't any money. I haven't seen any money for quite a while.

SABINA. Oh, you don't need money. They're taking anything you can give them. And I have some . . . some . . . Mrs. Antrobus, promise you won't tell anyone. It's a little against the law. But I'll give you some, too.

ANTROBUS. What is it?

SABINA. I'll give you some, too. Yesterday I picked up a lot of . . . of beef cubes!

(MRS. ANTROBUS *turns and says calmly:*)

MRS. ANTROBUS. But, Sabina, you know you ought to give that in to the Center downtown. They know who needs them most.

SABINA (*outburst*). Mrs. Antrobus, I didn't make this war. I didn't ask for it. And, in my opinion, after anybody's gone through what we've gone through, they have a right to grab what they can find. You're a very nice man, Mr. Antrobus, but you'd have got on better in the world if you'd realized that dog-eat-dog was the rule in the beginning and always will be. And most of all now.

(*In tears*)

Oh, the world's an awful place, and you know it is. I used to think something could be done about it; but I know better now. I hate it. I hate it.

(*She comes forward slowly and brings six cubes from the bag*)

All right. All right. You can have them.

ANTROBUS. Thank you, Sabina.

SABINA. Can I have . . . can I have one to go to the movies?

(ANTROBUS *in silence gives her one*)

Thank you.

ANTROBUS. Good night, Sabina.

SABINA. Mr. Antrobus, don't mind what I say. I'm just an ordinary girl, you know what I mean, I'm just an ordinary girl. But you're a bright man, you're a very bright man, and of course you invented the alphabet and the wheel and, my God, a lot of things . . . and if you've got any other plans, my God, don't let me upset them. Only every now and then I've got to go to the movies. I mean my nerves can't stand it. But if you have any ideas about improving the crazy old world, I'm really with you. I really am. Because it's . . . it's . . . Good night.

(*She goes out.* ANTROBUS *starts laughing softly with exhilaration.*)

ANTROBUS. Now I remember what three things always went together when I was able to see things most clearly: three things. Three things.

(*He points to where* SABINA *has gone out.*)

The voice of the people in their confusion and their need. And the thought of you and the children and this house . . . And . . . Maggie! I didn't dare ask you: my books! They haven't been lost, have they?

MRS. ANTROBUS. No. There are some of them right here. Kind of tattered.

ANTROBUS. Yes.—Remember, Maggie, we almost lost them once before? And when we finally did collect a few torn copies out of old cellars they ran in everyone's head like a fever. They as good as rebuilt the world.

(*Pauses, book in hand, and looks up*)

Oh, I've never forgotten for long at a time that living is struggle. I know that every good and excellent thing in the world stands moment by moment on the razor-edge of danger and must be fought for—whether it's a field, or a home, or a country. All I ask is the chance to build new worlds and God has always given us that. And has given us (*Opening the book.*) voices to guide us; and the memory of our mistakes to warn us. Maggie, you and I will remember in peacetime all the resolves that were so clear to us in the days of war. We've come a long ways. We've learned. We're learning. And the steps of our journey are marked for us here.

(*He stands by the table turning the leaves of a book*)

Sometimes out there in the war—standing all night on a hill—I'd try and remember some of the words in these books. Parts of them and phrases would come back to me. And after a while I used to give names to the hours of the night.

(*He sits, hunting for a passage in the book*)

Nine o'clock I used to call Spinoza. Where is it: "After experience had taught me—"

(*The back wall has disappeared, revealing the platform.* FRED BAILEY *carrying his numeral has started from left to right.* MRS. ANTROBUS *sits by the table sewing.*)

BAILEY. "After experience had taught me that the common occurrences of daily life are vain and futile; and I saw that all the objects of my desire and fear were in themselves nothing good nor bad save insofar as the mind was affected by them; I at length determined to search out whether there was something truly good and communicable to man."

(*Almost without break* HESTER, *carrying a large Roman numeral ten, starts crossing the platform.* GLADYS *appears at the kitchen door and moves toward her mother's chair.*)

HESTER. "Then tell me, O Critias, how will a man choose the ruler that shall rule over him? Will he not choose a man who has first established order in himself, knowing that any decision that has its spring from anger or pride or vanity can be multiplied a thousand-fold in its effects upon the citizens?"

(HESTER *disappears and* IVY, *as eleven o'clock starts speaking.*)

IVY. "This good estate of the mind possessing its object in energy we call divine. This we mortals have occasionally and it is this energy which is pleasantest and best. But God has it

always. It is wonderful in us; but in Him how much more wonderful."

(*As* MR. TREMAYNE *starts to speak,* HENRY *appears at the edge of the scene, brooding and unreconciled, but present.*)

TREMAYNE. "In the beginning, God created the Heavens and the earth; And the Earth was waste and void; And the darkness was upon the face of the deep. And the Lord said let there be light and there was light."

(*Sudden black-out and silence, except for the last strokes of the midnight bell. Then just as suddenly the lights go up, and* SABINA *is standing at the window, as at the opening of the play.*)

SABINA. Oh, oh, oh. Six o'clock and the master not home yet. Pray God nothing serious has happened to him crossing the Hudson River. But I wouldn't be surprised. The whole world's at sixes and sevens, and why the house hasn't fallen down about our ears long ago is a miracle to me.

(*She comes down to the footlights*)

This is where you came in. We have to go on for ages and ages yet.
You go home.
The end of this play isn't written yet.
Mr. and Mrs. Antrobus! Their heads are full of plans and they're as confident as the first day they began—and they told me to tell you: good night.

———◄•◄•►•►———

We considered *Oedipus Rex* as in some senses a parable about man's yearning for, his need for, and yet his difficulty in attaining, knowledge about himself and his world. *The Skin of Our Teeth* may be regarded as even more obviously a kind of parable, this one about the nature of the human endeavor. For example, the name Antrobus suggests the Greek name for man, *anthropos*, and the son of Mr. and Mrs. Antrobus, as we find out in the play, was originally called Cain—that is, he is the eldest son of Adam and Eve. (The word *Adam*, by the way, is simply the Hebrew word for man.) One of the things this play seems to be saying is that all times are essentially alike, and that the details of the particular peril that threatens the human race, whether of an advancing ice sheet, or a Noah's flood, or a devastating world war, are finally unimportant. What is important is that man is always being challenged and that it behooves him to make the proper response.

In a dozen different ways *The Skin of Our Teeth* manages to suggest this unchanging character of the human situation. For example, the play begins with a projection screen and an announcer—presumably a radio announcer—giving the news of the world in standard twentieth-century fashion, but the subject dominating the news is the advancing ice sheet, the catastrophe of 40,000 years ago. Soon a singing telegram (a popular "gimmick" in the 1930s) arrives, but the important information that the telegram contains is that Mr. Antrobus is making progress in perfecting the alphabet! Thus, there is a deliberate scrambling of epochs and a series of bewildering anachronisms. In spite of its realistic elements, *The Skin of Our Teeth* can best be described as an intellectual fantasy.

It may be useful at this point to sort out several aspects of the mode of presentation used in this play: (1) the playwright employs various kinds of symbolic shortcuts to set forth his theme; (2) the fantastic juxtapositions and startling anachronisms give rise to a special kind of comedy; and (3) the playwright makes free with the theatrical conventions, as when an actor breaks out of his or her part to criticize or comment on the play, or when the audience is taken into the author's confidence and let in on the workings of the play. Though the playwright may have some very profound thoughts about mankind, he evidently sees no need to be stuffy about them, and knows that his devices for condensing and pointing up the essentials of the human story will prove disastrously clumsy if they are not handled playfully and in a spirit of comedy.

The first character to speak, Sabina, the housemaid, provides a clue to the general tone. Sabina's normal speech is a hash of clichés: she tells us that "The whole world's at sixes and sevens" and observes that "In the midst of life we are in the midst of death, a truer word was never said." Her comments on the members of the Antrobus family—the announcer has called it a "typical American family"—are in the same vein. She remarks that if anything happened to Mr. Antrobus "we would certainly be inconsolable"; Mr. Antrobus is "an excellent husband and father, a pillar of the church." But Sabina manages, perhaps unconsciously, to undercut most of the vapidly laudatory things she is saying: after remarking that the loss of Mr. Antrobus would leave the family "inconsolable," she adds that they would "have to move into a less desirable residence district." That paragon, Mr. Antrobus, "has all the best interests of the community at heart," but rather inconsequentially Sabina notes that "Of course, every muscle [in him] goes tight every time he passes a policeman." As for Mrs. Antrobus, although she is "as fine a woman as you could hope to see," and lives "only for her children," Sabina makes it plain that, provided it benefited the children, Mrs. Antrobus would see "the rest of us stretched out dead at her feet without turning a hair."

In addition to providing some of the comic undercutting, Sabina is also used, and very early in the play, to call attention to its unrealistic character. In the first scene, she bursts out with the remark that "the author hasn't made up his silly mind as to whether we're all living back in caves or in New Jersey today." She doesn't understand the play. She says that she hates it. She finds it a comedown to have to accept a part in a piece of silly claptrap like this when she has acted in celebrated "straight" plays such as *Rain* and *The Barretts of Wimpole Street*.

Later on, however, Sabina suddenly catches on, and stepping out of her role as character "says in her own person as Miss Somerset, with surprise, 'Oh, *I* see what this part of the play means now!'" When Mr. Antrobus and the stage manager try to call her back to her proper role, she insists on speaking directly to the audience, crying out: "Ladies and gentlemen! Don't take this play serious. The world's not coming to an end. You know it's not. People exaggerate. Most people really have enough to eat and a roof over their heads. Nobody actually starves—you can always eat grass or something. That ice business—why, it was a long, long time ago. Besides they were only savages. Savages don't love their families—not like we do."

In the second act, Sabina refuses to play a scene because she has a friend in the audience who, thinking that her own situation was being referred to, might have her feelings hurt. At the very end of the play, Sabina speaks directly to the audience again, commenting on the fact that her last speech is identical with her first speech in the play, so that everything begins over again. The audience can go home now, but "the end of this play isn't written yet"—isn't written yet because the real play is the human endeavor in which all of us are caught up. In effect, Sabina is saying that the play is quite true and that the real play is still going on and cannot possibly end: the heads of the Antrobuses "are full of plans and they're as confident as the first day they began. . . ."

What does the playwright gain by exposing the theatrical conventions of the play in this fashion? Quite a number of things. By having Sabina express her bewilderment with the historical anachronisms, he indicates to his audience that they are deliberate and meaningful. By taking the audience from time to time *inside* the play instead of having to look at it from across the footlights, the playwright has found a way to call our attention to the mechanism—and the meaning—of his play. By having Sabina insist that it is just a play and later that it is not just a play, the playwright suggests that the real "play" with which he is concerned is continuous with life itself. This is the sort of effect achieved by Sabina's speech at the end of the play.

One way to view Sabina is to regard her as a sort of chorus. In *Oedipus Rex* we saw that the function of the chorus was to comment on the action, expressing the hopes, fears, anticipations, and anxieties of the audience as it watched the tragic spectacle. (*Murder in the Cathedral*, as we have seen, is another play with a formal chorus that has a somewhat similar, though not identical, function.) For all her goodnatured flightiness

and triviality, Sabina becomes an effective means for the author's commentary on the events which the audience is witnessing.

Sabina, however, is much more than a chorus. She is the temptress, the "other woman," the voice of banality, the flighty servant girl, the principal "comic." But she is only one of the many sources of comedy. The anachronisms, the scrambled history, the jangling of clichés, and most of all the foibles of the Antrobuses, are exploited for comic effect. At the very beginning of the play we are told that a wedding ring found in a movie house is inscribed "To Eva from Adam, Genesis II:18." The ring, of course, might have been lost by a twentieth-century Eva Smith, to whom it had been given by a certain Adam Jones, a young man who was a life-insurance agent, taught a Sunday school class, and thought it might be nice to cite the passage from Genesis in the ring. Such juxtapositions are not only amusing but, placed early in the play like this one, are hints as to what the real "time scheme" of the play is. The cleaning woman's discovery of the ring puts Adam and Eve in a new perspective, but it puts the modern inhabitants of New York City in a new perspective too.

Most of the people in the play, like Sabina, talk in platitudes and clichés. The announcer, giving his "News Events of the World," in which he features Mr. Antrobus as the discoverer of the wheel, describes Antrobus as a veteran of foreign wars, and says that he bears "a number of scars, front and back." The usual form of this oratorical phrase commends a person for having "all his scars in front," with the implication that he has never turned his back to the enemy. But the announcer, almost absent-mindedly, tells us the truth about Mr. Antrobus: he has fought some valiant battles and received honorable scars in the proper places, but like most of the rest of us, Mr. Antrobus has evidently sometimes run away in order to be able to fight another day.

The comedy characteristic of this play derives, however, from something deeper and more permanent than the mere temporary shock effect of startling juxtapositions between the life of cave men and life in suburban New Jersey of the 1940's, or the ragging and teasing of the expressions that we so constantly and thoughtlessly use. The essential comedy is based squarely upon human nature. Man remains, throughout the ages and in his various vicissitudes, much the same: amazing, cantankerous, foolish, and yet somehow a brave and admirable creature. Moreover, his folly and what, in an older America, would have been called his general "orneriness," are intimately tied up with his admirable qualities. Mr. Antrobus may occasionally break a law, but his respect for Moses the lawgiver and for law as the bedrock of civilization is genuine. He may have a foolish pride in his own accomplishments, but he is a genuine idealist, and his reverence for the great thinkers of Western civilization is profound. Mrs. Antrobus may focus her sympathies upon her own family—*her* husband and *her* son and *her* daughter, but she justifies the relative narrowness of her sympathies by her power to endure misfortune and hold the family together. Even Sabina has some admirable as well as amiable traits. One remembers her concern for the embittered Henry Antrobus at the end of Act 3. In this play, human nature and the human enterprise are seen in a comic light, but it is not a withering light that dries and shrivels the heroic qualities in man.

EXERCISES

1. May it be said that the playwright has divided his typical woman into two—into Mrs. Antrobus, the mother, the mate to whom her husband always finally returns, the basic prop of the family, and Sabina, the romantic attraction just across the fence from dull matrimony? Is Gladys, the daughter, to be taken as a third segment of the eternal woman? Why has the author not found it necessary to divide up his typical man in the same fashion? Or has he actually divided typical man by representing father and son in their potential rivalry?

2. Henry's past crime is obviously the principal skeleton in the Antrobus family closet. His original name, Cain, points back to the archetypal murderer, the son of Adam and Eve, who killed his brother Abel. Wilder uses the incident for various effects—the intractability of all boys and the desire of the family to conceal the blot on its good name—but Henry's Cain-like conduct evidently points to some more somber experience in the human story. Notice, for example, the effect on Mr. Antrobus when he hears that Henry has thrown a stone at the boy next door. Why should this boyish act have such a troubling effect on his father? Can you connect this general interpretation of Henry with the author's stage direction given in the middle of Act 3: "Throughout the following scene Henry is played, not as a misunderstood or misguided young man, but as a representation of strong unreconciled evil"?

3. What is the significance of the incident in Act 2 when Mrs. Antrobus, in her desperate attempt to find Henry, finally calls him by his original name, Cain? Is the point that, when the going gets really difficult enough, we drop our pretenses and call things by their true names? Or is the basic point that, murderer or not, the mother loves her son and means to save him even if she has to call him by the accursed name? Or do you have some other explanation for the effect and significance of the incident?

4. Is the happy ending of this play—even if it is to be regarded as only a temporary and provisional happy ending—based in good part on the fact that Henry and his father do become reconciled with each other? Notice Henry's speech to his father near the end of Act 3. What is the significance of Mr. Antrobus's speech—the one beginning "Wait a minute,"?

5. How do the faults and virtues of Mrs. Antrobus balance those of her husband? Is she less idealistic than her husband, or more idealistic? Is she more passionate, or more reasonable, or can one state the basic difference between this husband and wife in such terms as these? In this general connection, consider the end of Act 1. The refugees are invited in for coffee and warmth. It is Mr. Antrobus who has invited them in, and Mrs. Antrobus rather scolds her husband for having done so. Does this mean that Mrs. Antrobus is less kindhearted than her husband? Or what?

6. What do you think of the argument that Mrs. Antrobus makes about the nature of marriage toward the end of Act 2? What thing or combination of things brings Mr. Antrobus back to his wife and out of the snare that Sabina has woven for him?

7. What is the justification for the way in which Act 3 opens? The stage manager has to call the play to a halt, explain about the illness of some of the actors, work out substitutions, and have the substitute actors recite the opening and closing lines of their speeches to make sure that they know them. The stage manager tells the audience that for Mr. Antrobus "Each of the hours of the

night is a philosopher, or a great thinker. Eleven o'clock, for instance, is Aristotle. And nine o'clock is Spinoza." He goes on to apologize for this whimsy on Mr. Antrobus's part by saying: "I don't suppose it means anything. It's just a kind of poetic effect." After this little impromptu re-arrangement and partial rehearsal, Act 3 begins again and runs on through; but surely enough, at the end of the play when Mr. Antrobus finds that his books are safe, the substitute actors come forward to recite their passages from Spinoza, Plato, Aristotle, and the book of Genesis. Does the fact that these speeches have been anticipated diminish the effect they give us now? Or enhance it? What would be the difference of effect if, without this little business at the beginning of Act 3 to forewarn us, the actors simply walked on at the end of the play to recite their passages? Does this use of the philosophers, by the way, mean any-thing? Is it *just* a kind of "poetic effect"?

8. If, at the end of the play, the eloquent passages spoken by the hours do come with a very different effect, what is the nature of that effect? Do these passages from Spinoza and Plato and Aristotle and the Book of Genesis come with a special power, answering to and expressing the deeper poetry of the human experience? What is their special relevance to the underlying theme of the play?

9. What is the point about the substitute actors? Do they help "universalize" the play? Make it apply to all men? Is Wilder saying that in a sense any of us can find a part in this play?

10. What is the basic view of man implied by this play?

11. Would you say that the author of this play was optimistic about the future of mankind? Does he believe in progress? What does he seem to think is the most important thing about mankind? Does the fact that he sees the human enterprise in a comic light make his concern for it less serious or more serious?

12. Thus far the student has been asked to look at this play as constituting a kind of parable about mankind, and to be on the alert to see symbolic meanings and connections in the various incidents. But if generalizations about civilization were the only matter of importance, Thornton Wilder need not have written a play at all. He might have given us a little sheaf of comments and observations on the nature of the human animal, or a kind of exhortation, such as William Faulkner wrote in his Nobel Prize speech, expressing his belief that man will endure and, even if this planet is blown up, will not only endure, but "prevail." What does the play "say" that could not be "said" in a speech or an editorial, or any other piece of discursive prose?

13. If *The Skin of Our Teeth* may in some sense be read as a parable about man, how has the play-wright kept it from becoming a dull and rather empty parable? What is accomplished by the dra-matic form? As the playwright has managed matters, the very act of dramatizing the issues involves us as readers or spectators and makes us participate imaginatively in what the dramatist has to tell us about our lives. What is the perspec-tive in which we are asked to look at ourselves and our history? What is the tone of this play? Or, to put it in somewhat different terms, can you define and illustrate the precise kind of comedy which you find in *The Skin of Our Teeth*?

ACT WITHOUT WORDS I: A MIME FOR ONE PLAYER

Samuel Beckett (b. 1906)

Desert. Dazzling light.

The man is flung backwards on stage from right wing. He falls, gets up immediately, dusts himself, turns aside, reflects.

Whistle from right wing.

He reflects, goes out right.

Immediately flung back on stage, he falls, gets up immediately, dusts himself, turns aside, reflects.

Whistle from left wing.

He reflects, goes out left.

Immediately flung back on stage he falls, gets up immediately, dusts himself, turns aside, reflects.

Whistle from left wing.

He reflects, goes towards left wing, hesitates, thinks better of it, halts, turns aside, reflects.

A little tree descends from flies, lands. It has a single bough some three yards from ground and at its summit a meager tuft of palms casting at its foot a circle of shadow.

He continues to reflect.

Whistle from above.

He turns, sees tree, reflects, goes to it, sits down in its shadow, looks at his hands.

A pair of tailor's scissors descends from flies, comes to rest before tree, a yard from ground.

He continues to look at his hands.

Whistle from above.

He looks up, sees scissors, takes them and starts to trim his nails.

The palms close like a parasol, the shadow disappears.

He drops scissors, reflects.

A tiny carafe, to which is attached a huge label inscribed WATER, descends from flies, comes to rest some three yards from ground.

He continues to reflect.

Whistle from above.

He looks up, sees carafe, reflects, gets up, goes and stands under it, tries in vain to reach it, renounces, turns aside, reflects.

A big cube descends from flies, lands.

He continues to reflect.

Whistle from above.

He turns, sees cube, looks at it, at carafe, reflects, goes to cube, takes it up, carries it over and sets it down under carafe, tests its stability, gets up on it, tries in vain to reach carafe, renounces, gets down, carries cube back to its place, turns aside, reflects.

A second smaller cube descends from flies, lands.

He continues to reflect.

Whistle from above.

He turns, sees second cube, looks at it, at carafe, reflects, goes to cube, takes it up, carries it over and sets it down under carafe, tests its stability, gets up on it, tries in vain to reach carafe, renounces, gets down, takes up second cube to carry it back to its place, hesitates, thinks better of it, sets it down, goes to big cube, takes it up, carries it over and puts it on small one, tests their stability, gets up on them, the cubes collapse, he falls, gets up immediately, brushes himself, reflects.

He takes up small cube, puts it on big one, tests their stability, gets up on them and is about to reach carafe when it is pulled up a little way and comes to rest beyond his reach.

He gets down, reflects, carries cubes back to their place, one by one, turns aside, reflects.

A third still smaller cube descends from flies, lands.

He continues to reflect.

Whistle from above.

He turns, sees third cube, looks at it, reflects, turns aside, reflects.

The third cube is pulled up and disappears in flies.

Beside carafe a rope descends from flies, with knots to facilitate ascent.

He continues to reflect.

Whistle from above.

He turns, sees rope, reflects, goes to it, climbs up it and is about to reach carafe when rope is let out and deposits him back on ground.

He reflects, looks around for scissors, sees them, goes and picks them up, returns to rope and starts to cut it with scissors.

The rope is pulled up, lifts him off ground, he hangs on, succeeds in cutting rope, falls back on ground, drops scissors, falls, gets up again immediately, brushes himself, reflects.

The rope is pulled up quickly and disappears in flies.

With length of rope in his possession he makes a lasso with which he tries to lasso carafe.

The carafe is pulled up quickly and disappears in flies.

He turns aside, reflects.

He goes with lasso in his hand to tree, looks at bough, turns and looks at cubes, looks again at bough, drops lasso, goes to cubes, takes up small one, carries it over and sets it down under bough, goes back for big one, takes it up and carries it over under bough, makes to put it on small one, hesitates, thinks better of it, sets it down, takes up small one and puts it on big one, tests their stability, turns aside and stoops to pick up lasso.

The bough folds down against trunk.

He straightens up with lasso in his hand, turns and sees what has happened.

He drops lasso, turns aside, reflects.

He carries back cubes to their place, one by one, goes back for lasso, carries it over to cubes and lays it in a neat coil on small one.

He turns aside, reflects.

Whistle from right wing.

He reflects, goes out right.

Immediately flung back on stage he falls, gets up immediately, brushes himself, turns aside, reflects.

Whistle from left wing.

He does not move..

He looks at his hands, looks around for scissors, sees them, goes and picks them up, starts to trim his nails, stops, reflects, runs his finger along blade of scissors, goes and lays them on small cube, turns aside, opens his collar, frees his neck and fingers it.

The small cube is pulled up and disappears in flies, carrying away rope and scissors.

He turns to take scissors, sees what has happened.

He turns aside, reflects.

He goes and sits down on big cube.

The big cube is pulled from under him. He falls. The big cube is pulled up and disappears in flies.

He remains lying on his side, his face towards auditorium, staring before him.

The carafe descends from flies and comes to rest a few feet from his body.

He does not move.

Whistle from above.

He does not move.

The carafe descends further, dangles and plays about his face.

He does not move.

The carafe is pulled up and disappears in flies.

The bough returns to horizontal, the palms open, the shadow returns.

Whistle from above.

He does not move.

The tree is pulled up and disappears in flies.

He looks at his hands.

———————◆—·—◄►—·—◆———————

Act without Words I belongs to what has been called the theater of the absurd. Indeed, it is a simple and almost naked instance of that kind of play. In his book entitled *The Theater of the Absurd* (New York: Anchor Books, 1961), Martin Esslin locates the central impulse of that theater in a conviction that life is meaningless—in short, that the human enterprise itself makes no sense.

Now the notion that human existence is without purpose is, of course, scarcely new. It is often expressed by the writers of the latter part of the nineteenth century and, for that matter, it turns up at intervals throughout the course of human history. Examples are to be found in some of the poems and stories included in the preceding sections of this book. Ernest Hemingway's story "In Another Country" (sec. 8) implies—though it does not elaborate upon—such a world view. It turns upon the gallantry of despair with which the hero makes a desperate effort to redeem the incoherence and meaninglessness of the world in which he finds himself, or perhaps merely makes a gesture of courageous dignity, the more poignant because there is nothing out in the universe to sustain it or validate it. Isaac Babel's "Crossing into Poland" (sec. 2) is another story expressing the shocking brutality and senseless cruelty of which men are capable, though the stress in that story is not on the gallantry of despair, as with the Hemingway story, but on a hopeless attempt to sustain one's basic decency and humanity in an utterly inhuman world.

James Purdy's "Daddy Wolf" (sec. 10) also seems to reflect such a world view. The story consists of a monologue spoken by a man who evidently cannot cope with the situation in which he finds himself and who has no one to whom he can talk. In his desperation, he has picked a name at random from the telephone directory, and to the bewil-dered person at the other end of the line he pours out his anxieties and frustrations.

These examples from the fiction section imply human dignity and courage in the face of defeat. But the dramatists of the absurd accord their characters scant dignity. Believing that man's fate is absurd, they treat it so. The note that they sound is comic, and the laughter is frequently satiric. In our introduction to drama (sec. 20) we remarked that "in tragedy we stand side by side with the protagonist, even with a protagonist like Macbeth," but that "in comedy . . . our sympathies [are] with society itself, the laws or customs which the primary figure in comedy is breaking." But one must observe that in a modern play such as Eugene Ionesco's *The Bald Soprano*, society and its laws and conventions are the very subject of attack. The point of the play is to reveal to the audience the essential absurdity of society. Such, too, is the point of Bartheleme's "The Indian Uprising" (sec. 8). It seems plain that Bartheleme's story, if not actually influenced by the dramatists of the absurd, has at the least come out of a similar impulse and manifests the same general intent. As we put matters earlier, "By its incoherence, in the midst of hints of never specified coherences and logical relationships, it affirms that the modern world, for all its pretensions to science, rationality, system, and organization, is finally incomprehensible."

In the theater of the absurd, the dramatist's very presentation of his theme makes use of absurd means—by the lampooning of characters, the use of illogical actions and speeches, and stress upon unexpected turns and reversals. For example, in Beckett's play *Endgame* there is an almost continuous succession of inconsequential answers and non-sequiturs. When Clov refuses to carry out an order given by his master Hamm on the grounds that he has things to do in the kitchen, and Hamm asks in effect what these important tasks may be, Clov's answer is "I look at the wall." In *The Bald Soprano*, when the Smiths get into an argument, the Fire Chief says to them: "Everything's very simple really. Come on now, kiss and make up." To which Mrs. Smith replies: "But we kissed and made up only a few moments ago." This remark prompts another character to say: "Oh, they can kiss and make up tomorrow. They've all the time in the world."

Inconsequential answers, illogical motives, and sharp reversals occur, of course, in plays that have nothing to do with the theater of the absurd. Such devices are of the very stuff of comedy and are to be found in *Pygmalion*, for instance, and *The Skin of Our Teeth*. But in such matters as these the plays of Ionesco, Beckett, and Jean Genet go far beyond anything in the traditional theater.

Another "absurdist" feature is the flouting of realism, the use of fantastic settings, and a quite direct use of naked symbolism. *The Skin of Our Teeth* makes use of such strategies. As we have seen, historical epochs are scrambled, we are asked to accept anachronisms, the characters are not only individuals but frankly archetypal figures; for instance, the real name of Henry Antrobus is Cain. But Wilder's play remains in hailing distance of the realistic world of the twentieth century, whereas the settings of plays such as Ionesco's *The Chairs* or Beckett's *Endgame* and his *Waiting for Godot* are frankly placed in a country of the mind.

In *Act without Words I* Beckett has pared his cast down to one mute actor, and has kept even the gestures and actions that he allows that actor few and simple. Yet the essential absurdity of life, the lack of meaning in man's existence, is, nevertheless, powerfully presented. Beckett's having denied himself the use of words may even have served to enforce the more nakedly his basic theme. His failure to employ words here certainly does not come from any lack of power in constructing dialogue. Dialogue is his acknowledged strength.* It is as if here Beckett had tied his right arm behind his back to show what he could do with his left alone. The play is thus a *tour de force*—a champion's almost nonchalant display of his skill.

This tiny play may also be regarded as a piece of dramatic shorthand. The scene is

presumably the desert of modern life. Man finds himself, not in a land of green pastures through which he walks beside the still waters. There is little shade cast in this weary land, and such as it is is provided by a tree that is obviously a stage prop. But the rather transparent symbolism is not taken with full seriousness by the dramatist. A certain calculated flippancy is evident. The carafe of water that is let down to the thirst-tormented man in the desert has attached to it "a huge label inscribed WATER."

Since the man under his little tree has nothing to do but sit in the meager bit of shade and reflect—nothing to do except, as the phrase goes, to sit and pare his nails—an instrument proper for the purpose is conveniently let down to him. But if this sudden appearance of the tailor's shears looks like unexpected manna from heaven, the boon is immediately offset by a tiny disaster. The bit of shade disappears and the palm tree closes like a parasol. The universe that our hero inhabits is an absurd one indeed.

Beckett's hero, however, is a man not easily defeated. His notion of using the scissors, so miraculously let down to him, to cut the rope and to fabricate the cut portion into a lasso speaks well for his ingenuity and determination. But the powers—whatever they are—that control the absurd universe in which he finds himself do not play fair. When it appears that he may succeed in snaring the carafe, it is rapidly pulled up out of sight.

At this point, there occurs a crescendo of losses. The scissors, the cubes, and all are snatched away from him, but then the carafe is made to descend once more and "dangles and plays about his face." Now, however, the man refuses to respond. The fact that the bough returns to horizontal and the palm tree opens and again casts its bit of shade makes no difference to him. He refuses to respond to the whistle from above. Finally, the game of tantalizing him stops, at least temporarily. The tree itself disappears, and we have the man, as the playlet ends, sitting

---

* As one might infer from the fact that Beckett was a friend of James Joyce and regarded him as his literary master, Beckett himself commands all the resources of verbal wit, elaborate parody, literary allusion, and the mimicry of the clichés, banalities, and rhythms of everyday speech.

in an empty landscape, face to face with the ultimate nothingness, under the blazing desert sun, looking at his hands. Yet after all, he has learned something from his experience: he has learned that effort is pointless, that ingenuity and persistence will not get him the water that he craves, that anything other than an acceptance of the nothingness is a delusion.

EXERCISES

1. Our discussion of *Act without Words I* has perhaps insisted too much upon the meaning of the play (or alternatively on the "meaninglessness" of the universe portrayed). Is everything else subordinated to this theme? Is there any dramatic suspense? If so, how is it managed? Do you think that a skillful actor could, by the use of pauses, facial expression, and gesture, give depth and body to the rather stark outline of action?

2. We have suggested that this play is a commentary on knowledge and by what processes we acquire it. What are some of the ways in which Beckett has pointed this matter up? Note the stage directions that Beckett has provided.

3. Note the use of repetition in this play. Someone has remarked that the silences in Beckett's plays are often the most effective elements in them. Could one say something like this of the repetitions? If so, indicate specifically how they are used.

4. Does Beckett's hero learn what he learns by philosophical reasoning or by trial and error? Is he more like Socrates wrestling with an intellectual problem or like a white rat learning to run a maze? What is the evidence in the play?

5. The hero conceives the possibility of placing one cube on another so as to provide a platform that will bring him closer to the carafe. Experiments with apes have involved just such paraphernalia. The psychologist hangs a banana out of reach, but supplies the ape with sticks and boxes of various sizes, and then waits to see whether it will occur to the ape to put one box on another until he can reach his prize. Do you suppose that Beckett knew of such experiments? In any case, what is the point of introducing the business of building a platform of the cubes? What does it imply about man's reason? About man himself?

6. We have suggested earlier that *Oedipus Rex* is a play about man's ignorance and the difficulty of his acquiring knowledge. Compare *Oedipus Rex* with Beckett's play. Is there any resemblance whatever? Is what Oedipus learns at the end essentially what Beckett's hero learns? Or is there a difference? Do the two plays throw light on the difference between the classical Greek view of reality and a post–World War II view of reality?

7. Is *Act without Words I* a comedy? There are certainly comic effects—such as the palm tree fronds closing up like a parasol—and there are pratfalls aplenty. The actor might very well play up these comic effects. But upon whom is the joke? A character in another of Beckett's plays remarks that "Nothing is funnier than unhappiness," but the same character goes on to say that unhappiness is like a funny story that has been heard too often: "We still find it funny, but we don't laugh any more." Is this the point of *Act without Words I*?

8. Let us approach the issues raised in exercise 7 in another way. Is it possible to have a tragedy if the odds against the tragic hero are so heavy that he is defeated before he starts? Is it possible to receive a tragic effect from watching a bear trying to free his foot from a steel beartrap? Is it possible that a belief that the universe is truly absurd not only undermines the possibility of tragedy but the possibility of being fully human—at least as conceived in the past. In short, is *Act without Words I* neither tragic nor comic, but something beyond either?

GLOSSARY

This glossary does not attempt to give full or exhaustive definitions of the terms listed below. It does attempt to give a brief definition of the special sense or senses that the term has in literary criticism. In most cases, the term is treated rather fully in one of the introductory sections to the main divisions of this book.

ABSTRACT: Abstractions are qualities and characteristics isolated as pure ideas. A piece of sugar is a concrete substance with its own qualities, but we may *abstract* (literally "draw away") from the word *sugar* the ideas of whiteness, hardness, sweetness. Literature characteristically deals with the concrete rather than the abstract, and with the specific rather than the general. All of which is not to say that ideas that are capable of being stated abstractly—love, courage, justice—or very complex general truths are not involved in literature. Literature is, after all, an image of life, and life constantly involves abstractions; if we cannot arrive at abstractions, or at general ideas and principles, we cannot make sense of the process of living. But literature is not concerned with such things, in themselves, as *abstractions*. It is concerned with them as they grow out of, and affect, experience, as they are realized in the concreteness of life—in particular characters, events, feelings, objects, images. The general observations that one may abstract from the particulars of a story or poem—observations about human nature or life—are not to be taken as the equivalent of the story or poem. See also CONCRETE.

ACT: In drama, a division of a play which may comprehend one or more scenes. A SCENE usually represents an action occurring at a particular place and during one continuous period of time. What constitutes an *act* is more arbitrary and depends upon a unity felt by the playwright.

ALEXANDRINE: A line consisting of six iambic feet. See HEXAMETER.

ALLEGORY: An allegory is a kind of narrative in which the characters, objects, and events are to be taken, not as real, but as standing for some set of ideas. That is, each item in the narrative is equated with some item among the ideas. For example, in Bunyan's *Pilgrim's Progress* the character Christian, who leaves his home to go to the Celestial City, is not to be taken as a real person but as the type of all people who try to lead the Christian life, and each event that he encounters on his journey stands for some problem in the spiritual life. The chief danger in using allegory is that the system of equivalents may seem too complicated or too forced.

See also SYMBOL. The chief distinction between allegory and symbolism is that allegory characteristically consists of a thorough-going and mutually related *set*, or system, of equivalents, which have some sort of metaphoric function—e.g., PERSONIFICATION (which see). A symbol does not represent a system but a massive embodiment of meaning.

ALLITERATION: Identity of initial sounds, usually consonants, in a group of words.

AMBIGUITY: Multiplicity of meaning. In expository prose, ambiguity is a defect, for what is wanted is one clear, unequivocal meaning—not a doubtful or obscure statement. A more accurate term for poetic ambiguity is richness of meaning.

ANAPEST: A foot composed of two unaccented syllables followed by one accented syllable.

ANECDOTE: A brief narrative usually having to do with some detached and isolated event.

ANTICLIMAX: A break in the climactic order of events or effects; a falling off from the expected intensification of effect. See CLIMAX.

ASSONANCE: Identity of vowel sounds in accented syllables without the identity of the following consonants.

ATMOSPHERE: The general pervasive feeling aroused by the various factors such as setting, character, and theme in a piece of literature; the general effect on the reader of the handling of the total work. To be distinguished from SETTING and TONE (which see).

BALLAD: A ballad is a song that tells a story. A ballad such as "Sir Patrick Spens" (sec. 12) was originally sung, though now it is read like other poems. There are two general classes of ballads: (1) popular, or folk, and (2) literary.

"Sir Patrick Spens" is a folk ballad, for instance. Nobody knows who originally made up the poem or exactly what the original version was. But we do know how it was preserved. It was passed down by word of mouth (oral tradition), constantly being changed by the bad memory or the power of imagination of different people. A poem capable of being preserved in such a fashion would necessarily be simple in form. It would also tend to employ repetition and refrain, in part as aids to memory. There would be little or no comment or moralizing on the story, for the treatment would be objective and dramatic. The materials treated would be of a kind to appeal to a large number of rather simple people: a shipwreck in "Sir Patrick Spens," the murder of Johnny by his sweetheart in "Frankie and Johnny," and so on.

A literary ballad is an imitation of the method and the effect of the folk ballad by a professional poet, such as A. E. Housman, who wrote "The True Lover" (sec. 12). The literary ballad is preserved in the ordinary way, that is, by writing it down or by printing it. We note, however, that some poems, songs, and tales that begin as literary "creations"—that is, as the work of recognizable authors, in print, may enter so fully into the popular consciousness that they are regarded as folk song or folk tale. For instance, "Casey Jones." Here, again, as so often, we are not dealing with absolute distinction but with gradations.

BALLAD STANZA: The most common stanza in traditional ballads, a quatrain of alternate lines of four and three accents as in "Sir Patrick Spens." Often the term is used of more strictly metrical quatrains of alternate iambic tetrameter and iambic trimeter.

BLANK VERSE: Unrimed iambic pentameter verse.

CACOPHONY: Any unpleasant (literally "bad-sounding") verbal combination.

CAESURA: The main pause within a line of verse.

CHORUS: In ancient Greek drama, a singing and dancing group whose speeches comment upon or interpret the action. The chorus has occasionally been used in later plays (see *Murder in the Cathedral*, sec. 21), or a particular character may sometimes be said to have something of the interpretative function of a chorus (*e.g.,* Enobarbus in *Antony and Cleopatra:* note his speeches in Act 2, scene 2.

CHRONICLE: An account of events arranged in the order of the time of happening; sometimes applied to a story that has relatively light emphasis on the central situation. See also EPISODE.

CLICHÉ: A phrase that has lost its force because of continued use. See the analysis of "To Ianthe" (sec. 15). See also for a justifiable use of the cliché the analysis of "That the Night Come" (sec. 14). The cliché is one kind of appeal to a STOCK RESPONSE on the part of the reader. See SENTIMENTALITY.

CLIMAX: The highest point in an ascending series; in fiction or drama, for example, the point where the forces reach their moment of highest concentration.

COINCIDENCE: An accidental coming together of certain events. For the legitimate and the illegitimate use of coincidence in fiction, see section 1.

COMEDY: For discussions of this rich and complex term, and related terms such as *comic,* see section 21.

COMPLICATION: The interplay between character and event that builds up tension and develops a problem out of the situation given in the beginning of the story.

CONCRETE: Literature, especially poetry, fiction, and drama, aims, in large part, at being concrete and not abstract, particular and not general. It appeals to sensation, direct observation, perception, and experience. A novelist may wish to express an idea in his novel, but he does not give it to us in a series of general statements or in an argument; instead, he writes a novel, a long story that makes us feel the force of his idea. A poet, Robert Burns for instance, does not say merely, "I am in love." That would be a general, or an abstract, statement. Instead, he tries to convey to the reader the quality of his love by a set of particular comparisons. He says, "My Luve is like a red, red rose." Then he proceeds to give other comparisons, each of which adds to the concreteness of the poem. A piece of literature, to sum up, embodies, enacts, or dramatizes—to use terms most common in this connection—ideas, meanings, themes, truths. Literature does treat general ideas and abstractions, but it aims to express those ideas so that they can be felt immediately and will evoke an emotional resonance.

CONFLICT: Some kind of conflict is central to any piece of fiction or drama. The conflict is involved in the original situation and is developed in the action, and the concern with the outcome generates the basic suspense.

CONNOTATION: See DENOTATION.

CONSONANCE: Identity of consonants of words without identity of vowels.

CONVENTIONAL: A thing is said to be conventional when it is usual or expected: the term in particular carries the association of use in the past. For example, the fleetingness of beauty is a conventional theme in poetry, for poets in all ages have used it. So also certain forms, like the sonnet, for instance, are said to be conventional forms. To say that a theme or a form or a choice of words is conventional, however, is not necessarily to condemn it. Writers of literature have to work in terms of *conventions,* accepted ways of doing things. Most sound literature is to some extent conventional, but it uses its conventions for its purpose, freshening them and relating them to what is new. It does not—as in a mawkish poem, for instance—depend entirely upon them.

COUPLET: Two successive lines riming or unrimed.

DACTYL: A foot composed of one accented syllable followed by two unaccented syllables.

DENOTATION: The exact thing indicated by a word. It is opposed to CONNOTATION, which means the thing or things suggested by a word, or *associated* with it. In Coleridge's lines "In Xanadu did Kubla Khan / A stately pleasure-dome decree," the word *Xanadu denotes* a special place on the map, presumably, but it *connotes* something of remoteness, historical glamour, and Oriental splendor. The same applies to the name of the ruler, Kubla Khan. If a botanist uses the word *rose* in a professional discourse, he is concerned with denotation strictly. The beauty or freshness or salability of a rose has no place here. If instead of *rose* he uses the technical term "the genus *rosa,*" he has certainly given an unmistakable signal that denotation in a strict scientific sense is his concern. But imagine rewriting Robert Burns's line as "My Luve is like a red, red example of the genus *rosa.*" Poetry, and often fiction, too, works by a logic of connotations and suggestions, as when, in Sonnet 94, Shakespeare writes, "Lilies that fester smell far worse than weeds." Here a whole series of connotations are brought into conjunction—of *lilies, fester,* and *weeds,* each with its cluster of associations—to give an imagistic embodiment of the meaning of the poem.

DÉNOUEMENT: The untieing of the plot; the final resolution of the complications of the plot. It sometimes, but not always, coincides with the CLIMAX (which see).

DICTION: The choice of words in poetry or any other form of discourse. Critics sometimes refer to POETIC DICTION as if certain words are—or are supposed to be—especially poetical in themselves. In its most obvious form, this type of poetic diction appears as words associated with poetry of the past; so we find forms such as *o'er* instead of *over, thou* instead of *you, wight* instead of *man, lass* instead of *girl,* and *bark* instead of *boat,* forms that have been dropped from the living language. But another type of poetic diction appears in words that refer to objects or ideas that, in themselves, are thought to be privileged material for poetry, objects or ideas involving the pretty, the sweet, the holy, the romantic, and so on. The same fallacy appears here as above. As a preference for words "poetical" in themselves implies a repudiation of the living language, so a preference for words referring to poetical materials and connoting poetical associations implies a repudiation of the experience of life, for life involves many things beyond the pretty or the holy. There are, of course, no fixed rules to depend on in these matters. The choice of words in any given poem—or piece of fiction—must depend on the whole context.

DIMETER: A line consisting of two feet.

DIPODIC VERSE: A verse based on the regular alternation of basic and secondary stresses, to create a foot in which both a basic and a secondary stress occur; as in: |Go dówn to Kèw| in lílac-tìme.| See subsection 19.12.

DRAMATIC: This term is used with two meanings. The first, and more general, meaning implies the presence of a sharp struggle or conflict, or tension. The second, and more specific, meaning refers to the way in which a scene, in a short story, for instance, is presented when action and dialogue are given without interpretation or comment by the author in a direct form.

ELEGY: The term is used loosely for any poem of subjective and meditative nature, but more specially for a poem expressing grief.

END-STOPPED: A line of verse in which there is a definite pause at the end of the line.

ENJAMBEMENT: See RUN-ON.

EPIC: A long narrative poem dealing with persons of heroic proportions and actions of great significance: for example, Homer's *Iliad* or Milton's *Paradise Lost.*

EPILOGUE: In drama, a concluding speech (or even scene), not a part of the dramatic action proper. Shaw calls the last scene of *Saint Joan*—the time is twenty-five years after Joan's death—an epilogue. The term is used more loosely to refer to a part of a story or novel that winds up matters and falls outside the action proper.

EPISODE: A separate incident in a larger piece of action. The term *episodic* is used to describe a plot, for example, that is characterized by a rather loose linking together of separate incidents without much regard for cause and effect. In such cases one incident does not occur as a logical consequence of a previous incident, but merely follows it in time. See CHRONICLE.

EUPHONY: Any pleasant (literally "good-sounding") verbal combination. See CACOPHONY.

EXPOSITION: The process of providing the reader with necessary information.

FICTION: The term used to distinguish an unhistorical account from a historical one.

FICTIONAL POINT: The essential meaning of a piece of fiction; the basic theme brought into sharp focus. See THEME.

FEMININE ENDING: An ending in which a line closes with an extra unaccented syllable in addition to the normal accented syllable.

FEMININE RIME: A rime of two syllables of which the second is unstressed.

FIGURATIVE LANGUAGE: Expressions used not literally but rhetorically. Common examples are METAPHOR, SIMILE, PERSONIFICATION, and HYPERBOLE (which see).

FIRST-PERSON NARRATOR: See POINT OF VIEW.

FOCUS: The center around which the material of an imaginative work is organized.

FOOT: The smallest combination of unaccented and accented syllables occurring in verse.

FORCED PAUSE: A pause forced by the poet's handling of the various metrical elements in the line.

FORESHADOWING: The process of giving the reader an intimation of some event that is to follow.

FORM: The arrangement of various elements in a work of literature; the organization of various materials (ideas, images, characters, setting, and the like) to give a total effect. It may be said that a story is successful—that it has achieved form—when all of the elements are functionally related to each other, when each part contributes to the intended effect. Form is not to be thought of merely as a sort of container for the story; it is, rather, the total principle of organization and affects every aspect of the composition. It is the mode in which the story exists. *Structure* and *Style* are also used to indicate the author's arrangement of his materials to give his effect. *Structure,* however, is usually used with more special reference to the ordering of the larger elements such as episodes, scenes, and details of action, in contrast to the arrangement of words, for which the term *style* is ordinarily employed. In the fullest sense, both the terms become synonymous with form, but in this book *style* is used merely to refer to the selection and ordering of language.

FREE VERSE: Verse that does not conform to a fixed metrical pattern.

HEPTAMETER: A line consisting of seven feet.

HERO: The word *hero* is used to indicate the main character of a literary work. The word does not imply that the character is admirable.

HEROIC COUPLET: Two consecutive lines of iambic pentameter riming together.

HEXAMETER: A line consisting of six feet.

HYPERBOLE: An exaggerated or extravagant assertion used for rhetorical effect: "I could have slept for a month."

IAMB: A foot composed of an unaccented syllable followed by an accented syllable.

IMAGE: The representation of something sensed or perceived. The most important images in poetry are visual (verbal pictures of objects, events, and so forth) and auditory (verbal representations of sounds), but one may also find representations related to the senses of taste, smell, and touch. See CONCRETE. Images may also be used in FIGURATIVE LANGUAGE such as METAPHOR and SIMILE (which see) and an image may be endowed with symbolic power. See SYMBOL.

IMPERFECT FOOT: A metrical foot in which the unaccented syllable (or syllables) is lacking.

INEVITABILITY: The sense that the result presented is the only possible result of the situation already presented.

INTERNAL RIME: Rime occurring within a line unit.

IRONY. The term derives from the Greek word *eironeia,* which means dissembling or feigning ignorance. The term, as used here, always involves contrast, a discrepancy between the expected and the actual, between the apparent and the real. Such contrast may appear in many forms. A speaker uses irony, for example, when he deliberately says something which he does not mean, but indicates by his tone what he does mean. That is, we come back to the notion of dissembling. UNDERSTATEMENT—the saying of less than one feels the occasion would warrant—and PARADOX—the saying of something that is apparently untrue but that on examination proves to be true, or partially true—both of these are forms of irony. In addition to such forms of IRONY OF STATEMENT, there are also various forms of IRONY OF SITUATION. The irony of situation involves a discrepancy between what we expect the outcome of an action to be, to what would seem to be the fitting outcome, and the actual outcome. For instance, in *Oedipus Rex* (sec. 21) it is ironical that the hero, in seeking to discover the cause of the plague that lies on Thebes, moves, step by step and quite unwittingly, toward the discovery of himself as the criminal source of infection. The effect of the irony here is given an added dimension by the fact that, since the story was traditional, the Greek audience knew the end even as they watched Oedipus moving blindly toward his doom. In dealing with this term, the student should always remember that there are a thousand subtle shadings of irony, and must, therefore, not take it in too restricted a sense, for example, in the sense of obvious sarcasm. Irony can, in fact, be very light, delicate, or even playful, and it can merely be taken to imply an awareness of opposing options or ideas.

ITALIAN SONNET: A sonnet composed of an octet, riming a-b-b-a-a-b-b-a, and of a sestet riming c-d-e-c-d-e (or with a variation of the c-d-e rimes).

LINE: In the strict metrical sense, a separate unit composed of the number of feet called for in a specified pattern: for instance, an iambic pentameter line, a unit of five iambic feet. A line, in this sense, is equivalent to a VERSE (which see). In free verse, however, a line is simply the separate unit defined by typography. See subsection 19.13.

LOGIC: The relation of cause and effect that exists between character and character, or character and setting, in fiction or drama.

LYRIC: The term is used in two senses: (1) A short musical poem. This use is descriptive of the technique. (2) A poem (or other literary work) directly expressing the personality of the writer; that is, SUBJECTIVE rather than OBJECTIVE in emphasis, giving the personal vision of, or reaction to, the world. This use describes the subject matter or philosophy of a literary work.

MASCULINE ENDING: An ending in which a line closes with an accentuated syllable. See FEMININE ENDING.

MASCULINE RIME: The common form of rime, in which the rimed syllables are the last syllables of the riming words.

MELODRAMA: A play that depends largely on the plot suspense rather than on character.

METAPHOR: A figure of speech in which one object (or process) is identified with another; e.g., "my love is a rose" or "the journey of life." See section 15.

METER: The pattern on which rhythm is systematized in verse.

METRICAL VARIATION: Departure from the strict metrical pattern.

MONOMETER: A line consisting of one foot.

MOTIVATION: By *motive* we understand the purpose of a person's act. Motivation, therefore, is understood in fiction or drama as the purpose, or mixture of purposes, that determines a character's behavior.

NOVELETTE: Literally, a little novel. In a rough and ready way we call a piece of fiction a novelette when it runs from some 10,000 words to some 35,000. Anything longer than 35,000 words, more or less, we call a novel. But we may think of a novelette as being more than a long story. We may expect it to show something of the complication of a novel.

OBJECTIVE: This adjective, as applied to literature, indicates an attitude of detachment on the part of the author toward the facts he is presenting. He refrains from giving his personal interpretation or commentary; therefore, the term *impersonal* in this connection is often used as synonymous with *objective.* The method of a dramatist who merely presents his characters in dialogue is an objective method. A SUBJECTIVE description, on the other hand, is one which is highly colored by the author's personal feelings. Obviously, one will not find a completely objective attitude in literature, for that attitude belongs properly to science. The writer is never merely recording objective data and reasoning about them. The data he records—that is, his story or poem—constitute, finally, a creation; that is, no matter how much his material is drawn from objective observation, he inevitably manipulates it in accordance with his interpretation. One does find, however, relative degrees of objectivity in literature—and relative degrees of "apparent" or "dramatically assumed" objectivity.

OCTET: The first part (an eight-line unit) of an Italian sonnet.

ODE: A rather extended poem, usually complicated in metrical and stanzaic form, dealing with a serious theme.

OMNISCIENT NARRATOR: See POINT OF VIEW.

ONOMATOPOEIA: Imitation of sense by sound.

PACE: The rate of speed with which the various parts of a fiction are made to move, ranging from summary to fully reported scene.

PARABLE: A parable is a short, allegorical narrative. Our most famous parables are those found in the Bible, for instance, the parable of the sower in the Gospel according to Mark. See also ALLEGORY.

PARADOX: A statement, apparently untrue, which on closer examination is seen to be true in reality. For example, the poet Lovelace writes: "I could not love thee dear so much / Loved I not honor more." Keats writes: "Heard melodies are sweet, but those unheard / Are sweeter. . . ." Paradox is often used for effects of IRONY (which see).

PERSONAL ESSAY: An essay characterized by a familiar or informal or personal tone.

PERSONIFICATION: A figure of speech in which a thing or an abstraction is represented as having human traits. Thus, Thomas Gray writes "Let not Ambition mock their [the villagers'] useful toil. . . ."

PLOT: The structure of the action in fiction or drama.

POETIC DICTION: See DICTION.

POINT OF VIEW: The term is sometimes used, generally and loosely, to refer to the way in which a writer looks at his material. But used more strictly—as the editors will consistently use it in discussing the stories in this book—it refers to the mind through which the material of the story is presented.

Obviously a story does not exist without a point of view, for otherwise the action would have no structure or meaning; there would indeed be no story. What are some of the possible points of view that may be used? The story may be narrated in the FIRST PERSON. Thus, a writer of fiction may let a character speak in his own person to serve as the teller of the story. The character might be the hero telling his own story or he might be one of the minor characters reporting what he saw and heard.

But the writer may tell his story in the THIRD PERSON—either looking at his characters as an outside observer might do or entering into the minds and thoughts of such of them as he chooses to look at from the inside. We might call this latter point of view that of the OMNISCIENT, or all-knowing, narrator. But even the omniscient narrator does not present everything, for he selects the material for presentation in accordance with some plan in his own mind.

There are many possible variations of the point of view. In general, however, it is important to remember that by adopting a point of view the author is enabled to select and organize his material for fiction.

PROPAGANDA: Literature that tends to state the theme abstractly, which tends to insist on the "message" at the expense of other qualities, is called propaganda literature.

PROTAGONIST: The main character of a literary work. See HERO.

QUANTITATIVE VARIATION: See LENGTH VARIATION.

QUATRAIN: A stanza composed of four lines.

REALISTIC: Having a strong sense of fact or of actuality. The term is sometimes used as the opposite of *romantic*. A romantic attitude may be described very summarily here as being an attitude in which the sense of fact is weakened in favor of ideality or in which the object in question is suffused with emotion, particularly with warmth of emotion. No attempt is made in this text to go into the distinction between *romantic* and *classic*.

REFRAIN: A line (or phrase) that recurs (perhaps with slight variation) in a poem as a structural element. See "Lord Randall."

RHETORICAL VARIATION: Variation in the movement of a line dictated by considerations of the sense of particular words.

RHYTHM: Cadenced movement in sound. All spoken language has some rhythmic quality, but we tend not to notice it unless the recurrent beat is stressed.

RIME: Correspondence in two or more words between the sound of their last accented syllables (and whatever syllables follow them).

RIME SCHEME: The pattern of rime within a stanza.

ROMANTIC: See REALISTIC.

RUN-ON: A line of verse in which there is not a definite pause at the end of the line.

SCALE: The proportion of space allotted to the treatment of events in a piece of fiction.

SCENE: See ACT.

SECONDARY ACCENT: Stress on a normally unaccented syllable weaker than that of a primary accent but heavier than the light stress called for by strict metrical pattern.

SELECTIVITY: The choosing of the necessary and expressive elements and details which a writer thinks will best serve his purpose.

SENTIMENTALITY: A sentimental person is one who likes to "wallow in emotion" for its own sake without reference to the nature or force of the stimulus. Sentimentality in literature springs from the same attitude on the part of the writer and appeals to such an attitude in the reader. To state the matter more objectively, sentimentality in a literary work appears when there is an excess of emotion or when emotion has not been adequately prepared for by the work in question. The sentimental work appeals to automatic responses in the reader—to what is called a STOCK RESPONSE. There are many kinds of stock responses. For instance, some readers may respond automatically to patriotic subject matter, to religious subject matter, and so on.

SESTET: The second part (a six-line unit) of an Italian sonnet.

SETTING: The physical background, the element of place, in literature.

SHAKESPEARIAN SONNET: A sonnet composed of three quatrains and a couplet, riming a-b-a-b,c-d-c-d,e-f-e-f,g-g.

SIMILE: See IMAGERY.

SIMILE: A figure of speech in which one object or process is likened to another; e.g., "my love is like a rose" or "the night was black as pitch." See section 15.

SLANT RIME: An approximate rime.

SOLILOQUY: An utterance by a character who is talking to himself.

SONNET: A stanza of fourteen lines of iambic pentameter. For the common rime schemes, see subsection 19.11.

SPENSERIAN STANZA: A nine-line stanza of which the first eight lines are iambic pentameter; the ninth, iambic hexameter. The rime scheme is a-b-a-b-b-c-b-c-c.

STANZA: A pattern of lines usually repeated as a unit of composition in a poem.

STOCK RESPONSE: The automatic or conventionalized response of a reader to some word, phrase, situation, or subject in literature. See SENTIMENTALITY.

STRUCTURE: See FORM.

STYLE: See FORM.

SUBJECTIVE: See OBJECTIVE.

SYLLABLE TIME: Variation in the amount of time required to pronounce varying syllables.

SYMBOL: Generally speaking, an object, character, or incident that stands for—signifies—something else. But symbolism in literature is not primarily concerned with arbitrary and abstract symbols such as the letter *b*, which stands for a certain sound, or the figure *4*, which stands for a certain number of units; nor is literary symbolism specifically exemplified in such conventional symbols as the cross (as signifying Christianity) or the Stars and Stripes (as signifying the United States of America)—though a writer may obviously make use of such symbols in a poem or story. A literary symbol is an image (or complex of images) that on occasion has been endowed by the writer's shaping and development of the context in which it occurs. Such symbolization need not be systematic, as in ALLEGORY (which see). See also section 15.

TALE: A narrative, without overt complication, that gives the impression of being something "told."

TERCET: Specifically, a unit of three unrimed lines. But the term is sometimes used to refer to any stanza of three lines.

TERZA RIMA: Iambic pentameter tercets in linked rime.

TETRAMETER: A line composed of four feet.

THEME: The special view of life or special feeling about life or special sets of values that constitute the point or basic idea of a piece of literature.

THIRD-PERSON NARRATOR: See POINT OF VIEW.

TONE: The attitude (or attitudes) of the author as reflected in the form and structure of his work. In conversation, we often imply our attitude by the tone of voice that we use; and the tone of our utterance may very heavily qualify our literal statements. The skillful author is able, in an analogous way, to qualify what his work "says" by the way in which he "says" it. Indeed, if we are to understand a piece of literature, even on the simplest level, we must take into account its tone. See also SENTIMENTALITY.

TRAGEDY: For discussions of this rich and complex term, and related terms such as *tragic*, see section 21.

TRICK ENDING: In fiction, an ending that violates the laws of probability and fictional logic.

TRIMETER: A line composed of three feet.

TRIPLET: A unit of three lines, riming together. But the term is sometimes applied to three unrimed lines used as a unit. See TERCET.

TROCHEE: A foot composed of one accented syllable followed by one unaccented syllable.

UNITY: The sense of oneness—of having a total and final meaning.

UNDERSTATEMENT: Saying less than one might be expected to say; a sense of restraint that underplays the occasion. See IRONY.

VERS DE SOCIÉTÉ: Light verse, usually occasional and complimentary, that deals in a witty and elegant fashion with pleasantly trivial subjects.

VERSE: Rhythm patterned and systematized as a separate metrical unit. See LINE.

VERSE TEXTURE: The relation of the vowel and consonant sounds in verse.

INDEXES

AUTHORS

TITLES

FIRST LINES